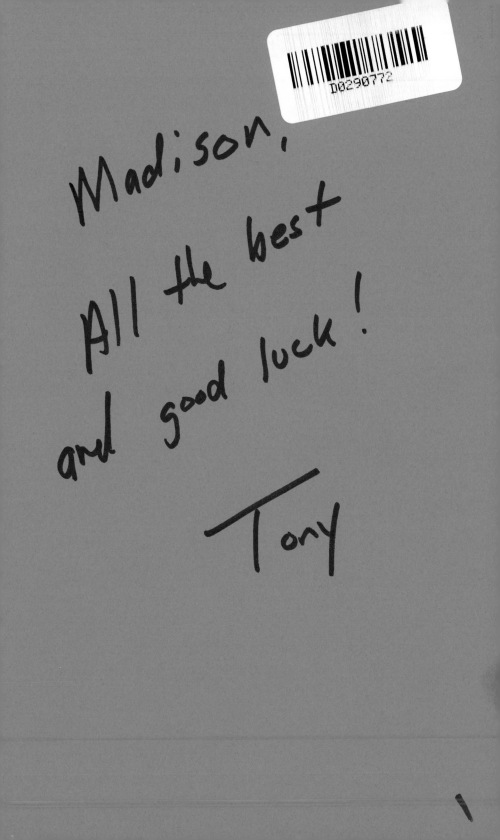

Madison,

All the best
and good luck!

Tony

WISCONSIN
· BLUE BOOK ·

2021 · 2022

Published biennially by
the Wisconsin Legislative Reference Bureau

To view a pdf of the 2021–2022 *Wisconsin Blue Book*, go to
http://legis.wisconsin.gov/lrb/blue-book

Wisconsin Legislative Reference Bureau
One East Main Street, Suite 200, Madison, WI 53703
http://legis.wisconsin.gov/lrb
©2021 Joint Committee on Legislative Organization, Wisconsin Legislature
All rights reserved. Published 2021.
Printed in the United States of America

ISBN: 978-1-7333817-1-0

Sold and distributed by:
Document Sales Unit
Department of Administration
2310 Darwin Road
Madison, WI 53704
608-243-2441, 800-362-7253
DOADocumentSalesInformation@wisconsin.gov

Front cover: Views of the Wisconsin State Capitol and its verdant 13.5-acre grounds in downtown Madison are stunning from any angle. Here, the capitol's granite dome and crowning statue, Wisconsin—a symbol of the state's motto, "Forward"—peek through the trees on a sunny fall day. GREG ANDERSON, LEGISLATIVE PHOTOGRAPHER

Back cover: The first state capitol built in Madison, portrayed in this 1853 engraving, was not only the seat of state government, but a busy public forum used as a dance hall, theater, and even, occasionally, a funeral parlor. After two governors were sworn into office in 1856, with each claiming to have won the 1855 gubernatorial election, citizens came to the capitol in droves to see how this drama—the subject of this book's feature article (see page 290)—would play out. WHS IMAGE ID 7042

Tony Evers
Office of the Governor

July 2021

Dear Readers:

This past year, our state, our country, and our world were ravaged by a pandemic that took the lives of thousands of our friends, neighbors, and loved ones. Nearly everything about our daily lives had to adapt to these circumstances, and we have been challenged in more ways than we ever could have imagined. It has been a year rife with worry, loss, and tragedy, and it challenged the depth of our empathy and the strength of our selflessness.

But it was also an extraordinary show of resilience, kindness, and community. We saw this in the retired healthcare professionals who returned to the workforce when we needed them most; in the school staff and community members who delivered meals to our kids learning at home; in the volunteers who provided comfort and company to isolated older adults. I have been overwhelmed—but frankly, not surprised—by the heart, grit, and determination of the people of this great state.

As I write this, the vaccine is being distributed across our state and country. But this pandemic underscored deficiencies and disparities in our state and our economy. Now, we are faced with a decision: we can go back to the way things were, or we can demand the future we dream. We must work in earnest to fix the problems this year brought to the forefront and to bounce back from this pandemic better than before. After all we've been through, we won't apologize for wanting more for each other and our state.

Each *Blue Book*—but especially this one—presents an opportunity for us to reflect; reminds us that we are more than the sum of our differences; and serves as a helpful resource to learn about, respect, and appreciate, not just our state, but each other.

Thank you for picking up a copy. Happy reading and On, Wisconsin!

Sincerely,

Tony Evers

Tony Evers
Governor

INTRODUCTION

Wisconsin faced its first major political crisis in 1856. On a bitterly cold day in early January, not one but two men were sworn in as governor: William Barstow, the Democratic incumbent, and Coles Bashford, his challenger and the first gubernatorial candidate of the newly formed Republican party. As days stretched into weeks, Wisconsinites nervously waited to see whether the standoff would end in civil strife. To their relief, the Wisconsin Supreme Court intervened with a ruling in *Bashford v. Barstow* that averted violence and charted a clear course forward.

The 2021–22 *Wisconsin Blue Book* feature article, "Dueling Governors: How the Wisconsin Supreme Court Resolved the State's First Political Crisis," revisits a moment when state institutions stood on shaky ground. Fierce partisan debate over slavery and immigration—coupled with unabashed corruption—threatened to upend what little stability existed in the new state. Against this backdrop, the court's decision in *Bashford v. Barstow* represented the triumph of the state's constitution over chaos. The court simultaneously settled the dispute over the rightful governor and asserted its authority to do so under the constitution. And thanks to its decisive action, Wisconsin not only weathered its first major political crisis but emerged stronger, with a clear separation of powers that has anchored state government ever since.

The 2021–22 *Blue Book* also contains the biographies of all legislators, descriptions of executive and judicial branch agencies, and vital statistics on Wisconsin. The *Blue Book* is an introduction to Wisconsin state and local government and the most comprehensive source for information about the State of Wisconsin. Composing the *Blue Book* requires agency-wide collaboration, involving all LRB staff, to write essays, update tables, and assemble and organize material about the legislature and state and local government. The LRB's legal and research expertise is unmatched, and three people deserve special recognition: Nancy Warnecke, Louisa Kamps, and Kira Langoussis Mochal. Their leadership has been invaluable, and I am grateful for their contributions.

Richard A. Champagne

Richard A. Champagne, Chief
Wisconsin Legislative Reference Bureau

TABLE OF CONTENTS

3 About Wisconsin

4 Statistics and Reference

1

ELECTED OFFICIALS

INDEX OF BIOGRAPHIES

Tony Evers, Governor
Democrat

Biography: Born Plymouth, Wisconsin, November 5, 1951; married; 3 children, 9 grandchildren. ▪ Graduate Plymouth High School, 1969; B.S. University of Wisconsin-Madison, 1973; M.S. University of Wisconsin-Madison, 1976; Ph.D. University of Wisconsin-Madison, 1986. ▪ Former teacher; technology coordinator; principal, Tomah; superintendent of schools, Oakfield, Verona; CESA 6 administrator, Oshkosh; deputy state superintendent of public instruction. ▪ Former member: Wisconsin Association of CESA Administrators; Wisconsin Association of School District Administrators; University of Wisconsin Board of Regents; Wisconsin Technical College System Board; Council of Chief State School Officers. ▪ Elected state superintendent 2009–17.

Current office: Elected governor 2018.

Contact: eversinfo@wisconsin.gov; 608-266-1212; PO Box 7863, Madison, WI 53707-7863.

Mandela Barnes, Lieutenant Governor
Democrat

Biography: Born Milwaukee, Wisconsin, December 1, 1986. ▪ Graduate John Marshall High School (Milwaukee), 2003; B.A. Media Communications, Alabama A&M University. ▪ Deputy Director of Strategic Engagement at the State Innovation Exchange; Lead Organizer of MICAH (Milwaukee Inner-city Congregations Allied for Hope). ▪ Member: National Lieutenant Governors Association; Democratic Lieutenant Governor's Association; NewDEAL Leader (Climate Policy Group cochair); NAACP Milwaukee Branch; Kappa Alpha Psi Fraternity, Inc.; La Follette Forum: Climate Policy Advisory Committee. ▪ Elected to Assembly 2012–15.

Current office: Elected lieutenant governor 2018.

Contact: ltgov@wisconsin.gov; 608-266-3516; PO Box 2043 Madison, WI 53701.

Joshua L. Kaul, Attorney General
Democrat

Biography: Born Mount Lebanon, Pennsylvania, February 2, 1981; married; 2 children. ▪ Graduate Goodrich High School (Fond du Lac) 1999; B.A. in Economics and History, Yale University, 2003; J.D., Stanford Law School, 2006. ▪ Former attorney; Assistant United States Attorney. ▪ Former president of Stanford Law Review.

Current office: Elected attorney general 2018. Member ex officio: Board of Commissioner of Public Lands.

Contact: 608-266-1221; PO Box 7857, Madison, WI 53707-7857.

Jill Underly, State Superintendent of Public Instruction
nonpartisan office

Biography: Born Hammond, Indiana, August 2, 1977; married; 2 children. ▪ Graduate Munster High School, Munster, Indiana, 1995; B.A. in History and Sociology, Indiana University, 1999; M.A. in Secondary Education Curriculum and Instruction, Indiana University-Purdue University, Indianapolis; Ph.D. in Educational Leadership and Policy Analysis, University of Wisconsin-Madison, 2012. ▪ Former school superintendent, middle school principal, high school principal, elementary principal, and director of instruction at Pecatonica Area School District, Blanchardville, Wisconsin; assistant director and education consultant, Wisconsin Department of Public Instruction; senior student services coordinator, College of Letters & Science, University of Wisconsin-Madison; high school social studies teacher, Munster High School, Munster, Indiana, and Community Schools of Frankfort, Frankfort, Indiana. ▪ Member: Wisconsin Association of School District Administrators (executive board); Wisconsin Association of Business Officials; Iowa County Humane Society. ▪ Former member: vestry, Trinity Episcopal Church, Mineral Point, Wisconsin; Fitchburg Optimists Club, Fitchburg, Wisconsin.

Current office: Elected state superintendent 2021. Member ex officio: University of Wisconsin Board of Regents; Wisconsin Technical College System Board; Education Commission of the States.

Contact: dpistatesuperintendent@dpi.wi.gov; 608-266-3390; 125 S. Webster Street, Madison, WI 53703.

Sarah Godlewski, State Treasurer
Democrat

Biography: Born Eau Claire, Wisconsin, November 9, 1981; married; 1 child. ▪ Graduate Eau Claire Memorial High School, 2000; B.A. in Peace and Conflict Resolution, George Mason University, 2004; Master of Public Administration candidate, University of Pennsylvania; National Security Fellow, Air War College, 2013; Certificates in Public Treasury Management and Finance, Pepperdine

Graziadio Business School and National Institute of Public Finance, 2017. ▪ Former national security project manager; director of strategy and performance; investor; entrepreneur. ▪ Member: National Association of State Treasurers (Midwestern Region vice president). ▪ Former member: UNICEF Advocacy Leadership Committee (chair); Congressional Bipartisan Post Traumatic Stress Disorder Task Force; U.S. Fund for UNICEF (board member); Arlington Academy of Hope (board secretary); George Mason University College of Visual and Performance Arts (board member).

Current office: Elected state treasurer 2018. Member ex officio: Board of Commissioners of Public Lands (chair); Wisconsin Insurance Security Fund.

Contact: Treasurer@wisconsin.gov; 608-266-1714; B38 West State Capitol, Madison, WI 53701.

Douglas J. La Follette, Secretary of State
Democrat

Biography: Single. ▪ B.S. in Chemistry, Marietta College, 1963; M.S. in Chemistry, Stanford University, 1964; Ph.D. in Organic Chemistry, Columbia University, 1967. ▪ Former director of training and development with an energy marketing company; assistant professor, University of Wisconsin-Parkside; public affairs director, Union of Concerned Scientists; owner and operator of a small business; research associate, University of Wisconsin-Madison. ▪ Member: American Solar Energy Society; Audubon Society; Friends of the Earth; Phi Beta Kappa. ▪ Former member: Council of Economic Priorities; American Federation of Teachers; Federation of American Scientists; Lake Michigan Federation; Southeastern Wisconsin Coalition for Clean Air; Clean Wisconsin (formerly Wisconsin Environmental Decade, founder). ▪ Elected to Senate 1972.

Current office: Elected secretary of state 1974 and 1982. Reelected since 1986. Member ex officio: Board of Commissioners of Public Lands.

Contact: doug.lafollette@wisconsin.gov; 608-266-8888 (press 3); PO Box 7848, Madison, WI 53707-7848.

Ann Walsh Bradley

Biography: Born Richland Center, Wisconsin, July 5, 1950; married; 4 children. ▪ Graduate Richland Center High School; B.A. Webster College (St. Louis, Missouri); J.D. University of Wisconsin-Madison (Knapp Scholar), 1976. ▪ Former high school teacher, practicing attorney, and Marathon County circuit court judge. ▪ Member: International Association of Women Judges (chair of the Board of Managerial Trustees); Global Network on Electoral Justice (founding member); American Law Institute (elected member); state coordinator for iCivics; Wisconsin Bench Bar Committee; University of Wisconsin Law School Board of Visitors; American Bar Association; State Bar of Wisconsin; lecturer for the American Bar Association's Asian Law Initiative, International Judicial Academy, U.S. Department of State, and Institute of International Education. ▪ Former member: International Judicial Academy (board of directors and vice chair); National Association of Women Judges (board of directors); American Judicature Society; National Conference on Uniform State Laws; Wisconsin Judicial College (associate dean and faculty); Wisconsin Rhodes Scholarship Committee (chair); Wisconsin Judicial Council; Wisconsin Equal Justice Task Force; Wisconsin Judicial Conference (executive committee, legislative committee, judicial education committee); Civil Law Committee (executive committee); Task Force on Children and Families; Wisconsin State Public Defender (board of directors); Committee on the Administration of Courts; Federal-State Judicial Council. ▪ Recipient: American Judicature Society's *Herbert Harley Award*; Business and Professional Woman of the Year; Business Woman of the Year *Athena Award*; Wisconsin Law Journal *Women in the Law Award*.

Current office: Elected to Supreme Court 1995. Reelected 2005 and 2015.

Patience Drake Roggensack

Biography: Born Joliet, Illinois, July 7; married; 3 children. ▪ Graduate Lockport Township High School; B.A. Drake University; J.D. University of Wisconsin-Madison Law School (cum laude). ▪ Former practicing attorney. ▪ Participation: Commissioner, Uniform Laws Commission; Fellow, American Bar Foundation; Wisconsin Judicial Council; Supreme Court Rules Procedure Committee;

Supreme Court Finance Committee; Committee for Public Trust and Confidence in the Courts; American Bar Association; State Bar Association of Wisconsin; Western District of Wisconsin Bar Association (past president); Dane County Bar Association, served on Personnel Review Board (supreme court delegate); 2005 Judicial Conference (cochair); 2005 Statewide Bench Bar Conference (cochair). ▪ Board service on: YMCA; YWCA; Wisconsin Center for Academically Talented Youth; Olbrich Botanical Society; International Women's Forum (past president); A Fund For Women; Friends of the Arboretum. ▪ Court of Appeals judge, District IV (1996–2003). Served on Judicial Conference (legislative liaison); Publication Committee for the Court of Appeals; State Court/Tribal Court Planning Committee (cochair); Personnel Review Board (appeals court delegate).

Current office: Elected to Supreme Court 2003. Reelected 2013. Elected chief justice 2015. Reelected as chief justice 2017 and 2019.

Annette Kingsland Ziegler, Chief Justice

Biography: Born Grand Rapids, Michigan, March 6, 1964; married with children. ▪ Graduate Forest Hills Central High School; B.A. in Business Administration and Psychology, Hope College (Holland, Michigan), 1986; J.D. Marquette University Law School, 1989. ▪ Former practicing attorney (civil litigation), 1989–95. Pro bono special assistant district attorney, Milwaukee County, 1992, 1996. Assistant U.S. attorney, Eastern District of Wisconsin, 1995–97. Washington County Circuit Court judge, 1997–2007. Court of Appeals District II (Judicial Exchange Program 1999). Deputy chief judge, Third Judicial District. Judicial faculty at various seminars. ▪ Member: State Bar of Wisconsin; American Bar Association; American Law Institute (elected member); American Bar Foundation (fellow); International Women's Forum; Washington County Bar Association; Milwaukee County Bar Association; Eastern District of Wisconsin Bar Association; Boys & Girls Club of Washington County (trustee board president); Marquette University Law School Advisory Board; Rotary Club West Bend. ▪ Former member: Uniform State Laws Commission; Wisconsin Judicial Council; State Bar of Wisconsin Bench & Bar Committee; Governor's Juvenile Justice Commission; Criminal Benchbook Committee; Criminal Jury

Instruction Committee; Legal Association for Women; James E. Doyle American Inn of Court.

Current office: Elected to Supreme Court 2007. Reelected 2017. Elected chief justice 2021.

Rebecca Grassl Bradley

Biography: Born Milwaukee, Wisconsin. ▪ Graduate Divine Savior Holy Angels High School; Honors B.S. in Business Administration and Business Economics, Marquette University, 1993; J.D. University of Wisconsin-Madison, 1996. ▪ Former practicing attorney, 1996–2012; Milwaukee County Circuit Court judge, appointed 2012, elected 2013; District I Court of Appeals judge, appointed 2015. ▪ Member: Supreme Court Finance Committee; Supreme Court Legislative Committee; Board of Advisors, Federalist Society, Milwaukee Lawyers Chapter; Wisconsin State Advisory Committee, U.S. Commission on Civil Rights. ▪ Former member: Board of Governors, St. Thomas More Lawyers Society; Wisconsin Juvenile Jury Instructions Committee; Wisconsin Juvenile Benchbook Committee; Milwaukee Trial Judges Association; Wisconsin Trial Judges Association. ▪ In private practice: American Arbitration Association arbitrator; chair, Business Law Section, State Bar of Wisconsin.

Current office: Appointed to Supreme Court October 2015 to fill vacancy created by death of Justice N. Patrick Crooks. Elected to full term 2016.

Rebecca Frank Dallet

Biography: Born Cleveland, Ohio, July 15, 1969; married, 3 children. ▪ Graduate B.A. in Economics summa cum laude with honors, The Ohio State University, 1991; J.D. summa cum laude, Case Western Reserve University School of Law, 1994. ▪ Law Clerk for U.S. Magistrate Judge Aaron Goodstein; Assistant District Attorney, Milwaukee County; Special Assistant United States Attorney, Eastern District of Wisconsin; Adjunct Law Professor, Marquette University Law School; Presiding Court Commissioner, Milwaukee County; Milwaukee County Circuit Court Judge. ▪ Member: Judicial Education Committee (chair); Access to Justice Commission (court liaison); National Institute on Domestic Violence (faculty); VoteRunLead (trainer); National Board of Trial Advocacy. ▪

Former member: Wisconsin Criminal Jury Instruction Committee; Wisconsin Judicial College (associate dean); Association of Women Lawyers (secretary); Milwaukee Trial Judges' Association (president); Eastern District of Wisconsin Bar Association (ex officio director); Milwaukee Jewish Federation (board member); Congregation Shalom (youth leader and educator). ▪ Recipient: Phi Beta Kappa; Merit Scholar, Case Western Reserve University School of Law; *Order of the Coif*; Whitehouse Leadership Project Women Rule! 2005; *Pasch Meritorious Service Award* 2005; Woman in the Law Honoree 2012; *Dallet Youth Award* 2014; 2019 *Woman of Influence;* Society of Benchers, Case Western Reserve University School of Law; Shaker Height High School Hall of Fame.

Current office: Elected to Supreme Court 2018.

Brian Hagedorn

Biography: Born Brookfield, Wisconsin, January 21, 1978; married; 5 children. ▪ Graduate Wauwatosa West High School, 1996; B.A. in Philosophy, Trinity International University, 2000; J.D. Northwestern University School of Law, 2003. ▪ Former attorney in private practice (2006–09); Wisconsin Supreme Court law clerk for Justice Michael Gableman (2009–10); Assistant Attorney General at Wisconsin Department of Justice (2010–11); Chief Legal Counsel for the Office of Governor Scott Walker (2010–15); Wisconsin Court of Appeals judge, District II (2015–19). ▪ Member: State Bar of Wisconsin Bench Bar Committee; State Claims Board; Wisconsin Judicial Commission; Federalist Society. ▪ Recipient: *Alumnus of the Year* 2014, Trinity International University.

Current office: Elected to Supreme Court 2019.

Jill J. Karofsky

Biography: Born Madison, Wisconsin, July 15, 1966; 2 children. ▪ Graduate Middleton High School, 1984; B.A. in Political Science and Spanish, Duke University, 1988; M.A. University of Wisconsin Robert M. La Follette School of Public Affairs, 1992; J.D. University of Wisconsin-Madison Law School, 1992. ▪ Former assistant district attorney and deputy district attorney for Dane County, 1992–2001; general counsel and director of education and human resources for the National Conference of Bar Examiners, 2001–10; adjunct law professor at University of Wisconsin, 2005–14; assistant state attorney general and Wisconsin's first Violence Against Women Prosecutor, 2010–11; executive director of Office of Crime Victim Services at Wisconsin Department of Justice, 2011–17, Dane County Circuit Court Judge, 2017–20. ▪ Member: Violence Against Women STOP Grant committee; Wisconsin State Bar; Dane County Bar Association. ▪ Former member: Governor's Council on Domestic Abuse; Wisconsin Child Abuse and Neglect Prevention Board; Wisconsin Crime Victims Council; Dane County Big Brothers/Big Sisters Board of Directors; Attorney General's Sexual Assault Response Team (cochair); James E. Doyle Inn of Court; Wisconsin Attorney General's Child Maltreatment Task Force; Madison Metropolitan School District Guiding Coalition Committee; Wisconsin Celebrate Children's Foundation; Wisconsin Legislative Committee on Criminal Penalties; Wisconsin Child Abuse Network Leadership Committee; Wisconsin Child Death Review Council; Wisconsin Task Force on Children in Need; Safe Harbor of Dane County; Wisconsin Judicial Education Committee. ▪ Recipient: Wisconsin Victim/Witness Professional Association *Professional of the Year*, Wisconsin Coalition Against Sexual Assault *Voices of Courage*, and Dane County Coordinated Community Response to Domestic Violence *Significant Impact*.

Current office: Elected to Supreme Court 2020.

Tammy Baldwin, U.S. Senator
Democrat

Biography: Born Madison, Wisconsin, February 11, 1962. Voting address: Madison, Wisconsin. ▪ Graduate Madison West High School; A.B. in Mathematics and Government, Smith College (Massachusetts), 1984; J.D. University of Wisconsin-Madison, 1989. ▪ Former practicing attorney, 1989–92. ▪ Madison City Council, 1986; Dane County Board, 1986–94. ▪ State legislative service: Elected to Assembly, 78th District, 1992–96 (served until January 4, 1999).

Congress: Elected to U.S. House of Representatives 1998. Reelected 2000–10. Elected to U.S. Senate since 2012. Committee assignments, 117th Congress: Appropriations and its subcommittees on Agriculture, Rural Development, Food and Drug Administration, and Related Agencies; on Department of Defense; on Department of Homeland Security; on Departments of Labor, Health and Human Services, and Education, and Related Agencies; on Energy and Water Development; and on Military Construction and Veterans Affairs, and Related Agencies. Commerce, Science, and Transportation and its subcommittees on Communications, Media, and Broadband; on Consumer Protection, Product Safety, and Data Security; on Oceans, Fisheries, Climate Change, and Manufacturing (chair); and on Surface Transportation, Maritime, Freight, and Ports. Health, Education, Labor, and Pensions and its subcommittees on Employment and Workplace Safety and on Primary Health and Retirement Security.

Contact: Washington—202-224-5653; 709 Hart Senate Office Building, Washington, D.C. 20510. Eau Claire—715-832-8424; 500 South Barstow Street, Suite LL2, Eau Claire, WI 54701. Green Bay—920-498-2668; 1039 West Mason Street, Suite 119, Green Bay, WI 54303. La Crosse—608-796-0045; 210 7th Street South, Suite 3, La Crosse, WI 54601. Madison—608-264-5338; 30 West Mifflin Street, Suite 700, Madison, WI 53703. Milwaukee—414-297-4451; 633 West Wisconsin Avenue, Suite 1300, Milwaukee, WI 53203. Ashland—715-450-3754; PO Box 61, Ashland, WI 54806.

Website: www.baldwin.senate.gov

Ron Johnson, U.S. Senator

Republican

Biography: Born Mankato, Minnesota, April 8, 1955; 3 children. Voting address: Oshkosh, Wisconsin. ▪ Graduate Edina High School, 1973; B.S.B. University of Minnesota, 1977. ▪ Former CEO, plastics manufacturing company. ▪ Former member: Partners in Education Council, Oshkosh Chamber of Commerce (business cochair); Oshkosh Opera House Foundation (treasurer); Lourdes Foundation (board president); Diocese of Green Bay Finance Council; Oshkosh Chamber of Commerce Board of Directors; Oshkosh Area Community Foundation Investment Council.

Congress: Elected to U.S. Senate 2010. Reelected 2016. Committee assignments, 117th Congress: Homeland Security and Governmental Affairs; its Permanent Subcommittee on Investigations; and its subcommittee on Government Operations and Border Management. Budget. Commerce, Science, and Transportation and its subcommittees on Communications, Media, and Broadband; on Oceans, Fisheries, Climate Change, and Manufacturing; on Surface Transportation, Maritime, Freight, and Ports; and on Tourism, Trade, and Export Promotion. Foreign Relations and its subcommittees on East Asia, the Pacific, and International Cybersecurity Policy; on Europe and Regional Security Cooperation; and on State Department and USAID Management, International Operations, and Bilateral International Development.

Contact: Washington—202-224-5323; 328 Hart Senate Office Building, Washington, D.C. 20510. Milwaukee—414-276-7282; 517 East Wisconsin Avenue, Suite 408, Milwaukee, WI 53202. Oshkosh—920-230-7250; 219 Washington Avenue, Suite 100, Oshkosh, WI 54901. Madison—608-240-9629; 5315 Wall Street, Suite 110; Madison, WI 53718.

Website: www.ronjohnson.senate.gov

U.S. Congressional Districts

Bryan Steil, U.S. Representative
Republican, 1st Congressional District

Biography: Born Janesville, Wisconsin, March 3, 1981. Voting address: Janesville, Wisconsin. ▪ Graduate Janesville Craig High School; B.S. in Business Administration, Georgetown University, 2003; J.D. University of Wisconsin-Madison, 2007. ▪ Former attorney; businessman. ▪ Member: St. John Vianney Parish. ▪ Former member: University of Wisconsin Board of Regents.

Congress: Elected to U.S. House of Representatives 2018. Committee assignments, 117th Congress: House Administration and its subcommittee on Elections. Financial Services and its subcommittees on Housing, Community Development and Insurance; and on Investor Protection, Entrepreneurship, and Capitol Markets.

Contact: Washington—202-225-3031; 1526 Longworth House Office Building, Washington, D.C. 20515. Janesville—608-752-4050; 20 South Main Street, Suite 10, Janesville, WI 53545. Kenosha—262-654-1901; Somers Village/Town Hall, 7511 12th Street, Somers, WI 53171. Racine—262-637-0510; Racine County Courthouse, Room 101; 730 Wisconsin Avenue, Racine, WI 53403.

Website: https://steil.house.gov

Mark Pocan, U.S. Representative
Democrat, 2nd Congressional District

Biography: Born Kenosha, Wisconsin, August 14, 1964; married. Voting address: Town of Vermont, Wisconsin. ▪ Graduate Mary D. Bradford High School (Kenosha); B.A. University of Wisconsin-Madison, 1986. ▪ Small businessperson. ▪ State legislative service: Elected to Assembly, 78th District, 1998–2010 (served until January 3, 2013).

Congress: Elected to U.S. House of Representatives 2012. Reelected since 2014. Committee assignments, 117th Congress: Appropriations and its subcommittees on Labor, Health and Human Services, Education, and Related Agencies; on Agriculture, Rural Development, Food and Drug Administration and Related Agencies; and on Financial Services and General Government. Joint Economic Committee. Education and Labor and its subcommittee on Higher Education and Workforce Investment.

Contact: Washington—202-225-2906; 1727 Longworth House Office Building, Washington, D.C. 20515. Beloit—608-365-8001; 100 State Street, 3rd floor, Beloit, WI 53511. Madison—608-258-9800; 10 East Doty Street, Suite 405, Madison, WI 53703.

Website: http://pocan.house.gov

Ron Kind, U.S. Representative
Democrat, 3rd Congressional District

Biography: Born La Crosse, Wisconsin, March 16, 1963; married; 2 children. Voting address: La Crosse, Wisconsin. ▪ Graduate Logan High School; B.A. Harvard University, 1985; M.A. London School of Economics (England); J.D. University of Minnesota Law School, 1990. ▪ Attorney. Former La Crosse County assistant district attorney and State of Wisconsin special

prosecutor. ▪ Member: U.S. Supreme Court Bar; State Bar of Wisconsin and La Crosse County Bar Association; Association of State Prosecutors; Democratic Party; Wisconsin Harvard Club (board of directors); Boys and Girls Club of Greater La Crosse (board of directors); Coulee Council on Alcohol and Other Drug Abuse (board of directors); Moose Club; Optimist Club.

Congress: Elected to U.S. House of Representatives 1996. Reelected since 1998. Committee assignments, 117th Congress: Ways and Means and its subcommittees on Health and on Trade.

Contact: Washington—202-225-5506; 1502 Longworth House Office Building, Washington, D.C. 20515-4906. Eau Claire—715-831-9214; 316 N. Barstow Street, Suite C, Eau Claire, WI 54703. La Crosse—608-782-2558; 205 5th Avenue South, Suite 400, La Crosse, WI 54601.

Website: https://kind.house.gov

Gwendolynne S. Moore

U.S. Representative

Democrat, 4th Congressional District

Biography: Born Racine, Wisconsin, April 18, 1951; 3 children. Voting address: Milwaukee, Wisconsin. ▪ Graduate North Division High School (Milwaukee); B.A. in Political Science, Marquette University, 1978; certification in Credit Union Management, Milwaukee Area Technical College, 1983. ▪ Former housing officer with Wisconsin Housing and Economic Development Authority; development specialist with Milwaukee City Development; program and planning analyst with Wisconsin Departments of Employment Relations and Health and Social Services. ▪ Member: National Black Caucus of State Legislators; National Conference of State Legislatures—Host Committee, Milwaukee 1995; National Black Caucus of State Legislators—Host Committee (chair) 1997; Wisconsin Legislative Black and Hispanic Caucus (chair since 1997). ▪ State legislative service: Elected to Assembly 1988 and 1990; elected to Senate 1992, 1996, and 2000. Senate President Pro Tempore 1997, 1995 (effective 7/15/96).

Congress: Elected to U.S. House of Representatives 2004. Reelected since 2006. Committee assignments, 117th Congress: Ways and Means and its subcommittees on Oversight; on Select Revenue Measures; and on Worker and Family Support. Science, Space, and Technology and its subcommittees on Research and Technology and on Investigations and Oversight.

Contact: Washington—202-225-4572; 2252 Rayburn House Office Building, Washington,

D.C. 20515. Milwaukee—414-297-1140; 250 East Wisconsin Avenue, Suite 950, Milwaukee, WI 53202.

Website: https://gwenmoore.house.gov

Scott Fitzgerald, U.S. Representative
Republican, 5th Congressional District

Biography: Born Chicago, Illinois; married; 3 children. Voting address: Juneau, Wisconsin. ▪ Graduate Hustisford High School, 1981; B.S. in Journalism, University of Wisconsin-Oshkosh, 1985; U.S. Army Armor Officer Basic Course, 1985; U.S. Army Command and General Staff College. ▪ Former associate newspaper publisher; U.S. Army Reserve Lieutenant Colonel (retired). ▪ Member: Dodge County Republican Party (chair, 1992–94); Juneau Lions Club; Reserve Officers Association; Knights of Columbus. ▪ State legislative service: Elected to Senate 1994. Reelected 1996–2018. Majority Leader 2019, 2017, 2015, 2013, 2011 (through 7/24/12); Minority Leader 2011 (effective 7/24/12), 2009, 2007; Majority Leader 9/17/04 to 11/10/04.

Congress: Elected to U.S. House of Representatives in 2020. Committee assignments, 117th Congress: Education and Labor and its subcommittees on Health, Employment, Labor, and Pensions; and on Civil Rights and Human Rights. Judiciary and its subcommittees on Antitrust, Commercial and Administrative Law; and on Crime, Terrorism, and Homeland Security. Small Business and its subcommittees on Contracting and Infrastructure and on Oversight, Investigations, and Regulations.

Contact: Washington—202-225-5101; 1507 Longworth House Office Building, Washington, D.C. 20515. Brookfield—262-784-1111; 120 Bishops Way, No. 154, Brookfield, WI 53005.

Website: https://fitzgerald.house.gov

Glenn Grothman, U.S. Representative
Republican, 6th Congressional District

Biography: Born Milwaukee, Wisconsin, July 3, 1955. Voting address: Glenbeulah, Wisconsin. ▪ Graduate Homestead High School (Mequon); B.B.A. and J.D. University of Wisconsin-Madison. ▪ Former practicing attorney. ▪ Member: ABATE of Wisconsin; Rotary Club of Fond du Lac. ▪ Recipient: The Association of Mature American Citizens *Friend of AMAC*;

International Food Distributors Association *Thomas Jefferson Award*; American Conservative Union *Award for Conservative Achievement*; FreedomWorks *Freedom Fighter Award*; *Asian American Hotel Owners Association Award*; U.S. Chamber of Commerce *Spirit of Enterprise Award*; National Retail Federation *Hero of Main Street*; Wisconsin Manufacturers and Commerce *Exemplar Award* for work on manufacturing tax credit; Wisconsin Farm Bureau's *Friend of Farm Bureau Award*; National Federation of Independent Business (NFIB) *Guardian of Small Business Award*; Motorcycle Riders Foundation *Champion of Motorcycle Rights and Safety*; Associated Builders and Contractors *Champion of the Merit Shop*; National Association of Mutual Insurance Companies *Benjamin Franklin Public Policy Award*; In Defense of Christians *Champion Award*; Family Research Council *True Blue Award*; Coalition for Medicare Choices *Medicare Advantage Champion*; National Association of Manufacturers *Manufacturing Legislative Excellence*; National Taxpayers Union *Taxpayers' Friend*; A-Team *A-Team All Star Award*; National Association of Home Builders *Defender of Housing*; Wisconsin Hemp Alliance *Hemp Hero Award* ▪ State legislative service: Elected to Assembly in December 1993 special election. Reelected 1994–2002. Elected to Senate 2004. Reelected 2008–12. Assistant Majority Leader 2013, 2011; Assistant Minority Leader 2009; Minority Caucus Chair 2007; Majority Caucus Vice Chair 2003, 2001, 1999.

Congress: Elected to U.S. House of Representatives since 2014. Committee assignments, 117th Congress: Budget. Education and Labor and its subcommittees on Early Childhood, Elementary, and Secondary Education; and on Higher Education and Workforce Investment. Oversight and Reform, and its subcommittee on National Security, Ranking Member.

Contact: Washington—202-225-2476; 1427 Longworth House Office Building, Washington, D.C. 20515. Fond du Lac—920-907-0624; 24 West Pioneer Road, Fond du Lac, WI 54935.

Website: https://grothman.house.gov

Tom Tiffany, U.S. Representative
Republican, 7th Congressional District

Biography: Born Wabasha, Minnesota, December 30, 1957; married; 3 children. Voting address: Town of Minocqua, Wisconsin. ▪ Graduate Elmwood High School, 1976; B.S. in Agricultural Economics, University of Wisconsin-River Falls, 1980. ▪ Dam tender, Wisconsin Valley Improvement Company. ▪ Member: NRA; Ruffed Grouse Society. ▪ Town of Little Rice supervisor, 2009–13. ▪ State legislative service: Elected to Assembly 2010. Elected to Senate 2012, 2014, 2016, 2018.

Congress: Elected to U.S. House of Representatives in May 2020 special election. Reelected November 2020. Committee assignments, 117th Congress: Judiciary and its subcommittees on Courts, Intellectual Property, and the Internet; on Crime, Terrorism, and Homeland Security; and on Immigration and Citizenship. Natural Resources and its subcommittees on National Parks, Forests, and Public Lands; and on Energy and Mineral Resources.

Contact: Washington—202-225-3365; 1719 Longworth House Office Building, Washington, D.C. 20515. Wausau—715-298-9344; 2620 Stewart Avenue, Suite 312, Wausau, WI 54401.

Website: https://tiffany.house.gov

Mike Gallagher, U.S. Representative
Republican, 8th Congressional District

Biography: Born Green Bay, Wisconsin, March 3, 1984. Voting address: Green Bay, Wisconsin. ▪ A.B. Princeton University; Master's in Security Studies, Georgetown University; Ph.D. in International Relations, Georgetown University. ▪ Iraq War Veteran, intelligence officer, served in U.S. Marine Corps 2006–13. ▪ Former staffer, U.S. Senate Foreign Relations Committee; senior global market strategist at a fuel management services company.

Congress: Elected to U.S. House of Representatives since 2016. Committee assignments, 117th Congress: Armed Services and its subcommittees on Seapower and Projection Forces; and on Cyber, Innovative Technologies, and Information Systems. Transportation and Infrastructure and its subcommittees on Aviation; on Coast Guard and Maritime Transportation; and on Highways and Transit.

Contact: Washington—202-225-5665; 1230 Longworth House Office Building, Washington, D.C. 20515. De Pere—920-301-4500; 1702 Scheuring Road, Suite B, De Pere, WI 54115.

Website: https://gallagher.house.gov

■ ■ ■

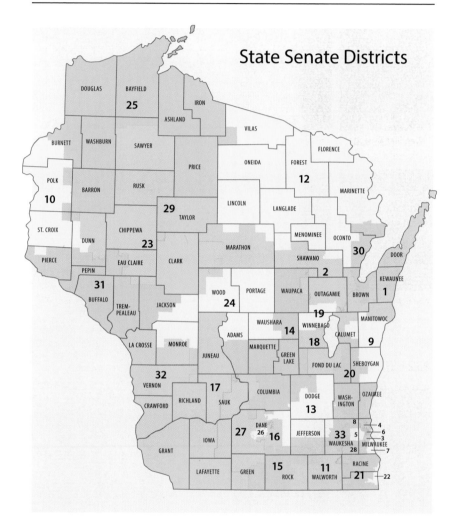

State Senate Districts

The Wisconsin Constitution requires the state legislature to redraw the state assembly and senate districts, based on population, following each U.S. Census. Accordingly, after the 2010 Census, 2011 Wisconsin Act 43 established the current districts. The legislature will create new districts using the 2020 U.S. Census data. The Wisconsin Constitution additionally requires that senate districts be "convenient contiguous territory" and that "no assembly district [be] divided in the formation of a senate district." Under 2011 Wisconsin Act 43, each senate district comprises three whole and contiguous assembly districts, numbered in consecutive order: for example, Senate District 1 is comprised of Assembly Districts 1, 2, and 3.

2021 State Senate Officers

President Kapenga

President Pro Tempore Testin

Majority Leader LeMahieu

Assistant Majority Leader Feyen

Minority Leader Bewley

Assistant Minority Leader Ringhand

Chief Clerk Queensland

Sergeant at Arms Engels

2021 State Assembly Officers

Speaker Vos

Speaker Pro Tempore August

Majority Leader Steineke

Assistant Majority Leader Petersen

Minority Leader Hintz

Assistant Minority Leader Hesselbein

Chief Clerk Blazel

Sergeant at Arms Tonnon Byers

Bay Moravian Church; Board of Directors, Door County Medical Center; Wisconsin Veterinary Medical Association; American Veterinary Medical Association; Sturgeon Bay Rotary Club. ▪ Former member: Sturgeon Bay Board of Education, 2000–14.

Legislature: Elected to Assembly since 2014. Committee assignments, 2021: Agriculture; Education (vice chair); Environment (chair); Housing and Real Estate; Tourism.

Contact: rep.kitchens@legis.wisconsin.gov; 608-266-5350; 888-482-0001 (toll free); 920-743-7990 (district); Room 220 North, State Capitol, PO Box 8952, Madison, WI 53708.

Shae Sortwell, Assembly District 2
Republican

Biography: Born Saratoga Springs, New York, August 3, 1985; married; 6 children. Voting address: Gibson, Wisconsin. ▪ B.A. in Public Administration, University of Wisconsin-Green Bay, 2006; Hazmat Tech certified, U.S. Army Chemical School, 2012. ▪ Former U.S. Army Sergeant, U.S. Army Reserve Chemical Corps, 2009–18; former Hazmat Technician and Emergency Response Team Member. ▪ Member: Disabled American Veterans; American Legion. ▪ Former Gibson Town Board Supervisor; former Green Bay City Council Member.

Legislature: Elected to Assembly since 2018. Committee assignments, 2021: Consumer Protection; Corrections; Criminal Justice and Public Safety; Judiciary; Regulatory Licensing Reform (chair); Sporting Heritage; Veterans and Military Affairs.

Contact: rep.sortwell@legis.wisconsin.gov; 608-266-9870; 888-534-0002 (toll free); Room 316 North, State Capitol, PO Box 8953, Madison, WI 53708.

Ron Tusler, Assembly District 3
Republican

Biography: Born Appleton, Wisconsin, March 21, 1984; married; 2 children. Voting address: Harrison, Wisconsin. ▪ Graduate Neenah High School, 2002; Degree in Urban Education, History, Honors from University of Wisconsin-Milwaukee, 2007; J.D. Marquette University Law School, 2010. ▪ Small business owner, law practice; attorney, private practice clients and Outagamie County Public Defender's Office; former attorney for Winnebago County District Attorney's Office and Outagamie County District Attorney's

Office; former student teacher, Milwaukee Public Schools.▪ Member: Appleton Area Jaycees (chair; president; treasurer); Heart of the Valley Chamber of Commerce; Republican Party of Outagamie County (chair; vice chair; communications director). ▪ Former Member: St. Thomas More Society (vice president); Native American Law Society (treasurer); Boy Scouts of America-Gathering Waters District (membership chair; executive officer).

Legislature: Elected to Assembly since 2016. Committee assignments, 2021: Campaigns and Elections; Environment (vice chair); Forestry, Parks and Outdoor Recreation; Insurance; Judiciary (chair); Sporting Heritage. Additional appointments: Commission on Uniform State Laws (chair).

Contact: rep.tusler@legis.wisconsin.gov; 608-266-5831; 888-534-0003 (toll free); 920-749-0400 (district); Room 22 West, State Capitol, PO Box 8953, Madison, WI 53708.

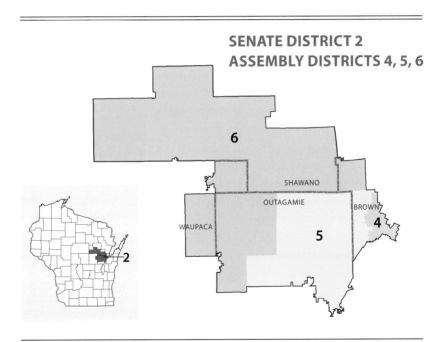

SENATE DISTRICT 2
ASSEMBLY DISTRICTS 4, 5, 6

Robert L. Cowles, Senate District 2
Republican

Biography: Born Green Bay, Wisconsin, July 31, 1950. Voting address: Green Bay, Wisconsin. ▪ B.S. University of Wisconsin-Green Bay, 1975; graduate work University of Wisconsin-Green Bay. ▪ Small business owner and legislator. Former director of an alternative energy division for a communications construction company. ▪ Member: Allouez Kiwanis; Friends of Whitefish Dunes State Park; Green Bay/

Brown County Professional Football Stadium District Board; National Caucus of Environmental Legislators; Salvation Army Volunteer; Trout Unlimited.

Legislature: Elected to Assembly 1982–86 (resigned 4/21/87). Elected to Senate in April 1987 special election. Reelected since 1988. Committee assignments, 2021: Natural Resources and Energy (chair); Transportation and Local Government (vice chair); Joint Legislative Audit Committee (cochair).

Contact: sen.cowles@legis.wisconsin.gov; 608-266-0484; 800-334-1465 (toll free); 920-448-5092 (district); Room 118 South, State Capitol, PO Box 7882, Madison, WI 53707-7882.

David Steffen, Assembly District 4
Republican

Biography: Born October 12, 1971; married; 1 child. Voting address: Howard, Wisconsin. ▪ Graduate Ashwaubenon High School, 1990; B.A. in Political Science, University of Wisconsin-Madison, 1995. ▪ Small business owner. ▪ Member: McPherson Eye Research Institute (advisory council member); U.S. Global Leadership Coalition (advisory council member); Howard Small Business Partnership (founder); Howard Go Green Save Green Initiative (founder, chair); Ashwaubenon Business Association (president); Prevent Blindness—Northeastern Wisconsin (president); Team Lambeau (executive director); Green Bay Area Chamber of Commerce State and Federal Issues Committee (chair). ▪ Village of Howard Board of Trustees, 2007–15; Brown County Board of Supervisors, 2012–15.

Legislature: Elected to Assembly since 2014. Committee assignments, 2021: Criminal Justice and Public Safety; Energy and Utilities (vice chair); Government Accountability and Oversight; Insurance (chair).

Contact: rep.steffen@legis.wisconsin.gov; 608-266-5840; 888-534-0004 (toll free); Room 323 North, State Capitol, PO Box 8953, Madison, WI 53708.

Jim Steineke, Assembly District 5
Republican

Biography: Born Milwaukee, Wisconsin, November 23, 1970; married; 3 children. Voting address: Kaukauna, Wisconsin. ▪ Graduate Wauwatosa West High School,

1989; attended University of Wisconsin-Milwaukee and University of Wisconsin-Oshkosh. ▪ Realtor; salesman. ▪ Member: Realtors Association of Northeast Wisconsin; Wisconsin Realtors Association. ▪ Town of Vandenbroek supervisor, 2005–07; town chair, 2007–11; Outagamie County supervisor, 2006–11.

Legislature: Elected to Assembly since 2010. Leadership positions: Majority Leader 2021, 2019, 2017, 2015; Assistant Majority Leader 2013. Committee assignments, 2021: Assembly Organization (vice chair); Employment Relations (vice chair); Rules (chair); Speaker's Task Force on Racial Disparities (cochair); Joint Committee on Employment Relations; Joint Committee on Legislative Organization; Joint Legislative Council.

Contact: rep.steineke@legis.wisconsin.gov; 608-266-2418; 888-534-0005 (toll free); Room 115 West, State Capitol, PO Box 8953, Madison, WI 53708.

Gary Tauchen, Assembly District 6
Republican

Biography: Born Rice Lake, Wisconsin, November 23, 1953; single. Voting address: Bonduel, Wisconsin. ▪ Graduate Bonduel High School, 1971; attended University of Wisconsin-Madison, 1971–72; B.S. in Animal Science, University of Wisconsin-River Falls, 1976. ▪ Dairy farmer. ▪ Member: Wisconsin Farm Bureau; Badger AgVest, LLC (former director); Professional  Dairy Producers of Wisconsin (former director); Dairy Business Association; Wisconsin Livestock Identification Consortium (former director, former chair); Brown, Shawano, Outagamie, Waupaca County Republican Party; Shawano Area Chamber of Commerce; Shawano County Dairy Promotions (former director); Cooperative Resources International (former vice chair); AgSource Cooperative Services (former chair); National Dairy Herd Improvement Association (former director); University of Wisconsin Center for Dairy Profitability (former chair); Shawano Rotary.

Legislature: Elected to Assembly since 2006. Leadership positions: Minority Caucus Sergeant at Arms 2009. Committee assignments, 2021: Agriculture (chair); Energy and Utilities; State Affairs; Tourism.

Contact: rep.tauchen@legis.wisconsin.gov; 608-266-3097; 888-529-0006 (toll free); Room 13 West, State Capitol, PO Box 8953, Madison, WI 53708.

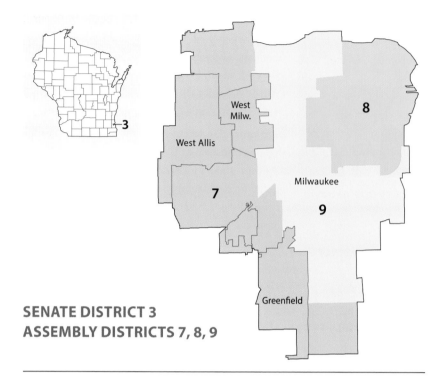

SENATE DISTRICT 3
ASSEMBLY DISTRICTS 7, 8, 9

Tim Carpenter, Senate District 3
Democrat

Biography: Born St. Francis Hospital, Milwaukee, Wisconsin; lifelong South Side resident. Voting address: Milwaukee, Wisconsin. ▪ Graduate Pulaski High School; B.A. in Political Science and History, University of Wisconsin-Milwaukee; M.A. in Public Policy and Public Administration, La Follette School of Public Affairs, University of Wisconsin-Madison; Milwaukee Police Department Citizen Academy, 2018. ▪ Full-time legislator. ▪ Member: Milwaukee Metropolitan Sewerage District Commission; Menominee Valley Partners; Friends of Hank Aaron State Trail; Friends of the Monarch Trail; Sierra Club; Jackson Park Neighborhood Association; Milwaukee VA Soldiers Home Advisory Council; Milwaukee LGBT Community Center; Wisconsin Humane Society. ▪ Recipient: Mothers Against Drunk Driving (MADD) *Legislator of the Year*; Wisconsin League of Conservation Voters *Conservation Champion*; several Wisconsin Environmental Decade *Clean 16* awards; Shepherd Express *Best State Legislator*; Wisconsin Public Health Association's *Champion of Public Health*;

Coalition of Wisconsin Aging Groups *Award for Service to Seniors*; Wisconsin Professional Fire Fighters *Legislator of the Year.*

Legislature: Elected to Assembly 1984–2000. Elected to Senate since 2002. Leadership positions: Senate President Pro Tempore, 2013, 2011; Assembly Speaker Pro Tempore, 1993–94. Committees assignments, 2021: Health; Transportation and Local Government; Veterans and Military Affairs and Constitution and Federalism; Joint Committee on Information Policy and Technology; Joint Legislative Audit Committee. Additional appointments: State Fair Park Board; Transportation Projects Commission; Wisconsin Economic Development Corporation Board.

Contact: sen.carpenter@legis.wisconsin.gov; 608-266-8535; Room 109 South, State Capitol, PO Box 7882, Madison, WI 53707.

Daniel G. Riemer, Assembly District 7
Democrat

Biography: Born Milwaukee, Wisconsin, December 10, 1986; married; 1 child. Voting address: Milwaukee, Wisconsin. ▪ Graduate Rufus King High School (Milwaukee), 2005; B.A. University of Chicago, 2009; J.D. University of Wisconsin Law School, 2013. ▪ Attorney. Captain, United States Army Reserve, Judge Advocate General's Corp. ▪ Member: Wisconsin State Bar Association; World Economic Forum: Global Shapers Alumni, Milwaukee Hub; Eisenhower Fellows; Milwaukee Jewish Federation—Weinstein Fellowship.

Legislature: Elected to Assembly since 2012. Committee assignments, 2021: Health; Insurance; Veterans and Military Affairs; Ways and Means.

Contact: rep.riemer@legis.wisconsin.gov; 608-266-1733; 888-529-0007 (toll free); Room 107 North, State Capitol, PO Box 8953, Madison, WI 53708.

Sylvia Ortiz-Velez, Assembly District 8
Democrat

Biography: Born Milwaukee, Wisconsin; widowed. Voting address: Milwaukee, Wisconsin. ▪ Graduate Bay View High School; B.A. in Political Science, University of Wisconsin-Milwaukee. ▪ Real estate broker.

Legislature: Elected to Assembly 2020. Committee assignments, 2021: Housing and Real Estate; Judiciary; Substance Abuse and Prevention; Transportation.

Contact: rep.ortiz-velez@legis.wisconsin.gov; 608-267-7669; 888-534-0008 (toll free); Room 11 North, State Capitol, PO Box 8953, Madison, 53708.

Marisabel Cabrera, Assembly District 9
Democrat

Biography: Born Milwaukee, Wisconsin, December 12, 1975; single. Voting address: Milwaukee, Wisconsin. ▪ Graduate Nathan Hale High School, 1993; B.A. in Spanish and Latin American Iberian Studies, University of Wisconsin-Madison, 1998; J.D. Michigan State University College of Law, 2002. ▪ Small business owner; immigration attorney. ▪ Member: Milwaukee Delegation of Democratic State Legislators (chair); National Hispanic Caucus of State Legislators (vice chair, Immigration Task Force); National Association of Elected and Appointed Officials; Voces de la Frontera; Democratic Party of Wisconsin; Democratic Party of Milwaukee County; State Bar of Wisconsin; State Bar of Florida. ▪ Former member: City of Milwaukee Fire and Police Commission (chair); Centro Hispano of Milwaukee Board of Directors; Latino Caucus of the Democratic Party of Wisconsin (chair). ▪ Recipient: Madison365 *Wisconsin's Most Powerful Latinos* 2018; Citizen Action of Wisconsin *Community Champion Award* 2018; Democratic Party of Milwaukee County's Rising Star 2016.

Legislature: Elected to Assembly since 2018. Committee assignments, 2021: Constitution and Ethics; Consumer Protection; Judiciary; Public Benefit Reform. Additional appointments: Women's Council.

Contact: rep.cabrera@legis.wisconsin.gov; 608-266-1707; 888-534-0009 (toll free); Room 16 West, State Capitol, PO Box 8952, Madison, WI 53708.

SENATE DISTRICT 4
ASSEMBLY DISTRICTS 10, 11, 12

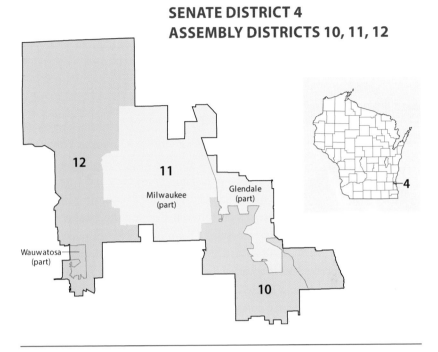

Lena C. Taylor, Senate District 4
Democrat

Biography: Born Milwaukee, Wisconsin, July 25, 1966; 1 child. Voting address: Milwaukee, Wisconsin. ▪ Graduate Rufus King High School (Milwaukee), 1984; B.A. in English, University of Wisconsin-Milwaukee, 1990; J.D. Southern Illinois University-Carbondale, 1993. ▪ Practicing Wisconsin attorney 1993–present; founding partner, Taylor & Associates Law Office, 1996–present. ▪ Member: Alpha Kappa Alpha Sorority Incorporated (former Wisconsin State Connection Coordinator); National Organization of Black Elected Legislative Women (Midwest Director); National Black Caucus of State Legislators (Midwest Director); NAACP (election chair).

Legislature: Elected to Assembly in April 2003 special election. Elected to Senate since 2004. Committee assignments, 2021: Agriculture and Tourism; Insurance, Licensing and Forestry; Judiciary and Public Safety; Joint Review Committee on Criminal Penalties; Joint Survey Committee on Tax Exemptions. Additional appointments: Commission on Uniform State Laws; Wisconsin Historical Society Board of Curators.

Contact: sen.taylor@legis.wisconsin.gov; Facebook: Senator Lena Taylor; Twitter: @sentaylor; 608-266-5810; 414-342-7176 (district); Room 5 South, State Capitol, PO Box 7882, Madison, WI 53707-7882.

David Bowen, Assembly District 10
Democrat

Biography: Born Milwaukee, Wisconsin, January 28, 1987; married. Voting address: Milwaukee, Wisconsin. ▪ Graduate MPS Bradley Technology High School, 2005; Scholar of Education Policy and Community Studies at the University of Wisconsin-Milwaukee. ▪ Member: Outreach Community Health Centers (board member); Beyond the Bell Milwaukee (steering committee); Black Youth Project 100; African American Breastfeeding Network (advisory board); State Innovation Exchange; People for the American Way Foundation (board); Young Elected Officials Network; National Black Caucus of State Legislators; National Conference of State Legislatures; Black Millennial Political Convention. ▪ Former member: American Legacy Foundation Activism Fellow; Democratic Party of Wisconsin (vice chair); Association of State Democratic Chairs (Midwest Caucus vice chair); Democratic National Committee State Leader (Super Delegate); Milwaukee County Juvenile Detention Alternative Initiative Advisory Committee. ▪ Recipient: Public Allies Alumni of the Year *Change Maker Award* 2013; Community Action Program Executive *Champion Against Poverty*; Young Elected Officials Network *Leader of the Year—Public Service Leadership Award*; Amani Neighborhood Award; Northwest Side CDC *Unsung Hero Award* 2014; Safe and Sound Borchert Field C.A.R.E.S. *Certificate for Outstanding Community Building Advocate*; Conservation Champion Award 2017–18, 2015–16. ▪ Milwaukee County Board of Supervisors, 2012–14.

Legislature: Elected to Assembly since 2014. Committee Assignments, 2021: Children and Families; Corrections; Criminal Justice and Public Safety; Jobs and the Economy.

Contact: rep.bowen@legis.wisconsin.gov; 608-266-7671; 888-534-0010 (toll free); Room 126 North, State Capitol, PO Box 8952, Madison, WI 53708.

Dora Drake, Assembly District 11
Democrat

Biography: Born Milwaukee, Wisconsin. ▪ Graduate: Eastbrook Academy (Milwaukee), 2011; B.A. Marquette University, 2015. ▪ Trauma-informed response

facilitator for criminal justice professionals; sales representative at Marcus Performing Arts Center. Former service coordinator, campaign manager, and pretrial case manager. ▪ Member: Young Democrats of Wisconsin; Emerge Wisconsin, Class of 2020. ▪ Former member: Wisconsin Delegate for Young Democrats of America; National Society of Black Engineers.

Legislature: Elected to Assembly 2020. Committee assignments, 2021: Criminal Justice and Public Safety; Family Law; Government Accountability and Oversight; Workforce Development.

Contact: rep.drake@legis.wisconsin.gov; 608-266-3756; 888-534-0011 (toll free); Room 19 North, State Capitol, PO Box 8952, Madison, WI 53708.

LaKeshia N. Myers, Assembly District 12
Democrat

Biography: Born Milwaukee, Wisconsin, May 21, 1984; single. Voting address: Milwaukee, Wisconsin. ▪ Graduate Rufus King High School, 2002; B.A. in Political Science, Alcorn State University, 2006; M.Ed. Strayer University, 2009; Ed.D. Argosy University, 2016. ▪ Educator; small business owner. Former subcommittee clerk, U.S. House of Representatives; former legislative aide, Wisconsin State Senate. ▪ Member: Alcorn State University National Alumni Association (Milwaukee Chapter vice president); Alpha Kappa Alpha Sorority, Inc.; Democratic Party of Wisconsin; Historically Black College/University Alumni United (president); Milwaukee Metropolitan Alliance of Black School Educators; National Education Association (NEA); NAACP; Wisconsin African American Chamber of Commerce. ▪ Former member: College Democrats of America (national membership director, 2005–06); Phi Delta Kappa International; National Council of Negro Women.

Legislature: Elected to Assembly since 2018. Committee assignments, 2021: Agriculture; Education; Public Benefit Reform; Tourism.

Contact: rep.myers@legis.wisconsin.gov; 608-266-5813; 888-534-0012 (toll free); 262-297-3291 (district); Room 3 North, State Capitol, PO Box 8953, Madison, WI 53708.

SENATE DISTRICT 5
ASSEMBLY DISTRICTS 13, 14, 15

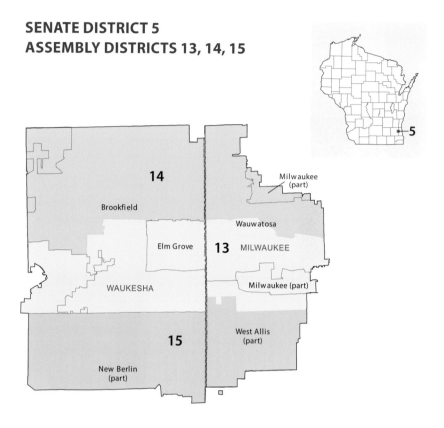

Dale Kooyenga, Senate District 5
Republican

Biography: Born Oak Lawn, Illinois, February 12, 1979; married; 4 children. Voting address: Brookfield, Wisconsin. ▪ Graduate Chicago Christian High School, 1997; A.A. Moraine Valley Community College, 2000; B.A. Lakeland College, 2000; M.B.A., Marquette University, 2007. ▪ Certified public accountant. Member U.S. Army Reserve, 2005–present. Iraq War veteran. ▪ Member: American Legion; American Institute of Certified Public Accountants; Wisconsin Institute of Certified Public Accountants.

Legislature: Elected to Assembly 2010–16. Elected to Senate since 2018. Committee assignments, 2021: Finance; Financial Institutions and Revenue (chair); Health (vice chair); Joint Committee on Finance; Joint Legislative Audit Committee. Additional appointments, 2021: State Capitol and Executive Residence Board.

Contact: sen.kooyenga@legis.wisconsin.gov; 608-266-2512; 866-817-6061 (toll free); Room 310 South, State Capitol, PO Box 7882, Madison, WI 53707.

Sara Rodriguez, Assembly District 13
Democrat

Biography: Born Milwaukee, Wisconsin, July 25, 1975; married; 2 children. Voting address: Brookfield, Wisconsin. ▪ Graduate Brookfield East High School, 1993; B.A. in Neuroscience, Illinois Wesleyan University, 1997; B.S. in Nursing, Johns Hopkins University, 2002; M.P.H and M.S. in Nursing, Johns Hopkins University, 2003. ▪ Owner, health care consulting company. Former healthcare executive for health care systems, health technology firms, and public health departments; Epidemic Intelligence Service Officer for the Centers for Disease Control and Prevention; Registered Nurse; Peace Corps Volunteer.

Legislature: Elected to Assembly 2020. Committee assignments, 2021: Energy and Utilities; Health; Insurance; Science, Technology and Broadband.

Contact: rep.srodriguez@legis.wisconsin.gov; 608-267-9836; 888-534-0013 (toll free); Room 4 West, State Capitol, PO Box 8953, Madison, WI 53708.

Robyn Dorianne Beckley Vining, Assembly District 14
Democrat

Biography: Born Wright Patterson Air Force Base, Ohio, November 11, 1976; married; 2 children. Voting address: Wauwatosa, Wisconsin. ▪ Attended Westlake High School, Austin, Texas; graduated James Madison High School, Vienna, Virginia, 1995; B.A. in Psychology and B.A. in Studio Art, James Madison University, 1999; M.A. in Religion, Trinity Evangelical Divinity School, 2002. ▪ Current small business owner and photographer. Former pastor; church planter; youth minister. ▪ Member: Wisconsin Legislative Children's

Caucus; cofounder of organization that combats child sex trafficking.

Legislature: Elected to Assembly since 2018. Committee assignments, 2021: Children and Families; Health; Mental Health; Small Business Development. Additional appointments: State Fair Park Board.

Contact: rep.vining@legis.wisconsin.gov; 608-266-9180; 888-534-0014 (toll free); Room 306 West, State Capitol, PO Box 8953, Madison, WI 53708.

Joe Sanfelippo, Assembly District 15
Republican

Biography: Born Milwaukee, Wisconsin, February 26, 1964; married; 3 children. Voting address: New Berlin, Wisconsin. ▪ Graduate Thomas More High School, 1982; attended Marquette University, 1982–84. ▪ Small businessman; currently operates a small Christmas tree farm, sod farm, and farm market. ▪ Member: St. John the Evangelist Parish, Greenfield. ▪ Milwaukee County Board of Supervisors, 2008–12.

Legislature: Elected to Assembly since 2012. Committee assignments, 2021: Campaigns and Elections (vice chair); Health (chair); Transportation.

Contact: rep.sanfelippo@legis.wisconsin.gov; 608-266-0620; 888-534-0015 (toll free); Room 314 North, State Capitol, PO Box 8953, Madison, WI 53708.

SENATE DISTRICT 6
ASSEMBLY DISTRICTS 16, 17, 18

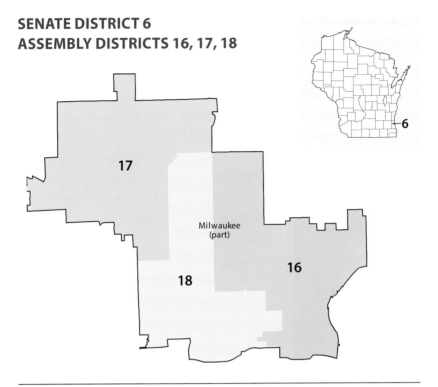

LaTonya Johnson, Senate District 6
Democrat

Biography: Born Somerville, Tennessee, June 22; 1 child. Voting address: Milwaukee, Wisconsin. ▪ Graduate Bay View High School, 1990; B.S. in Criminal Justice, Tennessee State University, 1997; attended University of Wisconsin-Milwaukee, 1990–92. ▪ Full-time legislator. Former family child care provider and owner, 2002–12; insurance agent, 2000–02; financial employment planner, 1997–2000. ▪ Member: American Federation of State, County and Municipal Employees (AFSCME) Wisconsin Child Care Providers Together Local 502 (former president); AFSCME District Council 32 (former vice president); AFSCME People; Emerge Wisconsin, Class of 2012; Coalition of Black Trade Unionists (CBTU); Milwaukee Democratic Legislative Caucus (former chair); Wisconsin Legislative Black Caucus; Wisconsin Center District (board member) Wisconsin Child Welfare Partnership Council; University of Wisconsin Population Health Institute (advisory board member); Midwestern Legislative Conference (executive committee member); Wisconsin Legislative

Children's Caucus (cochair); BLOC (Black Leaders Organizing for Communities) cofounder. ▪ Former Member: African American Chamber of Commerce; Wisconsin Women in Government (former board member).

Legislature: Elected to Assembly 2012 and 2014. Elected to Senate since 2016. Committee assignments, 2021: Education; Finance; Housing, Commerce and Trade; Human Services, Children and Families; Labor and Regulatory Reform; Joint Committee on Finance; Joint Legislative Council.

Contact: sen.johnson@legis.wisconsin.gov; 608-266-2500; 877-474-2000 (toll free); 414-313-1241 (district); Room 106 South, State Capitol, PO Box 7882, Madison, WI 53707-7882.

Kalan Haywood, Assembly District 16
Democrat

Biography: Born Milwaukee, Wisconsin, June 5, 1999; single. Voting address: Milwaukee, Wisconsin. ▪ Graduate Rufus King International Baccalaureate High School, 2017; B.A. in Business Administration, Cardinal Stritch University, 2017–present. ▪ Full-time legislator. Former nonprofit consultant. ▪ Member: City of Milwaukee Restorative Justice Advisory Committee (chair); BlackCEO Milwaukee Chapter (vice president); Determined Young Investors (president). ▪ Former member: City of Milwaukee Youth Council (president).

Legislature: Elected to Assembly since 2018. Committee assignments, 2021: Housing and Real Estate; Small Business Development; Speaker's Task Force on Racial Disparities; Tourism. Additional appointments: Wisconsin Center District Board; Wisconsin Housing and Economic Development Authority.

Contact: rep.haywood@legis.wisconsin.gov; 608-266-3786; 888-534-0016 (toll free); 608-266-3487 (district); Room 5 North, State Capitol, PO Box 8952, Madison, WI 53708.

Supreme Moore Omokunde, Assembly District 17
Democrat

Biography: Born Milwaukee, Wisconsin, August 22, 1979; single. Voting address: Milwaukee, Wisconsin. ▪ Graduate Riverside University High School (Milwaukee), 1997; attended Marquette University, 1997–2000, and the University of Wisconsin-Milwaukee. ▪ Full-time legislator. Former youth worker, Boys and Girls Club and YMCA; community organizer, Sherman Park Community Association; health care organizer, Citizen Action of Wisconsin. ▪ Member: Milwaukee

City County Task Force on Climate and Economic Equity (cocreator); Democratic Party of Wisconsin; Citizen Action Wisconsin (board member). ▪ Former member: Milwaukee Public Museum Board of Directors; Milwaukee County Human Rights Commission (workgroup member); Public Allies Milwaukee; TRUE Skool Board; 2016 Democratic National Convention (delegate for Bernie Sanders). ▪ Milwaukee County Board of Supervisors, 2015–20 (chair of Committee on Health and Human Needs and member finance committees).

Legislature: Elected to Assembly 2020. Committee assignments, 2021: Energy and Utilities; Mental Health; Regulatory Licensing Reform; Transportation.

Contact: rep.mooreomokunde@legis.wisconsin.gov; 608-266-5580; 888-534-0017 (toll free); Room 8 North, State Capitol, PO Box 8953, Madison, WI 53708

Evan Goyke, Assembly District 18
Democrat

Biography: Born Neenah, Wisconsin, November 24, 1982; married; 1 child. Voting address: Milwaukee, Wisconsin. ▪ Graduate Edgewood High School (Madison), 2001; B.A. in Political Science, St. John's University (Minnesota), 2005; J.D. Marquette University Law School, 2009. ▪ Attorney. Former state public defender. ▪ Member: Historic Concordia Neighborhood Association (board member); Progressive Community Health Center (former board member); State Bar of Wisconsin; Eagle Scout, Boy Scouts of America; Milwaukee Democratic Delegation (former chair); Milwaukee Young Lawyers Association (former board member). ▪ Former member: American Federation of Teachers Local 4822.

Legislature: Elected to Assembly since 2012. Committee assignments, 2021: Corrections; Finance; Joint Committee on Finance; Joint Legislative Council; Joint Review Committee on Criminal Penalties; Joint Survey Committee on Tax Exemptions.

Contact: rep.goyke@legis.wisconsin.gov; 608-266-0645; 888-534-0018 (toll free); Room 112 North, State Capitol, PO Box 8952, Madison, WI 53708.

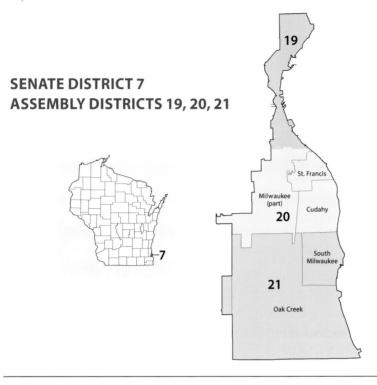

**SENATE DISTRICT 7
ASSEMBLY DISTRICTS 19, 20, 21**

Chris Larson, Senate District 7
Democrat

Biography: Born Milwaukee County, Wisconsin, November 12, 1980; married; 2 children. Voting address: Milwaukee, Wisconsin. ▪ Graduate Thomas More High School, 1999; degree in Finance, University of Wisconsin-Milwaukee, 2007. ▪ Full-time legislator. Former business manager. ▪ Member: ACLU; University of Wisconsin-Milwaukee Alumni Association; League of Conservation Voters; Bay View Neighborhood Association; Planned Parenthood Advocates of Wisconsin; Sierra Club; Humboldt Park Friends; South Side Business Club of Milwaukee; Bay View Historical Society; Arbor Day Foundation; TriWisconsin; Badgerland Striders; Bay View Lions Club; Lake Park Friends; MPTV Friends. ▪ Former member: Airport Area Economic Development Group; Young Elected Officials; Coalition to Save the Hoan Bridge (cofounder); Wisconsin Public Interest Research Group (WISPIRG) campus intern. ▪ Recipient: Wisconsin Conservation Voters *Conservation Champion* award, 2015–16; Shepherd Express *Legislator of the Year Award*, 2019; Mothers Against Drunk Driving *Legislator of the Year Award*, 2019; Wisconsin Freedom of Information Council

Political Openness Award, 2019; Shepherd Express *Legislator of the Year Award*, 2020, 2019. ▪ Milwaukee County Board of Supervisors, 2008–10.

Legislature: Elected to Senate since 2010. Leadership positions: Minority Leader 2013. Committee assignments, 2021: Administrative Rules; Education; Universities and Technical Colleges; Joint Committee for Review of Administrative Rules; Joint Committee on Information Policy and Technology; Joint Survey Committee on Retirement Systems.

Contact: sen.larson@legis.wisconsin.gov; 608-266-7505; 800-361-5487 (toll free); Room 20 South, State Capitol, PO Box 7882, Madison, WI 53707-7882.

Jonathan Brostoff, Assembly District 19
Democrat

Biography: Born September 25, 1983; married; 2 children. Voting address: Milwaukee, Wisconsin. ▪ B.A. in Political Science, University of Wisconsin-Milwaukee, 2011. ▪ Full-time legislator. Former district director for Senator Larson; backup shift supervisor, Pathfinders; program director, Social Development Commission Family Support Center; public ally, AmeriCorps; volunteer, Street Beat, Big Brothers Big Sisters, Casa Maria. ▪ Member: Bay View Neighborhood Association; Historic Water Tower Neighborhood Association; Planned Parenthood; Urban Ecology Center; Voces de la Frontera. ▪ Former board member: ACLU-Wisconsin; Tikkun Ha-Ir; Democratic Party of Milwaukee County; America's Black Holocaust Museum.

Legislature: Elected to Assembly since 2014. Committee assignments, 2021: Aging and Long-Term Care; Financial Institutions; Mental Health; Regulatory Licensing Reform.

Contact: rep.brostoff@legis.wisconsin.gov; 608-266-0650; 888-534-0019 (toll free); Room 15 North, State Capitol, PO Box 8952, Madison, WI 53708.

Christine Sinicki, Assembly District 20
Democrat

Biography: Born Milwaukee, Wisconsin, March 28, 1960; married; 2 children. Voting address: Milwaukee, Wisconsin. ▪ Graduate Bay View High School; Bow-hay Institute Fellow, La Follette School, University of Wisconsin-Madison, 2001; Flemming Fellow, Center for Policy Alternatives, 2003. ▪ Former small business manager. ▪ Member: Heroes for Healthcare (planning member); Respite Care Association of Wisconsin (board member); American Council of Young Political Leaders (Delegate

to Israel and Palestine, 2001); Milwaukee Committee on Domestic Violence and Sexual Assault; Major, Wisconsin Wing, Civil Air Patrol Legislative Squadron (official Auxiliary of the U.S. Air Force); Milwaukee City Council Parents and Teachers Association; Bay View Historical Society; Bay View Neighborhood Association; State Assembly Milwaukee Caucus (chair 2005, 2003). ▪ Former member: Delegate to U.S. President Electoral College, 2000; State Minimum Wage Council (governor's appointee), 2005; Assembly Democratic Task Force on Working Families (chair), 2003; State Committee to Celebrate the Centennial Anniversary of Wisconsin's Ratification (member), 2019. ▪ Recipient: Wisconsin Environmental Decade *Clean 16* 2000; Wisconsin Ob/Gyn Physicians *Legislator of the Year* 2000; Wisconsin Coalition Against Domestic Violence *DV Diva* 2003; Wisconsin Department of Veterans Affairs *Certificates of Commendation* 2006, 2005; Wisconsin League of Conservation Voters *Conservation Champion* 2019, 2017, 2015, 2013, 2011, 2009, 2007; Wisconsin Women's Alliance Legislation Award 2009–10; Professional Firefighters of Wisconsin *Legislator of the Year* 2010; Wisconsin Grocers Association *Friend of Grocers* 2010; Cudahy Veterans' *Service Award* 2010; AMVETS State Legislative *Advocacy Award* 2011; Mothers Against Drunk Driving *Legislator of the Year* 2018. ▪ Milwaukee School Board, 1991–98.

Legislature: Elected to Assembly since 1998. Leadership positions: Minority Caucus Sergeant at Arms 2019, 2017; Minority Caucus Secretary 2001. Committee assignments, 2021: Forestry, Parks and Outdoor Recreation; Labor and Integrated Employment; State Affairs; Veterans and Military Affairs; Workforce Development.

Contact: rep.sinicki@legis.wisconsin.gov; 608-266-8588; 888-534-0020 (toll free); Room 114 North, State Capitol, PO Box 8953, Madison, WI 53708.

Jessie Rodriguez, Assembly District 21
Republican

Biography: Born Puerto el Triunfo, El Salvador, July 5, 1977; married. Voting address: Oak Creek, Wisconsin. ▪ Graduate Alexander Hamilton High School (Milwaukee), 1996; B.A. Marquette University, 2002. ▪ Full-time legislator. Former analyst for a supermarket company; outreach coordinator for a nonprofit. ▪ Member: Wisconsin Wing, Civil Air Patrol Legislative Squadron (official Auxiliary of the U.S. Air Force).

Legislature: Elected to Assembly in November 2013 special election. Reelected since 2014. Leadership positions: Majority Caucus Secretary 2019, 2017, 2015. Committee assignments, 2021: Finance; Joint Committee on Finance.

Contact: rep.rodriguez@legis.wisconsin.gov; 608-266-0610; 888-534-0021 (toll free); Room 321 East, State Capitol, PO Box 8953, Madison, WI 53708.

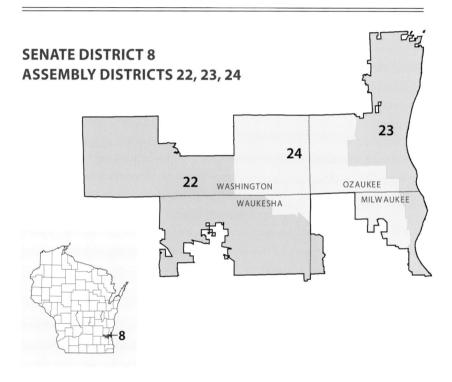

SENATE DISTRICT 8
ASSEMBLY DISTRICTS 22, 23, 24

Alberta Darling, Senate District 8
Republican

Biography: Born Hammond, Indiana, April 28; widowed; 2 children, 3 grandchildren. Voting address: River Hills, Wisconsin. ▪ Graduate University of Wisconsin-Madison; postgraduate work University of Wisconsin-Milwaukee. ▪ Former teacher and marketing director. ▪ Member: North Shore Rotary; College Savings Program Board (EdVest); Junior League of Milwaukee (former president); Wisconsin Children's Caucus (cofounder); Milwaukee Child Welfare Partnership Council; National Conference of State

Legislatures (NCSL) Task Force of State and Local Taxation; Fostering Futures Policy Advisory Council. ▪ Former member: Next Door Foundation; Public Policy Forum; Wisconsin Strategic Planning Council for Economic Development; Greater Milwaukee Committee; Goals for Greater Milwaukee 2000 Project (executive committee); United Way Board (chair, allocations committee); TEMPO Milwaukee, professional women's organization; Future Milwaukee (president); Milwaukee Forum; Children's Service Society of Wisconsin (board of directors); American Red Cross of Wisconsin (executive committee, board of directors); League of Women Voters; Today's Girl Tomorrow's Woman; Boys & Girls Club; NCSL Education Committee (chair); YMCA (board member). ▪ Recipient: Shining Star of Education Reform; Waterford Institute *Champion of Early Learning*; Wisconsin Academy of Family Physicians *Friend of Family Medicine*; Hispanic Chamber of Commerce *Government Advocates Award*; Greater Milwaukee Committee *Leadership Award*; Leukemia and Lymphoma Society *Legislative Leadership Award*; Wisconsin Manufacturers and Commerce *Working for Wisconsin*; American Conservative Union Foundation *Defender of Liberty Award*; *Iron Lady Award, Margaret Thatcher Award*; Coalition of Wisconsin Aging Groups *Tommy G. Thompson Award for Service*; *Wisconsin Charter Champion Award*; National MS Hall of Fame Inductee; American Cancer Society *Legislative Champion*; Fair Air Coalition *Friend of Education*; Metropolitan Milwaukee Association of Commerce *Champion of Commerce*; Wisconsin Head Start Directors Association *Award of Excellence*; National Association of Community Leadership *Leadership Award*; United Way *Gwen Jackson Leadership Award*; St. Francis Children's Center *Children Service Award*.

Legislature: Elected to Assembly in May 1990 special election. Reelected November 1990. Elected to Senate since 1992. Committee assignments, 2021: Education (chair); Elections, Election Process Reform and Ethics (vice chair); Judiciary and Public Safety; Universities and Technical Colleges; Joint Legislative Council; Joint Survey Committee on Retirement Systems. Additional appointments: Wisconsin Center District Board; Milwaukee Child Welfare Partnership Council; State Fair Park Board.

Contact: sen.darling@legis.wisconsin.gov; 608-266-5830; Room 122 South, State Capitol, PO Box 7882, Madison, WI 53707-7882.

Janel Brandtjen, Assembly District 22
Republican

Biography: Born Milwaukee, Wisconsin, March 27; married; 2 children. Voting address: Menomonee Falls, Wisconsin. ▪ Graduate Marshall High School; B.B.A.

in Finance and Marketing, University of Wisconsin-Milwaukee, 1988. ▪ Business owner. ▪ Member: Republican Party of Waukesha, Washington, and Milwaukee Counties; Republican Women of Waukesha, Washington, and Milwaukee Counties; NRA (life member); Immanuel Lutheran Church. ▪ Recipient: *Wisconsin Pro-Life Legislator of the Year* 2016; Wisconsin Family Action *Friend of Family, Life and Liberty* 2016; Associated Builders and Contractors *Building Wisconsin Award* 2020, 2018, 2016; Metropolitan Milwaukee Association of Commerce *Champion of Commerce* 2017–18, 2015–16; Wisconsin Dental Association *Dental Academy Award* 2019, 2017, 2015; Wisconsin Manufacturers and Commerce *Working for Wisconsin Award* 2017–18, 2015–16; ABATE of Wisconsin award for outstanding support of motorcyclists, 2018. ▪ Waukesha County supervisor, 2008–16.

Legislature: Elected to Assembly since 2014. Committee assignments, 2021: Campaigns and Elections (chair); Corrections; Government Accountability and Oversight (vice chair); Public Benefit Reform; Science, Technology and Broadband.

Contact: rep.brandtjen@legis.wisconsin.gov; 608-267-2367; 888-534-0022 (toll free); Room 12 West, State Capitol, PO Box 8952, Madison, WI 53708.

Deb Andraca, Assembly District 23
Democrat

Biography: Born Springfield, Massachusetts, April 10, 1970; married; 2 children. Voting address: Whitefish Bay, Wisconsin. ▪ Graduate B.A. Political Science and Public Relations, Syracuse University, 1992; M.A. Political Management, George Washington University, 1996; completed teacher licensure program at Alverno College, 2018. ▪ Substitute teacher. Former summer school math teacher, Bruce Guadalupe Community School; substitute teacher, Whitefish Bay School District; communications director and lobbyist, Environmental Law and Policy Center of the Midwest; vice-president, FleishmanHillard International Communications; executive assistant, Solar Energy Industries Association. ▪ Former member: Cumberland Elementary School PTO (president); Advocates for Education of Whitefish Bay (board member); Girl Scout Leader troops 1586 and 1305; Urban Ecology Center (fundraiser chair).

Legislature: Elected to Assembly 2020. Committee assignments, 2021: Energy and

Utilities; Forestry, Parks and Outdoor Recreation; Small Business Development; Workforce Development.

Contact: rep.andraca@legis.wisconsin.gov; 608-266-0486; 888-534-0023 (toll free); Room 21 North, State Capitol, PO Box 8953, Madison, WI 53708-8953.

Dan Knodl, Assembly District 24
Republican

Biography: Born Milwaukee, Wisconsin, December 14, 1958; 4 children, 4 grandchildren. Voting address: Germantown, Wisconsin. ▪ Graduate Menomonee Falls East High School, 1977; attended University of Wisconsin-Madison. ▪ Resort owner. ▪ Member: Ozaukee Washington Land Trust; Pike Lake Sportsmen's Club; Pike Lake Protection District (member 2000–present, secretary 2010–17, chair, 2017–19); Menomonee Falls Optimist Club; Knights of Columbus; St. Boniface Parish. ▪ Washington County Board, 2006–08.

Legislature: Elected to Assembly since 2008. Leadership positions: Majority Caucus Chair 2019, 2017. Assistant Majority Leader 2015, 2011. Committee assignments, 2021: Government Accountability and Oversight (chair); Labor and Integrated Employment; Regulatory Licensing Reform; Science, Technology and Broadband; State Affairs; Ways and Means; Joint Committee on Information Policy and Technology.

Contact: rep.knodl@legis.wisconsin.gov; 608-237-9124; 888-529-0024 (toll free); Room 218 North, State Capitol, PO Box 8952, Madison, WI 53708.

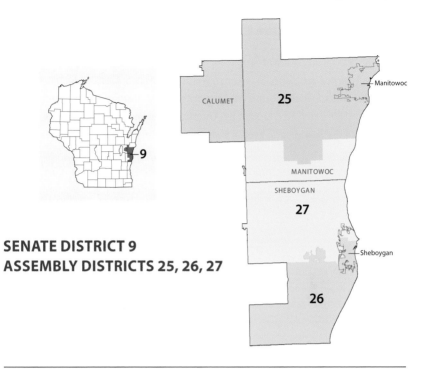

SENATE DISTRICT 9
ASSEMBLY DISTRICTS 25, 26, 27

Devin LeMahieu, Senate District 9
Republican

Biography: Born Sheboygan, Wisconsin, August 8, 1972; single. Voting address: Oostburg, Wisconsin. ▪ Graduate Sheboygan County Christian High School, 1991; B.A. in Business Administration and Political Science, Dordt College (Sioux Center, Iowa), 1995. ▪ Publisher/owner, Lakeshore Weekly. ▪ Member: Oostburg Chamber of Commerce; Sheboygan County Chamber of Commerce; Manitowoc County Chamber of Commerce; Bethel Orthodox Presbyterian Church (deacon); NRA (life member). ▪ Recipient: Wisconsin Wildlife Association *State Conservation Legislator of the Year*, 2015; League of Wisconsin Municipalities *Strong Municipal Supporter*, 2016; Wisconsin Cemetery and Cremation Association *Legislator of the Year*, 2016; Wisconsin Builders Association *Friend of Housing*, 2016; Wisconsin Academy of Family Physicians *Friend of Family Medicine*, 2016; Wisconsin Coalition for International Adoption *Friend of International Adoption*, 2016; Metropolitan Milwaukee Association of Commerce *Champion of Commerce*, 2017–18; Dairy Business Association *Legislative Excellence Award*, 2017–18; Wisconsin Nurses Association *Friend of*

Nursing Award, 2018; *Reining in Government Award*, 2018; Wisconsin Counties Association *Outstanding Legislator Award*, 2020, 2018, 2016; ABC of Wisconsin *Building Wisconsin Award*, 2020, 2018; Wisconsin Grocers Association *Friend of Grocers Award*, 2020, 2016; Wisconsin Manufacturers & Commerce *Working for Wisconsin Award*, 2020, 2018; The American Association of Nurse Practitioners *State Award for Excellence*, 2020; The American Legion, Department of Wisconsin *Legislator of the Year Award*, 2021. ▪ Sheboygan County Board supervisor, 2006–15, Human Resources Committee, 2006–15 (chair, 2010–14), Finance Committee, 2012–15, Executive Committee, 2010–12.

Legislature: Elected to Senate since 2014. Leadership positions: Majority Leader 2021. Committee assignments, 2021: Senate Organization (chair); Joint Committee on Employment Relations; Joint Committee on Legislative Organization; Joint Legislative Council. Additional appointments: Wisconsin Aerospace Authority Board.

Contact: sen.lemahieu@legis.wisconsin.gov; senatordevin.com; Facebook: Senator Devin LeMahieu; Twitter: @senatordevin; 608-266-2056; 888-295-8750 (toll free); Room 211 South, State Capitol, PO Box 7882, Madison, WI 53707-7882.

Paul Tittl, Assembly District 25
Republican

Biography: Born Delavan, Wisconsin, November 23, 1961; married; 2 children, 3 grandchildren. Voting address: Manitowoc, Wisconsin. ▪ Graduate Lincoln High (Manitowoc), 1980. ▪ Owner, vacuum and sewing center. ▪ Member: Faith Church Manitowoc (deacon); Lions Club of Manitowoc; NRA. ▪ Former member: Eagles Manitowoc; Manitowoc County Home Builders Association; Economic Development Corporation; Wastewater Treatment Facility Board; Manitowoc Crime Prevention Committee; Community Development Authority; Safety Traffic and Parking Commission; Wisconsin Utility Tax Association, 2009–13; Wisconsin Counties Association (WCA) Taxation and Finance Steering Committee, 2010–13; WCA Judicial and Public Safety Steering Committee, 2010–13. ▪ Manitowoc City Council, 2004–08 (president 2006–07); Manitowoc County Board of Supervisors, 2006–13 (chair 2010–12).

Legislature: Elected to Assembly since 2012. Committee assignments, 2021: Corrections; Forestry, Parks and Outdoor Recreation; Jobs and the Economy; Mental Health (chair); Rules; Sporting Heritage (vice chair); Tourism; Veterans and Military Affairs.

Contact: rep.tittl@legis.wisconsin.gov; 608-266-0315; 888-529-0025 (toll free); Room 219 North, State Capitol, PO Box 8953, Madison, WI 53708.

Terry Katsma, Assembly District 26
Republican

Biography: Born Sheboygan, Wisconsin, April 23, 1958; married; 3 children, 6 grandchildren. Voting address: Oostburg, Wisconsin. ▪ Graduate Sheboygan County Christian High School, 1976; B.A. in Business Administration, Dordt College (Sioux Center, Iowa), 1980; M.B.A. Marquette University, 1985. ▪ Full-time legislator. Former community bank president and CEO. ▪ Member: Oostburg State Bank Board of Directors (former president and CEO); Oostburg Chamber of Commerce (former president-elect); Oostburg Christian Reformed Church (elder); Random Lake Area Chamber of Commerce; Republican Party of Sheboygan County; NRA; Sheboygan County Chamber of Commerce; YMCA of Sheboygan County Board of Managers. ▪ Former member: Trinity Christian College Board of Trustees (Palos Heights, Illinois—treasurer); Dordt College Board of Trustees (vice chair); Sheboygan County Christian High School (board president); Oostburg Christian School Board (secretary); Oostburg Community Education Foundation; Oostburg Kiwanis Club (president); Workbound, Inc. (president).

Legislature: Elected to Assembly since 2014. Committee assignments, 2021: Finance; Financial Institutions (vice chair); Joint Committee on Finance. Additional appointments: Claims Board.

Contact: rep.katsma@legis.wisconsin.gov; 608-266-0656; 888-529-0026 (toll free); Room 306 East, State Capitol, PO Box 8952, Madison, WI 53708.

Tyler Vorpagel, Assembly District 27
Republican

Biography: Born Plymouth, Wisconsin, March 24, 1985; married; 1 child. Voting address: Plymouth, Wisconsin. ▪ Graduate Plymouth High School, 2003; B.A. in Political Science and B.S. in Public Administration, University of Wisconsin-Green Bay, 2007; completed 2016 Emerging Leader Program at University of Virginia Darden School of Business. ▪ Full-time legislator. Former district director, Congressman Tom Petri. ▪ Member: Plymouth Lions Club;

Sheboygan County Youth Apprenticeship Grant Advisory Committee; Sheboygan Elks #299; National Association of Parliamentarians; National Conference of State Legislatures (state chair); Republican Party of Sheboygan County (former member of executive committee); 6th District Republican Party (former vice chair); Republican Party of Wisconsin (former member of executive committee); Major, Wisconsin Wing, Civil Air Patrol Legislative Squadron (official Auxiliary of the U.S. Air Force). ▪ Former member: Plymouth Rotary; Exchange Club (president).

Legislature: Elected to Assembly since 2014. Committee assignments, 2021: Assembly Organization; Children and Families; Energy and Utilities; Mental Health; Rules; State Affairs (vice chair); Transportation; Joint Legislative Council (cochair).

Contact: rep.vorpagel@legis.wisconsin.gov; 608-266-8530; 888-529-0027 (toll free); Room 210 North, State Capitol, PO Box 8953, Madison, WI 53708.

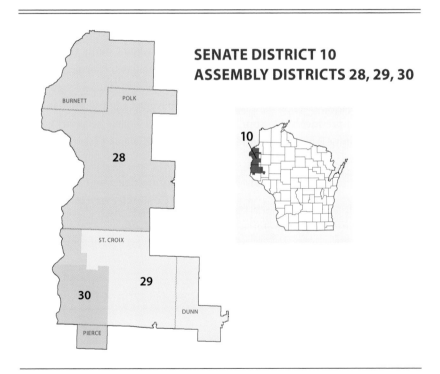

SENATE DISTRICT 10
ASSEMBLY DISTRICTS 28, 29, 30

Rob Stafsholt, Senate District 10
Republican

Biography: Lifelong resident of St. Croix County, Wisconsin; 1 child. Voting address: New Richmond, Wisconsin. ▪ Graduate New Richmond Public Schools;

attended University of Wisconsin-Eau Claire and University of Wisconsin-River Falls. ▪ Farmer; owner of waste disposal company; owner of residential rental and real estate investment company; volunteer coach for the New Richmond-Somerset High School trap team. Former co-owner of a salad and food dressings manufacturing and sales company; mortgage loan originator. ▪ Member: Farm Bureau; NRA (life member); New Richmond Chamber of Commerce. ▪ Former Member: Erin Prairie Township Planning Commission; Wisconsin Bear Hunters' Association (board of directors); Wisconsin Association of Mortgage Brokers.

Legislature: Elected to Assembly 2016–18. Elected to Senate 2020. Committee assignments, 2021: Financial Institutions and Revenue; Insurance, Licensing and Forestry (vice chair); Labor and Regulatory Reform; Sporting Heritage, Small Business and Rural Issues (chair); Universities and Technical Colleges. Additional apppointments: Small Business Environmental Council.

Contact: sen.stafsholt@legis.wisconsin.gov; 608-266-7745; Room 15 South, State Capitol, PO Box 7882, Madison, WI 53707.

Gae Magnafici, Assembly District 28
Republican

Biography: Born Amery, Wisconsin, July 14, 1952; married; 2 children, 3 grandchildren. Voting address: Dresser, Wisconsin. ▪ Graduate Amery High School, 1970; A.A. in Applied Science, Sauk Valley Community College (Dixon, Illinois), 1982. ▪ Small business owner. Former mental health technician; registered nurse.

Legislature: Elected to Assembly since 2018. Committee assignments, 2021: Aging and Long-Term Care; Constitution and Ethics; Family Law (chair); Health; Jobs and the Economy; Mental Health; Substance Abuse and Prevention (vice chair); Tourism.

Contact: rep.magnafici@legis.wisconsin.gov; 608-267-2365; 888-534-0028 (toll free); Room 7 West, State Capitol, PO Box 8953, Madison, WI 53708.

Clint Moses, Assembly District 29
Republican

Biography: Born Menomonie, Wisconsin, April 4, 1976; married; 4 children. Voting address: Menomonie, Wisconsin. ▪ Graduate: Menomonie High School, 1995; B.A. in Psychology, University of Wisconsin-Stout, 1999; B.S. in Human Biology, Northwestern College of Chiropractic, 2001; Doctor of Chiropractic, Northwestern College of Chiropractic, 2003. ▪ Chiropractor, small business owner, farmer. ▪ Member: Menomonie Rotary Club (past president); School District of the Menomonie Area (board clerk); Menomonie Chamber of Commerce; Wisconsin Farm Bureau. ▪ Former member: Community Foundation of Dunn County (past board president); Colfax Health & Rehabilitation Board; NRA; Boy Scouts of America (Eagle Scout and board member for the Tall Oaks District).

Legislature: Elected to the Assembly in 2020; Committee assignments, 2021: Agriculture; Colleges and Universities; Forestry, Parks and Outdoor Recreation; Health; Rural Development (vice chair).

Contact: rep.moses@legis.wisconsin.gov; 608-266-7683; 888-529-0029 (toll free); Room 16 West, State Capitol, PO Box 8953, Madison, WI 53708.

Shannon Zimmerman, Assembly District 30
Republican

Biography: Born Madison, Wisconsin, March 15, 1972; married; 2 children. Voting address: River Falls, Wisconsin. ▪ Attended Augusta High School; Chippewa Valley Technical College; University of Wisconsin-Milwaukee. ▪ Founder and CEO, language translation company; Wisconsin winery owner; small business owner. Coached youth football for 7 years. ▪ Former

member: University of Wisconsin-River Falls Foundation Board; University of Wisconsin-River Falls Chancellor's Advisory Committee; Rotary; Wisconsin Department of Workforce Development Board.

Legislature: Elected to Assembly since 2016. Committee assignments, 2021: Finance; Joint Committee on Finance; Joint Committee on Information Policy and Technology.

Contact: rep.zimmerman@legis.wisconsin.gov; 608-266-1526; 888-529-0030 (toll free); Room 324 East, State Capitol, PO Box 8953, Madison, WI 53708.

SENATE DISTRICT 11
ASSEMBLY DISTRICTS 31, 32, 33

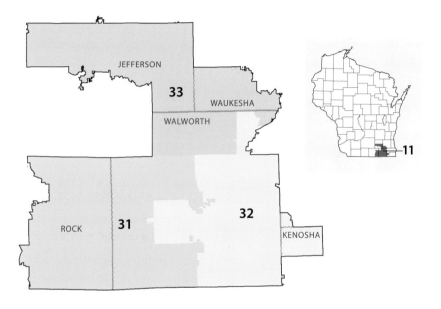

Stephen L. Nass, Senate District 11
Republican

Biography: Born Whitewater, Wisconsin, October 7, 1952. Voting address: Whitewater, Wisconsin.

■ Graduate Whitewater High School; B.S. University of Wisconsin-Whitewater, 1978; M.S. Ed. in School Business Management, University of Wisconsin-Whitewater, 1990. ■ Owner, rental property business. Former payroll benefits analyst and information analyst/negotiator. Member of Wisconsin Air National Guard (retired, CMSgt, 33 years of service), served in Middle East in Operations Desert Shield and Desert Storm. ■ Member: American Legion; VFW. ■ Former member: University of Wisconsin-Whitewater Board of Visitors, 1979–89. ■ Whitewater City Council, 1977–81.

Legislature: Elected to Assembly 1990–2012. Elected to Senate since 2014. Committee assignments, 2021: Administrative Rules (chair); Education; Labor and Regulatory Reform (chair); Universities and Technical Colleges (vice chair); Joint Committee for Review of Administrative Rules (cochair). Additional appointments: Midwestern Higher Education Commission.

Contact: sen.nass@legis.wisconsin.gov; 608-266-2635; Room 10 South, State Capitol, PO Box 7882, Madison, WI 53707-7882.

Amy Loudenbeck, Assembly District 31
Republican

Biography: Born Midland, Michigan, September 29, 1969; married. Voting address: Clinton, Wisconsin. ▪ Graduate Hinsdale Central High School (Hinsdale, Illinois), 1987; B.A. in Political Science, International Relations, University of Wisconsin-Madison, 1991; studied abroad in Kingston, Jamaica. ▪ Former chamber of commerce executive; former environmental/regulatory compliance project manager. ▪ Former member: Town of Linn Fire Department. ▪ Town of Clinton supervisor, 2010–12.

Legislature: Elected to Assembly since 2010. Committee assignments, 2021: Finance (vice chair); Joint Committee on Finance (vice cochair); Joint Committee on Information Policy and Technology (cochair). Additional appointments: State Capitol and Executive Residence Board (chair); State Fair Park Board.

Contact: rep.loudenbeck@legis.wisconsin.gov; 608-266-9967; 888-529-0031 (toll free); Room 304 East, State Capitol, PO Box 8952, Madison, WI 53708.

Tyler August, Assembly District 32
Republican

Biography: Born Wisconsin, January 26, 1983; single. Voting address: Lake Geneva, Wisconsin. ▪ Graduate Big Foot High School, 2001; attended University of Wisconsin-Eau Claire and University of Wisconsin-Madison; completed 2012 Emerging Leader Program at University of Virginia Darden School of Business. ▪ Full-time legislator. Former chief of staff to Representative Thomas Lothian. ▪ Member: Republican Party of Wisconsin (former board member); First Congressional District Republican Party (former chair);

Republican Party of Walworth County (former chair, vice chair); NRA. ▪ Recipient: American Conservative Union *Defender of Liberty* 2012; GOPAC *Emerging Leader* 2012.

Legislature: Elected to Assembly since 2010. Leadership positions: Speaker Pro Tempore 2021, 2019, 2017, 2015, 2013. Committee assignments, 2021: Administrative Rules (vice chair); Assembly Organization; Insurance; Rules; Joint Committee for Review of Administrative Rules; Joint Legislative Council; Joint Survey Committee on Tax Exemptions (cochair).

Contact: rep.august@legis.wisconsin.gov; 608-266-1190; Room 119 West, State Capitol, PO Box 8952, Madison, WI 53708.

Cody J. Horlacher, Assembly District 33
Republican

Biography: Born Burlington, Wisconsin, April 10, 1987; married; 2 children. Voting address: Mukwonago, Wisconsin. ▪ Graduate East Troy High School, 2006; B.A. in Marketing, University of Wisconsin-Whitewater, 2010; J.D. Marquette University Law School, 2014. ▪ Attorney; owner of Horlacher Law, LLC. Former special prosecutor, Walworth County; former assis-  tant district attorney, Walworth County. ▪ Member: Wisconsin Historical Society (Board of Curators); Mukwonago Area Chamber of Commerce; Sportsmen's Caucus; Carroll University President's Advisory Council; Wisconsin State Bar; National Conference of State Legislatures Occupational Licensing Consortium; Polish Heritage Alliance. ▪ Former member: Walworth County Republican Party (secretary, vice chair, chair); Federalist Society.

Legislature: Elected to Assembly since 2014. Committee assignments, 2021: Criminal Justice and Public Safety (vice chair); Energy and Utilities; Financial Institutions; Judiciary; Regulatory Licensing Reform; Science, Technology and Broadband.

Contact: rep.horlacher@legis.wisconsin.gov; 608-266-5715; 888-529-0033 (toll free); Room 214 North, State Capitol, PO Box 8952, Madison, WI 53708.

SENATE DISTRICT 12
ASSEMBLY DISTRICTS 34, 35, 36

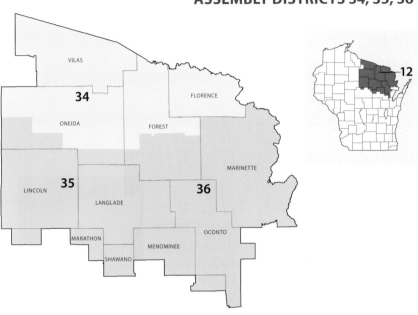

Mary J. Felzkowski, Senate District 12
Republican

Biography: Born Tomahawk, Wisconsin, September 25, 1963; married; 5 children, 4 grandchildren. Voting address: Tomahawk, Wisconsin. ▪ Graduate Tomahawk High School, 1981; B.S. in Finance and Economics, University of Wisconsin-River Falls, 1986. ▪ Insurance agency owner. ▪ Member: Tomahawk Main Street, Inc. (former president); Tomahawk Regional Chamber of Commerce; Tomahawk Child Care (former president); NRA (life member); Professional Insurance Agents of Wisconsin (former board member, secretary, treasurer, vice president, president, national director). ▪ Former member: National Alliance for Insurance Education and Research (board member).

Legislature: Elected to Assembly 2012–18. Elected to Senate 2020. Leadership positions: Assistant Majority Leader 2019. Committee assignments, 2021: Finance; Government Operations, Legal Review and Consumer Protection (vice chair); Insurance, Licensing and Forestry (chair); Natural Resources and Energy (vice chair); Joint Committee on Finance.

Contact: sen.felzkowski@legis.wisconsin.gov; 608-266-2509; Room 415 South, State Capitol, PO Box 7882, Madison, WI 53708.

Rob Swearingen, Assembly District 34
Republican

Biography: Born Oneida County, Wisconsin, July 23, 1963; married; 2 children. Voting address: Rhinelander, Wisconsin. ▪ Graduate Rhinelander High School, 1981. ▪ Restaurant owner and operator. ▪ Member: Tavern League of Wisconsin (former president, zone vice president, district director); American Beverage Licensees (former member, board of directors); Oneida County Tavern League (former president, vice president); Rhinelander Chamber of Commerce; Oneida County Republican Party; Rhinelander Rotary Club.

Legislature: Elected to Assembly since 2012. Committee assignments, 2021: Forestry, Parks and Outdoor Recreation; Small Business Development; State Affairs (chair); Tourism (vice chair); Joint Survey Committee on Tax Exemptions. Additional appointments: Building Commission (vice chair).

Contact: rep.swearingen@legis.wisconsin.gov; 608-266-7141; 888-534-0034 (toll free); Room 123 West, State Capitol, PO Box 8953, Madison, WI 53708.

Calvin Callahan, Assembly District 35
Republican

Biography: Born in Wausau, Wisconsin, March 2, 1999; single. Voting address: Tomahawk, Wisconsin. ▪ Graduate Tomahawk High School. Currently attending University of Wisconsin-Marathon County. ▪ Full-time legislator. ▪ Member: Lincoln County Republican Party (chairman 2018–20); Langlade County Republican Party; Marathon County Republican Party; NRA; Somo ATV Club; Somo Fish and Game Club; Wisconsin ATV/UTV Association; Wisconsin Bear Hunters Association; Wisconsin Trappers Association. ▪ Former member: Future Business Leaders of America (chief communications officer 2015–17). ▪ Lincoln County Board supervisor (2018–present); Town of Wilson supervisor (2019–21).

Legislature: Elected to Assembly 2020. Committee assignments, 2021: Corrections (vice chair); Criminal Justice and Public Safety; Forestry, Parks and Outdoor Recreation; Rural Development; Sporting Heritage; Transportation.

Contact: rep.callahan@legis.wisconsin.gov; 608-266-7694; 888-534-0035 (toll free); Room 15 West, State Capitol, PO Box 8952, Madison, WI 53708.

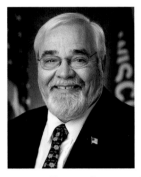

Jeffrey L. Mursau, Assembly District 36
Republican

Biography: Born Oconto Falls, Wisconsin, June 12, 1954; married; 4 children, 11 grandchildren. Voting address: Crivitz, Wisconsin. ▪ Graduate Coleman High School, 1972; attended University of Wisconsin-Oshkosh. ▪ Small business owner; electrical contractor. ▪ Member: Crivitz Ski Cats waterski team (advisor, former president); Crivitz Lions Club; Crivitz, Wisconsin–Crivitz, Germany Sister City Organization (former director); Wings Over Wisconsin; St. Mary's Catholic Church; Fourth Degree Knights of Columbus; Friends of Governor Thompson State Park; Master Loggers Certifying Board; Governor's Task Force on Broadband Access ▪ Recipient: Crivitz Business Association *Citizen of the Year* 1994. ▪ Crivitz Village President, 1991–2004.

Legislature: Elected to Assembly since 2004. Committee assignments, 2021: Agriculture; Education; Forestry, Parks and Outdoor Recreation (chair); Sporting Heritage; Tourism.

Contact: rep.mursau@legis.wisconsin.gov; 608-266-3780; 888-534-0036 (toll free); Room 113 West, State Capitol, PO Box 8953, Madison, WI 53708.

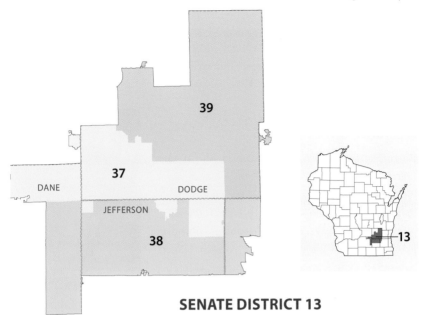

**SENATE DISTRICT 13
ASSEMBLY DISTRICTS 37, 38, 39**

John Jagler, Senate District 13

Republican

Biography: Born Louisville, Kentucky, November 4, 1969; married; 3 children. Voting address: Watertown, Wisconsin. ▪ Graduate Oak Creek High School, 1987; Trans-American School of Broadcasting (Madison), 1989; attended University of Wisconsin-Parkside, 1987–88. ▪ Realtor; owner, family-run natural dog treat company; owner, communications consulting company. Former radio morning show host, news anchor; communications director for Assembly Speaker Jeff Fitzgerald. ▪ Member: Honorable Order of Kentucky Colonels; Watertown Elks Club. ▪ Former member: Radio TV News Directors Association; Milwaukee Press Club.

Legislature: Elected to Assembly 2012–20. Elected to Senate in April 2021 special election. Committee assignments, 2021: Education; Financial Institutions and Revenue (vice chair); Housing, Commerce and Trade (chair); Insurance, Licensing and Forestry; Sporting Heritage, Small Business and Rural Issues; Joint Survey Committee on Tax Exemptions.

Contact: sen.jagler@legis.wisconsin.gov; 608-266-5660; Room 131 South, State Capitol, PO Box 7882, Madison, WI 53708.

Assembly District 37

This office was vacant at the time of publication. For complete information on the representative for this district, visit: https://legis.wisconsin.gov/lrb/blue-book/.

Barbara Dittrich, Assembly District 38
Republican

Biography: Born Milwaukee, Wisconsin, May 21, 1964; married; 3 children. Voting address: Oconomowoc, Wisconsin. ▪ Graduate Hamilton High School (Sussex), 1982; attended Waukesha County Technical College, 1983; attended University of Wisconsin-Milwaukee, 1986. ▪ Nonprofit leader (16 years). Former financial advisor (13 years); small business owner. ▪Member: Oconomowoc Area Chamber of Commerce; Crosspoint Community Church. ▪ Former member: Great Lakes Hemophilia Foundation (board of directors); Christian Council on Persons with Disabilities (board of directors); Lutheran Homes of Oconomowoc (personnel committee member); St. Catherine of Alexandria (parish council treasurer); Oconomowoc Area Chamber of Commerce (ambassador); NORD Rare Disease Day (ambassador).

Legislature: Elected to Assembly since 2018. Committee assignments, 2021: Children and Families; Consumer Protection (chair); Health; Jobs and the Economy; Mental Health; Rules; Ways and Means; Workforce Development (vice chair).

Contact: rep.dittrich@legis.wisconsin.gov; 608-266-8551; 888-534-0038 (toll free); Room 17 West, State Capitol, PO Box 8952, Madison, WI 53708.

Mark L. Born, Assembly District 39
Republican

Biography: Born Beaver Dam, Wisconsin, April 14, 1976; married; 1 child. Voting address: Beaver Dam, Wisconsin. ▪ Graduate Beaver Dam High School, 1994; B.A. in Political Science and History, Gustavus Adolphus College (St. Peter, Minnesota), 1998. ▪ Full-time legislator. Former corrections supervisor, Dodge County Sheriff's Department. ▪ Member: Downtown Beaver Dam, Inc.; Friends of Horicon Marsh; Dodge County Historical Society (vice president); Leadership Beaver Dam Steering Committee; Beaver Dam Lake Improvement Association (former vice president); Republican Party of Dodge

County (former chair); Beaver Dam Elks Lodge 1540. ▪ Beaver Dam Fire and Police Commission, 2003–05; Beaver Dam City Council, 2005–09.

Legislature: Elected to Assembly since 2012. Committee assignments, 2021: Audit; Employment Relations; Finance (chair); Joint Committee on Employment Relations; Joint Committee on Finance (cochair); Joint Legislative Audit Committee; Joint Legislative Council. Additional appointments: University of Wisconsin Hospitals and Clinics Authority.

Contact: rep.born@legis.wisconsin.gov; 608-266-2540; 888-534-0039 (toll free); Room 308 East, State Capitol, PO Box 8952, Madison, WI 53708.

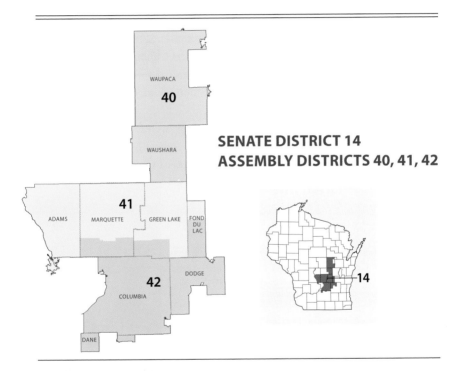

WAUPACA
40

WAUSHARA

**SENATE DISTRICT 14
ASSEMBLY DISTRICTS 40, 41, 42**

41

ADAMS   MARQUETTE   GREEN LAKE   FOND DU LAC

42   DODGE

COLUMBIA

DANE

14

Joan Ballweg, Senate District 14
Republican

Biography: Born Milwaukee, Wisconsin, March 16, 1952; married; 3 children, 3 grandchildren. Voting address: Markesan, Wisconsin. ▪ Graduate Nathan Hale High School (West Allis), 1970; attended University of Wisconsin-Waukesha; B.A. in Elementary Education, University of Wisconsin-Stevens Point, 1974.

▪ Co-owner of farm equipment business. Former first grade teacher. ▪ Member: Council of State Governments (chair 2021, 2020); Midwest Legislative Conference (chair 2016); Markesan Chamber of Commerce (former treasurer); Waupun Chamber of Commerce; Green Lake County Farm Bureau; Waupun Memorial Hospital (board of directors, former chair); Agnesian HealthCare Enterprises LLC management committee (former secretary); volunteer, Markesan District Schools; Markesan PTA (former president); Markesan American Field Service Chapter (hosting coordinator, president, former host family, liaison). ▪ Former member: FEMA V Regional Advisory Council. ▪ Markesan City Council, 1987–91; mayor of Markesan, 1991–97.

Legislature: Elected to Assembly 2004–18. Elected to Senate 2020. Leadership positions: Majority Caucus Chair 2013, 2011. Committee assignments, 2021: Agriculture and Tourism (chair); Finance; Human Services, Children and Families (vice chair); Natural Resources and Energy; Joint Committee on Finance. Additional appointments: Child Abuse and Neglect Prevention Board; Council on Tourism.

Contact: sen.ballweg@legis.wisconsin.gov; 608-266-0751; 888-534-0041 (toll free); Room 409 South, State Capitol, PO Box 8952, Madison, WI 53708.

Kevin David Petersen, Assembly District 40
Republican

Biography: Born Waupaca, Wisconsin, December 14, 1964; married; 2 children. Voting address: Waupaca, Wisconsin. ▪ Graduate Waupaca High School, 1983; B.S.M.E., University of New Mexico, 1989. ▪ Co-owner of family-run electronics corporation. Served in U.S. Navy sub service, 1983–94; Persian Gulf War veteran; U.S. Naval Reserve member, 1994–2008. ▪ Member: Waupaca County Republican Party; Waushara County Republican Party; VFW Post 1037 (life member); AMVETS Post 1887 (life member); American Legion Post 161; Waupaca Area Chamber of Commerce; New London Area Chamber of Commerce; NRA. ▪ Former Town of Dayton supervisor, 2001–07.

Legislature: Elected to Assembly since 2006. Leadership positions: Assistant Majority Leader 2021. Committee assignments, 2021: Assembly Organization; Energy and Utilities; Insurance (vice chair); Rules; Joint Committee on Legislative Organization.

Contact: rep.petersen@legis.wisconsin.gov; 608-237-9140; 888-947-0040 (toll free); Room 309 North, State Capitol, PO Box 8953, Madison, WI 53708.

Alex Dallman, Assembly District 41
Republican

Biography: Born Fond du Lac, Wisconsin, May 22, 1992; single. Voting address: Green Lake, Wisconsin. ▪ Graduate: Markesan High School, 2011; B.S., Edgewood College, 2015. ▪ Wisconsin Interscholastic Athletic Association (WIAA) licensed basketball official. Former outreach representative for U.S. Congressman Glenn Grothman. ▪ Member: Green Lake County Republican Party (former chair); Green Lake County Farm Bureau; Manchester Rod & Gun Club; NRA; St. John's Lutheran Church (Markesan).

Legislature: Elected to Assembly 2020. Committee assignments, 2021: Colleges and Universities (vice chair); Regulatory Licensing Reform; Science, Technology and Broadband; Sporting Heritage; Tourism.

Contact: rep.dallman@legis.wisconsin.gov; 608-266-8077; 888-534-0041 (toll free); Room 412 North, State Capitol, PO Box 8952, Madison, WI 53708.

Jon Plumer, Assembly District 42
Republican

Biography: Born Sterling, Illinois, March 1, 1955; married; 4 children, 8 grandchildren. Voting address: Lodi, Wisconsin. ▪ Graduate West High School, 1973. ▪ Small business owner, Plumer Karate America. Former route salesman for Kraft Foods for 30 years. ▪ Member: Lodi Optimist Club; Project SEARCH (board member); Lodi Knights of Columbus. ▪ Former member: Lodi Area EMS Commission; Lodi & Lake Wisconsin Chamber of Commerce (three-term president). ▪ Columbia County Board supervisor; former Town of Lodi Board supervisor.

Legislature: Elected to Assembly in June 2018 special election. Reelected since November 2018. Committee assignments, 2021: Aging and Long-Term Care; Agriculture; Family Law; Rules; Rural Development; Substance Abuse and Prevention; Tourism; Transportation (chair).

Contact: rep.plumer@legis.wisconsin.gov; 608-266-3404; 888-534-0042 (toll free); Room 317 North, State Capitol, PO Box 8953, Madison, WI 53708.

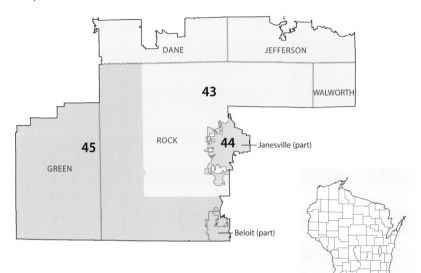

SENATE DISTRICT 15
ASSEMBLY DISTRICTS 43, 44, 45

Janis Ringhand, Senate District 15
Democrat

Biography: Born Madison, Wisconsin, February 13, 1950; married; 2 children, 5 grandchildren, 4 great-grandchildren. Voting address: Evansville, Wisconsin. ▪ Graduate Evansville High School, 1968; Associate Degree, Madison Area Technical College, 1985. ▪ Full-time legislator. Former accountant for small businesses; executive director of nonprofit. ▪ Member: Evansville Chamber of Commerce; Evansville Energy Independence Team. ▪ Former member: Stoughton Hospital Board (chair); Creekside Place, Inc. (board of directors); Evansville Community Partnership (secretary). ▪ Evansville City Council, 1998–2002, 2008–10; Mayor of Evansville, 2002–06.

Legislature: Elected to Assembly 2010–12. Elected to Senate since 2014. Leadership positions: Assistant Minority Leader, 2021; Minority Caucus Vice Chair 2019, 2017; Minority Caucus Secretary 2013. Committee assignments, 2021: Economic and Workforce Development; Financial Institutions and Revenue; Insurance, Licensing and Forestry; Senate Organization; Joint Committee on Legislative Organization; Joint Legislative Council. Additional appointments: Building Commission; Women's Council.

Contact: sen.ringhand@legis.wisconsin.gov; 608-266-2253; Room 108 South, State Capitol, PO Box 7882, Madison, WI 53707-7882.

Don Vruwink, Assembly District 43
Democrat

Biography: Born Auburndale, Wisconsin, June 12, 1952; married; 1 child. Voting address: Milton, Wisconsin. ▪ Graduate Auburndale High School, 1970; B.A. in Broad Field Social Studies, Political Science, and Coaching Minor, University of Wisconsin-Stevens Point, 1975; M.A. in History, University of Wisconsin-Whitewater, 1986. ▪ Full-time legislator; substitute teacher; softball and baseball umpire. Retired teacher, Milton School District; former Parks and Recreation Director, City of Milton; former Milton High School basketball, football, and softball coach. ▪ Member: Dairy Business Association; Greater Whitewater Committee; Milton Area Chamber of Commerce; Edgerton Chamber of Commerce; Farm Bureau; League of Conservation Voters. ▪ Recipient: Channel 3000 *Top Notch Teacher* 2011; Milton Athletic Hall of Fame, 2011; Wisconsin Fastpitch Coaches Hall of Fame, 2014; Milton Chamber of Commerce *Lifetime Achievement Award* 2014; Wisconsin Property Taxpayers *Property Taxpayer Champion Award* 2018; Wisconsin Educational Technology Leaders *Education Technology Appreciation Award* 2018; Wisconsin Builders Association *Friend of Housing Award* 2021. ▪ Milton City Council 2011–15 (president 2015); Milton School Board 2016–19 (acting president 2019).

Legislature: Elected to Assembly since 2016. Committee assignments, 2021: Agriculture; Education; Rural Development; Tourism.

Contact: rep.vruwink@legis.wisconsin.gov; 608-266-3790; 888-534-0043 (toll free); Room 6 North, State Capitol, PO Box 8953, Madison, WI 53708.

Sue Conley, Assembly District 44
Democrat

Biography: Born Galesburg, Illinois, February 19, 1960; married; 3 children. Voting address: Janesville, Wisconsin. ▪ Graduate Joseph A. Craig High School (Janesville); attended University of Wisconsin-Whitewater, University of Wisconsin-Rock County; Blackhawk Technical College. ▪ Full-time legislator. Former banker; YWCA Executive Director;

Community Foundation of Southern Wisconsin Executive Director; University of Wisconsin-Whitewater Rock County Foundation Executive Director. ▪ Janesville City Council, 2017–21 (president 2020–21).

Legislature: Elected to Assembly in 2020. Committee assignments, 2021: Family Law; Local Government; Public Benefit Reform; Ways and Means.

Contact: rep.conley@legis.wisconsin.gov; 608-266-7503; 888-947-0044 (toll free); Room 320 West, State Capitol, PO Box 8952, Madison, WI 53708.

Mark Spreitzer, Assembly District 45
Democrat

Biography: Born Evanston, Illinois, December 16, 1986; married. Voting address: Beloit, Wisconsin. ▪ Graduate Northside College Preparatory High School (Chicago, Illinois), 2005; B.A. in Political Science, Beloit College, 2009; Bowhay Institute for Legislative Leadership Development, 2017; State Legislative Leaders Foundation Emerging Leaders Program, 2017. ▪ Full-time legislator. Former assistant director of alumni and parent relations and annual support, Beloit College. ▪ Member: United Church of Beloit (finance and facilities board); Welty Environmental Center (board president); Young Democrats of Wisconsin; Young Elected Officials Network; National Caucus of Environmental Legislators; Great Lakes Legislative Caucus; Wisconsin Legislative Sportsmen's Caucus; Major, Wisconsin Wing, Civil Air Patrol Legislative Squadron (official Auxiliary of the U.S. Air Force). ▪ Former member: Community Action, Inc. of Rock and Walworth Counties (board member); City of Beloit Appointment Review Committee (chair). ▪ Recipient: Wisconsin League of Conservation Voters *Conservation Champion* 2017–18, 2015–16; Wisconsin Economic Development Association *Champion of Economic Development Award* 2019–20, 2017–18; Wisconsin Farmers Union *Friend of the Family Farmer* 2017; Rock River Coalition *Protector Award* 2017; Fair Wisconsin *Community Advocate of the Year* 2014. ▪ Beloit City Council, 2011–15 (president, 2014–15).

Legislature: Elected to Assembly since 2014. Leadership positions: Minority Caucus Chair 2021, 2019, 2017. Committee assignments, 2021: Agriculture; Assembly Organization; Campaigns and Elections; Local Government; Rules; Sporting Heritage.

Contact: rep.spreitzer@legis.wisconsin.gov; 608-266-1192; 888-534-0045 (toll free); Room 113 North, State Capitol, PO Box 8953, Madison, WI 53708.

SENATE DISTRICT 16
ASSEMBLY DISTRICTS 46, 47, 48

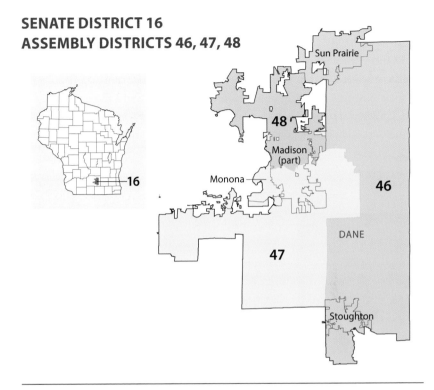

Melissa Agard, Senate District 16
Democrat

Biography: Born Madison, Wisconsin, March 28, 1969; 4 children. Voting address: Madison, Wisconsin. ▪ Graduate Madison East High School, 1987; B.A. University of Wisconsin-Madison, 1991. Graduate Bowhay Institute for Legislative Leadership Development (BILLD), 2014; Emerging Leaders Program, University of Virginia, 2014; Toll Fellowship, 2015. ▪ Former small business owner. ▪ Member: Women in Government; Women Legislators' Lobby (WiLL) and Women's Action for New Directions (WAND); Dane County Democratic Party; Democratic Party; Friends of Cherokee Marsh. ▪ Former member: Emerge Wisconsin (board of directors); Make Room for Youth; Boy Scouts of America Glacier's Edge Council (board of directors); Midwest Shiba Inu Dog Rescue (president); Gompers PTO (president). ▪ Recipient: National Federation of Women Legislators *Woman of Excellence*; WiLL *Pacesetter Award*; Arc *Dane County Elected Official of the Year* 2014; Citizen Action *Activist Achievement Award* 2014; *Eleanor Roosevelt Award* nominee 2013; Wisconsin League of Conservation

Voters *Conservation Champion* 2020, 2018, 2016, 2014; Brava *Women to Watch* 2018. ▪ Dane County Board of Supervisors, 2010–14.

Legislature: Elected to Assembly 2012–18. Elected to Senate 2020. Leadership positions: Senate Minority Caucus Vice Chair, 2020. Committee assignments, 2021: Financial Institutions and Revenue; Housing, Commerce and Trade; Human Services, Children and Families; Natural Resources and Energy; Joint Legislative Audit Committee. Additional appointments: State Capitol and Executive Residence Board.

Contact: sen.agard@legis.wisconsin.gov; 608-266-9170; Room 126 South, State Capitol, PO Box 7882, Madison, WI 53708.

Gary Alan Hebl, Assembly District 46
Democrat

Biography: Born Madison, Wisconsin, May 15, 1951; married; 3 children, 2 grandchildren. Voting address: Sun Prairie, Wisconsin. ▪ Graduate Sun Prairie High School, 1969; B.A. in Political Science, University of Wisconsin-Madison, 1973; Gonzaga University Law School, 1976; Bowhay Institute, 2008; Council of State Government 2018 Henry Toll Fellowship Program alumnus. ▪ Attorney and owner of a title insurance company. Former Sacred Hearts eighth grade basketball coach, 1980–99; former legal counsel for the Nature Conservancy and Operation Fresh Start, Inc. ▪ Member: National Caucus of Environmental Legislators (state lead 2021, 2019, 2018); Wisconsin League of Conservation Voters; Dane County Bar Association; Wisconsin Bar Association; Sun Prairie Optimist Club (former president); Sun Prairie Chamber of Commerce (former president); University of Wisconsin Flying Club (former board chair); Aircraft Owners and Pilots Association (AOPA); Experimental Aircraft Association (EAA) Young Eagles Program; Knights of Columbus (fourth degree member); Sun Prairie Cable Access Board; YMCA (former president); Sun Prairie Public Library Board (former president); Sacred Heart Parish Council (former trustee); Sun Prairie Quarterback Club (former president); Major, Wisconsin Wing, Civil Air Patrol Legislative Squadron (official Auxiliary of the U.S. Air Force). ▪ Recipient: State Bar of Wisconsin *Scales of Justice Award* 2009–10; Wisconsin Dietetic Association *Nutrition Champion Award* 2010; Pharmacy Society of Wisconsin *Legislator of the Year* 2010, 2009; Sun Prairie Star poll *Best Attorney in Sun Prairie* 2008–20; *James J. Reininger Award* for life-time achievement 2008; Wisconsin Association of PEG Channels *Friend of Access Award* 2010, 2007; Wisconsin League of Conservation Voters *Conservation Champion* 2019–20, 2017–18, 2015–16,

2013–14, 2011–12, 2009–10, 2005–06; Sun Prairie Exchange Club *Book of Golden Deeds Award* 2003; Chamber of Commerce *Judith Krivsky Business Person of the Year Award* 2002; Sun Prairie Business and Education Partnership *Outstanding Small Business of the Year* 2001; Sun Prairie High School Wall of Success 2015.

Legislature: Elected to Assembly since 2004. Committee assignments, 2021: Administrative Rules; Constitution and Ethics; Education; Environment; Forestry, Parks and Outdoor Recreation; Judiciary; Joint Committee for Review of Administrative Rules. Additional appointments: Commission on Uniform State Laws.

Contact: rep.hebl@legis.wisconsin.gov; 608-266-7678; Room 120 North, State Capitol, PO Box 8952, Madison, WI 53708.

Jimmy Anderson, Assembly District 47
Democrat

Biography: Born El Paso, Texas, August 26, 1986; raised in Patterson, California. Voting address: Fitchburg, Wisconsin. ▪ Graduate Patterson High School, 2004; B.A., summa cum laude, California State University, Monterey Bay, 2008; J.D. University of Wisconsin Law School, 2012. ▪ Nonprofit director. ▪ Member: Wisconsin State Bar Association.

Legislature: Elected to Assembly since 2016. Committee assignments, 2021: Colleges and Universities; Environment; Health; Science, Technology and Broadband.

Contact: rep.anderson@legis.wisconsin.gov; 608-266-8570; 888-302-0047 (toll free); Room 9 North, State Capitol, PO Box 8952, Madison, WI 53708.

Samba Baldeh, Assembly District 48
Democrat

Biography: Born Choya Village, The Gambia, September 10, 1971; married. Voting address: Madison, Wisconsin. ▪ Graduate: Armitage High School; associate's degree, Madison Area Technical College, 2006; attended University of The Gambia for B.A. in Education; Masters Certificate in Project Management, information technology, University of Wisconsin-Madison, 2017; Mandela Washington Fellowship Program for Young African Leaders, Young African Leaders Initiative, 2018. ▪ Software engineer, information technology project manager, and small business owner. ▪ Member: 100 Black Men of Madison; Dane County Democratic Party; YALI–UW Madison (Mandela Washington fellowship program for Young African Leaders Initiative) (board member); NAACP, Dane County; University of Wisconsin-Madison Community Advisory Council; New American Leaders, Elected Advisory Council (NAL–EAC); Center for Community Stewardship (C4CS); African Association of Madison (AAM). ∎ Former City of Madison alder, District 17, and Common Council president.

Legislature: Elected to Assembly 2020. Committee assignments, 2021: Local Government; Regulatory Licensing Reform; Rules; Science, Technology and Broadband; Small Business Development; Joint Committee on Information Policy and Technology.

Contact: rep.baldeh@legis.wisconsin.gov; 608-266-0960; 888-534-0048 (toll free); Room 11 North, State Capitol, PO Box 8952, Madison, WI 53708.

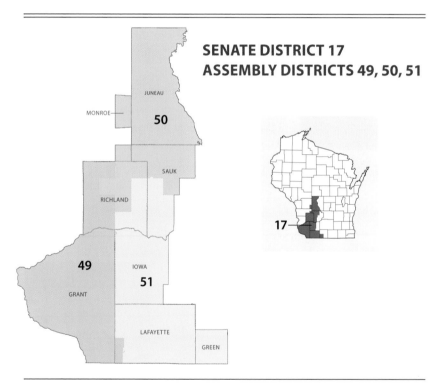

SENATE DISTRICT 17
ASSEMBLY DISTRICTS 49, 50, 51

Howard Marklein, Senate District 17
Republican

Biography: Born October 3, 1954; married; 2 children, 3 stepchildren, 5 grandchildren. Voting address: Spring Green, Wisconsin. ∎ Graduate River Valley High School (Spring Green), 1972; B.B.A. University of Wisconsin-Whitewater, 1976.

▪ Certified public accountant (CPA); certified fraud examiner (CFE). ▪ Member: St. John's Catholic Church Spring Green (finance committee member); NRA; Governor's Task Force on Broadband Access. ▪ Former member: Taliesin Preservation Inc. Board of Trustees (treasurer); University of Wisconsin-Whitewater National Alumni Association (president); University of Wisconsin-Whitewater Foundation (board of directors president); Fort HealthCare Board of Directors (chair, treasurer); Fort Atkinson Rotary Club (president); Fort Atkinson Chamber of Commerce (president); Whitewater Chamber of Commerce (president); Dodgeville Chamber of Commerce (vice president). ▪ Recipient: Wisconsin Manufacturers and Commerce *Working for Wisconsin Award* 2018, 2016, 2014, 2012; Metropolitan Milwaukee Association of Commerce *Champion of Commerce Award* 2018, 2016, 2014, 2012; Wisconsin Pork Association *Distinguished Service Award* 2019, 2013; Wisconsin Newspaper Association *Badger Award* 2013; Wisconsin Aquaculture Association *Legislator of the Year* 2013; Dairy Business Association *Legislative Excellence Award* 2018, 2016, 2012; Wisconsin Auto Collision Technicians Association *Legislator of the Year* 2016; Wisconsin Towns Association *Friend of Towns* 2016, 2020; Associated General Contractors *Legislator of the Year* 2016; Wisconsin Counties Association *Outstanding Legislator* 2018, 2016; Wisconsin Builders Association *Friend of Housing* 2018, 2016, 2015; Wisconsin Association of Local Health Departments and Boards & Wisconsin Public Health Association *Friend of Public Health* 2018, 2016; Wisconsin Hospitals Association *Health Care Advocate Award* 2018; Associated Builders and Contractors *Building Wisconsin Award* 2018, 2014; League of Wisconsin Municipalities *Municipal Champion Award* 2018, 2016; National Federation of Independent Businesses *Guardian of Small Business Award* 2018; University of Wisconsin-Platteville *Friend of the University Award* 2018; Wisconsin Grocers Association *Friend of Grocers* 2020, 2018; Wisconsin Agri-Business Association *Friend of Wisconsin Agri-Business* 2018; Wisconsin ATV/UTV Association *President's Award* 2017; Wisconsin State Telecommunications Association *Excellence in Legislative Leadership Award* 2018; Wisconsin Electric Cooperatives *Enlightened Legislator of the Year* 2018; Wisconsin Cooperative Network *Friend of Cooperatives* 2020.

Legislature: Elected to Assembly 2010–12. Elected to Senate since 2014. Leadership positions: Senate President Pro Tempore 2019, 2017. Committee assignments, 2021: Agriculture and Tourism (vice chair); Finance (chair); Joint Committee on Employment Relations; Joint Committee on Finance (cochair); Joint Legislative Audit Committee; Joint Legislative Council.

Contact: sen.marklein@legis.wisconsin.gov; 608-266-0703; Room 316 East, State Capitol, PO Box 7882, Madison, WI 53707-7882.

Travis Tranel, Assembly District 49
Republican

Biography: Born Dubuque, Iowa, September 12, 1985; married; 5 children. Voting address: Cuba City, Wisconsin. ▪ Graduate Wahlert Catholic High School (Dubuque, Iowa), 2004; B.A. Loras College (Dubuque, Iowa), 2007. ▪ Dairy farmer, small business owner. ▪ Member: St. Joseph Sinsinawa Parish Council, 2010–12 (president, 2011–12); Wisconsin Farm Bureau; Knights of Columbus; NRA; Platteville Regional Chamber of Commerce; Grant County Republican Party. ▪ Recipient: Associated Builders and Contractors of Wisconsin *Building Wisconsin Award* 2020; Dairy Business Association *Legislative Excellence Award* 2020, 2018, 2016, 2014, 2012; Wisconsin Manufacturers and Commerce *Working for Wisconsin Award* 2020, 2018, 2016, 2014, 2012; Metropolitan Milwaukee Association of Commerce *Champion of Commerce Award* 2014, 2012; Wisconsin Academy of Family Physicians *Friends of Family Medicine* 2014; Wisconsin Agricultural Tourism Association *Ambassador Award* 2015; University of Wisconsin-Platteville *Friend of the University Award* 2018; Wisconsin Economic Development Association *Champion of Economic Development Award* 2020, 2018; Wisconsin Water Alliance *Outstanding Water Legislator of the Year Award* 2020.

Legislature: Elected to Assembly since 2010. Committee assignments, 2021: Agriculture; Colleges and Universities; Energy and Utilities; Insurance; Small Business Development; Tourism (chair). Additional appointments: Council on Tourism.

Contact: rep.tranel@legis.wisconsin.gov; 608-266-1170; 888-872-0049 (toll free); Room 302 North, State Capitol, PO Box 8953, Madison, WI 53708.

Tony Kurtz, Assembly District 50
Republican

Biography: Born Columbus, Ohio, December 23, 1966. Voting address: Wonewoc, Wisconsin. ▪ B.S. in Professional Aeronautics, Embry-Riddle Aeronautical University, 1989; M.S. in International Relations, Troy State University (Troy, Alabama), 1997. ▪ Organic grain farmer. Former U.S. Army attack helicopter pilot 1985–2005, retired from active duty as a Chief Warrant

Officer Four (CW4); Persian Gulf War veteran; Iraq War veteran. ▪ Member: VFW (life member); Military Officers Association of America (life member); American Legion; Wisconsin Farm Bureau; Organic Farmers Association; Juneau County Republican Party.

Legislature: Elected to Assembly since 2018. Committee assignments, 2021: Finance; Joint Committee on Finance.

Contact: rep.kurtz@legis.wisconsin.gov; 608-266-8531; 888-534-0050; Room 320 East, State Capitol, PO Box 8952, Madison, WI 53708.

Todd Novak, Assembly District 51
Republican

Biography: Born Cobb, Wisconsin, April 23, 1965; 2 children. Voting address: Dodgeville, Wisconsin. ▪ Graduate Iowa-Grant High School, 1983; attended Southwest Technical College, 1983–85. ▪ Former government/associate newspaper editor, 1990–2014. ▪ Member: Wisconsin League of Municipalities; NRA; Wisconsin Farm Bureau. ▪ Former member: Iowa County Humane Society (founding member, treasurer); Wisconsin Newspaper Association; National Newspaper Association. ▪ Recipient: Gathering Waters *Policymaker of the Year* 2015; Wisconsin Community Action Program *William Steiger Human Services Award* 2016; Metropolitan Milwaukee Chamber of Commerce *Champion of Commerce* 2018, 2016; Wisconsin Manufacturers and Commerce *Working for Wisconsin Award* 2020, 2018, 2016; Foundation for Government Accountability *Champion of Work Award* 2018; Fair Wisconsin Education Fund *Advocate of the Year* 2015; Wisconsin Newspapers Association *Legislative Service Award* 2016; Wisconsin Counties Association *Outstanding Legislator Award* 2020, 2016; Wisconsin Primary Health Care Association *Friend of Community Health Centers* 2016; Wisconsin Academy of Family Physicians *Friend of Family Medicine Award* 2016; League of Wisconsin Municipalities *Municipal Champion Award*; Conservatives for a Clean Energy Future *Clean Energy Champion* 2018; University of Wisconsin-Platteville *Friend of the University Award* 2018; Wisconsin Public Health Association *Friend of Public Health* 2020; Wisconsin Towns Association *Friend of Towns* 2020; Wisconsin Grocers Association *Friend of Grocers* 2020; Wisconsin Water Alliance *Water Legislator of the Year* 2020. ▪ Southwest Regional Planning Commission, 2012–present; Mayor of Dodgeville, 2012–present.

Legislature: Elected to Assembly since 2014. Committee assignments, 2021;

Agriculture; Criminal Justice and Public Safety; Environment; Local Government (chair); Mental Health; Rural Development.

Contact: rep.novak@legis.wisconsin.gov; 608-266-7502; 888-534-0051 (toll free); Room 310 North, State Capitol, PO Box 8953, Madison, WI 53708.

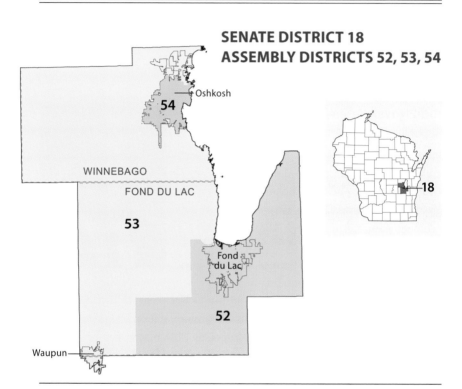

SENATE DISTRICT 18
ASSEMBLY DISTRICTS 52, 53, 54

Dan Feyen, Senate District 18
Republican

Biography: Born New Holstein, Wisconsin; married; 2 children. Voting address: Fond du Lac, Wisconsin. ▪ Graduate New Holstein High School, 1986; Diploma in Printing, Fox Valley Technical College, 1988. ▪ Print and bindery coordinator. ▪ Member: Knights of Columbus; Elks Club; Major, Wisconsin Wing, Civil Air Patrol Legislative Squadron (official Auxiliary of the U.S. Air Force); Fond du Lac County Republican Party (former chair); Fond du Lac Noon Rotary Club; 6th District Republican Party (former chair). ▪ Former member: Jaycees Fond du Lac County (past president); Fond du Lac Advisory Parks Board.

Legislature: Elected to Senate since 2016. Leadership positions: Assistant Majority Leader 2021, 2019. Committee assignments, 2021: Economic and Workforce Development (chair); Housing, Commerce and Trade (vice chair); Senate Organization; Universities and Technical Colleges; Joint Committee on Legislative Organization; Joint Survey Committee on Retirement Systems (cochair).

Contact: sen.feyen@legis.wisconsin.gov; 608-266-5300; Room 306 South, State Capitol, PO Box 7882, Madison, WI 53707-7882.

Jeremy Thiesfeldt, Assembly District 52
Republican

Biography: Born Fond du Lac, Wisconsin, November 22, 1966; married; 4 children. Voting address: Fond du Lac, Wisconsin. ▪ Graduate Kettle Moraine Lutheran High School (Jackson), 1985; B.S. in Elementary Education, Martin Luther College, 1989; attended University of Minnesota, 1992–93. ▪ Full-time legislator. Former teacher. ▪ Member: Fond du Lac Noon Rotary; Fond du Lac County Republican Party; Redeemer Lutheran Church; Thrivent Financial; NRA; Leadership Fond du Lac Alumni; Wisconsin Farm Bureau. ▪ Former Fond du Lac City Council member, 2005–10.

Legislature: Elected to Assembly since 2010. Committee assignments, 2021: Campaigns and Elections; Constitution and Ethics (vice chair); Education (chair); Government Accountability and Oversight; Judiciary; Transportation.

Contact: rep.thiesfeldt@legis.wisconsin.gov; 608-266-3156; 888-529-0052 (toll free); Room 223 North, State Capitol, PO Box 8953, Madison, WI 53708.

Michael Schraa, Assembly District 53
Republican

Biography: Born Fort Carson, Colorado, April 17, 1961; married; 3 children. Voting address: Oshkosh, Wisconsin. ▪ Graduate Oshkosh North High School, 1979; attended University of Wisconsin-Oshkosh, 1980–82. ▪ Restaurant owner. Former stock broker/investment advisor. ▪ Member: Winnebago County Republican Party (executive board); Fond du Lac County Republican Party; Calvary SonRise Church (Oshkosh); Wisconsin Independent Businesses; NRA; Winnebago County Farm Bureau; Fond du Lac County Farm

Bureau. ▪ Former member: Southwest Rotary; National Federation of Independent Businesses (NFIB); Oshkosh Jaycees; Big Brothers Big Sisters; Exchange Club.

Legislature: Elected to Assembly since 2012. Committee assignments, 2021: Corrections (chair); Criminal Justice and Public Safety; Labor and Integrated Employment; Public Benefit Reform (vice chair); Science, Technology and Broadband (vice chair); State Affairs.

Contact: rep.schraa@legis.wisconsin.gov; 608-267-7990; 888-534-0053 (toll free); Room 107 West, State Capitol, PO Box 8953, Madison, WI 53708.

Gordon Hintz, Assembly District 54
Democrat

Biography: Born Oshkosh, Wisconsin, November 29, 1973; married; 2 children. Voting address: Oshkosh, Wisconsin. ▪ Graduate Oshkosh North High School, 1992; B.A. Hamline University (St. Paul, Minnesota), 1996; M.P.A. University of Wisconsin-Madison, 2001. ▪ Municipal consultant. Former legislative staff assistant, U.S. Representative Jay Johnson, U.S. Senator Herb Kohl; management and budget analyst, City of Long Beach, California; former instructor, Political Science Department, University of Wisconsin-Oshkosh. ▪ Member: Oshkosh Rotary Club; First Congregational Church; Oshkosh Public Museum; Winnebagoland Housing Coalition; Winnebago County Safe Streets Committee; Winnebago County Democratic Party; Oshkosh Food Co-op; Wisconsin Family Impact Seminar. ▪ Former member: 2008 Presidential Elector for President Barack Obama and Vice President Joe Biden.

Legislature: Elected to Assembly since 2006. Leadership positions: Minority leader 2021, 2019, 2017. Committee assignments, 2021: Assembly Organization; Employment Relations; Rules; Joint Committee on Employment Relations; Joint Committee on Legislative Organization; Joint Legislative Council; Joint Survey Committee on Retirement Systems. Additional appointments: Wisconsin Economic Development Corporation Board.

Contact: rep.hintz@legis.wisconsin.gov; www.gordonhintz.com; Facebook: State Representative Gordon Hintz; Twitter: @GordonHintz; 608-266-2254; 888-534-0054 (toll free); 920-232-0805 (district); Room 201 West, State Capitol, PO Box 8952, Madison, WI 53708.

SENATE DISTRICT 19
ASSEMBLY DISTRICTS 55, 56, 57

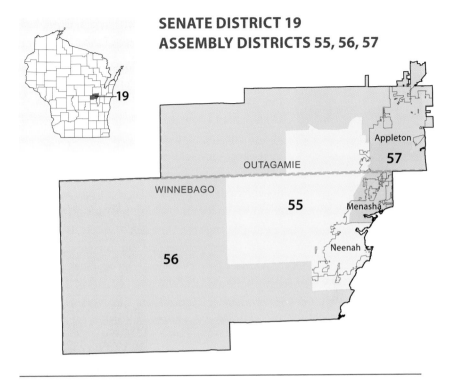

Roger Roth, Senate District 19
Republican

Biography: Born Appleton, Wisconsin; married; 5 children. Voting address: Appleton, Wisconsin. ▪ Graduate St. Mary Central High School (Menasha); B.S. in History, University of Wisconsin-Oshkosh. ▪ Self-employed home builder; Captain in the Wisconsin Air National Guard. Iraq War veteran. ▪ Member: American Legion; AMVETS; VFW.

Legislature: Elected to Assembly 2006–08. Elected to Senate since 2014. Leadership positions: President of the Senate 2019, 2017. Committee assignments, 2021: Housing, Commerce and Trade; Universities and Technical Colleges (chair); Utilities, Technology and Telecommunications (vice chair); Veterans and Military Affairs and Constitution and Federalism; Joint Committee on Information Policy and Technology; Joint Legislative Council. Additional appointments: State Capitol and Executive Residence Board.

Contact: sen.roth@legis.wisconsin.gov; 608-266-0718; Room 220 South, State Capitol, PO Box 7882, Madison, WI 53707-7882.

Rachael Cabral-Guevara, Assembly District 55
Republican

Biography: Born Appleton, Wisconsin, August 10, 1976; divorced; 4 children. Voting address: Appleton, Wisconsin. ▪ Graduate Machebeuf Catholic High School (Denver, Colorado); B.S. in Biology and Chemistry, Mount Mary University, 2000; B.S. in nursing, University of Wisconsin-Oshkosh, 2004; M.S. in Nursing, University of Wisconsin-Milwaukee, 2008. ▪ Owner, Nurse Practitioner Health Services LLC. Former senior lecturer in the College of Nursing, University of Wisconsin-Oshkosh and registered nurse. ▪ Member: Winnebago County Republican Party; Outagamie County Republican Party; ACES Xavier School System (parent volunteer); American Nurses Credentialing Center; Boy Scouts of America (parent volunteer); Fox Cities Morning Rotary Club; Fox Valley Health Professionals; Wisconsin Nurses Association; WNA, APRN Coalition. Former member: Sigma Theta Tau, Neenah Alliance School (parent volunteer), Wisconsin Express—Wisconsin AHEC (Area Health Education Centers) program.

Legislature: Elected to Assembly 2020. Committee assignments, 2021: Colleges and Universities; Health; Mental Health (vice chair); Public Benefit Reform; Regulatory Licensing Reform. Additional appointments: Women's Council.

Contact: rep.cabral-guevara@legis.wisconsin.gov; 608-266-5719; 888-534-0055 (toll free); Room 420 North, State Capitol, PO Box 8952, Madison, WI 53708.

Dave Murphy, Assembly District 56
Republican

Biography: Born Appleton, Wisconsin, November 26, 1954; married; 2 children. Voting address: Greenville, Wisconsin. ▪ Graduate Hortonville High School, 1972; University of Wisconsin-Fox Valley, 1972–74; Wisconsin School of Real Estate, 1975. ▪ Full-time legislator and farmer. Former owner, fitness center and agri-business; real estate broker. ▪ Member: Free Speech for Campus (board of directors); Greenville Lions Club; Immanuel Lutheran Church.

Legislature: Elected to Assembly since 2012. Committee assignments, 2021: Campaigns and Elections; Colleges and Universities (chair); Constitution and Ethics;

Financial Institutions; Health; Housing and Real Estate; Workforce Development. Additional appointments: Midwestern Higher Education Commission.

Contact: rep.murphy@legis.wisconsin.gov; 608-266-7500; 888-534-0056 (toll free); 318 North, State Capitol, PO Box 8953, Madison, WI 53708.

Lee Snodgrass, Assembly District 57
Democrat

Biography: Born Philadelphia, Pennsylvania, February 9, 1969; single; 2 children. Voting address: Appleton, Wisconsin. ▪ Graduate Preble High School (Green Bay), 1987; B.A. in English Literature, University of Wisconsin-Madison, 1991. ▪ Full-time legislator. Former communications director for Girl Scouts of the Northwestern Great Lakes; senior design project manager; sales manager for a paper corporation. ▪ Member: Democratic Freshman Caucus (chair); LBGTQ+ Caucus (chair); Democratic Party of Outagamie County (former chair); Democratic Party of Wisconsin (second vice chair).

Legislature: Elected to Assembly 2020. Committee assignments, 2021: Children and Families; Forestry, Parks and Outdoor Recreation; Tourism; Transportation.

Contact: rep.snodgrass@legis.wisconsin.gov; 608-266-3070; 888-534-0057 (toll free); Room 21 North, State Capitol, PO Box 8953, Madison, WI 53708.

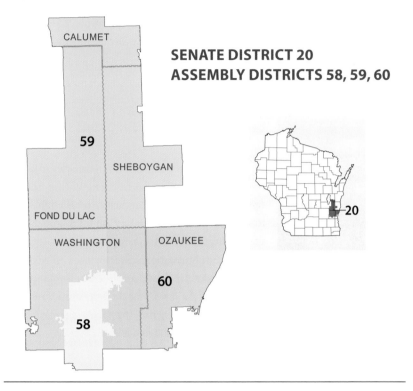

SENATE DISTRICT 20
ASSEMBLY DISTRICTS 58, 59, 60

Duey Stroebel, Senate District 20
Republican

Biography: Born Cedarburg, Wisconsin, September 1, 1959; married; 8 children. Voting address: Town of Cedarburg, Wisconsin. ▪ Graduate Cedarburg High School, 1978; B.B.A. University of Wisconsin-Madison, 1984; M.S. University of Wisconsin-Madison, 1987. ▪ Real estate. ▪ Member: Ozaukee Board of Realtors; Cedarburg Chamber of Commerce; Greater Cedarburg Foundation (former president); Concordia University President's Council; Farm Bureau; ABATE of Wisconsin; West Bend Chamber of Commerce; Saukville Chamber of Commerce. ▪ Former member: City of Cedarburg Downtown Ad Hoc Committee; Ozaukee Bank and Cornerstone Bank (board of directors). ▪ Town of Cedarburg Parks Commission, 2001–04; Town of Cedarburg Planning Commission, 2003–05; Cedarburg School Board, 2007–12.

Legislature: Elected to Assembly in May 2011 special election. Reelected 2012. Elected to Senate in April 2015 special election. Reelected since 2016. Committee assignments, 2021: Administrative Rules (vice chair); Elections, Election Process

Reform and Ethics; Finance (vice chair); Government Operations, Legal Review and Consumer Protection (chair); Joint Committee for Review of Administrative Rules; Joint Committee on Finance (vice cochair).

Contact: sen.stroebel@legis.wisconsin.gov; SenatorStroebel.com; Facebook: Senator Duey Stroebel; Twitter: @SenStroebel; 608-266-7513; 800-662-1227 (toll free); Room 18 South, State Capitol, PO Box 7882, Madison, WI 53707-7882.

Rick Gundrum, Assembly District 58
Republican

Biography: Born Nenno, Wisconsin, September 4; married; 2 stepchildren, 4 grandchildren. Voting address: Slinger, Wisconsin. ▪ Graduate Hartford Union High School; A.D. University of Wisconsin-Washington County; B.S. in Radio-TV-Film, University of Wisconsin-Oshkosh. ▪ Business owner in broadcast media. ▪ Member: St. Peter Catholic Church; Washington County Republican Party; Slinger Advancement Association; Washington County Agricultural & Industrial Society; Slinger Housing Authority; Village of Slinger Board of Trustees (2009–present). ▪ Former chair: East Wisconsin Counties Railroad Consortium; Washington County Aging & Disability Resource Board; Washington County Board of Health; Washington-Ozaukee County Joint Board of Health. ▪ Former Member: Waukesha-Ozaukee-Washington Workforce Development Board of Directors; Wisconsin Counties Association Board of Directors; Wisconsin Counties Utility Tax Association Board of Directors. ▪ Washington County Board of Supervisors (member 2006–18; chair 2016–18).

Legislature: Elected to Assembly in January 2018 special election. Reelected since 2018. Committee assignments, 2021: Aging and Long-Term Care (chair); Children and Families; Insurance; Labor and Integrated Employment; Local Government (vice chair); Substance Abuse and Prevention; Workforce Development.

Contact: rep.gundrum@legis.wisconsin.gov; 608-264-8486; 888-534-0058 (toll free); Room 312 North, State Capitol, PO Box 8952, Madison, WI 53708.

Timothy S. Ramthun, Assembly District 59
Republican

Biography: Born Kewaskum, Wisconsin, March 13, 1957; married; 2 children, 8 grandchildren. Voting address: Campbellsport, Wisconsin. ▪ Graduate Kewaskum school district, 1975; Manpower Business Training Institute, 1983; diplomas in

Project Management and Six Sigma (green), Project Management Institute, 1999; diplomas in Organizational Efficiency, Operational Quality, and Service Execution, American Management Association, 1994–96. ▪ Former executive business management consultant; vice president and directorship roles for multiple Fortune 100 and Fortune 500 companies that specialized in manufacturing, technology, finance, education, supply-chain service, and delivery and call center operations. ▪ Member: The Heritage Foundation. ▪ Kewaskum School District Board of Education (past president).

Legislature: Elected to Assembly since 2018. Committee assignments, 2021: Children and Families (vice chair); Constitution and Ethics; Education; Judiciary; Transportation; Ways and Means.

Contact: rep.ramthun@legis.wisconsin.gov; 608-266-9175; 888-534-0059 (toll free); Room 409 North, State Capitol, PO Box 8953, Madison, WI 53708.

Robert Brooks, Assembly District 60
Republican

Biography: Born Rockford, Illinois, July 13, 1965; married; 2 children. Voting address: Saukville, Wisconsin. ▪ Graduate Orfordville Parkview High School, 1983; attended University of Wisconsin-La Crosse, 1983–86. ▪ Real estate broker since 1990, restaurant/tavern owner. ▪ Former member: Stars and Stripes Honor Flight (board of directors); Wisconsin County Mutual (board of directors); Wisconsin Board of Realtors; Ozaukee County Tavern League (board of directors). ▪ Former commissioner, Southeastern Wisconsin Regional Planning Commission; Ozaukee County Board, 2000–14.

Legislature: Elected to Assembly since 2014. Leadership positions: Assistant Majority Leader 2017. Committee assignments, 2021: Housing and Real Estate; Insurance; Local Government; State Affairs; Transportation; Ways and Means; Joint Survey Committee on Retirement Systems.

Contact: rep.rob.brooks@legis.wisconsin.gov; 608-267-2369; 888-534-0060 (toll free); Room 216 North, State Capitol, PO Box 8952, Madison, WI 53708.

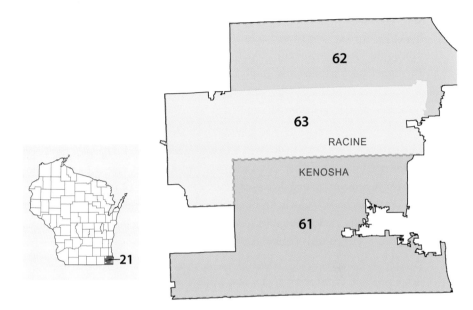

SENATE DISTRICT 21
ASSEMBLY DISTRICTS 61, 62, 63

Van H. Wanggaard, Senate District 21
Republican

Biography: Born Ft. Leavenworth, Kansas, April 1952; married; 2 children, 3 grandchildren. Voting address: Racine, Wisconsin. ▪ Graduate Racine Lutheran High School, 1970; Racine Police Academy; Wisconsin State Patrol Academy Accident Investigation; Northwestern University Traffic Institute—Reconstruction; U.S. Coast Guard National Search and Rescue School; attended John F. Kennedy University, California; University of Wisconsin-Extension; University of Wisconsin-Parkside; Green Bay Technical College; Milwaukee Area Technical College; Fox Valley Technical College. ▪ Retired traffic investigator, Racine Police Department; adjunct instructor, Gateway Technical College and Northwestern Traffic Institute; police liaison and security, Racine Unified School District. ▪ Member: NRA (life member); Racine County Line Rifle Club (board of directors); Racine Police Credit Union (former president, vice president); Major, Wisconsin Wing, Civil Air Patrol Legislative Squadron (official Auxiliary of the U.S. Air Force). ▪ Former member: Racine Zoological Society (board of directors); Racine Jaycees; Racine Police Explorers (advisor); Traffic Accident Consultants, Inc. (board of directors); Association of SWAT Personnel; Racine Innovative Youth Service (board); Hostage Negotiation Team, RAPD; Racine Junior Deputy Sheriffs Association; Racine Alateen (advisor); National Association for Search and Rescue (PSAR chair). ▪ Racine Police and Fire Commission, 2003–13 (chair, vice chair, secretary); Racine County Board, 2002–11.

Legislature: Elected to Senate 2010. Reelected since 2014. Leadership positions: Majority Caucus Vice Chair 2017, 2015; Majority Caucus Chair 2019, 2017. Committee assignments, 2021: Judiciary and Public Safety (chair); Labor and Regulatory Reform (vice chair); Utilities, Technology and Telecommunications; Joint Review Committee on Criminal Penalties (cochair). Additional appointments: Wisconsin Historical Society Board of Curators; Midwest Interstate Passenger Rail Commission.

Contact: sen.wanggaard@legis.wisconsin.gov; 608-266-1832; 866-615-7510 (toll free); Room 316 South, State Capitol, PO Box 7882, Madison, WI 53707-7882.

Samantha Kerkman, Assembly District 61
Republican

Biography: Born Burlington, Wisconsin, March 6, 1974; 2 children. Voting address: Village of Salem Lakes, Wisconsin. ▪ Graduate Wilmot High School; B.A. University of Wisconsin-Whitewater, 1996. ▪ Member: Kenosha Area Business Alliance; Twin Lakes Chamber and Area Business Association; Twin Lakes American Legion Auxiliary Post 544; St.  Alphonsus Catholic Church. ▪ Former member: Burlington Area Chamber of Commerce; Powers Lake Sportsmens Club; VFW Auxiliary, Bloomfield Center Post 5830.

Legislature: Elected to Assembly since 2000. Leadership positions: Majority Caucus Sergeant at Arms 2021, 2019, 2017, 2015, 2013, 2011. Committee assignments, 2021: Audit (chair); Children and Families; Judiciary (vice chair); Ways and Means; Joint Legislative Audit Committee (cochair).

Contact: rep.kerkman@legis.wisconsin.gov; 608-266-2530; 888-529-0061 (toll free); 262-279-1037 (district); Room 315 North, State Capitol, PO Box 8952, Madison, WI 53708; PO Box 156, Powers Lake, WI 53159 (district).

Robert O. Wittke, Jr., Assembly District 62
Republican

Biography: Born Racine, Wisconsin, September 23, 1957; married; 4 children. Voting address: Racine, Wisconsin. ▪ Graduate William Horlick High School (Racine, Wisconsin), 1975; B.A. University of Wisconsin-Eau Claire, 1980; Bowhay Institute of Legislative Leadership Development (BILLD), 2019. ▪ Tax professional for 35 years, specializing in corporate taxation. ▪ Recipient: *American Conservative Union Foundation Award*; Wisconsin Manufacturers and Commerce *Working for Wisconsin Award*. ▪ Racine Unified School District Board, 2016–19 (past president).

Legislature: Elected to the Assembly since 2018. Committee assignments, 2021: Colleges and Universities; Education; Jobs and the Economy (chair); Speaker's Task Force on Racial Disparities; Ways and Means (vice chair). Additional Appointments: Building Commission.

Contact: rep.wittke@legis.wisconsin.gov; 608-266-0731; 888-534-0062 (toll free); 262-417-0045 (district); Room 18 West, State Capitol, PO Box 8953, Madison, WI 53708.

Robin J. Vos, Assembly District 63
Republican

Biography: Born Burlington, Wisconsin, July 5, 1968. Voting address: Burlington, Wisconsin. ▪ Graduate Burlington High School, 1986; University of Wisconsin-Whitewater, 1991. ▪ Owner of several small businesses. Former congressional district director; former legislative assistant. ▪ Member: President of the National Conference of State Legislatures and the Vice Chair  of the State Legislative Leaders Foundation; Rotary Club (past president); Racine/Kenosha Farm Bureau; Knights of Columbus; Racine County Republican Party; Racine Area Manufacturers and Commerce; Union Grove Chamber of Commerce; Burlington Chamber of Commerce. ▪ University of Wisconsin Board of Regents, 1989–91; Racine County Board, 1994–2004 (former chair of Finance and Personnel committees).

Legislature: Elected to Assembly since 2004. Leadership positions: Speaker of the Assembly 2021, 2019, 2017, 2015, 2013; cochair of the Joint Committee on Finance

2011. Committee assignments, 2021: Assembly Organization (chair); Employment Relations (chair); Rules (vice chair); Joint Committee on Employment Relations (cochair); Joint Committee on Legislative Organization (cochair); Joint Legislative Council. Additional appointments: Wisconsin Economic Development Corporation Board.

Contact: rep.vos@legis.wisconsin.gov; SpeakerVos.com; 608-266-9171; 888-534-0063 (toll free); 608-282-3663 (fax); Room 217 West, State Capitol, PO Box 8953, Madison, WI 53708.

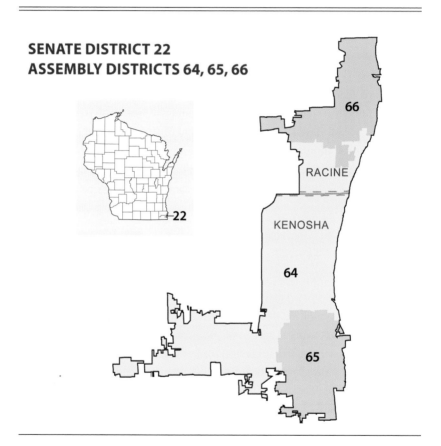

SENATE DISTRICT 22
ASSEMBLY DISTRICTS 64, 65, 66

Robert W. Wirch, Senate District 22
Democrat

Biography: Born Kenosha, Wisconsin, November 16, 1943; 2 children. Voting address: Somers, Wisconsin. ▪ Graduate Mary D. Bradford High School; B.A. University of Wisconsin-Parkside, 1970. ▪ Full-time legislator. ▪ Former factory

worker and liaison to Job Training Partnership Act (JPTA) programs; served in Army Reserve, 1965–71. ▪ Member: Danish Brotherhood; Kenosha Sport Fishing and Conservation Association; Democratic Party of Wisconsin. ▪ Former member: Kenosha Boys and Girls Club (board of directors). ▪ Kenosha County supervisor, 1986–94 (served on Health and Human Services Committee, Welfare Board, and Developmental Disabilities Board).

Legislature: Elected to Assembly 1992. Reelected 1994. Elected to Senate since 1996. Leadership positions: Minority Caucus Chair 2003. Committee assignments, 2021: Labor and Regulatory Reform; Natural Resources and Energy; Sporting Heritage, Small Business and Rural Issues; Veterans and Military Affairs and Constitution and Federalism.

Contact: sen.wirch@legis.wisconsin.gov; 608-267-8979; 262-694-7379 (district); 888-769-4724 (office hotline); Room 127 South, State Capitol, PO Box 7882, Madison, WI 53707-7882.

Tip McGuire, Assembly District 64
Democrat

Biography: Born Somers, Wisconsin. Voting address: Kenosha, Wisconsin. ▪ Graduate St. Catherine's High School (Racine), 2005; B.A. Marquette University, 2009; J.D., University of Wisconsin Law School, 2017. ▪ Attorney. Former legislative aide to Representative Peter Barca; Kenosha County special prosecutor; Milwaukee County assistant district attorney. ▪ Member: State Bar of Wisconsin. ▪ Former member: Kenosha Public Library Foundation Board (president of board of directors); National Alliance on Mental Illness (NAMI) of Kenosha County (board member).

Legislature: Elected to Assembly in April 2019 special election. Reelected in 2020. Committee assignments, 2021: Consumer Protection; Criminal Justice and Public Safety; State Affairs; Ways and Means.

Contact: rep.mcguire@legis.wisconsin.gov; 608-266-5504; 888-534-0064 (toll free); Room 321 West, State Capitol, PO Box 8953, Madison, WI 53708.

Tod Ohnstad, Assembly District 65
Democrat

Biography: Born Eau Claire, Wisconsin, May 21, 1952; married. Voting address: Kenosha, Wisconsin. ▪ Graduate Altoona Public High School, 1970; attended University of Wisconsin-Parkside. ▪ Former member: UAW Local 72 (chair of trustees, shop committeeman, bargaining committee, executive board). ▪ City of Kenosha alder, 2008–14.

Legislature: Elected to Assembly since 2012. Committee assignments, 2021: Jobs and the Economy; Labor and Integrated Employment; State Affairs; Ways and Means.

Contact: rep.ohnstad@legis.wisconsin.gov; 608-266-0455; 888-534-0065 (toll free); Room 128 North, State Capitol, PO Box 8953, Madison, WI 53708.

Greta Neubauer, Assembly District 66
Democrat

Biography: Born Racine, Wisconsin, September 13, 1991. Voting Address: Racine, Wisconsin. ▪ Graduate The Prairie School, 2010; B.A. in History, Middlebury College, 2015. ▪ Former legislative aide to State Representative Cory Mason; Fossil Fuel Divestment Student Network (director and cofounder); Divest Middlebury (cofounder and organizer); 350.org (fellow). ▪ Member: Racine Hospitality Center (board chair); Racine Interfaith Coalition; NAACP—Racine Branch; Great Lakes Legislative Caucus; National Caucus of Environmental Legislators; Young Elected Officials Network; Victory Institute; Democratic Party of Racine County. ▪ Former Member: Governor's Task Force on Climate Change; Mayor's Task Force on Police Reform ▪ Recipient: Racine Labor Council *Labor Person of the Year* 2019; Wisconsin Conservation Voters *Conservation Champion* 2019–20; RENEW Wisconsin *Legislative Leadership Award* 2020.

Legislature: Elected to Assembly in January 2018 special election. Reelected since November 2018. Committee assignments, 2021: Finance; Government Accountability and Oversight; Joint Committee on Finance; Joint Committee on Information Policy and Technology.

Contact: rep.neubauer@legis.wisconsin.gov; 608-266-0634; 888-534-0066 (toll free); Room 111 North, State Capitol, PO Box 8953, Madison, WI 53708.

SENATE DISTRICT 23
ASSEMBLY DISTRICTS 67, 68, 69

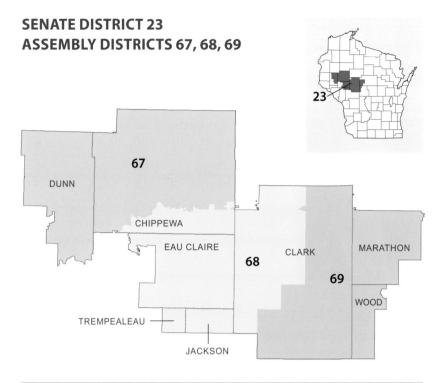

Kathy Bernier, Senate District 23
Republican

Biography: Born Eau Claire, Wisconsin, April 29, 1956; 3 children, 6 grandchildren. Voting address: Lake Hallie, Wisconsin. ▪ Graduate Chippewa Falls Senior High School, 1974; B.A. University of Wisconsin-Eau Claire, 1998; Certificate in Public Management Essentials, University of Wisconsin-Green Bay, 2005. ▪ Member: Lake Hallie Optimists Club; National Foundation for Women Legislators (State Director); American Legislative Exchange Council; Assembly of State Legislatures; National Conference of State Legislatures, Elections and Redistricting Committee; Wisconsin County Clerks Association (lifetime member). ▪ Former member: U.S. Elections Assistance Commission Board of Advisors; Wisconsin Women in Government; Wisconsin County Constitutional Officers; Chippewa County Humane Association; Kiwanis Noon Club. ▪ Chippewa County Clerk, 1999–2011; Village of Lake Hallie trustee, 2007–11 and 2015–16.

Legislature: Elected to Assembly 2010–16. Elected to Senate since 2018. Committee assignments, 2021: Agriculture and Tourism; Education (vice chair);

Elections, Election Process Reform and Ethics (chair); Finance; Joint Committee on Finance.

Contact: sen.bernier@legis.wisconsin.gov; 608-266-7511; Room 319 South, State Capitol, PO Box 7882, Madison, WI 53707.

Robert Summerfield, Assembly District 67
Republican

Biography: Born Eau Claire, Wisconsin, February 24, 1980; raised in Bloomer, Wisconsin; married; 3 children. Voting address: Bloomer, Wisconsin. ▪ Graduate Bloomer High School, 1998; B.S. in Business Administration, University of Wisconsin-Stout, 2002. ▪ Small business owner. ▪ Member: Bloomer Chamber of Commerce; Bloomer Community Lake Association; Bloomer Rod & Gun; Tavern League of Wisconsin; Chippewa County Tavern League; NRA; Good Shepherd Lutheran Church (Bloomer, Wisconsin).

Legislature: Elected to Assembly since 2016. Committee assignments, 2021: Colleges and Universities; Health (vice chair); Housing and Real Estate (chair); Rural Development; Science, Technology and Broadband (chair); Small Business Development; State Affairs; Tourism; Veterans and Military Affairs.

Contact: rep.summerfield@legis.wisconsin.gov; 608-266-1194; 888-534-0067 (toll free); Room 308 North, State Capitol, PO Box 8953, Madison, WI 53708.

Jesse James, Assembly District 68
Republican

Biography: Born Eau Claire, Wisconsin, April 16, 1972; married; 4 children, 1 grandchild. Voting address: Altoona, Wisconsin. ▪ Graduate Eau Claire North High School, 1990; Associate Degree in Police Science, Chippewa Valley Technical College (Eau Claire), 2001; Emergency Medical Responder, 2015; Entry level, Fire I, Fire II Firefighter, 2016; University of Wisconsin-

Madison Command College (Certified Public Manager), 2017. ▪ Small business owner; part-time police officer, Cadott Police Department; State of Wisconsin Firearms Instructor; Jacob's Well Security Team Advisor/Trainer. ▪ Served in the U.S. Army Air Defense, 1990–93; U.S. Army Reserves (Medic), 1993–96; Persian Gulf War veteran. ▪ Former warehouse specialist; SWAT team member; firefighter.

- Member: Solis Circle Housing Project—Altoona (community representative); American Veterans Association Post 0654.

Legislature: Elected to Assembly 2018. Reelected 2020. Committee assignments, 2021: Children and Families; Corrections; Criminal Justice and Public Safety; Family Law (vice chair); Mental Health; Small Business Development; Substance Abuse and Prevention (chair); Veterans and Military Affairs.

Contact: rep.james@legis.wisconsin.gov; 608-266-9172; 888-534-0068 (toll free); Room 9 West; State Capitol; PO Box 8952; Madison, WI 53708.

Donna Rozar, Assembly District 69
Republican

Biography: Born Lancaster, Pennsylvania, February 9, 1950; single; 5 children, 5 grandchildren. Voting address: Marshfield, Wisconsin. ▪ Graduated: Virginia Baptist Hospital School of Nursing, 1971; B.S. in Nursing, University of Tennessee, 1981; M.S. in Nursing, Viterbo University, 2008. ▪ Registered nurse; small business owner, residential and commercial rental property. ▪ Former nurse educator.

Legislature: Elected to Assembly 2020. Committee assignments, 2021: Aging and Long-Term Care; Campaigns and Elections; Education; Health; Jobs and the Economy; Small Business Development (vice chair); Transportation; Workforce Development.

Contact: rep.rozar@legis.wisconsin.gov; 608-267-0280; 888-534-0069 (toll free); Room 418 North, State Capitol, PO Box 8953, Madison, WI 53708.

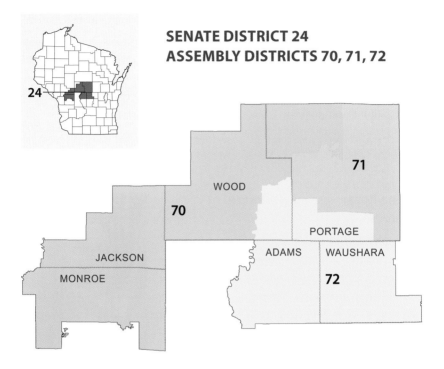

SENATE DISTRICT 24
ASSEMBLY DISTRICTS 70, 71, 72

Patrick Testin, Senate District 24
Republican

Biography: Born Madison, Wisconsin, June 9, 1988; married. Voting address: Stevens Point, Wisconsin. ▪ Graduate Marinette High School, 2006; B.S. in Political Science, University of Wisconsin-Stevens Point, 2011; Bowhay Institute for Legislative Leadership Development (BILLD) Fellow, 2018. ▪ Sales professional for a Wisconsin-based wine distributor.

▪ Member: Stevens Point Elk Lodge 641; Ignite Leadership Network of Portage County; Wisconsin Wing, Civil Air Patrol Legislative Squadron; Sportsman's Caucus (cochair). ▪ Recipient: American Conservative Union *Conservative Excellence Award* 2020, 2019, 2018, 2017; VFW Department of Wisconsin *Legislator of the Year* 2018; Dairy Business Association *Legislative Excellence Award* 2020, 2018; Wisconsin Water Alliance *Outstanding Legislator of the Year* 2020; Wisconsin Bear Hunters' Association *Hero Award* 2020, 2018; Americans for Prosperity (AFP) *Champion of Craft Beverage Freedom Award* 2017–18; Pharmacy Society of Wisconsin *Legislator of the Year* 2020; Wisconsin Counties Association *Outstanding*

Legislator of the Year 2020; Wisconsin Manufacturers and Commerce *Working for Wisconsin Award* 2019–20, 2017–18; Wisconsin Academy of Family Physicians *Friend of Family Medicine Award* 2019–20, 2017–18; Wisconsin Paper Council *Legislator of the Year* 2020; Wisconsin Economic Development Association *Champion of Economic Development Award* 2019–20, 2017–18; Wisconsin Grocers Association *Friend of Grocers* 2020; Cooperative Network *Friend of Cooperatives Award* 2018; Wisconsin Academy of Nutrition and Dietetics *Legislator of the Year* 2018; Whitetails of Wisconsin *Legislator of the Year* 2018; Wisconsin Public Health Association (WPHA) and Wisconsin Association of Local Health Departments and Boards (WALHDAB) *Friend of Public Health* 2019–20; Wisconsin Hemp Alliance *Hemp Hero Award* 2020; Wisconsin Child Support Enforcement Association (WCSEA) *Legislative Award*; Wisconsin Library Association *Wisconsin Library Champion* 2018.

Legislature: Elected to Senate since 2016. Leadership positions: Senate President Pro Tempore 2021; Majority Caucus Vice Chair 2019, 2017. Committee assignments, 2021: Agriculture and Tourism; Economic and Workforce Development (vice chair); Health (chair); Joint Committee on Information Policy and Technology; Joint Legislative Council; Joint Survey Committee on Tax Exemptions (cochair).

Contact: sen.testin@legis.wisconsin.gov; 608-266-3123; Room 8 South, State Capitol, PO Box 7882, Madison, WI 53707-7882.

Nancy Lynn VanderMeer, Assembly District 70
Republican

Biography: Born Evergreen Park, Illinois, December 15, 1958; married. Voting address: Tomah, Wisconsin. ▪ Graduate Evergreen Park Community High School, 1976; B.S. in Psychology, University of Wisconsin-La Crosse, 1988; Bowhay Institute for Legislative Leadership Development, 2017; National Conference of State Legislatures Early Learning Fellow, 2018. ▪ Small business owner; family dairy farmer. Former automobile dealer. ▪ Member: Vietnam Veterans of America (honorary life member); Jackson County Local Emergency Planning Commission; Farm Bureau; Gloria Dei Lutheran Church (former council president); Tomah Chamber of Commerce (former board of directors member); NRA; American Legion Auxiliary; board of directors of the nonprofit Handishop Industries; Monroe County Mental Health Coalition; American Association of University Women—Tomah Chapter. ▪ Former member:

Tomah Memorial Hospital board of directors (former officer); American Business Women's Association (former president). ▪ Recipient: Wisconsin Economic Development Corporation *Champion of Economic Development Award* 2019–20; Wisconsin Manufacturers and Commerce *Working for Wisconsin Award* 2019–20; Wisconsin Paper Council *Legislator of the Year Award* 2020; Sparta Area School District *Certificate of Recognition* 2015; Wisconsin Child Support Enforcement Association *Legislative Award* 2016; Wisconsin Academy of Family Physicians *Friend of Family Medicine* 2016; Dairy Business Association *Legislative Excellence Award* 2020, 2018, 2017, 2016; Wisconsin Library Association Wisconsin *Library Champion* 2016; National Foundation for Women Legislators *Elected Women of Excellence Award* 2017; U.S. Army War College Commandant's National Security Program *Certificate of Leader Development* 2017; Tomah American Association of University Women (AAUW) *Mary E. Wedin Women's History Month Award* 2018.

Legislature: Elected to Assembly since 2014. Committee assignments, 2021: Agriculture; Consumer Protection; Health; Labor and Integrated Employment (vice chair); Mental Health; Rural Development (chair); Tourism; Veterans and Military Affairs (vice chair). Additional appointments: Small Business Regulatory Review Board.

Contact: rep.vandermeer@legis.wisconsin.gov; 608-266-8366; 888-534-0070 (toll free); Room 11 West, State Capitol, PO Box 8953, Madison, WI 53708.

Katrina Shankland, Assembly District 71
Democrat

Biography: Born Wausau, Wisconsin, August 4, 1987; married. Voting address: Stevens Point, Wisconsin. ▪ Graduate Wittenberg-Birnamwood High School, 2005; attended University of Wisconsin-Marathon County, 2004–05, and Marquette University, 2005–06; B.A. in Political Science, University of Wisconsin-Madison, 2009; M.S. in Community and Organizational Leadership, University of Wisconsin-Stevens Point, 2019. ▪ Full-time legislator. Former nonprofit professional. ▪ Member: Born Learning Advocacy and Awareness Steering Committee; Wisconsin Legislative Children's Caucus; Wisconsin Legislative Sportsmen's Caucus; National Caucus of Environmental Legislators; Young Elected Officials Network; Council of State Governments Henry Toll Fellow, 2013; Major, Wisconsin Wing, Civil Air Patrol Legislative Squadron (official Auxiliary of the U.S. Air Force).

Legislature: Elected to Assembly since 2012. Leadership positions: Assistant Minority Leader 2015. Committee assignments, 2021: Agriculture; Colleges and Universities; Environment; Sporting Heritage; Workforce Development.

Contact: rep.shankland@legis.wisconsin.gov; 608-267-9649; 888-534-0071 (toll free); Room 304 West, State Capitol, PO Box 8953, Madison, WI 53708.

Scott S. Krug, Assembly District 72
Republican

Biography: Born Wisconsin Rapids, Wisconsin, September 16, 1975; married; 6 children. Voting address: Rome, Wisconsin. ▪ Graduate Lincoln High School, 1993; attended University of Wisconsin-Stevens Point; Associate Degree, Mid-State Technical College, 1999; B.A.S. in Psychology, University of Wisconsin-Green Bay, 2008. ▪ Realtor. Former Wood County Drug Court Coordinator, Jail Discharge Planner; Juneau County Sheriff's Deputy. ▪ Member: Heart of Wisconsin Chamber of Commerce; Wisconsin Rapids Rotary. ▪ Recipient: Wisconsin Paper Council *Legislator of the Year*; Wisconsin Industrial Energy Group *Legislator of the Year Award*; Child Support Enforcement Association *Legislator of the Year*; League of Conservation Voters *Honor Roll*; Dairy Business Association *Legislative Excellence Award*; Wisconsin Troopers Association *Legislator of the Year*; Wisconsin Counties Association *Outstanding Legislator*; Wisconsin Manufacturers and Commerce *Working for Wisconsin Award;* Wisconsin Grocers Association *Friend of Grocers Award*; Third Congressional District *State Legislator of the Year*; Milwaukee Metropolitan Association of Commerce *Champion of Commerce*; Wisconsin FORCE *Champion of the Second Amendment and the Rights of the People of Wisconsin*; Professional Firefighters of Wisconsin *Fire Safety Legislator of the Year*; Wisconsin Farmers Union *Friend of the Family Farm*; Wisconsin Building Association *Friend of Housing*; American Conservative Union Foundation *Defender of Liberty*.

Legislature: Elected to Assembly since 2010. Committee assignments, 2021: Colleges and Universities; Criminal Justice and Public Safety; Environment; Forestry, Parks and Outdoor Recreation (vice chair); Government Accountability and Oversight; Public Benefit Reform (chair).

Contact: rep.krug@legis.wisconsin.gov; 608-266-0215; 888-529-0072 (toll free); Room 207 North, State Capitol, PO Box 8952, Madison, WI 53708

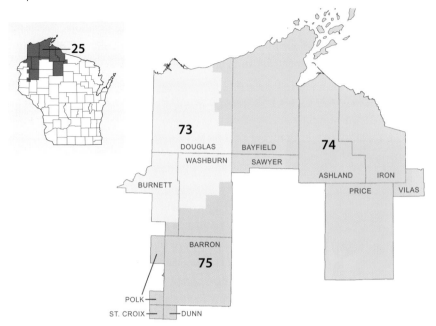

SENATE DISTRICT 25
ASSEMBLY DISTRICTS 73, 74, 75

Janet Bewley, Senate District 25
Democrat

Biography: Born Painesville, Ohio, November 10, 1951; married; 5 children, 5 grandchildren. Voting address: Mason, Wisconsin. ▪ Graduate James Ford Rhodes High School (Cleveland, Ohio), 1969; B.A. Case Western Reserve University, 1973; M. Ed. University of Maine, 1977. ▪ Full-time legislator. Former Community Relations Officer, Wisconsin Housing and Economic Development Authority; former Dean of Students, Northland College; former executive director, Mary H. Rice Foundation. ▪ Member: Lake Superior Big Top Chautauqua (original cast member); Rittenhouse Chamber Singers; Wisconsin Family Impact Seminar (advisory board member); Wisconsin Paper Caucus (vice chair); Democratic National Committee. ▪ Former Member: Governor's Task Force on Opioid Abuse; Fostering Futures Policy Advisory Committee. ▪ Recipient: Wisconsin Paper Council *Legislator of the Year Award* 2020; Wisconsin Realtors Association *Chairman Citation Award* 2020; Wisconsin

Association of Free & Charitable Clinics *Legislative Advocate of the Year* 2019; Professional Fire Fighters of Wisconsin *Legislator of the Year* 2018; Wisconsin Economic Development Association *Champion of Economic Development* 2020, 2018; Wisconsin Builders Association *Friend of Housing* 2020, 2018, 2016, 2014; Wisconsin Electric Cooperative Association *Enlightened Legislator of the Year* 2018; Wisconsin League of Conservation Voters *Conservation Champion* 2018, 2014, 2012; Wisconsin Brewers Guild *Friend of Wisconsin Craft Brewers* 2013. ▪ Ashland City Council, 2007–09.

Legislature: Elected to Assembly 2010–12. Elected to Senate since 2014. Leadership positions: Minority Leader 2021, 2020; Assistant Minority Leader 2017. Committee assignments, 2021: Senate Organization; Joint Committee on Employment Relations; Joint Committee on Legislative Organization; Joint Legislative Council. Additional appointments: Council on Forestry; Special Committee on State-Tribal Relations (vice chair); State Fair Park Board; Wisconsin Housing and Economic Development Authority.

Contact: sen.bewley@legis.wisconsin.gov; 608-266-3510; 800-469-6562 (toll free); Room 206 South, State Capitol, PO Box 7882, Madison, WI 53707-7882.

Nick Milroy, Assembly District 73
Democrat

Biography: Born Duluth, Minnesota, April 15, 1974; married; 3 children. Voting address: South Range, Wisconsin. ▪ Graduate Superior Senior High School, 1992; B.S. University of Wisconsin-Superior, 1998; attended University of Wisconsin-Eau Claire, 1999–2000. ▪ Full-time legislator; former fisheries biologist. Served in U.S. Navy, 1992–94, U.S. Naval Reserve,  1994–2000; deployed to Persian Gulf during Operation Southern Watch. ▪ Member: Great Lakes Legislative Caucus of the Council of State Governments; Wisconsin Chapter of the Congressional Sportsmen's Foundation (cochair); National Conference of Environmental Legislators; Douglas County Democratic Party (former secretary). ▪ Former member: Lake Superior Binational Forum; St. Louis River Watershed TMDL Partnership (board of directors); American Fisheries Society; Duluth-Superior Metropolitan Interstate Council (policy board member); Head of the Lakes Fair (board of directors). ▪ Superior City Council, 2005–09.

Legislature: Elected to Assembly since 2008. Committee assignments, 2021: Forestry, Parks and Outdoor Recreation; Rural Development; Sporting Heritage; Veterans and Military Affairs.

Contact: rep.milroy@legis.wisconsin.gov; 608-266-0640; 888-534-0073 (toll free); Room 104 North, State Capitol, PO Box 8953, Madison, WI 53708.

Beth Meyers, Assembly District 74
Democrat

Biography: Born Ashland, Wisconsin, May 29; married; 2 children. Voting address: Bayfield, Wisconsin. ▪ Graduate Bayfield High School; B.S. Northland College (Ashland, Wisconsin). ▪ Full-time legislator. Former executive director, CORE Community Resources, a nonprofit serving seniors. ▪ Member: Governor's Council on Forestry; Governor's Task Force on Broadband Access.

Legislature: Elected to Assembly since 2014. Leadership positions: Minority Caucus Secretary 2019, 2017, 2015. Committee assignments, 2021: Aging and Long-Term Care; Energy and Utilities; Financial Institutions; Rural Development. Additional appointments: Missing and Murdered Indigenous Women Task Force; University of Wisconsin-Madison Public Utility Institute Board.

Contact: rep.meyers@legis.wisconsin.gov; 608-266-7690; 888-534-0074 (toll free); Room 7 North, State Capitol, PO Box 8953, Madison, WI 53708.

David Armstrong, Assembly District 75
Republican

Biography: Born St. Paul, Minnesota, October 3, 1961; married; 4 children, 3 grandchildren. Voting address: Rice Lake, Wisconsin. ▪ Graduate St. Bernard's High School (St. Paul), 1979; attended Metropolitan State University (St. Paul). ▪ Executive director, Barron County Economic Development Corporation. Former business owner. ▪ Member: Law Enforcement Foundation of Barron County (board member); Pioneer Village-Barron County Historical Society (board member); Rice Lake Chamber of Commerce (board member); Rice Lake Tourism Commission (board member); Wisconsin Rural Partners. ▪ Former member: Community Connections to Prosperity (past vice president); Heart of the North Legislative Day (past chairperson); Law Enforcement Foundation of Barron County (past president); Rice Lake Cable Commission (past president).

Legislature: Elected to Assembly 2020. Committee assignments, 2021: Jobs and the Economy (vice chair); Rural Development; Small Business Development; Ways and Means; Workforce Development.

Contact: rep.armstrong@legis.wisconsin.gov; 608-266-2519; 888-534-0075 (toll free); Room 409 North, State Capitol, PO Box 8952, Madison, WI 53708.

SENATE DISTRICT 26
ASSEMBLY DISTRICTS 76, 77, 78

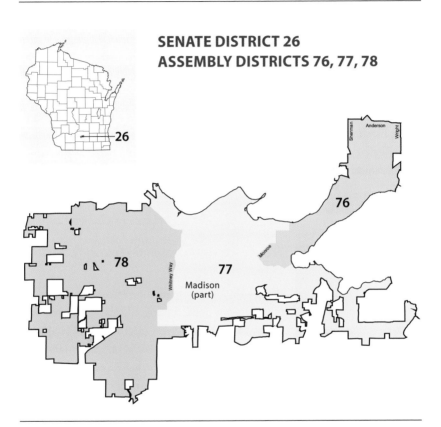

Kelda Helen Roys, Senate District 26
Democrat

Biography: Born Marshfield, Wisconsin, June 24, 1979; married; 2 children, 2 stepchildren. Voting address: Madison, Wisconsin. ▪ Graduate B.A. in Drama, Politics, and Cultural Studies, magna cum laude, New York University, 2000; J.D. University of Wisconsin Law School, magna cum laude, 2004. ▪ Attorney; small business owner. Former nonprofit

executive. ▪ Member: Clean Lakes Alliance (board member); Legal Association for Women; State Bar of Wisconsin; TEMPO Madison, professional women's organization (former board member and membership chair). ▪ Former member: ACLU of Wisconsin (board member); Coalition of Wisconsin Aging Groups (legislative advisory board); Citizen Action of Wisconsin (board member); Common Cause of Wisconsin (board member); Dane County Democratic Party (executive committee); Democratic Leadership Institute (board member); Emerge Wisconsin (advisory board); Madison Repertory Theatre (board member); Public Interest Law Foundation (board member); Wisconsin Bar Association (legal assistance committee); Sherman Neighborhood Association (board member); Women's Council (board member); Public Interest Law Foundation (board member).

Legislature: Elected to Assembly 2008–10. Leadership positions: Minority caucus chair 2011. Elected to Senate 2020. Committee assignments, 2021: Administrative Rules; Elections, Election Process Reform and Ethics; Government Operations, Legal Review and Consumer Protection; Judiciary and Public Safety; Universities and Technical Colleges; Joint Committee for Review of Administrative Rules.

Contact: sen.roys@legis.wisconsin.gov; 608-266-1627; Room 3 South, State Capitol, PO Box 7882, Madison, WI 53707.

Francesca Hong, Assembly District 76
Democrat

Biography: Born Madison, Wisconsin, November 4, 1988; 1 child. Voting address: Madison, Wisconsin. ▪ Graduate West High School (Madison), 2007; attended University of Wisconsin-Madison. ▪ Restaurant co-owner and co-chef. ▪ Member: Cook It Forward Madison (cofounder); Culinary Ladies Collective (cofounder and board president); Kennedy Heights Community Center (board); Madison Area Chefs Network.

Legislature: Elected to Assembly 2020. Committee assignments, 2021: Audit; Labor and Integrated Employment; Rural Development; Small Business Development; Joint Legislative Audit Committee.

Contact: rep.hong@legis.wisconsin.gov; 608-266-5342; 888-534-0076 (toll free); Room 122 North, State Capitol, PO Box 8952, Madison, WI 53708.

Shelia Stubbs, Assembly District 77
Democrat

Biography: Born Camden, Arkansas, February 22, 1971; married; 6 children. Voting

address: Madison, Wisconsin. ▪ Graduate: Beloit Memorial High School; B.A. in Political Science, Tougaloo College; B.S. in Criminal Justice Administration, magna cum laude, Mount Senario College; Masters of Science & Management, Cardinal Stritch University. ▪ Full-time legislator. Former special education teacher; adjunct professor; probation and parole agent; match support specialist. ▪ Member: Democratic Party of Wisconsin; Democratic Party of Wisconsin Black Caucus (former chair); Greater Madison Convention & Visitors (board of directors); Tamara D. Grigsby Office of Equity and Inclusion (advisory board); Alliant Energy Center Redevelopment Committee; Dane County Youth in Government (mentor); Wisconsin Legislative Black Caucus (chair); Vel Phillips Statute Advisory Taskforce; National Association of Counties (NACo) first African American woman to serve on a NACo committee representing Wisconsin; Women of NACo (WON) (secretary), Justice and Public Safety Steering Committee; National Association of Large Urban County Caucus (LUCC); National Association of Healthy Counties Initiative Advisory Board (HCAB); Community Justice Action Fund (CJAF) Policy Makers for Peace Midwestern (regional lead); Women's Legislative Network Governance Midwestern (regional member); National Conference of State Legislatures Law, Criminal Justice, and Public Safety Committee; Bridge-Lake Point Neighborhood Association (president); Madison Alumnae Chapter of Delta Sigma Theta Sorority, Inc.; NAACP Dane County Branch; End Time Ministries International (co-founder and ordained pastor); Wisconsin Women in Government (legislative board member); City of Madison Complete Count Committee (chair); Wisconsin State Complete Count Committee. ▪ Former member: Wisconsin Counties Association (board of directors, chair and vice chair of the Judicial and Public Safety Steering Committee, first African American woman to serve as steering committee chair); NAACP Madison Branch (first vice president); Wisconsin NAACP Conference of Branches (third vice president); Madison Youth Council of the NAACP (chartering member, youth advisor). ▪ Recipient: *2021 Rev. Dr. Martin Luther King Humanitarian Award*; *Who's Who Among High School Students*; Wisconsin Women of Color Network, Inc. *Woman of Achievement Award* 2014; National Dean's List; Broadway-Simpson-Waunona Neighborhood Center Fifth Annual Pride Festival *Spirit Award* 1998; Dane County Human Services *Friends of Joining Forces for Families Award*; "MISS NAACP" 1992 at Tougaloo College; NAACP Madison Branch *W.E.B. DuBois Advocates Award* 2004; Now Faith Ministries *100 Women in White Award*; *Genesis Social Services Corporation & The Black Women's Expo Award* 2008; *100 Black Men of Madison*

Award 2015; Democratic Party of Wisconsin *Eleanor Roosevelt Award* 2014; Madison 365 Black Power *The 44 Most Influential African Americans in Wisconsin* 2016; Community Building and Advocacy for Social Justice Building the Generation Gap *Community Leader Champion Award* 2018; Madison Metropolitan Chapter of the Links, Inc. *Community Award* 2017; Democratic Party of Dane County *Midge Miller Award for Outstanding Elected Official* 2019; YWCA *Woman of Distinction Award* 2019; BRAVA Magazine *Woman to Watch* 2020. ▪ Dane County Board of Supervisors, serving the 23rd district; first African American woman to chair a Dane County standing committee and to hold the leadership position of vice chair of the Board, currently serving on the following committees: Personnel & Finance Committee (chair); Dane County University of Wisconsin Extension Committee (cochair); Racial Disparities Subcommittee.

Legislature: Elected to Assembly since 2018. Committee assignments, 2021: Colleges and Universities; Corrections; Criminal Justice and Public Safety; Speaker's Task Force on Racial Disparities (cochair); Tourism.

Contact: rep.stubbs@legis.wisconsin.gov; 608-266-3784; 888-534-0077; Room 17 North, State Capitol, PO Box 8953, Madison, WI 53708.

Lisa Subeck, Assembly District 78
Democrat

Biography: Born Chicago, Illinois, June 17, 1971; single. Voting address: Madison, Wisconsin. ▪ Graduate Rich Central High School, 1989; B.A. University of Wisconsin-Madison, 1993. ▪ Full-time legislator. Former early childhood education/Head Start program manager; technical college instructor; nonprofit executive director. ▪ Member: National Foundation of Women Legislators (board member); National Association of Jewish Legislators (board member); National Caucus of Environmental Legislators; Women Legislators' Lobby (state director); Women's Legislative Network of the National Conference of State Legislatures. ▪ Former member: American Federation of Teachers. ▪ Recipient: National Foundation of Women Legislators *Woman of Excellence*; Wisconsin League of Conservation Voters *Conservation Champion*; Breastfeeding Coalition of South Central Wisconsin *Breastfeeding Advocate Award*; ARC Dane County *Elected Official Award*; Wisconsin Public Health Association and Wisconsin Association of Local Health Departments and Boards *Friend of Public Health*; Wisconsin Association for Home Health Care *Friend of Home Health Care*. ▪ City of Madison Common Council, 2011–15.

Legislature: Elected to Assembly since 2014. Committee assignments, 2021: Administrative Rules; Campaigns and Elections; Energy and Utilities; Health; Rules; Joint Committee for Review of Administrative Rules.

Contact: rep.subeck@legis.wisconsin.gov; 608-266-7521; 888-534-0078 (toll free); Room 109 North, State Capitol, PO Box 8953, Madison, WI 53708.

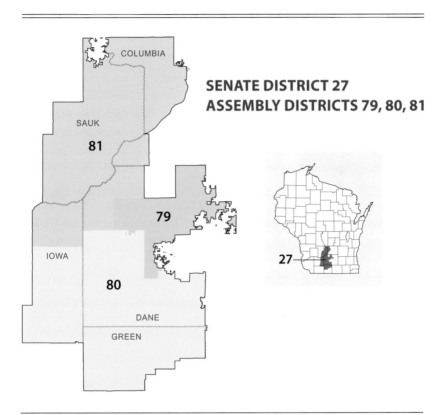

SENATE DISTRICT 27
ASSEMBLY DISTRICTS 79, 80, 81

Jon B. Erpenbach, Senate District 27
Democrat

Biography: Born Middleton, Wisconsin, January 28, 1961; married; 2 children. Voting address: West Point, Wisconsin. ▪ Graduate Middleton High School; attended University of Wisconsin-Oshkosh, 1979–81. ▪ Former communications director; legislative aide; radio personality; short order cook; meat packer; truck driver; City of Middleton recreation instructor.

Legislature: Elected to Senate since 1998. Leadership positions: Minority Leader

2003. Committee assignments, 2021: Agriculture and Tourism; Finance; Health; Universities and Technical Colleges; Joint Committee on Finance; Joint Legislative Council.

Contact: sen.erpenbach@legis.wisconsin.gov; 608-266-6670; 888-549-0027 (district, toll free); Room 130 South, State Capitol, PO Box 7882, Madison, WI 53707-7882.

Dianne Hesselbein, Assembly District 79
Democrat

Biography: Born Madison, Wisconsin, March 10, 1971; married; 3 children. Voting address: Middleton, Wisconsin. ▪ Graduate La Follette High School (Madison), 1989; B.S. University of Wisconsin-Oshkosh, 1993; M.A. Edgewood College, 1996. ▪ Full-time legislator. ▪ Member: Dane County Democratic Party; Friends of Pheasant Branch; Middleton Action Team; VFW Auxiliary Council. ▪ Former member: Parent Teacher Organization (president); Boy Scouts of America (cubmaster); Girl Scouts (troop leader); Monona Terrace Convention and Community Center Board; Clean Wisconsin. ▪ Middleton-Cross Plains Area School District Board, 2005–08; Dane County Board, 2008–14.

Legislature: Elected to Assembly since 2012. Leadership positions: Assistant Minority Leader 2021, 2019, 2017. Committee assignments, 2021: Assembly Organization; Audit; Colleges and Universities; Insurance; Rules; Sporting Heritage; Veterans and Military Affairs; Joint Committee on Legislative Organization; Joint Legislative Audit Committee; Joint Legislative Council.

Contact: rep.hesselbein@legis.wisconsin.gov; 608-266-5340; Room 119 North, State Capitol, PO Box 8952, Madison, WI 53708.

Sondy Pope, Assembly District 80
Democrat

Biography: Born Madison, Wisconsin, April 27, 1950; married. Voting address: Mount Horeb, Wisconsin. ▪ Graduate River Valley High School; attended Madison Area Technical College and Edgewood College. ▪ Former Associate Director of the Foundation for Madison's Public Schools. ▪ Member: National Caucus of Environmental Legislators; Wisconsin Congress of Parents and Teachers (honorary life member); Midwestern Higher Education

Compact Commission; Bowhay Institute, La Follette School, University of Wisconsin-Madison (fellow); Flemming Institute, Center for Policy Alternatives (fellow); Oakhill Correctional Institution Advisory Board; Women Legislators' Lobby (WiLL) and Women's Action for New Directions (WAND) National Women's Leadership. ▪ Former member: State Innovation Exchange; Agrace Hospice Care Patient and Family Partnership Council; Agrace Hospice Care Ethics Committee; Legislative Council Study Committee on School Data; DPI Parent Advisory Council; DPI Statewide Educator Effectiveness Coordinating Council; Improving Educational Opportunities in High School Task Force; Office of Educational Opportunity RFP Design Council; Rural Education Task Force; Urban Education Task Force; Common Core State Standards Task Force; Read to Lead Council; Water Quality Task Force; Blue Ribbon Commission on School Funding.

Legislature: Elected to Assembly since 2002. Committee assignments, 2021: Constitution and Ethics; Consumer Protection; Education; Rules; State Affairs.

Contact: rep.pope@legis.wisconsin.gov; 608-266-3520; 888-534-0080 (toll free); Room 118 North, State Capitol, PO Box 8953, Madison, WI 53708.

Dave Considine, Assembly District 81
Democrat

Biography: Born Janesville, Wisconsin, March 29, 1952; married; 5 children, 12 grandchildren. Voting address: Baraboo, Wisconsin. ▪ Graduate Mukwonago Union High School, 1970; B.S. in Education, University of Wisconsin-Whitewater, 1974; certificate in Emotional/Behavorial Disabilities, University of Wisconsin-Madison, 1990; M.A. in Education, Viterbo University, 2005; instructor certificate, autism spectrum, and enhanced verbal skills, Crisis Prevention Institute (Milwaukee), 2008, 2010, 2013. ▪ Full-time legislator. Former dairy goat farmer; special education teacher. ▪ Member: Columbia County Democratic Party; Pheasants Forever; Ducks Unlimited. ▪ Former member: Baraboo Education Association (president); American Dairy Goat Association (judge); Wisconsin Dairy Goat Association (president); Crisis Prevention Institute (instructor).

Legislature: Elected to Assembly since 2014. Committee assignments, 2021: Agriculture; Education; Mental Health; Rural Development; Transportation.

Contact: rep.considine@legis.wisconsin.gov; 608-266-7746; 888-534-0081 (toll free); Room 303 West, State Capitol, PO Box 8952, Madison, WI 53708.

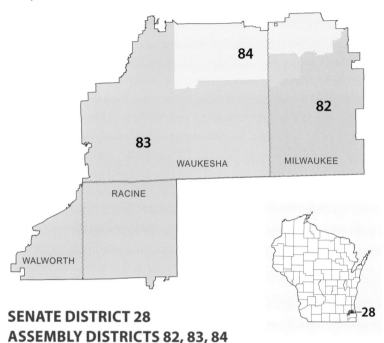

SENATE DISTRICT 28
ASSEMBLY DISTRICTS 82, 83, 84

Marc Julian Bradley, Senate District 28
Republican

Biography: Born Baltimore, Maryland, February 11, 1981. Voting address: Franklin, Wisconsin. ▪ Graduate B.S. in Political Science, University of Wisconsin-La Crosse, 2014; attended Temple University (Philadelphia), 2004–2005. ▪ Full-time legislator. ▪ Former employee of insurance and telecommunications companies. ▪ Former member: La Crosse County Republican Party (chair); 2015 Republican Party of Wisconsin Convention (chair); Third Congressional District Republican Party (vice chair); Together for Tots, Toys for Tots Drive (co-founder).

Legislature: Elected to Senate 2020. Committee assignments, 2021: Administrative Rules; Government Operations, Legal Review and Consumer Protection; Health; Judiciary and Public Safety; Utilities, Technology and Telecommunications (chair); Joint Committee on Information Policy and Technology (cochair); Joint Committee for Review of Administrative Rules.

Contact: sen.bradley@legis.wisconsin.gov; 608-266-5400; Room 323 South, State Capitol, PO Box 7882, Madison, WI 53707.

Ken Skowronski, Assembly District 82
Republican

Biography: Born Milwaukee, Wisconsin, May 31, 1938; widowed; 2 children, 5 grandchildren, 5 great-grandchildren. Voting address: Franklin, Wisconsin. ▪ Graduate Boys Tech High School, 1958; journeyman carpenter, Milwaukee Area Technical College, 1961; National Association of the Remodeling Industry (NARI) certified remodeler. ▪ General contractor. Served in Wisconsin Air National Guard, 128th Refueling, 1956–62. ▪ Member: Milwaukee/NARI Foundation (trustee, former president); Franklin Noon Lions Club (trustee, former president); Polish Heritage Alliance (immediate past president); Knights of Columbus (former deputy grand knight); NRA (benefactor life member); Ducks Unlimited (patron life member); Rocky Mountain Elk Foundation (life member); South Suburban Chamber of Commerce (former board member); Milwaukee/NARI Chapter (former president); NARI National (former president), NARI National Foundation/National Remodeling Foundation (former president); AmVets Post #60; American Legion Post #192; Army War College Foundation; Franklin Historical Society (life member); National Wild Turkey Federation. ▪ Former member: Franklin Lions Club (president); City of Franklin Plan Commission, Economic Development Commission (chair), Community Development Authority, and 50th Anniversary Committee (chair); Wisconsin DNR Hunter Safety Courses, chief instructor, 19 years. ▪ Recipient: City of Franklin *Distinguished Service Award* 1983; Lions Clubs International *Melvin Jones Fellowship Award* 1995; Remodeling Magazine *Big 50 Industry Impact Award* 1992; Milwaukee/NARI Chapter *Lifetime Achievement Award* 2002, 1997; VFW Department of Wisconsin *Legislator of the Year Award* 2018–19; National Guard Association of the United States *Patrick Henry Award* 2019; Polish National Alliance *Polish-American of the Year* 2019; Alzheimer Association *Leadership in Advocacy* 2018; Department of Defense *Certificate of Appreciation* 2018; Department of Defense *Vietnam War Commemoration* 2017; Polish American Congress *Zablocki Award* 2016; South Side Business Club *Person of the Year* 2016; Wisconsin Manufacturers and Commerce *Working for Wisconsin Award* 2020, 2018, 2016, 2014; ABC of Wisconsin *Building Wisconsin Award*, 2020, 2018, 2016; *Friend of Home Health Care* 2019–20. ▪ Alderman, City of Franklin 2005–14.

Legislature: Elected to Assembly in December 2013 special election. Reelected since 2014. Committee assignments, 2021: Consumer Protection; Health; Local Government; Small Business Development; Sporting Heritage; Transportation; Veterans and Military Affairs (chair).

Contact: rep.skowronski@legis.wisconsin.gov; 608-266-8590; 888-534-0082 (toll free); Room 209 North, State Capitol, PO Box 8953, Madison, WI 53708.

Chuck Wichgers, Assembly District 83
Republican

Biography: Born Milwaukee, Wisconsin, July 4, 1965; married; 8 children; grandfather. Voting address: Muskego, Wisconsin. ▪ Graduate Muskego High School, 1983; Waukesha County Technical College, 1984–85. ▪ Works in professional sales; formerly practiced medical sales offering conservative options for pain management. Coach for softball, basketball, football. Volunteer, along with wife and children, assisting nursing home residents to get to weekly religious services. Education curriculum watchdog. ▪ Member: Various pro-life groups across Wisconsin; church committees and organizations. ▪ Former Member: Muskego Hoops Booster Club (co-founder); Moose Club; Preserve Muskego (president); Janesville Road Reconstruction Advisory Committee. ▪ City of Muskego alderman, 1999–2002; Waukesha County supervisor, 1999–2002.

Legislature: Elected to Assembly since 2016. Committee assignments, 2021: Constitution and Ethics (chair); Education; Forestry, Parks and Outdoor Recreation; Health; Sporting Heritage.

Contact: rep.wichgers@legis.wisconsin.gov; 608-266-3363; 888-534-0083 (toll free); Room 306 North, State Capitol, PO Box 8953, Madison, WI 53708.

Michael Kuglitsch, Assembly District 84
Republican

Biography: Born Milwaukee, Wisconsin, February 3, 1960; married; 4 children. Voting address: New Berlin, Wisconsin. ▪ Graduate New Berlin West High School, 1978; B.A. in Business, University of Wisconsin-Whitewater, 1983. ▪ Business consultant. ▪ Former member: Wisconsin Restaurant Association (president); Bowling Centers Association of Wisconsin (president); New Berlin Chamber of Commerce (president).

Legislature: Elected to Assembly since 2010. Committee assignments, 2021: Energy and Utilities (chair); Environment; Government Accountability and Oversight; Rules; State Affairs; Joint Survey Committee on Retirement Systems (cochair).

Contact: rep.kuglitsch@legis.wisconsin.gov; 608-267-5158; 888-534-0084 (toll free); Room 129 West, State Capitol, PO Box 8952, Madison, WI 53708.

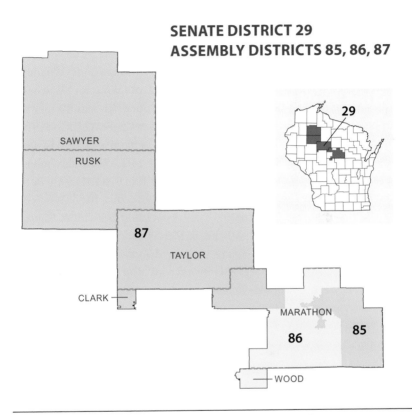

SENATE DISTRICT 29
ASSEMBLY DISTRICTS 85, 86, 87

Jerry Petrowski, Senate District 29
Republican

Biography: Born Wausau, Wisconsin, June 16, 1950; married; 4 children, 3 grandchildren. Voting address: Marathon, Wisconsin. ▪ Graduate Newman High School (Wausau); attended University of Wisconsin-Marathon County and Northcentral Technical College. ▪ Former ginseng, dairy, and beef farmer. Served in Army Reserve, 1968–74. ▪ Member: Seventh Congressional District, Marathon, Wood, Taylor, Rusk, Sawyer, Price, Lincoln, Portage, and Shawano County Republican Parties; Farm Bureau; NRA; Friends of Rib Mountain; Wausau Elks; Marathon Lions. ▪ Former member:

Wisconsin Rifle and Pistol Association; International Brotherhood of Electrical Workers Local #1791; Childcare Connection Board; Department of Transportation Law Enforcement Advisory Council; Marathon County Hunger Coalition. ∎ Recipient: American Heart Association *Legislator of the Year* 2018, 2016, 2014; End Domestic Abuse Wisconsin *Legislative Leader Award* 2014; Wisconsin VFW *Legislator of the Year* 2014; Wisconsin American Legion *Legislator of the Year* 2014; Wisconsin Vietnam Veterans *Legislator of the Year* 2002; Wisconsin Department of Veterans Affairs *Certificate of Commendation* 2005; Wisconsin Towns Association *Friend of Wisconsin Towns Award* 2016, 2014, 2011; Wisconsin Counties Association *Outstanding Legislator Award* 2014; Wisconsin Economic Development Association *Working for Wisconsin Award* 2018; Wisconsin Urban and Rural Transit Association *Legislative Statesman of the Year* 2014; Wisconsin Professional Police Association *Legislator of the Year* 2014; Wisconsin Troopers Association *Legislator of the Year* 2014, 2003; Center for Driver's License Recovery and Employability *Legislative Champion Award* 2014; State Bar of Wisconsin *Scales of Justice Award* 2014; Wisconsin Dental Association *Legislative Champion Award* 2013 and *Award of Honor* (Mission of Mercy) 2011; Wisconsin Academy of Family Physicians *Friend of Family Medicine Award* 2016, 2014; American Academy of Pediatrics *Childhood Legislative Advocate of the Year* 2005; Wisconsin Council on Physical Disabilities *Appreciation Award* 2014; Wisconsin Primary Health Care Association *Community Health Center Friend Award* 2018; Wisconsin Public Health Association *Friend of Public Health Award* 2016; Wisconsin Electric Cooperatives Association *Enlightened Legislator of the Year* 2013; Wisconsin Farm Bureau *Friend of Agriculture Award* 2006, 2004; Wisconsin Dairy Business Association *Legislative Excellence Award* 2018, 2014, 2012, 2010, 2008; Wisconsin Grocers Association *Friend of the Grocers Award* 2016, 2014, 2012, 2008, 2006; Wisconsin Pork Association *Distinguished Public Service Award* 2016; Wisconsin Builders Association *Friend of Housing Award* 2018, 2016, 2013, 2006; Associated Builders and Contractors of Wisconsin *Building Wisconsin Award* 2014; State Farm Insurance *Golden Car Seat Award* 2007; Chiropractic Society of Wisconsin *Legislator of the Year* 2014, *Champion for Chiropractic Award* 2018, 2017, 2016, 2015; 3M *Award of Appreciation* 2001; Wisconsin Paper Council *Champion of Paper Award* 2007; Wisconsin Technical College System *Legislator of the Year Award* 2016; Wisconsin Technical College District Boards Association *Legislator of the Year* 2016; University of Wisconsin-Stevens Point Paper Science Foundation *Friends of the Foundation Award* 2005; Wisconsin Manufacturers and Commerce *Working for Wisconsin Award* 2018, 2016, 2014, 2012, 2002, 2000; Metropolitan Milwaukee Association of Commerce *Champion of Commerce Award* 2016, 2014; The American Conservative Union *Defender of Liberty Award* 2013; Wisconsin

Ginseng Board *Assistance to the Wisconsin Ginseng Industry Award* 2005; Wisconsin Bear Hunters Association *Hero Award* 2014, 2012.

Legislature: Elected to Assembly 1998–2010. Elected to Senate in June 2012 special election. Reelected since 2014. Leadership positions: Majority Caucus Sergeant at Arms 2003–07. Committee assignments, 2021: Agriculture and Tourism; Sporting Heritage, Small Business and Rural Issues (vice chair); Transportation and Local Government (chair). Additional appointments: Building Commission.

Contact: sen.petrowski@legis.wisconsin.gov; 608-266-2502; Room 123 South, State Capitol, PO Box 7882, Madison, WI 53707-7882.

Patrick Snyder, Assembly District 85
Republican

Biography: Born Boone, Iowa, October 10, 1956; married; 2 children, 4 grandchildren. Voting address: Schofield, Wisconsin. ▪ Graduate Oelwein Community High School (Iowa), 1974; B.A. in Communications, University of Iowa, 1978. ▪ Former congressional staffer for Congressman Sean Duffy; radio host for WSAU. ▪ Member: Wausau Noon Rotary; Elks Club; United Way's Hunger Coalition and Housing and Homelessness Committee; Marathon County Health Department's Alcohol and Other Drugs (AOD) Committee. ▪ Former member: St. Therese Parish Council; Marathon County Department of Social Services Administrative Review Panel. ▪ Former alder for the City of Schofield.

Legislature: Elected to Assembly since 2016. Committee assignments, 2021: Children and Families (chair); Corrections; Family Law; Jobs and the Economy; Mental Health; Small Business Development; Substance Abuse and Prevention; Ways and Means. Additional appointments: Child Abuse and Neglect Prevention Board.

Contact: rep.snyder@legis.wisconsin.gov; 608-266-0654; 888-534-0085 (toll free); Room 307 North, State Capitol, PO Box 8953, Madison, WI 53708.

John Spiros, Assembly District 86
Republican

Biography: Born Akron, Ohio, July 28, 1961; married; 5 children, 4 grandchildren. Voting address: Marshfield, Wisconsin. ▪ Graduate Marietta High School (Marietta, Ohio), 1979; A.A.S. in Criminal Justice, Metropolitan Technical Community College (Omaha, Nebraska), 1985. ▪ Vice president, safety and claims management for a national trucking company in Marshfield, Wisconsin. Served in U.S. Air Force, 1979–85, member of the Strategic Air Command "Elite" guard. ▪ Trucking Industry Defense Association (president of the board of directors 2015–17; executive committee 2013–18); Wisconsin Farm Bureau; Marshfield Elks Club; American Trucking Association. ▪ City of Marshfield alder, 2005–13.

Legislature: Elected to Assembly since 2012. Committee assignments, 2021: Administrative Rules; Criminal Justice and Public Safety (chair); State Affairs; Transportation (vice chair); Joint Committee for Review of Administrative Rules; Joint Legislative Council; Joint Review Committee on Criminal Penalties (cochair).

Contact: rep.spiros@legis.wisconsin.gov; 608-266-1182; 888-534-0086 (toll free); Room 212 North, State Capitol, PO Box 8953, Madison, WI 53708.

James W. Edming, Assembly District 87
Republican

Biography: Born Ladysmith, Wisconsin, November 22, 1945; married; 3 sons, 2 granddaughters, 1 great-granddaughter. Voting address: Glen Flora, Wisconsin. ▪ Graduate Flambeau High School (Tony, Wisconsin), 1964; Teacher's Certificate, Taylor County Teacher's College, 1967; attended University of Wisconsin-Superior, University of Wisconsin-Eau Claire, University of Wisconsin-Menomonie, and University of Wisconsin-Barron County. ▪ Convenience store owner; metal stamping company owner; farmer. Former frozen pizza manufacturer. ▪ Member: 3rd degree Master Mason; 32nd degree Scottish Rite; Shriner; NRA (gun instructor); Model T Ford Club; Wisconsin Self Storage Association; St. Joseph's Hospital Advisory Council (Chippewa Falls) 2018–present; Rusk County Hospital Board, 1980–82, 2010–18. ▪ Rusk County Board of Supervisors, 1976–87.

Legislature: Elected to Assembly since 2014. Committee assignments, 2021: Consumer Protection (vice chair); Family Law; Forestry, Parks and Outdoor Recreation; Labor and Integrated Employment (chair); Rural Development; Small Business Development; Sporting Heritage; Veterans and Military Affairs; Workforce Development.

Contact: rep.edming@legis.wisconsin.gov; 608-266-7506; 888-534-0087 (toll free); Room 109 West, State Capitol, PO Box 8952, Madison, WI 53708.

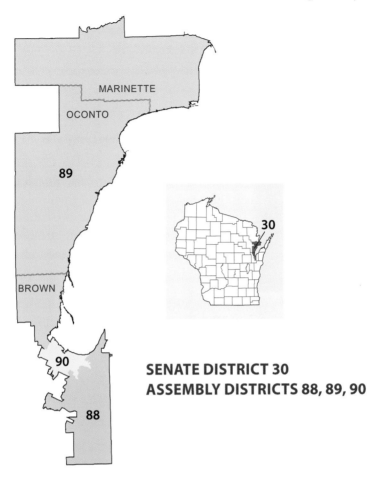

**SENATE DISTRICT 30
ASSEMBLY DISTRICTS 88, 89, 90**

Eric Wimberger, Senate District 30
Republican

Biography: Born Green Bay, Wisconsin, April 2, 1979; single. Voting address: Green Bay, Wisconsin. ▪ Graduate B.A in Criminal Justice, St. Cloud State University, 2001; J.D. Marquette University Law School, 2005. ▪ Attorney; owner, candy store in the district. Former Captain, U.S. Marine Corps, Judge Advocate General's Corp, 2006–10; former truck driver, bartender, factory worker, and retail employee.

Legislature: Elected to Senate 2020. Committee assignments, 2021: Human Services, Children and Families; Judiciary and Public Safety (vice chair); Transportation and Local Government; Veterans and Military Affairs and Constitution and Federalism (chair); Joint Legislative Council. Additional appointments: Commission on Uniform State Laws.

Contact: sen.wimberger@legis.wisconsin.gov; 608-266-5670; Room 104 South, State Capitol, PO Box 7882, Madison, WI 53707.

John J. Macco, Assembly District 88
Republican

Biography: Born Green Bay, Wisconsin, September 23, 1958; married; 2 children, 6 grandchildren. Voting address: De Pere, Wisconsin. ▪ Graduate Green Bay Southwest High School, 1976; attended Northeast Wisconsin Technical College and University of Wisconsin-Green Bay. ▪ Founder of regional financial planning group; founder of regional retail franchise; business consultant. ▪ Member: NRA. ▪ Former member: American Cancer Society of Wood County; Old Main Street Marshfield; Old Main Street De Pere; Old Main Street Green Bay; U.S. Ski Patrol; Aircraft Owners and Pilots Association; Central Church, Green Bay (deacon and church elder).

Legislature: Elected to Assembly since 2014. Committee assignments, 2021: Audit (vice chair); Consumer Protection; Jobs and the Economy; Local Government; Ways and Means (chair); Joint Legislative Audit Committee.

Contact: rep.macco@legis.wisconsin.gov; 608-266-0485; 888-534-0088 (toll free); Room 208 North, State Capitol, PO Box 8953, Madison, WI 53708.

Elijah Behnke, Assembly District 89
Republican

Biography: Born Oconto, Wisconsin, February 15, 1983; married; 2 children. Voting address: Oconto, Wisconsin. ▪ Graduate Oconto High School, 2001; associate's degree in Biblical Studies, Toccoa Falls College, 2005 (class chaplain). ▪ Entrepreneur. Former landscaper and farmer. ▪ Member: Oconto Gospel Chapel (ministry director). ▪ Former member: Town of Little River 4H Club (president).

Legislature: Elected to Assembly in April 2021 special election. Committee assignments, 2021: Education; Environment; Mental Health; Public Benefit Reform.

Contact: rep.behnke@legis.wisconsin.gov; 608-266-2343; 888-534-0089 (toll free); Room 308 North, State Capitol, PO Box 8952, Madison, WI 53707.

Kristina Shelton, Assembly District 90
Democrat

Biography: Born Pittsburgh, Pennsylvania, June 2, 1980; married; 2 children. Voting address: Green Bay, Wisconsin. ▪ Graduate North Hills High School (Pittsburgh, Pennsylvania), 1998; B.S. in Kinesiology, Pennsylvania State University, 2002; M.S. in Health Promotion Management, Marymount University (Arlington, Virginia), 2010. ▪ Certified health education specialist. Former health and physical education teacher, nonprofit director, community organizer. ▪ Member: Wisconsin Association of School Boards; Yoga Alliance; National Commission for Health Education Credentialing. ▪ Former member: American Public Health Association; The Society of Health and Physical Educators (SHAPE America). ▪ Green Bay School Board (vice president).

Legislature: Elected to Assembly 2020. Committee assignments, 2021: Aging and Long-Term Care; Jobs and the Economy; Sporting Heritage; Substance Abuse and Prevention; Transportation.

Contact: rep.shelton@legis.wisconsin.gov; 608-266-0616; 888-534-0090; Room 20 North, State Capitol, PO Box 8953, Madison, WI 53708.

SENATE DISTRICT 31
ASSEMBLY DISTRICTS 91, 92, 93

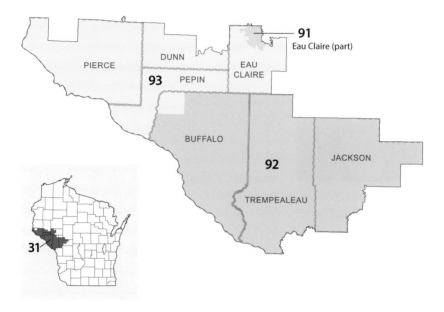

Jeff Smith, Senate District 31
Democrat

Biography: Born Eau Claire, Wisconsin, March 15, 1955; married; 2 children. Voting address: Town of Brunswick, Wisconsin. ▪ Graduate Eau Claire North High School, 1973. ▪ Former owner/operator of window cleaning business, 1973–2011; community organizer for Western Wisconsin Organizing Cooperative of Citizen Action, 2016–18. ▪ Member: Eau Claire Area Chamber of Commerce; Wisconsin Farmers Union. ▪ Former member: Valley Gospel Choir (president); Eau Claire Male Chorus; Eau Claire Kiwanis Club; Eau Claire Area School District Parent Advisory Committee (founder and chair); Eau Claire Family Resource Center (board member); Governor's Task Force for Educational Excellence; Wisconsin PTA state board; DPI Parent Leadership Corps; Wisconsin Alliance for Excellent Schools; Township Fire Department (vice president of board of directors); Tainter-Menomin Lake Improvement Association (board member); University of Wisconsin Extension Community Partner Advisory Group. ▪ Town of Brunswick chair, 2001–2007.

Legislature: Elected to Assembly 2006–08. Elected to Senate since 2018. Leadership positions: Minority Caucus Chair 2021. Committee assignments, 2021: Agriculture and Tourism; Education; Elections, Election Process Reform and Ethics; Government Operations, Legal Review and Consumer Protection; Sporting Heritage, Small Business and Rural Issues; Utilities, Technology and Telecommunications.

Contact: sen.smith@legis.wisconsin.gov; 608-266-8546; 715-600-3307 (district); Room 19 South, State Capitol, PO Box 7882, Madison, WI 53707.

Jodi Emerson, Assembly District 91
Democrat

Biography: Born Eau Claire, Wisconsin, August 3, 1972; married; 2 children. Voting address: Eau Claire, Wisconsin. ▪ Graduate Eau Claire Memorial High School, 1990; studied Biotechnology, University of Wisconsin-River Falls, 1990–92. ▪ Former anti-human trafficking advocate. ▪ Member: Wisconsin Anti-Human Trafficking Consortium. ▪ Former member: Wisconsin Human Trafficking Advisory Council; Wisconsin Anti-Human Trafficking Task Force; Wisconsin Parent Teacher Association; Girl Scouts; Eastside Hill Neighborhood Association Steering Committee.

Legislature: Elected to Assembly since 2018. Committee assignments, 2021: Campaigns and Elections; Colleges and Universities; Criminal Justice and Public Safety; Government Accountability and Oversight; Housing and Real Estate. Additional appointments: Women's Council.

Contact: rep.emerson@legis.wisconsin.gov; 608-266-7461; 888-534-0091 (toll free); 715-456-9355 (district); Room 322 West, State Capitol, PO Box 8952, Madison, WI 53708.

Treig E. Pronschinske, Assembly District 92
Republican

Biography: Born Eau Claire, Wisconsin, July 7, 1978; married; 1 child. Voting address: Mondovi, Wisconsin. ▪ Graduate Memorial High School, 1996; degree in Construction Management, Chippewa Valley Technical College, 1997. ▪ Small business owner; general construction contractor. ▪ Member: Mondovi Fire Department (volunteer firefighter); Gilmanton

Community Club. ▪ Former member: Mondovi Youth Baseball Association (president); Mondovi Ambulance Commission 2014–18; Big Brothers Big Sisters; Junior Achievement volunteer. ▪ Mayor of Mondovi, 2014–18.

Legislature: Elected to Assembly since 2016. Committee assignments, 2021: Aging and Long-Term Care; Agriculture; Children and Families; Forestry, Parks and Outdoor Recreation; Housing and Real Estate; Rural Development; Sporting Heritage (chair).

Contact: rep.pronschinske@legis.wisconsin.gov; 608-266-7015; 888-534-0092 (toll free); Room 127 West, State Capitol, PO Box 8953, Madison, WI 53708.

Warren Petryk, Assembly District 93
Republican

Biography: Born Eau Claire, Wisconsin, January 24, 1955; married. Voting address: Eau Claire County, Wisconsin. ▪ Graduate Badger Boys State, 1972; Boyceville High School, valedictorian, 1973; attended University of Wisconsin-Stout; B.A. with highest honors, University of Wisconsin-Eau Claire, 1978. ▪ Worked 15 years in community relations for United Cerebral Palsy of West Central Wisconsin; co-founder of musical entertainment group "The Memories" (started 1972). ▪ Member: Boy Scouts (Eagle Scout, November 1969); Eau Claire, Menomonie, Ellsworth, and Prescott Chambers of Commerce; NRA; Eau Galle-Rush River, Ellsworth, Durand, Rock Falls, and Arkansaw Sportsmen's Clubs; Wisconsin Farm Bureau; Sons of the American Legion; Cleghorn Lions Club; Chippewa Valley Council of Boy Scouts of America (board of directors). ▪ Recipient: VFW Wisconsin *Legislator of the Year* 2013; Wisconsin AMVETS Veteran's *Advocate of the Year* 2014; Wisconsin Electrical Cooperative Association *Most Enlightened Legislator* 2016; Wisconsin School Nutrition Association *Legislator of the Year* 2018, 2016; Wisconsin Manufacturers and Commerce *Working for Wisconsin Award* (every term); Dairy Business Association *Legislative Excellence Award* (every term); Wisconsin Economic Development Association *Champion of Economic Development Award* 2018; Wisconsin Town's Association *Friend of Towns Award*, 2020, 2018; Wisconsin Counties Association *Outstanding Legislator Award* 2020; Wisconsin Association for Talented and Gifted *Outstanding Legislator Award* 2020.

Legislature: Elected to Assembly since 2010. Committee assignments, 2021: Aging and Long-Term Care (vice chair); Colleges and Universities; Energy and Utilities; Financial Institutions; Insurance; Labor and Integrated Employment;

Substance Abuse and Prevention; Veterans and Military Affairs; Workforce Development (chair).

Contact: rep.petryk@legis.wisconsin.gov; 608-266-0660; 888-534-0093 (toll free); Room 103 West, State Capitol, PO Box 8953, Madison, WI 53708.

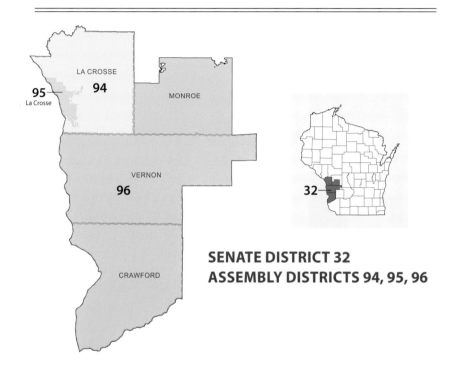

SENATE DISTRICT 32
ASSEMBLY DISTRICTS 94, 95, 96

Brad Pfaff, Senate District 32
Democrat

Biography: Born La Crosse, Wisconsin, December 7, 1967; married; 2 children. Voting address: Onalaska, Wisconsin. ▪ Graduate Melrose-Mindoro High School, 1986; B.S. University of Wisconsin-Green Bay, 1990; M.P.A. George Mason University, 2000. ▪ Full-time legislator. Former secretary-designee, Wisconsin Department of Agriculture, Trade and Consumer Protection; director, Business and Rural Development, Wisconsin Department of Administration; deputy administrator, Farm Programs, U.S. Department of Agriculture, Farm Service Agency; state executive director, U.S. Department of Agriculture, Farm Service Agency; staff of U.S. Representative Ron Kind and U.S.

Senator Herb Kohl. ▪ Member: Downtown La Crosse Rotary; Governor's Task Force on Broadband Access. ▪ La Crosse County Board of Supervisors, 2006–09.

Legislature: Elected to Senate 2020. Committee assignments, 2021: Agriculture and Tourism; Economic and Workforce Development; Transportation and Local Government; Universities and Technical Colleges; Utilities, Technology and Telecommunications.

Contact: sen.pfaff@legis.wisconsin.gov; 608-266-5490; 888-534-0094 (toll free); Room 22 South, State Capitol, PO Box 7882, Madison, WI 53707.

Steve Doyle, Assembly District 94
Democrat

Biography: Born La Crosse, Wisconsin, May 21, 1958; married; 2 children. Voting address: Onalaska, Wisconsin. ▪ Graduate Aquinas High School, 1976; B.A. University of Wisconsin-La Crosse, 1980; J.D. University of Wisconsin Law School, 1986. ▪ Attorney. Former instructor, University of Wisconsin-La Crosse. ▪ Former member: Family Resource Center (board member); Family and Children's Center (board member); Coulee Region Humane Society (board member, president). ▪ La Crosse County Board, 1986–present (chair 2002–11).

Legislature: Elected to Assembly in May 2011 special election. Reelected since 2012. Leadership positions: Minority Caucus Vice Chair 2019, 2017. Committee assignments, 2021: Family Law; Financial Institutions; Insurance; Jobs and the Economy.

Contact: rep.doyle@legis.wisconsin.gov; 608-266-0631; 888-534-0094 (toll free); Room 124 North, State Capitol, PO Box 8952, Madison, WI 53708.

Jill Billings, Assembly District 95
Democrat

Biography: Born Rochester, Minnesota, January 19, 1962; 2 children. Voting address: La Crosse, Wisconsin. ▪ Graduate Stewartville High School, 1980; B.A. Augsburg College (Minneapolis, MN), 1989; Council of State Governments: Bowhay Institute for Legislative Leadership Development (BILLD) Fellow 2012, Toll Fellow 2014; National Conference of State Legislatures Early Learning Fellow. ▪ Full-time legislator. Former teacher of English and Citizenship to Hmong adults. ▪ Member: Council of State Governments (member of Health and Human Services Committee; National Caucus of Environmental Legislators, Mississippi River Caucus; Wisconsin Legislative Children's Caucus (cochair); Wisconsin Family

Impact Seminar Advisors Committee; Viterbo University Board of Advisors; University of Wisconsin-La Crosse Chancellor's Community Council; League of Women Voters of the La Crosse Area; Preservation Alliance of La Crosse; La Crosse Alliance to HEAL (Halting the Effects of Addiction Locally). ▪ La Crosse County Board, 2004–12.

Legislature: Elected to Assembly in November 2011 special election. Reelected since 2012. Committee assignments, 2021: Children and Families; Substance Abuse and Prevention; Joint Legislative Council. Additional appointments: Building Commission; Child Abuse and Neglect Prevention Board; State Council on Alcohol and Other Drug Abuse; Historical Society Board of Curators; Wisconsin Mississippi River Parkway Commission.

Contact: rep.billings@legis.wisconsin.gov; 608-266-5780; 888-534-0095 (toll free); Room 307 West, State Capitol, PO Box 8952, Madison, WI 53708.

Loren Oldenburg, Assembly District 96
Republican

Biography: Born Viroqua, Wisconsin, September 8, 1965; married. Voting address: Viroqua, Wisconsin. ▪ Graduate Viroqua High School, 1984; attended University of Wisconsin-La Crosse, 1984–87. ▪ Small business owner, vacation rental owner, fourth-generation farmer. Former dairy farmer. ▪ Member: Chaseburg Cenex Co-op (19 years, former president of the board); Viroqua Church of Christ (trustee). ▪ Former member: Westby Co-op Creamery (board member and president). ▪ Former Harmony Town Board Supervisor; Harmony Town Board chair.

Legislature: Elected to Assembly since 2018. Committee assignments, 2021: Agriculture (vice chair); Energy and Utilities; Environment; Rural Development; Small Business Development (chair); Workforce Development. Additional appointments: Agricultural and Workforce Development Council.

Contact: rep.oldenburg@legis.wisconsin.gov; 608-266-3534; 888-534-0096 (toll free); Room 10 West, State Capitol, PO Box 8953, Madison, WI 53708.

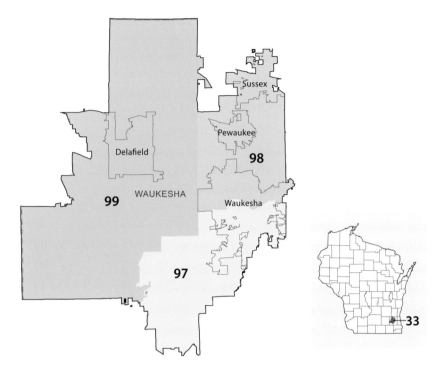

SENATE DISTRICT 33
ASSEMBLY DISTRICTS 97, 98, 99

Chris Kapenga, Senate District 33
Republican

Biography: Voting address: Delafield, Wisconsin. ▪ B.S. in Accountancy, Calvin College (Grand Rapids, Michigan), 1994. ▪ Business owner; certified public accountant.

Legislature: Elected to Assembly 2010–14. Elected to Senate in July 2015 special election. Reelected since 2018. Leadership positions: Senate President, 2021. Committee assignments, 2021: Senate Organization (vice chair); Joint Committee on Employment Relations (cochair); Joint Committee on Legislative Organization (cochair); Joint Legislative Council (cochair).

Contact: sen.kapenga@legis.wisconsin.gov; 608-266-9174; 800-863-8883 (toll free); Room 220 South, State Capitol, PO Box 7882, Madison, WI 53707-7882.

Scott Allen, Assembly District 97
Republican

Biography: Born Racine, Wisconsin, December 18, 1965; married; 2 adult children. Voting address: Waukesha, Wisconsin. ▪ Graduate Kettle Moraine High School; attended University of Wisconsin-Oshkosh, University of Wisconsin-Waukesha; B.A., University of Wisconsin-Milwaukee; Master of Public Administration and Master of Planning, University of Southern California. ▪ Realtor; sales and leadership speaker, trainer, and coach; co-owner of a printing and promotional products business. Former sales director; home builder; and risk management analyst. Served in U.S. Army Reserve, 1984–90. ▪ Member: Republican Party of Waukesha County; Spring Creek Church (Life Group leader); Carroll University President's Advisory Committee; La Casa de Esperanza Advisory Board; Greater Milwaukee Association of Realtors (former board member); Wisconsin Realtors Association. ▪ Waukesha County Community Development Block Grant Board, 2010–14; City of Waukesha alder, 1998–2001.

Legislature: Elected to Assembly since 2014. Committee assignments, 2021: Constitution and Ethics; Financial Institutions; Housing and Real Estate (vice chair); Public Benefit Reform; Regulatory Licensing Reform (vice chair); Veterans and Military Affairs.

Contact: rep.allen@legis.wisconsin.gov; 608-266-8580; 888-534-0097 (toll free); Room 105 West, State Capitol, PO Box 8952, Madison, WI 53708.

Adam Neylon, Assembly District 98
Republican

Biography: Born Elgin, Illinois, December 30, 1984; married; 3 children. Voting address: Pewaukee, Wisconsin. ▪ Graduate H.D. Jacobs High School, 2003; B.A. Carroll University, 2008; Council of State Governments, 2014 Bowhay Institute for Legislative Leadership Development (BILLD) Fellow. ▪ Small business owner. Former legislative staffer for U.S. Representa-

tive Jim Sensenbrenner and Republican leadership in the Wisconsin Assembly. ▪ Member: Wisconsin Future Caucus; 100th Anniversary Capitol Commemorative Commission; President's Advisory Council at Carroll University; Republican Party of Waukesha County (former youth chair); NRA. ▪ Recipient: RENEW Wisconsin *Energy Leadership Award* 2019–20; Wisconsin Economic Development

Association *Champion of Economic Development Award* 2017–18; Associated Builders and Contractors, Inc. *Building Wisconsin Award* 2018; Americans for Prosperity *Reining in Government Award* 2017–18; American Conservative Union *Conservative Achievement Award* 2020, 2019, 2018, 2017, 2016, 2015, 2013; Metropolitan Milwaukee Association of Commerce *Champion of Commerce Award* 2017–18, 2015–16, 2013–14; Wisconsin Dairy Business Association *Legislative Excellence Award* 2017–18, 2015–16; Wisconsin Manufacturers and Commerce *Working for Wisconsin Award* 2019–20, 2015–16, 2013–14; Wisconsin Family Action *Friend of Family, Life & Liberty Award* 2015–16.

Legislature: Elected to Assembly in April 2013 special election. Reelected since 2014. Committee assignments, 2021: Administrative Rules (chair); Energy and Utilities; Jobs and the Economy; Joint Committee for Review of Administrative Rules (cochair).

Contact: rep.neylon@legis.wisconsin.gov; 608-266-5120; 888-534-0098 (toll free); Room 204 North, State Capitol, PO Box 8953, Madison, WI 53708.

Cindi S. Duchow, Assembly District 99
Republican

Biography: Born Waukesha, Wisconsin; married; 2 children. Voting address: Pewaukee, Wisconsin. ▪ Graduate Catholic Memorial High School, 1977; B.S. University of Wisconsin-Madison, 1981. ▪ Former manager and fashion specialist for national retailers. ▪ Member: St. Anthony's Church; Republican Party of Waukesha County, Leadership Circle; Volunteer Service Club of Pewaukee Lake (former president); Kettle Moraine Curling Club; Pewaukee Yacht Club. ▪ Former member: Waukesha Youth Hockey Association board. ▪ Town of Delafield supervisor, 2013–16.

Legislature: Elected to Assembly in September 2015 special election. Reelected since 2016. Leadership positions: Majority Caucus Vice Chair, 2021. Committee assignments, 2021: Colleges and Universities; Criminal Justice and Public Safety; Education; Family Law; Financial Institutions (chair); Insurance; Local Government; Joint Legislative Council. Additional appointments: State Capitol and Executive Residence Board.

Contact: rep.duchow@legis.wisconsin.gov; 608-266-3007; 888-534-0099 (toll free); Room 221 North, State Capitol, PO Box 8952, Madison, WI 53708.

Chief Clerks and Sergeants at Arms

Michael Queensland, Senate Chief Clerk

Biography: Born Rochester, Minnesota, July 19, 1985; married; 2 children. Voting address: Monona, Wisconsin. ▪ Graduate Kingsland High School (Spring Valley, MN), 2003; B.S. in Public Administration, University of Wisconsin-La Crosse, 2007; J.D. University of Wisconsin Law School, 2011. ▪ Former attorney, Wisconsin Legislative Council, 2011–20. ▪ Member: American Society of Legislative Clerks and Secretaries; Research, Editorial, Legal and Committee Staff (director); National Conference of State Legislatures and its committee on Law, Criminal Justice, and Public Safety (vice chair).

Current office: Elected Senate Chief Clerk 2021.

Contact: 608-266-2517; Room B20 Southeast, State Capitol, PO Box 7882, Madison, WI 53707-7882.

Tom Engels, Senate Sergeant at Arms

Biography: Born Shullsburg, Wisconsin, January 1964; married; 3 children. Voting address: Cottage Grove, Wisconsin. ▪ Graduate Shullsburg High School, 1982; Madison Area Technical College, fire fighting and emergency medical service certification programs; currently majoring in history at the University of Wisconsin-Madison. ▪ Former Health Resources and Services Administration administrator,

U.S. Department of Health and Human Services; appointed member of White House Coronavirus Task Force. ▪ Member: Experimental Aircraft Association. ▪ Former member: Monona and Cottage Grove Volunteer Fire Departments firefighter; Monona and Deer Grove Emergency Medical Services volunteer emergency medical technician; Smithsonian Institute National Air and Space Museum volunteer.

Current office: Elected Senate Sergeant at Arms 2021.

Contact: tom.engels@legis.wisconsin.gov; 608-266-1801; Room B35 South, State Capitol, PO Box 7882, Madison, WI 53707-7882.

Edward (Ted) A. Blazel, Assembly Chief Clerk

Biography: Born Quincy, Illinois, June 14, 1972; married; 2 children. Voting address: Madison, Wisconsin. ▪ Graduate Quincy Senior High School, 1990; B.A. St. Norbert College (De Pere), 1994; M.A. Marquette University, 1998. ▪ Member: National Legislative Service and Security Association; Madison Area Youth Soccer Association (board member).

Previous service: Senate Sergeant at Arms, elected 2003–21. Current office: Elected Assembly Chief Clerk 2021.

Contact: 608-266-1801; Room B35 South, State Capitol, PO Box 7882, Madison, WI 53707-7882.

Anne Tonnon Byers
Assembly Sergeant at Arms

Biography: Born Green Bay, Wisconsin, December 14, 1968; married; 2 children. Voting address: McFarland, Wisconsin. ▪ Graduate Green Bay East High School, 1987; attended University of Wisconsin-Green Bay; B.S. University of Wisconsin-Madison, 1991; University of Wisconsin Certified Public Management Program, 2001. ▪ Former Assembly Assistant Sergeant at Arms, 1998–2010; office manager for Assembly Sergeant, 1993–98. Member: Boy Scout Troop 53.

Current office: Elected Assembly Sergeant at Arms 2011. Reelected since 2013.

Contact: anne.tonnonbyers@legis.wisconsin.gov; 608-266-1503; Room 411 West, State Capitol, PO Box 8952, Madison, WI 53708-8952.

2

UNITS OF STATE GOVERNMENT

THE LEGISLATURE

Officers of the Senate
President: Chris Kapenga
President pro tempore: Patrick Testin

Majority leader: Devin LeMahieu
Assistant majority leader: Dan Feyen
Majority caucus chair: Van H. Wanggaard
Majority caucus vice chair: Kathleen Bernier

Minority leader: Janet Bewley
Assistant minority leader: Janis Ringhand
Minority caucus chair: Jeff Smith
Minority caucus vice chair: Melissa Agard

Chief clerk: Michael Queensland
Sergeant at arms: Tom Engels

Officers of the Assembly
Speaker: Robin J. Vos
Speaker pro tempore: Tyler August

Majority leader: Jim Steineke
Assistant majority leader: Kevin Petersen
Majority caucus chair: Tyler Vorpagel
Majority caucus vice chair: Cindi Duchow
Majority caucus secretary: Jesse L. James
Majority caucus sergeant at arms: Samantha Kerkman

Minority leader: Gordon Hintz
Assistant minority leader: Dianne Hesselbein
Minority caucus chair: Mark Spreitzer
Minority caucus vice chair: Lisa Subeck
Minority caucus secretary: Beth Meyers
Minority caucus sergeant at arms: Kalan Haywood

Chief clerk: Edward A. Blazel
Sergeant at arms: Anne Tonnon Byers

Legislative hotline: 608-266-9960; 800-362-9472
Website: www.legis.wisconsin.gov
Number of employees: 205 (senate, includes the 33 senators); 317 (assembly, includes the 99 representatives)
Total budget 2019–21: $158,724,500 (includes the legislative service agencies)

Overview

Wisconsin's legislature makes the laws of the state. The legislature also controls the state's purse strings: no money can be paid out of the treasury unless the legislature enacts a law that specifically appropriates it. At the same time, the legislature is required to raise revenues sufficient to pay for the state's expenditures, and it is required to audit the state's accounts. The legislature can remove any elective office holder in state government, including the governor, from office for wrongdoing. It can also remove a judge or supreme court justice from office for any reason that, in its judgment, warrants it. The legislature can override the governor's veto of legislation. Finally, the legislature has charge of the two avenues by which the Wisconsin Constitution can be amended: the legislature can propose amendments for the people to vote on, and it can set in motion the process for calling a constitutional convention.

The legislature has two houses: the senate and the assembly. The senate is composed of 33 senators, each elected for a four-year term from a different senate district. The assembly is composed of 99 representatives, each elected for a two-year term from a different assembly district. Each senate district comprises the combined territory of three assembly districts. Elections are held in November of each even-numbered year. The terms of 17 senate seats expire in alternate even-numbered

The 2021 Wisconsin Legislature convenes on January 4, 2021, in the midst of the COVID-19 pandemic. Members of the state assembly taking their oath of office at the capitol observe social distancing and masking recommendations.

years from the terms of the other 16. If a midterm vacancy occurs in the office of senator or representative, it is filled through a special election called by the governor.

A new legislature is sworn in to office in January of each odd-numbered year, and it meets in continuous session for the full biennium until its successor is convened. The 2021 legislature is the 105th Wisconsin Legislature. It convened on January 4, 2021, and will continue until January 3, 2023.

Apparatus for conducting business

Rules. The Wisconsin Constitution prescribes a number of specific procedural requirements for the legislature (for example, that each house must keep and publish a journal of its proceedings and that a roll-call vote, rather than a voice vote, must be taken in certain circumstances). For the most part, however, the legislature determines for itself the manner in which it conducts its business. Each house of the legislature has adopted rules that codify its own practices, and the two houses have adopted joint rules that deal with relations between the houses and administrative proceedings common to both. Either house can change its own rules by passing a resolution, and the two houses can change the joint rules by passing a joint resolution.

Officers. Each house elects from among its members a presiding officer and an officer to stand in for the presiding officer as needed. The presiding officer or

Assembly Speaker Robin Vos is sworn in to office by Chief Justice Patience Roggensack on inauguration day.

JOE KOSHOLLEK, LEGISLATIVE PHOTOGRAPHER

stand-in chairs the house's meetings and authenticates the house's acts, orders, and proceedings. In the senate, these officers are the president and president pro tempore; in the assembly, they are the speaker and speaker pro tempore.

Each house also elects two individuals who are not legislators to serve as the house's chief clerk and sergeant at arms. The chief clerk is the clerk for the house's meetings. The chief clerk also manages the house's paperwork, records, and general operations. The sergeant at arms maintains order in and about the house's meeting chamber and supervises the house's messengers.

Within each house, the members from each political party organize as a caucus and elect officers to coordinate their activity. Caucus officers include the majority leader and assistant majority leader and the minority leader and assistant minority leader.

The senate majority leader and the assembly speaker play major, and roughly parallel, roles in guiding the activities of their houses as a result of special responsibilities that the rules in their houses assign to their offices. These responsibilities include appointing the members of committees, determining what business will be scheduled for the house's meetings, and making staffing and budget decisions for the house's operations.

Committees. The legislature does much of its work in committees. Legislative committees study proposed legislation to determine whether it should be given further consideration by the houses. They review the performance and expendi-

Senator Brad Pfaff (*left*) and Assembly Assistant Majority Leader Kevin Petersen (*right*) sign their respective houses' official registers on inauguration day—a tradition that started with statehood.

tures of state agencies. And they conduct inquiries to inform the public and the legislature about important issues facing the state.

Each committee is assigned a general area of responsibility or a particular matter to look into and, within the scope of its assignment, can hold hearings to gather information and executive sessions (deliberative meetings) to decide what recommendations and reports it will make. Some committees can do more than make recommendations and reports. (For example, the Joint Committee on Finance can approve requests from state agencies for supplemental funding.) With rare exceptions, all committee proceedings are open to the public.

Each house has its own committees, and the two houses together have joint committees. Usually, every member of the legislature serves on at least one committee. Each house committee includes members from the two major political parties, but more of the members are from the majority party. On a joint committee, which includes members from both houses, more of the members from each house are from the majority party in that house. For some members on some committees, membership is automatic and based on another office that they hold (ex officio membership), but otherwise, committee members are appointed. The senate majority leader and the assembly speaker make the appointments in their respective houses but honor the nominations of the minority leader for the minority party appointments. They also designate the committee chairs and the joint committee cochairs, except when those positions are held ex officio.

The standing committees in each house operate through the legislature's entire biennial session. They are created under or pursuant to the rules of the house and consist exclusively of legislators from the house. Most of the standing committees have responsibility for one or more specific subject areas—for example, "transportation" or "health." However, the Committee on Senate Organization has organizational responsibilities: it schedules and determines the agendas for the senate's meetings, and it decides matters pertaining to the senate's personnel, expenditures, and general operations. In the assembly, these organizational responsibilities fall, respectively, to the Assembly Committee on Rules and the Committee on Assembly Organization.

In addition to the standing committees in the houses, there are 10 joint standing committees, which likewise operate through the entire biennial session. These committees are created in the statutes rather than under the legislature's rules. Three of these committees include nonlegislators in addition to the legislators from both houses. The responsibilities of each of the joint standing committees are described on pages 148–65.

Special committees can also be appointed in either house or by the two houses jointly. Committees of this type are created to study a problem or conduct an investigation and report their findings to the house or the legislature. Special committees cease to exist when they have completed their assignments.

Meetings. Early in the biennial session, the legislature adopts a joint resolution to establish its session schedule. The session schedule specifies the floorperiods for the session. A floorperiod is a day or span of days that is reserved for meetings of the full houses. Committees can meet on any day, but generally do not meet on days when one or more of the full houses are meeting. When a house meets during a floorperiod, it meets in regular session.

The legislature can also call itself into extraordinary session for any day or span of days. The call requires a majority vote of the members of the committee on organization in each house, the adoption of a joint resolution in both houses, or a joint petition signed by a majority of the members of each house. In addition, the call must specify what business can be considered during the session. An extraordinary session can have the effect of extending a floorperiod so that it begins earlier or ends later than originally scheduled. An extraordinary session can also overlap a floorperiod, and a house can meet in extraordinary session and in regular session at different times during the same day.

The governor can call the legislature into special session at any time. When the legislature convenes in special session, it can act only upon the matters specified in the governor's call. Special sessions can occur during floorperiods and during extraordinary sessions, and a house can meet in special session and in regular or extraordinary session at different times during the same day.

Notices and records. Each house issues a calendar for each of its meetings. The calendar lists the business that the house will consider at the meeting.

The legislature publishes on the Internet a schedule of committee activities that indicates the time, place, and business scheduled for each committee meeting.

Each house keeps a record of its actions known as the daily journal.

The legislature issues the *Bulletin of the Proceedings of the Wisconsin Legislature* periodically during the biennial session. Each issue contains a cumulative record of actions taken on bills, resolutions, and joint resolutions; information on administrative rule changes; and a listing of statutes affected by acts.

Employees. Each house employs staff for its members and staff to take care of general administrative matters. In addition, the legislature maintains five service agencies to provide it with legal advice; bill drafting services; budgetary, economic, and fiscal analysis; public policy analysis; research and information services; committee staffing; auditing services; and information technology services.

Senator Janet Bewley, now in her second term as senate minority leader, is the fifth woman in state history to hold that leadership position.

GREG ANDERSON, LEGISLATIVE PHOTOGRAPHER

GREG ANDERSON, LEGISLATIVE PHOTOGRAPHER

As the senate's presiding officer, the senate president opens floor sessions by calling members to order and announcing the day's business. Here, Senate President Chris Kapenga chairs the senate's first meeting on inauguration day, January 4, 2021.

How a bill becomes a law

A bill is a formal document that proposes to make a new law or change an existing law. For a bill to become a law, two things must happen: (1) the bill must be enacted—that is, it must be passed in identical form by both houses of the legislature and either agreed to by the governor or passed again with a two-thirds vote by both houses over the governor's veto, and (2) the enacted bill must be published.

First reading. A bill takes the first step toward becoming a law when a member or committee of the legislature introduces it in the house of the member or committee. This is done by filing the bill with the chief clerk. The chief clerk then assigns the bill its bill number (for example, Assembly Bill 15), and the presiding officer refers the bill to a standing committee or joint standing committee.

A bill must be given three readings on three different days before the house can pass it. Each reading is followed by a different stage in the house's deliberation process. Introduction and referral to committee are considered a bill's first reading and are followed by committee review.

Committee review. When a bill is referred to a committee, it remains in the committee until the committee reports it out to the house, the bill is rereferred, or the house acts to withdraw it. The committee chair (or cochairs in a joint committee) determines whether the committee will meet to consider a bill and, if so, whether it will hold a hearing or an executive session or both. In the senate, though not in the assembly, a bill that has not received a public hearing cannot be placed on the calendar for a meeting of the full house unless the Committee on Senate Organization waives the public hearing requirement. And in both houses, a committee cannot report a bill out to the house unless it holds an executive session.

A committee holds a hearing on a bill to gather information from the public at large or from specifically invited persons. A committee holds an executive session on a bill to decide what recommendation it will make to the house. The committee can recommend passage of the bill as originally introduced, passage of the bill with amendments, passage of a substitute amendment, or rejection of the bill. Unless it recommends rejection, the committee reports the bill, together with its recommendation, out to the house. In limited circumstances (such as a tie vote), a committee can report out a bill without a recommendation.

If a bill is reported out by a committee, or if it is withdrawn from a committee by the house, it is generally sent to the house's scheduling committee—the Committee on Senate Organization or the Assembly Committee on Rules, depending on the house of origin—so that it can be scheduled for consideration at a meeting of that house. Sometimes, however, a bill is referred to another committee for that committee to review. In such cases, the bill remains in that other committee, just as it did in the previous committee, until it is reported out or withdrawn.

Scheduling. A bill that reaches a scheduling committee cannot advance further unless the scheduling committee schedules it for a meeting of the house or the house acts to withdraw it. The scheduling committee, however, is not required to schedule the bill for a meeting of the house. If the house withdraws a bill from the scheduling committee, the bill is automatically scheduled for a future meeting of the house. (In the senate, it is placed on the calendar for the senate's next succeeding meeting; in the assembly, it is placed on the calendar for the assembly's second succeeding meeting.) If a bill is scheduled for a meeting of the house, it can be given its second reading at that meeting.

Second reading. A bill's second reading is a formal announcement that the chief clerk makes just prior to the house considering the bill. Following this announcement, the house debates and votes on amendments and substitute amendments to the bill (any that the standing committee recommended and any that are offered by members). This stage ends if the house votes affirmatively to engross the bill. Such a vote means that the house has decided on the final form that the bill will take and is ready to consider passage of the bill in that final form. According to the house rules, the house cannot proceed to consider passage until the bill has been given its third reading—and this must be done on a different day. However, and this is often the case, the house can suspend this restriction by a unanimous voice vote or a two-thirds roll call vote. If the house suspends the restriction, the house may immediately proceed to the bill's third reading. If the house does not suspend the restriction, the bill is scheduled for a future meeting of the house. (In the senate, it is placed on the calendar for the senate's next succeeding meeting; in the assembly, it is placed on the calendar for the assembly's second succeeding meeting.)

Assembly Assistant Minority Leader Dianne Hesselbein (*left*) and Assembly Minority Caucus Chair Mark Spreitzer (*right*) confer on the floor during debate about Assembly Bill 1, relating to state government actions to address the COVID-19 pandemic.

Third reading. A bill's third reading, like its second, is a formal announcement that the chief clerk makes just prior to the house considering the bill. Following this announcement, the house debates whether the bill, in its final form previously determined by the house, should be passed. Members can speak only for or against passage; no further amendments can be offered. When debate on the bill ends, the members of the house vote. If the house passes the bill, it is ready to be messaged to the other house. Messaging occurs automatically following a reconsideration period specified in the rules of the house, unless, within that period, the house chooses to reconsider its action in passing the bill. (In the senate, the reconsideration period extends through the senate's next meeting; in the assembly, it extends through the seventh order of business at the assembly's next meeting.) Generally, only a member who voted for passage can make a motion for reconsideration. Alternatively, the house can suspend its rules to message the bill immediately, by a unanimous voice vote or a two-thirds roll call vote.

Action in the second house. When the bill is received in the other house, it goes through substantially the same process as in the first house. If the second house ultimately passes the bill, which it can do with or without additional amendments, it messages the bill back to the house of origin.

Subsequent action in the houses. If the second house adopted additional amendments, the house of origin must determine whether it agrees to those amendments. If the house of origin rejects or amends the amendments, it can message the bill back to the second house. The houses can message the bill back and forth repeatedly until it has been passed in identical form by both houses. Alternatively, the houses can create a conference committee to develop a compromise version of the bill. If the conference committee proposes a compromise version, the houses can vote on it but cannot adopt additional amendments. The compromise version is considered in the second house first; if it passes in the second house, it is messaged to the house of origin.

Action by the governor. If a bill is passed in identical form by both houses, it is sent to the governor. The governor has six days (excluding Sundays) in which to take action on a bill after receiving it. If the governor takes no action, the bill is enacted on the seventh day. If the governor signs the bill, the bill is enacted on the day it is signed. If the governor vetoes the bill, it goes back to the house of origin. If the governor signs the bill but vetoes part of it—which is permitted in the case of appropriation bills—the signed part is enacted on the day it is signed, and the vetoed part goes back to the house of origin.

(*below*) Senate Majority Leader Devin LeMahieu addresses the senate on February 18, 2021, and (*right*) on February 5, 2021, when the senate convened in extraordinary session to debate measures related to the state's pandemic response. The state legislature often meets in extraordinary session to focus attention on important public policy matters or to address unfinished legislative business after the last scheduled floorperiod ends.

GREG ANDERSON, LEGISLATIVE PHOTOGRAPHER

Publication and effective date. A bill or part of a bill that has been enacted is called an act. An act becomes a law when it is published in the manner prescribed by the legislature. The legislature has provided for each act to be published on the Internet no later than the day after its date of enactment. An act goes into effect on the second day after its date of enactment, unless the act specifies that it goes into effect on a different date.

Veto override. A bill or part of a bill that the governor has vetoed can become a law if the legislature passes it again over the governor's veto. The procedure is different from when the bill was passed the first time. The only question considered is passage, and this question can be taken up immediately; the three-readings process is not repeated, and amendments cannot be offered. In addition, passage requires a two-thirds vote in each house, rather than a simple majority vote. Any action on a veto begins in the house of origin. If a vote is taken in the house of origin and two-thirds of the members present and voting agree to pass the vetoed bill or vetoed part of a bill, the bill or part is messaged to the other house. If a vote is taken in the second house and two-thirds of the members present and voting agree to pass the bill or part, the bill or part is enacted on the day the vote is taken. The enacted bill or part is then published and becomes a law in the same way as other acts. If either house fails to take a vote or to muster a two-thirds vote to override the veto, the bill or part advances no further, and the governor's veto stands.

Senate standing committees

Administrative Rules Nass, *chair*; Stroebel, *vice chair*; Bradley; Roys, *ranking minority member*; Larson

Agriculture and Tourism Ballweg, *chair*; Marklein, *vice chair*; Testin, Petrowski, Bernier; Pfaff, *ranking minority member*; Erpenbach, Taylor, Smith

Economic and Workforce Development Feyen, *chair*; Testin, *vice chair*; Jacque; Ringhand, *ranking minority member*; Pfaff

Education Darling, *chair*; Bernier, *vice chair*; Nass, Jagler; Larson, *ranking minority member*; Smith, Johnson

Elections, Election Process Reform and Ethics Bernier, *chair*; Darling, *vice chair*; Stroebel; Smith, *ranking minority member*; Roys

Finance Marklein, *chair*; Stroebel, *vice chair*; Kooyenga, Felzkowski, Bernier, Ballweg; Erpenbach, *ranking minority member*; Johnson

Financial Institutions and Revenue Kooyenga, *chair*; Jagler, *vice chair*; Stafsholt; Ringhand, *ranking minority member*; Agard

Senate Majority Caucus Vice Chair Kathleen Bernier, chair of the Senate Committee on Elections, Election Process Reform and Ethics, speaks at a March committee hearing. The legislature does much of its work in committees, where legislators review introduced bills, hold hearings to gather information about proposals, and make recommendations on whether bills should be passed or rejected.

Government Operations, Legal Review and Consumer Protection Stroebel, *chair*; Felzkowski, *vice chair*; Bradley; Roys, *ranking minority member*; Smith

Health Testin, *chair*; Kooyenga, *vice chair*; Bradley; Erpenbach, *ranking minority member*; Carpenter

Housing, Commerce and Trade Jagler, *chair*; Feyen, *vice chair*; Roth; Agard, *ranking minority member*; Johnson

Human Services, Children and Families Jacque, *chair*; Ballweg, *vice chair*; Wimberger; Johnson, *ranking minority member*; Agard

Insurance, Licensing and Forestry Felzkowski, *chair*; Stafsholt, *vice chair*; Jagler; Taylor, *ranking minority member*; Ringhand

Judiciary and Public Safety Wanggaard, *chair*; Wimberger, *vice chair*; Darling, Jacque, Bradley; Taylor, *ranking minority member*; Roys

Labor and Regulatory Reform Nass, *chair*; Wanggaard, *vice chair*; Stafsholt; Wirch, *ranking minority member*; Johnson

Natural Resources and Energy Cowles, *chair*; Felzkowski, *vice chair*; Ballweg; Wirch, *ranking minority member*; Agard

Senate Organization LeMahieu, *chair*; Kapenga, *vice chair*; Feyen; Bewley, *ranking minority member*; Ringhand

Sporting Heritage, Small Business and Rural Issues Stafsholt, *chair*; Petrowski, *vice chair*; Jagler; Smith, *ranking minority member*; Wirch

Transportation and Local Government Petrowski, *chair*; Cowles, *vice chair*; Wimberger; Carpenter, *ranking minority member*; Pfaff

Universities and Technical Colleges Roth, *chair*; Nass, *vice chair*; Stafsholt, Feyen, Darling; Larson, *ranking minority member*; Erpenbach, Roys, Pfaff

Utilities, Technology and Telecommunications Bradley, *chair*; Roth, *vice chair*; Wanggaard; Pfaff, *ranking minority member*; Smith

Veterans and Military Affairs and Constitution and Federalism Wimberger, *chair*; Jacque, *vice chair*; Roth; Carpenter, *ranking minority member*; Wirch

Assembly standing committees

Administrative Rules Neylon, *chair*; August, *vice chair*; Spiros; Subeck, *ranking minority member*; Hebl

Aging and Long-Term Care Gundrum, *chair*; Petryk, *vice chair*; Magnafici, Plumer, Pronschinske, Rozar; Meyers, *ranking minority member*; Brostoff, Shelton

Agriculture Tauchen, *chair*; Oldenburg, *vice chair*; Tranel, Kitchens, VanderMeer, Mursau, Novak, Pronschinske, Plumer, Moses; Considine, *ranking minority member*; Shankland, Spreitzer, Vruwink, Myers

Assembly Organization Vos, *chair*; Steineke, *vice chair*; Petersen, August, Vorpagel; Hintz, *ranking minority member*; Hesselbein, Spreitzer

Audit Kerkman, *chair*; Macco, *vice chair*; Born; Hesselbein, *ranking minority member*; Hong

Campaigns and Elections Brandtjen, *chair*; Sanfelippo, *vice chair*; Tusler, Thiesfeldt, Murphy, Rozar; Spreitzer, *ranking minority member*; Subeck, Emerson

Children and Families Snyder, *chair*; Ramthun, *vice chair*; Kerkman, Vorpagel, Pronschinske, Gundrum, James, Dittrich; Billings, *ranking minority member*; Bowen, Vining, Snodgrass

Colleges and Universities Murphy, *chair*; Dallman, *vice chair*; Tranel, Duchow, Wittke, Summerfield, Krug, Petryk, Cabral-Guevara, Moses; Hesselbein, *ranking minority member*; Shankland, Anderson, Emerson, Stubbs

Constitution and Ethics Wichgers, *chair*; Thiesfeldt, *vice chair*; Allen, Ramthun, Magnafici, Murphy; Hebl, *ranking minority member*; Pope, Cabrera

Consumer Protection Dittrich, *chair*; Edming, *vice chair*; Skowronski, VanderMeer, Sortwell, Macco; Pope, *ranking minority member*; Cabrera, McGuire

Corrections Schraa, *chair*; Callahan, *vice chair*; Brandtjen, Snyder, James,

Assembly Minority Leader Gordon Hintz (*left*), seen here talking with Representative Robyn Vining (*right*), is responsible for guiding his party's policy agenda.

Representative Tyler August, seen here on inauguration day, is serving as the assembly's speaker pro tempore for a fifth session. Each house in the legislature elects presiding officers who chair meetings and ensure that business is conducted in accordance with the chamber's adopted rules.

Sortwell, Tittl; Bowen, *ranking minority member*; Goyke, Stubbs

Criminal Justice and Public Safety Spiros, *chair*; Horlacher, *vice chair*; Sortwell, Duchow, Novak, Schraa, Krug, James, Steffen, Callahan; McGuire, *ranking minority member*; Bowen, Emerson, Stubbs, Drake

Education Thiesfeldt, *chair*; Kitchens, *vice chair*; Wittke, Ramthun, Wichgers, Mursau, Duchow, Rozar, Behnke; Pope, *ranking minority member*; Hebl, Considine, Vruwink, Myers

Employment Relations Vos, *chair*; Steineke, *vice chair*; Born; Hintz, *ranking minority member*

Energy and Utilities Kuglitsch, *chair*; Steffen, *vice chair*; Tranel, Oldenburg, Petryk, Neylon, Vorpagel, Tauchen, Petersen, Horlacher; Meyers, *ranking minority member*; Subeck, Andraca, Moore Omokunde, S. Rodriguez

Environment Kitchens, *chair*; Tusler, *vice chair*; Oldenburg, Novak, Krug, Kuglitsch, Behnke; Hebl, *ranking minority member*; Shankland, Anderson

Family Law Magnafici, *chair*; James, *vice chair*; Plumer, Snyder, Edming, Duchow; Doyle, *ranking minority member*; Conley, Drake

Finance Born, *chair*; Loudenbeck, *vice chair*; Katsma, Zimmerman, J. Rodriguez, Kurtz; Goyke, *ranking minority member*; Neubauer

Financial Institutions Duchow, *chair*; Katsma, *vice chair*; Allen, Murphy, Petryk, Horlacher; Doyle, *ranking minority member*; Meyers, Brostoff

Forestry, Parks and Outdoor Recreation Mursau, *chair*; Krug, *vice chair*; Wichgers, Edming, Pronschinske, Tusler, Swearingen, Tittl, Moses, Callahan; Milroy, *ranking minority member*; Sinicki, Hebl, Andraca, Snodgrass

Government Accountability and Oversight Knodl, *chair*; Brandtjen, *vice chair*; Kuglitsch, Steffen, Thiesfeldt, Krug; Emerson, *ranking minority member*; Neubauer, Drake

Health Sanfelippo, *chair*; Summerfield, *vice chair*; Wichgers, VanderMeer, Skowronski, Murphy, Magnafici, Dittrich, Rozar, Moses, Cabral-Guevara; Subeck, *ranking minority member*; Riemer, Anderson, Vining, S. Rodriguez

Housing and Real Estate Summerfield, *chair*; Allen, *vice chair*; Brooks, Pronschinske, Murphy, Kitchens; Haywood, *ranking minority member*; Emerson, Ortiz-Velez

Insurance Steffen, *chair*; Petersen, *vice chair*; Duchow, Tusler, Brooks, Tranel, Petryk, Gundrum, August; Hesselbein, *ranking minority member*; Doyle, Riemer, S. Rodriguez

Jobs and the Economy Wittke, *chair*; Armstrong, *vice chair*; Snyder, Magnafici, Rozar, Macco, Dittrich, Neylon, Tittl; Ohnstad, *ranking minority member*; Bowen, Doyle, Shelton

Judiciary Tusler, *chair*; Kerkman, *vice chair*; Ramthun, Thiesfeldt, Horlacher, Sortwell; Cabrera, *ranking minority member*; Hebl, Ortiz-Velez

Labor and Integrated Employment Edming, *chair*; VanderMeer, *vice chair*; Knodl, Schraa, Petryk, Gundrum; Sinicki, *ranking minority member*; Ohnstad, Hong

Local Government Novak, *chair*; Gundrum, *vice chair*; Duchow, Skowronski, Brooks, Macco; Spreitzer, *ranking minority member*; Baldeh, Conley

Mental Health Tittl, *chair*; Cabral-Guevara, *vice chair*; James, Snyder, Novak, Vorpagel, Magnafici, Dittrich, VanderMeer, Behnke; Vining, *ranking minority member*; Brostoff, Considine, Moore Omokunde

Public Benefit Reform Krug, *chair*; Schraa, *vice chair*; Allen, Brandtjen, Cabral-Guevara, Behnke; Myers, *ranking minority member*; Cabrera, Conley

Regulatory Licensing Reform Sortwell, *chair*; Allen, *vice chair*; Horlacher, Knodl, Cabral-Guevara, Dallman; Brostoff, *ranking minority member*; Baldeh, Moore Omokunde

Rules Steineke, *chair*; Vos, *vice chair*; August, Petersen, Vorpagel, Kuglitsch, Tittl, Plumer, Dittrich; Hintz, *ranking minority member*; Hesselbein, Spreitzer, Subeck, Pope, Baldeh

Rural Development VanderMeer, *chair*; Moses, *vice chair*; Plumer, Edming, Novak, Oldenburg, Pronschinske, Summerfield, Armstrong, Callahan; Vruwink, *ranking minority member*; Milroy, Considine, Meyers, Hong

Science, Technology and Broadband Summerfield, *chair*; Schraa, *vice chair*; Brandtjen, Horlacher, Knodl, Dallman; Anderson, *ranking minority member*; Baldeh, S. Rodriguez

Small Business Development Oldenburg, *chair*; Rozar, *vice chair*; Snyder, Tranel, Swearingen, Skowronski, Edming, James, Summerfield, Armstrong; Vining, *ranking minority member*; Haywood, Andraca, Baldeh, Hong

Sporting Heritage Pronschinske, *chair*; Tittl, *vice chair*; Skowronski, Mursau, Sortwell, Wichgers, Tusler, Edming, Callahan, Dallman; Milroy, *ranking minority member*; Hesselbein, Shankland, Spreitzer, Shelton

Senate President Pro Tempore Patrick Testin (*left*) presides over a January senate session day while Senate Chief Clerk Michael Queensland (*right*) manages the house's administrative work.

State Affairs Swearingen, *chair;* Vorpagel, *vice chair;* Kuglitsch, Tauchen, Summerfield, Spiros, Knodl, Brooks, Schraa; Sinicki, *ranking minority member;* Pope, Ohnstad, McGuire

Substance Abuse and Prevention James, *chair;* Magnafici, *vice chair;* Snyder, Plumer, Petryk, Gundrum; Billings, *ranking minority member;* Ortiz-Velez, Shelton

Speaker's Task Force on Racial Disparities Steineke, *cochair;* Stubbs, *cochair;* Wittke, Haywood. **Subcommittees:** Education and Economic Development—Wittke, *cochair;* Haywood, *cochair.* Law Enforcement Policies and Standards—Steineke, *cochair;* Stubbs, *cochair.*

Tourism Tranel, *chair;* Swearingen, *vice chair;* VanderMeer, Tittl, Magnafici, Kitchens, Mursau, Summerfield, Tauchen, Plumer, Dallman; Stubbs, *ranking minority member;* Vruwink, Haywood, Myers, Snodgrass

Transportation Plumer, *chair;* Spiros, *vice chair;* Vorpagel, Sanfelippo, Thiesfeldt, Skowronski, Ramthun, Brooks, Callahan, Rozar; Considine, *ranking minority member;* Moore Omokunde, Ortiz-Velez, Shelton, Snodgrass

Veterans and Military Affairs Skowronski, *chair;* VanderMeer, *vice chair;* Edming, Sortwell, Tittl, Allen, James, Summerfield, Petryk; Riemer, *ranking minority member;* Sinicki, Milroy, Hesselbein

Assembly Majority Leader Jim Steineke (*left*) and Representative Shelia Stubbs (*right*) confer in the assembly. Representative Steineke and Representative Stubbs serve respectively as cochairs of the Speaker's Task Force on Racial Disparities.

Ways and Means Macco, *chair*; Wittke, *vice chair*; Kerkman, Knodl, Snyder, Dittrich, Ramthun, Brooks, Armstrong; McGuire, *ranking minority member*; Ohnstad, Riemer, Conley

Workforce Development Petryk, *chair*; Dittrich, *vice chair*; Gundrum, Edming, Murphy, Oldenburg, Rozar, Armstrong; Shankland, *ranking minority member*; Sinicki, Andraca, Drake

Joint legislative committees and commissions

Joint committees and commissions are created by statute and include members from both houses. Three joint committees include members who are not legislators. Commissions include gubernatorial appointees and, in two cases, the governor.

Joint Committee for Review of Administrative Rules

Senators: Nass, *cochair*; Stroebel, Bradley; Roys, *ranking minority member*; Larson
Representatives: Neylon, *cochair*; August, Spiros; Subeck, *ranking minority member*; Hebl
Senator Nass: sen.nass@legis.wisconsin.gov; 608-266-2635; Room 10 South, State Capitol, PO Box 7882, Madison, WI 53707-7882
Representative Neylon: rep.neylon@legis.wisconsin.gov; 608-266-5120; Room 204 North, State Capitol, PO Box 8953, Madison, WI 53708-8953

The Joint Committee for Review of Administrative Rules must review proposed rules and may object to the promulgation of rules as part of the legislative oversight of the rule-making process. It also may suspend rules that have been promulgated; suspend or extend the effective period of emergency rules; and order an agency to put policies in rule form. Following standing committee review, a proposed rule must be referred to the joint committee. The joint committee must meet to review proposed rules that receive standing committee objections, and may meet to review any rule received without objection. The joint committee generally has 30 days to review the rule, but that period may be extended in certain cases. The joint committee may concur or nonconcur in the standing committee's action or may on its own accord object to a proposed rule or portion of a rule. If it objects or concurs in a standing committee's objection, it must introduce bills concurrently in both houses to prevent promulgation of the rule. If either bill is enacted, the agency may not adopt the rule unless specifically authorized to do so by a subsequent legislative enactment. The joint committee may also request that an agency modify a proposed rule. The joint committee may suspend a rule that was previously promulgated after holding a public hearing. Within 30 days following the suspension, the joint committee must introduce bills concurrently in both houses to repeal the suspended rule. If either bill is enacted, the rule is repealed and the agency may not promulgate it again unless authorized by a subsequent legislative action. If both bills fail to pass, the rule remains in effect. The joint committee receives notice of any action in a circuit court for declaratory judgments about the validity of a rule and may intervene in the action with the consent of the Joint Committee on Legislative Organization. The joint committee is composed of five senators and five representatives, and the membership from each house must include representatives of both the majority and minority parties.

Senate Minority Caucus Chair Jeff Smith addresses his colleagues on the floor.

GREG ANDERSON, LEGISLATIVE PHOTOGRAPHER

State of Wisconsin Building Commission

Governor: Tony Evers, *chair*
Senators: Ringhand, Jacque, Petrowski
Representatives: Swearingen, *vice chair*; Billings, Wittke
Other members: Summer Strand (citizen member appointed by governor)
Nonvoting advisory members from Department of Administration: Naomi De Mers
(administrator, Division of Facilities Development), *commission secretary*; R. J. Binau,
Laura Larsen, David Erdman, Kevin Trinastic, Jillian Vessely
Contact: 608-266-1855; 101 East Wilson Street, 7th Floor, Madison, WI 53703; PO Box 7866,
Madison, WI 53707-7866

The State of Wisconsin Building Commission coordinates the state building program, which includes the construction of new buildings; the remodeling, renovation, and maintenance of existing facilities; and the acquisition of lands and capital equipment. The commission determines the projects to be incorporated into the building program and biennially makes recommendations concerning the building program to the legislature, including the amount to be appropriated in the biennial budget. The commission oversees all state construction, except highway development. In addition, the commission may authorize expenditures from the State Building Trust Fund for construction, remodeling, maintenance, and planning of future development. The commission has supervision over all matters relating to the contracting of state debt. All transactions for the sale of instruments that result in a state debt liability must be approved by official resolution of the commission. The eight-member commission includes three senators and three representatives. Both the majority and minority parties in each house must be represented, and one legislator from each house must also be a member of the State Supported Programs Study and Advisory Committee. The governor serves as chair. One citizen member serves at the pleasure of the governor. The Department of Administration provides staffing for the commission, and several department employees serve as nonvoting, advisory members.

Joint Review Committee on Criminal Penalties

Senators: Wanggaard, *cochair*; Taylor, *ranking minority member*
Representatives: Spiros, *cochair*; Goyke, *ranking minority member*
Other members: Josh Kaul (attorney general); Kevin A. Carr (secretary of corrections);
Kelli S. Thompson (state public defender); 2 vacancies (members appointed by the
supreme court); Bradley Gehring, Maury Straub (public members appointed by the
governor)

(right) On March 16, 2021, freshman Senator Melissa Agard formally addresses her new colleagues in the house for the first time while Senator Lena Taylor *(center)* captures the moment for posterity. For legislators in both houses, speaking on the floor for the first time is an important rite of passage.

JOE KOSHOLLEK, LEGISLATIVE PHOTOGRAPHER

Freshman Representative Donna Rozar (*left*) talks with Majority Leader Jim Steineke (*right*), now serving his sixth session in the assembly.

Senator Wanggaard: sen.wanggaard@legis.wisconsin.gov; 608-266-1832; Room 313 South, State Capitol, PO Box 7882, Madison, WI 53707-7882

Representative Spiros: rep.spiros@legis.wisconsin.gov; 608-266-1182; Room 212 North, State Capitol, PO Box 8953, Madison, WI 53708-8953

The Joint Review Committee on Criminal Penalties reviews any bill that creates a new crime or revises a penalty for an existing crime when requested to do so by the chair of a standing committee in the house of origin to which the bill was referred. The presiding officer in the house of origin may also request a report from the joint committee if the bill is not referred to a standing committee. Reports of the joint committee on bills submitted for its review concern the costs or savings to public agencies; the consistency of proposed penalties with existing penalties; whether alternative language is needed to conform the proposed penalties to existing penalties; and whether any acts prohibited by the bill are already prohibited under existing law. Once a report is requested for a bill, a standing committee may not vote on the bill and the house of origin may not pass the bill before the joint committee submits its report or before the 30th day after the request is made, whichever is earlier. The joint committee includes one majority and one minority party member from each house of the legislature; the members from the majority party serve as cochairs. The attorney general, secretary of corrections, and state public defender serve ex officio. The supreme court appoints one reserve judge residing somewhere within judicial adminis-

JOE KOSHOLLEK, LEGISLATIVE PHOTOGRAPHER

Freshman Representative Sara Rodriguez receives applause from her colleagues after she makes her first speech in the assembly in January 2021.

trative districts 1 to 5 and another residing within districts 7 to 10. The governor appoints two public members—an individual with law enforcement experience and an elected county official.

Joint Committee on Employment Relations

Senators: Kapenga, *cochair*; LeMahieu, Marklein; Bewley, *ranking minority member*
Representatives: Vos, *cochair*; Steineke, Born; Hintz, *ranking minority member*
Contact: Legislative Council Staff, 608-266-1304; 1 East Main Street, Suite 401, Madison, WI 53703-3382

The Joint Committee on Employment Relations approves all changes to the collective bargaining agreements that cover state employees represented by unions and the compensation plans for nonrepresented state employees. These plans and agreements include pay adjustments; fringe benefits; performance awards; pay equity adjustments; and other items related to wages, hours, and conditions of employment. The committee also approves the assignment of certain unclassified positions to the executive salary group ranges. The Division of Personnel Management in the Department of Administration submits the compensation plans for nonrepresented employees to the committee. One plan covers all nonrepresented classified employees and certain officials outside the classified service, including legislators, supreme court justices, court of appeals judges, circuit court judges, constitutional officers, district attorneys, heads of executive agencies, division

Assistant Majority Leader Dan Feyen (*center*) confers with Senator Robert Cowles (*left*) and President Pro Tempore Patrick Testin (*right*) during a break on the senate floor.

administrators, and others designated by law. The faculty and academic staff of the University of Wisconsin System are covered by a separate compensation plan, which is based on recommendations made by the University of Wisconsin Board of Regents. After public hearings on the nonrepresented employee plans, the committee may modify the plans, but the committee's modifications may be disapproved by the governor. The committee may set aside the governor's disapproval by a vote of six members. In the case of unionized employees, the Division of Personnel Management or, for University of Wisconsin bargaining units, the Board of Regents of the University of Wisconsin-Madison submits to the committee tentative agreements negotiated between it and certified labor organizations. If the committee disapproves an agreement, it is returned to the bargaining parties for renegotiation. When the committee approves an agreement for unionized employees it introduces those portions requiring legislative approval in bill form and recommends passage without change. If the legislature fails to pass the bill, the agreement is returned to the bargaining parties for renegotiation. The committee is composed of eight members: the presiding officers of each house; the majority and minority leaders of each house; and the cochairs of the Joint Committee on Finance. It is assisted in its work by the Legislative Council Staff and the Legislative Fiscal Bureau.

Joint Committee on Finance

Senators: Marklein, *cochair*; Stroebel, *vice cochair*; Kooyenga, Felzkowski, Bernier, Ballweg; Erpenbach, *ranking minority member*; Johnson
Representatives: Born, *cochair*; Loudenbeck, *vice cochair*; Katsma, Zimmerman, J. Rodriguez, Kurtz; Goyke, *ranking minority member*; Neubauer
Senator Marklein: sen.marklein@legis.wisconsin.gov; 608-266-0703; Room 316 East, State Capitol, PO Box 7882, Madison, WI 53707-7882
Representative Born: rep.born@legis.wisconsin.gov; 608-266-2540; Room 308 East, State Capitol, PO Box 8952, Madison, WI 53708-8952

The Joint Committee on Finance examines legislation that deals with state income and spending. The committee also gives final approval to a wide variety of state payments and assessments. Any bill introduced in the legislature that appropriates money, provides for revenue, or relates to taxation must be referred to the committee. The committee introduces the biennial budget as recommended by the governor. After holding a series of public hearings and executive sessions, it submits its own version of the budget as a substitute amendment to the governor's budget bill for consideration by the legislature. At regularly scheduled quarterly meetings, the committee considers agency requests to adjust their budgets. It may approve a request for emergency funds if it finds that the legislature has authorized the activities for which the appropriation is sought. It may also transfer funds between existing appropriations and change the number of positions authorized to an agency in the budget process. When required, the committee introduces legislation to pay claims against the state, resolve shortages in funds, and restore capital reserve funds of the Wisconsin Housing and Economic Development Authority to the required level. As an emergency measure, it may reduce certain state agency appropriations when there is a decrease in state revenues. The committee is composed of the eight senators on the Senate Finance Committee and the eight representatives on the Assembly Finance Committee. It includes members of the majority and minority parties in each house. The cochairs are appointed in the same manner as are the chairs of standing committees in their respective houses.

Joint Committee on Information Policy and Technology

Senators: Bradley, *cochair*; Roth, Testin; Larson, *ranking minority member*; Carpenter
Representatives: Loudenbeck, *cochair*; Knodl, Zimmerman; Neubauer, *ranking minority member*; Baldeh
Senator Bradley: sen.bradley@legis.wisconsin.gov; 608-266-5400; Room 323 South, State Capitol, PO Box 7882, Madison, WI 53707-7882
Representative Loudenbeck: rep.loudenbeck@legis.wisconsin.gov; 608-266-9967; Room 304 East, State Capitol, PO Box 8952, Madison, WI 53708-8952

The Joint Committee on Information Policy and Technology reviews information management practices and technology systems of state and local units of government to ensure economic and efficient service, maintain data security and integrity, and protect the privacy of individuals who are subjects of the databases. It studies the effects of proposals by the state to expand existing information technology or implement new technologies. With the concurrence of the Joint Committee on Finance, it may direct the Department of Administration to report on any information technology system project that could cost $1 million or more in the current or succeeding biennium. The committee may direct the Department of Administration to prepare reports or conduct studies and may make recommendations to the governor, the legislature, state agencies, or local governments based on this information. The University of Wisconsin Board of Regents is required to submit a report to the committee semiannually, detailing each information technology project in the University of Wisconsin System costing more than $1 million or deemed "high-risk" by the board. The committee may make recommendations on the identified projects to the governor and the legislature. The committee is composed of three majority and two minority party members from each house of the legislature.

Joint Legislative Audit Committee

Senators: Cowles, *cochair*; Marklein (cochair, Joint Committee on Finance), Kooyenga; Agard, *ranking minority member*; Carpenter

At a February 2021 public hearing held by the Joint Legislative Audit Committee, Representative Samantha Kerkman *(left)*, who has served in the assembly since 2001, and Senator Robert Cowles *(right)*, the committee's cochairs, hear testimony related to state recycling programs. Senator Cowles, who was inaugurated in 1987, is currently the senate's longest-serving member.

JOE KOSHOLLEK, LEGISLATIVE PHOTOGRAPHER

Representatives: Kerkman, *cochair*; Macco, Born (cochair, Joint Committee on Finance); Hesselbein, *ranking minority member*; Hong

Senator Cowles: sen.cowles@legis.wisconsin.gov; 608-266-0484; Room 118 South, State Capitol, PO Box 7882, Madison, WI 53707-7882

Representative Kerkman: rep.kerkman@legis.wisconsin.gov; 608-266-2530; Room 315 North, State Capitol, PO Box 8952, Madison, WI 53708-8952

The Joint Legislative Audit Committee advises the Legislative Audit Bureau, subject to general supervision of the Joint Committee on Legislative Organization. The committee is composed of the cochairs of the Joint Committee on Finance, plus two majority and two minority party members from each house of the legislature. The committee evaluates candidates for the office of state auditor and makes recommendations to the Joint Committee on Legislative Organization, which selects the auditor. The committee may direct the state auditor to undertake specific audits and review requests for special audits from individual legislators or standing committees, but no legislator or standing committee may interfere with the auditor in the conduct of an audit. The committee reviews each report of the Legislative Audit Bureau and then confers with the state auditor, other legislative committees, and the audited agencies on the report's findings. It may propose corrective action and direct that follow-up reports be submitted to it. The committee may hold hearings on audit reports, request the Joint Committee on Legislative Organization to investigate any matter within the scope of the audit, and request investigation of any matter relative to the fiscal and performance responsibilities of a state agency. If an audit report cites financial deficiencies, the head of the agency must report to the Joint Legislative Audit Committee on remedial actions taken. Should the agency head fail to report, the committee may refer the matter to the Joint Committee on Legislative Organization and the appropriate standing committees. When the committee determines that legislative action is needed, it may refer the necessary information to the legislature or a standing committee. It can also request information from a committee on action taken or seek advice of a standing committee on program portions of an audit. The committee may introduce legislation to address issues covered in audit reports.

Joint Legislative Council

Senators: Kapenga (senate president) *cochair*; LeMahieu (majority leader), Marklein (cochair, Joint Committee on Finance), Testin (president pro tempore), Darling, Wimberger, Roth; Bewley (minority leader), *ranking minority member*; Erpenbach (ranking minority member, Joint Committee on Finance), Ringhand, Johnson

Representatives: Vorpagel, *cochair*; Vos (assembly speaker), Steineke (majority leader), August (speaker pro tempore), Born (cochair, Joint Committee on Finance), Spiros,

JOE KOSHOLLEK, LEGISLATIVE PHOTOGRAPHER

GREG ANDERSON, LEGISLATIVE PHOTOGRAPHER

In both chambers, legislators and legislative staff took steps to help prevent the spread of COVID-19 during the 2021 session. (*above*) Minority Leader Gordon Hintz (*left*) of Oshkosh and freshman Representative Samba Baldeh of Madison (*right*) elbow-bump in the assembly. (*bottom*) Speaking via Skype from his office in the capitol, Senator Chris Larson (*foreground*) addresses his colleagues on the senate floor, including Senate President Chris Kapenga (*left background*) and Senate Chief Clerk Michael Queensland (*right background*), who follow social distancing safety guidelines on the floor.

Duchow; Hintz (minority leader), *ranking minority member*; Goyke (ranking minority member, Joint Committee on Finance); Hesselbein, Billings

Legislative Council Staff: Anne Sappenfield, *director*; Rachel Letzing and Daniel Schmidt, *deputy directors*; Scott Grosz, *rules clearinghouse director*; Margit Kelley, *rules clearinghouse assistant director*

Contact: leg.council@legis.wisconsin.gov; 608-266-1304; 1 East Main Street, Suite 401, Madison, WI 53703-3382

Website: http:// legis.wisconsin.gov/lc

Publications: *General Report of the Joint Legislative Council to the Legislature*; *State Agency Staff with Responsibilities to the Legislature*; *Directory of Joint Legislative Council Committees*; *Comparative Retirement Study*; *A Citizen's Guide to Participation in the Wisconsin State Legislature*; rules clearinghouse reports; staff briefs; memoranda on substantive issues considered by council committees; information memoranda and issue briefs; amendment and act memoranda.

Number of employees: 34.17

Total budget 2019–21: $8,207,000

The Joint Legislative Council creates special committees made up of legislators and members of the public to study various state and local government problems. Study topics are selected from requests presented to the council by law, joint resolution, and individual legislators. After research, expert testimony, and public hearings, the study committees draft proposals and submit them to the council, which must approve those drafts it wants introduced in the legislature as council bills. The council is assisted in its work by the Legislative Council Staff. The staff provides legal and research assistance to all of the legislature's substantive standing committees and joint statutory committees (except the Joint Committee on Finance) and assists individual legislators on request. The staff operates the rules clearinghouse to review proposed administrative rules and assists standing committees in their oversight of rulemaking. The staff also assists the legislature in identifying and responding to issues relating to the Wisconsin Retirement System. By law, the Legislative Council Staff must be strictly nonpartisan and must observe the confidential nature of the research and drafting requests it receives. The law requires that state agencies and local governments cooperate fully with the council staff to fulfill its statutory duties. The Joint Committee on Legislative Organization appoints the director of the Legislative Council Staff from outside the classified service and the director appoints the other staff members from outside the classified service. The council consists of 22 legislators. The majority of them serve ex officio, and the remainder are appointed in the same manner as are members of standing committees. The president of the senate and the speaker of the assembly serve as cochairs, but each may designate another member to serve as cochair and each may decline to serve on the council. The council operates two permanent statutory committees and various special committees appointed to study selected subjects.

PERMANENT COMMITTEES OF THE COUNCIL

Special Committee on State-Tribal Relations Representative Mursau, *chair*; Senator Bewley, *vice chair*; Senators Jacque, Smith; Representatives Considine, Edming; Dee Ann Allen (Lac du Flambeau Band of Lake Superior Chippewa Indians), Gary Besaw (Menominee Indian Tribe of Wisconsin), Ned Daniels Jr. (Forest County Potawatomi Community), Michael J. Decorah (St. Croix Chippewa Indians of Wisconsin), Lorraine Gouge (Lac Courte Oreilles Tribal Governing Board), Conroy Greendeer Jr. (Ho-Chunk Nation), Shannon Holsey (Stockbridge-Munsee Community), Lisa Liggins (Oneida Nation), Carmen McGeshick (Sokaogon Chippewa Community), Richard Peterson (Red Cliff Band of Lake Superior Chippewa Indians)

State-Tribal Relations Technical Advisory Committee Tom Bellavia (Department of Justice), Sandy Stankevich (Department of Transportation), David O'Connor (Department of Public Instruction), Michele Allness (Department of Natural Resources), Pam McGillivray (Department of Workforce Development), Holly Wilmer (Department of Revenue), Gail Nahwahquaw (Department of Health Services), Stephanie Lozano (Department of Children and Families)

The Special Committee on State-Tribal Relations is appointed by the Joint Legislative Council each biennium to study issues related to American Indians and the Indian tribes and bands in this state and develop specific recommendations and legislative proposals relating to such issues. Legislative membership includes not fewer than six nor more than 12 members, with at least one member of the majority and the minority party from each house. The council appoints no fewer than six and no more than 11 members from names submitted by federally recognized Wisconsin Indian tribes or bands or the Great Lakes Inter-Tribal Council. The council may not appoint more than one member recommended by any one tribe or band or the Great Lakes Inter-Tribal Council. The Technical Advisory Committee, consisting of representatives of eight major executive agencies, assists the Special Committee on State-Tribal Relations.

Law Revision Committee Senators Wimberger, *cochair*; Wanggaard, Smith, Roys; Representatives August, *cochair*; Petersen, Hebl, Riemer

The Law Revision Committee is appointed each biennium by the Joint Legislative Council. The membership of the committee is not specified, but it must include majority and minority party representation from each house. The committee reviews minor, remedial changes to the statutes as proposed by state agencies and reviews opinions of the attorney general and court decisions declaring a Wisconsin statute unconstitutional, ambiguous, or otherwise in need of revision. It considers proposals by the Legislative Reference Bureau to correct statutory language and session laws that conflict or need revision, and it may submit recommendations for major law revision projects to the Joint Legislative Council. It also serves as the repository for interstate compacts and

Senate Minority Leader Janet Bewley (*left*) speaks with Senator Tim Carpenter (*right*), who has been a member of the senate since 2003.

agreements and makes recommendations to the legislature regarding revision of such agreements.

SPECIAL COMMITTEES OF THE COUNCIL REPORTING IN 2020

Legislative Council Study Committee on Public Disclosure and Oversight of Child Abuse and Neglect Incidents Representative Snyder, *chair*; Senator Bernier, *vice chair*; Senators Jacque, Johnson; Representative Subeck

The study committee is directed to examine the requirements created by 2009 Wisconsin Act 78 relating to public disclosure of certain information when child abuse or neglect results in death or serious injury or when a child in out-of-home placement commits suicide or is sexually abused by a caregiver. Specifically, the committee determines whether those requirements effectively provide for public disclosure and legislative oversight of egregious incidents of child abuse and neglect. The committee also considers whether to modify the types of incidents prompting disclosure and reports and the timing of such. Finally, the committee examines the manner in which the legislature reviews the disclosures and reports and the scope of that review.

Joint Committee on Legislative Organization

Senators: Kapenga (senate president), *cochair*; LeMahieu (majority leader), Feyen (assistant majority leader); Bewley (minority leader), Ringhand (assistant minority leader)

Representatives: Vos (assembly speaker), *cochair*; Steineke (majority leader), Petersen (assistant majority leader); Hintz (minority leader), Hesselbein (assistant minority leader)

GREG ANDERSON, LEGISLATIVE PHOTOGRAPHER

Senator Lena Taylor emphasizes a point while speaking on the floor in January 2021.

Contact: Legislative Council Staff, 608-266-1304; 1 East Main Street, Suite 401, Madison, WI 53703-3382

The Joint Committee on Legislative Organization is the policy-making body for the Legislative Audit Bureau, the Legislative Fiscal Bureau, the Legislative Reference Bureau, and the Legislative Technology Services Bureau. In this capacity, it assigns tasks to each bureau, approves bureau budgets, and sets the salary of bureau heads. The committee selects the four bureau heads, but it acts on the recommendation of the Joint Legislative Audit Committee when appointing the state auditor. The committee also selects the director of the Legislative Council Staff. The committee may inquire into misconduct by members and employees of the legislature. It oversees a variety of operations, including the work schedule for the legislative session, computer use, space allocation for legislative offices and legislative service agencies, parking on the State Capitol Park grounds, and sale and distribution of legislative documents. The committee recommends which newspaper should serve as the official state newspaper for publication of state legal notices. It advises the Elections Commission and the Ethics Commission on their operations and, upon recommendation of the Joint Legislative Audit Committee, may investigate any problems the Legislative Audit Bureau finds during its audits. The committee may employ outside consultants to study ways to improve legislative staff services and organization. The 10-member committee consists of the presiding officers and party leadership of both houses. The committee has established a Subcommittee on Legislative Services to advise it on matters pertaining to the legislative institution, including the review of computer technology purchases. The Legislative Council Staff provides staff assistance to the committee.

Joint Survey Committee on Retirement Systems

Senators: Feyen, *cochair*; Darling; Larson
Representatives: Kuglitsch, *cochair*; Brooks; Hintz
Other members: Charlotte Gibson (assistant attorney general appointed by attorney general), Robert J. Conlin (secretary of employee trust funds), Mark V. Afable (insurance commissioner), Tim Pederson (public member appointed by governor)
Contact: Legislative Council Staff, 608-266-1304; 1 East Main Street, Suite 401, Madison, WI 53703-3382

The Joint Survey Committee on Retirement Systems makes recommendations on legislation that affects retirement and pension plans for public officers and employees, and its recommendations must be attached as an appendix to each retirement bill. Neither house of the legislature may consider such a bill until the committee submits a written report that describes the proposal's purpose, probable costs, actuarial effect, and desirability as a matter of public policy. The 10-member committee includes two majority party members and one minority party member from each house of the legislature. An experienced actuary from the Office of the Commissioner of Insurance may be designated to serve in the commissioner's place on the committee. The public member cannot be a participant in any public retirement system in the state and is expected to "represent the interests of the taxpayers." Appointed members serve four-year terms unless they lose the status upon which the appointment was based. The committee is assisted by the Legislative Council Staff in the performance of its duties, but may contract for actuarial assistance outside the classified service.

Joint Survey Committee on Tax Exemptions

Senators: Testin, *cochair*; Jagler; Taylor
Representatives: August, *cochair*; Swearingen; Goyke
Other members: Peter Barca (secretary of revenue), Brian Keenan (Department of Justice representative appointed by attorney general), Elizabeth Kessler (public member appointed by governor)
Contact: Legislative Council Staff, 608-266-1304; 1 East Main Street, Suite 401, Madison, WI 53703-3382

The Joint Survey Committee on Tax Exemptions considers all legislation related to the exemption of persons or property from state or local taxes. It is assisted by the Legislative Council Staff. Any legislative proposal that provides a tax exemption must be referred to the committee immediately upon introduction. Neither house of the legislature may consider the proposal until the committee has issued its report, attached as an appendix to the bill, describing the proposal's legality, desirability as public policy, and fiscal effect. In the course of its review, the committee is authorized to conduct investigations, hold hearings, and subpoena witnesses. For an executive budget bill that provides a tax exemption, the committee must prepare its report within 60 days. The committee includes two majority party members and one minority party member from each house of the legislature. The public member must be familiar with the tax problems of local government. Members' terms expire on January 15 of odd-numbered years.

Transportation Projects Commission

Governor: Tony Evers, *chair*
Senators: Cowles, Marklein, Petrowski; Carpenter, 1 vacancy
Representatives: Krug, Spiros, Spreitzer; Riemer, Plumer
Other members: Mark Servi, Allison Bussler, Timothy Hanna (citizen members appointed by governor)
Nonvoting member: Craig Thompson (transportation secretary-designee)
Commission secretary: Craig Thompson
Contact: bshp.dtim@dot.wi.gov; 608-267-7754; Bureau of State Highway Programs, 4822 Madison Yards Way, 6th Floor South, Madison, WI 53705

The Transportation Projects Commission includes three majority party and two minority party members from each house of the legislature. The commission reviews Department of Transportation recommendations for major highway projects. The department must report its recommendations to the commission by September 15 of each even-numbered year, and the commission, in turn, reports its recommendations to the governor or governor-elect, the legislature, and the Joint Committee on Finance before December 15 of each even-numbered year. The department must also provide the commission with a status report on major transportation projects every six months. The commission also approves the preparation of environmental impact or assessment statements for potential major highway projects.

Commission on Uniform State Laws

Members: Representative Tusler, *chair*; Aaron Gary (designated by Legislative Reference Bureau chief), *secretary*; Senators Wimberger, Taylor; Representative Hebl; Margit Kelley (designated by Legislative Council Staff director); former state senator Fred Risser, David Zvenvach (public members appointed by governor); former state representative David Cullen, former state senator Joanne B. Huelsman, Justice David T. Prosser, Jr. (ULC life members appointed by commission)

Contact: aaron.gary@legis.wisconsin.gov; 608-504-5850; 1 East Main Street, Suite 200, Madison, WI 53701-2037

The Commission on Uniform State Laws examines subjects on which interstate uniformity is desirable, cooperates with the national Uniform Law Commission, and advises the legislature on uniform laws and model laws. The commission consists of four current or former legislators, two public members, and two members representing legislative service agencies. The commission may also appoint as members individuals who have attained the status of Life Members of the national Uniform Law Commission.

Legislative service agencies

Legislative Audit Bureau

State auditor: Joe Chrisman
Deputy state auditor for financial audit: Carolyn Stittleburg
Deputy state auditor for performance evaluation: Dean Swenson

Representatives John Jagler (*left*) and Evan Goyke (*right*) share a laugh on a February 2021 session day when they realize that they both bought the same tie at the same store in Johnson Creek. After winning a special election in April 2021, Jagler moved to the senate, filling an open seat in that house.

JOE KOSHOLLEK, LEGISLATIVE PHOTOGRAPHER

Financial audit directors: Sherry Haakenson, Erin Scharlau
Assistant financial audit directors: Brian Geib, Lisa Kasel
Contact: asklab@legis.wisconsin.gov; 608-266-2818; 877-FRAUD-17 (fraud, waste, and mismanagement hotline); 22 East Mifflin Street, Suite 500, Madison, WI 53703-2512
Website: http://legis.wisconsin.gov/lab
Publications: Audit reports of individual state agencies and programs; biennial reports.
Number of employees: 86.80
Total budget 2019–21: $18,529,200

The Legislative Audit Bureau is responsible for conducting financial and program audits to assist the legislature in its oversight function. The bureau performs financial audits to determine whether agencies have conducted and reported their financial transactions legally and properly. It undertakes program audits to analyze whether agencies have managed their programs efficiently and effectively and have carried out the policies prescribed by law. The bureau's authority extends to executive, legislative, and judicial agencies; authorities created by the legislature; special districts; and certain service providers that receive state funds. The bureau may audit any county, city, village, town, or school district at the request of the Joint Legislative Audit Committee. The bureau provides an annual audit opinion on the state's comprehensive financial statements by the Department of Administration and prepares audits and reports on the financial transactions and records of state agencies at the state auditor's discretion or at the direction of the Joint Legislative Audit Committee. The bureau maintains a toll-free number to receive reports of fraud, waste, and mismanagement in state government. Typically, the bureau's program audits are conducted at the request of the Joint Legislative Audit Committee, initiated by the state auditor, or required by legislation. The reports are reviewed by the Joint Legislative Audit Committee, which may hold hearings on them and may introduce legislation in response to audit recommendations. The director of the bureau is the state auditor, who is appointed by the Joint Committee on Legislative Organization upon the recommendation of the Joint Legislative Audit Committee. Both the state auditor and the bureau's staff are appointed from outside the classified service and are strictly nonpartisan.

STATUTORY ADVISORY COUNCIL

Municipal Best Practices Reviews Advisory Council Steve O'Malley, Adam Payne (representing the Wisconsin Counties Association); Mark Rohloff (representing the League of Wisconsin Municipalities); Richard Nawrocki (representing the Wisconsin Towns Association).

The Municipal Best Practices Reviews Advisory Council advises the state auditor on the selection of county and municipal service delivery practices to be reviewed by the state auditor. The state auditor conducts periodic reviews of procedures and practices used by local governments in the delivery of governmental services; identifies variations in costs and effectiveness of such services between counties and municipalities; and recommends practices to save money or provide more effective service delivery. Council members are chosen and appointed by the state auditor from candidates submitted by the organizations represented.

Legislative Council Staff

Director: Anne Sappenfield
Deputy directors: Rachel Letzing, Dan Schmidt
Rules clearinghouse director: Scott Grosz
Rules clearinghouse assistant director: Margit Kelley
Contact: leg.council@legis.wisconsin.gov; 608-266-1304; 1 East Main Street, Suite 401, Madison, WI 53703-3382
Website: http://lc.legis.wisconsin.gov

GREG ANDERSON, LEGISLATIVE PHOTOGRAPHER

Senate Majority Caucus Chair Van Wanggaard addresses his colleagues in February 2021.

See the entry for the Joint Legislative Council, beginning on page 157.

Legislative Fiscal Bureau

Director: Robert Wm. Lang
Assistant director: David Loppnow
Program supervisors: Jere Bauer, Paul Ferguson, Charles Morgan, Sean Moran, Al Runde
Supervising analysts: Jon Dyck, Rachel Janke
Administrative assistant: Becky Hannah
Contact: fiscal.bureau@legis.wisconsin.gov; 608-266-3847; 1 East Main Street, Suite 301, Madison, WI 53703
Website: http://legis.wisconsin.gov/lfb
Publications: Biennial budget and budget adjustment summaries; summaries of state agency budget requests; cumulative and comparative summaries of the governor's proposals, Joint Committee on Finance provisions and legislative amendments, and separate summaries of legislative amendments when necessary; summary of governor's partial vetoes. Informational reports on various state programs, budget issue papers, and revenue estimates. (Reports and papers available on the Internet and upon request.)

GREG ANDERSON, LEGISLATIVE PHOTOGRAPHER

Senator Janis Ringhand of Evansville was elected assistant minority leader by her colleagues for the 2021 session.

Number of employees: 35.00
Total budget 2019–21: $8,239,400

The Legislative Fiscal Bureau develops fiscal information for the legislature, and its services must be impartial and non-partisan. One of the bureau's principal duties is to staff the Joint Committee on Finance and assist its members. As part of this responsibility, the bureau studies the state budget and its long-range implications, reviews state revenues and expenditures, suggests alternatives to the committee and the legislature, and prepares a report detailing earmarks in the budget bill. In addition, the bureau provides information on all other bills before the committee and analyzes agency requests for new positions and appropriation supplements outside of the budget process. The bureau provides fiscal information to any legislative committee or legislator upon request. On its own initiative, or at legislative direction, the bureau may conduct studies of any financial issue affecting the state. To aid the bureau in performing its duties, the director or designated employees are granted access to all state departments and to any records maintained by the agencies relating to their expenditures, revenues, operations, and structure. The Joint Committee on Legislative Organization is the policy-making body for the Legislative Fiscal Bureau, and it selects the bureau's director. The director is assisted by program supervisors responsible for broadly defined subject areas of government budgeting and fiscal operations. The director and all bureau staff are chosen outside the classified service.

Legislative Reference Bureau

Chief: Richard A. Champagne
Deputy chief: Cathlene M. Hanaman
Senior coordinating attorneys: Tamara Dodge, Michael Gallagher, Fern Knepp, Joe Kreye
Coordinating legislative analysts: Madeline Kasper, Jillian Slaight

Administrative services manager: Wendy L. Jackson

Contact: 608-504-5801 (legal); 608-504-5802 (research and analysis); 1 East Main Street, Suite 200, Madison; PO Box 2037, Madison, WI 53701-2037

Website: http://legis.wisconsin.gov/lrb

Publications: Wisconsin Statutes; Laws of Wisconsin; Wisconsin Administrative Code and Register; *Wisconsin Blue Book*; informational, legal, and research reports.

Number of employees: 60.00

Total budget 2019–21: $12,440,600

The Legislative Reference Bureau provides nonpartisan, confidential bill drafting and other legal services to the Wisconsin Legislature. The bureau employs a staff of attorneys and editors who serve the legislature and its members and who draft and prepare all legislation, including the executive budget bill, for introduction in the legislature. Bureau attorneys also draft legislation at the request of state agencies. The bureau publishes all laws enacted during each biennial legislative session and incorporates the laws into the Wisconsin Statutes. The bureau prints the Wisconsin Statutes every two years and continuously updates the Wisconsin Statutes on the Wisconsin Legislature's Internet site. The bureau publishes and updates the Wisconsin Administrative Code and the Wisconsin Administrative Register on the Wisconsin Legislature web site. The Legislative Reference Bureau employs research analysts who provide research and analysis services to the legislature. Bureau analysts and librarians also provide information services to the legislature and the public. The bureau publishes the Wisconsin Blue Book and informational, legal, and research reports. The bureau responds to inquiries from legislators, legislative staff, and the public on current law and pending legislation and the operations of the legislature and state government. The bureau operates a legislative library that contains an extensive collection of materials pertaining to Wisconsin government and politics. The bureau compiles and publishes the Assembly Rules, Senate Rules, and Joint Rules. The bureau maintains for public inspection the drafting records of all legislation introduced in the Wisconsin Legislature, beginning with the 1927 session. The Joint Committee on Legislative Organization is the policy-making body for the Legislative Reference Bureau, and it selects the bureau chief. The chief employs all bureau staff. The chief and the bureau staff serve outside the classified service.

Legislative Technology Services Bureau

Director: Jeff Ylvisaker

Deputy director: Nate Rohan

Enterprise operations manager: Matt Harned

Geographic information systems team lead and applications developer: Ryan Squires

Software development manager: Doug DeMuth

Technical services manager: Cade Gentry
Contact: 608-264-8582; 17 West Main Street, Suite 200, Madison, WI 53703
Website: http://legis.wisconsin.gov/ltsb
Number of employees: 43.00
Total budget 2019–21: $9,180,600

The Legislative Technology Services Bureau provides confidential, nonpartisan information technology services and support to the Wisconsin Legislature. The bureau creates, maintains, and enhances specialized software used for bill drafting, floor session activity, and committee activity, managing constituent interactions, producing the Wisconsin Statutes and the Wisconsin Administrative Code, and publishing the Wisconsin Blue Book. It supports the publication of legislative documents including bills and amendments, house journals, daily calendars, and the Bulletin of the Proceedings. The bureau also maintains network infrastructure, data center operations, electronic communications, desktops, laptops, printers, and other technology devices. It keeps an inventory of computer hardware and software assets and manages technology replacement schedules. It supports the redistricting project following each decennial U.S. Census and provides mapping services throughout the decade. The bureau also supports the legislature during floor sessions, delivers audio and video services, manages the technology for the Wisconsin Legislature's websites, and offers training services for legislators and staff in the use of information technology. The bureau's director is appointed by the Joint Committee on Legislative Organization and has overall management responsibilities for the bureau. The director appoints bureau staff; both the director and the staff serve outside the classified service.

Office of the Governor

Governor: Tony Evers
Chief of staff: Maggie Gau
Location: 115 East, State Capitol, Madison
Contact: eversinfo@wisconsin.gov; 608-266-1212; PO Box 7863, Madison, WI 53707-7863
Website: https://evers.wi.gov
Number of employees: 37.25
Total budget 2019–21: $8,099,200

The governor is the state's chief executive. Voters elect the governor and lieutenant governor on a joint ballot to a four-year term. Most of the individuals, commissions, and boards that head the major executive branch agencies are appointed by, and serve at the pleasure of, the governor, although many of these appointments require senate confirmation. The governor reviews all bills passed by the legislature and can veto an entire bill or veto parts of a bill containing an appropriation. A two-thirds vote of the members present in each house of the

Governor Tony Evers (*center*), along with VFW Commander Jason Johns (*left*) and Rolling Thunder State Liaison Mark Herrmann (*right*), unveils the POW/MIA Chair of Honor in the capitol's first-floor rotunda on September 18, 2020.

JOE KOSHOLLEK, LEGISLATIVE PHOTOGRAPHER

legislature is required to override the governor's veto. In addition, the governor can call the legislature into special session to deal with specific legislation.

If a vacancy occurs in the state senate or assembly, state law directs the governor to call a special election. Vacancies in elective county offices and judicial positions can be filled by gubernatorial appointment for the unexpired terms or until a successor is elected. The governor may dismiss sheriffs, district attorneys, coroners, and registers of deeds for cause.

Finally, the governor serves as commander in chief of the Wisconsin National Guard when it is called into state service during emergencies, such as natural disasters and civil disturbances.

Subordinate statutory boards, councils, and committees

STATE COUNCIL ON ALCOHOL AND OTHER DRUG ABUSE

The State Council on Alcohol and Other Drug Abuse coordinates and reviews the efforts of state agencies to control and prevent alcohol and drug abuse. It evaluates program effectiveness, recommends improved programming, educates people about the dangers of drug abuse, and allocates responsibility for various alcohol and drug abuse programs among state agencies. The council also reviews and provides an opinion to the legislature on proposed legislation that relates to alcohol and other drug abuse policies, programs, or services.

COUNCIL ON MILITARY AND STATE RELATIONS

The Council on Military and State Relations assists the governor by working with the state's military installations, commands and communities, state agencies, and economic development professionals to develop and implement strategies designed to enhance those installations. It advises and assists the governor on issues related to the location of military installations and assists and cooperates with state agencies to determine how those agencies can better serve military communities and families. It also assists the efforts of military families and their support groups regarding quality-of-life issues for service members and their families.

COUNCIL ON VETERANS EMPLOYMENT

The Council on Veterans Employment advises and assists the governor and state agencies with the recruitment and employment of veterans so as to increase veteran employment in state government.

Independent entities attached for administrative purposes

DISABILITY BOARD

Members: Tony Evers (governor), Annette K. Ziegler (chief justice of the supreme court), Senator Kapenga (senate president), Senator Bewley (senate minority leader), Representative Vos (assembly speaker), Representative Hintz (assembly minority leader), Robert Golden (dean, UW Medical School)

The Disability Board is authorized to determine when a temporary vacancy exists in the office of the governor, lieutenant governor, secretary of state, treasurer, state superintendent of public instruction, or attorney general because the incumbent is incapacitated due to illness or injury.

Nongovernmental entities with gubernatorial appointments

WISCONSIN HUMANITIES COUNCIL

Executive director: Dena Wortzel
Contact: contact@wisconsinhumanities.org; 608-262-0706; 3801 Regent Street, Madison, WI 53705
Website: www.wisconsinhumanities.org

The Wisconsin Humanities Council is an independent affiliate of the National Endowment for the Humanities. It is supported by state, federal, and private funding. Its mission is to create and support programs that use history, culture, and discussion to strengthen community life in Wisconsin. The governor appoints six members to the council. Other members are elected by the council.

THE MEDICAL COLLEGE OF WISCONSIN, INC.

President and CEO: John R. Raymond, Sr.
Contact: 414-955-8225; 8701 Watertown Plank Road, Milwaukee, WI 53226
Website: www.mcw.edu
State appropriation 2019–21: $21,899,900

The Medical College of Wisconsin, Inc., is a private nonprofit institution located in Milwaukee that operates a school of medicine, school of pharmacy, and graduate school of biomedical sciences. The college receives state funds for education, training, and research; for its family medicine residency program; and for cancer research. The college is required to fulfill certain reporting requirements concerning its finances, student body, and programs. The governor appoints two members to the board of trustees with the advice and consent of the senate.

Governor's special committees

The committees listed below were created by executive order to conduct studies and provide advice. Members serve at the governor's pleasure. These committees submit final reports to the governor or governor-elect prior to the beginning of a new gubernatorial term and, unless continued by executive order, expire on the fourth Monday in the January of the year in which a new gubernatorial term begins.

COUNCIL ON AUTISM

Aligned to: Department of Health Services; 1 West Wilson Street, Madison, WI 53703
Contact: Deborah Rathermel; deborah.rathermel@dhs.wisconsin.gov; 608-266-9366
Website: https://autismcouncil.wisconsin.gov

Created by Governor Jim Doyle in 2005 and continued by Governor Evers, the Council on Autism advises the Department of Health Services on strategies for implementing statewide support and services for children with autism. A majority of its members are parents of children with autism or autism spectrum disorders.

BICYCLE COORDINATING COUNCIL

Aligned to: Department of Transportation; 4822 Madison Yards Way, 6th Floor South, Madison, WI 53705
Contact: Jill Mrotek Glenzinski; jill.mrotekglenzinski@dot.wi.gov; 608-267-7757

Created by Governor Tommy G. Thompson in 1991 and continued most recently by Governor Evers, the Bicycle Coordinating Council's concerns include encouraging the use of the bicycle as an alternative means of transportation, promoting bicycle safety and education, promoting bicycling as a recreational and tourist activity, and disseminating information about state and federal funding for bicycle programs.

GOVERNOR'S TASK FORCE ON BROADBAND ACCESS

Aligned to: State Broadband Office, Public Service Commission; 4822 Madison Yards Way, Madison, WI 53705

Governor Evers created this task force in 2020 to research and recommend policies to address broadband needs and facilitate broadband access across the state. The task force must report to the governor and the legislature on recommendations for facilitating broadband expansion, measures for addressing gaps and inequities in broadband access, opportunities for coordination among various public and private entities, the role of broadband in specific sectors and industries, advances in broadband technology, and the extent to which certain institutions have access to federal broadband expansion funds.

GOVERNOR'S TASK FORCE ON CAREGIVING

Aligned to: Department of Health Services; 1 West Wilson Street, Madison, WI 53703
Contact: Lynn Gall; lynn.gall@dhs.wisconsin.gov; 608-266-5743
Website: https://gtfc.wisconsin.gov/

This task force was created by Governor Evers in 2019. It is charged with developing solutions and strategies for hiring and retaining a direct care workforce, increasing access to direct care services, developing a registry of home care providers, and supporting families providing such care.

DEPARTMENT OF TRANSPORTATION

Cyclists in Madison enjoy an energizing commute. The Bicycle Coordinating Council aims to improve the health of citizens and communities through its ongoing support of bicycling across Wisconsin.

2020 UNITED STATES CENSUS COMPLETE COUNT COMMITTEE

Aligned to: Department of Administration; 101 East Wilson Street, Madison, WI 53707

This committee was created by Governor Evers in 2019 to educate Wisconsinites on the importance of completing the 2020 census and to identify and reduce barriers that impede participation in the census. The committee is required to form a Hard-To-Count Populations Subcommittee to ensure that Wisconsin's hard-to-count populations are accurately and completely counted.

COMMITTEE TO CELEBRATE THE CENTENNIAL ANNIVERSARY OF WISCONSIN'S RATIFICATION OF THE 19TH AMENDMENT

Contact: Stefanie Weix; stephanie.weix@wisconsin.gov; 608-246-2022
Website: https://womenvotewi.wi.gov/

This committee was created by Governor Evers in April 2019 to educate the public and plan events related to Wisconsin becoming the first state to formally ratify the 19th Amendment, which granted women in the United States the right to vote.

GOVERNOR'S TASK FORCE ON CLIMATE CHANGE

Aligned to: Department of Administration; 101 East Wilson Street, Madison, WI 53707
Website: https://climatechange.wi.gov/pages/home.aspx

Created by Governor Evers in 2019, the Governor's Task Force on Climate Change advises and assists the governor in developing a strategy to mitigate and adapt to the effects of climate change. The task force must work closely with the Office of

Sustainability and Clean Energy in the Department of Administration to identify new, cost-effective conservation, sustainability, and efficiency strategies for Wisconsin and to prepare the state for climate change by incorporating climate adaptation strategies into existing planning.

WISCONSIN COASTAL MANAGEMENT COUNCIL

Aligned to: Department of Administration; 101 East Wilson Street, PO Box 8944, Madison, WI 53708-8944

Contact: Michael Friis; michael.friis@wisconsin.gov; coastal@wisconsin.gov; 608-267-7982

Website: https://doa.wi.gov/pages/localgovtsgrants/coastaladvisorycouncil.aspx

The Wisconsin Coastal Management Council was created by acting Governor Martin J. Schreiber in 1977 to comply with provisions of the federal Coastal Zone Management Act of 1972 and to implement Wisconsin's Coastal Management Program. It was continued most recently by Governor Evers. The council advises the governor with respect to Wisconsin's coastal management efforts.

CRIMINAL JUSTICE COORDINATING COUNCIL

Aligned to: Department of Justice; 608-266-1221; PO Box 7857, Madison, WI 53707-7857

Website: https://cjcc.doj.wi.gov

Created by Governor Walker in 2012, and continued by Governor Evers, the Criminal Justice Coordinating Council is tasked with assisting the governor in directing, collaborating with, and coordinating the services of state, local, and private actors in the criminal justice system to increase public safety and the system's efficiency and effectiveness. Members of the council represent various aspects of the state's criminal justice system.

GOVERNOR'S COMMITTEE FOR PEOPLE WITH DISABILITIES

Aligned to: Department of Health Services; 1 West Wilson Street, Room 551, Madison, WI 53703

Contact: Lisa Sobczyk; lisa.sobczyk@dhs.wisconsin.gov; 608-266-9354

Website: https://gcpd.wisconsin.gov/

The Governor's Committee for People with Disabilities, in its present form, was established in 1976 by Governor Patrick J. Lucey and has since been continued by each succeeding governor. The committee's functions include advising the governor on a broad range of issues affecting people with disabilities, including involvement in the workforce, reviewing legislation affecting people with disabilities, and promoting public awareness of the needs and abilities of people with disabilities.

EARLY CHILDHOOD ADVISORY COUNCIL

Aligned to: Department of Children and Families; 201 East Washington Avenue, 2nd Floor, PO Box 8916, Madison, WI 53708-8916

Contact: Priya Bhatia; priya.bhatia@wisconsin.gov; 414-270-4750
Website: https://dcf.wisconsin.gov/ecac

Governor Jim Doyle created the Early Childhood Advisory Council in 2008 in accordance with federal law, and Governor Evers has continued it. The council advises the governor on the development of a comprehensive statewide early childhood system by, among other things, conducting needs assessments, developing recommendations for increasing participation of children in early childhood services, assessing the capacity of higher education to support the development of early childhood professionals, and making recommendations for the improvement of early learning standards.

EARLY INTERVENTION INTERAGENCY COORDINATING COUNCIL

Aligned to: Department of Health Services; 1 West Wilson Street, Room 418, Madison, WI 53707
Contact: Deborah Rathermel; deborah.rathermel@dhs.wisconsin.gov; 608-266-9366
Website: https://b3icc.wisconsin.gov

First established by Governor Tommy G. Thompson in 1987, re-established by Governor Thompson in 1998, and continued most recently by Governor Evers, the Early Intervention Interagency Coordinating Council was created pursuant to federal law. The council assists the Department of Health Services in the development and administration of early intervention services, referred to as the "Birth to Three Program," for infants and toddlers with developmental delays and their families. The council's members include parents of children with disabilities.

On November 11, 2019, Governor Tony Evers signs 2019 Assembly Bill 52, now 2019 Wisconsin Act 22, joined by local advocates and legislators who supported the bipartisan measure. The act allows 17-year-olds who are homeless and unaccompanied by an adult to contract for admission at a shelter or transitional facility.

JOE KOSHOLLEK, LEGISLATIVE PHOTOGRAPHER

GOVERNOR'S COUNCIL ON FINANCIAL LITERACY AND CAPABILITY

Executive director: David Mancl
Aligned to: Department of Financial Institutions, Office of Financial Literacy; PO Box 8861, Madison, WI 53708-8861
Contact: david.mancl@dfi.wisconsin.gov; 608-261-9540
Website: https://www.wdfi.org/ofl/govcouncilfinlit/

Created by Governor Jim Doyle in 2005, this council was continued and renamed by Governor Evers. The Governor's Council on Financial Literacy and Capability works with state agencies, private entities, and nonprofit associations to improve financial literacy among Wisconsin citizens. The council promotes the financial literacy awareness and education campaign called Money Smart Week and identifies barriers to financial inclusion, such as systemic racism, in certain sectors.

GOVERNOR'S HEALTH EQUITY COUNCIL

Aligned to: Department of Health Services; 1 West Wilson Street, Madison, WI 53703
Contact: Cecilia Culp; dhshealthequitycouncil@dhs.wisconsin.gov; 608-590-7329
Website: https://www.dhs.wisconsin.gov/hec/index.htm

This council was created by Governor Evers in 2019. The council is tasked with developing a plan to reduce and eliminate health disparities in Wisconsin by the year 2030. The plan must address factors such as race, economic status, education, geography, and history of incarceration in health disparities.

HISTORICAL RECORDS ADVISORY BOARD

Aligned to: State Historical Society of Wisconsin; 816 State Street, Madison, WI 53706
Contact: Abbie Norderhaug; abbie.norderhaug@wisconsinhistory.org; 608-264-6480
Website: https://wisconsinhistory.org/records/article/cs3558

Continued most recently by Governor Evers, the Historical Records Advisory Board enables the state to participate in a grant program of the National Historical Publications and Records Commission. The board also promotes the availability and use of historic records as a key to understanding American culture.

HOMELAND SECURITY COUNCIL

Contact: 608-242-3075; 2400 Wright Street, PO Box 14587, Madison, WI 53708-0587
Website: http://hsc.wi.gov

Created by Governor Jim Doyle in 2003 and continued by Governor Evers, the Homeland Security Council advises the governor and coordinates the efforts of state and local officials concerning the prevention of and response to potential threats to the homeland security of Wisconsin.

INDEPENDENT LIVING COUNCIL OF WISCONSIN

Contact: ilcwinfo@gmail.com; 608-206-1581; 3810 Milwaukee Street, Madison, WI 53714
Website: https://ilcwis.org/

Governor Tommy G. Thompson created the Independent Living Council of Wisconsin in 1994; Governor Jim Doyle established the council as a nonprofit entity in 2004. Governor Evers has continued it. In coordination with the Division of Vocational Rehabilitation in the Department of Workforce Development, the council maintains the state's plan for independent living services for people with disabilities. The majority of the council's members are persons with disabilities. At least one member must be a director of a center for independent living, and at least one member must represent Native American vocational rehabilitation programs.

GOVERNOR'S INFORMATION TECHNOLOGY EXECUTIVE STEERING COMMITTEE

Aligned to: Department of Administration; 101 East Wilson Street, PO Box 7864, Madison, WI 53707

Created by Governor Walker in 2003 and continued by Governor Evers, the Governor's Information Technology Executive Steering Committee is responsible for the effective and efficient application of information technology assets across state agencies.

GOVERNOR'S JUDICIAL SELECTION ADVISORY COMMITTEE

Aligned to: Office of the Governor; Room 115 East, State Capitol, PO Box 7863, Madison, WI 53707-7863

Created by Governor Walker in 2011 and continued by Governor Evers, the Governor's Judicial Selection Advisory Committee recommends candidates to the governor to fill judicial vacancies in the state courts.

GOVERNOR'S JUVENILE JUSTICE COMMISSION

Aligned to: Department of Justice; PO Box 7857, Madison, WI 53707-7857
Contact: Allison Budzinski; budzinskiae@doj.state.wi.us

Governor Tommy G. Thompson created the Juvenile Justice Advisory Group in 1989. In 1991, he recreated it as the Governor's Juvenile Justice Commission, which was continued most recently by Governor Evers. The commission distributes federal grant moneys for the improvement of the juvenile justice system in the state. It also advises the governor and the legislature concerning juvenile justice issues.

PEOPLE'S MAPS COMMISSION

Aligned to: Department of Administration; 101 East Wilson Street, Madison WI 53707
Website: https://govstatus.egov.com/peoplesmaps

Created by Governor Evers in 2020, the People's Maps Commission is tasked with preparing congressional and state legislative redistricting maps based on the 2020 census for consideration by the legislature. Before drawing its maps, the Commission must hold at least one hearing in each of Wisconsin's eight congres-

OFFICE OF THE GOVERNOR

Governor Tony Evers delivers his third State of the State address remotely on January 12, 2021, while members of the senate staff look on.

sional districts. The redistricting maps the Commission prepares are required to be free from partisan bias and partisan political advantage.

GOVERNOR'S PARDON ADVISORY BOARD

Aligned to: Office of the Governor; Pardon Advisory Board, PO Box 7863, Madison, WI 53707

Website: https://evers.wi.gov/pages/pardon-information.aspx

Governor Lee Sherman Dreyfus originally created the Pardon Advisory Board in 1980; Governors Thompson, McCallum, and Doyle later recreated and restructured the board. Governor Evers recreated the board again in 2019. As recreated, the board consists of nine members appointed by the governor, including the governor's chief legal counsel or a designee, who serves as chair. Using applications provided by the Office of the Governor, the board receives and considers requests for clemency, as authorized under Article V, Section 6, of the Wisconsin Constitution.

JOINT ENFORCEMENT TASK FORCE ON PAYROLL FRAUD AND WORKER MISCLASSIFICATION

Aligned to: Department of Workforce Development; 201 East Washington Avenue, Madison, 53703; PO Box 7972, Madison, WI 53707-7972

Website: https://dwd.wisconsin.gov/misclassification/

The Joint Enforcement Task Force was created by Governor Evers to work with relevant agencies to coordinate the investigation and enforcement of worker misclassification issues, which can result in underpayment of wages, payroll taxes, unemployment insurance contributions and workers' compensation insurance.

PFAS COORDINATING COUNCIL

Aligned to: Department of Natural Resources; PO Box 7921, Madison, WI 53707-7921
Contact: dnrpfasinquiries@wisconsin.gov
Website: https://dnr.wi.gov/topic/contaminants/wispac.html

Governor Evers created the PFAS Coordinating Council in 2019 to assess the public health risks of Per- and Polyfluoroalkyl Substances (PFAS) and develop a state-wide plan to address those risks. The council's tasks include developing protocols to inform and engage the public on PFAS, best practices for identifying PFAS sources, and standard testing and treatment protocols. The council must also engage academic institutions and other experts to collaborate on joint projects and explore various avenues of public and private funding to support their efforts to address PFAS.

GOVERNOR'S COUNCIL ON PHYSICAL FITNESS AND HEALTH

Aligned to: Office of the Governor; Room 115 East, State Capitol, PO Box 7863, Madison, WI 53707-7863

Governor Anthony Earl established the Governor's Council on Physical Fitness and Health in 1983, and Governor Walker recreated it in 2012. It was continued by Governor Evers in 2019. The council develops policy recommendations to improve the status of and educate the public concerning children's health, physical fitness, and nutrition. The council also encourages obesity prevention for all state residents.

GOVERNOR'S TASK FORCE ON REDUCING PRESCRIPTION DRUG PRICES

Aligned to: Office of the Commissioner of Insurance; 125 South Webster Street, Madison, WI 53703, PO Box 7873, Madison, WI 53703-7873
Website: https://rxdrugtaskforce.wi.gov/pages/home.aspx

Created by Governor Evers in 2019, the Governor's Task Force on Reducing Prescription Drug Prices is chaired by the Commissioner of Insurance and advises and assists the governor in addressing excessive prescription drug prices and the financial burden that prescription drug prices place on Wisconsin residents.

STATE REHABILITATION COUNCIL

Aligned to: Department of Workforce Development, Division of Vocational Rehabilitation; 800-442-3477; 201 East Washington Avenue, PO Box 7852, Madison, WI 53707-7852
Website: https://dwd.wisconsin.gov/dvr/partners/wrc/

Created by Governor Tommy G. Thompson in 1999 and continued most recently by Governor Evers, the State Rehabilitation Council advises the Department of Workforce Development on a statewide vocational rehabilitation plan for disabled individuals that is required by federal law.

GOVERNOR'S TASK FORCE ON RETIREMENT SECURITY

Aligned to: Office of the State Treasurer; Room B38 West, State Capitol, PO Box 7871 Madison, WI 53707-7873

The Governor's Task Force on Retirement Security was created by Governor Evers in 2019 and is chaired by the state treasurer. It is tasked with developing recommendations for how the state can best address the retirement crisis for Wisconsinites who do not have a way to save for retirement; reducing the regulatory and operational burden on small businesses that want to offer payroll deduction retirement savings options to employees; encouraging younger Wisconsinites to save early in life; and developing other innovative reforms to help Wisconsinites retire in a financially secure manner.

GOVERNOR'S BLUE RIBBON COMMISSION ON RURAL PROSPERITY

Aligned to: Department of Administration; 101 East Wilson Street, Madison WI 53707
Website: https://wedc.org/rural-prosperity/

Created by Governor Evers in 2020, the Governor's Blue Ribbon Commission on Rural Prosperity is charged with holding listening sessions and meetings throughout the state to learn about the issues affecting farmers, the agricultural industry, and rural businesses and communities. The Commission is also required to gather input from stakeholders on current and future challenges facing them, ideas for

State Treasurer Sarah Godlewski (*back row, second from left*) chairs a January 2020 meeting of the Governor's Task Force on Retirement Security in Milwaukee.

OFFICE OF THE STATE TREASURER

addressing these challenges, and other means of partnering with and supporting the agricultural industry and rural businesses and communities. Based on the information it gathers, the Commission must develop a plan to invigorate the agricultural industry and rural businesses and communities throughout Wisconsin.

WISCONSIN SHARED SERVICES EXECUTIVE COMMITTEE

Aligned to: Department of Administration; 101 East Wilson Street, Madison WI 53707

The Wisconsin Shared Services Executive Committee was created by Governor Walker in 2018 and continued by Governor Evers in 2019. The committee is charged with establishing a shared services business model to deliver high-quality human resources and payroll and benefits services to all state agencies.

GOVERNOR'S TASK FORCE ON STUDENT DEBT

Aligned to: Department of Financial Institutions; 4822 Madison Yards Way, North Tower, Madison, WI 53705; PO Box 8861, Madison, WI 53708-8861
Contact: studentdebttasktorce@dfi.wisconsin.gov
Toll-free hotline: 833-589-0750
Website: https://lookforwardwi.gov/student-debt-task-force/

Created by Governor Evers in 2020, the Governor's Task Force on Student Debt is tasked with assessing student debt in Wisconsin and providing long-term strategies to reduce education-related debt, prevent abusive practices by loan companies, and improve financial literacy education.

WISCONSIN TECHNOLOGY COMMITTEE

Aligned to: Wisconsin Technology Council; 455 Science Drive, Suite 240, Madison, WI 53711
Contact: Angela Schlobohm; angela@wisconsintechnologycouncil.com; 608-442-7557
Website: http://wisconsintechnologycouncil.com

Created by Governor Walker in 2011 and continued by Governor Evers in 2019, the Wisconsin Technology Committee consists of the members of the Wisconsin Technology Council, a nonprofit corporation that was created by state legislation but later removed from the statutes. The committee provides a means by which the council can coordinate with state government. The council assists the state in promoting the creation, development, and retention of science-based and technology-based businesses.

TELECOMMUNICATIONS RELAY SERVICE COUNCIL

Aligned to: Public Service Commission; 4822 Madison Yards Way, Madison, WI 53705

Created by Governor Tommy G. Thompson in 1990 and continued most recently by Governor Evers, the Telecommunications Relay Service Council advises the state concerning telecommunications relay service, including with respect to rates and availability. The members include one speech-impaired person, one hearing-impaired person, one speech-impaired and hearing-impaired person, and one person not having a speech or hearing impairment.

GOVERNOR'S COUNCIL ON WORKFORCE INVESTMENT

Aligned to: Department of Workforce Development; 201 E. Washington Avenue, Madison, WI 53703; PO Box 7972, Madison, WI 53707-7972
Contact: 414-874-1680
Website: www.wi-cwi.org

Governor Tommy G. Thompson created the Governor's Council on Workforce Investment in 1999. Governor Scott Walker reconstituted the council in 2015 as a result of changes to federal law, and Governor Evers continued the council in 2019. The council is charged with carrying out certain duties and functions established under federal law governing state workforce development boards, including recommending strategies that align workforce development resources to support economic development, promoting programs to increase the number of skilled workers in the workforce and to provide resources to job seekers, and developing an online statewide workforce and labor market information system.

Office of the Lieutenant Governor

Lieutenant governor: Mandela Barnes
Chief of staff: Fred Ludwig
Location: 19 East, State Capitol, Madison

Lieutenant Governor Mandela Barnes (*center*) speaks at a ceremony held in the capitol rotunda on February 1, 2019, to mark the start of Black History Month. Members of the Wisconsin Legislative Black Caucus, including Representatives David Bowen (*left*) and Kalan Haywood (*right*), look on.

GREG ANDERSON, LEGISLATIVE PHOTOGRAPHER

Contact: ltgov@wisconsin.gov; 608-266-3516; PO Box 2043, Madison, WI 53701-2043
Website: www.ltgov.wisconsin.gov
Number of employees: 5.00
Total budget 2019–21: $847,800

The lieutenant governor is the state's second-ranking executive officer, a position analogous to that of the vice president of the United States. If the incumbent governor dies, resigns, or is removed from office, the lieutenant governor becomes governor for the balance of the unexpired term. The lieutenant governor serves as acting governor while the governor is unable to perform the duties of the office due to impeachment, incapacitation, or absence from the state. If there is a vacancy in the office of lieutenant governor, the governor must nominate a successor to serve, upon confirmation by both the senate and assembly, for the remainder of the unexpired term.

The governor may designate the lieutenant governor to represent the governor's office on any statutory board, commission, or committee on which the governor is entitled to membership; on any nonstatutory committee established by the governor; and on any intergovernmental body created to maintain relationships with federal, state, and local governments or regional agencies. The governor may ask the lieutenant governor to coordinate certain state services and programs that the governor is directed by law to coordinate.

Voters elect the governor and lieutenant governor on a joint ballot to four-year terms. Candidates are nominated independently in the partisan August primary, but voters cast a combined ballot for the two offices in the November election.

Department of Administration

Department secretary: Joel Brennan
Deputy secretary: Chris Patton
Location: State Administration Building, 101 East Wilson Street, Madison
Contact: 608-266-1741; PO Box 7864, Madison, WI 53707-7864
Website: www.doa.wi.gov
Number of employees: 1,436.08
Total budget 2019–21: $1,997,923,700

The Department of Administration is administered by a secretary who is appointed by the governor with the advice and consent of the senate.

The department provides a wide range of services to other state agencies, including personnel management, payroll, accounting systems, and legal services. The department administers the state civil service system. The department also administers the state's procurement policies and contracts, fleet transportation, and risk management. It oversees the state's buildings and leased office space, as well as statewide facilities project planning and analysis. The department also oversees the Capitol Police. It administers a federal and state funded low-income household energy assistance program and offers program assistance and funds to address homelessness and support affordable housing, public infrastructure, and economic development opportunities. It provides fiscal and policy analysis to the governor for development of executive budget proposals. It regulates racing, charitable gaming, and Indian gaming. The department advises the Building Commission and the governor on the issuance of state debt. It administers finances for the clean water revolving loan fund program. Finally, the department provides a variety of services to the public and state, local, and tribal governments.

Subordinate statutory boards, councils, and committees

COUNCIL ON AFFIRMATIVE ACTION

Chair: Adin Palau

Contact: nicole.guardiola@wisconsin.gov; 608-266-5709; 101 E. Wilson Street, 4th Floor, Madison, WI 53703

Website: https://dpm.wi.gov/pages/hr_admin/state-council-on-affirmative-action-diversity-awards.aspx

The Council on Affirmative Action advises the administrator of the Division of Personnel Management, evaluates affirmative action programs throughout the classified service, seeks compliance with state and federal regulations, and recommends improvements in state affirmative action efforts.

CERTIFICATION STANDARDS REVIEW COUNCIL

Chair: Kevin Freber

The Certification Standards Review Council reviews the Department of Natural Resources laboratory certification and registration program and makes recommendations on programs for testing water, wastewater, waste material, soil, and hazardous substances.

COUNCIL ON SMALL BUSINESS, VETERAN-OWNED BUSINESS AND MINORITY BUSINESS OPPORTUNITIES

Contact: wisdpwebapplication@wi.gov; Wisconsin Supplier Diversity Program, 101 E. Wilson St., 6th Floor, PO Box 7970, Madison, WI 53707-7970

The Council on Small Business, Veteran-Owned Business and Minority Business Opportunities advises the department on how to increase the participation of small businesses, veteran-owned businesses, and minority businesses in state purchasing.

STATE EMPLOYEES SUGGESTION BOARD

Contact: wiemployeesuggestionprogram@wisconsin.gov; State Employee Suggestion

Program, Division of Personnel Management, 101 E. Wilson St., 4th Floor, PO Box 7855, Madison, WI 53707-7855

Website: http://suggest.wi.gov

The State Employees Suggestion Board administers an awards program to encourage unusual and meritorious suggestions and accomplishments by state employees that promote economy and efficiency in government functions.

Independent entities attached for administrative purposes

BOARD ON AGING AND LONG-TERM CARE

Chair: Tanya L. Meyer

Executive director: Heather A. Bruemmer

Contact: boaltc@wisconsin.gov; 608-246-7013; Ombudsman Program, 800-815-0015; Medigap Helpline, 800-242-1060; Part D Helpline, 855-677-2783; 1402 Pankratz Street, Suite 111, Madison, WI 53704

Website: http://longtermcare.wi.gov

Number of employees: 44.50

Total budget 2019–21: $7,193,600

The Board on Aging and Long-Term Care reports to the governor and the legislature on matters relating to long-term care for the aged and disabled. The board monitors the development and implementation of federal, state, and local laws and regulations related to long-term care facilities and investigates complaints from people receiving long-term care. The board operates the Medigap Helpline, which provides information on insurance designed to supplement Medicare.

OFFICE OF BUSINESS DEVELOPMENT

Director: Tia Torhorst

Contact: doaobd@wisconsin.gov; 608-267-7873; PO Box 7864, Madison, WI 53707

Website: https://doa.wi.gov/obd

The Office of Business Development provides administrative support to the Small Business Regulatory Review Board.

CLAIMS BOARD

Chair: Corey Finkelmeyer

Secretary: Amy Kasper

Contact: patricia.reardon@wisconsin.gov; 608-264-9595; PO Box 7864, Madison, WI 53707-7864

Website: http://claimsboard.wi.gov/

Number of employees: 0.00

Total budget 2019–21: $75,000

The Claims Board investigates and makes recommendations on all money claims against the state for $10 or more. The findings and recommendations are reported to the legislature, and no claim may be considered by the legislature until the board has made its recommendation.

BOARD FOR PEOPLE WITH DEVELOPMENTAL DISABILITIES

Executive Director: Beth Swedeen
Chair: Elsa Diaz-Bautista
Contact: jennifer.neugart@wisconsin.gov; 608-266-7826; 101 East Wilson Street, Room 219, Madison, WI 53703
Website: http://wi-bpdd.org
Number of employees: 7.00
Total budget 2019–21: $3,194,400

The Board for People with Developmental Disabilities advises the department, other state agencies, the legislature, and the governor on matters related to developmental disabilities. The board also administers a program to foster the employment of individuals with disabilities and provide specific, targeted supports to businesses, school districts, and vocational agencies that demonstrate how coworkers can provide internal support to coworkers with disabilities.

ELECTRONIC RECORDING COUNCIL

Chair: Sharon Martin
Contact: sharon.martin@washcowisco.gov; 262-335-4318; Electronic Recording Council, c/o Secretary's Office, Department of Administration, 101 E. Wilson Street, PO Box 7864, Madison, WI 53707-7864
Website: http://ercwis.wi.gov/

The Electronic Recording Council adopts standards regarding the electronic recording of real estate documents to be promulgated by rule by the department.

DIVISION OF HEARINGS AND APPEALS

Administrator: Brian Hayes
Location: 4822 Madison Yards Way, 5th Floor North, Madison
Contact: dhamail@wisconsin.gov; 608-266-7709; PO Box 7875, Madison, WI 53707-7875
Website: www.doa.wi.gov/divisions/hearings-and-appeals
Number of employees: 88.65
Total budget 2019–21: $22,206,300

The Division of Hearings and Appeals decides contested proceedings for the Department of Natural Resources, cases arising under the Department of Justice's Crime Victim Compensation Program, and appeals related to actions of the Departments of Health Services, Children and Families, Safety and Professional Services, and Agriculture, Trade and Consumer Protection. It hears appeals from the Department of Transportation, including those related to motor vehicle dealer licenses, highway signs, motor carrier regulation, and disputes arising between motor vehicle dealers and manufacturers. The division conducts hearings for the Department of Corrections on probation, parole, and extended supervision revocation and juvenile aftercare supervision. It handles contested cases for the Department of Public Instruction, the Department of Employee Trust Funds, and the Low-Income Home Energy Assistance Program of the Department of Administration. Other agencies may request the division to conduct hearing services.

INTERAGENCY COUNCIL ON HOMELESSNESS

Director: Michael Basford
Contact: mike.basford@wisconsin.gov; 608-266-3633
Website: https://doa.wi.gov/pages/aboutdoa/ich.aspx

The Interagency Council on Homelessness is tasked with establishing and periodically reviewing a statewide policy with the purpose of preventing and ending homelessness in Wisconsin.

INCORPORATION REVIEW BOARD

Chair: Dawn Vick
Location: 101 East Wilson Street, 9th Floor, Madison
Contact: wimunicipalboundaryreview@wi.gov; 608-264-6102; PO Box 1645, Madison, WI 53701
Website: https://doa.wi.gov/pages/localgovtsgrants/incorporationreviewboard.aspx

The Incorporation Review Board reviews petitions for incorporating territory as a city or village to determine whether the petition meets certain statutory standards and is in the public interest.

LABOR AND INDUSTRY REVIEW COMMISSION

Chair: Michael Gillick
Location: Public Broadcasting Building, 3319 West Beltline Highway, Madison
Contact: lirc@wisconsin.gov; 608-266-9850; PO Box 8126, Madison, WI 53708-8126
Website: http://lirc.wisconsin.gov
Number of employees: 18.70
Total budget 2019–21: $5,353,100

The Labor and Industry Review Commission reviews the decisions of the Department of Workforce Development related to unemployment insurance, fair employment, and public accommodations and decisions of the Department of Workforce Development and the Division of Hearings and Appeals related to worker's compensation. The commission also hears appeals about discrimination in postsecondary education involving a person's physical condition or developmental disability.

NATIONAL AND COMMUNITY SERVICE BOARD

Chair: Christine Beatty
Executive director: Jeanne M. Duffy

Contact: servewisconsin@wisconsin.gov; 608-261-6716; 101 East Wilson Street, 6th Floor,
Madison, WI 53703-3405
Website: www.servewisconsin.wi.gov
Number of employees: 5.00
Total budget 2019–21: $8,699,300

The National and Community Service Board prepares a plan for providing national service programs (which must ensure outreach to organizations serving underrepresented populations) and provides a system to recruit and place participants in national service programs. The board receives and distributes funds from governmental and private sources and acts as an intermediary between the Corporation for National and Community Service and local agencies.

PUBLIC RECORDS BOARD

Chair: Paul Ferguson
Contact: 608-266-2996; 101 East Wilson Street, Madison, WI 53703
Website: http://publicrecordsboard.wi.gov

The Public Records Board is responsible for the preservation of important state records, the cost-effective management of records by state agencies, and the orderly disposition of state records that have become obsolete. State agencies must have written approval from the board to dispose of records they generate or receive.

SMALL BUSINESS REGULATORY REVIEW BOARD

Contact: doaobd@wisconsin.gov
Website: https://doa.wi.gov/pages/doingbusiness/sbrrb.aspx

The Small Business Regulatory Review Board reviews state agency rules and guidelines, proposed rules, and emergency rules to determine whether they place an unnecessary burden on small businesses.

STATE CAPITOL AND EXECUTIVE RESIDENCE BOARD

Members: Senator Agard, Senator Kooyenga, Senator Roth, Representative Loudenbeck, Representative Duchow, Representative Subeck, John Fernholz, Arlan Kay, Kathryn Neitzel, Marijo Reed, Lesley Sager, Ron Siggelkow, Cindy Torstveit, Paula Veltum, Christian Overland, Rafeeq Asad
Website: https://doa.wi.gov/pages/capitol/state-capitol-and-executive-residence-board-(scerb).aspx

The State Capitol and Executive Residence Board (SCERB) ensures the architectural and decorative integrity of the buildings, decorative furniture, furnishings, and grounds of the capitol and executive residence and directs the continuing and consistent maintenance of the properties. No renovations, repairs (except of an emergency nature), installation of fixtures, decorative items, or furnishings for the ground and buildings of the capitol or executive residence may be performed by or become the property of the state by purchase wholly or in part from state funds, or by gift, loan or otherwise, until approved by the board as to design, structure, composition, and appropriateness.

Increasing awareness of and concern for preserving and protecting the special nature of the people's buildings led to the creation of a mechanism for ensuring that the public interest and appropriate standards be carefully considered when altering or redecorating historic facilities. Building upon the State Capitol Restoration Guidelines prepared in 1980 by the Department of Administration's Division of State Facilities, the Legislature's Joint Committee on Legislative Organization in 1987 approved the Capitol Master Plan, which envisioned a full-scale renovation of the capitol, balancing the integrity of the building with the need to maintain it as a modern, functioning seat of government. After approval of the plan by SCERB and the State of Wisconsin Building Commission, renovation of the capitol, whose construction had been completed in 1917, commenced in 1990 and concluded in 2001. The project included extensive updating and improvements to the plumbing, electrical, and heating and cooling systems and largely restored office spaces to their original décor. The board is also responsible for overseeing the upkeep of the Classical Revival home on the shores of Lake Mendota in the Village of Maple Bluff that has served as the official residence of the governor's family for over 50 years.

Members of the capitol's gardening crew plant and tend one of the 15 spectacular flower beds on its 13.5-acre grounds in the heart of Madison.

JOE KOSHOLLEK, LEGISLATIVE PHOTOGRAPHER

STATE USE BOARD

Chair: Jean Zweifel

Contact: doawispro@wisconsin.gov; 608-266-5462 or 608-266-5669; Bureau of Procurement, Division of Enterprise Operations, State Use Program, PO Box 7867, Madison, WI 53707-7867

Website: http://stateuseprogram.wi.gov/

Number of employees: 1.50

Total budget 2019–21: $293,100

The State Use Board oversees state purchases of goods and services from charitable organizations or nonprofit institutions that employ individuals with severe disabilities for at least 75 percent of the direct labor used in providing the goods or services.

TAX APPEALS COMMISSION

Members: Elizabeth Kessler, Lorna Hemp Boll, Jessica Roulette

Contact: dorappeals@wisconsin.gov; 608-266-1391 (main line); 5005 University Avenue, Suite 110, Madison, WI 53705

Number of employees: 5.00

Total budget 2019–21: $1,170,500

The Tax Appeals Commission hears and decides appeals of assessments and determinations made by the Department of Revenue involving state-imposed taxes and state tax assessments of manufacturing property. The commission also adjudicates disputes between taxpayers and the Department of Transportation regarding certain motor vehicle taxes and fees. In addition, the commission has jurisdiction over cases involving the reasonableness of municipally imposed fees. The commission's decisions may be appealed to circuit court.

DIVISION OF TRUST LANDS AND INVESTMENTS

Executive secretary: Tom German

Deputy secretary: Jim DiUlio

Location: 101 East Wilson Street, 2nd Floor, Madison, WI 53703

Contact: bcplinfo@wisconsin.gov; 608-266-1370; PO Box 8943, Madison, WI 53708-8943

Website: http://bcpl.wisconsin.gov

The Division of Trust Lands and Investments assists the Board of Commissioners of Public Lands in its work and is under the direction and supervision of that board. The division is headed by an executive secretary who is appointed by the board. See the entry for the Board of Commissioners of Public Lands beginning on page 227.

WASTE FACILITY SITING BOARD

Chair: Dale Shaver

Executive director: Brian Hayes

Location: 4822 Madison Yards Way, 5th Floor North, Madison, WI 53705-9100
Contact: dhamail@wisconsin.gov; 608-266-7709; PO Box 7875, Madison, WI 53707-7875
Website: https://doa.wi.gov/pages/licenseshearings/dhawastefacilitysitingboard.aspx
Number of employees: 0.00
Total budget 2019–21: $91,000

The Waste Facility Siting Board supervises a mandated negotiation-arbitration procedure between applicants for new or expanded solid or hazardous waste facility licenses and local committees comprising representatives from the municipalities affected by proposed facilities. It is authorized to make final awards in arbitration hearings and can enforce legal deadlines and other obligations of applicants and local committees during the process.

WOMEN'S COUNCIL

Chair: Patty Cadorin
Executive director: Christine Lidbury
Contact: womenscouncil@wisconsin.gov; 608-266-2219; 101 East Wilson Street, 9th Floor, Madison, WI 53703
Website: http://womenscouncil.wi.gov
Number of employees: 1.00
Total budget 2019–21: $299,200

The Women's Council identifies barriers that prevent women in Wisconsin from participating fully and equally in all aspects of life. The council advises state agencies about how current and emerging state policies, laws, and rules have an impact on women; recommends changes to the public and private sectors and initiates legislation to further women's economic and social equality and improve this state's tax base and economy; and disseminates information on the status of women.

Department of Agriculture, Trade and Consumer Protection

Board of Agriculture, Trade and Consumer Protection: Miranda Leis, *chair*
Department secretary-designee: Randy Romanski
Assistant deputy secretary: Angela James
Location: 2811 Agriculture Drive, Madison
Contact: 608-224-5012; PO Box 8911, Madison, WI 53708-8911
Website: https://datcp.wi.gov
Number of employees: 633.29
Total budget 2019–21: $209,663,500

The Department of Agriculture, Trade and Consumer Protection is directed and supervised by the Board of Agriculture, Trade and Consumer Protection and is administered by a secretary. The members of the board and the secretary are appointed by the governor with the advice and consent of the senate.

The department regulates agriculture, trade, and commercial activity in Wisconsin for the protection of the state's citizens. It enforces the state's primary consumer protection laws, including those relating to deceptive advertising, unfair business practices, and consumer product safety. The department oversees the enforcement of Wisconsin's animal health and disease control laws and conducts a variety of programs to conserve and protect the state's vital land, water, and plant resources. The department licenses and inspects food-related businesses to ensure the safety of food produced or sold in Wisconsin. The department administers financial security programs to protect agricultural producers, facilitates the marketing of Wisconsin agricultural products in interstate and international markets, and promotes agricultural development.

Subordinate statutory boards, councils, and committees

AGRICULTURAL PRODUCER SECURITY COUNCIL

Contact: Eric Hanson; eric.hanson@wisconsin.gov; 608-224-4968

The Agricultural Producer Security Council advises the department on the administration and enforcement of the agricultural producer security program, which reimburses grain, milk, and vegetable producers and grain warehouse keepers if a purchaser defaults on payment.

FARM TO SCHOOL COUNCIL

Contact: April Lancer; april.lancer@wisconsin.gov, wifarmtoschool@wisconsin.gov; 608-224-5017

The Farm to School Council advises the department regarding the promotion and administration of farm to school programs and reports to the legislature on the needs of those programs.

FERTILIZER RESEARCH COUNCIL

Website: https://frc.soils.wisc.edu

The Fertilizer Research Council provides funding, with the department secretary's final approval, to the University of Wisconsin System for fertilizer-related research projects. The research projects are funded from a portion of the sales of fertilizer and soil or plant additives in Wisconsin.

VETERINARY EXAMINING BOARD

Chair: Hunter Lang

Contact: datcpveb@wi.gov; 608-224-4353

The Veterinary Examining Board determines the education and experience required for obtaining veterinary licenses and veterinary technician certifications and develops and evaluates examinations for obtaining these licenses and certifications. The board also establishes and enforces standards of professional conduct for veterinarians and veterinary technicians.

Independent entities attached for administrative purposes

LAND AND WATER CONSERVATION BOARD

Chair: Mark E. Cupp
Contact: Lisa Trumble; lisa.trumble@wi.gov; 608-224-4617

The Land and Water Conservation Board advises the secretary and department regarding soil and water conservation and animal waste management. It reviews and makes recommendations to the department on county land and water resource plans and funding allocations to county land conservation committees. The board also advises the University of Wisconsin System about needed research and education programs related to soil and water conservation and assists the Department of Natural Resources with issues related to runoff from agriculture and other rural sources of pollution.

LIVESTOCK FACILITY SITING REVIEW BOARD

Chair: Lee Engelbrecht
Contact: sitingboard@wisconsin.gov; 608-224-5026

The Livestock Facility Siting Review Board may review certain decisions made by political subdivisions relating to the siting or expansion of livestock facilities such as feedlots. An aggrieved person may challenge the decision of a city, village, town, or county government approving or disapproving the siting or expansion of a livestock facility by requesting that the board review the decision. If the board determines that a challenge is valid, it must reverse the decision of the governmental body. The decision of the board is binding on the governmental body, but either party may appeal the board's decision in circuit court.

Department of Children and Families

Department secretary: Emilie Amundson
Deputy secretary: Jeff Pertl
Assistant secretary: Nadya Perez-Reyes
Location: 201 East Washington Avenue, 2nd Floor, Madison
Contact: dcfweb@wisconsin.gov; 608-422-7000; PO Box 8916, Madison, WI 53703-8916
Website: https://dcf.wisconsin.gov
Number of employees: 788.16
Total budget 2019–21: $2,758,020,900

The Department of Children and Families is administered by a secretary who is appointed by the governor with the advice and consent of the senate.

The department provides or oversees county provision of various services to assist children and families, including services for children in need of protection or services, adoption and foster care services, the licensing of facilities that provide out-of-home care for children, background investigations of child caregivers, child abuse and neglect investigations, and community-based juvenile justice services. The

Department of Children and Families Secretary Emilie Amundson speaks at a press conference focused on human trafficking awareness.

department administers the Wisconsin Works (W-2) public assistance program, including the Wisconsin Shares child care subsidy program, the YoungStar child care quality improvement program, the child support enforcement and paternity establishment program, and programs related to the federal Temporary Assistance to Needy Families (TANF) income support program. The department also works to ensure that families have access to high quality and affordable early childhood care and education and administers the licensing and regulation of child care centers.

Subordinate statutory boards, councils, and committees

GOVERNOR'S COUNCIL ON DOMESTIC ABUSE
Contact: Sharon Lewandowski; 608-422-6965
Website: https://dcf.wisconsin.gov/domesticabuse

The Council on Domestic Abuse reviews applications for domestic abuse services grants, advises the department and the legislature on matters of domestic abuse policy, and, in conjunction with the Judicial Conference, develops forms for filing petitions for domestic abuse restraining orders and injunctions.

RATE REGULATION ADVISORY COMMITTEE

Contact: dcfcwlratereg@wisconsin.gov
Website: https://dcf.wisconsin.gov/ratereg

The Rate Regulation Advisory Committee advises the department regarding rates for child welfare agencies, residential care centers, and group homes.

Independent entities attached for administrative purposes

CHILD ABUSE AND NEGLECT PREVENTION BOARD

Chair: Vicki Tylka
Executive director: Rebecca K. Murray
Contact: preventionboard@wisconsin.gov; 608-266-6871; 110 East Main Street, Suite 810, Madison, WI 53703-3316
Website: https://preventionboard.wi.gov
Number of employees: 7.00
Total budget 2019–21: $6,444,000

The Child Abuse and Neglect Prevention Board administers the Children's Trust Fund, which was created to develop and fund strategies that prevent child maltreatment in Wisconsin. In addition, the board recommends to the governor, the legislature, and state agencies changes needed in state programs, statutes, policies, budgets, and rules to reduce child abuse and neglect and improve coordination among state agencies.

A Division of Milwaukee Child Protective Services employee receives a report of suspected child abuse or neglect.

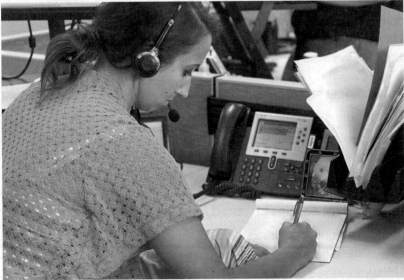

DEPARTMENT OF CHILDREN AND FAMILIES

MILWAUKEE CHILD WELFARE PARTNERSHIP COUNCIL

Chair: Michele Bria

Contact: Bridget Chybowski; dcfmilwaukeechildwelfare@wisconsin.gov; 414-343-5500;
635 North 26th Street, Milwaukee, WI 53233

Website: https://dcf.wisconsin.gov/mcps/partnership-council

The Milwaukee Child Welfare Partnership Council makes recommendations to the department and the legislature regarding policies and plans to improve the child welfare system in Milwaukee County.

Department of Corrections

Department secretary: Kevin A. Carr

Deputy secretary: Jared Hoy

Location: 3099 East Washington Avenue, Madison

Contact: 608-240-5000; PO Box 7925, Madison, WI 53707-7925

Website: www.doc.wi.gov

Number of employees: 10,213.92

Total budget 2019–21: $2,670,658,900

The Department of Corrections is administered by a secretary appointed by the governor with the advice and consent of the senate. The department administers Wisconsin's state prisons, community corrections programs, and juvenile corrections programs. It supervises the custody and discipline of all inmates and operates programs to rehabilitate offenders and reintegrate them into society. It also supervises offenders on probation, parole, and extended supervision; monitors compliance with deferred prosecution programs; and may make recommendations for pardons or commutations of sentence when requested by the governor. The department maintains the sex offender registry and monitors sex offenders and sexually violent persons who are subject to GPS tracking.

Subordinate statutory boards, councils, and committees

CORRECTIONS SYSTEM FORMULARY BOARD

The Corrections System Formulary Board establishes written guidelines, to be applied uniformly throughout the state's correctional institutions, for making therapeutic alternate drug selections for prisoners.

Independent entities attached for administrative purposes

INTERSTATE ADULT OFFENDER SUPERVISION BOARD

Chair: Joselyn Lopéz, *commissioner/compact administrator*

Contact: docdccic@wisconsin.gov, 608-240-5388 (Interstate Compact Office); joselyn.
lopez@wisconsin.gov, 608-240-5333; 3099 East Washington Avenue, Madison, WI 53704

Website: https://doc.wi.gov/pages/aboutdoc/communitycorrections/interstatecompact. aspx

The Interstate Adult Offender Supervision Board appoints the Wisconsin representative to the Interstate Commission for Adult Offender Supervision. The board advises and exercises oversight and advocacy concerning the state's participation in the Interstate Compact for Adult Offender Supervision and on the operation of the compact within this state.

COUNCIL ON OFFENDER REENTRY

Chair: Silvia Jackson
Contact: Sheree Rayford; sheree.rayford@wisconsin.gov; 608-240-5017
Website: https://doc.wi.gov/pages/aboutdoc/reentryunit.aspx (council annual reports)

The Council on Offender Reentry coordinates reentry initiatives across the state, including by promoting collaboration in the provision of transition services and training opportunities, identifying funding sources, and developing methods of information sharing.

PAROLE COMMISSION

Chair: John Tate II
Location: 3099 East Washington Avenue, Madison
Contact: parolecommission@wisconsin.gov; 608-240-7280; PO Box 7960, Madison, WI 53707-7960
Website: https://doc.wi.gov/pages/aboutdoc/parolecommission.aspx

The Parole Commission conducts regularly scheduled interviews to consider the parole of eligible inmates and is responsible for notifying victims and law enforcement about parole decisions.

PRISON INDUSTRIES BOARD

Members: David Hagemeir, *president*; Tracey Griffith, Todd Spencer, Aaron Zimmerman, James Meyer, Alacia Smith, Lenard Simpson, Jana Steinmetz, 1 vacancy
Location: 3099 East Washington Avenue, Madison
Contact: Wes Ray, wesley.ray@wi.gov; 608-240-5201; P.O. Box 8990, Madison, WI 53708
Website: http://www.shopbsi.com/; https://doc.wi.gov/pages/aboutdoc/adult institutions/bureauofcorrectionalenterprises.aspx

The Prison Industries Board develops a plan for the manufacture and marketing of prison industry products and the provision of prison industry services and research and development activities.

STATE BOARD FOR INTERSTATE JUVENILE SUPERVISION

Chair: Christopher Dee
Contact: Casey Gerber, *compact administrator/commissioner*, casey.gerber@wisconsin. gov; 608-240-5918

Website: https://doc.wi.gov/pages/aboutdoc/juvenilecorrections/interstatecompact. aspx; https://www.juvenile-compact.org/midwest/wisconsin

The State Board for Interstate Juvenile Supervision advises and exercises oversight and advocacy concerning the state's participation in the Interstate Compact for Juveniles and on the operation of the compact within this state.

Educational Communications Board

Chair: Rolf Wegenke
Executive director: Marta Bechtol
Contact: 608-264-9600; 3319 West Beltline Highway, Madison, WI 53713
Website: https://www.ecb.org
Number of employees: 55.18
Total budget 2019–21: $42,092,300

The Educational Communications Board oversees the statewide public broadcasting system. It maintains and operates the infrastructure necessary for the state's public radio and television networks; maintains infrastructure and oversees operation of the Emergency Alert System, the Amber Alert System, and National Weather Service transmitters; and provides broadcast engineering and transmission services. The board operates the statewide Wisconsin Public Radio and Wisconsin Public Television services in partnership with the University of Wisconsin-Madison and provides additional educational resources.

The Educational Communications Board maintains the infrastructure of the state's public broadcasting system, including this cell tower located near La Crosse.

Elections Commission

Commissioners: Ann S. Jacobs, *chair;*
Marge Bostelmann, Julie M. Glancey,
Dean Knudson, Robert F. Spindell, Jr.,
Mark L. Thomsen
Administrator: Meagan Wolfe
Location: 212 East Washington Avenue,
3rd Floor, Madison
Contact: elections@wi.gov; 608-266-8005;
866-VOTE-WIS (toll-free voter help line);
PO Box 7984, Madison, WI 53707-7984
Website: https://elections.wi.gov
Number of employees: 31.75
Total budget 2019–21: $11,257,300

The Elections Commission consists of six members and can include additional members in certain circumstances. The majority leader of the senate, the speaker of the assembly, and the minority leaders of the senate and assembly each appoint one member. The governor appoints two members who were formerly county or municipal clerks, selecting one each from lists prepared by the legislative leadership of the two major political parties. If another political party qualified for a separate ballot and received at least 10 percent of the vote in the most recent gubernatorial election, the governor must appoint an additional member selected from a list prepared by that party. The governor's appointees must be confirmed by a majority of the members of the senate, but they can serve on the commission prior to confirmation. The commission appoints an administrator to direct and supervise the commission's staff. This appointment must be confirmed by the senate, but the commission can select a person to serve as interim administrator while the confirmation is pending. The administrator serves as the chief election officer of the state. The commission is responsible for ensuring compliance with state election laws and with the federal Help America Vote Act of 2002, which established certain requirements regarding the conduct of federal elections in the state. In this capacity, the commission trains and certifies all municipal clerks and chief election inspectors in the state to promote uniform election procedures. In addition, the commission is responsible for the design and maintenance of the statewide voter registration system. Every municipality in the state must use this system to administer federal, state, and local elections.

Department of Employee Trust Funds

Employee Trust Funds Board: Wayne Koessl, *chair*
Department Secretary: John Voelker
Deputy Secretary: Shirley Eckes
Location: Hill Farms State Office Building, 8th Floor, 4822 Madison Yards Way, Madison
Contact: 608-266-3285; 877-533-5020 (toll free); PO Box 7931, Madison, WI 53707-7931
Website: http://etf.wi.gov
Number of employees: 274.20
Total budget 2019–21: $96,870,200

The Department of Employee Trust Funds is directed and supervised by the Employee Trust Funds Board. The board consists of 13 members, one of whom is the governor (or a designee). The department is administered by a secretary who is appointed by the board.

The department administers various benefit programs available to state and local public employees, including the Wisconsin Retirement System, health and life insurance programs for active and retired employees of the state and participating local governments, a deferred compensation program, and employee-funded reimbursement account plans. The department serves all state employees and teachers and most municipal employees, with the notable exceptions of employees of the City of Milwaukee and Milwaukee County.

The Employee Trust Funds Board sets policy for the department; appoints the department secretary; approves tables used for computing benefits, contribution rates, and actuarial assumptions; authorizes all annuities except for disability; approves or rejects the department's administrative rules; and generally oversees benefit programs administered by the department, except the group insurance and deferred compensation programs.

Subordinate statutory boards, councils, and committees

DEFERRED COMPENSATION BOARD

Website: http://etf.wi.gov/boards/board_dc.htm

The Deferred Compensation Board oversees the deferred compensation plans offered to state and local employees and contracts with deferred compensation plan providers.

GROUP INSURANCE BOARD

Website: http://etf.wi.gov/boards/board_gib.htm

The Group Insurance Board oversees the group health, life, income continuation, and other insurance programs offered to state employees, covered local employees, and retirees.

TEACHERS RETIREMENT BOARD

Website: http://etf.wi.gov/boards/board_tr.htm

The Teachers Retirement Board advises the Employee Trust Funds Board about retirement matters related to teachers, approves administrative rules related to teachers, authorizes the payment of disability annuities to teachers, and hears appeals of staff determinations regarding disability annuities for teacher participants.

WISCONSIN RETIREMENT BOARD

Website: http://etf.wi.gov/boards/board_wr.htm

The Wisconsin Retirement Board advises the Employee Trust Funds Board about retirement matters related to state and local general and protective employees and performs the same functions for these employees as the Teachers Retirement Board does for teachers.

Ethics Commission

Commissioners: Pat Strachota, *chair*, Paul Connell, Mac Davis, David R. Halbrooks, Scot Ross, Timothy Van Akkeren
Administrator: Daniel A. Carlton, Jr.
Location: 101 E. Wilson Street, Suite 127, Madison
Contact: ethics@wi.gov (general agency and code of ethics questions); campaign finance@wi.gov (campaign finance); ethlobbying@wi.gov (lobbying); 608-266-8123; PO Box 7125, Madison, WI 53707-7125
Website: https://ethics.wi.gov; https://cfis.wi.gov (Campaign Finance Information System); https://lobbying.wi.gov (Eye On Lobbying); https://sei.wi.gov (Statements of Economic Interests)
Number of employees: 8.00
Total budget 2019–21: $2,870,400

The Ethics Commission consists of six members and may include additional members in certain circumstances. The majority leader of the senate, the speaker of the assembly, and the minority leaders of the senate and assembly each appoint one member. The governor appoints two members who were formerly elected judges, selecting one each from lists prepared by the legislative leadership of the two major political parties. If another political party qualified for a separate ballot and received at least 10 percent of the vote in the most recent gubernatorial election, the governor must appoint an additional member selected from a list prepared by that party. The governor's appointees must be confirmed by a majority of the members of the senate, but they can serve on the commission prior to confirmation. The commission appoints an administrator to direct and supervise the commission's staff. The senate must confirm this appointment, but the commission may select a person to serve as interim administrator while the confirmation is pending.

The commission administers Wisconsin's campaign finance laws, lobbying laws, and ethics laws. The commission is the campaign finance filing officer for political organizations that are required to file campaign finance reports with the state, and provides forms, training materials, and assistance to local campaign filing officers (municipal, county, and school district clerks). Lobbyists must obtain a license from the commission; and organizations that employ a lobbyist must register and file reports with the commission detailing the time and money they spend on lobbying. State officials, candidates, and nominees must annually file with the commission statements detailing their economic interests.

Department of Financial Institutions

Department secretary: Kathy Blumenfeld
Deputy secretary: Cheryll Olson-Collins

DEPARTMENT OF FINANCIAL INSTITUTIONS

Members of the Governor's Council on Financial Literacy and Capability pose for a photo on February 19, 2020. In addition to promoting financial literacy and greater financial inclusion for all Wisconsin residents, the Council actively encourages saving for postsecondary education through Wisconsin's College Savings Program.

Contact: 608-261-9555; 4822 Madison Yards Way, North Tower, Madison, WI 53705
Website: www.wdfi.org
Number of employees: 141.54
Total budget 2019–21: $39,712,500

The Department of Financial Institutions is administered by a secretary who is appointed by the governor with the advice and consent of the senate. The department regulates state-chartered banks, savings banks, and savings and loan associations. The department also registers securities and securities industry members and regulates securities offerings, securities industry operations, corporate takeovers, and franchise offerings. It examines and files organizational documents and annual reports for corporations, limited liability companies, and other business entities. It also licenses and regulates the mortgage banking industry and other financial service providers, including payday lenders, high-interest consumer lenders, collection agencies, check cashing services, check sellers, credit counseling and debt settlement services, and automobile sales finance companies. The department administers the Uniform Commercial Code filing system and the Wisconsin Consumer Act. It also issues notary public commissions and registers trademarks, trade names, and brands. It registers and regulates charitable organizations, persons involved with solicitations on behalf of charitable organizations, and professional employer organizations. It also issues video service franchises to cable television operators.

Subordinate statutory boards, councils, and committees

BANKING INSTITUTIONS REVIEW BOARD

The Banking Institutions Review Board advises the Division of Banking in the department on matters related to banks, savings banks, and savings and loan associations, and reviews the division's administrative actions.

Independent entities attached for administrative purposes

COLLEGE SAVINGS PROGRAM BOARD

Administrator: James DiUlio
Location: 4822 Madison Yards Way, North Tower, Madison, WI
Contact: 608-264-7899; PO Box 8861, Madison, WI 53708-8861
Website: http://529.wi.gov

The College Savings Program Board administers the Edvest and Tomorrow's Scholar programs, which provide for tax-advantaged investment accounts used to pay higher education expenses. The Board also has continuing responsibility for a legacy college Tuition Units program.

OFFICE OF CREDIT UNIONS AND CREDIT UNION REVIEW BOARD

Director: Kim Santos
Location: 4822 Madison Yards Way, North Tower, Madison, WI
Contact: 608-261-9543; PO Box 14137, Madison, WI 53708-0137
Website: www.wdfi.org/fi/cu

The Office of Credit Unions regulates state-chartered credit unions. The Credit Union Review Board advises the Office of Credit Unions on matters relating to credit unions and reviews the office's administrative actions.

REMOTE NOTARY COUNCIL

The Remote Notary Council adopts standards for notaries public to perform notarial acts for remotely-located individuals, and these standards are then promulgated as rules by the department.

Department of Health Services

Secretary-designee: Karen Timberlake
Deputy secretary: Julie Willems Van Dijk
Location: Wilson Street State Human Services Building, 1 West Wilson Street, Madison
Contact: 608-266-1865; 1 West Wilson Street, Madison, WI 53703
Website: www.dhs.wisconsin.gov
Number of employees: 6,351.19
Total budget 2019–21: $26,094,873,500

The Department of Health Services is administered by a secretary who is appointed by the governor with the advice and consent of the senate.

The Department of Health Services administers a wide range of services to clients in the community and at state institutions; regulates certain care providers, including emergency medical services practitioners; oversees vital records, including birth, death, marriage, and divorce certificates; and supervises and consults with local public and voluntary agencies. The department promotes and protects public health in Wisconsin through various services and regulations addressing environmental and occupational health, family and community health, chronic and communicable disease prevention and control, and programs relating to maternal and child health. The department provides access to health care for low-income persons, the elderly, and people with disabilities and administers the Medical Assistance (Medicaid), BadgerCare Plus, SeniorCare, chronic disease aids, general relief, and FoodShare programs. Additionally, the department administers programs that provide long-term support for the elderly and people with disabilities, including Family Care, IRIS, Aging and Disability Resource Centers, and Pathways to Independence. The department licenses and regulates programs and facilities that provide health, long-term care, mental health, and substance abuse services, including assisted living facilities, nursing homes, home health agencies, and facilities serving people with developmental disabilities, including three state-operated centers for persons with developmental disabilities. The department administers programs to meet mental health disorder and substance abuse prevention, diagnosis, early intervention, and treatment needs in community and institutional settings, including two state-owned, inpatient mental health institutes, Mendota Mental Health Institute and Winnebago Mental Health Institute. Mendota Mental Health Institute houses a secure treatment unit to meet the mental health needs of male adolescents from the Department of Corrections' juvenile institutions. The department also operates the Wisconsin Resource Center as a maximum security facility for prison inmates whose mental health treatment needs cannot be met by the Department of Corrections and provides treatment at the Sand Ridge Secure Treatment Center for individuals civilly committed under the sexually violent persons law.

Subordinate statutory boards, councils, and committees

COUNCIL ON BIRTH DEFECT PREVENTION AND SURVEILLANCE

Contact: Peggy Helm-Quest; peggy.helmquest@dhs.wisconsin.gov; 608-267-2945
Website: https://cbdps.wisconsin.gov

The Council on Birth Defect Prevention and Surveillance makes recommendations to the department regarding the administration of the Wisconsin Birth Defects Registry, which documents diagnoses and counts the number of birth defects for children up to age two. The council advises what birth defects are to be reported and the content, format, and procedures for reporting.

COUNCIL ON BLINDNESS

Contact: Ann Sievert, *director*; dhsobvi@dhs.wisconsin.gov; 608-266-2536
Website: https://scob.wisconsin.gov

The Council on Blindness makes recommendations to the department and other state agencies on services, activities, programs, investigations, and research that affect persons who are blind or visually impaired.

COUNCIL FOR THE DEAF AND HARD OF HEARING

Contact: Hollie Barnes Spink, *director*; hollie.barnesspink@dhs.wisconsin.gov;
608-247-5343
Website: https://dhhcouncil.wisconsin.gov

The Council for the Deaf and Hard of Hearing advises the department on the provision of effective services to persons who are deaf, hard-of-hearing, or deaf-blind.

COUNCIL ON MENTAL HEALTH

Contact: wcmh@wisconsin.gov
Website: https://mhc.wisconsin.gov

The Council on Mental Health advises the department, governor, and legislature on mental health programs; provides recommendations on the expenditure of federal mental health block grants; reviews the department's plans for mental health services; and serves as an advocate for those who have mental illness.

PUBLIC HEALTH COUNCIL

Contact: dhspublichealthcouncil@wisconsin.gov
Website: https://publichealthcouncil.wisconsin.gov

The Public Health Council advises the department, the governor, the legislature, and the public on progress made in the implementation of the department's ten-year public health plan and coordination of responses to public health emergencies.

TRAUMA ADVISORY COUNCIL

Contact: Margaret Finco; margaret.finco@dhs.wisconsin.gov; 608-266-8282
Website: https://stac.wisconsin.gov

The Trauma Advisory Council advises the department on developing and implementing a statewide trauma care system.

Other statutorily required advisory entities

MEDICAID PHARMACY PRIOR AUTHORIZATION ADVISORY COMMITTEE

Website: https://www.forwardhealth.wi.gov/wiportal/content/provider/pac/index.htm

The Medicaid Pharmacy Prior Authorization Advisory Committee advises the department on issues related to prior authorization decisions concerning prescription drugs on behalf of Medical Assistance recipients.

NEWBORN SCREENING ADVISORY GROUP: UMBRELLA COMMITTEE

Contact: Tami Horzewski; tami.horzewski@dhs.wisconsin.gov; 608-266-8904
Website: http://www.slh.wisc.edu/clinical/newborn/program-information/
wisconsin-newborn-screening-advisory-group/

The Newborn Screening Advisory Umbrella Committee advises the department regarding a statutorily required program that generally requires that newborn infants receive blood or other diagnostic tests for congenital and metabolic disorders.

QUALITY ASSURANCE AND IMPROVEMENT COMMITTEE

Website: https://www.dhs.wisconsin.gov/regulations/qai/members.htm

The Quality Assurance and Improvement Committee makes recommendations for the disbursement of civil money penalties funds allocated for improving the quality of care in Wisconsin nursing homes.

Independent entities attached for administrative purposes

EMERGENCY MEDICAL SERVICES BOARD

Chair: Jerry Biggart
Contact: Amanda Bates; amanda.bates@dhs.wisconsin.gov; 608-261-6870
Website: https://www.dhs.wisconsin.gov/ems/boards/index.htm

The Emergency Medical Services Board appoints an advisory committee of physicians to advise the department on the selection of the state medical director for emergency medical services and to review that person's performance. The board also advises the director on medical issues; reviews emergency medical service statutes and rules concerning the transportation of patients; and recommends changes to the department and the Department of Transportation.

COUNCIL ON PHYSICAL DISABILITIES

Chair: Benjamin Barrett
Contact: ashley.walker@dhs.wisconsin.gov; 608-716-9212; TTY/TDD/Relay: WI Relay 711
Website: https://cpd.wisconsin.gov

The Council on Physical Disabilities develops and modifies the state plan for services to persons with physical disabilities. The council advises the secretary of health services, recommends legislation, encourages public understanding of the needs of persons with physical disabilities, and promotes programs to prevent physical disability.

Higher Educational Aids Board

Members: Stephen Willett, *chair*; Jennifer Kammerud, *vice chair*; Jeff Cichon, *secretary*;
  Brady Coulthard, Amy Christen, Angela Haney, Nathaniel Helm-Quest, Jeff Neubauer,
  Timothy Opgenorth, Justin Wesolek, Kyle M. Weatherly
Nonvoting members: Russell Swagger (president, Lac Courte Oreilles Ojibwa Community
  College), 1 vacancy
Executive secretary: Connie Hutchison
Location: 4822 Madison Yards Way, Seventh floor, Madison
Contact: heabmail@wi.gov; 608-267-2206; PO Box 7885, Madison, WI 53707-7885
Website: http://heab.state.wi.us
Number of employees: 10.00
Total budget 2019–21: $286,576,000

The Higher Educational Aids Board consists of the superintendent of public instruction and ten members appointed by the governor without senate confirmation. The board has added one nonvoting member to represent tribal colleges. The governor appoints the board's executive secretary. The board is responsible for administering the state's higher education student financial aid system and also enters into certain interstate agreements relating to higher education.

Independent entities attached for administrative purposes

DISTANCE LEARNING AUTHORIZATION BOARD

Members: Anny Morrobel-Sosa, *chair*, Morna Foy, *vice chair*, Rolf Wegenke, *secretary*,
  Dawn Crim, Russell Swagger
Contact: Connie Hutchison; connie.hutchison@wi.gov; 608-267-2206
Website: http://heab.wi.gov/dlab

The Distance Learning Authorization Board administers this state's participation in the State Authorization Reciprocity Agreement (SARA), an interstate agreement related to state authorization and oversight of postsecondary institutions that offer educational programs to students located in other states. As provided in SARA, the board reviews, authorizes, and monitors eligible postsecondary institutions with respect to their distance learning programs, such as online classes offered to out-of-state students.

State Historical Society of Wisconsin

Board of Curators: Greg Huber, *president*; Angela Bartell, *president-elect*; Brian Rude, *past
  president*; Walter Rugland, *treasurer*; Christian Overland, *secretary*, Representative
  Billings, Eric Borgerding, Mary Buestrin, Laura Cramer (president, Friends of the
  Wisconsin Historical Society), Ramona Gonzalez, Travis Gross (executive director,

Sheboygan County Historical Society and Museum), Mary Jane Herber, Representative Horlacher, Joanne Huelsman, Thomas Maxwell, Susan McLeod, Sherman Banker, Lowell Peterson, Theresa Richards (chair, Wisconsin Historical Foundation Board of Directors), Donald Schott, Thomas Shriner, Jr., Robert Smith, Leonard Sobczak, Greg Summers (designee of UW System president), John Thompson, Chia Youyee Vang, Senator Wanggaard, Rebecca Webster, Keene Winters, Terri Yoho, Cate Zeuske, Aharon Zorea, Senator Taylor

Director: Christian Overland

Location: 816 State Street, Madison (archives and library); 30 North Carroll Street, Madison (museum)

Contact: 608-264-6400 (general); 608-264-6535 (library); 608-264-6460 (archives); 608-264-6555 (museum); 608-264-6493 (historic preservation); 608-264-6456 (programs and outreach); 816 State Street, Madison, WI 53706

Website: www.wisconsinhistory.org

Number of employees: 181.54

Total budget 2019–21: $61,386,700

The State Historical Society of Wisconsin, also known as the Wisconsin Historical Society, is both a state agency and a membership organization. The society's Board of Curators includes eight statutory appointments and up to 30 members who are selected according to the society's constitution and bylaws. Three board members are appointed by the governor with the advice and consent of the senate. The board selects the society's director, who serves as administrative head and as secretary to the board.

The mission of the society is to help connect people to the past. The society has a statutory duty to collect and preserve historical and cultural resources related to Wisconsin and to make them available to the public. To meet these objectives, the society maintains a major history research collection in Madison and, in partnership with the University of Wisconsin System, operates 13 other area research centers, including the Northern Great Lakes Visitor Center. The society operates the Wisconsin Historical Museum in Madison and ten other museums and historic sites throughout the state. The society also leases Circus World Museum, which is operated by the Circus World Museum Foundation. The society provides statewide school services programs and public history programming such as National History Day, publishes a magazine and books related to Wisconsin history, and provides travelling exhibits and speakers on historical topics. The society also provides technical services and advice to approximately 400 affiliated local historical societies throughout the state. The society serves as the state's historic preservation office, which facilitates the preservation of historic structures and archaeological sites and administers the state and national registers of historic places. The society is also responsible for administering the state's Burial Sites Preservation Law.

The State Historical Society operates several historic sites and museums across the state. (*top*) A visitor to Old World Wisconsin in Eagle works with a historic trades coordinator to learn basic blacksmithing. (*below*) A birchbark cradle, made with dyed porcupine quills in the style of traditional Ojibwe bassinets, on display at the Madeline Island Museum.

Independent entities attached for administrative purposes

BURIAL SITES PRESERVATION BOARD

Members: Melinda Young, *chair*; Cynthia Stiles, *vice chair*; David J. Grignon, Jennifer Haas, Christian Overland, Katherine Stevenson, Corina Williams
Nonvoting members: Tyler Howe, Daina Penkiunas
Contact: Amy Rosebrough; amy.rosebrough@wisconsinhistory.org; 608-264-6494; 816 State Street, Madison, WI 53706
Website: https://www.wisconsinhistory.org/records/article/cs3252

The Burial Sites Preservation Board assists in the administration of the state's burial sites laws. The board's duties include reviewing decisions of the Wisconsin Historical Society director to record burial sites in the catalog or to remove land from the burial sites catalog, determining which Native American tribes in Wisconsin have an interest in cataloged burial sites, approving applicants for a registry of persons having an interest in cataloged burial sites, reviewing decisions on permit applications to disturb cataloged burial sites, reviewing decisions regarding the disposition of human remains and burial objects removed from burial sites, and approving the transfer of burial sites from the state or a political subdivision to private ownership.

HISTORIC PRESERVATION REVIEW BOARD

Members: Melinda Young, *chair*; Carol McChesney Johnson, *vice chair*; Kevin Pomeroy,

Sergio González, Carlen Hatala, Dan J. Joyce, Ray Reser, Neil Prendergast, Matt Sadowski, Amy Scanlon, Sissel Schroeder, Valentine Schute, Jr., Daniel J. Stephans, Paul Wolter, Donna Zimmerman

Contact: Peggy Veregin; peggy.veregin@wisconsinhistory.org; 608-264-6501; 816 State Street, Madison, WI 53706

Website: https://www.wisconsinhistory.org/records/article/cs3564

The Historic Preservation Review Board approves nominations to the Wisconsin State Register of Historic Places and the National Register of Historic Places upon recommendation of the state historic preservation officer. The board approves the distribution of federal grants-in-aid for preservation and approves the state preservation plan, advises the State Historical Society, and requests comments from planning departments of affected cities, villages, towns, counties, local landmark commissions, and local historical societies regarding properties being considered for nomination to the state and national registers.

Office of the Commissioner of Insurance

Commissioner: Mark V. Afable
Deputy commissioner: Nathan Houdek
Location: 125 South Webster Street, Madison
Contact: 608-266-3585; 800-236-8517 (toll free); PO Box 7873, Madison, WI 53707-7873
Website: https://oci.wi.gov
Email contacts by subject: https://oci.wi.gov/pages/aboutoci/emailadd.aspx
Number of employees: 134.83
Total budget 2019–2021: $361,907,100

The Office of the Commissioner of Insurance is administered by the commissioner of insurance, who is appointed by the governor with the advice and consent of the senate. The office supervises the insurance industry in Wisconsin. The office is responsible for examining insurance industry financial practices and market conduct, licensing insurance agents, reviewing policy forms for compliance with state insurance statutes and regulations, investigating consumer complaints, and providing consumer information.

The office administers two segregated insurance funds: the State Life Insurance Fund and the Injured Patients and Families Compensation Fund. The State Life Insurance Fund offers up to $10,000 of low-cost life insurance protection to any Wisconsin resident who meets prescribed risk standards. The Injured Patients and Families Compensation Fund provides medical malpractice coverage for qualified health care providers on claims in excess of a provider's underlying coverage. The office also oversees the Health Care Liability Insurance Plan, which provides liability coverage for hospitals, physicians, and other health care providers in Wisconsin.

Subordinate statutory boards, councils, and committees

BOARD OF GOVERNORS OF THE INJURED PATIENTS AND FAMILIES COMPENSATION FUND/ WISCONSIN HEALTH CARE LIABILITY INSURANCE PLAN

Board of governors: Mark V. Afable, Carla Borda, Bud Chumbly, Timothy Crummy, Jerome Hierseman, Kevin Martin, David Maurer, David R. Nelson, Linda Syth, Ralph Topinka, Jeffery Bingham, Greg Schroeder, 1 vacancy

Location: 125 South Webster Street, Madison

Contact: PO Box 7873, Madison, WI 53707-7873; Injured Patients and Families Compensation Fund: John Macy; ociipfcf@wisconsin.gov; 608-266-6830; Wisconsin Health Care Liability Insurance Plan: whclip@wausaumms.com; 715-841-1690

The Board of Governors of the Injured Patients and Families Compensation Fund/Wisconsin Health Care Liability Insurance Plan oversees the health care liability plan for licensed physicians and certified registered nurse anesthetists, medical partnerships and corporations, cooperative health care associations, ambulatory surgery centers, hospitals, some nursing homes, and certain other health care providers. The board also supervises the Injured Patients and Families Compensation Fund, which pays medical malpractice claims in excess of a provider's underlying coverage.

INJURED PATIENTS AND FAMILIES COMPENSATION FUND PEER REVIEW COUNCIL

The Injured Patients and Families Compensation Fund Peer Review Council reviews, within one year of the first payment on a claim, each claim for damages arising out of medical care provided by a health care provider or provider's employee, if the claim is paid by any of the following: the Injured Patients and Families Compensation Fund, the Wisconsin Health Care Liability Insurance Plan, a private health care liability insurer, or a self-insurer. The council can recommend adjustments in fees paid to the Injured Patients and Families Compensation Fund, premiums paid to the Wisconsin Health Care Liability Insurance Plan, or premiums paid to private insurers if requested by the insurer.

BOARD OF DIRECTORS OF THE INSURANCE SECURITY FUND

Chair: Scott Seymour

Contact: wisconsin@wisf-madison.org; 608-242-9473; 844-344-5484 (toll free); 2820 Walton Commons Lane, Suite 135, Madison, WI 53718-6797

Website: https://www.wilifega.org

The Board of Directors of the Insurance Security Fund administers a fund that protects certain insurance policyholders and claimants from excessive delay and loss in the event of insurer liquidation. The fund consists of accounts for life insurance, allocated annuities, disability insurance (includes health), HMO insurers, other insurance (includes property and casualty), and fund administration. The fund supports continuation of coverage under many life, annuity, and health policies. It is financed by assessments paid by most insurers in this state.

State of Wisconsin Investment Board

Chair: David Stein
Executive director/chief investment officer: Edwin Denson
Location: 121 East Wilson Street, Madison
Contact: info@swib.state.wi.us; 608-266-2381; PO Box 7842, Madison, WI 53707-7842
Website: www.swib.state.wi.us
Number of employees: 203.00
Total budget 2019–21: $124,889,400

The State of Wisconsin Investment Board consists of the secretary of administration or his or her designee and eight other members, six of whom are appointed by the governor with the advice and consent of the senate. The board appoints the executive director.

The board is responsible for investing the assets of the Wisconsin Retirement System and the State Investment Fund. The board's investments are managed by its own professional staff and by outside money managers. As of December 31, 2019, the board managed about $129 billion in assets. The largest portion of the assets managed by the board, almost $117 billion, is the trust funds of the Wisconsin Retirement System. For purposes of investment, the retirement system's assets are divided into two funds: the core fund, which is a broadly diversified portfolio that includes stocks, bonds, and other assets, and the variable fund, which is an all-stock fund. As of December 31, 2019, about $13 billion of the assets under management by the board are in the State Investment Fund, which is the state's cash management fund, and which is also available to local units of government through the Local Government Pooled-Investment Fund, a separate fund within the State Investment Fund. The board also manages the assets of the following trust funds, which together account for less than 1 percent of the board's total assets under management: the State Life Insurance Fund, the Historical Society Trust Fund, the Injured Patients and Families Compensation Fund, and the UW System Trust Funds.

Department of Justice

Attorney general: Joshua L. Kaul
Deputy attorney general: Eric Wilson
Location: 114 East, State Capitol (attorney general's office); 17 West Main Street, Madison (Department of Justice)

STATE OF WISCONSIN INVESTMENT BOARD

In honor of International Women's Day on March 8, 2020, the State of Wisconsin Investment Board (SWIB) recognizes the innovative, talented, and inspiring women who help make SWIB a trusted global investment organization.

Contact: 608-266-1221; PO Box 7857, Madison, WI 53707-7857
Website: www.doj.state.wi.us
Number of employees: 717.14
Total budget 2019–21: $289,032,600

The Department of Justice is headed by the attorney general, a constitutional officer who is elected on a partisan ballot to a four-year term. The department provides legal advice and representation, investigates criminal activity, and provides various law enforcement services for the state. The department appears for the state and prosecutes or defends civil and criminal actions and proceedings in the court of appeals or the supreme court in which the state is interested or a party. The department prosecutes or defends all civil cases sent or remanded to any circuit court in which the state is a party. The department also represents the state in criminal cases on appeal in federal court.

Subordinate statutory boards, councils, and committees

CRIME VICTIMS COUNCIL

Members: Michelle Arrowood, Tania M. Bonnett, Thomas Eagon, Jane E. Graham Jennings, Kurt D. Heuer, Scott L. Horne, Connie Klick, Dione Knop, Jennifer L. Noyes, Mallory E. O'Brien, Kari Sasso, 4 vacancies
Contact: ocvs@doj.state.wi.us
Website: https://www.doj.state.wi.us/ocvs/not-crime-victim/crime-victims-council

The Crime Victims Council provides advice and recommendations to the attorney general on the rights of crime victims, how to improve the criminal justice response to victims, and other issues affecting crime victims.

Independent entities attached for administrative purposes

CRIME VICTIMS RIGHTS BOARD

Director: Julie Braun
Members: Jen Dunn, Tania M. Bonnett, Amy Severt, Nela Kalpic, Paul Susienka
Contact: cvrb@doj.state.wi.us
Website: https://www.doj.state.wi.us/ocvs/victim-rights/crime-victims-rights-board

On May 16, 2019, Attorney General Joshua Kaul announces the filing of a lawsuit against Purdue Pharma, maker of the opioid OxyContin, alleging that deceptive marketing helped fuel opioid addiction across Wisconsin and the rest of the country.

The Crime Victims Rights Board has the authority to review complaints filed by a crime victim that allege that a public official, public employee, or public agency violated the victim's rights. The board may issue a private or public reprimand for a violation, seek appropriate equitable relief on behalf of a victim, or bring a civil action to assess a forfeiture for an intentional violation. The board may issue a report or recommendation concerning the rights of crime victims and the provision of services to crime victims.

LAW ENFORCEMENT STANDARDS BOARD

Chair: Christopher Domagalski
Members: Anthony Burrell, Todd Delain, Jean Galasinski, Timothy J. Gruenke, Robert Hughes, Casey Krueger, Scott Parks, Earnell R. Lucas, James Small, Charles Tubbs, Tina Virgil, Michelle Viste, Katie Rosenberg, Jessie Metoyer, Benjamin Bliven, Nicole R. Miller
Contact: wilenet@doj.state.wi.us
Website: https://wilenet.org

The Law Enforcement Standards Board sets minimum education and training standards for law enforcement and tribal law enforcement officers. The board certifies persons who meet professional standards as qualified to be law enforcement, tribal law enforcement, jail, or juvenile detention officers. The board consults with other government agencies regarding the development of training schools and courses, conducts research to improve law enforcement and performance, and evaluates governmental units for compliance with board standards.

The Curriculum Advisory Committee advises the Law Enforcement Standards Board on the establishment of curriculum requirements for training of law enforcement, tribal law enforcement, and jail and secure detention officers.

DEPARTMENT OF JUSTICE

Tutty, the Department of Justice's accelerant detection canine, awaits instruction at the scene of a potential crime. Tutty received advanced training at a federal facility in Virginia operated by the Bureau of Alcohol, Tobacco, Firearms and Explosives, and he is now one of only 55 canines in the country trained to detect the scent of explosives and explosives residue.

Department of Military Affairs

Commander in chief: Tony Evers (governor)
Adjutant general: Major General Paul E. Knapp
Deputy adjutant general support to civil authority: Brigadier General David O'Donahue
Deputy adjutant general for army: Brigadier General Joane Mathews
Deputy adjutant general for air: Brigadier General David W. May
Administrator, Division of Emergency Management: Darrell L. Williams, Ph.D
Location: 2400 Wright Street, Madison
Contact: 608-242-3000 (general); 800-335-5147 (toll free); 800-943-0003 (24-hour hotline for emergencies and hazardous materials spills); PO Box 7865, Madison, WI 53707-7865
Website: http://dma.wi.gov (Department of Military Affairs and Wisconsin National Guard); https://dma.wi.gov/dma/wem (Division of Emergency Management)
Number of state employees: 521.10
Total state budget 2019–21: $259,670,800 (Additional federal funding pays for National Guard salaries, benefits, and training.)

The governor is the commander in chief of the state's military forces, which are organized as the Wisconsin National Guard within the Department of Military Affairs. The department is directed by an adjutant general who is appointed by the governor without senate advice and consent. The department also includes the Division of Emergency Management, which is headed by an administrator who is appointed by the governor with the advice and consent of the senate.

The Wisconsin National Guard is maintained by both the federal and the state governments. (When it is called up in an active federal duty status, the president of the United States, rather than the governor, becomes its commander in chief.) The federal mission of the National Guard is to provide trained units to the U.S. Army and U.S. Air Force in time of war or national emergency. Its state mission is to assist civil authorities, protect life and property, and preserve peace, order, and public safety in times of natural or human-caused emergencies. The federal

(BOTH PHOTOS) DEPARTMENT OF MILITARY AFFAIRS

Wisconsin Army National Guard Soldiers display the Wisconsin flag while serving in California in September 2020. Two UH-60 Black Hawk helicopters and 15 crew members from the Madison-based 1st Battalion, 147th Aviation, deployed to California for more than a month to battle wildfires there.

government provides arms and ammunition, equipment and uniforms, and major outdoor training facilities and pays for military and support personnel, training, and supervision. The state provides personnel; conducts training as required under the National Defense Act; and shares the cost of constructing, maintaining, and operating armories and other military facilities.

Two Wisconsin National Guard members conduct COVID-19 testing in Milwaukee in October 2020. The Wisconsin National Guard administered more than one million COVID tests during the pandemic.

The Division of Emergency Management coordinates the development and implementation of the state emergency operations plan; provides assistance to local jurisdictions in the development of their programs and plans; administers private and federal disaster and emergency relief funds; administers the Wisconsin Disaster Fund; and maintains the state's 24-hour duty officer reporting and response system. The division also conducts training programs in emergency planning for businesses and state and local officials, as well as educational programs for the general public. It also prepares for off-site radiological emergencies at nuclear power plants and provides assistance for various emergencies such as prison disturbances and natural disasters.

Independent entities attached for administrative purposes

INTEROPERABILITY COUNCIL

Chair: Matthew Joski
Website: https://dma.wi.gov/dma/oec/programs/interop

The Interoperability Council develops strategies and makes recommendations on how to achieve and operate a statewide public safety interoperable communication system.

Department of Natural Resources

Natural Resources Board: Frederick Prehn, *chair*
Department secretary: Preston D. Cole
Deputy secretary: Beth Bier
Location: State Natural Resources Building (GEF 2), 101 South Webster Street, Madison
Contact: 888-936-7463 (TTY access via relay 711); PO Box 7921, Madison, WI 53707-7921
Website: http://dnr.wi.gov
Number of employees: 2521.60
Total budget 2019–21: $1,120,221,500

The Department of Natural Resources is directed and supervised by the Natural Resources Board and is administered by a secretary. The members of the board and the secretary are appointed by the governor with the advice and consent of the senate.

The department is responsible for implementing state and federal laws that protect and enhance Wisconsin's natural resources, including its air, land, water, forests, wildlife, fish, and plants. It coordinates the many state-administered programs that protect the environment and provides a full range of outdoor recreational opportunities for Wisconsin residents and visitors.

Subordinate statutory boards, councils, and committees

DRY CLEANER ENVIRONMENTAL RESPONSE COUNCIL (inactive)

The Dry Cleaner Environmental Response Council advises the department on matters relating to the Dry Cleaner Environmental Response Program, which is administered by the department and which provides awards to dry cleaning establishments for assistance in the investigation and cleanup of environmental contamination.

COUNCIL ON FORESTRY

The Council on Forestry advises the governor, legislature, department, and other state agencies on topics relating to forestry in Wisconsin, including protection from fire, insects, and disease; sustainable forestry; reforestation and forestry genetics; management and protection of urban forests; increasing the public's knowledge and awareness of forestry issues; forestry research; economic development and marketing of forestry products; legislation affecting forestry; and staff and funding needs for forestry programs.

METALLIC MINING COUNCIL (inactive)

The Metallic Mining Council advises the department on matters relating to the reclamation of mined land and the disposal of metallic mine-related waste.

NATURAL AREAS PRESERVATION COUNCIL

The Natural Areas Preservation Council advises the department on matters pertaining to the protection of natural areas that contain native biotic communities and habitats for rare species. It also makes recommendations about gifts or purchases for the state natural areas system.

NONMOTORIZED RECREATION AND TRANSPORTATION TRAILS COUNCIL

The Nonmotorized Recreation and Transportation Trails Council carries out studies and advises the governor, the legislature, the department, and the Department of Transportation on matters relating to nonmotorized recreation and transportation trails.

OFF-HIGHWAY MOTORCYCLE COUNCIL

The Off-Highway Motorcycle Council makes recommendations to the department on matters relating to off-highway motorcycle corridors and routes and the operation of off-highway motorcycles.

OFF-ROAD VEHICLE COUNCIL

The Off-Road Vehicle Council advises the department, the Department of Transportation, the governor, and the legislature on all matters relating to all-terrain vehicle trails and routes.

SMALL BUSINESS ENVIRONMENTAL COUNCIL

The Small Business Environmental Council advises the department on the effectiveness of assistance programs to small businesses that enable the businesses to comply with the federal Clean Air Act. It also advises on the fairness and effectiveness of air pollution rules promulgated by the department and the U.S. Environmental Protection Agency regarding their impact on small businesses.

SNOWMOBILE RECREATIONAL COUNCIL

The Snowmobile Recreational Council carries out studies and makes recommendations to the governor, the legislature, the department, and the Department of Transportation regarding all matters affecting snowmobiling.

SPORTING HERITAGE COUNCIL

The Sporting Heritage Council advises the governor, the legislature, and the Natural Resources Board about issues relating to hunting, trapping, fishing, and other types of outdoor recreation activities.

STATE TRAILS COUNCIL

The State Trails Council advises the department about the planning, acquisition, development, and management of state trails.

DEPARTMENT OF NATURAL RESOURCES

Visitors to Copper Falls State Park in Ashland County can walk the scenic 1.7-mile Doughboy's Trail, which winds along a rocky gorge where the Tyler Forks River joins the Bad River, and can take in dramatic views of several roaring waterfalls along the way.

WETLAND STUDY COUNCIL

The Wetland Study Council conducts research and develops recommendations on a range of topics involving wetland policy, procedures, regulations, and financing, including the implementation and effectiveness of statewide wetland mitigation programs; statewide incentive programs for creating, restoring, and enhancing wetlands; providing statewide wetland trainings; and methods of financing wetland mitigation requirements for local units of government.

Other advisory entities

FIRE DEPARTMENT ADVISORY COUNCIL

The Fire Department Advisory Council was chartered in 1994 as an official advisory council to the state forester. The purpose of the council is to strengthen partnerships between the department and the rural fire service in Wisconsin. The council advises and assists the state forester on operational issues relating to the department's forest fire management program to provide for an effective rural community fire protection program. In addition, the council provides fundamental guidance on the administration of the Forest Fire Protection Grant.

URBAN FORESTRY COUNCIL

The Urban Forestry Council advises the state forester and the department on the best ways to preserve, protect, expand, and improve Wisconsin's urban and community forest resources. The council gives awards to outstanding individuals, organizations, and communities that further urban forestry in Wisconsin.

Independent entities attached for administrative purposes

GROUNDWATER COORDINATING COUNCIL

Chair: James Zellmer

The Groundwater Coordinating Council advises state agencies on the coordination of nonregulatory programs relating to groundwater management. Member agencies exchange information regarding groundwater monitoring, budgets for groundwater programs, data management, public information efforts, laboratory analyses, research, and state appropriations for research.

INVASIVE SPECIES COUNCIL

Chair: Thomas Buechel

The Invasive Species Council conducts studies relating to controlling invasive species and makes recommendations to the department regarding a system for classifying invasive species under the department's statewide invasive species control program and regarding procedures for awarding grants to public and private agencies engaged in projects to control invasive species.

LAKE MICHIGAN COMMERCIAL FISHING BOARD

Members: Charles W. Henriksen, Richard R. Johnson, Michael LeClair, Mark Maricque, Dan Pawlitzke, Brett Schwarz, Todd Stuth

The Lake Michigan Commercial Fishing Board reviews applications for transfers of commercial fishing licenses between individuals, establishes criteria for allotting catch quotas to individual licensees, assigns catch quotas when the department establishes special harvest limits, and assists the department in establishing criteria for identifying inactive license holders.

LAKE SUPERIOR COMMERCIAL FISHING BOARD

Members: Bill Bodin, Maurine Halvorson, Craig Hoopman, Bob Nelson, 1 vacancy

The Lake Superior Commercial Fishing Board reviews applications for transfers of commercial fishing licenses between individuals, establishes criteria for allotting catch quotas to individual licensees, assigns catch quotas when the department establishes special harvest limits, and assists the department in establishing criteria for identifying inactive license holders.

LOWER WISCONSIN STATE RIVERWAY BOARD

Chair: Gerald Dorscheid
Executive Director: Mark E. Cupp
Contact: mark.cupp@wisconsin.gov; 608-739-3188; 202 N. Wisconsin Ave., P.O. Box 187, Muscoda, WI 53573
Website: http://lwr.state.wi.us/index.asp
Number of employees: 2.00
Total budget 2019–21: $494,600

The Lower Wisconsin State Riverway Board is responsible for protecting and preserving the scenic beauty and natural character of the riverway. The board reviews permit applications for buildings, walkways and stairways, timber harvests, nonmetallic mining, utility facilities, public access sites, bridges, and other structures in the riverway and issues permits for activities that meet established standards.

COUNCIL ON RECYCLING

Chair: David Keeling

The Council on Recycling promotes implementation of the state's solid waste reduction, recovery, and recycling programs; helps public agencies coordinate programs and exchange information; advises state agencies about creating administrative rules and establishing priorities for market development; and advises the department and the University of Wisconsin System about education and research relating to solid waste recycling. The council also works with the packaging industry on standards for recyclable packaging and works with counties, municipalities, and the auto service industry to promote the recycling of oil filters. The council advises the department about statewide public information activities and advises the governor and the legislature.

WISCONSIN WATERWAYS COMMISSION

Chair: Roger Walsh

The Wisconsin Waterways Commission conducts studies to determine the need for recreational boating facilities; approves financial aid to local governments for the development of recreational boating projects, including the acquisition of weed harvesters; and recommends administrative rules for the recreational facilities boating program.

Affiliated entity

CONSERVATION CONGRESS

The Conservation Congress is a publicly elected citizen advisory group, and its district leadership council advises the Natural Resources Board on all matters under the board's jurisdiction.

Office of the State Public Defender

Public Defender Board: Regina Dunkin, *chair*
State public defender: Kelli S. Thompson
Deputy state public defender: Jon Padgham
Location: 17 South Fairchild Street, 5th Floor, Madison
Contact: 608-266-0087; PO Box 7923, Madison, WI 53707-7923
Website: www.wispd.org
Number of employees: 614.85
Total budget 2019–21: $208,614,700

The Office of the State Public Defender provides legal representation to indigent persons and to persons otherwise entitled to such representation. The state public defender, who must be a member of the state bar, serves at the pleasure of the Public Defender Board. Board members are appointed by the governor with the advice and consent of the senate.

Attorneys are assigned by the state public defender to persons charged with a crime that may be sentenced with imprisonment and to other cases, such as cases involving paternity determinations, termination of parental rights, juvenile delinquency proceedings, emergency detentions, involuntary commitments, modification of bifurcated sentences, and certain appeals.

Department of Public Instruction

State superintendent of public instruction: Jill Underly
Deputy state superintendent: John Johnson
Location: State Education Building (GEF 3), 125 South Webster Street, Madison
Contact: 608-266-3390; 800-441-4563 (toll free); PO Box 7841, Madison, WI 53707-7841
Website: www.dpi.wi.gov; https://dpi.wi.gov/statesupt/councils-and-committees

Number of employees: 641.00
Total budget 2019–21: $15,457,871,700

The Department of Public Instruction is headed by the state superintendent of public instruction, a constitutional officer who is elected on the nonpartisan spring ballot for a term of four years. The department provides guidance and technical assistance to support public elementary and secondary education in Wisconsin. The department also administers the Milwaukee, Racine, and State-wide Parental Choice Programs; the Special Needs Scholarship Program; the open enrollment program; and a number of educational and other services for children and their families.

The department offers a broad range of programs and professional services to local school administrators and staff. It also reviews and approves educator preparation programs and licenses teachers, pupil services personnel, administrators, and library professionals. The department distributes state and federal aids to supplement local tax revenue, improve curriculum and school operations, ensure education for children with disabilities, offer professional guidance and counseling, and develop school and public library resources. The department also administers the Wisconsin Educational Services Program for the Deaf and Hard of Hearing and the Wisconsin Center for the Blind and Visually Impaired.

Finally, the department provides assistance for the development and improvement of public and school libraries. The department fosters interlibrary cooperation and resource sharing and promotes information and instructional technology in schools and libraries. The department also acts as a state-level clearinghouse for interlibrary loan requests; administers BadgerLink (https://badgerlink.dpi.wi.gov), the statewide full-text database project that allows access to thousands of magazines, newsletters, newspapers, pamphlets, and historical documents; and, in collaboration with other Wisconsin library organizations, manages BadgerLearn, the statewide portal that provides continuing education resources for library professionals.

Subordinate statutory boards, councils, and committees

STATE SUPERINTENDENT'S ADVISORY COUNCIL ON ALCOHOL AND OTHER DRUG ABUSE PROBLEMS

Contact: Brian Dean; brian.dean@dpi.wi.gov

The council advises the governor, the legislature, and state agencies about programs to prevent or reduce alcohol, tobacco, and other drug abuse.

BLIND AND VISUAL IMPAIRMENT EDUCATION COUNCIL

Contact: Amanda Jordan, amanda.jordan@wcbvi.k12.wi.us

The Blind and Visual Impairment Education Council provides advice on statewide activities that will benefit students who are blind or visually impaired; makes recommendations for improvements in services provided by the Wisconsin Center for the Blind and Visually Impaired; and proposes ways to improve the preparation of teachers and staff and coordination between the department and other agencies that offer services to the visually impaired.

DEAF AND HARD-OF-HEARING EDUCATION COUNCIL

Contact: Kathleen Lincoln; kathleen.lincoln@wsd.k12.wi.us
Website: http://wesp-dhh.wi.gov/advisory-council/

The Deaf and Hard-of-Hearing Education Council advises the state superintendent on issues related to pupils who are hearing impaired and informs the state superintendent about services, programs, and research that could benefit those pupils.

COUNCIL ON LIBRARY AND NETWORK DEVELOPMENT

Contact: Alison Hiam; 608-266-6439
Website: https://dpi.wi.gov/coland

The Council on Library and Network Development advises the state superintendent and the administrator of the Division for Libraries and Technology to ensure that all state citizens have access to library and information services.

PROFESSIONAL STANDARDS COUNCIL FOR TEACHERS

Contact: Ariana Baker; ariana.baker@dpi.wi.gov, 608-266-1879
Website: https://dpi.wi.gov/licensing/programs/psc

The Professional Standards Council for Teachers advises the state superintendent regarding licensing and evaluating teachers; the evaluation and approval of teacher education programs; the status of teaching in Wisconsin; school board practices to develop effective teaching; peer mentoring; evaluation systems; alternative dismissal procedures; and alternative procedures for the preparation and licensure of teachers.

SCHOOL DISTRICT BOUNDARY APPEAL BOARD

Contact: Janice Zmrazek; janice.zmrazek@dpi.wi.gov; 608-266-2803
Website: https://dpi.wi.gov/sms/school-district-boundary-appeal-board

Panels consisting of three or seven members of the School District Boundary Appeal Board hear appeals related to school district creation and dissolution, annexation, and boundary disputes.

COUNCIL ON SPECIAL EDUCATION

Contact: Jennifer Mims Howell; mimshjn@milwaukee.k12.wi.us; 414-438-3648; Pamela Hencke, pamelahenckeadvocacy@gmail.com
Website: https://dpi.wi.gov/sped/council

The Council on Special Education advises the state superintendent on matters related to meeting the needs and improving the education of children with disabilities.

Board of Commissioners of Public Lands

Members: Douglas J. La Follette (secretary of state), Sarah Godlewski (state treasurer), Joshua L. Kaul (attorney general)
Division of Trust Lands and Investments: Tom German, executive secretary; Richard Sneider, chief investment officer
Location: 101 East Wilson Street, 2nd Floor, Madison
Contact: 608-266-1370; PO Box 8943, Madison, WI 53708-8943
Website: https://bcpl.wisconsin.gov
Number of employees: 9.50
Total budget 2019–21: $3,552,500

The Board of Commissioners of Public Lands is a body established in the Wisconsin Constitution. The board is composed of the secretary of state, state treasurer, and attorney general. The board manages the state's remaining trust lands, manages trust funds primarily for the benefit of public education, and maintains the state's original 19th-century land survey and land sales records. The board is assisted in its work by the Division of Trust Lands and Investments, an entity attached to the Department of Administration for administrative purposes.

The board holds title to nearly 77,000 acres of school trust lands. These lands are managed for timber production, natural area preservation, and public use. The board manages four trust funds, totaling over $1 billion in assets. The largest of these is the Common School Fund. The principal of this fund continues to grow through the collection of fines and forfeitures that accrue to the state. The board invests the moneys of this fund in state and municipal bonds. It also loans moneys from this fund directly to Wisconsin municipalities and school districts through the State Trust Fund Loan Program. These loans are used for economic development, school repairs and improvements, local infrastructure and utilities, and capital equipment and vehicles. The net earnings of the Common School Fund are distributed annually by the Department of Public Instruction to all of Wisconsin's public school districts and provide the sole source of state aid for public school library media and resources. The other trust funds are used to support the University of Wisconsin and the state's general fund.

Public Service Commission

Members: Rebecca Cameron Valcq, *chair*; Ellen Nowak, Tyler Huebner
Executive assistant to the chair: Sally Mergen

PUBLIC SERVICE COMMISSION

Public Service Commission energy policy advisor Joe Fontaine (*right*) speaks at an electric vehicle workshop hosted by the commission.

Location: 4822 Madison Yards Way, North Tower, Sixth Floor, Madison

Contact: pscrecordsmail@wisconsin.gov (general); pscpublicrecordsrequest@wisconsin. gov (public records requests); 608-266-5481; 888-816-3831 (toll free); 608-266-2001 (consumer complaints); 800-225-7729 (consumer complaints, toll free); PO Box 7854, Madison, WI 53707-7854

Website: http://psc.wi.gov

Number of employees: 153.25

Total budget 2019–21: $103,260,000

The Public Service Commission consists of three commissioners appointed by the governor with the advice and consent of the senate for six-year terms. The governor appoints one of the commissioners as chair for a two-year term. A commissioner may not have a financial interest in a railroad, public utility, or water carrier; may not be a candidate for public office; and is subject to certain restrictions regarding political activity.

The commission is responsible for regulating Wisconsin's public utilities and ensuring that utility services are provided to customers safely, reliably, and at prices reasonable to both ratepayers and utility owners. The commission also regulates the rates and services of electric, natural gas distribution, water, and municipal combined water and sewer utilities. The commission's responsibilities include determining levels for adequate and safe service; overseeing compliance with renewable energy and energy conservation and efficiency requirements; approving public utility bond sales and stock offerings; and approving mergers, consolidations, and ownership changes regarding public utilities. The commission also considers applications for major construction projects, such as power plants, transmission lines, and wind farms. In addition to ensuring public utility compliance with statutes, administrative codes, and record-keeping requirements, commission staff investigates and mediates consumer complaints.

The commission has limited jurisdiction over landline telecommunications providers and services. The commission certifies various types of telecommunications providers; manages the Universal Service Fund; handles some wholesale disputes between telecommunications providers; and administers telephone numbering resources. In general, the commission has no jurisdiction over electric cooperatives, liquefied petroleum gas, fuel oil, wireless telephone, or cable television. Although the commission has no jurisdiction over Internet service, it does provide oversight for statewide broadband mapping and planning and makes grants for constructing broadband infrastructure in underserved areas. Also, the commission has the authority to enforce Digger's Hotline requirements involving natural gas or other hazardous materials.

Subordinate statutory boards, councils, and committees

UNIVERSAL SERVICE FUND COUNCIL

Contact: Holly O'Higgins, Universal Service Fund director; holly.ohiggins@wisconsin.gov; 608-267-9486; PO Box 7854, Madison, WI 53707-7854

The Universal Service Fund Council advises the commission on the administration of the Universal Service Fund. The purposes of the fund include assisting low-income customers, customers in areas where telecommunications service costs are relatively high, and customers with disabilities in obtaining affordable access to basic telecommunications services. The Universal Service Fund director acts as the liaison between the Public Service Commission and the council.

WIND SITING COUNCIL

The Wind Siting Council advises the commission on the promulgation of rules relating to restrictions that a political subdivision may impose on the installation or use of a wind energy system, including setback requirements that provide reasonable protection from any health effects. The council also surveys the peer-reviewed scientific research regarding the health impacts of wind energy systems and studies state and national regulatory developments regarding the siting of wind energy systems.

Independent entities attached for administrative purposes

OFFICE OF THE COMMISSIONER OF RAILROADS

Commissioner of railroads: Yash P. Wadhwa
Location: 4822 Madison Yards Way, Suite S633, Madison

Contact: 608-261-8221; PO Box 7854, Madison, WI 53707-7854
Website: http://ocr.wi.gov
Number of employees: 6.00
Total budget 2019–21: $1,204,600

The governor appoints the commissioner of railroads with the advice and consent of the senate for a six-year term. The commissioner may not have a financial interest in railroads or water carriers and may not serve on or under any committee of a political party. The Office of the Commissioner of Railroads enforces regulations related to railway safety and determines the safety of highway crossings, including the adequacy of railroad warning devices. The office also has authority over the rates and services of intrastate water carriers.

Department of Revenue

Department secretary: Peter Barca
Deputy secretary: David Casey
Location: 2135 Rimrock Road, Madison
Contact: 608-266-2772 (office phone); 608-266-5718 (fax); 608-266-2486 (individuals); 608-266-2776 (businesses); PO Box 8933, Mail Stop 624-A, Madison, WI 53708-8933
Website: www.revenue.wi.gov
Number of employees: 1,182.03
Total budget 2019–21: $445,939,000

The Department of Revenue is administered by a secretary who is appointed by the governor with the advice and consent of the senate. The department administers all major state tax laws except the insurance premiums tax and enforces the state's alcohol beverage and tobacco laws. It estimates state revenues, forecasts state economic activity, helps formulate tax policy, and administers the Wisconsin Lottery. The department also determines the equalized value of taxable property and assesses manufacturing and telecommunications company property for property tax purposes. It administers the tax incremental financing program, shared revenue, and other local financial assistance programs, and assists local governments in their property assessments and financial management. The department also oversees Wisconsin's Unclaimed Property program, which matches taxpayers with unclaimed financial assets.

Subordinate statutory boards, councils, and committees

STATE BOARD OF ASSESSORS

The State Board of Assessors investigates objections filed by manufacturers and municipalities to the amount, valuation, or taxability of real or personal manufacturing property, as well as objections to the penalties issued for late filing or nonfiling of required manufacturing property report forms.

FARMLAND ADVISORY COUNCIL

The Farmland Advisory Council advises the department on assessing agricultural land, implementing use-value assessment of agricultural land, and reducing the expansion of urban sprawl. It reports annually to the legislature on the usefulness of use-value assessment as a way to preserve farmland and reduce the conversion of farmland to other uses. The council also recommends changes to the shared revenue formula to compensate local governments and school districts adversely affected by use-value assessment.

Independent entities attached for administrative purposes

INVESTMENT AND LOCAL IMPACT FUND BOARD

Executive secretary: Dave Steines; 608-480-1307
Website: dorminingboard@wisconsin.gov

The Investment and Local Impact Fund Board administers the Investment and Local Impact Fund, created to help municipalities alleviate costs associated with social, educational, environmental, and economic impacts of metalliferous mineral mining. The board certifies to the Department of Administration the amount of the payments to be distributed to municipalities from the fund. It also provides funding to local governments throughout the development of a mining project, and distributes federal mining revenue received by the state to municipalities impacted by mining on federal land.

Department of Safety and Professional Services

Department secretary: Dawn B. Crim
Deputy secretary: Donna V. Moreland
Contact: 608-266-2112; 4822 Madison Yards Way, Madison, WI 53705
Website: http://dsps.wi.gov
Number of employees: 241.14
Total budget 2019–21: $118,950,400

The Department of Safety and Professional Services is administered by a secretary who is appointed by the governor with the advice and consent of the senate.

The department administers and enforces laws to ensure safe and sanitary conditions in public and private buildings, including by reviewing plans and performing inspections of commercial buildings and certain components and systems therein.

The department is also responsible for ensuring the safe and competent practice of various licensed occupations and businesses in Wisconsin. The department provides direct regulation or licensing of certain occupations and businesses. In addition, numerous boards are attached to the department that are responsible for regulating other occupations and businesses. In general, these boards determine the education and experience required for credentialing, develop and evaluate examinations, and establish standards for professional conduct. The department or the relevant board may reprimand a credential holder in a field that it regulates; limit, suspend, or revoke the credential of a practitioner who violates laws or rules; and, in some cases, impose forfeitures. The department provides administrative services to the boards and policy assistance in such areas as evaluating and establishing new professional licensing programs, creating routine procedures for legal proceedings, and adjusting policies in response to public needs. The department also investigates and prosecutes complaints against credential holders and assists with drafting administrative rules.

Under DSPS's Educational Approval Program, DSPS is also responsible for approving and overseeing most private, for-profit postsecondary schools offering educational programs or occupational training in this state; in-state private, nonprofit colleges and universities incorporated after 1991; and out-of-state postsecondary institutions offering distance education to Wisconsin residents if the institution is not located in a state participating in the State Authorization Reciprocity Agreement (see Distance Learning Authorization Board for more information on SARA).

Subordinate statutory boards, councils, and committees

AUTOMATIC FIRE SPRINKLER SYSTEM CONTRACTORS AND JOURNEYMEN COUNCIL

The Automatic Fire Sprinkler System Contractors and Journeymen Council advises the department on rules for credentials required for installing and maintaining automatic fire sprinkler systems.

COMMERCIAL BUILDING CODE COUNCIL

Contact: Jon Derenne; jon.derenne@wisconsin.gov; 608-266-2112

The Commercial Building Code Council advises the department on rules relating to public buildings and buildings that are places of employment. The council also reviews and makes recommendations pertaining to the department's rules for constructing, altering, adding to, repairing, and maintaining those types of buildings.

CONTROLLED SUBSTANCES BOARD

Contact: Christian Albouras; christian.albouras@wisconsin.gov; 608-261-5406

The Controlled Substances Board classifies controlled substances into schedules that regulate the prescription, use, and possession of controlled substances. The board also approves special use permits for controlled substances.

CONVEYANCE SAFETY CODE COUNCIL

Contact: Brian Rausch; brian.rausch@wisconsin.gov; 262-521-5444

The Conveyance Safety Code Council makes recommendations to the department pertaining to safety standards for elevators, escalators, and similar conveyances.

MANUFACTURED HOUSING CODE COUNCIL

The Manufactured Housing Code Council makes recommendations to the department pertaining to standards for the construction, installation, and sale of manufactured homes.

PLUMBERS COUNCIL

The Plumbers Council advises the department on rules for credentials required for plumbing.

SIGN LANGUAGE INTERPRETERS ADVISORY COMMITTEE

Contact: Christian Albouras; christian.albouras@wisconsin.gov; 608-261-5406

The Sign Language Interpreters Advisory Committee advises the department on rules for licensure and practice of sign language interpreters and consults with the department on the enforcement of laws related to sign language interpretation.

UNIFORM DWELLING CODE COUNCIL

Contact: Dale Kleven; dale2.kleven@wisconsin.gov; 608-266-2112

The Uniform Dwelling Code Council reviews and makes recommendations for department rules regarding the

Department of Safety and Professional Services Secretary Dawn Crim (*right*) accompanies Tim Condon (*left*), an occupational safety inspector with the department, as he inspects amusement rides at the Wisconsin State Fair midway.

DEPARTMENT OF SAFETY AND PROFESSIONAL SERVICES

construction and inspection of one-family and two-family dwellings and regarding continuing education, examinations, and financial responsibility for building contractors. The council also reviews complaints about building inspectors and recommends disciplinary action to the department. In addition, the council reviews and makes recommendations for department rules regarding modular homes.

Independent entities attached for administrative purposes

These are the occupation and business regulating boards described in the write-up of the department given above. (In each case, the occupations or businesses regulated are indicated by the entity's name.)

DEPARTMENT OF SAFETY AND PROFESSIONAL SERVICES

The Department of Safety and Professional Services helped set up an alternate care facility in the Wisconsin State Fair Park to treat COVID-19 patients. Here, Mike Schmidt, a specialist in the boiler and pressure vessels program, inspects part of the facility's bulk oxygen system.

ACCOUNTING EXAMINING BOARD
Chair: Gerald E. Denor
Contact: Valerie Payne; valerie.payne1@wisconsin.gov; 608-261-2378

EXAMINING BOARD OF ARCHITECTS, LANDSCAPE ARCHITECTS, PROFESSIONAL ENGINEERS, DESIGNERS AND PROFESSIONAL LAND SURVEYORS
Chair: Rosheen Styczinski
Architect section chair: Steven L. Wagner
Designer section chair: Michael J. Heberling
Engineer section chair: Kristine A. Cotharn
Landscape architect section chair: Rosheen M. Styczinski
Land surveyor section chair: Daniel Fedderly
Contact: Christian Albouras; christian.albouras@wisconsin.gov; 608-261-5406

ATHLETIC TRAINERS AFFILIATED CREDENTIALING BOARD (affiliated to Medical Examining Board)

Members: Jay J. Davide, Kurt A. Fielding, John J. Johnsen, Gregory S. Vergamini, Stephanie Atkins, Benjamin C. Wedro

Contact: Valerie Payne; valerie.payne1@wisconsin.gov; 608-261-2378

AUCTIONEER BOARD

Chair: Jerry L. Thiel

Contact: Christian Albouras; christian.albouras@wisconsin.gov; 608-261-5406

CEMETERY BOARD

Members: Patricia A. Grathen, Francis J. Groh, John F. Reinemann, Bernard G. Schroedl, E. Glen Porter III, Lloyd Shepherd

Contact: Christian Albouras: christian.albouras@wisconsin.gov; 608-261-5406

CHIROPRACTIC EXAMINING BOARD

Chair: Bryan R. Gerondale

Contact: Valerie Payne; valerie.payne1@wisconsin.gov; 608-261-2378

COSMETOLOGY EXAMINING BOARD

Chair: Megan A. Jackson

Contact: Christian Albouras; christian.albouras@wisconsin.gov; 608-261-5406

DENTISTRY EXAMINING BOARD

Chair: Matthew R. Bistan

Contact: Christian Albouras; christian.albouras@wisconsin.gov; 608-261-5406

DIETITIANS AFFILIATED CREDENTIALING BOARD (affiliated to Medical Examining Board)

Chair: Jill D. Hoyt

Contact: Valerie Payne; valerie.payne1@wisconsin.gov; 608-261-2378

FUNERAL DIRECTORS EXAMINING BOARD

Chair: Marc A. Eernisse

Contact: Christian Albouras; christian.albouras@wisconsin.gov; 608-261-5406

EXAMINING BOARD OF PROFESSIONAL GEOLOGISTS, HYDROLOGISTS AND SOIL SCIENTISTS

Chair: William N. Mode

Geologist section chair: William N. Mode

Hydrologist section chair: Kenneth Bradbury

Soil scientist section: (all seats currently vacant)
Contact: Valerie Payne; valerie.payne1@wisconsin.gov; 608-261-2378

HEARING AND SPEECH EXAMINING BOARD

Chair: Robert Broeckert
Contact: Valerie Payne; valerie.payne1@wisconsin.gov; 608-261-2378

MARRIAGE AND FAMILY THERAPY, PROFESSIONAL COUNSELING AND SOCIAL WORK EXAMINING BOARD

Chair: Lindsey E. Marsh
Marriage and family therapist section chair: Lisa D. Yee
Professional counselor section chair: Andrea L. Simon
Social worker section chair: Candace Coates
Contact: Christian Albouras; christian.albouras@wisconsin.gov; 608-261-5406

MASSAGE THERAPY AND BODYWORK THERAPY AFFILIATED CREDENTIALING BOARD (affiliated to Medical Examining Board)

Members: Robert Coleman Jr., Jeff A. Miller, Jaime L. Ehmer, Carla J. Hedtke, Gregory J. Quandt, Charisma J. Townsend, Ramona J. Trudeau
Contact: Valerie Payne; valerie.payne1@wisconsin.gov; 608-261-2378

MEDICAL EXAMINING BOARD

Chair: Sheldon A. Wasserman
Contact: Valerie Payne; valerie.payne1@wisconsin.gov; 608-261-2378
Advisory councils assisting the board: Council on Anesthesiologists Assistants, Michael L. Bottcher, *chair*; Perfusionists Examining Council, Shawn E. Mergen, *chair*; Council on Physician Assistants, Jennifer L. Jarrett, *chair*; Respiratory Care Practitioners Examining Council, Chris R. Becker, *chair*

BOARD OF NURSING

Chair: Peter J. Kallio
Contact: Valerie Payne; valerie.payne1@wisconsin.gov; 608-261-2378

NURSING HOME ADMINISTRATOR EXAMINING BOARD

Members: Susan Kinast-Porter, David L. Larson, Elizabeth Kaiser, Jessica Radtke, Patrick Shaughnessy, 5 vacancies
Contact: Valerie Payne; valerie.payne1@wisconsin.gov; 608-261-2378

OCCUPATIONAL THERAPISTS AFFILIATED CREDENTIALING BOARD (affiliated to Medical Examining Board)

Chair: Laura O'Brien
Contact: Valerie Payne; valerie.payne1@wisconsin.gov; 608-261-2378

OPTOMETRY EXAMINING BOARD

Chair: Robert C. Schulz
Contact: Valerie Payne; valerie.payne1@wisconsin.gov; 608-261-2378

PHARMACY EXAMINING BOARD

Chair: John G. Weitekamp
Contact: Christian Albouras; christian.albouras@wisconsin.gov; 608-261-5406

PHYSICAL THERAPY EXAMINING BOARD

Chair: John F. Greany
Contact: Valerie Payne; valerie.payne1@wisconsin.gov; 608-261-2378

PODIATRY AFFILIATED CREDENTIALING BOARD (affiliated to Medical Examining Board)

Members: Kerry Connelly, Jack W. Hutter, Robert M. Sage, Randal S. Kittleson
Contact: Valerie Payne; valerie.payne1@wisconsin.gov; 608-261-2378

PSYCHOLOGY EXAMINING BOARD

Members: Marcus P. Desmonde, John N. Greene, Mark A. Jinkins, Daniel A. Schroeder, Peter I. Sorce, David W. Thompson
Contact: Christian Albouras; christian.albouras@wisconsin.gov; 608-261-5406

RADIOGRAPHY EXAMINING BOARD

Chair: Donald A. Borst
Contact: Valerie Payne; valerie.payne1@wisconsin.gov; 608-261-2378

REAL ESTATE APPRAISERS BOARD

Chair: Carl N. Clementi
Contact: Valerie Payne; valerie.payne1@wisconsin.gov; 608-261-2378

REAL ESTATE EXAMINING BOARD

Chair: Thomas J. Richie
Contact: Christian Albouras; christian.albouras@wisconsin.gov; 608-261-5406
Advisory councils assisting the board: Council on Real Estate Curriculum and Examinations, Robert Blakely, *chair*

Office of the Secretary of State

Secretary of state: Douglas La Follette
Location: B41 West, State Capitol, Madison
Contact: statesec@wisconsin.gov; 608-266-8888; PO Box 7848, Madison, WI 53707-7848
Website: www.sos.state.wi.us
Number of employees: 2.00
Total budget 2019–21: $553,000

The secretary of state is a constitutional officer elected for a four-year term by partisan ballot in the November general election. The secretary of state maintains the official acts of the legislature and governor and keeps the Great Seal of the State of Wisconsin, affixing it to all official acts of the governor. Along with the attorney general and the state treasurer, the secretary of state serves on the Board of Commissioners of Public Lands. The secretary of state may also be called upon to act as governor under certain circumstances, for example, if the sitting governor dies or resigns and there is a vacancy in the office of lieutenant governor.

Office of the State Treasurer

State treasurer: Sarah Godlewski
Location: Room B38 West, State Capitol, Madison
Mailing address: PO Box 7871, Madison, WI 53707
Contact: treasurer@wisconsin.gov; 608-266-1714
Website: https://statetreasurer.wi.gov
Number of employees: 1.00
Total budget 2019–21: $233,400

The state treasurer is a constitutional officer elected for a four-year term by partisan ballot in the November general election. The state treasurer signs certain checks and financial instruments and helps to promote the state's unclaimed property program. Along with the attorney general and secretary of state, the state treasurer serves on the Board of Commissioners of Public Lands.

Technical College System

Technical College System Board: Becky Levzow, president
System president: Morna K. Foy
Location: 4622 University Avenue, Madison
Contact: communications@wtcsystem.edu; 608-266-1207; PO Box 7874, Madison, WI
    53707-7874
Website: https://wtcsystem.edu
Number of employees: 55.00
Total budget 2019–21: $1,139,790,000

The Technical College System Board is the agency that oversees the Technical College System. The governor, with the advice and consent of the senate, appoints 10 of the board's 13 members, 9 to serve six-year terms and a technical college student to serve a two-year term. The remaining board members are the state superintendent of public instruction, the secretary of workforce development, and the president of the Board of Regents of the University of Wisconsin System (but each of these officers may designate another individual to serve in his or her place).

The board establishes statewide policies for the educational programs and services provided by the state's 16 technical college districts. Each technical college district is governed by a district board that is responsible for the direct operation of that technical college, including setting academic and grading standards and hiring instructional staff for its programs.

The board defines, approves, evaluates, and reviews educational programs; provides guidance to the technical college districts in developing financial policies and standards; distributes state and federal aid; sets student fees; sets standards for and approves building projects; oversees district budgets and enrollments; coordinates state and federal grant programs and student financial aid; and supports services for students. The board also coordinates with the University of Wisconsin System on programming and college transfer courses and with other state agencies on vocational and technical education programs and apprentice training.

Department of Tourism

Acting secretary: Anne Sayers
Location: 201 West Washington Avenue, 2nd Floor, Madison
Contact: tourinfo@travelwisconsin.com; 800-432-8747; 608-266-7621; PO Box 8690, Madison, WI 53708-8690
Website: www.travelwisconsin.com (information for tourists); http://industry.travel wisconsin.com (information for the tourism industry)
Number of employees: 34.00
Total budget 2019–2021: $36,334,300

The Department of Tourism is administered by a secretary who is appointed by the governor with the advice and consent of the senate. The department formulates and implements a statewide marketing strategy to promote travel to Wisconsin's scenic, historic, natural, agricultural, educational, and recreational attractions. The department coordinates its efforts with public and private organizations and provides assistance to travel-related and recreational industries and their consumers. The department also does the following: (1) makes grants to local governments, American Indian organizations, and nonprofits for tourist information centers and marketing projects; (2) provides marketing services to state agencies; and (3) coordinates its economic development activities with the Wisconsin Economic Development Corporation and makes annual reports to the legislature assessing those activities.

Subordinate statutory boards, councils, and committees

ARTS BOARD

Chair: Kevin Miller
Executive director: George Tzougros

DEPARTMENT OF TOURISM

A family gets ready to kayak on Lake Kegonsa, located in Dane County, southeast of Madison. The lake has four public boat launches, including one in Lake Kegonsa State Park, which is a popular destination for swimming, fishing, kayaking, and canoeing.

Location: 201 West Washington Avenue, second floor, Madison
Contact: artsboard@wisconsin.gov; 608-266-0190; PO Box 8690, Madison, WI 53708-8690
Website: https://artsboard.wisconsin.gov
Number of employees: 4.00
Total budget 2019–21: $3,203,300

The Arts Board studies and assists artistic and cultural activities in the state, assists communities in developing their own arts programs, and plans and implements financial support programs for individuals and organizations engaged in the arts, including creation and presentation grants, folk art apprenticeships, creative communities grants, and challenge grants to organizations that exceed fundraising goals. The board also provides matching grants to local arts agencies and municipalities through the Wisconsin Regranting Program.

COUNCIL ON TOURISM

Chair: Joe Klimczak
Website: http://industry.travelwisconsin.com/about-the-department/
governors-council-on-tourism

The Council on Tourism advises the secretary on tourism, including assisting in the formulation of the statewide marketing strategy. The council also develops and adopts a plan for encouraging Wisconsin-based companies to promote the state in their advertisements.

Independent entities attached for administrative purposes

KICKAPOO RESERVE MANAGEMENT BOARD

Chair: Richard T. Wallin
Executive director: Marcy West
Contact: kickapoo.reserve@krm.state.wi.us; 608-625-2960; S3661 State Highway 131, La Farge, WI 54639
Website: http://kvr.state.wi.us
Number of employees: 4.00
Total budget 2019–21: $1,926,800

The Kickapoo Reserve Management Board manages the approximately 8,600-acre Kickapoo Valley Reserve through a joint management agreement with the Ho-Chunk Nation. The Kickapoo Valley Reserve exists to preserve and enhance the area's environmental, scenic, and cultural features and provides facilities for the use and enjoyment of visitors. Subject to the approval of the governor, the board may purchase land for inclusion in the reserve and may trade land in the reserve under certain conditions. The board also may lease land for purposes consistent with the management of the reserve or for agricultural purposes.

STATE FAIR PARK BOARD

Chair: John Yingling
Chief executive officer: Kathleen O'Leary
Contact: wsfp@wistatefair.com; 414-266-7000; 414-266-7100 (ticket office); 640 South 84th Street, West Allis, WI 53214
Website: https://wistatefair.com/wsfp/

A group of motorcyclists glides down the Great River Road, which covers a total 250 miles and winds through 33 historic river towns and villages along the Mississippi River. The Great River Road is one of 34 National Scenic Byways that have been recognized by U.S. Department of Transportation for their exceptional scenic, historical, and recreational qualities.

DEPARTMENT OF TOURISM

Number of employees: 47.00
Total budget 2019–21: $48,719,100

The State Fair Park Board manages the Wisconsin State Fair Park, including the development of new facilities. The park provides a permanent location for the annual Wisconsin State Fair and for major sports events, agricultural and industrial expositions, and other programs of civic interest.

Department of Transportation

Secretary-designee: Craig Thompson
Deputy secretary: Paul Hammer
Location: Hill Farms State Office Building, 4822 Madison Yards Way, Madison, WI 53705
Contact: information.dmv@dot.wi.gov; Office of Public Affairs, 608-266-3581; Driver
    Services and Vehicle Services, 608-264-7447; PO Box 7910, Madison, WI 53707-7910
Website: https://wisconsindot.gov
Number of employees: 3,244.11
Total budget 2019–21: $6,609,654,000

The Department of Transportation is administered by a secretary who is appointed by the governor with the advice and consent of the senate. The department is responsible for the planning, promotion, and protection of all transportation systems in the state. Its major responsibilities involve highways, motor vehicles, motor carriers, traffic law enforcement, railroads, waterways, mass transit, and aeronautics. The department issues vehicle titles and registrations and individual identification cards and examines and licenses drivers. The department works with several federal agencies in the administration of federal transportation aids. It also cooperates with departments at the state level in travel promotion, consumer protection, environmental analysis, and transportation services for elderly and handicapped persons.

(*left*) Cyclists ride along the Lake Michigan shoreline in Milwaukee. (*right*) Passengers commute to work, school, and recreation via bus.

The cargo ship BEATRIX, sailing under the flag of Netherlands, travels beneath the John A. Blatnik Bridge, which links Duluth, Minnesota, with Superior, Wisconsin.

Subordinate statutory boards, councils, and committees

COUNCIL ON HIGHWAY SAFETY

Acting chair: John Mesich
Location: 4822 Madison Yards Way, 9th Floor South, Madison, WI 53705
Contact: Diana Guinn; diana.guinn@dot.wi.gov; 608-709-0093

The Council on Highway Safety advises the department secretary about highway safety matters.

RUSTIC ROADS BOARD

Chair: Marion Flood
Contact: Liat Bonneville, Rustic Roads coordinator; wirusticroads@dot.wi.gov; 608-267-3614; 4822 Madison Yards Way, 6th Floor South, PO Box 7913, Madison, WI 53705
Website: https://wisconsindot.gov/pages/travel/road/rustic-roads/create.aspx

The Rustic Roads Board oversees the application and selection process of locally nominated county highways and local roads for inclusion in the Rustic Roads network system. The Rustic Roads program is a partnership between local officials and state government to showcase some of Wisconsin's most picturesque and lightly traveled roadways for the leisurely enjoyment of hikers, bikers, and motorists.

COUNCIL ON UNIFORMITY OF TRAFFIC CITATIONS AND COMPLAINTS
Chair: Sharon Olson
Location: 4822 Madison Yards Way, 2nd Floor South, Madison
Contact: Sharon Olson; sharon.olson@dot.wi.gov; 608-471-5731

The Council on Uniformity of Traffic Citations and Complaints recommends forms used for traffic violations citations.

University of Wisconsin System

Board of Regents: Robert Atwell, Scott Beightol, Amy Blumenfeld Bogost, Héctor Colón, Michael M. Grebe, Mike Jones, Tracey L. Klein, Becky Levzow (president, Technical College System Board), Edmund Manydeeds III, John W. Miller, Andrew S. Petersen, Cris Peterson, Ashok Rai, Corey Saffold, Brianna Tucker, Jill Underly (state superintendent of public instruction), Karen Walsh, Kyle M. Weatherly
Executive director and corporate secretary: Jess Lathrop
System Administration: Tommy G. Thompson, *interim president*
Contact: 608-262-2321; 1860 Van Hise Hall, 1220 Linden Drive, Madison, WI 53706
Website: www.wisconsin.edu
Number of employees: 36,273.16
Total budget 2019–21: $12,641,645,600

The University of Wisconsin System is governed by an 18-member Board of Regents, which consists of 14 citizen members, 2 student members, the president of the Technical College System Board or his or her designee, and the state superintendent of public instruction. The citizen and student members are appointed by the governor subject to senate confirmation. The Board of Regents appoints the president of the UW System, who has executive responsibility for system operation and management, and the chancellors for each four-year university.

The prime responsibilities of the UW System are teaching, public service, and research. The system provides postsecondary academic education for approximately 170,000 students, including approximately 150,000 undergraduates. The system consists of 13 four-year universities, an additional 13 branch campuses, and a statewide extension network with offices in every county. All of the four-year universities offer bachelor's degrees. Two of the four-year universities (UW-Madison and UW-Milwaukee) offer comprehensive master's and doctoral degree programs, including professional doctorate degrees. The remaining four-year universities (UW-Eau Claire, UW-Green Bay, UW-La Crosse, UW-Oshkosh, UW-Parkside, UW-Platteville, UW-River Falls, UW-Stevens Point, UW-Stout, UW-Superior, and UW-Whitewater) offer more limited master's degree programs, and some also offer associate degrees and clinical or professional doctorate degrees in select areas. The 13 branch campuses, aligned with seven of the four-year universities, offer Associate of Arts and Sciences (AAS) degrees, as well as transfer programs for students wishing to satisfy general education requirements and then transfer to a four-year university. Many branch campuses also offer bachelor's degrees in certain fields of study through collaboration with a four-year university. In addition, some campuses have partnered to offer an entirely online AAS degree program through UW College Courses Online. The system provides extension services, including access to system resources and research, through UW-Madison and the UW System administration. This system organization is the result of restructuring authorized by the Board of Regents in November 2017, and approved by the system's accreditor, the Higher Learning Commission, in June 2018.

UW-MADISON

Chancellor: Rebecca M. Blank
Contact: 608-262-9946; 500 Lincoln Drive, Madison, WI 53706
Website: www.wisc.edu

UW-MILWAUKEE

Chancellor: Mark Mone
Contact: 414-229-4331; PO Box 413, Milwaukee, WI 53201
Website: www.uwm.edu

The UW-La Crosse (UWL) Student Association presents interim UW System President Tommy Thompson with its annual 2020–21 Higher Education Advocate Award in May 2021. The award honors a person who empowers students to be active members in the community, and who strongly advocates for higher education across Wisconsin. "His leadership led the UW System through the COVID-19 pandemic and its challenges," said Cate Wiza, 2020–21 UWL Student Association president.

UW-LA CROSSE

(*left*) Dylan Pabrocki, a finance major at UW-Whitewater, holds one of the care bags that he and other students in the University Honors Program assembled to provide sustenance and encouragement to students suffering from COVID-19. The program raised donations and in-kind contributions from students, faculty, staff, parents, and area businesses during the 2020-21 school year. (*right*) Joseph Creanza, a junior soil and crop science major at UW-Platteville, scored first place at the 2020 Student Research and Innovation Showcase for his project using plant essential oils as a safe, natural way to control a soybean mold disease.

UW-EAU CLAIRE

Chancellor: James Schmidt
Contact: 715-836-2327; 105 Garfield Avenue, Eau Claire, WI 54701
Website: www.uwec.edu

UW-GREEN BAY

Chancellor: Michael Alexander
Contact: 920-465-2207; 2420 Nicolet Drive, Green Bay, WI 54311
Website: www.uwgb.edu

UW-LA CROSSE

Chancellor: Joe Gow
Contact: 608-785-8004; 1725 State Street, La Crosse, WI 54601
Website: www.uwlax.edu

UW-OSHKOSH

Chancellor: Andrew J. Leavitt
Contact: 920-424-0200; 800 Algoma Boulevard, Oshkosh, WI 54901
Website: www.uwosh.edu

UW-PARKSIDE

Chancellor: Deborah Ford
Contact: 262-595-2211; PO Box 2000, Kenosha, WI 53141-2000
Website: www.uwp.edu

UW-PLATTEVILLE

Chancellor: Dennis J. Shields
Contact: 608-342-1234; 1 University Plaza, Platteville, WI 53818
Website: www.uwplatt.edu

UW-RIVER FALLS

Interim Chancellor: Connie Foster
Contact: 715-425-3201; 410 South Third Street, River Falls, WI 54022
Website: www.uwrf.edu

UW-STEVENS POINT

Chancellor: Bernie L. Patterson
Contact: 715-346-2123; 2100 Main Street, Stevens Point, WI 54481
Website: www.uwsp.edu

UW-STOUT

Chancellor: Katherine P. Frank
Contact: 715-235-2441; 712 South Broadway, Menomonie, WI 54751
Website: www.uwstout.edu

UW-SUPERIOR

Chancellor: Renée Wachter
Contact: 715-394-8223; P. O. Box 2000, Superior, WI 54880
Website: www.uwsuper.edu

UW-WHITEWATER

Chancellor: Dwight C. Watson
Contact: 262-472-1918; 800 West Main Street, Whitewater, WI 53190
Website: www.uww.edu

Programs required by statute

OFFICE OF THE STATE CARTOGRAPHER

State cartographer: Howard Veregin
Contact: sco@wisc.edu; 608-262-3065; 384 Science Hall, 550 North Park Street, Madison, WI 53706
Website: www.sco.wisc.edu

GEOLOGICAL AND NATURAL HISTORY SURVEY

Director and state geologist: Ken Bradbury
Contact: 608-262-1705; 3817 Mineral Point Road, Madison, WI 53705
Website: http://wgnhs.wisc.edu

UW CENTER FOR AGRICULTURAL SAFETY AND HEALTH

Agricultural Safety and Health Specialist: Cheryl Skjolaas

Contact: 608-265-0568
Website: http://fyi.extension.wisc.edu/agsafety

WISCONSIN CENTER FOR ENVIRONMENTAL EDUCATION

Contact: wcee@uwsp.edu; 715-346-4973; WCEE—110 TNR, 800 Reserve Street, Stevens Point, WI 54481
Website: www.uwsp.edu/cnr-ap/wcee

AREA HEALTH EDUCATION CENTERS

Director: Elizabeth Bush
Contact: ahec@ahec.wisc.edu; 608-263-1712; 4251 Health Sciences Learning Center, 750 Highland Avenue, Madison, WI 53705
Website: www.ahec.wisc.edu

WISCONSIN STATE HERBARIUM

Director: Kenneth Cameron
Contact: kmcameron@wisc.edu; 608-262-2792; Birge Hall, 430 Lincoln Drive, Madison, WI 53706
Website: http://herbarium.wisc.edu

PSYCHIATRIC HEALTH EMOTIONS RESEARCH INSTITUTE

Director: Ned Kalin
Contact: 608-232-3171; 6001 Research Park Boulevard, Madison, WI 53719
Website: www.psychiatry.wisc.edu/research/heri/

ROBERT M. LA FOLLETTE SCHOOL OF PUBLIC AFFAIRS

Director: Susan Yackee
Contact: info@lafollette.wisc.edu; 608-262-3581; 1225 Observatory Drive, Madison, WI 53706
Website: www.lafollette.wisc.edu

STATE SOILS AND PLANT ANALYSIS LABORATORY

Director: Andrew Stammer
Contact: soil-lab@mailplus.wisc.edu; 715-387-2523; 2611 Yellowstone Drive, Marshfield, WI 54449
Website: https://uwlab.soils.wisc.edu

INSTITUTE FOR URBAN EDUCATION

Chair: Denise Ross
Contact: iue-info@uwm.edu; 414-251-9490; UW-Milwaukee, 2400 East Hartford Avenue, Room 568, Milwaukee, WI 53211
Website: https://uwm.edu/education/institute-urban-edu/

JAMES A. GRAASKAMP CENTER FOR REAL ESTATE

Executive director: Mark Eppli

Contact: mark.eppli@wisc.edu; 608-263-1000; Grainger Hall, 975 University Avenue, Madison, WI 53706

Website: https://bus.wisc.edu/centers/james-a-graaskamp-center-for-real-estate

SCHOOL OF VETERINARY MEDICINE

Dean: Mark D. Markel

Contact: 608-263-6716; 2015 Linden Drive West, Madison, WI 53706

Website: www.vetmed.wisc.edu

Subordinate statutory boards, councils, and committees

LABORATORY OF HYGIENE BOARD

Members: Chuck Warzecha, *chair;* James Morrison, *vice chair;* Robert Corliss, Gina Green-Harris, German Gonzalez, Barry Irmen, Gil Kelley, Jeff Kindrai, Richard Moss, Greg Pils, 1 vacancy

Nonvoting member and laboratory director: James Schauer

Contact: 608-890-0288 (administrative office); 608-262-6386 and 800-862-1013 (clinical laboratories); 608-224-6202 and 800-442-4618 (environmental health laboratory); 800-446-0403 (occupational health laboratory); 800-462-5261 (proficiency testing); 2601 Agriculture Drive, P.O. Box 7904, Madison, WI 53718

Website: www.slh.wisc.edu

Number of employees: 310.75

Total budget 2019–21: $68,056,200

UW-Eau Claire student researchers Aaron Ellefson (*right*) and Cuyler Monahan (*left*) are working to develop a clinical foam to protect cancer patients from radiation during treatment.

UW-EAU CLAIRE

The Laboratory of Hygiene Board oversees the Laboratory of Hygiene, which provides laboratory services in the areas of water quality, air quality, public health, and contagious diseases for state agencies, local health departments, physicians, veterinarians, and others to prevent and control diseases and environmental hazards. Attached to UW-Madison, the laboratory provides facilities for teaching and research in the fields of public health and environmental protection.

RURAL HEALTH DEVELOPMENT COUNCIL

Contact: Kevin Jacobson, 608-261-1888; 800-385-0005, Ext. 2; Wisconsin Office of Rural Health, 310 North Midvale Boulevard, Suite 301, Madison, WI 53705
Website: http://www.worh.org/rhdc

The Rural Health Development Council consists of 17 members appointed by the governor, with the advice and consent of the senate, for five-year terms and the secretary of health services or his or her designee. The council advises the Board of Regents on matters related to loan assistance programs for physicians, dentists, and other health care providers.

Independent entities attached for administrative purposes

PUBLIC LEADERSHIP BOARD

Members: Scott Jensen, Kimber Liedl, Gerard Randall, Dean Stensberg, Jason Thompson, Robin Vos
Thompson Center Director: Alexander Tahk
Contact: thompsoncenter@wisc.edu; 608-265-4087; 445 Henry Mall, Madison, WI 53706
Website: https://thompsoncenter.wisc.edu/

The Public Leadership Board appoints, upon joint recommendation of UW-Madison's chancellor and its dean of the College of Letters and Science, the director of the Tommy G. Thompson Center on Public Leadership at UW-Madison. The mission of the center, to be carried out in all the universities of the UW System, is to facilitate research, teaching, outreach, and policy reform regarding effective public leadership that improves American government. The board approves the center's budget and must allocate at least $500,000 annually for speaking engagements at campuses other than UW-Madison.

VETERINARY DIAGNOSTIC LABORATORY BOARD

Members: Charles Czuprynski, Casey Davis, Darlene Konkle, Paul Kunde, Sandra Madland, Mark Markel, Bob Steiner
Nonvoting member and laboratory director: Keith Poulsen
Contact: 608-262-5432; 800-608-8387; 445 Easterday Lane, Madison, WI 53706
Website: www.wvdl.wisc.edu
Number of employees: 94.50
Total budget 2019–21: $15,167,700

The Veterinary Diagnostic Laboratory Board oversees the Veterinary Diagnostic Laboratory, which provides animal health testing and diagnostic services on a statewide basis for all types of animals. The laboratory may also participate in research, education, and field services related to animal health.

Department of Veterans Affairs

Department secretary: Mary M. Kolar
Deputy secretary: James Bond
Board of Veterans Affairs: Curtis Schmitt Jr., *chair*
Location: 2135 Rimrock Road, Madison
Contact: 608-266-0517 (media inquiries); 1-800-WIS-VETS (toll free); PO Box 7843, Madison, WI 53707-7843
Website: https://dva.wi.gov
Number of employees: 1,269.36
Total budget 2019–21: $278,557,600

The Department of Veterans Affairs is administered by a secretary who must be a veteran and who is appointed by the governor with the advice and consent of the senate. The department includes the Board of Veterans Affairs, consisting of nine members who must be veterans and who are appointed by the governor with the advice and consent of the senate. The board advises the secretary on the promulgation of administrative rules necessary to carry out the powers and duties of the department.

The department administers an array of grants, benefits, programs, and services for eligible veterans, their families, and organizations that serve veterans. It operates the Wisconsin veterans homes at Chippewa Falls, King, and Union Grove, which provide short-term rehabilitation and long-term skilled nursing care to eligible veterans (and, to the extent of their resources, to the spouses and parents of veterans). The department also operates the Southern Wisconsin Veterans Memorial Cemetery at Union Grove, the Northern Wisconsin Veterans Memorial Cemetery near Spooner, and the Central Wisconsin Veterans Memorial Cemetery at King. Finally, the department operates the Wisconsin Veterans Museum in Madison.

Subordinate statutory boards, councils, and committees

COUNCIL ON VETERANS PROGRAMS

Chair: Larry Hill
Website: https://dva.wi.gov/pages/aboutwdva/councilonveteransprograms.aspx

The Council on Veterans Programs studies and presents policy alternatives and recommendations to the Board of Veterans Affairs and the Department of Veterans Affairs.

Department of Workforce Development

Department secretary-designee: Amy Pechacek
Deputy secretary: Robert Cherry Jr.
Location: 201 East Washington Avenue, Madison
Contact: 608-266-3131; PO Box 7946, Madison, WI 53707-7946
Website: https://dwd.wisconsin.gov
Number of employees: 1,606.05
Total budget 2019–21: $716,385,300

The Department of Workforce Development is administered by a secretary who is appointed by the governor with the advice and consent of the senate.

The department administers the unemployment insurance program and oversees the worker's compensation program. The department also operates the state's job center network (https://jobcenterofwisconsin.com); manages the Fast Forward worker training grant program; operates adult and youth apprenticeship programs; collects, analyzes, and distributes labor market information; monitors migrant workers services; provides vocational rehabilitation services to help people with disabilities achieve their employment goals; and offers comprehensive employment and training programs and services to youth and adults, including veterans with service-connected disabilities. Finally, the department enforces wage and hour laws; leave and benefits laws; child labor laws; civil rights laws; plant closing laws; and laws regulating migrant labor contractors and camps.

Subordinate statutory boards, councils, and committees

WISCONSIN APPRENTICESHIP ADVISORY COUNCIL

Cochairs: Terry Hayden, Henry Hurt
Contact: 608-266-3332; PO Box 7972, Madison, WI 53707-7972
Website: https://dwd.wisconsin.gov/apprenticeship/advisory-council.htm

The Wisconsin Apprenticeship Advisory Council advises the department on matters pertaining to Wisconsin's apprenticeship system.

COUNCIL ON MIGRANT LABOR

Contact: 608-266-0487; PO Box 7972, Madison, WI 53707-7972
Website: https://dwd.wisconsin.gov/jobservice/msfw/labor-council.htm

The Governor's Council on Migrant Labor advises the department and other state officials about matters affecting migrant workers.

SELF-INSURERS COUNCIL

Contact: 608-266-8327; PO Box 7901, Madison, WI 53707-7901
Website: https://dwd.wisconsin.gov/wc/councils/self-insured/

The Self-Insurers Council assists the department in administering the self-insurance program, under which an employer may be allowed to cover its worker's compensation costs directly rather than by purchasing insurance. The council ensures that those employers applying for self-insurance are financially viable and monitors the financial status of employers in the self-insurance pool.

UNEMPLOYMENT INSURANCE ADVISORY COUNCIL

Chair: Janell Knutson
Contact: 608-267-1405; PO Box 8942, Madison, WI 53708-8942
Website: https://dwd.wisconsin.gov/uibola/uiac/

The Unemployment Insurance Advisory Council provides advice and counsel to the department and the legislature about unemployment insurance matters, including by providing advice and recommendations with respect to proposed changes to the unemployment insurance law.

WORKER'S COMPENSATION ADVISORY COUNCIL

Chair: Steve Peters
Contact: 608-266-6841; PO Box 7901, Madison, WI 53707-7901
Website: https://dwd.wisconsin.gov/wc/councils/wcac/

The Council on Worker's Compensation provides advice and counsel to the department and the legislature about worker's compensation matters, including by providing advice and recommendations with respect to proposed changes to the worker's compensation law.

HEALTH CARE PROVIDER ADVISORY COMMITTEE

Chair: Steve Peters
Contact: 608-266-6841; PO Box 7901, Madison, WI 53707-7901
Website: https://dwd.wisconsin.gov/wc/councils/wcac//hcpac

The Health Care Provider Advisory Committee advises the department and the Council on Worker's Compensation on the standards that the department uses when it determines whether treatment provided to an injured employee was necessary treatment that is compensable by worker's compensation insurance.

Independent entities attached for administrative purposes

EMPLOYMENT RELATIONS COMMISSION

Chair: James J. Daley
Location: 2418 Crossroads Drive, Suite 1000, Madison, WI 53718-7896
Contact: werc@werc.state.wi.us; 608-243-2424
Website: http://werc.wi.gov
Number of employees: 6.0
Total budget 2019–21: $2,080,000

The Employment Relations Commission promotes collective bargaining and peaceful labor relations in the private and public sectors. The commission determines various types of labor relations cases and issues decisions arising from state employee civil service appeals. The commission also provides mediation and grievance arbitration services as well as training and assistance to parties interested in labor-management cooperation and a consensus approach to resolving labor relations issues.

Authorities

Wisconsin Aerospace Authority (inactive)

The Wisconsin Aerospace Authority is directed to promote and develop the state's space-related industry and coordinate these activities with governmental entities, the aerospace industry, businesses, educational organizations, and the Wisconsin Space Grant Consortium.

Wisconsin Economic Development Corporation

Board of directors chair: Henry C. Newell
Chief executive officer: Missy Hughes
Chief operating officer: Sam Rikkers
Location: 201 West Washington Avenue, Madison Contact: 608-210-6700; PO Box 1687, Madison, WI 53701
Website: https://wedc.org/
Total state appropriation 2019–21: $83,101,400

The Wisconsin Economic Development Corporation is a public corporation that develops, implements, and administers programs to provide business support and expertise and financial assistance to companies that are investing and creating jobs in Wisconsin and to promote new business start-ups and business expansion and growth in the state. The authority was established in 2011 and assumed many of the functions previously performed by the former Department of Commerce. WEDC is governed by an 18-member board that consists of six appointees of the governor, ten appointees of legislative leaders—four appointees each of the speaker of the assembly and senate majority leader and one appointee each of the minority leaders of both houses—and the secretaries of administration and revenue as nonvoting members. WEDC may issue bonds and incur other debt to achieve its public purposes. WEDC's bonds and other debt do not create a debt of the state.

Fox River Navigational System Authority

Board of directors chair: Ron Van De Hey
Chief executive officer: Jeremy Cords

Contact: 920-759-9833; 1008 Augustine Street, Kaukauna, WI 54130-1608
Website: www.foxlocks.org

The Fox River Navigational System Authority is a public corporation that is responsible for the rehabilitation, repair, and management of the navigation system on or near the Fox River, and it may enter into contracts with third parties to operate the system. The authority may charge fees for services provided to watercraft owners and users of navigational facilities, enter into contracts with nonprofit organizations to raise funds, and contract debt, but it may not issue bonds. Annually, the authority must submit an audited financial statement to the Department of Administration. The authority is governed by a nine-member board of directors. The nine members include six appointees of the governor, who appoints two each from Brown, Outagamie, and Winnebago Counties.

Wisconsin Health and Educational Facilities Authority

Board of directors: James Dietsche, *chair*
Executive director: Dennis P. Reilly
Contact: info@whefa.com; 262-792-0466; 18000 West Sarah Lane, Suite 300, Brookfield, WI 53045-5841
Website: www.whefa.com

The Wisconsin Health and Educational Facilities Authority is a public corporation governed by a seven-member board whose members are appointed by the governor with the advice and consent of the senate. No more than four of the members may be of the same political party. The governor appoints the chair annually.

WHEFA issues bonds on behalf of private nonprofit facilities to help them finance their capital costs.

The authority has no taxing power. WHEFA's bonds are not a debt, liability, or obligation of the State of Wisconsin or any of its subdivisions. The authority may issue bonds to finance any qualifying capital project, including new construction, remodeling, and renovation; expansion of current facilities; and purchase of new equipment or furnishings. WHEFA may also issue bonds to refinance outstanding debt.

Wisconsin Housing and Economic Development Authority

Board of directors chair: Ivan Gamboa
Executive director: Joaquin J. Altoro
Contact: info@wheda.com; 608-266-7884 or 800-334-6873 (Madison); 414-227-4039 or 800-628-4833 (Milwaukee); PO Box 1728, Madison, WI 53701-1728; 201 West Washington Avenue, Suite 700, Madison, WI 53701; 611 West National Avenue, Suite 110, Milwaukee, WI 53204 (Milwaukee office)
Website: www.wheda.com

The Wisconsin Housing and Economic Development Authority is a public corporation governed by a 12-member board that includes six appointees of the governor and four legislators representing both parties and both houses. WHEDA administers numerous loan programs and other programs and projects that provide housing and related assistance to Wisconsin residents, including single and multifamily housing for individuals and families of low and moderate income, and that promote and support home ownership. WHEDA also finances loan guarantees and administers other programs to support business and agricultural development in the state. WHEDA issues bonds to support its operations, which, however, do not create a debt of the state.

Lower Fox River Remediation Authority (inactive)

The Lower Fox River Remediation Authority is a public corporation that is authorized to issue assessment bonds for eligible waterway improvement costs, which generally include environmental investigation and remediation of the Fox River extending from Lake Winnebago to the mouth of the river in Lake Michigan, and including any portion of Green Bay in Lake Michigan that contains sediments discharged from the river.

University of Wisconsin Hospitals and Clinics Authority

Board of directors chair: Robert Golden
Chief executive officer: Alan Kaplan
Contact: 608-263-6400; 800-323-8942; 600 Highland Avenue, Madison, WI 53792
Website: www.uwhealth.org

The University of Wisconsin Hospitals and Clinics Authority is a public corporation governed by a 16-member board of directors that includes the cochairs of the Joint Committee on Finance and six appointees of the governor. The authority operates the UW Hospital and Clinics, including the American Family Children's Hospital, and related clinics and health care facilities. Through the UW Hospital and Clinics and its other programs, the authority delivers health care, including care for the indigent; provides an environment for instruction of physicians, nurses, and other health-related disciplines; sponsors and supports health care research; and assists health care programs and personnel throughout the state. The authority is self-financing. It derives much of its income from charges for clinical and hospital services. The authority also may issue bonds to support its operations, which, however, do not create a debt of the state, and may seek financing from the Wisconsin Health and Educational Facilities Authority.

Nonprofit corporations

Bradley Center Sports and Entertainment Corporation (inactive and dissolved)

The Bradley Center Sports and Entertainment Corporation is a public nonprofit corporation that was created as an instrumentality of the state to receive and operate the Bradley Center, a sports and entertainment facility located in Milwaukee County and donated by the Bradley Center Corporation. The Bradley Center was the home of the Milwaukee Bucks basketball team from 1988 to 2018 and hosted other sporting events as well as numerous entertainment shows and concerts. The Bradley Center has been replaced by a new facility, the Fiserv Forum, which is owned and operated by the Wisconsin Center District, a local governmental entity (see page 261). In 2019, the BCSEC submitted its final audited financial statements to state officials, announced completion of its business affairs, and transferred its remaining assets ($4.29 million) to the state.

Wisconsin Artistic Endowment Foundation (inactive)

The Wisconsin Artistic Endowment Foundation is a public nonprofit corporation that was created by the legislature for the purpose of supporting the arts, distributing funds, and facilitating the conversion of donated property into cash to support the arts. The foundation may not be dissolved except by an enactment of the legislature.

Regional planning commissions

Regional planning commissions advise cities, villages, towns, and counties on the planning and delivery of public services to the residents of a defined region, and they prepare and adopt master plans for the physical development of the region they serve.

The commissions may conduct research studies; make and adopt plans for the physical, social, and economic development of the region; provide advisory services to local governmental units and other public and private agencies; and coordinate local programs that relate to their objectives.

Currently, there are nine regional planning commissions serving all but five of the state's 72 counties. Their boundaries are based on factors including common topographical and geographical features; the extent of urban development; the existence of special or acute agricultural, forestry, or other rural problems; and the existence of physical, social, and economic problems of a regional character.

Regional planning commissions have developed and assisted with projects in areas including rail and air transportation, waste disposal and recycling, highways, air and water quality, farmland preservation and zoning, land conservation and reclamation, outdoor recreation, parking and lakefront studies, and land records modernization.

Membership of regional planning commissions varies according to conditions defined by statute. The commissions are funded through state and federal planning grants, contracts with local governments for special planning services, and a statutorily authorized levy of up to 0.003 percent of equalized real estate value charged to each local governmental unit.

Wisconsin's regional planning commissions have established the Association of Wisconsin Regional Planning Commissions. The association's purposes include assisting the study of common problems and serving as an information clearinghouse.

Bay-Lake Regional Planning Commission

Counties in region: Brown, Door, Florence, Kewaunee, Manitowoc, Marinette, Oconto, Sheboygan
Chair: Dan Koski
Executive director: Cindy J. Wojtczak
Contact: 920-448-2820; 425 South Adams Street, Suite 201, Green Bay, WI 54301
Website: www.baylakerpc.org

Capital Area Regional Planning Commission

Counties in region: Dane
Chair: Larry Palm
Agency director: Steve Steinhoff
Contact: info@capitalarearpc.org; 608-474-6017; 100 State Street, Suite 400, Madison, WI 53703
Website: www.capitalarearpc.org

East Central Wisconsin Regional Planning Commission

Counties in region: Calumet, Fond du Lac, Green Lake (not participating), Marquette (not participating), Menominee, Outagamie, Shawano, Waupaca, Waushara, Winnebago
Chair: Martin Farrell
Executive director: Melissa Kraemer-Badtke
Contact: 920-751-4770; 400 Ahnaip Street, Suite 100, Menasha, WI 54952-3100
Website: www.ecwrpc.org

Mississippi River Regional Planning Commission

Counties in region: Buffalo, Crawford, Jackson, La Crosse, Monroe, Pepin, Pierce, Trempealeau, Vernon

Regional planning commission areas

Chair: James Kuhn
Executive director: Dave Bonifas
Contact: plan@mrrpc.com; 608-785-9396; 1707 Main Street, Suite 435, La Crosse, WI 54601
Website: www.mrrpc.com

North Central Wisconsin Regional Planning Commission

Counties in region: Adams, Forest, Juneau, Langlade, Lincoln, Marathon, Oneida, Portage
(not participating), Vilas, Wood
Chair: Paul Millan
Executive director: Dennis L. Lawrence
Contact: info@ncwrpc.org; 715-849-5510; 210 McClellan Street, Suite 210, Wausau, WI 54403
Website: www.ncwrpc.org

Northwest Regional Planning Commission

Counties in region: Ashland, Bayfield, Burnett, Douglas, Iron, Price, Rusk, Sawyer, Taylor, Washburn
Participating tribal nations: Bad River, Lac Courte Oreilles, Lac du Flambeau, Red Cliff, St. Croix
Chair: Tom Mackie
Executive director: Sheldon Johnson
Contact: info@nwrpc.com; 715-635-2197; 1400 South River Street, Spooner, WI 54801
Website: www.nwrpc.com

Southeastern Wisconsin Regional Planning Commission

Counties in region: Kenosha, Milwaukee, Ozaukee, Racine, Walworth, Washington, Waukesha
Chair: Charles L. Colman
Executive director: Kevin Muhs
Contact: sewrpc@sewrpc.org; 262-547-6721; W239 N1812 Rockwood Drive, PO Box 1607, Waukesha, WI 53187-1607
Website: www.sewrpc.org

Southwestern Wisconsin Regional Planning Commission

Counties in region: Grant, Green, Iowa, Lafayette, Richland
Chair: Bob Keeney
Executive director: Troy Maggied
Contact: info@swwrpc.org; 608-342-1636; 20 South Court Street, Platteville, WI 53818
Website: www.swwrpc.org

West Central Wisconsin Regional Planning Commission

Counties in region: Barron, Chippewa, Clark, Dunn, Eau Claire, Polk, St. Croix
Chair: John L. Frank
Executive director: Lynn Nelson
Contact: wcwrpc@wcwrpc.org; 715-836-2918; 800 Wisconsin Street, Building D2, Room 401, Mail Box 9, Eau Claire, WI 54703
Website: www.wcwrpc.org

Other regional entities

Professional Football Stadium District

Board of directors chair: Chuck Lamine
Executive director: Patrick Webb
Contact: 920-965-6997; 1229 Lombardi Avenue, Green Bay, WI 54304

The Professional Football Stadium District is an owner and landlord of Lambeau

Field, the designated home of the Green Bay Packers football team. It is a local governmental unit that may acquire, construct, equip, maintain, improve, operate, and manage football stadium facilities or hire others to do the same. Maintenance and operation of the stadium is governed by provisions of the Lambeau Field Lease Agreement by and among the district; Green Bay Packers, Inc.; and the City of Green Bay. The district board consists of seven members who are appointed by local elected officials.

Southeast Wisconsin Professional Baseball Park District

Governing board chair: Don Smiley
Executive director: Michael R. Duckett
Contact: contact@wibaseballdistrict.com; 414-902-4040
Website: www.wibaseballdistrict.com

The Southeast Wisconsin Professional Baseball Park District is the majority owner of American Family Field the home of the Milwaukee Brewers Baseball Club. It is a local governmental unit that may acquire, construct, maintain, improve, operate, and manage baseball park facilities, which include parking lots, garages, restaurants, parks, concession facilities, entertainment facilities, and other related structures. The district is also authorized to issue bonds for certain purposes related to baseball park facilities. To pay off the bonds, the district may impose a sales tax and a use tax, known as the baseball stadium tax. As of April 1, 2020, however, retailers may no longer collect the baseball stadium tax; the district's board certified in March 2020 that the district's bonds had been paid and other required obligations had been met. A city or county within the district's jurisdiction may make loans or grants to the district, expend funds to subsidize the district, borrow money for baseball park facilities, or grant property to the state dedicated for use by a professional baseball park.

The district includes Milwaukee, Ozaukee, Racine, Washington, and Waukesha counties. The district's governing board consists of 13 members appointed by the governor and elected officials from within its jurisdiction. The governor appoints the chair of the governing board.

Wisconsin Center District

Board of directors chair: James Kanter
President and CEO: Marty Brooks
Contact: 414-908-6000; 555 West Wells Street, Milwaukee, WI 53203

The Wisconsin Center District is a local governmental unit that may acquire, construct, and operate an exposition center and related facilities; enter into contracts and grant concessions; mortgage district property and issue bonds; and invest funds as the district board considers appropriate. The Wisconsin Center District operates the University of Wisconsin-Milwaukee Panther Arena, the Miller High Life Theatre, and the Wisconsin Center. It also assists in the development and construction of sports and entertainment facilities, including a new arena for the Milwaukee Bucks, which opened in August 2018. The arena, known as the Fiserv Forum, is owned by the District, but operated, maintained, and managed by the Bucks organization. After the new sports and entertainment facilities were completed, the Wisconsin Center District oversaw the demolition of the Bradley Center, the previous large-event arena for the Milwaukee area. The demolition was completed in 2019.

The district is funded by operating revenue and special sales taxes on hotel rooms, restaurant food and beverages, and car rentals within its taxing jurisdiction. The district board has 17 members, including legislative leaders, local government finance officials, and members who are appointed by the governor, Milwaukee County executive, city of Milwaukee mayor, and city of Milwaukee common council president.

Interstate compacts

Wisconsin has entered with other states into various interstate compacts, under which the compacting states agree to coordinate their activities related to a particular matter according to uniform guidelines or procedures. Some of these compacts include provisions creating an interstate entity made up of representatives from the compacting states, while others do not.

Interstate entities created by interstate compacts

EDUCATION COMMISSION OF THE STATES

Wisconsin delegation: Tony Evers (governor) *Wisconsin delegation chair*, Derek Campbell, John Reinemann, Jill Underly (state superintendent of public instruction), Amy Traynor
Contact: 303-299-3600; 700 Broadway Street, Suite 810, Denver, CO 80203
Website: www.ecs.org

The Education Commission of the States was established to foster national cooperation among executive, legislative, educational, and lay leaders of the various states concerning education policy and the improvement of state and local education systems. The seven-member Wisconsin delegation includes the governor and the state superintendent of public instruction.

GREAT LAKES COMMISSION

Wisconsin delegation: Noah Roberts, *Wisconsin delegation chair;* Todd Ambs, *commission vice chair;* Stephen G. Galarneau, *alternate commissioner;* Dean Haen, Melonee Montano

Contact: 734-971-9135; 1300 Victors Way, Suite 1350, Ann Arbor, MI 48108
Website: www.glc.org

The Great Lakes Commission was established under the Great Lakes Basin Compact to promote the orderly, integrated, and comprehensive development, use, and conservation of the water and related natural resources of the Great Lakes basin and St. Lawrence River. Its members include the eight Great Lakes states of Illinois, Indiana, Michigan, Minnesota, New York, Ohio, Pennsylvania, and Wisconsin, with associate member status for the Canadian provinces of Ontario and Québec. A three-member delegation, appointed by the governor, represents Wisconsin on the commission. The commission develops and recommends the adoption of policy positions by its members and offers advice on issues such as clean energy, climate change, habitat and coastal management, control of aquatic invasive species, water quality, and water resources.

GREAT LAKES PROTECTION FUND

Wisconsin representatives to the board of directors: Kim Marotta, Kevin Shafer
Contact: 847-425-8150; 1560 Sherman Avenue, Suite 1370, Evanston, IL 60201
Website: www.glpf.org

The Great Lakes Protection Fund is a private nonprofit corporation, the members of which are the governors of Illinois, Michigan, Minnesota, New York, Ohio, Pennsylvania, and Wisconsin. The purpose of the corporation is to finance projects for the protection and cleanup of the Great Lakes. The corporation is managed by a board of directors composed of two representatives from each member state. The governor appoints the two Wisconsin representatives.

GREAT LAKES-ST. LAWRENCE RIVER BASIN WATER RESOURCES COUNCIL

Wisconsin members: Tony Evers (governor), *council chair*
Contact: gsgp@gsgp.org; 312-407-0177; 20 North Wacker Drive, Suite 2700, Chicago, IL
60606
Website: www.glslcompactcouncil.org

The Great Lakes-St. Lawrence River Basin Water Resources Council is charged with aiding, promoting, and coordinating the activities and programs of the Great Lakes states concerning water resources management in the Great Lakes-St. Lawrence River basin. The council may promulgate and enforce rules and regulations as may be necessary for the implementation and enforcement of the Great Lakes-St. Lawrence River Basin Water Resources Compact. The legally binding compact governs withdrawals, consumptive uses, conservation and efficient use, and diversions of basin water resources, and the council may initiate legal actions to compel compliance with the compact. In addition, the council must review and approve proposals from certain parties for the withdrawal, diversion, or consumptive use of water from the basin that is subject to the compact.

Under the compact, the governors from the states of Illinois, Indiana, Michigan, Minnesota, New York, Ohio, Pennsylvania, and Wisconsin jointly pursue intergovernmental cooperation and consultation to protect, conserve, restore, improve, and effectively manage the waters and water dependent natural resources of the basin. The governor serves as Wisconsin's representative on the council.

GREAT LAKES-ST. LAWRENCE RIVER WATER RESOURCES REGIONAL BODY

Wisconsin members: Tony Evers (governor)

Contact: gsgp@gsgp.org; 312-407-0177; 20 North Wacker Drive, Suite 2700, Chicago, IL 60606

Website: www.glslregionalbody.org

The Great Lakes-St. Lawrence River Water Resources Regional Body is an entity charged with aiding and promoting the coordination of the activities and programs of the Great Lakes states and provinces concerned with water resources management in the Great Lakes and St. Lawrence River basin. The regional body may develop procedures for the implementation of the Great Lakes-St. Lawrence River Basin Sustainable Water Resources Agreement, which is a good-faith agreement between Great Lakes states and provinces that governs the withdrawal, consumptive use, conservation and efficient use, and diversion of basin water resources. The regional body must review and approve proposals from certain parties for the withdrawal, diversion, or consumptive use of water from the basin that is subject to the agreement. The members of the regional body are the governors from the states of Illinois, Indiana, Michigan, Minnesota, New York, Ohio, Pennsylvania, and Wisconsin, and the premiers of Ontario and Québec. The members of the body jointly pursue intergovernmental cooperation and consultation to protect, conserve, restore, improve, and manage the waters and water dependent natural resources of the basin.

INTERSTATE COMMISSION FOR JUVENILES

Wisconsin members: Casey Gerber (commissioner, Department of Corrections, Division of Juvenile Corrections); Joy Swantz (deputy compact administrator, Department of Corrections, Division of Juvenile Corrections)

Contact: icjadmin@juvenilecompact.org; 859-721-1061; 836 Euclid Avenue, Suite 322, Lexington, KY 40502

Website: www.juvenilecompact.org

The Interstate Commission for Juveniles was established under the Interstate Compact for Juveniles. The compact is designed to coordinate the supervision of juveniles on probation and parole who move across state lines and assists states in returning youth who run away, escape, or abscond across state lines. The commission has the authority to promulgate rules that have the force of law and enforce compliance with the compact.

INTERSTATE COMMISSION OF NURSE LICENSURE COMPACT ADMINISTRATORS

Wisconsin member: Peter Kallio (chairperson, Wisconsin Board of Nursing)
Contact: info@ncsbn.org; 312-525-3600; 111 East Wacker Drive, Suite 2900, Chicago, IL 60601 Website: https://www.ncsbn.org/

The Interstate Commission of Nurse Licensure Compact Administrators was established under the Enhanced Nurse Licensure Compact. The compact authorizes a nurse licensed in a member state to practice nursing in any other member state without obtaining a license in that state. The commission administers the compact and has the authority to promulgate rules that have the force of law.

INTERSTATE INSURANCE PRODUCT REGULATION COMMISSION

Wisconsin member: Mark Afable (commissioner of insurance)
Contact: 202-471-3962; 444 North Capitol Street, NW, Hall of the States, Suite 700, Washington, DC 20001-1509
Website: www.insurancecompact.org

The Interstate Insurance Product Regulation Commission was established under the Interstate Insurance Product Regulation Compact. The compact's purposes are to promote and protect the interest of consumers of, and establish uniform standards for, annuity, life, disability income, and long-term care insurance products; establish a central clearinghouse for the review of those insurance products and related matters, such as advertising; and improve the coordination of regulatory resources and expertise among the various insurance agencies of the member states.

INTERSTATE MEDICAL LICENSURE COMPACT COMMISSION

Wisconsin members: Sheldon Wasserman, Clarence Chou
Contact: imlccexecutivedirector@imlcc.net; 303-997-9842; 5306 South Bannock Street #205, Littleton, CO 80120
Website: https://www.imlcc.org

The Interstate Medical Licensure Compact Commission was established under the Interstate Medical Licensure Compact. The compact provides an expedited process for physicians to become licensed to practice medicine in member states. The commission administers the compact and has the authority to promulgate rules that have the force of law.

INTERSTATE WILDLIFE VIOLATOR COMPACT BOARD OF ADMINISTRATORS

Wisconsin member: Jennifer McDonough (compact coordinator, Department of Natural Resources)

Contact: Wisconsin Department of Natural Resources; 608-267-0859; PO Box 7921, Madison, WI 53707-7921
Website: https://www.naclec.org/wvc#

The Interstate Wildlife Violator Compact is intended to promote compliance with laws and rules relating to the management of wildlife resources in the member states. The compact establishes a process for handling a wildlife resources law violation by a nonresident in a member state as if the violator were a resident of that state. The compact also requires each member state to recognize the revocation or suspension of an individual's wildlife resources privileges in another member state. The compact board of administrators resolves all matters relating to the operation of the compact.

LOWER ST. CROIX MANAGEMENT COMMISSION

Wisconsin member: Dan Baumann (designated by secretary of natural resources)
Contact: Department of Natural Resources, West Central Region; 715-839-3722; 1300 West Clairemont Avenue, Eau Claire, WI 54701

The Lower St. Croix Management Commission was created to provide a forum for discussion of problems and programs associated with the Lower St. Croix National Scenic Riverway. It coordinates planning, development, protection, and management of the riverway between Wisconsin, Minnesota, and the U.S. government.

MIDWEST INTERSTATE LOW-LEVEL RADIOACTIVE WASTE COMMISSION

Wisconsin member: Paul Schmidt (chief, Radiation Protection Section, Department of Health Services)
Contact: paul.schmidt@dhs.wisconsin.gov; 608-267-4792; PO Box 2659, Madison, WI 53701-2659
Website: www.midwestcompact.org

The Midwest Interstate Low-Level Radioactive Waste Commission administers the Midwest Interstate Low-Level Radioactive Waste Compact. The compact is an agreement between the states of Indiana, Iowa, Minnesota, Missouri, Ohio, and Wisconsin that provides for the cooperative and safe disposal of commercial low-level radioactive waste.

MIDWEST INTERSTATE PASSENGER RAIL COMMISSION

Wisconsin members: Arun Rao, *commission vice chair*; Scott Rogers, Senator Wanggaard, 1 vacancy
Contact: miprc@miprc.org; 630-925-1922; 701 East 22nd Street, Suite 110, Lombard, IL 60148
Website: www.miprc.org

The Midwest Interstate Passenger Rail Commission brings together state leaders from the members of the Midwest Interstate Passenger Rail Compact to advocate for passenger rail improvements. The commission also works to educate government officials and the public with respect to the advantages of passenger rail. The current members of the compact are Illinois, Indiana, Kansas, Michigan, Minnesota, Missouri, North Dakota, and Wisconsin.

MIDWESTERN HIGHER EDUCATION COMMISSION

Wisconsin members: Representative Murphy; Senator Nass; Connie Hutchison, Julie Underwood, Rolf Wegenke
Contact: 612-677-2777; 105 Fifth Avenue South, Suite 450, Minneapolis, Minnesota 55401
Website: www.mhec.org

The Midwestern Higher Education Commission was organized to further higher educational opportunities for residents of states participating in the Midwestern Higher Education Compact. The commission may enter into agreements with states, universities, and colleges to provide student programs and services. The commission also studies the compact's effects on higher education.

MILITARY INTERSTATE CHILDREN'S COMPACT COMMISSION

Wisconsin commissioner: Shelley Joan Weiss
Contact: mic3info@csg.org; 859-244-8000; 1776 Avenue of The States, Lexington, KY 40511
Website: www.mic3.net

The Military Interstate Children's Compact Commission oversees implementation of the Interstate Compact on Educational Opportunity for Military Children. The compact is intended to facilitate the education of children of military families and remove barriers to educational success due to frequent moves and parent deployment.

The commission is composed of one commissioner from each of the compacting states. In each compacting state, a council or other body in state government administers the compact within that state. In Wisconsin, the compact is administered by the State Council on the Interstate Compact on Educational Opportunity for Military Children.

MISSISSIPPI RIVER PARKWAY COMMISSION

Wisconsin commission chair: Sherry Quamme
Contact: mrpc@pilchbarnet.com; 866-763-8310; 701 East Washington Avenue, #202, Madison, WI 53703
Website: https://mrpcmembers.com

The Mississippi River Parkway Commission coordinates the development and preservation of Wisconsin's portion of the Great River Road corridor along the Mississippi River. It advises state and local agencies on maintaining and enhancing the scenic, historic, economic, and recreational assets within the corridor and works with similar commissions in other Mississippi River states and the province of Ontario. The 16-member Wisconsin commission includes 12 voting members. Four of these are legislative members who represent the two major political parties in each house, and eight others are appointed by the governor. The four nonvoting members are ex officio, consisting of the secretaries of tourism, natural resources, and transportation and the director of the historical society. The commission selects its own chair to act as Wisconsin's sole voting representative at national meetings of the Mississippi River Parkway Commission.

PHYSICAL THERAPY COMPACT COMMISSION
Wisconsin representative: Kathryn Zalewski
Contact: 703-562-8500; 124 West Street South, Third Floor, Alexandria, VA 22314
Website: http://ptcompact.org/

The Physical Therapy Compact Commission was established under the Physical Therapy Licensure Compact, which allows physical therapists and physical therapist assistants that are licensed in one state that is party to the compact to practice in other member states. The commission administers the compact and includes delegates from each member state's licensing board.

UPPER MISSISSIPPI RIVER BASIN ASSOCIATION
Wisconsin representative: Steve G. Galarneau; Jim Fischer, *alternate*
Contact: 651-224-2880; 7831 East Bush Lake Road, Suite 302, Bloomington, MN 55439
Website: www.umrba.org

The Upper Mississippi River Basin Association is a nonprofit regional organization created by Illinois, Iowa, Minnesota, Missouri, and Wisconsin to facilitate cooperative action regarding the basin's water and related land resources. The association consists of one voting member from each state and sponsors studies of river-related issues, cooperative planning for use of the region's resources, and an information exchange. The organization also enables the member states to develop regional positions on resource issues and to advocate for the basin states' collective interests before the U.S. Congress and federal agencies. The association is involved with programs related to commercial navigation, ecosystem restoration, water quality, aquatic nuisance species, hazardous spills, flood risk management, water supply, and other water resource issues. Six federal agencies with major water resources responsibilities serve as advisory members: the Environmental Protection Agency, the U.S. Army Corps of Engineers, and the U.S. departments of Agriculture, Homeland Security, the Interior, and Transportation.

Interstate compacts without interstate entities

INTERSTATE COMPACT ON ADOPTION AND MEDICAL ASSISTANCE

Requires each member state to cooperate with other states to ensure that children with special needs who were adopted in or from another member state receive medical and other benefits. The Department of Children and Families administers the compact in Wisconsin.

INTERSTATE COMPACT FOR ADULT OFFENDER SUPERVISION

Creates cooperative procedures for individuals placed on parole, probation, or extended supervision in one state to be supervised in another state if certain conditions are met. The Department of Corrections administers the compact in Wisconsin.

INTERSTATE CORRECTIONS COMPACT

Authorizes Wisconsin to contract with member states for the confinement of Wisconsin inmates in those states and to receive inmates from member states. The Department of Corrections administers the compact in Wisconsin.

INTERSTATE AGREEMENT ON DETAINERS

Allows a member state to obtain temporary custody of an individual incarcerated in another member state to conduct a trial on outstanding charges.

EMERGENCY MANAGEMENT ASSISTANCE COMPACT

Authorizes member states to provide mutual assistance to other states in an emergency or disaster declared by the governor of the affected state. Under the compact, member states cooperate in emergency-related training and formulate plans for interstate cooperation in responding to a disaster. The Division of Emergency Management in the Department of Military Affairs administers the compact in Wisconsin.

INTERSTATE COMPACT ON MENTAL HEALTH

Facilitates treatment of patients with mental illness and mental disabilities by the cooperative action of the member states, to the benefit of the patients, their families, and society.

NORTHERN EMERGENCY MANAGEMENT ASSISTANCE COMPACT

An international mutual aid agreement created to facilitate the sharing of resources between certain Midwestern states and Canadian provinces during major disasters and to allow for joint planning, exercising, and training for emergencies.

The Division of Emergency Management in the Department of Military Affairs administers the compact in Wisconsin.

INTERSTATE COMPACT ON THE PLACEMENT OF CHILDREN

Provides a uniform legal and administrative framework governing the interstate placement of abused, neglected, or dependent children, the interstate placement of children through independent or private adoption, and the interstate placement of any child into residential treatment facilities. The Department of Children and Families administers the compact in Wisconsin.

INTERSTATE AGREEMENT ON QUALIFICATION OF EDUCATIONAL PERSONNEL

Authorizes a state education official designated by each member state to contract with other member states to recognize the credentials of educators from those member states and facilitate the employment of qualified educational personnel.

Wisconsin Supreme Court

Justices: Annette Kingsland Ziegler, *chief justice*; Ann Walsh Bradley, Patience Drake Roggensack, Rebecca Grassl Bradley, Rebecca Frank Dallet, Brian Hagedorn, Jill J. Karofsky

Clerk of the supreme court: Sheila T. Reiff

Supreme court commissioners: Nancy Kopp, Julie Rich, David Runke, Mark Neuser

Location: Room 16 East, State Capitol, Madison (supreme court); 110 East Main Street, Suite 215, Madison (clerk)

Contact: 608-266-1880 (clerk); 608-266-7442 (commissioners); PO Box 1688, Madison, WI 53701-1688

Website: https://wicourts.gov/courts/supreme/index.htm

Number of employees: 38.50

Total budget 2019–21: $11,062,200

The Wisconsin Supreme Court is the highest court in Wisconsin's court system. It is the final authority on matters pertaining to the Wisconsin Constitution and the highest tribunal for all actions originating in the state court system, except those involving federal constitutional issues appealable to the U.S. Supreme Court. In addition, it has regulatory and administrative authority over all courts and the

Wisconsin's Supreme Court (*from left*): Justice Brian Hagedorn, Justice Rebecca Grassl Bradley, Justice Ann Walsh Bradley, former Chief Justice Patience Drake Roggensack, Chief Justice Annette Kingsland Ziegler, Justice Rebecca Frank Dallet, Justice Jill J. Karofsky.

STATE OF

CHIEF JUSTICE P.

TOM SHEEHAN, WISCONSIN SUPREME COURT

Chief Justice Patience Roggensack delivers the State of the Judiciary address at the 2019 Annual Meeting of the Wisconsin Judicial Conference held in Elkhart Lake.

practice of law in the state. In this capacity, it establishes procedural rules and codes of conduct for the courts and for the practice of law, and it regulates and disciplines attorneys, judges, and justices.

The supreme court consists of seven justices elected to 10-year terms. They are chosen in statewide elections on the nonpartisan April ballot and take office on the following August 1. The Wisconsin Constitution provides that only one justice can be elected in any single year. In the event of a vacancy, the governor may appoint a person to serve until an election can be held to fill the seat.

The justices elect one of themselves to be the chief justice for a term of two years. The chief justice serves as administrative head of the court system. Any four justices constitute a quorum for conducting court business.

The court decides which cases it will hear. The supreme court exercises its appellate jurisdiction to review a decision of a lower court if three or more justices approve a petition for review, if the court decides on its own motion to review a matter that has been appealed to the Wisconsin Court of Appeals, or if the court accepts a petition for bypass or a certification from the court of appeals. The majority of cases advance from the circuit court to the court of appeals before reaching the supreme court, but the supreme court can bypass the court of appeals, either on its own motion or at the request of the parties; in addition, the court of appeals may certify a case to the supreme court, asking the high court to take the case directly from the circuit court. The court accepts cases on bypass or on certification if four or more justices approve. Further, although rarely granted, a person may file a petition requesting the supreme court to exercise its superintending authority over actions and proceedings in the circuit courts and court of appeals. The supreme court may also exercise original jurisdiction as the first court to hear a case if four or more justices approve a petition requesting it to do so.

The supreme court does not take testimony. Instead, it decides cases on the basis of written briefs and oral argument. The court is required by statute to deliver its decisions in writing, and it may publish them as it deems appropriate.

Wisconsin Court of Appeals

Chief judge: Lisa S. Neubauer
Clerk of the court of appeals: Sheila T. Reiff
Location: 110 East Main Street, Suite 215, Madison (clerk)
Contact: 608-266-1880; PO Box 1688, Madison, WI 53701-1688
Website: https://wicourts.gov/courts/appeals/index.htm
Number of employees: 75.50
Total budget 2019–21: $22,682,400

In August 2020, the Wisconsin court system launched a voluntary eFiling pilot program for the Wisconsin Court of Appeals. The service, now available statewide, allows appellate practitioners to conveniently file and serve nearly all documents electronically and builds on a successful eFiling program already in place for the state's circuit courts.

Court of appeals districts

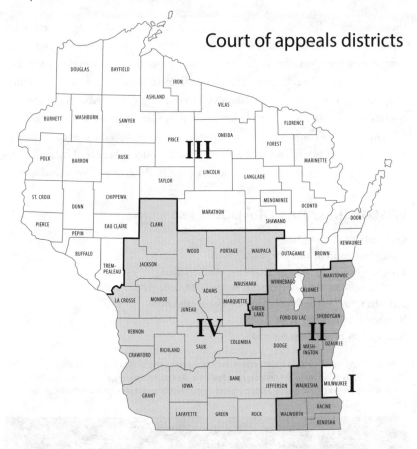

DISTRICT I

William W. Brash III, *presiding judge*; Timothy G. Dugan, M. Joseph Donald, Maxine A. White

Contact: 414-227-4680; 330 East Kilbourn Avenue, Suite 1020, Milwaukee, WI 53202-3161

DISTRICT II

Paul F. Reilly, *presiding judge*; Lisa S. Neubauer, Mark D. Gundrum, Shelley A. Grogan

Contact: 262-521-5230; 2727 North Grandview Boulevard, Suite 300, Waukesha, WI 53188-1671

DISTRICT III

Lisa K. Stark, *presiding judge*; Thomas M. Hruz, Mark A. Seidl

Contact: 715-848-1421; 2100 Stewart Avenue, Suite 310, Wausau, WI 54401

DISTRICT IV

Michael R. Fitzpatrick, *presiding judge*; Brian W. Blanchard, JoAnne F. Kloppenburg, Jennifer E. Nashold, Rachel A. Graham

Contact: 608-266-9250; 2921 Landmark Place, Suite 415, Madison, WI 53713-4248

The Wisconsin Court of Appeals consists of 16 judges serving in four districts. The Wisconsin Supreme Court appoints one of these judges to be the chief judge and to serve as administrative head of the court of appeals for a three-year term. The chief judge in turn appoints a presiding judge for each of the districts. The clerk of the supreme court serves as the clerk for the court of appeals. Court of appeals judges are elected to six-year terms in the nonpartisan April election and begin their terms of office on the following August 1. They must reside in the district from which they are elected. Only one court of appeals judge may be elected in a district in any one year. In the event of a vacancy, the governor may appoint a person to serve until an election can be held to fill the seat.

The court of appeals has appellate jurisdiction, as well as original jurisdiction to issue prerogative writs. The primary function of the court of appeals is to correct errors that occur at the circuit court level. The court also has supervisory authority over all actions and proceedings except those of the supreme court. The final judgments and orders of a circuit court may be appealed to the court of appeals as a matter of right. Other judgments or orders may be appealed upon leave of the appellate court.

The court of appeals usually sits as a three-judge panel to dispose of cases on their merits. However, a single judge may decide certain categories of cases, including juvenile cases; small claims actions; municipal ordinance and traffic regulation violations; and mental health, contempt, and misdemeanor cases. No testimony is taken in the appellate court. The court relies on the trial court record and written briefs in deciding a case, and it hears oral argument when the judges determine it is needed. Both oral argument and "briefs only" cases are placed on a regularly issued calendar. When it is possible to do so without undue delay of civil cases, the court gives preference on the calendar to expedited and criminal appeals, as well as to appeals statutorily required to be given scheduling preference.

Decisions of the appellate court are delivered in writing, and the court's publication committee determines which decisions will be published. Published opinions have precedential value and may be cited as controlling law in Wisconsin unless overruled by the Wisconsin Supreme Court.

Circuit Court

Website: https://wicourts.gov/courts/circuit/index.htm
Number of state-funded employees: 527.00
Total budget 2019–21: $209,042,400

DISTRICT 1

Mary E. Triggiano, *chief judge*; Holly Szablewski, *administrator*

Contact: 414-278-5115; Milwaukee County Courthouse, 901 North 9th Street, Room 609, Milwaukee, WI 53233-1425

DISTRICT 2

Jason A. Rossell, *chief judge*; Louis Moore, *administrator*

Contact: 262-636-3133; Racine County Courthouse, 730 Wisconsin Avenue, Racine, WI 53403-1274

DISTRICT 3

Jennifer Dorow, *chief judge*; Michael Neimon, *administrator*

Contact: 262-548-7209; Waukesha County Courthouse, 515 West Moreland Boulevard, Room C-359, Waukesha, WI 53188-2428

DISTRICT 4

Barbara Key, *chief judge*; Jon Bellows, *administrator*

Contact: 920-424-0027; District Court Administrator's Office, 415 Jackson Street, Room 510, Oshkosh, WI 54903-2808

DISTRICT 5

Thomas J. Vale, *chief judge*; Theresa Owens, *administrator*

Contact: 608-267-8820; Dane County Courthouse, 215 South Hamilton Street, Room 6111, Madison, WI 53703-3290

DISTRICT 6

District 6 was eliminated by supreme court order effective July 31, 2018.

DISTRICT 7

Robert P. VanDeHey, *chief judge*; Patrick Brummond, *administrator*

Contact: 608-785-9546; La Crosse County Law Enforcement Center, 333 Vine Street, Room 3504, La Crosse, WI 54601-3296

DISTRICT 8

James A. Morrison, *chief judge*; Thomas Schappa, *administrator*

Contact: 920-448-4281; District Court Administrator's Office, 414 East Walnut Street, Suite 100, Green Bay, WI 54301-5020

DISTRICT 9

Gregory B. Huber, *chief judge*; Susan Byrnes, *administrator*

Contact: 715-842-3872; District Court Administrator's Office, 2100 Stewart Avenue, Suite 310, Wausau, WI 54401

DISTRICT 10

Maureen D. Boyle, *chief judge*; Christopher Channing, *administrator*

Contact: 715-245-4104; District Court Administrator's Office, 1101 Carmichael Road, Suite 1260, Hudson, WI 54016

Judicial administrative districts

The circuit court is the trial court of general jurisdiction in Wisconsin. It has original jurisdiction in both civil and criminal matters unless exclusive jurisdiction is given to another court. It also reviews state agency decisions and hears appeals from municipal courts. Jury trials are conducted only in circuit courts. The circuit court consists of numerous judges serving in 69 circuits. Each circuit consists of the territory of a single county, except for three two-county circuits (Buffalo-Pepin, Florence-Forest, and Menominee-Shawano). Because of the varying size of their caseloads, some circuits have a single judge, while others have multiple judges. Each judge in a circuit holds court separately—circuit judges do not sit as a panel to hear cases—and each judgeship is called a "branch" of the circuit. As of August 1, 2021, there were a total of 253 circuit court branches in the state.

Circuit judges are elected to six-year terms on a nonpartisan basis in the April election and take office the following August 1. The governor may fill circuit court vacancies by appointment, and the appointees serve until a successor is

Grant County Circuit Court Judge Craig R. Day presides over a hearing as a court reporter takes the record using digital audio recording equipment.

elected. The state pays the salaries of circuit judges and court reporters. It also covers some of the expenses for interpreters, guardians ad litem, judicial assistants, court-appointed witnesses, and jury per diems. Counties bear the remaining expenses for operating the circuit courts.

The circuit court is divided into nine judicial administrative districts, each supervised by a chief judge appointed by the supreme court from the district's circuit judges. A judge usually cannot serve more than three successive two-year terms as chief judge. The chief judge has authority to assign judges, manage caseflow, supervise personnel, and conduct financial planning. The chief judge in each district appoints a district court administrator from a list of candidates supplied by the director of state courts. The administrator manages the nonjudicial business of the district at the direction of the chief judge.

Circuit court commissioners are appointed by the circuit court to assist the court, and they must be attorneys licensed to practice law in Wisconsin. They may be authorized by the court to conduct various civil, criminal, family, small claims, juvenile, and probate court proceedings. Their duties include issuing summonses, arrest warrants, or search warrants; conducting initial appearances; setting bail; conducting preliminary examinations and arraignments; imposing monetary penalties in certain traffic cases; conducting certain family, juvenile, and small claims court proceedings; hearing petitions for mental commitments; and conducting uncontested probate proceedings. On their own authority, court commissioners may perform marriages, administer oaths, take depositions, and issue subpoenas and certain writs.

The statutes require the circuit court for Milwaukee County to have full-time family, small claims, and probate court commissioners. In all other counties, the circuit court is required to have a family court commissioner.

Municipal Court

Website: https://wicourts.gov/courts/municipal/index.htm

The legislature has authorized cities, villages, and towns to establish municipal courts to exercise jurisdiction over municipal ordinance violations that have monetary penalties. Municipal courts also have the authority to handle first offense Operating While Under the Influence cases. In addition, municipal courts may rule on the constitutionality of municipal ordinances.

Municipal courts can have multiple branches (judges who hold court separately), and two or more municipalities can form a joint court. As of February 2021, there were 229 municipal courts and 232 municipal judges in Wisconsin. Seventy-nine of these courts are joint courts that serve from 2 to 18 municipalities. Milwaukee has the largest municipal court, with three full-time judges.

There are no jury trials in municipal court. All cases are decided by a judge. Upon convicting a defendant, the municipal court may order payment of a forfeiture plus costs, fees, and surcharges, or it may order community service in lieu of a forfeiture. In general, municipal courts may also order restitution up to $10,000. In certain cases, a municipal court may suspend or revoke a driver's license.

If a defendant fails to pay a forfeiture or make restitution, the municipal court may suspend the driver's license or order the defendant to jail. Municipal court decisions may be appealed to the circuit court for the county where the offense occurred.

Municipal judges are elected at the nonpartisan April election and take office on May 1. The term of office is four years, unless the municipality has adopted a charter ordinance designating a different term of at least two years, but less than four years. The governing body determines the judge's salary. There is no state requirement that the office be filled by an attorney, but a municipality may enact such a qualification by ordinance. If a municipal judge is ill, disabled, or temporarily absent, the municipal judge may temporarily designate another municipal judge to handle the matter, subject to an order of the chief judge of the judicial administrative district where the municipality is located. In other circumstances, such as when a judge is disqualified, the chief judge of the circuit court administrative district may designate another municipal judge to handle a matter. Finally, if a municipal judge is incompetent, is unable to act, or fails to act, the chief justice of the supreme court may assign cases to another municipal judge, a former municipal judge, or a former circuit court judge. If no judge is available, the chief justice may transfer a case from municipal court to circuit court.

Auxiliary entities

Office of the Director of State Courts

Director of state courts: Randy R. Koschnick
Deputy director for court operations: Diane M. Fremgen
Deputy director for management services: Caitlin M. Frederick
Location: Room 16 East, State Capitol, Madison (director); 110 East Main Street, Madison (staff)
Contact: 608-266-6828 (director); PO Box 1688, Madison, WI 53701-1688 (director); 110 East Main Street, Madison, WI 53703-3356 (staff)
Website: https://wicourts.gov/courts/offices/director.htm
Number of employees: 164.25
Total budget 2019–21: $45,772,000

The director of state courts is appointed by the supreme court and is the chief nonjudicial officer of the Wisconsin court system. The director is responsible for the management of the court system and advises the supreme court, particularly on matters relating to improvements to the court system. The director supervises most state-level court personnel; develops the court system's budget; and directs the courts' work on legislation, public information, and information systems. This office also controls expenditures; allocates space and equipment; supervises judicial education, interdistrict judicial assignments at the circuit court level, and planning and research; and administers the medical malpractice mediation system.

State Bar of Wisconsin

Board of governors, officer members: Cheryl Furstace Daniels, *president*; Margaret Wrenn Hickey, *president-elect*; Kathleen A. Brost, *past president*; Kristen Hardy, *secretary*; Eric L. Andrews, *treasurer*; Charles Stertz, *chair of the board*

Board of governors, district-elected members: Joseph M. Cardamone, III, Margaret Wrenn Hickey, Jennifer L. Johnson, Rochelle Johnson-Bent, Lisa M. Lawless, Odalo J. Ohiku, Amber Lane Raffeet August, Amy Elizabeth Wochos, Ryan M. Billings, Elizabeth K. Miles, Anna Frances Coyer Munoz, Krista G. LaFave Rosolino, Nicholas C. Zales, Renee Ann Read, Mary Lynne Donohue, Craig Steger, Jesse Blocher, John P. Macy, AnnMarie M. Sylla, Bradley Yanke, Joel D. Skinner, Jr., Jeff A. Goldman, David M. Gorwitz, Corey Gayle Lorenz, Mitch, Patricia Epstein Putney, Sam Wayne, Katie R. York, Starlyn Tourtillott Miller, Johanna R. Kirk, Jane E. Bucher, Robert G. Barrington, Sherry Coley, Brian P. Dimmer, Lawrence J. Wiesneske

Executive director: Larry J. Martin
Location: 5302 Eastpark Boulevard, Madison
Contact: service@wisbar.org; 608-257-3838 (general); 800-362-9082 (lawyer referral and information service); PO Box 7158, Madison, WI 53707-7158
Website: www.wisbar.org

The State Bar of Wisconsin is a mandatory professional association of all attorneys who hold a Wisconsin law license. In order to practice law in the state, attorneys must be admitted to practice by the full Wisconsin Supreme Court or by a single justice and must also join the State Bar. The governance and structure of the State Bar are established by the supreme court. The State Bar works to maintain and promote professional standards, improve the administration of justice and the delivery of legal services, and provide continuing legal education to lawyers. The State Bar conducts legal research in substantive law, practice, and procedure and develops related reports and recommendations. It also maintains the roll of attorneys, collects mandatory assessments imposed by the supreme court for supreme court boards and to fund civil legal services for the poor, and performs other administrative services for the judicial system.

David T. Prosser Jr. State Law Library

State law librarian: Amy Crowder
Location: 120 Martin Luther King, Jr. Blvd., 2nd Floor, Madison
Contact: wsll.ref@wicourts.gov (reference); 800-322-9755 (toll free); 608-266-1600 (circulation); 608-267-9696 (reference); PO Box 7881, Madison, WI 53707
Website: http://wilawlibrary.gov

The State Law Library is a public library open to all citizens of Wisconsin. The library supports the information needs of the officers and employees of the state, and of attorneys and the public. The library is administered by the supreme court, which appoints the state law librarian and determines the rules governing library access. The library acts as a consultant and resource for circuit court libraries throughout the state. Milwaukee County and Dane County contract with the State Law Library for management and operation of their courthouse libraries (the Milwaukee County Law Library and the Dane County Law Library).

The library's collection features session laws, statutory codes, case reporters, administrative rules, and legal indexes of the U.S. government, all 50 states, and U.S. territories. It also includes legal and bar periodicals and legal treatises and encyclopedias relevant to all major areas of law. As a federal depository library, it selects federal documents to complement the legal collection. The collection circulates to judges and court staff, attorneys, legislators, and government personnel. The library offers reference, legal research guidance, and document delivery services, as well as training in the use of legal research tools, databases, and websites.

Lawyer Regulation System

Office of Lawyer Regulation: Keith L. Sellen, *director*
Preliminary Review Committee: Robert Asti, *chair*
Special Preliminary Review Panel: Bruce Schultz, *chair*
Board of Administrative Oversight: Lori Kornblum, *chair*
Location: 110 East Main Street, Suite 315, Madison
Contact: 608-267-7274; 877-315-6941 (toll free); PO Box 1648, Madison, WI 53701-1648
Number of employees: 27.50
Website: https://www.wicourts.gov/courts/offices/olr.htm
Total budget 2019–21: $6,404,200

The Office of Lawyer Regulation assists the supreme court in supervising the practice of law and protecting the public from professional misconduct by persons practicing law in Wisconsin. The system includes several entities.

The Office of Lawyer Regulation receives and evaluates all complaints, inquiries, and grievances related to attorney misconduct or medical incapacity. The office is headed by a director who is appointed by the supreme court. If the allegations against an attorney are not within the office's jurisdiction, staff will close the file. A grievant may make a request for the director to review the decision; the director's decision is then final. The office must investigate any grievance that appears to support an allegation of possible attorney misconduct or incapacity, and the attorney in question must cooperate with the investigation. After investigation, the director decides whether the matter should be forwarded to the Preliminary Review Committee, be dismissed, or be diverted for alternative action. The director may also obtain the attorney's consent to a private or public reprimand. The director may refer a matter to a District Committee for assistance with the investigation.

If the director forwards a matter to the Preliminary Review Committee and a panel of that committee determines there is cause to proceed, the director may seek disciplinary action, ranging from agreement to a private reprimand to filing a formal complaint with the supreme court that requests private or public reprimand, license suspension or revocation, monetary payment, or imposing conditions on the continued practice of law. An attorney may be offered alternatives to formal disciplinary action, including mediation, fee arbitration, law office management assistance, evaluation and treatment for alcohol and other substance abuse, psychological evaluation and treatment, monitoring of the attorney's practice or trust account procedures, continuing legal education, ethics school, or the multistate professional responsibility examination.

Formal disciplinary actions for attorney misconduct are filed by the director with the supreme court, which appoints an attorney or reserve judge to be the

In 2019, in the Supreme Court Hearing Room at the capitol, Wisconsin Supreme Court Justice Rebecca Frank Dallet discusses the legal system and the role of the courts in with students from Whitefish Bay High School.

referee for each such action. Referees conduct hearings on complaints of attorney misconduct, petitions alleging attorney medical incapacity, and petitions for reinstatement. They make findings, conclusions, and recommendations and submit them to the supreme court for review and appropriate action. Only the supreme court has the authority to suspend or revoke a lawyer's license to practice law in Wisconsin.

If the director receives an allegation of misconduct or incapacity pertaining to an attorney who works in or is retained to assist the Lawyer Regulation System, the director must refer the matter to a special investigator. Special investigators are attorneys who are appointed by the supreme court and who are not currently working in or retained by the lawyer regulation system. The special investigator commences an investigation if he or she determines there is enough information to support a possible finding of cause to proceed on the allegation, but otherwise may close the matter. After an investigation, the special investigator can dismiss the matter or submit an investigative report to the Special Preliminary Review Panel. If this panel determines, after receiving an investigative report from a special investigator, that there is cause to proceed, the special investigator can proceed to file a complaint with the supreme court and prosecute the matter personally or may assign that responsibility to counsel retained by the director for such purposes.

The Board of Administrative Oversight monitors and assesses the performance of the lawyer regulation system and reports its findings to the supreme court. The board reviews with the supreme court the operation of the lawyer regulation system, proposes for consideration by the supreme court substantive and procedural rules related to the regulation of lawyers, and proposes to the supreme court the annual budget for the office of lawyer regulation, after consulting with the director of that office.

Board of Bar Examiners

Chairperson: Marc A. Hammer
Director: Jacquelynn B. Rothstein
Location: 110 East Main Street, Suite 715, Madison
Contact: bbe@wicourts.gov; 608-266-9760; PO Box 2748, Madison, WI 53701-2748
Website: https://wicourts.gov/courts/offices/bbe.htm
Number of employees: 6.00
Total budget 2019–21: $1,650,800

The Board of Bar Examiners administers all bar admissions; it writes and grades the bar examination, reviews motions for admission on proof of practice, and conducts character and fitness investigations of all candidates for admission to the bar, including diploma privilege graduates. The board also administers the Wisconsin mandatory continuing legal education requirement for attorneys.

Wisconsin Supreme Court Justice Annette Kingsland Ziegler (*standing*) discusses Marquette County's legal history during the court's 2019 Justice on Wheels outreach trip to Montello, where the court heard oral argument in three cases. In April 2021, Justice Ziegler was elected as the 27th Wisconsin Supreme Court chief justice, replacing Chief Justice Patience Drake Roggensack, who held the position from 2015 to 2021.

TOM SHEEHAN, WISCONSIN SUPREME COURT

Judicial Commission

Members: Yulonda Anderson, Mark Barrette, William W. Brash III, Eileen Burnett, William E. Cullinan, Frank J. Daily, Kendall M. Kelley, Steve C. Miller, Joseph L. Olson

Executive director: Jeremiah C. Van Hecke

Contact: judcmm@wicourts.gov; 608-266-7637; 110 East Main Street, Suite 700, Madison, WI 53703-3328

Website: https://wicourts.gov/judcom

Number of employees: 2.00

Total budget 2019–21: $632,200

The Judicial Commission conducts investigations regarding allegations that a justice, judge, or court commissioner has committed misconduct or has a permanent disability that substantially impairs his or her judicial performance. The commission's investigations are confidential. If the commission finds probable cause that a justice, judge, or court commissioner has engaged in misconduct or has a disability that substantially impairs his or her judicial performance, the commission must file a formal complaint of misconduct or a petition regarding disability with the supreme court.

The commission then prosecutes a proceeding against the judge before a three-judge panel or, if the commission so requested when it filed the complaint or petition, before a jury. The panel of judges, or a single judge to preside over a jury proceeding, is selected by the chief judge of the court of appeals. If the proceeding was held before a panel, the supreme court reviews the panel's findings of fact, conclusions of law, and recommended disposition and determines the appropriate discipline in cases of misconduct or appropriate action in cases of permanent disability. If the proceeding was held before a jury, the presiding judge files the jury verdict and his or her recommendations regarding appropriate discipline for misconduct or appropriate action for permanent disability with the supreme court for the court's review.

Judicial Conduct Advisory Committee

Members: Bryan Keberlein, *chair*; M. Joseph Donald, *vice chair*; Cynthia Davis, Todd Martens, Dennis Cimpl, Barbara Hart Key, Laura Mahan-Schmitz, Christine E. Ohlis, James R. Troupis

Contact: 608-266-6828; PO Box 1688, Madison, WI 53701-1688

Website: https://wicourts.gov/courts/committees/judicialconduct.htm

The Judicial Conduct Advisory Committee gives formal advisory opinions and informal advice to judges and judicial officers regarding whether actions contemplated by the officials comply with the Code of Judicial Conduct. It also makes recommendations to the supreme court about amending of the Code of Judicial Conduct or the rules governing the committee.

Judicial Conference

Website: https://wicourts.gov/courts/committees/judicialconf.htm

The Judicial Conference is composed of all supreme court justices, court of appeals judges, circuit court judges, and reserve judges; three municipal court judges designated by the Wisconsin Municipal Judges Association; three representatives from the tribal courts; one circuit court commissioner designated by the Family Court Commissioner Association; and one circuit court commissioner designated by the Judicial Court Commissioner Association.

The Judicial Conference meets at least once a year to consider and establish study committees to examine issues relating to the administration of justice and its improvement, consider the reports of such committees, and consider problems pertaining to the administration of justice and make recommendations for improvement; to conduct instructive programs and seminars; to consider and act on reports and recommendations from the committees; to conduct elections; and to consider any other matters and conduct other business included on the agenda.

The Judicial Conference has several standing committees, including committees to prepare model civil, criminal, and juvenile jury instructions. The Judicial Conference may also create additional study committees to examine particular topics. These study committees must report their findings and recommendations to the next annual meeting of the Judicial Conference. The Judicial Conference may also create other committees to perform duties not otherwise covered by the Judicial Conference bylaws.

Judicial Council

Members: William Gleisner, *chair* (designated by State Bar president-elect); Diane M. Fremgen (designated by director of state courts); Thomas R. Hruz (judge designated by court of appeals), Eugene A. Gasiorkiewicz, Robert P. VanDeHey, Hannah Dugan, Scott R. Needham (circuit court judges designated by Judicial Conference); Senator Wanggaard (chairperson, senate judicial committee); Representative Tusler (chair, assembly judicial committee); Steven C. Kilpatrick (designated by attorney general); Sarah Walkenhorst Barber (designated by Legislative Reference Bureau chief); Adam Stevenson (faculty member designated by UW Law School dean); Thomas L. Shriner, Jr. (faculty member designated by Marquette University Law School dean); Adam Plotkin (designated by state public defender); Sarah Zylstra, Margo Kirchner, John R. Orton (State Bar members selected by State Bar); Christian Gossett (district attorney appointed by governor); Benjamin J. Pliskie, Dennis Myers (public members appointed by governor), vacant (justice designated by supreme court)

Contact: 414-651-3182; 19125 Killarney Way, Brookfield, WI 53045

Website: http://wilawlibrary.gov/judicialcouncil/index.htm

Number of employees: 0.00

Total budget 2019–21: $0

The Judicial Council advises the supreme court, the governor, and the legislature on any matter affecting the administration of justice in Wisconsin, and it may recommend changes in the jurisdiction, organization, operation, or business methods of the courts that would result in a more effective and cost-efficient court system. The council studies the rules of pleading, practice, and procedure and advises the supreme court about changes that will simplify procedure and promote efficiency.

Judicial Education Committee

Members: Justice Rebecca F. Dallet, *chair*; Jini Jasti, Thomas Hammer, Randy Koshnick, Lisa K. Stark, Jay R. Tlusty, Eugene A. Gasiorkiewicz, Thomas R. Hruz, Mary E. Triggiano, Susan Crawford, Thomas Walsh, Gregory Strasser, Jodi Meier, Maria Lazar, Kelly Iselin, Jason Hanson

Director of Office of Judicial Education: Morgan Young

Contact: jed@wicourts.gov; 608-266-7807; Office of Judicial Education, 110 East Main Street, Suite 200, Madison, WI 53703-3328

Website: https://wicourts.gov/courts/committees/judicialed.htm

The Judicial Education Committee oversees continuing education programs for the judiciary. All supreme court justices and commissioners, appeals court judges and staff attorneys, and circuit court judges and commissioners must earn 60 credit hours of continuing education every six years in approved educational programs. Reserve judges and municipal court judges are subject to similar continuing education requirements. The committee monitors compliance with the continuing education requirements and refers instances of noncompliance to the supreme court. The committee works with the Office of Judicial Education in the Office of the Director of State Courts, which plans and conducts educational seminars for judges and tracks credits earned by judges.

Planning and Policy Advisory Committee

Chair: Annette Kingsland Ziegler (chief justice of the supreme court)

Contact: 608-266-3121; 110 East Main Street, Suite 410, Madison, WI 53703

Website: https://wicourts.gov/courts/committees/ppac.htm

The Planning and Policy Advisory Committee advises the Wisconsin Supreme Court and the director of state courts on planning and policy and assists in a continuing evaluation of the administrative structure of the court system. It participates in the budget process of the Wisconsin judiciary and appoints a subcommittee to confer with the supreme court and the director of state courts in the court's review of the budget. The committee meets at least quarterly, and the supreme court meets with the committee annually. The director of state courts participates in committee deliberations, with full floor and advocacy privileges, but is not a member of the committee and does not have a vote.

3

ABOUT WISCONSIN

Coles Bashford

DUELING GOVERNORS

HOW THE WISCONSIN SUPREME COURT RESOLVED THE STATE'S FIRST POLITICAL CRISIS

BY STACI DUROS, LOUISA KAMPS, AND JILLIAN SLAIGHT

William A. Barstow

O n January 7, 1856, Wisconsin held its third gubernatorial inauguration. It was a bitterly cold and snowy day in Madison. Nevertheless,
people flocked to the capital city to join in the elaborate inaugural
parade of Democratic Governor William A. Barstow, who was on
his way to be sworn in for his second term. Waving from a carriage
drawn by four black horses, Barstow led the parade down Washington Avenue,
then around Capitol Square, to the thunderous accompaniment of brass bands,
drums, and cannon fire. Later, inside the capitol, crowds packed into the senate
chambers to witness Barstow take his oath of office.[1]

But was the oath of office really his to take? Earlier that day, Barstow's challenger in the race, Republican Coles Bashford, slipped into the capitol with a
handful of his own close associates. In the Wisconsin Supreme Court Room,
the chief justice administered the governor's oath of office to Bashford, who was
sworn in without fanfare to serve as the state's third governor.[2]

Three weeks before Wisconsin acquired two governors, the State Board of Canvassers determined in mid-December that Barstow had defeated Bashford in the 1855 gubernatorial election, winning by a margin of only 157 votes out of more than 72,000 votes cast.[3] But even though Barstow had officially won, the election certification had occurred amid growing allegations of fraud and forgery as members of the board of canvassers—all Barstow's political allies—accepted and counted a flurry of late-arriving votes that leaned felicitously (and suspiciously) in Barstow's favor, pushing the incumbent to just over 50 percent. Barstow may have projected confidence during his inaugural parade and ceremony, but there was plenty of lingering doubt about the legitimacy of his reelection victory. And less than a week after both governors were sworn in, when Barstow refused to relinquish the governor's office, Bashford enlisted the state attorney general to file a suit seeking to remove Barstow from the governorship.

With both William Barstow and Coles Bashford asserting their right to govern the state, Wisconsin faced its first major political crisis. The conflict, unfolding in the already fractious period leading up to the Civil War, could have thrown the young state's government into chaos, or even resulted in violence—partisans for each side gathered arms while Bashford's lawsuit advanced. But in a remarkable turn of events, the matter was peacefully resolved before the Wisconsin Supreme Court. This resolution not only spared the state from bloodshed, but also helped establish a clear separation of powers in the newly established state. Moreover, the incident guided legislators as they worked to establish elections procedures that safeguarded the integrity of the vote. In short, the dueling inaugurations of William Barstow and Coles Bashford set in motion a series of events that shaped governmental norms that we take for granted today. The 2021 feature article recounts those events.

Part I introduces readers to the social and political landscape of Wisconsin in the years leading up to the 1855 gubernatorial election. Beginning in the 1840s, the territory's population surged as newcomers sought land and opportunity there. After Wisconsin achieved statehood in 1848, it achieved a measure of political stability—but contentious debate over slavery threatened to disrupt that stability. As Wisconsinites prepared to pick their third governor in 1855, this tension increased as new and old political parties jockeyed for power. In this charged environment, the stakes of the upcoming election were high.

Part II details the events of Election Day and describes the suspicion that mounted over the following weeks about Barstow's slim margin of victory. On November 6, 1855, Wisconsinites arrived, ballots in hand, at saloons, barns, and country stores to cast their votes. When the polls closed at sundown, election officials began the official canvass of votes under a system prone to error and

When the New York-based Colton map company published this map of Wisconsin townships in 1855, the new state teetered at the edge of political crisis. Two men both claimed to have won the 1855 gubernatorial election, setting off a legal battle.

abuse. It took until December 17 for the official results to be announced, by which time both political parties seemed poised to reject the results.

Part III returns to the two nearly simultaneous inaugurations that took place at the capitol on January 7, 1856, illustrating how partisan allies of each candidate depicted the day's events in radically different ways. It then outlines the charges laid out in Coles Bashford's lawsuit to unseat Governor Barstow.

Part IV delves into the tactics employed by Barstow's attorneys to quash the case. Instead of confronting allegations of elections tampering, they challenged the authority of the Wisconsin Supreme Court to intervene in elections. The case quickly became a dispute over the authority of the judicial branch and the proper separation of powers under the Wisconsin Constitution.

Finally, Part V outlines the startling evidence of ballot tampering that ultimately helped the court determine the rightful winner of the gubernatorial election of 1855.

Elections are competitive by nature, and close elections can heighten tensions between people with opposing interests. The intensely partisan election of 1855 put Wisconsin's fledgling legal system through a hard test. However, the Wisconsin Supreme Court's ruling in *Bashford v. Barstow* did not just provide clarity about who had won the governor's race and put a stop to saber-rattling in the capital; it also restored faith in the security of elections in the frontier state. Critically, at a time when all eyes were glued to the still-young supreme court, the justices deciding *Bashford v. Barstow* helped the judicial branch assert itself as coequal to the executive and legislative branches. The decision demonstrated the supreme court's authority, provided in the state constitution, to independently interpret law in Wisconsin—and in doing so, it helped to transform the court into the durably powerful institution it remains today.

I. THE YOUNG STATE'S POLITICAL LANDSCAPE

In the years following the establishment of statehood in 1848, Wisconsin was a place of change, where citizens witnessed a new system of government take shape and recognized their power to influence the unfolding path of politics. Waves of East Coast migrants and European immigrants arrived in the nation's thirtieth state, seeking land and the opportunities it provided. Lawyers followed close behind, eager to make their careers on the coattails of widespread land speculation. Many, in turn, became lawmakers and created code and courts to place the state on "sound legal footing."[4] Still, the terrain kept shifting underfoot. Politics transformed unpredictably around the issue of slavery, which dominated public debate and led to the creation (and collapse) of entire political parties. Wisconsinites also wrangled with nativist sentiments that challenged the cultural belonging and civic standing of new immigrants. This atmosphere of contention and uncertainty raised the stakes of the gubernatorial election of 1855. Would the newly formed state government coalesce or falter?

Between 1840 and 1860, Wisconsin's population multiplied 25 times.[5] By 1860, over a third of Wisconsinites hailed from foreign countries.[6] When economic and political instability drove many Europeans from home, they gravitated to

BIRTHPLACES OF WISCONSIN STATE LEGISLATORS

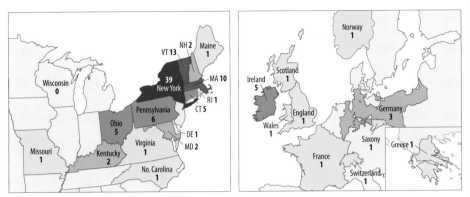

NH 2
VT 13
Maine 1
Wisconsin 0
39 New York
MA 10
RI 1
CT 5
Pennsylvania 6
Ohio 5
DE 1
MD 2
Missouri 1
Kentucky 2
Virginia 1
No. Carolina 1

Norway 1
Scotland 1
Ireland 5
England 1
Germany 3
Wales 1
Saxony 1
Greece 1
France 1
Switzerland 1

SOURCE: *MANUAL FOR THE USE OF THE ASSEMBLY OF THE STATE OF WISCONSIN FOR THE YEAR 1853* (MADISON, WI: BROWN AND CARPENTER, 1853), 85, *99.

Wisconsin for the promise of its ample, open land. As William Hodges of Pierce County wrote to a friend in June 1856, "There is a great many immigrants coming here this spring and a general rush for land."[7] Where land was available, working it was far from easy, as newcomer Gunleik Asmundson Bondal told his family back in Norway in 1854. All the same, Bondal reported that his family was in such good health that "we do not want to go back even if we were the owners of the best farm."[8]

Land also drew "Yankee settlers," a term often referring to New Englanders and New Yorkers of British descent. Lucy Hastings—who had moved to Oxford, Wisconsin, from Massachusetts—shared this assessment with her siblings back home: "We find it a very good way for poor folks out here, to go on to government land, make improvements, then sell, and after a while get to farming in good shape."[9] For migrants and immigrants alike, social events like "barn raisings, candle dippings, quilting parties, and corn huskings" provided welcome relief from their hard work on remote farms.[10]

Foreign-born immigrants accounted for about a third of Wisconsin's population in the 1850s. Newcomers like Aslak Olsen Lie, pictured here among family members in front of the home he built in 1849, came from Europe in search of land.

WHS IMAGE ID 27635

As new settlements dotted the state, law offices sprang up in cities like Madison to meet demand for land contracts, which became a "special niche" in Midwestern legal practice.[11] Lawyers accounted for a disproportionate share of Wisconsin's population because business abounded and no formal training was required to practice the profession. Most lawyers lacked legal degrees but made up for this deficit with hands-on training they acquired while drafting contracts and arguing cases. A man needed only three things to be successful: the first two—proof of residency and "good moral character"—were required by the Wisconsin Statutes of 1849.[12] Clients and courtroom audiences demanded the third quality: the power to command attention. With little other entertainment at their disposal, Wisconsinites in sparsely settled areas attended trials as a form of diversion. "Court days were the event of the season at the county seat," one lawyer later recalled, and "ability, learning and eloquence were exercised to serve clients and entertain spectators."[13]

Oratory trumped knowledge of the law—in part because the law was still very much in flux. In most early nineteenth-century legislatures, legal scholar Joseph Ranney notes, bills were handwritten, "put on a shelf" after passage, and "pulled out only in case of immediate need and otherwise forgotten."[14] Wisconsin legislators had only recently endeavored to organize enacted laws and make them accessible, completing the first compilation of territorial laws in 1839.[15]

With statehood, the courts—like the laws themselves—gained greater structure and continuity. The Wisconsin Constitution of 1848 created circuit courts whose judges served on a temporary state supreme court, and after a short "test period," the Wisconsin Supreme Court was officially established in 1853.[16] An air of excitement and unpredictability pervaded the high court in the mid-1850s, as new lawyers argued new laws before new justices. As one jurist reminisced, "the profession was not yet overwhelmed with whole libraries of precedents, [and] argument based upon general principles was still possible."[17] But the nascent court had yet to firmly establish its authority.

An opportunity came when the court placed itself at the center of contentious debates over slavery. Although few Wisconsinites had witnessed firsthand the horrors of human bondage, slavery had become an "explosive issue" that drove state politics.[18] Wisconsin's status as a free state mattered deeply to settlers who feared that the expansion of slavery spelled the demise of small farms like their own.[19] In 1854, Congress passed the Kansas-Nebraska Act, allowing each Western territory to decide for itself whether slavery would be allowed when the territory became a state. Although not directly affected, historian Michael McManus explains, "many concerned Northerners grimly concluded that slavery would likely take root in the West and eventually spread into the free states."[20] The March 1854 arrest of

Federal laws like the Fugitive Slave Act and the Kansas-Nebraska Act raised concerns that slavery would spread to free states. In a landmark 1854 decision, the Wisconsin Supreme Court asserted states' right to reject slavery.

LIBRARY OF CONGRESS, GEOGRAPHY AND MAP DIVISION

WHS IMAGE ID 1928

Joshua Glover—a man enslaved in Missouri who had escaped and established a new life in Wisconsin—stoked fears like these. The Fugitive Slave Act of 1850 exposed men and women like Glover to capture and reenslavement, even in free states. But in July 1854, the Wisconsin Supreme Court declared this law unconstitutional in a bold assertion of states' rights versus those of the federal government.[21] With this "act of defiance," the court placed itself on the map.[22]

Still, the court's rulings around this issue did little to quell anxieties about the fate of Wisconsin as a free state, and these anxieties in turn fueled political instability. At that time, the two main political parties—Democrats and Whigs—were constantly in flux. Democrats seemed to exercise a strong grip over the state, having elected more governors and members of Congress than the Whigs, but the party stumbled under the weight of internal divisions. Likewise, by 1855, the Whig Party had completely collapsed.[23] (See sidebar on page 298 for more on Wisconsin's political scene in the 1850s.) In this opening, the Republican Party was founded on the basis of opposition to slavery.[24] The creation of this new party marked the start of a gradual shift in power. By the late 1850s, the Republican Party

WISCONSIN'S EARLY POLITICAL PARTIES?

BIRTHPLACE
-∹ OF THE ∹-
REPUBLICAN PARTY
In this School House March 20th 1854 was held the first Mass Meeting, in this country that definitely and positively cut loose from old parties and advocated a new party under the name Republican.

On March 20, 1854, outraged Wisconsinites met at a Ripon schoolhouse and resolved to form a new political party to oppose the expansion of slavery.

In the early days of statehood, Wisconsin parties bucked the policy positions of their corresponding national parties. Wisconsin Whigs courted immigrant votes despite the national Whig Party's reputation for nativism. And in contrast to the national Democratic Party, Wisconsin Democrats opposed the expansion of slavery and supported federal investment in infrastructure projects. Although they hailed from different parties, all members of Wisconsin's Congressional delegation voted against the Fugitive Slave Act of 1850. A group of Wisconsinites eventually formed a new party to cast off the baggage associated with the national parties: the Republican Party. As established in 1854, the Republican Party brought together former Democrats and Whigs around the antislavery cause.

Source: Richard N. Current, *The History of Wisconsin*, vol. 2, The Civil War Era, 1848–1873 (Madison, WI: Wisconsin Historical Society Press, 2013), 197–230.

would become a major political force in the state.[25] But the party faced an uphill battle in the 1855 gubernatorial election, which was the first time a Republican challenged a Democrat in a statewide race.

Governor William Barstow, the Democratic incumbent, had moved from Connecticut to Prairieville (now known as Waukesha) in 1839, purchasing land and establishing a flour mill. Having cemented his reputation as a successful businessman—and "the handsomest man in Wisconsin" to boot—Barstow became active in local politics, serving as Prairieville's postmaster and a Milwaukee County Commissioner.[26] Barstow soon set his sights on higher office; he was elected as

Wisconsin's second secretary of state in 1849 and served in that office from 1850 to 1851.[27] Even in this short term, he faced allegations of bribery and corruption: specifically, Barstow was accused of not only awarding state printing contracts to his friends, but also underselling tracts of public lands to speculators without soliciting public bids. Lack of sufficient proof helped Barstow escape formal charges, but the allegations may have cost him his reelection bid in 1851.[28] Nevertheless, Barstow sought—and handily won—the governorship with 30,405 out of a total of 55,683 votes cast in November 1853.[29]

After Barstow began his two-year term in January 1854, the newly created Republican Party capitalized on Barstow's history of alleged malfeasance and eventually gained control of the assembly in the November 1854 election.[30] From there, the Republicans launched several legislative committees to investigate corruption within the Barstow administration. One such committee uncovered unfair bidding practices related to the state's contract for construction of a state insane asylum. Another investigation exposed grave mismanagement of certain state funds by members of Barstow's administration.[31] The leader of that particular investigation was the Republican who would challenge the governor in the 1855 election.

Like Barstow, Coles Bashford came to Wisconsin from the East Coast and rose quickly through the ranks of state politics. After he moved from New York to Oshkosh in 1850, Bashford attended the Whig state party convention as a delegate the following year, supporting the nomination of Leonard J. Farwell, who became the state's second governor. In 1852, Bashford ran successfully as a Whig candidate to represent Winnebago County in the state senate, where he served from 1853 to 1855.[32] As the issue of slavery in the West became increasingly charged, Bashford left the party to become a Republican, and nine months into his second term, he resigned from the senate to become the first Republican candidate for governor of Wisconsin.[33]

Republican prospects for the general election of 1855 looked promising. The party had performed well in the 1854 elections, despite being new to the political scene. Moreover, Bashford and his Republican senate colleagues had revealed the misdeeds of the Barstow administration, giving them fuel—or so they thought—to challenge incumbent Democrats in the upcoming election. But their embrace of prohibition, i.e., the strict curtailment of alcohol by law, exposed Republicans to charges of "Puritan bigotry."[34] As historian Tyler Abinder explains, nativist politicians often denounced saloons in a "thinly veiled attack" on their presumed customers: German and Irish immigrants.[35] These claims were an affront to foreign-born settlers, who already contended with more direct—and violent— nativist attacks. In one shocking instance, the brutal assault of a Bavarian farmer in West Bend, Wisconsin, pushed the man's community to exact violent retribution by lynching the perpetrator.[36] Against this backdrop, historian Richard Current notes, Wisconsin Democrats sprang at the opportunity "to exploit the resentment on the part of German and other immigrants."[37]

With this goal in mind, the Democratic Party recruited immigrant candidates and attempted to paint the top of the Republican ticket, Coles Bashford, as a member of the Know-Nothings, a semisecret, anti-Catholic nativist organization.[38] The Know-Nothings had dramatically risen to national prominence in 1854 with calls for immigration restrictions and the exclusion of foreign-born residents from voting or holding public office.[39] Weeks before the election of 1855, Democrat-aligned newspapers claimed to hold unimpeachable proof "that COLES BASHFORD IS A KNOW NOTHING."[40] One paper even alleged that Bashford also secretly disdained a core Republican constituency: abolitionists. According to the *Sauk Co. Democrat*, Bashford had purportedly remarked, "If there are any two creatures which I despise more than all others, they are the Irishmen and Abolitionists."[41]

The papers never corroborated these claims, but Republican-aligned papers still fired back. The *Mineral Point Tribune* reminded its Republican readers that their party—and Bashford's—supported "the equal rights of *all men*" and "[opposed] all secret organizations that favor proscription on account of birth place, religion, or color."[42] Taking a step further, the *Daily State Journal* charged that Barstow sought to win the election "with unrestrained and unmitigated whiskey on the one hand" and "midnight cabals on the other."[43]

This war of words arguably created more confusion than clarity with respect to the candidates' supposed nativist tendencies. As one reporter noted with exasperation, "The Know Nothings have created considerable panic, and both parties disown them. . . . We are totally ignorant of which party, if either, they give their support to, nor care but little."[44] Both candidates disavowed Know-Nothingism in letters later published in the press: Barstow wrote that "I do not now and never did belong to said order,"[45] and Bashford swore, "*I am not a member of the Order of Know Nothings and Never have been!!*"[46]

These emphatic denials underscored the fact that both parties eyed immigrants as a crucial voting bloc in the upcoming election. Article III of the 1848 Wisconsin Constitution granted the right to vote to every white male who was at least 21 years old and who had resided in the state for at least one year prior to an election. In short, U.S. citizenship was not required.[47] On the one hand, immigrant support at the ballot box could tip elections in favor of a political party. On the other hand, parties that catered to foreign-born voters (and distanced themselves from nativism) ran the risk of potentially alienating their native-born bases.[48]

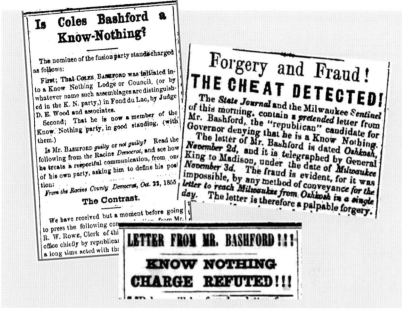

In an attempt to court immigrant votes, both Democrats and Republicans accused the opposing party's gubernatorial candidate of allying with the Know-Nothings, a semisecret nativist political organization. Shortly before the November 1855 election, the *Manitowoc Herald* (*top left*) and *Milwaukee Daily News* (*top right*) amplified rumors that Republican Coles Bashford was a Know-Nothing, whereas the *Mineral Point Tribune* published Bashford's letter rebutting these charges (*above*).

Whatever their strategic value, these accusations cultivated "an aura of intense paranoia" that persisted until the general election, as both parties encouraged Wisconsinites to doubt each gubernatorial candidate's true political allegiances.[49]

II. THE CONTESTED ELECTION OF 1855

The bitter campaign for the governorship frayed the nerves of voters. Rather than lay the conflict to rest, the election results heightened tensions. Forty days passed between Election Day and the official statewide vote count that determined the winner. This delay was not unusual at the time, because ballots were counted by hand and tallies were transported to Madison on horseback from isolated areas. Counting the votes took several weeks, allowing time for politically motivated operatives to attempt to manipulate the results. In this interval, accusations of vote tampering accumulated and threatened to undermine confidence in the integrity of the election. These allegations illuminated vulnerabilities in Wisconsin's nascent elections process and raised the possibility that people would contest the outcome.

This print depicts the boisterous atmosphere of an election day in nineteenth-century America, when it was common for voters to cast ballots in saloons or stables. John Sartain after George Caleb Bingham, *The Country Election*, 1854.

On Tuesday, November 6, 1855, the polls opened at nine o'clock in the morning. State law specified that they remain open "until sunset," with an hour-long adjournment of the polls permitted at noon.[50] At the time, a variety of public and private buildings doubled as polling places. In rural or frontier towns, for example, Americans voted in stores, saloons, barns, or the homes of well-known residents. In more populous areas, people cast their ballots in courthouses, hotels, factories, stables, and also saloons, where "cloth sheets would be raised around the area in which voting was done so that patrons could drink while the election was held."[51] As elections historian Richard Franklin Bensel notes, these circumstances rendered elections somewhat chaotic.

Rather than receive a ballot at the polls, each voter brought his own ballot, on which he wrote out the names of his preferred candidates in longform. (No voter submitted her ballot because the Wisconsin Constitution excluded women, as well as non-white men, from the franchise.) An eligible voter could also submit a printed "party ticket," clipped from his local partisan newspaper,[52] or a ballot containing partially printed and partially written choices.[53] Then the voter entered the polling place, making his way past "the throng of chanting, jostling partisans"

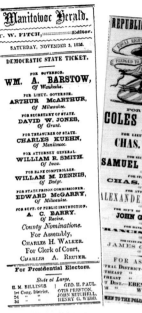

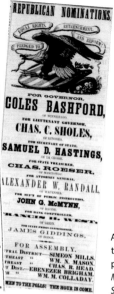

outside, and submitted his ballot.[54] Election officials then deposited the ballot into the ballot box.[55]

When the polls closed at sundown, some election officials faced a long night of counting ballots. They compared poll lists to correct mistakes, recorded the number of ballots the ballot box should contain, and counted sealed ballots in the ballot box to ensure they matched the number of voters on the poll list. Finally,

An eligible voter could either bring his own ballot to the polls or clip and submit a prefilled "party ticket" printed in the newspaper, like these tickets from the *Manitowoc Herald* (Nov. 3, 1855) and the *Wisconsin State Journal* (Nov. 6, 1855).

EXCLUDED AT THE POLLS: BLACK WISCONSINITES

While the Wisconsin Constitution of 1848 granted suffrage to white men, it took another 18 years before Black men could vote in the state. A referendum on extending suffrage to Black men appeared on the ballot in 1849. A majority of voters who responded approved the measure; however, the Board of Canvassers counted ballots that abstained on the referendum as votes against it, causing the measure to fail. Ezekiel Gillespie, a formerly enslaved man and a community leader in Milwaukee, attempted to vote in the 1865 general election and predictably was turned away at the polls. Gillespie and his attorneys took the matter to court, and in 1866, the state supreme court ruled that—regardless of how many voters responded to the 1849 referendum—Black men in Wisconsin had legally gained the right to vote in 1849.

Ezekiel Gillespie spearheaded the legal effort to enfranchise Black Wisconsinites.

WHS IMAGE ID 33364

Source: Christy Clark-Pujara, "Contested: Black Suffrage in Early Wisconsin," *Wisconsin Magazine of History*, Summer 2017, 21–27.

election officials proceeded to conduct the "canvass"—the official tally—of every valid vote cast.[56]

After counting all of the votes, local election officials wrote an official statement of the results, which contained the total number of votes for each office, as well as the total number of votes each candidate received. Then they transcribed, signed, and sealed shut official copies of this statement. The local clerk retained one copy, and the other was delivered to the county clerk within seven days. From these copies, county canvassers prepared their own official documentation of the total votes cast for each candidate for office.[57] Finally, signed and sealed copies of these documents were sent to the State Board of Canvassers, an entity composed of the secretary of state, attorney general, and state treasurer that was responsible for determining election results and announcing them to the public.[58]

A long paper trail built up between the time when voters cast their ballots on voting day and the time when the State Board of Canvassers received official county canvass records in Madison.[59] The extensive documentation had some advantages: multiple layers of authentication might shield the canvass from fraud. But hand-writing and hand-delivering these official papers could invite mistakes or manipulation. Fatigue alone likely caused clerical errors, as local election officials conducted the initial canvass late into the night without pause. Moreover, each canvass relied on the labor of elected politicians, who might be tempted to nudge the results in their party's favor. And most importantly, the gap between the election and official election results left plenty of time for rumors to circulate.

More than a month passed between election night and the last day permitted by law for filing of the official election results; no quicker pace was possible without cars, paved roads, or computers. The secretary of state received the first county canvass results on November 15, 1855, and announced the results on December 17.[60] But in the interim, unofficial and official election results circulated quickly by telegraph, mail, or gossip and were published in local newspapers. One week after the election, the *Daily State Journal* reported that election returns indicated that Democrats would hold the state assembly, but Republicans would control the senate.[61] Results in the gubernatorial race remained too close to call, and unofficial county tallies changed almost daily as new information was received and old information was corrected. Three weeks after the election, each party claimed that its candidate for governor won the election, resulting in statewide confusion.

With results uncertain, attention turned to the election returns for Waupaca County. In late November, rumors circulated that not one but *two* localities had claimed to be the county seat and thus issued county canvass results.[62] Reporting on the scuttlebutt, the Republican-leaning *Daily State Journal* initially acknowledged "the possibility of an unfair state canvass" but declined to entertain it.[63] The

Excluded at the Polls: Wisconsin Women

I WILL VOTE

WHS IMAGE ID 5158

The issue of women's suffrage was raised during Wisconsin's 1846 constitutional convention only as a cruel joke. One member moved to eliminate the word "white" from a provision describing which persons could vote, whereupon another member moved to eliminate the word "male"—a proposal meant to mock Black and indigenous suffrage by leveling it with the "preposterous" notion of women's suffrage. Unsurprisingly, the issue of women's suffrage was not revived during the next constitutional convention in 1847. Later, in 1855, famed abolitionist and suffragist Lucy Stone lectured throughout the state and encouraged audience members to petition the legislature to amend the constitution to grant women the right to vote. Some listeners answered her call, but the state senator who received their petitions during the 1856 legislative session took no action. Wisconsin women would not exercise full suffrage until 1920.

Sources: Louise Phelps Kellogg, "The Question Box," *Wisconsin Magazine of History*, December 1919, 227–30; Theodora W. Youmans, "How Wisconsin Women Won the Ballot," *Wisconsin Magazine of History*, September 1921, 3–32.

paper then reversed this position overnight after the newspaper's editors were denied their request to view the election returns. Where the *Journal* had dismissed suspicions, it now freely aired them: "Is not public suspicion justly aroused? It is an unheard of thing that citizens are refused a sight of public papers deposited in the state offices."[64] Days later, the *Journal* went further, suggesting that "notorious political intriguers" had produced a windfall of late-arriving election returns from Waupaca County that suspiciously favored the Democratic incumbent.[65] By December 6, the *Journal* openly alleged fraud, reporting that unnamed individuals had made "mysterious visits and midnight prowlings" to Waupaca County with the aim of "fixing things."[66]

Compounding Republicans' suspicions was the fact that the state canvass rested entirely in Democratic hands. Secretary of State Alexander Gray, Attorney General George Smith, and State Treasurer Edward Janssen were all Democrats and "warm personal and political friends" of Barstow.[67] Together, these three men would determine and announce a winner in the gubernatorial contest. With so much on the line, and with so much ill will between them, Democrats and Republicans eyed each other with considerable distrust by the time the State Board of Canvassers met in mid-December. Finally, on December 17, the board made its much-awaited announcement. The incumbent, Democrat William Barstow, had eked out a victory over Republican Coles Bashford by a mere 157 votes—a significant departure from his 8,500 vote margin in the 1853 gubernatorial race.[68] Out of a total of 72,553 votes cast, Barstow had won 36,355 votes against Bashford's 36,198; Barstow had been duly elected governor for the ensuing term.[69] Would Wisconsinites—already alerted to the possibility of fraud—accept this result? And, if not, who had the power to resolve a disputed election?

III. DUELING INAUGURATIONS

As suspicion about the legitimacy of Barstow's reelection victory was spreading among Bashford's Republican supporters, the Democratic State Central Committee arranged for a military escort to accompany Barstow to and from his second swearing-in at the capitol.[70] The committee called companies from Watertown and Milwaukee to Madison, an invitation that prompted even the Barstow-sympathizing *Daily State Journal* to note dryly that "if these warlike preparations are made lest a justly incensed people interfere with the progress of unblushing corruption and fraud, they are unnecessary."[71] The troops rolled into the Milwaukee & Mississippi Railroad Company's West Madison Depot shortly after four o'clock in the afternoon on January 7, 1856. Reports of what happened next varied widely between the partisan newspapers that described the events of inauguration day.

According to the *Argus and Democrat*, the troops marched gallantly up Washington Avenue (now West Washington Avenue) to collect Barstow from his house a few blocks from the capitol. Three military brass bands joined the procession as Barstow climbed into a luxurious carriage that carried him and

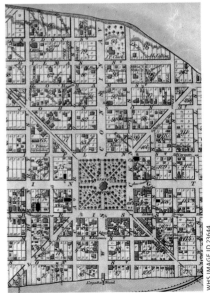

A military escort accompanied Barstow from his home to the capitol on the bitterly cold January day of his second swearing-in as governor.

several other state officers-elect back up to the capitol. Along the way, crowds of people stood at the roadside and raised cheer after cheer for their governor despite the bitter cold. In all, the *Argus* estimated that some 3,000 people had assembled to witness the spectacle.[72]

When Barstow and his party reached the capitol, cannons boomed in celebration. And after Barstow and his colleagues took turns being sworn in by a circuit court judge in the senate chambers, supporters crowded into the capitol called out loudly to each officer, asking him to say a few words. Governor Barstow's remarks were brief and unremarkable—he merely expressed gratitude for the honor of serving the people of Wisconsin in the executive office.[73] However, the state's new lieutenant governor, Arthur McArthur, was more expansive—and seemed ready to take aim at anyone doubting the election results. He and his fellow state officers came to the capitol that day "under the shadow of no intrigues" to assume the constitutional obligations that "the people had imposed upon them."[74] McArthur added for good measure that the inauguration that night "celebrated the rule of THE PEOPLE, *their* freedom, and *their* power."[75] After the officers were officially sworn into their seats, the capitol's stately halls remained open for hours, filled with people who danced and drank until well into the night.[76]

But papers that frequently sided with Republicans provided very different—and openly disdainful—accounts of Barstow's inauguration. According to the

In an example of newspaper partisanship, this cartoon, published in the Republican *Daily Wisconsin Patriot*, depicted Bashford flushing out Barstow's corrupt cronies with a hose.

Daily Wisconsin Patriot, the "frozen troops" who had accompanied Barstow to the capitol struggled through the streets "without order," vigorously rubbing their ears to ward off the cold in a gesture that the *Patriot* considered to be "the most military of their motions."[77] In its own biting account, the *Daily State Journal* described the soldiers pityingly, with "whiskers white with frost."[78] And as Barstow progressed toward the capitol, people "hurrahed repeatedly" for Bashford—not Barstow.[79]

To the "rub-a-dub of a single drum," the *Patriot* mocked, the "undisciplined rabble" made its way to the capitol.[80] And while Barstow took the governor's oath of office "amid the petty roar" of a miniature cannon, his military escort seemed more interested in drinking beer. The *Patriot* referred to Barstow as "little Bonaparte"—evoking the military leader who seized power over France by decidedly undemocratic means—and noted that he concluded his "usurpation" with a dance.[81] And by the end of the night, men with "rubicund countenances" who had come to the capitol to celebrate Barstow's inauguration "after copious drains upon the lager . . . slid down stairs on the bannisters."[82]

Given the highly partisan nature of newspapers in the mid-1800s, it is impossible to say with certainty whether Barstow's inauguration was a glorious celebration of the will of Wisconsinites or a cold and unruly affair. The truth may lie somewhere in between. But whatever the case, several hours before Barstow's inauguration, Coles Bashford slipped into the capitol for his own swearing-in ceremony. Only a few of Bashford's close associates had known that he would also be taking an oath to serve as Wisconsin's new governor that day. But word that the state's first Republican governor was going to be inaugurated "circulated with marvelous rapidity," and soon the Wisconsin Supreme Court Room "filled with spectators" who

Although the State Board of Canvassers had declared William Barstow the winner, Chief Justice Edward Whiton administered the oath of office to Coles Bashford, guaranteeing a dramatic confrontation.

Edward V. Whiton
1805–1859
Chief Justice – Supreme Court of Wisconsin, 1853–1859.

watched as Wisconsin Supreme Court Chief Justice Edward Whiton administered the governor's oath of office to Bashford.[83]

Chief Justice Whiton had previously served in Wisconsin's territorial legislature as a Whig, and since then, most Whigs—Bashford among them—had become Republicans. There is no way to know whether Whiton harbored any political agenda. However, the chief justice's personal history suggests that the state's laws—and the court established to interpret them—mattered more to him than the ascendance of any one political party. Whiton had codified Wisconsin's territorial laws, served on the state's first supreme court, and handed down that court's landmark decision regarding the Fugitive Slave Act.[84] As another justice later opined, "his history [became] the history of the bench itself."[85] Whatever motivation determined Whiton's decision to administer the oath of office to Bashford on the same day that Barstow would be sworn in, he would surely have understood that this decision would force a dramatic reckoning.

The next day, Bashford proceeded to the governor's executive chambers in the capitol to formally demand that Barstow give up his possession of the office. Barstow declined.[86]

But Bashford did not give up. Having confirmed that a polite request would not budge Barstow from the governor's office, he moved quickly to contest Barstow's right to the seat in the Wisconsin Supreme Court. On January 11, 1856, four days after the dual inaugurations, Bashford met with newly elected Attorney General William Smith in his office at the capitol to announce his intentions of contesting the election. Wisconsin law authorized Smith to challenge Barstow's right to the governorship by filing a *quo warranto* (Latin for "by what authority") action in the courts. Bashford and his attorneys believed that Smith, recently elected as a Democrat, would be favorable to Barstow's claim on the office. But they also hoped that Smith would decline to file Bashford's *quo warranto* action with the supreme court, thereby allowing Bashford's lawyers to file the action themselves. In the meantime, Bashford assented to Smith's request that he file his application for the *quo warranto* in writing.[87]

To this end, Bashford's attorneys drafted a lengthy document that alleged the falsifications of election results from six counties—Chippewa, Dunn, Monroe, Polk, Sheboygan, and Waupaca—from which the State Board of Canvassers had received suspiciously late-arriving returns.[88] The day after Bashford confronted Attorney General Smith, Smith attended a performance at Fairchild's Hall, a theater just blocks from the capitol that put on plays while the Wisconsin Legislature was in session.[89] That evening, one of Smith's companions gestured to a gentlemen at the entrance of their box. There stood attorney James Knowlton, who passed along a "packet of paper tied with tape," which Smith took before receding into

THE PRESS IN 1850S WISCONSIN

Throughout the nineteenth century, partisan newspapers proliferated across the United States. Starting in the 1830s, pioneering journalists in Wisconsin produced an array of papers that flattered the platforms and candidates of the political parties with which they were affiliated. In return, party and government officials in territorial Wisconsin often rewarded loyal newspaper editors with lucrative government printing contracts. In 1848, the adoption of article IV, section 25, of the state constitution sought to stop that practice by requiring that state printing contracts go to the lowest bidder. But as demonstrated by the insults that certain newspapers supporting Barstow and others supporting Bashford hurled back and forth vigorously, partisan journalism was still prevalent when the two men faced off in 1855.

the box.[90] This exchange likely attracted attention in the small theatre, which occupied a space of less than 1,500 square feet and catered to legislators.[91] In this conspicuous way, Bashford and his attorneys launched one of the most important legal proceedings in Wisconsin's history.

Attorney General Smith proceeded to file his own document with the supreme court. It stated that Barstow had "usurped, intruded into and unlawfully held and exercised" the office of governor "in contempt of the people of the State of Wisconsin" and that Barstow should "be made to answer" for his actions.[92] Yet, notably, Smith's brief made no mention of the instances of fraud that Bashford's counsel had detailed in their original application. To contemporary readers, Smith's language may seem harsh—as if he were abandoning party loyalties to accuse fellow Democrat Barstow of having stolen the governorship. But Bashford's lawyers recognized Smith's move as a politically motivated effort to control the proceedings and wrest any such control away from Bashford and his attorneys. By failing to describe any potential election tampering, the Democratic attorney general's filing almost certainly derailed the possibility of any substantive investigation into election fraud and thus hampered Bashford's ability to make his case. As a result, the court might have dismissed the case altogether.

For these reasons, Bashford and his attorneys asked the court if they could argue the case in lieu of the attorney general, who—they alleged—would seek only to delay or hinder the case. Speaking before the court on January 22, Knowlton stated that the information filed by Attorney General Smith was "calculated to delay and hinder [Bashford] in the prosecution of his rights."[93] Barstow's attorneys and Attorney General Smith, arguing on behalf of the state, objected—and the court found in their favor. The justices ruled that Bashford's counsel had no right to control the action or dictate the form of the information filed.[94] Smith represented the interests of the people of Wisconsin, and until he exhibited outright hostility to Bashford or failed to perform the duties that he assumed when he filed the information, the court would not interfere.[95]

Although Bashford's attorneys failed to convince the court on this point, they were correct in assuming that Barstow and his allies would attempt to delay the proceedings by any means possible.[96] After the court issued a summons ordering Barstow to appear on February 5, Barstow's counsel requested that the court bring the case to argument during the June term to give them enough time to prepare arguments.[97] Chief Justice Whiton denied the request, insistent that the case be brought to argument during the court's current term.[98] Whiton's colleague, Justice Abram Smith, stated that "no movement ought to be made for purposes of delay."[99]

Then, on February 2, Barstow's lead attorney, Jonathan Arnold, filed a formal motion to quash the summons and dismiss all proceedings based on the claim that the court had no jurisdiction to intervene in the contested election. Arnold also requested to delay proceedings for thirty days to prepare for the arguments concerning the court's jurisdiction, citing "the importance and novelty of the case" and "the weighty questions involved."[100] The court denied the request and fixed the date to hear the oral arguments on the dismissal motion for February 11, giving both sides just over a week to prepare.[101]

WHS IMAGE ID 118979

Attorney Jonathan Arnold argued that the Wisconsin Supreme Court could not intervene in contested elections—a challenge to the authority of the judicial branch.

As the case finally began, this friction between the contested governor and the court foreshadowed broader tensions between the executive and judicial branches themselves. The case was not just about who was the lawful governor, but about the authority of the state's courts and the wider balance of power in government.

IV. THE COURT'S AUTHORITY CHALLENGED

As their opening gambit, Barstow's counsel once again moved that the case be dismissed outright. In short, rather than argue their client's innocence against allegations of election fraud, they disputed the state supreme court's jurisdiction over any such allegations. This motion quickly transformed the case. Instead of only a dispute over the governorship, it became a dispute over the authority of the state supreme court. Could the court decide whether a governor legitimately held office? This question now eclipsed every other issue at stake in the case— including the alleged election fraud.

Towering figures in Wisconsin's legal world stood on both sides of the case.[102] Representing incumbent governor Barstow were Democrats Matthew Carpenter, Jonathan Arnold, and Harlow Orton.[103] Carpenter himself had been embroiled in a similar legal dispute months earlier: having lost his race for the office of Rock County District Attorney, Carpenter successfully argued that he had received more votes and that on this basis, a circuit court could overrule the canvassing board to determine the election's rightful winner.[104] Carpenter now set out to undermine his own claim, arguing that the supreme court could not decide the outcome of an election.[105]

Speaking on Bashford's behalf were attorneys James Knowlton, Timothy Howe, Alexander Randall, and Edward Ryan. Only three years earlier, Ryan had led the effort to impeach Supreme Court Justice Levi Hubbell in a trial akin to a "soap opera"[106] that tarnished the court's reputation.[107] Now he sought to elevate the court's standing. Although not a Republican, Ryan's deep-seated notion of "governmental integrity" trumped partisan politics.[108]

On February 11, Carpenter opened arguments by briefly summarizing the reasons the court should dismiss the case. Each branch of government, he explained, served as the "ultimate judge" of its members. Accordingly, the state supreme court could not determine the rightful governor: only the executive branch possessed this authority, and the governor and the executive branch were one and the same.[109]

Bashford's lawyers, including Edward G. Ryan, based their arguments on the theory of separation of powers, under which no man—even the governor—was above the law.

WHS IMAGE ID 24975

This argument departed from conventional notions of the separation of powers doctrine, wherein each of the three coequal branches of government acts independently but checks the powers of the other two branches. In Carpenter's estimation, the judicial branch was entitled to barely any power. Legal scholar Joseph Ranney notes that this position was "dated but by no means frivolous," as early Americans remained wary of powerful courts.[110] Carpenter and his colleagues frequently quoted Thomas Jefferson to illustrate the American founders' apparent mistrust of the judicial branch.[111]

In addition to the founders, Barstow's attorneys also alluded to European monarchs. Orton, for example, compared the governor to "a constitutional king"—"in him resides the power of the state, from him emanates the force of the state."[112] There was no distinction between the office of the governor and the man who occupied that office, Carpenter added. The constitution "breathed" executive power into Barstow, who "can no more separate himself from his official character than he can depart from his soul."[113] These points skirted dangerously close to theories of power that Americans had vehemently rejected in 1776 by declaring their independence from King George III of England.

Still, Barstow's attorneys continually referred to English and European history—rather than American history—to argue that the case against their client was unprecedented. To contemporary Americans, these frequent references to foreign, monarchical traditions might seem jarring in the context of a case about domestic democratic systems. But nineteenth-century lawyers in the United States regularly cited English case law and theory, and Barstow's legal team followed that tradition. No English court, Carpenter noted, had ever dethroned a monarch—although several had been violently overthrown.[114] He even suggested that violence was a more appropriate means to resolve disputes over executive authority. "What would Napoleon have done," Carpenter asked, if he had returned from battle and "found some jack-a-nape . . . calling himself Emperor?" Rather than "blubbering into a court of justice," Napoleon would have forcefully ejected the usurper.[115] Likewise, Bashford and his allies could unseat Barstow "only by force," because the Wisconsin Constitution provided no other solution.[116]

This proposition—that "might makes right"[117]—may have alarmed those in the courtroom who held faith in the rule of law. But Carpenter warned the court that its intervention in this case posed a more dangerous threat: "[I]f you remove Governor Barstow, you may remove any Governor, and place your friend or servant in his place."[118] On the basis of this precedent, he argued, nothing could stop a corrupt court from making the governor a mere extension of its power.

Bashford's counsel rejected these arguments and asserted the court's authority to intervene in the disputed election. The American founders, they said, envisioned a system of democracy that distributed power among three branches, each of which served as a check against the corruption of the other two.[119] This system did not concentrate "monstrous authority" in any one individual.[120] As Knowlton observed, the governor did not embody the executive branch, which could not "get drunk [or] go on a frolic" as he could.[121] No man—no matter his office or title—was above the law under the American system.

Bashford's attorneys argued that this new system likewise entitled all Wisconsinites to seek justice in the courts. To this point, Timothy Howe quoted article I, section 9, of the Wisconsin Constitution: "Every person is entitled to a certain remedy in the laws, for all injuries or wrongs which he may receive in his person, property, or character."[122] Just as the court could resolve a dispute between a landowner and a squatter, it could also offer a remedy to a candidate denied the office to which he had been elected.[123] Such an intervention posed no dangerous precedent, Howe argued. The court could not *make* Bashford governor: it could only "determine . . . his right to the office."[124] Such was the duty of the state supreme court as "the Court of last resort to determine to all time the rights of individuals and the State."[125] A fair process was all Bashford sought.

This process was a far cry from force, which was the only means of resolution that Barstow's attorneys had proposed. Addressing this point, Howe and his colleagues flatly rejected the notion that the framers of either the U.S. Constitution or the Wisconsin Constitution had intended for candidates to settle electoral disputes violently: "Revolutions have often been resorted to for the purpose of over-throwing governments, but never to get possession of an office under a government."[126] By deciding electoral disputes, the state supreme court could forestall chaos and assert order. Howe emphasized this point with his closing comment: "Here, we are to try our wager of law and not a wager of battle."[127]

These back-and-forth arguments on the motion to dismiss consumed three full days, interrupted only when the "trampling of feet" overhead—a rowdy group had gathered to address unrelated business in the assembly chambers above—drowned out the attorneys' arguments.[128] Although marathon in length, the arguments captured the attention of spectators and justices alike. Years later, Wisconsin Chief Justice John Bradley Winslow remarked admiringly on the "[t]rope and simile, metaphor and classic allusion, apt quotation and biting satire" that "abounded" in the attorneys' speeches.[129]

However, the ornate speeches from Barstow's counsel failed to sway the justices, who unanimously rejected the arguments brought forth by Barstow's counsel. On February 18, Chief Justice Whiton delivered the opinion of the court, which denied the motion to dismiss and affirmed the court's jurisdiction over the disputed election. After summarizing the questions before the court,

DECISIONS OF THE EARLY COURT

In the 1850s, the Wisconsin Supreme Court operated quite differently than it does today. The chief justice delivered the court's decision orally, and lawyers packed into the court to hear the ruling, since a written decision would not be published for weeks or months. To begin, the chief justice would state the facts of the case, which were usually "long, complicated and involved" but stated "without reference to any notes or memoranda." As Chief Justice John Bradley Winslow explained in 1912,

Chief Justice John Bradley Winslow, second from left, served on the court from 1891 to 1920 and published an extensive history of the court that included a chapter on the contested governorship.

WHS IMAGE ID 23436

"This marvelous exhibition of memory on the part of the chief justice was always a matter of wonder and of deep interest to the bar, and none of those who listened paid more rapt attention than his associates upon the bench." The other justices "made no sign by word or look" if they detected any error in the chief justice's delivery.

Source: John Bradley Winslow, *The Story of a Great Court; Being a Sketch History of the Supreme Court of Wisconsin, Its Judges and Their Times from the Admission of the State to the Death of Chief Justice Ryan* (Chicago, IL: T. H. Flood & Company, 1912), 61–62.

Whiton dismissed the notion that the governor alone should be the judge of his qualifications, finding no basis for this claim in either the constitution or the laws of the state. Instead, he cited article V, section 3, of the Wisconsin Constitution, which directly stated that the candidate receiving the highest number of votes from the qualified electors of the state must be elected governor.[130] On the basis of this clause, Barstow had "no legal right to the office" if he had not received the highest number of votes. Bashford, by contrast, had a "perfect right" to the office if it were proven that he received the highest number of votes.[131] The constitution established these rights, and the state supreme court simply enforced them as a "mere instrument" of the constitution.[132] By intervening in the disputed election, the court did not intrude on the powers of the executive branch, but rather was performing its duties and exercising the powers of the judicial branch as spelled out in the constitution.

By contrast, Governor Barstow had openly disobeyed the constitution, as Justice Smith noted in his concurring opinion. With his "bald, naked, successful usurpation of the office of governor," Barstow held office "in defiance of the constitution."[133] And in placing himself beyond the constitution, he forfeited any claim to its protection.

These statements represented a striking rebuke to Governor Barstow. Still, the justices chose their words carefully to avoid courting controversy—or worse. By this point, some observers feared that the situation would end in "armed conflict between the partisans of Barstow and Bashford."[134] Given this possible outcome, Justice Whiton framed the court's decision in conservative terms to minimize its "sweeping effect." The court intervened only out of solemn duty to the Wisconsin Constitution, and by no means relished in such an intervention.[135] Still, the court's work was not yet done. Having established its authority to do so, the court set out to answer the question before it: Who was the rightful governor of Wisconsin?

V. Wisconsin's rightful governor

After establishing its jurisdiction over the case, the court in late February directed both sides to present evidence supporting their client's claim to hold office as the rightful governor of Wisconsin. Whereas Bashford's attorneys welcomed this opportunity, Barstow's counsel consistently sought to wriggle out of this responsibility at every turn, and Barstow himself openly flouted the court's authority.

First, the governor's attorneys argued that they "ought not . . . be compelled to answer" to the court. The State Board of Canvassers had already determined the person elected governor, and on that basis, they argued, Barstow had lawfully assumed the governorship.[136] Asked to support this position, Barstow's attorneys stalled.[137] Only one of them, Harlow Orton, bothered to appear before the court when first ordered to do so. And even then, Orton felt "too weak to engage in the discussion alone" and requested a postponement.[138] Although Chief Justice Whiton initially relented,[139] his patience eventually wore thin. The court fixed March 8 as the final day for Barstow's counsel to prove their client's authority to serve as governor.[140]

When that day came, Barstow abruptly backed down. Standing before the court at ten o'clock in the morning on March 8, Matthew Carpenter announced to the court that Barstow had decided to withdraw from the case.[141] No evidence would be presented because none had been gathered. Instead, he delivered a letter from Barstow to the court.

In withdrawing, Barstow had not admitted defeat. Instead, he announced his intention to rebel against the judicial process rather than participate in it. He spelled out his intentions in the letter that Carpenter delivered to the court—but that the justices "refused to receive . . . on account of the indecent language in which it was couched."[142] Although the court refused to acknowledge this message, its contents circulated widely, since Barstow had enclosed it within another letter to the legislature.[143]

Barstow began by stating that he had hitherto cooperated out of respect for the court, although it had "no jurisdiction" over the dispute.[144] Now, however, the court seemed to demand his "full and unreserved submission"—which he summarily refused.[145] And, continuing in high dudgeon, he went on to formally protest the court's decision by announcing his "imperative duty to repel . . . any infringement upon the rights and powers which I exercise under the Constitution."[146]

Barstow would not speculate as to whether the court had been "reckless and partisan" or simply "misguided." But in his "warlike" communication, as historian Parker McCobb Reed later described it, Barstow denounced the court's decision as "a bold and dangerous assumption and usurpation of power."[147] He invited Wisconsinites to reject the court's decision, writing that "it is the duty of . . . every good citizen in the State to resist it to the last."[148] Moreover, he invited the legislature to reject the authority of the judicial branch and restore the "balance" of state government by asserting its own authority.[149]

To some observers, Barstow's letter implicitly promised "armed resistance" to any court decision declaring Bashford to be the rightful governor.[150] In it, he even seemed to entertain his attorneys' argument that force was the appropriate means to resolve the conflict. In fact, privately, Barstow briefly considered requesting the support of federal troops from U.S. President Franklin Pierce, but abandoned the plan as one likely to ruin his reputation.[151]

Arthur McArthur.

Born in Glasgow, Scotland, where he was educated; came to Milwaukee in 1848; elected city attorney for Milwaukee in '52; elected lieutenant-governor on the Democratic ticket in 1855; was acting governor four days after Barstow's resignation; he was elected circuit judge of the Milwaukee circuit in 1863, for the second time; appointed associate justice of the Supreme court for the District of Columbia by Gen. Grant, from which he retired in 1888, at the age of 73 years. He died in Washington in 1896.

WHS IMAGE ID 117534

In a last-ditch effort to prevent Bashford from becoming governor, Barstow resigned, whereupon Lieutenant Governor Arthur McArthur became governor—an office he held for four days.

Instead, Barstow settled on a more peaceful but still crafty scheme: he would resign, placing control of the governorship with a friend and fellow Democrat,

Lieutenant Governor Arthur McArthur. He predicted that the court would be inclined to drop the case, leaving control of the executive branch in Democratic hands.[152] On March 21, Barstow carried out this plan, resigning from office after serving only six weeks of his second term. In his resignation announcement, Barstow railed against the court case as an "extra-judicial proceeding" and characterized the eventual judgment against him as "a foregone conclusion."[153] Against this backdrop, he presented himself as sacrificing his own position for the safety of the state: "In this alarming and perilous emergency of the State government, the public demands a sacrifice, to save the State from the calamities of civil strife, and to preserve public peace."[154] Upon Barstow's resignation, Lieutenant Governor Arthur McArthur became the fourth Governor of Wisconsin.

Barstow was sorely mistaken: this peaceful transfer of power did not lay the case to rest. The court continued to hear evidence of election tampering on March 21 as if nothing had changed. In opening the proceedings, Chief Justice Whiton reminded Bashford's attorneys that "We assume the statement of the Board of Canvassers to be true, until it is disproved," but then proceeded as normal.[155] In subsequent days, Edward Ryan methodically set about casting suspicion on certain late-arriving election returns that materialized in mid-December 1855 and turned the tide of the election in Barstow's favor.

Most egregiously, Ryan began, certain late-arriving election returns came from nonexistent polling places. Although a town called Gilbert's Mill had produced 53 votes for Barstow and 14 for Bashford, the few inhabitants of the area—nearly all of them workers at Mr. Gilbert's sawmill—reported no knowledge of any election held there.[156] In fact, Mr. Gilbert himself said that "he thought of getting a poll established there, but he found his men would not vote to suit him, and he did not therefore procure it."[157] Casting further doubt on the authenticity of the returns, Representative Donald Cameron—whose district encompassed Gilbert's Mill and who had visited every voting precinct in his district before the election—had neither heard of the place nor any of the men who had signed its election returns.[158]

Late-arriving returns also came from parts of the state that were wholly uninhabited. One such place was referred to only as Township 25, near present-day Amherst. Representative Charles Burchard of Dodge said he had been "hunting up and locating land" in the area but had "neither saw nor heard of any settlers or improvement."[159] The county surveyor testified that the place was "uninhabited,"[160] and another witness described it as "a wilderness."[161] Still, the elusive inhabitants of Township 25 had managed to produce 83 votes for Barstow (and only seven votes for Bashford), edging Barstow ahead of Bashford in Waupaca County.[162] "I never heard there was any settlement in Town 25," witness Alfred Woodward said wryly, "until I heard about voting there," adding, "there used to be plenty of wolves there."[163] At this point, the justices pressed Ryan on whether it was possible that "men might camp out" in the wilderness and consequently vote there. To this Ryan quipped, "I do not see how there could be any voters, unless Mr. Woodward's wolves voted."[164]

Where polling places did exist, Ryan suggested that local election returns had been tampered with before they reached the State Board of Canvassers. To this end, he called firsthand witnesses of the local canvass. In Waupacca Village, for example, both the election and the canvass took place in Jeremiah Jones's tavern. Just before sundown, Jones stole a moment away from waiting tables to vote minutes before the polls closed. Then the canvass of votes began in his dining room. Later, as the dining room grew cold, Jones recalled, "[the canvassers] went

EARLY SETTLEMENT AND DISPLACEMENT

WHS IMAGE ID 3350

Depiction of Indians on Madeline Island, dated 1852.

In court, Coles Bashford's attorneys argued that certain supposed voting precincts were "uninhabited." But indigenous peoples had lived for centuries on lands that white settlers considered uninhabited or uninhabitable—catching fish, hunting game, and growing crops like corn and squash. Having survived the competition, disease, and displacement that began with the first arrival of Europeans in the Upper Midwest, Indians faced the U.S. government's aggressive attempts to "remove" them from Wisconsin and other Western territories in the nineteenth century. From the mid-1820s onward, the federal government often pressured Wisconsin tribes to cede their lands and sometimes forcefully relocated them altogether. Not satisfied with having dramatically circumscribed Native lands, the government later began a policy of allotment, i.e., dividing up tribal lands among individual members in a manner intended to "economically exploit Native lands and resources." Lands held by the Oneida tribe, for example, decreased by over 75 percent after the General Allotment Act of 1887.

Source: Patty Loew, *Indian Nations of Wisconsin: Histories of Endurance and Renewal* (Madison, WI: Wisconsin Historical Society Press, 2001).

Tabular Statement of the Votes polled for Governor, Lieutenant Governor, Secretary of State, Treasurer, State... Towns, Wards, and Election Precincts in the County of Waupaca, State of Wis...

NAME OF OFFICE.	GOVERNOR.			LIEUTENANT GOVERNOR.			SECRETARY OF STATE.			STATE T...
Towns, &c.	William A. Barstow.	Coles Bashford.	Scattering.	Arthur McArthur.	Charles C. Sholes.	Scattering.	David W. Jones.	Samuel D. Hastings.	Scattering.	Charles Kuehn.
Amherst	21	71		23	69			69	23	23
Belmont	4	19		4	19			19	4	4
Dayton	20	75		27	70			71	26	26
Farmington	58	41		58	42			43	58	59
Iola	1	28		2	27			27	2	2
Little Wolf	4	20		5	18			18	5	5
St. Lawrence	9	37		9	34			34	12	12
Scandinavia	63	28		63	29		1	29	62	63
Waupaca	543	59		544	58			56	545	555
	723	378		735	366		789	366	737	749
Precinct 25 RvE	83	7		84	6			84	6	90
	806	385		819	472			822	372	839

Before the court, Bashford's attorneys presented evidence that official election documentation—including the seals and tabular statement seen here—had been forged.

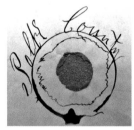

into the room where my wife and I slept." There, the election officials tallied votes until sunrise, and Jones periodically got up and "looked over their shoulders" to see how the candidates were faring.[165] After completing the canvass, election official John Chandler left behind some papers with the final tally: Barstow 288 to Bashford 219. To Jones' surprise, he read weeks later in the *Waupacca Spirit* that Barstow had won in Waupacca Village on a lopsided vote of 538 to 59.[166] Someone had meddled with the vote count before the final canvass by the State Board of Canvassers.

To this point, Ryan presented various proofs of amateurish forgery, directing the justices to closely examine certain returns with their magnifying glasses. "Though apparently written in a bold, free hand," Ryan noted, "they have been what is called *painted*, changing their original appearance."[167] Here, he drew attention to two copies of a document bearing the name "Henry Allen." On one copy, the name "Arthur Stewart" was faintly legible beneath "Henry Allen," despite apparent attempts to scratch it off with a knife. Neither name corresponded to a real person—but the forger had mistakenly employed two fictitious names in lieu of *one*, and sought to correct the error.[168]

Elsewhere, returns from disparate parts of the state bore suspicious similarities. Although purportedly produced one hundred miles apart, returns from Spring Creek and Gilbert's Mill contained identical errors—the word "inspector" had been scratched out and replaced with "clerk." Moreover, they were written on the same paper—stamped with the name "Plymouth"—and in the same handwriting. Or, as Ryan dramatically exclaimed to the court: "The same mistake, the same correction, and the same hand writing!"[169]

Though there were a variety of defects, all of these suspicious returns smiled more favorably on Barstow in comparison to the initial returns, which the state board received in the weeks immediately following the election. For example, the addition of supplemental returns for Spring Creek dramatically changed the total tally of votes in Polk County. Whereas the original tally stood at 42 votes for Barstow to seven votes for Bashford, Barstow shot ahead 149 to 20 with the addition of the late-arriving returns.[170]

Having presented all the evidence, Ryan concluded with some remarks on the significance of election tampering. He asserted that securing any office by this means—even the most humble elected office, like "fence-viewer or dog-killer"—constituted "a loud and crying insult to the public morality of the people of the State."[171] Using particularly colorful language, he proposed that it was far less offensive for someone to walk the streets naked than for a man "clothed with the ermine of office" to present himself in public "reeking with corruption and foul with vermin like this."[172] Finally, he noted that while he himself was practically "born a Democrat," the party had no future if it sacrificed all its principles.[173] For their part, Democrats disputed the testimony of witnesses like Jeremiah Jones as "puerile gossip."[174] However, in withdrawing from the case, Barstow and his attorneys had forfeited any opportunity to cross-examine the witnesses, challenge their credibility, and thereby undermine Ryan's narrative of election tampering.

The court adjourned on the evening of Friday, March 21, leaving Wisconsinites to wonder until Monday whether or how the court would weigh on the question of who was the rightful governor of Wisconsin. Some still feared that continued intervention on the court's part would provoke violence. In the wee hours of Monday, March 24, Justice Cole woke to "loud tapping at his window," finding a friend there "who seriously advised him not to go in with the court on the following day, as they would certainly be mobbed."[175]

At ten o'clock in the morning, Justice Cole delivered the opinion of the court and promised not to "say more than is required."[176] The decision began by referring at length to the statutes to underscore the fact that the election itself, not the board of canvassers, should determine the winner of an election. In this instance, Justice Cole continued, the state board had based its statement on election returns that were "wholly unauthorized"—and that turned the election in Barstow's favor.[177] The court declined to comment on whether such returns were "fraudulent." However, it concluded that if these returns were discounted, "the Relator was elected to the office of Governor by a plurality of votes."[178] More than four months after Wisconsin voters had cast their ballots, the court found that Republican Coles Bashford was the state's rightful governor.

In accordance with the court's judgment, Bashford strode into the capitol on March 25 to reclaim the governorship from Governor McArthur, who had occupied the executive chamber for less than a week. What transpired between the two men is not entirely clear. As they had done while covering Barstow's inauguration in January, leading partisan newspapers offered directly contradictory accounts. According to Republican papers, Bashford proudly and peacefully reclaimed his rightful position. Crowds of citizens—"unarmed, but strong in their reverence for justice"—gathered at the entrance of the capitol and followed Bashford into the building, packing into the rotunda and stairways.[179] Before these spectators, Bashford stated that he would take possession of the office "without the employment of force," and only by force "if necessary."[180] Inside, the "rush of people was so great," the *Daily State Journal* reported, that Bashford briefly shut the door of the executive chamber to converse with McArthur.[181] As they spoke privately, the *Daily Wisconsin Patriot* added, "anxious spectators" were soon joined by members of the senate, who took a recess to "to see the fun."[182] For nearly an hour, the "calm and quiet" crowd waited for someone—anyone—to emerge from the chamber.[183]

In sharp contrast to this triumphant scene, Democratic newspapers depicted a confrontation laden with the implicit threat of violence. According to the *Argus and Democrat*, a "mob of 50 to 60 men" followed on Bashford's heels as he marched to the executive office with a copy of the court's judgment and "demanded" possession of the office.[184] Blocking the doorway of the chamber, Bashford reportedly "threatened" to exercise the "force of the mob" to unseat MacArthur.[185]

On one point, all papers agreed: Governor McArthur made no last-ditch effort to remain in office. The prolonged fight to block Bashford from assuming office was officially over. As the *Argus and Democrat* explained, McArthur told Bashford that he had "no force for resistance" nor any "disposition to exercise it." He proceeded to sign a few bills and then "retired from the presence of *The Governor of the Supreme Court*."[186] Here, the paper took a sharp jab at Bashford, implying that the supreme court, rather than the electors themselves, had made him governor. Although Democrats had not managed to prevent the Republican from taking office, they would nevertheless seek to delegitimize him.

As if answering these attempts to undermine Bashford's authority, Republican papers depicted Wisconsin citizens as wholeheartedly embracing their new governor. According to the *Patriot*, members of the crowd rushed into the chamber following McArthur's departure, and "took the Governor by the hand, one by one" to congratulate him.[187] After Bashford dismissed them in order to get down to business, his admirers filed to the eastern end of the capitol, where they gave nine "long and loud cheers" which "moved the very night-caps of the old dome."[188]

In the coming days, legislators under "the old dome" would vote to recognize Bashford as the state's rightful governor and, in so doing, acknowledge the coequal authority of the judicial branch.[189] In the meantime, the people themselves signaled their acceptance of the supreme court's decision and the peaceful resolution to the crisis it had wrought. After the crowds at the capitol quietly dispersed, "bonfires were kindled" throughout Madison in a spontaneous celebration of Bashford's ascension.[190] According to the *Daily State Journal*, cheers for Bashford and his lawyers were so loud that people living as far as three miles from the city could distinctly hear them.[191] Accounts like these asserted Bashford's claim to represent the will of the people, as affirmed by the state supreme court.

Epilogue

Occurring at a time when political and social institutions in new frontier states were just beginning to emerge, the political crisis Wisconsin faced in 1855–56 could have played out differently. When the Bashford trial began in 1856, internecine warfare had already broken out in the Kansas territory over the issue of slavery. Even in well-established states like Rhode Island, where citizens formed a militia in 1842 to fight for broader voting rights, it was not uncommon for disputes over state and territorial law to end in bloodshed. In Wisconsin, either one of the state's two sworn-in governors could have mobilized troops to bring his opponent down. Alternatively, citizens could have taken to the streets to force Barstow or Bashford (or both) out of office, or the federal government could have intervened. Yet the political conflict and the lawsuit it triggered gave the Wisconsin Supreme Court an early opportunity to exercise the right to review the actions of other branches of government granted to it under the Wisconsin Constitution—and the court seized that opportunity. With its carefully considered ruling in *Bashford v. Barstow*, the court provided citizens with much needed stability and a clear path forward.

Bashford v. Barstow has become an essential touchstone in Wisconsin legal history. Like *Marbury v. Madison*, the 1803 U.S. Supreme Court case that affirmed the federal court's right of judicial review, the Wisconsin Supreme Court's ruling in *Bashford* clearly demonstrated the court's authority and, in the words of legal scholar Joseph Ranney, "permanently fixed the court's right to have the final say over interpretation of Wisconsin law."[192]

Any lawyer coming before the court or any justice sitting on the bench is likely to have pored over the ruling Chief Justice Whiton and his colleagues made in *Bashford v. Barstow*. For almost 160 years, the Wisconsin Supreme Court has cited important precedents set by the famous case in subsequent rulings. References to *Bashford* are a longstanding staple of state supreme court decisions in cases concerning election disputes. For example, the court's decision in *State ex rel McDill v. State Canvassers*, a case concerning canvass procedures, alluded to the near-sanctity of *Bashford*: "That decision, made, as it was, in a case of great public concern, and after the most mature deliberation by the court, we cannot overrule or disturb. Its influence in preserving the purity of the ballot box cannot well be overestimated."

The Wisconsin Supreme Court has also cited *Bashford* in rulings concerning the source of the court's authority and the powers of the legislative and executive departments. In *State v. Cannon* (1928), the court held that it possessed certain "inherent" powers, including the power to regulate its members' professional conduct. In his partial dissent, Justice Charles Crownhart firmly rejected this notion of inherent powers and, citing *Bashford*, reasoned that the powers of each branch of government flow from the constitution and nowhere else. As Crownhart observed, the *Bashford* ruling came at a time "shortly after our constitution was adopted, when its spirit pervaded the state." And so for Chief Justice Whiton and his colleagues, Crownhart continued, there was "no thought" of "inherent power outside the constitution," because the court "bottomed its power upon the constitution" and regarded it as its "efficient and only source of power."[193] Most recently, the court's holding in *SEIU v. Vos* (2020) referred to *Bashford* in its discussion of the separation of legislative and executive powers under the Wisconsin Constitution.

Wisconsin could have lost control of its new government in 1856, but instead, the ruling in *Bashford v. Barstow* allowed the state to resolve its first major political crisis through peaceful action and solidified the role of the court as a primary actor in Wisconsin's constitutional system. Justice Smith, rejecting Barstow's argument that the case could not go forward for lack of precedent, noted that the court already had a clear roadmap it could follow as it decided matters of great civic importance: the state constitution. That document, "adopted by the people of Wisconsin," was all the young state needed to continue finding its footing and forge its own path forward, Smith observed:

Let us then look to that constitution and endeavor to ascertain its true intent and meaning . . . [L]et it be remarked, that our conclusions must be guided and determined, not by theories of speculators upon the science of government, not by the opinion of jurists of other states reasoning upon philosophical abstractions or political postulates, but by the plain, simple, but authoritative and mandatory provisions of our own constitution.[194] 🔳

NOTES

1. "Wisconsin's Gala Day," *Weekly Argus and Democrat* (Madison, WI), January 15, 1856, 1.

2. "The Oath of Office, as Governor, Taken by Mr. Bashford," *Daily State Journal* (Madison, WI), January 8, 1856; "Another Scene in the Farce," *Weekly Argus and Democrat* (Madison, WI), January 15, 1856.

3. "Vote for Governor in General Elections Since 1848," *Wisconsin Blue Book* (Madison, WI: Wisconsin Legislative Reference Bureau, 2019), 476.

4. Joseph A. Ranney, *Wisconsin and the Shaping of American Law* (Madison, WI: The University of Wisconsin Press, 2017), 26.

5. Population figures drawn from the U.S. Census. See "Wisconsin," in chapter 10 of the U.S. Census (1940), 1157–80. https://www2.census.gov/library/publications/decennial/1940/population-volume-1/33973538v1ch10.pdf.

6. See "The People Who Came" in *Wisconsin: A Guide to the Badger State*, Writers' Program of the Works Projects Administration in the State of Wisconsin, comp., (New York: Duell, Sloan and Pearce, 1941), 46–50.

7. From William Hodges, June 11, 1856, *Letter, 1856*, SC 73, Wisconsin Historical Society, River Falls, WI, accessed from the UWDC State of Wisconsin Collection. http://digital.library.wisc.edu/1711.dl/WI.Hodges1i.

8. From Gunleik Asmundson Bondal, January 17, 1854, *Letter, 1854*, M94-396, Wisconsin Historical Society, Madison, WI, accessed from the UWDC State of Wisconsin Collection. http://digital.library.wisc.edu/1711.dl/WI.Bondal2m.

9. From Lucy Hastings, January 25, 1857, *Family correspondence, 1838, 1855–1874*, Eau Claire SC 35, Wisconsin Historical Society, accessed from the UWDC State of Wisconsin Collection. http://digicoll.library.wisc.edu/cgi-bin/WI/WI-idx?type=article&did=WI.Hastings1k.Hasti05&id=WI.Hastings1k&isize=M.

10. Lillian Krueger, "Social Life in Wisconsin: Pre-Territorial through the Mid-Sixties," *Wisconsin Magazine of History* 22 (December 1938), 156–76: 160.

11. Howard Feigenbaum, "The Lawyer in Wisconsin, 1836–1860: A Profile," *Wisconsin Magazine of History* 55, no. 2 (Winter, 1971–1972): 100–106, 103.

12. Wis. Rev. Stat. ch. 87 § 26 (1849).

13. William H. Seaman, speech, February 22, 1898, in *Report of the Meetings of State Bar*, 174–75. Quoted from the original in Ranney, *Wisconsin and the Shaping of American Law*, 25.

14. Ranney, *Shaping of American Law*, 25.

15. Ranney, 26. John Bradley Winslow, *The Story of a Great Court; Being a Sketch History of the Supreme Court of Wisconsin, Its Judges and Their Times from the Admission of the State to the Death of Chief Justice Ryan* (Chicago, IL: T. H. Flood & Company, 1912), 16.

16. Joseph A. Ranney, *Trusting Nothing to Providence: A History of Wisconsin's Legal System* (Madison, WI: University of Wisconsin Law School, Continuing Education and Outreach, 1999), 78.

17. Winslow, *Story of a Great Court*, 103.

18. Robert Booth Fowler, *Wisconsin Votes: An Electoral History* (Madison, WI: University of Wisconsin Press, 2008), 16.

19. Ranney, *Shaping of American Law*, 16–17. For a longer discussion of Western farmers' opposition to the plantation system and enslaved labor generally, see Adam Wesley Dean, "A Question of Slavery in the West" in *An Agrarian Republic: Farming, Antislavery Politics, and Nature Parks in the Civil War Era* (Chapel Hill, NC: University of North Carolina Press, 2016), 11–39.

20. Michael J. McManus, "'Freedom and Liberty First, and the Union Afterwards': State Rights and the Wisconsin Republican Party, 1854–1861," in David W. Blight and Brooks D. Simpson, eds., *Union & Emancipation: Essays on Politics and Race in the Civil War Era* (Kent, OH: Kent State University Press, 1997), 34.

21. McManus, "Freedom and Liberty First," 38–39. For a useful discussion of the case, see the Wisconsin Courts' summary of it. "In Re: Booth," *Famous Cases of the Supreme Court*, Wisconsin Court System, accessed October 16, 2020. https://www.wicourts.gov/courts/supreme/docs/famouscases01.pdf.

22. McManus, "Freedom and Liberty First," 40.

23. Richard N. Current, *The History of Wisconsin*, vol. 2, *The Civil War Era, 1848–1873* (Madison, WI: Wisconsin Historical Society Press, 2013), 197–230.

24. For a concise and helpful summary of the Kansas-Nebraska Act and its effect on Wisconsin politics, see Fowler, *Wisconsin Votes*, 15–16.

25. Fowler, *Wisconsin Votes*, 20–22. On the emergence of the Republican Party around opposition to slavery, see McManus, "Freedom and Liberty First."

26. "William Augustus Barstow" in *Portrait and Biographical Album of Racine and Kenosha Counties, Wisconsin* [. . .] (Chicago, IL: Lake City Publishing, 1892), 134.

27. "William Augustus Barstow," 133–34.

28. "Wisconsin's Former Governors" in M. G. Toepel and Hazel L. Kuehn, eds., *The Wisconsin Blue Book* (Madison, WI: State of Wisconsin, 1960), 80–82.

29. *Wisconsin Blue Book 2019–2020* (Madison, WI: Wisconsin Legislative Reference Bureau, 2019), 476.

30. "Wisconsin's Former Governors," in *The Wisconsin Blue Book* (Madison: State of Wisconsin, 1960), 80–82.

31. Current, *The History of Wisconsin*, 225.

32. *Portrait and Biographical Album of Rock County, Wisconsin* [. . .] (Chicago, IL: Acme Publishing, 1889), 137.

33. "Wisconsin's Former Governors," in M. G. Toepel and Hazel L. Kuehn, eds., *The Wisconsin Blue Book* (Madison: State of Wisconsin, 1960), 88–90; "Serving the State: Wisconsin Legislators, 1848–2019," Wisconsin History Project 1, no. 1 (Madison, WI: Wisconsin Legislative Reference Bureau), April 2019.

34. Current, *History of Wisconsin*, 225.

35. Tyler Anbinder, *Nativism and Slavery: The Northern Know Nothings and the Politics of the 1850s* (New York: Oxford University Press, 1992), 54.

36. Jennifer Depew, "'The Glorious American Banner Floating High Above the Ramparts': The Rise and Fall of Know-Nothingism in Wisconsin," *Oshkosh Scholar* 13 (December 2018): 8–9; "Lynch Law in Wisconsin," *New York Times*, August 16, 1855.

37. Current, *History of Wisconsin*, 226.

38. Current, *History of Wisconsin*, 226.

39. See, generally, Anbinder, *Nativism and Slavery*; Bruce Levine, "Conservatism, Nativism, and Slavery: Thomas R. Whitney and the Origins of the Know-Nothing Party," *Journal of American History* 88, no. 2 (Sept. 2001), 455–488.

40. "Sticking to It," *Weekly Argus and Democrat* (Madison, WI), October 23, 1855.

41. "Mass Meeting," *Sauk Co. Democrat* (Baraboo, WI), October 11, 1855.

42. "One Week More," *Tribune* (Mineral Point, WI), October 30, 1855.

43. "Rich Developments—K.N. Mevements," *Daily State Journal* (Madison, WI), August 21, 1855.

44. "Coles Bashford," *Waupaca Spirit* (Waupaca, WI), October 9, 1855.

45. "Know Nothingism," *Democratic Standard* (Janesville, WI), October 10, 1855.

46. Michael J. McManus, *Political Abolitionism in Wisconsin, 1840–1861* (Kent, OH: Kent State University Press, 1998), 252.

47. Fowler, *Wisconsin Votes*, 4–7.

48. Robert Carrington Nesbit and William F. Thompson, *Wisconsin: A History* (Madison, WI: University of Wisconsin Press, 2004), 239. See also McManus, *Political Abolitionism in Wisconsin*, 252.

49. Depew, "The Glorious American Banner," 12; Current, *History of Wisconsin*, 227.

50. Wis. Rev. Stat. ch. 6, § 26 (1849).

51. Richard Franklin Bensel, *The American Ballot Box in the Mid-Nineteenth Century* (New York: Cambridge University Press, 2004), 9–15.

52. Roy G. Saltman, *The History and Politics of Voting Technology: In Quest of Integrity and Public Confidence* (New York: Palgrave MacMillan, 2006). For more on the "ticket" system, see Bensel, American Ballot Box, 15–16, 30.

53. Wis. Rev. Stat. ch. 6, § 29 (1849).

54. Jon Grinspan, *The Virgin Vote: How Young Americans Made Democracy Social, Politics Personal, and Voting Popular in the Nineteenth Century* (Chapel Hill, NC: University of North Carolina Press, 2016), 66.

55. Wis. Rev. Stat. ch. 6, §§ 20–24 (1849).

56. These procedures are described under Wis. Rev. Stat. ch. 6, §§ 38–42 (1849).

57. Wis. Rev. Stat. ch. 6, §§ 47–48 (local canvass), ch. 6, §§ 51–52 (county canvass), ch. 6, §§ 67 (district canvass) (1849).

58. Wis. Rev. Stat. ch. 6 § 56 (1849).

59. Wis. Rev. Stat. ch. 6 § 79 (1849).

60. "The State Canvass," *Daily State Journal* (Madison, WI), December 18, 1855.

61. "The Legislature," *Daily State Journal* (Madison, WI), November 13, 1855.

62. "The Result of the Governor," *Daily State Journal* (Madison, WI), November 21, 1855.

63. "The Election News—Who Will Be Our Governor," *Daily State Journal* (Madison, WI), November 24, 1855.

64. "The Insolence of Office," *Daily State Journal* (Madison, WI), November 25, 1855.

65. "Waupaca County," *Daily State Journal* (Madison, WI), December 1, 1855.

66. "The Election Frauds in Waupacca County," *Daily State Journal* (Madison, WI), December 6, 1855.

67. Parker McCobb Reed, *The Bench and the Bar of Wisconsin: History and Biography, with Portrait Illustrations*, (Milwaukee, WI): P.M. Reed (1882), 481.

68. Barstow received 30,405 votes out of 55,683, over 8,500 votes more than his opponent. *Wisconsin Blue Book 2019–2020* (Madison, WI: Wisconsin Legislative Reference Bureau, 2019), 476.

69. See James R. Donoghue, *How Wisconsin Voted, 1848–1960* (Madison, WI: Bureau of Government, University of Wisconsin, 1962); Fowler, *Wisconsin Votes*.

70. "Inauguration of the State Officers," *Weekly Argus and Democrat* (Madison, WI), January 15, 1856.

71. "Barstow Celebration—The 'Milingtary,'" *Daily State Journal* (Madison, WI), January 1, 1856.

72. "Inauguration of the State Officers."

73. "Inauguration of the State Officers."

74. "Inauguration of the State Officers."

75. "Inauguration of the State Officers."

76. "Inauguration of the State Officers."

77. "The Barstow Pow-Wow," *Daily Wisconsin Patriot*, January 9, 1856.

78. "The Barstow Celebration Yesterday—The Military and the Festival," *Daily State Journal* (Madison, WI), January 8, 1856.

79. "Barstow Celebration Yesterday."

80. "Barstow Pow-Wow."

81. "Barstow Pow-Wow."

82. "Barstow Pow-Wow."

83. "The Oath of Office, as Governor, Taken by Mr. Bashford," Daily State Journal (Madison, WI), January 8, 1856.

84. "Justice Edward V. Whiton," Wisconsin Court System, accessed October 14, 2020, https://www.wicourts.gov/courts/supreme/justices/retired/whiton.htm. See also Winslow, "Personal Recollections of Whiton by Henry M. Lewis," in *Story of a Great Court*, 13–16, 59–66, 76–77. See also "Obituary: Chief Justice Edward Vernon Whiton"

in Abram Smith, *Reports of Cases Argued and Determined in the Supreme Court of the State of Wisconsin, Before June Term, 1859* (Madison: Atwood, Rublee & Reed, 1860), v–xiii.

85. Winslow, *Story of a Great Court*, 13.

86. *Biographical Album of Rock County*, 138.

87. Coles Bashford, *The Trial in the Supreme Court, of the Information in the Nature of a Quo Warranto Filed by the Attorney General, on the Relation of Coles Bashford vs. Wm. A. Barstow, Contesting the Right to the Office of Governor of Wisconsin* (Madison, WI: Calkins & Proudfit, and Atwood & Rublee, 1856), 31.

88. Bashford, *Trial in the Supreme Court*, 12–20.

89. David Mollenhoff, *Madison: A History of the Formative Years* (Madison, WI: University of Wisconsin Press, 2003), 22.

90. Bashford, *Trial in the Supreme Court*, 23.

91. Henry C. Youngerman, "Theater Buildings in Madison Wisconsin, 1836–1900," *Wisconsin Magazine of History*, March 1947, 274–5.

92. Bashford, *Trial in the Supreme Court*, 10.

93. Bashford, 9.

94. Bashford, 36–37.

95. Bashford, 37.

96. Reed, *Bench and the Bar*, 489.

97. Bashford, *Trial in the Supreme Court*, 39.

98. Bashford, 39.

99. Bashford, 39.

100. Bashford, 40.

101. Bashford, 40.

102. Nearly every last one of them became a state supreme court justice, governor, or U.S. senator. Ranney, *Trusting Nothing to Providence*, 84.

103. Ranney, 84.

104. These arguments proved successful before a circuit court and were eventually affirmed by the Wisconsin Supreme Court in June 1856. Carpenter v. Ely, 4 Wis. 420 (1856).

105. Current, *History of Wisconsin*, 228.

106. Ranney, *Trusting Nothing to Providence*, 81.

107. Ranney, *Shaping of American Law*, 28.

108. Ranney, *Trusting Nothing to Providence*, 84.

109. Bashford, *Trial in the Supreme Court*, 45.

110. Ranney, *Shaping of American Law*, 28.

111. See, for example, Bashford, *Trial in the Supreme Court*, 51, 78, 82.

112. Bashford, 75–76.

113. Bashford, 55.

114. Bashford, 43–44.

115. Bashford, 65.

116. Bashford, 85. See also, Bashford, 117.

117. Ranney, *Shaping of American Law*, 86.

118. Bashford, *Trial in the Supreme Court*, 53.

119. Bashford, 104.

120. Bashford, 101.

121. Bashford, 94.

122. Bashford, 107; Wis. Const. art. I, § 9 (1849).

123. Bashford, *Trial in the Supreme Court*, 100.

124. Bashford, 109.

125. Bashford, 72.

126. Bashford, 99.

127. Bashford, 110.

128. Bashford, 105.

129. Winslow, *Story of a Great Court*, 103.

130. Attorney Gen. ex rel. Bashford v. Barstow, 4 Wis. 567, 672 (1856).

131. Bashford at 672.

132. *Id.* at 672.

133. *Id.* at 677.

134. Winslow, *Story of a Great Court*, 107.

135. Ranney, *Shaping of American Law*, 29.

136. Bashford, *Trial in the Supreme Court*, 144–45.

137. Bashford, 161.

138. Bashford, 160.

139. Bashford, 162.

140. Bashford, 225.

141. Bashford, 226.

142. Bashford, 226.

143. Reed, *Bench and the Bar*, 487.

144. Bashford, *Trial in the Supreme Court*, 360.

145. Bashford, 361.

146. Bashford, 362.

147. Reed, *Bench and the Bar*, 487.

148. Bashford, 362.

149. Bashford, 362.

150. Winslow, *Story of a Great Court*, 105.

151. Ranney, *Trusting Nothing to Providence*, 86–87; Reed, *Bench and the Bar*, 490.

152. Reed, *Bench and the Bar*, 490.

153. Bashford, *Trial in the Supreme Court*, 363–64.

154. Bashford, 364.

155. Bashford, 288.

156. Bashford, 292–93.

157. Bashford, 330.

158. Bashford, 331–32.

159. Bashford, 319.

160. Bashford, 314.

161. Bashford, 319.

162. Bashford, 312.

163. Bashford, 327.

164. Bashford, 328.

165. Bashford, 320–321.

166. Bashford, 323.

167. Bashford, 295.

168. Bashford, 298.

169. Bashford, 297–300.

170. Bashford, 298.

171. Bashford, 342.

172. Bashford, 343.

173. Bashford, 343.

174. "The Evidence," *Weekly Argus and Democrat* (Madison, WI), March 25, 1856.

175. Reed, *Bench and the Bar*, 490.

176. Bashford, 344.

177. Bashford, 352.

178. Bashford, 353.

179. "Governor Bashford Instated," *Daily State Journal* (Madison, WI), March 26, 1856.

180. "Governor Bashford Instated."

181. "Governor Bashford Instated."

182. "The Finale of the Finality," *Daily Wisconsin Patriot*, March 26, 1856.

183. "Governor Bashford Instated," *Daily State Journal*, March 26, 1856.

184. "'Gov' Bashford in Office," *Weekly Argus and Democrat* (Madison, WI), April 1, 1856, 1.

185. "'Gov' Bashford in Office."

186. "'Gov' Bashford in Office."

187. "'Gov' Bashford in Office."

188. "'Gov' Bashford in Office."

189. The senate recognized Bashford on March 25, and after some deliberation, the Democrat-controlled assembly voted to recognize him on March 27 by a vote of 37 to 9. "The Matter Ended," *Daily Wisconsin Patriot*, March 27, 1856.

190. "A Popular Demonstration," *Daily State Journal* (Madison, WI), March 27, 1856.

191. "A Popular Demonstration."

192. Ranney, Shaping of American Law, 29.

193. State v. Cannon, 196 Wis. 534 at 543–45 (1928).

194. Attorney Gen. ex rel. Bashford v. Barstow, 4 Wis. 567, 785 (1856).

Elections in Wisconsin

Purposes and days

Wisconsin holds elections for a variety of purposes and, depending on the purpose, on a variety of days.

FILLING THE STATE'S ELECTIVE OFFICES

To fill its elective offices, Wisconsin holds elections on four regular election days.

The general election. On the Tuesday after the first Monday in November of every even-numbered year, Wisconsin elects individuals to fill its partisan elective offices. The elections held on this day are referred to collectively as the "general election."

The partisan offices in Wisconsin are U.S. senator, U.S. representative, state senator, state representative, governor, lieutenant governor, attorney general, secretary of state, state treasurer, and the county-level offices of district attorney, county clerk, sheriff, clerk of circuit court, register of deeds, treasurer, coroner (in counties that have one), and surveyor (in counties in which the office is elective).

The voters of the entire state elect Wisconsin's U.S. senators, governor, lieutenant governor, attorney general, secretary of state, and state treasurer. The voters of each congressional, senate, and assembly district elect that district's U.S. representative, state senator, or state representative. The voters of each county elect that county's clerk, sheriff, clerk of circuit court, register of deeds, treasurer, coroner, and surveyor and the district attorney for the prosecutorial unit serving the county. (For the prosecutorial unit that serves Menominee and Shawano Counties, the voters of both counties elect the district attorney.)

The terms of office for the partisan offices are not all the same length and do not all expire on the same day or in the same year. Accordingly, only some of the partisan offices will be up for election at any particular general election—those, namely, for which the currently running term of office will expire before the next general election is held.

The ballot at each general election lists the offices that are up for election and, under each office, the candidates for the office who have qualified to be listed. Next to each candidate's name, the ballot lists the name of the political party or, in the case of an independent candidate with no party affiliation, the principle that the candidate represents.

An individual who wishes to be listed as a candidate on the ballot must file, no later than the June 1 preceding the general election, 1) a declaration of candidacy indicating the office that the individual seeks and the political party or the principle that he or she proposes to represent and 2) nomination papers signed by a statutorily required number of voters residing in the governmental jurisdiction or election district that the office serves. In addition, the individual must win a partisan primary election if he or she proposes to represent one of the "recognized" political parties (see below). By contrast, an individual who does not propose to represent a recognized political party will be listed on the general election ballot without participating in a partisan primary election. Such an individual is called an "independent candidate."

The candidate who receives the most votes cast for a particular office at the general election fills that office when the currently running term of office expires.

The partisan primary. Prior to the general election, on the second Tuesday in August of every even-numbered year, Wisconsin holds primary elections to select the individuals who will be listed on the general election ballot as the candidates of the "recognized" political parties. The elections held on this day are referred to collectively as the "partisan primary."

A political party qualifies as a recognized political party in one of three situations:

- A candidate of the political party won at least 1 percent of the votes cast in Wisconsin, either for a statewide office at the last general election at which the office of governor was up for election or for U.S. president at the most recent general election, and the political party was a recognized political party for that election.
- An individual representing the political party as an independent candidate won at least 1 percent of the votes cast in Wisconsin, either for a statewide office at the last general election at which the office of governor was up for election or for U.S. president at the most recent general election, and the political party requests recognized status no later than the April 1 preceding the partisan primary.
- The political party submits, no later than the April 1 preceding the partisan primary, a petition requesting recognized status signed by at least 10,000 Wisconsin voters, including at least 1,000 from each of at least three congressional districts.

The ballot at the partisan primary is divided into sections, one for each recognized political party. Each party's section lists all of the offices that will be filled at the general election and, under each office, the individuals, if any, who have filed to be candidates for the office and have proposed, in their declarations of candidacy, to represent the party. A voter at the partisan primary can mark votes in only one of these ballot sections, but can pick any section for this purpose—voters in Wisconsin are not asked to declare a party affiliation when registering or voting and are not obliged in any other way to pick a particular party's section.

However, if a voter marks votes in more than one of the party sections, none of the voter's votes will be counted.

The individual who receives the most votes cast for a particular office in the ballot section for a particular party becomes that party's candidate for that office at the general election, and his or her name, together with the party's name, will be listed under the office on the general election ballot.

The partisan primary is the exclusive means by which a recognized political party can select a candidate to be listed on the general election ballot. The party must accept as its candidate the individual selected by the voters who vote on its section of the partisan primary ballot. Moreover, if no individual is listed under a particular office in that section (because no one who filed to be a candidate for the office proposed to represent that party), the party will not have a candidate for that office listed on the general election ballot.

The spring election. On the first Tuesday in April of every year, Wisconsin elects individuals to fill its nonpartisan elective offices. The elections held on this day are referred to collectively as the "spring election."

The nonpartisan offices in Wisconsin are state superintendent of public instruction; supreme court justice; court of appeals judge; circuit court judge; county executive (in counties that have one); county supervisor; county comptroller (in Milwaukee); every elective town, village, and city office; and school board member.

The voters of the entire state elect Wisconsin's state superintendent of public instruction and supreme court justices. The voters of each court of appeals district elect that district's judges. The voters of each county elect the county's county executive (if any) and county comptroller (in Milwaukee) and the circuit court judges for the circuit that serves the county. (For circuits that serve two counties, the voters of both counties elect the circuit court judges.) The voters of each county supervisory district elect that district's county supervisor. The voters of each town elect that town's officers. Village trustees and city alders can be elected at large by the voters of the entire village or city or from election districts by the voters residing in each election district. All other village and city officers are elected at large by the voters of the entire village or city. School board members can be elected at large by the voters of the entire school district, from election districts by the voters residing in each election district, or from election districts by the voters of the entire school district.

Just as with the partisan offices, the terms of office for the nonpartisan offices are not all the same length and do not all expire on the same day or in the same year. At each spring election, accordingly, the only nonpartisan offices up for election are those for which the currently running term of office will expire before the next spring election is held.

The ballot at each spring election lists the offices that are up for election and, under each office, the candidates for the office who have qualified to be listed. Ordinarily, no more than two candidates can be listed. The situation is different, however, when multiple, undifferentiated instances of the same office exist in a particular governmental jurisdiction or election district. In many villages, for example, the trustees who make up the village board are elected at large rather than from election districts, and no distinction is made between the "seat" occupied by one trustee and the "seat" occupied by another. In this situation, the ballot can list up to twice as many candidates for an office as the number of seats to be filled. The ballot would also include an instruction to vote for no more of those candidates than the number of seats to be filled.

An individual who wishes to be listed as a candidate on the ballot must file, no later than the first Tuesday in the January preceding the spring election, 1) a declaration of candidacy indicating the office that the individual seeks and 2) nomination papers signed by a required number of voters residing in the governmental jurisdiction or election district that the office serves. In addition, the individual must win a spring primary election (see below) if the total number of individuals who file to be candidates for the office is more than two or, if applicable, is more than twice the number of seats to be filled. By contrast, if the total number of individuals is less than two, or is less than twice the number of seats to be filled, each individual will be listed on the spring election ballot without participating in a spring primary election.[1]

The candidate who receives the most votes cast for a particular office at the spring election fills that office when the currently running term of office expires. If multiple seats are to be filled for a particular office, the candidates equal in number to the number of those seats who receive the most votes fill those seats when the currently running term of office expires.

The spring primary. Prior to the spring election, on the third Tuesday in February of every year, Wisconsin holds primary elections to select, for some of the offices that will be filled at the spring election, the individuals who will be listed as candidates on the spring election ballot. The elections held on this day are referred to collectively as the "spring primary."

The ballot at the spring primary lists only those offices for which more than two individuals or, if applicable, more individuals than twice the number of seats to be filled have filed to be candidates and, under each office, the individuals who have filed to be candidates for the office. The ballot also includes for each office an instruction to vote for not more than one individual or for not more individuals than the number of seats to be filled.

The two individuals, or the individuals equal in number to twice the number of seats to be filled, who receive the most votes cast for an office at a spring primary election will be listed as the candidates for that office on the spring election ballot.

ELECTING THE U.S. PRESIDENT AND VICE PRESIDENT

As part of the process by which the United States elects its president and vice president, Wisconsin holds two elections, each on one of the regular election days just discussed.

At the spring election. On the day of the spring election, in presidential election years, Wisconsin conducts its presidential preference primary.

This primary is advisory, rather than binding. Wisconsin's voters indicate which individual they would like a political party to select as its candidate for U.S. president, but Wisconsin law does not require the party's Wisconsin members to vote for that individual at the party's national convention. Rather, the party conducts its convention according to rules that it determines for itself, and it can select its presidential candidate using any mechanism it chooses.

A political party qualifies to participate in Wisconsin's presidential preference primary only if 1) it was a recognized political party (see above, page 332) at Wisconsin's last general election, 2) it had a candidate for governor at that election, and that candidate won at least 10 percent of the votes cast for that office, and 3) its state chair certifies to the Elections Commission, no later than the second Tuesday in the December preceding the presidential preference primary, that the party will participate.

The spring election ballot includes a separate section for the presidential preference primary of each participating political party. Each party's section lists the individuals who wish to be selected as the party's candidate for president and have qualified to be listed.

An individual can qualify to be listed on the ballot as a candidate in a party's presidential preference primary in two ways. The individual can be certified by a special committee that meets in the state capitol on the first Tuesday in the January preceding the presidential preference primary. This committee consists of the state chair, one national committeeman, and one national committeewoman of each participating political party; the speaker and the minority leader of the state assembly; the president and the minority leader of the state senate; and an additional member selected by the rest of the committee to be its chair. The committee identifies, for each of the participating political parties, the individuals who are generally recognized in the national media as the party's candidates for U.S. president and any additional individuals that the committee believes should be included as candidates on the party's ballot list. The committee must certify these candidates to the Elections Commission no later than the Friday following its meeting.

Alternatively, an individual can submit to the Elections Commission, no later than the last Tuesday in January, a petition requesting to be listed as a candidate in a party's presidential preference primary. The petition must be signed by a required number of voters from each of Wisconsin's congressional districts.

A voter at the spring election can cast votes in the presidential preference primary of just one of the participating political parties. As at the partisan primary, the voter can pick any party's section on the ballot to vote on and is not obliged, based on party affiliation or any other criteria, to pick the section of a particular party.

At the general election. In presidential election years, on the day of the general election, Wisconsin elects the slate of presidential electors that will be its delegation to the Electoral College, the nationwide body that actually elects the U.S. president and vice president.

The ballot at the general election does not list slates of would-be presidential electors. Rather, it lists the pairs of candidates who are running together, one for president and one for vice president, and who have qualified to be listed. Each of these candidate pairs has its own slate of would-be presidential electors, and a vote cast for a candidate pair is simultaneously a vote cast for its slate.

A pair of individuals can qualify to be listed on the general election ballot as candidates for U.S. president and vice president in two ways. They can be selected by a recognized political party (see above, page 332) to be its candidates. Each recognized political party selects its candidates at a national convention of party members conducted according to rules that the party determines for itself. The pair of individuals that a recognized political party selects will be listed on the general election ballot if 1) the party's state or national chair certifies to the Elections Commission, no later than the first Tuesday in the September preceding the general election, that the individuals are the party's candidates and 2) each of the individuals files a declaration of candidacy with the Elections Commission by the same deadline.

Alternatively, a pair of individuals can qualify to be listed as independent candidates. To do this, each of the individuals must file with the Elections Commission, no later than the first Tuesday in the August preceding the general election, a declaration of candidacy indicating the office that he or she seeks and the political party or principle that he or she proposes to represent, and the two individuals jointly must file nomination papers, signed by a required number of Wisconsin voters, nominating them as a pair.

The slate of presidential electors for each candidate pair must consist of ten individuals, one from each of Wisconsin's eight congressional districts and two more from anywhere in the state.

A slate can be determined in two ways. For the candidates of the recognized political parties, the slates are determined at a special convention held at the state capitol on the first Tuesday in the October preceding the general election. The convention consists of certain officials holding partisan elective offices in state government—the governor, lieutenant governor, attorney general, secretary of state, state treasurer, and those state senators whose seats are not up for election—together with the individuals who will be listed on the general election ballot as the candidates of the recognized political parties for the offices of state senator and state representative. The convention participants meet separately according to the parties they belong to, and each party designates a slate of presidential electors for its pair of candidates for president and vice president. The state chair of each party then certifies that party's slate to the Elections Commission.

By contrast, each pair of independent candidates for U.S. president and vice president designates its own slate of presidential electors in its nomination papers.

The slate of presidential electors of the candidate pair that wins the most votes at Wisconsin's general election becomes Wisconsin's delegation to the Electoral College. On the Monday after the second Wednesday in the December following the general election, this delegation assembles in the state capitol and casts its votes as members of that body.

FILLING A MIDTERM VACANCY

A "special election" can be held to fill a midterm vacancy in certain elective offices. This kind of election can be held on one of the four regular election days or on a different day.

A vacancy in the office of U.S. senator, U.S. representative, state senator, or state representative can be filled only by a special election called by the governor. A vacancy in the office of attorney general, state superintendent of public instruction, secretary of state, or state treasurer can be filled either by a special election called by the governor, if the vacancy occurs more than six months before the term of office expires, or by appointment by the governor, regardless of when the vacancy occurs. (A vacancy in the office of supreme court justice, court of appeals judge, circuit court judge, district attorney, sheriff, coroner, or register of deeds can be filled only by appointment by the governor.) In some county and municipal offices, a vacancy can be filled either by special election or by appointment, at the discretion of the local governing body.

An individual who wishes to be listed as a candidate on a special election ballot must file a declaration of candidacy and nomination papers and must also win a special primary election if one is required. For a partisan office, a special primary must be held for each of the recognized political parties if it is the case for any one of them that two or more individuals have proposed in their declarations of candidacy to represent it. For a nonpartisan office, a special primary must be held if three or more individuals file to be candidates.

RECALLING AN ELECTED OFFICIAL FROM OFFICE

A "recall election" can be held to decide whether an elected official will be recalled from office before his or her term of office expires and, if so, who will serve in the official's place for the remainder of the term. This kind of election can be held on one of the four regular election days or on a different day. However, a recall election cannot be held before an official has served one year of his or her term. In addition, no more than one recall election can be held for the same official during a single term of office.

A recall election is held only if voters of the governmental jurisdiction or election district that elected an official file a petition to recall the official. The petition must be signed by a number of voters equal to at least 25 percent of the vote cast for governor in the jurisdiction or district at the last election for governor. In addition, if the petition seeks the recall of a city, village, town, or school district official, it must assert a reason that is related to the duties of the office.

Other than the official named in the recall petition, an individual who wishes to be listed as a candidate on a recall election ballot must file a declaration of candidacy and nomination papers and might also have to win a recall primary election if one is required. The official named in the recall petition might similarly have to win a recall primary but otherwise will be listed on the recall election ballot automatically (unless he or she resigns).

For a partisan office, a recall primary must be held for each recognized political party for which it is the case that two or more individuals, who might include the official named in the recall petition, seek to be listed as its candidate on the recall election ballot. If only one individual seeks to be listed as a party's candidate, the individual will be listed as such without a primary being held for that party.

For a nonpartisan office, a recall primary must be held if three or more individuals, who might include the official named in the recall petition, seek to be listed as candidates on the recall election ballot. In contrast to other nonpartisan primaries, if one individual receives over 50 percent of the votes cast at the recall primary, no further election is held, and that individual fills the office for the remaining term.

APPROVING OR REJECTING A PROPOSAL

A "referendum" can be held in Wisconsin to approve or reject a proposal (rather than to choose an individual to fill an office). This kind of election can be held on one of the four regular election days or on a different day.

A referendum can be binding or nonbinding. In the former case, a proposal is implemented automatically if approved by a majority of the voters voting at the referendum; in the latter, the voters' approval or rejection of a proposal is merely advisory.

At the state level, binding referenda can be held on proposals 1) to amend the state constitution, 2) to extend the right to vote, 3) to allow the state to contract public debt in excess of the limit imposed by the state constitution, and 4) to permit an act of the legislature to take effect when the legislature has provided that the act's taking effect is contingent upon voter approval.

A referendum ballot presents the referendum proposal in the form of a yes-or-no question, and the voter votes the ballot by marking "yes" or "no." The question on the ballot summarizes the effect of the proposal. The full text of the proposal along with an explanation of its effect must be posted at the polling place.

Administration

The responsibility for administering elections is distributed across several levels of government.

Elections Commission. The state Elections Commission oversees and facilitates the performance of elections-related functions by officials at lower levels of government. The commission:

- Determines the format that must be used for ballots.
- Certifies all equipment and materials used to record votes at elections.
- Trains and certifies officials at lower levels of government.
- Maintains the electronic statewide voter registration list.

The Elections Commission also performs certain functions related to state and national elections. The commission:

- Determines which candidates for elective state and national offices qualify to be listed on the ballot. Such candidates must file with the commission their declarations of candidacy, nomination papers, and other documents that demonstrate that they are qualified.
- Certifies the tally of the votes cast in the state at each election held to fill a state or national office or to vote on a state referendum.

County clerk. The county clerk performs certain functions related to county, state, and national elections. The county clerk:

- Determines which candidates for elective offices in county government qualify to be listed on the ballot. Such candidates must file with the county clerk their declarations of candidacy, nomination papers, and other documents that demonstrate that they are qualified.

- Prepares the ballots for elections held to fill county, state, and national offices and to vote on county and state referenda and distributes these ballots to the municipalities (cities, villages, and towns) located within the county.

- Processes voter registrations for county residents who ask to register at the county clerk's office and forwards the information obtained to the municipal clerk of the municipality in which the registrant resides so that the municipal clerk can update the electronic statewide registration list.

- Tabulates the votes cast in the county at each election held to fill a county, state, or national office or to vote on a county or state referendum.

- Reports to the Elections Commission the votes cast in the county related to a state or national election.

In Wisconsin's most populous county, Milwaukee, a special commission performs these functions instead of a clerk.

Municipal clerk. The municipal clerk—i.e., the city, village, or town clerk—performs certain functions related to municipal, county, state, and national elections. The municipal clerk:

- Determines which candidates for elective offices in municipal government qualify to be listed on the ballot. Such candidates must file with the municipal clerk their declarations of candidacy, nomination papers, and other documents that demonstrate that they are qualified.

- Prepares the ballots for elections held to fill municipal offices and to vote on municipal referenda.

- Processes voter registrations for residents of the municipality and updates the electronic statewide registration list to reflect the information obtained. In some cases, a county clerk, by agreement with a municipal clerk, acts in place of the municipal clerk as that clerk's agent for the performance of all registration functions, including updating the statewide registration list.

- Provides the ballots for each election to the voters who desire to vote and receives the ballots back from those voters when they cast them. Only the municipal clerk provides ballots to voters and receives cast ballots back; county clerks and the Elections Commission do not.

- Operates polling places in the municipality on the day of an election. Only the municipal clerk operates polling places; county clerks and the Elections Commission do not.

- Tabulates the votes cast in the municipality at each election held to fill a municipal, county, state, or national office or to vote on a municipal, county, or state referendum.

- Reports to the county clerk of each county in which the municipality is located the votes cast in the municipality related to a county, state, or national election.

The municipal clerk also handles most matters related to elections held by school districts that are located in whole or part within the municipality. However, the school district clerk determines which candidates for school district elective offices qualify to be listed on the ballot, and such candidates must file with the school district clerk their declarations of candidacy, nomination papers, and other documents that demonstrate that they are qualified.

In Wisconsin's most populous city, Milwaukee, a special commission performs these functions instead of a clerk.

Voting

Eligibility. To vote at an election in Wisconsin, an individual must be a U.S. citizen, must be 18 years of age or older, and must reside in the governmental jurisdiction or election district for which the election is held. For example, an individual must reside in a particular county to vote at an election for that county's sheriff and must reside in a particular supervisory district within the county to vote at an election for that district's member of the county board of supervisors.

To establish residence for voting purposes, an individual must reside at the same address for at least 28 consecutive days prior to the election at which the individual wishes to vote.

An individual who moves to a new address in Wisconsin during the 28 days preceding an election is considered, for that election, to reside at his or her former address if the individual had established residence at the former address before the move. The individual can vote at the election only if the former address is located within the governmental jurisdiction or election district for which the election is held.

An individual who has resided in Wisconsin for less than 28 days but who is otherwise eligible to vote can vote for U.S. president and vice president only, under a special procedure.

Certain individuals are not eligible to vote at any election:

- An individual who has been convicted of treason, felony, or bribery, unless the individual has been pardoned or has completed his or her sentence—including any parole, probation, or extended supervision—for the crime.
- An individual who has been adjudicated incompetent by a court, unless the court has determined that the individual is competent to exercise the right to vote.

In addition, an individual is not eligible to vote at a particular election if the individual has bet upon the result of the election.

Registration. Registration is the means by which an individual demonstrates that the individual is eligible to vote. With limited exceptions, an individual must register to vote before being allowed to vote.

To register, an individual must fill out, sign, and submit a registration form and present acceptable proof of residence.

On the registration form, the individual must:

- Provide the individual's name and date of birth; current address; previous address; and the number and expiration date of the individual's Wisconsin driver's license or identification card, if any, or the last four digits of the individual's social security number, if any.
- Indicate whether the individual has been convicted of a felony for which the individual has not been pardoned and, if so, whether the individual is incarcerated or on parole, probation, or extended supervision.
- Indicate whether the individual is currently registered to vote at an address other than the current one.
- Certify that the individual is a U.S. citizen, will be 18 years of age or older on the day of the next election, and will have resided at his or her current address for at least 28 consecutive days prior to that day. Registrants are not asked to indicate a political party affiliation.

Documents that qualify as proof of residence include:

- A current and valid Wisconsin driver's license or identification card.
- A student identification card accompanied by a fee receipt dated within the preceding nine months.
- A property tax bill or receipt for the current or previous year.
- A bank statement.
- A utility bill for a period beginning no earlier than 90 days before the date of registration.

Through the third Wednesday preceding an election, an eligible voter can register in person at the office of the municipal clerk or county clerk, by mail with the municipal clerk, or via an electronic registration system maintained by the Elections Commission and accessible at myvote.wi.gov.[2] After that Wednesday and through the Friday preceding the election, an eligible voter can register only in person at the office of the municipal clerk (or of the county clerk, if the county clerk is acting as the municipal clerk's agent for registration purposes). After that Friday, an eligible voter who still has not registered and who wishes to vote at the election must register on the day of the election at his or her polling place.

The Elections Commission maintains an electronic list of all eligible voters who are registered to vote in Wisconsin. Every municipal clerk (or county clerk acting as the agent of a municipal clerk) who processes a registration for an eligible voter must update the list via an interface provided by the Elections Commission to reflect the information obtained. The list updates automatically to reflect registrations submitted via the electronic registration system.

An individual who has registered once does not need to register again, unless the individual changes his or her name or address. However, an individual's registration can be suspended if the individual has not voted for four years and fails to respond to a mailed postcard that asks whether the individual wishes to continue his or her registration. The Elections Commission sends out the post-cards to such voters every two years.

Military voters who are residents of Wisconsin, as well as their spouses and dependents who reside with or accompany them, are not required to register as a prerequisite to voting. In addition, an individual who has resided in Wisconsin for less than 28 days, but who is otherwise eligible to vote, can vote for U.S. president and vice president without being registered. Similarly, a former Wisconsin resident who has moved to another state and is not eligible to vote in the new state can, if the individual is otherwise eligible to vote, cast a Wisconsin absentee ballot for U.S. president and vice president without being registered for up to 24 months after the move.

Voter registration information is generally open to public inspection. However, voters who are victims of certain crimes, such as domestic abuse, sexual assault, and stalking, can request confidential voter status. If a voter qualifies for this status, the municipal clerk updates the electronic statewide registration list to indicate that the voter's registration must be kept confidential and issues a confidential voter identification card to the voter.

Photo identification. With few exceptions,[3] a registered voter (or an eligible voter exempt from registration) who wishes to vote at an election in Wisconsin must present acceptable proof of identification in order to obtain a ballot. In most cases, photo identification is required. Acceptable forms of photo identification include:

- A Wisconsin driver's license or identification card issued by the Wisconsin Department of Transportation.
- A U.S. passport.
- A Veterans Affairs identification card.
- An identification card issued by a federally recognized Indian tribe in Wisconsin.
- A photo identification card issued by a Wisconsin university, college, or technical college, if certain conditions are satisfied.

Individuals who have a religious objection to being photographed can obtain and present a Wisconsin driver's license or identification card issued without a photo. In addition, an individual who has had to surrender his or her driver's license to a law enforcement officer within 60 days of the election can present in place of the driver's license the citation or notice that the individual received. A confidential voter can present his or her confidential voter identification card instead of photo identification.

Voting at a polling place. Polling places are operated by the municipal clerk and are open for voting only on the day of an election. Each address in a municipality is served by a designated polling place, and a voter can vote only at the polling place that serves the voter's address. (If a registered voter has moved within Wisconsin during the 28 days preceding an election, the voter is considered to reside at his or her former address for that election and can vote only at the polling place that serves the former address.) Each polling place is staffed by poll workers who have been trained by the municipal clerk. Each polling place is supplied with duplicate "poll lists,"[4] which are generated from the electronic statewide registration list, of all eligible voters served by the polling place who registered before the day of the election. Each polling place is also supplied with ballots that are specific to the elections at which the voters served by the polling place are eligible to vote.

When an individual comes to a polling place to vote, a poll worker asks the individual to state his or her name and address and to present proof of identification. (A confidential voter can present a confidential voter identification card without stating anything or can state his or her name and the serial number of the card without presenting anything.) A poll worker confirms that the individual's name and address are listed in the poll list, that the name on the proof of identification is consistent with the name on the poll list, and that any photograph on the proof of identification reasonably resembles the individual.[5] The individual is then required to sign the poll list, unless the individual cannot sign due to a physical disability.

Following these preliminaries, the poll workers assign the individual a voter number, record the number on both copies of the poll list, and give the individual a paper ballot or a card that will permit the voter to access an electronic ballot on a voting machine.

The voter takes the ballot or card to a voting booth and marks the paper ballot, or marks an electronic ballot via an interface on a voting machine, to indicate the voter's votes. After marking a paper ballot, the voter casts it by depositing it through a slot into a locked ballot box or by feeding it into an optical scanning machine. (An optical scanning machine reads and tabulates electronically the votes marked on a paper ballot and stores the ballot in a locked compartment.)

After marking an electronic ballot, the voter verifies a record of the voter's votes that the voting machine prints on a paper tape. The voter then casts the ballot by giving a direction via the machine's interface. (A voting machine records a voter's votes in its electronic memory, tabulates them electronically, and advances the paper tape so that the paper record of the voter's votes is stored within a locked compartment.)

Voting by absentee ballot. A registered voter (or an eligible voter exempt from registration) who is unwilling or unable to vote at his or her polling place on the day of an election can vote by absentee ballot instead.

To obtain an absentee ballot, the voter must submit a written request to the municipal clerk. This can be done in person at the clerk's office or at an alternate site designated by the clerk. It can also be done by mail, email, or fax. In-person requests must be made prior to the Monday preceding the election; other requests, in most cases, must be made no later than the Thursday preceding the election.

An in-person requester must present acceptable proof of identification to the municipal clerk or an individual designated by the clerk before the requester will be issued a ballot. Most other requesters must submit a copy of their proof of identification with their request for a ballot.[6]

To cast an absentee ballot, the voter must mark his or her votes on the ballot and seal the marked ballot in a special envelope that is provided with the ballot. The voter must take these actions in the presence of a witness. The voter must also show the unmarked ballot to the witness prior to marking it and must make sure that no one, including the witness, sees how the voter marked the ballot. After the ballot is sealed in the special envelope, the voter and the witness must sign a certification that is printed on the special envelope—the voter to attest that the voter is eligible to cast the ballot, will not cast any other ballot at the election, and followed the required procedures in casting the ballot; and the witness to attest that the voter followed the required procedures in casting the ballot. If the voter requested the absentee ballot in person, the voter must return it before leaving the municipal clerk's office or alternate site. In these cases, the municipal clerk or an individual designated by the clerk serves as the witness. If the voter requested the absentee ballot in another way, the voter must seal the special envelope containing the ballot in a second envelope[7] and either mail it or deliver it in person to the municipal clerk so that it is received by the municipal clerk no later than the day of the election.

Campaign finance regulation

Wisconsin regulates campaign finance—the spending of money on campaigning and the giving of money to others to spend on campaigning—in several ways:

- Only a particular kind of entity, called a "committee," is allowed to use money that it has accepted from others to engage in campaign spending and campaign giving. If the amount of money exceeds a specified threshold, a committee must register and file reports of its financial activity.[8]
- Limits are placed on who can give money to a committee and how much money can be given.
- Limits are also placed on some campaign spending, and some campaign spending is subject to special disclosure requirements.

Three kinds of campaigning are covered by the regulations: 1) express advocacy related to a candidate for elective office in state or local government,[9] 2) campaigning related to a state or local referendum question, and 3) campaigning related to the recall of an elected official in state or local government.[10]

COMMITTEES

A "committee" is a group of two or more individuals that comes together, or an organization that is established, specifically for the purpose of accepting money from others and using that money for campaign spending or campaign giving.[11] An entity that is not formed specifically for that purpose—for example, a business or a social club—cannot accept money from others to use for campaign spending or campaign giving, and neither can an individual acting alone. However, such an entity or individual could set up a committee as a separate entity that would be able to undertake those activities.

Registration. A committee must register with a state or local filing officer before it accepts or disburses money above a specified threshold. Wisconsin's regulations distinguish seven types of committee (described below) and specify a threshold for each type. A committee must identify the type of committee it is when it registers. It must also identify a single depository account that it will use to accept and disburse money and an individual who will be in charge of the account.

A "candidate committee" is a committee formed by a candidate to accept contributions and make disbursements to support the candidate's election. A candidate cannot accept or disburse any money except through a candidate committee. In addition, a candidate can have only one candidate committee for any one office that the candidate seeks. However, the candidate can be the individual in charge of the candidate committee depository account. (For that matter, the candidate can be the sole member of the candidate committee—an exception to the rule that a committee consists of two or more individuals.) A candidate committee must register with the appropriate filing officer[12] as soon as the candidate qualifies[13] to be considered a candidate.

A "political party" is a committee that qualifies for a separate section on the partisan primary ballot—in other words, it is a "recognized" political party. (See page 332, above.) Local affiliates of a recognized political party that are authorized to operate under the same name are also considered political parties. A political party must register with the Ethics Commission before it accepts or disburses any money in a calendar year. (An entity that calls itself a political party, but that does not meet the criteria just described, would have to register as a different type of committee.)

A "legislative campaign committee" is a committee that is formed by state senators or state representatives of a particular political party to support candidates for legislative office by engaging in express advocacy on their behalf and by giving money to their candidate committees. A legislative campaign committee must register with the Ethics Commission before it accepts or disburses any money in a calendar year.

A "political action committee," or "PAC," is a committee, other than a candidate committee, political party, or legislative campaign committee, that 1) is formed to engage in express advocacy; 2) might do this independently or in coordination with a candidate, candidate committee, political party, or legislative campaign committee;[14] 3) might also campaign for and against referenda; and 4) might also give money to other committees. A PAC must register with the Ethics Commission if it accepts or disburses more than $2,500 in a calendar year.

An "independent expenditure committee," or "IEC," is a committee, other than a candidate committee, political party, or legislative campaign committee, that 1) is formed to engage in express advocacy; 2) will do this independently only and not in coordination with a candidate, candidate committee, political party, or legislative campaign committee; 3) might also campaign for and against referenda; and 4) might also give money to other committees, but will not give money to a candidate committee or to a committee that is able to give the money subsequently to a candidate committee. An IEC must register with the Ethics Commission if it accepts or disburses more than $2,500 in a calendar year.

A "referendum committee" is a committee that 1) is formed specifically to campaign for or against a referendum and 2) will not attempt to influence how voters vote with respect to a candidate. A referendum committee must register with the appropriate filing officer[15] if it accepts or disburses more than $10,000 in a calendar year.

A "recall committee" is a committee that is formed specifically to campaign for or against the recall of an elected official. A recall committee must register with the appropriate filing officer[16] if it accepts or disburses more than $2,000 in a calendar year. However, if a recall committee intends to gather signatures on a recall petition, it must register beforehand, regardless of whether it has accepted or disbursed any money.

Reporting financial activity. Each registered committee must file with its filing officer regular reports of its financial activity. Reports are due every January 15 and July 15. A report is also due on the fourth Tuesday in September of an even-numbered year if a committee accepts or disburses money for campaigning related to a partisan office or a referendum that will be held on the day of the partisan primary or general election. Other reports are required in advance of each primary and election with respect to which a committee accepts or disburses money. All of a committee's reports are made public within two days of their filing.

Each report must include, among other things:

- A listing of each gift of money received from an individual, specifying the amount and date of the gift and the name and address of the individual.
- A listing of each gift of money received from a committee, specifying the amount and date of the gift and the name and address of the committee.
- A listing of any other income received from any source, specifying the amount, date, and type of the income and the name and address of the source.
- A listing of each gift of money given to another committee, specifying the amount and date of the gift and the name and address of the committee.
- A listing of each other disbursement of money made to any individual or entity, specifying the amount, date, and purpose of the disbursement and the name and address of the individual or entity.

CAMPAIGN GIVING LIMITS

Campaign giving consists of giving money to a committee (necessarily, since an entity that is not a committee cannot use money given by others for campaigning). Wisconsin's regulations place limits on who can give money to a committee and how much money can be given. The limits apply simultaneously to the giver and the recipient; both are guilty if the latter accepts a gift that violates a limit.

Generally, only individuals and committees are allowed to give money to a committee. However, corporations, labor unions, cooperative associations, and federally recognized American Indian tribes can also give money in certain cases—but not to a candidate committee and not to a committee that is able to give the money subsequently to a candidate committee.

Giving to a candidate committee. An individual can give up to $20,000 to the candidate committee of a candidate for a statewide office (governor, lieutenant governor, attorney general, superintendent of public instruction, secretary of state, state treasurer, or supreme court justice). Other limits apply to other offices, including $2,000 for state senator and $1,000 for state representative.

A candidate committee can give to another candidate committee up to the same amount as an individual can give. However, the candidate committees of candidates who are running together for governor and lieutenant governor can give unlimited amounts to each other. A candidate can give unlimited amounts to his or her own candidate committee.

A political party or legislative campaign committee can give unlimited amounts to a candidate committee.

A PAC can give up to $86,000 to the candidate committee of a candidate for governor. Other limits apply to other offices, including $26,000 for lieutenant governor; $44,000 for attorney general; $18,000 for superintendent of public instruction, secretary of state, state treasurer, or supreme court justice; $2,000 for state senator; and $1,000 for state representative.

No other person may give money to a candidate committee.

Giving to a political party or legislative campaign committee. An individual, candidate committee, political party, or legislative campaign committee can give unlimited amounts to a political party or a legislative campaign committee. A PAC can give up to $12,000 in a calendar year to a political party or legislative campaign committee.

In addition to those amounts, an individual, candidate committee, political party, or legislative campaign committee can give unlimited amounts to a segregated fund established by a political party or legislative campaign committee to be used for purposes other than express advocacy or making contributions to a candidate committee. A PAC can give up to $12,000 in a calendar year to such a fund. A corporation, labor union, cooperative association, or American Indian tribe can also give up to $12,000 in a calendar year to such a fund, even though those entities cannot otherwise give money to a political party or legislative campaign committee.

No other person may give money to a political party or legislative campaign committee.

Giving to a PAC. An individual, candidate committee, political party, legislative campaign committee, or PAC can give unlimited amounts to a PAC. No other person may give money to a PAC.

Giving to an IEC. An individual, candidate committee, political party, legislative campaign committee, PAC, or IEC can give unlimited amounts to an IEC. A corporation, labor union, cooperative association, or American Indian tribe can also give unlimited amounts to an IEC. No other person may give money to an IEC.

Giving to a referendum committee. Individuals and committees can give unlimited amounts to a referendum committee. A corporation, labor union, cooperative association, or American Indian tribe can also give unlimited amounts to a referendum committee. No other person may give money to a referendum committee.

Giving to a recall committee. Individuals and committees other than IECs or referendum committees can give unlimited amounts to a recall committee. No other person may give money to a recall committee.

CAMPAIGN SPENDING LIMITS

Committees, entities that are not committees, and individuals can generally spend unlimited amounts on campaigning that they do themselves. The exception is spending on express advocacy that is coordinated with a candidate, candidate committee, political party, or legislative campaign committee.[17] Spending of this kind is treated as a gift given to the candidate committee of the candidate who is benefitted by the express advocacy. As such, it is subject to the limits that apply to giving to a candidate committee.

CAMPAIGN SPENDING SPECIAL DISCLOSURE REQUIREMENTS

Special disclosures are required for some kinds of campaign spending. These are the only disclosures that individuals and entities that are not committees must make about their campaign spending.[18] Committees, by contrast, must also report their campaign spending in the regular reports they file covering all of their financial activity.

Specific reporting of certain communications. If an individual, PAC, IEC, or entity that is not a committee spends $2,500 or more to make express advocacy communications during the 60 days preceding a primary or election, the individual, PAC, IEC, or entity must report that spending to the Ethics Commission within 72 hours after the first $2,500 has been spent and within 72 hours after any additional expenditure. Reports must specify the date, amount, recipient, and purpose of each expenditure, as well as the name of and office sought by any candidate who is the subject of the express advocacy. (However, these details are not required for the expenditures made prior to reaching the $2,500 threshold.) The reports are made public within two days of their filing.

Candidate committees, political parties, and legislative campaign committees are not required to report these expenditures other than in their regular financial activity reports.

Information required in certain communications. If an individual, committee, or other entity spends money to make an express advocacy communication or to make a communication to influence the outcome of a recall effort, the individual, committee, or entity must include in the communication the phrase, "Paid for by," followed by the name of the individual, committee, or other entity.[19] For individuals and entities that are not committees, this requirement applies only to a communication whose cost exceeds $2,500. ⚏

NOTES

1. An alternative mechanism exists by which an individual can qualify to be listed on the spring election ballot. A town or village (but no other type of governmental jurisdiction) can hold a special meeting called a "caucus" to select the individuals who will be the candidates at the spring election for the offices of the town or village. The caucus must be held on or between the January 2 and the January 21 preceding the spring election. The caucus is open to the public, but only the eligible voters of the town or village can participate. The caucus participants nominate one or more individuals to be the candidates for each office and vote, if the total number of nominated candidates for a particular office is more than two (or is more than twice the number of seats to be filled), to determine which ones will be the candidates. An individual who is selected at a caucus to be a candidate for a town or village office must subsequently file a declaration of candidacy in order to be listed on the spring election ballot.

2. To register via the electronic registration system, an individual must possess a current and valid Wisconsin driver's license or identification card. The system requires the individual to enter his or her name, address, and date of birth together with the number of the driver's license or identification card. If the system confirms that the individual's information matches the records of the state Department of Transportation pertaining to the driver's license or identification card, the system permits the individual to register by 1) filling out and submitting an electronic version of the registration form, 2) "signing" the form by authorizing the use of a copy of the signature that he or she provided when applying for the driver's license or identification card, and 3) using as proof of residence the number of his or her driver's license or identification card.

3. Military voters (members of a uniformed service who are residents of Wisconsin and their spouses and dependents who reside with or accompany them) and overseas voters (former Wisconsin residents who no longer reside in the U.S. but remain U.S. citizens) can obtain and cast a Wisconsin absentee ballot without providing proof of identification. Overseas voters are entitled to vote for offices in national government only (U.S. president, vice president, senator, and representative).

4. Some municipalities use electronic poll books as an alternative to creating paper copies of a poll list.

5. If an individual's name and address are not listed in the poll list or electronic poll book, the poll worker will determine whether the voter is at the wrong polling place or is at the correct polling place but not registered. In the one case, the poll worker will direct the voter to the correct polling place; in the other, the poll worker will tell the voter where to go so that the voter can register.

If an individual's name and address are listed in the poll list or the electronic poll book but a poll worker believes that the name on the proof of identification is not consistent with the name on the poll list or electronic poll book, or that a photograph on the proof of identification does not reasonably resemble the individual, the poll worker must challenge the individual as unqualified to vote. The individual must reply to the challenge under oath in order to obtain a ballot. If the poll worker does not withdraw the challenge, the individual must also take an oath that he or she is eligible to cast the ballot, and a poll worker must make a note in the poll list or electronic poll book and on the ballot before issuing it. The individual's votes will be considered valid unless the election officials responsible for counting the votes determine beyond a reasonable doubt, based on evidence presented, that the individual was not eligible to vote or was not properly registered.

If an individual's name and address are listed in the poll list or electronic poll book but the individual is unable or unwilling to present proof of identification, he or she is given an opportunity to cast a provisional ballot, rather than a regular ballot. The voter must sign a certification attesting that he or she is eligible to cast the ballot. The provisional ballot will not be counted unless the voter subsequently presents the proof of identification. The voter can return to the polling place to do this, until 8:00 p.m. when the polls close, or the voter can bring the proof of identification to the municipal clerk's office, until 4:00 p.m. on the Friday following the election.

6. Military and overseas voters are exempt from this requirement. (See note 3.)

7. If the voter requested the ballot by email or fax, the voter must also include in the second envelope a signed, printed copy of the request.

8. Another kind of entity, called a "conduit," is subject to similar requirements. Conduits do not spend money on campaigning themselves, nor do they give money to others to spend on campaigning. Rather, they hold money on behalf of givers and pass it on to a committee at the direction of those givers.

9. Express advocacy is communication that 1) uses words such as "vote for," "elect," "support," "vote against," "defeat," or "oppose" with reference to a clearly identified candidate and 2) unambiguously relates to the election or defeat of that candidate. Communication that refers to a candidate but that does not qualify as express advocacy

would not, by itself, subject the communicator to Wisconsin's regulations, even if the communication was intended to influence voters' opinion of the candidate.

10. Not covered by the regulations is campaigning related to a candidate for elective office in national government. That kind of campaigning is regulated under federal law. There is no national-level referendum or recall process.

11. The money that a committee accepts from others can consist exclusively of money provided by the committee's own members; the committee is an entity distinct from its individual members. A committee is formed, therefore, whenever individuals pool their money to engage in campaign spending or campaign giving, regardless of how informal their decision-making process is or how little campaign spending or giving they actually do.

12. The Ethics Commission, if the candidate is seeking office in state government, or a county, municipal, or school district clerk, if the candidate is seeking office in local government.

13. Based on one of the following criteria: 1) filing nomination papers, 2) being certified as the nominee of a political party or a village or town caucus, 3) accepting or disbursing any money in an effort to win a primary or election, or 4) being an incumbent elective office holder. See note 1 for details regarding village and town caucuses.

14. Under Wisconsin law, coordination exists in only two situations: 1) a candidate, candidate committee, political party, or legislative campaign committee communicates directly with an individual or with an entity other than a political party or legislative campaign committee to specifically request that the individual or entity make an expenditure for express advocacy, and the individual or entity explicitly assents before making the expenditure; or 2) a candidate, candidate committee, political party, or legislative campaign committee exercises control over an expenditure made for express advocacy by an individual or by an entity other than a political party or legislative campaign committee or exercises control over the content, timing, location, form, intended audience, number, or frequency of the express advocacy.

15. The Ethics Commission, for a statewide referendum, or a county, municipal, or school district clerk, for a local one.

16. The Ethics Commission, if the petition pertains to an official in state government, or a county, municipal, or school district clerk, if it pertains to an official in local government.

17. Also, some entities that enjoy tax-exempt status under federal law, based on the fact that they have limited themselves to specific activities, would lose that status if they were to spend money on campaigning. In addition, a registered committee cannot spend money on a kind of campaigning that is inconsistent with the type of committee that it has registered as. See note 14 for the criteria that define coordination.

18. Campaign giving is a different story. For every gift of money that an individual or entity makes to a committee, the individual or entity must disclose to the committee the information (such as name and address) that the committee needs to complete its financial activity reports, and those reports, in turn, are made public soon after they are filed.

19. An additional phrase—"Not authorized by any candidate or candidate's agent or committee"—must be included in an express advocacy communication that is made independently, rather than in coordination with a candidate, candidate committee, political party, or legislative campaign committee.

Local government in Wisconsin

Government in Wisconsin includes not only the state government, but also numerous local governments that exist and operate under the authority of the state government. Some local governments are "general purpose districts," which have broad authority to administer a particular locale, while others are "special purpose districts," whose authority is limited to the performance of a specific function.

General purpose districts

Counties and municipalities—towns, villages, and cities—are Wisconsin's general purpose districts. The territory of the state is divided into counties, and it is also divided into towns, villages, and cities. Towns lie entirely within the boundaries of counties, but villages and cities can lie across county boundaries.

Historically, counties were created to be administrative subdivisions of the state. Towns were created within counties to enable sparsely populated areas to provide basic services for themselves, whereas villages and cities were created to enable population centers, wherever they had formed, to govern their local affairs. Today, counties continue to act as the local arm of state government, and towns continue to be providers of basic services, but all general purpose districts have some authority to make decisions about their local affairs.

General purpose districts determine their own budgets and raise money to pay for their operations by establishing fees, imposing property taxes on real property within their boundaries, and incurring debt.

Counties. Wisconsin has 72 counties. County boundaries are drawn by the legislature and specified in state law. County boundary lines generally run north to south or east to west or follow major physical features (such as rivers).

The governing body of a county is the county board. The county board is composed of supervisors who are elected from election districts within the county for two-year terms at the nonpartisan spring election. Each county decides for itself how many supervisors it will have (subject to a statutory maximum that is based on a county's population) and whether their terms will be concurrent or staggered. In addition to the county board, counties are required to have a central administrative officer. For this purpose, a county can create the office of county executive or county administrator, or it can designate an individual holding an existing elective or appointive office (other than county supervisor) to serve also as the county's administrative coordinator.

A county executive is elected for a four-year term at the nonpartisan spring election. Twelve counties have a county executive, including Wisconsin's eight most populous counties. The county executive directs all administrative functions; proposes to the county board an annual budget for the county; appoints (subject to approval by the county board) members of boards and commissions and heads of departments; and can veto actions of the county board.

A county administrator is appointed by the county board. Thirty counties have county administrator positions. The powers and responsibilities of this office are similar to those of a county executive, but a county administrator has no veto power and can be removed by the county board.

A county administrative coordinator, finally, has only the powers and responsibilities assigned by the county board. These could be as extensive as those of a county administrator but need not be. An individual serving as county administrative coordinator has no veto power, and his or her service in this capacity can be terminated by the county board.

Apart from its supervisors and county executive (if any), the elected officers of a county, including the sheriff, district attorney, clerk, and treasurer, are elected for four-year terms at the partisan general election.

Counties administer state programs in a variety of ways. County district attorneys enforce the state's criminal laws, and county jails incarcerate many violators of those laws; county clerks and registers of deeds maintain state-mandated vital and property records; county clerks oversee elections; and county human services departments administer state family and human service programs. In performing these functions for the state, counties have a limited role in determining policy, because the state sets specific standards that counties must abide by.

At the same time, however, counties have some authority to determine policy on local matters. For example, counties can regulate land use in the county (though not within the territory of a city or village), operate county highway systems, and establish recreational programs and social services programs.

Generally, all counties have the same powers and duties, but the legislature has imposed special requirements on the state's most populous county, Milwaukee. Among other things, that county must utilize a specific budgeting procedure that includes various reports and notices and that limits certain types of expenditures; and it must use a county executive system rather than an appointed central administrative officer.

Towns. Wisconsin has 1,246 towns. Town boundaries can be drawn by a county or a circuit court, according to procedures authorized by the legislature, and also by the legislature directly. Town boundary lines, like those of counties, generally run north to south or east to west or follow major physical features. However, town boundary lines can vary from this pattern when part of a town has been incorporated as, or annexed to, a city or village.

The governing body of a town is the town board. This board is typically composed of three supervisors, but towns that meet certain criteria can opt to have up to five. Supervisors are elected at large for two-year terms at the non-partisan spring election. In towns that have four or five supervisors, the terms can be staggered. One of the supervisor seats is designated for the town board chair, and the supervisor elected to that seat presides over the board's meetings and acts on behalf of the board in certain matters. Towns do not have a separate elected executive officer, but a town can create the appointive position of town administrator to perform administrative functions. Other town officers include the town clerk, treasurer, surveyor, assessor, and constable. Each town can decide for itself whether these officers will be elected or appointed. If elected, they are elected for two-year terms at the nonpartisan spring election. Towns are also permitted to combine or abolish some of these offices.

A distinctive feature of the town form of government is the annual town meeting. The annual meeting is held on the third Tuesday of April (or another date set by the voters at the preceding town meeting). During the meeting all eligible voters of the town are entitled to debate and vote on certain matters, including major issues affecting the town, such as establishing the tax levy and authorizing bonding. Determinations of the town meeting are binding on the town board and cannot be overturned by it.

Towns are required to provide certain basic services, in particular fire protection and the maintenance of local roads, and are allowed to provide other basic services, such as law enforcement and garbage collection. Many towns, particularly less populous and more rural ones, do little more than this. However, towns can also make policy on local matters. In particular, a town can opt to exercise village powers (by approving a resolution at a town meeting), in which case it is permitted to take any of the actions a village can take, except actions relating to the structure of its government. The village powers that towns most often exercise are those related to land use regulation. (Towns are otherwise subject to county land use regulation.)

Cities and villages. Wisconsin has 190 cities and 415 villages. City and village boundaries do not follow any particular pattern and are determined when the residents of territory lying within one or more towns incorporate the territory as a city or village. Incorporation is authorized by state law, and several procedures are provided. Typically, residents who wish to incorporate territory file a petition with the circuit court. If the circuit court determines that the petition is formally sufficient and that requirements pertaining to size, population, and population density have been met, the petition is forwarded to the state's Incorporation Review Board. If that board determines that the incorporation is in the public interest, a referendum on the incorporation is held in the territory that is proposed to be incorporated. If the referendum is approved, the city or village is established.

The governing body of a city is the common council, which is composed of alders and, in cities that have one, a mayor. The alders are elected at the nonpartisan spring election. Each city decides for itself how many alders it will have, whether they will be elected at large or from election districts, what the term of office will be, and whether terms will be staggered or concurrent. The mayor is elected at large at the nonpartisan spring election for a term decided by the city. The mayor presides over meetings of the common council but has no vote, except to break a tie.

Cities use two forms of executive organization. In most cities, the mayor is the chief executive officer. The mayor can veto the council's actions and has a general responsibility to ensure that the laws are obeyed and that city officials and employees carry out their duties. Specific responsibilities, however, vary from city to city. In some cities, for example, the mayor proposes an annual budget for the city, but in others, the council develops the budget itself. Similarly, the mayor might have authority to appoint many or few of a city's appointive positions.

In place of a mayor, ten cities have created the position of city manager. A city manager is appointed (and can be removed) by the common council. A city manager can attend, but does not preside or vote at, meetings of the council and cannot veto its actions. The responsibilities of a city manager include proposing an annual budget and appointing department heads, unless the common council defines the position differently.

City officers other than alders and the mayor or city manager can be elected or appointed, as decided by the city. If elected, they are elected at the nonpartisan spring election.

The governing body of a village is the village board, which is composed of trustees and a village president. Trustees are elected at the nonpartisan spring election for staggered terms. Each village decides for itself how many trustees it will have, whether they will be elected at large or from election districts, and what the term of office will be. The village president is elected at large at the nonpartisan spring election, for a term decided by the village. The village president presides over meetings of the village board and votes as a trustee. The president also acts on behalf of the board in certain matters.

Villages do not have a separate elected executive officer, but 11 villages have created the position of village manager to perform much the same role as a city manager performs in a city. A village manager is appointed (and can be removed) by the village board.

Village officers other than the trustees, president, and village manager (if any) can be elected or appointed, as decided by the village. If elected, they are elected at the nonpartisan spring election.

Cities and villages, like towns, provide basic services. These include fire protection, road maintenance, and police service. To a greater extent than towns or counties, however, cities and villages have broad authority to make local policy. Some powers are granted expressly in state statutes. Among the most characteristic of these are powers related to land use regulation, including authority to make rules that limit land uses in particular areas and that limit the kinds of structures that can be built or maintained in the city or village and authority to grant exceptions to the rules.

Beyond the authority granted in the statutes, however, cities and villages possess "home rule" powers conferred by the state constitution. The home rule provision states that cities and villages have the authority to "determine their local affairs and government, subject only to this constitution and to such enactments of the legislature of statewide concern as with uniformity shall affect every city or every village." The extent of the powers conferred by the provision and the extent to which those powers may be restricted by the state have varied over time, based on judicial decisions. Typically, however, the provision has been understood to allow cities and villages to take action on local matters without specific authorization from the state. That is, conversely to the situation with towns or counties, cities and villages can take such action unless specifically prohibited from doing so.

An additional power exercised only by cities and villages is the power of annexation: the power to detach territory from a town and attach it to the city or village. There are several different procedures by which an annexation can take place. Usually, all of the owners of property in the territory to be annexed sign on to a petition for annexation that is filed with the annexing city or village. If the petition meets certain statutory requirements and the governing body of the city or village enacts an ordinance approving the annexation, the territory becomes part of the city or village. In most cases, a town has no power to prohibit an annexation of part of its territory (but it can challenge the legality of an annexation in court).

Although cities and villages ordinarily have the same powers and duties, the legislature has imposed special requirements on "1st class" cities, including specific standards for budgeting, public employment, and police and fire department administration. Milwaukee is Wisconsin's only 1st class city currently.

Special purpose districts

Wisconsin has over 1,100 special purpose districts. The legislature has created some special purpose districts directly, and it has also authorized general purpose districts to create certain types of special purpose districts. Although a special purpose district exists only to perform a special function, the scope of its authority and its impact on the people who reside within its jurisdiction can be great. For example, some school districts have jurisdiction over the education of tens of thousands of children and some metropolitan sewerage districts manage sewage for hundreds of thousands of people. Other special purpose districts, however, such as certain public inland lake protection and rehabilitation districts, have authority over a very small geographic area and directly affect only a very small number of people.

School districts. Wisconsin has 421 school districts, which collectively cover the entire territory of the state. District boundaries can be modified, including by subdividing or consolidating existing districts, so long as no territory of the state is left outside of a district. Boundary modifications are typically initiated by the affected districts and might require ratification by referendum. The governing body of a school district is the school board. School board members are elected at the nonpartisan spring election, usually to staggered three-year terms. The number of members on a school board varies between three and eleven, and school board members can be elected at large or from election districts. School districts operate primary and secondary schools and otherwise provide educational services to the children who reside in the district. School districts are authorized to levy property taxes and to incur debt.

Technical college districts. Wisconsin has 16 technical college districts, which collectively cover the entire territory of the state. The number of districts and their boundaries were originally determined by a predecessor of the state Technical College System Board, which now has the power to reorganize the districts. Technical college districts are governed by boards of nine members, who are appointed for staggered three-year terms. Depending on the district, the appointments are made by a committee composed of the county board chairs of the counties that lie within the district or by a committee composed of the school board presidents of the school districts that lie within the district. For the Milwaukee Area Technical College District, the appointing committee is composed of the Milwaukee county executive and the Milwaukee, Ozaukee, and Washington county board chairs. Technical college districts operate technical colleges that provide postsecondary education and occupational training to persons who enroll in their programs. Districts are authorized to charge tuition and other fees, levy property taxes, and incur debt.

Metropolitan sewerage districts. Wisconsin has seven metropolitan sewerage districts. The legislature created the Milwaukee Metropolitan Sewerage District (MMSD) in the Milwaukee area. State law authorizes general purpose districts in the rest of the state to create their own metropolitan sewerage districts. Sewerage districts plan, design, construct, maintain, and operate sewerage systems for the collection, transmission, disposal, and treatment of both sewage and storm water. An 11-member commission governs the MMSD, and commissions made up of five or nine members govern other sewerage districts. Commissioners of the MMSD are appointed to staggered three-year terms by officials of the municipalities located in Milwaukee County. Commissioners of the Madison Metropolitan Sewerage District are appointed to staggered three-year terms by officials of the municipalities included in the district. Commissioners of other sewerage districts are generally appointed to staggered five-year terms by the county board of the county in which the district is located. Funds for a district's projects and operations are generated from property taxes assessed against property located in the district, from the issuance of bonds, and from user fees that are paid by the individuals and businesses that use the district's services. A large district, like the MMSD, provides services both to people who live within its jurisdiction and to people whose municipalities have contracted with it for its services.

Professional sports team stadium districts. Wisconsin has three professional sports team stadium districts. The Southeast Wisconsin Professional Baseball Park District was created by the legislature in 1995 and was authorized to issue bonds to acquire, construct, own, and operate a baseball park and related facilities. The district built, and is the majority owner of, American Family Field, the home stadium of the Milwaukee Brewers baseball team. To pay off the bonds, and to pay for stadium maintenance, the district is authorized to impose a sales tax within the district's jurisdiction, which consists of the counties of Milwaukee, Ozaukee, Racine, Waukesha, and Washington. The tax, however, may not be collected after August 31, 2020. The district is governed by a board of 13 members: six appointed by the governor, three for two-year terms and three for four-year terms; two appointed by and serving at the pleasure of the Milwaukee county executive for indefinite terms; and one each appointed by and serving at the pleasure of the Racine county executive, Waukesha county executive, Ozaukee county board chair, Washington county board chair, and Milwaukee mayor.

The Professional Football Stadium District was created by the legislature in 1999 and was authorized to issue bonds to finance the renovation of Lambeau Field, the home stadium of the Green Bay Packers football team. To pay off the bonds, the district was authorized to impose a sales tax within the district's jurisdiction, which consists of Brown County. The sales tax was imposed until

September 2015, at which time sufficient money had been collected to repay the bonds and to set aside a required reserve fund. Although its purpose has been carried out, the district continues to exist. The district is governed by a board of seven members who are appointed for concurrent two-year terms by elected local officials, including the mayor of Green Bay and the Brown county executive.

The Wisconsin Center District was created in 1994 by the City of Milwaukee under a state law that permits general purpose districts in the state to create a kind of special purpose district called a local exposition district. The district was authorized to issue bonds to build, own, and operate certain entertainment facilities in Milwaukee. (These facilities are known today as the Miller High Life Theatre, Wisconsin Center, and UW-Milwaukee Panther Arena.) To pay off the bonds, the district is authorized to impose special sales taxes in Milwaukee County on hotel rooms, on food and beverages sold in restaurants and taverns, and on car rentals. Operating revenues of the facilities pay for the district's operations. In 2015, the legislature expanded the district's purpose, altered its governance structure, and authorized it to issue bonds to finance the development and construction of the Fiserv Forum, home arena of the Milwaukee Bucks basketball team. The state, the City of Milwaukee, and Milwaukee County are required to provide the district the money that the district will need to pay off the bonds. The district is governed by a board of 17 members, including the state assembly speaker and minority leader, the state senate majority leader and minority leader, and appointees of the governor, the Milwaukee mayor, the Milwaukee common council president, and the Milwaukee county executive.

Other special purpose districts. State law also authorizes the creation of other types of special purpose districts. These include agricultural drainage districts, sanitary districts, public inland lake protection and rehabilitation districts, sewer utility districts, solid waste management systems, long-term care districts, water utility districts, and mosquito control districts. ⬛

Public education in Wisconsin

rticle X, section 3 of the Wisconsin Constitution requires the legislature to make available to all children in the state a free uniform basic education. At the same time, the constitution does not prohibit the legislature from creating additional forms of publicly funded education; nor does it require the additional forms, if any, to be available to all children, to be entirely free, or to provide the same basic education as the legislature must make available to all children. This article describes first the general educational system that the legislature has established to meet its obligation under the constitution and then each of the currently existing additional forms of publicly funded education that the legislature has created. The article reflects education law as of July 1, 2020.

The general system

In Wisconsin, every child resides within a school district and is entitled to a free education at a public school operated by that school district. The education provided at the public school must conform to requirements specified in state law.

Wisconsin is organized into 421 school districts. Each school district is governed by a school board whose members are elected by the residents of the district. For the purpose of operating public schools, school districts can, among other things, own and lease property; employ teachers and other personnel; and contract for the provision of services. Funding for school district operations comes primarily from state aid and property taxes levied by each district, but also from federal aid and miscellaneous fees, sales, and interest earnings. The amount of general state aid that a school district receives is based on several factors, including the number of pupils enrolled in the district's schools. State law limits the total amount of revenue that a school district can raise each year from general state aid, the state aid it receives for computers, and the property taxes it levies. However, a school district can exceed its revenue limit if it obtains voter approval at a referendum. School districts also receive aid for specified purposes, known as categorical aids, that are not counted toward revenue limits.

State law sets out general educational goals for children attending public schools and requires school districts to provide educational programs that will enable students to attain those goals. State law requires school districts to specify the knowledge and skills that they intend students in each grade to acquire; to maintain curriculum plans; and to define criteria for promoting students to the fifth grade and the ninth grade and for awarding high school diplomas.

It requires school districts to schedule a minimum number of hours of direct student instruction in each grade. And it requires school districts to ensure that every teacher and professional staff member holds a certificate, license, or permit to teach issued by the state Department of Public Instruction (DPI), unless that teacher is a faculty member at an institution of higher education teaching in a high school. Within these parameters, and subject to further requirements, school districts have discretion to determine the specifics of their educational programs and policies.

Additional requirements under both state and federal law apply to how school districts provide education to children with disabilities. A school district must identify, locate, and evaluate children with disabilities who reside in the district. It must develop an individualized education program (IEP) for each child with a disability that describes the special education and related services that the child needs to make appropriate progress. As long as the child is enrolled in the district, the district must regularly reevaluate the child, review and revise the IEP, and offer the child an educational setting in which it will implement the IEP. In addition, the school district must make special education and related services available to a child with a disability beginning in the year the child turns three years old and continuing through the year in which the child turns 21.

For state oversight purposes, school districts are required to report various kinds of information to DPI and to administer annually certain standardized tests to public school students in specific grades. In addition, DPI is required to publish an annual report, called the school and school district accountability report, which evaluates the performance of every public school and school district. (The individual evaluations in the report are called school or school district "report cards.")

Additional forms of publicly funded education

FULL-TIME OPEN ENROLLMENT PROGRAM

Under the Full-Time Open Enrollment Program (open enrollment), a child can attend a public school in a school district other than the one in which the child resides. For each open enrollment student, the state transfers to the nonresident school district a set amount from the state aid that is allocated for the student's resident school district. This transfer is greater for students with disabilities and may vary based on the actual costs incurred to educate the student.

In most cases, a child must apply to participate in the open enrollment program in the school year preceding the school year for which the application is made. The nonresident school district in which the child wishes to enroll cannot deny the application except for certain reasons, such as that the nonresident school district does not have space for additional students; that the nonresident school district does not provide the special education or related services specified in the IEP of an applicant who is a child with a disability; that the child has been habitually truant from the nonresident school district in a prior school year; or that the child has been expelled from any school district in the previous three years because of specific behaviors. Under special circumstances, a child can apply to participate in the program immediately.

The nonresident school district must afford an open enrollment student the same educational opportunities and programs as it affords a student who resides in the district. If the open enrollment student is a child with a disability, the non-resident school district assumes, in place of the resident school district, the duties under state and federal law that apply to the education of such children. The parent, rather than the school district, is responsible for providing transportation to and from school for an open enrollment student who is not a child with a disability. However, parents can apply to DPI for financial assistance based on need.

PART-TIME OPEN ENROLLMENT PROGRAM

The Part-Time Open Enrollment Program allows a student who is attending a public high school to take up to two courses at one time in a public school in a nonresident school district. The student's resident school district may deny the student's application if the school district determines that the course conflicts with the IEP of a student with a disability. The student's resident district can also deny an application if the cost of the course the student wishes to take would impose an undue financial burden on the district. Lastly, a resident school district can reject an application for a course that does not satisfy graduation requirements in the resident school district.

In general, the resident school district pays the nonresident school district for a course that the student takes under part-time open enrollment. The amount of the payment is based on the total number of hours of instruction provided to the student in the particular course. Parents are responsible for transporting their student to and from the school in the other school district, unless a course is being taken to implement the student's IEP. Parents can apply to DPI for financial aid to offset the cost of transportation based on need.

EARLY COLLEGE CREDIT PROGRAM

The Early College Credit Program (ECCP) allows a student who is attending public or private high school to take college courses at a University of Wisconsin System institution, a tribally controlled college, or a private, nonprofit institution of higher education in Wisconsin. A student can indicate on their application whether they want to take the class for high school credit, college credit, or both. The ECCP does not include courses taken at a public or private high school for college credit, commonly known as dual enrollment.

If the course a student takes is for high school credit, and if the course is not comparable to a course offered by the school district or private school, then the student pays nothing. The Department of Workforce Development and the school district or private school split the cost. The student pays for each course that the student takes for college credit only, although this cost is reduced. The student also pays for each course that the school board or private school governing board finds to be comparable to an existing course at the student's school, or that the student does not successfully complete. Parents are responsible for providing transportation to and from courses under the ECCP, but can apply to DPI for financial assistance based on need.

TECHNICAL COLLEGE DUAL CREDIT

Wisconsin allows students who are attending a public school in grade 11 or 12 to take courses at a technical college. If the course is taken for high school credit and if the course is not comparable to a course at the student's high school but is eligible for credit, then the district will pay for the student's tuition, fees, and books. Parents are responsible for providing transportation to and from courses at the technical college, unless a course is being taken to implement a student's IEP. If a student with a disability applies to the program, they may be denied if the cost of their participation would impose an undue burden on the school district.

CHARTER SCHOOLS

A charter school is a type of public school that is operated by an organization that contracts with an entity that the legislature has empowered to authorize charter schools. Currently, all school districts and several other entities have this power. The contract describes the school's educational program and governance structure and specifies the facilities and funds that will be available to it. The authorizing entity can revoke a charter school contract if the charter school operator fails to comply with the terms of the contract. The authorizing entity can also revoke the contract if the children attending the charter school fail to make sufficient progress towards attaining the general educational goals set out in state law for children attending public schools. Like other public schools, charter schools are free to students.

In general, charter schools are largely exempt from state education laws that apply to other public schools. However, charter schools are not exempt from state education laws that pertain to public health and safety or any law that explicitly applies to charter schools. In addition, all professional employees of a charter school who have direct contact with students or involvement with the instructional program must hold a license or permit to teach issued by DPI, with two exceptions: teachers at virtual charter schools and high school grade teachers who are faculty at an institution of higher learning may not need licenses.

Charter school operators must report the same kinds of information to DPI as school districts and administer the same standardized tests to their students as school districts must administer to students in other public schools. In addition, DPI must include performance evaluations of charter schools in the annual school and school district accountability report.

As public schools, charter schools are subject to federal laws pertaining to education, the education of children with disabilities, and civil rights.

School district charter schools. A charter school established by a school district is a public school of that school district, even though the school district does not directly operate the charter school. As a result, a school district charter school is subject to school district policies, except as otherwise negotiated in the charter contract. A student who attends a school district charter school is enrolled in the school district just the same as if the student attended a school that the school district operated directly. The school district receives the same amount of state aid or the same full-time open enrollment transfer payment for the child, and the school district has the same duties to provide special education and related services. However, a school district cannot require a student to attend a charter school and must provide other public school attendance arrangements for a student who does not wish to attend a charter school. A school district that establishes a charter school pays the charter school operator an amount negotiated in the charter contract to operate the charter school.

A school district can also establish a "virtual" charter school, which is a kind of charter school at which all or a portion of the instruction is provided on the Internet. A virtual charter school is considered to be located in the school district that establishes it, even if it has no physical presence there. In contrast to a bricks-and-mortar school, it is feasible under the Full-Time Open Enrollment Program for children who reside anywhere in the state to attend a virtual charter school. A teacher for a virtual charter school is not required to have a license from DPI, if the teacher is licensed to teach the grade and subject they are teaching in the state from which the online course is provided.

Independent charter schools. Several entities other than school districts can authorize independent charter schools. This includes the chancellors of any institution in the University of Wisconsin System, the City of Milwaukee, any technical college district board, the county executive of Waukesha County, the College of Menominee Nation, the Lac Courte Oreilles Ojibwa Community College, and the Office of Educational Opportunity in the University of Wisconsin System.

An independent charter school established by one of these entities is not part of any school district. Accordingly, an independent charter school is not subject to any school district's policies. If a child with a disability attends an independent charter school, the charter school operator is subject to the same federal laws pertaining to the education of such children as a school district would be and must evaluate the child, develop an IEP, offer the child an educational setting in which it will provide the special education and services specified in the IEP, and regularly reevaluate the child and revise the IEP. None of the chartering entities may establish or contract with a virtual charter school.

The state pays an independent charter school operator a set amount for each student attending the independent charter school. However, for an independent charter school authorized by the College of Menominee Nation or the Lac Courte Oreilles Ojibwa Community College, the per student amount in each school year is tied to a type of federal aid provided to tribal schools.

PARENTAL CHOICE PROGRAMS

Under a parental choice program (sometimes called a "voucher" program), the state makes a payment to a private school, on behalf of a student's parent, for the student to attend the private school. There are three parental choice programs in Wisconsin: the Milwaukee Parental Choice Program, which has existed since 1989; the Racine Parental Choice Program, which was created in the 2011–13 biennial budget act; and the Statewide Parental Choice Program, which was created in the 2013–15 biennial budget act.

Each of these programs is available to children whose family income, at the time that the child first participates, is below a specified level (three times the federal poverty level for the Milwaukee and Racine programs and 2.2 times that level for the statewide program). A child must reside in the city of Milwaukee to participate in the Milwaukee program, in the Racine Unified School District to participate in the Racine program, and anywhere else in the state to participate in the statewide program. Except in certain circumstances, a child cannot participate in the Racine or statewide program if the child was attending a private school in the previous school year other than as a participant in one of those programs. In addition, a temporary limit has been imposed on the number of children from each school district who can participate in the statewide program. This limit was 5 percent of a school district's student membership in the 2020–21 school year.

The limit increases by one percentage point each school year until the 2025–26 school year and ceases to apply after that.

A private school that wishes to participate in a parental choice program must report to DPI, by the January 10 preceding each school year of participation, the number of spaces it has for choice students and pay an annual fee. Additional requirements apply to a private school that has been in continuous operation in this state for less than 12 consecutive months or provides education to fewer than 40 students divided into two or fewer grades.

A student who wishes to participate in a parental choice program must apply to a participating private school during specific enrollment periods. The private school may reject an applicant only if the spaces it has for choice students are full. If a private school rejects an application, the applicant can transfer his or her application to another participating private school. A private school must generally accept applicants on a random basis, but may give preference to applicants who participated in a parental choice program in the previous school year, siblings of such applicants, and siblings of applicants whom the private school has accepted for the current school year on a random basis.

A participating private school must satisfy all state health and safety laws and codes that are applicable to public schools and federal laws prohibiting discrimination on the basis of race, color, or national origin. It must satisfy at least one of four achievement standards to continue participating in the program, and it may not require a choice student to participate in any religious activity. The private school must also provide a prescribed minimum number of hours of direct student instruction in each grade. Additionally, all of the private school's teachers and administrators must have a bachelor's or higher degree, or a license issued by DPI, unless they are only teaching or administrating rabbinical courses.

Participating private schools must report the same kinds of information to DPI as school districts must report, but only with respect to the choice students attending them. They must also administer the same standardized tests to their choice students as school districts must administer to public school students. In addition, DPI must include an evaluation of each participating private school's performance with respect to its choice students in the annual school and school district accountability report.

A private school cannot charge tuition to a choice student unless the student's family income exceeds a set percentage of the federal poverty line. A private school can charge a choice student fees related to certain expenses (such as social and extracurricular activities, musical instruments, meals, and transportation) but cannot take adverse action against a choice student or the student's family if the fees are not paid.

SPECIAL NEEDS SCHOLARSHIP PROGRAM

Under the Special Needs Scholarship Program, the state makes a payment (the scholarship) to a private school, on behalf of the parent of a child with a disability, for the child to attend the private school. In the 2020–21 school year, the scholarship amount was $12,977. Beginning in the 2019–20 school year, if a student has participated in the program for a year, the scholarship amount can be the actual costs incurred by the private school in the previous year, if that is greater than the standard scholarship amount. There is no limit on the amount of additional tuition or fees a private school may charge a child who receives a scholarship under the program. A child with a disability is eligible for a scholarship under the program if three conditions are met. First, the child must have an IEP or services plan in effect. (A services plan outlines the services that a school district has agreed to provide to a child with a disability whose parent has enrolled the child in a private school rather than in the school district.) Second, the child's parent or guardian must consent to make the child available for reevaluation upon request of the child's school district of residence. And third, the private school that the child wishes to attend with the scholarship must be accredited or approved as a private school by DPI and must have notified DPI of its intent to participate in the program.

A private school that wishes to participate in the program must notify DPI of the number of spaces it has available for children who receive a scholarship under the program. A participating private school must accept applications under the program on a first-come, first-served basis, but may give preference to siblings of students who are already attending the private school if it receives more applications than the number of spaces it has available.

A participating private school must implement, for each child that receives a scholarship, either 1) the IEP or services plan that the child's school district of residence developed in its most recent evaluation of the child or 2) a modified version of that IEP or services plan agreed to between the private school and the child's parent. The private school must also provide the child with any related services agreed to between the private school and the child's parent that are not included in the child's IEP or services plan. A child with a disability who attends a private school under the program is not entitled to all the special education and related services to which he or she would be entitled under state and federal law if he or she attended a public school.

A participating private school must comply with all health and safety laws that apply to public schools; must provide each child who applies for a scholarship with a profile of the private school's special education program; and must submit to DPI an annual school financial information report.

Unless it is also participating in a parental choice program, a private school participating in the Special Needs Scholarship Program is not required to report to DPI the kinds of information that school districts must report or to administer to any of its students the standardized tests that school districts must administer to public school students, and no performance evaluation of the private school is included in the annual school and school district accountability report.

Once awarded, a scholarship continues until the child graduates from high school or until the end of the school term in which the child attains the age of 21, whichever comes first, unless, upon reevaluation by the child's school district of residence, it is determined that the child is no longer a child with a disability. In that case, the child can continue to receive a scholarship under the program, but the amount of the scholarship is reduced to the per student amount paid under the parental choice programs. ▣

The legislature and the state budget

The legislature has the power of the purse. In Wisconsin, the state government may not spend a single dollar without the legislature specifically authorizing the expenditure by law. The manner in which the legislature controls the expenditure of state funds is through its appropriation power, which is a power granted to the legislature under the Wisconsin Constitution. In the 1936 case *Finnegan v. Dammann*, the Wisconsin Supreme Court defined an appropriation as "the setting aside from the public revenue of a certain sum of money for a specified object, in such a manner that the executive officers of the government are authorized to use that money, and no more, for that object, and no other."[1] It is the legislature that directs the governor and the executive branch in determining what state moneys are to be spent and the purposes for which they may be spent.

The most consequential exercise of the legislature's appropriation power is the enactment of the state budget. The biennial budget bill is easily the most significant piece of legislation that is enacted during the entire legislative session. This is the case for two reasons. First, the biennial budget bill appropriates almost all dollars that will be spent by the state government during the two fiscal years covered by the bill. These dollars consist mostly of state taxes and revenues, program and license fees, and federal moneys allocated to Wisconsin. In 2019 Wisconsin Act 9, the state budget act for the 2019–21 fiscal biennium, the legislature authorized over $81 billion in total state government spending from all revenue sources. The second reason for the significance of the biennial budget bill is that it contains most of the governor's public policy agenda for the entire legislative session. The biennial budget bill is generally considered the one bill that "must pass" in order to sufficiently fund state government operations and programs during the fiscal years covered in the bill. As such, there is a strong incentive for the governor, as well as for legislators, to include in the biennial budget bill the major public policy items supported by the governor and the legislators. The state budget process is therefore unequaled in its significance for the operations of state government and for its effects on the people of Wisconsin.

The state budget process: core principles

There are several core principles to the state budget process in Wisconsin. First, the state budget is a biennial budget, covering two fiscal years of state government operations and programs, with each fiscal year beginning on July 1 and ending on June 30. Many states have a "drop-dead" date by which a new state budget must be enacted in order for state government to continue to operate. Wisconsin does not have such a deadline. In Wisconsin, if a new state budget is not enacted by June 30 of the odd-numbered year, state government continues to operate and its programs are funded, but only at the prior year's appropriation amounts. The governor and the legislature strive to enact the state budget bill before July 1 of the odd-numbered year, but there is little short-term fiscal impact if that deadline is not met.

Second, Wisconsin uses what is known as program budgeting, in which executive branch state agencies are assigned to different functional areas and generally lump-sum appropriations are made to the agencies to fund the programs. The biennial budget bill therefore lists the overall amounts appropriated for agency operations and programs, but does not contain the level of expenditure detail that one might find in a state that uses a "line-item" budget, in which each agency expenditure is specifically budgeted by line in the bill. Instead, this level of detail appears in accompanying budget documents, which are not law but which do capture the intentions of the governor and the legislature in budget deliberations. Consequently, that portion of the biennial bill that sets the expenditure levels of state operations and programs is roughly 200 pages in length, which is typically about 15 to 20 percent of the total number of pages of recent biennial budget bills.

Third, the Wisconsin Constitution requires that the legislature "provide for an annual tax sufficient to defray the estimated expenses of the state for each year."[2] What this means in practice is that Wisconsin has a balanced-budget requirement, in which state expenditures must equal revenues received by the state. Generally speaking, at each stage of the budget process, in which different versions of the budget are formulated and considered, each version of the budget must be balanced by having proposed state expenditures in any fiscal year be less than or equal to anticipated state revenues. This is a real constraint on state budgeting, one that is not found at the federal level.

Finally, the Wisconsin Constitution grants the governor partial veto power over appropriation bills. This partial veto power allows the governor to reduce amounts appropriated to state agencies for their operations and programs by writing in a lower amount and allows the governor, with limitations, to veto specific words and digits within newly created statutory text in appropriation bills. The governor can thus significantly alter the legislature's budget actions. While this power has been curtailed in recent years by amendments to the constitution as well as litigation, the governor still can reduce all state expenditures, or the expenditures of any specific state agency, with the stroke of a pen, subject only to an override of his or her actions by a two-thirds vote of each house of the legislature—an event that last occurred in 1985.

The state budget process: an overview of executive action

The provision for a biennial executive budget bill was created by Chapter 97, Laws of 1929,[3] and it has applied to all legislative sessions since 1931. Prior to that time, the governor was not responsible for submitting an executive budget bill to the legislature; individual bills were introduced for each department. The legislature delegated the biennial budget task to the governor for understandable reasons. As head of the executive branch, the governor can assess and coordinate the expenditure needs of each executive branch agency. In addition, the growth in state government in the twentieth century resulted in a level of public policy and budgetary expertise in the executive branch that is generally not available in the legislative branch, which has a much smaller professional staff. Requiring the governor to produce the budget bill allows the legislature to work from a document that may require modification, because of different legislative public policy or budgetary priorities, but which already contains numerous budgetary matters and details that the legislature need not address. The governor's budget is a solid foundation on which the legislature can build its version of the budget, a process which serves both the governor and the legislature well.

To begin the biennial budget process, in the summer of each even-numbered year, the State Budget Office in the Department of Administration submits budget instructions to executive branch agencies, establishing the manner of submitting budget requests and informing them of any broad fiscal or policy goals that the governor intends the state agencies to achieve. By September 15, state agencies must submit their budget requests to the State Budget Office for review by that office, the state budget director, and the governor. By November 20, the Department of Administration publishes a compilation and summation of the agency budget requests, as well as estimated revenues to the state for the current and forthcoming fiscal biennia. The State Budget Office oversees the preparation of legislation to achieve the governor's budget and policy recommendations. In this endeavor, the State Budget Office works closely with legal counsel at the Legislative Reference Bureau—the legislature's bill-drafting agency—to draft the statutory language that will ultimately be incorporated into the governor's budget bill. Throughout the process, the governor is briefed on individual items in the budget bill, and the bill is complete only when the governor has signed off on the items in the bill. The governor is then required to deliver the budget bill to the legislature no later than the last Tuesday in January of each odd-numbered year, though the legislature regularly moves this deadline back into February to allow the governor to make changes in the bill once more accurate revenue estimates for the current and forthcoming fiscal biennia are available in late January. When the budget bill is delivered to the legislature, the governor addresses the legislature on the proposals contained in the bill, which more often than not are the key public policy goals of the governor's administration for the entire legislative session.

The first thing to note about the production of the executive budget bill is the role of the State Budget Office. The State Budget Office is headed by the state budget director and consists of about 25 budget analysts who serve in classified civil service positions. These analysts serve both Republican and Democratic gubernatorial administrations in a strictly nonpartisan and highly professional manner and are able to provide independent review of state agency funding requirements, as well as fashion fiscal and nonfiscal policies to achieve the governor's political and public policy aims. The State Budget Office translates the governor's public policy goals into workable and funded programs.

The second thing to note about the production of the executive budget bill is that the State Budget Office works directly with nonpartisan legal counsel in the Legislative Reference Bureau to prepare statutory text that achieves the governor's policy goals. The Legislative Reference Bureau has about 20 licensed attorneys with subject matter and legal expertise in virtually all policy areas. This is significant. The governor's budget bill is drafted in a professional, nonpartisan manner, so that the legislators need only focus on the public policies in the bill and not worry about the bill's legal quality or effectiveness. In addition, when the legislature takes up the governor's budget bill, the Legislative Reference Bureau attorneys who originally drafted the governor's provisions in the bill will be the ones who draft the legislature's alternatives. In this way, often the very same attorneys are working on the same language in the bill throughout the process. The legislature can thus count on experienced and competent legal counsel to prepare its budget bill in an accurate, high-quality, and nonpartisan manner.

Finally, it is important to note the political uses of the executive budget bill. Given that it must pass, the budget bill is the primary tool by which a governor may advance his or her public policy agenda during the legislative session. Consequently, it is by far the longest and most complex bill before the legislature during the entire biennium. In recent years the bill has grown substantially in length. From 1961 to 1986, executive budget bills averaged 367 pages in length. From 1987 to 2019, in contrast, executive budget bills averaged 1,463 pages in length, roughly a fourfold increase in size. The governor uses the massive bill as a tool to garner public support for various policy changes.

The executive budget bill is now a blueprint for the legislature for taking up the governor's goals for public policy change. When the governor steps up to the assembly podium, usually in early or mid-February, to present the budget address to the legislature, an event that is televised throughout the state and broadcast live on the Internet, in many ways the political season commences in Wisconsin.

The state budget process: the role of the legislature

The Wisconsin Legislature is the policymaking body in this state and has the sole power to appropriate all moneys expended by the state. The biennial budget bill is, therefore, every bit as much of a product of legislative deliberation and action as it is a product of the governor's actions. The governor sets the agenda for legislative action on the budget, but the legislature examines, modifies or rejects, and altogether recreates what the governor originally had in the budget bill. In addition, the legislature will devise a few policies of its own, often from whole cloth, or it will refashion the governor's policies so that they are barely recognizable from their original form. Much of what the governor has proposed in the budget bill will survive the legislative process, but the document that emerges from the legislature is very much a product of the legislature.

When the governor presents the budget bill to the legislature, it is legally required to be introduced by the Joint Committee on Finance and referred to that committee. In 1885, a young congressional scholar by the name of Woodrow Wilson, then a professor at Bryn Mawr College, wrote that "Congress in session is Congress on public exhibition, whilst Congress in its committee rooms is Congress at work."[4] This applies perfectly to the Wisconsin Legislature. It is in its several committee rooms that the Wisconsin Legislature does its work, and no committee more exemplifies that work ethic than the Joint Committee on Finance.

The Joint Committee on Finance consists of eight senators and eight representatives to the assembly. All bills that affect revenues, taxes, or expenditures are referred to that committee and must be reported out of that committee before the legislature may take the bill up for consideration and passage. It is fair to say that this committee is the most powerful standing committee in the legislature and is a training ground for legislative leadership. Legislators on this committee work long hours.

The Joint Committee on Finance does not work alone, but is staffed by the Legislative Fiscal Bureau, a nonpartisan legislative service agency. The Legislative Fiscal Bureau has about the same number of analysts as the State Budget Office, each of whom has policy and budgetary expertise in specific areas of state government. The analysts perform their work in a professional, nonpartisan manner, serving both the majority and minority parties in the legislature. After the budget bill is introduced, Legislative Fiscal Bureau analysts prepare a lengthy, detailed summary document that contains an analysis of every single item in the bill. The summary is written in plain English, is precise and exhaustive in its presentation of the governor's policies, and is hundreds of pages in length. The Legislative Fiscal Bureau summary is the document that forms the basis on which the Joint Committee on Finance begins its work on the budget.

The Joint Committee on Finance will often hold hearings at different locations throughout the state to receive testimony from the general public and interest group representatives. Beginning in April and continuing into May, the Legislative Fiscal Bureau prepares papers on the items contained in the budget bill, laying out alternatives or even new ways to address the same items in the bill. The Legislative Fiscal Bureau derives its policy alternatives from its own public policy expertise and from committee member involvement. Sometimes working groups will form among members of the committee to consider and propose policy alternatives. During this time, the Joint Committee on Finance meets to approve items it will include in its version of the budget. These are lengthy, often contentious meetings that run late into the evening or early morning. It is not uncommon to see Joint Committee on Finance members and Legislative Fiscal Bureau analysts leaving the Capitol building in the bright light of early morning.

Once the committee has finished its work, the Legislative Fiscal Bureau oversees the production of a substitute amendment that incorporates the committee's version of the budget to replace the governor's budget bill. In this regard, the Legislative Fiscal Bureau gives drafting instructions to attorneys at the Legislative Reference Bureau, who also work around the clock to prepare the substitute amendment. While the executive branch often has six months or more to prepare the governor's budget bill, the Joint Committee on Finance will do its work in a much shorter time span, often only six to eight weeks.

The committee's substitute amendment is not always the final and complete version of the legislature's budget bill. Each house of the legislature has the option to further amend the substitute amendment to include items of its own design or to modify or reject items included by the Joint Committee on Finance. Whether this occurs, and the extent to which the substitute amendment will be modified, depends on a number of factors, such as whether the same political party is the majority party in both houses, whether legislators who do not serve on the Joint Committee on Finance believe that their interests and concerns have been addressed in the substitute amendment, and the likelihood of the convening of a conference committee on the bill to resolve differences between the two houses. These calculations are based on substantive factors, in that members will work to include items that benefit them or their constituents, as well as on strategic considerations, in that members will want to fortify their own house's position in conference committee negotiations with the other house.

Once the legislature passes its version of the budget bill, the bill is presented to the governor for signing. As mentioned earlier, the governor has partial veto power over appropriation bills and will use that power to modify what the legislature has passed. The governor can reduce appropriations, as well as modify some statutory text. The extent to which the governor will partially veto the bill also depends on a number of factors, such as the partisan makeup of the legislature, the degree to which the governor agrees with what the legislature has done, and whether the governor has made agreements in negotiations with the legislature over what can and cannot be vetoed. Once the governor has signed the bill into law, the budget-making process is concluded, as the only other possible step is for the legislature to override one or more of the governor's partial vetoes—an action, as mentioned earlier, that has not happened since 1985.

Concluding considerations

The state budget-making process is truly a year-long event, beginning in the summer of each even-numbered year when the State Budget Office sends budget instructions to the state agencies and concluding the following summer with the enactment of the biennial budget act. The process is characterized both by careful deliberation and by frenzied, all-night sessions and meetings. The budget bill is the work product of the governor, every elected member of the Senate and the Assembly, and numerous professional staff in both the executive and legislative branches. There is never an "easy" budget, as each fiscal biennium presents its own unique budgetary and political challenges. But there is never complete gridlock, as the legislature does complete its work. Sometimes the budget will be late, especially when the two houses are controlled by different political parties, but in the end Wisconsin will have a state budget. ▣

NOTES

1. Finnegan v. Dammann, 220 Wis. 143, 148, 264 N.W. 622 (1936).

2. Wisconsin Constitution, article VIII, section 5.

3. This would have been called Act 97 if it took effect today; before 1983, a bill that was enacted into law was called a "chapter" rather than an "act."

4. Woodrow Wilson, Congressional Government, A Study in American Politics (1885).

Significant enactments of the 2019 Legislature

Agriculture

Act 9 (AB-56) does the following:

1. Allows DATCP to request a supplemental appropriation to fund mental health assistance for farmers and farm families.
2. Authorizes $7,000,000 in bonding for cost-sharing grants under the soil and water resource management program.

Act 68 (SB-188) makes changes to the state hemp program so that it is consistent with the 2018 federal farm bill, including removing hemp from the list of Schedule I controlled substances; prohibiting a person convicted of a drug-related felony from producing hemp for ten years, with exceptions; and addressing negligent violations of the hemp program through enforcement of a compliance plan. The act also makes other changes, including changing the amount of THC in a driver's blood for OWI purposes from "any detectable amount" to one or more nanograms per milliliter; protecting a person from prosecution if he or she purchases a hemp product that is not more than 0.7 percent over the permissible THC limit for hemp; and prohibiting a person from mislabeling, making false claims, or knowingly selling a mislabeled hemp product.

Beverages

Act 6 (SB-83) removes the four-liter limit on distilled spirits sold for off-premises consumption by "Class B" licensed retailers (typically bars and restaurants) in municipalities that, by ordinance, allow "Class B" retailers to sell distilled spirits for off-premises consumption.

Children

Act 8 (AB-188) does all of the following:

1. Delays the closure of Lincoln Hills and Copper Lakes Schools and the opening of new state juvenile correctional facilities and county-run secured residential care centers for children and youth from January 1, 2021, to July 1, 2021.
2. Allows DOC to transfer juveniles between facilities until the new facilities are open.

Act 9 (AB-56) does the following:

1. Allows foster care payments to be made on behalf of a child who is placed in a qualifying residential family-based treatment facility with a parent.

2. Modifies the per-person daily rates that are assessed on counties for state-provided juvenile correctional services.

3. Increases the maximum reimbursement rate that DCF may set for Level I or Level II certified family child care providers from no more than 75 percent of the rate set for licensed child care to no more than 90 percent of that rate.

4. Authorizes DCF to award child care-related grants that target a geographic area with high-poverty levels in Milwaukee.

5. Beginning on January 1, 2020, increases by 4 percent the monthly age-related basic maintenance rates paid to foster parents and the monthly kinship care payments made to relatives who provide care for children.

Act 22 (AB-52) provides that a minor who is 17 and is an unaccompanied youth is presumed to be competent to contract for admission to a temporary place of lodging for individuals or families (shelter facility) or transitional living program under certain circumstances, and exempts this type of contract from the defense of infancy.

Act 109 (AB-47) creates a procedure and standards for the appointment of a guardian of a minor person. Under the act, any interested party, including a child age 12 or older, may file an action to establish a private guardianship of a child. The act creates four distinct types of guardianships:

1. A full guardianship, requiring a finding that the child's parents are unfit, unwilling, or unable to provide for the care, custody, and control of the child or other compelling facts and circumstances demonstrate that a full guardianship is necessary.

2. A limited guardianship, requiring a finding that the child's parents need assistance in providing for the care, custody, and control of the child.

3. A temporary guardianship, requiring a finding that the child's situation, including the inability of the child's parents to provide for the care, custody, and control of the child for a temporary period, requires the appointment of a temporary guardian.

4. An emergency guardianship, requiring a finding that the child's welfare requires the immediate appointment of an emergency guardian.

Temporary and emergency guardianships are time-limited. In each type of guardianship appointment, the parent retains all rights and duties that are not specifically assigned to the guardian.

Corrections

Act 123 (AB-30) creates the Council on Offender Employment, which may issue a certificate of qualification for employment to a person who has served a sentence for a nonviolent crime. A certificate of qualification for employment is a certificate that provides the person with relief from certain penalties, ineligibility, disability, or disadvantage that is related to employment or occupational licensing or certification that is a result of the person's criminal record.

Courts and civil actions

Act 30 (AB-59) allows certain pleadings and other papers to be served by e-mail to a designated e-mail address if an attorney or a party has consented in writing to accept service by e-mail. The act requires that the e-mail information provided to the court be kept current and provides that e-mail service is complete upon transmission unless the sender receives an indication that the message was not delivered.

Act 184 (AB-470) creates 12 additional circuit court branches that may be allocated by the director of state courts over the course of three years.

COVID-19 pandemic

Act 185 (AB-1038) is the response to the public health emergency related to the COVID-19 pandemic that was declared on March 12, 2020, by Executive Order 72. The following summaries for Act 185 use the term "COVID-19 public health emergency" to refer to that public health emergency and are organized by subheadings.

AGRICULTURE

The act suspends the requirement that an agricultural society, board, or association hold a fair each year to remain eligible in the next year for local fair aid from DATCP if the local fair is not held in 2020 because of the COVID-19 public health emergency.

CAMPAIGN FINANCE

The act allows state or local officeholders who are candidates for national, state, or local office to use public funds to pay for an unlimited number of communications related to the COVID-19 public health emergency during the public health emergency and for 30 days afterwards. Currently, such officeholders may not use public funds to pay for more than 49 pieces of substantially identical material during campaign season.

CHILDREN

The act credits federal Child Care and Development Fund block grant funds received by the state under the federal Coronavirus Aid, Relief, and Economic Security (CARES) Act of 2020 to federal block grant appropriations and subjects the expenditure of those funds to passive review by JCF.

CORRECTIONS

The act provides that, for the duration of the COVID-19 public health emergency, if an inmate of a correctional facility who has been diagnosed with COVID-19 dies, the coroner or medical examiner may perform a limited examination of the deceased inmate instead of a full autopsy, which may include an external examination of the body, a review of the inmate's medical records, or a review of the inmate's radiographs.

COURTS AND PROCEDURE

The act establishes immunity from civil liability for the death of or injury to an individual caused by emergency medical supplies for a manufacturer, distributor, or seller of emergency medical supplies who donates or sells the supplies to a charitable organization or governmental unit to respond to the COVID-19 public health emergency. A charitable organization that distributes these emergency medical supplies is also immune. The act defines "emergency medical supplies" to mean any medical equipment or supplies necessary to limit the spread of, or provide treatment for, a disease associated with the COVID-19 public health emergency.

ECONOMIC DEVELOPMENT

The act requires WEDC to submit to the governor and the legislature a plan for providing support to major industries in Wisconsin that have been adversely affected by the COVID-19 public health emergency.

EMPLOYMENT

The act does the following related to employment law:

1. Suspends the one-week waiting period that applies when receiving unemployment insurance benefits. The suspension applies to UI public benefit years beginning after March 12, 2020, and before February 7, 2021.

2. Provides that, for the purposes of worker's compensation, there is a rebuttable presumption that an injury caused to certain first responders by a COVID-19 diagnosis or positive test between the declaration of the COVID-19 public health emergency on March 12, 2020, and 30 days after its termination is caused by the individual's employment.

3. Provides that UI benefits for weeks occurring after March 12, 2020, and before December 31, 2020, will not be charged to individual employers but instead to certain other accounts. The act also requires the secretary of workforce development to seek advances (loans) to the state's UI trust fund from the federal government in order to keep UI contribution (tax) rates at their current levels.

4. Makes changes to the laws governing work-share plans, which are arrangements for reduced hours for a group of employees in lieu of layoffs while the employees receive partial UI benefits to compensate them for the reduction. The changes eliminate or reduce certain requirements governing work-share plans until December 31, 2020; allow plans during that time to go into effect more quickly; and require DWD to accept on-line plan applications and assist employers in submitting applications and developing plans.

5. During the COVID-19 public health emergency, eliminates the requirements that an employer provide an employee's personnel record within seven working days after receiving a request, that the inspection of the employee's records occur at a location near the employee's place of employment, and that the inspection occur during normal working hours.

The act does all the following related to public employment law:

1. Provides that, during the COVID-19 public health emergency, a state employee does not waive his or her right to appeal an adverse employment decision if the employee does not timely file the complaint.

2. Provides that, during the COVID-19 public health emergency, an appointing authority is not required to hold an in-person meeting with a state employee who has filed an employment grievance.

3. Allows a state employee to use annual leave during the COVID-19 public health emergency, even if the employee has not completed the first six months of the employee's probationary period. However, if the employee terminates employment before earning the leave used, the act allows the employer to deduct from the employee's final pay the cost of that leave.

4. Allows the director of the Bureau of Merit Recruitment and Selection in the Division of Personnel Management in DOA to adjust the number of hours a state employee in a limited term appointment may work during the COVID-19 public health emergency.

5. Allows an individual receiving an annuity from the WRS who is hired to a

critical position during the COVID-19 public health emergency by a public employer to not suspend his or her annuity for the duration of the public health emergency. The act also allows an individual receiving an annuity from the WRS to return to work for a public employer if at least 15 days, rather than the 75 days otherwise required, have elapsed since the individual retired from public employment.

6. For the purposes of group health insurance offered by the Group Insurance Board, an employee who returns from a leave of absence and who has not resumed active duty for at least 30 consecutive calendar days as of March 12, 2020, is deemed to have ended or interrupted the leave of absence on that date and may receive the employer contribution towards the premium for the insurance.

HEALTH

The act makes the following changes to health law:

1. Creates an exception to the law regarding cremation permits, providing that for the duration of the COVID-19 public health emergency, if a physician, coroner, or medical examiner signs a death certificate and lists COVID-19 as the cause of death, a coroner or medical examiner must (a) issue a cremation permit without viewing the corpse as otherwise would be required and (b) issue the permit within 48 hours after the death.

2. Prohibits DHS from requiring an instructional program for nurse aides to exceed the federal required minimum total training hours or minimum hours of supervised practical training.

3. During the COVID-19 public health emergency declared by the governor or the federal government, requires the entity that is under contract to collect and disseminate hospital data to prepare and publish a public health emergency dashboard.

4. Provides immunity from civil liability for certain health care professionals and providers for actions and omissions during the COVID-19 public health emergency, and the 60 days following its termination, if those actions and omissions do not involve reckless or wanton conduct or intentional misconduct and are for services provided in good faith or are substantially consistent with guidance from governmental officials or agencies.

5. During the COVID-19 public health emergency, and the 60 days following its termination, suspends credential renewal requirements for ambulance service providers, emergency medical services providers, and emergency medical responders.

6. Requires DHS to include coverage through the SeniorCare program of

vaccinations recommended for adults. The act requires DHS to provide payments to health care providers that administer the vaccinations. DHS must deduct amounts available from other sources from the amount DHS provides.

HOUSING

The act allows households to submit to DOA applications for heating assistance any time in 2020 instead of only before May 16 and after September 30.

INSURANCE

The act makes the following changes to insurance law:

1. During the COVID-19 public health emergency, and the 60 days after its termination, limits the amount an insured pays out-of-pocket for a service or supply provided by a provider that is out of the insured's health insurance network to the amount that the insured would pay if it was provided by a provider in the network; requires a certain amount of reimbursement of the out-of-network provider by the insurance plan; and requires an out-of-network provider to accept a certain amount as payment in full.

2. Prohibits certain insurance coverage discrimination based on a COVID-19 diagnosis, such as establishing eligibility rules, canceling coverage, setting rates, or refusing to honor premium grace periods.

3. Requires, before March 13, 2021, health insurance policies and self-insured governmental health plans to cover COVID-19 testing without copayment or coinsurance.

4. Prohibits health insurance policies, self-insured governmental health plans, and pharmacy benefit managers from requiring prior authorization for early prescription refills and imposing a limit on prescription drug quantities that are no more than 90-day supplies during the COVID public health emergency.

5. Specifies that during the COVID-19 public health emergency a physician or nurse anesthetist who is temporarily authorized to practice in Wisconsin may fulfill the financial responsibility requirement by filing a certificate of insurance for a policy from a certain jurisdiction and may elect to be covered by Wisconsin's health care liability laws.

LEGISLATURE

The act does the following relating to the legislature:

1. Permits JCF to transfer from sum-sufficient appropriations an amount up to $75,000,000 to other appropriations for expenditures related to the COVID-19 public health emergency.

2. Requires the Legislative Audit Bureau to review programs affected by Act 185 and expenditures authorized by Act 185 and to quarterly report the results of the review to the legislature and the Joint Legislative Audit Committee.

LOCAL GOVERNMENT

The act allows a municipal board of review to adjourn until a later date, without convening first, to consider property tax objections and allows a town to postpone its annual meeting so that it does not occur during the COVID-19 public health emergency.

MEDICAL ASSISTANCE

The act makes the following changes to the Medical Assistance program during the COVID-19 public health emergency:

1. Allows DHS to suspend compliance with current premium and health risk assessment requirements for childless adults, delay implementation of a community engagement requirement, and maintain continuous enrollment in order to qualify for an enhanced federal medical assistance percentage under federal law.

2. Suspends certain legislative oversight over the submission of requests for a waiver of federal law submitted by DHS during the COVID-19 public health emergency declared by the federal secretary of health and human services if the waiver request is any of the items specified in Act 185.

3. Requires DHS to develop a pay-for-performance system in the Medical Assistance program to incentivize participation in health information data sharing.

OCCUPATIONAL REGULATION

The act does all of the following during the COVID-19 public health emergency:

1. Authorizes certain health care providers holding valid, unexpired licenses or certificates granted by other states to practice within the scope of their credentials.

2. Authorizes persons who previously held a health care provider credential to practice within the scope of the person's previously held credential.

3. Creates a special provision governing a pharmacist's authority to extend prescription orders during the COVID-19 public health emergency and the 30 days after its conclusion. The provision exempts extensions during that period from certain requirements that otherwise apply to emergency extensions, and allows a pharmacist to dispense up to a 30-day supply using that authority during that period.

4. Authorizes DSPS to waive fees for applications for an initial credential and renewal of a credential for physicians, physician assistants, nurses, dentists, pharmacists, psychologists, and certain behavioral health providers.

5. Exempts certain health care workers from licensure renewal requirements during the period beginning March 12, 2020, and ending 60 days after the conclusion of the COVID-19 public health emergency.

PRIMARY AND SECONDARY EDUCATION

The act does all of the following relating to primary and secondary education:

1. In the 2019–20 school year, eliminates requirements to administer the Wisconsin Student Assessment System examinations to pupils in the fourth, eighth, ninth, tenth, and eleventh grades. These examinations include the Forward Exam, ACT ASPIRE, the ACT, and Dynamic Learning Maps.

2. In the 2019–20 school year, eliminates requirements to administer a third grade standardized reading test.

3. In the 2019–20 school year, prohibits the use of pupil performance on statewide assessments in the educator effectiveness system.

4. In the 2020–21 school year, prohibits DPI from publishing a school and school district accountability report for the 2019–20 school year.

5. During the period beginning on the first day of the COVID-19 public health emergency and ending on October 31, 2020, gives DPI the authority to do all of the following:

   a. Waive education statutes and administrative rules related to a parental choice program or the SNSP; private schools participating in a parental choice program or the SNSP; or independent charter schools.

   b. Establish alternate deadlines in education statutes or administrative rules if the original deadline occurs during, or is related to a date during, that same period of time.

6. Authorizes DPI to grant a request from a private school to waive required hours of instruction in the 2019–20 school year.

7. Extends application deadlines to attend a private school in the Wisconsin Parental Choice Program in the 2020–21 school year.

8. Extends application deadlines to attend a public school in a nonresident school district under the full-time open enrollment program in the 2020–21 school year.

9. Requires school boards to report to DPI information related to school closures during the public health emergency, including information related to virtual instruction, expenditure reductions, and staff layoffs. The act requires DPI to submit this information to the legislature.

10. Requires DPI to post best practices for transitioning back to in-person instruction on DPI's Internet site by June 30, 2020.

PUBLIC UTILITIES

The act authorizes the Board of Commissioners of Public Lands to make loans to municipal public utilities to ensure that those utilities can maintain liquidity during the COVID-19 public health emergency.

STATE GOVERNMENT

The act does the following relating to state government:

1. Allows a state entity to waive a requirement that an individual appear in person during the COVID-19 public health emergency if the state entity finds that the waiver assists in the state's response to the public health emergency or that enforcing the requirement may increase the public health risk.
2. Authorizes state agencies, local governments, the legislature, and the courts to suspend certain deadlines and training requirements during the COVID-19 public health emergency.
3. Authorizes an additional $725,000,000 in public debt to refund tax-supported or self-amortizing state general obligation debt. The current level of such authorized debt is $6,785,000,000; the new amount will be $7,510,000,000.
4. Authorizes the secretary of administration to transfer employees from one executive branch agency to another executive branch agency to provide service during the COVID-19 public health emergency. The transfers remain in effect until rescinded by the secretary or 90 days after the public health emergency terminates, whichever is earlier.

TAXATION

The act changes laws related to taxation as follows:

1. Allows counties and municipalities to provide, upon a finding of hardship, that any installment payment of property taxes due after April 1, 2020, that is received after its due date will not accrue interest or penalties if the total amount due is received on or before October 1, 2020. The act also allows taxpayers to retain their options under current law to contest their property taxes if payments received after the due date are received by October 1, 2020.
2. Authorizes DOR to waive, on a case-by-case basis, interest and penalties that accrue during the COVID-19 public health emergency for persons who fail to remit a variety of taxes during that period due to the pandemic's effects.
3. Adopts federal tax law changes made in response to the COVID-19 public

health emergency, including changes related to distributions from certain retirement accounts, deductions for charitable contributions, the treatment of paycheck protection loans to businesses and employees under the small business administration's loan guarantee program, and an exclusion from income certain student loan principal and interest payments made by an employer on behalf of an employee.

TRADE AND CONSUMER PROTECTION

The act prohibits retailers from accepting certain returns of food products, personal care products, cleaning products, and paper products during the COVID-19 public health emergency.

VITAL RECORDS

The act requires that, during the COVID-19 public health emergency, if the underlying cause of a death is determined to be COVID-19, the person signing the death certificate must provide an electronic signature on the certificate within 48 hours after the death.

Crime and law enforcement

Act 31 (AB-17) creates a mandatory minimum sentence of five years in prison for a person who is convicted of homicide by intoxicated use of a vehicle.

Act 108 (SB-50) requires law enforcement agencies that use body cameras to have a written policy on the use and storage of the cameras and the data recorded by the cameras. The act requires the law enforcement agencies to retain the data for at least 120 days and specifies circumstances in which the data must be retained longer. The act also specifies that the data are subject to the open records laws with exceptions to protect privacy and the identity of victims and minors.

Act 112 (AB-804) increases the penalty from a Class A misdemeanor to a Class G felony for intimidating a victim of a crime, or intimidating a witness to a crime, if the crime is domestic abuse.

Act 132 (AB-454) creates the crime of swatting. Under the act, it is a crime for a person to knowingly and intentionally convey false information that an emergency exists if the information elicits or could elicit a response from a specialized tactical (SWAT) team.

Act 144 (AB-734) creates the crime of mail theft, which is taking a letter, postcard, or package from a residence or other building without the owner's consent.

Act 161 (SB-368) creates the crime of money laundering. Under the act, it is a crime to engage in, supervise, or facilitate a transaction with illegally obtained property or items of value; to make property or items of value available to another with the intent to perpetuate illegal activity; or to engage in a transaction that is designed to conceal or disguise the nature, location, source, ownership, or control of property or items of value or to avoid a financial transaction reporting requirement under federal law.

Domestic relations

Act 95 (SB-158) does all of the following relating to paternity:

1. Creates a new presumption of paternity and a new way to conclusively determine paternity under the law using genetic testing.
2. Requires the court in a paternity action to order genetic testing.
3. Allows a court that determines that a judicial determination of whether a man is the father of the child is not in the best interest of the child to dismiss a paternity action with respect to that man, regardless of whether genetic tests have already been performed or what the results of those genetic tests were.

Education

HIGHER EDUCATION

Act 9 (AB-56) prohibits the Board of Regents from charging resident undergraduate academic fees in the 2019–20 and 2020–21 academic years that exceed those charged in the 2018–19 academic year.

Act 46 (AB-189) requires the Board of Regents and the WTCS board to enter into two agreements. The first agreement must promote and support agreements that articulate how the completion of requirements for specified programs of study transfer between institutions. The second agreement must identify at least 72 credits of core general education courses that are transferable between institutions beginning in the 2022–23 academic year. Former law required a similar agreement that was limited to at least 30 credits of core general education courses. As under former law, tribally controlled and private, nonprofit colleges in the state are allowed to participate in both of the agreements.

Act 149 (SB-537) requires HEAB to award tuition grants, not exceeding $2,000 per semester, to certain veterans or their dependents enrolled in private, nonprofit colleges. The grants are made for students who would have qualified for tuition remission under the Wisconsin GI Bill if they had attended a UW

System school or technical college. The grant amount must be matched by the college in which the student is enrolled.

Primary and secondary education

Act 9 (AB-56) does the following:

1. Provides a per pupil adjustment under school district revenue limits of $175 in the 2019–20 school year, $179 in the 2020–21 school year, and $0 in the 2021–22 school year and each school year thereafter.
2. Sets the low revenue adjustment under school district revenue limits at $9,700 per pupil in the 2019–20 school year and $10,000 per pupil in 2020–21 school year and each school year thereafter.
3. Beginning in the 2019–20 school year, increases the per pupil amount under the per pupil categorical aid program to $742 per pupil.
4. Creates the supplemental per pupil aid program.
5. Eliminates supplemental special education aid on July 1, 2020. Under prior law, DPI provided supplemental special education aid to a school district that in the previous year had revenue limit authority per pupil that was below the statewide average, that had expenditures for special education that were more than 16 percent of the school district's total expenditures, and that had a membership that was less than 2,000 pupils.
6. Eliminates school performance improvement grants effective July 1, 2020. Under prior law, beginning in the 2018–19 school year, DPI awarded a school performance improvement grant to an eligible school located in a first class city school district (currently only Milwaukee Public Schools) or in a school district that was in the lowest category on the school and school district accountability report (report card) if the eligible school developed a written school improvement plan to improve pupil performance and received a higher score on the report card than it did in the previous school year.
7. Makes changes to the Technology for Educational Achievement program, including the following: (a) continues the information technology block program for rural school districts through fiscal year 2021; (b) eliminates educational technology training grants for teachers; and (c) eliminates grants to school districts for technology-enhanced high school curriculum.

Act 43 (AB-195) creates an alternative method for meeting one requirement for obtaining a provisional teaching license based on the applicant having an out-of-state license, commonly known as a license based on reciprocity. Under the act, an applicant may satisfy the requirement by teaching under the out-of-state license for two semesters or by teaching in a public or private school in this state for two semesters while holding a DPI-issued teaching license, usually a tier 1 license with stipulations.

Act 83 (AB-528) creates a peer-to-peer suicide prevention grant program. Under the act, DPI provides grants to private, public, and tribal high schools to support existing or establish new peer-to-peer suicide prevention programs.

Act 176 (SB-437) creates an exception to the revenue ceiling freeze for a school district that had a failed operating referendum in the 2018–19 school year if the failed operating referendum was for the costs of operating a new school building and a capital referendum to build the new school building failed at the same election.

Employment

PUBLIC EMPLOYMENT

Act 9 (AB-56) does the following:
1. Authorizes DWD to enter into contracts under the Project SEARCH program to provide employment skills services to individuals with developmental disabilities. The act also requires DWD to allocate $250,000 in each year of the 2019–21 fiscal biennium to the program.
2. Requires DWD to allocate grants to DOC to create and operate job training centers at minimum and medium security prisons and to create and operate mobile classrooms.
3. Requires DWD to award grants of $75,000 per year of the 2019–21 fiscal biennium under its workforce training program, commonly referred to as the Fast Forward Program, for workforce training in county jail facilities. The grants are awarded without any matching-funds requirement and notwithstanding any otherwise applicable eligibility criteria.

Act 120 (AB-646) provides that a state employee is not subject to removal, suspension without pay, a reduction in base pay, or demotion without prior progressive discipline if the employee is under the influence of, or in possession of, a controlled substance or a controlled substance analog while on duty and the employee is using the controlled substance or analog as dispensed, prescribed, or recommended as part of medication-assisted treatment. Under former law, the employee would be subject to discipline without prior progressive discipline.

Environment

Act 9 (AB-56) does all of the following:

1. Requires the full $345 amount, rather than $95, of the annual concentrated animal feeding operation fee to be deposited into a new program revenue account for purposes of administering the concentrated animal feeding operation (CAFO) program.
2. Provides an additional $4,000,000 in bonding authority for dam safety grants.
3. Provides an additional $6,500,000 in bonding authority for rural nonpoint source water pollution abatement grants.
4. Provides an additional $4,000,000 in bonding authority for urban nonpoint source and storm water management and municipal flood control and riparian restoration programs.
5. Increases from $32,000,000 to $36,000,000 the amount of public debt the state may contract to fund removal of contaminated sediment.

Act 101 (SB-310) prohibits the use of fire fighting foams that contain intentionally added PFAS (perfluoroalkyl and polyfluoroalkyl substances), with exceptions provided for use during emergency fire fighting or fire prevention operations.

Act 151 (SB-91) creates a system for buying and selling water pollution credits through a central clearinghouse.

Financial institutions

Act 125 (AB-293) adopts, with modifications, the Revised Uniform Law on Notarial Acts, which allows a notary public, using technology, to notarize documents for persons not physically present with the notary public. The act also creates a remote notary council to adopt standards for performing notarial acts for remotely located individuals and requires DFI to maintain a database of notaries public who perform these remote notarizations.

Health and human services

HEALTH

Act 9 (AB-56) makes changes to health laws, including the following:
1. Combines funding for grants to assist rural hospitals in procuring infrastructure and increasing case volume to develop accredited graduate medical training programs with funding for grants to support existing graduate medical training programs and expands eligibility for both types of grants to all specialties rather than certain prescribed specialties.
2. Requires DHS to distribute grants to support "treatment programs." Recipients of the grants must use awards for supervision, training, and resources, including salaries, benefits, and other related costs. This provision was affected by a

partial veto, which changed a grant program from a qualified treatment trainee program to a "treatment program." The qualified treatment program would have provided opportunities for trainees to complete clinically supervised practice requirements to be credentialed and obtain specialized training in mental and behavioral health in children, youth, and families.

3. Requires DHS to award grants for residential lead hazard abatement.

Act 90 (AB-287) does the following:

1. Allows, unless a health care power of attorney instrument specifies otherwise, one physician and one qualified physician assistant or nurse practitioner to personally examine a principal and make a finding of incapacity upon which a health care power of attorney becomes effective.

2. Allows one physician and one qualified physician assistant or nurse practitioner to determine that a person is incapacitated for purposes of admission to a hospice.

Act 154 (SB-217) requires DHS to consult with DETF to develop and implement a plan to reduce the incidence of diabetes in Wisconsin, improve diabetes care, and control complications associated with diabetes. DHS may consult with DPI and DOC in developing the plan and must submit a biennial report to the legislature.

Medical assistance

Act 9 (AB-56) makes changes to the Medical Assistance program, including all of the following:

1. Increasing reimbursement rates for nursing homes, direct care, and personal care and payments under the rural critical care access supplement.

2. Expanding the definition of "telehealth services" for purposes of reimbursement under the Medical Assistance program and requiring DHS to develop a reimbursement method for providers.

3. Continuing the Medical Assistance reimbursement for the mental health clinical consultation program by eliminating the termination date.

4. Making changes to long-term care programs to reflect the statewide expansion of Family Care, elimination of the Community Options Program, and expansion of aging and disability resource center services to other programs such as IRIS.

5. For fiscal years 2019–20 and 2020–21, requiring DHS to pay hospitals that serve low-income patients an additional amount as the state share of Medical Assistance payments, and the matching federal share of payments. For fiscal

years 2019–20 and 2020–21, provided there is no conflict with federal rules, the act also increases from $4,600,000 to $9,600,000 the maximum payment that DHS may pay a single hospital that serves a disproportionate share of low-income patients.

Act 56 (SB-380) requires DHS to provide reimbursement for Medical Assistance benefits that are provided through interactive telehealth and requires DHS to include as a benefit and provide Medical Assistance reimbursement for additional forms of telehealth. Act 56 also prohibits DHS from setting certain additional requirements or limitations on services provided through telehealth or providers providing telehealth services.

Act 122 (AB-650) requires DHS to provide reimbursement under the Medical Assistance program for services provided by a peer recovery coach if the services meet the criteria established in the act. The act also requires DHS to include services provided by a peer recovery coach as a benefit under the Medical Assistance program.

Mental health and developmental disabilities

Act 9 (AB-56) makes changes to mental health laws, including all of the following:
1. Developing a comprehensive mental health consultation program.
2. Allowing opioid and methamphetamine treatment programs to offer methadone treatment.

Act 119 (AB-645) provides immunity for jailers, keepers of a jail, or persons designated with custodial authority by a jailer or keeper that administer naloxone or another opioid antagonist to a person believed to be undergoing an opioid overdose and that have the applicable training. The act also requires DHS, after consulting with DOC, to study the availability of medication-assisted treatment for opioid use disorder in each prison and county jail.

Act 120 (AB-646) requires recovery residences that promote recovery from a substance use disorder and that seek referrals or funding from DHS to register with DHS.

Act 122 (AB-650) requires DHS to establish and maintain a program related to referral and treatment services following a substance use overdose that includes that, among other requirements, overdose treatment providers coordinate and continue care and treatment after an overdose. The act requires DHS to seek any funding available from the federal government for the program.

Local government

Act 9 (AB-56) does the following:

1. Makes changes to the Technology for Educational Achievement program, including the following: (a) continues the information technology block program for rural public libraries through fiscal year 2021; and (b) eliminates educational technology training grants for librarians.
2. Requires cities, villages, and towns to reduce the quarterly fees they charge to video service providers by 0.5 percent beginning on January 1, 2020, and by an additional 1 percent beginning on January 1, 2021.

Act 14 (SB-239) creates a regulatory framework for what are commonly called 5G networks. The act imposes requirements on cities, villages, towns, counties, and the state regarding (a) permits for deploying wireless equipment and facilities; (b) placement of those items in rights-of-way; (c) access to certain governmental structures by wireless providers; and (d) resolution of disputes over the act's requirements. The act also allows cities, villages, towns, and counties to impose setback requirements for certain mobile service support structures.

Act 19 (SB-266) requires a city, village, town, or county, the state, the Board of Regents of the UW System, and Marquette University to pay health insurance premiums for the surviving spouse and dependent children of a law enforcement officer or emergency medical services practitioner who dies in the line of duty if the entity paid such premiums for the officer or practitioner while he or she was employed by the entity.

Act 126 (AB-310) allows a city, village, town, or county that uses a referendum to exceed the local levy limit to base the referendum question on either actual data or its best estimate, and requires that the question include the percentage increase for each fiscal year. The act also authorizes a city, village, town, or county to hold such a referendum in an odd-numbered year either by a special referendum or on the same schedule as certain school board referendums.

Natural resources

CONSERVATION

Act 9 (AB-56) reauthorizes the Warren Knowles-Gaylord Nelson Stewardship Program for two additional years, until June 30, 2022, at existing program bonding levels; authorizes the state to contract additional public debt in an amount up to $42,600,000 for that stewardship program; and authorizes DNR in fiscal year 2020–21 to obligate up to \$33,250,000 in unobligated amounts from prior fiscal years.

Navigable waters and wetlands

Act 9 (AB-56) authorizes the state to contract an additional public debt in an amount up to \$4,000,000 for financial assistance to counties, cities, villages, towns, and public inland lake protection and rehabilitation districts for dam safety projects.

Act 59 (SB-169) makes changes to requirements for wetland mitigation banks, including establishing geographic limits on a mitigation bank from which credits may be purchased, establishing financial assurance requirements for projects by mitigation banks, and allowing a mitigation bank to sell estimated credits before a project is completed.

Act 93 (SB-125) requires DNR to obligate up to \$5,200,000 in unobligated moneys under the Warren Knowles-Gaylord Nelson Stewardship 2000 Program to fund critical health- and safety-related water infrastructure projects and high-priority water infrastructure projects in state parks, prioritizing projects in those state parks with the highest demand.

Parks, forestry, and recreation

Act 141 (AB-692) increases from \$2,475,400 to \$5,475,400 aid to counties for snowmobile trails and areas, to cover costs such as purchasing land for trails, enforcing laws on trails, developing and maintaining trails, and improving bridges on trails.

Occupational regulation

Act 17 (AB-250) makes the following changes to the laws regulating sign language interpreters:

1. Replaces the former program for sign language interpreter licenses with four categories of licenses: sign language interpreter—intermediate hearing, sign language interpreter—advanced hearing, sign language interpreter—intermediate deaf, and sign language interpreter—advanced deaf.

2. Requires DSPS to promulgate rules defining the scope of practice of each category of sign language interpreter license.

Act 24 (AB-137) allows pharmacists to administer vaccines to children under age six if the vaccine is administered pursuant to a prescription order and the pharmacist completes a course that includes administering vaccines to children under age six. The act also generally allows pharmacists and pharmacy students to administer without a prescription order the vaccines listed in the immunization schedules published by the federal Centers for Disease Control and Prevention.

Act 100 (SB-390) enters Wisconsin into the Physical Therapy Licensure Compact, which allows physical therapists and physical therapist assistants that are licensed in one state that is a party to the compact to practice in other member states. The compact provides for the creation of the Physical Therapy Compact Commission, which is charged with administering the compact and includes delegates from each member state's licensing board. The act also contains provisions relating to implementation of the compact in Wisconsin.

Act 180 (SB-117) adopts, with some modifications, the Revised Uniform Athlete Agents Act, which makes changes to DSPS's registration program for athlete agents, including the following:

1. Prohibiting athlete agents from encouraging another person to engage in conduct the athlete agent is prohibited from doing.
2. Prohibiting a person from engaging in certain activities involving a student athlete, such as directly or indirectly attempting to influence a student athlete to choose an athlete agent or enter into an agency contract with an athlete agent, unless the person registers with DSPS as an athlete agent.
3. Requiring an agency contract to be accompanied by an acknowledgement by the student athlete that signing the contract may make the student ineligible to participate in athletics at an educational institution.

Real estate

Act 72 (SB-247) specifies that an owner of real estate may, with certain exceptions, use a surveillance device to observe or record an individual who is present for a private showing, open house, or other viewing of the real estate in connection with the owner's attempt to sell the real estate. The bill specifies that such use of a surveillance device is not an invasion of the individual's privacy under current state law recognizing the right of privacy.

Shared revenue

Act 9 (AB-56) provides state aid to municipalities to compensate for a reduction in video service provider fees.

State government

STATE BUILDING PROGRAM

Act 9 (AB-56) does all of the following:

1. Authorizes an additional $40,000,000 in general fund supported borrowing for grants to counties for the establishment of county-run, secured residential care centers for children and youth, bringing the total bonding authorization for that purpose to $80,000,000.

2. Authorizes $25,000,000 in general fund supported borrowing for construction projects having a public purpose, including $3,000,000 for a grant to the Incourage Community Foundation, Inc., to assist with constructing an economic and community hub.

3. Authorizes $15,000,000 in general fund supported borrowing for a "center." This provision was affected by a partial veto, which changed a center financed under the State Building Program from a northern Wisconsin regional crisis center to a "center."

4. Authorizes $10,000,000 in general fund supported borrowing to assist the Medical College of Wisconsin, Inc., in the construction of a cancer research facility.

STATE FINANCE

Act 9 (AB-56) transfers $25,000,000 from WEDC to the general fund.

GENERAL STATE GOVERNMENT

Act 9 (AB-56) requires DOA to award grants for alternative fuels from the Volkswagen settlement funds.

Taxation

Act 7 (AB-10) disallows any income tax deduction for moving expenses paid by a taxpayer to move the taxpayer's Wisconsin business operations, in whole or in part, to a location outside the state or to move the taxpayer's business operations outside the United States.

Act 9 (AB-56) changes laws related to taxation as follows:

1. Reduces from 5.84 percent to 5.21 percent the marginal individual income tax rate that applies to income that falls within the second income tax bracket.

2. Provides an exclusion from income for individuals and corporations for interest received on bonds or notes issued by the Wisconsin Health and Educational Facilities Authority if the bonds or notes are issued in an amount totaling $35,000,000 or less, to the extent such interest is not otherwise exempt.

3. Imposes an excise tax on vapor products, which are defined as noncombustible products that produce vapor or aerosol for inhalation from the application of a heating element, regardless of whether the liquid or other substance contains nicotine, at a rate of 5 cents per milliliter of the liquid or other substance.

Act 10 (AB-251) requires marketplace providers to collect and remit sales tax from third parties and reduces individual income tax rates based on the collection of sales and use tax from out-of-state retailers and marketplace providers. The act defines a "marketplace provider" as any person who facilitates the retail sales of a seller's products or services and who, by agreements with third parties, collects payment from the purchaser and transmits that payment to the seller.

Act 28 (AB-73) generally prohibits retailers and DOR from collecting sales and use taxes related to a local professional baseball park district (American Family Field) after August 31, 2020, or after the date on which the district board certifies that the district has paid off its bonds and established a special maintenance and capital improvements fund, whichever occurs earlier. The act also imposes legislative oversight of the district.

Act 136 (AB-532) reduces the amount of capital gains subject to income and franchise taxation for taxpayers who invest in Wisconsin opportunity zones.

Trade and consumer protection

Act 60 (SB-170) allows a minor to operate a temporary stand without a food license from DATCP if certain conditions are met and prohibits cities, villages, towns, and counties from enacting an ordinance that prohibits minors from operating such a stand.

Transportation

HIGHWAYS AND LOCAL ASSISTANCE

Act 9 (AB-56) does all of the following:

1. Adds major highway projects on I 43 and I 41 to the list of enumerated projects approved for construction.

2. Increases by $95,000,000 the authority to contract state debt for the reconstruction of the Zoo Interchange.

3. Increases by $27,000,000 the authority to contract state debt for major interstate bridge projects.

4. Decreases by $10,000,000 the authority to contract state debt for high-cost state highway bridge projects.

Act 69 (SB-447) modifies the supplemental general transportation aids program to require DOT to make supplemental general transportation aid payments to towns for which other general transportation aid payments are based on the number of miles of highway in the town and that have had their other general transportation aid payments limited by the requirement that a municipality not be paid an amount greater than 85 percent of its three-year average highway costs.

IMPAIRED DRIVING

Act 31 (AB-17) creates a mandatory minimum sentence of five years in prison for a person who is convicted of homicide by intoxicated use of a vehicle.

Act 106 (SB-6) imposes a mandatory minimum 18-month period of confinement in prison for fifth and sixth offenses of operating a motor vehicle while intoxicated.

MOTOR VEHICLES

Act 9 (AB-56) increases the registration fee for certain vehicles for which the fee is based on the vehicle's weight.

Act 163 (SB-523) expands an exception from the commercial driver license requirement for certain uses of commercial motor vehicles by farmers.

GENERAL TRANSPORTATION

Act 9 (AB-56) does all of the following:

1. Requires that a portion of petroleum inspection fees be deposited into the transportation fund.
2. Increases the amount of state aid payments for mass transit systems.
3. Appropriates an amount to DOT for "local grant." This provision was affected by a partial veto, which changed a local roads improvement discretionary supplemental grant program to a "local grant."
4. Allows DOT to make grants for intermodal freight facilities.
5. Requires that DOT expend in the 2019–21 fiscal biennium up to $9,080,000 from proceeds of transportation revenue bonds for administrative facility projects.

Act 11 (SB-152) authorizes the use of electric scooters on highways and requires operators of electric scooters to adhere to the rules of the road. The act also provides, with certain exceptions, that a local unit of government may regulate the rental and operation of electric scooters in the same way that it regulates bicycles.

Act 34 (AB-132) regulates the operation of electric bicycles.

Veterans and military affairs

Act 9 (AB-56) eliminates the veterans housing loan program and creates a veterans outreach and recovery program to provide outreach, mental health services, and support to Wisconsin veterans, national guard members, and members of the reserves who may have a mental health condition or substance use disorder.

Act 26 (AB-471) requires DMA to award grants to Wisconsin public safety answering points to purchase, upgrade, and maintain 911 equipment.

Constitutional amendments

Enrolled Joint Resolution 3 (SJR-2), proposed by the 2019 legislature on second consideration, expands the rights of crime victims under the Wisconsin Constitution. The amendment was ratified by the voters on April 7, 2020.

Survey of Significant Wisconsin Court Decisions, 2019–20

Surveyed below are the most significant Wisconsin court decisions during 2019 and 2020. In the last two years, the Wisconsin Supreme Court has broken new ground on a number of issues involving the ability of the legislature to call itself into extraordinary session, the governor's partial veto power, the governor's and the legislature's oversight of the state agency rulemaking process, and the involvement of the legislature in litigation handled by the attorney general. Rarely have so many cases involving the core and essential powers of the state's political institutions been on the court's docket.

The court has been active in other policy areas as well, issuing decisions on what constitutes a "mission" of a traffic stop, claims against firearm classified advertising, pretrial identification of crime suspects, involuntary medication of prisoners, provision of electronic documents under the state's public records law, and presumptions regarding implied consent to searches of incapacitated persons operating motor vehicles.

But, most importantly, during this period, the Wisconsin Supreme Court issued momentous decisions on matters involving the state government's response to the COVID-19 pandemic. The court struck down attempts by the secretary of health services to close nonessential businesses, prohibit private gatherings of non-household members, and forbid nonessential travel. In addition, the court also ruled that the governor, during a public health emergency, could not suspend statutes so as to prohibit in-person voting during the April 2020 elections.

The following survey prepared by attorneys at the Legislative Reference Bureau summarizes these critical and important judicial decisions. The LRB attorneys who prepared these summaries practice law, conduct research, and draft legislation in these issue areas. To be sure, each decision merits a much longer discussion because the issues confronted by the court in these cases touch on different and competing views of the legal authority of Wisconsin's political institutions and the role of government in society and the economy. The case summaries presented in this report serve as a concise introduction to the court's important activities in the last two years. Please contact us at the LRB offices if you would like a fuller discussion of any of these decisions, as well as of the significant issues litigated in these cases.

Emergency order issued under the COVID-19 pandemic

In *Wisconsin Legislature v. Palm*, 2020 WI 42, 391 Wis. 2d 497, 942 N.W.2d 900, the supreme court held that an emergency order issued by the state's secretary of health services-designee to address the 2020 COVID-19 pandemic constituted a "rule" within the meaning of the administrative procedure law and, as such, was required to be promulgated using the emergency rule process in order to be valid. Because that process had not been followed when the order was issued, the court declared the order unenforceable. The court also determined that parts of the order exceeded the authority granted by the statutes on which they relied.

The spring of 2020 saw the sudden emergence of the SARS-CoV-2 coronavirus pandemic around the world, and on March 12, 2020, Governor Tony Evers issued Executive Order 72, "Declaring a Health Emergency in Response to the COVID-19 Coronavirus." In addition to declaring a public health emergency for the state of Wisconsin, Executive Order 72 designated the Department of Health Services (DHS) as the lead agency to respond to the public health emergency and directed DHS to "take all necessary and appropriate measures to prevent and respond to incidents of COVID-19 in the State." Over the course of March 2020, Governor Evers and DHS issued a series of emergency orders ordering a number of actions in response to the pandemic, including a March 24, 2020, "Safer at Home" emergency order that directed all individuals present in Wisconsin to stay at their home or residence, with certain exceptions.

On April 16, 2020, DHS issued a similar, follow-up "Safer at Home" emergency order (Order 28) relying on certain powers granted to DHS under the laws governing communicable diseases. In contrast to some of the earlier orders, Order 28 did not purport to rely upon the governor's declaration of a public health emergency. DHS also, on April 20, 2020, issued a subsequent emergency order establishing criteria for lifting the measures put in place by Order 28. The orders were signed by secretary of health services-designee Andrea Palm. The legislature filed an emergency petition for original action related to Order 28 on April 21, 2020, and the court accepted the petition.

In a majority opinion authored by Chief Justice Patience D. Roggensack, the court first addressed the legislature's standing to seek judicial review of the order. Because, the majority wrote, the legislature claimed that the secretary was impinging upon the legislature's constitutional core power and functions, it had standing to proceed on the claims for which the court had granted review.

The court then moved to a discussion of whether Order 28 was required to be promulgated as a rule in order to be valid. Citing the definition of "rule" in Wis. Stat. ch. 227, and the court's opinion in *Citizens for Sensible Zoning, Inc. v.*

Wisconsin Department of Natural Resources, 90 Wis. 2d 804, 280 N.W.2d 702 (1979), the court concluded that Order 28 was a "general order of general application" that regulated all persons in Wisconsin at the time of issuance and all who would come into the state in the future. The court rejected an argument that Order 28 was not a rule because it was responding only to a specific, limited-in-time scenario, observing that the criteria for lifting the measures meant that the measures could continue indefinitely. The court further wrote that in order for a violation of Order 28 to constitute criminal conduct, as was provided in the order, the order would have to be promulgated as a rule. The court recognized that the governor had emergency powers, which were not being challenged in the case, but that the governor could not rely on those emergency powers indefinitely in confronting an emergency such as a pandemic. As such, the court wrote, DHS was required to follow the procedures for promulgating emergency rules in issuing Order 28, and, because it had not, Order 28 was unenforceable. Exempt from the court's order was a provision in Order 28 closing public and private k–12 schools.

The court also addressed more specifically the powers granted to DHS under the laws governing communicable diseases. Measures in Order 28 such as travel restrictions, the court wrote, were broader than what was permitted under the statute. Citing a legislative "canon of construction" against reading broad authority being implied in statutes, the court wrote that grants of authority to agencies were to be narrowly construed in the absence of explicit language granting such authority.

The court concluded by reiterating that Order 28 was invalid and unenforceable due to not having been promulgated as a rule and having exceeded DHS's statutory authority. The court also noted that the legislature had requested a stay of the court's order of at least six days. Citing the amount of time that had already passed since the court began consideration of the case, the majority declined to order a stay.

Chief Justice Roggensack also wrote a concurring opinion separate from her majority opinion. She wrote that although she joined the majority opinion, she also concluded that there was a legal basis for granting the legislature's request for a temporary stay of the court's order and that she would grant one. Justice Rebecca Grassl Bradley, joined by Justice Daniel Kelly, also concurred in the judgment, writing about the danger of concentrating governmental power in a single individual, in this case Palm, and against the erosion of constitutional rights during an emergency such as a pandemic. Justice Kelly also wrote separately, joined by Justice R.G. Bradley, emphasizing the limitations on the legislature's ability to delegate power to the executive branch and that, in his view, Order 28 went too far in making policy decisions in which the legislature need have a role.

Justice Ann Walsh Bradley, joined by Justice Rebecca Frank Dallet, wrote in dissent to criticize the chief justice's concurrence. The two justices concluded that the rulemaking procedures were incompatible with responding to the pandemic and observing that the statutes gave DHS broad authority to act. She further concluded that Order 28 was not a rule due to its being limited and not of future application, and that the legislature lacked standing to bring the claims. Justice Brian Hagedorn, joined in part by Justices A.W. Bradley and Dallet, offered a lengthy dissent further exploring some of the potential implications of the majority's decision. He wrote that Order 28 was ill-suited to the emergency rulemaking process, and that the majority's decision cast doubt on a host of other statutes that also provided for criminal violations.

Constitutionality of legislative extraordinary sessions

In *League of Women Voters of Wisconsin v. Evers*, 2019 WI 75, 387 Wis. 2d 511, 929 N.W.2d 209, the supreme court considered the constitutionality of extraordinary sessions held by the Wisconsin Legislature and, specifically, whether an extraordinary session convened by the legislature in December 2018 was constitutional. The court held that the December 2018 extraordinary session was constitutional, finding that the Wisconsin Constitution directs the legislature to meet at a time provided by law and that the legislature did so when it convened the extraordinary session.

Article IV, section 11, of the Wisconsin Constitution mandates that the legislature meet at such time "as shall be provided by law." The court has held that "provided by law" means statutory law. Article IV, section 8, of the Wisconsin Constitution further provides that "each house" of the legislature "may determine the rules of its own proceedings."

Under Wis. Stat. § 13.02 (3), "the joint committee on legislative organization shall meet and develop a work schedule for the legislative session, which shall include at least one meeting in January of each year, to be submitted to the legislature as a joint resolution."

In January 2017, the legislature adopted its work schedule for the 2017–18 legislature in 2017 Joint Resolution 1 (JR1). JR1 lists the dates of the 2017–18 session as January 3, 2017, to January 7, 2019. In December 2018, acting pursuant to JR1, the legislature convened an extraordinary session and passed three bills that were subsequently signed into law by then Governor Scott Walker as 2017 Wisconsin Act 368, 2017 Wisconsin Act 369, and 2017 Wisconsin Act 370. During the same extraordinary session, the senate confirmed 82 appointees that had been nominated by Governor Walker to various state authorities, boards, councils, and commissions.

In January 2019, the League of Women Voters of Wisconsin, along with several other plaintiffs (collectively, the League), filed an action in Dane County Circuit Court against Governor Tony Evers and officers of the Wisconsin Elections Commission (WEC) seeking a declaratory judgment and injunctive relief. The League sought a declaration that the three acts passed and 82 appointments confirmed during the extraordinary session were unconstitutional and unenforceable because they occurred during a constitutionally invalid session of the legislature. The legislature filed a motion to intervene in the case, which the circuit court granted. The WEC defendants and the legislature filed motions to dismiss, and the legislature requested a stay of any injunction the court might issue.

The parties agreed to dismiss the WEC defendants from the case. In March 2019, the circuit court denied the legislature's motion to dismiss, granted a temporary injunction, and denied the legislature's motion to stay the injunction. The legislature appealed. The League filed a petition requesting to bypass the court of appeals, which the supreme court granted.

In a majority opinion authored by Justice R.G. Bradley, the supreme court found that extraordinary sessions are not unconstitutional and that the extraordinary session held by the Wisconsin Legislature in December 2018 did not violate the Wisconsin Constitution. The court held "that extraordinary sessions do not violate the Wisconsin Constitution because the text of our constitution directs the Legislature to meet at times as 'provided by law,' and Wis. Stat. § 13.02 (3) provides the law giving the Legislature the discretion to construct its work schedule, including preserving times for it to meet in an extraordinary session." The court found that the plain language of Wis. Stat. § 13.02 (3), which directs a committee of the legislature to develop a work schedule for the legislative session, "satisfies the 'provided by law' requirement under Article IV, Section 11 of the Wisconsin Constitution."

The court noted that while "extraordinary sessions" are not expressly mentioned in Wis. Stat. § 13.02, terminology such as "floorperiods" and "extraordinary sessions" are terms used by the legislature in setting the work schedule and that "[t]he specific terminology [the legislature] chooses is not prescribed or limited by our constitution or by statute." The court rejected the argument that the legislature had terminated its 2017–18 session when it concluded the last general business floorperiod on March 22, 2018. The court held that "[t]he work schedule the Legislature formulated for its 2017–2018 biennial session established the beginning and end dates of the session period and specifically contemplated the convening of an extraordinary session, which occurred within the biennial session."

Finding that the circuit court "invaded the province of the Legislature in declaring the extraordinary session unconstitutional, enjoining enforcement of the three Acts, and vacating the 82 appointments," the supreme court vacated the circuit court's order and remanded the matter with directions to dismiss the League's complaint.

Justice Dallet, joined by Justices Shirley S. Abrahamson and A.W. Bradley, dissented, finding that the extraordinary session held by the legislature in December 2018 was unconstitutional and that, therefore, the three acts passed during those sessions (2017 Wisconsin Acts 368, 369, and 370) and the confirmation of 82 gubernatorial appointments were invalid.

Separation of powers and the constitutionality of post-election laws

In *Service Employees International Union (SEIU), Local 1 v. Vos*, 2020 WI 67, 393 Wis. 2d 38, 946 N.W.2d 35, the supreme court considered whether certain acts passed by the Wisconsin Legislature after the November 2018 election, but before a new administration took office, were unconstitutional as a violation of separation of powers. The court, through two separate majority opinions authored by different justices, held that 1) legislation relating to the authority of the governor and attorney general was facially constitutional, and 2) some provisions relating to "guidance documents" failed a facial constitutional analysis, while others survived.

The case arose from enactment of 2017 Wisconsin Act 369 and 2017 Wisconsin Act 370, which were passed by the legislature in December 2018, after the November election, and then signed by the governor before the new administration took office. Service Employees International Union (SEIU), Local 1, and other plaintiffs (collectively, SEIU) filed suit in Dane County Circuit Court against leaders of both houses of the legislature (collectively, the legislative defendants), the governor, and the attorney general, all in their official capacities, seeking declaratory and injunctive relief and moving for a temporary injunction. The legislative defendants moved to dismiss the complaint, arguing all provisions were consistent with the Wisconsin Constitution. While named as a defendant, the governor brought his own motion for a temporary injunction and sought to enjoin provisions not raised in SEIU's motion, while filing a cross-claim joining SEIU's complaint and requesting his own declaratory and injunctive relief regarding the provisions he challenged. The attorney general also largely supported SEIU and asked the circuit court to strike down multiple laws relating to his authority as attorney general.

The circuit court denied the legislative defendants' motion to dismiss while granting, in part, the motions for temporary injunction. The court enjoined laws concerning legislative involvement in state-related litigation, the ability for a legislative committee to suspend an administrative rule multiple times, and various provisions relating to agency communications referred to as guidance documents.

The legislative defendants appealed both the denial of the motion to dismiss and the order granting injunctive relief. The supreme court first assumed jurisdiction over the appeal of the temporary injunction and later assumed jurisdiction over and granted the interlocutory appeal of the denial of the motion to dismiss.

The supreme court reviewed the circuit court's denial of the legislative defendants' motion to dismiss and, therefore, had to determine whether the complaint stated a valid legal claim against the challenged laws, while assuming all allegations in the complaint were true. The court found that certain claims not enjoined by the circuit court were not sufficiently developed by the parties for the court to make a ruling, and the court issued no opinion about those provisions, indicating they could proceed in the ordinary course of litigation when the case was remanded to the circuit court.

In the first majority opinion, authored by Justice Hagedorn, the court noted that the constitutional challenge was a facial challenge, requiring a party to show "that all applications of the law are unconstitutional." The court rejected these facial challenges to several provisions, including provisions allowing legislative involvement in litigation and limiting the attorney general's ability to settle litigation; a provision regarding security at the capitol; a provision regarding multiple suspensions of administrative rules; and finally, a provision partially codifying the supreme court's ruling in *Tetra Tech EC, Inc. v. Wisconsin Department of Revenue*, 2018 WI 75, 382 Wis. 2d 496, 914 N.W.2d 21. The court held that there were at least some constitutionally valid applications of these provisions and that, as such, the facial challenge failed. The court vacated the temporary injunction and directed the circuit court to grant the motion to dismiss with respect to these provisions.

Justice Kelly authored a second majority opinion constituting the opinion of the court with regard to provisions of Act 369 that relate to guidance documents. The supreme court affirmed the circuit court's ruling that two provisions of Act 369 are facially unconstitutional because "they intrude on power the Wisconsin Constitution vests in the executive branch of the government." The court found that a provision requiring an agency to identify existing law that supports a guidance document's contents and a provision establishing a notice and comment procedure that an agency must follow when creating a guidance document are unconstitutional. The court found that "the creation and dissemination of guidance documents fall within the executive's core authority." The court reversed the circuit court on the other challenged guidance document-related provisions, finding, for purposes of a facial constitutional challenge, that it was not established that the remaining provisions would be unenforceable under any circumstances.

Chief Justice Roggensack concurred in part and dissented in part, concluding that Act 369's regulation of guidance documents "does not invade the executive's core powers." Chief Justice Roggensack found the majority opinion flawed in holding the creation of guidance documents to be a core power of the executive, instead concluding that interpreting the law is a shared power and that, for purposes of the facial challenge, it was not established that any of the guidance document provisions are unduly burdensome in all circumstances.

Justice Dallet also concurred in part and dissented in part, joined by Justice A.W. Bradley, finding that SEIU's complaint "plausibly suggests that the sweep of the 'Litigation Control' provisions" in Act 369 violates the constitutional separation of powers doctrine.

Justice Hagedorn wrote a separate opinion, concurring in part and dissenting in part, joined by Justice Annette Kingsland Ziegler, stating that he would hold that all of the guidance document provisions survive a facial challenge.

Governor's partial veto power

In *Bartlett v. Evers*, 2020 WI 68, 393 Wis. 2d 172, 945 N.W.2d 685, the supreme court held that three of the four partial vetoes that were challenged in the case were unconstitutional and invalid. In June 2019, the Wisconsin Legislature passed the 2019–21 biennial budget bill. Governor Tony Evers signed the bill with numerous partial vetoes. Three individual taxpayers sued to invalidate four of these partial vetoes.

In the first challenged veto, the budget bill had provided that certain funds were to be used to award grants to school boards for the replacement of school buses with energy efficient buses, including school buses that use alternative fuels. Governor Evers partially vetoed this language so that the sole remaining requirement was that the funds be used "for alternative fuels." In the second challenged veto, Governor Evers partially vetoed a provision that provided funds "for the local roads improvement discretionary supplemental grant program"—a program that provides money to local governments to improve deteriorating local roads—so that it allowed the funds to be used "for local grant [sic]," with no requirement that the money be used for road improvement. In the third challenged veto, the budget bill had changed the registration fees for four different weight classes of vehicles so that they were all the same—for two lighter weight classes the registration fee increased, and for two heavier classes the fee decreased. Governor Evers partially vetoed the decrease in fees for the heavier weight classes while leaving intact the increase in fees for the lighter weight classes. In the fourth challenged veto, Governor Evers vetoed language in the definition of "vapor product" so that a newly created tax on vapor products would apply not only to vaping devices but also to vaping fluid.

Under article V, section 10 (1) (b), of the Wisconsin Constitution, "[a]ppropriation bills may be approved in whole or in part by the governor, and the part approved shall become law." In deciding whether a governor's partial veto is valid, the supreme court previously applied an objective test of whether the resulting approved material resulted in a "complete, entire and workable law." The court had also previously discussed the notion that "the consequences of any partial veto must be a law that is germane to the topic or subject matter of the vetoed provisions."

In this case, a majority of the court held that the school bus modernization veto, the local roads improvement veto, and the vapor products tax veto were unconstitutional and invalid, and that the vehicle registration fee veto was constitutional and should be upheld. However, the court could not agree on a rationale for these holdings, and instead issued a per curium opinion with four separate writings and four separate rationales.

Chief Justice Roggensack's opinion elevated the germaneness requirement discussed in previous cases to a constitutional test that asks whether a partial veto has altered the legislative idea reflected in the text of the bill. Chief Justice Roggensack found the school bus modernization and the local road improvement vetoes to be unconstitutional because they resulted in topics or subject matters not found in the original bill: the part remaining after the school bus modernization veto related to reducing carbon emissions and had nothing to do with schools or buses; and the part remaining after the local road improvement veto created a general, undirected local fund and had nothing to do with road improvement. However, the chief justice held that the vapor products tax and vehicle registration fee vetoes were constitutional because they did not alter the topic or subject matter of the parts of the bill that were approved.

Justice Kelly, in an opinion joined by Justice R.G. Bradley, looked to the origination clause, amendment clause, and legislative passage clause of the Wisconsin Constitution and determined that the court's prior decisions on the partial veto had been wrongly decided. Justice Kelly concluded that, because the purpose of the partial veto power is to address the legislative practice of bundling several proposed laws into one bill, it followed that the smallest part of a bill that can be vetoed should be one of those proposed laws. Justice Kelly's opinion found that, "After exercising the partial veto, the remaining part of the bill must not only be a 'complete, entire, and workable law,' it must also be a law on which the legislature actually voted." Justice Kelly added that "the part or parts of the bill the governor did not approve must also comprise one or more 'complete, entire, and workable laws' that had passed the legislature." Applying this test, Justice Kelly found all four of the challenged vetoes to be invalid.

Justice Hagedorn, joined by Justice Ziegler, acknowledged that the governor may veto something less than an "item," but determined that he or she may not "selectively edit parts of a bill to create a new policy that was not proposed by the legislature. He may negate separable proposals actually made, but he may not create new proposals not presented in the bill." Applying this "policy" test, Justice Hagedorn held that, "with three of the challenges—the school bus modernization fund, the local road improvement fund, and the vapor products tax—the governor's vetoes went beyond negating legislative policy proposals; they created brand new ones." The vehicle registration fee veto, however, merely negated a policy proposal advanced by the legislature rather than creating a new policy and was therefore valid.

Justice A.W. Bradley, joined by Justice Dallet, supported applying the objective "complete, entire and workable law" test that the court had previously applied, under which all four of the challenged partial vetoes would be constitutional. Justice A.W. Bradley argued that none of the parties had argued or briefed the "legislative idea" test supported by Chief Justice Roggensack, the requirement that the vetoed material also be "complete, entire and workable" that was introduced by Justice Kelly, or the "policy" test proposed by Justice Hagedorn. Justice A.W. Bradley also argued that the "legislative idea" and "policy" tests were subjective and therefore difficult to apply. Finally, she rejected Justice Kelly's approach because it would overturn 85 years of jurisprudence; would ignore the difference between the words "part" and "item," even though the state constitution specifically authorizes a veto in "part" rather than a line-item veto; and would make article V, section 10 (1) (c), of the Wisconsin Constitution—which prohibits the governor from creating a new word by rejecting individual letters in the words of a bill or creating a new sentence by combining parts of two or more sentences of a bill—superfluous, because there would be no need for this constitutional provision if the constitution already limited the governor to vetoing an "item."

On the same day that it issued its opinion in *Bartlett*, the supreme court also decided *Wisconsin Small Business United, Inc. v. Brennan*, 2020 WI 69, 393 Wis. 2d 308, 946 N.W.2d 101. In that case, the court held that challenges to partial vetoes by Governor Walker in the 2017–19 biennial budget bill—which were not brought before the court until after the 2019–21 budget bill had been enacted— were brought too late and were therefore barred by the doctrine of laches. The merits of the case would have raised the question of whether the governor may partially veto individual numbers within a date, an issue that the court has never directly addressed.

Gubernatorial review of rules promulgated by the state superintendent of public instruction

In *Koschkee v. Taylor*, 2019 WI 76, 387 Wis. 2d 552, 929 N.W.2d 600, the supreme court held that provisions enacted under 2011 Wisconsin Act 21 that gave the governor and the secretary of administration certain authority over agency rulemaking were constitutional as applied to rules promulgated by the state superintendent of public instruction (SPI), a constitutional office established by article X, section 1, of the Wisconsin Constitution. Article X, section 1, establishes the SPI and provides that the "supervision of public instruction" shall be vested in the SPI and "such other officers as the legislature shall direct." The court's ruling in *Koschkee* overruled the court's earlier decision on substantially the same issue in *Coyne v. Walker*, 2016 WI 38, 368 Wis. 2d 444, 879 N.W.2d 520.

In May 2011, Governor Scott Walker signed 2011 Wisconsin Act 21 into law. Act 21 made numerous changes to provisions in Wis. Stat ch. 227 that delineate the process for state agencies to promulgate administrative rules. Among the changes in Act 21 were requirements that the governor approve agencies' initial "statements of scope" for proposed rulemaking and that the governor approve agencies' final drafts of proposed administrative rules. In *Coyne*, a number of parties (Coyne) filed suit, arguing that the provisions gave the governor and the secretary of administration equal or superior authority over the SPI and were therefore unconstitutional. The SPI sided with Coyne throughout the litigation. With a divided mandate split between multiple opinions, a majority of the court ruled in *Coyne* that the Act 21 requirements were unconstitutional as applied to the SPI and the Department of Public Instruction (DPI).

In August 2017, Governor Walker signed 2017 Wisconsin Act 57, also known as the REINS (Regulations from the Executive in Need of Scrutiny) Act into law. Act 57 made further changes to the rulemaking process, including requiring statements of scope for administrative rules to be first forwarded to the Department of Administration (DOA) for review before being submitted to the governor for approval. However, Act 57 preserved the gubernatorial approval requirements enacted in 2011 Wisconsin Act 21 that were the subject of *Coyne*. In *Koschkee*, the petitioners (Koschkee) filed a petition for an original action with the supreme court, seeking a declaratory judgment that then-SPI Tony Evers and DPI were required to submit statements of scope for administrative rules to DOA for review and approval by the governor. The court granted the petition, and the case was decided in June 2019.

With Chief Justice Roggensack writing for the majority, the court began by reiterating that administrative agencies are creations of the legislature and that the power to promulgate rules is a power delegated by the legislature, subject to limitations and conditions prescribed by the legislature. The court then moved to a discussion of article X, section 1, of the Wisconsin Constitution, concluding that the SPI was understood as having been given executive, not legislative, authority, with the SPI's duties to be further defined by the legislature. The constitution, the court concluded, vested the supervision of public instruction, an executive function, in the SPI. In contrast, the SPI's rulemaking authority was a delegation of legislative power and therefore was not the "supervision of public instruction" within the meaning of article X, section 1. The court rejected the argument, with which a majority of the court had agreed in *Coyne*, that the challenged provisions impermissibly elevated the governor to a position greater or equal to the SPI with regard to something the SPI does, calling it of no constitutional concern given that rulemaking is a legislative, not executive, power.

Justice R.G. Bradley concurred in the judgment to express her view that the majority was improperly acquiescing to delegations to administrative agencies and straying from original understandings of the separation of powers. Justice Kelly filed a separate concurring opinion. Justice A.W. Bradley wrote in dissent, joined by Justice Dallet, observing that *Coyne* was recently decided precedent by a court whose membership had since changed and concluding that *Coyne*, despite having had multiple opinions, had correctly held that the challenged provisions unconstitutionally infringed on the SPI's supervisory powers.

Justice Abrahamson withdrew from participation.

Suspending an election by executive order

In *Wisconsin Legislature v. Evers*, 2020 Wis. ___, the supreme court held that the governor could not by executive order suspend in-person voting on April 7, 2020, an action that would have resulted in modifying a number of election-related statutes outside of the lawmaking process. The court held that, although the governor's power during a public health emergency is substantial, it is not unlimited and not broad enough to suspend the operation of the statutes.

On March 12, 2020, Governor Tony Evers issued an executive order, "Declaring a Health Emergency in Response to the COVID-19 Coronavirus." Following that order, a number of parties filed lawsuits in federal court to modify or suspend certain election-related procedures for the upcoming spring election so that voters would be able to limit their exposure to the novel coronavirus while exercising their right to vote. The United States District Court for the Western District of Wisconsin, with Judge William M. Conley presiding, received three complaints which it consolidated into one case as *Democratic Nat'l Comm. v. Bostelmann*, 451 Supp. 3d 952 (2020). The parties seeking relief sought to enjoin a number of state statutory provisions regarding the conduct of elections, including the procedures for requesting and submitting absentee ballots and the photo identification requirement for voting. In addition, the parties asked the court to postpone the spring election. The parties noted that the governor himself had indicated that he did not believe he had the authority to issue an order postponing the spring election.

Judge Conley issued his decision and order on April 2, five days before the election. Although Judge Conley enjoined and modified certain absentee ballot procedures, he found that it was not in the court's purview to postpone the election. He also noted that delaying the election would create a different host of problems. For example, the WEC had already taken a number of actions in an attempt to conduct an election in as safe and efficient a manner as possible and that the commission administrator had testified that there were no good dates on which to move the election that would not hamper the administration of other elections.

On April 6, the day before the election, Governor Evers issued Executive Order 74, "Related to suspending in-person voting on April 7, 2020, due to the COVID-19 Pandemic." In addition to suspending the spring election and postponing it until June 9, the order also called the legislature into special session to commence at noon on April 7 for the purpose of considering legislation to determine a new date for holding the 2020 spring election. As a consequence of postponing the election, the order also extended the period for requesting, completing, and submitting absentee ballots and the terms of office for all local officials whose terms were, by statute, set to expire following the spring election. Those terms would continue until after the rescheduled election, when the terms for the newly elected officials would begin.

As authority for the order, the governor cited Wis. Stat. § 323.12 (4) (b), which provides that the governor may issue orders during an emergency "as he or she deems necessary for the security of persons and property." The governor also cited several provisions of the Wisconsin Constitution: the preamble, which provides, in part, that the people of Wisconsin establish the constitution in order to "form a more perfect government, insure domestic tranquility and promote the general welfare"; article IV, section 11, which authorizes the governor to convene the legislature into special session; article V, section 1, which provides that the executive power is vested in the governor; and article V, section 4, which authorizes the governor to convene the legislature at a location other than the seat of government due to "danger from the prevalence of contagious disease."

On the same day that the governor issued Executive Order 74, the legislature filed a petition with the supreme court to commence an original action challenging the legality of the order and seeking a temporary injunction. The court granted the petition and issued its decision that day. The court found that none of the authorities cited by the governor, with the exception of article IV, section 11, of the Wisconsin Constitution, pertaining to commencing a special session, allowed the governor to do what he intended under the order.

With regard to Wis. Stat. § 323.12 (4) (b), although it appears to provide a broad grant of executive power during an emergency, the court noted that it had to be construed in the context of the statute as a whole. For example, Wis. Stat. § 323.12 (4) (d) allows the governor to suspend "the provisions of any administrative rule if the strict compliance with that rule would prevent, hinder, or delay necessary actions to respond to the disaster," which is the subject of an emergency order. Other statutory provisions grant the governor the power during an emergency to engage in certain contracts and to waive fees for permits and licenses. Importantly, the court noted that nothing in Wis. Stat. § 323.12 (4) grants the governor the power to suspend the statutes or postpone an election during an emergency. In other words, if the legislature had intended to grant that power, it would have said so, just as it did with the authority to suspend the administrative rules.

Ultimately, the court enjoined the provisions of Executive Order 74, with the exception of calling the legislature into special session. The court held that failing to do otherwise would have allowed the governor "to invade the province of the Legislature by unilaterally suspending and rewriting laws without authority."

Justice A.W. Bradley, joined by Justice Dallet, dissented, opining that the power granted under Wis. Stat. § 323.12 (4) (b) to issue orders "necessary for the security of persons and property" is broad enough to allow the governor to postpone an election during a pandemic and to modify the operation of the various statutes that are implicated by that postponement.

Justice Kelly did not participate.

Indefinitely confined voters

In *Jefferson v. Dane County*, 2020 Wis. ___, the supreme court enjoined the Dane County clerk from advising all eligible voters in Dane County that they could designate themselves as "indefinitely confined" because of the governor's "Safer at Home" order and thereby request and receive an absentee ballot without having to provide photo identification.

On March 12, 2020, Governor Tony Evers issued Executive Order 72, "Declaring a Health Emergency in Response to the COVID-19 Coronavirus." On March 24, 2020, as an attempt to reduce the spread of the novel coronavirus, the secretary of health services-designee, Andrea Palm, issued Emergency Order 12, the "Safer at Home" order, which required all individuals present in the state to stay at their place of residence, with certain exceptions. For example, the order allowed individuals to leave their homes to buy groceries or household products. In addition, residents employed at essential businesses or providing essential services were allowed to leave their residence to go to work. Essential businesses and services included health care, infrastructure, construction, food production and distribution, law enforcement, and government. The order did not require that those who were ill from COVID-19 or at high-risk for becoming ill from it stay at home, but, instead, they were "urged to stay at their home or residence to the extent possible except as necessary to seek medical care." The order took effect at 8 a.m. on March 25, 2020, and was to remain in effect until 8 a.m. on April 24, 2020.

On March 25, 2020, Dane County Clerk Scott McDonnell posted a statement on his Facebook page indicating that, as a result of the executive order declaring a health emergency and the "Safer at Home" order, all eligible voters in Dane County could, as needed, declare themselves "indefinitely confined" for purposes of requesting and completing an absentee ballot for the upcoming spring election. He further urged absentee voters who were having difficulty presenting photo identification with their absentee ballot request to indicate that they were "indefinitely confined" in order to avoid that requirement.

Section 6.86 (2) (a) of the Wisconsin Statutes allows an eligible voter to automatically receive an absentee ballot for every election if the voter includes with his or her absentee ballot application a signed statement indicating that the voter is "indefinitely confined because of age, physical illness or infirmity or is disabled for an indefinite period." A voter who certifies himself or herself as "indefinitely confined" is not required to present photo identification to vote absentee if the individual who witnesses the voting of the ballot submits a statement that contains the voter's name and address and verifies that the voter's name and address are correct. A voter who certifies as "indefinitely confined" is required to notify the municipal clerk when the voter no longer qualifies as being "indefinitely confined."

Two days after the Dane County clerk's Facebook post, the Republican Party of Wisconsin and Mark Jefferson, its executive director, filed with the supreme court a petition for leave to commence an original action and a motion for a temporary injunction that would require the county clerk to remove his Facebook post from March 25, 2020, and issue a new statement that set forth the interpretation of Wis. Stat. § 6.86 (2) (a) proposed by the petitioners. On March 31, 2020, the court granted the motion for a temporary injunction, finding that the clerk's advice to the municipal clerks and voters of Dane County was "legally incorrect." The court also found that the clerk's subsequent posting of guidance from the WEC with regard to voters who certify themselves as "indefinitely confined" did not render the issue moot as that did not prevent the clerk from reposting the erroneous, misleading information or from the continued distribution of the original posting on the Internet. The court expressed its concern that eligible voters, relying on the clerk's incorrect advice, would be misled into thinking they could declare themselves "indefinitely confined" simply because of the public health emergency and the "Safer at Home" order and receive an absentee ballot without providing the photo identification that the law otherwise requires.

Consequently, the court ordered McDonnell to refrain from posting any advice regarding voters declaring themselves "indefinitely confined" that is inconsistent with WEC guidance. The court found that the WEC guidance provided an important clarification. Specifically, although the guidance indicated that the designation of "indefinitely confined" is a decision to be made by the voter on the basis or his or her current circumstances, the designation is not to be used solely as a means to avoid the photo identification requirement for voting. The WEC guidance also indicated that being "indefinitely confined" does not mean that the voter is either permanently or completely unable to travel outside the person's residence, but that the voter must be "indefinitely confined" because of age, physical illness or infirmity, or disability.

Justice Kelly did not participate in the decision.

On April 1, 2020, the court also granted the petition for leave to commence an original action. The petition set forth two questions for the court to resolve. The first question was whether the Dane County clerk had the authority to issue an interpretation of Wis. Stat. § 6.86 (2) (a) that would have allowed voters to request and return an absentee ballot without providing photo identification. The second question was whether all eligible Wisconsin voters could avoid the photo identification requirement for absentee ballots on the grounds that the "Safer at Home" order rendered them "indefinitely confined" because of age, physical illness or infirmity, or disability. The court heard oral argument on September 29, 2020.

On December 14, 2020, in a majority opinion authored by Chief Justice Patience D. Roggensack, the court held that the Dane County clerk's interpretation of Wis. Stat. § 6.86 (2) (a) was erroneous and that the "Safer at Home" order did not make all eligible Wisconsin voters "indefinitely confined" for the purpose of receiving absentee ballots without having to present photo identification. To reach that conclusion, the court determined that Wis. Stat. § 6.86 (2) allows each individual voter to make the determination as to whether he or she is "indefinitely confined" on the basis of age, physical illness or infirmity, or disability. All of the justices concurred in this part of the opinion.

However, the majority also held that the designation of being "indefinitely confined" could not be made on the basis of someone else's age, physical illness or infirmity, or disability. For example, an individual taking care of an eligible voter who is "indefinitely confined" may not claim that designation solely because the individual is the voter's caretaker. The court addressed this issue in response to arguments raised by Disability Rights Wisconsin, which the court had allowed to intervene. Justice A.W. Bradley and Justice Dallet filed separate dissents to this part of the decision and Justice Karofsky joined Justice Dallet's dissent. Justice A.W. Bradley objected to the majority "inserting its own words into the statutory text chosen by the legislature" in order to determine that a voter must determine whether he or she is "indefinitely confined" on the basis of his or her own age, illness, or disability. Justice Dallet objected to the majority reaching its determination by considering hypothetical voters in hypothetical situations and not on the facts before court.

Incapacitated driver provision of implied consent law is unconstitutional

In *State v. Prado*, 2020 WI App 42, 393 Wis. 2d 526, 947 N.W.2d 182, the court of appeals considered whether the implied consent that drivers are deemed to have given and are unable to withdraw due to incapacitation satisfies the Fourth Amendment to the U.S. Constitution. The court found that it does not and held the provision to be unconstitutional.

The implied consent law provides that a person operating a motor vehicle on a public highway has given consent to have a sample of his or her breath, blood, or urine subjected to a chemical test to determine the presence of alcohol, controlled substances, or other drugs. When a law enforcement officer requests a chemical test sample, the person may withdraw his or her consent. However, if the person is incapacitated, the person is presumed not to have withdrawn consent, and the officer may obtain a chemical test sample if the officer has probable cause to believe the person was operating a motor vehicle while intoxicated.

Dawn Prado was involved in a fatal car crash and was transported to a hospital. While Prado was unconscious, a law enforcement officer directed that a sample of Prado's blood be drawn for chemical testing. The officer did not obtain a warrant but instead relied on the incapacitated driver provision of the implied consent law.

Prado's blood sample revealed the presence of a controlled substance and a prohibited alcohol concentration. Prado moved to suppress the results of the blood test, arguing that the incapacitated driver provision upon which the officer relied is unconstitutional. The circuit court agreed, suppressing the results of the blood test, and the state appealed.

The court of appeals noted that it had certified the question of the constitutionality of the incapacitated driver provision to the Wisconsin Supreme Court on three prior occasions but had yet to see the issue definitively resolved. Indeed, the court of appeals stayed this appeal for over two years awaiting the outcome of other cases that raised the same issue. One of those appeals was taken up by the U.S. Supreme Court, which declined to directly address the issue, in *Mitchell v. Wisconsin*, 588 U.S. ___, 139 S. Ct. 2525 (2019).

In its consideration of the issue, the court of appeals provided a thorough review of relevant case law, including the most recent U.S. Supreme Court opinions. The court of appeals reasoned that collection of a blood sample is a search governed by the Fourth Amendment to the U.S. Constitution and may not be conducted without a warrant unless the search falls within one of the specifically established exceptions to the warrant requirement. Consent is one such exception, but the court held that implied consent that is not withdrawn does not meet the standards established by the U.S. Supreme Court in *Mitchell* and *Birchfield v. North Dakota*, 579 U.S. ___, 136 S. Ct. 2160 (2016). The court held that "implied consent" is not itself an established exception to the warrant requirement, nor does it satisfy the traditional warrant exception for voluntary consent.

The court of appeals held that the incapacitated driver provision of the implied consent statute authorizes warrantless searches that do not fit within any exception to the warrant requirement. Thus, the court held, any search conducted under that authority violates the Fourth Amendment to the U.S. Constitution. Ultimately, the court held the incapacitated driver provision to be unconstitutional.

However, the court noted that, while evidence obtained through unconstitutional searches should be excluded at trial, courts may deviate from this rule when law enforcement has acted in good faith reliance on settled law. The court held that the blood draw in this case occurred before *Birchfield* and *Mitchell* were decided and was therefore conducted in good-faith reliance on the incapacitated driver provision, which was settled law for decades. Thus, although the court found the provision to be unconstitutional, the court reversed the lower court's suppression of Prado's blood test result because the law enforcement officer was acting on a good faith understanding of the law.

Open records

In *Lueders v. Krug*, 2019 WI App 36, 388 Wis. 2d 147, 931 N.W.2d 898, the court of appeals held that Wisconsin's open records law requires a state representative to provide electronic, rather than paper, copies of emails when sought through an open records request.

In this case, Bill Lueders sent Representative Scott Krug a request to review correspondence sent to Krug's office during a certain period that related to specific topics and bills relating to the state's water laws. Krug provided Lueders with paper printouts of relevant emails. Lueders then sent Krug a request for all emails relating to changes in the state's water laws received by Krug's office within that same period, and requested that the records be provided in electronic form and not as printed copies. Krug declined, stating that he had already provided Lueders with printed copies of the requested emails, which satisfied the requirements of the open records law.

Wisconsin's open records law, Wis. Stat. § 19.35 (1) (b), provides that "any requester has a right to inspect a record and to make or receive a copy of a record." This provision also states the following: "If a requester appears personally to request a copy of a record that permits copying, the authority having custody of the record may, at its option, permit the requester to copy the record or provide the requester with a copy substantially as readable as the original."

The circuit court ordered Krug to provide electronic versions of the emails, and Krug appealed, arguing that the state's open records law required only that he provide copies of records that were substantially as readable as the originals.

The court of appeals first found that the provision under the open records law upon which Krug relied, which requires the custodian to provide the requester "with a copy substantially as readable as the original," applies only if "a requester appears personally to request a copy of a record." The provision did not apply in this case because Lueders did not appear personally, but instead submitted his open records requests by email.

The court of appeals next looked to *State ex rel. Milwaukee Police Ass'n v. Jones*, 2000 WI App 146, 237 Wis. 2d 840, 615 N.W.2d 190, in which the Milwaukee Police Department denied a request to provide a digital recording of a 911 call after the department had provided an analog copy of the call in response to a previous request. The court in that case held that the digital version of the recording would contain data not found in the analog version and that the requester was entitled to the digital copy. The court in that case noted that "[i]f a 'copy' differs in some significant way for purposes of responding to an open records request, then it is not truly an identical copy, but instead a different record."

In *Lueders*, the court held that the electronic copies of the emails that Lueders requested were substantially different from the printed copies he was provided because the electronic copies contained information not available on the printed versions, including metadata that showed when the emails were created and who created them. The court therefore concluded that providing paper versions of the emails was not a satisfactory response to Lueders's second request that specifically asked for digital versions of the emails and affirmed the circuit court's order requiring disclosure of the electronic versions of the emails.

Activities that are included in the mission of a traffic stop

In two cases before the Wisconsin Supreme Court, the court evaluated and applied the recent U.S. Supreme Court case *Rodriguez v. United States*, 575 U.S. 348 (2015), in which the U.S. Supreme Court held that the tolerable duration of police inquiries in the traffic-stop context is determined by the length of time reasonably required to complete the "mission" of the traffic stop.

The Fourth Amendment to the U.S. Constitution prohibits unreasonable seizures. A traffic stop is a type of seizure under the Fourth Amendment, and authority for a traffic stop seizure ends when the police officer completes, or reasonably should have completed, the "mission" of the traffic stop. The U.S. Supreme Court has explained that the mission includes 1) addressing the traffic violation that warranted the stop, 2) conducting ordinary inquiries incident to the stop, and 3) taking negligibly burdensome precautions to ensure officer safety. In addition, officers may make certain unrelated investigations as long as they do not measurably extend the duration of the traffic stop.

In *State v. Wright*, 2019 WI 45, 386 Wis. 2d 495, 926 N.W.2d 157, the Wisconsin Supreme Court considered whether a police officer unlawfully extended a traffic stop in violation of the Fourth Amendment to the U.S. Constitution when the officer asked the driver about the presence of weapons in the car and asked whether the driver held a valid permit to carry a concealed weapon (CCW permit).

In this case, police officers stopped the car John Patrick Wright was driving because the passenger-side headlight was out. Officer Kristopher Sardina asked Wright for his driver's license and asked several other questions, including whether Wright held a CCW permit and whether he had any weapons in the car. Wright admitted that he did not have a CCW permit and that he did have a firearm in the glove compartment. Officer Sardina took Wright's license back to the squad car, ran Wright's information, and ran a CCW permit check. Officer Sardina discovered that Wright did not hold a valid CCW permit and arrested him for carrying a concealed weapon.

Wright moved to suppress the firearm evidence on the basis that Officer Sardina unlawfully extended the traffic stop in violation of the Fourth Amendment to the U.S. Constitution when he asked questions about whether Wright held a CCW permit and about the presence of weapons. The circuit court granted Wright's motion to suppress, and the court of appeals affirmed.

In a unanimous opinion authored by Justice Abrahamson, the supreme court reversed. The court asked whether Officer Sardina's questions constituted part of the mission of the traffic stop. The court explained that, if the questions were part of the mission, they would not be considered an extension of the traffic stop, and, if the questions were not part of the mission, they would violate the Fourth Amendment to the U.S. Constitution only if they measurably extended the duration of the traffic stop.

The court quickly dispensed with the officer's question regarding the presence of weapons, concluding that the question was part of the mission of the traffic stop because the question was "a negligibly burdensome precaution taken to ensure officer safety." Because the question was part of the mission, it did not extend the traffic stop and did not violate the Fourth Amendment.

On the other hand, with respect to Officer Sardina's question regarding whether Wright held a CCW permit, the court held that the question and the CCW permit check were not part of the ordinary inquiries incident to the traffic stop. The court noted that ordinary inquiries typically involve checking the driver's license, determining whether there are outstanding warrants against the driver, and inspecting the automobile's registration and proof of insurance. Further, the question was not related to officer safety because it is the potential presence of a weapon that implicates the safety of the officer, not whether that weapon is being lawfully carried. Thus, in the absence of reasonable suspicion of criminal activity, the question and the CCW permit check were an investigation unrelated to the mission of the traffic stop.

Nevertheless, the court concluded that, in this case, there was no evidence that those activities had measurably extended the duration of the traffic stop. Because asking about the CCW permit and running a CCW permit check were conducted concurrently with mission-related activities, those unrelated investigations did not violate Wright's Fourth Amendment rights.

In *State v. Brown*, 2020 WI 63, 392 Wis. 2d 454, 945 N.W.2d 584, the supreme court considered whether a police officer unlawfully extended a traffic stop in violation of the Fourth Amendment to the U.S. Constitution when the officer, after writing a traffic ticket but before handing it to the driver, ordered the driver out of the car, led the driver to the front of the squad car, asked the driver if he had anything on his person that the officer should "be concerned about," and asked permission to search the driver.

In this case, Officer Christopher Deering pulled over the car Courtney Brown was driving for failing to make a complete stop at a stop sign. Officer Deering asked Brown multiple questions about his whereabouts and destination that evening and found Brown's story suspicious. Officer Deering ran a records search on Brown while writing him a ticket for failing to wear a seatbelt, then, with the completed ticket in hand, returned to Brown's vehicle. Officer Deering did not give Brown the ticket or return his driver's license. Instead, Officer Deering asked Brown to exit the car, led him back to the front of the squad car, and asked if there was anything on Brown's person that Officer Deering "needed to know about" or "be concerned about." Brown answered that he had nothing, but Officer Deering asked for consent to search Brown's person and proceeded to conduct the search, uncovering drugs and cash.

Brown was charged with possession with intent to deliver cocaine and moved to suppress the evidence of drugs and money on the grounds that the search was an unlawful extension of the traffic stop unsupported by reasonable suspicion. The circuit court denied the motion, and the court of appeals affirmed on other grounds.

In a majority opinion authored by Justice R.G. Bradley, the supreme court affirmed. The court examined each action taken by Officer Deering after writing the traffic ticket and returning to Brown's car, finding that the mission of the stop had not been completed and all of Officer Deering's actions were negligibly burdensome actions related to officer safety, which is part of the mission of the traffic stop.

With respect to the officer's request for Brown to exit the vehicle, the court held that the request was "of no constitutional moment" because courts decades ago established a bright-line rule in the interest of officer safety that officers may order a driver out of the vehicle during a lawful traffic stop without violating the Fourth Amendment to the U.S. Constitution. The court explained that, because the officer had not yet handed Brown the ticket, the mission of the traffic stop had not been completed. The court flatly rejected Brown's assertion that the stop reasonably should have been completed because "all that remained was handing the ticket to Brown and ending the seizure." The court stated that "the mission of the stop continued."

The court similarly disposed of Brown's challenge regarding Officer Deering walking Brown away from his car and back to the front of the squad car. The court noted the inherent danger of the driver and officer standing a few feet from passing traffic. The court concluded, "There is no distinction for Fourth Amendment purposes between law enforcement directing a driver to stand next to his car, at the curb, or behind his car, and leading a driver to the front of the officer's squad car."

Next, the court examined whether it was reasonable for Officer Deering to ask Brown whether he had anything on his person with which the officer should be concerned. The parties disagreed on the specific words Officer Deering used but agreed that he did not specifically ask about weapons. The court concluded that no "magic words" were required and, given the facts of the case, Officer Deering had a constitutionally reasonable safety concern regarding the presence of a weapon. The court essentially determined that the officer's question simultaneously asked two questions—one mission related, and one not. The court concluded that 1) the officer's question was negligibly burdensome and pursuant to the stop's mission because it concerned officer safety, and 2) the officer's question regarding possession of concerning items did not measurably extend the duration of the stop because it was posed concurrently with mission-related activities.

Finally, the court briefly considered Officer Deering's request to search Brown. The court noted that, while a search may be a severe intrusion, a *request* to search is not. The court summarily concluded that the request for consent to search "was constitutionally permissible as a negligibly burdensome inquiry related to officer safety." The court did not address the constitutionality of the actual search and did not address whether Brown actually gave consent for the search.

Justice R.G. Bradley also wrote a concurring opinion joined by Justice Kelly. Justice Dallet filed a dissenting opinion. Justices A.W. Bradley and Hagedorn did not participate.

Due process; fair identification requirement

In *State v. Roberson*, 2019 WI 102, 389 Wis. 2d 190, 935 N.W.2d 813, the supreme court held that pretrial identification of a crime suspect may be based on presenting the witness with a single photograph, overturning precedent that required the use of a photo array.

The case arose from an incident in which the victim, C.A.S., was shot over a drug deal that went wrong. In the days preceding the incident, C.A.S. spent a total of two-and-a-half to three hours over the course of three encounters with the man who shot him. When asked whether he could identify the shooter, C.A.S. initially responded with uncertainty. However, when a police officer showed C.A.S. a photograph of the defendant, Stephan I. Roberson, C.A.S. affirmatively identified Roberson as his shooter. The circuit court ordered the identification evidence to be suppressed on the basis that the investigators used a single photograph as opposed to a photo array. Previous supreme court precedent established that a "showup," or an identification based on showing a witness only one suspect, is inadmissible evidence unless, on the basis of the totality of the circumstances, the procedure was necessary.

In this case, the court of appeals, in an unpublished decision, reversed the circuit court's suppression, and the supreme court agreed. In a majority opinion authored by Chief Justice Roggensack, the court held that due process does not prohibit identification of a crime suspect on the basis of a showup, but rather requires that the identification evidence has a sufficient "indicia of reliability" to be admissible.

In reaching its conclusion, the supreme court overturned its 2005 decision in *State v. Dubose*, 2005 WI 126, 285 Wis. 2d 143, 699 N.W.2d 582. The court in Dubose had determined that identifications based on showups were unreliable because they were impermissibly suggestive and, therefore, allowing that identification evidence into the trial violated the defendant's right to due process under article I, section 8, of the Wisconsin Constitution. In its opinion in *Dubose*, the court acknowledged that the standard the court was adopting diverged from the standard that had been adopted by the U.S. Supreme Court in interpreting the due process clause of the Fourteenth Amendment to the U.S. Constitution. The U.S. Supreme Court has not interpreted the Fourteenth Amendment to prohibit identifications on the basis of showups, but rather requires an evaluation of the reliability of the identification testimony.

The court in *Roberson* criticized its decision in *Dubose* for its departure from past practice of interpreting the state's constitutional due process requirements as the same as federal constitutional due process requirements. In addition, the court disagreed with the reliance in *Dubose* on social science to evaluate the reliability of eyewitness identifications. Finally, the court noted several instances in which the standard set forth in *Dubose* was not followed. For these reasons, the court found that the decision in *Dubose* was unsound in principle and should be overturned.

After determining that *Dubose* was overturned, the court returned to the test employed to determine the reliability of an eyewitness identification pre-*Dubose*. Under the pre-*Dubose* standard, a criminal defendant bears the initial burden of demonstrating that a showup was impermissibly suggestive. If the defendant meets this burden, the state may still introduce the evidence if it proves that under the totality of the circumstances, the identification was reliable even though the confrontation procedure was suggestive. In *Roberson*, the court held that the state met its burden, and the identification based on a single photograph was allowed as evidence in the trial.

Justice R.G. Bradley filed a concurring opinion that was joined by Justice Kelly. Justice Hagedorn filed a separate concurring opinion. Justice Dallet, joined by Justice A.W. Bradley, dissented.

Claims against firearm classified advertising website barred by federal law

In *Daniel v. Armslist, LLC*, 2019 WI 47, 386 Wis. 2d 449, 926 N.W.2d 710, the supreme court held that the federal Communications Decency Act of 1996 (the CDA) barred claims asserted against the operator of a website that advertised a firearm for sale by a third party when an individual unlawfully purchased the gun and used it to commit a mass shooting.

In October 2012, a Wisconsin court granted Zina Daniel Haughton a restraining order against her husband Radcliffe Haughton after he assaulted her and threatened to kill her. Among other things, the restraining order prohibited Radcliffe from possessing a firearm for a period of four years. Within two days after the order was entered, Radcliffe used the firearm advertising website armslist. com to arrange to purchase a semiautomatic handgun and ammunition from

Devin Linn for $500. The following day, Radcliffe carried the handgun into the spa where Zina worked and fatally shot her and two other people, injured four others, and shot and killed himself.

Zina's daughter Yasmeen Daniel witnessed the shooting and brought this case against Armslist, LLC, the company that operated armslist.com, alleging negligence, wrongful death, and other claims on her own behalf and on behalf of her mother's estate. In her complaint, Daniel alleged that Armslist knew or should have known that its website would put firearms in the hands of dangerous, prohibited purchasers and that Armslist specifically designed its website to facilitate illegal transactions. Armslist moved to dismiss Daniel's complaint, arguing that Daniel's claims were barred under the CDA. The circuit court agreed and granted the motion to dismiss. The court of appeals reversed.

In an opinion written by Chief Justice Roggensack, the supreme court reversed the court of appeals's decision and affirmed the circuit court's dismissal of Daniel's complaint. The supreme court explained that the CDA was intended, in part, to prevent state and federal laws from interfering with the free exchange of information over the Internet. To that end, the CDA provides immunity from tort liability for "interactive computer service providers" for hosting third-party content. The question, then, came down to whether Armslist merely provided a platform for third parties to post information or whether Armslist, through the design and operation of its website, shared responsibility for the "creation or development" of the content that was posted.

The court noted that a website operator is considered to be responsible for developing content only if the operator materially contributed to the illegality of the content. In determining whether a website's design features materially contributed to the unlawfulness of third-party content, the court explained that, if a feature could be used for proper or improper purposes, it was a "neutral tool" and would generally not be considered to have contributed to the content's unlawfulness, even if the website operator knew that the neutral tools were being used for illegal purposes. Therefore, the court concluded, it was immaterial whether Armslist "knew or should have known," or even if Armslist intended, that its website would be used by third parties to facilitate illegal gun sales. Regardless of whether Armslist knew or intended that illegal content was being posted on the website, Armslist was not liable because it provided neutral tools and, thus, did not materially contribute to the content's illegality.

The court also rejected Daniel's claims because the CDA bars claims that treat an interactive computer service provider as the "publisher or speaker" of third-party content posted on a website. The court analyzed each of Daniel's claims and determined that, despite "artful pleading" by Daniel, all of the claims required that Armslist be treated as a publisher or speaker of information posted by third parties and therefore were barred by the CDA.

Justice A.W. Bradley dissented. Justice Abrahamson withdrew from participation in the case before oral argument.

Involuntary medication; finding of dangerousness

In *Winnebago County v. C.S.*, 2020 WI 33, 391 Wis. 2d 35, 940 N.W.2d 875, the supreme court held that an order for involuntary medication of a prisoner is unconstitutional when it is made without a finding of dangerousness.

Under Wisconsin statutes, involuntary commitment is generally allowed only if it is proved that the individual is mentally ill, a proper subject for treatment, and dangerous. However, if the individual is a prisoner, the standard for involuntary commitment does not require a finding that the individual is dangerous, but rather requires only that the court find that the individual is "in need of treatment."

Once an individual has been involuntarily committed, he or she generally has the right to refuse medication. A court may order an individual to be involuntarily medicated if the court finds that the individual is not competent to refuse medication or if medication is necessary to prevent serious physical harm to the individual or others. Because involuntary commitment is a prerequisite to involuntary medication, and involuntary commitment requires a finding of dangerousness for non-prisoners, an order for involuntary medication for non-prisoners will always include a finding of dangerousness. However, because involuntary commitment of a prisoner under the statutes does not require a finding of dangerousness, an order for involuntary medication for a prisoner may be entered without a finding of dangerousness.

C.S. was a prisoner who was subject to an involuntary commitment and involuntary medication order while he was incarcerated, without any finding or conclusions regarding dangerousness. C.S. sought post-commitment relief with the circuit court, arguing that the involuntary medication statute is unconstitutional for any inmate who is involuntarily committed without a finding of dangerousness. The circuit court denied the petition for post-commitment relief, concluding that involuntary medication is in the legitimate interests of both the county and C.S.

C.S. appealed the circuit court decision. The court of appeals found that the general welfare of a prisoner is a sufficiently legitimate reason for the state to involuntarily medicate and treat a prisoner even when there is no finding of dangerousness.

In an opinion authored by Justice Ziegler, the supreme court held that Wisconsin's involuntary medication statute violates the substantive due process rights of a prisoner who is involuntarily committed without a finding of dangerousness. The court grounded its analysis in a trilogy of U.S. Supreme Court cases, as well as Wisconsin precedent discussing a person's "significant liberty interest" in refusing medication.

In reaching its holding in this case, the Wisconsin Supreme Court distinguished between involuntary commitment and involuntary medication. While the supreme court previously held that the involuntary commitment statute was not unconstitutional because involuntary commitment of a prisoner is "reasonably related to the State's legitimate interest in providing care and assistance to inmates suffering from mental illness," the court recognized here that "[i]nvoluntary medication is much more invasive and must be justified by an overriding or essential [state] interest." The court concluded that incompetence to refuse medication alone is not an essential or overriding state interest and cannot justify involuntary medication.

Justice R.G. Bradley dissented, and Justice Hagedorn, joined by Chief Justice Roggensack, filed a separate dissenting opinion. Both opinions dissented on the basis of concerns relating to reliance on due process to guarantee specific substantive rights under the U.S. Constitution. ▣

4

STATISTICS AND REFERENCE

WISCONSIN STATE SYMBOLS

Over the years, the Wisconsin Legislature has officially recognized a wide variety of state symbols. In order of adoption, Wisconsin has designated an official seal, coat of arms, flag, song, flower, bird, tree, fish, state animal, wildlife animal, domestic animal, mineral, rock, symbol of peace, insect, soil, fossil, dog, beverage, grain, dance, ballad, waltz, fruit, tartan, pastry, dairy product, and herb. These symbols provide a focus for expanding public awareness of Wisconsin's history and diversity. They are listed and described in Section 1.10 of the Wisconsin Statutes.

COAT OF ARMS The large shield at the center of the coat of arms is divided into quarters on which appear symbols for agriculture (plow), mining (pick and shovel), manufacturing (arm and hammer), and navigation (anchor). At the center of the large shield, a small shield and the band that encircles it represent the United States coat of arms and symbolize Wisconsin's membership in and loyalty to the United States. Supporting the large shield from the sides are a sailor holding a coil of rope and a yeoman resting on a pick. These figures represent labor on water and land. At the base of the large shield, a horn of plenty represents prosperity and abundance, and a pyramid of 13 lead ingots represents mineral wealth and the 13 original states of the United States. Above the large shield appears a badger, the state animal, and above the badger appears the state motto, "Forward."

GREAT SEAL The great seal consists of the state coat of arms; the words "Great Seal of the State of Wisconsin" in a curve above; and a line of 13 stars, representing the 13 original states of the United States, in a curve below, all enclosed within an ornamental border. The great seal is used to authenticate the official acts of the governor other than the governor's approval of laws.

FLAG The state flag consists of the state coat of arms; the word "Wisconsin" in white letters above; and the statehood date "1848" in white numbers below, all centered on a royal blue field.

SONG "On, Wisconsin," music by William T. Purdy, words by Joseph S. Hubbard and Charles D. Rosa.

On, Wisconsin! On, Wisconsin! Grand old badger state! We, thy loyal sons and daughters, Hail thee, good and great. ▪ On, Wisconsin! On, Wisconsin! Champion of the right, "Forward", our motto—God will give thee might!

BALLAD "Oh Wisconsin, Land of My Dreams," words by Erma Barrett, music by Shari A. Sarazin.

Oh Wisconsin, land of beauty, with your hillsides and your plains, with your jack-pine and your birch tree, and your oak of mighty frame. ▪ Land of rivers, lakes and valleys, land of warmth and winter snows, land of birds and beasts and humanity, oh Wisconsin, I love you so. ▪ Oh Wisconsin, land of my dreams. Oh Wisconsin, you're all I'll ever need. A little heaven here on earth could you be? Oh Wisconsin, land of my dreams. ▪ In the summer, golden grain fields; in the winter, drift of white snow; in the springtime, robins singing; in the autumn, flaming colors show. ▪ Oh I wonder who could wander, or who could want to drift for long, away from all your beauty, all your sunshine, all your sweet song? ▪ Oh Wisconsin, land of my dreams. Oh Wisconsin, you're all I'll ever need. A little heaven here on earth could you be? Oh Wisconsin, land of my dreams. ▪ And when it's time, let my spirit run free in Wisconsin, land of my dreams.

WALTZ "The Wisconsin Waltz," words and music by Eddie Hansen.

Music from heaven throughout the years; the beautiful Wisconsin Waltz. Favorite song of the pioneers; the beautiful Wisconsin Waltz. ▪ Song of my heart on that last final day, when it is time to lay me away. One thing I ask is to let them play the beautiful Wisconsin Waltz. ▪ My sweetheart, my complete heart, it's for you when we dance together; the beautiful Wisconsin Waltz. I remember that September, before love turned into an ember, we danced to the Wisconsin Waltz. ▪ Summer ended, we intended that our lives then would both be blended, but somehow our planning got lost. ▪ Memory now sings a dream song, a faded love theme song; the beautiful Wisconsin Waltz.

TARTAN The thread count of the state tartan is 44 threads muted blue; 6 threads scarlet; 4 threads muted blue; 6 threads gray; 28 threads black; 40 threads dark green; 4 threads dark yellow; 40 threads dark green; 28 threads black; 22 threads muted blue; and 12 threads dark brown (half sett with full count at the pivots).

FLOWER
Wood violet *(Viola papilionacea)*

BIRD **Robin** *(Turdus migratorius)*

TREE
Sugar maple
(Acer saccharum)

FISH **Muskellunge**
(Esox masquinongy masquinongy Mitchell)

ANIMAL **Badger** *(Taxidea taxus)*

DOMESTIC ANIMAL
Dairy cow
(Bos taurus)

Holstein

Guernsey

INSECT **Honey bee** *(Apis mellifera)*

DOG **American water spaniel**

WILDLIFE ANIMAL
White-tailed deer *(Odocoileus virginianus)*

SYMBOL OF PEACE
Mourning dove
(Zenaidura macroura carolinensis Linnaeus)

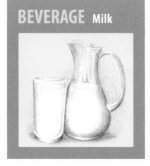

BEVERAGE Milk

SOIL Antigo silt loam
(Typic glossoboralf)

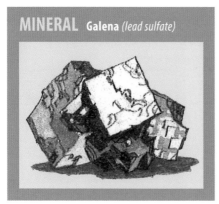

ROCK Red granite

MINERAL Galena *(lead sulfate)*

GRAIN Corn *(Zea mays)*

FOSSIL Trilobite *(Calymene celebra)*

FRUIT Cranberry
(Vaccinium macrocarpon)

PASTRY Kringle

HERB Ginseng *(Panax quinquefolius)*

DANCE Polka

DAIRY PRODUCT Cheese

Significant events in Wisconsin history

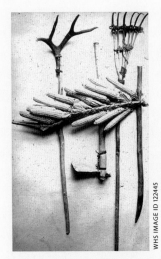

WHS IMAGE ID 122445

Indian agricultural implements.

First nations

Wisconsin's original residents were Native American hunters who arrived here about 14,000 years ago. The area's first farmers appear to have been the Hopewell people, who raised corn, squash, and pumpkins around 2,000 years ago. They were also hunters and fishers, and their trade routes stretched to the Atlantic Coast and the Gulf of Mexico. Later arrivals included the Chippewa, Ho-Chunk (Winnebago), Mohican/Munsee, Menominee, Oneida, Potawatomi, and Sioux.

Under the flag of France

The written history of the state began with the accounts of French explorers. The French explored areas of Wisconsin, named places, and established trading posts; however, they were interested in the fur trade, rather than agricultural settlement, and were never present in large numbers.

1600s

1634. Jean Nicolet became the first known European to reach Wisconsin.

1654–59. Pierre-Esprit Radisson and Médart Chouart des Groseilliers became the first known fur traders in Wisconsin.

1661. Father René Médard became the first missionary to set foot in Wisconsin.

1665. Father Claude Allouez founded a mission at La Pointe.

1668. Nicolas Perrot opened fur trade with Wisconsin Indians near Green Bay.

1672. Father Allouez and Father Louis André built the St. François Xavier mission at De Pere.

1673. Louis Jolliet and Father Jacques Marquette traveled the length of the Mississippi River.

1679. Daniel Greysolon Sieur du Lhut (Duluth) explored the western end of Lake Superior.

1689. Perrot asserted the sovereignty of France over various Wisconsin Indian tribes.

1690. Lead mines were discovered in Wisconsin and Iowa.

1700s

1701–38. The Fox Indian Wars occurred.

1755. Wisconsin Indians, under Charles Langlade, helped defeat British General Braddock during the French and Indian War.

1763. The Treaty of Paris was signed, making Wisconsin part of British colonial territory. ▪ Wisconsin Indians staged a revolt against the new and comparatively more hostile British regime.

1764. Charles Langlade—later known as the "Father of Wisconsin"—settled at Green Bay.

1766. Jonathan Carver explored various sites along the Mississippi River, including a Fox Indian settlement at Prairie du Chien.

1774. The Quebec Act made Wisconsin a part of the Province of Quebec.

1783. The second Treaty of Paris was signed, making Wisconsin a U.S. territory.

1787. Under the Northwest Ordinance of 1787, Wisconsin was made part of the Northwest Territory. The governing units for the Wisconsin area prior to statehood were:

1787–1800	Northwest Territory.
1800–1809	Indiana Territory.
1809–1818	Illinois Territory.
1818–1836	Michigan Territory.
1836–1848	Wisconsin Territory.

1795. Jacques Vieau established a trading post at Milwaukee and outposts at Kewaunee, Manitowoc, and Sheboygan.

Under the flag of Great Britain

Wisconsin experienced few changes under British control. It remained the western edge of European penetration into the American continent, important only as a source of valuable furs for export. French traders plied their trade, and British and colonial traders began to appear, but Europeans continued to be visitors rather than settlers.

Achieving territorial status

In spite of the second Treaty of Paris, Wisconsin remained British in all but title until after the War of 1812. In 1815, the American army established control. Gradually, the British extinguished Indian title to the southeastern half of the state. Lead mining brought the first heavy influx of settlers and ended the dominance of the fur trade in the economy of the area. The lead mining period ran from about 1824 to 1861. Almost half of the 11,683 people who lived in the territory in 1836 were residents of the lead mining district in the southwestern corner of the state.

1800s

1804. William Henry Harrison's treaty with Indians at St. Louis extinguished Indian title to land in the lead region, which eventually became a contributing cause of the Black Hawk War.

1815. The War of 1812 concluded, leading to the abandonment of Fort McKay (formerly Fort Shelby) by the British.

Fort Shelby, renamed Fort McKay.

1816. Astor's American Fur Company began operations in Wisconsin.

1819. Solomon Juneau bought Jacques Vieau's Milwaukee trading post.

1820. Rev. Jedediah Morse traveled to the Green Bay area to report on Indian tribes to the U.S. secretary of war.
■ Lewis Cass, James Duane Doty, and Henry Schoolcraft made an exploratory trip through Wisconsin.

1821. Oneida, Stockbridge, Munsee, and Brothertown tribes began migrating to Wisconsin from the New York area.

1822. The first mining leases in southwest Wisconsin were issued.

1825. A treaty concluded at Prairie du Chien established tribal boundaries.

1827. The Winnebago War began and quickly ended with the surrender of Chief Red Bird to the United States.

1832. The Black Hawk War occurred.

1833. The second Treaty of Chicago between the United States and the Potawatomi granted the U.S. government the land between Lake Michigan and Lake Winnebago. ■ The first Wisconsin newspaper, the *Green Bay Intelligencer*, was established.

1834. Land offices were established in Green Bay and Mineral Point. ■ The first public road was laid.

1835. The first steamboat arrived in

Wisconsin territory

Wisconsin's population had reached 305,000 by 1850. Newcomers were primarily migrants from New York and New England, or immigrants from England, Scotland, Ireland, Germany, and Scandinavia. New York's Erie Canal gave Wisconsin a water outlet to the Atlantic Ocean and a route for new settlers. Wheat was the primary cash crop for most of the newcomers.

State politics revolved around factions headed by James Doty and Henry Dodge. As political parties developed, the Democrats proved dominant throughout the period.

Early statehood

Heavy immigration continued, and the state remained largely agricultural. Slavery, banking laws, and temperance were the major political issues of the period. Despite the number of foreign immigrants, most political leaders continued to have ties to the northeastern United States, and New York state laws and institutions provided models for much of the activity of the early legislative sessions. Control shifted from the Democrats to the Republicans during this period.

Milwaukee. ▪ The first bank in Wisconsin obtained its charter and later opened in Green Bay.

1836. President Andrew Jackson signed the act creating the Territory of Wisconsin on April 20. (Provisions of the Ordinance of 1787 were made part of the act.) ▪ Henry Dodge was appointed governor by President Andrew Jackson. ▪ The first session of the legislature was held, and Madison was chosen as the permanent capital. (The capital had initially been located in Belmont.) ▪ Madison was surveyed and platted.

1837. Construction on the first capitol building began. ▪ The Panic of 1837 drove territorial banks to failure and initiated a five-year economic depression. ▪ The Winnebago Indians ceded all claims to land in Wisconsin. ▪ Imprisonment for debt was abolished.

1838. The territorial legislature met in Madison. ▪ The Milwaukee & Rock River Canal Company was chartered to create a canal connecting Lake Michigan to the Rock River and, accordingly, a waterway to the Mississippi River.

1841. James D. Doty was appointed governor by President John Tyler.

Yellow Thunder of the Winnebago tribe.

WHS IMAGE ID 27886

1842. Legislator James Vineyard shot and killed fellow legislator Charles Arndt in the capitol.

1844. Nathaniel P. Tallmadge was appointed governor by President Tyler. ▪ The Wisconsin Phalanx, a utopian commune, was established in Ceresco (later annexed by Ripon).

1845. Dodge was reappointed governor by President James Polk. ▪ Mormons settled in Voree (near Burlington). ▪ Swiss immigrants founded New Glarus.

1846. Congress passed the enabling act for the admission of Wisconsin as state. ▪ The first constitutional convention met in Madison.

1847. The first proposed state constitution was rejected by the people. A second constitutional convention was held.

1848. The second proposed state constitution was adopted. ▪ President Polk signed a bill on May

Governor Nelson Dewey.
WHS IMAGE ID 117519

29 making Wisconsin a state. ▪ The legislature met on June 5, and Governor Nelson Dewey was inaugurated June 7. ▪ The University of Wisconsin was founded. ▪ Large-scale German immigration began.

1849. A school code was adopted, and the first free, tax-supported, graded school with a high school was established in Kenosha. ▪ The first telegram reached Milwaukee.

The maturing commonwealth

After the Civil War, Wisconsin matured into a modern political and economic entity. Heavy immigration continued, with composition remaining similar to the antebellum period until the end of the century, when Poles arrived in larger numbers.

The Republican Party remained in control of state government throughout the period, but was challenged by Grangers, Populists, Socialists, and Temperance candidates in addition to the Democratic Party and dissidents within the Republican Party. Temperance, the use of foreign languages in schools, railroad regulation, and currency reform were major political issues in the state.

In the 1880s and 1890s, dairying surpassed wheat culture to become the state's primary agricultural activity, with the University of Wisconsin's agricultural school becoming a national leader in the field of dairy science. From the 1870s to the 1890s, lumbering prospered in the north, accounting for one-fourth of all wages paid in the state at its peak. During the same period, Milwaukee developed a thriving heavy machinery industry, and the paper industry emerged in the Fox River Valley. The tanning and the brewing industries were also prominent.

1850. The state opened the Wisconsin Institute for Education of the Blind at Janesville.

1851. The first railroad train ran from Milwaukee to Waukesha. ▪ The first state fair was held in Janesville.

1852. The Wisconsin School for the Deaf opened in Delavan. ▪ Prison construction begun at Waupun.

Art class at the State School for the Deaf.

WHS IMAGE ID 25774

1853. Capital punishment was abolished following the controversial execution of John McCaffary in 1851.

1854. The Republican Party formed in Ripon. ▪ The first class graduated from the University of Wisconsin. ▪ Joshua Glover, a fugitive slave, was arrested in Racine, and the Wisconsin Supreme Court, in a related matter, declared the Fugitive Slave Law of 1850 unconstitutional. ▪ The Milwaukee and Mississippi Railroad reached Madison.

1856. Two candidates claimed themselves winners of a contested gubernatorial race. Coles Bashford took office

only after acting Governor William Barstow was found to have committed election fraud.

1857. The first passenger train reached Prairie du Chien, connecting Milwaukee with the Mississippi River.

1858. Legislators uncovered bribery by former Governor Bashford and other members of the 1856 Legislature.

1859. Abraham Lincoln spoke at the state fair in Milwaukee.

1861. The U.S. Civil War began. ▪ A bank riot occurred in Milwaukee. ▪ The office of county superintendent of schools was created.

1862. Governor Louis P. Harvey drowned. ▪ Draft riots occurred.

1864. Chester Hazen founded the state's first cheese factory in Ladoga.

1865. The U.S. Civil War ends. Approximately 96,000 Wisconsin soldiers served in the war, and 12,216 died.

1866. The Platteville Normal School (University of Wisconsin-Platteville) opened as the first teacher preparation institution in the state. ▪ The legislature formally named the University of Wisconsin a land-grant institution and incorporated an agricultural department.

1871. The Peshtigo fire resulted in over 1,000 deaths—the most fatalities by fire in U.S. history.

1872. The Wisconsin Dairymen's Association organized in Watertown.

1873. Milwaukee newspaper publisher and Wisconsin legislator Christopher

The progressive era

The state's prominent role in the reform movements that swept the country at the beginning of the century gave Wisconsin national fame and its first presidential candidate. Republicans controlled the state legislature, but the Progressive and Stalwart factions fought continually for control of the party. Milwaukee consistently sent a strong Socialist contingent to the legislature.

Large-scale European immigration ended during this period, but ethnic groups retained strong individual identities and remained a significant force in the politics and culture of the state. Of those groups, Germans faced disproportionate suspicion and hostility during the two world wars.

Heavy machinery manufacturing, paper products, and dairying continued to drive the state economy. Meanwhile, lumbering faded in importance and brewing ground to a halt with the onset of Prohibition.

Latham Sholes invented the typewriter. ▪ The Patrons of Husbandry, an agricultural organization nicknamed the Grangers, helped elect William R. Taylor as governor.

1874. The Potter Law, which limited railroad rates, was enacted—only to be repealed two years later.

1875. A free high school law was enacted. ▪ The State Industrial School for Girls was established in Milwaukee. ▪ Republican Harrison Ludington defeated Governor Taylor. ▪ Oshkosh, a leader in the lumber trade, was almost destroyed by fire.

1876. The community of Hazel Green was destroyed by a tornado.

1877. John Appleby developed and later patented a device to bind bundles of grain with twine, a significant contribution to automating agricultural production.

1882. The Wisconsin Constitution was amended to make legislative sessions biennial. ▪ The world's first hydroelectric plant was built in Appleton.

World's first hydroelectric plant in Appleton.

1883. Fire at the Newhall House in Milwaukee killed 71—the country's most lethal hotel fire. ▪ The south wing of the capitol extension collapsed; seven were killed. ▪ The legislature established the Agricultural Experiment Station at the

University of Wisconsin. ▪ Wisconsin first observed Arbor Day.

1885. Gogebic iron range discoveries made Ashland a major shipping port.

1886. Strikes related to the eight-hour work day movement in Milwaukee culminated in confrontation with the militia at Bay View; five were killed. ▪ The University of Wisconsin established an agricultural short course.

1887. Marshfield was almost destroyed by fire.

1889. The Bennett Law, requiring classroom instruction in English, passed but was repealed two years later after bitter opposition from German Protestants and Catholics. ▪ In the "Edgerton Bible case," the Wisconsin Supreme Court prohibited reading and prayers from the King James Bible in public schools. ▪ Former Governor Jeremiah Rusk became the first U.S. secretary of agriculture.

1890. Stephen M. Babcock invented an easy and accurate test for milk butterfat content.

1893. The Wisconsin Supreme Court ordered the state treasurer to refund to the state interest on state deposits, which had customarily been retained by treasurers.

1897. Corrupt practices legislation was enacted to regulate caucuses and prohibit bribery of voters. ▪ The Wisconsin Tax Commission was created.

1898. Wisconsin sent 5,469 men to fight in the Spanish-American War, suffering 134 losses.

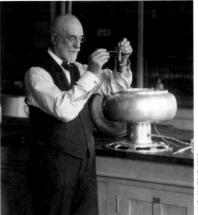

WHS IMAGE ID 5585

Dr. Stephen Babcock with butterfat tester.

1899. A new law prohibited railroads from giving public officials free rides. ▪ The New Richmond Tornado, the deadliest ever recorded in Wisconsin, killed 117 people.

1900s

1900. Interstate Park, Wisconsin's first state park, was established near St. Croix Falls.

1901. The first Wisconsin-born governor, Robert M. La Follette, was inaugurated. ▪ Agricultural education was introduced into rural schools. ▪ The Legislative Reference Library, which served as a model for other states and for the Library of Congress, was established and later renamed the Legislative Reference Bureau.

1904. A referendum vote approved popular election of primary candidates for state-level offices (in place of selection by party leaders). ▪ The state capitol burned down, destroying many records and state artifacts.

4610. Interstate Park, Dells of the St. Croix.

WHS IMAGE ID 109439

Wisconsin's first state park.

1905. The state civil service was established. ▪ An auto license law that required residents to register their automobiles and display license plates was enacted. ▪ A law was enacted that authorized the establishment of a state-owned sanitarium for tuberculosis patients. ▪ The Forestry Board and Railroad Commission were created.

1907. Construction on the current capitol building began.

1908. A referendum amended the Wisconsin Constitution to permit taxing the income of individuals and corporations.

1910. Milwaukee elected Emil Seidel as the first Socialist mayor of a major city in the United States. ▪ Eau Claire became the first Wisconsin city to adopt a commission form of government.

1911. The legislature enacted a bill to establish the state income tax. ▪ The Workmen's Compensation Act required employer compensation for on-the-job injuries. ▪ The legislature created a pension plan for public school teachers statewide. It also required every town,

city, or village with a population of over 5,000 to establish an industrial school. ▪ The State Highway Commission was created to regulate the construction and inspection of highways and bridges and to ensure highways would form continuous routes. ▪ The State Industrial Commission was formed to investigate and create administrative rules relating to industrial safety.

1913. Wisconsin ratified the Seventeenth Amendment, which provided that the people, rather than the state legislature, would directly elect U.S. senators.

1915. The Conservation Commission, the State Board of Agriculture, and the State Board of Education were created.

1917. The new capitol building was completed at a final cost of over $7 million. ▪ Wisconsin sent approximately 120,000 soldiers to serve during World War I, of which nearly 4,000 died. ▪ Wisconsin was the first state to meet national draft requirements.

1919. Wisconsin ratified the Eighteenth Amendment, which established Prohibition, and was the first state to deliver the ratification of the Nineteenth Amendment, which granted American women the right to vote.

1921. Laws establishing Prohibition and equal rights for women were enacted.

1923. Military training at the University of Wisconsin was made optional, rather than compulsory.

The middle years of the twentieth century

After the demise of the Progressives, the Democratic Party began a gradual resurgence and, by the late 1950s, became strongly competitive for the first time in over a century. As the black population grew in urban areas of the state, discrimination in housing and employment became matters of increasing concern. Other issues included the growth in the size of state government, radicalism on the university campuses, welfare programs, and environmental questions. Tourism emerged as a major industry during this period.

1924. Robert M. La Follette, Sr., ran for president as the Progressive Party candidate and won the state of Wisconsin.

1925. Professor Harry Steenbock developed a way to increase vitamin D in certain foods and prompted the formation of the Wisconsin Alumni Research Foundation to ensure that his patent would benefit the University of Wisconsin.

1929. The legislature repealed all Wisconsin laws enforcing Prohibition.

1933. Dairy farmers orchestrated strikes to protest low milk prices. ▪ Wisconsin voted for the repeal of the Eighteenth Amendment (Prohibition).

1935. A researcher from the Forest Products Laboratory in Madison helped convict the kidnapper and murderer of Charles Lindbergh's son in 1932.

1942. Governor-elect Orland Loomis died; the Wisconsin Supreme Court decided that Lieutenant Governor Walter Goodland would serve as acting governor.

1941–45. Wisconsin sent over 330,000 to serve in World War II (including approximately 9,000 enlisted women), of whom about 8,000 died.

1946. The Wisconsin Progressive Party dissolved and rejoined the Republican Party.

1948. Wisconsin's Centennial Year.

1949. The legislature enacted a new formula for the distribution of state educational aids and classified school districts for this purpose.

1950. Approximately 132,000 Wisconsinites served during the Korean Conflict, and 747 died.

Wisconsin Centennial postage stamp.

UNITED STATES POSTAGE
1848 1948
WISCONSIN-CENTENNIAL

WHS IMAGE ID 34700

WHS IMAGE ID 68083

Korean War Veteran Corporal Albert Griffin.

1951. Legislative districts were reapportioned to reflect the rapid growth of urban populations.

1957. A new law prohibited lobbyists from giving anything of value to a state employee.

1958. Professor Joshua Lederberg, a geneticist at the University of Wisconsin, won the Nobel Prize in Physiology or Medicine.

1959. Gaylord Nelson, the first Democratic governor since 1933, was inaugurated. ▪ The Circus World Museum was established in Baraboo. ▪ Famous Wisconsin architect Frank Lloyd Wright died.

1960. Dena Smith was elected state treasurer, becoming the first woman elected to statewide office in Wisconsin.

1961. The legislature initiated a long-range program of acquisition and improvement of state recreation facilities (the ORAP program). ▪ Menominee became Wisconsin's 72nd county when federal supervision of the Indian tribe terminated.

1962. Selective sales tax and income tax withholding were enacted. ▪ The Kohler Company recognized its workers'

union after a record-long strike that began in 1954.

1963. John Gronouski, the state tax commissioner, was appointed U.S. postmaster general. ▪ State expenditures from all funds for the 1963–64 fiscal year topped $1 billion for the first time.

1964. The Wisconsin Supreme Court redistricted the legislative districts after the legislature and the governor failed to agree on a plan. ▪ Two National Farmers Organization members were killed in a demonstration at a Bonduel stockyard. ▪ The legislature enacted property tax relief for the elderly. ▪ The office of county superintendent of schools was abolished, but Cooperative Educational Service Agencies (CESAs) were created to provide regional services.

1965. The school compulsory attendance age was raised to 18. ▪ All parts of the state were placed into vocational school districts. ▪ County boards were reapportioned on the basis of population. ▪ A new state law prohibited discrimination in housing. ▪ The capitol building, in use since 1917, was officially dedicated after extensive remodeling and cleaning.

1966. The 1965 Legislature held the first full even-year regular session since 1882. Governor Warren P. Knowles called the National Guard to keep order during civil rights demonstrations in Wauwatosa. ▪ The Wisconsin Supreme Court upheld the Milwaukee Braves baseball team's move to Atlanta. ▪ A grand jury investigation of illegal lobbying activities in the legislature resulted in 13 indictments.

State Treasurer Dena Smith.

1968. A constitutional amendment permitted the legislature to meet as provided by law rather than once per biennium. ▪ The State University of Wisconsin at Oshkosh expelled 94 black students who confronted administrators about civil rights issues. ▪ Doctors performed Wisconsin's first heart transplant at St. Luke's Hospital in Milwaukee. ▪ The first successful bone marrow transplant that was not between identical twins was performed by a team of scientists and surgeons at UW-Madison.

1969. Wisconsin implemented a general sales tax in place of elective sales taxes. ▪ Father James Groppi led protests at the capitol on the opening day of a special legislative session on welfare and urban aids. The National Guard was called, and Groppi was cited for contempt and jailed. ▪ Student strikes at UW-Madison demanded a black studies department, and the National Guard was again

1967. The executive branch was reorganized. ▪ Legislators repealed a ban on colored oleomargarine. ▪ Civil disturbances broke out in Milwaukee in late July. ▪ Activists advocated for a Milwaukee open housing ordinance. ▪ Anti-war protests at the University of Wisconsin-Madison culminated in violence.

The late twentieth century

Democrats lost control of the senate in 1993 for the first time since 1974, and in 1995 they lost control of the assembly for the first time since 1970. Women began to be widely represented in the legislature for the first time in the 1990s.

Health care reform, welfare, the state's business climate, taxation, education, and prisons were the chief concerns of policymakers in the 1990s.

California challenged Wisconsin's dominance of the dairy industry. After an economic downturn in the 1980s, the 1990s saw a robust economy throughout most of the state, with Madison leading the entire country in employment for several months. The farm sector and brewing industry continued to experience difficulties.

Litigation and demonstrations over off-reservation resource rights of the Chippewa Indians continued throughout the 1980s, to be replaced by controversy over Indian gaming in the 1990s and into the new century.

Father Groppi with civil rights activists.

WHS IMAGE ID 5295

the age of majority from 21 to 18, required an environmental impact statement for all legislation affecting the environment, repealed the railroad full crew law, and ratified the unsuccessful "equal rights" amendment to the U.S. Constitution.

1973. A state constitutional amendment permitting bingo was adopted. ▪ Barbara Thompson became the first woman to hold the elective office of state superintendent of public instruction. ▪ The 1954 Menominee Termination Act was repealed by the U.S. Congress. ▪ The legislature enacted a state ethics code, repealed an oleomargarine tax, funded programs for the education of all children with disabilities, and established procedures for the informal probate of simple estates.

1974. The legislature enacted a comprehensive campaign finance act and strengthened the open meetings law. ▪ Democrats swept all constitutional offices and gained control of both houses of the 1975 Legislature for the first time since 1893. ▪ Kathryn Morrison became the first woman elected to the state senate. ▪ The Hortonville School District fired striking teachers.

1964–75. 165,400 Wisconsinites served in Vietnam; at least 1,161 were killed.

1975. Menominee Indians occupied the Alexian Brothers Novitiate. ▪ The legislature made voter registration easier, established property tax levy limits on local governments, and eliminated statutory distinctions based on sex.

activated. ▪ Wisconsin Congressional Representative Melvin R. Laird was appointed U.S. secretary of defense. ▪ Wisconsin's portion of the Interstate Highway System was completed.

1970. Anti-war protestors bombed the Army Mathematics Research Building at UW-Madison, resulting in one death. ▪ "Old Main" at Wisconsin State University-Whitewater burned down in an apparent arson. ▪ State constitutional officers were elected to four-year terms for the first time in Wisconsin history following a constitutional amendment ratified in 1967. ▪ University of Wisconsin scientists, headed by Dr. Har Gobind Khorana, succeeded in the first total synthesis of a gene.

1971. The legislature enacted major shared tax redistribution, the merger of the University of Wisconsin and State University systems, and a revision of municipal employee relations laws.

1972. The legislature enacted comprehensive consumer protection, lowered

• UW-Madison scientist Dr. Howard Temin won the 1975 Nobel Prize in Physiology or Medicine. • Exxon discovered sulfide zinc and copper deposits near Crandon.

1976. A U.S. district court judge ordered the integration of Milwaukee public schools. • Ice storms caused $50.4 million in damages. • The legislature established a system for compensating crime victims. • Shirley S. Abrahamson was appointed the first woman on the Wisconsin Supreme Court.

1977. Governor Patrick Lucey was appointed as the ambassador to Mexico, and Lieutenant Governor Martin Schreiber became the acting governor. • The first state employees' union strike lasted 15 days, leaving the National Guard to run Wisconsin prisons. • Constitutional amendments authorized raffle games and revised the structure of the court system by creating a court of appeals. • Legislation enacted included public support of elections campaigns,

Shirley Abrahamson takes her oath of office.

WHS IMAGE ID 98857

no-fault divorce, and an implied consent law for drunk driving.

1978. Vel Phillips, elected as secretary of state, became Wisconsin's first black constitutional officer. • The legislature enacted a hazardous waste management program.

1979. The Wisconsin Supreme Court allowed cameras in state courtrooms. • A constitutional amendment removed the lieutenant governor from serving as the president of the senate. • A moratorium on tax collections gave state taxpayers a three-month "vacation" from taxes. • Shirley Abrahamson became the first woman elected to the Wisconsin Supreme Court after having served by appointment for three years. • The legislature established a school of veterinary medicine at UW-Madison.

1980. Eric Heiden of Madison broke several Olympic records when he won five gold medals for ice speed skating. • Fort McCoy housed 14,250 Cuban refugees following the Mariel boatlift. • Former Governor Patrick Lucey ran as an independent candidate for U.S. vice president. • A state revenue shortfall led to a 4.4 percent cut in state spending.

1981. The U.S. Supreme Court ruled against Wisconsin's historic open primary. • The legislature enacted stronger penalties for drunk driving and changes in mining taxes.

1982. State unemployment hit the highest levels since the Great Depression. • Voters endorsed the first statewide referendum in the nation calling for a freeze on nuclear weapons. • Stroh

Brewery Company of Detroit acquired the Schlitz Brewing Company and closed all Milwaukee operations.

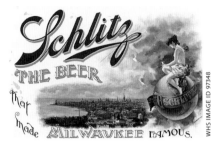

Schlitz Brewing Company.

1983. The continued recession resulted in a budget including a 10 percent tax surcharge and a pay freeze for state employees. ▪ A law raising the minimum drinking age to 19 passed (to become effective in 1985). ▪ Inmates at Waupun State Prison took 15 hostages but released them uninjured the same day. ▪ Laws enacted included a "lemon law" on motor vehicle warranties and changes in child support collection procedures. ▪ The UW-Madison School of Veterinary Medicine enrolled its first class.

1984. The most powerful U.S. tornado of 1984 destroyed Barneveld, killing nine residents. ▪ The Democratic Party chose presidential convention delegates in caucuses rather than by a presidential preference primary because of new Democratic National Committee rules. ▪ Economic conditions began to improve from the low point of the previous two years.

1985. A Milwaukee plane crash killed 31. ▪ A major consolidation of state banks by large holding companies occurred.

▪ A state tax amnesty program was implemented for the first time.

1986. Farm land values fell across the state. ▪ Exxon dropped plans to develop a copper mine near Crandon. ▪ Legislation raised the drinking age to 21 and limited damages payable in malpractice actions. ▪ Protests against Ojibwa spearfishing intensified, and some lawmakers proposed suspending or eliminating Indian hunting and fishing rights.

1987. Voters approved a constitutional amendment allowing pari-mutuel betting and a state lottery. ▪ Laws enacted included a mandatory seatbelt law, antitakeover legislation, a gradual end to the inheritance and gift taxes, and a "learnfare" program designed to keep children of families on welfare in school.

1988. The first state lottery games began. ▪ Chrysler Corporation's automobile assembly plant in Kenosha, the nation's oldest car plant, closed. ▪ Mandatory family leave for employees was enacted.

1989. The legislature created the Department of Corrections, the Lower Wisconsin State Riverway, and a statewide land stewardship program.

1990. More than 1,400 Wisconsin National Guard and Reserve soldiers were called to active duty in the Persian Gulf crisis, and 10 died. ▪ Milwaukee's homicide rate broke records, raising concerns about drugs and crime. ▪ Laws enacted included a major recycling law and a Milwaukee Parental Choice voucher program for public and nonsectarian private schools.

WHS IMAGE ID 97348

1991. The price of milk hit its lowest point since 1978. ▪ The first state-tribal gambling compacts were signed. ▪ Governor Tommy G. Thompson vetoed a record 457 items in the state budget.

1992. A train derailed, spilling toxic chemicals and forcing the evacuation of over 22,000 people in Superior. ▪ Protests at six abortion clinics in Milwaukee led to hundreds of arrests. ▪ Laws enacted included parental consent requirements for abortion, health care reform, and the creation of a three-member Gaming Commission.

1993. President Bill Clinton appointed Wisconsin Congressman Les Aspin as secretary of defense and UW-Madison Chancellor Donna Shalala as secretary of health and human services. ▪ Thousands in Milwaukee became ill as a result of cryptosporidium in the water supply. ▪ California passed Wisconsin in milk production. ▪ Republicans won control of the state senate for the first time since 1974. ▪ Laws enacted included a 1999 sunset for traditional welfare programs, a cap on school spending, and permission to organize limited liability companies.

1994. Laws enacted include the removal of about $1 billion in public school operating taxes from property taxes, to take effect by 1997; a new framework for the Public Service Commission's regulation of telecommunication utilities; and granting towns most of the same powers exercised by cities and villages.

1995. Republicans won control of the state assembly for the first time since 1970. ▪ Elk were reintroduced in northern Wisconsin. ▪ A July heat wave contributed to 152 deaths.

1996. Governor Thompson's welfare reform plan, known as Wisconsin Works (W-2), received national attention. ▪ A train derailment forced the evacuation of Weyauwega. ▪ Pabst Brewing closed its 152-year-old brewery in Milwaukee. ▪ Following his tie-breaking vote in favor of the new Brewers stadium, State Senator George Petak was removed from office in the first successful legislative recall election in state history.

1997. Workers broke ground on Miller Park, the future home of the Milwaukee Brewers.

1998. Tammy Baldwin became the first Wisconsin woman and first openly gay woman elected to U.S. Congress. ▪ The U.S. Supreme Court upheld the constitutionality of the extension of Milwaukee Parental Choice school vouchers to religious schools. ▪ Laws enacted

Artist's rendering of Miller Park Stadium.

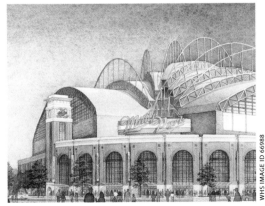

WHS IMAGE ID 66988

included a mining moratorium, new penalties for failure to pay child support, truth-in-sentencing, and penalties for substance abuse by expectant mothers.

1999. Laws enacted included requirements for local comprehensive plans, graduated drivers licensing, and a sales tax rebate. ▪ Supermax, the state's high security prison, opened at Boscobel. ▪ State unemployment reached a record low. ▪ The Department of Natural Resources began monitoring chronic wasting disease in the state's deer herd.

2000s

2000. The legislature approved a local sales tax and revenue bonds for the renovation of Lambeau Field, home of the Green Bay Packers.

2001. Governor Thompson ended a record 14 years in office and became U.S. secretary of health and human services. ▪ Lieutenant Governor Scott McCallum became governor and appointed State Senator Margaret Farrow as the first woman to serve as lieutenant governor. ▪ Extensive Mississippi River flooding occurred. ▪ Miller Park opened. ▪ Laws enacted included establishing a telemarketing "no call" list, wetland protection, and the "SeniorCare" prescription drug assistance plan.

2002. Barbara Lawton became the first woman elected lieutenant governor, and Peggy Lautenschlager became the first woman elected attorney general. ▪ The deadliest single traffic accident in state history killed 10 and injured almost 40 near Sheboygan. ▪ Several state legislators faced criminal charges following an investigation into legislative caucus staffs. ▪ Milwaukee County Board members resigned or were recalled over a pension scandal.

2003. Jim Doyle became the first Democratic governor in 16 years. ▪ Controversy over the Crandon mine ended when local Indian tribes purchased land and mining rights. ▪ The renovated Lambeau Field opened. ▪ State Senator Gary George became the second legislator in Wisconsin history to be recalled. ▪ Wisconsin National Guard and Reserve units were activated for service in the Iraq War. ▪ Wisconsin held its first mourning dove hunt.

2004. Louis Butler, Jr., became the first black justice of the Wisconsin Supreme Court. ▪ The state government reduced its automobile fleet after allegations of misuse. ▪ Significant legislation included a livestock facility siting law and a revision to clean air and water laws intended to spur job creation. ▪ Voter turnout in the fall election was 73 percent, the highest in many years.

2005. The state minimum wage was increased. ▪ Wisconsin experienced a record 62 tornadoes during the year, including a record 27 on August 18, when tornadoes hit Viola, Stoughton, and other communities, resulting in one death and 27 injuries. ▪ Several current and former members of the legislature were convicted of illegal campaign activities.

2006. Immigration reform and the Iraq War were potent, divisive issues. ▪ The legislature limited the use of condemnation power for the benefit of private individuals. ▪ Voters approved a constitutional amendment limiting marriage to persons of the opposite sex. ▪ An advisory referendum in favor of the death penalty was also approved by the voters.

2007. The legislature modified ethics laws and elections regulations. ▪ Milwaukee-based Miller Brewing Company merged with Denver's Coors Brewing Company. ▪ The state budget passed in late October as one of the latest budgets in state history.

2008. A sharp economic downturn led to rising unemployment and the closing of the General Motors plant in Janesville. ▪ Louis Butler, Jr., became the first sitting Wisconsin Supreme Court justice to be defeated at the polls in 40 years, losing to Michael Gableman. ▪ Severe flooding hit southern Wisconsin. ▪ Flooding caused Lake Delton to drain, destroying nearby homes. ▪ The Great Lakes Compact received state and federal approval, regulating the use of Great Lakes water outside its watershed.

2009. Democrats opened the 99th Legislature with control of the governor's office and both houses of the legislature for the first time since the 1985 session. ▪ The ongoing economic crisis resulted in a projected budget deficit of $6 billion for the next biennium. ▪ More than 3,000 members of the Wisconsin National Guard prepared for mobilization to Iraq. ▪ A severe influenza outbreak resulted in 47 deaths.

2010. Several powerful tornadoes hit southern Wisconsin, severely damaging the Old World Wisconsin historic site. ▪ Republicans swept the November elections, capturing the governor's office and both houses of the legislature—the first time in over 70 years that partisan control of all three switched in the same election. ▪ Governor-elect Scott Walker declined $810 million in federal funds to build a high speed rail line between Madison and Milwaukee.

2011. Governor Walker's proposal to curtail collective bargaining rights for public workers led 14 Democrats to leave the state in order to deny the senate a quorum. Thousands of protesters surrounded the capitol to oppose the legislation, which was delayed for weeks before being enacted. Wisconsin remained in a state of political agitation into the summer as nine senators were the subject of recall elections; two senators were recalled. ▪ The legislature enacted a legislative redistricting plan for the first time in three decades, revamped the state's economic development efforts, and expanded the parental school choice program.

2012. Governor Walker, Lieutenant Governor Rebecca Kleefisch, and four senators were the subject of recall elections in the wake of the 2011 collective bargaining law. ▪ Walker, Kleefisch, and two senators were retained; one senator resigned; and one senator was defeated, giving the Democrats control of the senate. ▪ A period of severe heat and drought occurred in June and July. ▪ Republican Paul Ryan was nominated for U.S. vice president. ▪ In November elections, Republicans regained control of the state senate, and Tammy Baldwin became the first Wisconsin woman and first openly gay woman elected to the U.S. Senate.

Vice Presidential candidate Paul Ryan.

2013. The legislature revised regulations for the mining of metallic ferrous minerals, easing the way for the construction of an iron mine in northern Wisconsin's Gogebic Range. ▪ Wisconsin's role as a major source of sand used in the "fracking" method of natural gas extraction presented questions for state and local quarry regulators. ▪ The winter of 2013–14 was the most severe in many years.

2014. Voters passed a constitutional amendment requiring that transportation fund resources be used only for transportation. ▪ Court rulings legalized same-sex marriage in Wisconsin. ▪ The deer harvest was the lowest in 30 years. ▪ Governor Walker denied the Menominee Nation permission to operate a casino in Kenosha.

2015. Senator Mary Lazich was elected president of the senate, becoming the

first woman to be elected presiding officer of either house of the legislature. ▪ Efforts to open an iron mine in the Gogebic Range were abandoned. ▪ The legislature enacted "Right to Work" legislation, raised the speed limit to 70 miles per hour on certain highways, and approved funding for a new Milwaukee Bucks arena. ▪ Voters approved a constitutional amendment requiring the Wisconsin Supreme Court to elect its chief justice by majority vote. ▪ Governor Walker announced his candidacy for U.S. president in July but dropped out of the race in late September. ▪ Congressman Paul Ryan was elected Speaker of the House.

2016. The Wisconsin Elections Commission and the Wisconsin Ethics Commission replaced the Wisconsin Government Accountability Board. ▪ An outbreak of Elizabethkingia meningoseptica killed 18 people. ▪ In the presidential election, Republican Donald Trump became the first Republican presidential candidate to win Wisconsin since President Reagan in 1984.

2017. A special session of the legislature was held to consider and pass legislation to curb the opioid epidemic in the state. ▪ The legislature voted to eliminate the forestry mill tax, Wisconsin's only state property tax. ▪ The legislature passed a $3 billion incentive package for Foxconn, a Taiwanese tech company that agreed to establish a large manufacturing facility in Mount Pleasant.

2018. Voters rejected a constitutional amendment eliminating the office of the state treasurer. ▪ After hearing oral arguments, the U.S. Supreme Court handed *Gill v. Whitford*—a case asking whether Wisconsin district lines were an unconstitutional partisan gerrymander—back to the lower courts. ▪ Wisconsin's unemployment rate reached a record low. ▪ Several areas of the state saw severe flooding following heavy storms. ▪ The legislature

A rainbow flag at the Capitol.

JOE KOSHOLLEK, LEGISLATIVE PHOTOGRAPHER

met in extraordinary session to enact legislation that was later challenged in court. ▪ Tony Evers was elected governor, defeating two-term incumbent Scott Walker.

2019. Mandela Barnes became the state's first black lieutenant governor. ▪ Milwaukee was chosen to host the 2020 Democratic National Convention. ▪ Heavy rainfall caused record-breaking water levels in the Great Lakes. ▪ A rainbow flag flew above the Wisconsin Capitol to commemorate LGBT Pride Month for the first time in state history. ▪ Dairy farmers struggled due to low milk prices and a continued trade war with China. ▪ The Wisconsin Institute for Law & Liberty launched a legal challenge to Governor Evers's use of the partial veto power. ▪ The state first observed Indigenous Peoples' Day on the second Monday of October.

2020. Governor Tony Evers declared a public health emergency in response to the COVID-19 pandemic; some related emergency orders, which closed schools and businesses, were invalidated by the Wisconsin Supreme Court. ▪ Unemployment rates reached record highs. ▪ Protests erupted across the state following the death of George Floyd in Minneapolis. ▪ COVID-19 led to the cancellation of in-person events at the 2020 Democratic National Convention in Milwaukee. ▪ Unrest rocked Kenosha following the shooting of Jacob Blake by police. ▪ The Wisconsin Supreme Court denied an attempt by the presidential campaign of Donald Trump to invalidate over 220,000 ballots cast in Wisconsin in the presidential election. ▪ COVID-19 claimed the lives of over 4,800 Wisconsinites. 𝐁𝐁

Wisconsin governors since 1848

	Party	Service	Residence[1]
Nelson Dewey	Democratic	6/7/1848–1/5/1852	Lancaster
Leonard James Farwell	Whig	1/5/1852–1/2/1854	Madison
William Augustus Barstow	Democratic	1/2/1854–3/21/1856	Waukesha
Arthur McArthur [2]	Democratic	3/21/1856–3/25/1856	Milwaukee
Coles Bashford	Republican	3/25/1856–1/4/1858	Oshkosh
Alexander William Randall	Republican	1/4/1858–1/6/1862	Waukesha
Louis Powell Harvey [3]	Republican	1/6/1862–4/19/1862	Shopiere
Edward Salomon	Republican	4/19/1862–1/4/1864	Milwaukee
James Taylor Lewis	Republican	1/4/1864–1/1/1866	Columbus
Lucius Fairchild	Republican	1/1/1866–1/1/1872	Madison
Cadwallader Colden Washburn	Republican	1/1/1872–1/5/1874	La Crosse
William Robert Taylor	Democratic	1/5/1874–1/3/1876	Cottage Grove
Harrison Ludington	Republican	1/3/1876–1/7/1878	Milwaukee
William E. Smith	Republican	1/7/1878–1/2/1882	Milwaukee
Jeremiah McLain Rusk	Republican	1/2/1882–1/7/1889	Viroqua
William Dempster Hoard	Republican	1/7/1889–1/5/1891	Fort Atkinson
George Wilbur Peck	Democratic	1/5/1891–1/7/1895	Milwaukee
William Henry Upham	Republican	1/7/1895–1/4/1897	Marshfield
Edward Scofield	Republican	1/4/1897–1/7/1901	Oconto
Robert Marion La Follette, Sr. [4]	Republican	1/7/1901–1/1/1906	Madison
James O. Davidson	Republican	1/1/1906–1/2/1911	Soldiers Grove
Francis Edward McGovern	Republican	1/2/1911–1/4/1915	Milwaukee
Emanuel Lorenz Philipp	Republican	1/4/1915–1/3/1921	Milwaukee
John James Blaine	Republican	1/3/1921–1/3/1927	Boscobel
Fred R. Zimmerman	Republican	1/3/1927–1/7/1929	Milwaukee
Walter Jodok Kohler, Sr.	Republican	1/7/1929–1/5/1931	Kohler
Philip Fox La Follette	Republican	1/5/1931–1/2/1933	Madison
Albert George Schmedeman	Democratic	1/2/1933–1/7/1935	Madison
Philip Fox La Follette	Progressive	1/7/1935–1/2/1939	Madison
Julius Peter Heil	Republican	1/2/1939–1/4/1943	Milwaukee
Walter Samuel Goodland [3, 5]	Republican	1/4/1943–3/12/1947	Racine
Oscar Rennebohm	Republican	3/12/1947–1/1/1951	Madison
Walter Jodok Kohler, Jr.	Republican	1/1/1951–1/7/1957	Kohler
Vernon Wallace Thomson	Republican	1/7/1957–1/5/1959	Richland Center
Gaylord Anton Nelson	Democratic	1/5/1959–1/7/1963	Madison
John W. Reynolds	Democratic	1/7/1963–1/4/1965	Green Bay
Warren Perley Knowles	Republican	1/4/1965–1/4/1971	New Richmond
Patrick Joseph Lucey [4]	Democratic	1/4/1971–7/6/1977	Madison
Martin James Schreiber	Democratic	7/6/1977–1/1/1979	Milwaukee
Lee Sherman Dreyfus	Republican	1/1/1979–1/3/1983	Stevens Point
Anthony Scully Earl	Democratic	1/3/1983–1/5/1987	Madison
Tommy George Thompson [4]	Republican	1/5/1987–2/1/2001	Elroy
Scott McCallum	Republican	2/1/2001–1/6/2003	Fond du Lac
James Edward Doyle, Jr.	Democratic	1/6/2003–1/3/2011	Madison
Scott Kevin Walker	Republican	1/3/2011–1/7/2019	Wauwatosa
Tony Evers	Democratic	1/7/2019–	Madison

Note: Prior to 1971, the term of office was two years rather than four. Prior to 1885, the term of office began in January of an even-numbered rather than an odd-numbered year.

1. Residence at the time of election.   2. Served as acting governor during dispute over outcome of gubernatorial election.
3. Died in office.   4. Resigned.   5. Served as acting governor for the 1943–44 term following the death of Governor-elect Orland Loomis.

Sources: "Wisconsin's Former Governors," 1960 *Wisconsin Blue Book*, pp. 69–206; *Blue Book* biographies.

Vote for governor in general elections since 1848

1848
Nelson Dewey[1]—D 19,875
John H. Tweedy[1]—W 14,621
Charles Durkee[1]—I 1,134
Total. 35,309

1849
Nelson Dewey—D 16,649
Alexander L. Collins—W . . 11,317
Warren Chase—I 3,761
Total. 31,759

1851
Leonard J. Farwell—W . . . 22,319
Don A. J. Upham—D 21,812
Total. 44,190

1853
William A. Barstow—D . . . 30,405
Edward D. Holton—FS . . . 21,886
Henry S. Baird—W 3,304
Total. 55,683

1855
William A. Barstow[2]—D . . 36,355
Coles Bashford—R 36,198
Total. 72,598

1857
Alexander W. Randall—R . 44,693
James B. Cross—D 44,239
Total. 90,058

1859
Alexander W. Randall—R . 59,999
Harrison C. Hobart—D . . . 52,539
Total. 112,755

1861
Louis P. Harvey—R 53,777
Benjamin Ferguson—D . . 45,456
Total. 99,258

1863
James T. Lewis—R 72,717
Henry L. Palmer—D 49,053
Total. 122,029

1865
Lucius Fairchild—R 58,332
Harrison C. Hobart—D . . . 48,330
Total. 106,674

1867
Lucius Fairchild—R 73,637
John J. Tallmadge—D . . . 68,873
Total. 142,522

1869
Lucius Fairchild—R 69,502
Charles D. Robinson—D . . 61,239
Total. 130,781

1871
Cadwallader C. Washburn—R
. 78,301
James R. Doolittle—D . . . 68,910
Total. 147,274

1873
William R. Taylor—D 81,599
Cadwallader C. Washburn—R
. 66,224
Total. 147,856

1875
Harrison Ludington—R . . 85,155
William R. Taylor—D 84,314
Total. 170,070

1877
William E. Smith—R. 78,759
James A. Mallory—D 70,486
Edward P. Allis—G. 26,216
Collin M. Campbell—S 2,176
Total. 178,122

1879
William E. Smith—R. . . . 100,535
James G. Jenkins—D 75,030
Reuben May—G. 12,996
Total. 189,005

1881
Jeremiah M. Rusk—R. . . . 81,754
N.D. Fratt—D. 69,797
T.D. Kanouse—Pro 13,225
Edward P. Allis—G 7,002
Total. 171,856

1884
Jeremiah M. Rusk—R. . . 163,214
N.D. Fratt—D. 143,945
Samuel D. Hastings—Pro . .8,545
William L. Utley—G. 4,274
Total. 319,997

1886
Jeremiah M. Rusk—R . . . 133,247
Gilbert M. Woodward—D 114,529
John Cochrane—PPop . . . 21,467
John Myers Olin—Pro . . . 17,089
Total. 286,368

1888
William D. Hoard—R . . . 175,696
James Morgan—D 155,423
E.G. Durant—Pro 14,373
D. Frank Powell—L 9,196
Total. 354,714

1890
George W. Peck—D 160,388
William D. Hoard—R . . . 132,068
Charles Alexander—Pro . . 11,246
Reuben May—UL 5,447
Total. 309,254

1892
George W. Peck—D 178,095
John C. Spooner—R . . . 170,497
Thomas C. Richmond—Pro 13,185
C.M. Butt—PPop. 9,638
Total. 371,559

1894
William H. Upham—R . . 196,150
George W. Peck—D. . . . 142,250
D. Frank Powell—PPop. . . 25,604
John F. Cleghorn—Pro . . . 11,240
Total. 375,449

1896
Edward Scofield—R. . . . 264,981
Willis C. Silverthorn—D . 169,257
Joshua H. Berkey—Pro. . . .8,140
Christ Tuttrop—SL 1,306
Robert Henderson—Nat. . . .407
Total. 444,110

1898
Edward Scofield—R. . . . 173,137
Hiram W. Sawyer—D . . . 135,353
Albinus A. Worsley—PPop. .8,518
Eugene W. Chafin—Pro . . .8,078
Howard Tuttle—SDA 2,544
Henry Riese—SL. 1,473
Total. 329,430

1900
Robert M. La Follette—R. 264,419
Louis G. Bomrich—D . . . 160,674
J. Burritt Smith—Pro 9,707
Howard Tuttle—SD 6,590
Frank R. Wilke—SL 509
Total. 441,900

1902
Robert M. La Follette—R. 193,417
David S. Rose—D 145,818
Emil Seidel—SD 15,970
Edwin W. Drake—Pro. 9,647
Henry E.D. Puck—SL 791
Total. 365,676

Vote for governor in general elections since 1848, continued

1904
Robert M. La Follette—R. 227,253
George W. Peck—D. . . . 176,301
William A. Arnold—SD . . . 24,857
Edward Scofield—NR. . . . 12,136
William H. Clark—Pro. 8,764
Charles M. Minkley—SL 249
Total. 449,570

1906
James O. Davidson—R . . 183,558
John A. Aylward—D . . . 103,311
Winfield R. Gaylord—SD. . 24,437
Ephraim L. Eaton—Pro. . . . 8,211
Ole T. Rosaas—SL 455
Total. 320,003

1908
James O. Davidson—R . . 242,935
John A. Aylward—D . . . 165,977
H.D. Brown—SD 28,583
Winfred D. Cox—Pro . . . 11,760
Herman Bottema—SL 393
Total. 449,656

1910
Francis E. McGovern—R . 161,619
Adolph H. Schmitz—D . . 110,442
William A. Jacobs—SD . . . 39,547
Byron E. Van Keuren—Pro . . 7,450
Fred G. Kremer—SL 430
Total. 319,522

1912
Francis E. McGovern—R . 179,360
John C. Karel—D 167,316
Carl D. Thompson—SD. . . 34,468
Charles L. Hill—Pro 9,433
William H. Curtis—SL. 3,253
Total. 393,849

1914
Emanuel L. Philipp—R . . 140,787
John C. Karel—D 119,509
John J. Blaine—I. 32,560
Oscar Ameringer—SD . . . 25,917
David W. Emerson—Pro . . . 6,279
John Vierthaler—I. 352
Total. 325,430

1916
Emanuel L. Philipp—R . . 229,889
Burt Williams—D 164,555
Rae Weaver—Soc 30,649
George McKerrow—Pro . . . 9,193
Total. 434,340

1918
Emanuel L. Philipp—R . . 155,799
Henry A. Moehlenpah—D 112,576
Emil Seidel—SD 57,523
William C. Dean—Pro. . . . 5,296
Total. 331,582

1920
John J. Blaine—R 366,247
Robert McCoy—D. 247,746
William Coleman—S 71,126
Henry H. Tubbs—Pro 6,047
Total. 691,294

1922
John J. Blaine—R 367,929
Arthur A. Bentley—ID . . . 51,061
Louis A. Arnold—S 39,570
M.L. Welles—Pro. 21,438
Arthur A. Dietrich—ISL. . . . 1,444
Total. 481,828

1924
John J. Blaine—R 412,255
Martin L. Lueck—D 317,550
William F. Quick—S 45,268
Adolph R. Bucknam—Pro . 11,516
Severi Alanne—IW 4,107
Farrand K. Shuttleworth—IPR 4,079
Jose Snover—SL. 1,452
Total. 796,432

1926
Fred R. Zimmerman—R . 350,927
Charles Perry—I 76,507
Virgil H. Cady—D 72,627
Herman O. Kent—S 40,293
David W. Emerson—Pro . . . 7,333
Alex Gorden—SL 4,593
Total. 552,912

1928
Walter J. Kohler, Sr—R . . 547,738
Albert G. Schmedeman—D 394,368
Otto R. Hauser—S. 36,924
Adolph R. Bucknam—Pro . 6,477
Joseph Ehrhardt—IL 1,938
Alvar J. Hayes—IW 1,420
Total. 989,143

1930
Philip F. La Follette—R . . 392,958
Charles E. Hammersley—D 170,020
Frank B. Metcalfe—S 25,607
Alfred B. Taynton—Pro. . . 14,818
Fred B. Blair—IC 2,998
Total. 606,825

1932
Albert G. Schmedeman—D
. . . . 590,114
Walter J. Kohler, Sr—R . . 470,805
Frank B. Metcalfe—S 56,965
William C. Dean—Pro. . . . 3,148
Fred B. Blair—Com 2,926
Joe Ehrhardt—SL 398
Total. 1,124,502

1934
Philip F. La Follette—P . . 373,093
Albert G. Schmedeman—D
. . . . 359,467
Howard Greene—R 172,980
George A. Nelson—S 44,589
Morris Childs—IC 2,454
Thomas W. North—IPro 857
Joe Ehrhardt—ISL. 332
Total. 953,797

1936
Philip F. La Follette—P . . 573,724
Alexander Wiley—R. . . . 363,973
Arthur W. Lueck—D. . . . 268,530
Joseph F. Walsh—U 27,934
Joseph Ehrhardt—SL. 1,738
August F. Fehlandt—Pro. . . 1,008
Total. 1,237,095

1938
Julius P. Heil—R 543,675
Philip F. La Follette—P . . 353,381
Harry W. Bolens—D. 78,446
Frank W. Smith—U 4,564
John Schleier, Jr—ISL. 1,459
Total. 981,560

1940
Julius P. Heil—R 558,678
Orland S. Loomis—P . . . 546,436
Francis E. McGovern—D . 264,985
Fred B. Blair—Com 2,340
Louis Fisher—SL. 1,158
Total. 1,373,754

1942
Orland S. Loomis—P . . . 397,664
Julius P. Heil—R 291,945
William C. Sullivan—D . . . 98,153
Frank P. Zeidler—S 11,295
Fred Bassett Blair—IC 1,092
Georgia Cozzini—ISL. 490
Total. 800,985

Vote for governor in general elections since 1848, continued

1944
Walter S. Goodland—R . . 697,740
Daniel W. Hoan—D 536,357
Alexander O. Benz—P . . . 76,028
George A. Nelson—S 9,183
Georgia Cozzini—I (ISL) . . . 1,122
Total. 1,320,483

1946
Walter S. Goodland—R . . 621,970
Daniel W. Hoan—D 406,499
Walter H. Uphoff—S 8,996
Sigmund G. Eisenscher—IC 1,857
Jerry R. Kenyon—ISL 959
Total. 1,040,444

1948
Oscar Rennebohm—R . . 684,839
Carl W. Thompson—D . . 558,497
Henry J. Berquist—PP . . . 12,928
Walter H. Uphoff—S 9,149
James E. Boulton—ISW 356
Georgia Cozzini—ISL 328
Total. 1,266,139

1950
Walter J. Kohler, Jr—R . . 605,649
Carl W. Thompson—D . . 525,319
M. Michael Essin—PP. 3,735
William O. Hart—S 3,384
Total. 1,138,148

1952
Walter J. Kohler, Jr—R . 1,009,171
William Proxmire—D . . . 601,844
M. Michael Essin—I 3,706
Total. 1,615,214

1954
Walter J. Kohler, Jr—R . . 596,158
William Proxmire—D . . . 560,747
Arthur Wepfer—I 1,722
Total. 1,158,666

1956
Vernon W. Thomson—R . 808,273
William Proxmire—D . . . 749,421
Total. 1,557,788

1958
Gaylord A. Nelson—D . . 644,296
Vernon W. Thomson—R . 556,391
Wayne Leverenz—I 1,485
Total. 1,202,219

1960
Gaylord A. Nelson—D . . 890,868
Philip G. Kuehn—R 837,123
Total. 1,728,009

1962
John W. Reynolds—D. . . 637,491
Philip G. Kuehn—R 625,536
Adolf Wiggert—I 2,477
Total. 1,265,900

1964
Warren P. Knowles—R . . 856,779
John W. Reynolds—D. . . 837,901
Total. 1,694,887

1966
Warren P. Knowles—R . . 626,041
Patrick J. Lucey—D 539,258
Adolf Wiggert—I 4,745
Total. 1,170,173

1968
Warren P. Knowles—R . . 893,463
Bronson C. La Follette—D 791,100
Adolf Wiggert—I 3,225
Robert Wilkinson—I 1,813
Total. 1,689,738

1970
Patrick J. Lucey—D 728,403
Jack B. Olson—R. 602,617
Leo J. McDonald—A 9,035
Georgia Cozzini—I (SL). . . . 1,287
Samuel K. Hunt—I (SW) 888
Myrtle Kastner—I (PLS) 628
Total. 1,343,160

1974
Patrick J. Lucey—D 628,639
William D. Dyke—R. . . . 497,189
William H. Upham—A . . . 33,528
Crazy Jim[3]—I 12,107
William Hart—I (DS) 5,113
Fred Blair—I (C) 3,617
Georgia Cozzini—I (SL). . . . 1,492
Total. 1,181,685

1978
Lee S. Dreyfus—R 816,056
Martin J. Schreiber—D. . 673,813
Eugene R. Zimmerman—C . 6,355
John C. Doherty—I 2,183
Adrienne Kaplan—I (SW) . . 1,548
Henry A. Ochsner—I (SL) . . . 849
Total. 1,500,996

1982
Anthony S. Earlv—D . . . 896,872
Terry J. Kohler—R 662,738
Larry Smiley—Lib 9,734
James P. Wickstrom—Con . . 7,721
Peter Seidman—I (SW). . . . 3,025
Total. 1,580,344

1986
Tommy G. Thompson—R
. . . . 805,090
Anthony S. Earl—D 705,578
Kathryn A. Christensen—LF 10,323
Darold E. Wall—I. 3,913
Sanford Knapp—I. 1,668
Total. 1,526,573

1990
Tommy G. Thompson—R
. . . . 802,321
Thomas A. Loftus—D. . . 576,280
Total. 1,379,727

1994
Tommy G. Thompson—R 1,051,326
Charles J.Chvala—D . . . 482,850
David S. Harmon—Lib . . . 11,639
Edward J. Frami—Tax. 9,188
Michael J. Mangan—I 8,150
Total. 1,563,835

1998
Tommy G. Thompson—R
. . . . 1,047,716
Ed Garvey—D 679,553
Jim Mueller—Lib 11,071
Edward J. Frami—Tax. . . . 10,269
Mike Mangan—I. 4,985
A-Ja-mu Muhammad—I . . . 1,604
Jeffrey L. Smith—WG. 14
Total. 1,756,014

2002
Jim Doyle—D 800,515
Scott McCallum—R 734,779
Ed Thompson—Lib 185,455
Jim Young—WG 44,111
Alan D. Eisenberg—I 2,847
Ty A. Bollerud—I. 2,637
Mike Mangan—I. 1,710
Aneb Jah Rasta Sensas-Utcha
Nefer-I—I 929
Total. 1,775,349

2006
Jim Doyle—D 1,139,115
Mark Green—R 979,427
Nelson Eisman—WG 40,709
Total. 2,161,700

2010
Scott Walker—R 1,128,941
Tom Barrett—D 1,004,303
Jim Langer—I 10,608
James James—I 8,273
Total[4]. 2,160,832

Vote for governor in general elections since 1848, continued

June 5, 2012 recall election	2014	2018
Scott Walker—R 1,335,585	Scott Walker—R 1,259,706	Tony Evers—D 1,324,307
Tom Barrett—D 1,164,480	Mary Burke—D 1,122,913	Scott Walker—R 1,295,080
Hari Trivedi—I 14,463	Robert Burke—I (Lib) 18,720	Phillip Anderson—Lib . . . 20,225
Total. 2,516,065	Dennis Fehr—I (Peo) 7,530	Maggie Turnbull—I 18,884
	Total. 2,410,314	Michael J. White—WG . . . 11,087
		Arnie Enz—I (Wis) 2,745
		Total. 2,673,308

Note: A candidate whose party did not receive 1% of the vote for a statewide office in the previous election or who failed to meet the alternative requirement of section 5.62, Wis. Stats., is listed on the Wisconsin ballot as "independent." When a candidate's party affiliation is listed as "I," followed by a party designation in parentheses, "independent" was the official ballot listing, but a party designation was found by the Wisconsin Legislative Reference Bureau in newspaper reports.

Totals include scattered votes for other candidates.

A—American	IPro—Independent Prohibition	Pro—Prohibition
C—Conservative	ISL—Independent Socialist Labor	R—Republican
Com—Communist	ISW—Independent Socialist Worker	S—Socialist
Con—Constitution	IW—Independent Worker	SD—Social Democrat
D—Democrat	L—Labor	SDA—Social Democrat of America
DS—Democratic Socialist	LF—Labor-Farm/Laborista-Agrario	SL—Socialist Labor
FS—Free Soil	Lib—Libertarian	SW—Socialist Worker
G—Greenback	Nat—National	Tax—U.S. Taxpayers
I—Independent	NR—National Republic	U—Union
IC—Independent Communist	P—Progressive	UL—Union Labor
ID—Independent Democrat	Peo—People's	W—Whig
IL—Independent Labor	PLS—Progressive Labor Socialist	WG—Wisconsin Green
IPR—Independent Prohibition Republic	PP—People's Progressive	Wis—Wisconsin Party
	PPop—People's (Populist)	

1. Votes for Dewey and Tweedy are from 1874 *Blue Book*; Durkee vote is based on county returns, as filed in the Office of the Secretary of State, but returns from Manitowoc and Winnebago Counties were missing. Without these 2 counties, Dewey had 19,605 votes and Tweedy had 14,514 votes.   2. Barstow's plurality was set aside in *Atty. Gen. ex rel. Bashford v. Barstow*, 4 Wis. 567 (1855) because of irregularities in the election returns.   3. Legal name.   4. Total includes 6,780 votes for the Libertarian ticket, which had a candidate for lieutenant governor, but no candidate for governor.

Source: Canvass reports and Wisconsin Elections Commission records.

Wisconsin lieutenant governors since 1848

	Party	Service	Residence[1]
John E. Holmes	Democratic	1848–1850	Jefferson
Samuel W. Beall	Democratic	1850–1852	Taycheedah
Timothy Burns.	Democratic	1852–1854	La Crosse
James T. Lewis.	Republican	1854–1856	Columbus
Arthur McArthur[2]	Democratic	1856–1858	Milwaukee
Erasmus D. Campbell	Democratic	1858–1860	La Crosse
Butler G. Noble	Republican	1860–1862	Whitewater
Edward Salomon[3]	Republican	1862–1864	Milwaukee
Wyman Spooner	Republican	1864–1870	Elkhorn
Thaddeus C. Pound	Republican	1870–1872	Chippewa Falls
Milton H. Pettit[4]	Republican	1872–3/23/73	Kenosha
Charles D. Parker	Democratic	1874–1878	Pleasant Valley
James M. Bingham	Republican	1878–1882	Chippewa Falls
Sam S. Fifield	Republican	1882–1887	Ashland
George W. Ryland.	Republican	1887–1891	Lancaster
Charles Jonas	Democratic	1891–1895	Racine
Emil Baensch	Republican	1895–1899	Manitowoc
Jesse Stone	Republican	1899–1903	Watertown
James O. Davidson[5]	Republican	1903–1907	Soldiers Grove
William D. Connor	Republican	1907–1909	Marshfield

Wisconsin lieutenant governors since 1848, continued

	Party	Service	Residence[1]
John Strange	Republican	1909–1911	Oshkosh
Thomas Morris	Republican	1911–1915	La Crosse
Edward F. Dithmar	Republican	1915–1921	Baraboo
George F. Comings	Republican	1921–1925	Eau Claire
Henry A. Huber	Republican	1925–1933	Stoughton
Thomas J. O'Malley	Democratic	1933–1937	Milwaukee
Henry A. Gunderson[6]	Progressive	1937–10/16/37	Portage
Herman L. Ekern[7]	Progressive	5/16/38–1939	Madison
Walter S. Goodland[8]	Republican	1939–1945	Racine
Oscar Rennebohm[9]	Republican	1945–1949	Madison
George M. Smith	Republican	1949–1955	Milwaukee
Warren P. Knowles	Republican	1955–1959	New Richmond
Philleo Nash	Democratic	1959–1961	Wisconsin Rapids
Warren P. Knowles	Republican	1961–1963	New Richmond
Jack Olson	Republican	1963–1965	Wisconsin Dells
Patrick J. Lucey	Democratic	1965–1967	Madison
Jack Olson	Republican	1967–1971	Wisconsin Dells
Martin J. Schreiber[10]	Democratic	1971–1979	Milwaukee
Russell A. Olson	Republican	1979–1983	Randall
James T. Flynn	Democratic	1983–1987	West Allis
Scott McCallum[11]	Republican	1987–2/1/01	Fond du Lac
Margaret A. Farrow[12]	Republican	5/9/01–2003	Pewaukee
Barbara Lawton	Democratic	2003–2011	Green Bay
Rebecca Kleefisch	Republican	2011–2019	Oconomowoc
Mandela Barnes	Democratic	2019–	Milwaukee

Note: Prior to 1971, the term of office was two years rather than four. Prior to 1885, the term of office began in January of an even-numbered rather than an odd-numbered year. Prior to 1979, lieutenant governors did not cease to hold the office of lieutenant governor while acting in place of a governor who had died or resigned.

1. Residence at the time of election. 2. Served as acting governor 3/21/1856 to 3/25/1856 during dispute over outcome of gubernatorial election. 3. Became acting governor on the death of Governor Harvey, 4/19/1862. 4. Died in office. 5. Became acting governor when Governor La Follette resigned, 1/1/1906. 6. Resigned. 7. Appointed to serve the rest of Gunderson's term. 8. Became acting governor on the death of Governor-elect Orland Loomis, 1/1/1943. 9. Became acting governor on the death of Governor Goodland, 3/12/1947. 10. Became acting governor when Governor Lucey resigned, 7/6/1977. 11. Became governor when Governor Thompson resigned, 2/1/2001. 12. Appointed to serve the rest of McCallum's term.

Source: Wisconsin Legislative Reference Bureau, *Wisconsin Blue Book*, various editions, and bureau records.

Wisconsin attorneys general since 1848

	Party	Service	Residence[1]
James S. Brown	Democratic	1848–1850	Milwaukee
S. Park Coon	Democratic	1850–1852	Milwaukee
Experience Estabrook	Democratic	1852–1854	Geneva
George B. Smith	Democratic	1854–1856	Madison
William R. Smith	Democratic	1856–1858	Mineral Point
Gabriel Bouck	Democratic	1858–1860	Oshkosh
James H. Howe[2]	Republican	1860–1862	Green Bay
Winfield Smith[3]	Republican	1862–1866	Milwaukee
Charles R. Gill	Republican	1866–1870	Watertown
Stephen Steele Barlow	Republican	1870–1874	Dellona
Andrew Scott Sloan	Republican	1874–1878	Beaver Dam
Alexander Wilson	Republican	1878–1882	Mineral Point
Leander F. Frisby	Republican	1882–1887	West Bend
Charles E. Estabrook	Republican	1887–1891	Manitowoc
James L. O'Connor	Democratic	1891–1895	Madison
William H. Mylrea	Republican	1895–1899	Wausau

Wisconsin attorneys general since 1848, continued

	Party	Service	Residence[1]
Emmett R. Hicks	Republican	1899–1903	Oshkosh
Lafayette M. Sturdevant	Republican	1903–1907	Neillsville
Frank L. Gilbert	Republican	1907–1911	Madison
Levi H. Bancroft	Republican	1911–1913	Richland Center
Walter C. Owen[4]	Republican	1913–1918	Maiden Rock
Spencer Haven[5]	Republican	1918–1919	Hudson
John J. Blaine	Republican	1919–1921	Boscobel
William J. Morgan	Republican	1921–1923	Milwaukee
Herman L. Ekern	Republican	1923–1927	Madison
John W. Reynolds	Republican	1927–1933	Green Bay
James E. Finnegan	Democratic	1933–1937	Milwaukee
Orlando S. Loomis	Progressive	1937–1939	Mauston
John E. Martin[2]	Republican	1939–6/1/48	Madison
Grover L. Broadfoot[6]	Republican	6/5/48–11/12/48	Mondovi
Thomas E. Fairchild[7]	Democratic	11/12/48–1951	Verona
Vernon W. Thomson	Republican	1951–1957	Richland Center
Stewart G. Honeck	Republican	1957–1959	Madison
John W. Reynolds	Democratic	1959–1963	Green Bay
George Thompson	Republican	1963–1965	Madison
Bronson C. La Follette	Democratic	1965–1969	Madison
Robert W. Warren[2]	Republican	1969–10/8/74	Green Bay
Victor A. Miller[8]	Democratic	10/8/74–11/25/74	St. Nazianz
Bronson C. La Follette[9]	Democratic	11/25/74–1987	Madison
Donald J. Hanaway	Republican	1987–1991	Green Bay
James E. Doyle	Democratic	1991–2003	Madison
Peggy A. Lautenschlager	Democratic	2003–2007	Fond du Lac
J.B. Van Hollen	Republican	2007–2015	Waunakee
Brad D. Schimel	Republican	2015–2019	Waukesha
Josh Kaul	Democratic	2019–	Madison

Note: Prior to 1971, the term of office was two years rather than four. Prior to 1885, the term of office began in January of an even-numbered rather than an odd-numbered year.

1. Residence at the time of election. 2. Resigned. 3. Appointed 10/7/1862 to serve the rest of Howe's term. 4. Resigned 1/7/1918. 5. Appointed to serve the rest of Owen's term. 6. Appointed to serve the rest of Martin's term. Resigned. 7. Attorney General-elect Fairchild appointed to serve the rest of Martin's term. 8. Appointed to serve the rest of Warren's term. Resigned. 9. Attorney General-elect La Follette appointed to serve the rest of Warren's term.

Source: Wisconsin Legislative Reference Bureau, *Wisconsin Blue Book*, various editions, and bureau records.

Wisconsin superintendents of public instruction since 1849

	Service	Residence[1]
Eleazer Root	1849–1852	Waukesha
Azel P. Ladd	1852–1854	Shullsburg
Hiram A. Wright	1854–1855	Prairie du Chien
A. Constantine Barry	1855–1858	Racine
Lyman C. Draper	1858–1860	Madison
Josiah L. Pickard	1860–1864	Platteville
John G. McMynn	1864–1868	Racine
Alexander J. Craig	1868–1870	Madison
Samuel Fallows	1870–1874	Milwaukee
Edward Searing	1874–1878	Milton
William Clarke Whitford	1878–1882	Milton
Robert Graham	1882–1887	Oshkosh
Jesse B. Thayer	1887–1891	River Falls
Oliver Elwin Wells	1891–1895	Appleton

Wisconsin superintendents of public instruction since 1849, continued

	Service	Residence[1]
John Q. Emery	1895–1899	Albion
Lorenzo D. Harvey	1899–1903	Milwaukee
Charles P. Cary	1903–1921	Delavan
John Callahan	1921–1949	Madison
George Earl Watson	1949–1961	Wauwatosa
Angus B. Rothwell[2]	1961–7/1/66	Manitowoc
William C. Kahl[3]	7/1/66–1973	Madison
Barbara Thompson	1973–1981	Madison
Herbert J. Grover[4]	1981–4/9/93	Cottage Grove
John T. Benson	1993–2001	Marshall
Elizabeth Burmaster	2001–2009	Madison
Tony Evers	2009–2019	Madison
Carolyn Stanford Taylor[5]	2019–2021	Madison
Jill Underly	2021–	Hollandale

Note: Prior to 1971, the term of office was two years rather than four. Prior to 1885, the term of office began in January of an even-numbered rather than an odd-numbered year. From 1905 onward, the term of office began in July rather than in January and the office was filled at the nonpartisan spring election rather than at the November general election.

1. Residence at the time of election. 2. Resigned. 3. Appointed to serve the rest of Rothwell's term. 4. Resigned. Lee Sherman Dreyfus was appointed to serve as "interim superintendent" for the rest of Grover's term but did not officially become superintendent. 5. Appointed to serve the rest of Evers's term.

Source: Wisconsin Legislative Reference Bureau, *Wisconsin Blue Book*, various editions, and bureau records.

Wisconsin state treasurers since 1848

	Party	Service	Residence[1]
Jarius C. Fairchild	Democratic	1848–1852	Madison
Edward H. Janssen	Democratic	1852–1856	Cedarburg
Charles Kuehn	Democratic	1856–1858	Manitowoc
Samuel D. Hastings	Republican	1858–1866	Trempealeau
William E. Smith	Republican	1866–1870	Fox Lake
Henry Baetz	Republican	1870–1874	Manitowoc
Ferdinand Kuehn	Democratic	1874–1878	Milwaukee
Richard Guenther	Republican	1878–1882	Oshkosh
Edward C. McFetridge	Republican	1882–1887	Beaver Dam
Henry B. Harshaw	Republican	1887–1891	Oshkosh
John Hunner	Democratic	1891–1895	Eau Claire
Sewell A. Peterson	Republican	1895–1899	Rice Lake
James O. Davidson	Republican	1899–1903	Soldiers Grove
John J. Kempf[2]	Republican	1903–7/30/04	Milwaukee
Thomas M. Purtell[3]	Republican	7/30/04–1905	Cumberland
John J. Kempf	Republican	1905–1907	Milwaukee
Andrew H. Dahl	Republican	1907–1913	Westby
Henry Johnson	Republican	1913–1923	Suring
Solomon Levitan	Republican	1923–1933	Madison
Robert K. Henry	Democratic	1933–1937	Jefferson
Solomon Levitan	Progressive	1937–1939	Madison
John M. Smith[4]	Republican	1939–8/17/47	Shell Lake
John L. Sonderegger[5]	Republican	8/19/47–9/30/48	Madison
Clyde M. Johnston (appointed from staff)[5]	X	10/1/48–1949	Madison
Warren R. Smith[4]	Republican	1949–12/4/57	Milwaukee
Mrs. Dena A. Smith[5]	Republican	12/5/57–1959	Milwaukee
Eugene M. Lamb	Democratic	1959–1961	Milwaukee
Mrs. Dena A. Smith[4]	Republican	1961–2/20/68	Milwaukee

Wisconsin state treasurers since 1848, continued

	Party	Service	Residence[1]
Harold W. Clemens[5]	Republican	2/21/68–1971	Oconomowoc
Charles P. Smith	Democratic	1971–1991	Madison
Cathy S. Zeuske	Republican	1991–1995	Shawano
Jack C. Voight	Republican	1995–2007	Appleton
Dawn Marie Sass	Democratic	2007–2011	Milwaukee
Kurt W. Schuller	Republican	2011–2015	Eden
Matt Adamczyk	Republican	2015–2019	Wauwatosa
Sarah Godlewski	Democratic	2019–	Madison

Note: Prior to 1971, the term of office was two years rather than four. Prior to 1885, the term of office began in January of an even-numbered rather than an odd-numbered year.

X—Not applicable.

1. Residence at the time of election. 2. Vacated office by failure to give the required bond. 3. Appointed to serve the rest of Kempf's term. 4. Died in office. 5. Appointed.

Source: Wisconsin Legislative Reference Bureau, *Wisconsin Blue Book*, various editions, and bureau records.

Wisconsin secretaries of state since 1848

	Party	Service	Residence[1]
Thomas McHugh	Democratic	1848–1850	Delavan
William A. Barstow	Democratic	1850–1852	Waukesha
Charles D. Robinson	Democratic	1852–1854	Green Bay
Alexander T. Gray	Democratic	1854–1856	Janesville
David W. Jones	Democratic	1856–1860	Belmont
Lewis P. Harvey	Republican	1860–1862	Shopiere
James T. Lewis	Republican	1862–1864	Columbus
Lucius Fairchild	Republican	1864–1866	Madison
Thomas S. Allen	Republican	1866–1870	Mineral Point
Llywelyn Breese	Republican	1870–1874	Portage
Peter Doyle	Democratic	1874–1878	Prairie du Chien
Hans B. Warner	Republican	1878–1882	Ellsworth
Ernst G. Timme	Republican	1882–1891	Kenosha
Thomas J. Cunningham	Democratic	1891–1895	Chippewa Falls
Henry Casson	Republican	1895–1899	Viroqua
William H. Froehlich	Republican	1899–1903	Jackson
Walter L. Houser	Republican	1903–1907	Mondovi
James A. Frear	Republican	1907–1913	Hudson
John S. Donald	Republican	1913–1917	Mt. Horeb
Merlin Hull	Republican	1917–1921	Black River Falls
Elmer S. Hall	Republican	1921–1923	Green Bay
Fred R. Zimmerman	Republican	1923–1927	Milwaukee
Theodore Dammann	Republican	1927–1935	Milwaukee
Theodore Dammann	Progressive	1935–1939	Milwaukee
Fred R. Zimmerman[2]	Republican	1939–12/14/54	Milwaukee
Louis Allis[3]	Republican	12/16/54–1/3/55	Milwaukee
Mrs. Glenn M. Wise[4]	Republican	1/3/55–1957	Madison
Robert C. Zimmerman	Republican	1957–1975	Madison
Douglas J. La Follette	Democratic	1975–1979	Kenosha
Mrs. Vel R. Phillips	Democratic	1979–1983	Milwaukee
Douglas J. La Follette	Democratic	1983–	Madison

Note: Prior to 1971, the term of office was two years rather than four. Prior to 1885, the term of office began in January of an even-numbered rather than an odd-numbered year.

1. Residence at the time of election. 2. Died after being reelected for a new term but before the new term began. 3. Appointed to serve the rest of Zimmerman's unfinished term. 4. Appointed to serve Zimmerman's new term.

Source: Wisconsin Legislative Reference Bureau, *Wisconsin Blue Book*, various editions, and bureau records.

Justices of the Wisconsin Supreme Court since 1836

	Service	Residence[1]
Judges during the territorial period		
Charles Dunn (Chief Justice)[2]	1836–1848	NA
William C. Frazier	1836–1838	NA
David Irvin	1836–1838	NA
Andrew G. Miller	1836–1848	NA
Circuit judges who served as justices 1848–1853[3]		
Alexander W. Stow	1848–1851 (C.J.)	Fond du Lac
Levi Hubbell	1848–1853 (C.J. 1851)	Milwaukee
Edward V. Whiton	1848–1853 (C.J. 1852–53)	Janesville
Charles H. Larrabee	1848–1853	Horicon
Mortimer M. Jackson	1848–1853	Mineral Point
Wiram Knowlton	1850–1853	Prairie du Chien
Timothy O. Howe	1851–1853	Green Bay
Justices since 1853		
Edward V. Whiton	1853–1859 (C.J.)	Janesville
Samuel Crawford	1853–1855	New Diggings
Abram D. Smith	1853–1859	Milwaukee
Orsamus Cole	1855–1892 (C.J. 1880–92)	Potosi
Luther S. Dixon[4]	1859–1874 (C.J.)	Portage
Byron Paine[4]	1859–1864, 1867–71	Milwaukee
Jason Downer[4]	1864–1867	Milwaukee
William P. Lyon[4]	1871–1894 (C.J. 1892–94)	Racine
Edward G. Ryan[4]	1874–1880 (C.J.)	Racine
David Taylor	1878–1891	Sheboygan
Harlow S. Orton	1878–1895 (C.J. 1894–95)	Madison
John B. Cassoday[4]	1880–1907 (C.J. 1895–07)	Janesville
John B. Winslow[4]	1891–1920 (C.J. 1907–20)	Racine
Silas U. Pinney	1892–1898	Madison
Alfred W. Newman	1894–1898	Trempealeau
Roujet D. Marshall[4]	1895–1918	Chippewa Falls
Charles V. Bardeen[4]	1898–1903	Wausau
Joshua Eric Dodge[4]	1898–1910	Milwaukee
Robert G. Siebecker[5]	1903–1922 (C.J. 1920–22)	Madison
James C. Kerwin	1905–1921	Neenah
William H. Timlin	1907–1916	Milwaukee
Robert M. Bashford[4]	Jan.–June 1908	Madison
John Barnes	1908–1916	Rhinelander
Aad J. Vinje[4]	1910–1929 (C.J. 1922–29)	Superior
Marvin B. Rosenberry[4]	1916–1950 (C.J. 1929–50)	Wausau
Franz C. Eschweiler[4]	1916–1929	Milwaukee
Walter C. Owen	1918–1934	Maiden Rock
Burr W. Jones[4]	1920–1926	Madison
Christian Doerfler[4]	1921–1929	Milwaukee
Charles H. Crownhart[4]	1922–1930	Madison
E. Ray Stevens	1926–1930	Madison
Chester A. Fowler[4]	1929–1948	Fond du Lac
Oscar M. Fritz[4]	1929–1954 (C.J. 1950–54)	Milwaukee
Edward T. Fairchild[4]	1929–1957 (C.J. 1954–57)	Milwaukee
John D. Wickhem[4]	1930–1949	Madison
George B. Nelson[4]	1930–1942	Stevens Point
Theodore G. Lewis[4]	Nov. 15–Dec. 5, 1934	Madison
Joseph Martin[4]	1934–1946	Green Bay
Elmer E. Barlow[4]	1942–1948	Arcadia
James Ward Rector[4]	1946–1947	Madison
Henry P. Hughes	1948–1951	Oshkosh
John E. Martin[4]	1948–1962 (C.J. 1957–62)	Green Bay
Grover L. Broadfoot[4]	1948–1962 (C.J. Jan.–May 1962)	Mondovi
Timothy Brown[4]	1949–1964 (C.J. 1962–64)	Madison

Justices of the Wisconsin Supreme Court since 1836, continued

	Service	Residence[1]
Edward J. Gehl	1950–1956	Hartford
George R. Currie[4]	1951–1968 (C.J. 1964–68)	Sheboygan
Roland J. Steinle[4]	1954–1958	Milwaukee
Emmert L. Wingert[4]	1956–1959	Madison
Thomas E. Fairchild	1957–1966	Verona
E. Harold Hallows[4]	1958–1974 (C.J. 1968–74)	Milwaukee
William H. Dieterich	1959–1964	Milwaukee
Myron L. Gordon	1962–1967	Milwaukee
Horace W. Wilkie[4]	1962–1976 (C.J. 1974–76)	Madison
Bruce F. Beilfuss	1964–1983 (C.J. 1976–83)	Neillsville
Nathan S. Heffernan[4]	1964–1995 (C.J. 1983–95)	Sheboygan
Leo B. Hanley[4]	1966–1978	Milwaukee
Connor T. Hansen[4]	1967–1980	Eau Claire
Robert W. Hansen	1968–1978	Milwaukee
Roland B. Day[4]	1974–1996 (C.J. 1995–96)	Madison
Shirley S. Abrahamson[4]	1976–2019 (C.J. 1996–2015)	Madison
William G. Callow	1978–1992	Waukesha
John L. Coffey	1978–1982	Milwaukee
Donald W. Steinmetz	1980–1999	Milwaukee
Louis J. Ceci[4]	1982–1993	Milwaukee
William A. Bablitch	1983–2003	Stevens Point
Jon P. Wilcox[4]	1992–2007	Wautoma
Janine P. Geske[4]	1993–1998	Milwaukee
Ann Walsh Bradley	1995–	Wausau
N. Patrick Crooks	1996–2015	Green Bay
David T. Prosser, Jr.[4]	1998–2016	Appleton
Diane S. Sykes[4]	1999–2004	Milwaukee
Patience D. Roggensack	2003– (C.J. 2015–2021)	Madison
Louis B. Butler, Jr.[4]	2004–2008	Milwaukee
Annette K. Ziegler	2007– (C.J. 2021–)	West Bend
Michael J. Gableman	2008–2018	Webster
Rebecca Grassl Bradley[4]	2015–	Milwaukee
Daniel Kelly[4]	2016–	North Prairie
Rebecca Frank Dallet	2018–	Whitefish Bay
Brian Hagedorn	2019–	Oconomowoc
Jill Karofsky	2020–	Madison

Note: The structure of the Wisconsin Supreme Court has varied. There were three justices during the territorial period. From 1848 to 1853, circuit judges acted as supreme court justices—five from 1848 to 1850 and six from 1850 to 1853. From 1853 to 1877, there were three elected justices. The number was increased to five in 1877, and to seven in 1903.

C.J.—Chief justice; NA—Not available.

1. Residence at the time of election or appointment. 2. Before 1889, the chief justice was elected or appointed to the position. From 1889 to 2015, the most senior justice seved as chief justice. From 2015 onward, the justices have elected one of themselves to be chief justice for a two-year term. 3. Circuit judges acted as supreme court justices from1848 to 1853. 4. Initially appointed to the court. 5. Siebecker was elected April 7, 1903, but prior to inauguration for his elected term was appointed April 9, 1903, to fill the vacancy caused by the death of Justice Bardeen.

Sources: Wisconsin Legislative Reference Bureau, *Wisconsin Blue Book*, 1935, 1944, 1977; Wisconsin Elections Commission; Wisconsin Supreme Court, *Wisconsin Reports*, various volumes.

Senate presidents, or presidents pro tempore, and assembly speakers since 1848

Session	Senate presidents or presidents pro tempore[1]	Residence[2]	Assembly speakers	Residence[2]
1848	X	X	Ninian E. Whiteside—D	Lafayette County

Senate presidents, or presidents pro tempore, and assembly speakers since 1848, continued

Session	Senate presidents or presidents pro tempore[1]	Residence[2]	Assembly speakers	Residence[2]
1849.	X	X	Harrison C. Hobart—D	Sheboygan
1850.	NA	NA	Moses M. Strong—D	Mineral Point
1851.	NA	NA	Frederick W. Horn—D	Cedarburg
1852.	E.B. Dean, Jr.—D	Madison	James M. Shafter—W	Sheboygan
1853.	Duncan C. Reed—D	Milwaukee	Henry L. Palmer—D	Milwaukee
1854.	Benjamin Allen—D	Hudson	Frederick W. Horn—D	Cedarburg
1855.	Eleazor Wakeley—D	Whitewater	Charles C. Sholes—R	Kenosha
1856.	Louis Powell Harvey—R	Shopiere	William Hull—D	Grant County
1857.	X	X	Wyman Spooner—R	Elkhorn
1858.	Hiram H. Giles—R	Stoughton	Frederick S. Lovell—R	Kenosha County
1859.	Dennison Worthington—R	Summit	William P. Lyon—R	Racine
1860.	Moses M. Davis—R	Portage	William P. Lyon—R	Racine
1861.	Alden I. Bennett—R	Beloit	Amasa Cobb—R	Mineral Point
1862.	Frederick O. Thorp—D	West Bend	James W. Beardsley—UD	Prescott
1863.	Wyman Spooner—R	Elkhorn	J. Allen Barber—R	Lancaster
1864.	Smith S. Wilkinson—R	Prairie du Sac	William W. Field—U	Fennimore
1865.	Willard H. Chandler—U	Windsor	William W. Field—U	Fennimore
1866.	Willard H. Chandler—U	Windsor	Henry D. Barron—U	St. Croix Falls
1867.	George F. Wheeler—U	Nanuapa	Angus Cameron—U	La Crosse
1868.	Newton M. Littlejohn—R	Whitewater	Alexander M. Thomson—R	Janesville
1869.	George C. Hazelton—R	Boscobel	Alexander M. Thomson—R	Janesville
1870.	David Taylor—R	Sheboygan	James M. Bingham—R	Palmyra
1871.	Charles G. Williams—R	Janesville	William E. Smith—R	Fox Lake
1872.	Charles G. Williams—R	Janesville	Daniel Hall—R	Watertown
1873.	Henry L. Eaton—R	Lone Rock	Henry D. Barron—R	St. Croix Falls
1874.	John C. Holloway—R	Lancaster	Gabriel Bouck—D	Oshkosh
1875.	Henry D. Barron—R	St. Croix Falls	Frederick W. Horn—R	Cedarburg
1876.	Robert L.D. Potter—R	Wautoma	Sam S. Fifield—R	Ashland
1877.	William H. Hiner—R	Fond du Lac	John B. Cassoday—R	Janesville
1878.	Levi W. Barden—R	Portage	Augustus R. Barrows—GB	Chippewa Falls
1879.	William T. Price—R	Black River Falls	David M. Kelly—R	Green Bay
1880.	Thomas B. Scott—R	Grand Rapids	Alexander A. Arnold—R	Galesville
1881.	Thomas B. Scott—R	Grand Rapids	Ira B. Bradford—R	Augusta
1882.	George B. Burrows—R	Madison	Franklin L. Gilson—R	Ellsworth
1883.	George W. Ryland—R	Lancaster	Earl P. Finch—D	Oshkosh
1885.	Edward S. Minor—R	Sturgeon Bay	Hiram O. Fairchild—R	Marinette
1887.	Charles K. Erwin—R	Tomah	Thomas B. Mills—R)	Millston
1889.	Thomas A. Dyson—R	La Crosse	Thomas B. Mills—R	Millston
1891.	Frederick W. Horn—D	Cedarburg	James J. Hogan—D	La Crosse
1893.	Robert J. MacBride—D	Neillsville	Edward Keogh—D	Milwaukee
1895.	Thompson D. Weeks—R	Whitewater	George B. Burrows—R	Madison
1897.	Lyman W. Thayer—R	Ripon	George A. Buckstaff—R	Oshkosh
1899.	Lyman W. Thayer—R	Ripon	George H. Ray—R	La Crosse
1901.	James J. McGillivray—R	Black River Falls	George H. Ray—R	La Crosse
1903–05 . .	James J. McGillivray—R	Black River Falls	Irvine L. Lenroot—R	West Superior
1907.	James H. Stout—R	Menomonie	Herman L. Ekern—R	Whitehall
1909.	James H. Stout—R	Menomonie	Levi H. Bancroft—R	Richland Center
1911.	Harry C. Martin—R	Darlington	C.A. Ingram—R	Durand
1913.	Harry C. Martin—R	Darlington	Merlin Hull—R	Black River Falls
1915.	Edward T. Fairchild—R	Milwaukee	Lawrence C. Whittet—R	Edgerton
1917.	Timothy Burke—R	Green Bay	Lawrence C. Whittet—R	Edgerton
1919.	Willard T. Stevens—R	Rhinelander	Riley S. Young—R	Darien
1921.	Timothy Burke—R	Green Bay	Riley S. Young—R	Darien
1923.	Henry A. Huber—R	Stoughton	John L. Dahl—R	Rice Lake
1925.	Howard Teasdale—R	Sparta	Herman Sachtjen[3]—R	Madison
			George A. Nelson[3]—R	Milltown
1927.	William L. Smith—R	Neillsville	John W. Eber—R	Milwaukee

Senate presidents, or presidents pro tempore, and assembly speakers since 1848, continued

Session	Senate presidents or presidents pro tempore[1]	Residence[2]	Assembly speakers	Residence[2]
1929.	Oscar H. Morris—R	Milwaukee	Charles B. Perry—R	Wauwatosa
1931.	Herman J. Severson—P	Iola	Charles B. Perry—R	Wauwatosa
1933.	Orland S. Loomis—R	Mauston	Cornelius T. Young—D	Milwaukee
1935.	Harry W. Bolens—D	Port Washington	Jorge W. Carow—P	Ladysmith
1937.	Walter J. Rush—P	Neillsville	Paul R. Alfonsi—P	Pence
1939.	Edward J. Roethe—R	Fennimore	Vernon W. Thomson—R	Richland Center
1941–43 . .	Conrad Shearer—R	Kenosha	Vernon W. Thomson—R	Richland Center
1945.	Conrad Shearer—R	Kenosha	Donald C. McDowell—R	Soldiers Grove
1947.	Frank E. Panzer—R	Brownsville	Donald C. McDowell—R	Soldiers Grove
1949.	Frank E. Panzer—R	Brownsville	Alex L. Nicol—R	Sparta
1951–53 . .	Frank E. Panzer—R	Brownsville	Ora R. Rice—R	Delavan
1955.	Frank E. Panzer—R	Brownsville	Mark Catlin, Jr.—R	Appleton
1957.	Frank E. Panzer—R	Brownsville	Robert G. Marotz—R	Shawano
1959.	Frank E. Panzer—R	Brownsville	George Molinaro—D	Kenosha
1961.	Frank E. Panzer—R	Brownsville	David J. Blanchard—R	Edgerton
1963.	Frank E. Panzer—R	Brownsville	Robert D. Haase—R	Marinette
1965.	Frank E. Panzer—R	Brownsville	Robert T. Huber—D	West Allis
1967–69 . .	Robert P. Knowles—R	New Richmond	Harold V. Froehlich—R	Appleton
1971.	Robert P. Knowles—R	New Richmond	Robert T. Huber[4]—D	West Allis
			Norman C. Anderson[4]—D	Madison
1973.	Robert P. Knowles—R	New Richmond	Norman C. Anderson—D	Madison
1975.	Fred A. Risser—D	Madison	Norman C. Anderson—D	Madison
1977–81 . .	Fred A. Risser—D	Madison	Edward G. Jackamonis—D	Waukesha
1983–89 . .	Fred A. Risser—D	Madison	Thomas A. Loftus—D	Sun Prairie
1991.	Fred A. Risser—D	Madison	Walter J. Kunicki—D	Milwaukee
1993.	Fred A. Risser[5]—D	Madison	Walter J. Kunicki—D	Milwaukee
	Brian D. Rude[5]—R	Coon Valley		
1995.	Brian D. Rude[6]—R	Coon Valley	David T. Prosser, Jr.—R	Appleton
	Fred A. Risser[6]—D	Madison		
1997.	Fred A. Risser[7]—D	Madison	Ben Brancel[8]—R	Endeavor
	Brian D. Rude[7]—R	Coon Valley	Scott R. Jensen[8]—R	Waukesha
1999.	Fred A. Risser—D	Madison	Scott R. Jensen—R	Waukesha
2001.	Fred A. Risser—D	Madison	Scott R. Jensen—R	Waukesha
2003–05 . .	Alan J. Lasee—R	De Pere	John Gard—R	Peshtigo
2007.	Fred A. Risser—D	Madison	Michael D. Huebsch—R	West Salem
2009.	Fred A. Risser—D	Madison	Michael J. Sheridan—D	Janesville
2011.	Michael G. Ellis[9]—R	Neenah	Jeff Fitzgerald—R	Horicon
	Fred A. Risser[9]—D	Madison		
2013.	Michael G. Ellis—R	Neenah	Robin J. Vos—R	Burlington
2015.	Mary A. Lazich—R	New Berlin	Robin J. Vos—R	Burlington
2017–19 . .	Roger Roth—R	Appleton	Robin J. Vos—R	Burlington
2021.	Chris Kapenga—R	Delafield	Robin J. Vos—R	Rochester

Note: Political party indicated is for session elected and is obtained from newspaper accounts for some early legislators.

X–Not applicable. No permanent president pro tempore; NA–Not available; D–Democrat; GB–Greenback; P–Progressive; R–Republican; U–Union; UD–Union Democrat; W–Whig.

1. Prior to May 1, 1979, the president pro tempore is listed because the lieutenant governor, rather than a legislator, was the president of the senate under the constitution until that time.   2. Residence at the time of election.   3. Nelson was elected to serve at special session, 4/15/26 to 4/16/26, as Sachtjen had resigned.   4. Anderson was elected speaker 1/18/72 after Huber resigned   5. A new president was elected on 4/20/93 after a change in party control following two special elections.   6. A new president was elected on 7/9/96 after a change in party control following a recall election.   7. A new president was elected on 4/21/98 after a change in party control following a special election.   8. Jensen was elected speaker 11/4/97 after Brancel resigned.   9. A new president was elected on 7/17/12 after a change in party control following a recall election.

Sources: Senate and Assembly Journals; Wisconsin Legislative Reference Bureau records.

Majority and minority leaders of the legislature since 1937

Session	Senate majority	Senate minority	Assembly majority	Assembly minority
1937 . . .	Maurice Coakley—R	NA	NA	NA
1939 . . .	Maurice Coakley—R	Philip Nelson—P	NA	Paul Alfonsi—P
1941 . . .	Maurice Coakley—R	Cornelius Young—D	Mark Catlin, Jr.—R	Andrew Biemiller—P
				Robert Tehan—D
1943 . . .	Warren Knowles[1]—R	NA	Mark Catlin, Jr.—R	Elmer Genzmer—D
	John Byrnes[1]—R			Lyall Beggs—P
1945 . . .	Warren Knowles—R	Anthony Gawronski—D	Vernon Thomson—R	Lyall Beggs—P
				Leland McParland—D
1947 . . .	Warren Knowles—R	Robert Tehan—D	Vernon Thomson—R	Leland McParland—D
1949 . . .	Warren Knowles—R	NA	Vernon Thomson—R	Leland McParland—D
1951 . . .	Warren Knowles—R	Gaylord Nelson—D	Arthur Mockrud—R	George Molinaro—D
1953 . . .	Warren Knowles—R	Henry Maier—D	Mark Catlin, Jr.—R	George Molinaro—D
1955 . . .	Paul Rogan[2]—R	Henry Maier—D	Robert Marotz—R	Robert Huber—D
1957 . . .	Robert Travis—R	Henry Maier—D	Warren Grady—R	Robert Huber—D
1959 . . .	Robert Travis—R	Henry Maier—D	Keith Hardie—D	David Blanchard—R
1961 . . .	Robert Travis—R	William Moser[3]—D	Robert Haase—R	Robert Huber—D
1963 . . .	Robert Knowles—R	Richard Zaborski—D	Paul Alfonsi—R	Robert Huber—D
1965 . . .	Robert Knowles—R	Richard Zaborski—D	Frank Nikolay—D	Robert Haase[4]—R
				Paul Alfonsi[4]—R
1967 . . .	Jerris Leonard—R	Fred Risser—D	J. Curtis McKay—R	Robert Huber—D
1969 . . .	Ernest Keppler—R	Fred Risser—D	Paul Alfonsi—R	Robert Huber—D
1971 . . .	Ernest Keppler—R	Fred Risser—D	Norman Anderson[5]—D	Harold Froehlich—R
			Anthony Earl[5]—D	
1973 . . .	Raymond Johnson—R	Fred Risser—D	Anthony Earl—D	John Shabaz—R
1975 . . .	Wayne Whittow[6]—D	Clifford Krueger—R	Terry Willkom—D	John Shabaz—R
	William Bablitch[6]—D			
1977 . . .	William Bablitch—D	Clifford Krueger—R	James Wahner—D	John Shabaz—R
1979 . . .	William Bablitch—D	Clifford Krueger—R	James Wahner[7]—D	John Shabaz—R
			Gary Johnson[7]—D	
1981 . . .	William Bablitch[9]—D	Walter Chilsen—R	Thomas Loftus—D	John Shabaz[8]—R
	Timothy Cullen[9]—D			Tommy Thompson[8]—R
1983 . . .	Timothy Cullen—D	James Harsdorf—R	Gary Johnson—D	Tommy Thompson—R
1985 . . .	Timothy Cullen—D	Susan Engeleiter—R	Dismas Becker—D	Tommy Thompson—R
1987 . . .	Joseph Strohl—D	Susan Engeleiter—R	Thomas Hauke—D	Betty Jo Nelsen—R
1989 . . .	Joseph Strohl—D	Michael Ellis—R	Thomas Hauke—D	David Prosser—R
1991 . . .	David Helbach—D	Michael Ellis—R	David Travis—D	David Prosser—R
1993 . . .	David Helbach[10]—D	Michael Ellis[10]—R	David Travis—D	David Prosser—R
	Michael Ellis[10]—R	David Helbach[10,11]—D		
		Robert Jauch[11]—D		
1995 . . .	Michael Ellis[13]—R	Robert Jauch[12]—D	Scott Jensen—R	Walter Kunicki—D
		Charles Chvala[12,13]—D		
	Charles Chvala[13]—D	Michael Ellis[13]—R		
1997 . . .	Charles Chvala[14]—D	Michael Ellis[14]—R	Steven Foti—R	Walter Kunicki[15]—D
	Michael Ellis[14]—R	Charles Chvala[14]—D		Shirley Krug[15]—D
1999 . . .	Charles Chvala—D	Michael Ellis[16]—R	Steven Foti—R	Shirley Krug—D
		Mary Panzer[16]—R		
2001 . . .	Charles Chvala—D	Mary Panzer—R	Steven Foti—R	Shirley Krug—D
	Russell Decker[17]—D			Spencer Black[18]—D
	Fred Risser[17]—D			
	Jon Erpenbach[17]—D			
2003 . . .	Mary Panzer[19]—R	Jon Erpenbach—D	Steven Foti—R	James Kreuser—D
	Scott Fitzgerald[19]—R			
	Dale Schultz[20]—R	Judith Robson[20]—D		
2005 . . .	Dale Schultz—R	Judith Robson—D	Michael Huebsch—R	James Kreuser—D
2007 . . .	Judith Robson—D	Scott Fitzgerald—R	Jeff Fitzgerald—R	James Kreuser—D
	Russell Decker[21]—D			
2009 . . .	Russell Decker[22]—D	Scott Fitzgerald—R	Thomas Nelson—D	Jeff Fitzgerald—R
	Dave Hansen[22]—D			
2011 . . .	Scott Fitzgerald—R	Mark Miller—D	Scott Suder—R	Peter Barca—D
	Mark Miller[23]—D	Scott Fitzgerald[23]—R		

Majority and minority leaders of the legislature since 1937, continued

Session	Senate majority	Senate minority	Assembly majority	Assembly minority
2013. . .	Scott Fitzgerald—R	Chris Larson—D	Scott Suder[24]—R Bill Kramer[25]—R Pat Strachota—R	Peter Barca—D
2015. . .	Scott Fitzgerald—R	Jennifer Shilling—D	Jim Steineke—R	Peter Barca—D
2017. . .	Scott Fitzgerald—R	Jennifer Shilling—D	Jim Steineke—R	Peter Barca[26]—D Gordon Hintz[27]—D
2019. . .	Scott Fitzgerald—R	Jennifer Shilling[28]—D Janet Bewley[28]—D	Jim Steineke—R	Gordon Hintz—D
2021. . .	Devin LeMahieu—R	Janet Bewley—D	Jim Steineke—R	Gordon Hintz—D

Note: Majority and minority leaders, who are chosen by the party caucuses in each house, were first recognized officially in the senate and assembly rules in 1963. Prior to the 1977 session, these positions were also referred to as "floor leader."

NA–Not available. D–Democrat; P–Progressive; R–Republican.

1. Knowles granted leave of absence to return to active duty in U.S. Navy; Byrnes chosen to succeed him on 4/30/1943. 2. Resigned after sine die adjournment. 3. Resigned 1/30/1962. 4. Haase resigned 9/15/1965; Alfonsi elected 10/4/1965. 5. Earl elected 1/18/1972 to succeed Anderson who became assembly speaker. 6. Whittow resigned 4/30/1976; Bablitch elected 5/17/1976. 7. Wahner resigned 1/28/1980; Johnson elected 1/28/1980. 8. Shabaz resigned 12/18/1981; Thompson elected 12/21/1981. 9. Bablitch resigned 5/26/1982; Cullen elected 5/26/1982. 10. Democrats controlled senate from 1/4/1993 to 4/20/1993 when Republicans assumed control after a special election. 11. Helbach resigned 5/12/1993; Jauch elected 5/12/1993. 12. Jauch resigned 10/17/1995; Chvala elected 10/24/1995. 13. Republicans controlled senate from 1/5/1995 to 6/13/1996 when Democrats assumed control after a recall election. 14. Democrats controlled the senate from 1/6/1997 to 4/21/1998 when Republicans assumed control after a special election. 15. Kunicki resigned 6/3/1998; Krug elected 6/3/1998. 16. Ellis resigned 1/25/2000; Panzer elected 1/25/2000. 17. Decker and Risser elected co-leaders 10/22/2002. Erpenbach elected leader 12/4/2002. 18. Black elected 5/1/2001. 19. Panzer resigned 9/17/2004; Fitzgerald elected 9/17/2004. 20. Schultz elected 11/9/2004; Robson elected 11/9/2004. 21. Decker elected 10/24/2007. 22. Hansen replaced Decker as leader, 12/15/2010. 23. After a resignation on 3/16/12 resulted in a 16–16 split, Fitzgerald and Miller served as co-leaders. A recall election gave Democrats control of the senate as of 7/17/12. 24. Suder resigned 9/3/13; Kramer elected 9/4/13. 25. Kramer removed 3/4/14; Strachota elected 3/4/14. 26. On 9/19/17, Barca resigned as Minority Leader, effective 9/30/17. 27. On 9/19/17, Hintz elected Minority Leader, effective 10/1/17. 28. Shilling resigned 4/24/20; Bewley elected 4/24/20.

Sources: *Wisconsin Blue Book*, various editions; Senate and Assembly Journals; newspaper accounts.

Chief clerks and sergeants at arms of the legislature since 1848

Session	Senate		Assembly	
	Chief clerk	Sergeant at arms	Chief clerk	Sergeant at arms
1848.	Henry G. Abbey	Lyman H. Seaver	Daniel N. Johnson	John Mullanphy
1849.	William R. Smith	F. W. Shollner	Robert L. Ream	Felix McLinden
1850.	William R. Smith	James Hanrahan	Alex T. Gray	E. R. Hugunin
1851.	William Hull	E. D. Masters	Alex T. Gray	C. M. Kingsbury
1852.	John K. Williams	Patrick Cosgrove	Alex T. Gray	Elisha Starr
1853.	John K. Williams	Thomas Hood	Thomas McHugh	Richard F. Wilson
1854.	Samuel G. Bugh	J. M. Sherwood	Thomas McHugh	William H. Gleason
1855.	Samuel G. Bugh	William H. Gleason	David Atwood	William Blake
1856.	Byron Paine	Joseph Baker	James Armstrong	Egbert Mosely
1857.	William H. Brisbane	Alanson Filer	William C. Webb	William C. Rogers
1858.	John L. V. Thomas	Nathaniel L. Stout	L. H. D. Crane	Francis Massing
1859.	Hiram Bowen	Asa Kinney	L. H. D. Crane	Emmanual Munk
1860.	J. H. Warren	Asa Kinney	L. H. D. Crane	Joseph Gates
1861.	J. H. Warren	J. A. Hadley	L. H. D. Crane	Craig B. Peebe
1862.	J. H. Warren	B. U. Caswell	John S. Dean	A. A. Huntington
1863.	Frank M. Stewart	Luther Bashford	John S. Dean	A. M. Thompson
1864.	Frank M. Stewart	Nelson Williams	John S. Dean	A. M. Thompson
1865.	Frank M. Stewart	Nelson Williams	John S. Dean	Alonzo Wilcox
1866.	Frank M. Stewart	Nelson Williams	E. W. Young	L. M. Hammond
1867.	Leander B. Hills	Asa Kinney	E. W. Young	Daniel Webster

Chief clerks and sergeants at arms of the legislature since 1848,
continued

Session	Senate		Assembly	
	Chief clerk	Sergeant at arms	Chief clerk	Sergeant at arms
1868.	Leander B. Hills	W. H. Hamilton	E. W. Young	C. L. Harris
1869.	Leander B. Hills	W. H. Hamilton	E. W. Young	Rolin C. Kelly
1870.	Leander B. Hills	E. M. Rogers	E. W. Young	Ole C. Johnson
1871.	O. R. Smith	W. W. Baker	E. W. Young	Sam S. Fifield
1872.	J. H. Waggoner	W. D. Hoard	E. W. Young	Sam S. Fifield
1873.	J. H. Waggoner	Albert Emonson	E. W. Young	O. C. Bissel
1874.	J. H. Waggoner	O. U. Aiken	George W. Peck	Joseph Deuster
1875.	Fred A. Dennett	O. U. Aiken	R. M. Strong	J. W. Brackett
1876.	A. J. Turner	E. T. Gardner	R. M. Strong	Elisha Starr
1877.	A. J. Turner	C. E. Bullard	W. A. Nowell	Thomas B. Reid
1878.	A. J. Turner[1]	L. J. Brayton	Jabez R. Hunter	Anton Klaus
	Charles E. Bross[1]			
1879.	Charles E. Bross	Chalmers Ingersoll	John E. Eldred	Miletus Knight
1880.	Charles E. Bross	Chalmers Ingersoll	John E. Eldred	D. H. Pulcifer
1881.	Charles E. Bross	W. W. Baker	John E. Eldred	G. W. Church
1882.	Charles E. Bross	A. T. Glaze	E. D. Coe	D. E. Welch
1883.	Charles E. Bross	A. D. Thorp	I. T. Carr	Thomas Kennedy
1885.	Charles E. Bross	Hubert Wolcott	E. D. Coe	John M. Ewing
1887.	Charles E. Bross	T. J. George	E. D. Coe	William A. Adamson
1889.	Charles E. Bross	T. J. George	E. D. Coe	F. E. Parsons
1891.	J. P. Hume	John A. Barney	George W. Porth	Patrick Whelan
1893.	Sam J. Shafer	John B. Becker	George W. Porth	Theodore Knapstein
1895.	Walter L. Houser	Charles Pettibone	W. A. Nowell	B. F. Millard
1897.	Walter L. Houser	Charles Pettibone	W. A. Nowell	C. M. Hambright
1899.	Walter L. Houser	Charles Pettibone	W. A. Nowell	James H. Agen
1901.	Walter L. Houser	Charles Pettibone	W. A. Nowell	A. M. Anderson
1903.	Theodore W. Goldin	Sanfield McDonald	C. O. Marsh	A. M. Anderson
1905.	L .K. Eaton	R. C. Falconer	C. O. Marsh	Nicholas Streveler
1907.	A. R. Emerson	R. C. Falconer	C. E. Shaffer	W. S. Irvine
1909.	F. E. Andrews	R. C. Falconer	C. E. Shaffer	W. S. Irvine
1911–13 . . .	F. M. Wylie	C. A. Leicht	C. E. Shaffer	W. S. Irvine
1915.	O. G. Munson	F. E. Andrews	C. E. Shaffer	W. S. Irvine
1917.	O. G. Munson	F. E. Andrews	C. E. Shaffer	T. G. Cretney
1919.	O. G. Munson	John Turner	C. E. Shaffer	T. G. Cretney
1921.	O. G. Munson	Vincent Kielpinski	C. E. Shaffer	T. G. Cretney
1923.	F. W. Schoenfeld	C. A. Leicht	C. E. Shaffer	T. W. Bartingale
1925.	F. W. Schoenfeld	C. A. Leicht	C. E. Shaffer	C. E. Hanson
1927–29 . .	O. G. Munson	George W. Rickeman	C. E. Shaffer	C. F. Moulton
1931.	R. A. Cobban	Emil A. Hartman	C. E. Shaffer	Gustave Rheingans
1933.	R. A. Cobban	Emil A. Hartman	John J. Slocum	George C. Faust
1935–37 . . .	Lawrence R. Larsen	Emil A. Hartman	Lester R. Johnson	Gustave Rheingans
1939.	Lawrence R. Larsen	Emil A. Hartman	John J. Slocum	Robert A. Merrill
1941–43 . . .	Lawrence R. Larsen	Emil A. Hartman	Arthur L. May	Norris J. Kellman
1945.	Lawrence R. Larsen	Harold E. Damon	Arthur L. May	Norris J. Kellman
1947–53 . . .	Thomas M. Donahue	Harold E. Damon	Arthur L. May	Norris J. Kellman
1955–57 . . .	Lawrence R. Larsen	Harold E. Damon	Arthur L. May	Norris J. Kellman
1959.	Lawrence R. Larsen	Harold E. Damon	Norman C. Anderson	Thomas H. Browne
1961.	Lawrence R. Larsen	Harold E. Damon	Robert G. Marotz	Norris J. Kellman
1963.	Lawrence R. Larsen	Harold E. Damon	Kenneth E. Priebe	Norris J. Kellman
1965.	Lawrence R. Larsen[2]	Harold E. Damon	James P. Buckley	Thomas H. Browne
	William P. Nugent[2]			
1967.	William P. Nugent	Harry O. Levander	Arnold W. F. Langner[3]	Louis C. Romell
			Wilmer H. Struebing[3]	
1969.	William P. Nugent	Kenneth Nicholson	Wilmer H. Struebing	Louis C. Romell
1971.	William P. Nugent	Kenneth Nicholson	Thomas P. Fox	William F. Quick
1973.	William P. Nugent	Kenneth Nicholson	Thomas S. Hanson	William F. Quick
1975.	Glenn E. Bultman	Robert M. Thompson	Everett E. Bolle	Raymond J. Tobiasz

Chief clerks and sergeants at arms of the legislature since 1848, continued

Session	Senate		Assembly	
	Chief clerk	Sergeant at arms	Chief clerk	Sergeant at arms
1977.	Donald J. Schneider	Robert M. Thompson	Everett E. Bolle	Joseph E. Jones
1979.	Donald J. Schneider	Daniel B. Fields	Marcel Dandeneau	Joseph E. Jones
1981.	Donald J. Schneider	Daniel B. Fields	David R. Kedrowski	Lewis T. Mittness
1983.	Donald J. Schneider	Daniel B. Fields	Joanne M. Duren	Lewis T. Mittness
1985.	Donald J. Schneider	Daniel B. Fields	Joanne M. Duren	Patrick Essie
1987.	Donald J. Schneider	Daniel B. Fields	Thomas T. Melvin	Patrick Essie
1989–91 . . .	Donald J. Schneider	Daniel B. Fields	Thomas T. Melvin	Robert G. Johnston
1993.	Donald J. Schneider	Daniel B. Fields[4] Jon H. Hochkammer[4]	Thomas T. Melvin	Robert G. Johnston
1995.	Donald J. Schneider	Jon H. Hochkammer	Thomas T. Melvin[5] Charles R. Sanders[5]	John A. Scocos
1997.	Donald J. Schneider	Jon H. Hochkammer	Charles R. Sanders	John A. Scocos[6] Denise L. Solie[6]
1999.	Donald J. Schneider	Jon H. Hochkammer	Charles R. Sanders	Denise L. Solie
2001.	Donald J. Schneider	Jon H. Hochkammer[7]	John A. Scocos[7]	Denise L. Solie
2003.	Donald J. Schneider[8] Robert J. Marchant[8]	Edward A. Blazel	Patrick E. Fuller	Richard A. Skindrud
2005–07 . . .	Robert J. Marchant	Edward A. Blazel	Patrick E. Fuller	Richard A. Skindrud
2009.	Robert J. Marchant	Edward A. Blazel	Patrick E. Fuller	William M. Nagy
2011.	Robert J. Marchant[9]	Edward A. Blazel	Patrick E. Fuller	Anne Tonnon Byers
2013–19 . . .	Jeffrey Renk	Edward A. Blazel	Patrick E. Fuller	Anne Tonnon Byers
2021.	Michael Queensland	Tom Engels	Edward A. Blazel	Anne Tonnon Byers

1. Bross elected 2/6/78; Turner resigned 2/7/78. 2. Larsen died 3/2/65; Nugent elected 3/31/65. 3. Langner resigned 5/2/67; Struebing elected 5/16/67. 4. Fields served until 8/2/93. Randall Radtke served as acting sergeant from 8/3/93 to 11/3/93. Hochkammer elected 1/25/94. 5. Melvin retired 1/31/95; Sanders elected 5/24/95. 6. Scocos resigned 9/25/97; Solie elected 1/15/98. 7. Scocos resigned 2/25/02. Hochkammer resigned 9/2/02. No replacement was elected for either. 8. Schneider resigned 7/4/03; Marchant elected 1/20/04. 9. Marchant resigned 1/2/12.

Sources: Wisconsin Legislative Reference Bureau, *Wisconsin Blue Book*, various editions; journals and organizing resolutions of each house.

Political composition of the legislature since 1885

Session[1]	Senate[2]					Assembly[3]				
	D	R	P	S	SD	D	R	P	S	SD
1885.	13	20	—	—	—	39	61	—	—	—
1887.	6	25	—	—	—	30	57	—	—	—
1889.	6	24	—	—	—	29	71	—	—	—
1891.	19	14	—	—	—	66	33	—	—	—
1893.	26	7	—	—	—	56	44	—	—	—
1895.	13	20	—	—	—	19	81	—	—	—
1897.	4	29	—	—	—	8	91	—	—	—
1899.	2	31	—	—	—	19	81	—	—	—
1901.	2	31	—	—	—	18	82	—	—	—
1903.	3	30	—	—	—	25	75	—	—	—
1905.	4	28	—	—	1	11	85	—	—	4
1907.	5	27	—	—	1	19	76	—	—	5
1909.	4	28	—	—	1	17	80	—	—	3
1911.	4	27	—	—	2	29	59	—	—	12
1913.	9	23	—	—	1	37	57	—	—	6
1915.	11	21	—	—	1	29	63	—	—	8
1917.	6	24	—	3	—	14	79	—	7	—
1919.	2	27	—	4	—	5	79	—	16	—

Political composition of the legislature since 1885, continued

Session[1]	Senate[2]					Assembly[3]				
	D	R	P	S	SD	D	R	P	S	SD
1921.	2	27	—	4	—	2	92	—	6	—
1923.	—	30	—	3	—	1	89	—	10	—
1925.	—	30	—	3	—	1	92	—	7	—
1927.	—	31	—	2	—	3	89	—	8	—
1929.	—	31	—	2	—	6	90	—	3	—
1931.	1	30	—	2	—	2	89	—	9	—
1933.	9	23	—	1	—	59	13	24	3	—
1935.	13	6	14	—	—	35	17	45	3	—
1937.	9	8	16	—	—	31	21	46	2	—
1939.	6	16	11	—	—	15	53	32	—	—
1941.	3	24	6	—	—	15	60	25	—	—
1943.	4	23	6	—	—	14	73	13	—	—
1945.	6	22	5	—	—	19	75	6	—	—
1947.	5	27	1	—	—	11	88	—	—	—
1949.	3	27	—	—	—	26	74	—	—	—
1951.	7	26	—	—	—	24	75	—	—	—
1953.	7	26	—	—	—	25	75	—	—	—
1955.	8	24	—	—	—	36	64	—	—	—
1957.	10	23	—	—	—	33	67	—	—	—
1959.	12	20	—	—	—	55	45	—	—	—
1961.	13	20	—	—	—	45	55	—	—	—
1963.	11	22	—	—	—	46	53	—	—	—
1965.	12	20	—	—	—	52	48	—	—	—
1967.	12	21	—	—	—	47	53	—	—	—
1969.	10	23	—	—	—	48	52	—	—	—
1971.	12	20	—	—	—	67	33	—	—	—
1973.	15	18	—	—	—	62	37	—	—	—
1975.	18	13	—	—	—	63	36	—	—	—
1977.	23	10	—	—	—	66	33	—	—	—
1979.	21	10	—	—	—	60	39	—	—	—
1981.	19	14	—	—	—	59	39	—	—	—
1983.	17	14	—	—	—	59	40	—	—	—
1985.	19	14	—	—	—	52	47	—	—	—
1987.	19	11	—	—	—	54	45	—	—	—
1989.	20	13	—	—	—	56	43	—	—	—
1991.	19	14	—	—	—	58	41	—	—	—
1993[4].	15	15	—	—	—	52	47	—	—	—
1995[4].	16	17	—	—	—	48	51	—	—	—
1997[4].	17	16	—	—	—	47	52	—	—	—
1999.	17	16	—	—	—	44	55	—	—	—
2001.	18	15	—	—	—	43	56	—	—	—
2003.	15	18	—	—	—	41	58	—	—	—
2005.	14	19	—	—	—	39	60	—	—	—
2007.	18	15	—	—	—	47	52	—	—	—
2009.	18	15	—	—	—	52	46	—	—	—
2011[5].	14	19	—	—	—	38	60	—	—	—
2013.	15	18	—	—	—	39	59	—	—	—
2015.	14	18	—	—	—	36	63	—	—	—
2017.	13	20	—	—	—	35	64	—	—	—
2019.	14	19	—	—	—	36	63	—	—	—
2021.	12	20	—	—	—	38	60	—	—	—

Note: The number of assembly districts was reduced from 100 to 99 beginning in 1973. There have been 33 senate districts since 1862. Any deviation of a session's total from these numbers indicates vacant seats.

— Represents zero; D–Democrat; P–Progressive; R–Republican; S–Socialist; SD–Social Democrat.

1. Political composition at inauguration.   2. Miscellaneous affiliations for senate seats not shown in the table are: one Independent and one People's (1887); one Independent and 2 Union Labor (1889).   3. Miscellaneous affiliations for assembly seats not shown: 3 Independent, 4 Independent Democrat, and 6 People's (1887); one Union Labor (1891); one Fusion (1897);

one Independent (1929, 2009, 2011); one Independent Republican (1933). 4. In the 1993, 1995, and 1997 Legislatures, majority control of the senate shifted during the session. On 4/20/93, vacancies were filled resulting in a total of 16 Democrats and 17 Republicans; on 6/16/96, there were 17 Democrats and 16 Republicans; on 4/19/98, there were 16 Democrats and 17 Republicans. 5. A series of recall elections during the session resulted in a switch in majority control of the senate, with 17 Democrats and 16 Republicans as of 7/16/12.

Sources: Pre-1943 data compiled from the Secretary of State, *Officers of Wisconsin: U.S., State, Judicial, Congressional, Legislative and County Officers*, 1943 and prior editions, and the *Wisconsin Blue Book*, various editions. Later data compiled from Wisconsin Legislative Reference Bureau records.

Wisconsin legislative sessions since 1848

	Opening/final adjournment	Days	Measures introduced Bills	Joint res.	Res.	Bills vetoed[1] (overridden)	Laws enacted
1848.	6/5–8/21	78	217	—	—	—	155
1849.	1/10–4/2	83	428	—	—	2(1)	220
1850.	1/9–2/11	34	438	—	—	1	284
1851.	1/8–3/17	69	707	—	—	9	407
1852.	1/14–4/19	97	813	—	—	3(1)	504
1853.	1/12–7/13	183	1,145	—	—	6	521
1854.	1/11–4/3	83	880	—	—	2	437
1855.	1/10–4/2	83	955	—	—	6	500
1856.	1/9–10/14	288	1,242	—	—	1	688
1857.	1/14–3/9	55	895	—	—	—	517
1858.	1/13–5/17	125	1,364	157	342	28	436
1859.	1/12–3/21	69	986	113	143	9	680
1860.	1/11–4/2	83	1,024	69	246	2	489
1861.	1/9–4/17	99	857	100	235	2	387
1861 SS.	5/15–5/27	13	28	24	34	—	15
1862.	1/8–6/17	161	1,008	125	207	36[2](8)	514
1862 SS.	9/10–9/26	17	43	25	37	—	17
1863.	1/14–4/2	79	895	101	157	10(1)	383
1864.	1/13–4/4	83	835	66	141	—	509
1865.	1/11–4/10	90	1,132	82	190	2	565
1866.	1/10–4/12	93	1,107	64	208	5	733
1867.	1/9–4/11	93	1,161	97	161	2	790
1868.	1/8–3/6	59	987	73	119	2(2)	692
1869.	1/13–3/11	58	887	52	81	14(1)	657
1870.	1/12–3/17	65	1,043	54	89	2	666
1871.	1/11–3/25	74	1,066	55	82	4	671
1872.	1/10–3/26	77	709	79	124	2	322
1873.	1/8–3/20	72	611	62	122	4	308
1874.	1/14–3/12	58	688	91	111	2	349
1875.	1/13–3/6	53	637	39	93	2	344
1876.	1/12–3/14	63	715	57	115	2	415
1877.	1/10–3/8	58	720	59	95	4	384
1878.	1/9–3/21	72	735	79	134	2	342
1878 SS.	6/4–6/7	4	6	14	10	—	5
1879.	1/8–3/5	57	610	49	105	—	256
1880.	1/14–3/17	64	669	58	93	3	323
1881.	1/12–4/4	83	780	104	100	6	334
1882.	1/11–3/31	80	728	57	90	6	330
1883.	1/10–4/4	85	705	75	100	2	360
1885.	1/14–4/13	90	963	97	108	8	471
1887.	1/12–4/15	94	1,293	114	60	10	553
1889.	1/9–4/19	101	1,355	136	82	6(1)	529
1891.	1/14–4/25	102	1,216	137	91	10(1)	483
1892 SS.	6/28–7/1	4	4	7	16	—	1
1892 SS.	10/17–10/27	11	8	6	14	—	2
1893.	1/11–4/21	101	1,124	135	86	6	312

Wisconsin legislative sessions since 1848, continued

	Opening/final adjournment	Days	Measures introduced			Bills vetoed[1] (overridden)	Laws enacted
			Bills	Joint res.	Res.		
1895.	1/9–4/20	102	1,154	139	88	—	387
1896 SS.	2/18–2/28	11	3	11	15	—	1
1897.	1/13–8/20	220	1,077	155	39	19(1)	381
1899.	1/11–5/4	114	910	113	40	3	357
1901.	1/9–5/15	127	1,091	81	39	24	470
1903.	1/14–5/23	130	1,115	65	81	23	451
1905.	1/11–6/21	162	1,357	134	101	22	523
1905 SS.	12/4–12/19	16	24	15	26	—	17
1907.	1/9–7/16	189	1,685	205	84	28(1)	677
1909.	1/13–6/18	157	1,567	213	49	22	550
1911.	1/11–7/15	186	1,710	267	37	15	665
1912 SS.	4/30–5/6	7	41	7	6	—	22
1913.	1/8–8/9	214	1,847	175	79	24	778
1915.	1/13–8/24	224	1,560	220	79	15	637
1916 SS.	10/10–10/11	2	2	8	4	—	2
1917.	1/10–7/16	188	1,439	229	115	18	679
1918 SS.	2/19–3/9	19	27	22	28	2	16
1918 SS.	9/24–9/25	2	2	6	9	—	2
1919.	1/8–7/30	204	1,350	268	100	39	703
1919 SS.	9/4–9/8	5	7	4	6	—	7
1920 SS.	5/25–6/4	11	46	10	22	2	32
1921.	1/12–7/14	184	1,199	207	93	41(1)	591
1922 SS.	3/22–3/28	7	10	7	12	1	4
1923.	1/10–7/14	186	1,247	215	93	52	449
1925.	1/14–6/29	167	1,144	200	115	73	454
1926 SS.	4/15–4/16	2	1	8	12	—	1
1927.	1/12–8/13	214	1,341	235	167	90(2)	542
1928 SS.	1/24–2/4	12	20	35	23	—	5
1928 SS.	3/6–3/13	8	13	9	17	—	2
1929.	1/9–9/20	255	1,366	278	185	44	530
1931.	1/14–6/27	165	1,429	291	160	56	487
1931 SS.	11/24/31–2/5/32	74	99	93	83	2	31
1933.	1/11–7/25	196	1,411	324	157	15	496
1933 SS.	12/11/33–2/3/34	55	45	160	53	—	20
1935.	1/9–9/27	262	1,662	346	190	27	556
1937.	1/13–7/2	171	1,404	228	127	10	432
1937 SS.	9/15–10/16	32	28	18	23	—	15
1939.	1/11–10/6	269	1,559	268	133	22	535
1941.	1/8–6/6	150	1,368	160	109	17	333
1943.	1/13/43–1/22/44	375	1,153	202	136	39(20)	577
1945.	1/10–9/6	240	1,156	208	109	30(5)	590
1946 SS.	7/29–7/30	2	2	6	14	—	2
1947.	1/8–9/11	247	1,220	195	97	10(1)	615
1948 SS.	7/19–7/20	2	—	5	11	—	—
1949.	1/12–9/13	245	1,432	188	86	17(2)	643
1951.	1/10–6/14	156	1,559	157	73	18	735
1953.	1/14–11/6	297	1,593	175	70	31(3)	687
1955.	1/12–10/21	283	1,503	256	74	38	696
1957.	1/9–9/27	262	1,512	246	71	35(1)	706
1958 SS.	6/11–6/13	3	3	7	13	—	3
1959.	1/14/59–5/27/60	500	1,769	272	84	36(4)	696
1961.	1/11/61–1/9/63	729	1,592	295	68	70(2)	689
1963.	1/9/63–1/13/65	736	1,619	241	110	72(4)	580
1963 SS.	12/10–12/12	3	8	10	10	—	3
1965 [3].	1/13/65–1/2/67	720	1,818	293	86	24(1)	666
1967.	1/11/67–1/6/69	727	1,700	215	61	18	355
1969.	1/6/69–1/4/71	729	2,014	232	101	34(1)	501
1969 SS [4].	9/29/69–1/17/70	111	5	5	8	—	1

Wisconsin legislative sessions since 1848, continued

	Opening/final adjournment	Days	Measures introduced			Bills vetoed[1] (overridden)	Laws enacted
			Bills	Joint res.	Res.		
1970 SS	12/22	1	—	1	5	—	—
1971.	1/4/71–1/1/73	729	2,568	291	121	32(3)	336
1972 SS	4/19–4/28	10	9	4	4	—	6
1973.	1/1/73–1/6/75	736	2,501	277	126	13	332
1973 SS	12/17–12/21	5	3	2	6	—	2
1974 SS	4/29–6/13	46	12	1	4	—	6
1974 SS	11/19–11/20	2	2	—	—	—	1
1975.	1/6/75–1/3/77	729	2,325	169	88	36(6)	414
1975 SS	12/9–12/11	3	13	1	2	1	6
1976 SS	5/18	1	2	2	3	—	1
1976 SS	6/15–6/17	3	13	4	3	—	9
1976 SS	9/8	1	4	1	4	—	2
1977.	1/3/77–1/3/79	730	2,053	182	48	21(4)	442
1977 SS	6/30	1	—	1	2	—	—
1977 SS	11/7–11/11	5	6	4	2	—	5
1978 SS	6/13–6/15	3	2	5	2	—	2
1978 SS	12/20	1	2	4	2	—	2
1979[5]	1/3/79–1/5/81	734	1,920	203	40	19(3)	350
1979 SS	9/5	1	10	3	2	—	5
1980 SS	1/22–1/25	4	8	3	2	—	—
1980 SS	6/3–7/3	31	20	14	2	—	7
1981[6]	1/5/81–1/3/83	729	1,987	176	70	10(2)	381
1981 SS	11/4–11/17	14	6	3	2	—	3
1982 SS	4/6–5/20	45	4	2	2	1	1
1982 SS	5/26–5/28	3	13	7	2	—	9
1983.	1/3/83–1/7/85	736	1,902	173	50	3	521
1983 SS	1/4–1/6	3	2	2	1	—	2
1983 SS	4/12–4/14	3	1	1	—	—	1
1983 SS	7/11–7/14	4	5	3	1	—	4
1983 SS	10/18–10/28	11	12	1	—	—	11
1984 SS	2/2–4/4	63	2	1	—	—	—
1984 SS	5/22–5/24	3	12	5	1	—	11
1985.	1/7/85–1/5/87	729	1,624	171	41	7	293
1985 SS	3/19–3/21	3	6	1	—	—	3
1985 SS	9/24–10/19	26	22	1	—	—	17
1985 SS	10/31	1	1	3	—	—	1
1985 SS	11/20	1	24	2	—	—	12
1986 SS	1/27–5/30	124	1	4	—	—	1
1986 SS	3/24–3/26	3	1	1	—	—	1
1986 SS	5/20–5/29	10	44	3	—	—	12
1986 SS	7/15	1	3	1	—	—	2
1987[7]	1/5/87–1/3/89	730	1,631	196	21	35	413
1987 SS	9/15–9/16	2	2	1	—	—	2
1987 SS	11/18/87–6/7/88	203	19	3	—	3	5
1988 SS	6/30	1	4	1	3	—	2
1989[8]	1/3/89–1/7/91	735	1,557	244	45	35	361
1989 SS	10/10/89–3/22/90	164	52	6	—	—	7
1990 SS	5/15/90	1	7	1	—	—	—
1991[9]	1/7/91–1/4/93	729	1,676	244	32	33	318
1991 SS	1/29–7/4	157	16	1	—	—	2
1991 SS	10/15/91–5/21/92	220	9	2	—	—	1
1992 SS	4/14–6/4	52	7	1	2	—	2
1992 SS	6/1	1	—	2	—	—	—
1992 SS	8/25–9/15	22	1	1	2	—	1
1993[10].	1/1/93–1/3/95	730	2,147	207	47	8	491
1994 SS	5/18–5/19	2	6	1	—	—	3
1994 SS	6/7–6/23	17	3	4	—	—	3
1995.	1/3/95–1/6/97	735	1,780	163	38	4	467

Wisconsin legislative sessions since 1848, continued

	Opening/final adjournment	Days	Measures introduced			Bills vetoed[1] (overridden)	Laws enacted
			Bills	Joint res.	Res.		
1995 SS	1/4	1	1	1	—	—	1
1995 SS	9/5–10/12	36	1	1	—	—	1
1997[11]	1/6/97–1/4/99	729	1,508	183	30	3	333
1998 SS	4/21–5/21	31	13	2	2	—	5
1999[12]	1/4/99–1/3/01	731	1,498	168	52	5	196
1999 SS	10/27–11/11	16	3	1	—	—	1
2000 SS	5/4–5/9	8	2	2	1	—	1
2001	1/3/01–1/6/03	734	1,436	174	75	—	106
2001 SS	5/1–5/3	3	1	—	—	—	1
2002 SS	1/22–7/8	168	1	2	7	—	1
2002 SS	5/13–5/15	3	2	—	—	—	1
2003 [13]	1/6/03–1/3/05	729	1,567	164	78	54	326
2003 SS	1/30–2/20	22	1	—	—	—	1
2005[14]	1/3/05–1/3/07	731	1,967	196	76	47	489
2005 SS	1/12–1/20	9	2	—	—	—	1
2006 SS	2/14–3/7	22	2	—	—	—	1
2007	1/3/07–1/5/09	733	1,574	230	50	1	239
2007 SS	1/11–2/1	22	2	1	—	—	1
2007 SS	10/15–10/23	9	2	—	—	—	—
2007 SS	12/11/07–5/14/08	156	1	1	—	—	—
2008 SS	3/12–5/14	65	1	4	2	—	1
2008 SS	4/17–5/15	29	1	4	2	—	1
2009[15]	1/5/09–1/3/11	729	1,720	221	44	6	406
2009 SS	6/24–6/27	4	1	—	—	—	—
2009 SS	12/16–3/4/10	79	2	—	—	—	—
2011 [16]	1/3/11–1/7/13	735	1,325	211	48	—	267
2011 SS	1/4–9/27	267	27	1	3	—	12
2011 SS	9/29–12/8	71	48	—	—	—	7
2013	1/7/13–1/5/15	730	1,627	214	37	1	373
2013 SS	10/10–11/12	34	8	—	—	—	4
2013 SS	12/2–12/19	18	2	—	—	—	1
2014 SS	1/23–3/20	57	4	—	—	—	2
2015[17]	1/5/15–1/3/17	730	1,830	236	45	2	392
2017[18]	1/3/17–1/7/19	735	1,960	237	39	—	349
2017 SS	1/5–6/14	161	22	—	—	—	11
2017 SS	8/1–9/15	46	2	—	1	—	1
2018 SS	1/18–2/27	41	20	—	—	—	9
2018 SS	3/15–3/29	15	6	—	—	—	—
2019[19]	1/7/19–1/4/21	729	1,970	264	29	20	186
2019 SS	11/7	1	—	—	—	—	—
2020 SS	1/28–4/14	78	16	—	—	—	—
2020 SS	2/11–2/25	15	—	—	—	—	—
2020 SS	4/4–4/8	5	—	—	—	—	—
2020 SS	4/7–4/8	2	—	—	—	—	—
2020 SS	8/31–12/22	114	—	—	—	—	—

— Represents zero; Res.–Resolution; SS–Special session.

1. Partial vetoes not included. See executive vetoes table. 2. Does not include 18 bills that the lieutenant governor asserted had been vetoed by pocket veto when the governor, to whom they had been sent, died without signing them. 3. Although 1965 Legislature adjourned to 1/11/67, terms automatically expired on 1/2/67. 4. Senate adjourned the special session 11/15/69; assembly, 1/17/70. 5. Extraordinary session held in January 1980. 6. Extraordinary session held in December 1981. 7. Extraordinary sessions held in February, September, and November 1987 and April, May, and June 1988. 8. Extraordinary session held in May 1990. 9. Extraordinary session held in April 1992. 10. Extraordinary session held in June 1994. 11. Extraordinary session held in April 1998. 12. Extraordinary session held in May 2000. 13. Extraordinary sessions held in February, July, August, and December 2003 and March, May, and July 2004. 14. Extraordinary sessions held in July 2005 and April 2006. 15. Extraordinary sessions held in February, May, June, and December 2009 and December 2010. 16. Extraordinary sessions held in June and July 2011. 17. Extraordinary sessions held in February, July, and November 2015. 18. Extraordinary sessions held in March, April, November, and December 2018. 19. Extraordinary sessions held in February 2019 and April 2020.

Sources: *Bulletin of the Proceedings of the Wisconsin Legislature*, various editions; Senate and Assembly Journals.

Executive vetoes since 1931

Session	Bills vetoed (overridden)	Bills partially vetoed (overridden)	Biennial budget bill partial vetoes[1] (overridden)
1931	58	2	12
1933	15	1	12
1935	27	4	—
1937	10	1	—
1939[2]	22	4	1
1941	17	1	1
1943	39 (20)	1 (1)	—
1945	30 (5)	2 (1)	1
1947	10 (1)	1	1
1949	17 (2)	2 (1)	—
1951	18	—	—
1953[3]	31 (3)	4	2
1955	38	—	—
1957	35 (1)	3	2
1959	36 (4)	1	—
1961	70 (2)	3	2
1963	72 (4)	1	—
1965	24 (1)	4	1
1967	18	5	—
1969	34 (1)	11	27
1971	32 (3)	8	12
1973	13	18 (3)	38 (2)
1975	37 (6)	22 (4)	42 (5)
1977	21 (4)	16 (3)	67 (21)
1979	19 (3)	9 (2)	45 (1)
1981[4]	11 (2)	11 (1)	121
1983	3	11 (1)	70 (6)
1985	7	7 (1)	78 (2)
1987	38	20	290
1989	35	28	208
1991	33	13	457
1993	8	24	78
1995	4	21	112
1997	3	8	152
1999	5	10	255
2001	—	3	315
2003	54	10	131
2005	47	2	139
2007	1	4	33
2009	6	5	81
2011	—	3	50
2013	1	4	57
2015	2	5	104
2017	—	4	98
2019	20	2	78

— Represents zero.

1. The number of individual veto statements in the governor's veto message.   2. Attorney general ruled veto of 1939 SB-43 was void and it became law (see Vol. 28, *Opinions of the Attorney General*, p. 423).   3. 1953 AB-141, partially vetoed in two separate sections by separate veto messages, is counted as one.   4. Attorney general ruled several vetoes "ineffective" because the governor failed to express his objections (see Vol. 70, *Opinions of the Attorney General*, p. 189).

Source: *Bulletin of the Proceedings of the Wisconsin Legislature*, various editions; Senate and Assembly Journals.

History of proposed constitutional amendments since 1854

Article	Section	Subject	Election result	Vote totals	Date	Proposed amendment
IV	4	Assemblymen, 2-year terms	rejected	6,549–11,580	Nov. 1854	1854 Ch. 89
IV	5	Senators, 4-year terms	rejected	6,348–11,885	Nov. 1854	1854 Ch. 89
IV	11	Biennial legislative sessions	rejected	6,752–11,589	Nov. 1854	1854 Ch. 89
V	5	Governor's salary, changed from $1,250 to $2,500 a year	rejected	14,519–32,612	Nov. 1862	1862 JR 6
IV	21	Change legislators' pay to $350 a year	ratified	58,363–24,418	Nov. 1867	1866 JR 3
V	5	Change governor's salary from $1,250 to $5,000 a year	ratified	47,353–41,764	Nov. 1869	1869 JR 2
V	9	Change lieutenant governor's salary to $1,000 a year	ratified	47,353–41,764	Nov. 1869	1869 JR 2
I	8	Grand jury system modified	ratified	48,894–18,606	Nov. 1870	1870 JR 3
IV	31, 32	Private and local laws, prohibited on 9 subjects	ratified	54,087–3,675	Nov. 1871	1871 JR 1
VII	4	Supreme court, 1 chief and 4 associate justices	rejected	16,272–29,755	Nov. 1872	1872 JR 8
XI	3	Indebtedness of municipalities limited to 5%	ratified	66,061–1,509	Nov. 1874	1873 JR 4
VII	4	Supreme court, 1 chief and 4 associate justices	ratified	79,140–16,763	Nov. 1877	1877 JR 1
VIII	2	Claims against state, 6-year limit	ratified	33,046–3,371	Nov. 1877	1877 JR 4
IV	4, 5, 11	Biennial sessions; assemblymen 2-year, senators 4-year terms	ratified	53,532–13,936	Nov. 1881	1881 AJR 7[1]
IV	21	Change legislators' pay to $500 a year	ratified	53,532–13,936	Nov. 1881	1881 AJR 7[1]
III	1	Voting residence 30 days; in municipalities voter registration	ratified	36,223–5,347	Nov. 1882	1882 JR 5
VI	4	County officers except judicial, vacancies filled by appointment	ratified	60,091–8,089	Nov. 1882	1882 JR 3
VII	12	Clerk of court, full term election	ratified	60,091–8,089	Nov. 1882	1882 JR 3
XIII	1	Political year; biennial elections	ratified	60,091–8,089	Nov. 1882	1882 JR 3
X	1	State superintendent, qualifications and pay fixed by legislature	rejected	12,967–18,342	Nov. 1888	1887 JR 4
VII	4	Supreme court, composed of 5 justices of supreme court.	ratified	125,759–14,712	Apr. 1889	1889 JR 3
IV	31	Cities incorporated by general law	ratified	15,718–9,015	Nov. 1892	1891 JR 4
X	1	State superintendent, pay fixed by law	rejected	38,752–56,506	Nov. 1896	1895 JR 2
VIII	7	Circuit judges, additional in populous counties	ratified	45,823–41,513	Apr. 1897	1897 JR 9
X	1	State superintendent, nonpartisan 4-year term, pay fixed by law	ratified	71,550–57,411	Nov. 1902	1901 JR 3
XI	4	General banking law authorized	ratified	64,836–44,620	Nov. 1902	1901 JR 2
XI	5	Banking law referenda requirement repealed	ratified	64,836–44,620	Nov. 1902	1901 JR 2
XIII	11	Free passes prohibited	ratified	67,781–40,697	Nov. 1902	1901 JR 9
VII	4	Supreme court, 7 justices, 10-year terms	ratified	51,377–39,857	Apr. 1903	1903 JR 7
III	1	Suffrage for full citizens only.	ratified	85,838–36,733	Nov. 1908	1907 JR 25
V	10	Governor's approval of bills in 6 days	ratified	85,958–27,270	Nov. 1908	1907 JR 13
VIII	1	Income tax	ratified	85,696–37,729	Nov. 1908	1907 JR 29
VIII	10	Highways, appropriations for	ratified	116,421–46,739	Nov. 1908	1907 JR 18
IV	3	Apportionment after each federal census.	ratified	54,932–52,634	Nov. 1910	1909 JR 55

History of proposed constitutional amendments since 1854, continued

Article	Section	Subject	Election result	Vote totals	Date	Proposed amendment
IV	21	Change legislators' pay to $1,000 a year.	rejected	44,153–76,278	Nov. 1910	1909 JR 7
VIII	10	Water power and forests, appropriations for [2]	rejected	62,468–45,924 [2]	Nov. 1910	1909 Ch. 514
VII	10	Judges' salaries, time of payment.	ratified	44,855–34,865	Nov. 1912	1911 JR 24
XI	3	City or county debt for lands, discharge within 50 years.	ratified	46,369–34,975	Nov. 1912	1911 JR 42
XI	3a	Public parks, playgrounds, etc.	ratified	48,424–33,931	Nov. 1912	1911 JR 48
IV	1	Initiative and referendum	rejected	84,934–148,536	Nov. 1914	1913 JR 22
IV	21	Change legislators' pay to $600 a year, 2 cents a mile for additional round trips	rejected	68,907–157,202	Nov. 1914	1913 JR 24
VII	6,7	Judicial circuits, decreased number, additional judges.	rejected	63,311–154,827	Nov. 1914	1913 JR 26
VIII	—	State annuity insurance.	rejected	59,909–170,338	Nov. 1914	1913 JR 35
VIII	—	State insurance.	rejected	58,490–165,966	Nov. 1914	1913 JR 12
XI	—	Home rule of cities and villages.	rejected	86,020–141,472	Nov. 1914	1913 JR 21
XII	—	Municipal power of condemnation.	rejected	61,122–154,945	Nov. 1914	1913 JR 25
XII	1	Constitutional amendments, submission after 3/5 approval by one legislature	rejected	71,734–160,761	Nov. 1914	1913 JR 17
XII	—	Constitution amended upon petition	rejected	68,435–150,215	Nov. 1914	1913 JR 22
XIII	—	Recall of civil officers.	rejected	81,628–144,386	Nov. 1914	1913 JR 15
IV	21	Legislators' pay fixed by law	rejected	126,243–132,258	Apr. 1920	1919 JR 37
VII	6,7	Judicial circuits, decreased number, additional judges.	rejected	113,786–116,436	Apr. 1920	1919 JR 92
I	5	Jury verdict, 5/6 in civil cases	ratified	171,433–156,820	Nov. 1922	1921 JR 17
VI	4	Sheriffs, no limit on successive terms	rejected	161,832–207,594	Nov. 1922	1921 JR 36
XI	—	Municipal indebtedness for public utilities	rejected	105,234–219,639	Nov. 1922	1921 JR 37
IV	21	Change legislators' pay to $750 a year.	rejected	189,635–250,236	Apr. 1924	1923 JR 18
VII	7	Circuit judges, additional in populous counties	ratified	240,207–226,562	Nov. 1924	1923 JR 64
VIII	10	Forestry, appropriations for	ratified	336,360–173,563	Nov. 1924	1923 JR 57
XI	3	Home rule for cities and villages	ratified	299,792–190,165	Nov. 1924	1923 JR 34
V	5	Governor's salary fixed by law	ratified	202,156–188,302	Nov. 1926	1925 JR 52
XIII	12	Recall of elective officials.	ratified	205,868–201,125	Nov. 1926	1925 JR 16
IV	21	Change legislators' pay to $1,000 for session.	rejected	151,786–199,260	Apr. 1927	1927 JR 12
VIII	1	Severance tax: forests, minerals.	ratified	179,217–141,888	Apr. 1927	1927 JR 13
IV	21	Legislators' salary repealed; to be fixed by law	ratified	237,250–212,846	Apr. 1929	1929 JR 6
VI	4	Sheriffs succeeding themselves for 2 terms	ratified	259,881–210,964	Apr. 1929	1929 JR 13
V	10	Item veto on appropriation bills	ratified	252,655–153,703	Nov. 1930	1929 JR 43
V	5	Governor's salary provision repealed; fixed by law	ratified	452,605–275,175	Nov. 1932	1931 JR 52
V	5	Lieutenant governor's salary repealed; fixed by law	ratified	427,768–267,120	Nov. 1932	1931 JR 53
VII	1	Wording of section corrected	ratified	436,113–221,563	Nov. 1932	1931 JR 58

Art.	Sec.	Amendment	Result	Vote	Election	Joint Resolution
XI	3	Municipal indebtedness for public utilities	ratified	401,194–279,631	Nov. 1932	1931 JR 71
III	1	Women's suffrage	ratified	411,088–166,745	Nov. 1934	1933 JR 76
XIII	11	Free passes, permitted as specified	ratified	365,971–361,799	Nov. 1936	1935 JR 98
VIII	1	Installment payment of real estate taxes	ratified	330,971–134,808	Apr. 1941	1941 JR 18
VIII	15	Justice of peace, abolish office in first class cities	ratified	160,965–113,408	Apr. 1945	1945 JR 2
VIII	10	Aeronautical program	ratified	187,111–101,169	Apr. 1945	1945 JR 3
VI	4	Sheriffs, no limit on successive terms	rejected	121,144–170,131	Apr. 1946	1945 JR 47
IV	33	Auditing of state accounts	ratified	480,938–308,072	Nov. 1946	1945 JR 73
VI	2	Auditing (part of same proposal)	ratified	480,938–308,072	Nov. 1946	1945 JR 73
X	3	Public transportation of school children to any school	rejected	437,817–545,475	Nov. 1946	1945 JR 78
XI	2	Repeal; relating to exercise of eminent domain by municipalities	rejected	210,086–807,318	Nov. 1948	1947 JR 48
II	2	Prohibition on taxing federal lands repealed	rejected	245,412–297,237	Apr. 1949	1949 JR 2
VIII	10	Allow internal improvement debt for veterans' housing	ratified	311,576–290,736	Apr. 1949	1949 JR 1
II	2	Prohibition on taxing federal lands repealed	ratified	305,612–186,284	Apr. 1951	1951 JR 7
XI	2	City debt limit 8% for combined city and school purposes	ratified	313,739–191,897	Apr. 1951	1951 JR 6
IV	3, 4, 5	Apportionment based on area and population[3]	rejected	433,043–406,133 [3]	Apr. 1953	1953 JR 9
VII	9	Judicial elections to full terms	ratified	386,972–345,094	Apr. 1953	1953 JR 12
VII	24	Judges: qualifications, retirement	ratified	380,214–177,929	Apr. 1955	1955 JR 14
XI	3	School debt limit, equalized value	ratified	320,376–228,641	Apr. 1955	1955 JR 12
IV	26	Teachers' retirement benefits	ratified	365,560–255,284	Apr. 1956	1955 JR 17
VI	4	Sheriffs, no limit on successive terms	rejected	269,722–328,603	Apr. 1956	1955 JR 53
XI	3a	Municipal acquisition of land for public purposes	ratified	376,692–193,544	Apr. 1956	1955 JR 36
XIII	11	Free passes, not for public use	rejected	188,715–380,207	Apr. 1956	1955 JR 54
VIII	10	Port development	ratified	472,177–451,045	Apr. 1960	1959 JR 15
XI	3	Debt limit in populous counties, 5% of equalized valuation	ratified	686,104–529,467	Nov. 1960	1959 JR 32
IV	26	Salary increases during term for various public officers	rejected	297,066–307,575	Apr. 1961	1961 JR 11
IV	34	Continuity of civil government	ratified	498,869–132,728	Apr. 1961	1961 JR 10
VI	4	Sheriffs, no limit on successive terms	rejected	283,495–388,238	Apr. 1961	1961 JR 9
VIII	1	Personal property classified for tax purposes	ratified	381,881–220,434	Apr. 1961	1961 JR 13
XI	2	Municipal eminent domain, abolished jury verdict of necessity	ratified	348,406–259,566	Apr. 1961	1961 JR 12
XI	3	Debt limit 10% of equalized valuation for integrated aid school district	ratified	409,963–224,783	Apr. 1961	1961 JR 8
IV	23	"Indians not taxed" exclusion removed from apportionment formula	ratified	631,296–259,577	Nov. 1962	1961 JR 32
IV	4	County executive: 4-year term	ratified	527,075–331,393	Nov. 1962	1961 JR 64
IV	23a	County executive: 2-year terms	ratified	527,075–331,393	Nov. 1962	1961 JR 64
IV	3	County executive veto power	ratified	524,240–319,378	Nov. 1962	1961 JR 64
IV	26	Time for apportionment of seats in the state legislature	rejected	232,851–277,014	Apr. 1963	1963 JR 9
IV	3	Salary increases during term for justices and judges	rejected	216,205–335,774	Apr. 1963	1963 JR 7
XI	26	Equalized value debt limit	ratified	285,296–231,702	Apr. 1963	1963 JR 8
VIII	10	Maximum state appropriation for forestry increased	rejected	440,978–536,724	Apr. 1964	1963 JR 32

History of proposed constitutional amendments since 1854, continued

Article	Section	Subject	Election result	Vote totals	Date	Proposed amendment
XI	3	Property valuation for debt limit adjusted	rejected	336,994–572,276	Apr. 1964	1963 JR 33
XII	1	Constitutional amendments, submission of related items in a single proposition	rejected	317,676–582,045	Apr. 1964	SS 1963 JR 1
VI	4	Coroner and surveyor abolished in counties of 500,000	ratified	380,059–215,169	Apr. 1965	1965 JR 5
IV	24	Lotteries, definition revised	ratified	454,390–194,327	Apr. 1965	1965 JR 2
IV	13	Legislators on active duty in armed forces	ratified	362,935–189,641	Apr. 1966	1965 JR 14
VII	2	Establishment of inferior courts	ratified	321,434–216,341	Apr. 1966	1965 JR 50
VII	15	Justices of the peace abolished	ratified	321,434–216,341	Apr. 1966	1965 JR 50
XI	3	Special district public utility debt limit	ratified	307,502–199,919	Apr. 1966	1965 JR 51
						1965 JR 58
I	23	Transportation of children to private schools	ratified	494,236–377,107	Apr. 1967	1967 JR 13
IV	26	Judicial salary increased during term	ratified	489,989–328,292	Apr. 1967	1967 JR 17
V	1m, 1n	4-year term for governor and lieutenant governor	ratified	534,368–310,478	Apr. 1967	1967 JR 10
V	3	Joint election of governor and lieutenant governor	ratified	507,339–312,267	Apr. 1967	1967 JR 11
VI	1m	4-year term for secretary of state	ratified	520,326–311,974	Apr. 1967	1967 JR 14
VI	1n	4-year term for state treasurer	ratified	514,280–314,873	Apr. 1967	1967 JR 10
VI	1p	4-year term for attorney general	ratified	515,962–311,603	Apr. 1967	1967 JR 10
VI	4	Sheriffs, no limit on successive terms	ratified	508,242–324,544	Apr. 1967	1967 JR 12
VII	11	Legislative sessions, more than one permitted in biennium	ratified	670,757–267,997	Apr. 1968	1967 JR 48
VII	24	Uniform retirement date for justices and circuit judges	ratified	734,046–215,455	Apr. 1968	1967 JR 56
VII	24	Temporary appointment of justices and circuit judges	ratified	678,249–245,807	Apr. 1968	1967 JR 56
VIII	10	Forestry appropriation from sources other than property tax	ratified	652,705–286,512	Apr. 1968	1967 JR 25
VIII	23	Uniform county government modified	ratified	326,445–321,851	Apr. 1969	1969 JR 2
IV	23a	County executive to have veto power	ratified	326,445–321,851	Apr. 1969	1969 JR 2
VIII	7	State public debt for specified purposes allowed	ratified	411,062–258,366	Apr. 1969	1969 JR 3
I	24	Private use of school buildings	ratified	871,707–298,016	Apr. 1972	1971 JR 27
IV	23	County government systems authorized	ratified	571,285–515,255	Apr. 1972	1971 JR 13
VI	4	Coroner/medical examiner option	ratified	795,497–323,930	Apr. 1972	1971 JR 21
X	3	Released time for religious instruction	ratified	595,075–585,511	Apr. 1972	1971 JR 28
I	25	Equality of the sexes	rejected	447,240–520,936	Apr. 1973	1973 JR 5
IV	24	Charitable bingo authorized	ratified	645,544–391,499	Apr. 1973	1973 JR 3
IV	26	Increased benefits for retired public employees	ratified	396,051–315,545	Apr. 1974	1973 JR 15
VII	13	Removal of judges by 2/3 vote of legislature for cause	ratified	493,496–193,867	Apr. 1974	1973 JR 25
VIII	1	Taxation of agricultural lands	ratified	353,377–340,518	Apr. 1974	1973 JR 29

Art.	Sec.	Description	Vote	Result	Date	Reference
VIII	3, 7	Public debt for veterans' housing[5]	385,915-300,232	ratified	Apr. 1975	1975 JR 3
VIII	7, 10	Internal improvements for transportation facilities[5]	342,396-341,291[5]	rejected	Apr. 1975	1975 JR 2
XI	3	Exclusion of certain debt from municipal debt limit	310,434-337,925	ratified	Apr. 1975	1973 JR 133
XIII	2	Dueling: repeal of disenfranchisement[5]	395,616-282,726	ratified	Apr. 1975	1975 JR 4
XI	3	Municipal indebtedness increased up to 10% of equalized valuation	328,097-715,420	rejected	Apr. 1976	1975 JR 6
VIII	7(2)(a), 10	Internal improvements for transportation facilities[5]	722,658-935,152	rejected	Nov. 1976[5]	1975 JR 2
IV	24	Charitable raffle games authorized	483,518-300,473	ratified	Apr. 1977	1977 JR 6
VII	2	Unified court system [also affected I 21; IV 17, 26; VII 3–11, 14, 16–23; XIV 16(1)–(4)]	490,437-215,939	ratified	Apr. 1977	1977 JR 7
VII	5	Court of appeals created [also affected I 21(1); VII 2, 3(3); XIV 16(5)]	455,350-229,316	ratified	Apr. 1977	1977 JR 7
VII		Court system disciplinary proceedings	565,087-151,418	ratified	Apr. 1977	1977 JR 7
VII	11, 13	Retirement age for justices and judges set by law	506,207-244,170	ratified	Apr. 1977	1977 JR 7
IV	24	Town government uniformity	179,011-383,395	rejected	Apr. 1978	1977 JR 18
V	23	Gubernatorial succession	538,959-187,440	ratified	Apr. 1979	1979 JR 3
XIII	7, 8	Lieutenant governor vacancy	540,186-181,497	ratified	Apr. 1979	1979 JR 3
IV	10	Senate presiding officer	372,734-327,008	ratified	Apr. 1979	1979 JR 3
V	9	4-year constitutional officer terms (improved wording) [also affected V 1m, 1n; VI 1, 1m, 1n, 1p]	533,620-164,768	ratified	Apr. 1979	1979 JR 3
—	1	Right to bail[6]	505,092-185,405[6]	ratified	Apr. 1981	1981 JR 8
XI	8	Obsolete corporation and banking provisions	418,997-186,898	ratified	Apr. 1981	1981 JR 9
XI	1, 4	Indebtedness period for sewage collection or treatment systems.	386,792-250,866	ratified	Apr. 1981	1981 JR 7
XIII	3	Primaries in recall elections	366,635-259,820	ratified	Apr. 1981	1981 JR 6
VI	12	Counties responsible for acts of sheriff	316,156-219,752	ratified	Apr. 1982	1981 JR 15
—	4	Gender-neutral wording [also affected X 1, 2]	771,267-479,053	ratified	Nov. 1982	1981 JR 29
IV	1, 18	Military personnel treatment in redistricting.	834,188-321,331	ratified	Nov. 1982	1981 JR 29
IV	3	Obsolete 1881 amendment reference.	919,349-238,884	ratified	Nov. 1982	1981 JR 29
XIII	4, 5	Elections by legislature	977,438-193,679	ratified	Nov. 1982	1981 JR 29
X	30	Obsolete reference to election and term of superintendent of public instruction.	934,236-215,961	ratified	Nov. 1982	1981 JR 29
X	1	Obsolete reference to military draft exemption purchase; school fund	887,488-295,693	ratified	Nov. 1982	1981 JR 29
XIV	3	Obsolete transition from territory to statehood [also affected XIV 4–12; XIV 14, 15].	926,875-223,213	ratified	Nov. 1982	1981 JR 29
XIV	16(1)	Obsolete transitional provisions of 1977 court reorganization [also affected XIV 16(2), (3), (5)].	882,091-237,698	ratified	Nov. 1982	1981 JR 29
XIV	16(4)	Terms on supreme court effective date provision	960,540-190,366	ratified	Nov. 1982	1981 JR 29
—	1	Rewording to parallel Declaration of Independence	419,699-65,418	ratified	Apr. 1986	1985 JR 21
III	1–6	Revision of suffrage defined by general law	401,911-83,183	ratified	Apr. 1986	1985 JR 14
XIII	1	Modernizing constitutional text	404,273-82,512	ratified	Apr. 1986	1985 JR 14
XIII	5	Obsolete suffrage right on Indian land	381,339-102,090	ratified	Apr. 1986	1985 JR 14
IV	24(5)	Permitting pari-mutuel on-track betting	580,089-529,729	ratified	Apr. 1987	1987 JR 3
IV	24(6)	Authorizing the creation of a state lottery	739,181-391,942	ratified	Apr. 1987	1987 JR 4
V	1	Authorizing income tax credits or refunds for property or sales taxes	405,765-406,863	rejected	Apr. 1989	1989 JR 2
V	10	Redefining the partial veto power of the governor.	387,068-252,481	ratified	Apr. 1990	1989 JR 39
VIII	10	Providing housing for persons of low or moderate income	295,823-402,921	rejected	Apr. 1991	1991 JR 2

History of proposed constitutional amendments since 1854, continued

Article	Section	Subject	Election result	Vote totals	Date	Proposed amendment
VIII	7(2)(a)1	Railways and other railroad facilities [also created VIII 10].	ratified	650,592–457,690	Apr. 1992	1991 JR 9
IV	26	Legislative and judiciary compensation, effective date	ratified	736,832–348,645	Apr. 1992	1991 JR 13
VIII	1	Residential property tax reduction.	rejected	675,876–1,536,975	Nov. 1992	1991 JR 14
I	9m	Crime victims	ratified	861,405–163,087	Apr. 1993	1993 JR 2
IV	24	Gambling, limiting "lottery"; divorce under general law [also affected IV 31, 32].	ratified	623,987–435,180	Apr. 1993	1993 JR 3
I	3	Removal of unnecessary references to masculine gender [also affected I 3, 7, 9, 19, 21(2); IV 6, 12, 13, 23a; V 4, 6; VI 2; VII 1, 12; XI 3a; XIII 4, 11, 12(6)].	rejected	412,032–498,801	Apr. 1995	1995 JR 3
IV	24(6)(a)	Authorizing sports lottery dedicated to athletic facilities	rejected	348,818–618,377	Apr. 1995	1995 JR 2
VII	10(1)	Removal of restriction on judges holding nonjudicial public office after resignation during the judicial term.	rejected	390,744–503,239	Apr. 1995	1995 JR 4
XIII	3	Eligibility to seek or hold public office if convicted of a felony or a misdemeanor involving violation of a public trust	ratified	1,292,934–543,516	Nov. 1996	1995 JR 28
I	25	Guaranteeing the right to keep and bear arms	ratified	1,205,873–425,052	Nov. 1998	1997 JR 21
VI	4(1), (3), (5), (6)	4-year term for sheriff; sheriffs permitted to hold nonpartisan office; allowed legislature to provide for election to fill vacancy during term.	ratified	1,161,942–412,508	Nov. 1998	1997 JR 18
IV	24(3), (5), (6)	Distributing state lottery, bingo and pari-mutuel proceeds for property tax	ratified	648,903–105,976	Apr. 1999	1999 JR 2
IV	26	Right to fish, hunt, trap, and take game.	ratified	668,459–146,182	Apr. 2003	2003 JR 8
VI	4(1), (3), (4)	4-year term for county clerks, treasurers, clerks of circuit court, district attorneys, coroners, elected surveyors, and registers of deeds [also affected VII 12]	ratified	534,742–177,037	Apr. 2005	2005 JR 2
XIII	13	Marriage between one man and one woman	ratified	1,264,310–862,924	Nov. 2006	2005 JR 30
V	10(1)(c)	Gubernatorial partial veto power.	ratified	575,582–239,613	Apr. 2008	2007 JR 26
IV	9(2)	Department of transportation and transportation fund [also created VIII 11].	ratified	1,733,101–434,806	Nov. 2014	2013 JR 1
VIII	1	Election of chief justice of the supreme court	ratified	433,533–384,503	Apr. 2015	2015 JR 2
VI	1,3	Elimination of state treasurer [also affected X 7, 8 and XIV 17]	rejected	363,562–586,134	Apr. 2018	2017 JR 7
I	9m	Crime victims	ratified	1,107,067–371,013	Apr. 2020	2019 JR 3

Note: To amend the Wisconsin Constitution, two consecutive legislatures must adopt an identical amendment (known as "first consideration" and "second consideration") and a majority of the electorate must ratify the amendment at a subsequent election. See Art. XII, Sec. 1. Since the adoption of the Wisconsin Constitution in 1848, the electorate has voted 146 out of 198 times to amend the constitution, including a vote that was later resubmitted by the legislature and two votes that were declared invalid by the courts.

AJR–Assembly Joint Resolution; Ch.–Chapter; JR–Joint resolution; SS–Special session.

1. No other number was assigned to this joint resolution.   2. Ratified but declared invalid by Supreme Court in *State ex rel. Owen v. Donald*, 160 Wis. 21 (1915).   3. Ratified but declared invalid by Supreme Court in *State ex rel. Thomson v. Zimmerman*, 264 Wis. 644 (1953).   4. Special session December 1964.   5. Recount resulted in rejection (342,132 to 342,309). However, the Dane County Circuit Court ruled the recount invalid due to election irregularities and required that the referendum be resubmitted to the electorate. Resubmitted to the electorate November 1976 by the 1975 Wisconsin Legislature through Ch. 224, s.145r, Laws of 1975.   6. As a result of a Dane County Circuit Court injunction, vote totals were certified April 7, 1982, by the Board of State Canvassers.

Sources: Official records of the Wisconsin Elections Commission; *Laws of Wisconsin*, 2017 and prior volumes.

Statewide referenda other than constitutional amendments since 1849

Subject	Election result	Vote totals	Date	Submitting law
Extend suffrage to colored persons [1]	Approved	5,265–4,075	Nov. 1849	1849 Ch. 137
State banks; advisory	Approved	31,289–9,126	Nov. 1851	1851 Ch. 143
General banking law.	Approved	32,826–8,711	Nov. 1852	1852 Ch. 479
Liquor prohibition; advisory	Approved	27,519–24,109	Nov. 1853	1853 Ch. 101
Extend suffrage to colored persons	Rejected	28,235–41,345	Nov. 1857	1857 Ch. 44
Amend general banking law; redemption of bank notes	Approved	27,267–2,837	Nov. 1858	1858 Ch. 98
Amend general banking law; circulation of bank notes	Approved	57,646–2,515	Nov. 1861	1861 Ch. 242
Amend general banking law; interest rate 7% per year	Approved	46,269–7,794	Nov. 1862	1862 Ch. 203
Extend suffrage to colored persons [1]	Rejected	46,588–55,591	Nov. 1865	1865 Ch. 414
Amend general banking law; taxing shareholders	Approved	49,714–19,151	Nov. 1866	1866 Ch. 102
Amend general banking law; winding up circulation.	Approved	45,796–11,842	Nov. 1867	1866 Ch. 143; 1867 JR 12
Abolish office of bank comptroller	Approved	15,499–1,948	Nov. 1868	1868 Ch. 28
Incorporation of savings banks and savings societies	Approved	4,029–3,069	Nov. 1876	1876 Ch. 384
Women's suffrage upon school matters	Approved	43,581–38,998	Nov. 1886	1885 Ch. 211
Revise 1897 banking law; banking department under commission	Rejected	86,872–92,607	Nov. 1898	1897 Ch. 303
Primary election law.	Approved	130,366–80,102	Nov. 1904	1903 Ch. 451
Pocket ballots and coupon voting systems.	Rejected	45,958–111,139	Apr. 1906	1905 Ch. 522
Women's suffrage	Rejected	135,545–227,024	Nov. 1912	1911 Ch. 227
Soldiers' bonus financed by 3-mill property tax and income tax	Approved	165,762–57,324	Sept. 1919	1919 Ch. 667
Wisconsin prohibition enforcement act.	Approved	419,309–199,876	Nov. 1920	1919 Ch. 556
U.S. prohibition act (Volstead Act); memorializing Congress to amend	Approved	349,443–177,603	Nov. 1926	1925 JR 47
Repeal of Wisconsin prohibition enforcement act; advisory	Approved	350,337–196,402	Nov. 1926	1925 JR 47
Modification of Wisconsin prohibition enforcement act; advisory.	Approved	321,688–200,545	Apr. 1929	1929 JR 16
County distribution of auto licenses; advisory	Rejected	183,716–368,674	Apr. 1931	1931 JR 11
Sunday blue law repeal; advisory.	Approved	396,436–271,786	Apr. 1932	1931 JR 114
Old-age pensions; advisory	Approved	531,915–154,729	Apr. 1934	SS 1933 JR 64
Teacher tenure law repeal; advisory	Approved	403,782–372,524	Apr. 1940	1939 JR 100
Property tax levy for high school aid; 2 mills of assessed valuation	Rejected	131,004–410,315	Apr. 1944	1943 Ch. 525
Daylight saving time; advisory.	Rejected	313,091–379,740	Apr. 1947	1947 JR 4
3% retail sales tax for veterans bonus; advisory	Rejected	258,497–825,990	Nov. 1948	1947 JR 62
4-year term for constitutional officers; advisory.	Rejected	210,821–328,613	Apr. 1951	1951 JR 13
Apportionment of legislature by area and population; advisory.	Rejected	689,615–753,092	Nov. 1952	1951 Ch. 728
New residents entitled to vote for president and vice president.	Approved	550,056–414,680	Nov. 1954	1953 Ch. 76

Statewide referenda other than constitutional amendments since 1849, continued

Subject	Election result	Vote totals	Date	Submitting law
Statewide educational television tax-supported; advisory	Rejected	308,385–697,262	Nov. 1954	1953 JR 66
Daylight saving time	Approved	578,661–480,656	Apr. 1957	1957 Ch. 6
Ex-residents entitled to vote for president and vice president	Approved	627,279–229,375	Nov. 1962	1961 Ch. 512
Gasoline tax increase for highway construction; advisory	Rejected	150,769–889,364	Apr. 1964	SS 1963 JR 3
New residents entitled to vote after 6 months	Approved	582,389–256,246	Nov. 1966	1965 Chs. 88,89
State control and funding of vocational education; advisory	Rejected	292,560–409,789	Apr. 1969	1969 JR 4
Recreational lands bonding; advisory	Approved	361,630–322,882	Apr. 1969	1969 JR 5
Water pollution abatement bonding; advisory	Approved	446,763–246,968	Apr. 1969	1969 JR 5
New residents entitled to vote after 10 days	Approved	1,017,887–660,875	Nov. 1976	1975 Ch. 85
Presidential voting revised	Approved	782,181–424,386	Nov. 1978	1977 Ch. 394
Overseas voting revised	Approved	658,289–524,029	Nov. 1978	1977 Ch. 394
Public inland lake protection and rehabilitation districts	Approved	1,210,452–355,024	Nov. 1980	1979 Ch. 299
Nuclear weapons moratorium and reduction; advisory	Approved	641,514–205,018	Sept. 1982	1981 JR 38
Nuclear waste site locating; advisory	Rejected	78,327–628,414	Apr. 1983	1983 JR 5
Gambling casinos on excursion vessels; advisory	Rejected	465,432–604,289	Apr. 1993	1991 WisAct 321
Gambling casino restrictions; advisory	Approved	646,827–416,722	Apr. 1993	1991 WisAct 321
Video poker and other forms of video gambling allowed; advisory	Rejected	358,045–702,864	Apr. 1993	1991 WisAct 321
Pari-mutuel on-track betting continuation; advisory	Approved	548,580–507,403	Apr. 1993	1991 WisAct 321
State-operated lottery continuation; advisory	Approved	773,306–287,585	Apr. 1993	1991 WisAct 321
Extended suffrage in federal elections to adult children of U.S. citizens living abroad	Approved	1,293,458–792,975	Nov. 2000	1999 WisAct 182
Death penalty; advisory	Approved	1,166,571–934,508	Nov. 2006	2005 JR 58

Note: Statewide referendum questions are submitted to the electorate by the Wisconsin Legislature: 1) to ratify a law extending the right of suffrage (as required by the state constitution); 2) to ratify a law that has been passed contingent on voter approval; or 3) to seek voter opinion through an advisory referendum. Since 1848, the Wisconsin Legislature has presented 53 referendum questions to the Wisconsin electorate through the passage of acts or joint resolutions; 39 were ratified. Prior to statehood, the territorial legislature sent four questions to the electorate, as follows: Formation of a state government, submitted by Territorial Laws 1846, page 5 (Jan.31), approved April 1846, 12,334 votes for, 2,487 against; Ratification of first constitution, submitted by Art. XIX, Sec. 9 of 1846 Constitution, rejected April 1847, 14,119 votes for, 20,231 against; Extend suffrage to colored persons, submitted by supplemental resolution to 1846 Constitution, rejected April 1847, 7,664 votes for, 14,615 against; Ratification of second constitution, submitted by Art. XIV, Sec. 9 of 1848 Constitution, approved March 1848, 16,799 votes for, 6,384 against.

Ch.–Chapter; JR–Joint resolution; SS–Special session.

1. In *Gillespie v. Palmer*, 20 Wis. 544 (1866), the Wisconsin Supreme Court ruled that Chapter 137, Laws of 1849, extending suffrage to colored persons, was ratified November 6, 1849.

Sources: Official records of the Wisconsin Elections Commission; *Laws of Wisconsin*, 2015 and prior volumes.

Wisconsin vote in presidential elections since 1848

1848—4 electoral votes
Lewis Cass—D 15,001
Zachary Taylor—W 13,747
Martin Van Buren—FS . . . 10,418
Total. **39,166**

1852—5 electoral votes
Franklin Pierce—D 33,658
Winfield Scott—W 22,210
John P. Hale—FS. 8,814
Total. **64,682**

1856—5 electoral votes
John C. Fremont—R 66,090
James Buchanan—D 52,843
Millard Fillmore—A. 579
Total. **119,512**

1860—5 electoral votes
Abraham Lincoln—R 86,113
Stephen A. Douglas—D . . 65,021
John C. Breckinridge—SoD . . 888
John Bell—CU 161
Total. **152,183**

1864—8 electoral votes
Abraham Lincoln—R 83,458
George B. McClellan—D . . 65,884
Total. **149,342**

1868—8 electoral votes
Ulysses S. Grant—R 108,857
Horatio Seymour—D 84,707
Total. **193,564**

1872—10 electoral votes
Ulysses S. Grant—R 104,994
Horace Greeley—D & LR . . 86,477
Charles O'Conor—D 834
Total. **192,305**

1876—10 electoral votes
Rutherford B. Hayes—R . 130,668
Samuel J. Tilden—D . . . 123,927
Peter Cooper—G 1,509
Green Clay Smith—Pro. 27
Total. **256,131**

1880—10 electoral votes
James A. Garfield—R . . . 144,398
Winfield S. Hancock—D . 114,644
James B. Weaver—G 7,986
John W. Phelps—A 91
Neal Dow—Pro 68
Total. **267,187**

1884—11 electoral votes
James G. Blaine—R 161,157
Grover Cleveland—D. . . 146,477
John P. St. John—Pro 7,656
Benjamin F. Butler—G 4,598
Total. **319,888**

1888—11 electoral votes
Benjamin Harrison—R   176,553
Grover Cleveland—D. . . 155,232
Clinton B. Fisk—Pro. 14,277
Alson J. Streeter—UL. 8,552
Total. **354,614**

1892—12 electoral votes
Grover Cleveland—D. . . 177,325
Benjamin Harrison—R . . 171,101
John Bidwell—Pro 13,136
James B. Weaver—PPop . . 10,019
Total. **371,581**

1896—12 electoral votes
William McKinley—R . . . 268,135
William J. Bryan—D. . . . 165,523
Joshua Levering—Pro 7,507
John M. Palmer—ND 4,584
Charles H. Matchett—SL. . .1,314
Charles E. Bentley—Nat 346
Total. **447,409**

1900—12 electoral votes
William McKinley—R . . . 265,760
William J. Bryan—D. . . . 159,163
John G. Wooley—Pro. . . . 10,027
Eugene V. Debs—SD 7,048
Joseph F. Malloney—SL 503
Total. **442,501**

1904—13 electoral votes
Theodore Roosevelt—R . 280,164
Alton B. Parker—D 124,107
Eugene V. Debs—SD 28,220
Silas C. Swallow—Pro 9,770
Thomas E. Watson—PPop . . . 530
Charles H. Corregan—SL . . . 223
Total. **443,014**

1908—13 electoral votes
William H. Taft—R. 247,747
William J. Bryan—D. . . . 166,632
Eugene V. Debs—SD 28,164
Eugene W. Chafin—Pro . . 11,564
August Gillhaus—SL 314
Total. **454,421**

1912—13 electoral votes
Woodrow Wilson—D . . . 164,230
William H. Taft—R. 130,596
Theodore Roosevelt—P . . 62,448
Eugene V. Debs—SD 33,476
Eugene W. Chafin—Pro . . .8,584
Arthur E. Reimer—SL. 632
Total. **399,966**

1916—13 electoral votes
Charles E. Hughes—R . . 220,822
Woodrow Wilson—D . . . 191,363
Allan Benson—S. 27,631
J. Frank Hanly—Pro 7,318
Total. **447,134**

1920—13 electoral votes
Warren G. Harding—R . . 498,576
James M. Cox—D 113,422
Eugene V. Debs—S 80,635
Aaron S. Watkins—Pro 8,647
Total. **701,280**

1924—13 electoral votes
Robert M. La Follette—P . 453,678
Calvin Coolidge—R. . . . 311,614
John W. Davis—D 68,096
William Z. Foster—Wrk. . . .3,834
Herman P. Faris—Pro 2,918
Total. **840,140**

1928—13 electoral votes
Herbert Hoover—R 544,205
Alfred E. Smith—D 450,259
Norman Thomas—S 18,213
William F. Varney—Pro 2,245
William Z. Foster—Wrk. . . .1,528
Verne L. Reynolds—SL 381
Total. **1,016,831**

1932—12 electoral votes
Franklin D. Roosevelt—D 707,410
Herbert Hoover—R 347,741
Norman Thomas—S 53,379
William Z. Foster—Com . . .3,112
William D. Upshaw—Pro . . .2,672
Verne L. Reynolds—SL 494
Total. **1,114,808**

1936—12 electoral votes
Franklin D. Roosevelt—D 802,984
Alfred M. Landon—R . . . 380,828
William Lemke—U 60,297
Norman Thomas—S 10,626
Earl Browder—Com. 2,197
David L. Calvin—Pro 1,071
John W. Aiken—SL 557
Total. **1,258,560**

Wisconsin vote in presidential elections since 1848, continued

1940—12 electoral votes
Franklin D. Roosevelt—D   704,821
Wendell Willkie—R 679,206
Norman Thomas—S 15,071
Earl Browder—Com. 2,394
Roger Babson—Pro. 2,148
John W. Aiken—SL 1,882
Total. 1,405,522

1944—12 electoral votes
Thomas Dewey—R 674,532
Franklin D. Roosevelt—D 650,413
Norman Thomas—S 13,205
Edward Teichert—I 1,002
Total. 1,339,152

1948—12 electoral votes
Harry S Truman—D 647,310
Thomas Dewey—R 590,959
Henry Wallace—PP 25,282
Norman Thomas—S 12,547
Edward Teichert—I 399
Farrell Dobbs—ISW 303
Total. 1,276,800

1952—12 electoral votes
Dwight D. Eisenhower—R 979,744
Adlai E. Stevenson—D . . 622,175
Vincent Hallinan—IP 2,174
Farrell Dobbs—ISW. 1,350
Darlington Hoopes—IS . . .1,157
Eric Hass—ISL 770
Total. 1,607,370

1956—12 electoral votes
Dwight D. Eisenhower—R 954,844
Adlai E. Stevenson—D . . 586,768
T. Coleman Andrews—I (Con)
. 6,918
Darlington Hoopes—I (S) . . . 754
Eric Hass—I (SL) 710
Farrell Dobbs—I (SW) 564
Total. 1,550,558

1960—12 electoral votes
Richard M. Nixon—R . . . 895,175
John F. Kennedy—D . . . 830,805
Farrell Dobbs—I (SW) 1,792
Eric Hass—I (SL) 1,310
Total. 1,729,082

1964—12 electoral votes
Lyndon B. Johnson—D 1,050,424
Barry M. Goldwater—R. . 638,495
Clifton DeBerry—I (SW) . . .1,692
Eric Hass—I (SL) 1,204
Total. 1,691,815

1968—12 electoral votes
Richard M. Nixon—R . . . 809,997
Hubert H. Humphrey—D 748,804
George C. Wallace—I (A). 127,835
Henning A. Blomen—I (SL) .1,338
Frederick W. Halstead
—I (SW) 1,222
Total. 1,689,196

1972—11 electoral votes
Richard M. Nixon—R . . . 989,430
George S. McGovern—D. 810,174
John G. Schmitz—A. 47,525
Benjamin M. Spock—I (Pop)
. 2,701
Louis Fisher—I (SL) 998
Gus Hall—I (Com) 663
Evelyn Reed—I (SW) 506
Total. 1,851,997

1976—11 electoral votes
Jimmy Carter—D 1,040,232
Gerald R. Ford—R 1,004,987
Eugene J. McCarthy—I. . . 34,943
Lester Maddox—A 8,552
Frank P. Zeidler—I (S). 4,298
Roger L. MacBride—I (Lib). .3,814
Peter Camejo—I (SW) 1,691
Margaret Wright—I (Pop) . . . 943
Gus Hall—I (Com) 749
Lyndon H. LaRouche, Jr—
I (USL) 738
Jules Levin—I (SL). 389
Total. 2,104,175

1980—11 electoral votes
Ronald Reagan—R . . . 1,088,845
Jimmy Carter—D 981,584
John Anderson—I. 160,657
Ed Clark—I (Lib) 29,135
Barry Commoner—I (Cit) . .7,767
John Rarick—I (Con) 1,519
David McReynolds—I (S) . . . 808
Gus Hall—I (Com) 772
Deidre Griswold—I (WW) . . . 414
Clifton DeBerry—I (SW) 383
Total. 2,273,221

1984—11 electoral votes
Ronald Reagan—R . . . 1,198,800
Walter F. Mondale—D . . 995,847
David Bergland—Lib 4,884
Bob Richards—Con 3,864
Lyndon H. LaRouche, Jr—I 3,791
Sonia Johnson—I (Cit) 1,456
Dennis L. Serrette—I (WIA) .1,007
Larry Holmes—I (WW) 619
Gus Hall—I (Com) 597
Melvin T. Mason—I (SW). . . . 445
Total. 2,212,018

1988—11 electoral votes
Michael S. Dukakis—D
. 1,126,794
George Bush—R. 1,047,499
Ronald Paul—I (Lib). 5,157
David E. Duke—I (Pop). . . .3,056
James Warren—I (SW) 2,574
Lyndon H. LaRouche, Jr—I (NER)
. 2,302
Lenora B. Fulani—I (NA) . . .1,953
Total. 2,191,612

1992—11 electoral votes
Bill Clinton—D. 1,041,066
George Bush—R. 930,855
Ross Perot—I. 544,479
Andre Marrou—Lib. 2,877
James Gritz—I (AFC) 2,311
Ron Daniels—LF. 1,883
Howard Phillips—I (Tax) . . .1,772
J. Quinn Brisben—I (S) 1,211
John Hagelin—NL. 1,070
Lenora B. Fulani—I (NA) 654
Lyndon H. LaRouche, Jr—I (ER)
. 633
Jack Herer—I (Gr) 547
Eugene A. Hem—3rd. 405
James Warren—I (SW) 390
Total. 2,531,114

1996—11 electoral votes
Bill Clinton—D. 1,071,971
Bob Dole—R 845,029
Ross Perot—Rfm 227,339
Ralph Nader—I (WG) 28,723
Howard Phillips—Tax. 8,811
Harry Browne—Lib 7,929
John Hagelin—I (NL) 1,379
Monica Moorehead—I (WW)
. 1,333
Mary Cal Hollis—I (S) 848
James E. Harris—I (SW) 483
Total. 2,196,169

2000—11 electoral votes
Al Gore—D 1,242,987
George W. Bush—R. . . 1,237,279
Ralph Nader—WG 94,070
Pat Buchanan—I (Rfm). . . 11,446
Harry Browne—Lib 6,640
Howard Phillips—Con 2,042
Monica G. Moorehead—I (WW)
. 1,063
John Hagelin—I (Rfm) 878
James Harris—I (SW) 306
Total. 2,598,607

Wisconsin vote in presidential elections since 1848, continued

2004—10 electoral votes
John F. Kerry—D. 1,489,504
George W. Bush—R . . . 1,478,120
Ralph Nader—I (TBL). . . . 16,390
Michael Badnarik—Lib. . . .6,464
David Cobb—WG 2,661
Walter F. Brown—I (SPW) . . . 471
James Harris—I (SW) 411
Total. 2,997,007

2008—10 electoral votes
Barack Obama—D . . . 1,677,211
John McCain—R. 1,262,393
Ralph Nader—I 17,605
Bob Barr—Lib 8,858
Chuck Baldwin—I (Con) . . .5,072
Cynthia McKinney—WG . . .4,216
Jeffrey J. Wamboldt—I (WtP) . 764
Brian Moore—I (SocUSA) . . . 540
Gloria La Riva—I (S&L) 237
Total. 2,983,417

2012—10 electoral votes
Barack Obama—D . . . 1,620,985
Mitt Romney—R. 1,407,966
Gary Johnson—I (Lib) . . . 20,439
Jill Stein—I (Grn) 7,665
Virgil Goode—Con 4,930
Jerry White—I (SE) 553
Gloria La Riva—I (S&L) 526
Total. 3,068,434

2016—10 electoral votes
Donald J. Trump—R . . 1,405,284
Hillary Clinton—D. . . . 1,382,536
Gary Johnson—Lib 106,674
Jill Stein—WG 31,072
Darrell L. Castle—Con . . . 12,162
Monica Moorehead—I (WW)
. 1,770
Rocky Roque De La Fuente—I (AD)
. 1,502
Total. 2,976,150

2020—10 electoral votes
Joseph R. Biden—D . . 1,630,866
Donald J. Trump—R . . 1,610,184
Jo Jorgensen—I (Lib) . . . 38,491
Brian Carroll—I (ASP) 5,259
Don Blankenship—Con . . .5,146
Total. 3,298,041

Note: The party designation listed for a candidate is taken from the Congressional Quarterly, *Guide to U.S. Elections*. A candidate whose party did not receive 1% of the vote for a statewide office in the previous election or who failed to meet the alternative requirement of section 5.62, Wis. Stats., must be listed on the Wisconsin ballot as "independent." In this listing, candidates whose party affiliations appear as "I," followed by a party designation in parentheses, were identified on the ballot simply as "independent" although they also provided a party designation or statement of principle.

Under the Electoral College system, each state is entitled to electoral votes equal in number to its total congressional delegation of U.S. Senators and U.S. Representatives.

Some totals include scattered votes for other candidates.

A—American (Know Nothing)	**LF**—Labor–Farm/Laborista–	**S&L**—Party for Socialism and
AD—American Delta	Agrario	Liberation
AFC—America First Coalition	**Lib**—Libertarian	**SocUSA**—Socialist Party USA
ASP—American Solidarity Party	**LR**—Liberal Republican	**SoD**—Southern Democrat
Cit—Citizens	**NA**—New Alliance	**SPW**—Socialist Party of Wis.
Com—Communist	**Nat**—National	**SW**—Socialist Worker
Con—Constitution	**ND**—National Democrat	**Tax**—U.S. Taxpayers
CU—Constitutional Union	**NER**—National Economic	**TBL**—The Better Life
D—Democrat	Recovery	**3rd**—Third Party
ER—Independents for Economic	**NL**—Natural Law	**U**—Union
Recovery	**P**—Progressive	**UL**—Union Labor
FS—Free Soil	**Pop**—Populist	**USL**—U.S. Labor
G—Greenback	**PP**—People's Progressive	**W**—Whig
Gr—Grassroots	**PPop**—People's (Populist)	**WG**—Wisconsin Green
Grn—Green	**Pro**—Prohibition	**WIA**—Wis. Independent Alliance
I—Independent	**R**—Republican	**Wrk**—Workers
IP—Independent Progressive	**Rfm**—Reform	**WtP**—We, the People
IS—Independent Socialist	**S**—Socialist	**WW**—Worker's World
ISL—Independent Socialist Labor	**SD**—Social Democrat	
ISW—Independent Socialist	**SE**—Socialist Equality	
Worker	**SL**—Socialist Labor	

Sources: Official records of the Wisconsin Elections Commission and Congressional Quarterly, *Guide to U.S. Elections*, 1994.

Wisconsin members of the U.S. Senate since 1848

Class 1			Class 3		
	Term			**Term**	
Henry Dodge—D	1848–1857		Isaac P. Walker—D.	1848–1855	
James R. Doolittle—R	1857–1869		Charles Durkee—UR	1855–1861	
Matthew H. Carpenter—R.	1869–1875		Timothy O. Howe—UR.	1861–1879	
Angus Cameron[1]—R	1875–1881		Matthew H. Carpenter—R.	1879–1881	
Philetus Sawyer—R.	1881–1893		Angus Cameron[1]—R	1881–1885	
John Lendrum Mitchell—D	1893–1899		John C. Spooner—R	1885–1891	
Joseph Very Quarles—R	1899–1905		William F. Vilas—D	1891–1897	
Robert M. La Follette, Sr.[2]—R.	1906–1925		John C. Spooner—R	1897–1907	
Robert M. La Follette, Jr.[3]—R.	1925–1935		Isaac Stephenson[5]—R	1907–1915	
Robert M. La Follette, Jr.—P.	1935–1947		Paul O. Husting—D.	1915–1917	
Joseph R. McCarthy—R	1947–1957		Irvine L. Lenroot[6]—R.	1918–1927	
William Proxmire[4]—D	1957–1989		John J. Blaine—R	1927–1933	
Herbert H. Kohl—D.	1989–2013		F. Ryan Duffy—D	1933–1939	
Tammy Baldwin—D.	2013–		Alexander Wiley—R.	1939–1963	
			Gaylord A. Nelson—D	1963–1981	
			Robert W. Kasten, Jr.—R	1981–1993	
			Russell D. Feingold—D.	1993–2011	
			Ron Johnson—R.	2011–	

Note: Each state has two U.S. Senators, and each serves a six-year term. They were elected by their respective state legislatures until passage of the 17th Amendment to the U.S. Constitution on April 8, 1913, which provided for popular election. Article I, Section 3, Clause 2, of the U.S. Constitution divides senators into three classes so that one-third of the senate is elected every two years. Wisconsin's seats were assigned to Class 1 and Class 3 at statehood.

D–Democrat; P–Progressive; R–Republican; UR–Union Republican.

1. Not a candidate for reelection to Class 1 seat, but elected 3/10/1881 to fill vacancy caused by death of Class 3 Senator Carpenter on 2/24/1881. 2. Elected 1/25/1905 but continued to serve as governor until 1/1/1906. 3. Elected 9/29/1925 to fill vacancy caused by death of Robert La Follette, Sr., on 6/18/1925. 4. Elected 8/27/1957 to fill vacancy caused by death of McCarthy on 5/2/1957. 5. Elected 5/17/1907 to fill vacancy caused by resignation of Spooner on 4/30/1907. 6. Elected 5/2/1918 to fill vacancy caused by death of Husting on 10/21/1917.

Source: Wisconsin Legislative Reference Bureau records.

Wisconsin members of the U.S. House of Representatives since 1848

	Party	District	Term	Residence
Adams, Henry C.	Rep.	2	1903–1906	Madison
Amlie, Thomas R	Rep., Prog.	1	1931–1933; 1935–1939	Elkhorn
Aspin, Les	Dem.	1	1971–1993	East Troy
Atwood, David	Rep.	2	1870–1871	Madison
Babbitt, Clinton	Dem.	1	1891–1893	Beloit
Babcock, Joseph W.	Rep.	3	1893–1907	Necedah
Baldus, Alvin.	Dem.	3	1975–1981	Menomonie
Baldwin, Tammy	Dem.	2	1999–2013	Madison
Barber, J. Allen	Rep.	3	1871–1875	Lancaster
Barca, Peter W.	Dem.	1	1993–1995	Kenosha
Barnes, Lyman E	Dem.	8	1893–1895	Appleton
Barney, Samuel S	Rep.	5	1895–1903	West Bend
Barrett, Thomas M	Dem.	5	1993–2003	Milwaukee
Barwig, Charles	Dem.	2	1889–1895	Mayville
Beck, Joseph D	Rep.	7	1921–1929	Viroqua
Berger, Victor L	Soc.	5	1911–1913; 1919; 1923–1929	Milwaukee
Biemiller, Andrew J.	Dem.	5	1945–1947; 1949–1951	Milwaukee
Billinghurst, Charles	Rep.	3	1855–1859	Juneau
Blanchard, George W	Rep.	1	1933–1935	Edgerton

Wisconsin members of the U.S. House of Representatives since 1848, continued

	Party	District	Term	Residence
Boileau, Gerald J	Rep., Prog.	8, 7	1931–1939	Wausau
Bolles, Stephen	Rep.	1	1939–1941	Janesville
Bouck, Gabriel	Dem.	6	1877–1881	Oshkosh
Bragg, Edward S	Dem.	5, 2	1877–1883; 1885–1887	Fond du Lac
Brickner, George H	Dem.	5	1889–1895	Sheboygan Falls
Brophy, John C	Rep.	4	1947–1949	Milwaukee
Brown, James S	Dem.	1	1863–1865	Milwaukee
Brown, Webster E	Rep.	9, 10	1901–1907	Rhinelander
Browne, Edward E	Rep.	8	1913–1931	Waupaca
Burchard, Samuel D	Dem.	5	1875–1877	Beaver Dam
Burke, Michael E	Dem.	6, 2	1911–1917	Beaver Dam
Bushnell, Allen R	Dem.	3	1891–1893	Madison
Byrnes, John W	Rep.	8	1945–1973	Green Bay
Cannon, Raymond J	Dem.	4	1933–1939	Milwaukee
Cary, William J	Rep.	4	1907–1919	Milwaukee
Caswell, Lucien B	Rep.	2, 1	1875–1883; 1885–1891	Fort Atkinson
Cate, George W	Reform	8	1875–1877	Stevens Point
Clark, Charles B	Rep.	6	1887–1891	Neenah
Classon, David G	Rep.	9	1917–1923	Oconto
Cobb, Amasa	Rep.	3	1863–1871	Mineral Point
Coburn, Frank P	Dem.	7	1891–1893	West Salem
Cole, Orasmus	Whig	2	1849–1851	Potosi
Cook, Samuel A	Rep.	6	1895–1897	Neenah
Cooper, Henry Allen	Rep.	1	1893–1919; 1921–1931	Racine
Cornell, Robert J	Dem.	8	1975–1979	De Pere
Dahle, Herman B	Rep.	2	1899–1903	Mount Horeb
Darling, Mason C	Dem.	2	1848–1849	Fond du Lac
Davidson, James H	Rep.	6, 8	1897–1913; 1917–1918	Oshkosh
Davis, Glenn R	Rep.	2, 9	1947–1957; 1965–1975	Waukesha
Deuster, Peter V	Dem.	4	1879–1885	Milwaukee
Dilweg, La Vern R	Dem.	8	1943–1945	Green Bay
Doty, James D	Dem.	3	1849–1853	Neenah
Duffy, Sean P	Rep.	7	2011–2019	Wausau
Durkee, Charles	Free Soil	1	1849–1853	Kenosha
Eastman, Ben C	Dem.	2	1851–1855	Platteville
Eldredge, Charles A	Dem.	4, 5	1863–1875	Fond du Lac
Esch, John Jacob	Rep.	7	1899–1921	La Crosse
Fitzgerald, Scott	Rep.	5	2021–	Clyman
Flynn, Gerald T	Dem.	1	1959–1961	Racine
Frear, James A	Rep.	10, 9	1913–1935	Hudson
Froehlich, Harold V	Rep.	8	1973–1975	Appleton
Gallagher, Mike	Rep.	8	2017–	Allouez
Gehrmann, Bernard J	Prog.	10	1935–1943	Mellen
Green, Mark A	Rep.	8	1999–2007	Green Bay
Griffin, Michael	Rep.	7	1894–1899	Eau Claire
Griswold, Harry W	Rep.	3	1939–1941	West Salem
Grothman, Glenn	Rep.	6	2015–	Glenbeulah
Guenther, Richard W	Rep.	6, 2	1881–1889	Oshkosh
Gunderson, Steven	Rep.	3	1981–1997	Osseo
Hanchett, Luther	Rep.	2	1861–1862	Plover
Haugen, Nils P	Rep.	8, 10	1887–1895	Black River Falls
Hawkes, Charles, Jr	Rep.	2	1939–1941	Horicon
Hazelton, George C	Rep.	3	1877–1883	Boscobel
Hazelton, Gerry W	Rep.	2	1871–1875	Columbus
Henney, Charles W	Dem.	2	1933–1935	Portage
Henry, Robert K	Rep.	2	1945–1947	Jefferson
Hopkins, Benjamin F	Rep.	2	1867–1870	Madison
Hudd, Thomas R	Dem.	5	1886–1889	Green Bay

Wisconsin members of the U.S. House of Representatives since 1848, continued

	Party	District	Term	Residence
Hughes, James	Dem.	8	1933–1935	De Pere
Hull, Merlin	Prog.	7, 9	1929–1931; 1935–1953	Black River Falls
Humphrey, Herman L	Rep.	7	1877–1883	Hudson
Jenkins, John J	Rep.	10, 11	1895–1909	Chippewa Falls
Johns, Joshua L	Rep.	8	1939–1943	Appleton
Johnson, Jay	Dem.	8	1997–1999	New Franken
Johnson, Lester R.	Dem.	9	1953–1965	Black River Falls
Jones, Burr W	Dem.	3	1883–1885	Madison
Kading, Charles A.	Rep.	2	1927–1933	Watertown
Kagen, Steve.	Dem.	8	2007–2011	Appleton
Kasten, Robert W., Jr	Rep.	9	1975–1979	Waukesha
Kastenmeier, Robert W	Dem.	2	1959–1991	Sun Prairie
Keefe, Frank B	Rep.	6	1939–1951	Oshkosh
Kersten, Charles J.	Rep.	5	1947–1949; 1951–1955	Whitefish Bay
Kimball, Alanson M.	Rep.	6	1875–1877	Waushara
Kind, Ron.	Dem.	3	1997–	La Crosse
Kleczka, Gerald D	Dem.	4	1984–2005	Milwaukee
Kleczka, John C	Rep.	4	1919–1923	Milwaukee
Klug, Scott L	Rep.	2	1991–1999	Madison
Konop, Thomas F	Dem.	9	1911–1917	Kewaunee
Kopp, Arthur W	Rep.	3	1909–1913	Platteville
Kustermann, Gustav	Rep.	9	1907–1911	Green Bay
La Follette, Robert M., Sr	Rep.	3	1885–1891	Madison
Laird, Melvin R	Rep.	7	1953–1969	Marshfield
Lampert, Florian	Rep.	6	1918–1930	Oshkosh
Larrabee, Charles H	Dem.	3	1859–1861	Horicon
Lenroot, Irvine L	Rep.	11	1909–1918	Superior
Lynch, Thomas	Dem.	9	1891–1895	Antigo
Lynde, William Pitt	Dem.	1, 4	1848–1849; 1875–1879	Milwaukee
Macy, John B.	Dem.	3	1853–1855	Fond du Lac
Magoon, Henry S	Rep.	3	1875–1877	Darlington
McCord, Myron H.	Rep.	9	1889–1891	Merrill
McDill, Alexander S	Rep.	8	1873–1875	Plover
McIndoe, Walter D	Rep.	6	1863–1867	Wausau
McMurray, Howard J	Dem.	5	1943–1945	Milwaukee
Miller, Lucas M	Dem.	6	1891–1893	Oshkosh
Minor, Edward S	Rep.	8, 9	1895–1907	Sturgeon Bay
Mitchell, Alexander	Dem.	1, 4	1871–1875	Milwaukee
Mitchell, John L	Dem.	4	1891–1893	Milwaukee
Monahan, James G.	Rep.	3	1919–1921	Darlington
Moody, James P.	Dem.	5	1983–1993	Milwaukee
Moore, Gwen S	Dem.	4	2005–	Milwaukee
Morse, Elmer A	Rep.	10	1907–1913	Antigo
Murphy, James W.	Dem.	3	1907–1909	Platteville
Murray, Reid F.	Rep.	7	1939–1953	Ogdensburg
Nelson, Adolphus P	Rep.	11	1918–1923	Grantsburg
Nelson, John Mandt	Rep.	2, 3	1906–1919; 1921–1933	Madison
Neumann, Mark W	Rep.	1	1995–1999	Janesville
Obey, David R	Dem.	7	1969–2011	Wausau
O'Konski, Alvin E	Rep.	10	1943–1973	Mercer
O'Malley, Thomas D. P	Dem.	5	1933–1939	Milwaukee
Otjen, Theobald.	Rep.	4	1895–1907	Milwaukee
Paine, Halbert E.	Rep.	1	1865–1871	Milwaukee
Peavey, Hubert H	Rep.	11, 10	1923–1935	Washburn
Petri, Thomas E	Rep.	6	1979–2015	Fond du Lac
Pocan, Mark	Dem.	2	2013–	Black Earth
Potter, John F	Rep.	1	1857–1863	East Troy

Wisconsin members of the U.S. House of Representatives
since 1848, continued

	Party	District	Term	Residence
Pound, Thaddeus C.	Rep.	8	1877–1883	Chippewa Falls
Price, Hugh H	Rep.	8	1887	Black River Falls
Price, William T	Rep.	8	1883–1886	Black River Falls
Race, John A.	Dem.	6	1965–1967	Fond du Lac
Randall, Clifford E.	Rep.	1	1919–1921	Kenosha
Rankin, Joseph	Dem.	5	1883–1886	Manitowoc
Reilly, Michael K.	Dem.	6	1913–1917; 1930–1939	Fond du Lac
Reuss, Henry S.	Dem.	5	1955–1983	Milwaukee
Ribble, Reid J.	Rep.	8	2011–2017	Appleton
Roth, Toby	Rep.	8	1979–1997	Appleton
Rusk, Jeremiah M.	Rep.	6, 7	1871–1877	Viroqua
Ryan, Paul	Rep.	1	1999–2019	Janesville
Sauerhering, Edward	Rep.	2	1895–1899	Mayville
Sauthoff, Harry	Prog.	2	1935–1939; 1941–1945	Madison
Sawyer, Philetus	Rep.	5, 6	1865–1875	Oshkosh
Schadeberg, Henry C	Rep.	1	1961–1965; 1967–1971	Burlington
Schafer, John C	Rep.	4	1923–1933; 1939–1941	Milwaukee
Schneider, George J	Rep., Prog.	9, 8	1923–1933; 1935–1939	Appleton
Sensenbrenner, F. James, Jr.	Rep.	9, 5	1979–2021	Menomonee Falls
Shaw, George B	Rep.	7	1893–1894	Eau Claire
Sloan, A. Scott.	Rep.	3	1861–1863	Beaver Dam
Sloan, Ithamar C	Rep.	2	1863–1867	Janesville
Smith, Henry.	Union Labor	4	1887–1889	Milwaukee
Smith, Lawrence H	Rep.	1	1941–1959	Racine
Somers, Peter J	Dem.	4	1893–1895	Milwaukee
Stafford, William H	Rep.	5	1903–1911; 1913–1919; 1921–1923; 1929–1933	Milwaukee
Stalbaum, Lynn E	Dem.	1	1965–1967	Racine
Steiger, William A.	Rep.	6	1967–1978	Oshkosh
Steil, Bryan.	Rep.	1	2019–	Janesville
Stephenson, Isaac	Rep.	9	1883–1889	Marinette
Stevenson, William H	Rep.	3	1941–1949	La Crosse
Stewart, Alexander.	Rep.	9	1895–1901	Wausau
Sumner, Daniel H.	Dem.	2	1883–1885	Waukesha
Tewes, Donald E	Rep.	2	1957–1959	Waukesha
Thill, Lewis D.	Rep.	5	1939–1943	Milwaukee
Thomas, Ormsby B	Rep.	7	1885–1891	Prairie du Chien
Thomson, Vernon W	Rep.	3	1961–1975	Richland Center
Tiffany, Tom	Rep	7	2020–	Minocqua
Van Pelt, William K	Rep.	6	1951–1963	Fond du Lac
Van Schaick, Isaac W	Rep.	4	1885–1887; 1889–1891	Milwaukee
Voigt, Edward	Rep.	2	1917–1927	Sheboygan
Washburn, Cadwallader C	Rep.	2 6	1855–1861; 1867–1871	Mineral Point, La Crosse
Wasielewski, Thaddeus F	Dem.	4	1941–1947	Milwaukee
Weisse, Charles H.	Dem.	6	1903–1911	Sheboygan Falls
Wells, Daniel, Jr	Dem.	1	1853–1857	Milwaukee
Wells, Owen A.	Dem.	6	1893–1895	Fond du Lac
Wheeler, Ezra	Dem.	5	1863–1865	Berlin
Williams, Charles G.	Rep.	1	1873–1883	Janesville
Winans, John	Dem.	1	1883–1885	Janesville
Withrow, Gardner R	Rep., Prog.	7, 3	1931–1939; 1949–1961	La Crosse
Woodward, Gilbert M	Dem.	7	1883–1885	La Crosse
Zablocki, Clement J	Dem.	4	1949–1983	Milwaukee

Dem.–Democrat; Prog.–Progressive; Rep.–Republican; Soc.–Socialist.

Sources: Wisconsin Legislative Reference Bureau, *Wisconsin Blue Book*, various editions; *Congressional Quarterly, Guide to U.S. Elections*, 1985; and official election records.

Wisconsin members of the U.S. House of Representatives since 1941, by district

District		Party	Term	Residence
1	Lawrence H. Smith	Rep.	1941–1959	Racine
	Gerald T. Flynn	Dem.	1959–1961	Racine
	Henry C. Schadeberg	Rep.	1961–1965; 1967–1971	Burlington
	Lynn E. Stalbaum	Dem.	1965–1967	Racine
	Les Aspin[1]	Dem.	1971–1993	East Troy
	Peter W. Barca[1]	Dem.	1993–1995	Kenosha
	Mark W. Neumann	Rep.	1995–1999	Janesville
	Paul Ryan	Rep.	1999–2019	Janesville
	Bryan Steil	Rep.	2019–	Janesville
2	Harry Sauthoff	Prog.	1941–1945	Madison
	Robert K. Henry	Rep.	1945–1947	Jefferson
	Glenn R. Davis	Rep.	1947–1957	Waukesha
	Donald E. Tewes	Rep.	1957–1959	Waukesha
	Robert W. Kastenmeier	Dem.	1959–1991	Sun Prairie
	Scott L. Klug	Rep.	1991–1999	Madison
	Tammy Baldwin	Dem.	1999–2013	Madison
	Mark Pocan	Dem.	2013–	Black Earth
3	William H. Stevenson	Rep.	1941–1949	La Crosse
	Gardner R. Withrow	Rep.	1949–1961	La Crosse
	Vernon W. Thomson	Rep.	1961–1975	Richland Center
	Alvin Baldus	Dem.	1975–1981	Menomonie
	Steven Gunderson	Rep.	1981–1997	Osseo
	Ron Kind	Dem.	1997–	La Crosse
4[3]	Thaddeus F. Wasielewski	Dem.	1941–1947	Milwaukee
	John C. Brophy	Rep.	1947–1949	Milwaukee
	Clement J. Zablocki[2]	Dem.	1949–1983	Milwaukee
	Gerald D. Kleczka[2]	Dem.	1984–2005	Milwaukee
	Gwen S. Moore	Dem.	2005–	Milwaukee
5[3]	Howard J. McMurray	Dem.	1943–1945	Milwaukee
	Andrew J. Biemiller	Dem.	1945–1947; 1949–1951	Milwaukee
	Charles J. Kersten	Rep.	1947–1949; 1951–1955	Whitefish Bay
	Henry S. Reuss	Dem.	1955–1983	Milwaukee
	James P. Moody	Dem.	1983–1993	Milwaukee
	Thomas M. Barrett	Dem.	1993–2003	Milwaukee
	F. James Sensenbrenner, Jr.	Rep.	2003–2021	Menomonee Falls
	Scott Fitzgerald	Rep.	2021–	Clyman
6	Frank B. Keefe	Rep.	1939–1951	Oshkosh
	William K. Van Pelt	Rep.	1951–1965	Fond du Lac
	John A. Race	Dem.	1965–1967	Fond du Lac
	William A. Steiger[4]	Rep.	1967–1978	Oshkosh
	Thomas E. Petri[4]	Rep.	1979–2015	Fond du Lac
	Glenn Grothman	Rep.	2015–	Glenbeulah
7	Reid F. Murray	Rep.	1939–1953	Ogdensburg
	Melvin R. Laird[5]	Rep.	1953–1969	Marshfield
	David R. Obey[5]	Dem.	1969–2011	Wausau
	Sean P. Duffy[6]	Rep.	2011–2019	Wausau
	Tom Tiffany[6]	Rep.	2020–	Minocqua
8	La Vern R. Dilweg	Dem.	1943–1945	Green Bay
	John R. Byrnes	Rep.	1945–1973	Green Bay
	Harold V. Froehlich	Rep.	1973–1975	Appleton
	Robert J. Cornell	Dem.	1975–1979	De Pere
	Toby Roth	Rep.	1979–1997	Appleton
	Jay Johnson	Dem.	1997–1999	New Franken
	Mark A. Green	Rep.	1999–2007	Green Bay

Wisconsin members of the U.S. House of Representatives since 1941, by district, continued

District		Party	Term	Residence
	Steve Kagen	Dem.	2007–2011	Appleton
	Reid J. Ribble	Rep.	2011–2017	Appleton
	Mike Gallagher	Rep.	2017–	Allouez
9[3,7] . . .	Merlin Hull	Prog.	1935–1953	Black River Falls
	Lester R. Johnson	Dem.	1953–1965	Black River Falls
	Glenn R. Davis	Rep.	1965–1975	Waukesha
	Robert W. Kasten	Rep.	1975–1979	Thiensville
	F. James Sensenbrenner, Jr.	Rep.	1979–2003	Menomonee Falls
10[8]	Alvin E. O'Konski	Rep.	1943–1973	Rhinelander

Dem.–Democrat; Prog.–Progressive; Rep.–Republican.

1. Aspin resigned 1/20/1993, to become U.S. Secretary of Defense. Barca was elected in a special election, 5/4/1993.
2. Zablocki died 12/3/1983. Kleczka was elected in a special election, 4/3/1984.   3. In the congressional reapportionment following the 2000 census, Wisconsin's delegation was reduced from nine to eight members. The previous 4th, 5th, and 9th districts were reconfigured into the new 4th and 5th districts.   4. Steiger died 12/4/1978, following his November 1978 election. Petri was elected in a special election, 4/3/1979.   5. Laird resigned 1/21/1969, to become U.S. Secretary of Defense. Obey was elected in a special election, 4/1/1969.   6. Duffy resigned 9/23/2019. Tiffany was elected in a special election, 5/12/2020.   7. In the congressional redistricting following the 1960 census, the previous 9th District in western Wisconsin ceased to exist and a new 9th District was created in the Waukesha-Milwaukee metropolitan area.   8. In the congressional reapportionment following the 1970 census, Wisconsin's delegation was reduced from ten members to nine members.

Sources: 1944 *Wisconsin Blue Book* and Wisconsin Legislative Reference Bureau records.

POPULATION AND POLITICAL SUBDIVISIONS

Wisconsin population since 1840

Year	Population	% increase	Rural	Urban (%)[1]	Density[2]
1840	30,945	X	30,945	—	0.6
1850	305,391	886.9	276,768	28,623 (9.4)	5.6
1860	775,881	154.1	664,007	111,874 (14.4)	14.1
1870	1,054,670	35.9	847,471	207,099 (19.6)	19.2
1880	1,315,497	24.7	998,293	317,204 (24.1)	24.0
1890	1,693,330	28.7	1,131,044	562,286 (33.2)	30.9
1900	2,069,042	22.2	1,278,829	790,213 (38.2)	37.4
1910	2,333,860	12.8	1,329,540	1,004,320 (43.0)	42.6
1920	2,632,067	12.8	1,387,209	1,244,858 (47.3)	47.6
1930	2,939,006	11.7	1,385,163	1,553,843 (52.9)	53.0
1940	3,137,587	6.7	1,458,443	1,679,144 (53.5)	57.3
1950	3,434,575	9.5	1,446,687	1,987,888 (57.9)	62.7
1960	3,951,777	15.1	1,429,598	2,522,179 (63.8)	72.2
1970	4,417,821	11.8	1,507,313	2,910,418 (65.9)	81.3
1980	4,705,642	6.5	1,685,035	3,020,732 (64.2)	86.6
1990	4,891,769	4.0	1,679,813	3,211,956 (65.7)	90.1
2000	5,363,715	9.6	1,700,032	3,663,643 (68.3)	98.8
2010	5,686,986	6.0	1,697,348	3,989,638 (70.2)	105.0

—Represents zero; X–Not applicable.

1. The "urban" definition was revised beginning with the 1950 census.   2. Population per square mile of land area.

Sources: U.S. Department of Commerce, U.S. Census Bureau; Wisconsin Department of Administration, Demographic Services Center, *Time Series of The Final Official Population Estimates and Census Counts for Wisconsin Counties*, October 10, 2016.

Wisconsin population by race, 1890 to 2019

Year	Total	White (%)	Black (%)	American Indian[1] (%)	Asian[2] (%)	Some other race (%)	Two or more races[3] (%)
1890	1,693,330	1,680,828 (99.3)	2,444 (0.1)	9,930 (0.6)	128 (Z)	—	X
1900	2,069,042	2,057,911 (99.5)	2,542 (0.1)	8,372 (0.4)	217 (Z)	—	X
1910	2,333,860	2,320,555 (99.4)	2,900 (0.1)	10,142 (0.4)	260 (Z)	3 (Z)	X
1920	2,632,067	2,616,938 (99.4)	5,201 (0.2)	9,611 (0.4)	314 (Z)	3 (Z)	X
1930	2,939,006	2,916,255 (99.2)	10,739 (0.4)	11,548 (0.4)	451 (Z)	13 (Z)	X
1940	3,137,587	3,112,752 (99.2)	12,158 (0.4)	12,265 (0.4)	388 (Z)	24 (Z)	X
1950	3,434,575	3,392,690 (98.8)	28,182 (0.8)	12,196 (0.4)	1,119 (Z)	388 (Z)	X
1960	3,951,777	3,858,903 (97.6)	74,546 (1.9)	14,297 (0.4)	2,836 (0.1)	1,195 (Z)	X
1970[4]	4,417,933	4,258,959 (96.4)	128,224 (2.9)	18,924 (0.4)	6,557 (0.2)	5,067 (0.1)	X
1980[4]	4,705,642	4,443,035 (94.4)	182,592 (3.9)	29,320 (0.6)	22,043 (0.3)	41,788 (0.9)	X
1990	4,891,769	4,512,523 (92.2)	244,539 (5.0)	39,387 (0.8)	53,583 (1.2)	42,538 (0.9)	X
2000	5,363,675	4,769,857 (88.9)	304,460 (5.7)	47,228 (0.9)	90,393 (1.7)	84,842 (1.6)	66,895 (1.2)
2010	5,686,986	4,902,067 (86.2)	359,148 (6.3)	54,526 (1.0)	131,061 (2.3)	135,867 (2.4)	104,317 (1.8)
2019	5,822,434	4,963,354 (85.2)	374,747 (6.4)	54,577 (0.9)	171,640 (3.0)	121,082 (2.1)	137,034 (2.4)

Note: Wisconsin's total population (census data by year) for Hispanic or Latino origins is as follows: 1970–62,875; 1980–62,782; 1990–93,194; 2000–192,921; 2010–336,056; 2019-412,769. The 1990 data on Hispanic/Spanish origin are generally comparable with those for the 1980 Census, but not the 1970 Census. Starting in the 2000 Census, "Hispanic or Latino Origin" represents ethnicity and includes people of Cuban, Mexican, Puerto Rican, South or Central American, or other Spanish culture or origin, regardless of race.

Z–Less than 0.1%; —Represents zero; X–Not applicable.

1. Aleut and Eskimo populations included beginning in 1960. 2. Native Hawaiian and other Pacific Islanders are grouped with Asian. 3. Beginning with the 2000 Census, individuals were allowed to select more than one race. 4. Total has been corrected by the U.S. Census Bureau. Details not adjusted to revised total.

Sources: U.S. Census Bureau, decennial census data and *2019 American Community Survey 1-Year Estimates, ACS Demographic and Housing Estimates*, September 2020.

Wisconsin population by race, 2019

	Total	Percent
One race	5,685,400	97.6
White	4,963,354	85.2
Black or African American	374,747	6.4
American Indian and Alaska Native	54,577	0.9
Asian	167,420	2.9
Asian Indian	36,049	0.6
Chinese	22,622	0.4
Filipino	12,668	0.2
Japanese	2,893	0
Korean	7,999	0.1
Vietnamese	6,660	0.1
Other Asian[1]	78,529	1.3
Native Hawaiian and Other Pacific Islander	4,220	0.1
Native Hawaiian	1,191	0
Guamanian or Chamorro	533	0
Samoan	510	0
Other Pacific Islander[2]	1,986	0
Some other race	121,082	2.1
Two or more races	137,034	2.4

1. Other Asian alone, or two or more Asian categories. 2. Other Pacific Islander alone, or two or more Native Hawaiian and Other Pacific Islander categories.

Source: U.S. Census Bureau, *2019 American Community Survey 1-Year Estimates, ACS Demographic and Housing Estimates*, September 2020.

Wisconsin population by Hispanic and non-Hispanic origin, 2019

	Total	Percent
Not Hispanic or Latino[1]	5,409,665	92.9
One race	5,296,607	91
White	4,704,609	80.8
Black or African American	366,735	6.3
American Indian and Alaska Native	49,093	0.8
Asian	166,443	2.9
Native Hawaiian and Other Pacific Islander	3,903	0.1
Some other race	5,824	0.1
Two or more races	113,058	1.9
Hispanic or Latino[1] (of any race)	412,769	7.1
Mexican	290,079	5
Puerto Rican	64,506	1.1
Cuban	5,412	0.1
Other Hispanic or Latino	52,772	0.9

1. "Hispanic or Latino" refers to a person of Cuban, Mexican, Puerto Rican, South or Central American, or other Spanish culture or origin regardless of race.

Source: U.S. Census Bureau, *2019 American Community Survey 1-Year Estimates, ACS Demographic and Housing Estimates*, September 2020.

Wisconsin 2010 census by sex, race, and Hispanic origin

County	Total population	Male	Female	White	Black or African American	American Indian/ Alaska Native	Asian or Pacific Islander	Some other race	Two or more races	Hispanic origin (any race)
Adams . . .	20,875	11,221	9,654	19,409	633	205	86	266	276	783
Ashland. . .	16,157	8,082	8,075	13,662	48	1,791	63	56	537	302
Barron. . . .	45,870	22,814	23,056	44,076	407	406	226	236	519	862
Bayfield . . .	15,014	7,716	7,298	13,024	46	1,435	49	29	431	158
Brown. . . .	248,007	122,658	125,349	214,415	5,491	6,715	6,828	9,155	5,403	17,985
Buffalo . . .	13,587	6,859	6,728	13,253	37	38	28	122	109	237
Burnett . . .	15,457	7,806	7,651	14,163	81	718	55	67	373	194
Calumet . .	48,971	24,543	24,428	46,187	246	203	1,047	705	583	1,690
Chippewa . .	62,415	32,404	30,011	59,504	982	310	788	182	649	800
Clark.	34,690	17,577	17,113	33,338	80	174	135	773	190	1,292
Columbia. .	56,833	28,935	27,898	54,468	717	277	330	441	600	1,444
Crawford . .	16,644	8,575	8,069	16,080	296	39	66	36	127	150
Dane	488,073	241,411	246,662	413,631	25,347	1,730	23,201	12,064	12,100	28,925
Dodge . . .	88,759	46,679	42,080	83,294	2,381	385	513	1,309	877	3,522
Door.	27,785	13,679	14,106	26,839	144	162	116	249	275	671
Douglas. . .	44,159	22,087	22,072	41,166	486	868	384	82	1,173	494
Dunn	43,857	22,133	21,724	41,545	220	168	1,158	228	538	626
Eau Claire. .	98,736	48,351	50,385	91,946	874	471	3,328	519	1,598	1,804
Florence . .	4,423	2,262	2,161	4,306	10	31	14	14	48	37
Fond du Lac	101,633	49,926	51,707	95,674	1,305	471	1,169	1,700	1,314	4,368
Forest	9,304	4,724	4,580	7,690	76	1,256	24	32	226	138
Grant	51,208	26,636	24,572	49,655	588	103	317	221	324	649
Green	36,842	18,241	18,601	35,593	140	65	209	490	345	1,033
Green Lake	19,051	9,509	9,542	18,428	88	52	91	268	124	743
Iowa	23,687	11,878	11,809	23,127	87	36	134	102	201	336
Iron	5,916	2,959	2,957	5,790	3	36	18	13	56	35
Jackson . . .	20,449	10,874	9,575	18,258	400	1,271	73	144	303	519
Jefferson . .	83,686	41,638	42,048	78,632	681	257	578	2,479	1,059	5,555
Juneau . . .	26,664	14,029	12,635	25,077	557	398	122	188	322	687
Kenosha . .	166,426	82,444	83,982	139,416	11,052	814	2,482	7,880	4,782	19,592
Kewaunee .	20,574	10,460	10,114	19,955	69	77	65	219	189	463
La Crosse. .	114,638	55,961	58,677	105,540	1,610	493	4,770	371	1,854	1,741
Lafayette . .	16,836	8,582	8,254	16,292	39	48	58	303	96	522
Langlade . .	19,977	10,032	9,945	19,267	72	191	63	100	284	324
Lincoln . . .	28,743	14,412	14,331	27,929	157	100	134	131	292	340
Manitowoc	81,442	40,489	40,953	76,402	442	450	2,060	1,069	1,019	2,565
Marathon. .	134,063	67,308	66,755	122,446	841	634	7,178	1,223	1,741	2,992
Marinette. .	41,749	20,758	20,991	40,559	108	238	227	176	441	522
Marquette .	15,404	7,808	7,596	14,920	77	86	68	126	127	391
Menominee	4,232	2,098	2,134	451	19	3,701	1	6	54	178
Milwaukee .	947,735	457,717	490,018	574,656	253,764	6,808	32,785	51,429	28,293	126,039
Monroe . . .	44,673	22,648	22,025	41,940	512	510	329	764	618	1,661
Oconto . . .	37,660	19,194	18,466	36,418	73	467	116	198	388	519
Oneida . . .	35,998	17,993	18,005	34,787	152	323	193	82	461	385
Outagamie	176,695	88,130	88,565	161,238	1,736	2,982	5,294	2,728	2,717	6,359
Ozaukee . .	86,395	42,340	44,055	82,010	1,177	208	1,529	483	988	1,956
Pepin	7,469	3,780	3,689	7,337	21	19	14	35	43	72
Pierce	41,019	20,420	20,599	39,614	232	151	308	201	513	623
Polk	44,205	22,177	22,028	42,807	96	454	166	226	456	656
Portage. . .	70,019	34,984	35,035	65,981	383	265	1,983	546	861	1,853
Price	14,159	7,180	6,979	13,750	39	54	126	42	148	153

Wisconsin 2010 census by sex, race, and Hispanic origin, continued

County	Total popu- lation	Male	Female	White	Black or African Amer- ican	Amer- ican Indian/ Alaska Native	Asian or Pacific Islander	Some other race	Two or more races	Hispanic origin (any race)
Racine. . . .	195,408	96,771	98,637	155,731	21,767	781	2,174	10,046	4,909	22,546
Richland . .	18,021	9,042	8,979	17,540	82	46	99	119	135	360
Rock.	160,331	78,815	81,516	140,513	7,978	516	1,669	5,948	3,707	12,124
Rusk	14,755	7,371	7,384	14,398	61	74	42	37	143	173
St. Croix. . .	84,345	42,218	42,127	80,914	552	313	923	483	1,160	1,692
Sauk.	61,976	30,848	31,128	58,588	357	769	350	1,156	756	2,675
Sawyer . . .	16,557	8,393	8,164	13,123	77	2,757	49	42	509	268
Shawano . .	41,949	20,921	21,028	37,254	143	3,172	193	366	821	905
Sheboygan	115,507	58,010	57,497	103,861	1,684	444	5,345	2,297	1,876	6,329
Taylor	20,689	10,559	10,130	20,248	58	43	64	128	148	316
Trempealeau	28,816	14,638	14,178	27,230	62	63	127	1,086	248	1,667
Vernon . . .	29,773	14,854	14,919	29,085	109	61	99	145	274	394
Vilas	21,430	10,861	10,569	18,658	35	2,370	62	45	260	268
Walworth. .	102,228	51,237	50,991	93,935	980	308	888	4,604	1,513	10,578
Washburn .	15,911	7,924	7,987	15,343	36	186	65	49	232	208
Washington	131,887	65,393	66,494	126,317	1,155	401	1,445	1,052	1,517	3,385
Waukesha .	389,891	191,355	198,536	363,963	4,914	1,066	10,852	4,041	5,055	16,123
Waupaca . .	52,410	26,447	25,963	50,916	154	258	200	425	457	1,307
Waushara. .	24,496	12,893	11,603	23,012	454	131	108	509	282	1,329
Winnebago	166,994	83,952	83,042	154,445	2,975	1,036	3,880	2,188	2,470	5,784
Wood	74,749	36,777	37,972	71,048	393	587	1,328	593	800	1,680
Total.	**5,686,986**	**2,822,400**	**2,864,586**	**4,902,067**	**359,148**	**54,526**	**131,061**	**135,867**	**104,317**	**336,056**

Sources: U.S. Department of Commerce, U.S. Census Bureau, P.L. 94-171 Redistricting File, processed by Wisconsin Demographic Services Center and the Applied Population Laboratory of UW-Madison, May 2011.

Wisconsin American Indian population

Year	Total	Male	Female
1900.	8,372	4,321	4,051
1910.	10,142	5,231	4,911
1920.	9,611	4,950	4,661
1930.	11,548	5,951	5,597
1940.	12,265	6,354	5,911
1950.	12,196	6,274	5,922
1960.	14,297	7,195	7,102
1970.	18,924	9,251	9,673
1980.	29,320	14,489	14,831
1990.	38,986	19,240	19,746
2000[1].	47,228	23,462	23,766
2010.	54,526	27,212	27,314
2019.	51,392	26,632	24,760

1. Beginning with the 2000 Census, individuals were allowed to select more than one race.

Source: U.S. Census Bureau, *2015–2019 American Community Survey*, 2010 Census Summary File 1, July 2011, and prior issues.

Wisconsin voting age population

County	2020 estimate	2010 census	White	Black/ African American	American Indian/ Alaska Native	Asian	Pacific Islander	Some other	Two or more	2010 Hispanic or Latino
Adams . . .	17,531	17,454	15,935	598	203	90	6	8	26	588
Ashland. . .	12,356	12,413	10,718	39	1,416	44	4	7	18	167
Barron. . . .	36,726	35,720	34,325	291	392	177	7	10	24	494
Bayfield. . .	12,578	12,161	10,812	22	1,170	43	4	9	10	91
Brown. . . .	201,194	186,184	162,483	3,705	5,076	4,470	92	96	196	10,066
Buffalo . . .	10,777	10,566	10,306	18	60	26	1	17	2	136
Burnett . . .	12,577	12,375	11,496	46	660	41	6	8	11	107
Calumet . .	38,832	35,733	33,709	167	248	665	12	15	16	901
Chippewa . .	50,621	47,706	45,395	864	361	535	11	11	26	503
Clark.	24,951	24,599	23,527	52	141	87	10	3	9	770
Columbia. .	44,385	43,566	41,505	621	270	247	27	15	16	865
Crawford . .	13,127	12,920	12,441	247	68	47	6	5	10	96
Dane	430,627	381,989	324,503	17,235	1,901	18,629	189	450	845	18,237
Dodge . . .	71,108	69,180	63,961	2,241	441	369	38	30	46	2,054
Door.	23,850	22,709	21,902	92	196	89	4	7	18	401
Douglas. . .	35,235	34,694	32,579	376	1,047	336	14	20	38	284
Dunn	36,000	34,798	33,112	200	225	786	16	13	38	408
Eau Claire. .	83,076	77,864	73,172	653	572	2,232	35	40	82	1,078
Florence . .	3,738	3,649	3,560	7	41	20	2	—	—	19
Fond du Lac	81,869	78,589	73,638	937	549	754	23	34	57	2,597
Forest	7,265	7,261	6,222	58	863	13	15	3	8	79
Grant	42,052	40,322	38,922	513	140	265	6	13	21	442
Green	28,354	27,889	26,912	101	83	140	8	15	14	616
Green Lake	14,964	14,663	14,027	57	65	63	5	3	13	430
Iowa.	18,219	17,798	17,377	58	63	100	8	12	8	172
Iron	4,999	4,935	4,845	5	48	15	—	—	4	18
Jackson . . .	16,332	15,818	14,148	379	878	46	19	8	15	325
Jefferson . .	65,444	63,829	59,160	502	318	470	16	32	40	3,291
Juneau . . .	21,764	20,991	19,592	513	343	94	4	8	9	428
Kenosha . .	128,473	123,597	101,744	7,217	769	2,031	80	144	255	11,357
Kewaunee .	16,058	15,725	15,256	49	102	40	5	14	14	245
La Crosse. .	95,802	90,176	83,999	1,149	576	3,172	33	58	100	1,089
Lafayette . .	12,778	12,487	12,053	18	53	37	—	—	4	322
Langlade . .	16,051	15,762	15,264	58	213	51	2	4	4	166
Lincoln . . .	22,811	22,441	21,916	63	136	104	15	16	9	182
Manitowoc	64,026	63,232	59,800	272	439	1,247	25	33	50	1,366
Marathon. .	104,986	101,194	94,081	527	625	4,105	43	41	97	1,675
Marinette. .	33,217	33,182	32,221	85	293	203	18	15	17	330
Marquette .	12,475	12,319	11,900	57	93	51	—	4	3	211
Menominee	2,916	2,853	423	10	2,338	1	—	—	1	80
Milwaukee .	718,676	711,358	433,061	168,280	5,644	23,660	331	790	2,476	77,116
Monroe . . .	35,104	33,003	31,038	366	420	229	34	13	22	881
Oconto . . .	30,526	29,228	28,308	50	450	95	5	12	11	297
Oneida . . .	29,990	29,359	28,454	134	373	150	16	7	10	215
Outagamie	142,423	132,271	121,384	1,180	2,390	3,410	60	65	119	3,663
Ozaukee . .	70,211	66,023	62,520	878	239	1,123	26	32	65	1,140
Pepin	5,780	5,765	5,658	13	24	15	2	4	2	47
Pierce	33,425	31,860	30,766	187	185	280	6	17	17	402
Polk	34,491	33,705	32,677	77	394	119	5	23	26	384
Portage. . .	57,458	55,472	52,322	325	309	1,325	20	31	49	1,091
Price	11,631	11,460	11,164	13	103	52	36	7	1	84
Racine. . . .	149,276	146,898	115,625	15,037	867	1,693	54	113	220	13,289
Richland . .	14,020	13,821	13,417	52	65	67	2	8	5	205
Rock.	121,645	120,148	105,720	5,460	646	1,331	54	80	135	6,722

The header note: 2010 not Hispanic or Latino,[1] by race

Wisconsin voting age population, continued

County	2020 estimate	2010 census	White	Black/ African American	American Indian/ Alaska Native	Asian	Pacific Islander	Some other	Two or more	2010 Hispanic or Latino
					2010 not Hispanic or Latino,[1] by race					
Rusk	11,698	11,440	11,158	28	97	40	2	1	6	108
St. Croix. . .	67,190	61,462	59,021	394	358	638	19	36	44	952
Sauk	48,903	47,209	44,473	254	557	292	13	30	30	1,560
Sawyer . . .	13,568	13,103	10,799	64	2,046	38	2	5	5	144
Shawano . .	32,670	32,387	29,227	84	2,371	155	18	4	25	503
Sheboygan	90,260	87,925	79,347	1,305	499	3,064	32	48	78	3,552
Taylor	15,893	15,600	15,269	27	65	48	7	3	6	175
Trempealeau	23,093	21,831	20,622	40	71	95	3	5	7	988
Vernon . . .	22,723	21,895	21,414	76	89	75	7	8	12	214
Vilas	18,151	17,621	15,816	33	1,533	66	3	9	4	157
Walworth. .	80,846	78,228	70,164	769	352	682	34	35	56	6,136
Washburn .	12,923	12,679	12,231	22	246	46	2	2	7	123
Washington	105,707	99,510	95,331	765	414	1,022	22	51	66	1,839
Waukesha .	313,146	296,081	273,899	3,256	1,160	7,769	112	143	256	9,486
Waupaca . .	40,890	40,540	39,216	111	303	152	7	9	10	732
Waushara. .	19,884	19,662	18,231	440	158	82	9	6	1	735
Winnebago	134,905	130,862	121,239	2,336	1,105	2,655	58	62	132	3,275
Wood	59,043	57,745	55,161	240	503	857	16	17	30	921
Total.	4,536,293	4,347,494	3,753,673	242,398	47,511	93,260	1,826	2,897	6,107	199,822

Note: The voting age population is 18 and older.

—Represents zero.

1. "Hispanic or Latino" represents ethnicity and includes people of Cuban, Mexican, Puerto Rican, South or Central American, or other Spanish culture or origin, regardless of race.

Sources: U.S. Census Bureau, P.L. 94–171 Redistricting File, as processed by the Wisconsin Legislative Technology Services Bureau, May 2011; Wisconsin Department of Administration, Demographic Services Center, *Official Final Estimates, 1/1/2020, Wisconsin Counties, with Comparison to Census 2010*, October 2020.

Wisconsin population by age group

Age (years)	Male 2010 census	Male 2019 estimate	Female 2010 census	Female 2019 estimate	Total 2010 census	Total 2019 estimate
Under 5.	183,391	168,701	175,052	161,795	358,443	330,496
5–9.	188,286	177,736	180,331	169,504	368,617	347,240
10–14	192,232	187,556	183,695	179,235	375,927	366,791
15–19	204,803	192,751	194,406	184,817	399,209	377,568
20–24	196,897	198,773	189,655	191,799	386,552	390,572
25–29	189,349	195,545	182,998	184,099	372,347	379,644
30–34	178,120	184,962	171,227	176,616	349,347	361,578
35–39	174,619	188,602	170,709	184,899	345,328	373,501
40–44	191,738	172,101	188,600	167,473	380,338	339,574
45–49	218,539	172,582	219,088	170,402	437,627	342,984
50–54	218,303	186,105	217,823	186,120	436,126	372,225
55–59	192,952	208,601	193,034	213,639	385,986	422,240
60–64	155,756	197,840	158,069	202,938	313,825	400,778
65–69	109,168	165,387	117,861	173,229	227,029	338,616
70–74	81,067	123,090	92,400	133,042	173,467	256,132
75–79	62,181	80,196	79,071	95,092	141,252	175,288

Wisconsin population by age group, continued

Age (years)	Male 2010 census	Male 2019 estimate	Female 2010 census	Female 2019 estimate	Total 2010 census	Total 2019 estimate
80–84	47,549	51,385	69,512	67,513	117,061	118,898
85 and over	37,450	45,296	81,055	83,013	118,505	128,309
All ages.	**2,822,400**	**2,897,209**	**2,864,586**	**2,925,225**	**5,686,986**	**5,822,434**

Note: The median age was 38.5 in 2010 and 39.8 in 2019. The median age for males was 37.3 in 2010 and 38.8 in 2019. The median age for females was 39.6 in 2010 and 40.9 in 2019.

Source: U.S. Census Bureau, Population Division, *Annual Estimates of the Resident Population for Selected Age Groups by Sex for the United States, States, Counties and Puerto Rico Commonwealth and Municipios: April 1, 2010 to July 1, 2019*, June 2020.

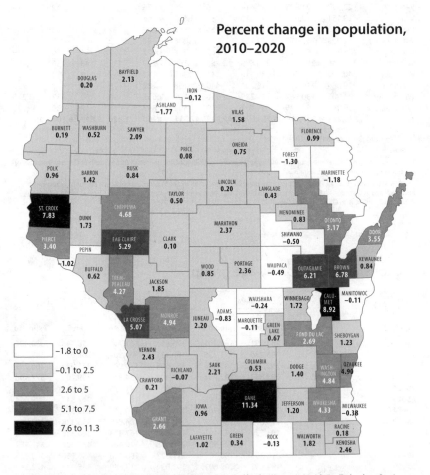

Percent change in population, 2010–2020

Sources: U.S. Census Bureau, P.L. 94–171 Redistricting File, as processed by the Wisconsin Legislative Technology Services Bureau, May 2011; Wisconsin Department of Administration, Demographic Services Center, Official Final Estimate, 1/1/2020 Wisconsin Counties, with Comparison to Census 2010, October 2020.

Wisconsin births, 2019

County	Births	County	Births	County	Births
Adams	161	Iron	38	Price	101
Ashland	157	Jackson	262	Racine	2,333
Barron	473	Jefferson	764	Richland	163
Bayfield	113	Juneau	245	Rock	1,832
Brown	3,104	Kenosha	1,836	Rusk	136
Buffalo	112	Kewaunee	183	St. Croix	992
Burnett	106	La Crosse	1,124	Sauk	747
Calumet	481	Lafayette	221	Sawyer	138
Chippewa	661	Langlade	211	Shawano	426
Clark	582	Lincoln	244	Sheboygan	1,199
Columbia	570	Manitowoc	780	Taylor	218
Crawford	159	Marathon	1,515	Trempealeau	389
Dane	5,765	Marinette	349	Vernon	423
Dodge	749	Marquette	153	Vilas	181
Door	196	Menominee	84	Walworth	945
Douglas	413	Milwaukee	13,062	Washburn	135
Dunn	417	Monroe	551	Washington	1,285
Eau Claire	1,111	Oconto	380	Waukesha	3,724
Florence	30	Oneida	302	Waupaca	544
Fond du Lac	1,023	Outagamie	2,228	Waushara	201
Forest	93	Ozaukee	838	Winnebago	1,741
Grant	567	Pepin	86	Wood	787
Green	331	Pierce	372	**Total**	**63,280**
Green Lake	194	Polk	377		
Iowa	236	Portage	618		

Note: Wisconsin resident births are reported by mother's county of residence. Total includes 13 births in unspecified counties.
Source: Wisconsin Department of Health Services, Division of Public Health, Office of Health Informatics departmental data.

Wisconsin deaths and death rates, 2018

Age (years)	Total		Male		Female	
	Deaths	Rate[1]	Deaths	Rate[1]	Deaths	Rate[1]
0–4	458	711.0	269	814.4	189	602.2
5–9	27	10.1	14	10.2	13	9.9
10–14	60	17.2	30	16.9	30	17.6
15–17	73	19.9	48	25.5	25	13.9
18–19	84	37.5	62	54.3	22	20.1
20–24	304	199.5	224	287.8	80	107.3
25–29	458	116.4	321	160.8	137	70.7
30–34	514	138.1	354	184.3	160	88.9
35–39	570	158.1	377	205.8	193	108.8
40–44	598	161.9	401	214.7	197	108.0
45–49	1,005	303.7	631	377.3	374	228.6
50–54	1,546	441.3	949	538.3	597	343.0
55–59	2,665	695.6	1,637	856.8	1,028	535.3
60–64	3,589	847.3	2,230	1,064.2	1,359	635.0
65–69	4,324	1,100.8	2,570	1,325.6	1,754	881.7
70–74	5,165	1,577.0	2,913	1,818.4	2,252	1,346.0
75–79	5,848	2,424.4	3,224	2,783.7	2,624	2,092.5
80–84	7,040	4,183.9	3,510	4,575.5	3,530	3,855.8

Wisconsin deaths and death rates, 2018, continued

Age (years)	Total Deaths	Total Rate[1]	Male Deaths	Male Rate[1]	Female Deaths	Female Rate[1]
85–89	8,276	7,164.2	3,738	7,499.1	4,538	6,910.0
90–94	7,069	5,523.6	2,641	5,934.4	4,428	5,304.5
All ages[2]	53,680	928.6	27,165	944.8	26,515	912.4

1. Per 100,000 population in the age group. 2. Includes ages 95 and higher.

Source: Wisconsin Department of Health Services, Division of Public Health, Office of Health Informatics, *Annual Wisconsin Death Report, 2018*, P-01170-20, December 2020.

Wisconsin mortality rates, 2018

County	Deaths	Mortality rate[1]	County	Deaths	Mortality rate[1]
Adams	266	78.7	Marathon.	1,261	71.7
Ashland.	204	98.3	Marinette.	555	76.8
Barron.	553	73.5	Marquette	210	84.4
Bayfield	178	68.8	Menominee	45	95.9
Brown.	2,059	70.6	Milwaukee	8,684	86.8
Buffalo	130	64.4	Monroe	443	77.2
Burnett	199	77.4	Oconto	366	71.9
Calumet	377	68.7	Oneida	475	72.5
Chippewa	608	74.3	Outagamie.	1,516	71.9
Clark.	362	77.8	Ozaukee	826	61.1
Columbia.	562	74.3	Pepin	71	60
Crawford	176	67.7	Pierce	287	67.7
Dane	3,453	62.4	Polk	469	77.2
Dodge	985	74.7	Portage.	535	61.7
Door.	339	59.9	Price.	174	66.7
Douglas.	452	80.7	Racine.	1,865	76.9
Dunn	386	72.5	Richland	212	74
Eau Claire.	896	72.8	Rock.	1,596	80.4
Florence	60	81.2	Rusk	200	77.7
Fond du Lac	983	66.2	St. Croix.	619	71.4
Forest	112	86.8	Sauk	638	74.3
Grant	471	61.8	Sawyer	203	79
Green	387	75.1	Shawano	497	77.7
Green Lake.	234	72.5	Sheboygan.	1,151	72.3
Iowa	185	60.1	Taylor	190	62.9
Iron	83	68.7	Trempealeau	297	74.4
Jackson.	201	71.3	Vernon	294	66.8
Jefferson	725	73.3	Vilas	306	78
Juneau	285	70.9	Walworth.	981	73.4
Kenosha	1,504	83.4	Washburn	196	68.9
Kewaunee	190	61.9	Washington	1,172	65.2
La Crosse	1,043	67.2	Waukesha	3,661	63
Lafayette	146	69.1	Waupaca	721	74.9
Langlade	198	57.6	Waushara.	293	74.1
Lincoln	337	68.3	Winnebago	1,597	73.5
Manitowoc.	874	70.4	Wood	856	73.6

1. Per 10,000 population. Rates are adjusted for differences in age distributions.

Source: Wisconsin Department of Health Services, Division of Public Health, Office of Health Informatics, *Annual Wisconsin Death Report, 2018*, P-01170-20, December 2020.

Basic data on Wisconsin counties

County (year created)[1]	County seat	Full value 2019 assessment ($1,000)[2]	Population 2020 estimate	% change[3]	2020 rank	Land area in sq. miles[4]	2020 population/ sq. mile
Adams (1848)	Friendship	2,825,953	20,701	-0.83	53	645.7	32.1
Ashland (1860)	Ashland	1,252,163	15,871	-1.77	61	1,045.0	15.2
Barron (1859)	Barron	4,502,277	46,522	1.42	31	862.7	53.9
Bayfield (1845)	Washburn	2,714,849	15,334	2.13	64	1,477.9	10.4
Brown (1818)	Green Bay	23,181,417	264,821	6.78	4	529.7	499.9
Buffalo (1853)	Alma	1,228,183	13,671	0.62	67	671.6	20.4
Burnett (1856)	Meenon	2,845,710	15,486	0.19	62	821.9	18.8
Calumet (1836)	Chilton	4,490,140	53,338	8.92	27	318.2	167.6
Chippewa (1845)	Chippewa Falls	6,046,130	65,339	4.68	24	1,008.4	64.8
Clark (1853)	Neillsville	2,289,783	34,725	0.10	41	1,209.8	28.7
Columbia (1846)	Portage	5,863,531	57,134	0.53	26	765.5	74.6
Crawford (1818)	Prairie du Chien	1,257,908	16,679	0.21	59	570.7	29.2
Dane (1836)	Madison	69,928,054	543,408	11.34	2	1,197.2	453.9
Dodge (1836)	Juneau	6,971,933	90,005	1.40	19	875.6	102.8
Door (1851)	Sturgeon Bay	7,532,357	28,770	3.55	45	482.0	59.7
Douglas (1854)	Superior	3,654,146	44,246	0.20	34	1,304.1	33.9
Dunn (1854)	Menomonie	3,354,244	44,788	2.12	32	850.1	52.7
Eau Claire (1856)	Eau Claire	9,220,492	103,959	5.29	16	638.0	162.9
Florence (1881)	Florence	647,308	4,467	0.99	71	488.2	9.1
Fond du Lac (1836)	Fond du Lac	8,046,438	104,370	2.69	14	719.6	145.0
Forest (1885)	Crandon	1,172,743	9,183	-1.30	68	1,014.1	9.1
Grant (1836)	Lancaster	3,411,037	52,572	2.66	28	1,146.9	45.8
Green (1836)	Monroe	3,263,247	36,967	0.34	39	584.0	63.3
Green Lake (1858)	Green Lake	2,387,399	19,178	0.67	55	349.4	54.9
Iowa (1829)	Dodgeville	2,197,456	23,915	0.96	48	762.6	31.4
Iron (1893)	Hurley	983,071	5,909	-0.12	70	758.2	7.8
Jackson (1853)	Black River Falls	1,723,496	20,828	1.85	50	987.7	21.1
Jefferson (1836)	Jefferson	7,725,723	84,692	1.20	20	556.5	152.2
Juneau (1856)	Mauston	2,309,017	27,250	2.20	46	766.9	35.5
Kenosha (1850)	Kenosha	16,831,339	170,514	2.46	7	272.0	626.9
Kewaunee (1852)	Kewaunee	1,788,280	20,746	0.84	52	342.5	60.6
La Crosse (1851)	La Crosse	10,552,445	120,447	5.07	12	451.7	266.7
Lafayette (1846)	Darlington	1,225,243	17,007	1.02	57	633.6	26.8
Langlade (1879)	Antigo	1,807,505	20,063	0.43	54	870.6	23.0
Lincoln (1874)	Merrill	2,541,239	28,800	0.20	44	879.0	32.8
Manitowoc (1836)	Manitowoc	5,737,214	81,349	-0.11	21	589.1	138.1
Marathon (1850)	Wausau	11,639,161	137,237	2.37	11	1,545.0	88.8
Marinette (1879)	Marinette	4,002,461	41,255	-1.18	37	1,399.4	29.5
Marquette (1836)	Montello	1,669,514	15,387	-0.11	63	455.6	33.8
Menominee (1961)	Keshena	327,200	4,267	0.83	72	357.6	11.9
Milwaukee (1834)	Milwaukee	67,178,450	944,099	-0.38	1	241.4	3,910.9
Monroe (1854)	Sparta	3,579,764	46,882	4.94	30	900.8	52.0
Oconto (1851)	Oconto	4,102,238	38,853	3.17	38	998.0	38.9
Oneida (1885)	Rhinelander	7,226,435	36,268	0.75	40	1,113.0	32.6
Outagamie (1851)	Appleton	16,570,537	187,661	6.21	6	637.5	294.4
Ozaukee (1853)	Port Washington	12,995,888	90,630	4.90	18	233.1	388.8
Pepin (1858)	Durand	646,927	7,393	-1.02	69	232.0	31.9
Pierce (1853)	Ellsworth	3,624,907	42,413	3.40	35	573.8	73.9
Polk (1853)	Balsam Lake	5,090,558	44,628	0.96	33	914.0	48.8
Portage (1836)	Stevens Point	6,353,475	71,670	2.36	23	800.7	89.5
Price (1879)	Phillips	1,440,978	14,170	0.08	66	1,254.4	11.3
Racine (1836)	Racine	16,475,065	195,766	0.18	5	332.5	588.8
Richland (1842)	Richland Center	1,209,046	18,034	0.07	56	586.2	30.8
Rock (1836)	Janesville	12,364,513	160,120	-0.13	9	718.1	223.0
Rusk (1901)	Ladysmith	1,278,969	14,879	0.84	65	913.6	16.3
St. Croix (1840)	Hudson	10,620,318	90,949	7.83	17	722.3	125.9

Basic data on Wisconsin counties, continued

County (year created)[1]	County seat	Full value 2019 assessment ($1,000)[2]	Population 2020 estimate	% change[3]	2020 rank	Land area in sq. miles[4]	2020 population/ sq. mile
Sauk (1840)	Baraboo	7,715,950	63,343	2.21	25	830.9	76.2
Sawyer (1883)	Hayward	3,695,423	16,903	2.09	58	1,257.3	13.4
Shawano (1853)	Shawano	3,324,247	41,739	-0.50	36	893.1	46.7
Sheboygan (1836) . .	Sheboygan	10,142,962	116,924	1.23	13	511.3	228.7
Taylor (1875)	Medford	1,509,079	20,793	0.50	51	974.9	21.3
Trempealeau (1854) .	Whitehall	2,402,213	30,047	4.27	43	733.0	41.0
Vernon (1851)	Viroqua	2,098,674	30,496	2.43	42	791.6	38.5
Vilas (1893)	Eagle River	7,223,863	21,769	1.58	49	856.6	25.4
Walworth (1836) . . .	Elkhorn	15,706,735	104,086	1.82	15	555.1	187.5
Washburn (1883) . . .	Shell Lake	2,644,186	15,993	0.52	60	797.1	20.1
Washington (1836) . .	West Bend	16,155,740	138,268	4.84	10	430.7	321.0
Waukesha (1846) . . .	Waukesha	59,540,913	406,785	4.33	3	549.6	740.1
Waupaca (1851)	Waupaca	4,336,539	52,155	-0.49	29	747.7	69.8
Waushara (1851) . . .	Wautoma	2,709,640	24,436	-0.24	47	626.2	39.0
Winnebago (1840) . .	Oshkosh	14,203,070	169,861	1.72	8	434.5	390.9
Wood (1856)	Wisconsin Rapids	5,557,615	75,381	0.85	22	793.1	95.0
Total		580,872,723,300	5,854,594	2.95		54,157.8	108.1

1. Counties are created by legislative act. Depending on the date, Wisconsin counties were created by the Michigan Territorial Legislature (1818–1836), the Wisconsin Territorial Legislature (1836–1848), or the Wisconsin State Legislature (after 1848).
2. Reflects actual market value of all taxable general property, including personal property and real estate, as determined by the Wisconsin Department of Revenue.   3. Change from 2010 U.S. census.   4. Determined by 2010 census.

Sources: Wisconsin Department of Revenue, Division of State and Local Finance, *Town, Village, and City Taxes Levied 2019—Collected 2020*; Wisconsin Department of Administration, Demographic Services Center, *County Final Population Estimates, October 2020*; U.S. Census Bureau, *Census 2010 Summary File 1*, March 2015.

Population of legislative districts as created by 2011 Wisconsin Act 43[1]

District	2010 Population	Deviation from ideal[2] Total	Percent	District	2010 Population	Deviation from ideal[2] Total	Percent
SD-1	172,313	-20	-0.01	AD-14 . .	57,597	153	0.27
AD-1 . . .	57,220	-224	-0.39	AD-15 . .	57,372	-72	-0.13
AD-2 . . .	57,649	205	0.36	SD-6	172,292	-41	-0.02
AD-3 . . .	57,444	0	0.00	AD-16 . .	57,458	14	0.02
SD-2	172,461	128	0.07	AD-17 . .	57,354	-90	-0.16
AD-4 . . .	57,486	42	0.07	AD-18 . .	57,480	36	0.06
AD-5 . . .	57,470	26	0.04	SD-7	172,423	90	0.05
AD-6 . . .	57,505	61	0.11	AD-19 . .	57,546	102	0.18
SD-3	171,977	-356	-0.21	AD-20 . .	57,428	-16	-0.03
AD-7 . . .	57,498	54	0.09	AD-21 . .	57,449	5	0.01
AD-8[1] . .	57,196	-248	-0.43	SD-8	172,356	23	0.01
AD-9[1] . .	57,283	-161	-0.28	AD-22 . .	57,495	51	0.09
SD-4	172,425	92	0.05	AD-23 . .	57,579	135	0.23
AD-10 . .	57,428	-16	-0.03	AD-24 . .	57,282	-162	-0.28
AD-11 . .	57,503	59	0.10	SD-9	172,439	106	0.06
AD-12 . .	57,494	50	0.09	AD-25 . .	57,322	-122	-0.21
SD-5	172,421	88	0.05	AD-26 . .	57,581	137	0.24
AD-13 . .	57,452	8	0.01	AD-27 . .	57,536	92	0.16

Population of legislative districts as created by 2011 Wisconsin Act 43[1], continued

District	2010 Population	Deviation from ideal[2] Total	Percent	District	2010 Population	Deviation from ideal[2] Total	Percent
SD-10	172,245	−88	−0.05	SD-22	172,270	−63	−0.04
AD-28 . .	57,467	23	0.04	AD-64 . .	57,270	−174	−0.30
AD-29 . .	57,537	93	0.16	AD-65 . .	57,455	11	0.02
AD-30 . .	57,241	−203	−0.35	AD-66 . .	57,545	101	0.18
SD-11	172,329	−4	0.00	SD-23	172,149	−184	−0.11
AD-31 . .	57,240	−204	−0.36	AD-67 . .	57,239	−205	−0.36
AD-32 . .	57,524	80	0.14	AD-68 . .	57,261	−183	−0.32
AD-33 . .	57,565	121	0.21	AD-69 . .	57,649	205	0.36
SD-12	172,381	48	0.03	SD-24	172,520	187	0.11
AD-34 . .	57,387	−57	−0.10	AD-70 . .	57,552	108	0.19
AD-35 . .	57,562	118	0.20	AD-71 . .	57,519	75	0.13
AD-36 . .	57,432	−12	−0.02	AD-72 . .	57,449	5	0.01
SD-13	172,387	54	0.03	SD-25	172,409	76	0.04
AD-37 . .	57,507	63	0.11	AD-73 . .	57,453	9	0.02
AD-38 . .	57,493	49	0.08	AD-74 . .	57,494	50	0.09
AD-39 . .	57,387	−57	−0.10	AD-75 . .	57,462	18	0.03
SD-14	171,988	−345	−0.20	SD-26	172,596	263	0.15
AD-40 . .	57,366	−78	−0.14	AD-76 . .	57,617	173	0.30
AD-41 . .	57,337	−107	−0.19	AD-77 . .	57,433	−11	−0.02
AD-42 . .	57,285	−159	−0.28	AD-78 . .	57,546	102	0.18
SD-15	172,496	163	0.09	SD-27	172,449	116	0.07
AD-43 . .	57,443	−1	0.00	AD-79 . .	57,461	17	0.03
AD-44 . .	57,395	−49	−0.09	AD-80 . .	57,585	141	0.24
AD-45 . .	57,658	214	0.37	AD-81 . .	57,403	−41	−0.07
SD-16	172,429	96	0.06	SD-28	172,218	−115	−0.07
AD-46 . .	57,458	14	0.02	AD-82 . .	57,430	−14	−0.02
AD-47 . .	57,465	21	0.04	AD-83 . .	57,423	−21	−0.04
AD-48 . .	57,506	62	0.11	AD-84 . .	57,365	−79	−0.14
SD-17	172,550	217	0.13	SD-29	172,292	−41	−0.02
AD-49 . .	57,346	−98	−0.17	AD-85 . .	57,480	36	0.06
AD-50 . .	57,624	180	0.31	AD-86 . .	57,454	10	0.02
AD-51 . .	57,580	136	0.24	AD-87 . .	57,358	−86	−0.15
SD-18	171,722	−611	−0.35	SD-30	172,798	465	0.27
AD-52 . .	57,232	−212	−0.37	AD-88 . .	57,556	112	0.19
AD-53 . .	57,240	−204	−0.36	AD-89 . .	57,634	190	0.33
AD-54 . .	57,250	−194	−0.34	AD-90 . .	57,608	164	0.28
SD-19	172,576	243	0.14	SD-31	172,338	5	0.00
AD-55 . .	57,493	49	0.08	AD-91 . .	57,359	−85	−0.15
AD-56 . .	57,582	138	0.24	AD-92 . .	57,431	−13	−0.02
AD-57 . .	57,501	57	0.10	AD-93 . .	57,548	104	0.18
SD-20	172,003	−330	−0.19	SD-32	172,122	−211	−0.12
AD-58 . .	57,227	−217	−0.38	AD-94 . .	57,266	−178	−0.31
AD-59 . .	57,391	−53	−0.09	AD-95 . .	57,372	−72	−0.13
AD-60 . .	57,385	−59	−0.10	AD-96 . .	57,484	40	0.07
SD-21	172,324	−9	−0.01	SD-33	172,288	−45	−0.03
AD-61 . .	57,614	170	0.30	AD-97 . .	57,279	−165	−0.29
AD-62 . .	57,345	−99	−0.17	AD-98 . .	57,513	69	0.12
AD-63 . .	57,365	−79	−0.14	AD-99 . .	57,496	52	0.09

1. This table reflects modifications made to Assembly Districts 8 and 9 by the U.S. District Court for the Eastern District of Wisconsin in its decision in *Baldus vs. Members of the Wisconsin Government Accountability Board*, Case No. 11-CV-562, April 11, 2012. 2. Ideal senate district: 172,333. Ideal assembly district: 57,444.

Sources: U.S. Census Bureau, 2010 Census Redistricting Data (Public Law 94-171) Summary File, March 2011; Appendix to: 2011 Wisconsin Act 43. Assembly districts 8 and 9 population and deviations calculated by the Wisconsin Legislative Reference Bureau.

Wisconsin population by county and municipality

	2010 census	2020 estimate	% change		2010 census	2020 estimate	% change
Adams	20,875	20,701	-0.83	Haugen, village	287	279	-2.79
Adams, city	1,967	1,907	-3.05	Lakeland, town	975	1,003	2.87
Adams, town	1,345	1,358	0.97	Maple Grove, town	979	966	-1.33
Big Flats, town	1,018	1,031	1.28	Maple Plain, town	803	833	3.74
Colburn, town	223	230	3.14	New Auburn, village (part)	20	33	65.00
Dell Prairie, town	1,590	1,622	2.01	Oak Grove, town	948	962	1.48
Easton, town	1,130	1,106	-2.12	Prairie Farm, town	573	600	4.71
Friendship, village	725	749	3.31	Prairie Farm, village	473	456	-3.59
Jackson, town	1,003	981	-2.19	Prairie Lake, town	1,532	1,530	-0.13
Leola, town	308	303	-1.62	Rice Lake, city	8,419	8,788	4.38
Lincoln, town	296	299	1.01	Rice Lake, town	3,060	3,101	1.34
Monroe, town	398	410	3.02	Sioux Creek, town	655	670	2.29
New Chester, town	2,254	1,944	-13.75	Stanfold, town	719	736	2.36
New Haven, town	655	682	4.12	Stanley, town	2,546	2,575	1.14
Preston, town	1,393	1,400	0.50	Sumner, town	798	816	2.26
Quincy, town	1,163	1,182	1.63	Turtle Lake, town	624	644	3.21
Richfield, town	158	159	0.63	Turtle Lake, village (part)	957	941	-1.67
Rome, town	2,720	2,816	3.53	Vance Creek, town	669	662	-1.05
Springville, town	1,318	1,297	-1.59				
Strongs Prairie, town	1,150	1,164	1.22	**Bayfield**	15,014	15,334	2.13
Wisconsin Dells, city (part)	61	61	0.00	Ashland, city (part)	0	0	0.00
				Barksdale, town	723	725	0.28
Ashland	16,157	15,871	-1.77	Barnes, town	769	772	0.39
Agenda, town	422	422	0.00	Bayfield, city	487	484	-0.62
Ashland, city (part)	8,216	7,985	-2.81	Bayfield, town	680	704	3.53
Ashland, town	594	581	-2.19	Bayview, town	487	484	-0.62
Butternut, village	375	359	-4.27	Bell, town	263	281	6.84
Chippewa, town	374	374	0.00	Cable, town	825	829	0.48
Gingles, town	778	781	0.39	Clover, town	223	218	-2.24
Gordon, town	283	286	1.06	Delta, town	273	275	0.73
Jacobs, town	722	713	-1.25	Drummond, town	463	433	-6.48
La Pointe, town	261	269	3.07	Eileen, town	681	691	1.47
Marengo, town	390	386	-1.03	Grand View, town	468	471	0.64
Mellen, city	731	710	-2.87	Hughes, town	383	394	2.87
Morse, town	493	496	0.61	Iron River, town	1,123	1,170	4.19
Peeksville, town	141	139	-1.42	Kelly, town	463	472	1.94
Sanborn, town	1,331	1,307	-1.80	Keystone, town	378	368	-2.65
Shanagolden, town	125	123	-1.60	Lincoln, town	287	289	0.70
White River, town	921	940	2.06	Mason, town	315	324	2.86
				Mason, village	93	93	0.00
Barron	45,870	46,522	1.42	Namakagon, town	246	249	1.22
Almena, town	858	851	-0.82	Orienta, town	122	121	-0.82
Almena, village	677	641	-5.32	Oulu, town	527	533	1.14
Arland, town	789	819	3.80	Pilsen, town	210	213	1.43
Barron, city	3,423	3,356	-1.96	Port Wing, town	368	379	2.99
Barron, town	873	866	-0.80	Russell, town	1,279	1,465	14.54
Bear Lake, town	659	659	0.00	Tripp, town	231	239	3.46
Cameron, village	1,783	1,865	4.60	Washburn, city	2,117	2,102	-0.71
Cedar Lake, town	948	990	4.43	Washburn, town	530	556	4.91
Chetek, city	2,221	2,187	-1.53				
Chetek, town	1,644	1,688	2.68	**Brown**	248,007	264,821	6.78
Clinton, town	879	899	2.28	Allouez, village	13,975	13,734	-1.72
Crystal Lake, town	757	775	2.38	Ashwaubenon, village	16,963	16,961	-0.01
Cumberland, city	2,170	2,174	0.18	Bellevue, village	14,570	15,706	7.80
Cumberland, town	876	867	-1.03	De Pere, city	23,800	24,595	3.34
Dallas, town	565	581	2.83	Denmark, village	2,123	2,271	6.97
Dallas, village	409	348	-14.91	Eaton, town	1,508	1,674	11.01
Dovre, town	849	882	3.89	Glenmore, town	1,135	1,125	-0.88
Doyle, town	453	479	5.74	Green Bay, city	104,057	105,599	1.48

Wisconsin population by county and municipality, continued

	2010 census	2020 estimate	% change		2010 census	2020 estimate	% change
Green Bay, town	2,035	2,158	6.04	Siren, village	806	788	-2.23
Hobart, village	6,182	10,454	69.10	Swiss, town	790	783	-0.89
Holland, town	1,519	1,576	3.75	Trade Lake, town	823	838	1.82
Howard, village (part)	17,399	20,209	16.15	Union, town	340	340	0.00
Humboldt, town	1,311	1,347	2.75	Webb Lake, town	311	315	1.29
Lawrence, town	4,284	6,020	40.52	Webster, village	653	646	-1.07
Ledgeview, town	6,555	8,444	28.82	West Marshland, town	367	372	1.36
Morrison, town	1,599	1,605	0.38	Wood River, town	953	944	-0.94
New Denmark, town	1,541	1,556	0.97				
Pittsfield, town	2,608	2,769	6.17	**Calumet**	**48,971**	**53,338**	**8.92**
Pulaski, village (part)	3,321	3,514	5.81	Appleton, city (part)	11,088	11,670	5.25
Rockland, town	1,734	1,848	6.57	Brillion, city	3,148	3,257	3.46
Scott, town	3,545	3,657	3.16	Brillion, town	1,486	1,562	5.11
Suamico, village	11,346	12,796	12.78	Brothertown, town	1,329	1,321	-0.60
Wrightstown, town	2,221	2,350	5.81	Charlestown, town	775	782	0.90
Wrightstown, village (part)	2,676	2,853	6.61	Chilton, city	3,933	3,956	0.58
				Chilton, town	1,143	1,165	1.92
Buffalo	**13,587**	**13,671**	**0.62**	Harrison, town	10,839	0	-100.00
Alma, city	781	777	-0.51	Harrison, village (part)[1]	NA	13,185	NA
Alma, town	297	307	3.37	Hilbert, village	1,132	1,183	4.51
Belvidere, town	396	390	-1.52	Kaukauna, city (part)	0	0	0.00
Buffalo, town	705	697	-1.13	Kiel, city (part)	309	330	6.80
Buffalo City, city	1,023	1,005	-1.76	Menasha, city (part)	2,209	2,833	28.25
Canton, town	305	316	3.61	New Holstein, city	3,236	3,210	-0.80
Cochrane, village	450	437	-2.89	New Holstein, town	1,508	1,516	0.53
Cross, town	377	384	1.86	Potter, village	253	248	-1.98
Dover, town	486	503	3.50	Rantoul, town	798	816	2.26
Fountain City, city	859	840	-2.21	Sherwood, village	2,713	3,152	16.18
Gilmanton, town	426	426	0.00	Stockbridge, town	1,456	1,513	3.91
Glencoe, town	485	494	1.86	Stockbridge, village	636	651	2.36
Lincoln, town	162	180	11.11	Woodville, town	980	988	0.82
Maxville, town	309	315	1.94				
Milton, town	534	560	4.87	**Chippewa**	**62,415**	**65,339**	**4.68**
Modena, town	354	354	0.00	Anson, town	2,076	2,266	9.15
Mondovi, city	2,777	2,751	-0.94	Arthur, town	759	781	2.90
Mondovi, town	469	476	1.49	Auburn, town	697	742	6.46
Montana, town	284	290	2.11	Birch Creek, town	517	533	3.09
Naples, town	691	698	1.01	Bloomer, city	3,539	3,582	1.22
Nelson, town	571	636	11.38	Bloomer, town	1,050	1,108	5.52
Nelson, village	374	358	-4.28	Boyd, village	552	540	-2.17
Waumandee, town	472	477	1.06	Cadott, village	1,437	1,444	0.49
				Chippewa Falls, city	13,661	14,405	5.45
Burnett	**15,457**	**15,486**	**0.19**	Cleveland, town	864	877	1.50
Anderson, town	398	394	-1.01	Colburn, town	856	900	5.14
Blaine, town	197	195	-1.02	Cooks Valley, town	805	840	4.35
Daniels, town	649	654	0.77	Cornell, city	1,467	1,462	-0.34
Dewey, town	516	511	-0.97	Delmar, town	936	980	4.70
Grantsburg, town	1,136	1,135	-0.09	Eagle Point, town	3,053	3,241	6.16
Grantsburg, village	1,341	1,318	-1.72	Eau Claire, city (part)	1,981	2,043	3.13
Jackson, town	773	793	2.59	Edson, town	1,089	1,068	-1.93
La Follette, town	536	527	-1.68	Estella, town	433	430	-0.69
Lincoln, town	309	315	1.94	Goetz, town	762	808	6.04
Meenon, town	1,163	1,160	-0.26	Hallie, town	161	183	13.66
Oakland, town	827	851	2.90	Howard, town	798	801	0.38
Roosevelt, town	199	205	3.02	Lafayette, town	5,765	6,179	7.18
Rusk, town	409	418	2.20	Lake Hallie, village	6,448	7,121	10.44
Sand Lake, town	531	535	0.75	Lake Holcombe, town	1,031	1,041	0.97
Scott, town	494	504	2.02	New Auburn, village (part)	528	515	-2.46
Siren, town	936	945	0.96	Ruby, town	494	505	2.23

Wisconsin population by county and municipality, continued

	2010 census	2020 esti- mate	% change		2010 census	2020 esti- mate	% change
Sampson, town	892	953	6.84	Caledonia, town	1,378	1,419	2.98
Sigel, town	1,044	1,053	0.86	Cambria, village.	767	756	−1.43
Stanley, city (part)	3,602	3,624	0.61	Columbus, city (part) . .	4,991	5,187	3.93
Tilden, town	1,485	1,530	3.03	Columbus, town	646	653	1.08
Wheaton, town	2,701	2,815	4.22	Courtland, town	525	532	1.33
Woodmohr, town.	932	969	3.97	Dekorra, town.	2,311	2,343	1.38
				Doylestown, village . . .	297	290	−2.36
Clark	**34,690**	**34,725**	**0.10**	Fall River, village	1,712	1,793	4.73
Abbotsford, city (part). .	1,616	1,727	6.87	Fort Winnebago, town. .	825	824	−0.12
Beaver, town.	885	879	−0.68	Fountain Prairie, town. .	887	910	2.59
Butler, town	96	97	1.04	Friesland, village	356	346	−2.81
Colby, city (part)	1,354	1,305	−3.62	Hampden, town	574	582	1.39
Colby, town	874	897	2.63	Leeds, town	774	765	−1.16
Curtiss, village.	216	209	−3.24	Lewiston, town	1,225	1,220	−0.41
Dewhurst, town.	323	337	4.33	Lodi, city	3,050	3,139	2.92
Dorchester, village (part)	871	852	−2.18	Lodi, town	3,273	3,312	1.19
Eaton, town	712	716	0.56	Lowville, town.	1,008	1,010	0.20
Foster, town	95	96	1.05	Marcellon, town	1,102	1,107	0.45
Fremont, town	1,265	1,281	1.26	Newport, town	586	583	−0.51
Grant, town	916	938	2.40	Otsego, town	693	690	−0.43
Granton, village.	355	350	−1.41	Pacific, town	2,707	2,742	1.29
Green Grove, town	756	755	−0.13	Pardeeville, village	2,115	2,067	−2.27
Greenwood, city	1,026	1,009	−1.66	Portage, city	10,324	10,132	−1.86
Hendren, town	499	503	0.80	Poynette, village	2,528	2,534	0.24
Hewett, town	293	297	1.37	Randolph, town.	769	757	−1.56
Hixon, town	808	810	0.25	Randolph, village (part).	472	461	−2.33
Hoard, town	841	833	−0.95	Rio, village	1,059	1,078	1.79
Levis, town.	492	495	0.61	Scott, town.	905	923	1.99
Longwood, town	858	856	−0.23	Springvale, town	520	528	1.54
Loyal, city.	1,261	1,232	−2.30	West Point, town	1,955	2,008	2.71
Loyal, town.	826	832	0.73	Wisconsin Dells, city (part)	2,440	2,382	−2.38
Lynn, town.	861	885	2.79	Wyocena, town	1,666	1,696	1.80
Mayville, town.	961	935	−2.71	Wyocena, village	768	729	−5.08
Mead, town	321	337	4.98				
Mentor, town	584	577	−1.20	**Crawford**	**16,644**	**16,679**	**0.21**
Neillsville, city	2,463	2,362	−4.10	Bell Center, village	117	114	−2.56
Owen, city	940	913	−2.87	Bridgeport, town	990	1,037	4.75
Pine Valley, town	1,157	1,160	0.26	Clayton, town	958	921	−3.86
Reseburg, town	776	784	1.03	De Soto, village (part) . .	108	97	−10.19
Seif, town.	172	167	−2.91	Eastman, town	739	747	1.08
Sherman, town	882	917	3.97	Eastman, village	428	419	−2.10
Sherwood, town	220	230	4.55	Ferryville, village	176	193	9.66
Stanley, city (part)	6	6	0.00	Freeman, town	686	715	4.23
Thorp, city	1,621	1,588	−2.04	Gays Mills, village.	491	494	0.61
Thorp, town	808	824	1.98	Haney, town	309	320	3.56
Unity, town	878	888	1.14	Lynxville, village	132	130	−1.52
Unity, village (part). . . .	139	136	−2.16	Marietta, town	470	492	4.68
Warner, town	669	673	0.60	Mount Sterling, village .	211	206	−2.37
Washburn, town	290	285	−1.72	Prairie du Chien, city. . .	5,911	5,840	−1.20
Weston, town	699	688	−1.57	Prairie du Chien, town. .	1,073	1,058	−1.40
Withee, town	966	988	2.28	Scott, town.	462	494	6.93
Withee, village	487	500	2.67	Seneca, town	866	938	8.31
Worden, town	666	705	5.86	Soldiers Grove, village. .	592	561	−5.24
York, town	886	871	−1.69	Steuben, village.	131	122	−6.87
				Utica, town.	661	684	3.48
Columbia	**56,833**	**57,134**	**0.53**	Wauzeka, town	422	412	−2.37
Arlington, town.	806	802	−0.50	Wauzeka, village	711	685	−3.66
Arlington, village	819	834	1.83				

Wisconsin population by county and municipality, continued

	2010 census	2020 esti- mate	% change		2010 census	2020 esti- mate	% change
				Vienna, town	1,482	1,539	3.85
Dane	488,073	543,408	11.34	Waunakee, village	12,097	14,399	19.03
Albion, town	1,951	1,997	2.36	Westport, town	3,950	4,038	2.23
Belleville, village (part)	1,848	1,949	5.47	Windsor, village[2]	6,345	8,240	29.87
Berry, town	1,127	1,165	3.37	York, town	652	650	-0.31
Black Earth, town	483	491	1.66				
Black Earth, village	1,338	1,428	6.73	**Dodge**	88,759	90,005	1.40
Blooming Grove, town	1,815	1,616	-10.96	Ashippun, town	2,559	2,644	3.32
Blue Mounds, town	968	1,016	4.96	Beaver Dam, city	16,214	16,890	4.17
Blue Mounds, village	855	966	12.98	Beaver Dam, town	3,962	4,041	1.99
Bristol, town	3,765	4,347	15.46	Brownsville, village	581	607	4.48
Brooklyn, village (part)	936	1,007	7.59	Burnett, town	904	897	-0.77
Burke, town	3,284	3,303	0.58	Calamus, town	1,048	1,036	-1.15
Cambridge, village (part)	1,348	1,484	10.09	Chester, town	687	688	0.15
Christiana, town	1,235	1,256	1.70	Clyman, town	774	784	1.29
Cottage Grove, town	3,875	3,889	0.36	Clyman, village	422	411	-2.61
Cottage Grove, village	6,192	6,716	8.46	Columbus, city (part)	0	0	0.00
Cross Plains, town	1,507	1,564	3.78	Elba, town	996	997	0.10
Cross Plains, village	3,538	4,010	13.34	Emmet, town	1,302	1,306	0.31
Dane, town	990	997	0.71	Fox Lake, city	1,519	1,550	2.04
Dane, village	995	1,100	10.55	Fox Lake, town	2,465	2,492	1.10
DeForest, village	8,936	10,624	18.89	Hartford, city (part)	0	7	N/A
Deerfield, town	1,585	1,634	3.09	Herman, town	1,108	1,130	1.99
Deerfield, village	2,319	2,489	7.33	Horicon, city	3,655	3,768	3.09
Dunkirk, town	1,945	1,910	-1.80	Hubbard, town	1,774	1,785	0.62
Dunn, town	4,931	4,852	-1.60	Hustisford, town	1,373	1,376	0.22
Edgerton, city (part)	97	138	42.27	Hustisford, village	1,123	1,107	-1.42
Fitchburg, city	25,260	30,391	20.31	Iron Ridge, village	929	920	-0.97
Madison, city	233,209	257,197	10.29	Juneau, city	2,814	2,634	-6.40
Madison, town	6,279	6,228	-0.81	Kekoskee, village[3]	916	919	0.33
Maple Bluff, village	1,313	1,285	-2.13	Lebanon, town	1,659	1,638	-1.27
Marshall, village	3,862	3,899	0.96	Leroy, town	1,002	977	-2.50
Mazomanie, town	1,090	1,084	-0.55	Lomira, town	1,137	1,152	1.32
Mazomanie, village	1,652	1,681	1.76	Lomira, village	2,430	2,528	4.03
McFarland, village	7,808	8,952	14.65	Lowell, town	1,190	1,216	2.18
Medina, town	1,376	1,380	0.29	Lowell, village	340	326	-4.12
Middleton, city	17,442	21,050	20.69	Mayville, city	5,154	5,069	-1.65
Middleton, town	5,877	6,614	12.54	Neosho, village	574	565	-1.57
Monona, city	7,533	7,920	5.14	Oak Grove, town	1,080	1,057	-2.13
Montrose, town	1,081	1,095	1.30	Portland, town	1,079	1,091	1.11
Mount Horeb, village	7,009	7,387	5.39	Randolph, village (part)	1,339	1,324	-1.12
Oregon, town	3,184	3,240	1.76	Reeseville, village	708	713	0.71
Oregon, village	9,231	10,270	11.26	Rubicon, town	2,207	2,276	3.13
Perry, town	729	730	0.14	Shields, town	554	556	0.36
Pleasant Springs, town	3,154	3,203	1.55	Theresa, town	1,075	1,079	0.37
Primrose, town	731	748	2.33	Theresa, village	1,262	1,258	-0.32
Rockdale, village	214	214	0.00	Trenton, town	1,293	1,297	0.31
Roxbury, town	1,794	1,899	5.85	Watertown, city (part)	8,459	8,566	1.26
Rutland, town	1,966	2,012	2.34	Waupun, city (part)	7,864	8,112	3.15
Shorewood Hills, village	1,565	2,363	50.99	Westford, town	1,228	1,216	-0.98
Springdale, town	1,904	2,021	6.14				
Springfield, town	2,734	2,935	7.35	**Door**	27,785	28,770	3.55
Stoughton, city	12,611	12,954	2.72	Baileys Harbor, town	1,022	1,075	5.19
Sun Prairie, city	29,364	35,895	22.24	Brussels, town	1,136	1,129	-0.62
Sun Prairie, town	2,326	2,383	2.45	Clay Banks, town	382	388	1.57
Vermont, town	819	834	1.83	Egg Harbor, town	1,342	1,424	6.11
Verona, city	10,619	12,737	19.95	Egg Harbor, village	201	206	2.49
Verona, town	1,948	1,993	2.31	Ephraim, village	288	288	0.00

Wisconsin population by county and municipality, continued

	2010 census	2020 esti-mate	% change		2010 census	2020 esti-mate	% change
Forestville, town	1,096	1,109	1.19	Rock Creek, town	1,000	1,023	2.30
Forestville, village	430	424	–1.40	Sand Creek, town.	570	574	0.70
Gardner, town.	1,194	1,233	3.27	Sheridan, town	454	472	3.96
Gibraltar, town	1,021	1,068	4.60	Sherman, town	849	892	5.06
Jacksonport, town	705	731	3.69	Spring Brook, town. . . .	1,558	1,658	6.42
Liberty Grove, town . . .	1,734	1,786	3.00	Stanton, town	791	800	1.14
Nasewaupee, town. . . .	2,061	2,119	2.81	Tainter, town.	2,319	2,423	4.48
Sevastopol, town	2,628	2,742	4.34	Tiffany, town.	618	619	0.16
Sister Bay, village	876	966	10.27	Weston, town	594	589	–0.84
Sturgeon Bay, city	9,144	9,542	4.35	Wheeler, village.	348	343	–1.44
Sturgeon Bay, town . . .	818	825	0.86	Wilson, town.	531	526	–0.94
Union, town	999	997	–0.20				
Washington, town	708	718	1.41	**Eau Claire**	**98,736**	**103,959**	**5.29**
				Altoona, city.	6,706	8,099	20.77
Douglas	**44,159**	**44,246**	**0.20**	Augusta, city.	1,550	1,518	–2.06
Amnicon, town	1,155	1,205	4.33	Bridge Creek, town. . . .	1,900	1,924	1.26
Bennett, town.	597	624	4.52	Brunswick, town	1,624	1,947	19.89
Brule, town.	656	671	2.29	Clear Creek, town.	821	844	2.80
Cloverland, town	210	201	–4.29	Drammen, town	783	807	3.07
Dairyland, town.	184	183	–0.54	Eau Claire, city (part). . .	63,950	66,386	3.81
Gordon, town	636	634	–0.31	Fairchild, town	343	361	5.25
Hawthorne, town.	1,136	1,098	–3.35	Fairchild, village.	550	535	–2.73
Highland, town	311	305	–1.93	Fall Creek, village.	1,315	1,269	–3.50
Lake Nebagamon, village	1,069	1,087	1.68	Lincoln, town	1,096	1,160	5.84
Lakeside, town	693	717	3.46	Ludington, town	1,063	1,077	1.32
Maple, town	744	762	2.42	Otter Creek, town	500	489	–2.20
Oakland, town	1,136	1,189	4.67	Pleasant Valley, town . .	3,044	3,419	12.32
Oliver, village	399	436	9.27	Seymour, town	3,209	3,361	4.74
Parkland, town	1,220	1,235	1.23	Union, town	2,663	2,828	6.20
Poplar, village	603	615	1.99	Washington, town	7,134	7,441	4.30
Solon Springs, town . . .	910	927	1.87	Wilson, town.	485	494	1.86
Solon Springs, village . .	600	593	–1.17				
Summit, town	1,063	1,078	1.41	**Florence**	**4,423**	**4,467**	**0.99**
Superior, city	27,244	26,986	–0.95	Aurora, town	1,036	1,057	2.03
Superior, town	2,166	2,235	3.19	Commonwealth, town. .	399	409	2.51
Superior, village.	664	703	5.87	Fence, town	192	190	–1.04
Wascott, town	763	762	–0.13	Fern, town	159	160	0.63
				Florence, town	2,002	2,003	0.05
Dunn	**43,857**	**44,788**	**2.12**	Homestead, town	336	342	1.79
Boyceville, village.	1,086	1,080	–0.55	Long Lake, town	157	159	1.27
Colfax, town	1,186	1,283	8.18	Tipler, town	142	147	3.52
Colfax, village	1,158	1,095	–5.44				
Downing, village	265	262	–1.13	**Fond du Lac**	**101,633**	**104,370**	**2.69**
Dunn, town	1,524	1,515	–0.59	Alto, town	1,045	1,072	2.58
Eau Galle, town	757	774	2.25	Ashford, town	1,747	1,791	2.52
Elk Mound, town	1,792	1,930	7.70	Auburn, town	2,352	2,395	1.83
Elk Mound, village	878	871	–0.80	Brandon, village	879	863	–1.82
Grant, town	385	392	1.82	Byron, town	1,634	1,657	1.41
Hay River, town	558	561	0.54	Calumet, town	1,470	1,495	1.70
Knapp, village	463	458	–1.08	Campbellsport, village .	2,016	1,825	–9.47
Lucas, town	764	770	0.79	Eden, town.	1,028	1,042	1.36
Menomonie, city	16,264	16,461	1.21	Eden, village.	875	908	3.77
Menomonie, town	3,366	3,512	4.34	Eldorado, town	1,462	1,468	0.41
New Haven, town.	677	690	1.92	Empire, town	2,797	2,784	–0.46
Otter Creek, town	501	497	–0.80	Fairwater, village	371	362	–2.43
Peru, town	242	246	1.65	Fond du Lac, city	43,021	44,279	2.92
Red Cedar, town	2,086	2,204	5.66	Fond du Lac, town	3,015	3,967	31.58
Ridgeland, village	273	268	–1.83	Forest, town	1,080	1,069	–1.02

Wisconsin population by county and municipality, continued

	2010 census	2020 estimate	% change		2010 census	2020 estimate	% change
Friendship, town	2,675	2,675	0.00	Hickory Grove, town . . .	455	525	15.38
Kewaskum, village (part)	0	0	0.00	Jamestown, town.	2,076	2,264	9.06
Lamartine, town	1,737	1,792	3.17	Lancaster, city	3,868	3,757	-2.87
Marshfield, town	1,138	1,164	2.28	Liberty, town	553	556	0.54
Metomen, town.	741	736	-0.67	Lima, town.	805	802	-0.37
Mount Calvary, village. .	762	534	-29.92	Little Grant, town.	283	291	2.83
North Fond du Lac, village	5,014	5,181	3.33	Livingston, village (part)	657	646	-1.67
Oakfield, town.	703	718	2.13	Marion, town	572	605	5.77
Oakfield, village.	1,075	1,104	2.70	Millville, town	166	169	1.81
Osceola, town.	1,865	1,865	0.00	Montfort, village (part) .	622	627	0.80
Ripon, city	7,733	7,839	1.37	Mount Hope, town. . . .	300	300	0.00
Ripon, town	1,400	1,409	0.64	Mount Hope, village . . .	225	222	-1.33
Rosendale, town	695	699	0.58	Mount Ida, town	561	559	-0.36
Rosendale, village	1,063	1,024	-3.67	Muscoda, town	769	774	0.65
Springvale, town	707	713	0.85	Muscoda, village (part) .	1,249	1,202	-3.76
St. Cloud, village	477	473	-0.84	North Lancaster, town. .	509	541	6.29
Taycheedah, town	4,205	4,591	9.18	Paris, town	702	734	4.56
Waupun, city (part). . . .	3,476	3,476	0.00	Patch Grove, town	339	347	2.36
Waupun, town	1,375	1,400	1.82	Patch Grove, village . . .	198	197	-0.51
				Platteville, city.	11,224	12,262	9.25
Forest.	**9,304**	**9,183**	**-1.30**	Platteville, town.	1,509	1,563	3.58
Alvin, town.	157	154	-1.91	Potosi, town	849	855	0.71
Argonne, town	512	519	1.37	Potosi, village	688	674	-2.03
Armstrong Creek, town .	409	402	-1.71	Smelser, town	794	812	2.27
Blackwell, town	332	323	-2.71	South Lancaster, town. .	843	846	0.36
Caswell, town	91	88	-3.30	Tennyson, village	355	361	1.69
Crandon, city	1,920	1,805	-5.99	Waterloo, town	550	590	7.27
Crandon, town	650	662	1.85	Watterstown, town. . . .	330	349	5.76
Freedom, town	345	347	0.58	Wingville, town	357	374	4.76
Hiles, town	311	315	1.29	Woodman, town	185	199	7.57
Laona, town	1,212	1,194	-1.49	Woodman, village	132	126	-4.55
Lincoln, town	955	962	0.73	Wyalusing, town	346	355	2.60
Nashville, town	1,064	1,082	1.69				
Popple River, town	44	42	-4.55	**Green**.	**36,842**	**36,967**	**0.34**
Ross, town	136	133	-2.21	Adams, town	530	534	0.75
Wabeno, town.	1,166	1,155	-0.94	Albany, town	1,106	1,141	3.16
				Albany, village.	1,018	995	-2.26
Grant	**51,208**	**52,572**	**2.66**	Belleville, village (part) .	537	524	-2.42
Bagley, village.	379	372	-1.85	Brodhead, city (part). . .	3,203	3,181	-0.69
Beetown, town	777	787	1.29	Brooklyn, town	1,083	1,147	5.91
Bloomington, town . . .	350	365	4.29	Brooklyn, village (part) .	465	452	-2.80
Bloomington, village . .	735	725	-1.36	Browntown, village . . .	280	278	-0.71
Blue River, village.	434	427	-1.61	Cadiz, town	815	797	-2.21
Boscobel, city	3,231	3,219	-0.37	Clarno, town.	1,166	1,162	-0.34
Boscobel, town	376	371	-1.33	Decatur, town	1,767	1,773	0.34
Cassville, town	416	403	-3.13	Exeter, town	2,023	2,159	6.72
Cassville, village	947	919	-2.96	Jefferson, town	1,217	1,224	0.58
Castle Rock, town.	248	256	3.23	Jordan, town	641	624	-2.65
Clifton, town.	385	401	4.16	Monroe, city	10,827	10,641	-1.72
Cuba City, city (part) . . .	1,877	1,892	0.80	Monroe, town	1,245	1,286	3.29
Dickeyville, village	1,061	1,061	0.00	Monticello, village	1,217	1,205	-0.99
Ellenboro, town.	525	546	4.00	Mount Pleasant, town . .	598	609	1.84
Fennimore, city	2,497	2,501	0.16	New Glarus, town.	1,335	1,402	5.02
Fennimore, town	612	601	-1.80	New Glarus, village. . . .	2,172	2,085	-4.01
Glen Haven, town	417	416	-0.24	Spring Grove, town . . .	874	918	5.03
Harrison, town	495	490	-1.01	Sylvester, town	1,004	1,034	2.99
Hazel Green, town	1,132	1,097	-3.09	Washington, town	809	825	1.98
Hazel Green, village (part)	1,243	1,239	-0.32	York, town	910	971	6.70

Wisconsin population by county and municipality, continued

	2010 census	2020 estimate	% change		2010 census	2020 estimate	% change
Green Lake	**19,051**	**19,178**	**0.67**	Montreal, city	807	795	−1.49
Berlin, city (part)	5,435	5,512	1.42	Oma, town	289	305	5.54
Berlin, town	1,140	1,133	−0.61	Pence, town	163	161	−1.23
Brooklyn, town	1,826	1,864	2.08	Saxon, town	324	318	−1.85
Green Lake, city	960	1,005	4.69	Sherman, town	290	290	0.00
Green Lake, town	1,154	1,152	−0.17				
Kingston, town	1,064	1,095	2.91	**Jackson**	**20,449**	**20,828**	**1.85**
Kingston, village	326	324	−0.61	Adams, town	1,342	1,388	3.43
Mackford, town	560	551	−1.61	Albion, town	1,210	1,238	2.31
Manchester, town	1,022	1,046	2.35	Alma, town	1,044	1,112	6.51
Markesan, city	1,476	1,417	−4.00	Alma Center, village	503	506	0.60
Marquette, town	531	543	2.26	Bear Bluff, town	138	138	0.00
Marquette, village	150	150	0.00	Black River Falls, city	3,622	3,573	−1.35
Princeton, city	1,214	1,179	−2.88	Brockway, town	2,828	2,890	2.19
Princeton, town	1,434	1,443	0.63	City Point, town	182	181	−0.55
St. Marie, town	351	358	1.99	Cleveland, town	481	505	4.99
Seneca, town	408	406	−0.49	Curran, town	343	309	−9.91
				Franklin, town	448	458	2.23
Iowa	**23,687**	**23,915**	**0.96**	Garden Valley, town	422	433	2.61
Arena, town	1,456	1,518	4.26	Garfield, town	638	699	9.56
Arena, village	834	829	−0.60	Hixton, town	652	672	3.07
Avoca, village	637	612	−3.92	Hixton, village	433	425	−1.85
Barneveld, village	1,231	1,270	3.17	Irving, town	751	786	4.66
Blanchardville, village (part)	177	175	−1.13	Knapp, town	299	312	4.35
				Komensky, town	509	533	4.72
Brigham, town	1,034	1,091	5.51	Manchester, town	704	722	2.56
Clyde, town	306	314	2.61	Melrose, town	470	506	7.66
Cobb, village	458	464	1.31	Melrose, village	503	487	−3.18
Dodgeville, city	4,693	4,681	−0.26	Merrillan, village	542	515	−4.98
Dodgeville, town	1,708	1,720	0.70	Millston, town	159	166	4.40
Eden, town	355	370	4.23	North Bend, town	488	514	5.33
Highland, town	750	785	4.67	Northfield, town	639	658	2.97
Highland, village	842	836	−0.71	Springfield, town	623	615	−1.28
Hollandale, village	288	281	−2.43	Taylor, village	476	487	2.31
Linden, town	847	840	−0.83				
Linden, village	549	532	−3.10	**Jefferson**	**83,686**	**84,692**	**1.20**
Livingston, village (part)	7	7	0.00	Aztalan, town	1,457	1,453	−0.27
Mifflin, town	585	596	1.88	Cambridge, village (part)	109	107	−1.83
Mineral Point, city	2,487	2,488	0.04	Cold Spring, town	727	799	9.90
Mineral Point, town	1,033	1,074	3.97	Concord, town	2,072	2,063	−0.43
Montfort, village (part)	96	96	0.00	Farmington, town	1,380	1,378	−0.14
Moscow, town	576	608	5.56	Fort Atkinson, city	12,368	12,395	0.22
Muscoda, village (part)	50	39	−22.00	Hebron, town	1,094	1,101	0.64
Pulaski, town	400	400	0.00	Ixonia, town	4,385	4,965	13.23
Rewey, village	292	280	−4.11	Jefferson, city	7,973	7,935	−0.48
Ridgeway, town	568	579	1.94	Jefferson, town	2,178	2,185	0.32
Ridgeway, village	653	647	−0.92	Johnson Creek, village	2,738	3,029	10.63
Waldwick, town	473	477	0.85	Koshkonong, town	3,692	3,658	−0.92
Wyoming, town	302	306	1.32	Lac La Belle, village (part)	1	1	0.00
				Lake Mills, city	5,708	6,066	6.27
Iron	**5,916**	**5,909**	**−0.12**	Lake Mills, town	2,070	2,130	2.90
Anderson, town	58	59	1.72	Milford, town	1,099	1,141	3.82
Carey, town	163	159	−2.45	Oakland, town	3,100	3,124	0.77
Gurney, town	159	162	1.89	Palmyra, town	1,186	1,174	−1.01
Hurley, city	1,547	1,506	−2.65	Palmyra, village	1,781	1,742	−2.19
Kimball, town	498	503	1.00	Sullivan, town	2,208	2,225	0.77
Knight, town	211	206	−2.37	Sullivan, village	669	660	−1.35
Mercer, town	1,407	1,445	2.70	Sumner, town	832	803	−3.49

Wisconsin population by county and municipality, continued

	2010 census	2020 estimate	% change		2010 census	2020 estimate	% change
Waterloo, city	3,333	3,341	0.24	Franklin, town	993	999	0.60
Waterloo, town	909	907	-0.22	Kewaunee, city	2,952	2,870	-2.78
Watertown, city (part) . .	15,402	15,234	-1.09	Lincoln, town	948	933	-1.58
Watertown, town	1,975	2,017	2.13	Luxemburg, town	1,469	1,521	3.54
Whitewater, city (part) . .	3,240	3,059	-5.59	Luxemburg, village	2,515	2,620	4.17
				Montpelier, town	1,306	1,320	1.07
Juneau	**26,664**	**27,250**	**2.20**	Pierce, town	833	833	0.00
Armenia, town	699	760	8.73	Red River, town	1,393	1,411	1.29
Camp Douglas, village. .	601	619	3.00	West Kewaunee, town. .	1,296	1,356	4.63
Clearfield, town.	728	755	3.71	**La Crosse**	**114,638**	**120,447**	**5.07**
Cutler, town	326	329	0.92	Bangor, town	615	629	2.28
Elroy, city	1,442	1,333	-7.56	Bangor, village	1,459	1,535	5.21
Finley, town	97	93	-4.12	Barre, town	1,234	1,350	9.40
Fountain, town	555	603	8.65	Burns, town	947	955	0.84
Germantown, town . . .	1,471	1,742	18.42	Campbell, town	4,314	4,282	-0.74
Hustler, village	194	191	-1.55	Farmington, town	2,061	2,125	3.11
Kildare, town	681	717	5.29	Greenfield, town	2,060	2,155	4.61
Kingston, town	91	89	-2.20	Hamilton, town	2,436	2,498	2.55
Lemonweir, town.	1,743	1,752	0.52	Holland, town	3,701	4,266	15.27
Lindina, town	718	711	-0.97	Holmen, village	9,005	10,662	18.40
Lisbon, town.	912	928	1.75	La Crosse, city	51,320	52,282	1.87
Lyndon, town	1,384	1,419	2.53	Medary, town	1,461	1,528	4.59
Lyndon Station, village .	500	483	-3.40	Onalaska, city	17,736	19,330	8.99
Marion, town	426	427	0.23	Onalaska, town	5,623	5,846	3.97
Mauston, city	4,423	4,475	1.18	Rockland, village (part) .	594	738	24.24
Necedah, town	2,327	2,438	4.77	Shelby, town.	4,715	4,686	-0.62
Necedah, village	916	908	-0.87	Washington, town	558	535	-4.12
New Lisbon, city	2,554	2,605	2.00	West Salem, village. . . .	4,799	5,045	5.13
Orange, town	570	565	-0.88				
Plymouth, town.	597	597	0.00	**Lafayette**	**16,836**	**17,007**	**1.02**
Seven Mile Creek, town .	358	361	0.84	Argyle, town	436	465	6.65
Summit, town	646	672	4.02	Argyle, village	857	834	-2.68
Union Center, village . .	200	195	-2.50	Belmont, town	767	820	6.91
Wisconsin Dells, city (part)	2	0	-100.00	Belmont, village	986	1,000	1.42
Wonewoc, town.	687	691	0.58	Benton, town	504	519	2.98
Wonewoc, village.	816	792	-2.94	Benton, village	973	966	-0.72
				Blanchard, town	264	287	8.71
Kenosha	**166,426**	**170,514**	**2.46**	Blanchardville, village			
Brighton, town	1,456	1,466	0.69	(part)	648	635	-2.01
Bristol, village	4,914	5,139	4.58	Cuba City, city (part) . . .	209	221	5.74
Genoa City, village (part).	6	6	0.00	Darlington, city	2,451	2,378	-2.98
Kenosha, city	99,218	98,891	-0.33	Darlington, town	875	918	4.91
Paddock Lake, village . .	2,992	3,176	6.15	Elk Grove, town	551	585	6.17
Paris, town	1,504	1,516	0.80	Fayette, town	376	420	11.70
Pleasant Prairie, village .	19,719	22,456	13.88	Gratiot, town	550	559	1.64
Randall, town	3,180	3,189	0.28	Gratiot, village	236	226	-4.24
Salem Lakes, village[4]. . .	14,478	14,679	1.39	Hazel Green, village (part)	13	13	0.00
Somers, town	9,597	1,263	-86.84	Kendall, town	454	485	6.83
Somers, village[5].	NA	9,182	NA	Lamont, town	314	311	-0.96
Twin Lakes, village	5,989	6,189	3.34	Monticello, town	133	131	-1.50
Wheatland, town	3,373	3,362	-0.33	New Diggings, town . . .	502	521	3.78
				Seymour, town	446	447	0.22
Kewaunee	**20,574**	**20,746**	**0.84**	Shullsburg, city	1,226	1,196	-2.45
Ahnapee, town	940	932	-0.85	Shullsburg, town	354	349	-1.41
Algoma, city	3,167	3,105	-1.96	South Wayne, village. . .	489	477	-2.45
Carlton, town	1,014	1,036	2.17	Wayne, town.	490	493	0.61
Casco, town	1,165	1,212	4.03	White Oak Springs, town	118	123	4.24
Casco, village	583	598	2.57				

Wisconsin population by county and municipality, continued

	2010 census	2020 esti- mate	% change		2010 census	2020 esti- mate	% change
Willow Springs, town . .	758	774	2.11	Manitowoc, town.	1,083	1,114	2.86
Wiota, town	856	854	–0.23	Manitowoc Rapids, town	2,150	2,179	1.35
				Maple Grove, town. . . .	835	830	–0.60
Langlade.	**19,977**	**20,063**	**0.43**	Maribel, village	351	355	1.14
Ackley, town.	524	519	–0.95	Meeme, town	1,446	1,458	0.83
Ainsworth, town	469	460	–1.92	Mishicot, town	1,289	1,293	0.31
Antigo, city.	8,234	8,289	0.67	Mishicot, village	1,442	1,442	0.00
Antigo, town.	1,412	1,390	–1.56	Newton, town.	2,264	2,315	2.25
Elcho, town	1,233	1,245	0.97	Reedsville, village	1,206	1,181	–2.07
Evergreen, town	495	507	2.42	Rockland, town	1,001	1,023	2.20
Langlade, town	473	475	0.42	St. Nazianz, village	783	760	–2.94
Neva, town.	902	890	–1.33	Schleswig, town	1,963	2,031	3.46
Norwood, town.	913	900	–1.42	Two Creeks, town.	437	433	–0.92
Parrish, town	91	91	0.00	Two Rivers, city	11,712	11,364	–2.97
Peck, town	349	367	5.16	Two Rivers, town	1,795	1,843	2.67
Polar, town.	984	1,007	2.34	Valders, village	962	952	–1.04
Price, town.	228	224	–1.75	Whitelaw, village	757	753	–0.53
Rolling, town	1,504	1,523	1.26				
Summit, town	163	160	–1.84	**Marathon**	**134,063**	**137,237**	**2.37**
Upham, town	676	678	0.30	Abbotsford, city (part). .	694	650	–6.34
Vilas, town	233	227	–2.58	Athens, village	1,105	1,116	1.00
White Lake, village	363	352	–3.03	Bergen, town	641	635	–0.94
Wolf River, town	731	759	3.83	Berlin, town	945	957	1.27
				Bern, town	591	616	4.23
Lincoln	**28,743**	**28,800**	**0.20**	Bevent, town	1,118	1,138	1.79
Birch, town.	594	539	–9.26	Birnamwood, village (part)	16	20	25.00
Bradley, town	2,408	2,465	2.37	Brighton, town	612	607	–0.82
Corning, town.	883	887	0.45	Cassel, town	911	937	2.85
Harding, town.	372	375	0.81	Cleveland, town.	1,488	1,524	2.42
Harrison, town	833	840	0.84	Colby, city (part)	498	554	11.24
King, town	855	895	4.68	Day, town	1,085	1,093	0.74
Merrill, city.	9,661	9,661	0.00	Dorchester, village (part)	5	4	–20.00
Merrill, town.	2,980	3,027	1.58	Easton, town.	1,111	1,150	3.51
Pine River, town.	1,869	1,869	0.00	Eau Pleine, town	773	759	–1.81
Rock Falls, town.	618	640	3.56	Edgar, village	1,479	1,466	–0.88
Russell, town	677	680	0.44	Elderon, town	606	619	2.15
Schley, town.	934	936	0.21	Elderon, village	179	177	–1.12
Scott, town.	1,432	1,433	0.07	Emmet, town	931	961	3.22
Skanawan, town	391	396	1.28	Fenwood, village	152	153	0.66
Somo, town	114	116	1.75	Frankfort, town	670	652	–2.69
Tomahawk, city	3,397	3,299	–2.88	Franzen, town.	578	590	2.08
Tomahawk, town	416	431	3.61	Green Valley, town	541	557	2.96
Wilson, town.	309	311	0.65	Guenther, town	341	346	1.47
				Halsey, town.	651	672	3.23
Manitowoc	**81,442**	**81,349**	**–0.11**	Hamburg, town.	918	926	0.87
Cato, town	1,566	1,599	2.11	Harrison, town	374	382	2.14
Centerville, town	645	651	0.93	Hatley, village	574	637	10.98
Cleveland, village.	1,485	1,502	1.14	Hewitt, town.	606	637	5.12
Cooperstown, town . . .	1,292	1,304	0.93	Holton, town	873	883	1.15
Eaton, town	833	848	1.80	Hull, town	750	746	–0.53
Francis Creek, village . .	669	658	–1.64	Johnson, town	985	990	0.51
Franklin, town.	1,264	1,263	–0.08	Knowlton, town.	1,910	1,972	3.25
Gibson, town	1,344	1,362	1.34	Kronenwetter, village . .	7,210	8,158	13.15
Kellnersville, village . . .	332	329	–0.90	Maine, village[6]	2,588	2,619	1.20
Kiel, city (part).	3,429	3,600	4.99	Marathon, town	1,048	1,037	–1.05
Kossuth, town.	2,090	2,088	–0.10	Marathon City, village . .	1,524	1,588	4.20
Liberty, town	1,281	1,292	0.86	Marshfield, city (part) . .	900	1,108	23.11
Manitowoc, city.	33,736	33,527	–0.62				

Wisconsin population by county and municipality, continued

	2010 census	2020 esti- mate	% change		2010 census	2020 esti- mate	% change
McMillan, town	1,968	2,043	3.81	Montello, city	1,495	1,447	-3.21
Mosinee, city	3,988	4,124	3.41	Montello, town	1,033	1,039	0.58
Mosinee, town	2,174	2,206	1.47	Moundville, town	552	570	3.26
Norrie, town	976	994	1.84	Neshkoro, town	561	548	-2.32
Plover, town	689	698	1.31	Neshkoro, village	434	420	-3.23
Reid, town	1,215	1,242	2.22	Newton, town	547	555	1.46
Rib Falls, town	993	999	0.60	Oxford, town	885	895	1.13
Rib Mountain, town	6,825	7,001	2.58	Oxford, village	607	583	-3.95
Rietbrock, town	981	991	1.02	Packwaukee, town	1,416	1,400	-1.13
Ringle, town	1,711	1,771	3.51	Shields, town	550	554	0.73
Rothschild, village	5,269	5,328	1.12	Springfield, town	830	834	0.48
Schofield, city	2,169	2,201	1.48	Westfield, town	866	883	1.96
Spencer, town	1,581	1,640	3.73	Westfield, village	1,254	1,232	-1.75
Spencer, village	1,925	1,913	-0.62				
Stettin, town	2,554	2,595	1.61	**Menominee**	**4,232**	**4,267**	**0.83**
Stratford, village	1,578	1,610	2.03	Menominee, town	4,232	4,267	0.83
Texas, town	1,615	1,598	-1.05				
Unity, village (part)	204	197	-3.43	**Milwaukee**	**947,735**	**944,099**	**-0.38**
Wausau, city	39,106	38,884	-0.57	Bayside, village (part)	4,300	4,201	-2.30
Wausau, town	2,229	2,364	6.06	Brown Deer, village	11,999	12,518	4.33
Weston, town	639	695	8.76	Cudahy, city	18,267	18,007	-1.42
Weston, village	14,868	15,646	5.23	Fox Point, village	6,701	6,826	1.87
Wien, town	825	861	4.36	Franklin, city	35,451	36,514	3.00
				Glendale, city	12,872	12,463	-3.18
Marinette	**41,749**	**41,255**	**-1.18**	Greendale, village	14,046	14,335	2.06
Amberg, town	726	731	0.69	Greenfield, city	36,720	36,659	-0.17
Athelstane, town	504	509	0.99	Hales Corners, village	7,692	7,555	-1.78
Beaver, town	1,146	1,168	1.92	Milwaukee, city (part)	594,833	587,072	-1.30
Beecher, town	724	734	1.38	Oak Creek, city	34,451	36,529	6.03
Coleman, village	724	716	-1.10	River Hills, village	1,597	1,553	-2.76
Crivitz, village	984	939	-4.57	St. Francis, city	9,365	9,658	3.13
Dunbar, town	1,094	627	-42.69	Shorewood, village	13,162	13,472	2.36
Goodman, town	619	622	0.48	South Milwaukee, city	21,156	20,622	-2.52
Grover, town	1,768	1,814	2.60	Wauwatosa, city	46,396	48,478	4.49
Lake, town	1,135	1,172	3.26	West Allis, city	60,411	59,517	-1.48
Marinette, city	10,968	10,720	-2.26	West Milwaukee, village	4,206	4,120	-2.04
Middle Inlet, town	840	834	-0.71	Whitefish Bay, village	14,110	14,000	-0.78
Niagara, city	1,624	1,564	-3.69				
Niagara, town	853	864	1.29	**Monroe**	**44,673**	**46,882**	**4.94**
Pembine, town	889	906	1.91	Adrian, town	762	823	8.01
Peshtigo, city	3,502	3,382	-3.43	Angelo, town	1,296	1,758	35.65
Peshtigo, town	4,057	4,149	2.27	Byron, town	1,342	1,353	0.82
Porterfield, town	1,971	2,019	2.44	Cashton, village	1,102	1,101	-0.09
Pound, town	1,425	1,420	-0.35	Clifton, town	690	714	3.48
Pound, village	377	370	-1.86	Glendale, town	667	687	3.00
Silver Cliff, town	491	506	3.05	Grant, town	495	513	3.64
Stephenson, town	3,006	3,101	3.16	Greenfield, town	707	719	1.70
Wagner, town	681	704	3.38	Jefferson, town	819	937	14.41
Wausaukee, town	1,066	1,121	5.16	Kendall, village	472	453	-4.03
Wausaukee, village	575	563	-2.09	La Grange, town	2,007	1,990	-0.85
				Lafayette, town	396	430	8.59
Marquette	**15,404**	**15,387**	**-0.11**	Leon, town	1,086	1,161	6.91
Buffalo, town	1,221	1,258	3.03	Lincoln, town	835	850	1.80
Crystal Lake, town	484	491	1.45	Little Falls, town	1,523	1,620	6.37
Douglas, town	725	737	1.66	Melvina, village	104	102	-1.92
Endeavor, village	468	458	-2.14	New Lyme, town	168	182	8.33
Harris, town	790	795	0.63	Norwalk, village	638	631	-1.10
Mecan, town	686	688	0.29	Oakdale, town	772	799	3.50

Wisconsin population by county and municipality, continued

	2010 census	2020 estimate	% change		2010 census	2020 estimate	% change
Oakdale, village	297	290	-2.36	Monico, town	309	306	-0.97
Ontario, village (part)	0	0	0.00	Newbold, town	2,719	2,752	1.21
Portland, town	808	839	3.84	Nokomis, town	1,371	1,466	6.93
Ridgeville, town.	501	547	9.18	Pelican, town	2,764	2,799	1.27
Rockland, village (part) .	0	0	0.00	Piehl, town.	86	89	3.49
Scott, town	135	130	-3.70	Pine Lake, town	2,740	2,752	0.44
Sheldon, town.	727	781	7.43	Rhinelander, city	7,798	7,783	-0.19
Sparta, city.	9,522	10,056	5.61	Schoepke, town.	387	387	0.00
Sparta, town.	3,128	3,275	4.70	Stella, town	650	639	-1.69
Tomah, city	9,093	9,385	3.21	Sugar Camp, town	1,694	1,698	0.24
Tomah, town	1,400	1,446	3.29	Three Lakes, town	2,131	2,146	0.70
Warrens, village.	363	362	-0.28	Woodboro, town	813	838	3.08
Wellington, town	621	662	6.60	Woodruff, town	1,987	1,992	0.25
Wells, town.	519	562	8.29	**Outagamie . . . .**	**176,695**	**187,661**	**6.21**
Wilton, town.	1,027	1,099	7.01	Appleton, city (part) . . .	60,045	61,317	2.12
Wilton, village	504	486	-3.57	Bear Creek, village	448	439	-2.01
Wyeville, village.	147	139	-5.44	Black Creek, town	1,259	1,254	-0.40
				Black Creek, village. . . .	1,316	1,299	-1.29
Oconto	**37,660**	**38,853**	**3.17**	Bovina, town	1,145	1,189	3.84
Abrams, town	1,856	1,974	6.36	Buchanan, town	6,755	7,055	4.44
Bagley, town.	291	298	2.41	Center, town.	3,402	3,648	7.23
Brazeau, town	1,284	1,299	1.17	Cicero, town	1,103	1,107	0.36
Breed, town	712	732	2.81	Combined Locks, village	3,328	3,592	7.93
Chase, town	3,005	3,263	8.59	Dale, town	2,731	2,894	5.97
Doty, town	260	263	1.15	Deer Creek, town	637	659	3.45
Gillett, city	1,386	1,323	-4.55	Ellington, town	2,758	3,133	13.60
Gillett, town	1,043	1,019	-2.30	Freedom, town	5,842	6,088	4.21
How, town	516	535	3.68	Grand Chute, town. . . .	20,919	23,227	11.03
Lakewood, town	816	836	2.45	Greenville, town[7]	10,309	12,267	18.99
Lena, town	727	716	-1.51	Harrison, village (part)[8] .	NA	0	NA
Lena, village	564	552	-2.13	Hortonia, town	1,097	1,090	-0.64
Little River, town	1,094	1,122	2.56	Hortonville, village. . . .	2,711	2,911	7.38
Little Suamico, town . . .	4,799	5,460	13.77	Howard, village (part) . .	0	0	0.00
Maple Valley, town	662	661	-0.15	Kaukauna, city (part). . .	15,462	16,363	5.83
Morgan, town	984	1,013	2.95	Kaukauna, town	1,238	1,335	7.84
Mountain, town.	822	820	-0.24	Kimberly, village	6,468	7,137	10.34
Oconto, city	4,513	4,598	1.88	Liberty, town	867	880	1.50
Oconto, town	1,335	1,369	2.55	Little Chute, village . . .	10,449	11,947	14.34
Oconto Falls, city	2,891	2,806	-2.94	Maine, town	866	880	1.62
Oconto Falls, town	1,265	1,288	1.82	Maple Creek, town	619	609	-1.62
Pensaukee, town	1,381	1,397	1.16	New London, city (part) .	1,610	1,720	6.83
Pulaski, village (part). . .	0	0	0.00	Nichols, village	273	279	2.20
Riverview, town.	725	729	0.55	Oneida, town	4,678	4,739	1.30
Spruce, town	835	846	1.32	Osborn, town	1,170	1,234	5.47
Stiles, town	1,489	1,526	2.48	Seymour, city	3,451	3,415	-1.04
Suring, village	544	534	-1.84	Seymour, town	1,193	1,207	1.17
Townsend, town	979	964	-1.53	Shiocton, village	921	923	0.22
Underhill, town	882	910	3.17	Vandenbroek, town	1,474	1,591	7.94
Oneida	**35,998**	**36,268**	**0.75**	Wrightstown, village (part)	151	233	54.30
Cassian, town	985	982	-0.30				
Crescent, town	2,033	2,048	0.74	**Ozaukee . . . .**	**86,395**	**90,630**	**4.90**
Enterprise, town	315	315	0.00	Bayside, village (part) . .	89	89	0.00
Hazelhurst, town	1,273	1,272	-0.08	Belgium, town.	1,415	1,434	1.34
Lake Tomahawk, town. .	1,043	1,056	1.25	Belgium, village.	2,245	2,448	9.04
Little Rice, town.	306	317	3.59	Cedarburg, city	11,412	12,147	6.44
Lynne, town	141	140	-0.71	Cedarburg, town	5,760	6,006	4.27
Minocqua, town	4,453	4,491	0.85	Fredonia, town	2,172	2,186	0.64

Wisconsin population by county and municipality, continued

	2010 census	2020 esti- mate	% change		2010 census	2020 esti- mate	% change
Fredonia, village	2,160	2,199	1.81	Black Brook, town	1,325	1,359	2.57
Grafton, town	4,053	4,227	4.29	Bone Lake, town	717	730	1.81
Grafton, village	11,459	11,989	4.63	Centuria, village	948	946	-0.21
Mequon, city	23,132	24,806	7.24	Clam Falls, town	596	609	2.18
Newburg, village (part) .	97	95	-2.06	Clayton, town	975	981	0.62
Port Washington, city . .	11,250	11,954	6.26	Clayton, village	571	559	-2.10
Port Washington, town .	1,643	1,647	0.24	Clear Lake, town	899	906	0.78
Saukville, town	1,822	1,843	1.15	Clear Lake, village	1,070	1,090	1.87
Saukville, village	4,451	4,396	-1.24	Dresser, village	895	906	1.23
Thiensville, village	3,235	3,164	-2.19	Eureka, town.	1,649	1,687	2.30
				Farmington, town	1,836	1,908	3.92
Pepin	**7,469**	**7,393**	**-1.02**	Frederic, village.	1,137	1,119	-1.58
Albany, town	676	693	2.51	Garfield, town.	1,692	1,704	0.71
Durand, city	1,931	1,841	-4.66	Georgetown, town. . . .	977	995	1.84
Durand, town	742	747	0.67	Johnstown, town.	534	520	-2.62
Frankfort, town	343	360	4.96	Laketown, town.	961	973	1.25
Lima, town.	702	692	-1.42	Lincoln, town	2,208	2,233	1.13
Pepin, town	721	746	3.47	Lorain, town	284	290	2.11
Pepin, village	837	788	-5.85	Luck, town	930	933	0.32
Stockholm, town	197	204	3.55	Luck, village	1,119	1,087	-2.86
Stockholm, village	66	66	0.00	McKinley, town	347	361	4.03
Waterville, town	831	823	-0.96	Milltown, town	1,226	1,237	0.90
Waubeek, town	423	433	2.36	Milltown, village	917	908	-0.98
				Osceola, town.	2,855	2,941	3.01
Pierce	**41,019**	**42,413**	**3.40**	Osceola, village	2,568	2,698	5.06
Bay City, village	500	491	-1.80	St. Croix Falls, city. . . .	2,133	2,113	-0.94
Clifton, town.	2,012	2,134	6.06	St. Croix Falls, town. . . .	1,165	1,179	1.20
Diamond Bluff, town. . .	469	462	-1.49	Sterling, town	790	776	-1.77
El Paso, town	681	721	5.87	Turtle Lake, village (part)	93	91	-2.15
Ellsworth, town	1,146	1,175	2.53	West Sweden, town . . .	699	710	1.57
Ellsworth, village	3,284	3,365	2.47				
Elmwood, village	817	789	-3.43	**Portage**.	**70,019**	**71,670**	**2.36**
Gilman, town	959	1,014	5.74	Alban, town	885	885	0.00
Hartland, town	827	865	4.59	Almond, town.	680	670	-1.47
Isabelle, town	281	293	4.27	Almond, village.	448	424	-5.36
Maiden Rock, town. . . .	589	608	3.23	Amherst, town	1,325	1,365	3.02
Maiden Rock, village. . .	119	116	-2.52	Amherst, village	1,035	1,097	5.99
Martell, town	1,185	1,213	2.36	Amherst Junction, village	377	397	5.31
Oak Grove, town	2,150	2,318	7.81	Belmont, town	616	630	2.27
Plum City, village	599	600	0.17	Buena Vista, town	1,198	1,212	1.17
Prescott, city.	4,258	4,217	-0.96	Carson, town	1,305	1,331	1.99
River Falls, city (part). . .	11,851	12,626	6.54	Dewey, town.	932	985	5.69
River Falls, town.	2,271	2,314	1.89	Eau Pleine, town	908	993	9.36
Rock Elm, town	485	491	1.24	Grant, town	1,906	1,955	2.57
Salem, town	510	528	3.53	Hull, town	5,346	5,468	2.28
Spring Lake, town	563	586	4.09	Junction City, village. . .	439	435	-0.91
Spring Valley, village (part)	1,346	1,332	-1.04	Lanark, town.	1,527	1,562	2.29
Trenton, town	1,829	1,875	2.52	Linwood, town	1,121	1,148	2.41
Trimbelle, town	1,679	1,679	0.00	Milladore, village (part) .	0	0	0.00
Union, town	609	601	-1.31	Nelsonville, village	155	161	3.87
				New Hope, town	718	715	-0.42
Polk	**44,205**	**44,628**	**0.96**	Park Ridge, village	491	499	1.63
Alden, town	2,786	2,812	0.93	Pine Grove, town	937	925	-1.28
Amery, city.	2,902	2,856	-1.59	Plover, town	1,701	1,744	2.53
Apple River, town.	1,146	1,172	2.27	Plover, village	12,123	13,486	11.24
Balsam Lake, town	1,411	1,380	-2.20	Rosholt, village	506	496	-1.98
Balsam Lake, village . . .	1,009	1,013	0.40	Sharon, town	1,982	2,078	4.84
Beaver, town.	835	846	1.32				

Wisconsin population by county and municipality, continued

	2010 census	2020 esti-mate	% change
Stevens Point, city	26,717	26,269	-1.68
Stockton, town	2,917	3,062	4.97
Whiting, village	1,724	1,678	-2.67
Price.	**14,159**	**14,170**	**0.08**
Catawba, town	269	270	0.37
Catawba, village	110	107	-2.73
Eisenstein, town	630	628	-0.32
Elk, town	988	1,026	3.85
Emery, town	297	291	-2.02
Fifield, town	901	893	-0.89
Flambeau, town.	489	484	-1.02
Georgetown, town	171	168	-1.75
Hackett, town	169	175	3.55
Harmony, town	222	221	-0.45
Hill, town	333	340	2.10
Kennan, town	356	355	-0.28
Kennan, village	135	132	-2.22
Knox, town	341	352	3.23
Lake, town	1,128	1,132	0.35
Ogema, town	713	727	1.96
Park Falls, city	2,462	2,472	0.41
Phillips, city	1,478	1,426	-3.52
Prentice, town.	475	468	-1.47
Prentice, village.	660	642	-2.73
Spirit, town	277	282	1.81
Worcester, town.	1,555	1,579	1.54
Racine	**195,408**	**195,766**	**0.18**
Burlington, city (part) . .	10,464	10,911	4.27
Burlington, town	6,502	6,478	-0.37
Caledonia, village.	24,705	25,131	1.72
Dover, town	4,051	4,197	3.60
Elmwood Park, village . .	497	486	-2.21
Mount Pleasant, village .	26,197	26,922	2.77
North Bay, village.	241	236	-2.07
Norway, town	7,948	7,991	0.54
Racine, city.	78,860	76,709	-2.73
Raymond, village[2]	3,870	4,015	3.75
Rochester, village.	3,682	3,854	4.67
Sturtevant, village	6,970	6,633	-4.84
Union Grove, village . . .	4,915	5,227	6.35
Waterford, town	6,344	6,489	2.29
Waterford, village.	5,368	5,664	5.51
Wind Point, village	1,723	1,676	-2.73
Yorkville, village[2]	3,071	3,147	2.47
Richland	**18,021**	**18,034**	**0.07**
Akan, town.	403	404	0.25
Bloom, town.	512	510	-0.39
Boaz, village	156	155	-0.64
Buena Vista, town	1,869	1,907	2.03
Cazenovia, village (part)	314	302	-3.82
Dayton, town	693	697	0.58
Eagle, town	531	520	-2.07
Forest, town	352	362	2.84
Henrietta, town	493	491	-0.41
Ithaca, town	619	643	3.88
Lone Rock, village	888	879	-1.01

	2010 census	2020 esti-mate	% change
Marshall, town	567	575	1.41
Orion, town	579	596	2.94
Richland, town	1,379	1,354	-1.81
Richland Center, city. . .	5,184	5,144	-0.77
Richwood, town	533	533	0.00
Rockbridge, town	734	725	-1.23
Sylvan, town.	555	580	4.50
Viola, village (part)	477	462	-3.14
Westford, town	530	538	1.51
Willow, town.	579	587	1.38
Yuba, village.	74	70	-5.41
Rock.	**160,331**	**160,120**	**-0.13**
Avon, town.	608	601	-1.15
Beloit, city	36,966	36,162	-2.17
Beloit, town	7,662	7,658	-0.05
Bradford, town	1,121	1,066	-4.91
Brodhead, city (part) . . .	90	94	4.44
Center, town.	1,066	1,058	-0.75
Clinton, town	930	938	0.86
Clinton, village	2,154	2,097	-2.65
Edgerton, city (part) . . .	5,364	5,504	2.61
Evansville, city.	5,012	5,487	9.48
Footville, village	808	825	2.10
Fulton, town.	3,252	3,443	5.87
Harmony, town	2,569	2,582	0.51
Janesville, city.	63,575	63,403	-0.27
Janesville, town.	3,434	3,537	3.00
Johnstown, town	778	765	-1.67
La Prairie, town	834	811	-2.76
Lima, town	1,280	1,282	0.16
Magnolia, town	767	764	-0.39
Milton, city.	5,546	5,585	0.70
Milton, town.	2,923	2,988	2.22
Newark, town.	1,541	1,519	-1.43
Orfordville, village	1,442	1,476	2.36
Plymouth, town.	1,235	1,166	-5.59
Porter, town	945	962	1.80
Rock, town.	3,196	3,131	-2.03
Spring Valley, town. . . .	746	751	0.67
Turtle, town	2,388	2,356	-1.34
Union, town	2,099	2,109	0.48
Rusk.	**14,755**	**14,879**	**0.84**
Atlanta, town	592	586	-1.01
Big Bend, town	358	380	6.15
Big Falls, town.	140	140	0.00
Bruce, village	779	752	-3.47
Cedar Rapids, town . . .	41	40	-2.44
Conrath, village	95	96	1.05
Dewey, town	545	563	3.30
Flambeau, town.	1,059	1,075	1.51
Glen Flora, village	92	88	-4.35
Grant, town	813	809	-0.49
Grow, town	427	438	2.58
Hawkins, town	153	164	7.19
Hawkins, village.	305	314	2.95
Hubbard, town	204	203	-0.49
Ingram, village	78	80	2.56

Wisconsin population by county and municipality, continued

	2010 census	2020 esti-mate	% change		2010 census	2020 esti-mate	% change
Ladysmith, city	3,414	3,327	-2.55	Bear Creek, town	595	639	7.39
Lawrence, town	311	307	-1.29	Cazenovia, village (part)	4	13	225.00
Marshall, town	688	700	1.74	Dellona, town	1,552	1,629	4.96
Murry, town	277	281	1.44	Delton, town	2,391	2,468	3.22
Richland, town	232	239	3.02	Excelsior, town	1,575	1,574	-0.06
Rusk, town	525	551	4.95	Fairfield, town	1,077	1,108	2.88
Sheldon, village	237	234	-1.27	Franklin, town	652	666	2.15
South Fork, town	120	118	-1.67	Freedom, town	447	457	2.24
Strickland, town	280	297	6.07	Greenfield, town	932	938	0.64
Stubbs, town	579	586	1.21	Honey Creek, town	733	737	0.55
Thornapple, town	774	820	5.94	Ironton, town	660	660	0.00
Tony, village	113	108	-4.42	Ironton, village	253	253	0.00
True, town	296	295	-0.34	La Valle, town	1,302	1,342	3.07
Washington, town	339	360	6.19	La Valle, village	367	351	-4.36
Weyerhaeuser, village	238	240	0.84	Lake Delton, village	2,914	2,900	-0.48
Wilkinson, town	40	42	5.00	Lime Ridge, village	162	158	-2.47
Willard, town	505	526	4.16	Loganville, village	300	292	-2.67
Wilson, town	106	120	13.21	Merrimac, town	942	1,011	7.32
				Merrimac, village	420	428	1.90
St. Croix	**84,345**	**90,949**	**7.83**	North Freedom, village	701	657	-6.28
Baldwin, town	928	957	3.13	Plain, village	773	756	-2.20
Baldwin, village	3,957	3,993	0.91	Prairie du Sac, town	1,144	1,136	-0.70
Cady, town	821	871	6.09	Prairie du Sac, village	3,972	4,193	5.56
Cylon, town	683	695	1.76	Reedsburg, city	9,200	9,678	5.20
Deer Park, village	216	209	-3.24	Reedsburg, town	1,293	1,266	-2.09
Eau Galle, town	1,139	1,245	9.31	Rock Springs, village	362	292	-19.34
Emerald, town	853	867	1.64	Sauk City, village	3,410	3,443	0.97
Erin Prairie, town	688	678	-1.45	Spring Green, town	1,697	1,716	1.12
Forest, town	629	620	-1.43	Spring Green, village	1,628	1,623	-0.31
Glenwood, town	785	791	0.76	Sumpter, town	1,191	1,183	-0.67
Glenwood City, city	1,242	1,210	-2.58	Troy, town	794	819	3.15
Hammond, town	2,102	2,359	12.23	Washington, town	1,007	1,026	1.89
Hammond, village	1,922	1,868	-2.81	West Baraboo, village	1,414	1,654	16.97
Hudson, city	12,719	14,091	10.79	Westfield, town	571	557	-2.45
Hudson, town	8,461	8,689	2.69	Winfield, town	856	872	1.87
Kinnickinnic, town	1,722	1,818	5.57	Wisconsin Dells, city (part)	175	309	76.57
New Richmond, city	8,375	9,741	16.31	Woodland, town	790	826	4.56
North Hudson, village	3,768	3,847	2.10				
Pleasant Valley, town	515	547	6.21	**Sawyer**	**16,557**	**16,903**	**2.09**
Richmond, town	3,272	3,782	15.59	Bass Lake, town	2,377	2,440	2.65
River Falls, city (part)	3,149	3,487	10.73	Couderay, town	401	409	2.00
Roberts, village	1,651	1,872	13.39	Couderay, village	88	88	0.00
Rush River, town	508	500	-1.57	Draper, town	204	210	2.94
St. Joseph, town	3,842	4,119	7.21	Edgewater, town	519	534	2.89
Somerset, town	4,036	4,401	9.04	Exeland, village	196	193	-1.53
Somerset, village	2,635	2,939	11.54	Hayward, city	2,318	2,370	2.24
Spring Valley, village (part)	6	12	100.00	Hayward, town	3,567	3,582	0.42
Springfield, town	932	988	6.01	Hunter, town	678	687	1.33
Stanton, town	900	892	-0.89	Lenroot, town	1,279	1,364	6.65
Star Prairie, town	3,504	3,622	3.37	Meadowbrook, town	131	142	8.40
Star Prairie, village	561	552	-1.60	Meteor, town	158	155	-1.90
Troy, town	4,705	5,398	14.73	Ojibwa, town	249	256	2.81
Warren, town	1,591	1,773	11.44	Radisson, town	405	413	1.98
Wilson, village	184	186	1.09	Radisson, village	241	237	-1.66
Woodville, village	1,344	1,330	-1.04	Round Lake, town	977	1,016	3.99
				Sand Lake, town	813	835	2.71
Sauk	**61,976**	**63,343**	**2.21**	Spider Lake, town	351	362	3.13
Baraboo, city	12,048	12,008	-0.33	Weirgor, town	332	334	0.60
Baraboo, town	1,672	1,705	1.97				

Wisconsin population by county and municipality, continued

	2010 census	2020 estimate	% change		2010 census	2020 estimate	% change
Winter, town	960	966	0.63	Oostburg, village	2,887	3,059	5.96
Winter, village	313	310	–0.96	Plymouth, city	8,445	8,715	3.20
				Plymouth, town	3,195	3,244	1.53
Shawano	**41,949**	**41,739**	**–0.50**	Random Lake, village . .	1,594	1,570	–1.51
Almon, town	584	586	0.34	Rhine, town	2,134	2,140	0.28
Angelica, town	1,793	1,836	2.40	Russell, town	377	373	–1.06
Aniwa, town	541	537	–0.74	Scott, town	1,836	1,808	–1.53
Aniwa, village	260	252	–3.08	Sheboygan, city	49,288	48,756	–1.08
Bartelme, town	819	807	–1.47	Sheboygan, town	7,271	8,029	10.42
Belle Plaine, town	1,855	1,832	–1.24	Sheboygan Falls, city . .	7,775	8,396	7.99
Birnamwood, town	763	779	2.10	Sheboygan Falls, town .	1,718	1,780	3.61
Birnamwood, village (part)	802	793	–1.12	Sherman, town	1,505	1,525	1.33
Bonduel, village	1,478	1,462	–1.08	Waldo, village	503	492	–2.19
Bowler, village	302	289	–4.30	Wilson, town	3,330	3,367	1.11
Cecil, village	570	572	0.35				
Eland, village	202	202	0.00	**Taylor**	**20,689**	**20,793**	**0.50**
Fairbanks, town	616	609	–1.14	Aurora, town	422	429	1.66
Germania, town	332	343	3.31	Browning, town	905	942	4.09
Grant, town	991	985	–0.61	Chelsea, town	806	818	1.49
Green Valley, town	1,089	1,094	0.46	Cleveland, town	268	269	0.37
Gresham, village	586	579	–1.19	Deer Creek, town	768	772	0.52
Hartland, town	904	896	–0.88	Ford, town	268	273	1.87
Herman, town	776	767	–1.16	Gilman, village	410	373	–9.02
Hutchins, town	600	588	–2.00	Goodrich, town	510	519	1.76
Lessor, town	1,263	1,281	1.43	Greenwood, town	638	639	0.16
Maple Grove, town	972	960	–1.23	Grover, town	256	253	–1.17
Marion, city (part)	25	25	0.00	Hammel, town	713	726	1.82
Mattoon, village	438	426	–2.74	Holway, town	973	963	–1.03
Morris, town	453	455	0.44	Jump River, town	375	371	–1.07
Navarino, town	446	443	–0.67	Little Black, town	1,140	1,146	0.53
Pella, town	865	886	2.43	Lublin, village	118	115	–2.54
Pulaski, village (part). . .	218	217	–0.46	Maplehurst, town	335	338	0.90
Red Springs, town	925	955	3.24	McKinley, town	458	460	0.44
Richmond, town	1,864	1,874	0.54	Medford, city	4,326	4,321	–0.12
Seneca, town	558	557	–0.18	Medford, town	2,606	2,690	3.22
Shawano, city	9,305	9,129	–1.89	Molitor, town	324	327	0.93
Tigerton, village	741	714	–3.64	Pershing, town	180	178	–1.11
Washington, town	1,895	1,949	2.85	Rib Lake, town	852	870	2.11
Waukechon, town	1,021	1,051	2.94	Rib Lake, village	910	868	–4.62
Wescott, town	3,183	3,183	0.00	Roosevelt, town	473	468	–1.06
Wittenberg, town	833	827	–0.72	Stetsonville, village . . .	541	531	–1.85
Wittenberg, village	1,081	999	–7.59	Taft, town	430	435	1.16
				Westboro, town	684	699	2.19
Sheboygan	**115,507**	**116,924**	**1.23**				
Adell, village	516	506	–1.94	**Trempealeau**	**28,816**	**30,047**	**4.27**
Cascade, village	709	691	–2.54	Albion, town	653	676	3.52
Cedar Grove, village . . .	2,113	2,112	–0.05	Arcadia, city	2,925	3,051	4.31
Elkhart Lake, village . . .	967	1,019	5.38	Arcadia, town	1,779	1,830	2.87
Glenbeulah, village . . .	463	469	1.30	Blair, city	1,366	1,342	–1.76
Greenbush, town	2,565	2,579	0.55	Burnside, town	511	523	2.35
Herman, town	2,151	2,057	–4.37	Caledonia, town	920	947	2.93
Holland, town	2,239	2,247	0.36	Chimney Rock, town . . .	241	245	1.66
Howards Grove, village .	3,188	3,285	3.04	Dodge, town	389	392	0.77
Kohler, village	2,120	2,078	–1.98	Eleva, village	670	675	0.75
Lima, town	2,982	2,965	–0.57	Ettrick, town	1,237	1,295	4.69
Lyndon, town	1,542	1,564	1.43	Ettrick, village	524	522	–0.38
Mitchell, town	1,304	1,314	0.77	Gale, town	1,695	1,772	4.54
Mosel, town	790	784	–0.76	Galesville, city	1,481	1,565	5.67

Wisconsin population by county and municipality, continued

	2010 census	2020 esti-mate	% change		2010 census	2020 esti-mate	% change
Hale, town	1,037	1,077	3.86	Manitowish Waters, town	566	582	2.83
Independence, city	1,336	1,340	0.30	Phelps, town	1,200	1,259	4.92
Lincoln, town	823	863	4.86	Plum Lake, town	491	502	2.24
Osseo, city	1,701	1,699	-0.12	Presque Isle, town	618	636	2.91
Pigeon, town	891	912	2.36	St. Germain, town	2,085	2,062	-1.10
Pigeon Falls, village	411	409	-0.49	Washington, town	1,451	1,465	0.96
Preston, town	953	1,006	5.56	Winchester, town	383	387	1.04
Strum, village	1,114	1,085	-2.60	**Walworth**	**102,228**	**104,086**	**1.82**
Sumner, town	810	859	6.05	Bloomfield, town	6,278	1,611	-74.34
Trempealeau, town	1,756	1,939	10.42	Bloomfield, village[5]	NA	4,798	NA
Trempealeau, village	1,529	1,952	27.67	Burlington, city (part)	0	1	NA
Unity, town	506	515	1.78	Darien, town	1,693	1,722	1.71
Whitehall, city	1,558	1,556	-0.13	Darien, village	1,580	1,574	-0.38
Vernon	**29,773**	**30,496**	**2.43**	Delavan, city	8,463	8,270	-2.28
Bergen, town	1,364	1,374	0.73	Delavan, town	5,285	5,168	-2.21
Chaseburg, village	284	284	0.00	East Troy, town	4,021	4,073	1.29
Christiana, town	931	973	4.51	East Troy, village	4,281	4,500	5.12
Clinton, town	1,358	1,436	5.74	Elkhorn, city	10,084	9,968	-1.15
Coon, town	728	763	4.81	Fontana-on-Geneva Lake,			
Coon Valley, village	765	742	-3.01	village	1,672	1,712	2.39
De Soto, village (part)	179	184	2.79	Geneva, town	4,993	5,085	1.84
Forest, town	634	653	3.00	Genoa City, village (part)	3,036	3,002	-1.12
Franklin, town	1,140	1,198	5.09	Lafayette, town	1,979	2,042	3.18
Genoa, town	789	797	1.01	La Grange, town	2,454	2,476	0.90
Genoa, village	253	250	-1.19	Lake Geneva, city	7,651	8,233	7.61
Greenwood, town	847	857	1.18	Linn, town	2,383	2,459	3.19
Hamburg, town	973	987	1.44	Lyons, town	3,698	3,710	0.32
Harmony, town	755	823	9.01	Mukwonago, village (part)	101	210	107.92
Hillsboro, city	1,417	1,382	-2.47	Richmond, town	1,884	1,887	0.16
Hillsboro, town	807	818	1.36	Sharon, town	907	901	-0.66
Jefferson, town	1,143	1,193	4.37	Sharon, village	1,605	1,561	-2.74
Kickapoo, town	626	678	8.31	Spring Prairie, town	2,181	2,217	1.65
La Farge, village	746	702	-5.90	Sugar Creek, town	3,943	3,933	-0.25
Liberty, town	252	270	7.14	Troy, town	2,353	2,395	1.78
Ontario, village (part)	554	540	-2.53	Walworth, town	1,702	1,685	-1.00
Readstown, village	415	414	-0.24	Walworth, village	2,816	2,829	0.46
Stark, town	363	389	7.16	Whitewater, city (part)	11,150	11,976	7.41
Sterling, town	633	630	-0.47	Whitewater, town	1,471	1,474	0.20
Stoddard, village	774	825	6.59	Williams Bay, village	2,564	2,614	1.95
Union, town	700	731	4.43	**Washburn**	**15,911**	**15,993**	**0.52**
Viola, village (part)	222	220	-0.90	Barronett, town	442	451	2.04
Viroqua, city	4,362	4,491	2.96	Bashaw, town	946	978	3.38
Viroqua, town	1,718	1,733	0.87	Bass Lake, town	505	524	3.76
Webster, town	778	825	6.04	Beaver Brook, town	713	721	1.12
Westby, city	2,200	2,208	0.36	Birchwood, town	478	493	3.14
Wheatland, town	561	587	4.63	Birchwood, village	442	436	-1.36
Whitestown, town	502	539	7.37	Brooklyn, town	254	255	0.39
Vilas	**21,430**	**21,769**	**1.58**	Casey, town	353	361	2.27
Arbor Vitae, town	3,316	3,326	0.30	Chicog, town	234	232	-0.85
Boulder Junction, town	933	950	1.82	Crystal, town	267	269	0.75
Cloverland, town	1,029	1,040	1.07	Evergreen, town	1,135	1,132	-0.26
Conover, town	1,235	1,239	0.32	Frog Creek, town	130	130	0.00
Eagle River, city	1,398	1,510	8.01	Gull Lake, town	186	187	0.54
Lac du Flambeau, town	3,441	3,463	0.64	Long Lake, town	624	632	1.28
Land O'Lakes, town	861	877	1.86	Madge, town	508	515	1.38
Lincoln, town	2,423	2,471	1.98	Minong, town	917	933	1.74

Wisconsin population by county and municipality, continued

	2010 census	2020 estimate	% change		2010 census	2020 estimate	% change
Minong, village	527	540	2.47	New Berlin, city	39,584	40,600	2.57
Sarona, town	384	380	−1.04	North Prairie, village	2,141	2,234	4.34
Shell Lake, city	1,347	1,347	0.00	Oconomowoc, city	15,759	17,501	11.05
Spooner, city	2,682	2,576	−3.95	Oconomowoc, town	8,408	8,706	3.54
Spooner, town	706	731	3.54	Oconomowoc Lake, village	595	598	0.50
Springbrook, town	445	447	0.45	Ottawa, town	3,859	3,936	2.00
Stinnett, town	246	244	−0.81	Pewaukee, city	13,195	14,775	11.97
Stone Lake, town	508	515	1.38	Pewaukee, village	8,166	7,883	−3.47
Trego, town	932	964	3.43	Summit, village[2]	4,674	4,974	6.42
Washington	**131,887**	**138,268**	**4.84**	Sussex, village	10,518	11,373	8.13
Addison, town	3,495	3,485	−0.29	Vernon, village[9]	7,601	7,621	0.26
Barton, town	2,637	2,721	3.19	Wales, village	2,549	2,616	2.63
Erin, town	3,747	3,824	2.05	Waukesha, city	70,718	71,952	1.74
Farmington, town	4,014	4,085	1.77	Waukesha, town[10]	9,133	9,329	2.15
Germantown, town	254	251	−1.18				
Germantown, village	19,749	20,686	4.74	**Waupaca**	**52,410**	**52,155**	**−0.49**
Hartford, city (part)	14,223	15,863	11.53	Bear Creek, town	823	826	0.36
Hartford, town	3,609	3,534	−2.08	Big Falls, village	61	60	−1.64
Jackson, town	4,134	4,564	10.40	Caledonia, town	1,627	1,700	4.49
Jackson, village	6,753	7,199	6.60	Clintonville, city	4,559	4,447	−2.46
Kewaskum, town	1,053	1,085	3.04	Dayton, town	2,748	2,753	0.18
Kewaskum, village (part)	4,004	4,177	4.32	Dupont, town	738	747	1.22
Milwaukee, city (part)	0	0	0.00	Embarrass, village	404	385	−4.70
Newburg, village (part)	1,157	1,169	1.04	Farmington, town	3,974	3,778	−4.93
Polk, town	3,937	4,040	2.62	Fremont, town	597	603	1.01
Richfield, village	11,300	11,948	5.73	Fremont, village	679	679	0.00
Slinger, village	5,068	5,845	15.33	Harrison, town	468	483	3.21
Trenton, town	4,732	4,800	1.44	Helvetia, town	636	637	0.16
Wayne, town	2,169	2,267	4.52	Iola, town	971	990	1.96
West Bend, city	31,078	32,058	3.15	Iola, village	1,301	1,250	−3.92
West Bend, town	4,774	4,667	−2.24	Larrabee, town	1,381	1,371	−0.72
				Lebanon, town	1,665	1,675	0.60
Waukesha	**389,891**	**406,785**	**4.33**	Lind, town	1,579	1,599	1.27
Big Bend, village	1,290	1,491	15.58	Little Wolf, town	1,424	1,425	0.07
Brookfield, city	37,920	40,044	5.60	Manawa, city	1,371	1,317	−3.94
Brookfield, town	6,116	6,744	10.27	Marion, city (part)	1,235	1,203	−2.59
Butler, village	1,841	1,803	−2.06	Matteson, town	936	933	−0.32
Chenequa, village	590	588	−0.34	Mukwa, town	2,930	2,978	1.64
Delafield, city	7,085	7,181	1.35	New London, city (part)	5,685	5,716	0.55
Delafield, town	8,400	8,503	1.23	Ogdensburg, village	185	182	−1.62
Dousman, village	2,302	2,353	2.22	Royalton, town	1,434	1,445	0.77
Eagle, town	3,507	3,586	2.25	St. Lawrence, town	710	713	0.42
Eagle, village	1,950	2,104	7.90	Scandinavia, town	1,066	1,087	1.97
Elm Grove, village	5,934	5,857	−1.30	Scandinavia, village	363	362	−0.28
Genesee, town	7,340	7,379	0.53	Union, town	806	815	1.12
Hartland, village	9,110	9,286	1.93	Waupaca, city	6,069	6,004	−1.07
Lac La Belle, village (part)	289	296	2.42	Waupaca, town	1,173	1,222	4.18
Lannon, village	1,107	1,264	14.18	Weyauwega, city	1,900	1,878	−1.16
Lisbon, town	10,157	10,564	4.01	Weyauwega, town	583	570	−2.23
Menomonee Falls, village	35,626	38,948	9.32	Wyoming, town	329	322	−2.13
Merton, town	8,338	8,469	1.57				
Merton, village	3,346	3,711	10.91	**Waushara**	**24,496**	**24,436**	**−0.24**
Milwaukee, city (part)	0	0	0.00	Aurora, town	985	1,008	2.34
Mukwonago, town	7,959	7,979	0.25	Berlin, city (part)	89	89	0.00
Mukwonago, village (part)	7,254	7,916	9.13	Bloomfield, town	1,052	1,081	2.76
Muskego, city	24,135	25,271	4.71	Coloma, town	753	749	−0.53
Nashotah, village	1,395	1,350	−3.23	Coloma, village	450	458	1.78
				Dakota, town	1,227	1,225	−0.16

Wisconsin population by county and municipality, continued

	2010 census	2020 esti- mate	% change		2010 census	2020 esti- mate	% change
Deerfield, town	737	744	0.95	Winchester, town	1,763	1,824	3.46
Hancock, town	528	540	2.27	Winneconne, town	2,350	2,436	3.66
Hancock, village	417	410	−1.68	Winneconne, village	2,383	2,499	4.87
Leon, town	1,439	1,436	−0.21	Wolf River, town	1,189	1,195	0.50
Lohrville, village	402	390	−2.99				
Marion, town	2,038	2,033	−0.25	**Wood**	**74,749**	**75,381**	**0.85**
Mount Morris, town	1,097	1,114	1.55	Arpin, town	929	963	3.66
Oasis, town	389	405	4.11	Arpin, village	333	328	−1.50
Plainfield, town	550	544	−1.09	Auburndale, town	860	850	−1.16
Plainfield, village	862	850	−1.39	Auburndale, village	703	714	1.56
Poy Sippi, town	931	912	−2.04	Biron, village	839	819	−2.38
Redgranite, village	2,149	2,116	−1.54	Cameron, town	511	474	−7.24
Richford, town	612	650	6.21	Cary, town	424	419	−1.18
Rose, town	640	652	1.88	Cranmoor, town	168	164	−2.38
Saxeville, town	986	988	0.20	Dexter, town	359	359	0.00
Springwater, town	1,274	1,271	−0.24	Grand Rapids, town	7,646	7,771	1.63
Warren, town	668	672	0.60	Hansen, town	690	698	1.16
Wautoma, city	2,218	2,127	−4.10	Hewitt, village	828	841	1.57
Wautoma, town	1,278	1,294	1.25	Hiles, town	167	172	2.99
Wild Rose, village	725	678	−6.48	Lincoln, town	1,564	1,599	2.24
				Marshfield, city (part)	18,218	18,370	0.83
Winnebago	**166,994**	**169,861**	**1.72**	Marshfield, town	764	788	3.14
Algoma, town	6,822	6,939	1.72	Milladore, town	690	683	−1.01
Appleton, city (part)	1,490	1,478	−0.81	Milladore, village (part)	276	274	−0.72
Black Wolf, town	2,410	2,446	1.49	Nekoosa, city	2,580	2,516	−2.48
Clayton, town	3,951	4,193	6.13	Pittsville, city	874	868	−0.69
Fox Crossing, village[11]	18,498	19,090	3.20	Port Edwards, town	1,427	1,415	−0.84
Menasha, city (part)	15,144	14,635	−3.36	Port Edwards, village	1,818	1,779	−2.15
Neenah, city	25,501	26,333	3.26	Remington, town	268	260	−2.99
Neenah, town	3,237	3,632	12.20	Richfield, town	1,628	1,580	−2.95
Nekimi, town	1,429	1,422	−0.49	Rock, town	855	882	3.16
Nepeuskun, town	710	743	4.65	Rudolph, town	1,028	1,028	0.00
Omro, city	3,517	3,584	1.91	Rudolph, village	439	426	−2.96
Omro, town	2,116	2,325	9.88	Saratoga, town	5,142	5,252	2.14
Oshkosh, city	66,083	66,595	0.77	Seneca, town	1,120	1,107	−1.16
Oshkosh, town	2,475	2,480	0.20	Sherry, town	803	820	2.12
Poygan, town	1,301	1,327	2.00	Sigel, town	1,051	1,067	1.52
Rushford, town	1,561	1,612	3.27	Vesper, village	584	573	−1.88
Utica, town	1,299	1,337	2.93	Wisconsin Rapids, city	18,367	18,721	1.93
Vinland, town	1,765	1,736	−1.64	Wood, town	796	801	0.63

NA–Not available.

1. This part of this village was created from part of the town of the same name after April 1, 2010. 2. This village was created from the entire town of the same name after April 1, 2010; the 2010 figure reflects the data for the previously existing town. 3. The town of Williamstown was attached to the village of Kekoskee on October 5, 2018; the 2010 figure reflects the sum of the data for the previously existing town and village. 4. The town of Salem and the village of Silver Lake merged to become the village of Salem Lakes on February 14, 2017; the 2010 figure reflects the sum of the data for the previously existing town and village. 5. This village was created from part of the town of the same name after April 1, 2010. 6. The town of Maine became the village of Maine on December 8, 2015. The village of Brokaw attached to the village of Maine on September 10, 2018. The 2010 figure reflects the sum of the data for the previously existing town of Maine and village of Brokaw. 7. Part of the town of Greenville became the village of Greenville on January 12, 2021. 8. This part of this village was created from part of the town of Buchanan after April 1, 2010. 9. Became the village of Vernon on June 4, 2020. 10. Became the village of Waukesha on May 12, 2020. 11. The village of Fox Crossing was created on April 20, 2016, from part of the town of Menasha. Subsequently, the village annexed the remainder of the town, except for three parcels that were annexed by the city of Menasha. The 2010 figure reflects the data for the previously existing town.

Sources: Wisconsin Department of Administration, Demographic Services Center, *Official Final Estimates, 1/1/2020, Wisconsin Municipalities, with Comparison to Census 2010, Official Final Estimates, 1/1/2020, Wisconsin Counties, with Comparison to Census 2010, and Official Final Estimates, 1/1/2020, Wisconsin Municipalities with Territory in Multiple Counties,* October 2020; Wisconsin Department of Administration, Municipal Data System, Municipality changes since January 2000, January 2021.

Wisconsin cities, January 1, 2020

City	Year incorporated	County	2010 census	2020 estimate	% change
One first class city (150,000 or more)[1]					
Milwaukee	1846	Milwaukee, Washington, Waukesha	594,833	587,072	–1.30
15 second class cities (39,000–149,999)[1]					
Appleton	1857	Calumet, Outagamie, Winnebago	72,623	74,465	2.54
Eau Claire[2]	1872	Chippewa, Eau Claire	65,931	68,429	3.79
Fond du Lac[2] . . .	1852	Fond du Lac	43,021	44,279	2.92
Green Bay	1854	Brown	104,057	105,599	1.48
Janesville[2]	1853	Rock	63,575	63,403	–0.27
Kenosha	1850	Kenosha	99,218	98,891	–0.33
La Crosse	1856	La Crosse	51,320	52,282	1.87
Madison	1856	Dane	233,209	257,197	10.29
Oshkosh[2]	1853	Winnebago	66,083	66,595	0.77
Racine	1848	Racine	78,860	76,709	–2.73
Sheboygan	1853	Sheboygan	49,288	48,756	–1.08
Waukesha	1895	Waukesha	70,718	71,952	1.74
Wausau	1872	Marathon	39,106	38,884	–0.57
Wauwatosa	1897	Milwaukee	46,396	48,478	4.49
West Allis	1906	Milwaukee	60,411	59,517	–1.48
33 third class cities (10,000–38,999)[1]					
Baraboo	1882	Sauk	12,048	12,008	–0.33
Beaver Dam	1856	Dodge	16,214	16,890	4.17
Beloit[2]	1857	Rock	36,966	36,162	–2.17
Brookfield	1954	Waukesha	37,920	40,044	5.60
Burlington	1900	Racine, Walworth	10,464	10,912	4.28
Chippewa Falls . .	1869	Chippewa	13,661	14,405	5.45
Cudahy	1906	Milwaukee	18,267	18,007	–1.42
De Pere	1883	Brown	23,800	24,595	3.34
Fort Atkinson[2] . . .	1878	Jefferson	12,368	12,395	0.22
Franklin	1956	Milwaukee	35,451	36,514	3.00
Glendale	1950	Milwaukee	12,872	12,463	–3.18
Greenfield	1957	Milwaukee	36,720	36,659	–0.17
Hartford	1883	Dodge, Washington	14,223	15,870	11.58
Kaukauna	1885	Calumet, Outagamie	15,462	16,363	5.83
Manitowoc	1870	Manitowoc	33,736	33,527	–0.62
Marinette	1887	Marinette	10,968	10,720	–2.26
Marshfield	1883	Marathon, Wood	19,118	19,478	1.88
Menasha	1874	Calumet, Winnebago	17,353	17,468	0.66
Middleton	1963	Dane	17,442	21,050	20.69
Muskego	1964	Waukesha	24,135	25,271	4.71
Neenah	1873	Winnebago	25,501	26,333	3.26
New Berlin	1959	Waukesha	39,584	40,600	2.57
Oak Creek	1955	Milwaukee	34,451	36,529	6.03
Oconomowoc . . .	1875	Waukesha	15,759	17,501	11.05
Pewaukee	1999	Waukesha	13,195	14,775	11.97
River Falls	1875	Pierce, St. Croix	15,000	16,113	7.42
Stevens Point . . .	1858	Portage	26,717	26,269	–1.68
Sun Prairie	1958	Dane	29,364	35,895	22.24
Superior	1858	Douglas	27,244	26,986	–0.95
Two Rivers[2]	1878	Manitowoc	11,712	11,364	–2.97
Watertown	1853	Dodge, Jefferson	23,861	23,800	–0.26
West Bend	1885	Washington	31,078	32,058	3.15
Wisconsin Rapids	1869	Wood	18,367	18,721	1.93
141 fourth class cities (Under 10,000)[1]					
Abbotsford	1965	Clark, Marathon	2,310	2,377	2.90
Adams	1926	Adams	1,967	1,907	–3.05
Algoma	1879	Kewaunee	3,167	3,105	–1.96

Wisconsin cities, January 1, 2020, continued

City	Year incorporated	County	2010 census	2020 estimate	% change
Alma.	1885	Buffalo	781	777	-0.51
Altoona.	1887	Eau Claire.	6,706	8,099	20.77
Amery.	1919	Polk	2,902	2,856	-1.59
Antigo	1885	Langlade	8,234	8,289	0.67
Arcadia	1925	Trempealeau	2,925	3,051	4.31
Ashland.	1887	Ashland, Bayfield.	8,216	7,985	-2.81
Augusta.	1885	Eau Claire.	1,550	1,518	-2.06
Barron.	1887	Barron.	3,423	3,356	-1.96
Bayfield.	1913	Bayfield.	487	484	-0.62
Berlin	1857	Green Lake, Waushara.	5,524	5,601	1.39
Black River Falls. .	1883	Jackson.	3,622	3,573	-1.35
Blair	1949	Trempealeau	1,366	1,342	-1.76
Bloomer	1920	Chippewa	3,539	3,582	1.22
Boscobel	1873	Grant	3,231	3,219	-0.37
Brillion	1944	Calumet	3,148	3,257	3.46
Brodhead.	1891	Green, Rock	3,293	3,275	-0.55
Buffalo City	1859	Buffalo	1,023	1,005	-1.76
Cedarburg	1885	Ozaukee	11,412	12,147	6.44
Chetek	1891	Barron.	2,221	2,187	-1.53
Chilton	1877	Calumet	3,933	3,956	0.58
Clintonville.	1887	Waupaca	4,559	4,447	-2.46
Colby	1891	Clark, Marathon.	1,852	1,859	0.38
Columbus	1874	Columbia, Dodge.	4,991	5,187	3.93
Cornell	1956	Chippewa	1,467	1,462	-0.34
Crandon	1898	Forest	1,920	1,805	-5.99
Cuba City.	1925	Grant, Lafayette.	2,086	2,113	1.29
Cumberland.	1885	Barron.	2,170	2,174	0.18
Darlington	1877	Lafayette.	2,451	2,378	-2.98
Delafield	1959	Waukesha	7,085	7,181	1.35
Delavan.	1897	Walworth.	8,463	8,270	-2.28
Dodgeville.	1889	Iowa.	4,693	4,681	-0.26
Durand	1887	Pepin	1,931	1,841	-4.66
Eagle River.	1937	Vilas	1,398	1,510	8.01
Edgerton	1883	Dane, Rock.	5,461	5,642	3.31
Elkhorn.	1897	Walworth.	10,084	9,968	-1.15
Elroy.	1885	Juneau	1,442	1,333	-7.56
Evansville.	1896	Rock.	5,012	5,487	9.48
Fennimore	1919	Grant	2,497	2,501	0.16
Fitchburg.	1983	Dane	25,260	30,391	20.31
Fountain City	1889	Buffalo	859	840	-2.21
Fox Lake	1938	Dodge	1,519	1,550	2.04
Galesville.	1942	Trempealeau	1,481	1,565	5.67
Gillett	1944	Oconto	1,386	1,323	-4.55
Glenwood City	1895	St. Croix.	1,242	1,210	-2.58
Green Lake.	1962	Green Lake.	960	1,005	4.69
Greenwood	1891	Clark.	1,026	1,009	-1.66
Hayward	1915	Sawyer	2,318	2,370	2.24
Hillsboro	1885	Vernon	1,417	1,382	-2.47
Horicon.	1897	Dodge	3,655	3,768	3.09
Hudson.	1857	St. Croix.	12,719	14,091	10.79
Hurley.	1918	Iron	1,547	1,506	-2.65
Independence.	1942	Trempealeau	1,336	1,340	0.30
Jefferson	1878	Jefferson	7,973	7,935	-0.48
Juneau	1887	Dodge	2,814	2,634	-6.40

Wisconsin cities, January 1, 2020, continued

City	Year incorporated	County	2010 census	2020 estimate	% change
Kewaunee	1883	Kewaunee	2,952	2,870	-2.78
Kiel	1920	Calumet, Manitowoc.	3,738	3,930	5.14
Ladysmith	1905	Rusk.	3,414	3,327	-2.55
Lake Geneva. . . .	1883	Walworth.	7,651	8,233	7.61
Lake Mills[2]	1905	Jefferson	5,708	6,066	6.27
Lancaster.	1878	Grant	3,868	3,757	-2.87
Lodi	1941	Columbia.	3,050	3,139	2.92
Loyal	1948	Clark.	1,261	1,232	-2.30
Manawa	1954	Waupaca	1,371	1,317	-3.94
Marion	1898	Shawano, Waupaca	1,260	1,228	-2.54
Markesan.	1959	Green Lake.	1,476	1,417	-4.00
Mauston	1883	Juneau	4,423	4,475	1.18
Mayville.	1885	Dodge	5,154	5,069	-1.65
Medford	1889	Taylor	4,326	4,321	-0.12
Mellen	1907	Ashland.	731	710	-2.87
Menomonie	1882	Dunn	16,264	16,461	1.21
Mequon	1957	Ozaukee	23,132	24,806	7.24
Merrill.	1883	Lincoln	9,661	9,661	0.00
Milton.	1969	Rock.	5,546	5,585	0.70
Mineral Point . . .	1857	Iowa.	2,487	2,488	0.04
Mondovi	1889	Buffalo	2,777	2,751	-0.94
Monona	1969	Dane	7,533	7,920	5.14
Monroe.	1882	Green	10,827	10,641	-1.72
Montello	1938	Marquette	1,495	1,447	-3.21
Montreal	1924	Iron	807	795	-1.49
Mosinee	1931	Marathon.	3,988	4,124	3.41
Neillsville.	1882	Clark.	2,463	2,362	-4.10
Nekoosa	1926	Wood	2,580	2,516	-2.48
New Holstein . . .	1926	Calumet	3,236	3,210	-0.80
New Lisbon	1889	Juneau	2,554	2,605	2.00
New London. . . .	1877	Outagamie, Waupaca	7,295	7,436	1.93
New Richmond . .	1885	St. Croix.	8,375	9,741	16.31
Niagara	1992	Marinette.	1,624	1,564	-3.69
Oconto	1869	Oconto	4,513	4,598	1.88
Oconto Falls	1919	Oconto	2,891	2,806	-2.94
Omro	1944	Winnebago	3,517	3,584	1.91
Onalaska	1887	La Crosse	17,736	19,330	8.99
Osseo	1941	Trempealeau	1,701	1,699	-0.12
Owen	1925	Clark.	940	913	-2.87
Park Falls	1912	Price.	2,462	2,472	0.41
Peshtigo	1903	Marinette.	3,502	3,382	-3.43
Phillips	1891	Price.	1,478	1,426	-3.52
Pittsville	1887	Wood	874	868	-0.69
Platteville[2]	1876	Grant	11,224	12,262	9.25
Plymouth.	1877	Sheboygan.	8,445	8,715	3.20
Port Washington .	1882	Ozaukee	11,250	11,954	6.26
Portage	1854	Columbia.	10,324	10,132	-1.86
Prairie du Chien. .	1872	Crawford	5,911	5,840	-1.20
Prescott.	1857	Pierce	4,258	4,217	-0.96
Princeton.	1920	Green Lake	1,214	1,179	-2.88
Reedsburg	1887	Sauk.	9,200	9,678	5.20
Rhinelander	1894	Oneida	7,798	7,783	-0.19
Rice Lake	1887	Barron.	8,419	8,788	4.38
Richland Center. .	1887	Richland	5,184	5,144	-0.77
Ripon	1858	Fond du Lac	7,733	7,839	1.37

Wisconsin cities, January 1, 2020, continued

City	Year incorporated	County	2010 census	2020 estimate	% change
St. Croix Falls . . .	1958	Polk	2,133	2,113	−0.94
St. Francis	1951	Milwaukee.	9,365	9,658	3.13
Schofield	1951	Marathon.	2,169	2,201	1.48
Seymour	1879	Outagamie.	3,451	3,415	−1.04
Shawano	1874	Shawano	9,305	9,129	−1.89
Sheboygan Falls .	1913	Sheboygan.	7,775	8,396	7.99
Shell Lake	1961	Washburn	1,347	1,347	0.00
Shullsburg	1889	Lafayette	1,226	1,196	−2.45
South Milwaukee	1897	Milwaukee	21,156	20,622	−2.52
Sparta.	1883	Monroe.	9,522	10,056	5.61
Spooner	1909	Washburn	2,682	2,576	−3.95
Stanley	1898	Chippewa, Clark	3,608	3,630	0.61
Stoughton	1882	Dane	12,611	12,954	2.72
Sturgeon Bay . . .	1883	Door.	9,144	9,542	4.35
Thorp	1948	Clark.	1,621	1,588	−2.04
Tomah	1883	Monroe.	9,093	9,385	3.21
Tomahawk	1891	Lincoln	3,397	3,299	−2.88
Verona	1977	Dane	10,619	12,737	19.95
Viroqua	1885	Vernon	4,362	4,491	2.96
Washburn	1904	Bayfield.	2,117	2,102	−0.71
Waterloo	1962	Jefferson	3,333	3,341	0.24
Waupaca	1875	Waupaca	6,069	6,004	−1.07
Waupun	1878	Dodge, Fond du Lac	11,340	11,588	2.19
Wautoma.	1901	Waushara	2,218	2,127	−4.10
Westby	1920	Vernon	2,200	2,208	0.36
Weyauwega	1939	Waupaca	1,900	1,878	−1.16
Whitehall.	1941	Trempealeau	1,558	1,556	−0.13
Whitewater[2]	1885	Jefferson, Walworth	14,390	15,035	4.48
Wisconsin Dells . .	1925	Adams, Columbia, Juneau, Sauk.	2,678	2,752	2.76

1. A city is initially classified according to its population when it incorporates. If its population changes, a city can take action to change its classification, but if it does not take such action, its classification remains unchanged.   2. One of ten cities with a city manager.

Sources: Wisconsin Department of Administration, Demographic Services Center, *Official Final Estimates, 1/1/2020, Wisconsin Municipalities, with Comparison to Census 2010,* October 2020; League of Wisconsin Municipalities, *2020 Directory of Wisconsin City and Village Officials* at http://lwm-info.org/1236/Directory-of-Cities-Villages; and data compiled by Wisconsin Legislative Reference Bureau.

Wisconsin villages, January 1, 2020

Village	Year incorporated	County	2010 census	2020 estimate	% change
Adell.	1918	Sheboygan.	516	506	−1.94
Albany	1918	Green	1,018	995	−2.26
Allouez	1986	Brown.	13,975	13,734	−1.72
Alma Center	1902	Jackson	503	506	0.60
Almena	1945	Barron.	677	641	−5.32
Almond.	1905	Portage.	448	424	−5.36
Amherst	1899	Portage.	1,035	1,097	5.99
Amherst Junction	1912	Portage.	377	397	5.31
Aniwa	1899	Shawano	260	252	−3.08
Arena	1923	Iowa	834	829	−0.60

Wisconsin villages, January 1, 2020, continued

Village	Year incorporated	County	2010 census	2020 estimate	% change
Argyle.	1903	Lafayette	857	834	-2.68
Arlington	1945	Columbia.	819	834	1.83
Arpin	1978	Wood	333	328	-1.50
Ashwaubenon[1]	1977	Brown.	16,963	16,961	-0.01
Athens	1901	Marathon.	1,105	1,116	1.00
Auburndale	1881	Wood	703	714	1.56
Avoca	1870	Iowa.	637	612	-3.92
Bagley.	1919	Grant	379	372	-1.85
Baldwin.	1875	St. Croix.	3,957	3,993	0.91
Balsam Lake	1905	Polk	1,009	1,013	0.40
Bangor	1899	La Crosse	1,459	1,535	5.21
Barneveld	1906	Iowa	1,231	1,270	3.17
Bay City	1909	Pierce	500	491	-1.80
Bayside[1]	1953	Milwaukee, Ozaukee	4,389	4,290	-2.26
Bear Creek	1902	Outagamie.	448	439	-2.01
Belgium.	1922	Ozaukee	2,245	2,448	9.04
Bell Center	1901	Crawford	117	114	-2.56
Belleville	1892	Dane, Green	2,385	2,473	3.69
Bellevue	2003	Brown.	14,570	15,706	7.80
Belmont	1894	Lafayette	986	1,000	1.42
Benton	1892	Lafayette	973	966	-0.72
Big Bend	1928	Waukesha	1,290	1,491	15.58
Big Falls.	1925	Waupaca	61	60	-1.64
Birchwood	1921	Washburn	442	436	-1.36
Birnamwood.	1895	Marathon, Shawano	818	813	-0.61
Biron	1910	Wood	839	819	-2.38
Black Creek	1904	Outagamie.	1,316	1,299	-1.29
Black Earth.	1901	Dane	1,338	1,428	6.73
Blanchardville.	1890	Iowa, Lafayette	825	810	-1.82
Bloomfield[2]	2011	Walworth.	NA	4,798	NA
Bloomington	1880	Grant	735	725	-1.36
Blue Mounds	1912	Dane	855	966	12.98
Blue River	1916	Grant	434	427	-1.61
Boaz.	1939	Richland	156	155	-0.64
Bonduel	1916	Shawano	1,478	1,462	-1.08
Bowler	1923	Shawano	302	289	-4.30
Boyceville	1922	Dunn	1,086	1,080	-0.55
Boyd.	1891	Chippewa	552	540	-2.17
Brandon	1881	Fond du Lac	879	863	-1.82
Bristol.	2009	Kenosha	4,914	5,139	4.58
Brooklyn	1905	Dane, Green	1,401	1,459	4.14
Brown Deer[1]	1955	Milwaukee.	11,999	12,518	4.33
Brownsville	1952	Dodge	581	607	4.48
Browntown	1890	Green	280	278	-0.71
Bruce	1901	Rusk	779	752	-3.47
Butler	1913	Waukesha	1,841	1,803	-2.06
Butternut.	1903	Ashland.	375	359	-4.27
Cadott	1895	Chippewa	1,437	1,444	0.49
Caledonia	2005	Racine.	24,705	25,131	1.72
Cambria	1866	Columbia.	767	756	-1.43
Cambridge.	1891	Dane, Jefferson	1,457	1,591	9.20
Cameron	1894	Barron.	1,783	1,865	4.60
Campbellsport	1902	Fond du Lac	2,016	1,825	-9.47
Camp Douglas	1893	Juneau	601	619	3.00
Cascade.	1914	Sheboygan.	709	691	-2.54
Casco	1920	Kewaunee	583	598	2.57
Cashton.	1901	Monroe	1,102	1,101	-0.09
Cassville	1882	Grant	947	919	-2.96

Wisconsin villages, January 1, 2020, continued

Village	Year incorporated	County	2010 census	2020 estimate	% change
Catawba	1922	Price	110	107	−2.73
Cazenovia	1902	Richland, Sauk	318	315	−0.94
Cecil	1905	Shawano	570	572	0.35
Cedar Grove	1899	Sheboygan	2,113	2,112	−0.05
Centuria	1904	Polk	948	946	−0.21
Chaseburg	1922	Vernon	284	284	0.00
Chenequa	1928	Waukesha	590	588	−0.34
Clayton	1909	Polk	571	559	−2.10
Clear Lake	1894	Polk	1,070	1,090	1.87
Cleveland	1958	Manitowoc	1,485	1,502	1.14
Clinton	1882	Rock	2,154	2,097	−2.65
Clyman	1924	Dodge	422	411	−2.61
Cobb	1902	Iowa	458	464	1.31
Cochrane	1910	Buffalo	450	437	−2.89
Coleman	1903	Marinette	724	716	−1.10
Colfax	1904	Dunn	1,158	1,095	−5.44
Coloma	1939	Waushara	450	458	1.78
Combined Locks	1920	Outagamie	3,328	3,592	7.93
Conrath	1915	Rusk	95	96	1.05
Coon Valley	1907	Vernon	765	742	−3.01
Cottage Grove	1924	Dane	6,192	6,716	8.46
Couderay	1922	Sawyer	88	88	0.00
Crivitz	1974	Marinette	984	939	−4.57
Cross Plains	1920	Dane	3,538	4,010	13.34
Curtiss	1917	Clark	216	209	−3.24
Dallas	1903	Barron	409	348	−14.91
Dane	1899	Dane	995	1,100	10.55
Darien	1951	Walworth	1,580	1,574	−0.38
Deerfield	1891	Dane	2,319	2,489	7.33
Deer Park	1913	St. Croix	216	209	−3.24
DeForest	1891	Dane	8,936	10,624	18.89
Denmark	1915	Brown	2,123	2,271	6.97
De Soto	1886	Crawford, Vernon	287	281	−2.09
Dickeyville	1947	Grant	1,061	1,061	0.00
Dorchester	1901	Clark, Marathon	876	856	−2.28
Dousman	1917	Waukesha	2,302	2,353	2.22
Downing	1909	Dunn	265	262	−1.13
Doylestown	1907	Columbia	297	290	−2.36
Dresser	1919	Polk	895	906	1.23
Eagle	1899	Waukesha	1,950	2,104	7.90
Eastman	1909	Crawford	428	419	−2.10
East Troy	1900	Walworth	4,281	4,500	5.12
Eden	1912	Fond du Lac	875	908	3.77
Edgar	1898	Marathon	1,479	1,466	−0.88
Egg Harbor	1964	Door	201	206	2.49
Eland	1905	Shawano	202	202	0.00
Elderon	1917	Marathon	179	177	−1.12
Eleva	1902	Trempealeau	670	675	0.75
Elkhart Lake	1894	Sheboygan	967	1,019	5.38
Elk Mound	1909	Dunn	878	871	−0.80
Ellsworth	1887	Pierce	3,284	3,365	2.47
Elm Grove[1]	1955	Waukesha	5,934	5,857	−1.30
Elmwood	1905	Pierce	817	789	−3.43
Elmwood Park	1960	Racine	497	486	−2.21
Embarrass	1895	Waupaca	404	385	−4.70
Endeavor	1946	Marquette	468	458	−2.14
Ephraim	1919	Door	288	288	0.00

Wisconsin villages, January 1, 2020, continued

Village	Year incorporated	County	2010 census	2020 estimate	% change
Ettrick.	1948	Trempealeau	524	522	-0.38
Exeland.	1920	Sawyer	196	193	-1.53
Fairchild	1880	Eau Claire.	550	535	-2.73
Fairwater.	1921	Fond du Lac	371	362	-2.43
Fall Creek.	1906	Eau Claire.	1,315	1,269	-3.50
Fall River	1903	Columbia.	1,712	1,793	4.73
Fenwood.	1904	Marathon.	152	153	0.66
Ferryville	1912	Crawford	176	193	9.66
Fontana-on-Geneva Lake	1924	Walworth.	1,672	1,712	2.39
Footville	1918	Rock.	808	825	2.10
Forestville	1960	Door.	430	424	-1.40
Fox Crossing[1,3]	2016	Winnebago	18,498	19,090	3.20
Fox Point[1]	1926	Milwaukee.	6,701	6,826	1.87
Francis Creek	1960	Manitowoc.	669	658	-1.64
Frederic.	1903	Polk.	1,137	1,119	-1.58
Fredonia	1922	Ozaukee	2,160	2,199	1.81
Fremont	1882	Waupaca	679	679	0.00
Friendship	1907	Adams	725	749	3.31
Friesland	1946	Columbia.	356	346	-2.81
Gays Mills	1900	Crawford	491	494	0.61
Genoa.	1935	Vernon	253	250	-1.19
Genoa City.	1901	Kenosha, Walworth	3,042	3,008	-1.12
Germantown	1927	Washington	19,749	20,686	4.74
Gilman	1914	Taylor.	410	373	-9.02
Glenbeulah	1913	Sheboygan.	463	469	1.30
Glen Flora	1915	Rusk.	92	88	-4.35
Grafton	1896	Ozaukee	11,459	11,989	4.63
Granton.	1916	Clark.	355	350	-1.41
Grantsburg.	1887	Burnett	1,341	1,318	-1.72
Gratiot	1891	Lafayette	236	226	-4.24
Greendale[1].	1939	Milwaukee.	14,046	14,335	2.06
Greenville[4]	2021	Outagamie	NA	9,617	NA
Gresham	1908	Shawano	586	579	-1.19
Hales Corners	1952	Milwaukee.	7,692	7,555	-1.78
Hammond	1880	St. Croix.	1,922	1,868	-2.81
Hancock	1902	Waushara.	417	410	-1.68
Harrison[5].	2013	Calumet, Outagamie.	NA	13,185	NA
Hartland	1891	Waukesha	9,110	9,286	1.93
Hatley.	1912	Marathon.	574	637	10.98
Haugen.	1918	Barron.	287	279	-2.79
Hawkins	1922	Rusk.	305	314	2.95
Hazel Green	1867	Grant, Lafayette.	1,256	1,252	-0.32
Hewitt.	1973	Wood	828	841	1.57
Highland	1873	Iowa.	842	836	-0.71
Hilbert	1898	Calumet	1,132	1,183	4.51
Hixton.	1920	Jackson.	433	425	-1.85
Hobart	2003	Brown.	6,182	10,454	69.10
Hollandale.	1910	Iowa.	288	281	-2.43
Holmen.	1946	La Crosse.	9,005	10,662	18.40
Hortonville.	1894	Outagamie.	2,711	2,911	7.38
Howard.	1959	Brown, Outagamie	17,399	20,209	16.15
Howards Grove	1967	Sheboygan.	3,188	3,285	3.04
Hustisford	1870	Dodge	1,123	1,107	-1.42
Hustler	1914	Juneau	194	191	-1.55
Ingram	1907	Rusk.	78	80	2.56
Iola.	1892	Waupaca	1,301	1,250	-3.92

Wisconsin villages, January 1, 2020, continued

Village	Year incorporated	County	2010 census	2020 estimate	% change
Iron Ridge	1913	Dodge	929	920	-0.97
Ironton	1914	Sauk	253	253	0.00
Jackson	1912	Washington	6,753	7,199	6.60
Johnson Creek	1903	Jefferson	2,738	3,029	10.63
Junction City	1911	Portage	439	435	-0.91
Kekoskee[6]	1958	Dodge	161	919	0.33
Kellnersville	1971	Manitowoc	332	329	-0.90
Kendall	1894	Monroe	472	453	-4.03
Kennan	1903	Price	135	132	-2.22
Kewaskum	1895	Fond du Lac, Washington	4,004	4,177	4.32
Kimberly	1910	Outagamie	6,468	7,137	10.34
Kingston	1923	Green Lake	326	324	-0.61
Knapp	1905	Dunn	463	458	-1.08
Kohler	1912	Sheboygan	2,120	2,078	-1.98
Kronenwetter	2002	Marathon	7,210	8,158	13.15
La Farge	1899	Vernon	746	702	-5.90
La Valle	1883	Sauk	367	351	-4.36
Lac La Belle	1931	Jefferson, Waukesha	290	297	2.41
Lake Delton	1954	Sauk	2,914	2,900	-0.48
Lake Hallie	2003	Chippewa	6,448	7,121	10.44
Lake Nebagamon	1907	Douglas	1,069	1,087	1.68
Lannon	1930	Waukesha	1,107	1,264	14.18
Lena	1921	Oconto	564	552	-2.13
Lime Ridge	1910	Sauk	162	158	-2.47
Linden	1900	Iowa	549	532	-3.10
Little Chute	1899	Outagamie	10,449	11,947	14.34
Livingston	1914	Grant, Iowa	664	653	-1.66
Loganville	1917	Sauk	300	292	-2.67
Lohrville	1910	Waushara	402	390	-2.99
Lomira	1899	Dodge	2,430	2,528	4.03
Lone Rock	1886	Richland	888	879	-1.01
Lowell	1894	Dodge	340	326	-4.12
Lublin	1915	Taylor	118	115	-2.54
Luck	1905	Polk	1,119	1,087	-2.86
Luxemburg	1908	Kewaunee	2,515	2,620	4.17
Lyndon Station	1903	Juneau	500	483	-3.40
Lynxville	1899	Crawford	132	130	-1.52
Maiden Rock	1887	Pierce	119	116	-2.52
Maine[6]	2015	Marathon	2,337	2,619	1.20
Maple Bluff	1930	Dane	1,313	1,285	-2.13
Marathon City	1884	Marathon	1,524	1,588	4.20
Maribel	1963	Manitowoc	351	355	1.14
Marquette	1958	Green Lake	150	150	0.00
Marshall	1905	Dane	3,862	3,899	0.96
Mason	1925	Bayfield	93	93	0.00
Mattoon	1901	Shawano	438	426	-2.74
Mazomanie	1885	Dane	1,652	1,681	1.76
McFarland	1920	Dane	7,808	8,952	14.65
Melrose	1914	Jackson	503	487	-3.18
Melvina	1922	Monroe	104	102	-1.92
Menomonee Falls[1]	1892	Waukesha	35,626	38,948	9.32
Merrillan	1881	Jackson	542	515	-4.98
Merrimac	1899	Sauk	420	428	1.90
Merton	1922	Waukesha	3,346	3,711	10.91
Milladore	1933	Portage, Wood	276	274	-0.72
Milltown	1910	Polk	917	908	-0.98
Minong	1915	Washburn	527	540	2.47

Wisconsin villages, January 1, 2020, continued

Village	Year incorporated	County	2010 census	2020 estimate	% change
Mishicot	1950	Manitowoc	1,442	1,442	0.00
Montfort	1893	Grant, Iowa	718	723	0.70
Monticello	1891	Green	1,217	1,205	−0.99
Mount Calvary	1962	Fond du Lac	762	534	−29.92
Mount Hope	1919	Grant	225	222	−1.33
Mount Horeb	1899	Dane	7,009	7,387	5.39
Mount Pleasant	2003	Racine	26,197	26,922	2.77
Mount Sterling	1936	Crawford	211	206	−2.37
Mukwonago	1905	Walworth, Waukesha	7,355	8,126	10.48
Muscoda	1894	Grant, Iowa	1,299	1,241	−4.46
Nashotah	1957	Waukesha	1,395	1,350	−3.23
Necedah	1870	Juneau	916	908	−0.87
Nelson	1978	Buffalo	374	358	−4.28
Nelsonville	1913	Portage	155	161	3.87
Neosho	1902	Dodge	574	565	−1.57
Neshkoro	1906	Marquette	434	420	−3.23
New Auburn	1902	Barron, Chippewa	548	548	0.00
Newburg	1973	Ozaukee, Washington	1,254	1,264	0.80
New Glarus	1901	Green	2,172	2,085	−4.01
Nichols	1967	Outagamie	273	279	2.20
North Bay	1951	Racine	241	236	−2.07
North Fond du Lac	1903	Fond du Lac	5,014	5,181	3.33
North Freedom	1893	Sauk	701	657	−6.28
North Hudson	1912	St. Croix	3,768	3,847	2.10
North Prairie	1919	Waukesha	2,141	2,234	4.34
Norwalk	1894	Monroe	638	631	−1.10
Oakdale	1988	Monroe	297	290	−2.36
Oakfield	1903	Fond du Lac	1,075	1,104	2.70
Oconomowoc Lake	1959	Waukesha	595	598	0.50
Ogdensburg	1912	Waupaca	185	182	−1.62
Oliver	1917	Douglas	399	436	9.27
Ontario	1890	Vernon, Monroe	554	540	−2.53
Oostburg	1909	Sheboygan	2,887	3,059	5.96
Oregon	1883	Dane	9,231	10,270	11.26
Orfordville	1900	Rock	1,442	1,476	2.36
Osceola	1886	Polk	2,568	2,698	5.06
Oxford	1912	Marquette	607	583	−3.95
Paddock Lake	1960	Kenosha	2,992	3,176	6.15
Palmyra	1866	Jefferson	1,781	1,742	−2.19
Pardeeville	1894	Columbia	2,115	2,067	−2.27
Park Ridge	1938	Portage	491	499	1.63
Patch Grove	1921	Grant	198	197	−0.51
Pepin	1860	Pepin	837	788	−5.85
Pewaukee	1876	Waukesha	8,166	7,883	−3.47
Pigeon Falls	1956	Trempealeau	411	409	−0.49
Plain	1912	Sauk	773	756	−2.20
Plainfield	1882	Waushara	862	850	−1.39
Pleasant Prairie	1989	Kenosha	19,719	22,456	13.88
Plover	1971	Portage	12,123	13,486	11.24
Plum City	1909	Pierce	599	600	0.17
Poplar	1917	Douglas	603	615	1.99
Port Edwards	1902	Wood	1,818	1,779	−2.15
Potosi	1887	Grant	688	674	−2.03
Potter	1980	Calumet	253	248	−1.98
Pound	1914	Marinette	377	370	−1.86
Poynette	1892	Columbia	2,528	2,534	0.24
Prairie du Sac	1885	Sauk	3,972	4,193	5.56

Wisconsin villages, January 1, 2020, continued

Village	Year incorporated	County	2010 census	2020 estimate	% change
Prairie Farm	1901	Barron	473	456	-3.59
Prentice	1899	Price	660	642	-2.73
Pulaski	1910	Brown, Oconto, Shawano	3,539	3,731	5.43
Radisson	1953	Sawyer	241	237	-1.66
Randolph	1870	Columbia, Dodge	1,811	1,785	-1.44
Random Lake	1907	Sheboygan	1,594	1,570	-1.51
Raymond[8]	2019	Racine	3,870	4,015	3.75
Readstown	1898	Vernon	415	414	-0.24
Redgranite	1904	Waushara	2,149	2,116	-1.54
Reedsville	1892	Manitowoc	1,206	1,181	-2.07
Reeseville	1899	Dodge	708	713	0.71
Rewey	1902	Iowa	292	280	-4.11
Rib Lake	1902	Taylor	910	868	-4.62
Richfield	2008	Washington	11,300	11,948	5.73
Ridgeland	1921	Dunn	273	268	-1.83
Ridgeway	1902	Iowa	653	647	-0.92
Rio	1887	Columbia	1,059	1,078	1.79
River Hills[1]	1930	Milwaukee	1,597	1,553	-2.76
Roberts	1945	St. Croix	1,651	1,872	13.39
Rochester	1912	Racine	3,682	3,854	4.67
Rockdale	1914	Dane	214	214	0.00
Rockland	1919	La Crosse, Monroe	594	738	24.24
Rock Springs	1894	Sauk	362	292	-19.34
Rosendale	1915	Fond du Lac	1,063	1,024	-3.67
Rosholt	1907	Portage	506	496	-1.98
Rothschild	1917	Marathon	5,269	5,328	1.12
Rudolph	1960	Wood	439	426	-2.96
St. Cloud	1909	Fond du Lac	477	473	-0.84
St. Nazianz	1956	Manitowoc	783	760	-2.94
Salem Lakes[9]	2017	Kenosha	14,478	14,679	1.39
Sauk City	1854	Sauk	3,410	3,443	0.97
Saukville	1915	Ozaukee	4,451	4,396	-1.24
Scandinavia	1894	Waupaca	363	362	-0.28
Sharon	1892	Walworth	1,605	1,561	-2.74
Sheldon	1917	Rusk	237	234	-1.27
Sherwood	1968	Calumet	2,713	3,152	16.18
Shiocton	1903	Outagamie	921	923	0.22
Shorewood[1]	1900	Milwaukee	13,162	13,472	2.36
Shorewood Hills	1927	Dane	1,565	2,363	50.99
Siren	1948	Burnett	806	788	-2.23
Sister Bay	1912	Door	876	966	10.27
Slinger	1869	Washington	5,068	5,845	15.33
Soldiers Grove	1888	Crawford	592	561	-5.24
Solon Springs	1920	Douglas	600	593	-1.17
Somers[2]	2015	Kenosha	NA	9,182	NA
Somerset	1915	St. Croix	2,635	2,939	11.54
South Wayne	1911	Lafayette	489	477	-2.45
Spencer	1902	Marathon	1,925	1,913	-0.62
Spring Green	1869	Sauk	1,628	1,623	-0.31
Spring Valley	1895	Pierce, St. Croix	1,352	1,344	-0.59
Star Prairie	1900	St. Croix	561	552	-1.60
Stetsonville	1949	Taylor	541	531	-1.85
Steuben	1900	Crawford	131	122	-6.87
Stockbridge	1908	Calumet	636	651	2.36
Stockholm	1903	Pepin	66	66	0.00
Stoddard	1911	Vernon	774	825	6.59
Stratford	1910	Marathon	1,578	1,610	2.03

Wisconsin villages, January 1, 2020, continued

Village	Year incorporated	County	2010 census	2020 estimate	% change
Strum	1948	Trempealeau	1,114	1,085	−2.60
Sturtevant	1907	Racine.	6,970	6,633	−4.84
Suamico	2003	Brown.	11,346	12,796	12.78
Sullivan.	1915	Jefferson	669	660	−1.35
Summit[8]	2010	Waukesha	4,674	4,974	6.42
Superior	1949	Douglas.	664	703	5.87
Suring.	1914	Oconto	544	534	−1.84
Sussex.	1924	Waukesha	10,518	11,373	8.13
Taylor	1919	Jackson	476	487	2.31
Tennyson.	1940	Grant	355	361	1.69
Theresa	1898	Dodge	1,262	1,258	−0.32
Thiensville	1910	Ozaukee	3,235	3,164	−2.19
Tigerton	1896	Shawano	741	714	−3.64
Tony	1911	Rusk	113	108	−4.42
Trempealeau	1867	Trempealeau	1,529	1,952	27.67
Turtle Lake.	1898	Barron, Polk	1,050	1,032	−1.71
Twin Lakes	1937	Kenosha	5,989	6,189	3.34
Union Center	1913	Juneau	200	195	−2.50
Union Grove	1893	Racine.	4,915	5,227	6.35
Unity	1903	Clark, Marathon.	343	333	−2.92
Valders	1919	Manitowoc.	962	952	−1.04
Vernon[10]	2020	Waukesha	7,601	7,621	0.26
Vesper.	1948	Wood	584	573	−1.88
Viola.	1899	Richland, Vernon	699	682	−2.43
Waldo.	1922	Sheboygan.	503	492	−2.19
Wales	1922	Waukesha	2,549	2,616	2.63
Walworth.	1901	Walworth.	2,816	2,829	0.46
Warrens.	1973	Monroe.	363	362	−0.28
Waterford	1906	Racine.	5,368	5,664	5.51
Waukesha[10]	2020	Waukesha	9,133	9,329	2.15
Waunakee.	1893	Dane	12,097	14,399	19.03
Wausaukee.	1924	Marinette.	575	563	−2.09
Wauzeka	1890	Crawford	711	685	−3.66
Webster.	1916	Burnett	653	646	−1.07
West Baraboo	1956	Sauk	1,414	1,654	16.97
Westfield	1902	Marquette	1,254	1,232	−1.75
West Milwaukee	1906	Milwaukee	4,206	4,120	−2.04
Weston	1996	Marathon.	14,868	15,646	5.23
West Salem	1893	La Crosse	4,799	5,045	5.13
Weyerhaeuser.	1906	Rusk	238	240	0.84
Wheeler.	1922	Dunn	348	343	−1.44
Whitefish Bay[1]	1892	Milwaukee	14,110	14,000	−0.78
White Lake.	1926	Langlade	363	352	−3.03
Whitelaw	1958	Manitowoc.	757	753	−0.53
Whiting	1947	Portage.	1,724	1,678	−2.67
Wild Rose.	1904	Waushara.	725	678	−6.48
Williams Bay	1919	Walworth.	2,564	2,614	1.95
Wilson.	1911	St. Croix.	184	186	1.09
Wilton.	1890	Monroe.	504	486	−3.57
Wind Point.	1954	Racine.	1,723	1,676	−2.73
Windsor[8]	2015	Dane	6,345	8,240	29.87
Winneconne.	1887	Winnebago	2,383	2,499	4.87
Winter.	1973	Sawyer	313	310	−0.96
Withee.	1901	Clark.	487	500	2.67
Wittenberg.	1893	Shawano	1,081	999	−7.59
Wonewoc	1878	Juneau	816	792	−2.94

Wisconsin villages, January 1, 2020, continued

Village	Year incorporated	County	2010 census	2020 estimate	% change
Woodman	1917	Grant	132	126	−4.55
Woodville	1911	St. Croix.	1,344	1,330	−1.04
Wrightstown.	1901	Brown, Outagamie	2,827	3,086	9.16
Wyeville	1923	Monroe	147	139	−5.44
Wyocena	1909	Columbia.	768	729	−5.08
Yorkville[8]	2018	Racine.	3,071	3,147	2.47
Yuba	1935	Richland	74	70	−5.41

Note: There are 415 villages in Wisconsin as of March 1, 2021.

NA–Not available.

1. One of 11 villages with a village manager.   2. This village was created from part of the town of the same name after April 1, 2010.   3. The village of Fox Crossing was created on April 20, 2016, from part of the town of Menasha; the 2010 figure shows the population of the previously existing town.   4. The village of Greenville was created from part of the town of the same name on January 12, 2021; the 2020 population estimate comes from the village's certificate of incorporation.   5. This village was created from parts of two towns after April 1, 2010.   6. The town of Williamstown was attached to the village of Kekoskee on October 5, 2018; the 2010 figure includes the population of the previously existing town.   7. The town of Maine became the village of Maine on December 8, 2015, and the village of Brokaw attached to the village of Maine on September 10, 2018; the 2010 figure shows the combined population of the previously existing town of Maine and village of Brokaw.   8. This village was created from the entire town of the same name after April 1, 2010; the 2010 figure shows the population of the previously existing town.   9. The town of Salem and the village of Silver Lake merged to become the village of Salem Lakes on February 14, 2017; the 2010 figure shows the combined population of the previously existing town and village.   10. This village was created from the entire town of the same name after January 1, 2020; the 2010 and 2020 figures show the population of the previously existing town.

Sources: Wisconsin Department of Administration, Demographic Services Center, *Official Final Estimates, 1/1/2020, Wisconsin Municipalities, with Comparison to Census 2010*, October 2020; Wisconsin Department of Administration, Municipal Data System, *Municipality changes since January 2000*, January 2021; Wisconsin Secretary of Administration Joel T. Brennan, *Certificate of Incorporation: Village of Greenville*, January 12, 2021; League of Wisconsin Municipalities, *2020 Directory of Wisconsin City and Village Officials* at http://lwm-info.org/1236/Directory-of-Cities-Villages; and data compiled by Wisconsin Legislative Reference Bureau.

Wisconsin cities and villages over 10,000 population, January 1, 2020

City or village (county)	2020 estimate[1]	2010 census	% change	2020 rank	2010 non-white,[2] non-Hispanic	2010 Hispanic or Latino origin[3]
Cities						
Milwaukee (Milwaukee, Washington, Waukesha)	587,072	594,833	−1.30	1	271,607	103,007
Madison (Dane).	257,197	233,209	10.29	2	40,798	15,948
Green Bay (Brown)	105,599	104,057	1.48	3	13,912	13,896
Kenosha (Kenosha).	98,891	99,218	−0.33	4	14,121	16,130
Racine (Racine)	76,709	78,860	−2.73	5	20,362	16,309
Appleton (Calumet, Outagamie, Winnebago) . .	74,465	72,623	2.54	6	7,124	3,643
Waukesha (Waukesha)	71,952	70,718	1.74	7	5,321	8,529
Eau Claire (Chippewa, Eau Claire)	68,429	65,931	3.79	8	5,116	1,268
Oshkosh (Winnebago).	66,595	66,083	0.77	9	5,539	1,770
Janesville (Rock)	63,403	63,575	−0.27	10	3,689	3,421
West Allis (Milwaukee).	59,517	60,411	−1.48	11	5,094	5,770
La Crosse (La Crosse).	52,282	51,320	1.87	12	4,885	1,012
Sheboygan (Sheboygan)	48,756	49,288	−1.08	13	6,314	4,866
Wauwatosa (Milwaukee)	48,478	46,396	4.49	14	4,361	1,450
Fond du Lac (Fond du Lac)	44,279	43,021	2.92	15	2,695	2,742
New Berlin (Waukesha)	40,600	39,584	2.57	16	2,256	1,036
Brookfield (Waukesha)	40,044	37,920	5.60	17	3,545	853
Wausau (Marathon)	38,884	39,106	−0.57	19	5,891	1,149
Greenfield (Milwaukee)	36,659	36,720	−0.17	20	3,043	3,087

Wisconsin cities and villages over 10,000 population, January 1, 2020, continued

City or village (county)	2020 estimate[1]	2010 census	% change	2020 rank	2010 non-white,[2] non-Hispanic	2010 Hispanic or Latino origin[3]
Oak Creek (Milwaukee)	36,529	34,451	6.03	21	3,282	2,582
Franklin (Milwaukee)	36,514	35,451	3.00	22	4,168	1,592
Beloit (Rock)	36,162	36,966	-2.17	23	7,149	6,332
Sun Prairie (Dane)	35,895	29,364	22.24	24	3,749	1,253
Manitowoc (Manitowoc)	33,527	33,736	-0.62	25	2,486	1,695
West Bend (Washington)	32,058	31,078	3.15	26	1,049	1,213
Fitchburg (Dane)	30,391	25,260	20.31	27	4,464	4,341
Superior (Douglas)	26,986	27,244	-0.95	28	2,166	382
Neenah (Winnebago)	26,333	25,501	3.26	30	1,163	967
Stevens Point (Portage)	26,269	26,717	-1.68	31	1,946	696
Muskego (Waukesha)	25,271	24,135	4.71	32	529	545
Mequon (Ozaukee)	24,806	23,132	7.24	34	1,760	467
De Pere (Brown)	24,595	23,800	3.34	35	1,207	511
Watertown (Dodge, Jefferson)	23,800	23,861	-0.26	36	706	1,731
Middleton (Dane)	21,050	17,442	20.69	38	1,764	984
South Milwaukee (Milwaukee)	20,622	21,156	-2.52	40	1,100	1,699
Marshfield (Marathon, Wood)	19,478	19,118	1.88	42	796	452
Onalaska (La Crosse)	19,330	17,736	8.99	43	1,539	276
Wisconsin Rapids (Wood)	18,721	18,367	1.93	45	1,186	535
Cudahy (Milwaukee)	18,007	18,267	-1.42	46	1,142	1,769
Oconomowoc (Waukesha)	17,501	15,759	11.05	47	422	559
Menasha (Calumet, Winnebago)	17,468	17,353	0.66	48	954	1,204
Beaver Dam (Dodge)	16,890	16,214	4.17	50	502	1,210
Menomonie (Dunn)	16,461	16,264	1.21	51	1,176	276
Kaukauna (Calumet, Outagamie)	16,363	15,462	5.83	52	654	407
River Falls (Pierce, St. Croix)	16,113	15,000	7.42	53	673	270
Hartford (Dodge, Washington)	15,870	14,223	11.58	54	425	686
Whitewater (Jefferson, Walworth)	15,035	14,390	4.48	57	1,009	1,372
Pewaukee (Waukesha)	14,775	13,195	11.97	58	667	281
Chippewa Falls (Chippewa)	14,405	13,661	5.45	60	605	221
Hudson (St. Croix)	14,091	12,719	10.79	63	539	347
Stoughton (Dane)	12,954	12,611	2.72	69	554	230
Verona (Dane)	12,737	10,619	19.95	71	617	258
Glendale (Milwaukee)	12,463	12,872	-3.18	73	2,499	465
Fort Atkinson (Jefferson)	12,395	12,368	0.22	74	315	1,128
Platteville (Grant)	12,262	11,224	9.25	75	535	179
Cedarburg (Ozaukee)	12,147	11,412	6.44	76	367	197
Baraboo (Sauk)	12,008	12,048	-0.33	77	487	446
Port Washington (Ozaukee)	11,954	11,250	6.26	79	457	347
Waupun (Dodge, Fond du Lac)	11,588	11,340	2.19	82	1,651	217
Two Rivers (Manitowoc)	11,364	11,712	-2.97	84	536	224
Burlington (Racine, Walworth)	10,912	10,464	4.28	85	327	898
Marinette (Marinette)	10,720	10,968	-2.26	86	271	149
Monroe (Green)	10,641	10,827	-1.72	88	252	526
Portage (Columbia)	10,132	10,324	-1.86	92	811	414
Sparta (Monroe)	10,056	9,522	5.61	93	345	643
Villages						
Menomonee Falls (Waukesha)	38,948	35,626	9.32	18	2,789	697
Mount Pleasant (Racine)	26,922	26,197	2.77	29	2,714	2,181
Caledonia (Racine)	25,131	24,705	1.72	33	1,563	1,303
Pleasant Prairie (Kenosha)	22,456	19,719	13.88	37	1,141	1,332
Germantown (Washington)	20,686	19,749	4.74	39	1,334	400
Howard (Brown, Outagamie)	20,209	17,399	16.15	41	919	410
Fox Crossing (Winnebago)[4]	19,090	18,498	3.20	44	1,030	1,131
Ashwaubenon (Brown)	16,961	16,963	-0.01	49	1,375	471

Wisconsin cities and villages over 10,000 population, January 1, 2020, continued

City or village (county)	2020 estimate[1]	2010 census	% change	2020 rank	2010 non-white,[2] non-Hispanic	2010 Hispanic or Latino origin[3]
Bellevue (Brown)	15,706	14,570	7.80	55	970	1,359
Weston (Marathon)	15,646	14,868	5.23	56	1,670	301
Salem Lakes (Kenosha)[5]	14,679	14,478	1.39	59	330	644
Waunakee (Dane)	14,399	12,097	19.03	61	416	269
Greendale (Milwaukee)	14,335	14,046	2.06	62	805	667
Whitefish Bay (Milwaukee)	14,000	14,110	-0.78	64	1,060	399
Allouez (Brown)	13,734	13,975	-1.72	65	1,252	383
Plover (Portage)	13,486	12,123	11.24	66	684	393
Shorewood (Milwaukee)	13,472	13,162	2.36	67	1,416	447
Harrison (Calumet, Outagamie)[6]	13,185	NA	NA	68	NA	NA
Suamico (Brown)	12,796	11,346	12.78	70	242	112
Brown Deer (Milwaukee)	12,518	11,999	4.33	72	4,358	471
Grafton (Ozaukee)	11,989	11,459	4.63	78	421	266
Richfield (Washington)	11,948	11,300	5.73	80	304	162
Little Chute (Outagamie)	11,947	10,449	14.34	81	337	327
Sussex (Waukesha)	11,373	10,518	8.13	83	431	249
Holmen (La Crosse)	10,662	9,005	18.40	87	827	96
DeForest (Dane)	10,624	8,936	18.89	89	467	325
Hobart (Brown)	10,454	6,182	69.10	90	1,261	140
Oregon (Dane)	10,270	9,231	11.26	91	344	204

NA–Not available.

1. Population estimates are based on the corrected 2010 Census totals. Race and ethnicity data have not been adjusted since the 2010 Census.   2. In the 2010 Census, respondents were allowed to choose more than one race. The column "nonwhite" includes all who chose at least one race other than white.   3. "Hispanic or Latino Origin" represents ethnicity and includes people of Cuban, Mexican, Puerto Rican, South or Central American, or other Spanish culture or origin, regardless of race. 4. The village of Fox Crossing was created on April 20, 2016, from part of the town of Menasha. The village subsequently annexed the remainder of the town, except for three parcels that were annexed by the city of Menasha. The 2010 figures reflect the data for the previously existing town.   5. The village of Salem Lakes was created on February 14, 2017, by the merger of the village of Silver Lake and the town of Salem. The 2010 figures reflect the combined data for the previously existing village and town.   6. This village was created from parts of two towns after the date reflected by the 2010 data.

Sources: Wisconsin Department of Administration, Demographic Services Center, *Official Final Estimates, 1/1/2020, Wisconsin Municipalities, with Comparison to Census 2010*, October 2020, and *Population and Hispanic & Non-Hispanic Data, Wisconsin Municipalities, Census 2000 and 2010 Comparisons, Based on Census 2010 Geography*, March 2011; and Wisconsin Department of Administration, Municipal Data System, *Municipality changes since January 2000*, January 2021.

Wisconsin towns over 2,500 population, January 1, 2020

Town (county)	2020 estimate	2010 census	% change	Town (county)	2020 estimate	2010 census	% change
Addison (Washington) . .	3,485	3,495	-0.29	Burlington (Racine)	6,478	6,502	-0.37
Alden (Polk)	2,812	2,786	0.93	Campbell (La Crosse) . . .	4,282	4,314	-0.74
Algoma (Winnebago) . .	6,939	6,822	1.72	Cedarburg (Ozaukee) . . .	6,006	5,760	4.27
Arbor Vitae (Vilas)	3,326	3,316	0.30	Center (Outagamie)	3,648	3,402	7.23
Ashippun (Dodge)	2,644	2,559	3.32	Chase (Oconto)	3,263	3,005	8.59
Barton (Washington) . . .	2,721	2,637	3.19	Clayton (Winnebago) . . .	4,193	3,951	6.13
Beaver Dam (Dodge)	4,041	3,962	1.99	Cottage Grove (Dane) . . .	3,889	3,875	0.36
Beloit (Rock)	7,658	7,662	-0.05	Dale (Outagamie)	2,894	2,731	5.97
Bristol (Dane)	4,347	3,765	15.46	Dayton (Waupaca)	2,753	2,748	0.18
Brockway (Jackson)	2,890	2,828	2.19	Delafield (Waukesha) . . .	8,503	8,400	1.23
Brookfield (Waukesha) . .	6,744	6,116	10.27	Delavan (Walworth)	5,168	5,285	-2.21
Buchanan (Outagamie) . .	7,055	6,755	4.44	Dover (Racine)	4,197	4,051	3.60
Burke (Dane)	3,303	3,284	0.58	Dunn (Dane)	4,852	4,931	-1.60

Wisconsin towns over 2,500 population, January 1, 2020, continued

Town (county)	2020 estimate	2010 census	% change	Town (county)	2020 estimate	2010 census	% change
Eagle (Waukesha)	3,586	3,507	2.25	Oakland (Jefferson)	3,124	3,100	0.77
Eagle Point (Chippewa) . .	3,241	3,053	6.16	Oconomowoc (Waukesha)	8,706	8,408	3.54
East Troy (Walworth). . . .	4,073	4,021	1.29	Onalaska (La Crosse). . . .	5,846	5,623	3.97
Ellington (Outagamie). . .	3,133	2,758	13.60	Oneida (Outagamie). . . .	4,739	4,678	1.30
Empire (Fond du Lac) . . .	2,784	2,797	−0.46	Oregon (Dane)	3,240	3,184	1.76
Erin (Washington)	3,824	3,747	2.05	Osceola (Polk)	2,941	2,855	3.01
Farmington (Washington)	4,085	4,014	1.77	Ottawa (Waukesha)	3,936	3,859	2.00
Farmington (Waupaca) . .	3,778	3,974	−4.93	Pacific (Columbia)	2,742	2,707	1.29
Fond du Lac (Fond du Lac)	3,967	3,015	31.58	Pelican (Oneida)	2,799	2,764	1.27
Freedom (Outagamie). . .	6,088	5,842	4.21	Peshtigo (Marinette). . . .	4,149	4,057	2.27
Friendship (Fond du Lac) .	2,675	2,675	0.00	Pine Lake (Oneida)	2,752	2,740	0.44
Fulton (Rock)	3,443	3,252	5.87	Pittsfield (Brown)	2,769	2,608	6.17
Genesee (Waukesha) . . .	7,379	7,340	0.53	Pleasant Springs (Dane). .	3,203	3,154	1.55
Geneva (Walworth)	5,085	4,993	1.84	Pleasant Valley (Eau Claire)	3,419	3,044	12.32
Grafton (Ozaukee)	4,227	4,053	4.29	Plymouth (Sheboygan) . .	3,244	3,195	1.53
Grand Chute (Outagamie)	23,227	20,919	11.03	Polk (Washington)	4,040	3,937	2.62
Grand Rapids (Wood) . . .	7,771	7,646	1.63	Randall (Kenosha)	3,189	3,180	0.28
Greenbush (Sheboygan) .	2,579	2,565	0.55	Rib Mountain (Marathon)	7,001	6,825	2.58
Greenville (Outagamie)[1]	12,267	10,309	18.99	Rice Lake (Barron)	3,101	3,060	1.34
Harmony (Rock).	2,582	2,569	0.51	Richmond (St. Croix). . . .	3,782	3,272	15.59
Hartford (Washington) . .	3,534	3,609	−2.08	Rock (Rock)	3,131	3,196	−2.03
Hayward (Sawyer)	3,582	3,567	0.42	Rome (Adams)	2,816	2,720	3.53
Holland (La Crosse).	4,266	3,701	15.27	St. Joseph (St. Croix)	4,119	3,842	7.21
Hudson (St. Croix)	8,689	8,461	2.69	Saratoga (Wood)	5,252	5,142	2.14
Hull (Portage)	5,468	5,346	2.28	Scott (Brown)	3,657	3,545	3.16
Ixonia (Jefferson)	4,965	4,385	13.23	Sevastopol (Door)	2,742	2,628	4.34
Jackson (Washington). . .	4,564	4,134	10.40	Seymour (Eau Claire). . . .	3,361	3,209	4.74
Janesville (Rock)	3,537	3,434	3.00	Sheboygan (Sheboygan) .	8,029	7,271	10.42
Koshkonong (Jefferson). .	3,658	3,692	−0.92	Shelby (La Crosse)	4,686	4,715	−0.62
Lac du Flambeau (Vilas). .	3,463	3,441	0.64	Somerset (St. Croix)	4,401	4,036	9.04
Lafayette (Chippewa) . . .	6,179	5,765	7.18	Sparta (Monroe)	3,275	3,128	4.70
Lawrence (Brown)	6,020	4,284	40.52	Springfield (Dane)	2,935	2,734	7.35
Ledgeview (Brown)	8,444	6,555	28.82	Stanley (Barron).	2,575	2,546	1.14
Lima (Sheboygan)	2,965	2,982	−0.57	Star Prairie (St. Croix) . . .	3,622	3,504	3.37
Lisbon (Waukesha).	10,564	10,157	4.01	Stephenson (Marinette). .	3,101	3,006	3.16
Little Suamico (Oconto). .	5,460	4,799	13.77	Stettin (Marathon)	2,595	2,554	1.61
Lodi (Columbia).	3,312	3,273	1.19	Stockton (Portage)	3,062	2,917	4.97
Lyons (Walworth).	3,710	3,698	0.32	Sugar Creek (Walworth). .	3,933	3,943	−0.25
Madison (Dane).	6,228	6,279	−0.81	Taycheedah (Fond du Lac)	4,591	4,205	9.18
Medford (Taylor)	2,690	2,606	3.22	Trenton (Washington) . . .	4,800	4,732	1.44
Menominee (Menominee)	4,267	4,232	0.83	Troy (St. Croix)	5,398	4,705	14.73
Menomonie (Dunn)	3,512	3,366	4.34	Union (Eau Claire)	2,828	2,663	6.20
Merrill (Lincoln)	3,027	2,980	1.58	Vernon (Waukesha)[2]	7,621	7,601	0.26
Merton (Waukesha)	8,469	8,338	1.57	Washington (Eau Claire). .	7,441	7,134	4.30
Middleton (Dane).	6,614	5,877	12.54	Waterford (Racine)	6,489	6,344	2.29
Milton (Rock)	2,988	2,923	2.22	Waukesha (Waukesha)[3] . .	9,329	9,133	2.15
Minocqua (Oneida).	4,491	4,453	0.85	Wescott (Shawano).	3,183	3,183	0.00
Mukwa (Waupaca)	2,978	2,930	1.64	West Bend (Washington) .	4,667	4,774	−2.24
Mukwonago (Waukesha) .	7,979	7,959	0.25	Westport (Dane)	4,038	3,950	2.23
Neenah (Winnebago) . . .	3,632	3,237	12.20	Wheatland (Kenosha) . . .	3,362	3,373	−0.33
Newbold (Oneida)	2,752	2,719	1.21	Wheaton (Chippewa) . . .	2,815	2,701	4.22
Norway (Racine)	7,991	7,948	0.54	Wilson (Sheboygan)	3,367	3,330	1.11

1. On January 12, 2021, part of the town of Greenville became a village. 2. On June 4, 2020, the town of Vernon became a village. 3. On May 12, 2020, the town of Waukesha became a village.

Source: Wisconsin Department of Administration, Demographic Services Center, *Official Final Estimates, 1/1/2020, Wisconsin Municipalities, with Comparison to Census 2010*, October 2020; and Wisconsin Department of Administration, Municipal Data System, *Municipality changes since January 2000*, January 2021.

Democratic presidential primary vote, by county, April 7, 2020

	Joe Biden	Bernie Sanders	Elizabeth Warren	Uninstructed delegation	Total
Adams	1,932	560	13	9	2,630
Ashland	1,560	941	32	8	2,629
Barron	3,618	1,214	53	29	5,131
Bayfield	2,519	1,360	52	15	4,064
Brown	21,495	9,447	391	127	32,666
Buffalo	1,246	405	18	13	1,772
Burnett	1,293	370	22	19	1,802
Calumet	4,446	1,878	85	39	6,791
Chippewa	6,075	2,126	98	43	8,692
Clark	2,061	681	25	15	2,925
Columbia	6,819	2,921	132	40	10,292
Crawford	1,620	713	24	9	2,467
Dane	92,892	67,424	4,002	462	168,758
Dodge	6,488	2,603	136	46	9,691
Door	4,691	1,523	90	26	6,546
Douglas	4,931	1,759	79	18	7,013
Dunn	3,570	1,701	56	29	5,625
Eau Claire	11,202	6,672	275	68	18,913
Florence	331	117	6	1	471
Fond du Lac	7,914	3,041	113	56	11,644
Forest	743	244	15	7	1,052
Grant	4,285	1,600	91	28	6,261
Green	4,537	1,939	91	23	6,847
Green Lake	1,351	475	26	7	1,948
Iowa	3,270	1,366	66	14	4,862
Iron	814	273	11	7	1,155
Jackson	1,711	656	23	13	2,529
Jefferson	7,825	3,710	185	49	12,250
Juneau	1,923	752	29	9	2,858
Kenosha	13,553	6,897	269	68	21,458
Kewaunee	1,762	589	27	11	2,519
La Crosse	12,688	6,797	275	78	20,496
Lafayette	1,674	488	35	9	2,295
Langlade	1,519	410	27	9	2,050
Lincoln	2,558	841	38	21	3,599
Manitowoc	6,739	2,394	115	42	9,752
Marathon	11,929	4,669	233	66	17,549
Marinette	3,263	959	55	29	4,478
Marquette	1,343	466	14	8	1,883
Menominee	167	111	3	0	293
Milwaukee	89,400	55,737	2,606	534	153,031
Monroe	3,218	1,328	58	31	4,864
Oconto	2,922	1,000	44	18	4,142
Oneida	4,100	1,453	76	28	5,868
Outagamie	16,752	8,263	358	122	26,499
Ozaukee	10,964	4,139	211	66	15,999
Pepin	671	192	20	0	924
Pierce	3,341	1,530	67	29	5,180
Polk	3,544	1,206	52	37	5,099
Portage	7,669	4,303	152	39	12,583
Price	1,440	565	24	10	2,135

Democratic presidential primary vote, by county, April 7, 2020, continued

	Joe Biden	Bernie Sanders	Elizabeth Warren	Uninstructed delegation	Total
Racine.	18,336	7,886	321	109	27,658
Richland	1,670	682	42	10	2,511
Rock.	16,078	7,341	293	90	24,595
Rusk.	1,130	347	13	13	1,567
St. Croix.	7,689	2,744	93	42	11,054
Sauk.	7,749	3,365	166	54	11,753
Sawyer	1,593	683	22	7	2,399
Shawano.	2,558	1,035	50	27	3,850
Sheboygan.	10,264	4,217	178	84	15,371
Taylor.	1,172	342	19	15	1,639
Trempealeau	2,587	945	46	25	3,789
Vernon	2,796	1,685	48	24	4,713
Vilas.	2,478	806	29	18	3,459
Walworth.	8,439	3,805	189	60	13,018
Washburn	1,622	496	22	14	2,261
Washington	10,870	4,360	203	89	16,239
Waukesha	41,662	16,962	769	222	62,186
Waupaca.	3,848	1,580	58	26	5,776
Waushara.	1,821	593	32	13	2,582
Winnebago	15,825	8,096	375	123	25,529
Wood	6,898	2,663	94	41	10,136
Total.	**581,463**	**293,441**	**14,060**	**3,590**	**925,065**

Note: County totals include scattered votes.

Source: Official records of the Wisconsin Elections Commission.

Republican presidential primary vote, by county, April 7, 2020

	Donald J. Trump	Uninstructed delegation	Total
Adams	2,834	24	2,871
Ashland.	1,324	15	1,342
Barron.	5,592	63	5,670
Bayfield.	2,047	38	2,086
Brown.	24,328	436	24,882
Buffalo	1,734	33	1,772
Burnett.	2,338	40	2,379
Calumet	6,505	112	6,638
Chippewa	7,795	134	7,941
Clark.	4,084	50	4,145
Columbia.	6,500	111	6,630
Crawford	1,605	26	1,631
Dane	27,680	945	28,898
Dodge	12,423	210	12,633
Door.	4,007	108	4,135
Douglas.	3,661	49	3,723
Dunn	4,510	80	4,590
Eau Claire.	8,638	213	8,893
Florence	919	0	921
Fond du Lac	13,538	220	13,776

Republican presidential primary vote, by county, April 7, 2020, continued

	Donald J. Trump	Uninstructed delegation	Total
Forest	1,512	24	1,541
Grant	4,499	117	4,633
Green	3,573	74	3,654
Green Lake.	2,851	38	2,894
Iowa.	2,187	39	2,241
Iron	1,267	12	1,279
Jackson.	1,948	19	1,967
Jefferson	10,911	173	11,108
Juneau	3,308	25	3,352
Kenosha	13,730	245	14,030
Kewaunee	2,823	33	2,856
La Crosse.	8,828	216	9,044
Lafayette.	1,824	39	1,865
Langlade.	2,895	32	2,928
Lincoln	3,777	46	3,831
Manitowoc.	9,896	1	10,051
Marathon.	17,617	214	17,870
Marinette.	6,055	91	6,146
Marquette	2,303	29	2,334
Menominee	85	2	88
Milwaukee.	48,609	1,294	50,181
Monroe.	4,712	80	4,804
Oconto	6,152	59	6,211
Oneida	5,430	78	5,522
Outagamie.	20,336	437	20,773
Ozaukee	15,723	308	16,101
Pepin	885	7	892
Pierce	3,861	56	3,921
Polk	6,109	84	6,194
Portage.	6,971	111	7,113
Price.	2,465	28	2,493
Racine.	22,697	444	23,235
Richland	1,641	33	1,676
Rock.	10,913	263	11,240
Rusk.	2,067	24	2,092
St. Croix.	9,596	163	9,811
Sauk.	6,940	127	7,067
Sawyer	2,354	27	2,385
Shawano.	5,726	78	5,804
Sheboygan.	16,411	245	16,701
Taylor	3,186	26	3,213
Trempealeau	2,708	0	2,757
Vernon	3,004	72	3,081
Vilas.	4,004	42	4,053
Walworth.	13,538	281	13,875
Washburn	2,568	34	2,606
Washington	28,373	391	28,764
Waukesha	76,192	1,364	77,886
Waupaca.	7,341	113	7,465
Waushara.	3,620	43	3,663
Winnebago	18,275	420	18,778
Wood	10,424	138	10,573
Total.	**616,782**	**11,246**	**630,198**

Note: County totals include scattered votes. Write-in candidate Adam Nicholas Paul received a total of 246 votes.

Source: Official records of the Wisconsin Elections Commission.

Democratic National Convention delegates, August 17–20, 2020, Milwaukee, Wisconsin

Joe Biden delegates and residence

Party leaders and elected officials
Mandela Barnes. . . . . Milwaukee
Tom Barrett . . . . Milwaukee
Jim Doyle. . . . . Verona
Sarah Godlewski . . . . Madison
Gordon Hintz . . . . Oshkosh
Joshua Kaul . . . . Madison
Satya Rhodes-Conway. . . . . . Madison

At-large
Kathleen Arciszewski . . . . Milwaukee
Stephanie Bloomingdale . . . . . Milwaukee
Marisabel Cabrera . . . . Milwaukee
Michael Childers (alternate) . . . La Pointe
David Crowley. . . . . Milwaukee
Ada Deer . . . . Fitchburg
Jason Fields . . . . Milwaukee
Alicia Halvensleben . . . . Waukesha
Frances Huntley-Cooper . . . . . Fitchburg
Shelly Moore Krajacic . . . . Kenosha
Ronald Martin. . . . . Eau Claire
Cory Mason . . . . Racine
Thelma Sias . . . . Milwaukee
Sequanna Taylor . . . . Milwaukee

First congressional district
John Collins . . . . Kenosha
Trevor Jung . . . . Racine
Connie Cobb Madsen . . . . Racine
Sally Simpson . . . . Kenosha

Second congressional district
Laura Beutel. . . . . Montrose
David Boetcher . . . . Waunakee
Farah Famouri. . . . . Madison
Awais Khaleel . . . . Madison
Elizabeth Miller . . . . Madison
Shawn Reents . . . . Janesville
John Smallwood . . . . Madison
Shelia Stubbs (alternate) . . . . . Madison

Third congressional district
Bobbi Green . . . . Eau Claire
Gary Hawley . . . . Stevens Point
Lance Tryggestad (alternate). . . La Crosse
Nicholas Webber . . . . Eau Claire
Margaret Wood . . . . La Crosse

Fourth congressional district
Sachin Chheda (alternate) . . . . Milwaukee
Megan Holbrook . . . . Milwaukee
Craig Mastantuono. . . . . Milwaukee
LaKeshia Myers . . . . Milwaukee
Deiadra Queary . . . . Milwaukee
Christopher Walton . . . . Milwaukee

Fifth congressional district
Lynn Carey. . . . . Germantown
Nick Katers. . . . . Menomonee Falls
Donald Placidi. . . . . Greenfield
Lauren Yoder . . . . Waukesha

Sixth congressional district
Debra Dassow. . . . . Cedarburg
Thomas Kitchen. . . . . Fond du Lac
Ryan Sorenson . . . . Sheboygan
Marcia Steele . . . . Oshkosh
Kyle Whelton (alternate) . . . . . Sheboygan

Seventh congressional district
Kay Gruling . . . . Wausau
Preston Pagel . . . . Mosinee
Melissa Schroeder . . . . Merrill
Ann Stevning-Roe (alternate) . . Marshfield
Vik Verma. . . . . Merrill

Eighth congressional district
David Hayes . . . . Sturgeon Bay
Amaad Rivera-Wagner. . . . . . . Green Bay
Jill Swenson . . . . Appleton
Katie Van Zeeland . . . . Appleton

Bernie Sanders delegates and residence

Party leaders and elected officials
David Bowen . . . . Milwaukee
Thomas Nelson . . . . Appleton
Marcelia Nicholson. . . . . Milwaukee

At-large
Randy Bryce . . . . Racine
Angelina Cruz . . . . Racine
Sarah Lloyd . . . . Wisconsin Dells
Fabi Maldonado . . . . Racine
Amy Mizialko . . . . Milwaukee
Peter Rickman . . . . Milwaukee
Kamryn Yelk (alternate) . . . . . . Milwaukee

First congressional district
Steven Doelder . . . . Genoa City
Susan Sheldon . . . . Burlington

Second congressional district
Essie Lenchner . . . . Madison
Michael Morgan . . . . Madison
Charlie Ryan . . . . Verona
Laura Valderrama. . . . . Madison

Third congressional district
Erin Ford . . . . Viroqua
Jeremy Gragert . . . . Eau Claire

Democratic National Convention delegates, August 17–20, 2020, Milwaukee, Wisconsin, continued

Bernie Sanders delegates and residence, continued

Fourth congressional district
Alexander Kostal . . . . Milwaukee
Tommy Molina . . . . Milwaukee
Noel Ray . . . . Milwaukee
Corinne Rosen. . . . . Milwaukee

Fifth congressional district
Naimeh Mohammad. . . . . . . Greenfield
William Walter. . . . . Germantown

Sixth congressional district
Michael Beardsley . . . . Oshkosh
Isabel Klemmer . . . . Mequon

Seventh congressional district
Lauren Henkelman. . . . . Wausau

Eighth congressional district
Jasmine Neosh . . . . Shawano
Justice Peche . . . . Green Bay

Unpledged delegates and residence

Tammy Baldwin. . . . . Madison
Janet Bewley . . . . Mason
Tony Evers . . . . Madison
Ron Kind . . . . La Crosse
Martha Love . . . . Milwaukee
Felesia Martin . . . . Madison
Mahlon Mitchell . . . . Madison

Gwen Moore. . . . . Milwaukee
Khary Penebaker . . . . Hartland
Mark Pocan . . . . Madison
Jason Rae. . . . . Glendale
Andrew Werthmann . . . . Eau Claire
Ben Wikler . . . . Madison

Source: Democratic Party of Wisconsin.

Republican National Convention delegates, August 24–27, 2020, Charlotte, North Carolina

Donald Trump delegates and residence

At-large
Candee Arndt . . . . Brookfield
Tyler August (alternate) . . . . . . Lake Geneva
Kim Bliss . . . . Darien
Nick Boerke (alternate) . . . . . Mequon
Mary Buestrin . . . . Mequon
Rachael Campos-Duffy . . . . . . Wausau
Kristan Collins (alternate) . . . . Waunakee
Brad Courtney. . . . . Whitefish Bay
Sean Duffy . . . . Wausau
Dan Feyen . . . . Fond Du Lac
Scott Fitzgerald . . . . Juneau
Jim Geldreich . . . . West Bend
Keith Gilkes (alternate) . . . . . Waunakee
Andrew Hitt . . . . Appleton
Mike Huebsch (alternate). . . . . West Salem
Rebecca Kleefisch . . . . Sullivan
Don Lee (alternate). . . . . Franklin
Domingo Leguizamon (alternate) Hillpoint
Julie Leschke (alternate) . . . . . Oshkosh
Michelle Litjens-Vos . . . . Burlington
Sue Lynch . . . . Kenosha
Katie McCallum (alternate) . . . . Middleton
Bill McCoshen (alternate) . . . . . Fitchburg
Jean Merry (alternate) . . . . . . Germantown

Barbara Michels (alternate). . . . Hartland
Tim Michels . . . . Hartland
Mark Mingo (alternate) . . . . . . Bayside
Van Mobley (alternate) . . . . . Franklin
Robin Moore (alternate). . . . . Brookfield
Reggie Newson . . . . Milwaukee
Kevin Nicholson . . . . Pewaukee
John Nygren (alternate). . . . . . Marinette
Gerard Randall . . . . Milwaukee
Charlotte Rasmussen . . . . . . Stanley
Greg Reiman (alternate). . . . . . Whitefish Bay
Brian Reisinger (alternate) . . . . Madison
Judith Rhodes (alternate). . . . . Cottage Grove
Brandon Rosner (alternate). . . . Waukesha
Lane Ruhland . . . . Waunakee
Brian Schimming (alternate) . . . Fitchburg
Tom Schreibel. . . . . Hartland
Dean Stensberg (alternate). . . . Middleton
Ruth Streck. . . . . Neenah
Jenny Toftness (alternate) . . . . Madison
Kim Travis . . . . Williams Bay
Rachel VerVelde (alternate). . . . Columbus
Robin Vos. . . . . Burlington
Leah Vukmir . . . . Brookfield
Scott Walker . . . . Pewaukee

Republican National Convention delegates, August 24–27, 2020, Charlotte, North Carolina, continued

Donald Trump delegates and residence, continued

Tonette Walker	Pewaukee
Heather Weininger (alternate) . .	Green Bay
Ladd Wiley	Appleton
Carmala Zager.	Franklin

First congressional district

Carol Brunner	Franklin
Erin Decker.	Silver Lake
Richard Frazier	Racine
Annette Guye-Kordus (alternate)	Lake Geneva
Gabriele Nudo (alternate).	Kenosha
Mary Patterson (alternate)	Racine

Second congressional district

Al Exner (alternate).	La Valle
Scott Grabins	Verona
Navin Jarugumilli.	Madison
Billie Johnson (alternate)	Madison
Scott Kowalski (alternate).	Madison
Howard Marklein	Spring Green

Third congressional district

William Feehan (alternate)	La Crosse
Kathryn Heitman	Lyndon Station
Charles Krueger.	Menomonie
Maripat Krueger	Menomonie
Jacalyn Szehner (alternate). . . .	Plover
Larry Vangen (alternate)	La Crosse

Fourth congressional district

John Graber Jr. (alternate)	Milwaukee
Patricia Reiman	Whitefish Bay
Robert Spindell	Milwaukee
Carol Pociecha-Palm (alternate).	Milwaukee

Cindy Werner (alternate)	Milwaukee
Laurie Wolf.	Milwaukee

Fifth congressional district

Terrence Dittrich (alternate) . . .	Hartland
Jennie Frederick	Jackson
David Karst (alternate).	Greenfield
Mark Kelly	Hartland
Kathleen Kiernan	Richfield
James Schildbach (alternate) . .	Watertown

Sixth congressional district

Kathleen Broghammer	Mequon
Katherine Horan (alternate) . . .	Neenah
Tim Lakin.	Fond Du Lac
Denise Solie (alternate)	Columbus
Carl Toepel	Howards Grove
Donald Zimmer (alternate). . . .	Manitowoc

Seventh congressional district

Dave Anderson	Wausau
Carol Cady	Arbor Vitae
Jim Miller (alternate).	Hayward
Jeanie Moore (alternate)	Marshfield
Travis Nez	Phillips
Pamela Travis (alternate)	Neillsville

Eighth congressional district

Barbara Finger (alternate)	Oconto
Julie Frees (alternate)	Green Bay
Jerome Murphy.	Appleton
Kelly Ruh (alternate)	De Pere
Patricia Schick.	Hobart
William Vanevenhoven	De Pere

Source: Republican Party of Wisconsin.

Presidential vote by county and municipality, November 3, 2020 general election

	Joe Biden/ Kamala Harris (Dem.)	Donald J. Trump/ Mike Pence (Rep.)		Joe Biden/ Kamala Harris (Dem.)	Donald J. Trump/ Mike Pence (Rep.)
Adams	**4,329**	**7,362**	New Chester, town . . .	174	351
Adams, city	322	458	New Haven, town	168	243
Adams, town	263	465	Preston, town	291	494
Big Flats, town	190	358	Quincy, town	309	438
Colburn, town	44	97	Richfield, town	27	75
Dell Prairie, town	358	630	Rome, town	849	1,390
Easton, town	184	377	Springville, town	269	508
Friendship, village	113	173	Strongs Prairie, town . .	269	438
Jackson, town	262	406	Wisconsin Dells, city (part)	9	16
Leola, town	35	132			
Lincoln, town	71	140	**Ashland**	**4,801**	**3,841**
Monroe, town	122	173	Agenda, town	65	191

Presidential vote by county and municipality, November 3, 2020 general election, continued

	Joe Biden/ Kamala Harris (Dem.)	Donald J. Trump/ Mike Pence (Rep.)		Joe Biden/ Kamala Harris (Dem.)	Donald J. Trump/ Mike Pence (Rep.)
Ashland, city (part)	2,660	1,518	Barnes, town	321	346
Ashland, town	152	159	Bayfield, city	314	57
Butternut, village	74	110	Bayfield, town	399	158
Chippewa, town	75	147	Bayview, town	227	137
Gingles, town	239	254	Bell, town	182	82
Gordon, town	67	113	Cable, town	270	339
Jacobs, town.	116	249	Clover, town	118	88
La Pointe, town	236	52	Delta, town	120	132
Marengo, town	110	113	Drummond, town	196	168
Mellen, city	173	170	Eileen, town	211	258
Morse, town	158	175	Grand View, town	160	192
Peeksville, town.	34	64	Hughes, town	160	189
Sanborn, town	442	85	Iron River, town	366	440
Shanagolden, town . . .	38	45	Kelly, town	108	157
White River, town.	162	396	Keystone, town	89	143
			Lincoln, town	76	114
Barron	**9,194**	**15,803**	Mason, town	82	108
Almena, town	171	405	Mason, village.	24	32
Almena, village	85	246	Namakagon, town	113	151
Arland, town.	123	215	Orienta, town	44	58
Barron, city.	683	837	Oulu, town.	178	200
Barron, town.	109	304	Pilsen, town	85	65
Bear Lake, town.	174	266	Port Wing, town	148	126
Cameron, village	298	615	Russell, town	601	91
Cedar Lake, town	256	525	Tripp, town	64	82
Chetek, city	415	718	Washburn, city	944	320
Chetek, town	462	713	Washburn, town	256	143
Clinton, town	121	272			
Crystal Lake, town	147	320	**Brown**.	**65,511**	**75,871**
Cumberland, city	492	681	Allouez, village	4,475	3,805
Cumberland, town	169	315	Ashwaubenon, village. .	4,635	5,459
Dallas, town	82	225	Bellevue, village	4,053	4,694
Dallas, village	44	137	De Pere, city	7,021	7,070
Dovre, town	144	297	Denmark, village	436	820
Doyle, town	98	214	Eaton, town	323	725
Haugen, village	60	90	Glenmore, town	180	493
Lakeland, town	214	401	Green Bay, city	25,036	21,125
Maple Grove, town. . . .	118	371	Green Bay, town	379	1,011
Maple Plain, town	219	291	Hobart, village	2,500	3,314
New Auburn, village (part)	5	5	Holland, town	302	703
Oak Grove, town	189	343	Howard, village (part) . .	5,068	6,948
Prairie Farm, town	105	221	Humboldt, town	230	610
Prairie Farm, village . . .	66	147	Lawrence, town	1,518	2,423
Prairie Lake, town.	285	683	Ledgeview, town	2,326	2,901
Rice Lake, city	1,925	2,292	Morrison, town	196	768
Rice Lake, town	674	1,039	New Denmark, town . .	324	689
Sioux Creek, town	111	251	Pittsfield, town	525	1,336
Stanfold, town	129	274	Pulaski, village (part). . .	655	1,218
Stanley, town	476	1,017	Rockland, town	408	787
Sumner, town	145	308	Scott, town	1,024	1,505
Turtle Lake, town	108	244	Suamico, village	2,894	5,333
Turtle Lake, village (part)	161	273	Wrightstown, town . . .	445	1,053
Vance Creek, town	131	248	Wrightstown, village (part)	558	1,081
Bayfield	**6,147**	**4,617**	**Buffalo**	**2,860**	**4,834**
Ashland, city (part). . . .	0	0	Alma, city.	213	254
Barksdale, town.	291	241	Alma, town	82	96

Presidential vote by county and municipality, November 3, 2020 general election, continued

	Joe Biden/ Kamala Harris (Dem.)	Donald J. Trump/ Mike Pence (Rep.)		Joe Biden/ Kamala Harris (Dem.)	Donald J. Trump/ Mike Pence (Rep.)
Belvidere, town	84	194	Harrison, town	0	0
Buffalo, town	201	283	Harrison, village (part)	3,247	4,325
Buffalo City, city	275	356	Hilbert, village	133	459
Canton, town	56	115	Kaukauna, city (part)	0	0
Cochrane, village	91	136	Kiel, city (part)	64	115
Cross, town	78	150	Menasha, city (part)	894	962
Dover, town	98	161	New Holstein, city	703	1,107
Fountain City, city	222	224	New Holstein, town	243	651
Gilmanton, town	77	162	Potter, village	29	126
Glencoe, town	75	169	Rantoul, town	95	368
Lincoln, town	47	78	Sherwood, village	891	1,263
Maxville, town	44	152	Stockbridge, town	297	704
Milton, town	146	223	Stockbridge, village	126	310
Modena, town	72	98	Woodville, town	123	419
Mondovi, city	465	842			
Mondovi, town	83	195	**Chippewa**	**13,983**	**21,317**
Montana, town	45	110	Anson, town	555	947
Naples, town	122	289	Arthur, town	115	284
Nelson, town	105	240	Auburn, town	130	295
Nelson, village	69	93	Birch Creek, town	122	222
Waumandee, town	110	214	Bloomer, city	656	1,322
			Bloomer, town	167	421
Burnett	**3,569**	**6,462**	Boyd, village	90	204
Anderson, town	69	190	Cadott, village	259	412
Blaine, town	37	106	Chippewa Falls, city	3,556	3,497
Daniels, town	128	282	Cleveland, town	156	375
Dewey, town	92	216	Colburn, town	115	370
Grantsburg, town	208	465	Cooks Valley, town	110	327
Grantsburg, village	247	447	Cornell, city	257	475
Jackson, town	299	400	Delmar, town	152	376
La Follette, town	143	189	Eagle Point, town	817	1,264
Lincoln, town	47	147	Eau Claire, city (part)	615	511
Meenon, town	195	467	Edson, town	142	348
Oakland, town	299	381	Estella, town	56	201
Roosevelt, town	36	93	Goetz, town	159	309
Rusk, town	99	185	Hallie, town	63	53
Sand Lake, town	144	183	Howard, town	173	280
Scott, town	203	248	Lafayette, town	1,683	2,276
Siren, town	209	410	Lake Hallie, village	1,628	2,195
Siren, village	154	262	Lake Holcombe, town	167	451
Swiss, town	206	258	New Auburn, village (part)	72	193
Trade Lake, town	197	404	Ruby, town	56	195
Union, town	88	158	Sampson, town	182	394
Webb Lake, town	148	187	Sigel, town	211	397
Webster, village	123	196	Stanley, city (part)	332	636
West Marshland, town	54	168	Tilden, town	342	646
Wood River, town	144	420	Wheaton, town	664	1,011
			Woodmohr, town	181	430
Calumet	**12,116**	**18,156**			
Appleton, city (part)	3,245	2,754	**Clark**	**4,524**	**10,002**
Brillion, city	561	1,114	Abbotsford, city (part)	237	401
Brillion, town	240	694	Beaver, town	81	221
Brothertown, town	214	648	Butler, town	18	45
Charlestown, town	140	355	Colby, city (part)	197	359
Chilton, city	705	1,236	Colby, town	76	223
Chilton, town	166	546	Curtiss, village	17	36

Presidential vote by county and municipality, November 3, 2020 general election, continued

	Joe Biden/ Kamala Harris (Dem.)	Donald J. Trump/ Mike Pence (Rep.)		Joe Biden/ Kamala Harris (Dem.)	Donald J. Trump/ Mike Pence (Rep.)
Dewhurst, town	76	155	Leeds, town	226	280
Dorchester, village (part)	84	234	Lewiston, town	323	423
Eaton, town	80	216	Lodi, city	1,205	761
Foster, town	25	53	Lodi, town	1,131	1,153
Fremont, town	124	424	Lowville, town	298	387
Grant, town	128	289	Marcellon, town	233	360
Granton, village	60	103	Newport, town	167	259
Green Grove, town	59	160	Otsego, town	180	247
Greenwood, city	197	332	Pacific, town	851	978
Hendren, town	79	125	Pardeeville, village	503	603
Hewett, town	73	131	Portage, city	2,571	1,914
Hixon, town	71	156	Poynette, village	736	677
Hoard, town	60	201	Randolph, town	92	371
Levis, town	71	181	Randolph, village (part)	88	178
Longwood, town	63	179	Rio, village	305	307
Loyal, city	213	408	Scott, town	146	251
Loyal, town	62	213	Springvale, town	139	201
Lynn, town	79	203	West Point, town	794	669
Mayville, town	93	274	Wisconsin Dells, city (part)	607	617
Mead, town	39	103	Wyocena, town	489	588
Mentor, town	69	179	Wyocena, village	172	194
Neillsville, city	457	705			
Owen, city	182	293	**Crawford**	**3,953**	**4,620**
Pine Valley, town	205	476	Bell Center, village	27	25
Reseburg, town	74	117	Bridgeport, town	229	399
Seif, town	38	81	Clayton, town	279	256
Sherman, town	78	277	De Soto, village (part)	24	17
Sherwood, town	75	89	Eastman, town	170	259
Stanley, city (part)	2	0	Eastman, village	58	156
Thorp, city	250	484	Ferryville, village	70	71
Thorp, town	80	245	Freeman, town	236	244
Unity, town	80	261	Gays Mills, village	125	144
Unity, village (part)	11	52	Haney, town	84	97
Warner, town	64	166	Lynxville, village	33	48
Washburn, town	35	129	Marietta, town	102	190
Weston, town	91	232	Mount Sterling, village	53	40
Withee, town	92	221	Prairie du Chien, city	1,303	1,228
Withee, village	82	147	Prairie du Chien, town	239	301
Worden, town	70	192	Scott, town	127	138
York, town	127	231	Seneca, town	232	309
			Soldiers Grove, village	132	153
Columbia	**16,410**	**16,927**	Steuben, village	23	38
Arlington, town	252	288	Utica, town	196	163
Arlington, village	230	290	Wauzeka, town	82	151
Caledonia, town	541	466	Wauzeka, village	129	193
Cambria, village	191	203			
Columbus, city (part)	1,724	1,349	**Dane**	**260,185**	**78,800**
Columbus, town	147	255	Albion, town	662	593
Courtland, town	89	208	Belleville, village (part)	872	386
Dekorra, town	784	883	Berry, town	466	357
Doylestown, village	63	88	Black Earth, town	204	166
Fall River, village	441	501	Black Earth, village	583	341
Fort Winnebago, town	230	336	Blooming Grove, town	789	263
Fountain Prairie, town	249	303	Blue Mounds, town	396	238
Friesland, village	48	124	Blue Mounds, village	399	171
Hampden, town	165	215	Bristol, town	1,478	1,308

Presidential vote by county and municipality, November 3, 2020 general election, continued

	Joe Biden/ Kamala Harris (Dem.)	Donald J. Trump/ Mike Pence (Rep.)		Joe Biden/ Kamala Harris (Dem.)	Donald J. Trump/ Mike Pence (Rep.)
Brooklyn, village (part) .	392	206	Beaver Dam, town	1,048	1,335
Burke, town	1,297	808	Brownsville, village. . . .	96	294
Cambridge, village (part)	663	401	Burnett, town	150	396
Christiana, town	414	376	Calamus, town	235	352
Cottage Grove, town. . .	1,647	1,017	Chester, town	106	290
Cottage Grove, village. .	2,919	1,421	Clyman, town	103	369
Cross Plains, town	643	442	Clyman, village	51	138
Cross Plains, village . . .	1,748	801	Columbus, city (part) . .	0	0
Dane, town	244	333	Elba, town	269	412
Dane, village.	341	298	Emmet, town	214	645
Deerfield, town	566	451	Fox Lake, city	268	519
Deerfield, village	894	562	Fox Lake, town	214	569
DeForest, village	4,088	2,310	Hartford, city (part). . . .	1	4
Dunkirk, town.	782	545	Herman, town	125	667
Dunn, town	2,289	1,264	Horicon, city.	723	1,260
Edgerton, city (part) . . .	28	38	Hubbard, town	358	793
Fitchburg, city.	13,011	3,229	Hustisford, town	201	704
Madison, city	136,007	23,122	Hustisford, village. . . .	143	492
Madison, town	2,360	309	Iron Ridge, village	144	387
Maple Bluff, village. . . .	778	302	Juneau, city	396	660
Marshall, village.	1,093	871	Kekoskee, village	137	457
Mazomanie, town	394	340	Lebanon, town	260	738
Mazomanie, village . . .	650	399	Leroy, town	119	478
McFarland, village	4,224	1,698	Lomira, town	129	566
Medina, town	439	435	Lomira, village.	382	982
Middleton, city	11,001	2,699	Lowell, town	172	489
Middleton, town	3,095	1,668	Lowell, village.	51	111
Monona, city	4,798	1,116	Mayville, city.	996	1,884
Montrose, town.	495	272	Neosho, village	94	279
Mount Horeb, village . .	3,245	1,462	Oak Grove, town	197	456
Oregon, town	1,458	774	Portland, town	250	419
Oregon, village	4,908	2,063	Randolph, village (part) .	230	429
Perry, town.	349	172	Reeseville, village.	129	218
Pleasant Springs, town .	1,323	932	Rubicon, town	265	1,188
Primrose, town	336	166	Shields, town	112	256
Rockdale, village	81	47	Theresa, town	136	527
Roxbury, town.	661	540	Theresa, village	195	591
Rutland, town	862	540	Trenton, town	207	551
Shorewood Hills, village	1,504	128	Watertown, city (part) . .	1,781	2,987
Springdale, town	885	541	Waupun, city (part). . . .	866	1570
Springfield, town	1,096	828	Westford, town	334	511
Stoughton, city	5,627	2,433			
Sun Prairie, city	14,158	5,835	**Door.**	**10,044**	**9,752**
Sun Prairie, town	903	651	Baileys Harbor, town . .	550	370
Vermont, town	429	203	Brussels, town	217	454
Verona, city	6,467	2,233	Clay Banks, town	120	131
Verona, town	906	475	Egg Harbor, town	527	544
Vienna, town	503	506	Egg Harbor, village. . . .	167	89
Waunakee, village	5,958	3,325	Ephraim, village.	159	102
Westport, town	1,923	1,113	Forestville, town	229	422
Windsor, village.	3,212	2,069	Forestville, village	95	178
York, town	242	208	Gardner, town	282	529
			Gibraltar, town	557	376
Dodge	**16,356**	**31,355**	Jacksonport, town	290	320
Ashippun, town	425	1,380	Liberty Grove, town . . .	972	641
Beaver Dam, city	4,044	4,002	Nasewaupee, town . . .	564	729

Presidential vote by county and municipality, November 3, 2020 general election, continued

	Joe Biden/ Kamala Harris (Dem.)	Donald J. Trump/ Mike Pence (Rep.)		Joe Biden/ Kamala Harris (Dem.)	Donald J. Trump/ Mike Pence (Rep.)
Sevastopol, town	982	1,090	Stanton, town.	148	357
Sister Bay, village	500	314	Tainter, town.	693	921
Sturgeon Bay, city	3,084	2,379	Tiffany, town.	96	289
Sturgeon Bay, town . . .	231	304	Weston, town	109	241
Union, town	226	455	Wheeler, village.	43	90
Washington, town	292	325	Wilson, town	115	172
Douglas	**13,218**	**10,923**	**Eau Claire**	**31,620**	**25,341**
Amnicon, town	342	376	Altoona, city.	2,417	2,054
Bennett, town	177	249	Augusta, city.	237	466
Brule, town	219	172	Bridge Creek, town . . .	221	459
Cloverland, town	62	80	Brunswick, town	547	682
Dairyland, town	25	101	Clear Creek, town	185	292
Gordon, town	190	319	Drammen, town	174	297
Hawthorne, town	273	397	Eau Claire, city (part). . .	21,653	13,254
Highland, town	125	118	Fairchild, town	35	135
Lake Nebagamon, village	353	398	Fairchild, village.	76	155
Lakeside, town	196	230	Fall Creek, village.	361	441
Maple, town	234	196	Lincoln, town	223	443
Oakland, town	372	357	Ludington, town	231	411
Oliver, village	142	123	Otter Creek, town . . .	85	173
Parkland, town	380	306	Pleasant Valley, town . .	1,060	1,440
Poplar, village	139	233	Seymour, town	937	1,207
Solon Springs, town . . .	282	395	Union, town	774	849
Solon Springs, village . .	179	217	Washington, town	2,355	2,411
Summit, town	345	303	Wilson, town	49	172
Superior, city	7,999	5,083	**Florence**	**781**	**2,133**
Superior, town	688	749	Aurora, town	152	442
Superior, village.	242	193	Commonwealth, town .	64	201
Wascott, town	254	328	Fence, town	25	100
			Fern, town	24	101
Dunn	**9,897**	**13,173**	Florence, town	407	911
Boyceville, village.	169	325	Homestead, town	64	189
Colfax, town	262	456	Long Lake, town	29	102
Colfax, village	263	292	Tipler, town	16	87
Downing, village	28	94			
Dunn, town	381	498	**Fond du Lac**	**20,588**	**35,754**
Eau Galle, town	135	332	Alto, town	100	563
Elk Mound, town	344	669	Ashford, town	247	896
Elk Mound, village	195	223	Auburn, town	325	1,356
Grant, town	99	152	Brandon, village	123	366
Hay River, town	107	228	Byron, town	275	807
Knapp, village.	63	180	Calumet, town	265	660
Lucas, town	145	325	Campbellsport, village .	296	797
Menomonie, city	3,867	2,980	Eden, town	159	519
Menomonie, town	807	1,098	Eden, village.	102	349
New Haven, town	112	264	Eldorado, town	228	653
Otter Creek, town	101	206	Empire, town	649	1,269
Peru, town	40	97	Fairwater, village	44	138
Red Cedar, town	525	838	Fond du Lac, city	9,490	11,226
Ridgeland, village	44	80	Fond du Lac, town	872	1,446
Rock Creek, town	232	351	Forest, town	142	528
Sand Creek, town	115	220	Friendship, town	474	1,007
Sheridan, town	81	196	Kewaskum, village (part)	0	0
Sherman, town	219	367	Lamartine, town	293	835
Spring Brook, town . . .	359	632	Marshfield, town	188	532

Presidential vote by county and municipality, November 3, 2020 general election, continued

	Joe Biden/ Kamala Harris (Dem.)	Donald J. Trump/ Mike Pence (Rep.)		Joe Biden/ Kamala Harris (Dem.)	Donald J. Trump/ Mike Pence (Rep.)
Metomen, town	96	347	Lancaster, city	805	1,111
Mount Calvary, village. .	87	221	Liberty, town	70	194
North Fond du Lac, village	1,129	1,387	Lima, town	161	214
Oakfield, town	113	317	Little Grant, town	49	112
Oakfield, village.	199	460	Livingston, village (part)	168	179
Osceola, town	252	977	Marion, town	93	180
Ripon, city	1,820	2,019	Millville, town	42	53
Ripon, town	300	569	Montfort, village (part) .	139	147
Rosendale, town	126	320	Mount Hope, town . . .	29	66
Rosendale, village	175	447	Mount Hope, village . . .	42	53
St. Cloud, village	83	234	Mount Ida, town	86	216
Springvale, town	121	322	Muscoda, town	123	244
Taycheedah, town	1,011	2,140	Muscoda, village (part) .	275	292
Waupun, city (part). . . .	587	1,354	North Lancaster, town .	102	199
Waupun, town	217	693	Paris, town	167	276
			Patch Grove, town	61	115
Forest.	**1,721**	**3,285**	Patch Grove, village . . .	38	50
Alvin, town	30	73	Platteville, city	2,782	1,968
Argonne, town	73	229	Platteville, town	436	447
Armstrong Creek, town .	72	185	Potosi, town	161	329
Blackwell, town	15	44	Potosi, village	145	242
Caswell, town	10	43	Smelser, town	213	272
Crandon, city	266	552	South Lancaster, town .	138	239
Crandon, town	112	250	Tennyson, village	68	131
Freedom, town	79	166	Waterloo, town	110	209
Hiles, town	93	180	Watterstown, town . . .	80	120
Laona, town	216	451	Wingville, town	79	100
Lincoln, town	240	341	Woodman, town	25	69
Nashville, town	276	387	Woodman, village	12	35
Popple River, town	9	16	Wyalusing, town	77	121
Ross, town	11	70	**Green**.	**10,851**	**10,169**
Wabeno, town	219	298	Adams, town	170	172
			Albany, town	349	381
Grant	**10,998**	**14,142**	Albany, village.	300	233
Bagley, village.	75	114	Belleville, village (part) .	205	114
Beetown, town	75	266	Brodhead, city (part). . .	702	796
Bloomington, town . . .	56	160	Brooklyn, town	429	353
Bloomington, village . .	136	230	Brooklyn, village (part) .	172	78
Blue River, village.	92	117	Browntown, village . . .	47	82
Boscobel, city	584	713	Cadiz, town	165	313
Boscobel, town	81	129	Clarno, town	270	444
Cassville, town	56	160	Decatur, town	460	590
Cassville, village	188	251	Exeter, town	831	536
Castle Rock, town	61	92	Jefferson, town	243	451
Clifton, town	62	72	Jordan, town	139	200
Cuba City, city (part) . . .	517	465	Monroe, city	2,893	2,420
Dickeyville, village	260	322	Monroe, town	330	402
Ellenboro, town	97	233	Monticello, village	385	285
Fennimore, city	517	691	Mount Pleasant, town .	192	222
Fennimore, town	90	155	New Glarus, town	545	396
Glen Haven, town	57	162	New Glarus, village. . . .	945	422
Harrison, town	95	176	Spring Grove, town . . .	170	356
Hazel Green, town	317	355	Sylvester, town	270	388
Hazel Green, village (part)	296	331	Washington, town	261	257
Hickory Grove, town . .	60	126	York, town	378	278
Jamestown, town	450	839			

Presidential vote by county and municipality, November 3, 2020 general election, continued

	Joe Biden/ Kamala Harris (Dem.)	Donald J. Trump/ Mike Pence (Rep.)		Joe Biden/ Kamala Harris (Dem.)	Donald J. Trump/ Mike Pence (Rep.)
Green Lake	**3,344**	**7,168**	Kimball, town	132	209
Berlin, city (part)	925	1,543	Knight, town	50	81
Berlin, town	180	576	Mercer, town	413	747
Brooklyn, town	467	837	Montreal, city	197	268
Green Lake, city.	248	362	Oma, town	96	157
Green Lake, town	211	610	Pence, town	52	67
Kingston, town	77	234	Saxon, town	73	156
Kingston, village	54	140	Sherman, town	76	149
Mackford, town	60	249			
Manchester, town	98	305	**Jackson**.	**4,256**	**5,791**
Markesan, city.	215	527	Adams, town	357	495
Marquette, town	84	235	Albion, town	280	414
Marquette, village	32	70	Alma, town	182	327
Princeton, city.	242	453	Alma Center, village . . .	114	114
Princeton, town	322	659	Bear Bluff, town	11	89
St. Marie, town	61	179	Black River Falls, city . . .	867	811
Seneca, town	68	189	Brockway, town	511	361
			City Point, town.	41	72
Iowa.	**7,828**	**5,909**	Cleveland, town	81	192
Arena, town	522	410	Curran, town	72	106
Arena, village	256	218	Franklin, town	76	107
Avoca, village	109	127	Garden Valley, town . . .	77	165
Barneveld, village.	433	310	Garfield, town	130	273
Blanchardville, village			Hixton, town	109	223
(part)	66	44	Hixton, village.	84	154
Brigham, town	451	278	Irving, town	155	235
Clyde, town	131	75	Knapp, town	56	144
Cobb, village.	137	116	Komensky, town	146	30
Dodgeville, city	1,646	989	Manchester, town	152	320
Dodgeville, town	613	446	Melrose, town	78	156
Eden, town	118	121	Melrose, village	124	160
Highland, town	194	224	Merrillan, village	115	119
Highland, village	221	236	Millston, town	35	66
Hollandale, village	95	58	North Bend, town	111	155
Linden, town	176	254	Northfield, town	125	245
Linden, village.	126	112	Springfield, town	94	148
Livingston, village (part)	0	2	Taylor, village	73	110
Mifflin, town	122	161			
Mineral Point, city	979	516	**Jefferson**.	**19,904**	**27,208**
Mineral Point, town . . .	263	331	Aztalan, town	339	536
Montfort, village (part) .	31	24	Cambridge, village (part)	44	20
Moscow, town	213	180	Cold Spring, town	185	291
Muscoda, village (part) .	8	8	Concord, town	414	935
Pulaski, town	77	119	Farmington, town	282	698
Rewey, village.	69	51	Fort Atkinson, city	3,389	2,911
Ridgeway, town	235	137	Hebron, town	219	458
Ridgeway, village.	211	144	Ixonia, town	867	2,257
Waldwick, town	158	139	Jefferson, city	1,876	2,070
Wyoming, town	168	79	Jefferson, town	465	824
			Johnson Creek, village. .	718	1,040
Iron	**1,533**	**2,438**	Koshkonong, town	897	1,398
Anderson, town	21	23	Lac La Belle, village (part)	0	0
Carey, town	32	67	Lake Mills, city.	2,030	1,698
Gurney, town	50	46	Lake Mills, town	753	713
Hurley, city.	341	468	Milford, town	260	459
			Oakland, town	1,157	988

Presidential vote by county and municipality, November 3, 2020 general election, continued

	Joe Biden/ Kamala Harris (Dem.)	Donald J. Trump/ Mike Pence (Rep.)		Joe Biden/ Kamala Harris (Dem.)	Donald J. Trump/ Mike Pence (Rep.)
Palmyra, town	262	576	**Kewaunee**	**3,976**	**7,927**
Palmyra, village	303	660	Ahnapee, town	207	304
Sullivan, town	441	1,051	Algoma, city	825	819
Sullivan, village	128	265	Carlton, town	166	478
Sumner, town	235	341	Casco, town	193	521
Waterloo, city	860	936	Casco, village	84	250
Waterloo, town	233	336	Franklin, town	174	422
Watertown, city (part) . .	2,731	4,490	Kewaunee, city	640	893
Watertown, town	350	947	Lincoln, town	167	360
Whitewater, city (part) . .	466	310	Luxemburg, town	202	757
			Luxemburg, village. . . .	433	963
Juneau	**4,746**	**8,749**	Montpelier, town	246	650
Armenia, town	139	295	Pierce, town	186	282
Camp Douglas, village. .	93	213	Red River, town	264	635
Clearfield, town	138	330	West Kewaunee, town .	189	593
Cutler, town	53	167			
Elroy, city	251	327	**La Crosse**.	**37,846**	**28,684**
Finley, town	17	50	Bangor, town	134	213
Fountain, town	103	241	Bangor, village	363	421
Germantown, town . . .	344	700	Barre, town	269	511
Hustler, village	45	56	Burns, town	221	349
Kildare, town	134	252	Campbell, town	1,489	1,135
Kingston, town	1	19	Farmington, town	509	754
Lemonweir, town	330	589	Greenfield, town	643	696
Lindina, town	195	260	Hamilton, town	623	943
Lisbon, town	182	350	Holland, town	1,257	1,513
Lyndon, town	344	437	Holmen, village.	3,113	2,696
Lyndon Station, village .	95	132	La Crosse, city	17,441	8,715
Marion, town	65	191	Medary, town	586	519
Mauston, city	790	989	Onalaska, city	5,920	5,040
Necedah, town	365	1,017	Onalaska, town	1,724	1,953
Necedah, village	177	288	Rockland, village (part) .	161	228
New Lisbon, city	206	472	Shelby, town	1,850	1,382
Orange, town	79	211	Washington, town	155	157
Plymouth, town	130	228	West Salem, village. . . .	1,388	1,459
Seven Mile Creek, town .	73	129			
Summit, town	109	260	**Lafayette**.	**3,647**	**4,821**
Union Center, village . .	29	89	Argyle, town	119	133
Wisconsin Dells, city (part)	0	0	Argyle, village	215	195
Wonewoc, town	122	240	Belmont, town	160	198
Wonewoc, village.	137	217	Belmont, village	221	273
			Benton, town	88	197
Kenosha	**42,193**	**44,972**	Benton, village	274	228
Brighton, town	279	718	Blanchard, town	102	80
Bristol, village	1,099	2,194	Blanchardville, village		
Genoa City, village (part)	0	0	(part)	210	137
Kenosha, city	26,159	19,566	Cuba City, city (part) . . .	78	69
Paddock Lake, village . .	586	1,087	Darlington, city	542	482
Paris, town	310	709	Darlington, town	196	324
Pleasant Prairie, village .	5,836	7,261	Elk Grove, town	79	154
Randall, town	650	1,366	Fayette, town	76	141
Salem Lakes, village . . .	2,882	5,489	Gratiot, town	107	208
Somers, town	236	354	Gratiot, village	48	68
Somers, village	2,244	2,659	Hazel Green, village (part)	6	7
Twin Lakes, village	1,229	2,183	Kendall, town	61	130
Wheatland, town	683	1,386	Lamont, town	70	95

Presidential vote by county and municipality, November 3, 2020 general election, continued

	Joe Biden/ Kamala Harris (Dem.)	Donald J. Trump/ Mike Pence (Rep.)		Joe Biden/ Kamala Harris (Dem.)	Donald J. Trump/ Mike Pence (Rep.)
Monticello, town	15	59	Cooperstown, town . . .	221	570
New Diggings, town . .	95	176	Eaton, town	145	407
Seymour, town	45	129	Francis Creek, village . .	133	248
Shullsburg, city	285	293	Franklin, town	187	560
Shullsburg, town	69	108	Gibson, town	262	547
South Wayne, village. . .	60	139	Kellnersville, village . . .	69	104
Wayne, town	55	192	Kiel, city (part).	740	1,298
White Oak Springs, town	17	56	Kossuth, town	389	861
Willow Springs, town . .	151	267	Liberty, town	226	597
Wiota, town	203	283	Manitowoc, city.	7,510	8,911
			Manitowoc, town	233	438
Langlade.	**3,704**	**7,330**	Manitowoc Rapids, town	507	1,037
Ackley, town	94	211	Maple Grove, town . . .	94	397
Ainsworth, town	75	240	Maribel, village	54	127
Antigo, city.	1,529	2,203	Meeme, town	283	655
Antigo, town	258	590	Mishicot, town	220	540
Elcho, town	269	530	Mishicot, village	284	534
Evergreen, town	80	233	Newton, town	396	1,039
Langlade, town	97	207	Reedsville, village	180	413
Neva, town	150	376	Rockland, town	133	447
Norwood, town	159	407	St. Nazianz, village	104	266
Parrish, town	19	53	Schleswig, town	431	849
Peck, town	48	154	Two Creeks, town	83	168
Polar, town	180	460	Two Rivers, city	2,532	3,288
Price, town	49	82	Two Rivers, town	377	728
Rolling, town	257	598	Valders, village	149	377
Summit, town	28	66	Whitelaw, village	131	312
Upham, town	169	361	**Marathon . . . .**	**30,808**	**44,624**
Vilas, town	26	106	Abbotsford, city (part). .	52	97
White Lake, village	63	98	Athens, village	171	413
Wolf River, town	154	355	Bergen, town	182	317
			Berlin, town	167	437
Lincoln	**6,261**	**10,017**	Bern, town	67	185
Birch, town	97	164	Bevent, town	258	445
Bradley, town	623	975	Birnamwood, village (part)	6	6
Corning, town	146	358	Brighton, town	50	235
Harding, town	84	175	Cassel, town	173	408
Harrison, town	229	390	Cleveland, town	234	658
King, town	277	411	Colby, city (part)	106	148
Merrill, city.	2,044	2,497	Day, town	189	461
Merrill, town	583	1,167	Dorchester, village (part)	0	2
Pine River, town	386	798	Easton, town	195	569
Rock Falls, town	145	294	Eau Pleine, town	112	297
Russell, town	123	250	Edgar, village	298	523
Schley, town	130	402	Elderon, town	102	268
Scott, town	307	589	Elderon, village	28	64
Skanawan, town	131	157	Emmet, town	194	389
Somo, town	27	58	Fenwood, village	20	69
Tomahawk, city	753	976	Frankfort, town	86	250
Tomahawk, town	102	205	Franzen, town	86	229
Wilson, town	74	151	Green Valley, town	112	247
			Guenther, town	67	171
Manitowoc	**16,818**	**27,218**	Halsey, town	57	244
Cato, town	282	716	Hamburg, town	132	352
Centerville, town	135	269	Harrison, town	50	150
Cleveland, village.	328	515			

Presidential vote by county and municipality, November 3, 2020 general election, continued

	Joe Biden/ Kamala Harris (Dem.)	Donald J. Trump/ Mike Pence (Rep.)		Joe Biden/ Kamala Harris (Dem.)	Donald J. Trump/ Mike Pence (Rep.)
Hatley, village	106	245	Silver Cliff, town	118	248
Hewitt, town	87	292	Stephenson, town	687	1,561
Holton, town	100	324	Wagner, town	135	298
Hull, town	72	260	Wausaukee, town	232	514
Johnson, town	99	302	Wausaukee, village. . . .	70	169
Knowlton, town	429	823			
Kronenwetter, village . .	1,930	2,956	**Marquette . . . .**	**3,239**	**5,719**
Maine, village	620	1,087	Buffalo, town	237	397
Marathon, town	163	475	Crystal Lake, town	135	212
Marathon City, village . .	306	598	Douglas, town	196	334
Marshfield, city (part) . .	245	239	Endeavor, village	72	126
McMillan, town	518	776	Harris, town	167	325
Mosinee, city	872	1,584	Mecan, town	177	289
Mosinee, town	460	933	Montello, city	350	394
Norrie, town	200	394	Montello, town	243	490
Plover, town	117	295	Moundville, town	107	181
Reid, town	256	496	Neshkoro, town	97	258
Rib Falls, town	144	452	Neshkoro, village	74	159
Rib Mountain, town . . .	1,977	2,716	Newton, town	83	191
Rietbrock, town	134	376	Oxford, town	168	380
Ringle, town	402	727	Oxford, village.	114	177
Rothschild, village	1,494	1,649	Packwaukee, town	300	560
Schofield, city	587	571	Shields, town	128	241
Spencer, town	277	637	Springfield, town	176	331
Spencer, village	315	630	Westfield, town	196	333
Stettin, town	559	1,074	Westfield, village	219	341
Stratford, village	269	596			
Texas, town	339	702	**Menominee . . . .**	**1,303**	**278**
Unity, village (part). . . .	22	83	Menominee, town	1,303	278
Wausau, city	10,234	8,673			
Wausau, town	490	924	**Milwaukee. . . . .**	**317,270**	**134,357**
Weston, town	142	265	Bayside, village (part) . .	2,185	866
Weston, village	3,510	4,532	Brown Deer, village . . .	5,324	2,011
Wien, town	139	304	Cudahy, city	5,146	4,227
			Fox Point, village	3,492	1,429
Marinette	**7,366**	**15,304**	Franklin, city.	10,046	11,870
Amberg, town	130	333	Glendale, city	6,312	2,326
Athelstane, town	97	256	Greendale, village	4,784	4,513
Beaver, town	160	493	Greenfield, city	10,804	9,891
Beecher, town	126	341	Hales Corners, village . .	2,240	2,479
Coleman, village	104	286	Milwaukee, city (part) . .	194,661	48,414
Crivitz, village	162	359	Oak Creek, city	9,850	10,562
Dunbar, town	103	251	River Hills, village.	715	535
Goodman, town	132	235	St. Francis, city	3,381	2,237
Grover, town	234	793	Shorewood, village. . . .	7,700	1,460
Lake, town	200	517	South Milwaukee, city. .	5,639	5,346
Marinette, city.	1,900	2,828	Wauwatosa, city	20,882	10,104
Middle Inlet, town	152	359	West Allis, city.	15,899	12,681
Niagara, city	264	521	West Milwaukee, village	1,130	539
Niagara, town	148	394	Whitefish Bay, village . .	7,080	2,867
Pembine, town	162	354			
Peshtigo, city	559	1,015	**Monroe. . . . .**	**8,433**	**13,775**
Peshtigo, town	914	1,652	Adrian, town	137	335
Porterfield, town	371	787	Angelo, town	230	514
Pound, town	173	613	Byron, town	204	430
Pound, village	33	127	Cashton, village.	204	301
			Clifton, town	81	157

Presidential vote by county and municipality, November 3, 2020 general election, continued

	Joe Biden/ Kamala Harris (Dem.)	Donald J. Trump/ Mike Pence (Rep.)		Joe Biden/ Kamala Harris (Dem.)	Donald J. Trump/ Mike Pence (Rep.)
Glendale, town	106	257	Riverview, town	221	345
Grant, town	65	204	Spruce, town	143	399
Greenfield, town	119	297	Stiles, town	257	656
Jefferson, town	115	197	Suring, village	58	182
Kendall, village	86	129	Townsend, town	255	483
La Grange, town	408	818	Underhill, town	151	344
Lafayette, town	62	133			
Leon, town	215	454	**Oneida**	**10,105**	**13,671**
Lincoln, town	120	366	Cassian, town	299	458
Little Falls, town	283	562	Crescent, town	615	768
Melvina, village	17	32	Enterprise, town	62	186
New Lyme, town	30	88	Hazelhurst, town	398	518
Norwalk, village	86	133	Lake Tomahawk, town	280	467
Oakdale, town	112	302	Little Rice, town	86	171
Oakdale, village	42	97	Lynne, town	24	63
Ontario, village (part)	0	0	Minocqua, town	1,423	2,093
Portland, town	164	293	Monico, town	47	133
Ridgeville, town	104	172	Newbold, town	825	1,098
Rockland, village (part)	0	0	Nokomis, town	411	597
Scott, town	9	45	Pelican, town	752	945
Sheldon, town	59	215	Piehl, town	18	27
Sparta, city	2,058	2,234	Pine Lake, town	753	927
Sparta, town	728	1,097	Rhinelander, city	2,007	1,775
Tomah, city	1,768	2,398	Schoepke, town	105	190
Tomah, town	289	556	Stella, town	168	223
Warrens, village	78	186	Sugar Camp, town	422	816
Wellington, town	116	168	Three Lakes, town	578	1,121
Wells, town	107	243	Woodboro, town	225	348
Wilton, town	83	193	Woodruff, town	607	747
Wilton, village	123	122			
Wyeville, village	25	47	**Outagamie**	**47,667**	**58,385**
			Appleton, city (part)	18,562	14,234
Oconto	**6,715**	**16,226**	Bear Creek, village	54	102
Abrams, town	368	908	Black Creek, town	176	583
Bagley, town	40	161	Black Creek, village	231	483
Brazeau, town	236	664	Bovina, town	202	530
Breed, town	103	324	Buchanan, town	1,854	2,463
Chase, town	518	1,374	Center, town	753	1,730
Doty, town	87	159	Cicero, town	206	423
Gillett, city	188	432	Combined Locks, village	985	1,302
Gillett, town	108	511	Dale, town	511	1,308
How, town	79	259	Deer Creek, town	60	249
Lakewood, town	203	411	Ellington, town	475	1,483
Lena, town	104	336	Freedom, town	1,143	2,690
Lena, village	83	202	Grand Chute, town	6,545	6,916
Little River, town	158	458	Greenville, town	2,771	4,864
Little Suamico, town	927	2,446	Harrison, village (part)	0	0
Maple Valley, town	87	303	Hortonia, town	197	497
Morgan, town	157	512	Hortonville, village	590	1,113
Mountain, town	203	362	Howard, village (part)	0	0
Oconto, city	810	1,379	Kaukauna, city (part)	4,084	4,784
Oconto, town	220	567	Kaukauna, town	213	640
Oconto Falls, city	464	890	Kimberly, village	1,971	2,185
Oconto Falls, town	226	526	Liberty, town	133	397
Pensaukee, town	261	633	Little Chute, village	2,811	3,483
Pulaski, village (part)	0	0	Maine, town	141	364

Presidential vote by county and municipality, November 3, 2020 general election, continued

	Joe Biden/ Kamala Harris (Dem.)	Donald J. Trump/ Mike Pence (Rep.)		Joe Biden/ Kamala Harris (Dem.)	Donald J. Trump/ Mike Pence (Rep.)
Maple Creek, town	73	275	Plum City, village	91	185
New London, city (part) .	261	504	Prescott, city	1,066	1,299
Nichols, village	28	105	River Falls, city (part) . . .	3,036	2,177
Oneida, town	1,030	1,207	River Falls, town	720	779
Osborn, town	233	544	Rock Elm, town	96	162
Seymour, city	692	1,196	Salem, town	89	174
Seymour, town	178	547	Spring Lake, town	114	250
Shiocton, village	129	322	Spring Valley, village (part)	315	410
Vandenbroek, town . . .	301	737	Trenton, town	389	682
Wrightstown, village (part)	74	125	Trimbelle, town	326	709
			Union, town	94	258
Ozaukee	**26,517**	**33,912**			
Bayside, village (part) . .	59	33	**Polk**	**9,370**	**16,611**
Belgium, town	335	664	Alden, town	611	1,169
Belgium, village.	406	1,006	Amery, city	710	830
Cedarburg, city	4,032	4,013	Apple River, town	228	437
Cedarburg, town	1,653	2,832	Balsam Lake, town	308	607
Fredonia, town	284	1,073	Balsam Lake, village . . .	170	334
Fredonia, village	412	946	Beaver, town	172	343
Grafton, town	1,149	1,935	Black Brook, town	259	594
Grafton, village	3,442	4,404	Bone Lake, town	164	267
Mequon, city	8,419	8,781	Centuria, village	114	235
Newburg, village (part) .	9	46	Clam Falls, town	114	198
Port Washington, city . .	3,607	3,909	Clayton, town	190	362
Port Washington, town .	359	675	Clayton, village	58	167
Saukville, town	350	933	Clear Lake, town	112	399
Saukville, village	920	1,536	Clear Lake, village	174	403
Thiensville, village	1,081	1,126	Dresser, village	140	313
			Eureka, town	337	731
Pepin	**1,489**	**2,584**	Farmington, town	387	814
Albany, town	140	215	Frederic, village.	242	322
Durand, city	339	616	Garfield, town	337	657
Durand, town	99	313	Georgetown, town . . .	244	381
Frankfort, town	75	116	Johnstown, town	135	164
Lima, town	105	215	Laketown, town	218	390
Pepin, town	179	276	Lincoln, town	487	907
Pepin, village	235	226	Lorain, town	59	138
Stockholm, town	83	71	Luck, town	186	397
Stockholm, village	31	29	Luck, village	238	355
Waterville, town	116	335	McKinley, town	72	147
Waubeek, town	87	172	Milltown, town	266	482
			Milltown, village	148	320
Pierce	**9,796**	**12,815**	Osceola, town	655	1,233
Bay City, village	75	161	Osceola, village	647	848
Clifton, town	675	817	St. Croix Falls, city.	635	621
Diamond Bluff, town . .	115	198	St. Croix Falls, town . . .	255	465
El Paso, town	144	280	Sterling, town	127	279
Ellsworth, town	243	464	Turtle Lake, village (part)	10	32
Ellsworth, village	643	964	West Sweden, town . . .	161	270
Elmwood, village	144	267			
Gilman, town	246	364	**Portage**.	**20,428**	**19,299**
Hartland, town	146	373	Alban, town	206	332
Isabelle, town	48	103	Almond, town	124	315
Maiden Rock, town . . .	124	242	Almond, village	63	134
Maiden Rock, village. . .	35	47	Amherst, town	418	506
Martell, town	301	448	Amherst, village	312	316
Oak Grove, town	521	1,002			

Presidential vote by county and municipality, November 3, 2020 general election, continued

	Joe Biden/ Kamala Harris (Dem.)	Donald J. Trump/ Mike Pence (Rep.)		Joe Biden/ Kamala Harris (Dem.)	Donald J. Trump/ Mike Pence (Rep.)
Amherst Junction, village	82	143	Norway, town	1,406	4,026
Belmont, town	129	259	Racine, city	21,321	10,499
Buena Vista, town	234	501	Raymond, village	778	1,934
Carson, town	320	560	Rochester, village	743	1,821
Dewey, town	265	390	Sturtevant, village	1,287	1,500
Eau Pleine, town	236	414	Union Grove, village	916	1,725
Grant, town	408	783	Waterford, town	1,230	3,201
Hull, town	1,751	1,755	Waterford, village	1,157	2,228
Junction City, village	86	111	Wind Point, village	694	606
Lanark, town	396	567	Yorkville, village	629	1,452
Linwood, town	292	450			
Milladore, village (part)	4	3	**Richland**	**3,995**	**4,871**
Nelsonville, village	67	42	Akan, town	92	141
New Hope, town	279	219	Bloom, town	106	153
Park Ridge, village	240	140	Boaz, village	36	29
Pine Grove, town	145	267	Buena Vista, town	355	490
Plover, town	374	561	Cazenovia, village (part)	78	85
Plover, village	3,932	3,522	Dayton, town	166	216
Rosholt, village	105	153	Eagle, town	87	165
Sharon, town	521	890	Forest, town	104	94
Stevens Point, city	8,078	4,381	Henrietta, town	127	125
Stockton, town	772	1,129	Ithaca, town	143	205
Whiting, village	589	456	Lone Rock, village	186	225
			Marshall, town	120	217
Price	**3,032**	**5,394**	Orion, town	146	163
Catawba, town	51	106	Richland, town	285	406
Catawba, village	24	52	Richland Center, city	1,186	1,207
Eisenstein, town	155	232	Richwood, town	132	155
Elk, town	253	443	Rockbridge, town	200	207
Emery, town	71	137	Sylvan, town	79	157
Fifield, town	226	385	Viola, village (part)	118	100
Flambeau, town	117	242	Westford, town	117	156
Georgetown, town	27	61	Willow, town	114	157
Hackett, town	34	90	Yuba, village	18	18
Harmony, town	39	106			
Hill, town	55	176	**Rock**	**46,658**	**37,138**
Kennan, town	56	114	Avon, town	115	249
Kennan, village	28	50	Beloit, city	8,728	5,620
Knox, town	77	134	Beloit, town	2,091	2,377
Lake, town	304	460	Bradford, town	219	380
Ogema, town	117	304	Brodhead, city (part)	45	29
Park Falls, city	517	637	Center, town	357	339
Phillips, city	293	408	Clinton, town	159	366
Prentice, town	82	170	Clinton, village	419	632
Prentice, village	105	202	Edgerton, city (part)	1,968	1,115
Spirit, town	63	142	Evansville, city	2,130	1,080
Worcester, town	338	743	Footville, village	232	256
			Fulton, town	1,170	1,135
Racine	**50,159**	**54,479**	Harmony, town	897	819
Burlington, city (part)	2,606	3,251	Janesville, city	19,559	13,490
Burlington, town	1,293	2,676	Janesville, town	1,265	1,255
Caledonia, village	6,851	9,222	Johnstown, town	194	293
Dover, town	651	1,553	La Prairie, town	201	296
Elmwood Park, village	153	174	Lima, town	320	349
Mount Pleasant, village	8,348	8,542	Magnolia, town	211	227
North Bay, village	96	69	Milton, city	1,823	1,484

Presidential vote by county and municipality, November 3, 2020 general election, continued

	Joe Biden/ Kamala Harris (Dem.)	Donald J. Trump/ Mike Pence (Rep.)		Joe Biden/ Kamala Harris (Dem.)	Donald J. Trump/ Mike Pence (Rep.)
Milton, town	949	1,030	Glenwood City, city	176	468
Newark, town	336	623	Hammond, town	444	1,047
Orfordville, village	370	391	Hammond, village	423	589
Plymouth, town	295	468	Hudson, city	4,689	4,013
Porter, town	378	283	Hudson, town	2,401	3,232
Rock, town	713	794	Kinnickinnic, town	494	685
Spring Valley, town	168	264	New Richmond, city	2,306	2,821
Turtle, town	601	960	North Hudson, village	1,207	1,292
Union, town	745	534	Pleasant Valley, town	127	214
			Richmond, town	824	1,506
Rusk	**2,517**	**5,257**	River Falls, city (part)	1,225	1,021
Atlanta, town	101	259	Roberts, village	456	616
Big Bend, town	102	208	Rush River, town	106	214
Big Falls, town	31	53	St. Joseph, town	1,212	1,584
Bruce, village	141	247	Somerset, town	955	1,888
Cedar Rapids, town	7	21	Somerset, village	537	908
Conrath, village	17	19	Spring Valley, village (part)	2	7
Dewey, town	114	210	Springfield, town	182	397
Flambeau, town	162	405	Stanton, town	206	353
Glen Flora, village	13	26	Star Prairie, town	707	1,498
Grant, town	125	269	Star Prairie, village	129	237
Grow, town	34	191	Troy, town	1,665	2,113
Hawkins, town	22	44	Warren, town	396	704
Hawkins, village	53	115	Wilson, village	31	74
Hubbard, town	31	75	Woodville, village	240	454
Ingram, village	8	27			
Ladysmith, city	611	886	**Sauk**	**18,108**	**17,493**
Lawrence, town	37	119	Baraboo, city	3,585	2,702
Marshall, town	47	197	Baraboo, town	602	579
Murry, town	49	76	Bear Creek, town	166	196
Richland, town	44	73	Cazenovia, village (part)	5	5
Rusk, town	123	245	Dellona, town	426	657
Sheldon, village	29	94	Delton, town	645	723
South Fork, town	25	45	Excelsior, town	443	597
Strickland, town	70	106	Fairfield, town	350	382
Stubbs, town	116	208	Franklin, town	196	231
Thornapple, town	102	350	Freedom, town	114	174
Tony, village	15	37	Greenfield, town	332	322
True, town	54	117	Honey Creek, town	235	228
Washington, town	79	160	Ironton, town	104	199
Weyerhaeuser, village	48	77	Ironton, village	36	89
Wilkinson, town	8	29	La Valle, town	361	587
Willard, town	79	203	La Valle, village	57	139
Wilson, town	20	66	Lake Delton, village	723	699
			Lime Ridge, village	42	49
St. Croix	**23,190**	**32,199**	Loganville, village	61	94
Baldwin, town	173	429	Merrimac, town	418	399
Baldwin, village	872	1,294	Merrimac, village	170	142
Cady, town	146	354	North Freedom, village	140	164
Cylon, town	103	302	Plain, village	231	253
Deer Park, village	28	95	Prairie du Sac, town	341	362
Eau Galle, town	230	518	Prairie du Sac, village	1,646	980
Emerald, town	148	348	Reedsburg, city	2,213	2,442
Erin Prairie, town	149	298	Reedsburg, town	271	432
Forest, town	82	289	Rock Springs, village	48	122
Glenwood, town	119	337			

Presidential vote by county and municipality, November 3, 2020 general election, continued

	Joe Biden/ Kamala Harris (Dem.)	Donald J. Trump/ Mike Pence (Rep.)		Joe Biden/ Kamala Harris (Dem.)	Donald J. Trump/ Mike Pence (Rep.)
Sauk City, village	1,319	736	Lessor, town	160	631
Spring Green, town	604	561	Maple Grove, town	152	418
Spring Green, village	690	304	Marion, city (part)	1	10
Sumpter, town	245	207	Mattoon, village	53	118
Troy, town	216	263	Morris, town	82	166
Washington, town	139	259	Navarino, town	71	191
West Baraboo, village	395	365	Pella, town	123	422
Westfield, town	103	210	Pulaski, village (part)	31	72
Winfield, town	206	340	Red Springs, town	328	210
Wisconsin Dells, city (part)	52	57	Richmond, town	303	856
Woodland, town	178	243	Seneca, town	87	217
			Shawano, city	1,770	2,310
Sawyer	**4,498**	**5,909**	Tigerton, village	106	256
Bass Lake, town	831	632	Washington, town	317	778
Couderay, town	101	85	Waukechon, town	128	449
Couderay, village	26	29	Wescott, town	661	1,335
Draper, town	62	84	Wittenberg, town	148	336
Edgewater, town	127	267	Wittenberg, village	168	264
Exeland, village	36	68			
Hayward, city	469	661	**Sheboygan**	**27,101**	**37,609**
Hayward, town	933	1,132	Adell, village	55	220
Hunter, town	217	240	Cascade, village	117	311
Lenroot, town	402	516	Cedar Grove, village	295	1,000
Meadowbrook, town	16	79	Elkhart Lake, village	360	386
Meteor, town	31	67	Glenbeulah, village	123	171
Ojibwa, town	63	129	Greenbush, town	300	662
Radisson, town	83	175	Herman, town	285	774
Radisson, village	34	55	Holland, town	361	1,226
Round Lake, town	317	472	Howards Grove, village	755	1,328
Sand Lake, town	267	352	Kohler, village	689	779
Spider Lake, town	147	192	Lima, town	472	1,424
Weirgor, town	60	161	Lyndon, town	298	715
Winter, town	224	408	Mitchell, town	224	597
Winter, village	52	105	Mosel, town	173	319
			Oostburg, village	357	1,599
Shawano	**7,131**	**15,173**	Plymouth, city	2,202	2,835
Almon, town	68	256	Plymouth, town	710	1,349
Angelica, town	259	840	Random Lake, village	270	697
Aniwa, town	78	240	Rhine, town	572	978
Aniwa, village	30	86	Russell, town	56	178
Bartelme, town	260	88	Scott, town	233	955
Belle Plaine, town	337	767	Sheboygan, city	12,160	10,236
Birnamwood, town	122	278	Sheboygan, town	2,268	2,863
Birnamwood, village (part)	123	229	Sheboygan Falls, city	2,136	2,832
Bonduel, village	198	573	Sheboygan Falls, town	344	776
Bowler, village	51	88	Sherman, town	227	752
Cecil, village	106	256	Waldo, village	83	210
Eland, village	63	64	Wilson, town	976	1,437
Fairbanks, town	72	281			
Germania, town	72	140	**Taylor**	**2,693**	**7,657**
Grant, town	95	448	Aurora, town	34	152
Green Valley, town	133	466	Browning, town	90	402
Gresham, village	110	152	Chelsea, town	105	324
Hartland, town	79	346	Cleveland, town	29	104
Herman, town	108	319	Deer Creek, town	61	294
Hutchins, town	78	217	Ford, town	31	114

Presidential vote by county and municipality, November 3, 2020 general election, continued

	Joe Biden/ Kamala Harris (Dem.)	Donald J. Trump/ Mike Pence (Rep.)		Joe Biden/ Kamala Harris (Dem.)	Donald J. Trump/ Mike Pence (Rep.)
Gilman, village	67	134	Coon, town	227	245
Goodrich, town	58	212	Coon Valley, village. . . .	230	225
Greenwood, town	88	294	De Soto, village (part) . .	76	69
Grover, town	32	120	Forest, town	102	180
Hammel, town	90	320	Franklin, town	242	380
Holway, town	61	238	Genoa, town	222	227
Jump River, town	45	112	Genoa, village.	83	64
Little Black, town	142	441	Greenwood, town	85	146
Lublin, village	14	40	Hamburg, town	250	334
Maplehurst, town	36	179	Harmony, town	157	212
McKinley, town	29	201	Hillsboro, city	283	385
Medford, city	803	1,306	Hillsboro, town	114	247
Medford, town	306	1,102	Jefferson, town	304	390
Molitor, town	52	142	Kickapoo, town	143	135
Pershing, town	34	52	La Farge, village.	172	200
Rib Lake, town	110	318	Liberty, town	115	87
Rib Lake, village.	112	283	Ontario, village (part) . .	77	129
Roosevelt, town	53	134	Readstown, village	76	113
Stetsonville, village . . .	73	194	Stark, town	115	118
Taft, town	41	114	Sterling, town	113	219
Westboro, town	97	331	Stoddard, village	221	231
			Union, town	112	120
Trempealeau	**6,285**	**8,833**	Viola, village (part)	39	59
Albion, town	128	256	Viroqua, city	1,508	949
Arcadia, city	348	491	Viroqua, town	508	602
Arcadia, town	308	646	Webster, town	203	170
Blair, city	247	306	Westby, city	650	581
Burnside, town	105	136	Wheatland, town	163	202
Caledonia, town	222	332	Whitestown, town	98	164
Chimney Rock, town . .	63	101			
Dodge, town	107	157	**Vilas**	**5,903**	**9,261**
Eleva, village.	147	191	Arbor Vitae, town	899	1,366
Ettrick, town	329	443	Boulder Junction, town .	328	493
Ettrick, village	128	157	Cloverland, town	275	532
Gale, town	393	647	Conover, town	313	628
Galesville, city	415	447	Eagle River, city	387	523
Hale, town	212	411	Lac du Flambeau, town .	977	634
Independence, city. . . .	198	302	Land O'Lakes, town . . .	240	440
Lincoln, town	145	197	Lincoln, town	592	1,165
Osseo, city	432	494	Manitowish Waters, town	179	372
Pigeon, town	149	233	Phelps, town	266	609
Pigeon Falls, village . . .	107	94	Plum Lake, town	162	261
Preston, town	171	299	Presque Isle, town	250	332
Strum, village	260	294	St. Germain, town	507	909
Sumner, town	187	322	Washington, town	395	772
Trempealeau, town . . .	522	687	Winchester, town	133	225
Trempealeau, village. . .	486	585			
Unity, town	112	203	**Walworth**	**22,789**	**33,851**
Whitehall, city.	364	402	Bloomfield, town	333	465
			Bloomfield, village	728	1,586
Vernon	**7,457**	**8,218**	Burlington, city (part) . .	1	0
Bergen, town	374	459	Darien, town	279	639
Chaseburg, village	70	86	Darien, village.	278	460
Christiana, town	225	347	Delavan, city	1,854	1,902
Clinton, town	100	143	Delavan, town	1,196	1,872

Presidential vote by county and municipality, November 3, 2020 general election, continued

	Joe Biden/ Kamala Harris (Dem.)	Donald J. Trump/ Mike Pence (Rep.)		Joe Biden/ Kamala Harris (Dem.)	Donald J. Trump/ Mike Pence (Rep.)
East Troy, town	807	1,990	Erin, town	726	2,064
East Troy, village	957	1,741	Farmington, town	523	1,967
Elkhorn, city	2,082	2,879	Germantown, town . . .	64	114
Fontana-on-Geneva Lake, village.	578	717	Germantown, village . .	5,203	8,275
Geneva, town	1,341	2,055	Hartford, city (part). . . .	2,973	5,804
Genoa City, village (part)	511	951	Hartford, town	535	1,874
Lafayette, town	461	903	Jackson, town	734	2,438
La Grange, town	589	1,039	Jackson, village	1,343	3,094
Lake Geneva, city.	2,047	2,186	Kewaskum, town	167	624
Linn, town	626	963	Kewaskum, village (part)	676	1,875
Lyons, town	728	1,427	Milwaukee, city (part) . .	0	0
Mukwonago, village (part)	44	67	Newburg, village (part) .	155	510
Richmond, town	467	722	Polk, town	650	2,185
Sharon, town	181	369	Richfield, village	2,348	6,208
Sharon, village	270	462	Slinger, village.	1,012	2,559
Spring Prairie, town . . .	388	1,106	Trenton, town.	778	2,517
Sugar Creek, town	854	1,547	Wayne, town	279	1,206
Troy, town	503	1,101	West Bend, city	6,522	11,316
Walworth, town	304	729	West Bend, town	976	2,380
Walworth, village.	600	803	**Waukesha**	**103,906**	**159,649**
Whitewater, city (part). .	2,541	1,626	Big Bend, village	263	683
Whitewater, town	412	538	Brookfield, city	12,462	14,807
Williams Bay, village . . .	829	1,006	Brookfield, town	1,979	2,580
			Butler, village	424	588
Washburn	**3,867**	**6,334**	Chenequa, village	120	281
Barronett, town	91	169	Delafield, city	1,991	2,970
Bashaw, town	210	475	Delafield, town	2,065	3,917
Bass Lake, town	106	240	Dousman, village.	512	941
Beaver Brook, town . . .	175	314	Eagle, town	720	1,773
Birchwood, town	114	301	Eagle, village	335	1,024
Birchwood, village	82	143	Elm Grove, village	2,188	2,323
Brooklyn, town	82	129	Genesee, town	1,693	3,617
Casey, town	130	187	Hartland, village	2,342	3,528
Chicog, town	86	129	Lac La Belle, village (part)	83	157
Crystal, town	52	117	Lannon, village	330	540
Evergreen, town	287	453	Lisbon, town	2,228	5,013
Frog Creek, town	27	52	Menomonee Falls, village	11,077	13,882
Gull Lake, town	64	80	Merton, town	1,777	4,288
Long Lake, town	184	278	Merton, village	645	1,587
Madge, town	157	239	Milwaukee, city (part) . .	0	0
Minong, town	269	383	Mukwonago, town . . .	1,457	3,805
Minong, village	101	163	Mukwonago, village (part)	1,651	3,122
Sarona, town	71	181	Muskego, city	5,578	11,400
Shell Lake, city	386	396	Nashotah, village.	348	620
Spooner, city	534	674	New Berlin, city	11,350	15,994
Spooner, town	184	315	North Prairie, village. . .	437	1,072
Springbrook, town . . .	93	208	Oconomowoc, city	4,563	6,929
Stinnett, town	33	90	Oconomowoc, town . .	1,935	4,340
Stone Lake, town.	103	231	Oconomowoc Lake, village	111	323
Trego, town	246	387	Ottawa, town	873	1,855
			Pewaukee, city	3,837	6,662
Washington	**26,650**	**60,237**	Pewaukee, village	2,086	2,990
Addison, town	481	1,773	Summit, village	1,269	2,268
Barton, town	505	1,454	Sussex, village.	2,781	4,422

Presidential vote by county and municipality, November 3, 2020 general election, continued

	Joe Biden/ Kamala Harris (Dem.)	Donald J. Trump/ Mike Pence (Rep.)		Joe Biden/ Kamala Harris (Dem.)	Donald J. Trump/ Mike Pence (Rep.)
Vernon, town	1,464	3,935	Plainfield, town	73	221
Wales, village	720	1,228	Plainfield, village	151	232
Waukesha, city	18,130	20,247	Poy Sippi, town	118	427
Waukesha, village	2,082	3,938	Redgranite, village	142	312
Waupaca	**9,703**	**18,952**	Richford, town	61	201
Bear Creek, town	73	349	Rose, town	167	243
Big Falls, village	11	30	Saxeville, town	217	433
Caledonia, town	318	765	Springwater, town	340	553
Clintonville, city.	718	1,177	Warren, town	119	257
Dayton, town	648	1,068	Wautoma, city.	341	485
Dupont, town	88	268	Wautoma, town	282	546
Embarrass, village	51	132	Wild Rose, village.	176	217
Farmington, town	918	1,323	**Winnebago**	**44,060**	**47,796**
Fremont, town	120	319	Algoma, town	2,034	2,467
Fremont, village	129	347	Appleton, city (part) . . .	299	166
Harrison, town	83	205	Black Wolf, town	652	1,032
Helvetia, town	121	323	Clayton, town	1,001	1,862
Iola, town	199	431	Fox Crossing, village . . .	4,865	5,622
Iola, village.	300	417	Menasha, city (part) . . .	3,831	3,538
Larrabee, town	214	542	Neenah, city	7,881	6,955
Lebanon, town	291	683	Neenah, town	1,080	1,291
Lind, town	250	687	Nekimi, town	262	625
Little Wolf, town	190	657	Nepeuskun, town.	139	325
Manawa, city	170	433	Omro, city	752	1,186
Marion, city (part)	159	458	Omro, town	527	1,044
Matteson, town	142	460	Oshkosh, city	17,012	14,248
Mukwa, town	617	1,243	Oshkosh, town	714	1,015
New London, city (part) .	997	1,701	Poygan, town	236	613
Ogdensburg, village . . .	26	75	Rushford, town	274	747
Royalton, town	225	652	Utica, town.	270	596
St. Lawrence, town . . .	134	312	Vinland, town	495	791
Scandinavia, town	282	435	Winchester, town	379	821
Scandinavia, village . . .	84	124	Winneconne, town. . . .	602	1,193
Union, town	104	343	Winneconne, village . . .	531	1,044
Waupaca, city	1,409	1,557	Wolf River, town	224	615
Waupaca, town	230	477	**Wood**	**16,365**	**24,308**
Weyauwega, city	274	567	Arpin, town	152	362
Weyauwega, town	79	251	Arpin, village	42	102
Wyoming, town	49	141	Auburndale, town	110	372
Waushara	**4,388**	**9,016**	Auburndale, village . . .	134	248
Aurora, town	159	438	Biron, village.	198	273
Berlin, city (part)	19	42	Cameron, town	102	210
Bloomfield, town	165	503	Cary, town	75	182
Coloma, town	138	282	Cranmoor, town	43	62
Coloma, village	73	183	Dexter, town.	75	158
Dakota, town	197	424	Grand Rapids, town . . .	1,990	2,908
Deerfield, town	169	279	Hansen, town	119	324
Hancock, town	101	226	Hewitt, village.	200	319
Hancock, village	79	141	Hiles, town.	21	73
Leon, town	287	641	Lincoln, town	341	687
Lohrville, village	64	149	Marshfield, city (part) . .	4,458	5,021
Marion, town	436	887	Marshfield, town	161	351
Mount Morris, town . . .	248	514	Milladore, town	115	270
Oasis, town	66	180	Milladore, village (part) .	58	93

Presidential vote by county and municipality, November 3, 2020 general election, continued

	Joe Biden/ Kamala Harris (Dem.)	Donald J. Trump/ Mike Pence (Rep.)		Joe Biden/ Kamala Harris (Dem.)	Donald J. Trump/ Mike Pence (Rep.)
Nekoosa, city	429	753	Saratoga, town	993	2,045
Pittsville, city	137	305	Seneca, town	256	398
Port Edwards, town . . .	283	489	Sherry, town	129	323
Port Edwards, village . .	447	577	Sigel, town	214	416
Remington, town.	48	103	Vesper, village.	96	205
Richfield, town	273	644	Wisconsin Rapids, city. .	4,059	4,715
Rock, town.	143	397	Wood, town	151	333
Rudolph, town	210	426	**State totals**	**1,630,673**	**1,610,065**
Rudolph, village	103	164			

Note: Other president/vice president tickets received the following votes: Don Blankenship/William Mohr (Constitution)—5,146; Jo Jorgensen/Jeremy Spike Cohen (Ind.)—38,491; Brian Carroll/Amar Patel (Ind.)—5,259; Kasey Wells (write-in)—25; Jade Simmons/Claudeliah J. Roze (write-in)—36; President R19 Boddie (write-in)—5; Howie Hawkins/Angela Walker (write-in)—1,089; Gloria La Riva/Sunil Freeman (write-in)—110; Kanye West/Michelle Tidball (write-in)—411; Mark Charles/Adrian Wallace (write-in)—52.

Source: Official records of the Wisconsin Elections Commission.

Political parties qualifying for ballot status as of November 2020

in the order they will be listed on the ballot

Democratic Party of Wisconsin

PO Box 1686, Madison, Wisconsin 53701; 608-255-5172; www.wisdems.org

Executive director . . . . Nellie Sires
Senior elections director . . . . .Devin Remiker
Senior operations adviser . . . . Greg Diamond
Senior digital director. . . . . Bhavik Lathia
Organizing director . . . . Anna Surrey
Political director . . . . Nicholas J. Truog
Finance director . . . . Jade Tacka

State Administrative Committee

Party officers . . . . Ben Wikler, Madison, *chair*; Felesia Martin, Milwaukee, *first vice chair*; Lee Snodgrass, Appleton, *second vice chair*; Meg Andrietsch, Racine, *secretary*; Randy Udell, Madison, *treasurer*
National committee members. . . . . Martha Love, Milwaukee; Andrew Werthmann, Eau Claire; Khary Penebaker, Hartland; Janet Bewley, Mason; Jason Rae, Glendale; Mahlon Mitchell, Fitchburg
College Democrats representative . . . . Cecelia McDermott, Appleton, *chair*
Young Democrats representative. . . . . Charles Myers, Middleton, *chair*
High School Democrats representative . . . . Ethan Jackowski, Walworth, *chair*
Milwaukee County chair . . . . .Christopher Walton, Milwaukee
At-large members . . . . Rey Villar, Sturtevant; Gretchen Lowe, Madison; Haben Goitom, Fitchburg; Sean Elliot, Madison; Ryan Greendeer, Black River Falls; Wayde Lawler, Viola; Michelle Bryant, Milwaukee; Marcia Steele, Oshkosh; Sherrie Richards-Francar, Manitowoc; Mary Arnold, Columbus; Michael Childers, La Pointe; Yee Leng Xiong, Wausau; Lisa Noel, Greenleaf
County Chairs Association chair. . . . . Sandy Rindy, New Glarus
Assembly representative . . . . Sara Rodriguez, Brookfield
Senate representative. . . . . Janis Ringhand, Evansville
CD 1 representatives. . . . . Mary Jonker, Franklin, *chair*; Matt Mareno, Muskego
CD 2 representatives. . . . . Noah Lieberman, Madison, *chair*; Kriss Marion, Blanchardville

Political parties qualifying for ballot status as of November 2020, continued

Democratic Party of Wisconsin, continued

CD 3 representatives. . . . . Bobbi Greene, Eau Claire, *chair*; Gary Hawley, Stevens Point
CD 4 representatives. . . . . Terrell Martin, Milwaukee, *chair*; Carmen Cabrera, Milwaukee
CD 5 representatives. . . . . Justin Koestler, Waukesha, *chair*; Colleen Schulz, Oconomowoc
CD 6 representatives. . . . . Ryan Sorenson, Sheboygan, *chair*; Debra Dassow, Cedarburg
CD 7 representatives. . . . . Kim Butler, Balsam Lake, *chair*; Steve Okonek, Marshfield
CD 8 representatives. . . . . Mary Ginnebaugh, Green Bay, *chair*; Thomas Mandi, Peshtigo

Republican Party of Wisconsin

148 E Johnson Street, Madison, WI 53703; 608-257-4765; www.wisgop.org

Executive director . . . . Mark Jefferson
Political and data director . . . . Jordan Moskowitz
Research director. . . . . Alesha Guenther
Communications director . . . . Anna Kelly
Finance coordinator . . . . Sabrina Stencil
African American outreach director . . . . .Khenzer Senat
Grassroots engagement directors . . . . .Nicholas Perryman, Nathan Trueblood
Telemarketing manager. . . . . .Rich Dickie

Executive Committee

Party officers . . . . .Andrew Hitt, Appleton, *chair*; Maripat Krueger, Menomonie, *first vice chair*;
Katie McCallum, Middleton, *second vice chair*; Jesse Garza, Hudson, *third vice chair*;
Andrew Davis, Milwaukee, *fourth vice chair*; Tyler August, Lake Geneva, *party secretary*;
Brian Westrate, Fall Creek, *party treasurer*; Tom Schreibel, Madison, *national committeeman*;
Mary Buestrin, River Hills, *national committeewoman*
Immediate past chair . . . . Brad Courtney, Whitefish Bay
At-large member. . . . . Brian Schimming, Fitchburg
Wisconsin African American Council chair . . . . .Gerard Randall, Milwaukee
Wisconsin Republican Labor Council chair . . . . Van Wanggaard, Racine
Wisconsin Hispanic Heritage Council chair . . . . Domingo Leguizamon, Hillpoint
CD 1 representatives. . . . . Kim Travis, Williams Bay, *chair*; Carol Brunner, Franklin, *vice chair*
CD 2 representatives. . . . . Kim Babler, Madison, *chair*; Tim McCumber, Merrimac, *vice chair*
CD 3 representatives. . . . . .Bill Feehan, La Crosse, *chair*; Hannah Testin, Stevens Point, *vice chair*
CD 4 representatives. . . . . Bob Spindell, Milwaukee, *chair*; Doug Haag, Milwaukee, *vice chair*
CD 5 representatives. . . . . Kathy Kiernan, Richfield, *chair*; Keith Best, Waukesha, *vice chair*
CD 6 representatives. . . . . .Darryl Carlson, Sheboygan, *chair*; Al Ott, Forest Junction, *vice chair*
CD 7 representatives. . . . . Jim Miller, Hayward, *chair*; Jesse Garza, Hudson, *vice chair*
CD 8 representatives. . . . . .Kelly Ruh, Green Bay, *chair*; Bill Berglund, Sturgeon Bay, *vice chair*

Constitution Party of Wisconsin

PO Box 070344, Milwaukee, WI 53207; 608-561-7996; constitutionpartyofwisconsin@gmail.com;
www.constitutionpartyofwisconsin.com

Executive Committee

Party officers . . . . Andrew Zuelke, Ripon, *chair*; Glenn E. L. Petroski, Kenosha, *vice chair*;
Douglas Lindee, Deer Park, *director of communications*; Nigel Brown, Janesville, *secretary*;
Robert DesJarlais, Mishicot, *treasurer*
CD 1 representatives. . . . . Michaeljon Murphy, Waukesha; Don Hilbig, Muskego

Political parties qualifying for ballot status as of November 2020, continued

Constitution Party of Wisconsin, continued

CD 2 representatives. . . . . Dan Herro, Beloit; *vacant*
CD 3 representatives. . . . . Matthew J. Kloskowski, Wisconsin Rapids; *vacant*
CD 4 representatives. . . . . .Colin Hudson, Milwaukee; Kent Steffke, Milwaukee
CD 5 representatives. . . . . *vacant*
CD 6 representatives. . . . .*vacant*
CD 7 representatives. . . . . .Elizabeth Lindee, Deer Park; *vacant*
CD 8 representatives. . . . . .Mark Gabriel, Appleton; Brian Farmer, Appleton
At-large representatives . . Jason Murphy, Waukesha; Michelle Gabriel, Appleton; Robert Heine, Muskego

Note: Parties qualifying for ballot status are those that fulfill the definition of "recognized political party" under Wis. Stat. s. 5.02 (16m). Independent candidates may list a party or principle along with their name on the ballot under s. 5.64 (1) (e) 1. and (es).

CD–Congressional district.

Sources: Democratic Party of Wisconsin, Republican Party of Wisconsin, Constitution Party of Wisconsin.

Seventh Congressional District vote for U.S. representative, February 18, 2020 special primary

	Republican		Democrat	
County	Jason Church	Tom Tiffany	Lawrence Dale	Tricia Zunker
Ashland.	474	600	180	1,236
Barron.	2,144	2,050	241	1,728
Bayfield.	687	941	179	2,068
Burnett	725	828	81	716
Chippewa (part)	1,277	997	122	784
Clark.	1,467	1,516	169	847
Douglas.	1,335	1,612	391	2,718
Florence	207	351	31	121
Forest	420	754	47	320
Iron	239	567	63	405
Jackson (part)	122	94	14	70
Juneau (part)	265	356	41	174
Langlade.	748	1,853	107	871
Lincoln	1,417	2,544	187	1,515
Marathon.	6,556	8,818	745	7,079
Monroe (part)	248	202	44	135
Oneida	2,014	4,163	297	2,751
Polk	1,552	1,927	240	1,732
Price.	794	1,381	148	866
Rusk	967	671	87	596
Sawyer	919	1,047	93	1,162
St. Croix.	2,869	3,112	354	3,090
Taylor	1,186	1,561	81	541
Vilas	1,295	3,011	158	1,729
Washburn	828	1,005	116	899
Wood (part)	1,584	1,753	172	1,424
Total.	**32,339**	**43,714**	**4,388**	**35,577**

Source: Official records of the Wisconsin Elections Commission.

Seventh Congressional District vote for U.S. representative, May 12, 2020 special election

County	Tom Tiffany (Rep.)	Tricia Zunker (Dem.)
Ashland	1,503	2,473
Barron	6,769	4,447
Bayfield	2,290	3,821
Burnett	2,501	1,665
Chippewa (part)	3,622	2,057
Clark	4,029	2,089
Douglas	4,066	6,166
Florence	1,006	432
Forest	1,640	852
Iron	1,134	882
Jackson (part)	274	146
Juneau (part)	785	394
Langlade	3,683	1,972
Lincoln	5,005	3,510
Marathon	22,768	16,042
Monroe (part)	499	249
Oneida	7,322	6,114
Polk	5,825	4,220
Price	2,615	1,903
Rusk	2,266	1,246
Sawyer	2,867	2,335
St. Croix	10,653	8,946
Taylor	3,635	1,368
Vilas	5,227	3,392
Washburn	2,783	2,089
Wood (part)	4,731	3,325
Total	**109,498**	**82,135**

Dem.–Democrat; Rep.–Republican.
Source: Official records of the Wisconsin Elections Commission.

District vote for U.S. representatives, August 11, 2020 partisan primary

First congressional district

County	Josh Pade (Dem.)	Roger Polack (Dem.)	Bryan Steil* (Rep.)
Kenosha	5,285	5,502	5,407
Milwaukee (part)	3,302	5,131	7,386
Racine	4,774	7,286	9,793
Rock (part)	3,447	5,088	2,356
Walworth (part)	1,957	2,831	5,545
Waukesha (part)	1,843	2,860	9,786
Total	**20,608**	**28,698**	**40,273**

Second congressional district

County	Mark Pocan* (Dem.)	Peter Theron (Rep.)
Dane	103,132	10,755
Green	2,857	1,359
Iowa	2,423	831

District vote for U.S. representatives, August 11, 2020 partisan primary, continued

Second congressional district, continued

County	Mark Pocan* (Dem.)	Peter Theron (Rep.)
Lafayette	807	1,185
Richland (part)	191	212
Rock (part)	6,321	1,922
Sauk	4,622	2,548
Total.	**120,353**	**18,812**

Third congressional district

County	Ron Kind* (Dem.)	Mark Neumann (Dem.)	Jessi Ebben (Rep.)	Derrick Van Orden (Rep.)
Adams	1,099	360	1,012	1,195
Buffalo	770	136	431	821
Chippewa (part)	2,628	449	869	1,751
Crawford	1,544	356	428	749
Dunn	2,795	600	1,089	2,995
Eau Claire.	8,595	1,867	2,184	4,186
Grant	2,543	674	1,141	1,956
Jackson (part)	1,219	153	441	823
Juneau (part)	884	259	883	975
La Crosse	11,922	2,989	2,157	5,533
Monroe (part)	2,173	366	2,009	2,403
Pepin	465	70	298	487
Pierce	2,749	653	810	2,493
Portage.	6,129	1,679	1,448	3,199
Richland (part)	834	281	424	695
Trempealeau	1,827	362	715	1,421
Vernon	2,391	810	1,022	2,368
Wood (part)	2,497	701	1,474	2,345
Total.	**53,064**	**12,765**	**18,835**	**36,395**

Fourth congressional district

County	Gwen S. Moore* (Dem.)	Tim Rogers (Rep.)	Cindy Werner (Rep.)
Milwaukee (part)	68,898	6,685	6,598
Waukesha (part)	0	0	0
Total.	**68,898**	**6,685**	**6,598**

Fifth congressional district

County	Tom Palzewicz (Dem.)	Cliff DeTemple (Rep.)	Scott Fitzgerald (Rep.)
Dodge (part).	1,285	1,036	3,775
Jefferson	4,786	1,784	5,299
Milwaukee (part)	14,002	2,280	8,010
Walworth (part).	561	97	277
Washington	5,292	4,243	13,902
Waukesha (part)	17,784	8,389	29,413
Total.	**43,710**	**17,829**	**60,676**

District vote for U.S. representatives, August 11, 2020 partisan primary, continued

Sixth congressional district

County	Michael G. Beardsley (Dem.)	Matthew L. Boor (Dem.)	Jessica J. King (Dem.)	Glenn Grothman* (Rep.)
Columbia.	835	340	3,495	3,105
Dodge (part).	380	175	1,792	3,043
Fond du Lac.	639	294	5,136	6,893
Green Lake.	133	143	609	2,772
Manitowoc.	743	582	3,365	4,437
Marquette.	193	115	611	2,068
Milwaukee (part).	66	20	193	137
Ozaukee.	1,390	683	5,730	9,942
Sheboygan.	1,479	1,035	5,293	6,350
Waushara.	189	163	994	2,210
Winnebago (part).	1,849	615	10,825	11,290
Total.	7,896	4,165	38,043	52,247

Seventh congressional district

County	Tricia Zunker (Dem.)	Tom Tiffany* (Rep.)
Ashland.	1,586	630
Barron.	2,714	3,318
Bayfield.	2,993	1,034
Burnett.	1,224	1,869
Chippewa (part).	1,447	1,768
Clark.	1,104	2,869
Douglas.	4,127	1,843
Florence.	247	961
Forest.	507	805
Iron.	741	599
Jackson (part).	110	218
Juneau (part).	308	632
Langlade.	1,112	1,960
Lincoln.	1,762	2,785
Marathon.	9,349	10,383
Monroe (part).	196	504
Oneida.	3,440	3,439
Polk.	2,910	5,071
Price.	1,052	1,043
Rusk.	841	1,355
Sawyer.	1,260	1,885
St. Croix.	6,394	8,486
Taylor.	720	1,903
Vilas.	1,752	2,609
Washburn.	1,247	1,646
Wood (part).	1,996	2,527
Total.	51,139	62,142

Eighth congressional district

County	Amanda Stuck (Dem.)	Mike Gallagher* (Rep.)
Brown.	18,543	16,036
Calumet.	2,553	3,067
Door.	3,287	2,906
Kewaunee.	986	1,315
Marinette.	1,951	4,513

District vote for U.S. representatives, August 11, 2020 partisan primary, continued

Eighth congressional district, continued

County	Amanda Stuck (Dem.)	Mike Gallagher* (Rep.)
Menominee	128	36
Oconto	1,707	3,303
Outagamie	10,963	10,614
Shawano	1,696	2,922
Waupaca	2,389	4,183
Winnebago (part)	590	1,281
Total	**44,793**	**50,176**

Note: County totals include scattered votes.

*Incumbent. Dem.–Democrat; Rep.–Republican.

Source: Official records of the Wisconsin Elections Commission.

District vote for U.S. representatives, November 3, 2020 general election

First congressional district

County	Bryan Steil* (Rep.)	Roger Polack (Dem.)
Kenosha	48,524	38,337
Milwaukee (part)	32,032	23,566
Racine	59,331	45,091
Rock (part)	20,845	21,871
Walworth (part)	34,497	18,057
Waukesha (part)	43,042	16,248
Total	**238,271**	**163,170**
% of total vote[1]	**59.31**	**40.61**

Second congressional district

County	Mark Pocan* (Dem.)	Peter Theron (Rep.)
Dane	253,784	83,066
Green	11,060	9,874
Iowa	8,063	5,595
Lafayette	3,836	4,454
Richland (part)	786	962
Rock (part)	22,604	17,296
Sauk	18,390	17,059
Total	**318,523**	**138,306**
% of total vote[1]	**69.67**	**30.25**

Third congressional district

County	Ron Kind* (Dem.)	Derrick Van Orden (Rep.)
Adams	4,639	6,910
Buffalo	3,457	4,282
Chippewa (part)	10,332	10,587
Crawford	4,551	4,055

District vote for U.S. representatives, November 3, 2020 general election, continued

Third congressional district, continued

County	Ron Kind* (Dem.)	Derrick Van Orden (Rep.)
Dunn	10,667	12,616
Eau Claire.	33,210	24,260
Grant	11,967	13,114
Jackson (part)	4,508	4,507
Juneau (part)	4,063	5,957
La Crosse.	40,504	26,698
Monroe (part)	8,684	11,001
Pepin	1,682	2,425
Pierce.	10,208	12,871
Portage.	21,626	18,276
Richland (part)	3,513	3,588
Trempealeau	7,154	8,086
Vernon	8,557	7,260
Wood (part)	10,548	13,031
Total.	**199,870**	**189,524**
% of total vote[1]	**51.30**	**48.64**

Fourth congressional district

County	Gwen S. Moore* (Dem.)	Tim Rogers (Rep.)	Robert R. Raymond (Ind.)
Milwaukee (part)	232,668	70,769	7,911
Waukesha (part)	0	0	0
Total.	**232,668**	**70,769**	**7,911**
% of total vote[1]	**74.65**	**22.70**	**2.54**

Fifth congressional district

County	Scott Fitzgerald (Rep.)	Tom Palzewicz (Dem.)
Dodge (part).	15,293	6,310
Jefferson	27,605	19,282
Milwaukee (part)	34,243	45,404
Walworth (part).	1,750	2,438
Washington	62,039	24,841
Waukesha (part)	124,504	77,627
Total.	**265,434**	**175,902**
% of total vote[1]	**60.11**	**39.83**

Sixth congressional district

County	Glenn Grothman* (Rep.)	Jessica J. King (Dem.)
Columbia.	16,971	15,837
Dodge (part).	16,175	9,709
Fond du Lac	36,176	20,191
Green Lake.	7,313	3,218
Manitowoc.	27,663	16,164
Marquette	5,692	3,211

District vote for U.S. representatives, November 3, 2020 general election, continued

Sixth congressional district, continued

County	Glenn Grothman* (Rep.)	Jessica J. King (Dem.)
Milwaukee (part)	627	686
Ozaukee	36,259	24,272
Sheboygan	38,901	25,993
Waushara	9,033	4,342
Winnebago (part)	44,064	40,616
Total	**238,874**	**164,239**
% of total vote[1]	**59.23**	**40.72**

Seventh congressional district

County	Tom Tiffany* (Rep.)	Tricia Zunker (Dem.)
Ashland	3,746	4,795
Barron	15,936	9,119
Bayfield	4,589	6,107
Burnett	6,497	3,499
Chippewa (part)	9,722	4,751
Clark	9,968	4,672
Douglas	10,962	13,266
Florence	2,149	752
Forest	3,212	1,777
Iron	2,396	1,542
Jackson (part)	764	326
Juneau (part)	2,403	1,040
Langlade	7,413	3,676
Lincoln	10,123	6,129
Marathon	46,096	29,770
Monroe (part)	1,839	796
Oneida	13,877	9,979
Polk	16,701	9,271
Price	5,327	3,116
Rusk	5,172	2,553
Sawyer	5,917	4,448
St. Croix	33,296	22,354
Taylor	7,843	2,683
Vilas	9,499	5,761
Washburn	6,385	3,846
Wood (part)	10,216	6,713
Total	**252,048**	**162,741**
% of total vote[1]	**60.73**	**39.21**

Eighth congressional district

County	Mike Gallagher* (Rep.)	Amanda Stuck (Dem.)
Brown	87,044	55,344
Calumet	20,138	10,303
Door	11,255	8,778
Kewaunee	8,614	3,413
Marinette	16,514	6,275
Menominee	411	1,110
Oconto	17,375	5,644

District vote for U.S. representatives, November 3, 2020 general election, continued

Eighth congressional district, continued

County	Mike Gallagher* (Rep.)	Amanda Stuck (Dem.)
Outagamie.	64,985	41,690
Shawano	15,970	6,379
Waupaca	20,252	8,459
Winnebago (part).	5,615	2,163
Total.	268,173	149,558
% of total vote[1]	64.18	35.79

*Incumbent. Dem.–Democrat; Rep.–Republican; Ind.–Independent.

1. Percentages do not add up to 100, as scattered and write-in votes have been omitted.

Source: Official records of the Wisconsin Elections Commission.

County vote for superintendent of public instruction, February 16, 2021 spring primary

	Sheila Briggs	Joe Fenrick	Troy Gunderson	Shandowlyon Hendricks- Williams	Deborah Kerr	Steve Krull	Jill Underly	Total
Adams . . .	150	65	121	60	249	78	247	972
Ashland. . .	168	45	81	74	161	45	317	900
Barron. . . .	279	69	179	123	512	103	440	1,707
Bayfield. . .	238	58	89	153	226	62	579	1,409
Brown. . . .	1,959	725	1,356	1,218	4,584	1,175	4,362	15,435
Buffalo . . .	56	30	193	18	142	41	124	606
Burnett . . .	106	47	82	43	257	69	193	797
Calumet . .	282	164	231	213	847	211	615	2,568
Chippewa .	394	139	399	162	810	167	604	2,684
Clark.	141	71	203	54	495	65	281	1,315
Columbia. .	615	117	237	250	825	184	774	3,019
Crawford . .	92	20	146	48	132	53	217	710
Dane	15,780	1,136	1,626	6,203	6,064	2,107	17,607	50,627
Dodge . . .	527	373	507	552	1,881	502	963	5,305
Door.	364	81	138	167	534	112	669	2,073
Douglas. . .	357	87	166	205	635	179	648	2,286
Dunn	297	75	579	134	765	152	703	2,705
Eau Claire. .	728	116	538	364	1,312	182	1,668	4,916
Florence . .	32	16	19	13	71	40	60	251
Fond du Lac	735	2,007	651	599	2,290	588	1,163	8,041
Forest	60	54	53	38	135	80	105	525
Grant	239	89	221	121	355	129	636	1,792
Green	757	212	422	273	911	366	1,341	4,302
Green Lake.	77	68	60	55	255	43	198	757
Iowa.	201	40	101	121	208	64	765	1,503
Iron	89	25	39	27	143	37	142	503
Jackson. . .	103	23	465	39	237	65	184	1,116
Jefferson . .	567	266	361	625	1,709	496	1,211	5,267
Juneau . . .	125	83	167	83	346	87	264	1,160
Kenosha . .	1,251	357	432	1,080	2,106	630	2,011	7,918
Kewaunee .	125	70	87	68	336	82	244	1,017
La Crosse . .	1,129	256	4,741	709	1,288	456	1,884	10,521
Lafayette . .	80	17	58	34	214	62	345	810
Langlade . .	120	42	60	70	404	65	237	998
Lincoln . . .	167	71	102	61	452	102	359	1,318

County vote for superintendent of public instruction, February 16, 2021 spring primary, continued

	Sheila Briggs	Joe Fenrick	Troy Gunderson	Shandowlyon Hendricks-Williams	Deborah Kerr	Steve Krull	Jill Underly	Total
Manitowoc.	446	255	296	299	1,679	266	984	4,237
Marathon. .	949	260	580	542	2,541	435	1,790	7,126
Marinette. .	278	243	295	180	928	293	494	2,711
Marquette .	109	71	65	63	260	68	130	772
Menominee	8	0	4	5	11	3	8	39
Milwaukee .	5,979	1,009	1,459	9,095	9,872	2,706	13,848	44,101
Monroe. . .	172	58	667	83	488	88	270	1,831
Oconto . . .	237	210	241	150	865	264	484	2,451
Oneida . . .	307	94	157	147	663	129	679	2,186
Outagamie.	1,118	448	677	839	2,692	810	2,562	9,146
Ozaukee . .	575	170	228	750	2,027	305	1,361	5,436
Pepin	36	8	94	10	85	15	79	327
Pierce	261	53	203	115	454	88	442	1,619
Polk	185	67	171	111	713	100	429	1,776
Portage. . .	673	159	325	368	859	238	1,314	3,945
Price.	82	39	74	42	233	51	182	703
Racine. . . .	805	194	394	825	2,068	365	1,564	6,238
Richland . .	135	29	95	40	194	45	273	812
Rock.	1,211	335	300	667	1,346	443	2,135	6,452
Rusk.	112	33	93	47	219	59	134	699
St. Croix. . .	541	175	420	325	1,366	214	1,209	4,261
Sauk.	700	137	336	270	955	241	1,081	3,720
Sawyer . . .	103	40	101	91	258	91	289	978
Shawano . .	240	116	229	139	694	272	434	2,124
Sheboygan.	937	396	540	808	2,562	453	1,966	7,696
Taylor	91	80	85	43	400	61	156	916
Trempealeau	129	25	510	61	310	45	266	1,347
Vernon . . .	109	39	414	143	321	61	387	1,477
Vilas	153	50	124	87	379	76	352	1,228
Walworth. .	671	234	299	462	1,438	338	972	4,441
Washburn .	131	74	65	50	219	46	250	836
Washington	561	408	549	885	3,308	542	1,341	7,594
Waukesha .	2,330	891	1,146	3,592	8,726	1,286	4,828	22,900
Waupaca . .	284	142	287	241	964	254	685	2,862
Waushara. .	134	69	84	79	358	86	249	1,059
Winnebago	1,119	570	548	858	2,620	603	2,125	8,468
Wood	514	212	387	281	1,208	224	884	3,727
Total.	50,815	14,507	27,452	36,850	86,174	20,543	88,796	326,074

Note: County totals include scattered votes.
Source: Official records of the Wisconsin Elections Commission.

County vote for superintendent of public instruction, April 6, 2021 spring election

	Deborah Kerr	Jill Underly	Total
Adams	1,346	1,699	3,047
Ashland.	1,071	1,769	2,852
Barron.	3,644	3,492	7,139
Bayfield.	1,502	2,939	4,444
Brown.	17,391	21,705	39,143
Buffalo	844	1,056	1,907

County vote for superintendent of public instruction, April 6, 2021 spring election, continued

	Deborah Kerr	Jill Underly	Total
Burnett	1,629	1,251	2,880
Calumet	4,407	4,391	8,808
Chippewa	3,807	4,039	7,857
Clark	2,269	1,976	4,254
Columbia	3,793	5,216	9,026
Crawford	803	1,458	2,264
Dane	23,464	94,819	118,443
Dodge	7,429	6,636	14,065
Door	2,266	3,978	6,255
Douglas	2,247	3,191	5,457
Dunn	3,026	3,537	6,563
Eau Claire	5,735	9,657	15,412
Florence	638	515	1,153
Fond du Lac	9,048	8,355	17,425
Forest	736	783	1,522
Grant	2,481	4,083	6,570
Green	2,927	5,364	8,300
Green Lake	1,386	1,379	2,769
Iowa	1,188	3,039	4,231
Iron	721	780	1,501
Jackson	1,384	2,049	3,433
Jefferson	6,768	7,560	14,365
Juneau	1,529	1,717	3,254
Kenosha	9,997	12,046	22,117
Kewaunee	1,666	1,704	3,374
La Crosse	5,976	12,192	18,204
Lafayette	1,253	1,816	3,069
Langlade	2,045	1,988	4,033
Lincoln	2,381	2,464	4,857
Manitowoc	7,037	7,448	14,511
Marathon	12,393	12,135	24,570
Marinette	3,644	3,856	7,500
Marquette	1,241	1,175	2,421
Menominee	43	117	160
Milwaukee	31,520	71,432	103,190
Monroe	2,400	2,712	5,122
Oconto	3,796	3,994	7,790
Oneida	3,041	3,777	6,826
Outagamie	12,254	15,583	27,837
Ozaukee	10,655	9,005	19,695
Pepin	488	597	1,085
Pierce	2,521	2,775	5,315
Polk	3,590	3,335	6,925
Portage	4,043	6,539	10,609
Price	1,237	1,292	2,529
Racine	12,495	12,610	25,163
Richland	1,208	1,994	3,202
Rock	7,153	12,232	19,423
Rusk	1,200	1,063	2,266
St. Croix	6,188	6,083	12,307
Sauk	4,119	6,507	10,626
Sawyer	1,392	1,360	2,759
Shawano	3,000	3,114	6,114
Sheboygan	9,734	9,702	19,454
Taylor	2,713	2,071	4,789
Trempealeau	1,422	2,023	3,452
Vernon	1,779	2,853	4,635
Vilas	2,203	2,427	4,640

County vote for superintendent of public instruction, April 6, 2021 spring election, continued

	Deborah Kerr	Jill Underly	Total
Walworth.	8,530	8,080	16,655
Washburn	1,389	1,349	2,741
Washington	15,135	8,423	23,558
Waukesha	46,925	32,894	79,938
Waupaca	3,690	4,044	7,749
Waushara.	1,641	1,600	3,241
Winnebago	10,685	13,855	24,605
Wood	5,242	5,707	10,974
Total.	**386,543**	**526,406**	**914,369**

Note: County totals include scattered votes.
Source: Official records of the Wisconsin Elections Commission.

District vote for state senators, partisan and special primaries

Senate district	Assembly districts	Party	Candidates	Vote
August 11, 2020 partisan primary				
2	4, 5, 6	Democratic	Tony Lee	286
		Republican	Robert L. Cowles*	11,224
4	10, 11, 12	Democratic	Lena C. Taylor*	16,898
6	16, 17, 18	Democratic	LaTonya Johnson*	14,462
		Democratic	Michelle Bryant	3,515
		Republican	Alciro Deacon	782
8	22, 23, 24	Democratic	Neal Plotkin	17,569
		Republican	Alberta Darling*	16,172
10	28, 29, 30	Democratic	Patty Schachtner*	13,306
		Republican	Rob Stafsholt	12,603
		Republican	Cherie Link.	6,828
12	34, 35, 36	Democratic	Ed Vocke	10,348
		Republican	Mary Czaja-Felzkowski	15,936
14	40, 41, 42	Democratic	Joni D. Anderson	9,380
		Republican	Ken Van Dyke, Sr.	4,982
		Republican	Joan A. Ballweg	11,096
16	46, 47, 48	Democratic	Melissa Agard Sargent.	27,734
		Democratic	Andrew McKinney	8,328
		Republican	Scott Barker	4,150
18	52, 53, 54	Democratic	Aaron M. Wojciechowski	11,240
		Republican	Dan Feyen*	11,131
20	58, 59, 60	Republican	Duey Stroebel*	19,471
22	64, 65, 66	Democratic	Robert W. Wirch*	11,412
24	70, 71, 72	Democratic	Paul Piotrowski	13,604
		Republican	Patrick Testin*	14,257
26	76, 77, 78	Democratic	Aisha Moe	3,632
		Democratic	Nada Elmikashfi.	13,220
		Democratic	Amani Latimer Burris	4,370
		Democratic	Brian Benford	4,699

District vote for state senators, partisan and special primaries, continued

Senate district	Assembly districts	Party	Candidates	Vote
		Democratic	Kelda Helen Roys	19,801
		Democratic	William Henry Davis III.	408
		Democratic	John Imes	3,074
28	82, 83, 84	Democratic	Adam Murphy	12,556
		Republican	Steve Bobowski	4,692
		Republican	Dan Griffin	4,177
		Republican	Jim Engstrand	1,543
		Republican	Julian Bradley	8,263
		Republican	Marina Croft	1,623
30	88, 89, 90	Democratic	Sandra Ewald	5,055
		Democratic	Jonathon Hansen	8,390
		Republican	Eric Wimberger	10,785
32	94, 95, 96	Democratic	Jayne Swiggum	6,558
		Democratic	Paul Michael Weber	934
		Democratic	Brad Pfaff	12,631
		Republican	Dan Kapanke	8,395
February 16, 2021 special primary				
13	37, 38, 39	Democratic	Melissa Winker	4,552
		Republican	John Jagler	6,034
		Republican	Don Pridemore	3,343
		Republican	Todd Menzel	1,204

*Incumbent.
Source: Official records of the Wisconsin Elections Commission.

District vote for state senators, general and special elections

Senate district	Assembly districts	Party	Candidates	Vote	% of total[1]
November 3, 2020 general election					
2	4, 5, 6	Republican	Robert L. Cowles*	80,602	98.33
4	10, 11, 12	Democratic	Lena C. Taylor*	62,405	98.34
6	16, 17, 18	Democratic	LaTonya Johnson*	60,057	88.51
		Republican	Alciro Deacon	7,555	11.13
		Independent	Michelle Bryant (write-in)	142	0.21
8	22, 23, 24	Democratic	Neal Plotkin	54,693	45.70
		Republican	Alberta Darling*	64,906	54.24
10	28, 29, 30	Democratic	Patty Schachtner*	41,410	40.07
		Republican	Rob Stafsholt	61,914	59.91
12	34, 35, 36	Democratic	Ed Vocke	35,386	34.27
		Republican	Mary Czaja-Felzkowski	67,800	65.66
14	40, 41, 42	Democratic	Joni D. Anderson	33,459	35.08
		Republican	Joan A. Ballweg	61,883	64.87
16	46, 47, 48	Democratic	Melissa Agard Sargent	83,526	73.43
		Republican	Scott Barker	30,121	26.48
18	52, 53, 54	Democratic	Aaron M. Wojciechowski	36,274	40.84
		Republican	Dan Feyen*	52,490	59.09
20	58, 59, 60	Republican	Duey Stroebel*	87,715	98.69

District vote for state senators, general and special elections,
continued

Senate district	Assembly districts	Party	Candidates	Vote	% of total[1]
22	64, 65, 66	Democratic	Robert W. Wirch*	55,214	96.22
24	70, 71, 72	Democratic	Paul Piotrowski	41,419	43.51
		Republican	Patrick Testin*	53,720	56.43
26	76, 77, 78	Democratic	Kelda Helen Roys	102,569	98.16
28	82, 83, 84	Democratic	Adam Murphy	43,391	40.31
		Republican	Julian Bradley	64,179	59.62
30	88, 89, 90	Democratic	Jonathon Hansen	39,711	45.26
		Republican	Eric Wimberger	47,948	54.65
32	94, 95, 96	Democratic	Brad Pfaff	48,877	50.26
		Republican	Dan Kapanke	48,295	49.67
April 6, 2021 special election					
13	37, 38, 39	Democrat	Melissa Winker	16,364	43.62
		Republican	John Jagler	19,125	50.99
		Independent	Spencer Zimmerman	1,702	4.54
		Independent	Ben Schmitz	194	0.52

*Incumbent.

1. Percentages do not add up to 100, as scattered votes have been omitted.

Source: Official records of the Wisconsin Elections Commission.

District vote for representatives to the assembly, partisan and special elections

Assem. district	Party	Candidates	Vote
August 11, 2020 partisan primary			
1	Dem.	Kim Delorit Jensen	4,743
	Rep.	Joel C. Kitchens*	4,863
2	Dem.	Mark Kiley	3,146
	Rep.	Shae Sortwell*	3,671
3	Dem.	Emily Voight	3,370
		Ron Tusler*	3,261
4	Dem.	Kathy A. Hinkfuss	4,711
	Rep.	David Steffen*	4,129
5	Rep.	Jim Steineke*	3,341
6	Dem.	Simon A. Moesch	910
	Dem.	Richard Sarnwick	1,421
	Rep.	Gary Tauchen*	3,623
7	Dem.	Daniel G. Riemer*	4,491
8	Dem.	Sylvia Ortiz-Velez	901
	Dem.	JoAnna Bautch	793
	Rep.	Ruben Velez	103
	Rep.	Angel C. Sanchez	116
9	Dem.	Christian Saldivar	1,118
	Dem.	Marisabel Cabrera*	1,851
	Rep.	Veronica Diaz	493
10	Dem.	David Bowen*	7,112

Assem. district	Party	Candidates	Vote
11	Dem.	Curtis Cook II	824
	Dem.	Dora Drake	2,471
	Dem.	Tomika S. Vukovic	1,632
	Dem.	Carl Gates	287
	Rep.	Orlando Owens	406
12	Dem.	LaKeshia N. Myers*	4,861
	Rep.	Ozell Cox	624
13	Dem.	Sara Rodriguez	5,593
	Rep.	Rob Hutton*	4,656
14	Dem.	Robyn Vining*	7,056
	Rep.	Bonnie Lee	5,127
	Rep.	Steven Shevey	839
	Rep.	Linda Boucher	1,428
15	Dem.	Jessica Katzenmeyer	3,894
	Rep.	Joe Sanfelippo*	4,033
16	Dem.	Kalan Haywood*	4,450
17	Dem.	Mike Brox	1,157
	Dem.	Supreme Moore Omokunde	3,457
	Dem.	Chris Walton	2,553
	Rep.	Abie Eisenbach	465
18	Dem.	Evan Goyke*	5,106
19	Dem.	Jonathan Brostoff*	9,426
	Rep.	Helmut Fritz	905

District vote for representatives to the assembly, partisan and special elections, continued

Assem. district	Party	Candidates	Vote
20	Dem.	Christine M. Sinicki*	6,243
21	Dem.	Erik Brooks	4,190
	Rep.	Jessie Rodriguez*	2,899
22	Rep.	Janel Brandtjen*	6,405
23	Dem.	Deb Andraca	7,855
	Rep.	Jim Ott*	4,796
24	Dem.	Emily Siegrist	6,166
	Rep.	Dan Knodl*	4,928
25	Dem.	Kerry Trask	2,903
	Rep.	Paul Tittl*	3,085
26	Dem.	Mary Lynne Donohue	3,687
	Rep.	Terry Katsma*	3,467
27	Rep.	Tyler Vorpagel*	3,216
28	Dem.	Kim Butler	3,615
	Rep.	Gae Magnafici*	6,503
29	Dem.	John Rocco Calabrese	3,870
	Rep.	Neil R. Kline	1,998
	Rep.	Ryan Sherley	1,807
	Rep.	Clint Moses	2,355
30	Dem.	Sarah Yacoub	5,522
	Rep.	Shannon Zimmerman*	5,446
31	Dem.	Elizabeth Lochner-Abel	4,046
	Rep.	Amy Loudenbeck*	2,802
32	Dem.	Katherine Gaulke	2,802
	Rep.	Tyler August*	3,269
33	Dem.	Mason Becker	3,235
	Rep.	Cody J. Horlacher*	4,162
34	Dem.	Kirk Bangstad	4,812
	Rep.	Rob Swearingen*	6,623
35	Dem.	Tyler E. Ruprecht	3,126
	Rep.	Calvin Callahan	4,446
	Rep.	Donald Nelson	1,726
36	Rep.	Jeffrey L. Mursau*	4,672
37	Dem.	Abigail Lowery	3,781
	Rep.	John Jagler*	4,125
38	Dem.	Melissa Winker	4,416
	Rep.	Barbara Dittrich*	5,347
39	Dem.	Izzy Hassey Nevarez	2,284
	Rep.	Mark L. Born*	4,905
40	Dem.	Deb Silver	2,676
	Rep.	Kevin Petersen*	4,777
41	Dem.	Nate Zimdars	3,098
	Rep.	Alex A. Dallman	3,411
	Rep.	Luke Dretske	1,125
	Rep.	Chuck Harsh	973
	Rep.	Gary A. Will	1,400
42	Dem.	Melisa Arndt	3,638
	Rep.	Jon Plumer*	3,929

Assem. district	Party	Candidates	Vote
43	Dem.	Don Vruwink*	5,219
	Rep.	Beth Drew	1,882
44	Dem.	Sue Conley	5,892
	Rep.	DuWayne Severson	1,435
45	Dem.	Mark Spreitzer*	3,482
	Rep.	Tawny Gustina	1,195
46	Dem.	Gary Alan Hebl*	8,932
	Rep.	Terry Lyon	1,604
47	Dem.	Jimmy Anderson*	10,751
	Rep.	Phil Anderson	1,289
48	Dem.	Lindsay Lemmer	5,215
	Dem.	Samba Baldeh	7,305
	Dem.	Jason Vangalis	665
	Dem.	Walter Stewart	1,578
	Rep.	Samuel Anderson	1,184
49	Dem.	Shaun Murphy-Lopez	3,325
	Rep.	Travis Tranel*	3,449
50	Dem.	Mark Waldon	2,994
	Rep.	Tony Kurtz*	4,225
51	Dem.	Kriss Marion	4,212
	Rep.	Todd Novak*	3,109
52	Dem.	Julie Schroeder	3,296
	Rep.	Jeremy Thiesfeldt*	3,336
53	Rep.	Michael Schraa*	4,043
54	Dem.	Gordon Hintz*	5,539
	Rep.	Pete Kohlhoff	1,402
	Rep.	Donny Herman	2,739
55	Dem.	Daniel Schierl	4,073
	Rep.	Lauri Asbury	1,401
	Rep.	Jay Schroeder	1,069
	Rep.	Rachael Cabral-Guevara	3,481
56	Dem.	Diana Lawrence	3,982
	Rep.	Dave Murphy*	4,721
57	Dem.	Lee Snodgrass	4,240
	Rep.	Eric J. Beach	2,190
58	Rep.	Rick Gundrum*	6,401
59	Rep.	Timothy S. Ramthun*	5,537
60	Dem.	Brian Adams	30
	Rep.	Chris Reimer	2,198
	Rep.	Robert Brooks*	6,958
61	Dem.	Steve Kundert	3
	Rep.	Samantha Kerkman*	2,562
62	Dem.	August Schutz	3,681
	Rep.	Robert Wittke*	3,425
63	Dem.	Joel Jacobsen	3,490
	Rep.	Robin Vos*	3,302
64	Dem.	Tip McGuire*	4,479
	Rep.	Ed Hibsch	1,589

District vote for representatives to the assembly, partisan and special elections, continued

Assem. district	Party	Candidates	Vote
65	Dem.	Tod Ohnstad*	4,087
	Rep.	Crystal J. Miller	1,169
66	Dem.	Greta Neubauer*	2,801
	Rep.	Will Leverson	833
67	Dem.	Chris Kapsner	3,868
	Rep.	Rob Summerfield*	4,465
68	Dem.	Emily Berge	3,644
	Rep.	Jesse James*.	4,264
69	Dem.	Brian Giles	2,803
	Rep.	Donna M. Rozar.	3,040
	Rep.	Michael V. Smith	906
	Rep.	Matthew F. Windheuser.	240
	Rep.	Tim Miller	1,550
70	Dem.	John Iver Baldus	3,513
	Rep.	Nancy Lynn VanderMeer*.	5,526
71	Dem.	Katrina Shankland*	6,423
	Rep.	Scott C. Soik	3,318
72	Dem.	Criste Greening	3,909
	Rep.	Scott S. Krug*	5,179
73	Dem.	Nick Milroy*	5,263
	Rep.	Keith Kern	3,015
74	Dem.	Beth Meyers*	6,934
	Rep.	James Bolen	3,531
75	Dem.	John C. Ellensen	3,478
	Rep.	David Armstrong	4,463
76	Dem.	Heather Driscoll.	2,780
	Dem.	Dewey Bredeson	143
	Dem.	Tyrone Cratic Williams.	3,810
	Dem.	Francesca Hong.	4,793
	Dem.	Nicki Vander Meulen.	1,586
	Dem.	Marsha A. Rummel.	2,803
	Dem.	Ali Maresh	1,099
	Rep.	Patrick Hull.	302
77	Dem.	Shelia Stubbs*.	14,985
78	Dem.	Lisa B. Subeck*	14,092
	Dem.	Rob Slamka.	1,321
79	Dem.	Dianne Hesselbein*	9,942
	Rep.	Victoria Fueger	1,810
80	Dem.	Kimberly Smith	3,221
	Dem.	Sondy Pope*.	6,668
	Rep.	Chase Binnie.	1,564
81	Dem.	Dave Considine*	5,096
	Rep.	David J. Dahlke	2,331
82	Dem.	Jacob Malinowski.	3,809
	Dem.	Paul McCreary.	2,045

Assem. district	Party	Candidates	Vote
	Rep.	Ken Skowronski*	4,897
	Rep.	Theodore D. Kafkas.	938
83	Dem.	Alan R. DeYoung	3,278
	Rep.	Chuck Wichgers*	7,151
84	Rep.	Mike Kuglitsch*	5,078
85	Dem.	Jeff Johnson.	3,051
	Dem.	Aaron A. LaFave.	1,629
	Rep.	Patrick Snyder*	3,599
86	Rep.	John Spiros*	4,739
87	Dem.	Richard Pulcher	2,648
	Rep.	James W. Edming*	5,201
88	Dem.	Kristin Lyerly.	4,910
	Rep.	John Macco*.	3,702
89	Dem.	Karl Jaeger.	3,076
	Rep.	Andi Rich.	1,032
	Rep.	John Nygren*	5,189
90	Dem.	Staush Gruszynski*.	971
	Dem.	Kristina Shelton.	3,620
	Rep.	Drew Kirsteatter	1,716
91	Dem.	Jodi Emerson*.	5,868
	Dem.	Charlie Walker.	2,063
92	Dem.	Amanda WhiteEagle.	3,803
	Rep.	Treig E. Pronschinske*.	3,997
93	Dem.	Charlene Charlie Warner	4,534
	Rep.	Warren Petryk*	5,180
94	Dem.	Steve Doyle*.	6,549
	Rep.	Kevin Hoyer	4,424
95	Dem.	Jill Billings*.	7,419
	Rep.	Jerome Gundersen.	2,351
96	Dem.	Tucker Gretebeck.	2,494
	Dem.	Josefine Jaynes	3,127
	Rep.	Loren Oldenburg*	5,571
97	Dem.	Aaron D. Perry.	3,107
	Rep.	Scott Allen*	4,235
98	Rep.	Rob Ochoa.	1,788
	Rep.	Adam Neylon*	4,941
99	Rep.	Cindi Duchow*	5,917

February 16, 2021 special primary

Assem. district	Party	Candidates	Vote
89	Dem.	Karl Jaeger.	1,376
	Rep.	Michael T. Kunesh	875
	Rep.	Michael Schneider	264
	Rep.	Elijah Behnke	1,691
	Rep.	David J. Kamps	160
	Rep.	Debbie Jacques.	789

*Incumbent. Assem.–Assembly; Dem.–Democrat; Rep.–Republican.
Source: Official records of the Wisconsin Elections Commission.

District vote for representatives to the assembly, general and special elections

Assembly district	Party	Candidates	Vote	% of total[1]
November 3, 2020 general election				
1	Democratic	Kim Delorit Jensen	14,462	38.14
	Republican	Joel Kitchens*	23,441	61.82
2	Democratic	Mark Kiley	12,970	36.80
	Republican	Shae Sortwell*	22,244	63.11
3	Democratic	Emily Voight	14,703	40.82
	Republican	Ron Tusler*	21,316	59.17
4	Democratic	Kathy A. Hinkfuss	15,804	46.99
	Republican	David Steffen*	17,811	52.96
5	Republican	Jim Steineke*	29,401	99.40
	Independent	Dominic Jessy McClain (write-in)	4	0.01
6	Democratic	Richard Sarnwick	9,378	30.58
	Republican	Gary Tauchen*	21,283	69.40
7	Democratic	Daniel G. Riemer*	19,431	97.11
8	Democratic	Sylvia Ortiz-Velez	8,914	78.70
	Republican	Angel C. Sanchez	2,375	20.97
9	Democratic	Marisabel Cabrera*	11,981	72.77
	Republican	Veronica Diaz	4,458	27.08
10	Democratic	David Bowen*	22,208	98.97
11	Democratic	Dora Drake	18,329	84.64
	Republican	Orlando Owens	3,299	15.24
12	Democratic	LaKeshia N. Myers*	18,539	81.67
	Republican	Ozell Cox	4,117	18.14
13	Democratic	Sara Rodriguez	19,318	50.93
	Republican	Rob Hutton*	18,583	49.00
14	Democratic	Robyn Vining*	21,370	53.99
	Republican	Bonnie Lee	18,186	45.95
	Independent	Linda Boucher (write-in)	1	0
15	Democratic	Jessica Katzenmeyer	14,134	45.15
	Republican	Joe Sanfelippo*	17,133	54.72
16	Democratic	Kalan Haywood*	17,664	88.91
	Independent	Dennis C. Walton	2,153	10.84
17	Democratic	Supreme Moore Omokunde	22,418	85.93
	Republican	Abie Eisenbach	3,638	13.94
18	Democratic	Evan Goyke*	18,775	99.00
19	Democratic	Jonathan Brostoff*	27,552	78.41
	Republican	Helmut Fritz	7,535	21.44
20	Democratic	Christine M. Sinicki*	22,750	96.84
21	Democratic	Erik Brooks	14,708	45.30
	Republican	Jessie Rodriguez*	17,729	54.61
22	Republican	Janel Brandtjen*	29,508	96.51
23	Democratic	Deb Andraca	21,052	51.59
	Republican	Jim Ott*	19,728	48.34
24	Democratic	Emily Siegrist	18,924	48.50
	Republican	Dan Knodl*	20,075	51.45
25	Democratic	Kerry Trask	10,703	35.31
	Republican	Paul Tittl*	19,593	64.63
26	Democratic	Mary Lynne Donohue	12,675	40.99
	Republican	Terry Katsma*	18,224	58.93

District vote for representatives to the assembly, general and special elections, continued

Assembly district	Party	Candidates	Vote	% of total[1]
27	Republican	Tyler Vorpagel*	26,223	97.30
28	Democratic	Kim Butler	12,230	36.06
	Republican	Gae Magnafici*	21,678	63.93
29	Democratic	John Rocco Calabrese	12,509	39.73
	Republican	Clint Moses	18,961	60.23
30	Democratic	Sarah Yacoub	16,322	44.04
	Republican	Shannon Zimmerman*	20,711	55.88
31	Democratic	Elizabeth Lochner-Abel	13,551	40.40
	Republican	Amy Loudenbeck*	19,962	59.51
32	Democratic	Katherine Gaulke	12,460	38.15
	Republican	Tyler August*	20,164	61.74
	Independent	Jacquelyn Rose Romando (write-in)	1	0
33	Democratic	Mason Becker	13,228	38.06
	Republican	Cody Horlacher*	21,496	61.85
34	Democratic	Kirk Bangstad	14,267	36.62
	Republican	Rob Swearingen*	24,652	63.27
35	Democratic	Tyler E. Ruprecht	11,105	34.68
	Republican	Calvin Callahan	20,913	65.31
36	Republican	Jeffrey L. Mursau*	26,932	99.92
37	Democratic	Abigail Lowery	14,142	40.87
	Republican	John Jagler*	19,406	56.08
	Independent	Stephen W. Ratzlaff, Jr.	1,041	3.01
38	Democratic	Melissa Winker	16,163	41.47
	Republican	Barbara Dittrich*	22,786	58.47
39	Democratic	Izzy Hassey Nevarez	10,049	31.27
	Republican	Mark L. Born*	22,085	68.73
40	Democratic	Deb Silvers	9,654	30.58
	Republican	Kevin Petersen*	21,902	69.38
41	Democratic	Nate Zimdars	10,428	33.94
	Republican	Alex A. Dallman	18,604	60.55
	Independent	Jean Bartz	1,680	5.47
42	Democratic	Melisa Arndt	13,381	40.79
	Republican	Jon Plumer*	19,404	59.15
43	Democratic	Don Vruwink*	17,643	55.24
	Republican	Beth Drew	14,263	44.66
44	Democratic	Sue Conley	17,205	60.11
	Republican	DuWayne Severson	11,335	39.60
	Independent	Reese Wood (write-in)	13	0.05
45	Democratic	Mark Spreitzer*	14,451	54.80
	Republican	Tawny Gustina	11,895	45.11
46	Democratic	Gary Alan Hebl*	25,919	67.70
	Republican	Terry Lyon	12,331	32.21
47	Democratic	Jimmy Anderson*	27,947	74.89
	Republican	Phil Anderson	9,331	25.00
48	Democratic	Samba Baldeh	30,074	79.63
	Republican	Samuel Anderson	7,650	20.25
49	Democratic	Shaun Murphy-Lopez	11,528	40.76
	Republican	Travis Tranel*	16,741	59.19
50	Democratic	Mark Waldon	10,872	36.68
	Republican	Tony Kurtz*	18,757	63.29

District vote for representatives to the assembly, general and special elections, continued

Assembly district	Party	Candidates	Vote	% of total[1]
51	Democratic	Kriss Marion	14,679	47.93
	Republican	Todd Novak*	15,937	52.04
52	Democratic	Julie Schroeder	11,674	38.02
	Republican	Jeremy Thiesfeldt*	19,028	61.98
53	Republican	Michael Schraa*	19,758	68.49
	Independent	Joseph Connelly	9,054	31.39
54	Democratic	Gordon Hintz*	15,487	54.18
	Republican	Donny Herman	13,063	45.70
55	Democratic	Daniel Schierl	15,658	45.06
	Republican	Rachael Cabral-Guevara	19,056	54.84
56	Democratic	Diana Lawrence	15,054	39.47
	Republican	Dave Murphy*	23,083	60.52
57	Democratic	Lee Snodgrass	15,972	56.52
	Republican	Eric J. Beach	12,277	43.44
58	Republican	Rick Gundrum*	28,272	100
59	Republican	Timothy Ramthun*	29,123	99.78
60	Republican	Robert Brooks*	28,853	96.77
61	Democratic	Steve Kundert (write-in)	8	0.03
	Republican	Samantha Kerkman*	28,254	96.26
62	Democratic	August Schutz	14,463	41.28
	Republican	Robert Wittke*	20,540	58.63
63	Democratic	Joel Jacobsen	14,132	41.46
	Republican	Robin J. Vos*	19,919	58.44
64	Democratic	Tip McGuire*	16,364	56.00
	Republican	Ed Hibsch	12,813	43.85
65	Democratic	Tod Ohnstad*	14,356	60.25
	Republican	Crystal J. Miller	9,444	39.63
66	Democratic	Greta Neubauer*	14,522	70.17
	Republican	Will Leverson	6,131	29.63
67	Democratic	Chris Kapsner	11,923	36.02
	Republican	Rob Summerfield*	21,172	63.97
68	Democratic	Emily Berge	12,162	39.03
	Republican	Jesse James*	18,993	60.95
69	Democratic	Brian Giles	9,606	34.07
	Republican	Donna M. Rozar	18,568	65.85
70	Democratic	John Iver Baldus	10,318	33.23
	Republican	Nancy Lynn VanderMeer*	20,708	66.70
71	Democratic	Katrina Shankland*	17,753	55.51
	Republican	Scott C. Soik	14,206	44.42
72	Democratic	Criste Greening	12,623	39.63
	Republican	Scott S. Krug*	19,208	60.31
73	Democratic	Nick Milroy*	16,625	50.21
	Republican	Keith Kern	16,486	49.79
74	Democratic	Beth Meyers*	18,163	51.46
	Republican	James Bolen	17,119	48.51
75	Democratic	John C. Ellenson	12,141	37.64
	Republican	David Armstrong	20,108	62.33
76	Democratic	Francesca Hong	35,731	88.02
	Republican	Patrick Hull	4,779	11.77

District vote for representatives to the assembly, general and special elections, continued

Assembly district	Party	Candidates	Vote	% of total[1]
77	Democratic	Shelia Stubbs*	30,741	98.80
78	Democratic	Lisa B. Subeck*	34,576	97.96
79	Democratic	Dianne H. Hesselbein*	29,719	67.14
	Republican	Victoria Fueger	14,507	32.77
80	Democratic	Sondy Pope*	26,526	64.48
	Republican	Chase Binnie	14,590	35.47
81	Democratic	Dave Considine*	18,914	56.90
	Republican	David J. Dahlke	14,314	43.06
82	Democratic	Jacob Malinowski	15,925	46.50
	Republican	Ken Skowronski*	17,205	50.24
	Independent	Marc Adam Ciske	1,098	3.21
83	Democratic	Alan R. DeYoung	11,748	30.28
	Republican	Chuck Wichgers*	27,019	69.63
84	Republican	Mike Kuglitsch*	25,031	96.18
85	Democratic	Jeff Johnson	13,515	44.85
	Republican	Patrick Snyder*	16,599	55.09
86	Republican	John Spiros*	28,267	97.97
87	Democratic	Richard Pulcher	8,887	29.15
	Republican	James W. Edming*	21,595	70.83
88	Democratic	Kristin Lyerly	15,673	47.63
	Republican	John Macco*	17,214	52.31
89	Democratic	Karl Jaeger	10,374	31.24
	Republican	John Nygren*	22,823	68.73
90	Democratic	Kristina Shelton	12,756	60.14
	Republican	Drew Kirsteatter	8,429	39.74
91	Democratic	Jodi Emerson*	18,758	61.86
	Republican	Charlie Walker	11,530	38.03
92	Democratic	Amanda WhiteEagle	12,220	41.38
	Republican	Treig E. Pronschinske*	17,301	58.58
93	Democratic	Charlene Charlie Warner	13,773	38.29
	Republican	Warren Petryk*	22,179	61.65
94	Democratic	Steve Doyle*	19,186	52.44
	Republican	Kevin Hoyer	16,526	45.17
	Independent	Leroy Brown II	868	2.37
95	Democratic	Jill Billings*	19,684	65.63
	Republican	Jerome Gundersen	10,271	34.25
96	Democratic	Josefine Jaynes	13,059	43.71
	Republican	Loren Oldenburg*	16,812	56.27
97	Democratic	Aaron D. Perry	12,770	40.72
	Republican	Scott Allen*	18,556	59.16
98	Republican	Adam Neylon*	28,221	96.93
99	Republican	Cindi Duchow*	31,741	97.66
April 6, 2021 special election				
89	Democratic	Karl Jaeger	4,732	36.77
	Republican	Elijah Behnke	8,129	63.17

*Incumbent.

1. Percentages do not add up to 100, as scattered votes have been omitted.

Source: Official records of the Wisconsin Elections Commission.

Personal data on Wisconsin legislators, 2011–21 sessions

	2011 Sen.	Rep.[1]	2013 Sen.	Rep.	2015 Sen.	Rep.	2017 Sen.	Rep.	2019 Sen.	Rep.	2021 Sen.	Rep.[2]
Party affiliation												
Democratic	14	38	15	39	14	36	13	35	15	35	12	38
Republican	19	60	18	60	19	63	20	64	18	64	21	60
Previous legislative service												
Senate	26	0	30	0	27	0	30	0	28	0	24	0
Assembly	23	69	25	74	24	74	24	83	26	82	24	81
Most prior sessions in same house	24	14	25	13	26	14	27	12	28	10	17	11
Occupations												
Full-time legislator. .	11	32	12	35	11	34	24	56	22	48	14	35
Attorney	3	8	3	7	2	7	2	6	2	8	3	8
Farmer	2	6	2	4	1	6	1	7	1	6	1	8
Other	16	53	16	53	19	52	6	30	9	39	15	47
Education												
High school only . . .	0	4	1	5	1	4	0	5	0	8	1	5
Beyond high school .	33	95	32	94	32	95	5	20	7	19	5	28
Bachelor's or associate degree. . .	29	73	28	72	28	69	18	48	17	47	18	38
Advanced degree . .	10	27	9	27	9	24	10	26	9	25	9	27
Experience on local governing body												
County board	6	16	7	18	9	19	9	26	7	19	5	21
Municipal board . . .	9	29	11	30	9	29	16	49	14	41	6	35
Age (years)[3]												
Oldest	83	72	85	72	87	76	89	78	91	80	77	82
Youngest.	30	25	32	25	34	24	36	26	31	19	32	21
Average	56	49	57	49	57	48	58	49	58	49	56	51
Veterans	2	13	2	10	3	7	7	10	7	9	6	9
Women	8	23	9	24	11	22	9	22	8	28	10	31

Sen.–Senators; Rep.–Representatives.

1. Includes one Independent.   2. Data does not include Assembly District 37, which was vacant at time of publication.
3. Ages for 2021 session calculated as of 1/31/2021.

Source: Data collected from legislative surveys by Wisconsin Legislative Reference Bureau, June 2021.

County vote for supreme court justice, February 18, 2020 spring primary

	Daniel Kelley*	Jill J. Karofsky	Ed Fallone	Total
Adams	1,474	754	213	2,443
Ashland.	892	937	264	2,100
Barron.	3,633	1,755	536	6,024
Bayfield.	1,355	1,707	402	3,470
Brown.	12,442	7,604	2,660	22,738
Buffalo	795	491	128	1,414
Burnett	1,418	669	183	2,270
Calumet	3,160	1,651	569	5,387
Chippewa	3,547	2,151	635	6,333
Clark.	2,466	989	307	3,762
Columbia.	3,285	2,373	840	6,512
Crawford	750	636	186	1,572

County vote for supreme court justice, February 18, 2020 spring primary, continued

	Daniel Kelley*	Jill J. Karofsky	Ed Fallone	Total
Dane	17,482	55,609	14,298	87,519
Dodge	6,236	2,804	730	9,770
Door	1,552	1,706	359	3,619
Douglas	2,506	2,103	442	5,063
Dunn	2,249	1,591	659	4,499
Eau Claire	4,149	4,275	1,920	10,366
Florence	497	142	47	686
Fond du Lac	6,158	2,395	888	9,442
Forest	977	343	104	1,425
Grant	2,131	1,314	631	4,078
Green	1,803	1,723	440	3,971
Green Lake	1,154	422	159	1,736
Iowa	1,249	1,409	441	3,103
Iron	684	414	108	1,208
Jackson	1,014	746	159	1,919
Jefferson	5,643	2,927	986	9,564
Juneau	1,587	681	200	2,471
Kenosha	7,004	5,836	1,378	14,253
Kewaunee	1,223	450	186	1,859
La Crosse	4,652	6,702	1,395	12,749
Lafayette	992	595	238	1,827
Langlade	2,273	879	267	3,419
Lincoln	3,042	1,489	401	4,939
Manitowoc	4,603	2,029	685	7,381
Marathon	13,109	7,042	1,852	22,038
Marinette	2,376	984	282	3,642
Marquette	1,208	449	179	1,842
Menominee	43	45	11	99
Milwaukee	44,088	47,432	25,963	117,875
Monroe	2,762	1,624	313	4,708
Oconto	2,305	853	273	3,431
Oneida	4,641	2,450	829	7,930
Outagamie	10,434	6,906	2,343	19,683
Ozaukee	9,327	3,911	1,403	14,658
Pepin	310	201	69	580
Pierce	1,660	1,110	332	3,102
Polk	3,208	1,634	427	5,269
Portage	3,958	3,807	976	8,765
Price	1,753	814	267	2,834
Racine	12,121	6,490	2,284	20,939
Richland	845	572	352	1,770
Rock	5,867	6,044	1,530	13,463
Rusk	1,429	632	188	2,249
St. Croix	4,917	2,565	790	8,284
Sauk	3,384	2,933	908	7,225
Sawyer	1,713	1,002	297	3,063
Shawano	2,464	835	270	3,569
Sheboygan	8,280	4,009	966	13,263
Taylor	2,446	672	182	3,300
Trempealeau	1,175	915	213	2,310
Vernon	1,510	1,331	391	3,235
Vilas	3,345	1,531	558	5,450
Walworth	6,851	3,254	931	11,058
Washburn	1,646	889	215	2,760
Washington	14,161	3,563	1,045	18,769
Waukesha	44,999	14,409	5,344	64,830
Waupaca	3,206	1,464	428	5,105
Waushara	1,626	631	213	2,470

County vote for supreme court justice, February 18, 2020 spring primary, continued

	Daniel Kelley*	Jill J. Karofsky	Ed Fallone	Total
Winnebago	7,367	5,311	1,608	14,318
Wood	6,265	3,168	908	10,361
Total.	**352,876**	**261,783**	**89,184**	**705,138**

Note: County totals include scattered votes.
*Incumbent.
Source: Official records of the Wisconsin Elections Commission.

County vote for supreme court justice, April 7, 2020 spring election

	Jill J. Karofsky	Daniel Kelly*	Total
Adams	2,568	2,912	5,481
Ashland	2,351	1,468	3,826
Barron	4,902	5,882	10,785
Bayfield	3,750	2,237	5,988
Brown	29,966	27,503	57,506
Buffalo	1,747	1,841	3,588
Burnett	1,697	2,407	4,104
Calumet	6,312	7,176	13,498
Chippewa	8,061	8,316	16,389
Clark	2,835	4,211	7,046
Columbia	9,625	7,232	16,873
Crawford	2,378	1,741	4,119
Dane	159,735	36,427	196,293
Dodge	9,402	12,989	22,391
Door	6,273	4,399	10,678
Douglas	6,204	4,175	10,393
Dunn	5,244	4,850	10,094
Eau Claire	17,384	10,186	27,593
Florence	493	858	1,351
Fond du Lac	10,762	14,755	25,517
Forest	1,060	1,497	2,559
Grant	6,123	4,676	10,803
Green	6,507	4,044	10,556
Green Lake	1,949	2,905	4,854
Iowa	4,749	2,336	7,090
Iron	1,112	1,228	2,340
Jackson	2,405	2,115	4,520
Jefferson	11,618	11,986	23,615
Juneau	2,880	3,298	6,187
Kenosha	19,911	15,108	35,054
Kewaunee	2,343	3,044	5,387
La Crosse	19,622	9,950	29,572
Lafayette	2,242	1,940	4,183
Langlade	1,971	3,041	5,012
Lincoln	3,402	4,020	7,430
Manitowoc	9,067	10,842	19,923
Marathon	16,598	19,027	35,651
Marinette	4,620	5,936	10,556
Marquette	1,897	2,295	4,194
Menominee	246	121	367
Milwaukee	134,949	65,122	200,308
Monroe	4,655	5,043	9,710

County vote for supreme court justice, April 7, 2020 spring election, continued

	Jill J. Karofsky	Daniel Kelly*	Total
Oconto	4,154	6,176	10,330
Oneida	5,682	5,719	11,412
Outagamie	24,567	22,803	47,370
Ozaukee	14,201	18,054	32,271
Pepin	869	956	1,825
Pierce	4,856	4,155	9,017
Polk	4,834	6,340	11,174
Portage	11,597	8,060	19,674
Price	2,037	2,523	4,560
Racine	24,902	25,819	50,769
Richland	2,413	1,814	4,228
Rock	23,138	12,690	35,861
Rusk	1,501	2,111	3,613
St. Croix	10,091	10,342	20,456
Sauk	11,245	7,540	18,785
Sawyer	2,222	2,426	4,653
Shawano	3,879	5,853	9,732
Sheboygan	13,925	18,050	31,985
Taylor	1,597	3,293	4,892
Trempealeau	3,539	2,980	6,523
Vernon	4,519	3,272	7,796
Vilas	3,338	4,152	7,495
Walworth	12,146	14,607	26,773
Washburn	2,177	2,607	4,785
Washington	14,483	30,660	45,143
Waukesha	54,360	86,775	141,211
Waupaca	5,727	7,535	13,273
Waushara	2,554	3,727	6,281
Winnebago	23,703	19,970	43,726
Wood	9,702	10,986	20,700
Total	**855,573**	**693,134**	**1,549,697**

Note: County totals include scattered votes.

*Incumbent.

Source: Official records of the Wisconsin Elections Commission.

Vote for circuit judges, February 18, 2020 spring primary

Counties in circuit	Branch	Candidates	Vote
Milwaukee	5	Brett Blomme	37,889
		Paul Dedinsky*	34,695
		Zach Whitney	30,453

*Incumbent.

Source: Official records of the Wisconsin Elections Commission.

Vote for circuit judges, April 7, 2020 spring election

Counties in circuit	Branch	Candidates	Vote
Barron	2	J. Michael Bitney*	8,981
	3	Maureen D. Boyle*	8,962
Brown	8	Beau G. Liegeois*	29,035
		Andy Williams	23,079

Vote for circuit judges, April 7, 2020 spring election, continued

Counties in circuit	Branch	Candidates	Vote
Chippewa	3	Benjamin Lane	8,839
		Sharon Gibbs McIlquham	6,774
Dane	7	William E. Hanrahan*	127,673
Dodge	1	Brian A. Pfitzinger*	16,773
	4	Kristine A. Snow	10,351
		James T. Sempf	10,017
Dunn	1	James M. Peterson*	8,283
Eau Claire	2	Michael Schumacher*	20,246
Florence, Forest	—	Leon D. Stentz*	2,189
		Robert A. Kennedy, Jr.	1,770
Fond du Lac	1	Dale L. English*	20,170
Iron	—	Anthony J. Stella, Jr.*	1,927
Juneau	1	Paul S. Curran*	5,282
Kenosha	3	Bruce E. Schroeder*	26,063
Marathon	3	LaMont K. Jacobson*	26,455
Marinette	1	Jane Kopish Sequin	5,397
		Mike Perry	5,123
Menominee, Shawano	1	Tony A. Kordus	7,420
Milwaukee	2	Milton L. Childs, Sr.*	127,585
	5	Brett Blomme	99,091
		Paul Dedinsky*	70,005
	7	Thomas J. McAdams*	123,474
	16	Brittany Grayson*	126,151
	24	Janet C. Protasiewicz*	125,239
	27	Kevin E. Martens*	123,248
	29	Rebecca Kiefer	122,798
		Dan Gabler*	50,602
	32	Laura Gramling Perez	126,227
Oneida	1	Patrick F. O'Melia*	9,210
Outagamie	2	Emily I. Lonergan*	35,172
	3	Mitchell J. Metropulos*	35,126
St. Croix	1	Scott J. Norstrand*	15,250
Washburn	—	Angeline E. Winton*	4,034
Washington	2	James K. Muehlbauer*	31,757
Waukesha	5	Jack Melvin	67,792
		Sarah A. Ponath	53,059
Waupaca	2	Vicki L. Clussman*	10,664
Wood	1	Gregory J. Potter*	16,270

Note: William E. Hanrahan and Tony A. Kordus both ended their campaigns prior to election day, and Governor Evers went on to appoint their seats.

*Incumbent. — Means the circuit has only one branch.

Source: Official records of the Wisconsin Elections Commission.

Vote for circuit judges, February 16, 2021 spring primary

Counties in circuit	Branch	Candidates	Vote
Fond du Lac	3	Andrew J. Christenson	3,419
		Laura Lavey	2,408
		Catherine A. Block	1,300
		Dawn M. Sabel	1,210
Green	1	Jane Bucher	1,962
		Faun Marie Phillipson	1,086
		Peter B. Kelly	1,053
		Daniel R. Bartholf	731

Vote for circuit judges, February 16, 2021 spring primary, continued

Counties in circuit	Branch	Candidates	Vote
Kenosha	6	Angela D. Cunningham	3,616
		Angelina Gabriele	2,780
		Elizabeth Pfeuffer	1,905

Source: Official records of the Wisconsin Elections Commission.

Vote for circuit judges, April 6, 2021 spring election

Counties in circuit	Branch	Candidates	Vote
Adams		Daniel Glen Wood*	2,509
Bayfield	—	John P. Anderson*	3,664
		Vincent Scott Kurta	908
Brown	1	Donald R. Zuidmulder*	30,018
	4	Kendall M. Kelley*	21,400
		Rachel Maes	15,467
	5	Marc A. Hammer*	28,919
Calumet	2	Carey John Reed	4,762
		Kimberly A. Tenerelli	3,781
Chippewa	2	James M. Isaacson*	6,283
Columbia	1	Todd J. Hepler*	7,007
Dane	2	Josann M. Reynolds*	77,472
	6	Nia Trammell*	78,255
	7	Mario D. White*	77,787
	9	Jacob B. Frost*	77,148
	10	Juan B. Colás*	78,472
	12	Chris Taylor*	80,833
	13	Julie Genovese*	76,883
	17	David Conway*	75,096
Douglas	1	Kelly J. Thimm*	4,678
	2	George L. Glonek*	4,581
Dunn	2	Christina Mayer	3,496
		Nicholas P. Lange	3,013
	3	Luke M. Wagner	5,070
Fond Du Lac	3	Andrew J. Christenson	9,142
		Laura Lavey	8,625
Grant	2	Craig R. Day*	5,660
Green	1	Faun Marie Phillipson	4,142
		Jane Bucher	4,057
	2	Tom Vale*	6,585
Jackson	1	Anna L. Becker*	2,959
	2	Daniel Diehn	2,189
		Robyn R. Matousek	1,371
Kenosha	1	Gerad Dougvillo	10,720
		Larisa V. Benitez-Morgan*	10,364
	5	David P. Wilk*	15,789
	6	Angelina Gabriele	11,745
		Angela D. Cunningham	10,218
	8	Chad G. Kerkman*	15,476
La Crosse	5	Gloria L. Doyle*	13,828
Lafayette	—	Duane M. Jorgenson*	2,852
Langlade	—	John Rhode*	3,531
Marathon	1	Suzanne C. O'Neill*	17,564

Vote for circuit judges, April 6, 2021 spring election, continued

Counties in circuit	Branch	Candidates	Vote
	6	Scott M. Corbett	13,772
		Daniel T. Cveykus	9,865
Menominee, Shawano	1	Katie Sloma*	5,133
Milwaukee	1	Jack L. Dávila*	62,459
	3	Katie Kegel	60,089
		Susan Roth	32,299
	6	Ellen R. Brostrom*	62,100
	12	David L. Borowski*	62,165
	15	J.D. Watts*	62,074
	19	Kori L. Ashley*	62,654
	22	Timothy Witkowiak*	61,264
	30	Jon Richards*	62,942
	37	Christopher Dee*	61,445
	42	Reyna Morales*	62,906
	46	David A. Feiss*	61,130
Outagamie	6	Vincent R. Biskupic*	20,313
Ozaukee	1	Paul V. Malloy*	13,513
	3	Sandy A. Williams*	13,434
Racine	6	David W. Paulson*	16,757
	8	Faye Flancher*	16,877
Rock	5	Mike Haakenson*	14,416
Sawyer	—	John M. Yackel*	2,304
Sheboygan	1	Samantha Bastil	14,162
	4	Rebecca Persick*	14,283
Taylor	—	Ann N. Knox-Bauer*	4,397
Walworth	3	Kristine E. Drettwan*	12,238
Washington	4	Sandra J. Giernoth*	16,283
Waukesha	7	Maria S. Lazar*	48,711
	8	Michael P. Maxwell*	48,406
	9	Michael J. Aprahamian*	48,795
	10	Paul Bugenhagen Jr.*	48,458
Wood	3	Todd P. Wolf*	8,958

*Incumbent. — Means the circuit has only one branch.

Source: Official records of the Wisconsin Elections Commission.

State officers appointed by the governor, May 15, 2021

911 Subcommittee
Dena Clark. . . . . .expires 7/1/21
John Cummings 7/1/21
Rodney D. Olson 7/1/21
Jean M. Pauk 7/1/21
Mark Podoll 7/1/21
Marcie R. Rainbolt 7/1/21
Andrew Faust 7/1/22
Brad Jorgenson. 7/1/22
Steven R. Kutsch 7/1/22
Kristina Page 7/1/22
Matt Sparks 7/1/22
Robert C. Whitaker 7/1/22
Melvin Frank 7/1/23
Jamey Lysne. 7/1/23
Danielle Miller 7/1/23
Kinnyetta Patterson 7/1/23
2 vacancies

Accounting Examining Board[1] ($25/day[2])
Gerald Denor . . . . .expires 7/1/17
Robert Misey 7/1/21
John Reinemann 7/1/21
David K. Schlichting. 7/1/22
Michael Friedman 7/1/23
Joan Phillips 7/1/23
Susan Strautmann[3] 7/1/24

Adjutant General (group 6 salary[2])
Major Gen. Paul E. Knapp . . . . . . expires 3/4/2025

Administration, Department of, secretary[1] (group 8 salary[2])
Joel T. Brennan . . . . expires at governor's pleasure

Adult Offender Supervision Board, Interstate
Michael Bohren . . . . .expires 5/1/21
Veronica Figueroa-Velez 5/1/23
Kari S. Ives 5/1/23
LaKeshia Nicole Myers 5/1/23

Adult Offender Supervision Board, Interstate Compact Administrator
Joselyn Lopez . . . . .expires 5/1/21

Aerospace Authority, Wisconsin[1] (inactive)

Affirmative Action, Council on
Carlene Bechen. . . . . .expires 7/1/22
Jacquelyn Boggess 7/1/22
Janice Crump 7/1/22
Alenka Dries. 7/1/22
Fabiola Hamdan 7/1/22
Joshua Hargrove 7/1/22
Shandowlyon Hendricks-Williams 7/1/22
Lisa Mortenson 7/1/22
Nia Trammell 7/1/22
Yee Leng Xiong. 7/1/22
Philomena Kebec 7/1/23

Aging and Long-Term Care, Board on[1]
Valerie A. Palarski . . . . .expires 5/1/21

Barbara Bechtel 5/1/22
Abigail Lowery 5/1/22
Tanya L. Meyer 5/1/22
Michael Brooks 5/1/23
James Surprise 5/1/23
Dale B. Taylor 5/1/25

Agriculture, Trade and Consumer Protection, Board of[1] (not to exceed $35/day nor $1,000/year[2])
Paul M. Bauer . . . . .expires 5/1/23
Andrew S. Diercks 5/1/23
Miranda Leis 5/1/23
Patty Edelburg 5/1/25
Daniel G. Smith. 5/1/25
Carla Washington 5/1/25
Clare Hintz[3] 5/1/27
Paul Palmby[3] 5/1/27
Doug Rebout[3] 5/1/27

Agriculture, Trade and Consumer Protection, Department of, secretary[1] (group 6 salary[2])
Randy J. Romanski[3] . expires at governor's pleasure

Alcohol and Other Drug Abuse, State Council on
Michael R. Knetzger . . . . .expires 7/1/21
Thai Vue 7/1/21
Mary Ann Gerrard 7/1/23
Sandy Hardie 7/1/23
Terry Schemenauer 7/1/23
Jessica Geschke. . . . expires at governor's pleasure
Christine A. Ullstrup . . . . governor's pleasure

Architects, Landscape Architects, Professional Engineers, Designers and Professional Land Surveyors, Examining Board of[1] ($25/day[2])
Michael J. Kinney . . . . .expires 7/1/12
Daniel Fedderly 7/1/13
Rosheen Styczinski 7/1/13
Steven Hook 7/1/14
Andrew Gersich 7/1/15
Kenneth D. Arneson. 7/1/18
Michael J. Heberling 7/1/19
Christina C. Martin. 7/1/19
Kristine Cotharn 7/1/21
Karl Linck 7/1/21
Dennis Myers 7/1/21
Steven Wagner 7/1/21
Gregory Douglas 7/1/23
Colleen M. Scholl. 7/1/23
Steven Tweed[3] 7/1/24
Nathan Vaughn[3] 7/1/24
9 vacancies . . . .

Artistic Endowment Foundation[1] (inactive)

Arts Board
Robert Wagner . . . . .expires 5/1/21
La'Ketta D. Caldwell 5/1/22
Karen A. Hoffman 5/1/22
Susan Lipp. 5/1/22
Kevin M. Miller 5/1/22

State officers appointed by the governor, May 15, 2021, continued

Mary K. Reinders 5/1/22
Lynn Richie 5/1/22
Jennifer Schwarzkopf 5/1/22
Matthew J. Wallock 5/1/22
Jayne Herring .5/1/23
John Johnson .5/1/23
Brian Kelsey 5/1/23
Leah Kolb 5/1/23
John H. Potter .5/1/24
Gerard Randall 5/1/24

Athletic Trainers Affiliated Credentialing Board[1]
($25/day[2])
Jay J. Davide . . . . .expires 7/1/18
Kurt Fielding .7/1/19
Gregory Vergamini 7/1/20
Jack J. Johnsen 7/1/21
Stephanie Atkins 7/1/23
Benjamin Wedro 7/1/23

Auctioneer Board[1] ($25/day[2])
Heather Berlinski . . . . .expires 5/1/16
Jerry Thiel 5/1/18
Stanley D. Jones 5/1/22
Deana M. Zentner 5/1/23
Bryce L. Hansen[3] 5/1/24
Randy J. Stockwell[3] 5/1/24
vacancy

Banking Institutions Review Board[1] ($25/day, not
to exceed $1,500/year[2])
Debra R. Lins . . . . expires 5/1/19
Thomas J. Pamperin 5/1/20
Thomas E. Spitz 5/1/22
Scot Thompson[3] 5/1/22
Robert C. Gorsuch 5/1/23

Bradley Center Sports and Entertainment
Corporation, Board of Directors of the[1] (inactive)

Building Commission
Summer Strand . . . . expires at governor's pleasure

Burial Sites Preservation Board ($25/day[2])
Jennifer R. Haas . . . . .expires 7/1/21
Katherine P. Stevenson 7/1/22
Corina Williams 7/1/22
David Grignon 7/1/23
Cynthia Stiles .7/1/23
Melinda Young 7/1/24

Cemetery Board[1] ($25/day[2])
Francis J. Groh . . . . .expires 7/1/20
John Reinemann 7/1/20
Bernard Schroedl 7/1/21
Patricia Grathen 7/1/22
Edward G. Porter III 7/1/23
Lloyd Shepherd 7/1/24

Child Abuse and Neglect Prevention Board
Molly J. Jasmer . . . . .expires 5/1/22
Jennifer Kleven 5/1/22
Michael McHorney 5/1/22
Michael Meulemans 5/1/22
Jennifer L. Noyes 5/1/22
Teri B. Zywicki 5/1/22

Paula J. Breese 5/1/23
Quincey Daniels, Jr. 5/1/23
William Olivier 5/1/23
Vicki M. Tylka .5/1/23
Jameelah A. Love . . . expires at governor's pleasure

Children and Families, Department of, Secretary[1]
(group 6 salary[2])
Emilie Amundson . . expires at governor's pleasure

Chiropractic Examining Board[1] ($25/day[2])
Scott D. Bautch . . . . .expires 7/1/21
Bryan R. Gerondale 7/1/21
Carl R. Kugler 7/1/21
James M. Damrow 7/1/23
Eugene Yellen-Shiring[3] 7/1/23
Kathleen A. Hendrickson[3] 7/1/24

Circus World Museum Foundation[1]
David Hoffman . . . expires at governor's pleasure

Claims Board
Ryan Nilsestuen . . . expires at governor's pleasure

College Savings Program Board[1]
Alberta Darling . . . . .expires 5/1/21
Kimberly Shaul 5/1/21
Susan M. Bauer 5/1/23
William L. Oemichen 5/1/23
Ashleigh Edgerson[3] 5/1/24
LaTonya Johnson[3] 5/1/25

Commercial Building Code Council
Kevin Bierce . . . . .expires 7/1/17
Irina Ragozin .7/1/17
Steven Howard 7/1/18
Brian J. Rinke 7/1/18
Jennifer Emberson Acker 7/1/22
Michael Adamavich 7/1/22
Steven Harms 7/1/22
William Hebert 7/1/22
Matthew Marciniak 7/1/22
Richard P. Paur 7/1/22

Controlled Substances Board
Subhadeep Barman . . . . .expires 5/1/19
Alan Bloom 5/1/20

Conveyance Safety Code Council
Steven L. Ketelboeter . . . . .expires 7/1/17
Ronald P. Mueller 7/1/17
Jennie L. Macaluso 7/1/18
Keith S. Misustin 7/1/18
Paul S. Rosenberg 7/1/19
Kenneth R. Smith 7/1/19
Harold A. Thurmer 7/1/19
vacancy

Corrections, Department of, Secretary[1] (group 8
salary[2])
Kevin A. Carr . . . . . expires at governor's pleasure

Cosmetology Examining Board[1] ($25/day[2])
Georgianna Halverson . . . . .expires 7/1/23
Ann Hoeppner 7/1/23
Megan Jackson 7/1/23

State officers appointed by the governor, May 15, 2021, continued

Kristin N. Lee 7/1/23
Daisy Quintal 7/1/23
Nickolas Raehsler[3] 7/1/23
Kayla Cwojdzinski 7/1/24
Charity Faith Fazel[3] 7/1/24
vacancy

Credit Union Review Board[1] ($25/day, not to
exceed $1,500 per year[2])
Sheila Schinke[3] . . . . .expires 5/1/21
Colleen Woggon 5/1/22
Lisa M. Greco 5/1/23
Sally Dischler[3] 5/1/25
Liza Edinger[3] 5/1/25

Credit Unions, Office of, Director (group 3 salary[2])
Kim Santos . . . . . . expires at governor's pleasure

Crime Victims Rights Board
Nela Kalpic . . . . .expires 5/1/23

Criminal Penalties, Joint Review Committee on
2 vacancies

Deaf and Hard of Hearing, Council for the
Nicole Everson . . . . expires 7/1/21
Christopher Rawlings 7/1/21
Katy M. Schmidt 7/1/21
David H. Seligman 7/1/21
Peggy J. Troller 7/1/21
Christine Koemeter 7/1/23
Thomas O'Connor 7/1/23
Gregory Puhlmann 7/1/23
Steven Smart 7/1/23

Deferred Compensation Board[1] ($25/day[2])
Jason A. Rothenberg . . . . expires 7/1/21
Arthur Zimmerman 7/1/21
Gail Hanson[3] 7/1/22
Terrance L. Craney 7/1/23
Connie Haberkorn[3] 7/1/24

Dentistry Examining Board[1] ($25/day[2])
Matthew R. Bistan . . . . expires 7/1/21
Leonardo Huck 7/1/21
Wendy M. Pietz 7/1/21
Lisa Bahr 7/1/22
Shaheda Govani 7/1/22
Herbert Michael Kaske 7/1/22
Katherine F. Schrubbe 7/1/22
Peter Sheild 7/1/22
Deb Kolste .7/1/24
Diana Whalen[3] 7/1/24
vacancy

Developmental Disabilities, Board for People with
($50/day[2])
Pam Malin . . . . expires 7/1/21
Hector H. Portillo 7/1/21
Gregory A. Meyer 7/1/22
Elsa Diaz Bautista 7/1/23
Gail M. Bovy 7/1/23
Kedibonye Carpenter 7/1/23
Pamela K. Delap 7/1/23
Patrick Friedrich 7/1/23
Desi Kluth .7/1/23

Ashley Mathy 7/1/23
Stephanie J. Mlodzik 7/1/23
Nathan E. Ruffolo 7/1/23
Andy Thain .7/1/23
Tricia Thompson 7/1/23
Christopher J. Wood. 7/1/23
Houa Yang. .7/1/23
George Zaske 7/1/23
Sydney Badeau 7/1/24
Cheryl Funmaker 7/1/24
King Hall 7/1/24
Shannon Mattox 7/1/24
Kelly Weyer .7/1/24

Dietitians Affiliated Credentialing Board[1] ($25/
day[2]) . . . .
David Joe . . . . .expires 7/1/18
Scott Krueger 7/1/19
Jill D. Hoyt .7/1/21
Tara LaRowe. 7/1/22

Distance Learning Authorization Board
Russell Swagger . . . . governor's pleasure

Domestic Abuse, Council on[1]
Melissa Baldauff[3] . . . . .expires 7/1/22
Kathy Flores .7/1/22
Susan M. Perry 7/1/22
Tammie Xiong 7/1/22
Nela Kalpic .7/1/23
Rosalind McClain 7/1/23
Justine Rufus 7/1/23
Susan Sippel 7/1/23
Alena A. Taylor 7/1/23

Dry Cleaner Environmental Response Council
(inactive)

**Economic Development Corp. Authority,
Wisconsin[1]**
John J. Brogan . . . . expires at governor's pleasure
Rebecca Cooke[3] . . . . governor's pleasure
Joe Kirgues . . . . governor's pleasure
Eugenia Podestá Losada . . . . . governor's pleasure
Henry Newell[3] . . . . governor's pleasure
Thelma Sias . . . . governor's pleasure

**Economic Development Corporation Authority,
Wisconsin, Chief Executive Officer[1]**
Melissa L. Hughes[3] .expires at governor's pleasure[4]

Education Commission of the States
John Reinemann . . . expires at governor's pleasure
Amy Traynor . . . . governor's pleasure
vacancy

Educational Communications Board[1]
Tara Grace Ann Senter . . . . .expires 5/1/21
Alyssa Kenney[3] 5/1/23
Rolf Wegenke 5/1/23
Leah R. Lechleiter-Luke 5/1/24
Eileen Littig . . . . . . expires at governor's pleasure

Elections Commission[1] ($115/day[2])
Marge R. Bostelmann . . . . .expires 5/1/24
Julie M. Glancey[3] 5/1/26

State officers appointed by the governor, May 15, 2021, continued

Electronic Recording Council
Margo C. Katterhagen . . . . .expires 7/1/21
Katharine Marlin 7/1/22
Sharon A. Martin 7/1/22
Sally Spanel 7/1/22
Natalie A. Strohmeyer 7/1/22
John F. Wilcox 7/1/22
Trista Mayer 7/1/23

Emergency Management Division, Administrator of[1] (group 3 salary[2])
Darrell L. Williams . . expires at governor's pleasure

Emergency Medical Services Board
Laura Albert . . . . .expires 5/1/22
Timothy A. Bantes 5/1/22
Steven Zils 5/1/22
Amanda Bates 5/1/23
Jerry R. Biggart 5/1/23
Justin Pluess .5/1/23
Dustin E. Ridings 5/1/23
Gregory Neal West 5/1/23
Michael Clark 5/1/24
Christopher M. Eberlein 5/1/24
Brian Litza 5/1/24

Employee Trust Funds Board[1] ($25/day[2])
Stephen Arnold . . . . .expires 5/1/23
Katy Lounsbury . . . expires at governor's pleasure

Employment Relations Commission[1] (group 5 salary[2])
James Daley . . . . .expires 3/1/23

Ethics Commission[1] ($115/day[2])
Timothy M. Van Akkeren . . . . .expires 5/1/24
David J. Wambach[3] 5/1/26

Federal-State Relations Office, Director (group 3 salary[2])
vacancy

Financial Institutions, Department of, Secretary[1] (group 6 salary[2])
Kathy Blumenfeld . . expires at governor's pleasure

Forestry, Council on
Thomas Hittle . . . . .expires 1/1/21
Heather Berklund . . expires at governor's pleasure
Janet Bewley . . . . governor's pleasure
Michael H. Bolton . . . . governor's pleasure
Matt Dallman . . . . governor's pleasure
James Hoppe . . . . governor's pleasure
Buddy Huffaker . . . . governor's pleasure
James R. Kerkman . . . . governor's pleasure
Rebekah Luedtke . . . . governor's pleasure
Beth Meyers . . . . governor's pleasure
Jeffrey Mursau . . . . governor's pleasure
Kenneth Price . . . . governor's pleasure
Adena Rissman . . . . governor's pleasure
Henry Schienebeck . . . . governor's pleasure
Jason Sjostrom . . . . governor's pleasure
Jordan Skiff . . . . governor's pleasure
Paul Strong . . . . governor's pleasure
William Van Lopik . . . . governor's pleasure
2 vacancies

Fox River Navigational System Authority[1]
Tim Short . . . . .expires 7/1/21
Ronald Van De Hey 7/1/21
Kathryn A. Curren 7/1/22
John L. Vette .7/1/22
H. Bruce Enke 7/1/23
Jeffery Feldt .7/1/23

Funeral Directors Examining Board[1] ($25/day[2])
Eric Lengell . . . . .expires 7/1/16
Marla Michaelis 7/1/21
Marc A. Eernisse 7/1/22
Dawn Adams 7/1/23
Joseph B. Schinkten 7/1/23
vacancy

Geologists, Hydrologists and Soil Scientists, Examining Board of Professional[1] ($25/day[2])
Brenda Halminiak . . . . .expires 7/1/12
Randall Hunt 7/1/12
Kenneth Bradbury 7/1/13
William Mode 7/1/13
Stephanie Williams 7/1/17
Ann Hirekatur[3] 7/1/24
Trevor Nobile[3] 7/1/24
5 vacancies

Great Lakes Commission
Todd Ambs . . . . .expires 7/1/23
Melonee Montano 7/1/24
Noah Roberts . . . . . expires at governor's pleasure

Great Lakes Protection Fund[1]
Kevin L. Shafer . . . . .expires 1/12/16
Kim Marotta . . two-year term, at governor's pleasure thereafter

Groundwater Coordinating Council
Steve Diercks . . . . .expires 7/1/17

Group Insurance Board ($25/day[2])
Herschel Day . . . . .expires 5/1/21
Harper Donahue, IV 5/1/21
Dan B. Fields 5/1/21
Walter E. Jackson 5/1/21
Nancy L. Thompson 5/1/21
Katy Lounsbury . . . expires at governor's pleasure
vacancy

Health and Educational Facilities Authority, Wisconsin[1]
Billie Jo Higgins . . . . .expires 7/1/21
Pamela Stanick 7/1/22
James K. Oppermann 7/1/23
Renee E. Anderson 7/1/24
Tim K. Size 7/1/25
James Allen Dietsche 7/1/26
Robert Van Meeteren[3] 7/1/27

Health Care Liability Insurance Plan/Injured Patients and Families Compensation Fund Board of Governors ($50/day[2])
Carla Borda . . . . .expires 5/1/21
Jeffery Bingham 5/1/22
Greg Schroeder 5/1/23
vacancy

State officers appointed by the governor, May 15, 2021, continued

Health Services, Department of, Secretary[1] (group 8 salary[2])
Karen E. Timberlake[3] expires at governor's pleasure

Hearing and Speech Examining Board[1] ($25/day[2])
Steven Klapperich . . . . .expires 7/1/19
Robert R. Broeckert 7/1/20
Barbara Johnson 7/1/21
Thomas J. Krier 7/1/21
Michael Harris 7/1/23
Kathleen A. Pazak 7/1/23
David H. Seligman 7/1/23
Catherine Denison Kanter[3] 7/1/24
2 vacancies

Higher Educational Aids Board
Stephen D. Willett . . . . .expires 5/1/18
Amy L. Christen 5/1/22
Angela Haney 5/1/22
Justin Wesolek 5/1/23
Jeff Cichon 5/1/23
Brady Coulthard 5/1/23
Nathaniel Helm-Quest 5/1/23
Jeff Neubauer 5/1/23
Timothy Opgenorth 5/1/23
Kyle M. Weatherly 5/1/23

Higher Educational Aids Board, Executive Secretary (group 3 salary[2])
Connie L. Hutchison. expires at governor's pleasure

Highway Safety, Council on
J.D. Lind . . . . expires 7/1/18
Richard G. Van Boxtel 7/1/18
Joseph C. Gonnering 7/1/19
John P. Mesich 7/1/19
Yash Wadhwa 7/1/19
Brian Dean 7/1/20
Robert D. Hinds 7/1/20
Donald Gutkowski 7/1/21
William Neitzel 7/1/21
Kurt Schultz 7/1/21

Historic Preservation Review Board
Paul Wolter . . . . .expires 7/1/18
Sissel Schroeder 7/1/21
Sergio M. González 7/1/22
Carol Johnson 7/1/22
Kevin Pomeroy 7/1/22
Neil Prendergast 7/1/22
Ray Reser 7/1/22
Matthew G. Sadowski 7/1/22
Amy L. Scanlon 7/1/22
Melinda J. Young 7/1/22
Carlen I. Hatala 7/1/23
Daniel J. Joyce 7/1/23
Valentine Schute, Jr. 7/1/23
Daniel J. Stephans 7/1/23
Donna Zimmerman 7/1/23

Housing and Economic Development Authority, Wisconsin[1]
Raynetta R. Hill . . . . .expires 1/1/22
Victoria Parmentier 1/1/22
Ivan Gamboa 1/1/23

Diane House[3] 1/1/23
Jeffrey L. Skrenes 1/1/24
Ranell G. Washington[3] 1/1/24

Housing and Economic Development Authority, Wisconsin, Executive Director[1] (group 6 salary[2])
Joaquín J. Altoro[3] . . . . .expires 1/3/23

Insurance, Commissioner of[1] (group 6 salary[2])
Mark V. Afable . . . . expires at governor's pleasure

Interoperability Council
Steven Hansen . . . . .expires 5/1/13
Matthew Joski 5/1/15
James D. Formea 5/1/19
Kirk A. Gunderson 5/1/21
Sean Marschke 5/1/21
Michael J. Woodzicka 5/1/23
Kyle Mirehouse 5/1/24
3 vacancies

Interstate Juvenile Supervision, State Board for
T. Christopher Dee . . . . .expires 7/1/19
4 vacancies

Invasive Species Council
Thomas Bressner . . . . .expires 7/1/22
Gregory Long 7/1/22
Mark Renz 7/1/23
Douglas Cox 7/1/24
Jennifer A. Hauxwell 7/1/24
Hannah Spaul 7/1/24
Thomas Buechel 7/1/25

Investment and Local Impact Fund Board
Edward Brandis . . . . .expires 5/1/15
Kelly Klein 5/1/15
David Pajula 5/1/15
Robert Walesewicz 5/1/16
Leslie Kolesar 5/1/18
Emmer Shields, Jr. 5/1/18
Rick J. Hermus 5/1/20
2 vacancies

Investment Board, State of Wisconsin[1] ($50/day[2])
Esther Ancel . . . . .expires 5/1/21
Mark Doll 5/1/21
Barbara Nick 5/1/21
Kristi Palmer .5/1/23
Timothy R. Sheehy 5/1/23
David Stein 5/1/23

Judicial Commission[1] ($25/day[2])
Mark Barrette . . . . .expires 8/1/14
Eileen Burnett 8/1/14
William Cullinan 8/1/14
Steven C. Miller 8/1/17
Yulonda M. Anderson 8/1/22

Judicial Council
Dennis Myers . . . . .expires 7/1/18
Benjamin J. Pliskie 7/1/19
Christian Gossett . . expires at governor's pleasure

Kickapoo Reserve Management Board[1] ($25/day[2])
Adlai Mann . . . . .expires 5/1/13

State officers appointed by the governor, May 15, 2021, continued

Paul Hayes. 5/1/21
Reggie Nelson 5/1/21
Tina Brown. 5/1/22
Susan C. Cushing. 5/1/22
Travis M. Downing. 5/1/22
David M. Maxwell 5/1/22
Julie Van Aman Hoel. 5/1/22
Scott Lind .5/1/23
William L. Quackenbush 5/1/23
Richard T. Wallin 5/1/23

Labor and Industry Review Commission[1] (group 5 salary[2])
Georgia E. Maxwell . . . . .expires 3/1/23
Michael Gillick[3]. 3/1/25
Marilyn Townsend[3] 3/1/27

Labor and Industry Review Commission, general counsel
Anita Krasno. . . . . . expires at governor's pleasure

Laboratory of Hygiene Board
Robert Corliss. . . . . .expires 5/1/22
Barry E. Irmen. 5/1/22
James Morrison. 5/1/22
German Gonzalez 5/1/23
Gina Green-Harris 5/1/23
Jeffery A. Kindrai 5/1/23
vacancy

Lake Michigan Commercial Fishing Board
Charles W. Henriksen expires at governor's pleasure
Richard R. Johnson . . . . governor's pleasure
Michael Le Clair . . . . governor's pleasure
Mark Maricque . . . . governor's pleasure
Dan Pawlitzke . . . . governor's pleasure
Brett Schwarz . . . . governor's pleasure
Todd Stuth . . . . governor's pleasure

Lake States Wood Utilization Consortium (inactive)

Lake Superior Commercial Fishing Board
William Bodin . . . . expires at governor's pleasure
Maurine Halvorson . . . . governor's pleasure
Craig Hoopman . . . . governor's pleasure
Robert J. Nelson . . . . governor's pleasure
vacancy

Land and Water Conservation Board[1] ($25/day[2])
Eric D. Birschbach . . . . .expires 5/1/21
Andrew J. Buttles. 5/1/23
Ronald Grasshoff. 5/1/23
Bobbie Webster 5/1/23
Mark E. Cupp 5/1/24

Law Enforcement Standards Board
Jessie Metoyer . . . . .expires 5/1/22
Scott R. Parks 5/1/22
Katie Rosenberg 5/1/23
Benjamin Bliven 5/1/23
James Small 5/1/23
Charles A. Tubbs, Sr. 5/1/23
Todd Delain 5/1/24
Jean Galasinski 5/1/24

Timothy J. Gruenke 5/1/25
Earnell R. Lucas. 5/1/25
Nicole R. Miller 5/1/25

Library and Network Development, Council on
Bryan McCormick . . . . .expires 7/1/21
Dennis Myers 7/1/21
Joan Robb .7/1/21
Amy Bahena-Ettner 7/1/22
Jaime Healy-Plotkin 7/1/22
Svetha S. Hetzler 7/1/22
Joshua L. Klingbeil. 7/1/22
Ellen Kupfer 7/1/22
Anna Lewis 7/1/22
Jennifer Stoltz. 7/1/22
Martha A. Van Pelt 7/1/22
Kristi A. Williams 7/1/22
Terrence Berres 7/1/23
Nick Dimassis 7/1/23
Miriam M. Erickson 7/1/23
Joan Schneider 7/1/23
Charmaine Sprengelmeyer-Podein 7/1/23
Cigdem Unal 7/1/23
vacancy

Lower Fox River Remediation Authority[1] (inactive)

Lower Wisconsin State Riverway Board[1] ($25/day[2])
Ritchie Brown. . . . . .expires 5/1/17
Richard McFarlane 5/1/21
Gerald Dorscheid 5/1/22
Randall H. Poelma 5/1/22
Steve Wetter 5/1/22
Steve A. Williamson 5/1/22
James Czajkowski 5/1/23
Gretchen F.G. LaBudde 5/1/23
vacancy

Marriage and Family Therapy, Professional Counseling, and Social Work, Examining Board of[1] ($25/day[2])
Bridget Ellingboe . . . . .expires 7/1/20
Elizabeth A. Krueger 7/1/20
Tammy H. Scheidegger. 7/1/20
Kathleen M. Miller 7/1/21
Nancy Unzueta Saiz[3] 7/1/23
Cynthia Adell 7/1/23
Cynthia Brown 7/1/23
Candace E. Coates 7/1/23
Andrea L. Simon 7/1/23
Lisa Yee. 7/1/23
Lindsey E. Marsh[3] 7/1/24
Abike Sanyaolu[3] 7/1/24
vacancy

Massage Therapy and Bodywork Therapy Affiliated Credentialing Board[1] ($25/day[2])
Robert Coleman, Jr. . . . . .expires 7/1/23
Jaime Ehmer 7/1/23
Carla Hedtke 7/1/23
Jeff A. Miller 7/1/23
Charisma Townsend. 7/1/23
Ramona J. Trudeau 7/1/23
Gregory J. Quandt 7/1/23

State officers appointed by the governor, May 15, 2021, continued

Medical College of Wisconsin, Incorporated, Board of Trustees of the[1]
Ted Kellner. . . . . expires 6/30/21
Jon Hammes 6/30/23

Medical Education Review Committee (inactive)

Medical Examining Board[1] ($25/day[2])
David Anthony Bryce . . . . .expires 7/1/21
Padmaja Doniparthi. 7/1/21
David Roelke .7/1/21
Milton Bond, Jr. 7/1/23
Clarence Chou 7/1/23
Sumeet Goel 7/1/23
Michael Parish[3]. 7/1/23
Sheldon A. Wasserman 7/1/23
Diane Gerlach[3] 7/1/24
Carmen Lerma[3]. 7/1/24
Rachel E. Sattler[3]. 7/1/24
Lemuel G. Yerby III[3] 7/1/24
Emily Yu[3]. .7/1/24

Mental Health, Council on
Richard Immler . . . . .expires 7/1/18
Holly Audley 7/1/20
Tracey Hassinger 7/1/20
Lea D. Collins-Worachek 7/1/21
Dennis Hanson. 7/1/21
Carol Keen .7/1/21
Jerolynn Bell-Scaggs 7/1/22
Rebecca Collins. 7/1/22
Kimberlee M. Coronado 7/1/22
Inshirah Farhoud. 7/1/22
Lynn A. Harrigan. 7/1/22
Crystal A. Hester 7/1/22
Kevin Kallas 7/1/22
Radha K. Karthik 7/1/22
Dawn Shelton-Williams. 7/1/22
Sheryl L. Smith 7/1/22
May Yer Thao 7/1/22
Peter Thao .7/1/22
Kristin Welch 7/1/22
Ana Winton 7/1/22

Midwest Interstate Low-Level Radioactive Waste Commission, Wisconsin Commissioner[1] ($25/day[2])
Paul Schmidt[3]. . . . . expires at governor's pleasure

Midwest Interstate Passenger Rail Commission
Scott Rogers. . . . . .expires 1/2/23
Arun Rao . . . . expires at governor's pleasure

Midwestern Higher Education Commission
Connie L. Hutchison. . . . . .expires 7/1/21
Rolf Wegenke 7/1/23
Julie Underwood. . . expires at governor's pleasure

Migrant Labor, Council on
Kate Lambert . . . . .expires 7/1/22
Lupe G. Martinez 7/1/22
Jeanine M. McCain. 7/1/22
Guadalupe Rendon 7/1/22
Erica L. Sweitzer-Beckman 7/1/22
John I. Bauknecht 7/1/23
Aimee Jo Castleberry 7/1/23

Erica A. Kunze 7/1/23
Jose Martinez. 7/1/23
Nancy Quezada 7/1/23
Laura Waldvogel. 7/1/23
vacancy

Military and State Relations, Council on
Linda Fournier . . . . expires at governor's pleasure
vacancy

Milwaukee Child Welfare Partnership Council
Michele M. Bria. . . . . .expires 7/1/21
Victor E. Barnett 7/1/22
Bria Grant .7/1/22
Christine Holmes. 7/1/22
Willie Johnson, Jr. 7/1/22
Patti R. Logsdon 7/1/22
Jameelah A. Love. 7/1/22
Mark Mertens. 7/1/22
Mallory O'Brien 7/1/22
Carmen M. Pitre 7/1/22
Anthony E. Shields 7/1/22
Sequanna Taylor 7/1/22
vacancy

Mississippi River Parkway Commission
Jill Billings . . . . .expires 2/1/24
Dennis Donath 2/1/24
Jean Galasinski 2/1/24
Howard Marklein 2/1/24
Lee Nerison .2/1/24
Loren Oldenburg 2/1/24
Sherry Quamme 2/1/24
John J. Rosenow 2/1/24
Rosalie Schnick. 2/1/24
Jeff Smith 2/1/24
Kathleen Sweeney. 2/1/24
Thomas Vondrum 2/1/24

National and Community Service Board
Laura M. Doolin . . . . .expires 5/1/20
Paula Horning 5/1/21
Angela Ahlgrim. 5/1/22
Christine Beatty 5/1/22
Anthony F. Hallman 5/1/22
Kate Jaeger .5/1/22
Ibrahim Jalloh 5/1/22
Leah R. Lechleiter-Luke. 5/1/22
Benjamin P. Lehner 5/1/22
Margaret Jane Moore. 5/1/22
Susan Schwartz. 5/1/22
Yolanda D. Shelton-Morris 5/1/22
Patricia Takamine 5/1/22
Theresa Clark 5/1/23
Adam Riley .5/1/24

Natural Resources, Department of, Secretary[1]
(group 7 salary[2])
Preston D. Cole . . . . expires at governor's pleasure

Natural Resources Board[1]
William Bruins . . . . .expires 5/1/23
Terry N. Hilgenberg 5/1/23
Gregory J. Kazmierski. 5/1/23

State officers appointed by the governor, May 15, 2021, continued

William H. Smith 5/1/25
Marcy West 5/1/25
Sharon Adams[3]. 5/1/27
Sandra Dee Naas[3] 5/1/27

Nonmotorized Recreation and Transportation Trails Council
Michael Arrowood. . expires at governor's pleasure
Rod Bartlow . . . . governor's pleasure
William Hauda . . . . governor's pleasure
William Johnson . . . . governor's pleasure
Anne Murphy . . . . governor's pleasure
Joel Patenaude . . . . governor's pleasure
William Pennoyer . . . . governor's pleasure
David Phillips . . . . governor's pleasure
Ben Popp . . . . governor's pleasure
Geoffrey Snudden . . . . governor's pleasure
Blake Theisen . . . . governor's pleasure

Nursing, Board of [1] ($25/day[2])
Jennifer L. Eklof. . . . . .expires 7/1/21
Luann Skarlupka. 7/1/21
Rosemary P. Dolatowski 7/1/22
Peter Kallio 7/1/22
Christian Saldivar Frias[3] 7/1/23
Lisa Pisney. 7/1/23
Robert Weinman. 7/1/23
Emily Zentz 7/1/23
Janice Ann Edelstein[3] 7/1/24

Nursing Home Administrator Examining Board[1] ($25/day[2])
Susan Kinast-Porter . . . . .expires 7/1/09
Bryan Bee .7/1/23
Lizzy Kaiser[3]. 7/1/23
David L. Larson[3] 7/1/23
Patrick Shaughnessy[3]. 7/1/23
Diane Lynch-Decombhs[3] 7/1/24
3 vacancies

Occupational Therapists Affiliated Credentialing Board[1] ($25/day[2])
Amy Summers . . . . .expires 7/1/18
Laura O'Brien 7/1/19
Teresa L. Black. 7/1/23
Terry Erickson. 7/1/23
Randi Hanson. 7/1/23
2 vacancies

Off-Highway Motorcycle Council
Mitch Winder . . . . .expires 3/1/22
Craig A. Johnson. 3/1/24
Bryan T. Much. 3/1/24
Robert B. McConnell 3/1/24
Phillip Smage. 3/1/24

Off-Road Vehicle Council
Adam Harden . . . . expires 3/1/21
Rob McConnell 3/1/21
Michael Biese. 3/1/22
Robert A. Donahue 3/1/22
Daniel Thole. 3/1/22
David Traczyk 3/1/23
James Wisneski 3/1/23

Offender Reentry, Council on
Michael R. Knetzger. . . . . .expires 7/1/18
Robert P. Koebele 7/1/19
Angela M. Mancuso 7/1/19
Jonathon W. Nejedlo 7/1/19
Antwayne M. Robertson 7/1/19
Mary B. Davies 7/1/21
Jon Padgham 7/1/21
Eric Boulanger 7/1/22
Angela Eggers 7/1/22
Awais Khaleel 7/1/22

Optometry Examining Board[1] ($25/day[2])
Mark Jinkins. . . . . .expires 7/1/16
Robert C. Schulz 7/1/20
John L. Sterling 7/1/21
Jeffrey J. Clark. 7/1/23
Lisa Slaby .7/1/23
Peter I. Sorce 7/1/23
Emmylou Wilson. 7/1/23

Parole Commission, Chairperson[1] (group 2 salary[2])
John Tate II[3] . . . . .expires 3/1/23

Perfusionists Examining Council ($25/day[2])
David F. Cobb . . . . .expires 7/1/13
Jeffery P. Edwards 7/1/14
Shawn E. Mergen 7/1/14
Gary Tsarovsky 7/1/16
vacancy

Pharmacy Examining Board[1] ($25/day[2])
Philip J. Trapskin . . . . .expires 7/1/21
Cathy Winters. 7/1/21
John Weitekamp 7/1/22
Tony D. Peterangelo 7/1/23
Shana Weiss 7/1/23
Tiffany O'Hagan[3] 7/1/24
Michael Walsh 7/1/24

Physical Disabilities, Council on
Gabriel M. Schlieve . . . . .expires 7/1/18
Roberto Escamilla II 7/1/21
Benjamin Barrett 7/1/22
Jeff Fox 7/1/22
Jackie Gordon. 7/1/22
Nicole Herda 7/1/22
Kathleen A. Johnson 7/1/22
Karen E. Secor. 7/1/22
Artrell M. Mason 7/1/23
Jason S. Ostrowski 7/1/23
Charles H. Vandenplas 7/1/23
Noah Roberts. . . . . . expires at governor's pleasure
2 vacancies

Physical Therapy Examining Board[1] ($25/day[2])
Shari Berry. . . . . .expires 7/1/20
Barbara A. Carter. 7/1/21
Todd McEldowney. 7/1/21
Kathryn R. Zalewski 7/1/21
John F. Greany 7/1/23

Physician Assistants, Council on
vacancy

State officers appointed by the governor, May 15, 2021, continued

Podiatry Affiliated Credentialing Board[1] ($25/day[2])
Kerry Connelly . . . . .expires 7/1/22
Jack W. Hutter. 7/1/23
Randal Kittleson 7/1/23
Robert M. Sage. 7/1/24

Prison Industries Board[1]
David Hagemeier . . . . .expires 5/1/23
James M. Langdon[3] 5/1/23
Lenard Simpson 5/1/23
Alacia Smith 5/1/23
Aaron Zimmerman 5/1/23
Tracey Griffith. 5/1/24
James Meyer 5/1/24
Todd Spencer 5/1/24
vacancy

Psychology Examining Board[1] ($25/day[2])
Daniel Schroeder . . . . .expires 7/1/19
Peter I. Sorce 7/1/20
Marcus P. Desmonde 7/1/21
Mark A. Jinkins 7/1/22
David Thompson. 7/1/22
John N. Greene 7/1/23

Public Defender Board[1]
James Brennan . . . . .expires 5/1/22
Anthony B. Cooper, Sr.[3] 5/1/22
Regina Dunkin 5/1/22
Ellen Thorn 5/1/22
Mai N. Xiong 5/1/22
Patrick Fiedler[3] 5/1/23
John J. Hogan. 5/1/23
Ingrid Jagers 5/1/23
Joseph T. Miotke 5/1/23

Public Health Council
Ann H. Hoffman . . . . .expires 7/1/16
William Keeton 7/1/16
Terry Brandenburg 7/1/17
Mary Dorn 7/1/17
Gary D. Gilmore 7/1/17
Alan Schwartzstein 7/1/17
Dale Hippensteel 7/1/18
Eric Krawczyk. 7/1/18
Robert Leischow 7/1/18
Joan Theurer 7/1/18
Tatiana Maida. 7/1/22
Paula P. Morgen 7/1/22
Catoya M. Roberts 7/1/22
Laura Rose. 7/1/22
Darlene M. Weis 7/1/22
8 vacancies

Public Leadership Board[1]
Scott R. Jensen . . . . .expires 5/1/23
Kimberly Liedl 5/1/23
Dean Stensberg 5/1/23
Jason Thompson. 5/1/23
Robin J. Vos 5/1/23

Public Records Board
James A. Friedman. . expires at governor's pleasure

Staci M. Hoffman. . . . . governor's pleasure
Julie A. Laundrie . . . . governor's pleasure
vacancy

Public Service Commission[1] (group 5 salary[2])
Ellen Nowak. . . . . .expires 3/1/23
Rebecca Cameron Valcq 3/1/25
Tyler Huebner[3] 3/1/27

Radiography Examining Board[1] ($25/day[2])
Heidi Nichols . . . . .expires 7/1/20
Donald Borst 7/1/21
Paul J. Grebe 7/1/23
Rachael Julson[3] 7/1/24
Timothy Peter Szczykutowicz[3] 7/1/24
2 vacancies

Railroads, Commissioner of[1] (group 5 salary[2])
Yash Wadhwa . . . . .expires 3/1/23

Real Estate Appraisers Board[1] ($25/day[2])
Jennifer M. Espinoza-Coates . . . . .expires 5/1/19
Carl Clementi 5/1/20
Dennis Myers 5/1/21
Thomas Kneesel 5/1/22
David J. Wagner[3] 5/1/22
2 vacancies

Real Estate Curriculum and Examinations, Council on
Kathryne Kuhl . . . . .expires 7/1/15
Robert G. Blakely 7/1/20
Kathy S. Zimmermann 7/1/20
Elizabeth Anne Lauer. 7/1/22
Anne M. Blood 7/1/23
2 vacancies

Real Estate Examining Board[1] ($25/day[2])
Dennis Pierce . . . . .expires 7/1/13
Robert R. Larson 7/1/21
Elizabeth Anne Lauer. 7/1/22
Cathy Lacy[3] 7/1/21
Thomas J. Richie 7/1/22
Sonya Mays[3] 7/1/24
vacancy

Recycling, Council on
Mark A. Walter . . . . .expires 1/5/23
Barb Worcester 1/5/23
Carsten Jarrod Holter 1/5/24
David F. Keeling 1/5/24
David Pellitteri 1/5/24
Heidi Woelfel 1/5/24
Jeff Zillich 1/5/24

Remote Notary Council
Cheri Hipenbecker. . . . . .expires 5/1/23
Mark Ladd. 5/1/23
Jessica J. Shrestha 5/1/23
Philip Suckow. 5/1/23

Respiratory Care Practitioners Examining Council[1] ($25/day[2])
vacancy

State officers appointed by the governor, May 15, 2021, continued

Retirement Board, Wisconsin ($25/day[2])
Wayne E. Koessl . . . . .expires 5/1/09
Herbert Stinski .5/1/12
Mary Von Ruden 5/1/13
Julie Wathke .5/1/18
John David 5/1/23
Steven Wilding 5/1/24
2 vacancies

Retirement Systems, Joint Survey Committee on
vacancy

Revenue, Department of, Secretary[1] (group 7 salary[2])
Peter W. Barca . . . . . expires at governor's pleasure

Rural Health Development Council[1]
Hendrik Lai . . . . .expires 7/1/24
Rian Podein 7/1/24
Nicole Schweitzer[3] 7/1/25
14 vacancies

Safety and Professional Services, Department of, Secretary[1] (group 6 salary[2])
Dawn B. Crim[3] . . . . expires at governor's pleasure

Small Business Environmental Council
Jody A. Jansen . . . . .expires 7/1/19
Amy Litscher .7/1/20
vacancy

Small Business Regulatory Review Board
Peggy Gunderson . . . . .expires 5/1/22
Brian Cummins 5/1/23
Hana Cutler .5/1/23
Mickey Judkins 5/1/23
Elizabeth Krause 5/1/23
Alycann Taylor 5/1/23
Ruth Zahm 5/1/23

Snowmobile Recreational Council[1]
Thomas Chwala . . . . .expires 7/1/21
Joel Enking .7/1/21
Dale Mayo 7/1/21
Lee Van Zeeland 7/1/21
Beverly A. Dittmar 7/1/22
Abigail Haas .7/1/22
Michael F. Holden 7/1/22
Erica Keehn .7/1/22
Don Mrotek .7/1/22
Sue Smedegard 7/1/22
Gary Hilgendorf[3] 7/1/23
Samuel J. Landes[3] 7/1/23
Robert B. Lang[3] 7/1/23
Andrew F. Malecki[3] 7/1/23
Leon Wolfe[3] .7/1/23

Southeast Wisconsin Professional Baseball Park District Board[1]
Anthony Berndt . . . . .expires 7/1/21
Troy A. Dennhof 7/1/21
Donald A. Smiley 7/1/21
Frank J. Busalacchi 7/1/23
Deb C. Dassow 7/1/23
John T. Zapfel 7/1/23

Sporting Heritage Council
Reggie Hayes . . . . .expires 7/1/22

State Capitol and Executive Residence Board
Kathryn Neitzel . . . . .expires 5/1/23
Marijo Reed .5/1/23
Rafeeq Asad .5/1/26
Lesley Sager .5/1/26
Ronald L. Siggelkow 5/1/26
Jay Fernholz .5/1/27
Arlan K. Kay .5/1/27

State Employees Suggestion Board
Paul Ruby . . . . .expires 5/1/17
2 vacancies

State Fair Park Board[1] ($10/day, not to exceed $600/year[2])
Becky Merwin . . . . .expires 5/1/22
Susan Crane .5/1/23
Dan Devine .5/1/24
Paul M. Ziehler 5/1/24
Kelly H. Grebe 5/1/25
John Yingling .5/1/25
Jayme L. Buttke[3] 5/1/26

State Historical Society of Wisconsin Board of Curators[1]
Cate Zeuske . . . . .expires 7/1/21
Sherman Banker 7/1/22
Keene Winters 7/1/23

State Trails Council
Roy Atkinson . . . . .expires 7/1/21
Bryan T. Much 7/1/21
Kendal Neitzke 7/1/21
Ben L. Popp .7/1/21
John Siegert .7/1/21
James White .7/1/21
Steve Falter .7/1/23
Randy Harden 7/1/24
Kristin Jewett .7/1/24
Luana Schneider 7/1/24
Holly Tomlanovich 7/1/24

State Use Board
Bill Smith . . . . expires 5/1/11
Jean L. Zweifel 5/1/19
Amy C. Grotzke 5/1/21
Jana Steinmetz 5/1/21
Nickolas C. George 5/1/23
3 vacancies

Tax Appeals Commission[1] (group 4 salary[2])
Lorna Hemp Boll . . . . .expires 3/1/23
Elizabeth Kessler 3/1/25
Jessica Roulette[3] 3/1/27

Tax Exemptions, Joint Survey Committee on
Elizabeth Kessler . . . . .expires 1/15/23

Teachers Retirement Board ($25/day[2])
David Schalow . . . . .expires 5/1/24
3 vacancies

State officers appointed by the governor, May 15, 2021, continued

Technical College System Board[1] ($100/year[2])
Megan E. Bahr[3] . . . . .expires 5/1/23
Quincey Daniels, Jr.[3]. 5/1/23
Rodney Pasch. 5/1/23
Stephen D. Willett 5/1/23
Douglas A. Holton, Sr. 5/1/25
Terrance McGowan 5/1/25
Mark Tyler 5/1/25
R. Paul Buhr[3] 5/1/27
Sara J. Rogers[3] 5/1/27
Eric G. Williams[3] 5/1/27

Tourism, Council on
Deborah T. Archer . . . . .expires 7/1/21
Robert Davis 7/1/21
Kathy Kopp 7/1/21
Mary McPhetridge. 7/1/21
Darren S. Bush 7/1/22
Genyne Edwards. 7/1/22
Arlan Frels 7/1/22
Michelle Martin 7/1/22
Ben L. Popp 7/1/22
Krystal Westfahl 7/1/22
Deborah Carey 7/1/23
Nathan Gordon. 7/1/23
Missy Tracy 7/1/23
Luke Zahm 7/1/23

Tourism, Department of, Secretary[1] (group 6
salary[2])
vacancy

Transportation, Department of, Secretary[1] (group
7 salary[2])
Craig M. Thompson[3]   expires at governor's pleasure

Transportation Projects Commission
Allison Bussler . . . . expires at governor's pleasure
Timothy M. Hanna . . . . governor's pleasure
Mark Servi . . . . governor's pleasure

Uniform Dwelling Code Council
Daniel E. Wald. . . . . .expires 7/1/19
Abe Degnan. 7/1/20
W. Scott Satula 7/1/20
Mark Etrheim 7/1/21
Brian Wert 7/1/21
Donald Brunner 7/1/22
Brian Juarez. 7/1/22
Joseph Lotegeluaki 7/1/22
Dawn McIntosh 7/1/22
Virge Temme 7/1/22
Edmund Weaver, Jr. 7/1/22

Uniform State Laws, Commission on
Vladlen David Zvenyach . . . . .expires 5/1/21
Fred Risser. 5/1/23

**University of Wisconsin Hospitals and Clinics
Authority[1]**
John W. Litscher . . . . .expires 7/1/21
Pablo Sanchez 7/1/22
Karen Menéndez Coller 7/1/24
Annette Miller 7/1/24

Candice Owley[3] 7/1/25
Paul Seidenstricker[3]. 7/1/25

**University of Wisconsin System, Board of Regents
of the[1]**
Michael M. Grebe . . . . .expires 5/1/22
Andrew Petersen 5/1/22
Corey Saffold[3] 5/1/22
Scott C. Beightol 5/1/23
Tracey Klein 5/1/23
Brianna Tucker[3] 5/1/23
Robert B. Atwell 5/1/24
Michael T. Jones 5/1/24
Héctor Colón[3] 5/1/25
Cris Peterson 5/1/25
Edmund Manydeeds III. 5/1/26
Karen Walsh. 5/1/26
Amy Blumenfeld Bogost[3] 5/1/27
Kyle M. Weatherly[3]. 5/1/27
John W. Miller[3] 5/1/28
Ashok Rai[3] 5/1/28

Veterans Affairs, Board of[1]
Tonnetta D. Carter[3] . . . . .expires 5/1/23
Curtis L. Schmitt, Jr.[3] 5/1/23
William R. Schrum 5/1/23
Chris J. Cornelius[3] 5/1/25
Mark Grams[3] 5/1/25
Christopher Hanson[3] 5/1/25
Vern L. Larson[3] 5/1/25
Jason Maloney[3]. 5/1/25
Mark Mathwig[3]. 5/1/25

Veterans Affairs, Department of, Secretary[1] (group
6 salary[2])
Mary M. Kolar. . . . . expires at governor's pleasure

Veterinary Diagnostic Laboratory Board
Sandra C. Madland . . . . .expires 5/1/20
Laurence Baumann 5/1/22
Robert Steiner 5/1/22
Rory Meyer 5/1/23
Rebecca Suchla. 5/1/24
Paul Kunde . . . . . . expires at governor's pleasure

Veterinary Examining Board[1] ($25/day[2])
Robert Forbes . . . . .expires 7/1/21
Hunter Lang. 7/1/23
Diane Dommer Martin 7/1/23
Lisa Weisensel Nesson 7/1/23
Lyn M. Schuh 7/1/23
Arden M. Sherpe 7/1/24
Alan Holter 7/1/24
Amanda Reese 7/1/24

Waste Facility Siting Board[1] ($35/day[2])
James Schuerman . . . . expires 5/1/2013
Jeanette P. DeKeyser 5/1/18
Dale R. Shaver 5/1/20

Waterways Commission, Wisconsin[1]
Ralph C. Brzezinski. . . . . .expires 3/1/21
Roger E. Walsh 3/1/23
Bruce J. Neeb[3] 3/1/24

State officers appointed by the governor, May 15, 2021, continued

Janeau Allman .3/1/25
Korin Doering[3] 3/1/25

Wetland Study Council
Thomas Larson . . . . expires 7/1/21
Carol McCoy. 7/1/21
Paul Kent. 7/1/22
Karen Gefvert. .7/1/23
Tracy Hames. 7/1/24
Matthew Howard 7/1/25
Tim Andryk 7/1/26
Stacy Jepson 7/1/26

Wisconsin Compensation Rating Bureau
Daniel Burazin . . . . expires at governor's pleasure
Chris Reader . . . . governor's pleasure

Women's Council
Lisa L. Armaganian . . . . .expires 7/1/21
Denise Gaumer Hutchison. 7/1/21
Chantia A. Lewis 7/1/21
Rosalyn L. McFarland 7/1/21
Nerissa Nelson .7/1/21
Ze Xiong Yang .7/1/21
Patricia M. Cadorin 7/1/23

**Workforce Development, Department of,
Secretary[1] (group 7 salary[2])**
Amy Pechacek[3] . . . . expires at governor's pleasure

Note: List includes only appointments made by the governor. Additional members frequently serve ex officio or are appointed by other means. The governor also appoints members of intrastate regional agencies and nonstatutory committees and makes temporary appointments under chapter 17, Wis. Stats., to elected state and county offices when vacancies occur.

Terms are specified by the following statute sections or as otherwise provided by law: s. 15.05 (1)—secretaries; s. 15.06 (1)—commissioners; s. 15.07 (1)—governing boards and attached boards; s. 15.08 (1)—examining boards and councils; s. 15.09 (1)—councils.

1. Nominated by the governor and appointed with the advice and consent of the senate. Senate confirmation is required for secretaries of departments, members of commissions and commissioners, governing boards, examining boards, and other boards as designated by statute. 2. Members of boards and councils are reimbursed for actual and necessary expenses incurred in performing their duties. In addition, examining board members receive $25 per day for days worked, and members of certain other boards under section 15.07 (5), Wis. Stats., receive a per diem as noted in the table. Section 20.923, Wis. Stats., places state officials in one of 10 executive salary groups (ESG) for which salary ranges have been established. Group salary ranges for the period January 6, 2019, through June 19, 2021, are: Group 1: $62,858–$107,952; Group 2: $67,850–$116,605; Group 3: $73,299–$125,923; Group 4: $79,165–$136,011; Group 5: $85,467–$146,931; Group 6: $92,331–$158,704; Group 7: $99,715–$171,413; Group 8: $107,682–$185,141; Group 9: $116,293–$199,950; Group 10: $125,611–$215,987. 3. Nominated by governor but not yet confirmed by senate. 4. Compensation set by Economic Development Corporation Board.

Source: Appointment lists maintained by governor's office and received by the Legislative Reference Bureau on or before May 15, 2021.

Circuit court judges, April 6, 2021

Counties in circuit	Branch	Court location	Judges	Term expires July 31
Adams	—	Friendship	Daniel Glen Wood[1]	2021
Ashland.	—	Ashland	Kelly J. McKnight	2024
Barron.	1	Barron	James C. Babler	2022
	2	Barron	J. Michael Bitney	2026
	3	Barron	Maureen D. Boyle.	2026
Bayfield.	—	Washburn	John P. Anderson[1]	2021
Brown.	1	Green Bay	Donald R. Zuidmulder[1]	2021
	2	Green Bay	Thomas J. Walsh	2024
	3	Green Bay	Tammy Jo Hock	2025
	4	Green Bay	Kendall M. Kelley[1]	2021
	5	Green Bay	Marc A. Hammer[1].	2021
	6	Green Bay	John P. Zakowski	2024
	7	Green Bay	Timothy A. Hinkfuss	2025
	8	Green Bay	Beau G. Liegeois	2026
Buffalo, Pepin	—	Alma	Thomas W. Clark	2024
Burnett	—	Siren	Melissia R. Mogen	2023
Calumet[3]	—	Chilton	Jeffrey S. Froehlich	2024
Chippewa	1	Chippewa Falls	Steven H. Gibbs	2024
	2	Chippewa Falls	James M. Isaacson[1].	2021
	3	Chippewa Falls	Benjamin J. Lane	2026

Circuit court judges, April 6, 2021, continued

Counties in circuit	Branch	Court location	Judges	Term expires July 31
Clark.	—	Neillsville	Lyndsey Boon Brunette	2024
Columbia.	1	Portage	Todd J. Hepler[1]	2021
	2	Portage	W. Andrew Voigt	2023
	3	Portage	Troy D. Cross.	2024
Crawford	—	Prairie du Chien	Lynn Marie Rider	2022
Dane	1	Madison	Susan M. Crawford	2024
	2	Madison	Josann M. Reynolds[1]	2021
	3	Madison	Valerie L. Bailey-Rihn.	2022
	4	Madison	Everett Mitchell	2022
	5	Madison	Nicholas J. McNamara	2022
	6	Madison	Nia Trammell[1, 2]	2021
	7	Madison	Mario D. White[1, 2]	2021
	8	Madison	Frank D. Remington	2024
	9	Madison	Jacob B. Frost[1, 2]	2021
	10	Madison	Juan B. Colas[1]	2021
	11	Madison	Ellen K. Berz	2024
	12	Madison	Chris Taylor[1, 2]	2021
	13	Madison	Julie Genovese[1]	2021
	14	Madison	John D. Hyland	2022
	15	Madison	Stephen Ehlke.	2022
	16	Madison	Rhonda L. Lanford	2025
	17	Madison	David Conway[1, 2]	2021
Dodge	1	Juneau	Brian A. Pfitzinger	2026
	2	Juneau	Martin J. De Vries	2023
	3	Juneau	Joseph G. Sciascia	2025
	4	Juneau	Kristine A. Snow	2026
Door.	1	Sturgeon Bay	D. Todd Ehlers	2024
	2	Sturgeon Bay	David L. Weber	2023
Douglas.	1	Superior	Kelly J. Thimm[1]	2021
	2	Superior	George L. Glonek[1]	2021
Dunn[3].	1	Menomonie	James M. Peterson	2026
	2	Menomonie	Rod W. Smeltzer[4]	2021
Eau Claire.	1	Eau Claire	John F. Manydeeds.	2022
	2	Eau Claire	Michael A. Schumacher	2026
	3	Eau Claire	Emily M. Long	2024
	4	Eau Claire	Jon M. Theisen	2024
	5	Eau Claire	Sarah Harless	2024
Florence, Forest. . . .	—	Crandon	Leon D. Stenz	2026
Fond du Lac	1	Fond du Lac	Dale L. English	2026
	2	Fond du Lac	Peter L. Grimm	2022
	3	Fond du Lac	Richard J. Nuss[5]	2021
	4	Fond du Lac	Tricia L. Walker[2]	2022
	5	Fond du Lac	Paul G. Czisny[2]	2023
Grant	1	Lancaster	Robert P. Van De Hey.	2023
	2	Lancaster	Craig R. Day[1].	2021
Green	1	Monroe	James R. Beer[6].	2021
	2	Monroe	Thomas J. Vale[1]	2021
Green Lake.	—	Green Lake	Mark Slate	2023
Iowa.	—	Dodgeville	Margaret M. Koehler.	2022
Iron	—	Hurley	Anthony J. Stella, Jr.	2026
Jackson[3]	—	Black River Falls	Anna L. Becker[1]	2021
Jefferson	1	Jefferson	William V. Gruber.	2025
	2	Jefferson	William F. Hue	2025
	3	Jefferson	Robert F. Dehring, Jr..	2024
	4	Jefferson	Bennett J. Brantmeier	2023
Juneau	1	Mauston	Stacy A. Smith.	2024
	2	Mauston	Paul S. Curran	2026
Kenosha	1	Kenosha	Larisa Benitez-Morgan[2, 7]	2021
	2	Kenosha	Jason A. Rossell	2024

Circuit court judges, April 6, 2021, continued

Counties in circuit	Branch	Court location	Judges	Term expires July 31
	3	Kenosha	Bruce E. Schroeder	2026
	4	Kenosha	Anthony J. Milisauskas	2023
	5	Kenosha	David P. Wilk[1]	2021
	6	Kenosha	Mary K. Wagner[8]	2021
	7	Kenosha	Jodi L. Meier	2023
	8	Kenosha	Chad G. Kerkman[1]	2021
Kewaunee	—	Kewaunee	Keith A. Mehn	2022
La Crosse	1	La Crosse	Ramona A. Gonzalez	2025
	2	La Crosse	Elliott Levine	2025
	3	La Crosse	Todd Bjerke	2025
	4	La Crosse	Scott L. Horne	2025
	5	La Crosse	Gloria L. Doyle[1]	2021
Lafayette	—	Darlington	Duane M. Jorgenson[1]	2021
Langlade	—	Antigo	John B. Rhode[1]	2021
Lincoln	1	Merrill	Jay R. Tlusty	2022
	2	Merrill	Robert R. Russell	2025
Manitowoc	1	Manitowoc	Mark R. Rohrer	2025
	2	Manitowoc	Jerilyn M. Dietz	2024
	3	Manitowoc	Robert P. Dewane	2023
Marathon[3]	1	Wausau	Suzanne C. O'Neill[1, 2]	2021
	2	Wausau	Gregory B. Huber	2022
	3	Wausau	Lamont K. Jacobson	2026
	4	Wausau	Gregory J. Strasser	2023
	5	Wausau	Michael K. Moran	2023
Marinette	1	Marinette	Jane M. Sequin	2026
	2	Marinette	James A. Morrison	2025
Marquette	—	Montello	Chad A. Hendee	2025
Menominee, Shawano	1	Shawano	Katherine Sloma[1, 2]	2021
	2	Shawano	William F. Kussel, Jr.	2024
Milwaukee	1	Milwaukee	Jack L. Dávila[1, 2]	2021
	2	Milwaukee	Milton L. Childs	2026
	3	Milwaukee	Clare L. Fiorenza[9]	2021
	4	Milwaukee	Michael J. Hanrahan	2023
	5	Wauwatosa	Brett R. Blomme	2026
	6	Wauwatosa	Ellen R. Brostrom[1]	2021
	7	Milwaukee	Thomas J. McAdams	2026
	8	Milwaukee	William Sosnay	2024
	9	Milwaukee	Paul R. Van Grunsven	2023
	10	Milwaukee	Michelle A. Havas	2023
	11	Milwaukee	David C. Swanson	2025
	12	Milwaukee	David L. Borowski[1]	2021
	13	Milwaukee	Mary Triggiano	2023
	14	Milwaukee	Christopher R. Foley	2022
	15	Milwaukee	Jonathan D. Watts[1]	2021
	16	Wauwatosa	Brittany C. Grayson	2026
	17	Milwaukee	Carolina Maria Stark	2024
	18	Milwaukee	Pedro Colón	2023
	19	Milwaukee	Kori L. Ashley[1, 2]	2021
	20	Milwaukee	Joseph R. Wall	2024
	21	Milwaukee	Cynthia M. Davis	2023
	22	Milwaukee	Timothy M. Witkowiak[1]	2021
	23	Milwaukee	Lindsey C. Grady	2024
	24	Milwaukee	Janet C. Protasiewicz	2026
	25	Milwaukee	Stephanie G. Rothstein	2022
	26	Milwaukee	William S. Pocan	2025
	27	Milwaukee	Kevin E. Martens	2026
	28	Milwaukee	Mark A. Sanders	2024
	29	Milwaukee	Rebecca A. Kiefer	2026
	30	Milwaukee	Jonathan D. Richards[1, 2]	2021

Circuit court judges, April 6, 2021, continued

Counties in circuit	Branch	Court location	Judges	Term expires July 31
	31	Milwaukee	Hannah C. Dugan	2022
	32	Milwaukee	Laura Gramling Perez	2026
	33	Milwaukee	Carl Ashley	2023
	34	Milwaukee	Glenn H. Yamahiro	2022
	35	Milwaukee	Frederick C. Rosa	2023
	36	Wauwatosa	Laura A. Crivello	2025
	37	Milwaukee	T. Christopher Dee[1]	2021
	38	Milwaukee	Jeffrey A. Wagner	2024
	39	Milwaukee	Jane V. Carroll	2024
	40	Milwaukee	Danielle L. Shelton	2025
	41	Wauwatosa	Audrey K. Skwierawski	2025
	42	Wauwatosa	Reyna Morales[1,2]	2021
	43	Wauwatosa	Marshall B. Murray	2024
	44	Wauwatosa	Gwendolyn G. Connolly	2022
	45	Milwaukee	Jean M. Kies	2022
	46	Milwaukee	David A. Feiss[1]	2021
	47	Wauwatosa	Kristy Yang	2023
Monroe	1	Sparta	Todd L. Ziegler	2025
	2	Sparta	Mark L. Goodman	2022
	3	Sparta	Rick Radcliffe	2024
Oconto	1	Oconto	Michael T. Judge	2023
	2	Oconto	Jay N. Conley	2022
Oneida	1	Rhinelander	Patrick F. O'Melia	2026
	2	Rhinelander	Michael H. Bloom	2024
Outagamie	1	Appleton	Mark J. McGinnis	2023
	2	Appleton	Emily I. Lonergan	2026
	3	Appleton	Mitchell J. Metropulos	2026
	4	Appleton	Gregory B. Gill, Jr.	2024
	5	Appleton	Carrie A. Schneider	2024
	6	Appleton	Vincent Biskupic[1]	2021
	7	Appleton	Mark G. Schroeder[2]	2022
Ozaukee	1	Port Washington	Paul V. Malloy[1]	2021
	2	Port Washington	Steven M. Cain	2025
	3	Port Washington	Sandy A. Williams[1]	2021
Pierce	—	Ellsworth	Elizabeth Rohl[2]	2022
Polk	1	Balsam Lake	Daniel J. Tolan	2023
	2	Balsam Lake	Jeffrey L. Anderson	2023
Portage	1	Stevens Point	Thomas B. Eagon	2024
	2	Stevens Point	Robert J. Shannon	2022
	3	Stevens Point	Patricia Baker[2]	2022
Price	—	Phillips	Kevin G. Klein	2024
Racine	1	Racine	Wynne Laufenberg	2024
	2	Racine	Eugene A. Gasiorkiewicz	2022
	3	Racine	Maureen Martinez	2025
	4	Racine	Mark F. Nielsen	2022
	5	Racine	Kristin M. Cafferty[2]	2022
	6	Racine	David W. Paulson[1]	2021
	7	Racine	Jon E. Fredrickson	2025
	8	Racine	Faye M. Flancher[1]	2021
	9	Racine	Robert S. Repischak	2024
	10	Racine	Timothy D. Boyle	2024
Richland	—	Richland Center	Andrew Sharp	2024
Rock	1	Janesville	Karl R. Hanson	2025
	2	Janesville	Derrick A. Grubb	2025
	3	Janesville	Jeffrey S. Kuglitsch	2024
	4	Janesville	Daniel T. Dillon	2025
	5	Janesville	Michael A. Haakenson[1]	2021
	6	Janesville	John M. Wood	2023
	7	Janesville	Barbara W. McCrory	2024

Circuit court judges, April 6, 2021, continued

Counties in circuit	Branch	Court location	Judges	Term expires July 31
Rusk.	—	Ladysmith	Steven P. Anderson	2022
St. Croix.	1	Hudson	Scott J. Nordstrand.	2026
	2	Hudson	Edward F. Vlack III.	2025
	3	Hudson	Scott R. Needham	2024
	4	Hudson	R. Michael Waterman	2022
Sauk.	1	Baraboo	Michael P. Screnock	2022
	2	Baraboo	Wendy J. N. Klicko	2022
	3	Baraboo	Patricia A. Barrett	2024
Sawyer	—	Hayward	John M. Yackel[1]	2021
Sheboygan.	1	Sheboygan	L. Edward Stengel[10]	2021
	2	Sheboygan	Kent Hoffmann	2023
	3	Sheboygan	Angela Sutkiewicz	2023
	4	Sheboygan	Rebecca L. Persick[1]	2021
	5	Sheboygan	Daniel J. Borowski	2023
Taylor	—	Medford	Ann Knox-Bauer[1, 2]	2021
Trempealeau	—	Whitehall	Rian W. Radtke	2023
Vernon	—	Viroqua	Darcy J. Rood	2023
Vilas	—	Eagle River	Neal A. Nielsen	2022
Walworth.	1	Elkhorn	Phillip A. Koss	2024
	2	Elkhorn	Daniel S. Johnson.	2022
	3	Elkhorn	Kristine E. Drettwan[1]	2021
	4	Elkhorn	David M. Reddy	2022
Washburn	—	Shell Lake	Angeline E. Winton	2026
Washington	1	West Bend	James G. Pouros	2023
	2	West Bend	James K. Muehlbauer	2026
	3	West Bend	Todd K. Martens	2023
	4	West Bend	Sandra J. Giernoth[1, 2]	2021
Waukesha	1	Waukesha	Michael O. Bohren	2025
	2	Waukesha	Jennifer Dorow	2024
	3	Waukesha	Ralph M. Ramirez	2023
	4	Waukesha	Lloyd V. Carter	2023
	5	Waukesha	J. Arthur Melvin, III	2026
	6	Waukesha	Brad D. Schimel	2025
	7	Waukesha	Maria S. Lazar[1]	2021
	8	Waukesha	Michael P. Maxwell[1]	2021
	9	Waukesha	Michael J. Aprahamian[1]	2021
	10	Waukesha	Paul Bugenhagen, Jr.[1]	2021
	11	Waukesha	William Domina	2023
	12	Waukesha	Laura Lau	2024
Waupaca	1	Waupaca	Troy L. Nielsen.	2023
	2	Waupaca	Vicki L. Clussman	2026
	3	Waupaca	Raymond S. Huber	2024
Waushara.	—	Wautoma	Guy D. Dutcher	2023
Winnebago	1	Oshkosh	Teresa S. Basiliere.	2024
	2	Oshkosh	Scott C. Woldt	2023
	3	Oshkosh	Barbara Hart Key	2022
	4	Oshkosh	LaKeisha D. Haase[2]	2022
	5	Oshkosh	John A. Jorgensen	2022
	6	Oshkosh	Daniel J. Bissett	2023
Wood	1	Wisconsin Rapids	Gregory J. Potter	2026
	2	Wisconsin Rapids	Nicholas J. Brazeau, Jr.	2024
	3	Wisconsin Rapids	Todd P. Wolf[1].	2021

— Means the circuit has only one branch.

1. Reelected on April 6, 2021, for a six-year term to commence on August 1, 2021.   2. Appointed by the governor.   3. Under 2019 Act 184, four counties selected by the director of state courts may add new circuit court branches effective August 1, 2021. Judges were elected on April 6, 2021, for six-year terms to commence on August 1, 2021. Carey John Reed was elected to serve as Calumet County Circuit Court Judge Branch 2; Luke M. Wagner was elected to serve as Dunn County Circuit Court Judge Branch 3; Daniel Diehn was elected to serve as Jackson County Circuit Court Judge Branch 2; and Scott M. Corbett was elected to serve as Marathon County Circuit Court Judge Branch 6.   4. Christina Mayer was newly elected on April 6, 2021, for a

six-year term to commence on August 1, 2021.   5. Andrew J. Christenson was newly elected on April 6, 2021, for a six-year term to commence on August 1, 2021.   6. Faun Marie Phillipson was newly elected on April 6, 2021, for a six-year term to commence on August 1, 2021.   7. Gerad Dougvillo was newly elected on April 6, 2021, for a six-year term to commence on August 1, 2021.   8. Angelina Gabriele was newly elected on April 6, 2021, for a six-year term to commence on August 1, 2021.   9. Katie Kegel was newly elected on April 6, 2021, for a six-year term to commence on August 1, 2021.   10. Samantha Bastil was newly elected on April 6, 2021, for a six-year term to commence on August 1, 2021.

Sources: 2019–2020 Wisconsin Statutes; Wisconsin Elections Commission, department data, April 2021; governor's appointment notices; Wisconsin Court System, Circuit court judges and court websites, April 2021.

Wisconsin county officers: county clerks, April 2021

	Clerk	Website
Adams	Cheryl Kroening (R)	www.co.adams.wi.us
Ashland	Heather Schutte (D)	www.co.ashland.wi.us
Barron	DeeAnn Cook (R)	www.barroncountywi.gov
Bayfield	Lynn Divine (D)	www.bayfieldcounty.org
Brown	Patrick W. Moynihan, Jr. (R)	www.co.brown.wi.us
Buffalo	Roxann Halverson (D)	www.buffalocounty.com
Burnett	Wanda Hinrichs (D)	www.burnettcounty.com
Calumet	Beth Hauser (R)	www.co.calumet.wi.us
Chippewa	Jaclyn Sadler (D)	www.co.chippewa.wi.us
Clark	Christina Jensen (R)	www.clarkcounty.wi.gov
Columbia	Susan Moll (R)	www.co.columbia.wi.us
Crawford	Roberta Fisher (D)	www.crawfordcountywi.org
Dane	Scott McDonell (D)	www.countyofdane.com
Dodge	Karen Gibson (R)	www.co.dodge.wi.gov
Door	Jill Lau (R)	www.co.door.wi.gov
Douglas	Susan Sandvick (D)	www.douglascountywi.org
Dunn	Vacant	www.co.dunn.wi.us
Eau Claire	Sue McDonald (D)	www.co.eau-claire.wi.us
Florence	Donna Trudell (R)	www.florencecountywi.com
Fond du Lac	Lisa Freiberg (R)	www.fdlco.wi.gov
Forest	Nora Matuszewski (R)	www.co.forest.wi.gov
Grant	Tonya White (R)	www.co.grant.wi.gov
Green	Arianna L. Voegeli (D)	www.co.green.wi.gov
Green Lake	Elizabeth Otto (R)	www.co.green-lake.wi.us
Iowa	Kristy Spurley (D)	www.iowacounty.org
Iron	Michael Saari (D)	www.co.iron.wi.gov
Jackson	Cindy M. Altman (D)	www.co.jackson.wi.us
Jefferson	Audrey McGraw (R)	www.jeffersoncountywi.gov
Juneau	Terri Treptow (R)	www.co.juneau.wi.gov
Kenosha	Regi Bachochin (D)	www.co.kenosha.wi.us
Kewaunee	Jamie Annoye (D)	www.kewauneeco.org
La Crosse	Ginny Dankmeyer (D)	www.lacrossecounty.org
Lafayette	Carla Jacobson (R)	www.lafayettecountywi.org
Langlade	Judy Nagel (R)	www.co.langlade.wi.us
Lincoln	Christopher Marlowe (R)	www.co.lincoln.wi.us
Manitowoc	Jessica Backus (R)	www.co.manitowoc.wi.us
Marathon	Kim Trueblood (R)	www.co.marathon.wi.us
Marinette	Kathy Brandt (R)	www.marinettecounty.com
Marquette	Kiley Lloyd (R)	www.co.marquette.wi.us
Menominee	Laure Pecore (D)	www.co.menominee.wi.us
Milwaukee	George L. Christenson (D)	https://county.milwaukee.gov
Monroe	Shelley Bohl (R)	www.co.monroe.wi.us
Oconto	Kim Pytleski (R)	www.co.oconto.wi.us
Oneida	Tracy Hartman (R)	www.co.oneida.wi.us
Outagamie	Jeff King (R)	www.outagamie.org
Ozaukee	Julianne B. Winkelhorst (R)	www.co.ozaukee.wi.us
Pepin	Audrey Bauer (R)	www.co.pepin.wi.us
Pierce	Jamie Feuerhelm (I)	www.co.pierce.wi.us
Polk	Lisa Ross (R)	www.co.polk.wi.us

Wisconsin county officers: county clerks, April 2021, continued

	Clerk	Website
Portage	Kayla R. Filen (D)	www.co.portage.wi.us
Price	Jean Gottwald (D)	www.co.price.wi.us
Racine	Wendy Christensen (R)	https://racinecounty.com
Richland	Victor V. Vlasak (R)	www.co.richland.wi.us
Rock	Lisa Tollefson (D)	www.co.rock.wi.us
Rusk	Connie Meyer (R)	www.ruskcounty.org
St. Croix	Cindy Campbell (D)	www.sccwi.gov
Sauk	Rebecca Evert (R)	www.co.sauk.wi.us
Sawyer	Lynn Fitch (R)	www.sawyercountygov.org
Shawano	Pamela Schmidt (R)	www.co.shawano.wi.us
Sheboygan	Jon Dolson (R)	www.sheboygancounty.com
Taylor	Andria Farrand (R)	www.co.taylor.wi.us
Trempealeau	Paul L. Syverson (D)	https://co.trempealeau.wi.us
Vernon	Jody Audetat (R)	www.vernoncounty.org
Vilas	David R. Alleman (R)	www.vilascountywi.gov
Walworth	Kimberly Bushey (R)	www.co.walworth.wi.us
Washburn	Lolita Olson (R)	www.co.washburn.wi.us
Washington	Ashley Reichert (R)	www.co.washington.wi.us
Waukesha	Meg Wartman (R)	www.waukeshacounty.gov
Waupaca	Jill Lodewegen (R)	www.co.waupaca.wi.us
Waushara	Megan Kapp (R)	www.co.waushara.wi.us
Winnebago	Susan Ertmer (R)	www.co.winnebago.wi.us
Wood	Trent Miner (R)	www.co.wood.wi.us

Note: County clerks are elected at the general election for four-year terms.

D–Democrat; I–Independent; R–Republican.

Source: Data collected from county clerks by Wisconsin Legislative Reference Bureau, April 2021.

Wisconsin county officers: county board chair; executive (or alternative); treasurer, April 2021

	County board chair (# of supervisors)	Executive, administrator, administrative coordinator	Treasurer
Adams	John West (20)	Jim Bialecki (interim AC)	Jani Zander (D)
Ashland	Richard Pufall (21)	Clark Schroeder (CA)	Tracey Hoglund (D)
Barron	Louie Okey (29)	Jeff French (CA)	Yvonne Ritchie (R)
Bayfield	Dennis M. Pocernich (13)	Mark Abeles-Allison (CA)	Jenna Galligan (D)
Brown	Patrick J. Buckley (26)	Troy Streckenbach (CE)	Paul Zeller (R)
Buffalo	Dennis Bork (14)	Sonya Hansen (AC)	Tina Anibas (R)
Burnett	Donald Taylor (21)	Nathan Ehalt (CA)	Judith Dykstra (R)
Calumet	Alice Connors (21)	Todd Romenesko (CA)	Mike Schlaak (R)
Chippewa	Dean Gullickson (15)	Randy Scholz (CA)	Patricia Schimmel (D)
Clark	Wayne Hendrickson (29)	Christina Jensen (AC)	Renee Schoen (R)
Columbia	Vern Gove (28)	Susan Moll (AC)	Stacy L. Opalewski (R)
Crawford	Tom Cornford (17)	Dan McWilliams (AC)	Deanne Lutz (D)
Dane	Analiese Eicher (37)	Joe Parisi (CE)	Adam Gallagher (D)
Dodge	Russell Kottke (33)	Jim Mielke (CA)	Patti Hilker (R)
Door	David Lienau (21)	Ken Pabich (CA)	Ryan Schley (R)
Douglas	Mark Liebaert (21)	Ann Doucette (CA)	Carol Jones (D)
Dunn	David Bartlett (29)	Paul R. Miller (CM)	Vacant
Eau Claire	Nick Smiar (29)	Kathryn Schauf (CA)	Glenda J. Lyons (D)
Florence	Jeanette Bomberg (12)	Donna Trudell (AC)	Donna Liebergen (R)
Fond du Lac	Martin F. Farrell (25)	Allen J. Buechel (CE)	Brenda A. Schneider (R)
Forest	Cindy Gretzinger (21)	Nora Matuszewski (AC)	Christy Conley (R)
Grant	Robert C. Keeney (17)	Shane Drinkwater (AC)	Carrie Eastlick (R)

Wisconsin county officers: county board chair; executive (or alternative); treasurer, April 2021, continued

	County board chair (# of supervisors)	Executive, administrator, administrative coordinator	Treasurer
Green	Arthur F. Carter (31)	Arianna L. Voegeli (AC)	Sherri Hawkins (R)
Green Lake	Harley Reabe (19)	Catherine Schmit (CA)	Amanda R. Toney (R)
Iowa	John M. Meyers (21)	Larry Bierke (CA)	Connie Johnson (D)
Iron	Joe Pinardi (15)	Michael Saari (AC)	Clara Maki (D)
Jackson	Ray Ransom (19)	Cindy M. Altman (AC)	Tabitha Chonka-Michaud (D)
Jefferson	Steven J. Nass (30)	Ben Wehmeier (CA)	John E. Jensen (R)
Juneau	Alan K. Peterson (21)	None	Denise Giebel (R)
Kenosha	John J. O'Day (23)	Jim Kreuser (CE)	Teri Jacobson (D)
Kewaunee	Daniel A. Olson (20)	Scott Feldt (CA)	Michelle Dax (R)
La Crosse	Monica Kruse (29)	Steve O'Malley (CA)	Amy Twitchell (D)
Lafayette	Jack Sauer (16)	Jack Sauer (AC)	Lisa Black (R)
Langlade	Ben Pierce (21)	Jason Hilger (CM)	Tammy Wilhelm (D)
Lincoln	Kevin Koth (22)	Cate Wylie (AC)	Diana Petruzates (R)
Manitowoc	Jim Brey (25)	Bob Ziegelbauer (CE)	Amy Kocian (R)
Marathon	Kurt Gibbs (38)	Lance Leonhard (CA)	Connie Beyersdorff (R)
Marinette	John M. Guarisco (30)	John Lefebvre (CA)	Bev A. Noffke (R)
Marquette	Robert C. Miller (17)	Gary Sorensen (AC)	Jody Myers (R)
Menominee	Elizabeth Moses (7)	Jeremy Weso (AC)	Mary Beth Pecore (D)
Milwaukee	Marcelia Nicholson (18)	David Crowley (CE)	David Cullen (D)
Monroe	Cedric Schnitzler (16)	Tina Osterberg (CA)	Debra Carney (R)
Oconto	Paul Bednarik (31)	Kevin Hamann (CA)	Tanya Peterson (R)
Oneida	David Hintz (21)	Lisa Charbarneau (AC)	Tara Ostermann (R)
Outagamie	Jeff Nooyen (36)	Tom Nelson (CE)	Trenten Woelfel (R)
Ozaukee	Lee Schlenvogt (26)	Jason Dzwinel (CA)	Joshua H. Morrison (R)
Pepin	Tom Milliren (12)	Pamela Hansen (AC)	Patricia Scharr (R)
Pierce	Jeff Holst (17)	Jason Matthys (AC)	Kathy Fuchs (R)
Polk	Chris Nelson (15)	Vince Netherland (CA)	Amanda Nissen (D)
Portage	Allen Haga, Jr. (25)	Chris Holman (CE)	Pamela R. Przybelski (D)
Price	Robert Kopisch (13)	Nicholas Trimner (CA)	Lynn Neeck (D)
Racine	Thomas Roanhouse (21)	Jonathan Delagrave (CE)	Jeff Latus (R)
Richland	Marty Brewer (21)	Clinton Langreck (CA)	Julie Keller (R)
Rock	Richard Bostwick (29)	Joshua Smith (CA)	Michelle Roettger (D)
Rusk	David Willingham (19)	Andy Albarado (AC)	Verna Nielsen (R)
St. Croix	David Peterson (19)	Ken Witt (CA)	Denise Anderson (R)
Sauk	Tim McCumber (31)	Brent Miller (AC)	Elizabeth Geoghegan (R)
Sawyer	Tweed Shuman (15)	Thomas Hoff (CA)	Dianne Ince (R)
Shawano	Thomas Kautza (27)	James Davel (AC)	Debra Wallace (R)
Sheboygan	Vern Koch (25)	Adam Payne (CA)	Laura Henning-Lorenz (D)
Taylor	Jim Metz (17)	Marie Koerner (AC)	Sarah Holtz (R)
Trempealeau	John Aasen (17)	Paul L. Syverson (AC)	Laurie Halama (D)
Vernon	Justin Running (29)	Cari Redington (CA)	Karen DeLap (R)
Vilas	Ronald De Bruyne (21)	David R. Alleman (AC)	Paulette Sarnicki (R)
Walworth	Nancy Russell (11)	Mark W. Luberda (CA)	Valerie Etzel (R)
Washburn	Thomas Mackie (21)	Lolita Olson (AC)	Nicole Tims (R)
Washington	Donald Kriefall (26)	Joshua Schoemann (CE)	Scott M. Henke (R)
Waukesha	Paul Decker (25)	Paul Farrow (CE)	Pamela Reeves (R)
Waupaca	Dick Koeppen (27)	Amanda Welch (AC)	Mark Sether (R)
Waushara	Donna Kalata (11)	Vacant	Jessica Jaeger (R)
Winnebago	Shiloh Ramos (36)	Jon Doemel (CE)	Mary Krueger (R)
Wood	Lance A. Pliml (19)	Lance A. Pliml (AC)	Heather Gehrt (D)

Note: The county board is composed of supervisors who are elected at the nonpartisan spring election for two-year terms. The county board elects one of its members to be its chair. County executives are elected at the nonpartisan spring election for four-year terms. In lieu of electing a county executive, a county can choose to appoint a county administrator or to designate a county official to serve as the county's administrative coordinator. Treasurers are elected at the general election for four-year terms.

AC–Administrative coordinator; CA–County administrator; CE–County executive; CM–County manager; D–Democrat; R–Republican.

Source: Data collected from county clerks by Wisconsin Legislative Reference Bureau, April 2021.

Wisconsin county officers: clerk of circuit court; register of deeds; surveyor, April 2021

	Clerk of circuit court	Register of deeds	Surveyor[1]
Adams	Lori L. Banovec (D)	Jodi Helgeson (R)	Jerol Smart
Ashland	Sandra Paitl (D)	Julie Gleeson (D)	Patrick McKuen
Barron	Sharon Millermon (R)	Margo Katterhagen (R)	Mark Netterlund
Bayfield	Kay L. Cederberg (D)	Dan Heffner (D)	Patrick McKuen
Brown	John A. Vander Leest (R)	Cheryl Berken (R)	Ryan Duckart
Buffalo	Roselle Schlosser (R)	Carol Burmeister (D)	Auth Consulting
Burnett	Jacqueline O. Baasch (D)	Jeanine Chell (D)	Jason Towne
Calumet	Connie Daun (R)	Tamara Alten (R)	Bradley Buechel
Chippewa	Karen Hepfler (D)	Melanie K. McManus (D)	Sam Wenz
Clark	Heather Bravener (D)	Mary Denk (R)	Wade Pettit
Columbia	Susan Raimer (R)	Lisa Krintz (R)	Jim Grothman
Crawford	Nancy Dowling (A)	Melissa Nagel (D)	Rich Marks
Dane	Carlo Esqueda (D)	Kristi Chlebowski (D)	Dan Frick
Dodge	Lynn Hron (R)	Chris Planasch (R)	Dave Addison
Door	Connie DeFere (R)	Carey Petersilka (R)	None
Douglas	Michele L. Wick (D)	Tracy Middleton (D)	Matt Johnson
Dunn	Katie Schalley (R)	Heather Kuhn (D)	Thomas Carlson
Eau Claire	Susan Schaffer (D)	Tina Pommier (D)	Dean Roth
Florence	Tanya Neuens (R)	Laurie J. Boren (R)	None
Fond du Lac	Ramona Geib (R)	James M. Krebs (R)	Peter Kuen
Forest	Penny Carter (D)	Cortney Britten Cleereman (D)	None
Grant	Tina McDonald (R)	Andrea Noethe (R)	Jay P. Adams
Green	Barbara Miller (R)	Cynthia Meudt (R)	None
Green Lake	Amy Thoma (R)	Renee Thiem-Korth (R)	Don Lenz
Iowa	Lia Leahy (R)	Taylor Campbell (D)	None
Iron	Karen Ransanici (D)	Daniel Soine (D)	Todd Maki
Jackson	Jan Moennig (D)	Shari Marg (D)	Cody Brommerich
Jefferson	Cindy Hamre Incha (R)	Staci M. Hoffman (R)	Jim Morrow
Juneau	Lori J. Lowe (R)	Stacy Havill (R)	Gary Dechant
Kenosha	Rebecca Matoska-Mentink (D)	JoEllyn M. Storz (D)	Robert W. Merry
Kewaunee	Rebecca Deterville (D)	Germaine Bertrand (D)	Mau & Associates, LLP
La Crosse	Pamela Radtke (R)	Cheryl McBride (R)	Bryan Meyer
Lafayette	Trisha Rowe (R)	Cathy Paulson (R)	Aaron Austin
Langlade	Marilyn Baraniak (D)	Chet Haatvedt (D)	None
Lincoln	Marie Peterson (D)	Sarah Koss (R)	Anthony Dallman
Manitowoc	Lynn Zigmunt (D)	Kristi L. Tuesburg (R)	Jason Bolz
Marathon	Shirley Lang (R)	Dean Stratz (R)	Dave Decker
Marinette	Sheila M. Dudka (R)	Renee Miller (R)	None
Marquette	Shari Rudolph (R)	Bette Krueger (R)	Jerry Smart
Menominee	Delsy Kakwich (D)	Menomin Hawpetoss (D)	None
Milwaukee	John Barrett (D)	Israel Ramón (D)	Robert W. Merry
Monroe	Shirley Chapiewsky (R)	Deb Brandt (R)	Gary Dechant
Oconto	Trisha L. LeFebre (R)	Laurie Wusterbarth (R)	Brian Gross
Oneida	Brenda Behrle (R)	Kyle Franson (R)	Michael Romportl
Outagamie	Barb Bocik (R)	Sarah R. Van Camp (R)	Paul Nordwig
Ozaukee	Mary Lou Mueller (R)	Ronald A. Voigt (R)	None
Pepin	Audrey Lieffring (R)	Monica J. Bauer (R)	Cedar Corporation
Pierce	Kerry Feuerhelm (R)	Julie Hines (D)	James Filkins
Polk	Sharon Jorgenson (R)	Sally Spanel (R)	Steve Geiger
Portage	Lisa M. Roth (D)	Cynthia A. Wisinski (D)	Thomas J. Trzinski
Price	Penny Huck (D)	Sylvia Kerner (D)	Alfred Schneider
Racine	Samuel A. Christensen (R)	Karie Pope (R)	None
Richland	Stacy Kleist (R)	Susan Triggs (D)	Todd Rummler
Rock	Jackie Gackstatter (D)	Sandy Disrud (D)	Brad Heuer
Rusk	Lori Gorsegner (R)	Mary Berg (R)	None
St. Croix	Kristi Severson (R)	Beth Pabst (D)	Brian Halling
Sauk	Carrie Wastlick (R)	Brent Bailey (R)	Patrick Dederich
Sawyer	Marge Kelsey (R)	Paula Chisser (R)	Dan Pleoger
Shawano	Ethan Schmidt (R)	Amy Dillenburg (R)	David Yurk

Wisconsin county officers: clerk of circuit court; register of deeds; surveyor, April 2021, continued

	Clerk of circuit court	Register of deeds	Surveyor[1]
Sheboygan.	Melody Lorge (I)	Ellen Schleicher (D)	Jeremy Hildebrand
Taylor	Rose Thums (R)	Jaymi S. Kohn (R)	Robert Meyer
Trempealeau	Michelle Weisenberger (D)	Rose Ottum (D)	Joe Nelson
Vernon	Sheila Olson (R)	Marilyn Hauge (R)	Laurence Johns
Vilas	Beth Soltow (R)	Sherry Bierman (R)	Thomas Boettcher (R)
Walworth.	Kristina Secord (R)	Michele Jacobs (R)	SEWRPC
Washburn	Shannon Anderson (R)	Renee Bell (R)	Lucas Meier
Washington	Theresa Russell (R)	Sharon Martin (R)	Scott Schmidt
Waukesha	Monica Paz (A)	James Behrend (R)	Robert W. Merry
Waupaca	Terrie Tews-Liebe (R)	Michael Mazemke (R)	Joseph Glodowski
Waushara.	Melissa Zamzow (R)	Heather Schwersenska (R)	Jerry Smart
Winnebago	Melissa Pingel (R)	Natalie Strohmeyer (R)	None
Wood	Cindy Joosten (R)	Tiffany Ringer (R)	Kevin Boyer

Note: Clerks of circuit court, registers of deeds, and surveyors are elected at the general election for four-year terms. In lieu of electing a surveyor, a county can choose to appoint one.

A–Appointed to fill a vacancy; D–Democrat; I–Independent; R–Republican.

1. Surveyors are appointed unless party designation is shown.

Source: Data collected from county clerks by Wisconsin Legislative Reference Bureau, April 2021.

Wisconsin county officers: district attorney; sheriff; coroner (or alternative), April 2021

	District attorney	Sheriff	Coroner/medical examiner
Adams	Tania M. Bonnett (I)	Brent R. York (R)	Marilyn Rogers (ME)
Ashland.	David Meany (I)	Mick Brennan (D)	Barbara Beeksma (R)
Barron.	Brian Wright (R)	Chris Fitzgerald (D)	Nate Dunston (ME)
Bayfield.	Kimberly Lawton (D)	Paul Susienka (D)	Thomas Renz (D)
Brown.	David L. Lasee (R)	Todd J. Delain (R)	Vincent Tranchida (ME)
Buffalo	Tom Bilski (R)	Mike Schmidtknecht (R)	Cindy Giese (R)
Burnett	James Jay Rennicke (R)	Tracy Finch (I)	Mike Maloney (ME)
Calumet	Nathan F. Haberman (R)	Mark Wiegert (R)	Michael Klaeser (ME)
Chippewa	Wade C. Newell (R)	James L. Kowalczyk (D)	Ronald Patten (R)
Clark.	Melissa Inlow (D)	Scott Haines (R)	Richard J. Schleifer (R)
Columbia.	Brenda Yaskal (D)	Roger Brandner (R)	Katelyn Schara (Acting ME)
Crawford	Lukas Steiner (A)	Dale McCullick (D)	Joe Morovits (D)
Dane	Ismael R. Ozanne (D)	Kalvin Barrett (A)	Vincent Tranchida (ME)
Dodge	Kurt Klomberg (R)	Dale J. Schmidt (R)	Patrick Schoebel (ME)
Door.	Colleen Nordin (R)	Tammy Sternard (D)	Vincent Tranchida (ME)
Douglas.	Mark Fruehauf (D)	Thomas Dalbec (D)	Darrell Witt (ME)
Dunn	Andrea Nodolf (R)	Kevin Bygd (R)	Marcie Rosas (ME)
Eau Claire.	Gary King (D)	Ron D. Cramer (R)	Marcie Rosas (ME)
Florence	Doug Drexler (D)	Dan Miller (R)	Jeff Rickaby (R)
Fond du Lac	Eric Toney (R)	Ryan F. Waldschmidt (R)	Adam Covach (ME)
Forest	Charles Simono (D)	John Dennee (R)	Crystal Schaub (ME)
Grant	Lisa Riniker (R)	Nate Dreckman (R)	Phyllis Fuerstenberg (R)
Green	Craig Nolen (R)	Jeff Skatrud (D)	Monica Hack (D)
Green Lake.	Vacant	Mark Podoll (R)	Vacant
Iowa	Matthew C. Allen (D)	Steven R. Michek (R)	Wendell F. Hamlin (R)
Iron	Matthew Tingstad (R)	Paul Samardich (D)	Diane Simonich (D)
Jackson	Daniel Diehn (I)	Duane Waldera (D)	Bonnie Kindschy (ME)
Jefferson	Monica J. Hall (D)	Paul Milbrath (R)	Nichol Tesch (ME)
Juneau	Kenneth Hamm (R)	Brent Oleson (R)	Myron Oestreich (ME)
Kenosha	Michael Graveley (D)	David Beth (R)	Patrice Hall (ME)
Kewaunee	Andrew Naze (D)	Matthew Joski (R)	Rory Groessl (D)

Wisconsin county officers: district attorney; sheriff; coroner (or alternative), April 2021, continued

	District attorney	Sheriff	Coroner/medical examiner
La Crosse	Tim Gruenke (D)	Jeff Wolf (R)	Tim Candahl (ME)
Lafayette	Jenna Gill (R)	Reginald Gill (R)	Linda Gebhardt (D)
Langlade	Elizabeth R. Gebert (R)	Mark Westen (R)	Larry Shadick (R)
Lincoln	Galen Bayne-Allison (D)	Ken Schneider (R)	Paul Proulx (R)
Manitowoc	Jacalyn LaBre (R)	Daniel Hartwig (R)	Curtis Green (D)
Marathon	Theresa Wetzsteon (D)	Scott Parks (R)	Jessica Blahnik (ME)
Marinette	DeShea D. Morrow (R)	Jerry Sauve (R)	Kalynn Van Ermen (ME)
Marquette	Brian Juech (I)	Joseph Konrath (R)	Thomas Wastart II (R)
Menominee[1]	Gregory Parker (R)	Rebecca Smith (I)	Patrick Roberts (ME)
Milwaukee	John T. Chisholm (D)	Earnell R. Lucas (D)	Brian L. Peterson (ME)
Monroe	Kevin Croninger (R)	Wesley D. Revels (R)	Robert Smith (ME)
Oconto	Ed Burke (R)	Todd Skarban (R)	Barry Irmen (ME)
Oneida	Michael Schiek (R)	Grady Hartman (R)	Crystal Schaub (ME)
Outagamie	Melinda Tempelis (R)	Clint C. Kriewaldt (R)	Douglas A. Bartelt (R)
Ozaukee	Adam Y. Gerol (R)	James G. Johnson (R)	Timothy J. Deppisch (R)
Pepin	Jon D. Seifert (R)	Joel D. Wener (R)	Joan Huppert (R)
Pierce	Halle Hatch (D)	Nancy Hove (D)	John Worsing (ME)
Polk	Jeffrey L. Kemp (R)	Brent A. Waak (R)	John Dinnies (ME)
Portage	Louis J. Molepske, Jr. (D)	Michael Lukas (D)	Scott W. Rifleman (ME)
Price	Karl Kelz (Write-In)	Brian Schmidt (R)	James Dalbesio, III (D)
Racine	Patricia J. Hanson (R)	Christopher Schmaling (R)	Michael Payne (ME)
Richland	Jennifer M. Harper (R)	James Bindl (R)	James C. Rossing (I)
Rock	David J. O'Leary (D)	Troy Knudson (D)	Barry E. Irmen (ME)
Rusk	Annette Barna (D)	Jeffery Wallace (R)	Jim Rassbach (ME)
St. Croix	Karl Anderson (R)	Scott Knudson (R)	Patty Schachtner (ME)
Sauk	Michael X. Albrecht (I)	Chip Meister (R)	Greg L. Hahn (R)
Sawyer	Bruce R. Poquette (R)	Doug Mrotek (R)	John Froemel (R)
Shawano[1]	Gregory Parker (R)	Adam Bieber (R)	Brian Westfahl (R)
Sheboygan	Joel Urmanski (R)	Cory Roeseler (R)	Chris Nehring (ME)
Taylor	Kristi Tlusty (D)	Larry Woebbeking (R)	Scott Perrin (ME)
Trempealeau	John Sacia (D)	Brett Semingson (D)	Bonnie Kindschy (D)
Vernon	Timothy Gaskell (R)	John B. Spears (R)	Betty Nigh (R)
Vilas	Martha Milanowski (R)	Joseph A. Fath (R)	Crystal Schaub (ME)
Walworth	Zeke Wiedenfeld (R)	Kurt Picknell (R)	Gina Carver (ME)
Washburn	Aaron Marcoux (D)	Dennis Stuart (R)	Angela Pank (R)
Washington	Mark Bensen (R)	Martin Schulteis (R)	Robert Schafer (ME)
Waukesha	Susan L. Opper (R)	Eric J. Severson (R)	Lynda Biedrzycki (ME)
Waupaca	Veronica Isherwood (R)	Timothy R. Wilz (R)	Catherine Wegener (ME)
Waushara	Matthew Leusink (R)	Walter Zuehlke (R)	Amanda Thoma (ME)
Winnebago	Christian Gossett (R)	John Matz (R)	Cheryl Brehmer (A)
Wood	Craig Lambert (I)	Shawn Becker (R)	Scott Brehm (R)

Note: District attorneys, sheriffs, and coroners are elected at the general election for four-year terms. In lieu of electing a coroner, a county can choose to appoint a medical examiner.

A–Appointed to fill a vacancy; D–Democrat; I–Independent; ME–medical examiner; R–Republican.

1. Menominee and Shawano counties comprise a single prosecutorial unit, served by a single district attorney.

Source: Data collected from county clerks by Wisconsin Legislative Reference Bureau, April 2021.

Tribal chairs and contact information, April 2021

Tribe and chair	Contact information
Bad River Band of Lake Superior Chippewa Mike Wiggins, Jr. (chair)	P.O. Box 39, Odanah 54861-0039 715-682-7111; www.badriver-nsn.gov
Forest County Potawatomi Ned Daniels, Jr. (chair)	P.O. Box 340, Crandon 54520-0346 715-478-7200; www.fcpotawatomi.com

Tribal chairs and contact information, April 2021, continued

Tribe and chair	Contact information
Ho-Chunk Nation . . . . Marlon WhiteEagle (president)	P.O. Box 667, Black River Falls 54615-0667 715-284-9343; www.ho-chunknation.com
Lac Courte Oreilles Band of Lake Superior Chippewa . . Louis Taylor, Sr. (chair)	13394 W. Trepania Road, Hayward 54843-2186 715-634-8934; www.lcotribe.com
Lac du Flambeau Band of Lake Superior Chippewa. . . . John Johnson (president)	P.O. Box 67, Lac du Flambeau 54538-0067 715-588-3303; www.ldftribe.com
Menominee Indian Tribe of Wisconsin . . . . Gunnar Peters (chair)	P.O. Box 910, Keshena 54135-0910 715-799-5114; www.menominee-nsn.gov
Oneida Nation . . . . Tehassi Hill (chair)	P.O. Box 365, Oneida 54155-0365 920-869-4380; www.oneida-nsn.gov
Red Cliff Band of Lake Superior Chippewa . . . . Richard Peterson (chair)	88455 Pike Road, Bayfield 54814-0529 715-779-3700; www.redcliff-nsn.gov
St. Croix Chippewa Indians of Wisconsin . . . . Susan Lowe (chair)	24663 Angeline Avenue, Webster 54893-9246 715-349-2195; https://stcroixojibwensn.gov
Sokaogon Chippewa Community . . . . Robert VanZile, Jr. (chair)	3051 Sand Lake Road, Crandon 54520-8815 715-478-7500; www.sokaogonchippewa.com
Stockbridge-Munsee Band of Mohican Indians . . . . . . Shannon Holsey (president)	P.O. Box 70, Bowler 54416-9801 715-793-4111; www.mohican.com

Sources: Wisconsin State Tribal Relations Initiative, http://witribes.wi.gov [April 2021] and individual tribal websites.

Wisconsin full-time equivalent state government positions

Type of funding	Number of positions[1]
General purpose revenue.	35,479.27
Program revenue.	20,716.07
Federal appropriations	10,756.72
Segregated funds	4,877.13
Total.	**71,829.19**

1. Positions authorized by the legislature, or under procedures authorized by the legislature, as of June 30, 2020. Includes all branches of state government and the UW System.
Source: Wisconsin Department of Administration, Division of Executive Budget and Finance, departmental data.

Wisconsin executive branch employees

Status	Number of employees[1]
Permanent.	29,247
Unclassified	1,222
Limited term.	2,876
Project	242
Seasonal	7
Elected	74
Total.	**33,668**

1. Employees working on a full–time or part–time basis for the executive branch only, as of June 30, 2020.
Source: Wisconsin Department of Administration, Division of Executive Budget and Finance, departmental data, April 2021.

Wisconsin state and local government employment and payrolls, March 2019

	Number of employees			
Function	Full-time	Part-time	Full-time equivalent[1]	Total payroll ($1,000)
Air and water transport	386	59	405	2,172
Corrections	12,506	948	13,020	64,051
Education	134,428	90,755	168,238	799,640
Elementary and secondary	98,614	42,444	119,209	525,699
Higher education institutions.	34,929	48,020	47,962	268,384
Other.	885	291	1,067	5,557
Fire protection	4,372	5,219	4,999	30,586
Government administration	9,700	12,659	11,809	57,133
Health and hospitals.	9,782	3,522	11,500	55,664
Highways.	9,557	1,475	10,012	51,107
Housing and community development	1,018	358	1,156	5,129
Judicial and legal.	5,413	1,087	5,818	32,693
Libraries	1,638	3,230	2,961	10,416
Natural resources.	2,908	1,395	3,420	16,156
Parks and recreation.	2,341	3,402	3,236	13,612
Police protection	15,111	2,812	15,936	96,102
Public welfare and social insurance administration	12,711	3,710	14,856	64,544
Sewerage.	1,825	713	1,936	10,310
Solid waste management.	1,335	995	1,445	6,415
Transit.	1,870	155	1,959	8,365
Utilities (electric and water supply).	2,258	320	2,354	12,503
Other	6,735	3,669	7,477	38,677
Total.	**235,894**	**136,483**	**282,537**	**1,375,277**

1. Full-time equivalent (FTE) is a derived statistic that provides an estimate of a government's total full-time employment by converting part-time employees to a full-time amount.

Source: U.S. Census Bureau, "2019 Government Employment and Payroll Tables," https://www.census.gov/programs-surveys/apes/data/datasetstables/2019.html [November 2020].

Wisconsin state and local government employment and payrolls

	Employees (full-time equivalents)			Monthly payroll ($1,000)		
	State	Local	Total	State	Local	Total
2007.	68,714	212,931	281,645	295,616	788,590	1,084,207
2008.	69,019	214,332	283,351	308,878	813,054	1,121,932
2009.	70,457	211,564	282,021	322,316	841,573	1,163,889
2010.	72,428	211,407	283,835	326,643	851,380	1,178,022
2011.	70,891	208,623	279,514	328,658	855,316	1,183,974
2012.	70,543	208,485	279,028	321,601	863,452	1,185,053
2013.	72,347	202,153	274,500	333,226	862,139	1,195,365
2014.	72,551	208,108	280,659	344,334	884,405	1,228,738
2015.	74,383	211,442	285,825	357,334	901,925	1,259,259
2016.	72,676	212,640	285,316	356,014	926,005	1,282,019
2017.	72,751	211,335	284,086	362,146	950,653	1,312,800
2018.	71,253	212,400	283,653	365,007	960,546	1,325,553
2019.	71,640	210,897	282,537	380,251	995,026	1,375,277

Source: U.S. Census Bureau, "2019 Government Employment & Payroll Tables" and prior years, at https://www.census.gov/programs-surveys/apes/data/datasetstables/2019.html [February 2021].

Wisconsin state classified service profile, 2018

Category	Number	Percent
Permanent classified employees	29,240	100
Persons with disabilities[1]	1,523	5.2
Women	15,112	51.7
Racial/ethnic minorities	3,910	13.4
Black	2,015	6.9
Hispanic	880	3
Asian	839	2.9
American Indian	176	0.6

Note: Data excludes unclassified, temporary, judicial, and legislative employees and employees in the UW System. Data may not be comparable to prior Blue Book tables.

1. Includes persons with severe disabilities. Disabilities are voluntarily self-reported.

Source: Wisconsin Department of Administration, Division of Personnel Management, *State of Wisconsin Classified Workforce & Affirmative Action Report: Fiscal Years 2017 and 2018*.

Wisconsin state revenues and expenditures

Fiscal year	General fund[1] Revenues ($1,000)	Expenditures ($1,000)	Other funds[2] Revenues ($1,000)	Expenditures ($1,000)	Total—all funds Revenues ($1,000)	Expenditures ($1,000)	Net surplus or deficit[3] ($1,000)
1971...	1,790,957	1,780,703	929,124	726,545	2,720,081	2,507,247	34,840
1972...	2,096,084	2,031,896	961,970	697,144	3,058,054	2,729,040	116,914
1973...	2,480,748	2,296,679	1,112,600	791,657	3,593,347	3,088,337	217,404
1974...	2,687,517	2,729,854	1,114,326	865,724	3,801,842	3,595,577	241,359
1975...	2,966,532	3,148,968	1,252,422	924,455	4,218,954	4,073,423	78,120
1976...	3,476,690	3,439,062	1,677,155	1,283,467	5,153,846	4,722,529	86,473
1977...	3,807,748	3,712,595	1,887,150	1,376,726	5,694,898	5,089,322	166,587
1978...	4,240,298	3,994,220	1,875,978	1,446,286	6,116,277	5,440,486	407,770
1979...	4,622,611	4,696,263	2,200,365	1,620,899	6,822,976	6,317,162	280,561
1980...	4,900,275	5,027,130	2,481,324	1,809,840	7,381,599	6,836,970	72,627
1981...	5,335,427	5,452,247	2,738,491	1,922,648	8,073,918	7,374,895	14,065
1982...	5,564,585	5,520,811	2,757,388	2,021,266	8,321,974	7,542,078	70,811
1983...	6,036,016	6,302,575	3,905,944	2,288,804	9,941,961	8,591,379	-182,126
1984...	6,966,282	6,360,657	3,614,895	2,528,273	10,581,177	8,888,930	383,085
1985...	7,160,174	7,237,716	4,908,582	2,743,287	12,068,756	9,981,002	314,084
1986...	7,798,367	7,757,063	6,380,605	2,774,683	14,178,972	10,531,747	279,744
1987...	8,133,265	8,205,100	5,061,597	2,693,737	13,194,863	10,898,836	232,733
1988...	8,432,698	8,427,084	3,566,763	2,790,038	11,999,461	11,217,121	216,963
1989...	9,030,466	8,809,189	5,778,125	3,094,116	14,808,591	11,903,305	375,016
1990...	9,418,918	9,464,483	5,483,442	3,287,809	14,902,360	12,752,292	306,452
1991...	10,184,183	10,350,332	5,930,658	3,706,452	16,114,839	14,056,784	113,609
1992...	11,033,948	11,082,220	7,786,483	4,218,565	18,820,431	15,300,785	73,681
1993...	11,828,599	11,708,360	8,192,793	4,596,981	20,021,392	16,305,341	153,540
1994...	12,442,349	12,323,509	5,812,805	4,756,564	18,255,154	17,080,073	234,877
1995...	13,259,772	13,094,450	9,823,810	4,963,553	23,083,582	18,058,003	400,881
1996...	13,804,399	13,648,601	10,038,961	5,057,062	23,843,360	18,705,663	581,690
1997...	14,669,320	14,932,404	12,741,438	5,144,002	27,410,758	20,076,406	386,558
1998...	15,701,212	15,509,615	13,896,719	6,071,649	29,597,931	21,581,264	533,240
1999...	16,252,539	16,098,587	11,847,678	6,864,567	28,100,217	22,963,154	737,748
2000...	18,185,980	18,333,634	14,687,330	8,111,005	32,873,310	26,444,639	574,416
2001...	19,285,734	19,448,417	2,990,770	8,719,341	22,276,504	28,167,758	445,999
2002...	20,850,074	21,248,608	5,920,241	10,395,514	26,770,315	31,644,122	44,469
2003...	20,683,921	20,956,485	10,598,486	11,025,745	31,282,407	31,982,230	-163,608
2004...	22,040,940	21,716,332	19,544,497	12,177,401	41,585,437	33,893,733	127,369
2005...	21,191,600	21,488,178	15,827,541	10,772,231	37,019,141	32,260,409	-131,675
2006...	22,321,870	22,148,049	17,611,450	11,636,031	39,933,320	33,784,080	35,014
2007...	23,123,424	23,205,243	23,140,557	11,329,591	46,263,981	34,534,834	36,467
2008...	23,997,838	24,103,773	4,668,268	12,195,449	28,666,106	36,299,222	110,424
2009...	25,078,246	25,280,016	-4,760,111	13,216,367	20,318,135	38,496,383	-37,167
2010...	26,918,079	26,933,345	19,320,601	13,214,942	46,238,680	40,148,287	99,873
2011...	28,926,518	28,951,824	27,574,543	13,974,915	56,501,061	42,926,739	305,584
2012...	28,557,414	27,379,001	11,959,996	14,158,805	40,517,410	41,537,806	1,115,672
2013...	29,435,181	28,400,745	20,586,682	14,164,382	50,021,863	42,565,127	1,987,605
2014...	29,765,921	30,028,018	26,166,710	15,060,009	55,932,631	45,088,027	1,669,233
2015...	30,622,404	30,861,201	14,096,474	15,437,387	44,718,878	46,298,588	1,359,156
2016...	31,172,186	30,852,156	12,752,252	15,034,976	43,924,438	45,887,132	1,656,065
2017...	32,390,154	31,891,665	23,285,943	15,099,934	55,676,097	46,991,599	2,254,454

Wisconsin state revenues and expenditures, continued

Fiscal year	General fund[1] Revenues ($1,000)	Expenditures ($1,000)	Other funds[2] Revenues ($1,000)	Expenditures ($1,000)	Total—all funds Revenues ($1,000)	Expenditures ($1,000)	Net surplus or deficit[3] ($1,000)
2018...	32,850,441	32,685,469	20,506,458	15,513,335	53,356,899	48,198,804	1,744,973
2019...	35,034,907	34,173,937	20,229,339	16,069,377	55,264,246	50,243,314	2,437,987
2020...	37,984,891	35,684,286	17,996,210	16,149,772	55,981,101	51,834,058	4,109,663

1. Includes general purpose revenue (GPR), program revenue, and federal funding. 2. Includes special revenue funds (such as conservation and transportation), federal funding, debt service, capital projects, pension and retirement funds, trust and agency funds, and others. 3. Unappropriated (unreserved) balance of the general fund for the fiscal year.

Source: Wisconsin Department of Administration, State Controller's Office, *2020 Annual Fiscal Report*, October 15, 2020, and prior editions.

Wisconsin state budget allocations

Revenue type and allocation	Fiscal year 2019–20 ($)	Fiscal year 2020–21 ($)	Fiscal biennium ($)	% of total budget allocations
GENERAL PURPOSE REVENUE	18,314,860,600	19,190,025,700	37,504,886,300	46.06
State operations	4,304,949,100	4,528,680,000	8,833,629,100	10.85
Local assistance	9,263,259,900	9,405,160,700	18,668,420,600	22.93
Aids to individuals and organizations	4,746,651,600	5,256,185,000	10,002,836,600	12.29
PROGRAM REVENUE—TOTAL	16,932,256,200	17,162,013,400	34,094,269,600	41.88
State operations	7,454,737,200	7,552,236,800	15,006,974,000	18.43
Local assistance	1,450,540,300	1,301,918,100	2,752,458,400	3.38
Aids to individuals and organizations	8,026,978,700	8,307,858,500	16,334,837,200	20.06
Program Revenue—federal	10,637,382,100	10,797,082,100	21,434,464,200	26.33
State operations	2,532,761,000	2,631,488,400	5,164,249,400	6.34
Local assistance	1,380,956,800	1,231,867,900	2,612,824,700	3.21
Aids to individuals and organizations	6,723,664,300	6,933,725,800	13,657,390,100	16.77
Program Revenue—service	927,616,400	927,348,000	1,854,964,400	2.28
State operations	717,027,300	720,865,100	1,437,892,400	1.77
Local assistance	38,420,600	38,407,300	76,827,900	0.09
Aids to individuals and organizations	172,168,500	168,075,600	340,244,100	0.42
Program Revenue—other	5,367,257,700	5,437,583,300	10,804,841,000	13.27
State operations	4,204,948,900	4,199,883,300	8,404,832,200	10.32
Local assistance	31,162,900	31,642,900	62,805,800	0.08
Aids to individuals and organizations	1,131,145,900	1,206,057,100	2,337,203,000	2.87
SEGREGATED REVENUE—TOTAL	4,916,574,300	4,902,599,500	9,819,173,800	12.06
State operations	2,666,896,200	2,653,747,300	5,320,643,500	6.53
Local assistance	1,477,816,000	1,505,056,900	2,982,872,900	3.66
Aids to individuals and organizations	771,862,100	743,795,300	1,515,657,400	1.86
Segregated Revenue—federal	948,378,300	943,482,400	1,891,860,700	2.32
State operations	750,463,900	745,568,000	1,496,031,900	1.84
Local assistance	191,625,700	191,625,700	383,251,400	0.47
Aids to individuals and organizations	6,288,700	6,288,700	12,577,400	0.02
Segregated Revenue—local	115,325,600	115,325,600	230,651,200	0.28
State operations	7,452,900	7,452,900	14,905,800	0.02
Local assistance	99,678,500	99,678,500	199,357,000	0.24
Aids to individuals and organizations	8,194,200	8,194,200	16,388,400	0.02
Segregated Revenue—service	145,846,900	145,846,900	291,693,800	0.36
State operations	123,846,900	123,846,900	247,693,800	0.30
Aids to individuals and organizations	22,000,000	22,000,000	44,000,000	0.05
Segregated Revenue—other	3,707,023,500	3,697,944,600	7,404,968,100	9.09
State operations	1,785,132,500	1,776,879,500	3,562,012,000	4.37
Local assistance	1,186,511,800	1,213,752,700	2,400,264,500	2.95

Wisconsin state budget allocations, continued

Revenue type and allocation	Fiscal year 2019–20 ($)	Fiscal year 2020–21 ($)	Fiscal biennium ($)	% of total budget allocations
Aids to individuals and organizations . .	735,379,200	707,312,400	1,442,691,600	1.77
FEDERAL REVENUE—TOTAL	**11,585,760,400**	**11,740,564,500**	**23,326,324,900**	**28.65**
State operations	3,283,224,900	3,377,056,400	6,660,281,300	8.18
Local assistance	1,572,582,500	1,423,493,600	2,996,076,100	3.68
Aids to individuals and organizations . . .	6,729,953,000	6,940,014,500	13,669,967,500	16.79
TOTAL—ALL SOURCES	**40,163,691,100**	**41,254,638,600**	**81,418,329,700**	**100.00**
State operations	14,426,582,500	14,734,664,100	29,161,246,600	35.82
Local assistance	12,191,616,200	12,212,135,700	24,403,751,900	29.97
Aids to individuals and organizations . . .	13,545,492,400	14,307,838,800	27,853,331,200	34.21

Definitions: **General purpose revenue**—general taxes, miscellaneous receipts, and revenues collected by state agencies that are paid into the general fund, lose their identity, and are available for appropriation by the legislature. **Program revenue**—revenues paid into the general fund and credited by law to an appropriation used to finance a specific program or agency. **Segregated fund revenue**—revenues deposited, by law, into funds other than the general fund and available only for the purposes for which such funds were created. **Federal revenue**—money received from the federal government (may be disbursed either through a segregated fund or through the general fund). **Service revenue**—money transferred between or within state agencies for reimbursement for services rendered or materials purchased. **State operations**—amounts budgeted to operate programs carried out by state government. **Local assistance**—amounts budgeted as state aids to assist programs carried out by local governmental units in Wisconsin.

Source: Wisconsin Department of Administration, State Budget Office, departmental data, March 2021.

Annual appropriation obligations of the state of Wisconsin

Category	Amount of debt issued[1] ($1,000)	Amount outstanding December 15, 2020 ($1,000)
General fund annual appropriation bonds	3,252,620	2,977,575
Master lease obligations	139,645	73,676
Total.	3,392,265	3,051,251

Note: Appropriation obligations are not general obligations of the state, and they do not constitute "public debt" of the state as that term is used in the Wisconsin Constitution and in the Wisconsin Statutes. The payment of the principal of, and interest on, appropriation obligations is subject to annual appropriation. The state has no legal obligation to make these appropriations and incurs no liability to the owners of the appropriation obligations if it does not do so.

1. Amounts do not include refunding bonds, which do not count against the respective authorizations.

Source: Wisconsin Department of Administration, Division of Executive Budget and Finance, departmental data, March 2021.

Wisconsin state revenues, all funds

	Fiscal year 2017–18 ($1,000)	Fiscal year 2018–19 ($1,000)	Fiscal year 2019–20 ($1,000)
REVENUES FROM TAXES.	**17,393,056**	**18,576,414**	**18,760,189**
General fund	16,168,750	17,369,028	17,558,529
General purpose revenues	16,144,167	17,341,387	17,532,124
Income taxes.	9,373,042	10,332,159	10,350,139
Individual	8,479,150	8,994,096	8,742,266
Corporation.	893,892	1,338,063	1,607,873
Sales and excise taxes	6,128,097	6,357,466	6,515,718
General sales and use.	5,448,118	5,695,548	5,836,215
Cigarette	538,898	514,273	523,557

Wisconsin state revenues, all funds, continued

	Fiscal year 2017–18 ($1,000)	Fiscal year 2018–19 ($1,000)	Fiscal year 2019–20 ($1,000)
Other tobacco products	80,202	85,521	91,364
Vapor products.	—	—	1,319
Liquor and wine	51,970	53,600	54,776
Malt beverage (beer)	8,909	8,524	8,487
Public utility taxes.	365,343	364,941	357,152
Private light, heat, and power.	235,390	231,474	225,411
Municipal light, heat, and power.	3,065	2,695	2,729
Telephone.	63,591	67,197	66,173
Pipeline	45,531	44,884	44,513
Electric cooperative.	12,464	13,353	12,752
Municipal electric	4,802	4,714	4,445
Conservation and regulation	434	601	473
Utility tax (refunds) interest and penalties	66	23	656
Inheritance and estate taxes	-33	6	41
Miscellaneous taxes	277,718	286,815	309,074
Insurance companies (premiums)	186,273	194,356	217,381
Real estate transfer fee	76,600	77,388	77,430
Lawsuits (courts).	14,795	15,023	14,263
Other.	50	48	—
Program revenues	24,583	27,641	26,405
Fire dues	20,570	22,398	23,122
Pari-mutuel taxes	—	—	—
County expo tax administration	905	985	776
Baseball park administration fee.	480	507	390
Business trust regulation fee	2,133	3,153	1,439
Other.	495	598	678
Transportation fund.			
Motor fuel tax	1,065,936	1,066,310	1,022,464
Air-carrier tax	6,176	7,375	7,047
Railroad tax.	40,765	42,960	42,020
Aviation fuel tax.	1,338	1,315	1,264
Other taxes.	9,005	10,136	9,325
Conservation fund.			
Forestry mill tax	22,335	-21	-796
Forest crop taxes	1,318	497	1,289
Motor fuel tax	1	—	—
Dry cleaner fund	619	561	533
Mediation fund.	1	1	1
Petroleum inspection tax	51,073	51,262	83,892
Historical Preservation Partnership Trust	—	9	—
Economic development fund temporary service charges	25,739	26,981	34,621
DEPARTMENT REVENUES.	**34,461,277**	**34,947,248**	**35,839,304**
Intergovernmental revenue.	11,149,472	12,115,331	15,033,737
Licenses and permits	1,779,406	1,867,293	1,960,681
Charges for goods and services	4,457,319	4,512,950	4,404,752
Contributions	3,827,381	3,774,485	3,831,957
Interest and investment income	8,849,596	8,284,624	5,511,010
Gifts and donations	667,540	685,800	660,447
Proceeds from sale of bonds	703,623	447,615	1,052,808
Other revenues.	2,627,829	2,942,375	3,006,119
Other transactions.	399,111	316,775	377,793
TRANSFERS	**1,502,566**	**1,740,584**	**1,381,608**
TOTAL REVENUES	**53,356,899**	**55,264,246**	**55,981,101**

—Represents zero.

Source: Wisconsin Department of Administration, State Controller's Office, *2020 Annual Fiscal Report*, October 15, 2020.

Revenue bonds of the state of Wisconsin

Program funded	Amount of debt authorized ($1,000)	Amount issued[1] ($1,000)	Amount outstanding December 15, 2020 ($1,000)
Transportation facilities and highway projects.	4,197,628	3,968,817	1,670,565
Clean Water/Environmental Improvement Fund.	2,526,700	1,916,245	307,760
Petroleum environmental cleanup	436,000	387,550	—
Total.	**7,160,328**	**6,272,612**	**1,978,325**

Note: Revenue bonds are issued for purposes and amounts specifically authorized by the legislature. This debt is not a legal obligation of the state and is not subject to existing debt limitations.

—Represents zero.

1. Amounts do not include refunding bonds, which do not count against the respective authorizations.

Source: Wisconsin Department of Administration, Division of Executive Budget and Finance, departmental data, March 2021.

Wisconsin state government expenditures

Function	Fiscal year 2018–19 Amount ($1,000)	Percent	Fiscal year 2019–20 Amount ($1,000)	Percent
Executive total	**45,301,841**	**90.16**	**46,713,948**	**90.12**
Administration	860,086	1.71	1,123,939	2.17
Agriculture, Trade and Consumer Protection	104,047	0.21	104,925	0.20
Board on Aging and Long Term Care	3,400	0.01	3,491	0.01
Board for People with Developmental Disabilities	3,404	0.01	1,907	0.00
Child Abuse and Neglect Prevention Board	3,481	0.01	2,674	0.01
Children and Families.	2,154,800	4.29	2,296,578	4.43
Corrections	1,249,783	2.49	1,300,385	2.51
District attorneys.	48,445	0.10	52,256	0.10
Educational Communications Board.	17,988	0.04	17,779	0.03
Elections Commission	5,078	0.01	8,617	0.02
Employee Trust Funds	7,937,002	15.80	8,004,833	15.44
Employment Relations Commission.	905	0.00	930	0.00
Environmental Improvement Program	113,954	0.23	78,833	0.15
Ethics Commission	1,065	0.00	1,202	0.00
Financial Institutions	17,833	0.04	19,665	0.04
Fox River Navigation System Authority	125	0.00	125	0.00
Governor	3,827	0.01	3,843	0.01
Health Services.	12,845,410	25.57	13,720,485	26.47
Higher Education Aids Board	141,481	0.28	137,120	0.26
Historical Society	29,836	0.06	27,874	0.05
Insurance Commissioner.	55,785	0.11	46,562	0.09
Investment Board	47,092	0.09	58,477	0.11
Justice	222,860	0.44	220,158	0.42
Kickapoo Reserve Management Board	1,119	0.00	1,054	0.00
Labor and Industry Review Commission	2,269	0.00	2,240	0.00
Lieutenant Governor	377	0.00	441	0.00
Lower Wisconsin Riverway.	221	0.00	224	0.00
Medical College of Wisconsin	10,134	0.02	10,408	0.02
Military Affairs	121,091	0.24	134,089	0.26
Natural Resources	630,676	1.26	632,144	1.22
Public Defender	89,211	0.18	90,181	0.17
Public Instruction	7,002,797	13.94	7,184,833	13.86
Public Lands Board	1,531	0.00	1,454	0.00
Public Service Commission	30,433	0.06	50,029	0.10

Wisconsin state government expenditures, continued

| | Fiscal year 2018–19 | | Fiscal year 2019–20 | |
| | Amount | | Amount | |
Function	($1,000)	Percent	($1,000)	Percent
Revenue.	642,222	1.28	666,090	1.29
Safety and Professional Services	57,041	0.11	55,671	0.11
Secretary of State	251	0.00	264	0.00
State Fair Park.	31,119	0.06	29,899	0.06
Technical College System Board	551,187	1.10	562,927	1.09
Tourism	17,558	0.03	13,518	0.03
Transportation	3,208,999	6.39	3,154,801	6.09
Treasurer.	135	0.00	122	0.00
University of Wisconsin.	6,498,925	12.93	6,406,848	12.36
Veterans Affairs.	159,553	0.32	122,337	0.24
Wisconsin Economic Development Corporation	41,551	0.08	40,551	0.08
Workforce Development	335,755	0.67	321,165	0.62
Total judicial.	143,404	0.29	148,000	0.29
Total legislative.	73,209	0.15	75,475	0.15
Shared revenue and tax relief	2,813,112	5.60	2,862,194	5.52
Miscellaneous appropriations.	154,339	0.31	206,876	0.40
Program supplements	70,615	0.14	(26,341)	-0.05
Public debt	961,641	1.91	1,029,589	1.99
Building Commission	21,824	0.04	23,066	0.04
Building programs.	703,328	1.40	801,250	1.55
Total.	50,243,313	100.00	51,834,057	100.00

Source: Wisconsin Department of Administration, State Controller's Office, *Appendix to Annual Fiscal Report (Budgetary Basis)*, 2019 and 2020.

Debt of the state of Wisconsin, 1980–2019

| | | Amount incurred during calendar year | | Amount outstanding January 1 | | |
	Annual debt limit[1] ($1,000)	Total ($1,000)	% of debt limit	Total ($1,000)	Per capita ($)	% of state as- sessed value
1980.	813,604	123,500	15.2	1,916,177	407	1.77
1985.	922,661	440,955	47.8	2,153,152	508	1.96
1990.	1,060,277	484,099	45.7	2,566,496	568	1.97
1995.	1,511,536	368,322	24.4	3,244,079	637	1.64
2000.	2,147,411	538,795	25.1	3,942,659	735	1.49
2001.	2,343,628	485,645	20.7	4,270,718	790	1.42
2002.	2,514,949	481,000	19.1	4,452,626	819	1.40
2003.	2,705,327	499,030	18.5	4,682,045	855	1.33
2004.	2,933,909	664,435	22.6	4,794,398	871	1.31
2005.	3,209,502	571,990	17.8	5,116,439	924	1.27
2006.	3,517,374	891,285	25.3	5,445,615	980	1.26
2007.	3,734,403	483,280	12.9	5,898,647	1,053	1.18
2008.	3,857,955	493,635	12.8	5,893,590	1,047	1.19
2009.	3,839,340	542,765	14.1	6,146,978	1,087	1.27
2010.	3,719,281	809,293	21.8	6,481,010	1,139	1.49
2011.	3,651,482	896,260	24.5	7,407,431	1,298	1.62
2012.	3,533,194	735,585	20.8	7,878,628	1,377	1.78
2013.	3,506,269	642,295	18.3	8,385,973	1,462	1.78
2014.	3,596,100	598,170	16.6	8,344,531	1,451	1.70
2015.	3,679,519	750,475	20.4	8,134,099	1,412	1.68

Debt of the state of Wisconsin, 1980–2019, continued

	Annual debt limit[1] ($1,000)	Amount incurred during calendar year		Amount outstanding January 1		
		Total ($1,000)	% of debt limit	Total ($1,000)	Per capita ($)	% of state assessed value
2016...............	3,788,432	713,305	18.8	8,238,759	1,427	1.66
2017...............	3,944,844	607,975	15.4	8,389,198	1,448	1.55
2018...............	4,121,495	547,290	13.3	8,155,030	1,403	1.48
2019...............	4,356,545	539,415	12.4	8,212,806	1,411	1.41

1. The debt limit for each calendar year is derived through a formula specified in section 18.05, Wis. Stats.

Source: Wisconsin Department of Administration, Division of Executive Budget and Finance, departmental data, March 2021.

Debt of the state of Wisconsin, December 2020

Type	Amount outstanding ($1,000)
Tax supported debt	5,480,843
General fund	3,892,195
Segregated funds[1].	1,588,648
Revenue supported debt[2]	1,925,932
Total.	**7,406,775**

1. Includes the Transportation Fund and certain administrative facilities for the Wisconsin Department of Natural Resources.
2. Revenue supported debt includes debt that is issued with initial expectation that revenues and other proceeds from the operation of the programs or facilities financed will amortize the debt without recourse to the general fund.

Source: Wisconsin Department of Administration, Division of Executive Budget and Finance, departmental data, March 2021.

Debt of Wisconsin state authorities

Authority	Amount outstanding ($1,000)
Wisconsin Health and Educational Facilities Authority.	9,115,688[1]
Wisconsin Housing and Economic Development Authority.	1,969,626[2]

Note: State authority debt is not an obligation of the State of Wisconsin.

1. As of 6/30/20.   2. As of 12/31/20.

Source: Data provided by the respective authorities.

Debt of Wisconsin local governments

Year (Dec. 31)	Counties (mil. dol.)	Cities (mil. dol.)	Villages (mil. dol.)	Towns (mil. dol.)	Total (mil. dol.)
1965.......................	192.5	548.1	22.5	9.2	772.3
1975.......................	261.0	598.7	69.8	26.2	955.7
1985.......................	532.5	1,320.4	227.6	75.2	2,155.7
1995.......................	1,221.6	2,082.8	418.7	193.8	3,916.9
2005.......................	1,753.7	3,718.5	1,098.0	308.5	6,878.8
2010.......................	2,444.8	4,468.2	1,440.1	374.6	8,727.7

Debt of Wisconsin local governments, continued

Year (Dec. 31)	Counties (mil. dol.)	Cities (mil. dol.)	Villages (mil. dol.)	Towns (mil. dol.)	Total (mil. dol.)
2015	2,378.1	4,713.3	1,560.9	338.6	8,990.9
2016	2,352.8	5,026.9	1,632.0	341.0	9,352.6
2017	2,553.3	5,139.0	1,773.7	350.7	9,816.6
2018	2,590.6	5,399.0	1,858.9	376.9	10,225.5
2019	2,610.2	5,607.8	2,032.6	429.8	10,680.4

Sources: Wisconsin Department of Revenue, *Indebtedness 1981* and prior editions; Wisconsin Department of Revenue, Division of State and Local Finance, Bureau of Local Government Services, *County and Municipal Revenues and Expenditures 2019*, and prior editions.

Debt of Wisconsin school districts and technical college districts

Year (June 30)	School districts (mil. dol.)	Technical college districts (mil. dol.)	Total (mil. dol)
1965	336.6	X	336.6
1975	798.7	97.2	895.9
1985	448.7	64.7	513.4
1995	2,104.9	192.8	2,297.7
2005	5,335.5	461.4	5,796.9
2010	4,863.7	510.2	5,373.9
2015	4,916.4	886.4	5,802.8
2016	4,989.8	913.4	5,903.2
2017	5,763.2	916.2	6,679.4
2018	6,307.8	934.8	7,242.6
2019	7,468.5	908.8	8,377.4
2020	7,552.1	907.4	8,459.5

X–Not applicable. Technical college districts did not have authority to incur debt prior to 1967.
Sources: Wisconsin Department of Public Instruction, departmental data, March 2021; Wisconsin Technical College System Board, departmental data, March 2021.

Federal aids to Wisconsin

Agency administering aid	Aid received by Wisconsin ($1,000)		Disbursed to local governments ($1,000)		Aid to individuals and organizations ($1,000)	
	Fiscal year 2018–19	Fiscal year 2019–20	Fiscal year 2018–19	Fiscal year 2019–20	Fiscal year 2018–19	Fiscal year 2019–20
Administration	168,803	2,177,532	142,038	142,491	15,279	16,332
Agriculture, Trade and Consumer Protection	14,600	14,899	—	—	—	—
Child Abuse and Neglect Prevention Board	491	521	—	—	516	382
Children and Families	619,883	733,486	113,655	112,367	414,372	425,790
Clean Water Fund Program[1]	54,878	75,768	58,865	67,028	—	—
Corrections	1,991	3,282	—	—	—	—
Elections Commission	505	15,905	—	—	—	—
Government Accountability Board	1	—	—	—	—	—

Federal aids to Wisconsin, continued

Agency administering aid	Aid received by Wisconsin ($1,000)		Disbursed to local governments ($1,000)		Aid to individuals and organizations ($1,000)	
	Fiscal year 2018–19	Fiscal year 2019–20	Fiscal year 2018–19	Fiscal year 2019–20	Fiscal year 2018–19	Fiscal year 2019–20
Health Services	7,086,726	7,792,851	158,556	158,539	6,166,663	6,416,430
Historical Society	1,193	1,178	—	—	—	—
Insurance, Commissioner of . . .	—	8	—	—	—	—
Justice	52,407	49,766	32,194	36,322	1,478	1,975
Military Affairs.	72,777	84,653	15,232	25,855	689	487
Natural Resources	166,356	164,886	7,415	9,392	—	—
People with Developmental Disabilities, Board for	1,240	1,848	—	—	561	447
Public Instruction.	814,986	775,752	687,055	700,357	60,385	60,445
Public Lands Board.	55	59	51	55	—	—
Public Service Commission. . . .	4,925	3,721	—	—	—	—
Revenue	—	—	—	—	—	—
Safety and Professional Services	65	308	—	—	—	—
Supreme Court	665	576	—	—	—	—
Technical College System Board	28,796	30,973	23,264	24,296	1,272	847
Tourism.	915	66	—	—	620	714
Transportation	1,039,065	1,095,460	191,562	166,739	6,676	6,112
University of Wisconsin System .	1,622,962	1,632,790	—	—	—	—
Veterans Affairs	2,698	2,536	—	—	—	—
Workforce Development	209,651	203,744	—	—	79,040	63,158
Total.	**11,966,630**	**14,862,568**	**1,429,888**	**1,443,441**	**6,747,552**	**6,993,117**

Note: Aid is not necessarily disbursed in the same fiscal year in which it is received by the agency. In some cases, aid is received as reimbursement for previous expenditures.

—Represents zero.

1. Federal aid received by Wisconsin for Clean Water Fund (Environmental Improvement Program, DOA) also includes safe drinking water loan program appropriations.

Source: Wisconsin Department of Administration, State Controller's Office, *Annual Fiscal Report—Appendix*, 2019 and 2020.

State payments to local units of government, fiscal year 2020

County[1]	School levy tax credit[2] ($)	Shared revenue payments[3] ($)	Exempt property aid[4] ($)	Personal property aid[5] ($)	Total ($)	Per capita[6] Amount ($)	Rank
Adams	4,269,102	1,278,417	35,167	101,543	5,684,229	274.59	64
Ashland.	2,233,244	6,031,702	57,769	189,816	8,512,531	536.36	1
Barron.	7,872,702	6,928,081	185,926	437,439	15,424,147	331.55	31
Bayfield.	3,688,447	1,494,557	6,912	51,742	5,241,659	341.83	24
Brown.	36,751,791	26,943,119	5,389,664	3,460,488	72,545,061	273.94	65
Buffalo	2,229,838	2,908,040	64,433	99,403	5,301,714	387.81	10
Burnett	3,802,314	1,180,060	20,970	43,363	5,046,708	325.89	35
Calumet	6,913,565	3,712,154	438,541	387,121	11,451,381	214.69	72
Chippewa . . .	8,705,913	10,886,376	774,525	792,837	21,159,650	323.84	39
Clark.	3,436,224	8,115,421	76,953	487,711	12,116,308	348.92	19
Columbia. . . .	9,861,729	7,871,676	202,007	636,996	18,572,408	325.07	36
Crawford	2,159,738	3,545,942	100,133	290,956	6,096,769	365.54	14
Dane	122,510,828	26,113,050	16,880,920	8,878,254	174,383,051	320.91	40
Dodge	11,268,610	12,847,967	442,012	1,365,598	25,924,186	288.03	58
Door.	7,237,538	1,500,430	134,238	338,110	9,210,315	320.14	41
Douglas.	6,568,881	11,125,873	129,904	723,287	18,547,946	419.20	6

State payments to local units of government, fiscal year 2020, continued

County[1]	School levy tax credit[2] ($)	Shared revenue payments[3] ($)	Exempt property aid[4] ($)	Personal property aid[5] ($)	Total ($)	Per capita[6] Amount ($)	Rank
Dunn	5,382,998	8,029,864	187,514	910,812	14,511,189	324.00	37
Eau Claire. . . .	14,240,180	13,358,687	1,213,018	1,215,677	30,027,561	288.84	56
Florence	1,034,946	339,013	5,382	25,448	1,404,790	314.48	44
Fond du Lac . .	13,244,232	15,020,867	1,090,943	1,530,621	30,886,663	295.93	52
Forest	2,061,370	985,232	17,072	24,585	3,088,259	336.30	27
Grant	6,160,883	12,382,265	157,665	358,621	19,059,435	362.54	16
Green	5,979,543	3,917,377	600,642	468,348	10,965,911	296.64	51
Green Lake. . .	3,414,412	3,147,976	92,168	369,648	7,024,206	366.26	13
Iowa.	4,017,174	2,265,258	625,567	585,847	7,493,846	313.35	45
Iron	1,307,826	1,369,098	4,202	35,849	2,716,975	459.80	3
Jackson	3,053,341	3,109,543	90,914	712,849	6,966,647	334.48	29
Jefferson	12,719,098	9,403,191	924,640	768,897	23,815,825	281.21	61
Juneau	3,825,080	4,966,846	64,070	146,883	9,002,879	330.38	32
Kenosha	26,705,606	20,361,765	2,981,053	5,171,866	55,220,291	323.85	38
Kewaunee . . .	2,904,727	3,191,714	60,847	216,850	6,374,138	307.25	49
La Crosse. . . .	18,619,091	18,011,241	2,580,998	2,306,611	41,517,941	344.70	23
Lafayette	2,142,417	5,376,570	23,040	267,499	7,809,526	459.19	4
Langlade	2,595,254	4,126,868	108,831	119,297	6,950,250	346.42	21
Lincoln	3,949,721	5,682,726	194,788	228,414	10,055,649	349.15	18
Manitowoc. . .	9,032,867	17,345,760	601,487	685,299	27,665,413	340.08	25
Marathon. . . .	19,426,564	19,713,368	2,311,040	1,969,129	43,420,102	316.39	43
Marinette. . . .	6,299,017	9,790,956	220,810	411,630	16,722,413	405.34	7
Marquette . . .	2,564,860	1,036,450	55,358	88,722	3,745,390	243.41	68
Menominee . .	534,363	645,236	3,058	2,415	1,185,072	277.73	62
Milwaukee . . .	121,566,391	312,025,975	31,267,186	9,536,249	474,395,802	502.49	2
Monroe.	5,165,237	8,328,155	152,226	678,284	14,323,903	305.53	50
Oconto	6,116,581	4,532,159	78,954	198,531	10,926,224	281.22	60
Oneida	9,929,559	1,932,350	135,796	524,040	12,521,745	345.26	22
Outagamie. . .	24,614,450	22,372,039	2,649,792	2,428,589	52,064,871	277.44	63
Ozaukee	19,828,099	6,601,064	810,708	685,695	27,925,566	308.13	48
Pepin	1,289,269	1,367,825	15,550	123,287	2,795,932	378.19	11
Pierce	6,372,262	5,171,858	104,317	380,453	12,028,890	283.61	59
Polk	8,459,392	4,160,919	89,493	445,195	13,154,999	294.77	53
Portage.	8,593,404	7,658,065	1,094,696	861,889	18,208,054	254.05	67
Price	2,357,667	3,036,043	53,855	74,329	5,521,895	389.69	8
Racine.	28,370,330	34,119,037	3,287,441	2,349,492	68,126,300	348.00	20
Richland	1,986,984	3,775,044	54,670	64,025	5,880,723	326.09	34
Rock.	18,864,226	32,826,293	1,711,098	2,523,888	55,925,505	349.27	17
Rusk.	2,532,113	3,740,586	70,867	117,934	6,461,501	434.27	5
St. Croix.	16,394,176	3,790,088	281,731	799,992	21,265,987	233.82	70
Sauk.	11,385,143	4,951,566	567,864	1,399,737	18,304,310	288.97	55
Sawyer	4,471,272	1,112,334	22,596	75,086	5,681,289	336.11	28
Shawano	5,549,003	5,255,210	111,049	276,733	11,191,994	268.14	66
Sheboygan. . .	16,344,377	17,214,911	1,957,166	1,071,912	36,588,365	312.92	47
Taylor	2,482,759	3,558,611	162,181	439,727	6,643,278	319.50	42
Trempealeau. .	4,131,349	6,320,506	208,308	291,242	10,951,405	364.48	15
Vernon	3,612,123	5,979,585	119,846	308,056	10,019,611	328.55	33
Vilas	7,773,237	562,201	27,624	107,160	8,470,221	389.10	9
Walworth. . . .	26,554,408	6,661,530	478,869	1,066,105	34,760,912	333.96	30
Washburn . . .	3,941,900	1,285,736	70,647	113,905	5,412,188	338.41	26
Washington . .	23,042,477	5,583,801	1,060,569	1,260,835	30,947,682	223.82	71
Waukesha . . .	95,777,707	10,932,788	6,242,177	6,628,561	119,581,234	293.97	54
Waupaca	7,505,837	8,207,739	301,573	321,397	16,336,546	313.23	46
Waushara. . . .	3,875,377	1,745,155	51,382	167,423	5,839,338	238.96	69
Winnebago . .	21,169,636	22,013,704	4,200,523	1,571,994	48,955,857	288.21	57

State payments to local units of government, fiscal year 2020, continued

County[1]	School levy tax credit[2] ($)	Shared revenue payments[3] ($)	Exempt property aid[4] ($)	Personal property aid[5] ($)	Total ($)	Per capita[6] Amount ($)	Rank
Wood	9,217,219	15,573,735	1,451,124	1,555,887	27,797,965	368.77	12
State	940,000,000	888,457,352	98,047,059	75,354,115	2,001,858,526	314.93	X

X–Not applicable.

1. Some cities and villages are located in more than one county. In these cases, payments are attributed to the "primary" county, as determined by the Wisconsin Department of Revenue. For example, payments to the city of Appleton are attributed to Outagamie County even though parts of Appleton are located in Calumet and Winnebago Counties. 2. Distributed July 2020. 3. Total of amounts (excluding deductions) distributed July and November 2019. 4. Includes exempt computer aid distributed July 2019. 5. May 2020 payment. 6. Based on 2020 population estimates.

Sources: Wisconsin Department of Revenue, Division of State and Local Finance, Local Government Services Bureau, departmental data, March 2021; Wisconsin Department of Administration, Demographic Services Center, *Official Final Estimates, January 1, 2020*, October 2020.

Wisconsin general property assessments and tax levies

	Full-value assess-ment of all property (mil. dol.)	% change	Total state and local property taxes levied (mil. dol)	% change	State property tax relief (mil. dol.)	Average full-value tax rate per $1,000	% change	Average net tax rate per $1,000 after state tax relief	% change
1900. . . .	630	X	19	X	NA	31.00	X	NA	X
1910. . . .	2,743	X	31	X	NA	11.18	X	NA	X
1920. . . .	4,571	X	96	X	NA	21.06	X	NA	X
1930. . . .	5,896	X	121	X	NA	20.49	X	NA	X
1940. . . .	4,354	X	110	X	NA	25.26	X	NA	X
1950. . . .	9,201	X	226	X	NA	24.52	X	NA	X
1960. . . .	18,844	X	481	X	NA	25.55	X	NA	X
1970. . . .	34,790	X	1,179	X	140	33.88	X	NA	X
1980. . . .	108,480	X	2,210	X	309	20.37	X	NA	X
1990. . . .	141,370	X	4,388	X	319	31.04	X	28.78	X
2000. . . .	286,321	X	6,605	X	469	23.06	X	21.42	X
2001. . . .	312,484	9.1	7,044	6.7	469	22.54	-2.3	21.03	-1.8
2002. . . .	335,326	7.3	7,364	4.5	469	21.95	-2.6	20.55	-2.3
2003. . . .	360,710	7.6	7,687	4.4	469	21.31	-3.0	20.01	-2.7
2004. . . .	391,188	8.4	8,151	6.0	469	20.83	-2.2	19.63	-1.9
2005. . . .	427,934	9.4	8,327	2.2	469	19.45	-6.6	18.36	-6.5
2006. . . .	468,983	9.6	8,706	4.6	593	18.56	-4.6	17.29	-5.8
2007. . . .	497,920	6.2	9,251	6.3	672	18.57	0.1	17.22	-0.4
2008. . . .	514,394	3.3	9,667	4.5	747	18.79	1.2	17.34	0.6
2009. . . .	511,912	-0.5	10,106	4.5	747	19.74	5.0	18.28	5.4
2010. . . .	495,904	-3.1	10,365	2.6	747	20.90	5.9	19.39	6.1
2011. . . .	486,864	-1.8	10,385	0.2	747	21.33	2.1	19.79	2.1
2012. . . .	471,093	-3.2	10,470	0.8	747	22.22	4.2	20.63	4.3
2013. . . .	467,503	-0.8	10,606	1.3	747	22.68	2.1	21.08	2.2
2014. . . .	479,024	2.5	10,384	-2.1	747	21.67	4.4	20.11	4.6
2015. . . .	490,603	2.4	10,620	2.3	853	21.65	0.1	19.91	1.0
2016. . . .	505,124	3.0	10,792	1.6	853	21.37	1.3	19.68	1.2
2017. . . .	525,985	4.1	11,016	2.1	940	20.94	2.0	19.16	2.6
2018. . . .	549,533	4.5	11,199	1.7	940	20.38	-2.7	18.67	-2.6
2019. . . .	580,873	5.7	11,618	3.7	940	20.00	-1.9	18.38	-1.6

NA–Not available; X–Not applicable.

Source: Wisconsin Department of Revenue, Division of State and Local Finance, *2019 Town, Village, and City Taxes: Taxes Levied 2019—Collected 2020*, and prior issues.

General property assessments, taxes, and rates, 2019

County	Full-value assessment[1] ($)	Total property tax[2] ($)	State property tax credit[3] ($)	Average full-value tax rate per $1,000[4]	
				Gross ($)	Net ($)
Adams	2,825,953,400	53,928,718	4,194,197	19.08	17.60
Ashland	1,252,163,400	28,555,947	2,251,739	22.81	21.01
Barron	4,502,277,100	90,434,886	8,110,182	20.09	18.29
Bayfield	2,714,849,300	39,868,755	3,632,669	14.69	13.35
Brown	23,181,417,300	462,096,330	37,002,700	19.93	18.34
Buffalo	1,228,183,300	25,185,686	2,250,285	20.51	18.67
Burnett	2,845,710,000	39,303,254	3,719,812	13.81	12.50
Calumet	4,490,140,000	91,239,221	6,832,657	20.32	18.80
Chippewa	6,046,130,300	100,913,883	8,910,190	16.69	15.22
Clark	2,289,782,500	49,393,490	3,426,741	21.57	20.07
Columbia	5,863,531,000	115,913,400	9,958,181	19.77	18.07
Crawford	1,257,908,400	30,184,162	2,212,776	24.00	22.24
Dane	69,928,053,700	1,516,756,787	126,243,497	21.69	19.88
Dodge	6,971,933,100	143,857,319	11,414,118	20.63	19.00
Door	7,532,357,400	104,149,452	7,212,130	13.83	12.87
Douglas	3,654,146,000	70,757,227	6,512,856	19.36	17.58
Dunn	3,354,243,900	70,054,664	5,288,534	20.89	19.31
Eau Claire	9,220,492,300	179,058,771	14,341,709	19.42	17.86
Florence	647,308,000	12,447,824	1,078,423	19.23	17.56
Fond du Lac	8,046,438,000	172,613,515	12,906,970	21.45	19.85
Forest	1,172,743,300	20,554,819	2,038,531	17.53	15.79
Grant	3,411,037,100	72,215,090	6,279,823	21.17	19.33
Green	3,263,247,100	73,806,145	6,128,820	22.62	20.74
Green Lake	2,387,398,800	42,108,940	3,273,805	17.64	16.27
Iowa	2,197,456,200	52,068,687	4,139,731	23.69	21.81
Iron	983,071,000	16,224,667	1,289,560	16.50	15.19
Jackson	1,723,495,700	35,125,205	3,048,938	20.38	18.61
Jefferson	7,725,722,500	156,340,822	12,907,323	20.24	18.57
Juneau	2,309,017,300	47,399,732	3,731,019	20.53	18.91
Kenosha	16,831,339,100	361,483,353	26,719,037	21.48	19.89
Kewaunee	1,788,279,900	37,381,887	2,886,443	20.90	19.29
La Crosse	10,552,445,000	225,841,181	18,597,003	21.40	19.64
Lafayette	1,225,242,500	29,546,681	2,242,793	24.11	22.28
Langlade	1,807,505,300	32,213,269	2,560,929	17.82	16.41
Lincoln	2,541,238,500	51,271,603	4,029,346	20.18	18.59
Manitowoc	5,737,214,100	117,779,718	8,773,352	20.53	19.00
Marathon	11,639,160,900	252,054,643	19,581,435	21.66	19.97
Marinette	4,002,460,800	70,486,944	6,230,395	17.61	16.05
Marquette	1,669,513,800	32,091,666	2,495,393	19.22	17.73
Menominee	327,199,900	6,486,108	507,345	19.82	18.27
Milwaukee	67,178,449,700	1,766,028,378	116,998,689	26.29	24.55
Monroe	3,579,764,100	71,035,231	5,132,990	19.84	18.41
Oconto	4,102,238,100	71,682,839	6,253,057	17.47	15.95
Oneida	7,226,434,800	94,780,521	9,928,899	13.12	11.74
Outagamie	16,570,536,900	313,246,042	24,409,747	18.90	17.43
Ozaukee	12,995,887,800	214,043,087	19,947,535	16.47	14.94
Pepin	646,926,700	13,988,541	1,290,652	21.62	19.63
Pierce	3,624,907,300	74,112,854	6,395,314	20.45	18.68
Polk	5,090,558,200	90,465,265	8,370,990	17.77	16.13
Portage	6,353,475,400	129,308,405	8,689,029	20.35	18.98
Price	1,440,977,900	28,400,516	2,265,972	19.71	18.14
Racine	16,475,064,700	354,029,616	28,555,750	21.49	19.76
Richland	1,209,046,400	25,662,692	1,993,606	21.23	19.58
Rock	12,364,512,600	284,753,670	19,059,785	23.03	21.49
Rusk	1,278,969,200	25,294,647	2,463,664	19.78	17.85
St. Croix	10,620,318,200	185,223,025	17,255,663	17.44	15.82

General property assessments, taxes, and rates, 2019, continued

County	Full-value assessment[1] ($)	Total property tax[2] ($)	State property tax credit[3] ($)	Average full-value tax rate per $1,000[4] Gross ($)	Net ($)
Sauk.	7,715,950,200	148,550,205	11,477,084	19.25	17.76
Sawyer	3,695,423,300	42,361,427	4,437,309	11.46	10.26
Shawano	3,324,246,600	65,268,831	5,541,679	19.63	17.97
Sheboygan.	10,142,962,300	205,805,231	16,082,692	20.29	18.70
Taylor	1,509,078,800	31,721,198	2,430,812	21.02	19.41
Trempealeau.	2,402,213,100	54,538,364	4,179,742	22.70	20.96
Vernon	2,098,673,500	45,167,887	3,539,336	21.52	19.84
Vilas	7,223,863,100	77,173,829	7,721,524	10.68	9.61
Walworth.	15,706,734,800	276,779,935	26,442,862	17.62	15.94
Washburn	2,644,185,500	42,012,368	3,993,034	15.89	14.38
Washington	16,155,740,400	253,271,621	23,352,340	15.68	14.23
Waukesha	59,540,912,600	944,480,181	95,244,479	15.86	14.26
Waupaca	4,336,538,900	90,427,078	7,543,386	20.85	19.11
Waushara.	2,709,640,200	47,759,127	3,752,629	17.63	16.24
Winnebago	14,203,069,600	299,309,900	21,139,420	21.07	19.59
Wood	5,557,615,200	122,366,895	9,148,968	22.02	20.37
Total.	**580,872,723,300**	**11,618,243,857**	**940,000,025**	**20.00**	**18.38**

1. Reflects actual market value of all taxable general property, as determined by the Wisconsin Department of Revenue independent of locally assessed values, which can vary substantially from full value.   2. Includes taxes and special charges levied by schools, counties, cities, villages, towns, special purpose districts, and the State of Wisconsin. It does not include special assessments or other charges.   3. Total amount of school levy tax credit paid by the state to taxing districts and credited to taxpayers on their tax bills. The credit is considered part of the tax payment.   4. A county's average tax rate per $1,000 of assessed valuation (determined by dividing total taxes by equalized value and multiplying by 1,000) is the preferred figure for comparison purposes, rather than the general local property tax rate because the average is based on full market value. Net tax rate per $1,000 reflects the effect of state property tax relief.

Source: Wisconsin Department of Revenue, Division of State and Local Finance, *Town, Village, and City Taxes—2019: Taxes Levied 2019— Collected 2020.*

Municipal property taxes levied in Wisconsin

	Total (mil. dol.)	% Residential	% Commercial	% Manufacturing	% Agricultural	% Personal[1]	% Other[2]
1960.	481.4	47.5	13.5	10.7	11.2	16.5	0.6
1965.	664.1	48.4	14.4	10.3	10.6	15.8	0.6
1970.	1,179.0	47.3	15.2	10.4	9.7	16.9	0.5
1975.	1,601.3	50.5	16.8	5.7	10.1	16.2	0.7
1980.	2,210.0	57.7	16.2	4.8	12.5	7.5	1.3
1985.	3,203.5	58.9	17.7	4.7	12.4	4.8	1.6
1990.	4,388.2	60.4	20.2	4.1	8.4	5.5	1.3
1995.	5,738.9	64.8	18.8	3.6	6.7	4.9	1.1
1996.	5,378.0	65.7	18.9	3.6	3.6	4.6	3.7
1997.	5,635.9	66.2	18.7	3.6	3.3	4.5	3.7
1998.	5,975.0	66.5	18.7	3.6	2.9	4.5	3.9
1999.	6,190.9	67.3	18.8	3.7	2.7	3.5	4.0
2000.	6,604.5	67.9	18.9	3.7	1.7	3.4	4.3
2001.	7,043.7	68.1	19.0	3.6	1.6	3.4	4.4
2002.	7,363.6	69.0	18.9	3.5	0.8	3.2	4.6
2003.	7,687.3	69.7	18.8	3.4	0.6	2.9	4.7

Municipal property taxes levied in Wisconsin, continued

	Total (mil. dol.)	% Residential	% Commercial	% Manufacturing	% Agricultural	% Personal[1]	% Other[2]
2004	8,150.8	70.3	18.8	3.2	0.5	2.7	4.5
2005	8,326.7	71.0	18.7	3.0	0.5	2.6	4.2
2006	8,706.4	71.4	18.7	2.8	0.5	2.5	4.2
2007	9,250.3	71.4	18.9	2.7	0.4	2.4	4.2
2008	9,677.1	70.9	19.2	2.7	0.4	2.6	4.2
2009	10,105.7	70.4	19.6	2.7	0.4	2.6	4.3
2010	10,364.6	70.4	19.6	2.8	0.4	2.6	4.3
2011	10,384.8	70.2	19.7	2.8	0.4	2.5	4.3
2012	10,469.9	69.6	20.2	2.9	0.4	2.6	4.3
2013	10,605.5	69.0	20.5	3.0	0.4	2.7	4.3
2014	10,383.7	68.8	20.8	3.0	0.4	2.8	4.2
2015	10,620.2	68.6	21.0	3.0	0.4	2.7	4.2
2016	10,792.1	68.3	21.3	3.0	0.4	2.8	4.2
2017	11,016.1	68.1	21.7	3.0	0.4	2.7	4.1
2018	11,198.9	68.7	22.0	3.0	0.4	1.9	4.1
2019	11,618.2	68.8	22.0	3.0	0.4	1.9	4.0

Note: Percentages may not add up to 100 due to rounding.

1. An exemption for "Line A" business property was phased in beginning in 1977. "Line A" property was completely exempted by 1981.   2. Beginning in 1996, "Other" includes agricultural property not considered agricultural land for purposes of use-value assessment.

Sources: Wisconsin Department of Revenue, Division of State and Local Finance, Local Government Services, *2019 Town, Village and City Taxes: Taxes Levied 2019—Collected 2020*, and prior issues; for 1980, 1975, and 1970 data, *Property Tax*, 1981 and prior issues; 1960 and 1965 data are from the Wisconsin Department of Taxation.

Wisconsin general property tax levies, 2019

Type of property	Towns ($)	Villages ($)	Cities ($)	Total ($)
Real estate	3,351,597,362	2,095,581,276	5,955,441,462	11,402,620,100
Residential	2,631,231,876	1,557,116,662	3,804,334,964	7,992,683,502
Commercial	195,110,593	445,523,705	1,917,229,024	2,557,863,322
Manufacturing	35,469,476	79,968,888	228,250,180	343,688,544
Forest lands	124,043,350	2,228,189	707,901	126,979,440
Agricultural	40,974,632	1,099,167	508,854	42,582,653
Ag forest	55,961,114	975,733	363,878	57,300,725
Undeveloped	33,908,428	1,398,538	795,900	36,102,866
Other land and improvements	234,897,893	7,270,395	3,250,762	245,419,050
Personal property	25,591,686	34,736,023	155,295,955	215,623,664
Furniture, fixtures, equipment	7,638,548	19,246,200	86,927,506	113,812,254
Machinery, tools, patterns	6,066,980	8,598,627	29,510,596	44,176,203
Boats and other watercraft	149,627	35,984	128,053	313,664
All other personal property	11,736,531	6,855,212	38,729,801	57,321,544
Total general property taxes	3,377,189,009	2,130,317,335	6,110,737,513	11,618,243,857
Total state tax credit	331,920,842	173,461,017	434,618,166	940,000,025
Total effective taxes	3,045,268,167	1,956,856,318	5,676,119,347	10,678,243,832

Note: The sums of some columns and rows may differ slightly from the reported totals because the Department of Revenue truncates (rather than rounds) amounts under $1 for individual units of government.

Source: Wisconsin Department of Revenue, Division of State and Local Finance, *Town, Village, and City Taxes—2019: Taxes Levied 2019—Collected 2020*.

Wisconsin Conservation Fund revenues and expenditures, 2013-2017

	FY 2013–14 ($)	FY 2014–15 ($)	FY 2015–16 ($)	FY 2016–17 ($)
Opening cash balance	39,267,307	37,191,298	42,685,686	60,473,125
Revenues	**286,915,608**	**292,932,526**	**311,640,899**	**303,038,659**
User fees (licenses, registration)	102,118,589	104,820,956	113,182,781	125,634,380
Forestry mill tax	79,399,769	81,350,401	83,306,027	85,760,413
Federal aids	45,486,239	45,687,437	44,928,485	43,064,052
Motor fuel tax formula	22,842,478	23,574,182	23,681,894	23,086,512
Severance tax	8,985,347	9,263,069	10,555,268	10,150,721
Other revenues (sales, services)	28,083,186	28,236,481	35,986,444	15,342,581
Expenditures	**288,991,617**	**287,438,138**	**293,853,460**	**291,600,806**
Land and forestry—state	93,368,808	89,769,542	95,214,571	96,581,448
Land and forestry—federal	15,146,341	17,111,226	16,228,694	16,442,572
Enforcement/science—state	22,554,512	22,986,382	22,797,824	22,489,837
Enforcement/science—federal	11,257,421	11,246,443	10,166,126	10,324,407
Water management—state	21,704,213	22,638,169	22,601,306	20,970,586
Water management—federal	5,736,280	5,180,222	5,064,936	5,298,995
Conservation aids—state	29,955,985	32,205,061	31,619,966	34,876,037
Conservation aids—federal	4,250,563	4,867,250	6,309,235	6,613,623
Environmental aids—state	6,722,852	6,287,498	5,892,225	6,316,021
Development/debt service—state . . .	21,065,928	21,958,417	22,218,355	22,854,570
Development/debt service—federal . .	6,539,906	3,413,936	6,368,552	1,567,312
Administrative services—state	3,729,519	2,577,149	2,170,431	2,302,533
Administrative services—federal	1,337,961	621,125	437,401	342,926
CAES[1] management—state	24,318,420	24,934,968	26,409,465	26,150,748
CAES[1] management—federal	6,015,817	6,931,415	6,196,326	5,515,622
Other activities—state	15,287,091	14,709,335	14,158,047	12,953,569
Fund Balance	**37,191,298**	**42,685,686**	**60,473,125**	**71,910,978**

FY–Fiscal year.

1. Customer and Employee Services Division.

Source: Wisconsin Department of Administration, Division of Executive Budget and Finance, State Controller's Office, *2017 Annual Fiscal Report (Budgetary Basis) Appendix*, and prior editions.

Wisconsin Conservation Fund revenues and expenditures, 2017-20

	FY 2017–18 ($)	FY 2018–19 ($)	FY 2019–20 ($)
Opening cash balance	71,910,978	105,999,248	132,085,902
Revenues	**338,539,046**	**340,176,062**	**338,811,825**
User fees (licenses, registrations, recreational fees) . . .	118,204,889	114,683,192	115,386,597
Forestry mill tax	22,334,529	—	—
GPR transfer for forestry mill tax[1]	89,259,577	93,255,699	98,574,101
Federal aids	39,856,736	72,477,080	66,183,985
Motor fuel tax formula	22,362,031	21,172,548	20,716,368
Severance tax	1,318,170	—	—
Gifts, donations and private support	1,730,300	2,119,743	1,462,418
Other revenues (sales, services)	43,472,814	36,467,800	36,488,356
Expenditures	**304,450,776**	**314,089,408**	**320,640,101**
Fish, wildlife, and parks—state	60,188,152	58,739,616	62,793,867
Fish, wildlife, and parks—federal	30,820,435	30,045,014	27,535,596
Forestry—state	50,217,824	53,148,340	54,761,432
Forestry—federal	3,495,496	3,380,625	1,651,113
Enforcement—state	23,450,604	23,634,039	27,980,261

Wisconsin Conservation Fund revenues and expenditures, 2017–20, continued

	FY 2017–18 ($)	FY 2018–19 ($)	FY 2019–20 ($)
Enforcement—federal.	6,083,611	5,878,387	5,909,881
Environmental management—state	1,964,993	2,061,757	2,620,947
Conservation aids—state	30,854,146	36,474,315	33,709,146
Conservation aids—federal	6,010,268	7,640,628	8,528,438
Environmental aids—state	7,229,769	5,947,944	6,907,555
Development/debt service—state	22,677,941	25,897,070	25,182,892
Development/debt service—federal.	1,993,275	2,503,522	1,496,042
Administration—state.	1,991,523	3,085,914	3,457,124
Administration—federal	423,126	1,233,470	1,149,511
Internal and external services—state	35,457,689	31,833,402	36,343,776
Internal and external services—federal	6,926,777	8,725,168	5,541,017
Other activities—state	14,665,147	13,860,197	15,071,503
Fund balance	**105,999,248**	**132,085,902**	**150,257,626**

Note: Because of reorganization of the Department of Natural Resources, expenditure categories since 2017–18 are not comparable to those of prior years.

FY–Fiscal year; —Represents zero.

1. The forestry mill tax sunset as of January 1, 2017, property tax assessments. 2017 Wisconsin Act 59 provides for a GPR transfer to the conservation fund in an amount comparable to what would have been provided from the tax.

Source: Wisconsin Department of Administration, Division of Executive Budget and Finance, State Controller's Office, *2020 Annual Fiscal Report (Budgetary Basis) Appendix*, and prior editions.

Wisconsin Transportation Fund revenues and expenditures

	Fiscal year 2018–19		Fiscal year 2019–20	
	State funds ($)	Federal, local, and agency funds ($)	State funds ($)	Federal, local, and agency funds ($)
Opening balance	350,907,692	-1,229,822,382	367,815,644	-1,435,803,905
Revenues	1,777,027,793	1,283,077,375	1,900,707,730	1,326,796,477
Motor fuel taxes.	1,063,953,155	X	1,018,543,126	X
Vehicle registration[1]	493,155,213	X	622,946,749	X
Drivers license fees.	40,564,420	X	39,043,092	X
Motor carrier fees.	2,378,111	X	2,672,877	X
Other motor vehicle fees	26,927,238	X	23,497,398	X
Overweight/oversize permits	6,849,053	X	6,919,302	X
Investment earnings.	8,957,899	X	6,367,872	X
Aeronautical taxes and fees	2,002,922	X	1,764,918	X
Public utility tax revenues (aeronautics and railroads)	50,334,795	X	49,066,726	X
Transfers-in[2]	75,482,468	X	111,311,203	X
Miscellaneous	6,422,519	4,011,228	18,574,467	1,663,748
Service center operations.	X	32,351,444	X	24,458,496
State and local highway facilities— federal.	X	929,016,900	X	948,198,908
State and local highway facilities—local	X	88,343,494	X	107,042,031
Major highway development revenue bonds	X	102,800,990	X	74,257,373
Highway administration and planning— federal.	X	1,847,720	X	2,184,089
Aeronautics—federal	X	39,155,560	X	65,387,219
Aeronautics—local.	X	5,418,310	X	19,766,869

Wisconsin Transportation Fund revenues and expenditures, continued

	Fiscal year 2018–19		Fiscal year 2019–20	
	State funds ($)	Federal, local, and agency funds ($)	State funds ($)	Federal, local, and agency funds ($)
Railroad assistance—federal	X	2,950,329	X	2,578
Railroad assistance—local	X	3,790,056	X	10,384
Railroad passenger service—federal . . .	X	530,917	X	637,325
Railroad passenger service—local	X	7,354	X	119,076
Transit assistance—federal	X	21,904,176	X	33,386,769
Transit assistance—local	X	743,481	X	2,307,744
Congestion mitigation air quality—federal	X	1,707,042	X	3,406,695
Congestion mitigation air quality—local	X	539,321	X	62,317
Harbors assistance—federal	X	—	X	509
Harbors assistance—local	X	9,600	X	—
Transportation alternatives program—federal	X	5,686,188	X	8,098,342
Transportation alternatives program—local	X	1,680,366	X	410,237
General administration and planning—federal	X	28,518,334	X	25,665,333
General administration and planning—local	X	1,290,737	X	2,838
Administrative facilities—revenue bonds	X	2,902,370	X	3,881,756
Highway safety—federal	X	7,612,237	X	5,513,621
Gifts and grants	X	259,221	X	332,220
Expenditures[3]	**1,760,119,841**	**1,489,058,901**	**1,762,892,000**	**1,223,557,684**
Local assistance	676,247,479	236,853,236	698,312,603	393,657,147
Highway aids	477,162,128	—	496,929,474	—
Local bridge and highway improvement	50,769,631	157,863,539	37,785,461	234,619,189
Mass transit	126,577,832	12,402,362	130,916,624	60,209,433
Railroads	2,485,075	-316,866	3,155,131	1,718,888
Aeronautics	16,348,413	63,545,121	19,070,429	84,071,533
Highway safety	—	3,359,009	—	5,698,783
Rail passenger service	2,467,655	71	4,960,798	-4
Harbors	-46,583	—	5,356,115	7,339,325
Multimodal transportation studies	—	—	-40,000	—
Transportation alternatives program . .	483,328	—	178,571	—
Aids to individuals and organizations . .	8,578,914	7,781,076	6,402,495	12,017,763
Transportation facilities economic assistance and development	3,306,217	-17,978	592,294	1,237,304
Railroad crossings	3,874,251	4,805,785	4,227,909	3,850,401
Elderly and disabled	1,398,446	3,494,126	1,582,292	5,297,626
Freight rail	—	-500,857	—	1,632,432
State operations	1,054,119,815	1,244,424,589	1,037,460,534	817,882,774
Highway improvements	390,409,561	1,039,593,416	380,780,604	693,560,054
Major highway development—revenue bonds	—	122,333,054	—	52,838,965
Highway maintenance, repair, and traffic operations	289,686,852	9,577,451	277,068,138	14,061,333
Highway administration and planning	12,451,264	1,755,896	13,945,075	1,745,707
Traffic enforcement and inspection . . .	65,713,362	7,208,932	74,304,955	4,500,710
Transportation safety	1,462,338	3,516,095	1,844,430	5,405,757
General administration and planning .	69,536,490	14,887,509	67,136,221	13,056,628
Administrative facilities—revenue bonds		13,231,803	—	4,540,000

Wisconsin Transportation Fund revenues and expenditures,
continued

	Fiscal year 2018–19		Fiscal year 2019–20	
	State funds ($)	Federal, local, and agency funds ($)	State funds ($)	Federal, local, and agency funds ($)
Vehicle registration and drivers licensing.	73,455,315	433,231	74,814,347	196,493
Vehicle inspection and maintenance . .	2,595,960	—	2,809,050	—
Debt repayment and interest[4]	146,739,741	—	142,956,962	—
Service centers	—	25,699,872	—	26,609,038
Congestion mitigation air quality	—	5,404,444	—	306,816
Miscellaneous	2,068,932	782,886	1,800,752	1,061,273
Conservation Fund transfers	21,173,633	—	20,716,368	—
Closing balance	**367,815,644**	**-1,435,803,908**	**505,631,374**	**-1,332,565,112**

X–Not applicable; — Represents zero.

1. Section 84.59, Wis. Stats., provides that vehicle registration revenues derived under s. 341.25 are deposited with a trustee in a fund outside the state treasury. Only those revenues not required for the repayment of revenue bond obligations are considered income to the transportation fund. The trustee retained $211.1 million during FY 2019 and $216.3 million during FY 2020. 2. Transfer-in amount for FY 2019 includes $41.6 million general fund, $30.3 million petroleum inspection fund, $0.4 million conservation fund, and $3.2 million intrafund transfer from s. 20.395 (2)(bw); and for FY 2020 includes $43.3 million general fund, $61.3 million petroleum inspection fund, and $0.4 million conservation fund. 3. The amounts exclude financial activity relating to general obligation bond funded projects that are reimbursed by the capital improvement fund. 4. 2017 Wisconsin Act 59 (the 2017–19 biennial budget act) authorized $26.1 million in general obligation bond funding for railroad and harbor improvements. Debt service will be funded by the transportation fund. 2017 Wisconsin Act 58 authorized, contingent upon the receipt of federal moneys for certain purposes, up to $252.4 million in general obligation bond funding for southeast Wisconsin freeway megaprojects.

Source: Wisconsin Department of Administration, Division of Executive Budget and Finance, State Controller's Office, *2020 Annual Fiscal Report (Budgetary Basis) Appendix*.

Value added by manufacturing in Wisconsin

Industry group	2014 ($1,000)	2015 ($1,000)	2016 ($1,000)	2018 ($1,000)	2019 ($1,000)
Food manufacturing.	13,456,814	13,804,143	15,323,526	16,204,355	16,994,632
Machinery manufacturing	11,199,129	10,820,344	10,201,491	10,862,682	11,292,087
Fabricated metal product manufacturing. .	8,178,266	7,907,890	7,693,146	9,426,449	9,681,743
Paper manufacturing	6,193,379	6,360,489	6,120,441	6,324,080	6,746,369
Transportation equipment manufacturing	3,817,121	4,014,721	4,095,890	5,499,361	5,584,262
Plastics and rubber products manufacturing	3,946,250	4,061,013	4,422,525	4,675,909	4,747,464
Chemical manufacturing	5,788,557	6,061,961	6,231,740	4,917,573	4,736,544
Computer and electronic product manufacturing	4,792,239	4,488,886	4,709,640	4,459,958	4,555,884
Electrical equipment, appliance, and component manufacturing	3,913,824	3,920,074	4,100,086	4,211,280	4,112,518
Printing and related support activities	2,903,377	2,809,449	2,924,793	2,857,374	2,670,177
Primary metal manufacturing	3,172,064	3,067,135	2,919,110	2,832,312	2,642,089
Wood product manufacturing	1,650,465	1,713,280	2,029,390	1,837,367	2,030,744
Miscellaneous manufacturing	1,771,675	1,752,515	1,732,885	1,975,016	2,011,031
Nonmetallic mineral product manufacturing	2,286,320	2,335,148	2,446,309	2,072,172	1,936,192
Furniture and related product manufacturing	1,564,026	1,618,473	1,667,070	1,729,338	1,749,314
Beverage and tobacco product manufacturing	1,039,866	990,464	1,101,301	983,618	898,090
Petroleum and coal products manufacturing	D	D	863,111	215,066	209,741
Textile mills	D	D	162,570	195,485	189,179
Leather and allied product manufacturing .	D	D	111,021	128,451	116,295
Textile product mills	D	D	81,406	107,567	72,402
Apparel manufacturing	D	D	34,234	40,796	36,787
Total[1]	82,959,072	80,588,078	78,971,684	81,556,209	83,013,544

Note: U.S. Census Bureau data for 2017 was not available when this table was compiled.

D–Figure withheld to avoid disclosure.

1. Total may not add due to the exclusion of manufacturing categories beneath the top 20 highest values.

Source: U.S. Census Bureau, "Annual Survey of Manufactures: Geographic Area Statistics: Summary Statistics for Industry Groups and Industries in the U.S. and States: 2019 and 2018" and prior editions, at https://www.census.gov/programs-surveys/asm.html [March 8, 2021].

Value of Wisconsin exports by category

	2018 ($1,000)	2019 ($1,000)	2020 ($1,000)	% change 2019 to 2020
Top 20 categories[1] in 2020	18,472,555	17,668,795	16,963,843	-4.00
Industrial machinery, including computers . .	5,736,785	5,619,251	5,249,492	-6.58
Medical and scientific instruments.	2,153,969	2,048,391	2,038,832	-0.47
Electric machinery.	2,572,927	2,398,430	2,018,141	-15.86
Vehicles and parts (not railway).	1,412,195	1,458,357	1,337,406	-8.29
Plastics	1,146,069	1,147,667	1,165,771	1.58

Value of Wisconsin exports by category, continued

	2018 ($1,000)	2019 ($1,000)	2020 ($1,000)	% change 2019 to 2020
Paper and paperboard	888,717	814,010	723,254	-11.15
Aircraft, spacecraft, and parts	729,701	554,322	575,307	3.79
Miscellaneous chemical products	429,654	460,232	530,600	15.29
Iron and steel products.	456,205	392,617	385,337	-1.85
Miscellaneous edible preparations.	366,214	344,706	343,227	-0.43
Pharmaceutical products	393,934	351,226	315,746	-10.10
Prepared vegetables, fruits, and nuts	354,800	361,834	315,595	-12.78
Organic chemicals	197,459	207,288	277,993	34.11
Dairy, eggs, honey, etc.	282,263	237,869	263,402	10.73
Starch, glue, enzymes.	159,877	201,983	256,953	27.21
Printed matter	272,384	241,083	245,725	1.93
Wood products.	269,773	237,260	244,272	2.96
Essential oils, perfumes.	221,236	217,820	231,802	6.42
Prepared meats and fish	245,735	223,257	224,240	0.44
Prepared cereal, flour, starch	182,658	151,192	220,748	46.00
All categories	**22,709,323**	**21,668,455**	**20,504,334**	**-5.37**

1. Export categories based on U.S. Census Bureau commodity codes.

Source: Wisconsin Economic Development Corporation, "Top Products Exported from Wisconsin," at https://wedc.org/wp-content/uploads/2021/03/WI-Exports-by-Product-Top-Products.pdf [March 8, 2021].

Value of Wisconsin exports by market

	2018 ($1,000)	2019 ($1,000)	2020 ($1,000)	% change 2019 to 2020
Top 20 markets in 2020	**19,303,347**	**18,392,498**	**17,099,144**	**-7.03**
Canada.	7,026,881	6,753,896	6,226,130	-7.81
Mexico	3,452,912	3,281,841	2,554,048	-22.18
China	1,633,403	1,373,152	1,553,608	13.14
Germany.	814,002	760,020	726,290	-4.44
Japan	734,269	704,443	686,149	-2.60
United Kingdom	792,216	804,559	625,725	-22.23
Australia	572,808	576,227	567,959	-1.43
South Korea.	591,401	544,564	508,524	-6.62
Netherlands.	448,529	451,766	429,416	-4.95
Belgium	397,824	418,578	381,309	-8.90
France	497,963	434,923	372,998	-14.24
Hong Kong	290,796	212,381	360,969	69.96
Chile	187,439	228,996	355,014	55.03
Brazil	392,802	299,408	302,491	1.03
Thailand	267,223	328,220	290,399	-11.52
Italy	319,084	312,328	262,127	-16.07
Singapore	221,133	235,197	253,630	7.84
Saudi Arabia	186,121	156,264	234,238	49.90
India	280,252	289,097	206,773	-28.48
Taiwan	196,287	226,638	201,347	-11.16
All markets	**22,709,323**	**21,668,455**	**20,504,334**	**-5.37**

Source: Wisconsin Economic Development Corporation, "Top Destinations for Wisconsin Exports," at https://wedc.org/wp-content/uploads/2021/03/WI-Exports-by-Country-Top-Destinations.pdf [March 8, 2021].

Basic data on Wisconsin corporations

Year[2]	Transactions[1]			Fees ($)			
	Domestic			Fees for articles of incorporation	Fees for foreign cor- poration[4]	Other corporation fees[5]	Total fees collected
	Articles of incorpora- tion filed[3]	Amdts. and restated articles	Foreign corporations licensed				
Calendar							
1905	98	NA	95	NA	NA	NA	69,312
1915	1,043	382	112	28,287	3,743	89,695	121,725
1925	1,438	896	198	57,614	11,139	78,153	146,906
1935	1,272	439	176	30,839	8,956	41,631	81,426
1945	1,120	680	131	31,823	4,826	113,963	150,612
1955	2,537	874	287	89,951	31,146	175,973	297,070
1965	4,063	1,320	401	344,906	120,506	193,844	659,256
Fiscal							
1975	5,976	1,483	663	361,013	386,061	594,498	1,341,572
1980	7,334	1,978	753	373,220	753,461	788,204	1,914,885
1985	7,605	2,359	1,018	485,835	1,142,129	1,371,476	2,999,440
1990	8,387	2,525	1,408	546,550	2,368,900	1,491,104	4,406,554
1995	10,031	2,716	1,507	829,555	4,208,178	2,538,521	7,576,254
2000	21,133	3,088	2,464	2,265,455	6,403,447	3,548,264	12,217,166
2005	33,589	3,595	2,787	4,092,782	6,043,400	5,509,178	15,645,000
2010	27,349	2,231	2,495	5,247,361	8,311,900	5,291,939	18,851,200
2011	28,535	2,210	2,706	10,303,300	7,696,300	723,400	18,723,000
2012	30,014	2,166	2,817	10,599,880	8,345,500	700,200	19,645,500
2013	34,045	2,907	3,100	10,911,200	8,701,600	751,900	20,364,700
2014	35,955	2,917	3,400	11,206,000	9,379,000	784,100	21,369,100
2015	36,576	2,804	3,523	11,746,200	7,820,600	844,400	20,411,200
2016	38,304	3,203	3,701	13,643,500	6,659,700	748,700	21,051,900
2017	39,933	3,208	3,771	12,534,100	9,957,900	729,000	23,221,100
2018	43,179	3,430	4,116	13,165,800	9,822,300	782,700	23,770,800
2019	44,584	3,263	4,561	13,791,900	11,539,400	798,900	26,130,200
2020	45,943	3,080	4,283	14,489,000	9,416,100	946,500	24,851,600

Amdts.– Amendments; NA–Not available.

1. Includes only corporate entities for which the reporting agency is the office of record. 2. Since 1975, data is computed on a fiscal year basis, ending June 30 of year shown. 3. Beginning in 1997, includes limited liability companies. 4. Since 1975, totals include fees for foreign corporation annual reports. 5. Includes fees for filing annual reports and corporation charter documents other than articles of incorporation.

Sources: Wisconsin Department of Financial Institutions, departmental data for 2000–20 [February 2021]; prior data from the Office of the Wisconsin Secretary of State.

Financial institutions operating in Wisconsin

Year[1]	Number	Total deposits (mil. dol.)	Year[1]	Number	Total deposits (mil. dol.)
1900.	349	$125	1990.	504	37,589
1910.	630	269	2000.	365	75,379
1920.	976	768	2010.	299	126,660
1930.	936	935	2011.	296	128,628
1940.	574	993	2012.	295	132,812
1950.	556	2,966	2013.	285	129,714
1960.	561	4,386	2014.	278	136,508
1970.	602	8,751	2015.	269	140,261
1980.	634	24,764	2016.	257	143,504

Financial institutions operating in Wisconsin, continued

Year[1]	Number	Total deposits (mil. dol.)	Year[1]	Number	Total deposits (mil. dol.)
2017.	241	155,034	2019.	226	151,229
2018.	236	150,114	2020.	216	179,312

1. Beginning in 1994, data include federal charter savings associations and state-chartered savings associations, supervised by the U.S. Office of Thrift Supervision, and institutions operating in Wisconsin but headquartered outside the state. Deposits for these years are rounded to nearest thousands of dollars.

Sources: 1950 and earlier: Board of Governors of the Federal Reserve System, All-Bank Statistics, U.S., 1959; 1960: Wisconsin Commissioner of Banks, agency data, December 1965; 1970: Federal Deposit Insurance Corporation, Assets and Liabilities—Commercial and Mutual Savings Banks, June 1971; 1980: Federal Deposit Insurance Corporation, corporate data; 1990: Federal Deposit Insurance Corporation, Data Book: Operating Banks and Branches, Book 3, June 30, 1993; 2000 to date: Federal Deposit Insurance Corporation, Summary of Deposits, "State Totals by Charter Class for All Institution Deposits, Deposits of All FDIC-Insured Institutions Operating in Wisconsin," June 30, 2020, and prior issues.

Wisconsin financial institutions, June 30, 2020

	Insured commercial banks and trust companies				Insured savings institutions		
			State charter				
Type of institution or branch	Total	National charter	FRS member	FRS non-member	Total	Federal charter	State charter
Headquartered in state	183	20	16	123	24	10	14
Headquartered outside of state	33	12	4	14	3	3	0
Total institutions	216	32	20	137	27	13	14
Total offices	1,855	906	116	690	143	78	65
Total deposits (mil. dol.).	179,312	118,231	12,259	40,064	8,757	5,001	3,756

FRS–Federal Reserve System.

Source: Federal Deposit Insurance Corporation, Summary of Deposits, "Deposits of all FDIC-Insured Institutions: State Totals by Charter Class" at www.fdic.gov/regulations/resources/call/sod.html [June 30, 2020].

FDIC-insured institutions operating in Wisconsin, June 30, 2020

	Commercial banks			Savings institutions		
County	Institutions	Offices	Deposits (mil. dol.)	Institutions	Offices	Deposits (mil. dol.)
Adams	4	5	222	1	1	5
Ashland.	4	9	409	—	—	—
Barron.	9	21	998	1	1	134
Bayfield.	4	11	324	—	—	—
Brown.	17	62	9,148	1	6	174
Buffalo	4	10	358	—	—	—
Burnett	3	7	386	—	—	—
Calumet	7	11	584	1	1	31
Chippewa	10	21	856	1	1	25
Clark.	6	9	334	2	4	171
Columbia.	10	23	1,549	—	—	—
Crawford	6	11	439	—	—	—
Dane	32	145	19,782	4	7	1,429

FDIC-insured institutions operating in Wisconsin, June 30, 2020, continued

County	Commercial banks			Savings institutions		
	Institutions	Offices	Deposits (mil. dol.)	Institutions	Offices	Deposits (mil. dol.)
Dodge	12	30	1,266	2	2	125
Door	3	12	797	1	2	92
Douglas	5	9	578	1	1	59
Dunn	8	15	459	—	—	—
Eau Claire	15	32	2,396	1	1	3
Florence	2	4	135	—	—	—
Fond du Lac	9	33	2,162	1	1	183
Forest	2	6	199	—	—	—
Grant	11	38	1,315	—	—	—
Green	9	16	1,104	—	—	—
Green Lake	6	12	764	—	—	—
Iowa	7	13	519	—	—	—
Iron	2	3	91	—	—	—
Jackson	3	9	274	—	—	—
Jefferson	12	26	1,455	—	—	—
Juneau	6	14	492	—	—	—
Kenosha	10	34	2,864	1	3	68
Kewaunee	3	11	492	—	—	—
La Crosse	14	37	2,656	—	—	—
Lafayette	8	12	390	—	—	—
Langlade	4	5	104	—	—	—
Lincoln	4	6	326	1	2	139
Manitowoc	9	19	2,004	—	—	—
Marathon	17	49	3,930	3	5	213
Marinette	7	17	950	1	1	8
Marquette	6	9	238	—	—	—
Milwaukee	21	190	52,472	8	42	2,230
Monroe	8	17	826	—	—	—
Oconto	4	7	252	1	3	53
Oneida	7	15	958	—	—	—
Outagamie	18	36	3,863	3	8	259
Ozaukee	12	33	2,885	3	4	136
Pepin	3	3	250	—	—	—
Pierce	8	12	649	—	—	—
Polk	11	13	663	—	—	—
Portage	12	22	2,039	2	2	44
Price	2	2	55	2	4	215
Racine	12	42	5,507	2	6	203
Richland	6	7	247	—	—	—
Rock	17	34	2,888	—	—	—
Rusk	4	5	291	1	1	56
St. Croix	12	26	1,748	1	1	65
Sauk	5	7	504	—	—	—
Sawyer	9	14	583	—	—	—
Shawano	15	37	2,531	—	—	—
Sheboygan	14	24	1,549	—	—	—
Taylor	3	4	271	2	2	190
Trempealeau	9	19	658	—	—	—
Vernon	7	14	551	—	—	—
Vilas	10	14	584	—	—	—
Walworth	14	34	1,910	—	—	—
Washburn	5	7	348	—	—	—
Washington	14	39	3,314	1	1	111
Waukesha	26	141	13,619	8	22	1,592

FDIC-insured institutions operating in Wisconsin, June 30, 2020, continued

County	Commercial banks			Savings institutions		
	Institutions	Offices	Deposits (mil. dol.)	Institutions	Offices	Deposits (mil. dol.)
Waupaca	6	19	916	—	—	—
Waushara.	7	8	314	—	—	—
Winnebago	13	30	2,360	2	2	68
Wood	9	21	1,599	4	6	677
Total[1]	189	1,712	170,554	27	143	8,757

Note: Menominee County did not report separately.

— Represents zero.

1. Total number of institutions is an unduplicated total for institutions operating in more than one county. Deposit figures do not add to state totals due to rounding.

Source: Federal Deposit Insurance Corporation, "Deposits of all FDIC-Insured Institutions: State Totals by County," at www.fdic. gov/regulations/resources/call/sod.html [June 30, 2020].

Wisconsin state-chartered credit unions

	Number of credit unions	Total members (% chg. from prior yr.)	Total assets in mil. dols. (% chg. from prior yr.)
1930.	22	4,659 (NA)	0.5 (NA)
1935.	383	57,847 (NA)	2.9 (NA)
1940.	592	153,849 (NA)	-11.2 (NA)
1945.	536	144,524 (NA)	19.1 (NA)
1950.	542	193,296 (NA)	42.9 (NA)
1955.	696	292,552 (NA)	120.6 (NA)
1960.	733	363,444 (NA)	206.4 (NA)
1965.	781	493,399 (NA)	346.6 (NA)
1970.	766	628,543 (NA)	480.4 (NA)
1975.	673	805,123 (NA)	875.5 (NA)
1980.	618	1,060,292 (NA)	1,403.8 (NA)
1985.	550	1,261,407 (NA)	2,831.4 (NA)
1990.	440	1,485,109 (4.3)	4,148.7 (8.6)
1995.	384	1,744,696 (1.8)	6,179.2 (7.4)
2000.	340	1,918,729 (1.7)	9,425.9 (7.9)
2005.	280	2,047,031 (2.8)	14,805.3 (8.2)
2010.	223	2,186,471 (1.0)	20,685.4 (4.9)
2011.	203	2,225,892 (1.8)	21,915.6 (5.9)
2012.	187	2,264,788 (1.7)	23,353.8 (6.6)
2013.	171	2,335,239 (3.1)	24,517.9 (5.0)
2014.	160	2,460,025 (5.3)	26,324.6 (7.4)
2015.	150	2,613,667 (6.2)	28,797.1 (9.4)
2016.	143	2,790,644 (6.8)	31,453.3 (9.2)
2017.	129	2,938,267 (5.3)	34,157.2 (8.6)
2018.	125	3,081,193 (4.9)	37,012.0 (8.4)
2019.	121	3,196,907 (3.8)	41,069.5 (11.0)
2020.	118	3,307,029 (3.4)	49,524.8 (20.6)

NA–Not available.

Source: Wisconsin Department of Financial Institutions, Office of Credit Unions, 2020 Year End Credit Union Bulletin, at https://www.wdfi.org/_resources/indexed/site/fi/cu/QuarterlyReports/2020/2020%20Year%20End%20Bulletin.pdf [March 2021], and prior editions.

Wisconsin's tribal gaming facilities

Casino	Location	Tribe
Legendary Waters Resort and Casino	Bayfield	Red Cliff Band (Lake Superior Chippewa)
Bad River Casino	Odanah	Bad River Band (Lake Superior Chippewa)
Lake of the Torches Resort Casino	Lac du Flambeau	Lac du Flambeau Band (Lake Superior Chippewa)
Sevenwinds Casino	Hayward	Lac Courte Oreilles Band (Lake Superior Chippewa)
Grindstone Creek Casino	Hayward	Lac Courte Oreilles Band (Lake Superior Chippewa)
St. Croix Casino Danbury	Danbury	St. Croix Band (Lake Superior Chippewa)
St. Croix Casino Hertel	Hertel	St. Croix Band (Lake Superior Chippewa)
St. Croix Casino Turtle Lake	Turtle Lake	St. Croix Band (Lake Superior Chippewa)
Mole Lake Casino	Crandon	Sokaogon Chippewa Community
Potawatomi Carter Casino and Hotel	Carter	Forest County Potawatomi Community
Menominee Casino Resort	Keshena	Menominee Tribe
The Thunderbird Mini-Casino	Keshena	Menominee Tribe
North Star Mohican Casino Resort	Bowler	Stockbridge-Munsee Community
Ho-Chunk Gaming Wittenberg	Wittenberg	Ho-Chunk Nation
Ho-Chunk Gaming Black River Falls	Black River Falls	Ho-Chunk Nation
Ho-Chunk Gaming Nekoosa	Nekoosa	Ho-Chunk Nation
Ho-Chunk Gaming Tomah	Tomah	Ho-Chunk Nation
Ho-Chunk Gaming Wisconsin Dells	Baraboo	Ho-Chunk Nation
Potawatomi Bingo Casino	Milwaukee	Forest County Potawatomi Community
Oneida Main Casino	Green Bay	Oneida Nation
IMAC Casino/Bingo	Green Bay	Oneida Nation
Oneida Mason Street Casino	Green Bay	Oneida Nation
Oneida One-Stop Packerland	Green Bay	Oneida Nation
Oneida Casino Travel Center	Oneida	Oneida Nation

Note: Only Class III gaming facilities regulated by tribal compact are included, pursuant to P.L. 100-497, the Indian Gaming Regulatory Act, which divides gambling into three classes. An additional Ho-Chunk casino in Madison offers Class II gaming. Class I games are social games played solely for prizes of minimal value or traditional forms of Indian gaming played in connection with tribal ceremonies or celebrations. Class II includes bingo or bingo-type games, pull-tabs and punch-boards, and certain nonbanking card games, such as poker. Class III covers all other forms of gaming.

Source: Wisconsin Legislative Fiscal Bureau, "Informational Paper 87: Tribal Gaming in Wisconsin," January 2021, at https://docs.legis.wisconsin.gov/misc/lfb/informational_papers/january_2021/0087_tribal_gaming_in_wisconsin_informational_paper_87.pdf.

EMPLOYMENT AND INCOME

Employment trends in Wisconsin

	Labor force (1,000)	Employed (1,000)	Unem-ployed (1,000)	Unem-ployment rate (%)	Total non-farm em-ployment (1,000)	Service providing (1,000)	Goods producing (1,000)	Manu-facturing (1,000)	Trade, trans-portation, and utilities (1,000)
2000	2,985.6	2,884.7	100.9	3.4	2,832.3	2,107.6	724.7	595.8	551.1
2001	3,017.7	2,884.3	133.4	4.4	2,812.2	2,120.9	691.3	562.1	545.7
2002	3,016.8	2,856.2	160.5	5.3	2,780.1	2,122.0	658.1	530.2	534.7
2003	3,045.3	2,874.0	171.3	5.6	2,771.8	2,138.0	633.9	506.0	534.2
2004	3,034.6	2,883.6	151.0	5.0	2,802.3	2,166.9	635.4	504.8	536.7
2005	3,029.7	2,885.7	144.0	4.8	2,836.0	2,197.5	638.5	507.0	540.9
2006	3,066.3	2,923.6	142.7	4.7	2,859.1	2,219.6	639.4	508.0	542.0
2007	3,087.6	2,938.9	148.7	4.8	2,875.7	2,242.4	633.3	503.7	544.4
2008	3,098.9	2,945.9	153.1	4.9	2,868.2	2,251.0	617.2	495.4	538.1
2009	3,112.5	2,833.3	279.2	9.0	2,741.2	2,197.6	543.6	438.9	514.7
2010	3,082.9	2,820.6	262.3	8.5	2,725.0	2,194.6	530.5	433.0	505.5
2011	3,072.2	2,840.0	232.2	7.6	2,751.8	2,208.6	543.2	447.4	507.9
2012	3,070.0	2,857.2	212.9	6.9	2,780.8	2,225.6	555.2	458.2	509.5
2013	3,077.8	2,872.0	205.8	6.7	2,809.6	2,247.3	562.3	460.1	514.8
2014	3,078.0	2,913.8	164.2	5.3	2,852.9	2,277.9	575.0	467.3	521.5
2015	3,084.2	2,947.0	137.2	4.4	2,893.7	2,310.1	583.6	470.0	528.4
2016	3,110.5	2,988.7	121.7	3.9	2,929.3	2,345.3	584.0	467.7	536.4
2017	3,122.3	3,020.2	102.1	3.3	2,951.9	2,359.7	592.2	470.5	539.1
2018	3,106.5	3,012.8	93.7	3.0	2,980.1	2,373.5	606.7	479.6	540.1
2019	3,094.3	2,993.0	101.3	3.3	2,987.7	2,375.5	612.1	483.5	535.4
2020	3,065.4	2,872.6	192.8	6.3	2,818.0	2,230.8	587.2	459.7	518.2
2021	3,044.4	2,902.0	142.4	4.7	2,783.3	2,207.8	575.5	464.0	521.3

Note: Data are estimates that are revised monthly and annually and are seasonally adjusted. Industry classifications in this table are defined by the North American Industry Classification System (NAICS).

Sources: Wisconsin Department of Workforce Development, WisConomy, Wisconsin Labor Market Information Data Access, "Local Area Unemployment Statistics" and "Current Employment Estimates by Industry" at https://www.jobcenterofwisconsin.com/wisconomy/query [March 2021].

Annual employment in Wisconsin

Industry	2016	2017	2018	2019	2020
Labor force.	3,110,466	3,122,309	3,106,532	3,094,325	3,065,402
Unemployment.	121,722	102,141	93,731	101,300	192,793
Unemployment rate	3.9	3.3	3.0	3.3	6.3
Employment.	2,988,744	3,020,168	3,012,801	2,993,025	2,872,609
Total nonfarm	2,929,300	2,951,900	2,980,100	2,987,700	2,818,000
Service providing	2,345,300	2,359,700	2,373,500	2,375,500	2,230,800
Goods producing.	584,000	592,200	606,700	612,100	587,200
Trade, transportation, and utilities	536,400	539,100	540,100	535,400	518,200
Manufacturing	467,700	470,500	479,600	483,500	459,700
Educational and health services.	445,100	451,300	457,300	464,100	449,900
Professional and business services	322,600	325,800	328,200	326,600	309,500
Local government	287,200	283,300	285,300	282,900	265,600
Leisure and hospitality	275,900	280,300	282,400	285,500	226,000
Finance	151,900	152,900	153,000	154,500	152,200
Other services.	149,900	151,400	152,200	152,700	143,900
Construction	112,600	117,400	122,300	124,500	124,000

Annual employment in Wisconsin, continued

Industry	2016	2017	2018	2019	2020
State government	98,200	98,800	98,800	97,600	89,800
Information	49,100	47,900	47,200	47,100	44,900
Federal government	29,000	29,000	29,100	29,300	30,800
Mining and logging	3,800	4,300	4,700	4,200	3,500

Note: Industry classifications in this table are defined by the North American Industry Classification System (NAICS).

Source: Wisconsin Department of Workforce Development, WisConomy, Wisconsin Labor Market Information Data Access, "Local Area Unemployment Statistics" and "Current Employment Estimates by Industry" at https://www.jobcenterofwisconsin.com/wisconomy/query [March 2021].

Manufacturing employment in Wisconsin

Industry group	2016	2017	2018	2019	2020
Durable goods	280,000	280,300	287,200	289,100	269,300
Fabricated metal product manufacturing	72,900	73,600	76,500	77,900	71,400
Machinery manufacturing	65,500	65,100	66,900	67,400	63,200
Transportation equipment manufacturing	26,700	26,800	26,200	26,000	24,000
Electrical equipment and appliances	23,700	23,800	24,300	24,900	24,000
Wood product manufacturing	17,500	17,600	17,900	17,700	16,800
Nondurable goods	187,700	190,100	192,400	194,400	190,300
Food manufacturing	68,500	70,900	72,800	74,500	75,800
Plastics and rubber products manufacturing . . .	32,200	32,800	33,600	33,600	32,100
Paper manufacturing	30,400	29,900	29,600	29,300	28,000
Printing and related support activities	29,700	29,000	28,200	28,000	25,700
Total	**467,700**	**470,400**	**479,600**	**483,500**	**459,600**

Source: Wisconsin Department of Workforce Development, WisConomy, Wisconsin Labor Market Information Data Access, "Current Employment Estimates by Industry" at https://www.jobcenterofwisconsin.com/wisconomy/query [March 2021].

Wisconsin personal income

	Personal income (mil. dol.)[1]	Per capita personal income[2]		
		Amount (dol.)	State rank	% of national average
1940	1,723.3	548	21	92
1945	3,527.0	1,191	22	96
1950	5,209.0	1,515	24	100
1955	6,955.7	1,891	21	98
1960	8,994.3	2,270	20	99
1965	11,798.4	2,788	22	98
1970	17,648.8	3,988	25	95
1975	27,872.0	6,099	26	96
1980	47,282.0	10,034	23	99
1985	66,276.7	13,960	27	95
1990	90,431.2	18,438	24	94
1995	119,327.1	23,015	21	98
2000	159,326.0	29,648	19	97
2005	190,975.8	34,434	23	96
2010	221,909.7	38,997	24	96
2015	269,952.1	46,859	24	96
2016	274,764.7	47,598	23	95

Wisconsin personal income, continued

	Personal income (mil. dol.)[1]	Per capita personal income[2]		
		Amount (dol.)	State rank	% of national average
2017.	285,249.9	49,264	23	95
2018.	299,827.0	51,628	23	95
2019.	309,909.3	53,227	24	94

1. Personal income includes all forms of income received by persons from business establishments; federal, state, and local governments; households and institutions; and foreign countries. Allowance is made for "in-kind" income not received as cash. 2. Per capita personal income is total personal income divided by total midyear population.

Source: U.S. Department of Commerce, Bureau of Economic Analysis, Regional Data, "SAINC1: Personal Income Summary: Personal Income, Population, Per Capita Personal Income," 2019 and prior editions at https://apps.bea.gov/itable/iTable. cfm?ReqID=70&step=1 [March 2021].

Wisconsin personal income, by industry

Industry	2015 (mil.dol.)	2016 (mil.dol.)	2017 (mil.dol.)	2018 (mil.dol.)	2019 (mil.dol.)
Services[1]	63,989	66,541	68,814	72,617	75,417
Manufacturing	34,933	34,248	35,696	37,324	38,522
Government and government enterprises	28,457	28,665	28,865	29,778	30,832
Finance and insurance	11,428	12,146	12,720	13,025	13,451
Retail trade.	11,320	11,444	11,727	12,038	12,330
Construction	11,245	11,661	12,523	13,224	13,744
Wholesale trade	9,865	10,040	10,648	11,279	11,212
Transportation and warehousing	6,915	6,936	7,242	7,563	8,023
Information	4,506	4,474	4,586	4,825	5,225
Farm earnings.	2,697	1,835	1,745	1,739	2,507
Real estate and rental and leasing	2,996	3,152	2,933	3,077	3,241
Utilities	1,635	1,568	1,647	1,653	1,656
Forestry, fishing, and related activities.	629	656	642	612	657
Mining, quarrying, and oil and gas extraction	312	262	309	407	365
Total[2]	269,952	274,765	285,250	299,827	309,909

1. Services includes the following NAICS classification categories: professional, scientific and technical services; management of companies and enterprises; administrative and waste management services; educational services; health care and social assistance; arts, entertainment, and recreation; accommodation and food services; and other services (except government). 2. Total may not add due to rounding.

Source: U.S. Department of Commerce, Bureau of Economic Analysis, Regional Data, "SAINC5: Personal Income by Major Component and Earnings by Industry" at https://apps.bea.gov/itable/iTable.cfm?ReqID=70&step=1 [March 2021].

Wisconsin adjusted gross income

County	2019 AGI[1] ($)	per return AGI					2019 rank[2]
		2015 ($)	2016 ($)	2017 ($)	2018 ($)	2019 ($)	
Adams	395,474,678	35,544	36,292	38,307	38,287	39,659	70
Ashland.	319,821,794	36,628	37,658	38,219	41,038	41,616	68
Barron.	1,159,266,874	43,293	44,329	46,537	49,036	48,424	47
Bayfield.	404,312,647	46,466	44,402	46,050	52,404	51,205	39
Brown.	9,263,166,900	59,421	61,239	62,528	65,652	68,385	7
Buffalo	334,961,044	40,732	40,861	41,796	43,518	48,778	45
Burnett	359,944,765	38,158	39,356	40,392	44,341	47,878	52

Wisconsin adjusted gross income, continued

County	2019 AGI[1] ($)	per return AGI					2019 rank[2]
		2015 ($)	2016 ($)	2017 ($)	2018 ($)	2019 ($)	
Calumet	1,675,041,878	62,299	62,718	63,548	66,857	71,461	6
Chippewa	1,686,171,432	47,585	49,686	51,372	54,180	53,308	34
Clark.	742,908,648	42,578	40,838	45,156	47,758	49,056	44
Columbia.	1,779,242,455	50,928	52,614	55,170	55,429	57,771	20
Crawford	344,607,020	39,526	41,574	43,320	45,035	43,704	66
Dane	23,079,067,093	68,051	70,303	72,928	75,399	79,597	3
Dodge	2,389,985,479	49,139	49,596	51,596	53,324	55,255	26
Door.	949,438,297	50,845	51,463	54,808	57,215	59,608	15
Douglas.	1,074,513,235	44,577	45,106	45,675	48,685	49,560	42
Dunn	1,106,632,171	46,468	46,967	50,807	53,201	54,061	31
Eau Claire.	3,235,857,431	57,602	54,543	57,056	60,409	62,437	10
Florence	100,934,054	40,881	44,776	43,900	46,318	47,409	54
Fond du Lac	3,057,967,955	53,402	53,666	56,779	57,867	58,791	16
Forest	177,583,647	35,160	35,742	37,544	39,583	40,059	69
Grant	1,110,927,174	41,690	41,841	43,177	45,684	47,500	53
Green	1,102,935,070	52,928	52,040	55,858	56,107	58,199	19
Green Lake.	489,149,531	51,836	44,759	46,745	48,141	50,449	41
Iowa	690,878,913	50,263	50,837	52,209	54,019	57,041	23
Iron	143,487,956	37,477	38,702	39,836	41,191	45,037	60
Jackson	453,797,659	40,717	43,113	43,116	44,187	48,618	46
Jefferson	2,371,340,481	50,124	50,421	56,012	55,556	56,634	25
Juneau	571,685,011	38,654	39,136	41,147	42,821	44,586	64
Kenosha	4,845,644,974	51,439	52,410	53,570	56,076	57,680	21
Kewaunee	576,787,162	48,885	48,394	50,956	51,533	55,074	27
La Crosse	3,492,436,293	53,781	54,610	56,217	57,861	58,753	17
Lafayette	377,732,451	41,924	42,075	42,904	48,950	48,396	48
Langlade	440,209,224	39,353	40,203	41,182	43,061	44,696	61
Lincoln	719,863,780	46,188	44,994	46,158	48,081	49,279	43
Manitowoc.	2,198,864,135	49,208	48,594	54,314	53,267	53,848	32
Marathon.	4,345,789,540	55,310	57,027	57,099	59,993	62,278	11
Marinette.	947,122,220	40,965	41,483	42,162	44,447	44,680	62
Marquette	365,200,990	38,216	40,010	42,631	44,876	46,701	58
Menominee	47,033,256	19,003	17,164	7,415	20,261	23,423	72
Milwaukee	25,758,031,107	48,533	49,692	50,516	53,380	54,920	29
Monroe	1,031,009,202	42,927	43,661	45,432	46,561	47,093	56
Oconto	1,012,451,722	47,394	48,296	49,069	51,963	53,700	33
Oneida	1,064,784,864	46,809	51,505	48,710	52,711	55,008	28
Outagamie.	6,496,997,390	58,774	60,762	62,398	63,894	65,444	8
Ozaukee	5,169,647,308	99,050	99,649	102,425	107,155	111,890	1
Pepin	193,806,712	50,151	48,706	52,444	60,523	54,348	30
Pierce	1,289,816,465	58,918	57,791	58,999	63,918	64,867	9
Polk	1,159,063,450	46,111	46,335	47,955	50,873	52,135	37
Portage	1,991,153,674	51,402	51,056	52,738	54,930	56,738	24
Price	308,972,187	39,992	40,348	40,992	43,133	43,851	65
Racine.	5,687,998,345	52,380	53,002	54,073	56,886	57,265	22
Richland	350,960,450	39,631	40,139	42,415	45,081	44,657	63
Rock.	5,033,875,821	48,142	50,800	54,847	57,144	60,720	12
Rusk	263,335,927	35,734	36,261	37,534	39,993	39,475	71
St. Croix.	3,411,381,937	68,133	68,823	70,628	75,912	75,165	4
Sauk.	1,852,159,992	47,398	47,658	49,560	53,335	53,229	35
Sawyer	362,758,033	38,373	40,562	40,509	43,398	43,595	67
Shawano	942,732,828	41,421	41,340	44,768	45,731	47,222	55
Sheboygan.	3,540,202,389	53,311	53,418	55,348	56,875	58,237	18
Taylor	445,516,575	44,184	43,706	45,345	46,552	47,915	51
Trempealeau.	755,042,516	48,587	44,875	46,649	48,979	50,478	40
Vernon	648,712,129	42,168	42,004	43,827	45,477	47,052	57
Vilas	562,188,827	40,998	45,135	43,819	48,453	48,170	50
Walworth.	3,135,844,088	54,723	53,804	55,567	58,923	60,527	14

Wisconsin adjusted gross income, continued

County	2019 AGI[1] ($)	per return AGI					2019 rank[2]
		2015 ($)	2016 ($)	2017 ($)	2018 ($)	2019 ($)	
Washburn	413,177,445	40,835	39,664	41,880	48,457	48,376	49
Washington	5,043,052,467	64,558	65,642	68,180	70,403	71,594	5
Waukesha	19,482,706,753	83,021	85,796	86,671	90,062	92,569	2
Waupaca	1,395,643,659	47,009	46,361	48,262	49,760	52,148	36
Waushara.	523,803,405	40,600	40,765	42,483	43,253	45,280	59
Winnebago	5,233,908,266	54,613	55,890	59,145	58,908	60,701	13
Wood	2,006,154,098	46,653	48,418	48,470	50,108	51,573	38
Total[3]	194,341,461,432	54,227	55,267	56,698	59,423	61,003	

1. "Wisconsin adjusted gross income" (AGI) is Wisconsin income as reported to the Wisconsin Department of Revenue for income tax purposes and is based on the federal income tax definition of gross income as modified by certain additions and subtractions required by state law.   2. Rankings calculated by Wisconsin Legislative Reference Bureau.   3. State totals and state per return figures include amounts not allocated to a particular county.

Source: Wisconsin Department of Revenue, "Wisconsin Municipal Income Per Return Report for 2019" and prior reports at https://www.revenue.wi.gov/Pages/Report/WI-Muni-AGI.aspx [March 2021].

Distribution of Wisconsin business establishments, March 2018

Industry	Total employees[1]	Number of establishments by employment size						
		Total	1 to 19	20 to 49	50 to 99	100 to 249	250 to 499	500 or more
Agriculture, forestry, fishing, and hunting	3,484	567	543	19	Z	Z	Z	Z
Mining, quarrying, and oil and gas extraction	8,251	166	110	32	14	7	Z	Z
Utilities	13,175	355	234	59	32	21	6	3
Construction	116,757	13,960	12,886	741	201	92	28	10
Manufacturing	468,493	8,749	5,141	1,520	921	778	253	136
Wholesale trade	122,285	6,935	5,525	890	310	163	39	8
Retail trade.	314,377	18,533	15,077	2,217	653	476	102	6
Transportation and warehousing . .	104,853	5,733	4,710	613	232	128	27	23
Information	57,690	2,616	2,204	237	87	58	18	12
Finance and insurance	144,468	8,872	8,042	488	158	104	45	35
Real estate and rental and leasing .	28,047	5,052	4,816	175	38	18	4	Z
Professional, scientific, and technical services	114,003	11,503	10,464	677	213	113	20	16
Management of companies and enterprises	82,079	1,023	597	165	100	87	24	50
Administrative, support, waste management, and remediation services	153,375	7,267	6,117	559	268	219	68	36
Educational services	57,001	1,653	1,245	272	75	34	9	18
Health care and social assistance . .	411,238	16,064	12,662	2,003	729	459	124	87
Arts, entertainment, and recreation	47,886	2,848	2,381	278	100	60	23	5
Accommodation and food services.	250,817	14,905	10,779	3,158	827	117	14	10
Other services (except public administration)	103,708	14,718	13,757	764	140	50	6	Z
Industries not classified.	161	147	145	Z	Z	Z	Z	Z
Total.	2,602,148	141,666	117,437	14,867	5,099	2,986	812	465

Z—Two or fewer establishments.

1. Number of employees for the week including March 12, 2018. Excludes most government and railroad employees and self-employed persons. Totals are provided by the U.S. Census Bureau and may not equal the sum of columns or rows due to incomplete data.

Source: U.S. Census Bureau, "County Business Patterns" at https://census.gov/programs-surveys/cbp/data/tables.2018.html [March 18, 2021].

Wisconsin Works (W-2) benefits

County	2019		2020	
	Avg. mo. paid caseload	Avg. mo. benefit payment ($)	Avg. mo. paid caseload	Avg. mo. benefit payment ($)
Adams	7	422	5	461
Ashland	10	248	14	481
Barron	19	360	17	489
Bayfield	5	320	4	401
Brown	181	285	122	513
Buffalo	2	457	2	522
Burnett	10	459	12	516
Calumet	9	402	13	494
Chippewa	32	315	36	511
Clark	12	379	11	526
Columbia	19	446	10	468
Crawford	7	377	5	522
Dane	199	400	170	471
Dodge	23	427	14	462
Door	9	377	9	511
Douglas	35	454	40	531
Dunn	29	404	29	551
Eau Claire	49	331	60	511
Florence	1	53	—	—
Fond du Lac	66	314	43	426
Forest	1	509	1	282
Grant	24	358	20	568
Green	8	346	2	647
Green Lake	14	321	8	474
Iowa	10	394	8	597
Iron	1	105	1	407
Jackson	6	329	6	476
Jefferson	16	462	16	519
Juneau	9	511	12	508
Kenosha	207	338	160	467
Kewaunee	14	365	14	596
La Crosse	24	298	22	419
Lafayette	2	262	2	727
Langlade	14	322	6	555
Lincoln	11	429	5	539
Manitowoc	32	293	26	464
Marathon	47	334	28	478
Marinette	16	341	10	492
Marquette	7	484	5	524
Menominee	8	255	5	368
Milwaukee	3,293	368	3,445	522
Monroe	10	285	5	412
Oconto	11	273	6	537
Oneida	19	492	16	567
Outagamie	61	323	49	474
Ozaukee	4	229	2	301
Pepin	1	295	1	503
Pierce	10	484	13	521
Polk	10	497	16	509
Portage	19	319	16	496

Wisconsin Works (W-2) benefits, continued

| | 2019 | | 2020 | |
County	Avg. mo. paid caseload	Avg. mo. benefit payment ($)	Avg. mo. paid caseload	Avg. mo. benefit payment ($)
Price.	4	307	2	554
Racine.	231	386	256	497
Richland	6	362	11	523
Rock.	150	382	107	524
Rusk.	5	398	3	568
St. Croix.	13	494	16	509
Sauk.	20	399	11	477
Sawyer	10	296	9	457
Shawano	21	315	20	507
Sheboygan.	88	384	61	490
Taylor	2	42	3	345
Trempealeau	4	292	4	414
Vernon	3	134	5	494
Vilas.	3	381	2	369
Walworth.	25	407	31	479
Washburn	3	375	4	510
Washington	13	335	13	366
Waukesha	47	457	70	477
Waupaca	15	372	14	542
Waushara.	9	384	13	489
Winnebago	122	293	100	471
Wood	57	384	32	529
Total.	**5,478**	**365**	**5,329**	**512**

—Represents zero.

Source: Wisconsin Department of Children and Families, departmental data, March 2021.

Wisconsin Works (W-2) expenditures

W-2 contract agency	Counties served	2019 expenditures ($)	2020 expenditures ($)
Ross IES (www.rossprov.com)	Northern Milwaukee	10,278,571	7,383,506
MAXIMUS (www.maximus.com)	West central Milwaukee	4,681,345	4,200,346
America Works of Wisconsin (www.americaworks.com)	East central Milwaukee	7,341,831	5,236,403
UMOS (www.umos.org)	Southern Milwaukee	5,639,722	4,191,874
Forward Service Corporation (www.fsc-corp.org)	Adams, Brown, Calumet, Columbia, Dane, Dodge, Door, Florence, Fond du Lac, Forest, Grant, Green, Green Lake, Iowa, Jefferson, Juneau, Kewaunee, Lafayette, Langlade, Lincoln, Manitowoc, Marathon, Marinette, Marquette, Menominee, Oconto, Oneida, Outagamie, Portage, Price, Richland, Rock, Sauk, Shawano, Sheboygan, Taylor, Vilas, Waupaca, Waushara, Winnebago, Wood	11,789,694	11,287,995
ResCare (www.rescare.com)	Kenosha, Ozaukee, Racine, Walworth, Washington, Waukesha	4,088,989	3,974,894

Wisconsin Works (W-2) expenditures, continued

W-2 contract agency	Counties served	2019 expenditures ($)	2020 expenditures ($)
Workforce Connections (www.workforceconnections.org)	Buffalo, Crawford, Jackson, La Crosse, Monroe, Pepin, Trempealeau, Vernon	723,783	896,118
Workforce Resource, Inc. (www.workforceresource.org) . . .	Ashland, Barron, Bayfield, Burnett, Chippewa, Clark, Douglas, Dunn, Eau Claire, Iron, Pierce, Polk, Rusk, Sawyer, St Croix, Washburn	2,385,933	2,066,169
Total.		46,929,869	39,237,307

Source: Wisconsin Department of Children and Families, departmental data, March 2021.

Wisconsin Medicaid and BadgerCare

County	Recipients[1] Fiscal yr. 2019	Fiscal yr. 2020	% of 2020 population	Rank[3]	Expenditures[2] Fiscal yr. 2019	Fiscal yr. 2020	Per 2020 recipient Amount	Rank[3]
Adams	5,421	5,335	25.77	18	$28,632,503	$30,473,757	$5,712.04	65
Ashland. . . .	5,865	5,782	36.43	3	39,074,782	40,173,765	6,948.07	14
Barron.	12,793	12,969	27.88	11	76,044,081	78,692,724	6,067.76	53
Bayfield. . . .	3,900	3,839	25.04	22	23,934,558	25,004,019	6,513.16	32
Brown.	58,463	59,386	22.42	35	327,388,362	350,298,793	5,898.68	60
Buffalo	2,636	2,668	19.52	53	16,940,236	16,796,929	6,295.70	45
Burnett	4,547	4,532	29.27	8	21,757,016	22,990,242	5,072.87	70
Calumet . . .	5,896	6,057	11.36	70	32,176,153	34,710,873	5,730.70	64
Chippewa . .	14,600	14,700	22.50	32	100,928,947	101,623,676	6,913.18	15
Clark.	7,620	7,517	21.65	40	47,969,303	48,616,232	6,467.50	36
Columbia. . .	10,247	10,124	17.72	60	73,104,509	73,710,350	7,280.75	9
Crawford . . .	4,071	4,063	24.36	25	24,891,380	25,443,912	6,262.35	48
Dane	83,203	85,666	15.76	66	598,406,268	638,746,342	7,456.24	7
Dodge	15,639	15,544	17.27	64	109,214,580	106,009,072	6,819.94	18
Door.	5,064	5,055	17.57	62	30,020,711	31,834,635	6,297.65	44
Douglas. . . .	10,890	11,054	24.98	23	68,374,856	71,262,393	6,446.75	38
Dunn	9,931	9,794	21.87	39	61,478,412	64,336,249	6,568.95	27
Eau Claire. . .	23,087	23,264	22.38	36	137,557,704	140,339,634	6,032.48	55
Florence . . .	1,064	1,072	24.00	27	5,886,593	5,990,661	5,588.30	67
Fond du Lac .	19,534	19,790	18.96	56	126,543,443	133,781,359	6,760.05	20
Forest	2,811	2,904	31.62	5	14,952,608	15,974,204	5,500.76	69
Grant	9,870	10,003	19.03	55	62,323,457	65,252,210	6,523.26	31
Green	6,642	6,598	17.85	59	41,675,839	44,092,772	6,682.75	24
Green Lake. .	3,944	3,934	20.51	45	22,725,001	24,790,625	6,301.63	43
Iowa.	4,274	4,227	17.68	61	26,682,881	28,279,571	6,690.22	23
Iron	1,695	1,714	29.01	9	10,976,441	11,834,542	6,904.63	16
Jackson. . . .	5,146	5,234	25.13	21	31,045,651	30,562,394	5,839.20	62
Jefferson . . .	15,450	15,555	18.37	57	115,899,245	122,445,913	7,871.80	4
Juneau	7,149	7,393	27.13	16	44,371,464	49,841,559	6,741.72	21
Kenosha . . .	42,785	42,544	24.95	24	243,053,877	255,643,511	6,008.92	56

Wisconsin Medicaid and BadgerCare, continued

	Recipients[1]				Expenditures[2]			
County	Fiscal yr. 2019	Fiscal yr. 2020	% of 2020 population	Rank[3]	Fiscal yr. 2019	Fiscal yr. 2020	Per 2020 recipient Amount	Rank[3]
Kewaunee . .	3,499	3,463	16.69	65	23,853,044	24,852,963	7,176.71	11
La Crosse . . .	24,148	23,938	19.87	50	169,613,635	173,737,184	7,257.80	10
Lafayette . . .	3,282	3,392	19.94	48	15,944,085	16,750,230	4,938.16	71
Langlade . . .	5,916	6,016	29.99	7	34,052,662	35,852,403	5,959.51	57
Lincoln	6,341	6,356	22.07	38	45,906,474	46,462,824	7,310.07	8
Manitowoc. .	15,849	16,142	19.84	51	102,792,395	109,666,168	6,793.84	19
Marathon. . .	28,531	28,710	20.92	43	180,401,751	185,735,984	6,469.38	35
Marinette. . .	10,771	10,941	26.52	17	67,632,402	69,782,744	6,378.10	39
Marquette . .	3,667	3,714	24.14	26	23,356,961	24,622,354	6,629.61	26
Menominee .	2,812	2,971	69.63	1	16,716,882	17,548,724	5,906.67	59
Milwaukee . .	377,250	379,735	40.22	2	2,386,432,923	2,493,122,807	6,565.43	28
Monroe	10,528	10,530	22.46	34	66,615,300	68,020,689	6,459.70	37
Oconto	7,460	7,568	19.48	54	45,593,290	47,598,811	6,289.48	46
Oneida	8,415	8,353	23.03	29	50,434,692	51,212,656	6,131.05	51
Outagamie. .	31,955	32,418	17.27	63	193,665,835	204,420,512	6,305.77	42
Ozaukee . . .	8,571	8,692	9.59	72	71,092,581	76,614,710	8,814.39	2
Pepin	1,445	1,498	20.26	46	8,794,699	8,899,205	5,940.72	58
Pierce	6,150	6,198	14.61	67	38,202,060	40,454,296	6,526.99	30
Polk	10,165	10,203	22.86	30	57,431,696	63,849,327	6,257.90	49
Portage	13,270	13,145	18.34	58	73,166,675	76,145,968	5,792.77	63
Price	3,888	3,915	27.63	14	24,861,509	26,057,640	6,655.85	25
Racine.	54,160	54,559	27.87	12	350,733,290	375,440,308	6,881.36	17
Richland . . .	4,580	4,537	25.16	20	35,194,241	36,052,243	7,946.27	3
Rock.	44,099	44,175	27.59	15	225,343,794	245,141,524	5,549.33	68
Rusk.	4,605	4,607	30.96	6	26,124,581	27,170,323	5,897.62	61
St. Croix. . . .	12,281	12,378	13.61	68	75,158,544	78,509,418	6,342.66	41
Sauk.	13,912	14,127	22.30	37	84,681,322	90,003,600	6,371.03	40
Sawyer	5,647	5,629	33.30	4	32,837,418	34,690,939	6,162.90	50
Shawano . . .	9,600	9,815	23.52	28	62,777,464	64,344,061	6,555.69	29
Sheboygan. .	23,004	23,525	20.12	47	140,232,870	147,670,955	6,277.19	47
Taylor	4,502	4,428	21.30	41	24,325,917	25,261,888	5,705.03	66
Trempealeau	6,779	6,796	22.62	31	42,935,273	44,002,011	6,474.69	34
Vernon	6,568	6,393	20.96	42	45,040,480	45,555,361	7,125.82	12
Vilas	5,972	6,020	27.65	13	26,759,295	28,834,722	4,789.82	72
Walworth. . .	20,505	20,728	19.91	49	125,713,617	134,623,093	6,494.75	33
Washburn . .	4,681	4,554	28.47	10	32,034,866	31,692,674	6,959.30	13
Washington .	16,028	16,505	11.94	69	117,584,353	123,518,232	7,483.69	6
Waukesha . .	40,820	41,662	10.24	71	309,202,367	325,902,986	7,822.55	5
Waupaca . . .	11,074	10,904	20.91	44	97,336,564	101,596,764	9,317.38	1
Waushara . .	5,535	5,490	22.47	33	32,549,406	33,224,761	6,051.87	54
Winnebago .	33,195	33,598	19.78	52	198,397,467	205,473,821	6,115.66	52
Wood	18,710	19,027	25.24	19	119,897,000	127,841,202	6,718.94	22
Total.	**1,315,697**	**1,326,645**	**22.66**	**NA**	**$8,465,452,539**	**$8,877,512,004**	**$6,691.70**	**X**

X–Not applicable.

1. If an individual resided in multiple counties during the year, the individual is counted only in the recipient tally for the last county of residence to avoid double-counting in the statewide total.   2. The expenditure totals include benefits issued and individuals eligible under BadgerCare+/MA and subprograms CORE, BASIC, Family Planning Only Services, and Medicaid Waiver. Costs include: Managed Care Capitation Payments, Fee For Service Payment to providers, and Long Term Care waiver program payments.   3. Rankings calculated by Wisconsin Legislative Reference Bureau.

Sources: Wisconsin Department of Health Services, departmental data, March 2021; Wisconsin Department of Administration, Division of Intergovernmental Relations, Demographic Services Center, *County Population Estimates, January 1, 2020.*

BadgerCare and Medical Assistance in Wisconsin

Fiscal year	Long-term care				Hospitals				Physicians and clinics		Drugs		Home care[1]		Managed care[2]		Other noninstitutional fee-for-service[3]		Total provider payments[4,5]	
	Nursing homes		State centers		Inpatient		Outpatient													
	Amt (mil. $)	% of total	Amt (mil. $)	% of total	Amt (mil. $)	% of total	Amt (mil. $)	% of total	Amt (mil. $)	% of total	Amt (mil. $)	% of total	Amt (mil. $)	% of total	Amt (mil. $)	% of total	Amt (mil. $)	% of total	Amt (mil. $)	Annual % change
1999–2000	906.3	29.8	135.9	4.5	270.6	8.9	55.3	1.8	63.2	2.1	336.5	11.1	498.8	16.4	394.4	13.0	251.8	8.3	3,044.0	NA
2000–01	916.2	27.8	115.3	3.5	297.8	9.0	58.7	1.8	72.4	2.2	373.6	11.4	522.2	15.9	523.6	15.9	280.1	8.5	3,291.8	8.1
2001–02	980.6	26.5	126.9	3.4	333.2	9.0	69.6	1.9	78.7	2.1	432.5	11.7	528.4	14.3	681.8	18.4	319.2	8.6	3,700.9	12.4
2002–03	990.6	25.7	123.9	3.2	332.0	8.6	75.6	2.0	85.2	2.2	494.7	12.9	592.6	15.4	657.9	17.1	334.5	8.7	3,849.2	4.0
2003–04	972.2	21.3	143.0	3.1	338.0	7.4	91.6	2.0	116.9	2.6	700.5	15.4	636.8	14.0	1,013.6	22.2	381.8	8.4	4,558.9	18.4
2004–05	963.8	20.2	117.7	2.5	388.6	8.1	103.7	2.2	133.2	2.8	772.0	16.2	754.9	15.8	873.7	18.3	487.2	10.2	4,777.1	4.8
2005–06	940.1	20.7	111.5	2.5	357.0	7.9	85.8	1.9	104.9	2.3	459.6	10.1	789.2	17.4	1,068.0	23.5	424.2	9.3	4,546.3	-4.8
2006–07	878.2	18.3	111.4	2.3	372.6	7.7	81.6	1.7	111.0	2.3	389.7	8.1	773.6	16.1	1,307.5	27.2	472.3	9.8	4,809.4	5.8
2007–08	837.2	16.3	117.1	2.3	409.7	8.0	85.1	1.7	157.2	3.1	466.3	9.1	812.5	15.8	1,422.3	27.7	599.3	11.7	5,137.5	6.8
2008–09	890.7	14.4	92.0	1.5	602.2	9.7	162.2	2.6	152.6	2.5	621.5	10.0	747.9	12.1	2,089.3	33.8	637.2	10.3	6,188.6	20.5
2009–10	909.5	12.8	148.1	2.1	459.9	6.5	152.8	2.1	188.5	2.6	660.7	9.3	604.5	8.5	2,358.5	33.2	760.2	10.7	7,114.6	15.0
2010–11	842.9	11.2	112.5	1.5	502.5	6.7	188.2	2.5	151.9	2.0	617.6	8.2	599.5	8.0	3,457.1	46.0	1,050.7	14.0	7,522.8	5.7
2011–12	818.8	11.7	127.1	1.8	440.0	6.3	196.3	2.8	166.8	2.4	610.6	8.7	659.0	9.4	2,691.3	38.5	1,288.5	18.4	6,998.4	-7.0
2012–13	819.4	10.8	133.5	1.8	580.6	7.7	208.6	2.8	143.9	1.9	625.8	8.3	784.4	10.4	3,024.3	40.0	1,207.0	16.0	7,553.1	7.9
2013–14	770.0	9.5	128.3	1.6	519.5	6.4	202.5	2.5	187.9	2.3	710.6	8.8	889.1	11.0	3,272.7	40.4	1,355.4	16.7	8,105.8	7.3
2014–15	762.8	9.0	112.5	1.3	564.1	6.6	230.0	2.7	158.3	1.9	876.0	10.3	925.5	10.9	3,531.5	41.5	1,350.5	15.9	8,511.2	5.0
2015–16	713.3	8.2	120.1	1.4	525.9	6.1	201.7	2.3	141.4	1.6	996.0	11.5	920.6	10.6	3,759.2	43.3	1,301.6	15.0	8,680.0	2.0
2016–17	708.0	8.3	108.4	1.3	567.0	6.6	206.8	2.4	170.2	2.0	1,061.9	12.4	903.3	10.6	3,909.4	45.7	917.4	10.7	8,552.5	-1.5
2017–18	685.7	7.7	114.5	1.3	576.4	6.5	194.7	2.2	158.9	1.8	1,139.2	12.8	978.0	11.0	4,043.0	45.4	1,019.6	11.4	8,910.1	4.2
2018–19	680.1	7.2	117.2	1.2	522.2	5.5	174.1	1.8	146.6	1.6	1,203.8	12.8	973.9	10.3	4,495.4	47.7	1,119.7	11.9	9,433.0	5.9
2019–20	672.4	6.3	120.8	1.1	519.7	4.9	177.1	1.7	168.7	1.6	1,355.1	12.7	1,057.5	9.9	5,512.8	51.6	1,091.9	10.2	10,676.1	13.2

Note: Enrollments in BadgerCare began in July 1999, and expenditures for the program are included in the Medical Assistance figures above. Medical Assistance expenditure data prior to BadgerCare can be found in previous Blue Books.

NA–Not available.

1. Home Care includes HCBS waivers. 2. Managed Care includes all capitated programs (BC/BS+, HMOs, CCF/WAM, SSI managed care, PACE/Partnership, Family Care). 3. All noninstitutional fee-for-service acute care includes acute fee-for-service, PACE/Partnership, Family Care. 3. All noninstitutional fee-for-service acute care not otherwise captured plus local government plus Medicare crossovers. 4. Does not include offsetting recoveries and collections, such as estate recoveries, drug rebates, etc. 5. Total includes expenditures not listed separately.

Source: Wisconsin Department of Health Services, departmental data, March 2021. Data prior to 2006 is from the Wisconsin Legislative Fiscal Bureau.

CORRECTIONAL AND TREATMENT FACILITIES

State corrections populations

	2020		Average daily population (fiscal year)					
Institutions	Avg. pop.	Capac- ity[1]	1970	1980	1990	2000	2010	2019
Maximum security (men)	**5,228**	**3,838**	**1,709**	**1,833**	**2,986**	**4,513**	**5,161**	**5,303**
Assessment and evaluation[2]	NA	904	NA	NA	NA	NA	1,214	NA
Columbia Correctional Institution . . .	812	541	NA	NA	477	808	820	812
Dodge Correctional Institution[2]	1,630	1,165	NA	88	551	1,377	341	1,649
Green Bay Correctional Institution . . .	1,066	749	755	658	832	1,002	1,089	1,098
Wisconsin Secure Program Facility . . .	478	501	NA	NA	NA	101	461	481
Waupun Correctional Institution	1,242	882	954	1,087	1,126	1,225	1,237	1,263
Medium security	**11,767**	**9,430**	**846**	**938**	**1,771**	**7,281**	**11,242**	**11,895**
Fox Lake Correctional Institution	1,337	979	553	570	785	1,112	1,046	1,347
Jackson Correctional Institution.	985	837	NA	NA	NA	971	977	994
Kettle Moraine Correctional Institution	1,177	783	293	368	542	1,233	1,160	1,186
New Lisbon Correctional Institution . .	1,036	950	NA	NA	NA	NA	1,009	1,046
Oshkosh Correctional Institution	2,035	1,494	NA	NA	444	1,859	2,031	2,051
Prairie du Chien Correctional Institution	513	326	NA	NA	NA	297	500	517
Racine Correctional Institution	1,666	1,171	NA	NA	NA	1,414	1,553	1,694
Racine Youthful Offender Correctional Facility.	447	400	NA	NA	NA	395	445	458
Redgranite Correctional Institution . .	1,008	990	NA	NA	NA	NA	1,013	1,022
Stanley Correctional Institution	1,563	1,500	NA	NA	NA	NA	1,509	1,581
Minimum security	**3,316**	**2,230**	**390**	**474**	**1,439**	**2,380**	**3,332**	**3,394**
Chippewa Valley Correctional Treatment Center.	455	450	NA	NA	NA	NA	465	486
Fox Lake Correctional Institution	NA	NA	NA	NA	NA	NA	280	NA
Oakhill Correctional Institution	745	344	NA	198	368	564	677	759
Sturtevant Transitional Facility	140	150	NA	NA	NA	NA	261	145
Wisconsin Correctional Center System (WCCS)[4].	1,976	1,286	390	276	1,071	1,816	1,649	2,004
Detention facility	**924**	**460**	**998**	**NA**	**NA**	**NA**	**956**	**1,043**
Milwaukee Secure Detention Facility. .	924	460	998	NA	NA	NA	956	1,043
Wisconsin Women's Correctional System[3].	**1,454**	**937**	**141**	**123**	**203**	**644**	**1,262**	**1,514**
Taycheedah Correctional Institution (med./max.)	902	653	141	123	203	644	579	946
Correctional centers (min.)	552	284	NA	NA	NA	NA	683	568
Contract facilities	**522**	**545**	**NA**	**NA**	**78**	**4,665**	**690**	**522**
Intergovernmental contract	32	NA	NA	NA	NA	NA	30	32
In–state.	490	NA	NA	NA	NA	NA	660	490
Other adults.	**66,189**	**NA**	**8,859**	**19,842**	**30,172**	**64,409**	**68,123**	**66,322**
Community residential confinement. .	NA	NA	NA	NA	48	NA	NA	NA
Division of Intensive Sanctions	NA	NA	NA	NA	NA	412	NA	NA
Extended supervision and parole. . . .	22,711	NA	4,329	3,045	4,217	8,951	19,783	21,949
Probation.	43,478	NA	4,530	16,797	25,907	55,046	48,340	44,373
Unknown offender type	NA	NA	NA	NA	NA	NA	NA	NA
Juvenile corrections.	**118**	**560**	**446**	**575**	**572**	**904**	**437**	**142**
Copper Lake School[4]	16	29	NA	NA	NA	NA	NA	16
Ethan Allen School[4]	NA	NA	365	306	320	438	207	NA
Lincoln Hills School[4].	98	519	NA	245	252	330	176	122
Southern Oaks Girls School[4]	NA	NA	NA	NA	NA	87	49	NA
Youth Leadership Training Center[5] . . .	NA	NA	NA	NA	NA	40	NA	NA

State corrections populations, continued

Institutions	2020 Avg. pop.	Capac- ity[1]	Average daily population (fiscal year) 1970	1980	1990	2000	2010	2019
Sprite program[6].	NA	NA	NA	NA	NA	9	5	NA
Grow Academy[6]	4	12	NA	NA	NA	NA	NA	4
Juvenile correctional camp system. . .	NA	NA	81	24	NA	NA	NA	NA
Other juveniles.	80	NA	NA	NA	NA	308	265	104
Juvenile aftercare.	NA	NA	NA	NA	NA	NA	76	NA
Alternate care.	20	NA	NA	NA	NA	174	49	27
Corrective sanctions.	NA	NA	NA	NA	NA	134	140	NA
Home supervision	38	NA	NA	NA	NA	NA	NA	48
Alternate care supervision	22	NA	NA	NA	NA	NA	NA	29
Total.	89,598	NA	12,391	23,785	37,221	84,796	91,840	90,239

NA–Not available.

1. DOC "rated capacity" is the original design capacity, based on industry standards, plus modifications and expansions. It excludes beds and multiple bunking to accommodate crowding. DHS Care and Treatment Facilities' capacity is "staffed capacity," based on staffing and other budgetary resources rather than number of beds.   2. Dodge CI serves as the assessment and evaluation (A&E) center for sentenced adult male felons. A&E for sentenced adult female felons moved from Dodge CI to Taycheedah CI in December 2004.   3. In July 2005, DOC designated the institutions for female offenders as the Wisconsin Women's Correctional System, which now includes Taycheedah CI and two of the minimum security correctional centers.   4. Ethan Allen and Southern Oaks closed in June 2011; Copper Lake opened in June 2011.   5. Youth Leadership Training Camp program, formerly at Camp Douglas and closed in February 2002, is now part of the program at Lincoln Hills.   6. The Sprite program was eliminated in March 2010. Grow Academy opened in June 2014.

Sources: Wisconsin Department of Corrections, Fiscal Year Summary Report of Population Movement for 1991 and prior issues, and departmental data, February 2021 and prior years.

State health service institutions populations

Institutions	2020 Avg. pop.	Capac- ity[1]	Average daily population (fiscal year) 1970	1980	1990	2000	2010	2019
Mental health institutions (MHI). . . .	1,185	1,344	1,354	666	693	1,053	1,273	1,224
Mendota MHI	287	288	522	202	266	238	240	284
Winnebago MHI	168	184	574	310	266	279	291	175
Mendota Juvenile Treatment Center . .	23	29	NA	NA	NA	43	29	25
Sand Ridge Secure Treatment Center .	310	400	NA	NA	NA	72	286	326
Central State Hospital	NA	NA	258	154	NA	NA	NA	NA
Wisconsin Resource Center.	397	443	NA	NA	161	421	427	414
Centers for developmentally disabled (CDD)	324	440	3,698	2,142	1,677	843	448	336
Central Wisconsin CDD	189	255	1,070	731	606	380	258	197
Northern Wisconsin CDD	13	25	1,421	676	495	189	12	15
Southern Wisconsin CDD	122	160	1,207	735	576	274	178	124
Total.	1,509	1,784	5,052	2,808	2,370	1,896	1,721	1,560

NA–Not available.

Source: Wisconsin Department of Health Services, departmental data, February 2021 and prior years.

MILITARY AND VETERANS AFFAIRS

Wisconsin veterans benefits

		Grants			Loans		
Fiscal year	Total benefits	Economic	Educational	Full-time educational grants	Economic assistance	Personal loans	General obligation bond housing loans
1993. . . .	$22,446,997	$472,302	$512,770	$167,838	$2,673,585	X	$18,620,502
1994. . . .	36,893,647[1]	451,666	716,858	667	2,567,053	X	33,157,403
1995. . . .	114,984,938[1]	552,893	754,052	X	2,544,584	X	111,133,409
1996. . . .	80,581,789	601,030	1,609,350	X	3,189,625	X	75,181,784
1997. . . .	99,984,937	937,294	1,797,649	X	2,401,548	X	94,848,446
1998. . . .	160,760,389	783,664	1,680,881	X	666,575[2]	$10,215,928[2]	147,413,341
1999. . . .	140,457,525	2,263,317	1,447,882	X	X	11,837,974	124,908,352
2000. . . .	143,192,551	3,226,128	1,786,205	X	X	10,802,068	127,378,150
2001. . . .	73,390,596	1,205,846	1,768,452	X	X	9,034,356	61,381,942
2002. . . .	88,227,531	1,925,094	2,822,134	X	X	15,780,270	67,700,033
2003. . . .	83,866,773	1,752,733	2,909,812	X	X	19,792,680	59,411,548
2004. . . .	95,593,212	1,296,310	4,384,642	X	X	11,808,566	78,103,694
2005. . . .	37,428,288	413,564	5,698,107	X	X	2,271,942	29,044,675
2006. . . .	23,935,069	1,052,493	4,751,263	X	X	4,113,262	14,018,050
2007. . . .	48,026,312	678,109	3,715,648	X	X	5,933,810	37,698,745
2008. . . .	59,388,229	1,028,788	2,276,489	X	X	5,081,986	51,000,967
2009. . . .	43,587,113	961,497	1,694,312	X	X	2,764,736	38,166,568
2010. . . .	15,859,166	426,535	1,726,307	X	X	3,133,961	10,572,363
2011. . . .	4,011,393	682,235	1,271,083	X	X	2,058,075	X
2012. . . .	2,531,220	577,061	1,044,751	X	X	909,397	X
2013. . . .	1,242,884	443,312	799,572	X	X	NA	X
2014. . . .	1,181,380	713,279	468,101	X	X	NA	X
2015. . . .	2,450,024	2,005,365	444,659	X	X	NA	X
2016. . . .	2,099,056	1,843,991	255,065	X	X	NA	X
2017. . . .	2,459,211	2,074,031	385,180	X	X	NA	X
2018. . . .	2,674,808	2,562,378	112,430	X	X	NA	X
2019. . . .	2,560,050	2,503,224	56,826	X	X	NA	X
2020. . . .	2,475,928	2,420,420	55,508	X	X	NA	X

NA–Not available; X–Not applicable.

1. Includes $21,444,166 (FY94) and $11,024,956 (FY95) in consumer loans under the Veterans Trust Fund stabilization provision of 1993 Wisconsin Act 16.   2. Personal Loan Program replaced economic assistance loans.

Source: Wisconsin Department of Veterans Affairs, departmental data, March 2021.

Wisconsin Veterans Homes membership, 1888–1974

	Civil and Indian Wars	Spanish-American	World War I		World War II		Korean Conflict		Total
			Men	Women	Men	Women	Men	Women	
1888.	72	X	X	X	X	X	X	X	72
1890.	139	X	X	X	X	X	X	v	139
1900.	680	X	X	X	X	X	X	X	680
1910.	699	X	X	X	X	X	X	X	699
1920.	532	X	X	X	X	X	X	X	532
1930.	254	108	10	14	X	X	X	X	386
1940.	89	196	101	130	X	X	X	X	516
1950.	27	156	189	93	5	1	X	X	471
1960.	4	74	203	94	40	5	X	X	450
1961.	3	66	221	88	39	8	X	X	427

Wisconsin Veterans Homes membership, 1888–1974, continued

	Civil and Indian Wars	Spanish-American	World War I		World War II		Korean Conflict		Total
			Men	Women	Men	Women	Men	Women	
1962.........	3	66	223	82	52	9	X	X	431
1963.........	3	67	235	87	57	10	X	X	459
1964.........	3	63	237	105	61	16	X	X	485
1965.........	2	62	247	112	77	16	X	X	516
1966.........	1	56	258	112	86	21	X	X	534
1967.........	1	46	272	120	93	20	X	X	555
1968.........	1	48	253	123	93	16	X	X	534
1969.........	1	43	253	145	101	14	X	X	560
1970.........	1	35	279	146	153	20	1	—	635
1971.........	1	39	316	160	184	31	2	—	723
1972.........	—	28	279	155	199	39	2	—	702
1973.........	—	25	285	108	199	37	—	1	715
1974.........	—	21	279	175	185	37	—	2	699

X–Not applicable; —Represents zero.
Source: Wisconsin Department of Veterans Affairs, departmental data, March 2021.

Wisconsin Veterans Homes membership, 1975–2020

	Spanish-American		World War I		World War II		Korean Conflict		Vietnam		Other eras[1]		Total
	Vets.	Deps.	Vets.	Deps.	Vets.	Deps.	Vets.	Deps.	Vets.	Deps.	Vets.	Deps.	
1975......	1	18	272	171	198	40	3	2	—	—	—	—	705
1976......	1	14	254	167	209	40	2	2	—	—	—	—	689
1977......	1	13	270	164	205	41	4	2	—	—	—	—	700
1978......	1	11	261	158	218	38	3	2	—	—	—	—	692
1979......	1	11	244	146	227	37	4	1	—	—	—	—	672
1980......	1	8	242	144	241	36	5	1	—	—	—	—	678
1981......	—	8	224	139	264	40	8	2	—	—	—	—	685
1982......	—	7	189	124	282	43	11	2	—	—	—	—	658
1983......	—	5	171	111	297	42	14	2	1	—	—	—	643
1984......	—	4	144	97	316	47	21	2	3	—	—	—	634
1985......	—	4	129	102	329	54	28	—	5	—	—	—	651
1986......	—	4	117	92	348	56	35	5	7	—	—	—	664
1987......	—	2	108	84	384	60	36	4	8	—	—	—	686
1988......	—	1	84	76	395	55	45	7	8	—	—	—	671
1989......	—	2	62	75	399	67	50	7	9	1	—	—	672
1990......	—	2	49	65	431	76	62	8	10	1	3	—	707
1991......	—	2	43	57	440	74	69	10	10	2	3	—	710
1992......	—	1	33	44	442	77	82	10	12	1	2	—	704
1993......	—	1	23	41	463	73	94	9	11	1	2	—	718
1994......	—	1	14	33	488	83	99	11	12	2	1	—	744
1995......	—	1	8	31	484	84	99	12	16	2	1	—	738
1996......	—	1	4	24	489	79	103	12	25	1	1	—	739
1997......	—	1	3	20	479	82	107	11	38	1	3	—	744
1998......	—	—	1	17	460	83	123	12	39	1	9	—	745
1999......	—	—	—	12	445	87	128	11	41	3	13	1	741
2000......	—	—	—	10	423	94	132	12	47	4	21	2	745
2001[2]....	—	—	—	9	414	95	133	10	51	3	25	2	742
2002......	—	—	—	8	404	103	130	11	54	3	29	2	744
2003......	—	—	—	7	433	105	140	13	67	3	35	2	805
2004......	—	—	—	3	416	99	148	15	72	3	40	2	798

Wisconsin Veterans Homes membership, 1975–2020, continued

	Spanish-American		World War I		World War II		Korean Conflict		Vietnam		Other eras[1]		Total
	Vets.	Deps.	Vets.	Deps.	Vets.	Deps.	Vets.	Deps.	Vets.	Deps.	Vets.	Deps.	
2005	—	—	—	2	350	103	144	15	71	3	40	2	730
2006	—	—	—	1	407	119	164	17	87	5	50	4	854
2007	—	—	—	1	475	135	173	26	100	8	3	—	921
2008	—	—	—	1	417	123	177	26	115	7	4	—	870
2009	—	—	—	1	389	130	193	21	122	8	8	—	947
2010	—	—	—	1	356	127	176	22	122	8	10	—	892
2011	—	—	—	1	339	124	170	19	154	12	12	—	904
2012	—	—	—	1	330	121	180	32	178	11	19	2	953
2013[3]	—	—	—	1	412	145	286	53	276	16	44	2	1,235
2014	—	—	—	1	259	128	215	34	262	11	98	4	1,012
2015	—	—	—	—	308	114	269	49	338	11	43	1	1,133
2016	—	—	—	—	248	107	255	46	364	14	45	3	1,082
2017	—	—	—	—	207	93	217	49	376	17	39	9	1,007
2018	—	—	—	—	157	79	224	46	382	13	44	2	947
2019	—	—	—	—	85	26	144	26	222	11	94	8	616
2020	—	—	—	—	44	31	101	23	281	10	118	8	616

—Represents zero. Deps.–Dependents; Vets.–Veterans.

1. Other periods of hostilities for which expeditionary medals were awarded.   2. The Wisconsin Veterans Home at King was established in 1887, and the home at Union Grove opened in 2001. Data starting in 2001 includes both homes.   3. Veterans Home at Chippewa Falls opened in 2013. Data starting in 2013 includes veterans homes at King, Union Grove, and Chippewa Falls.

Source: Wisconsin Department of Veterans Affairs, departmental data, March 2021.

Wisconsin National Guard

JOINT UNITS
Joint Force Headquarters Wisconsin
Joint Force Headquarters Detachment Madison
54th Civil Support Team (WMD) - Madison

ARMY UNITS
Headquarters, Wisconsin Army National Guard–
  Madison

Joint Force Headquarters Separate Units
Recruiting and Retention Battalion–Madison
Det. 1, Recruiting and Retention Battalion–Madison
Det. 2, Recruiting and Retention Battalion–
  Milwaukee

32nd Infantry Brigade Combat Team
Headquarters and Headquarters Co.–Camp
  Douglas

1st Battalion, 120th Field Artillery
Headquarters and Headquarters Battery*–
  Wisconsin Rapids
Det. 1, Headquarters and Headquarters Company–
  Berlin
Battery A–Marshfield
Battery B–Stevens Point
Battery C–Oconomowoc

3rd Battalion, 126th Infantry (Michigan Army
  National Guard)

2nd Battalion, 127th Infantry
Headquarters and Headquarters Co.*–Appleton
Det. 1, Headquarters Co.–Clintonville
Company A*–Waupun
Det. 1, Co. A–Ripon
Company B–Green Bay
Company C–Fond du Lac
Company D–Marinette

1st Battalion, 128th Infantry
Headquarters and Headquarters Co.*–Eau Claire
Det. 1, Headquarters Co.–Abbotsford
Company A–Menomonie
Company B*–New Richmond
Det. 1, Company B–Rice Lake
Company C*–Arcadia
Det. 1, Company C–Onalaska
Company D–River Falls

132nd Brigade Support Battalion
Headquarters and Headquarters Co.–Portage
Company A* (Distribution)–Janesville
Det. 1, Company A–Elkhorn
Company B (Maintenance)–Mauston
Company C (Medical)–Racine
Company D (Forward Support)–Madison
Company E (Forward Support)–Antigo
Company F (Forward Support)–Mosinee
Company G (Forward Support)–Waupaca
Company H (Forward Support)–Neillsville

Wisconsin National Guard, continued

173rd Brigade Engineer Battalion
Headquarters and Headquarters Co.–Wausau
Company A*–Tomahawk
Det. 1, Co. A–Rhinelander
Company B–Onalaska
Company C (Signal)–Camp Douglas
Company D* (Military Intelligence)–Madison
Det. 1, Company D (TUAS)–Camp Douglas

1st Squadron, 105th Cavalry (Reconnaissance, Surveillance and Target Acquisition)
Headquarters and Headquarters Troop–Madison
Troop A–Fort Atkinson
Troop B–Watertown
Troop C–Reedsburg

64th Troop Command
Headquarters–Madison
Wisconsin Medical Detachment–Camp Douglas

732nd Combat Sustainment Support Battalion
Headquarters and Headquarters Company–Tomah
107th Maintenance Co.*–Sparta
Det. 1, 107th Maintenance Co.–Viroqua
1157th Transportation Co.–Oshkosh
1158th Transportation Co.*–Beloit
Det. 1, 1158th Trans. Co.–Black River Falls

1st Battalion, 147th Aviation Regiment
Headquarters and Headquarters Co.*–Madison
Company A–Madison
Det. 1, Company C–Madison
Company D*–Madison
Company E*–Madison
Det. 1, Company B, 248th Aviation Support Bn.–West Bend
Company C* 1st Battalion, 168th Aviation–West Bend
Det. 1, Company G, 2nd Battalion, 104th Aviation–West Bend
Det. 2, Co. D, 1st Battalion, 112th Aviation Regiment–West Bend
Det. 5, Company A, 2nd Battalion, 641st Aviation–Madison
54th Civil Support Team–Madison

641st Troop Command Battalion
Headquarters and Headquarters Detachment/Wisconsin CERFP Command and Control Element–Madison
135th Medical Company–Waukesha
1967th Contingency Contracting Team–Camp Douglas
273rd Engineer Company (Wheeled Sapper)/CERFP Search and Extraction–Medford
457th Chemical Co./CERFP Decontamination*–Hartford
Det. 1, 457th Chemical Company–Burlington
112th Mobile Public Affairs Det.–Madison
132nd Army Band–Madison
Det. 1, Cyber Protection Team–Madison
505th Trial Defense Team–Madison

157th Maneuver Enhancement Brigade
Headquarters and Headquarters Co.–Milwaukee
32nd Military Police Company*–Milwaukee
924th Engineer Det. (Facilities)– Milwaukee
357th Signal Network Support Co.– Milwaukee

1st Battalion, 121st Field Artillery (HIMARS)
Headquarters and Headquarters Battery (HIMARS), 121st Field Artillery – Oak Creek
Battery A (HIMARS)–Sussex
Battery B (HIMARS)–Plymouth
108th Forward Support Company–Sussex

724th Engineer Battalion
Headquarters and Headquarters Co.–Chippewa Falls
Company A (Forward Support Company)–Hayward
106th Engineer Det. (Quarry Team)–Tomah
229th Engineer Co.* (Horizontal)–Prairie du Chien
Det. 1, 229th Engineer Company–Platteville
824th Engineer Det. (Concrete)– Tomah
829th Engineer Co. (Vertical)*–Spooner
Det. 1, 829th Engineer Co.–Ashland 950th Engineer Co. (Clearance)–Superior

426th Regiment–Regional Training Institute (Wisconsin Military Academy)
Headquarters and Headquarters Det.–Fort McCoy
1st Battalion, 426th Regiment (Field Artillery)–Fort McCoy
2nd Battalion, 426th Regiment (Modular Training)–Fort McCoy

AIR UNITS
Headquarters, Wisconsin Air National Guard–Madison

115th Fighter Wing–Truax Field, Madison
115th Operations Group
176th Fighter Squadron
115th Operations Support Flight
115th Maintenance Group
115th Aircraft Maintenance Squadron
115th Maintenance Squadron
115th Maintenance Operations Flight
115th Mission Support Group
115th Logistics Readiness Squadron
115th Security Forces Squadron
115th Force Support Squadron
115th Civil Engineer Squadron
115th Communications Flight
15th Medical Group
Det. 1–CERFP Medical

128th Air Refueling Wing–Mitchell Field, Milwaukee
128th Operations Group
126th Air Refueling Squadron
128th Operations Support Flight
128th Maintenance Group
128th Aircraft Maintenance Squadron
128th Maintenance Squadron

128th Air Refueling Wing–Mitchell Field,
Milwaukee (continued)
128th Maintenance Operations Flight 1
128th Mission Support Group
128th Logistics Readiness Squadron
128th Security Forces Squadron
128th Mission Support Flight
128th Services Flight

128th Civil Engineer Squadron
128th Communications Flight
128th Medical Group

Volk Field Combat Readiness Training Center–
Camp Douglas

128th Air Control Squadron–Camp Douglas
126th Weather Flight

Bold Face–Major Command
*Headquarters of a split unit
Bn.–Battalion
Co.–Company
Det.–Detachment
HIMARS–High-Mobility Artillery Rocket System

Trans.–Transportation
TUAS–Tactical Unmanned Aircraft System
WMD–Weapons of mass destruction
CERFP–Chemical, Biological, Radiological, Nuclear Enhanced
Response Force Package

Source: Wisconsin Department of Military Affairs, departmental data, May 2021.

Wisconsin's military service

Military action	Number Served	Number Killed
Civil War	91,379[1]	12,216
Spanish–American War	5,469	134[2]
Mexican Border Service	4,168	NA
World War I	122,215	3,932
World War II	332,200	8,390
Korean Conflict	132,000	729
Vietnam	165,400	1,239
Lebanon/Grenada	400	1
Panama	520	1
Operations Desert Shield/Desert Storm	10,400	11
Somalia	426	2
Bosnia/Kosovo	678	NA
Military and civilian personnel deployed since September 11, 2001	36,941[3]	128[4]

Note: Includes Wisconsin residents who served on active duty during declared wars and officially designated periods of hostilities.

NA–Not available.

1. Total includes some who enlisted more than once. The net number of soldiers recruited in Wisconsin was about 80,000. 2. Casualties only from Wisconsin 1st, 2nd, 3rd, and 4th Regiments. No details available for Wisconsin residents serving in federal units. 3. Includes the total personnel deployed through December 2018. The U.S. Department of Defense stopped reporting the number of personnel deployed from a particular state after that date. 4. Includes one killed in attack on Pentagon on September 11, 2001.

Sources: U.S. Veterans Administration; U.S. Department of Defense; and Wisconsin Department of Military Affairs, departmental data, April 2021.

EDUCATION

University of Wisconsin System fall enrollment

Institution	2014–15	2015–16	2016–17	2017–18	2018–19	2019–20	2019–20 detail Female	Male
Universities	**166,807**	**165,019**	**163,792**	**162,908**	**171,636**	**167,688**	**91,263**	**76,425**
Eau Claire.	10,692	10,531	10,705	10,825	11,547	11,184	6,896	4,288
Undergraduate	10,167	9,956	10,043	10,104	10,831	10,519	6,517	4,002
Graduate	525	575	662	721	716	665	379	286
Green Bay	6,921	6,779	7,030	7,178	8,581	8,796	5,575	3,221
Undergraduate	6,668	6,528	6,758	6,815	8,204	8,400	5,324	3,076
Graduate	253	251	272	363	377	396	251	145
La Crosse.	10,664	10,486	10,624	10,534	10,579	10,604	6,002	4,602
Undergraduate	9,815	9,702	9,737	9,691	9,708	9,649	5,415	4,234
Graduate	849	784	887	843	871	955	587	368
Madison	42,865	43,064	42,994	43,450	44,116	44,993	23,264	22,592
Undergraduate	30,990	31,365	31,407	31,872	32,381	33,165	17,092	16,073
Graduate	11,875	11,699	11,587	11,578	11,735	11,828	6,172	5,656
Milwaukee.	28,013	27,119	26,011	25,381	27,444	26,139	14,281	11,858
Undergraduate . . .	23,079	22,284	21,375	20,750	22,767	21,509	11,474	10,035
Graduate	4,934	4,835	4,636	4,631	4,677	4,630	2,807	1,823
Oshkosh	14,542	14,059	13,955	13,935	16,424	15,520	9,449	6,071
Undergraduate	13,312	12,710	12,479	12,412	15,111	14,266	8,624	5,642
Graduate	1,230	1,349	1,476	1,523	1,313	1,254	825	429
Parkside	4,584	4,443	4,399	4,308	4,325	4,420	2,384	2,036
Undergraduate	4,448	4,300	4,276	4,168	4,090	3,938	2,153	1,785
Graduate	136	143	123	140	235	482	231	251
Platteville.	8,901	8,950	8,782	8,558	8,966	8,281	3,136	5,145
Undergraduate	8,047	7,983	7,865	7,621	8,134	7,489	2,786	4,703
Graduate	854	967	917	937	832	792	350	442
River Falls.	6,184	5,958	5,931	6,110	6,139	5,977	3,864	2,113
Undergraduate	5,721	5,507	5,482	5,678	5,725	5,581	3,573	2,008
Graduate	463	451	449	432	414	396	291	105
Stevens Point	9,322	9,255	8,627	8,208	9,107	8,325	4,639	3,686
Undergraduate	8,998	8,857	8,297	7,880	8,792	7,830	4,274	3,556
Graduate	324	398	330	328	315	495	365	130
Stout	9,371	9,535	9,619	9,401	8,748	8,393	3,849	4,544
Undergraduate	8,254	8,388	8,398	8,116	7,555	7,289	3,111	4,178
Graduate	1,117	1,147	1,221	1,285	1,193	1,104	738	366
Superior	2,589	2,489	2,487	2,590	2,601	2,608	1,677	931
Undergraduate	2,455	2,362	2,365	2,368	2,294	2,257	1,428	829
Graduate	134	127	122	222	307	351	249	102
Whitewater	12,159	12,351	12,628	12,430	13,059	12,448	6,247	6,201
Undergraduate	10,971	11,142	11,380	11,128	11,722	11,020	5,429	5,591
Graduate	1,188	1,209	1,248	1,302	1,337	1,428	818	610
Branch campuses	**14,172**	**13,552**	**12,033**	**11,608**	**9,741**	**7,399**	**3,953**	**3,446**
Baraboo/Sauk County (UW-Platteville)	567	538	523	461	494	360	200	160
Barron (UW-Eau Claire) . . .	613	578	497	512	642	454	267	187
Fond du Lac (UW-Oshkosh)	627	594	523	563	579	444	256	188
Fox Valley (UW-Oshkosh) . .	1,702	1,557	1,367	1,286	1,629	1,134	562	572
Manitowoc (UW-Green Bay)	461	478	364	334	311	237	126	111
Marinette (UW-Green Bay) .	495	465	292	289	306	203	121	82
Marshfield (UW-Stevens Point)	623	649	535	541	545	431	275	156
Richland (UW-Platteville) . .	567	528	278	273	366	159	84	75
Rock County (UW-Whitewater)	1,152	1,155	1,038	908	975	862	457	405

University of Wisconsin System fall enrollment, continued

Institution	2014–15	2015–16	2016–17	2017–18	2018–19	2019–20	2019–20 detail Female	Male
Sheboygan (UW-Green Bay)	770	727	637	560	581	381	178	203
Washington County (UW-Milwaukee).........	937	869	760	730	744	605	294	311
Waukesha (UW-Milwaukee)	2,261	2,085	1,868	1,740	1,767	1,542	776	766
Wausau (UW-Stevens Point)	1,107	978	841	779	802	587	357	230
UW Colleges Online	2,290	2,351	2,510	2,632	—	—	—	—
System total..........	180,979	178,571	175,825	174,516	181,377	175,087	95,216	79,871

— Represents zero.

Source: University of Wisconsin System, Office of Policy Analysis and Research, Education Reports and Statistics, "Enrollment" at https://www.wisconsin.edu/education-reports-statistics/enrollments/ [March 2021].

University of Wisconsin System budgeted faculty positions, 2020–21

Institution	Professor	Associate professor	Assistant professor	Instructor	Total faculty
Eau Claire.	160	107	88	—	355
Green Bay	44	91	64	2	200
La Crosse	100	131	164	—	395
Madison	1,174	491	581	—	2,246
Milwaukee	252	379	107	—	739
Oshkosh	136	127	81	—	344
Parkside	28	62	36	—	126
Platteville.	93	78	95	—	266
River Falls.	99	33	71	—	203
Stevens Point	134	91	60	—	285
Stout	101	63	93	—	256
Superior	35	32	31	1	99
Whitewater	105	159	129	2	395
System total.	2,460	1,843	1,599	5	5,907

Notes: Full-time equivalent (FTE) data used. Positions at branch campuses are included with their afilitated university. Includes vacant positions. Does not include student assistants. Numbers may not add due to rounding.

—Represents zero.

Source: University of Wisconsin System, Office of Budget and Planning, departmental data, May 2021.

Wisconsin private institutions of higher education fall enrollment

Institution (location)	2015	2016	2017	2018	2019
Universities and colleges	52,293	49,827	48,403	55,350	54,400
Alverno College (Milwaukee).	2,209	2,017	1,942	1,851	1,744
Beloit College (Beloit)	1,358	1,394	1,402	1,275	1,143
Cardinal Stritch University (Milwaukee)	3,176	2,464	2,355	2,148	1,896
Carroll University (Waukesha)	3,508	3,491	3,452	3,352	3,449
Carthage College (Kenosha)	2,978	2,930	2,860	2,872	2,742
Concordia University Wisconsin (Mequon)	8,268	7,721	7,288	6,374	5,777
Edgewood College (Madison)	2,678	2,552	2,221	2,190	2,038
Lakeland College (Sheboygan)	3,677	3,230	2,679	2,497	2,511
Lawrence University (Appleton)	1,557	1,528	1,467	1,463	1,442

Wisconsin private institutions of higher education fall enrollment, continued

Institution (location)	2015	2016	2017	2018	2019
Marian University (Fond du Lac)	2,099	1,974	1,971	1,819	1,656
Marquette University (Milwaukee)	11,491	11,294	11,426	11,605	11,819
Mount Mary University (Milwaukee)	1,313	1,404	1,399	1,339	1,246
Northland College (Ashland)	541	582	635	582	609
Ripon College (Ripon)	794	793	756	807	787
Saint Norbert College (De Pere)	2,180	2,211	2,165	2,228	2,081
Silver Lake College (Manitowoc)	522	429	475	444	448
Viterbo University (La Crosse)	2,756	2,699	2,796	2,598	2,592
Wisconsin Lutheran College (Milwaukee)	1,188	1,114	1,114	1,248	1,148
Technical and professional	**8,873**	**8,466**	**8,208**	**8,658**	**9,272**
Bellin College of Nursing (Green Bay)	371	430	440	477	649
Columbia College of Nursing	154	141	122	122	122
Herzing University[1] (WI campuses)	3,503	3,038	2,700	2,994	3,327
Medical College of Wisconsin (Milwaukee)	1,217	1,297	1,385	1,413	1,477
Milwaukee Institute of Art & Design (Milwaukee)	627	630	660	756	870
Milwaukee School of Engineering (Milwaukee)	2,906	2,846	2,823	2,820	2,746
Wisconsin School of Professional Psychology (Milwaukee)	95	84	78	76	81
Theological seminaries	**1,247**	**1,291**	**1,321**	**1,220**	**1,147**
Maranatha Baptist University (Watertown)	1,059	1,118	1,139	1,035	985
Nashotah House (Nashotah)	96	88	73	65	57
Sacred Heart School of Theology (Franklin)	92	85	109	120	105
Tribal colleges	**804**	**682**	**496**	**468**	**530**
College of Menominee Nation (Keshena)	433	394	285	237	191
Lac Courte Oreilles Ojibwa Community College (Hayward)	371	288	211	231	339
Total	**63,217**	**60,266**	**58,428**	**65,696**	**65,349**

1. For-profit institution.

Sources: National Center for Education Statistics, Integrated Postsecondary Education Data System at https://nces.ed.gov/ipeds/datacenter; U.S. Department of Education, Office of Postsecondary Education, Database of Accredited Postsecondary Institutions and Programs, accredited by the Higher Learning Commission of the North Central Association of Colleges and Schools at https://www.hlcommission.org/Directory-of-HLC-Institutions.html [March 2021].

Wisconsin Technical College System enrollment, 2007–2020

School year	Total[1]	Associate arts & associate science[2]	Applied associate degree[3]	Technical diploma	Vocational adult	Non-post secondary	Community services
2007–08	397,748	22,274	125,044	39,148	203,493	70,585	9,113
2008–09	385,297	24,119	132,128	39,612	182,713	73,198	8,760
2009–10	393,993	27,222	145,547	39,759	178,257	76,325	10,082
2010–11	383,671	28,052	149,249	36,911	167,135	72,176	13,181
2011–12	378,240	27,796	148,017	35,401	166,463	65,506	14,112
2012–13	362,252	26,532	148,548	34,546	149,628	61,552	14,929
2013–14	348,747	25,590	144,915	32,416	143,943	51,902	15,339
2014–15	329,407	23,996	140,380	32,164	134,203	50,782	12,704
2015–16	326,153	22,729	135,593	31,406	134,796	48,794	13,831
2016–17	307,607	21,721	134,543	30,789	119,921	45,885	11,804
2017–18	314,835	21,103	137,562	31,359	124,974	43,325	12,121
2018–19	307,849	21,543	140,767	32,134	114,970	41,771	11,672
2019–20	286,381	20,862	138,658	31,397	98,484	41,090	9,313

1. Unduplicated student headcount. 2. Includes courses that transfer to four-year institutions. Prior to 2019, the Technical College System labeled this column "Liberal arts transfer." 3. In the 2019 *Wisconsin Blue Book* and prior editions, this column was labeled "Associate degree."

Source: Wisconsin Technical College System, *Fact Book: Student Data 2019–2020*, January 2021, at https://www.wtcsystem.edu/impact/publications/fact-book-student-data/ [January 2021] and prior issues.

Wisconsin Technical College enrollment, 2019

Technical college	Total[1]	Associate arts & associate science[2]	Applied associate degree[3]	Technical diploma	Vocational adult	Non-post secondary	Community services
Blackhawk	8,290	—	5,514	784	2,188	879	71
Chippewa Valley . . .	17,094	1,197	10,185	2,268	4,768	2,482	—
Fox Valley.	47,595	—	17,191	3,468	26,411	2,103	1,092
Gateway	19,998	—	12,508	3,084	4,308	2,433	—
Lakeshore	8,901	—	3,869	1,145	3,793	920	45
Madison Area	31,139	9,183	14,434	2,679	6,190	5,017	3,915
Mid-State.	8,026	—	4,391	995	2,597	1,667	212
Milwaukee Area. . . .	31,227	9,039	16,391	3,104	3,906	10,904	49
Moraine Park	14,412	—	6,677	1,842	4,145	2,815	1,111
Nicolet Area	4,586	655	1,203	349	2,135	597	543
Northcentral.	17,797	—	8,760	1,277	7,494	3,620	328
Northeast Wisconsin	24,604	—	13,869	3,873	8,402	899	267
Southwest Wisconsin	6,525	—	3,016	970	3,040	1,109	—
Waukesha County . .	17,836	—	9,324	2,365	6,223	2,042	739
Western.	12,113	1,029	7,061	1,461	2,978	2,839	—
Wisconsin Indianhead	16,238	—	4,265	1,733	9,906	764	941
Total.	**286,381**	**21,103**	**138,658**	**31,397**	**98,484**	**41,090**	**9,313**

—Represents zero.

1. Unduplicated student headcount.   2. Includes courses that transfer to four-year institutions. Prior to 2019, the Technical College System labeled this column "Liberal arts transfer."   3. In the 2019 *Wisconsin Blue Book* and prior editions, this column was labeled "Associate degree."

Sources: Wisconsin Technical College System, *Fact Book: Student Data 2019–2020* at https://www.wtcsystem.edu/impact/publications/fact-book-student-data, January 2021, and prior issues.

Wisconsin public high school completion rates, 2019–2020

CESA[2]	Students (rate) Total[3]	Female	Male	American Indian	Asian	Black	Hispanic	White	2 or more
1	16,541 (85.4)	8,428 (88.0)	8,113 (82.9)	NA	756	2,976	2,677	9,266	415
2	11,019 (91.7)	5,542 (93.3)	5,477 (90.2)	11	293	495	1,423	7,824	307
3	1,392 (96.1)	646 (96.4)	715 (95.8)	NA	NA	NA	NA	724	NA
4	2,336 (93.6)	1,119 (95.8)	1,201 (91.6)	16	80	30	70	1,480	46
5	3,689 (94.2)	1,814 (96.0)	1,875 (92.5)	19	50	8	183	2,717	19
6	7,189 (93.3)	3,580 (94.7)	3,609 (91.9)	NA	187	105	474	5,574	79
7	6,043 (92.7)	2,977 (94.1)	3,053 (91.4)	71	249	177	588	4,161	54
8	1,357 (91.9)	631 (92.5)	696 (91.0)	110	NA	NA	NA	822	18
9	2,429 (94.9)	1,207 (96.0)	1,205 (93.8)	35	133	NA	42	1,639	37
10	2,410 (91.4)	1,174 (91.9)	1,223 (90.7)	NA	68	NA	22	1,493	26
11	3,448 (93.6)	1,687 (94.5)	1,719 (92.7)	8	10	18	58	2,539	49
12	999 (90.7)	471 (93.1)	516 (88.4)	76	NA	6	NA	600	22
Total. . .	**58,860 (90.6)**	**29,353 (92.3)**	**29,507 (88.9)**	**647**	**2,213**	**4,251**	**6,239**	**43,705**	**1,771**
Rate				**-86.3**	**-92.7**	**-70.9**	**-83.9**	**-94.3**	**-86.9**

Header note for race section: Student detail by race[1] or Hispanic origin

Notes: Percent completion calculated by number of combined completions (diplomas, HSED, certificate) divided by number of students in the 4-year cohort. This table is based on 4-year adjusted cohort completion rates, as required by federal law, and may not be comparable to tables in prior Blue Books. Details may not sum to totals due to privacy rules.

NA–Not available. Includes only students who are identified by race in DPI report. Not all students can be identified by race due to privacy rules relating to small groups.

1. Pacific Islander state total (rate): 34 (85.0).   2. Cooperative Educational Service Agency.   3. Includes students who have completed high school with a diploma, HSED, or other method.

Source: Wisconsin Department of Public Instruction, Wisconsin Information System for Education Data Dashboard at https://dpi.wi.gov/wisedash/download-files [March 2021].

Enrollment in Wisconsin elementary and secondary public schools

Grade level	2011–12	2012–13	2013–14	2014–15	2015–16	2016–17	2017–18	2018–19	2019–20	2020–21
Pre-kinder-garten[1] .	54,438	55,008	56,777	55,830	55,907	55,435	55,186	56,096	56,338	47,126
Kindergar-ten	60,875	62,422	61,522	60,424	58,078	57,331	56,832	56,915	56,756	53,961
1	60,572	61,037	62,479	61,498	60,459	58,224	57,517	57,236	56,992	55,037
2	60,984	60,585	60,999	62,311	61,405	60,523	58,370	57,706	57,345	55,579
3	60,216	61,243	60,697	60,885	62,322	61,749	60,783	58,744	57,949	56,227
4	60,094	60,670	61,393	60,795	60,999	62,407	61,911	61,157	59,044	56,975
5	60,958	60,253	60,768	61,459	60,924	61,207	62,743	62,329	61,357	58,194
6	61,818	61,369	60,505	60,843	61,677	61,264	61,549	63,275	62,482	60,555
7	61,442	62,310	61,814	60,795	61,047	62,170	61,582	62,193	63,739	61,928
8	61,413	61,857	62,721	62,029	61,077	61,428	62,353	61,964	62,455	63,374
9	67,542	67,699	67,985	68,043	67,036	65,847	65,959	66,758	65,849	65,807
10	65,510	64,507	64,958	65,290	65,841	65,137	64,298	64,687	65,459	64,702
11	66,851	66,346	65,450	65,019	64,546	65,269	64,505	63,643	63,903	64,842
12	68,392	67,130	66,346	65,431	65,819	65,832	66,542	66,130	65,291	65,628
Total[2] . . .	871,105	872,436	874,414	870,652	867,137	863,823	860,130	858,833	854,959	829,935

1. Includes K3 and K4. 2. Totals do not include students with unknown grade levels.

Source: Wisconsin Department of Public Instruction, Wisconsin Information System for Education Data Dashboard at http://dpi.wi.gov/wisedash/download-files [March 2021].

Enrollment in Wisconsin elementary and secondary private schools

Grade level	2010–11	2011–12	2012–13	2013–14	2014–15	2015–16	2016–17	2017–18	2018–19	2019–20
Pre-kinder-garten[1] . .	14,737	14,793	14,982	14,204	14,516	14,226	13,572	14,456	14,153	14,150
Kindergar-ten	9,893	9,797	9,994	9,841	9,796	9,529	9,336	9,346	9,381	9,259
1	9,810	9,767	9,492	9,600	9,929	9,658	9,459	9,198	9,384	9,258
2	9,744	9,703	9,487	9,325	9,822	9,855	9,532	9,327	9,201	9,314
3	9,648	9,635	9,462	9,327	9,541	9,769	9,733	9,432	9,347	9,069
4	9,659	9,542	9,320	9,153	9,494	9,425	9,677	9,609	9,444	9,133
5	9,927	9,587	9,450	9,139	9,285	9,403	9,291	9,481	9,598	9,251
6	9,486	9,555	9,233	9,012	9,114	9,105	9,142	9,164	9,400	9,349
7	9,223	9,192	9,157	8,750	8,853	8,827	8,723	8,782	9,030	8,922
8	9,072	9,078	8,909	8,702	8,802	8,747	8,711	8,547	8,731	8,667
9	6,089	5,939	6,159	6,026	6,328	6,389	6,313	6,410	6,406	6,321
10	5,789	5,866	5,917	5,766	5,926	6,072	6,039	6,010	6,177	6,200
11	5,796	5,534	5,677	5,590	5,682	5,795	5,844	5,781	5,889	5,885
12	5,583	5,442	5,217	5,190	5,233	5,250	5,344	5,505	5,536	5,352
Ungraded elem. and secondary	916	1,238	493	176	783	1,087	784	788	863	575
Total.	125,372	124,668	122,949	119,801	123,104	123,137	121,500	121,836	122,540	120,705

1. Includes K4.

Source: Wisconsin Department of Public Instruction, Wisconsin Information System for Education Data Dashboard at http://dpi.wi.gov/wisedash/download-files [March 2021].

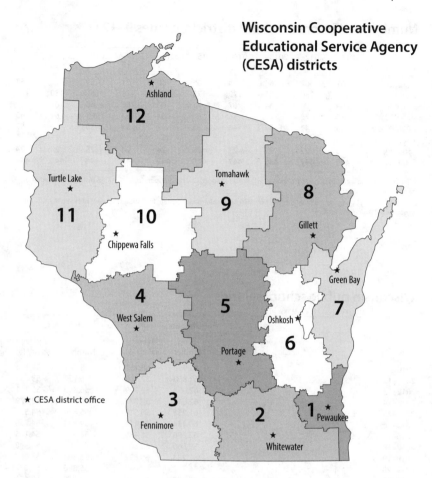

Wisconsin Cooperative Educational Service Agency (CESA) districts

★ CESA district office

Number of Wisconsin school districts, all grades

# of pupils[1]	2011– 12	2012– 13	2013– 14	2014– 15	2015– 16	2016– 17	2017– 18	2018– 19	2019– 20	2020– 21
1–499	120	123	125	129	130	123	125	126	124	128
500–999 . .	121	122	123	116	117	117	118	120	118	121
1,000–1,999	99	98	96	97	96	98	98	94	100	98
2,000–2,999	33	29	31	31	32	31	29	32	27	26
3,000–3,999	30	32	29	29	29	28	30	26	29	27
4,000–4,999	10	11	13	13	11	12	10	13	13	12
5,000–9,999	21	21	22	22	23	23	23	23	23	24
10,000 and above . . .	11	11	10	10	10	10	10	10	9	8
Total.	445	447	449	447	448	442	443	444	443	444

1. Enrollment data includes charter schools not sponsored by a school district.

Source: Wisconsin Department of Public Instruction, Wisconsin Information System for Education Data Dashboard data at https://dpi.wi.gov/wisedash/download-files [March 2021].

Number of Wisconsin school districts, grades 9–12

# of pupils[1]	2011–12	2012–13	2013–14	2014–15	2015–16	2016–17	2017–18	2018–19	2019–20	2020–21
0[2]	61	62	64	64	65	60	61	59	57	57
1–299	174	180	181	179	173	178	178	182	180	180
300–499 . .	69	64	64	67	71	64	66	65	67	66
500–999 . .	73	72	71	66	63	64	63	63	62	65
1,000–1,999	45	47	47	48	51	52	51	50	53	52
2,000 and above . . .	23	22	22	23	25	24	24	25	24	24
Total.	**445**	**447**	**449**	**447**	**448**	**442**	**443**	**444**	**443**	**444**

1. Enrollment data includes nondistrict-sponsored charter schools. 2. This group includes the K3-8 districts, which do not have secondary level students.

Source: Wisconsin Department of Public Instruction, Wisconsin Information System for Education Data Dashboard at https://dpi. wi.gov/wisedash/download-files.

Wisconsin public school salaries

	Instructional staff		Teachers	
	Number	Average salary ($)	Number	Average salary ($)
2010–11	63,948	58,159	58,041	54,195
2011–12	61,850	57,649	56,180	53,792
2012–13	62,698	58,999	56,800	55,171
2013–14	62,612	57,777	56,835	53,679
2014–15	61,251	58,518	55,624	54,535
2015–16	60,434	59,111	54,893	54,766
2016–17	62,986	58,485	56,937	54,115
2017–18	59,866	59,561	54,401	54,998
2018–19	61,284	59,632	55,501	58,007
2019–20	66,722	60,027	55,850	58,277
2020–21	67,048	61,177	55,960	59,431

Source: National Education Association, *Rankings of the States 2020 and Estimates of School Statistics 2021* at http://www.nea. org/rankings-and-estimates, April 2021 and prior issues.

State and local expenditures for Wisconsin public education

Agency/program	2015–16 (mil. dol.)	2016–17 (mil. dol.)	2017–18 (mil. dol.)	2018–19 (mil. dol.)	2019–20 (mil. dol.)
Public elementary and secondary schools[1].	11,057.5	11,274.4	11,557.2	11,900.0	12,184.6
Department of Public Instruction.	129.5	132.5	137.8	139.5	131.6
University of Wisconsin System	6,005.4	6,055.9	6,201.7	6,498.9	6,406.8
Wisconsin Technical College System Board.	543.6	550.4	551.1	551.2	562.9
Public libraries (local expenditures)[2]	248.5	284.0	291.0	NA	NA

State and local expenditures for Wisconsin public education, continued

Agency/program	2015–16 (mil. dol.)	2016–17 (mil. dol.)	2017–18 (mil. dol.)	2018–19 (mil. dol.)	2019–20 (mil. dol.)
Other:					
Educational Communications Board	16.6	17.5	19.3	18	17.8
Higher Educational Aids Board	140.4	146.7	142.0	141.5	137.1
Medical College of Wisconsin, Inc. (state funding) .	8.6	10.2	9.8	10.1	10.4
State Historical Society	23.4	25.5	27.5	29.8	27.9
Total.	**18,173.5**	**18,497.1**	**18,937.4**	**19,289.0**	**19,479.1**
Per capita expenditures[3] (dollars)	3,159	3,203	3,275	3,316	3,349

NA–Not available.

1. Includes the gross costs of general operations, special projects, debt service, and food service; the net capital projects; and the costs of CESA and County Children with Disabilities Education Board operations.   2. Expenditures are for calendar year ending in the fiscal year shown.   3. Based on total state population. Wisconsin population estimate for 2015: 5,753,324; 2016: 5,775,120; 2017: 5,783,278.

Sources: Wisconsin Department of Administration, *Annual Fiscal Report, Appendix (Budgetary Basis)* 2020, and previous issues; Wisconsin Department of Administration, Demographic Services Center, Time Series Population Estimates: County Totals [March 2020]; Wisconsin Department of Public Instruction, Library Service Data 2017, and previous data; Wisconsin Department of Public Instruction, departmental data.

Wisconsin school district financial data

Fiscal year	State school aid Amount (mil. dol.)	State school aid % change	Gross school levy Amount (mil. dol.)	Gross school levy % change	Total school costs Amount (mil. dol.)	Total school costs % change	Cost per pupil Amount ($)	Cost per pupil % change
1999–00	4,226	5.9	2,795	2.2	7,535	3.9	8,679	3.9
2000–01	4,463	5.6	2,928	4.7	7,900	4.8	9,087	4.7
2001–02	4,602	3.1	3,072	4.9	8,349	5.7	9,583	5.5
2002–03	4,775	3.8	3,192	3.9	8,750	4.8	10,035	4.7
2003–04	4,806	0.7	3,368	5.5	8,911	1.8	10,228	1.9
2004–05	4,858	1.1	3,611	7.2	9,216	3.4	10,605	3.7
2005–06	5,159	6.2	3,592	-0.5	9,539	3.5	10,989	3.6
2006–07	5,294	2.6	3,788	5.4	9,903	3.8	11,413	3.9
2007–08	5,340	0.9	4,067	7.4	10,265	3.7	11,894	4.2
2008–09	5,462	2.3	4,279	5.2	10,623	3.5	12,346	3.8
2009–10	5,315	-2.7	4,538	6.0	10,834	2.0	12,624	2.3
2010–11	5,325	0.2	4,693	3.4	11,162	3.0	13,020	3.1
2011–12	4,894	-8.1	4,647	-1.0	10,585	-5.2	12,375	-5.0
2012–13	4,964	1.4	4,656	0.2	10,568	-0.2	12,343	-0.3
2013–14	5,079	2.3	4,694	0.8	10,750	1.7	12,546	1.6
2014–15	5,242	3.2	4,754	1.3	10,972	2.1	12,842	2.4
2015–16	5,244	0.0	4,855	2.1	11,058	0.8	12,942	0.8
2016–17	5,445	3.8	4,858	0.1	11,274	2.0	13,182	1.9
2017–18	5,730	5.2	4,945	1.8	11,557	2.5	13,505	2.5
2018–19	5,900	3.0	4,988	0.9	11,900	3.0	13,913	3.0
2019–20	6,073	2.9	5,209	4.4	NA	NA	NA	NA
2020–21	6,295	3.7	5,380	3.3	NA	NA	NA	NA

NA–Not available.

Source: Wisconsin Legislative Fiscal Bureau, Informational Paper #27, *State Aid to School Districts*, January 2021, at https://docs.legis.wisconsin.gov/misc/lfb/informational_papers/january_2021/0027_state_aid_to_school_districts_informational_paper_27.pdf.

Wisconsin home-based private educational enrollments

Grade level	2010– 11	2011– 12	2012– 13	2013– 14	2014– 15	2015– 16	2016– 17	2017– 18	2018– 19	2019– 20
1	1,127	1,136	1,158	1,197	1,183	1,175	1,214	1,304	1,210	1,196
2	1,164	1,142	1,060	1,144	1,144	1,084	1,133	1,199	1,142	1,150
3	1,179	1,076	1,106	1,077	1,160	1,136	1,147	1,228	1,114	1,112
4	1,098	1,137	1,062	1,095	1,136	1,081	1,191	1,211	1,179	1,130
5	1,155	1,050	1,123	1,087	1,095	1,037	1,118	1,247	1,077	1,177
6	1,189	1,078	1,085	1,089	1,171	1,046	1,131	1,206	1,242	1,174
7	1,160	1,070	1,102	1,035	1,171	1,069	1,119	1,167	1,154	1,207
8	1,149	1,027	1,018	1,053	1,078	983	1,068	1,134	1,165	1,104
9	1,042	1,038	989	996	1,080	933	1,071	1,144	1,076	1,098
10	1,144	917	1,030	996	1,041	936	1,017	1,135	1,056	1,043
11	1,064	1,004	840	993	964	845	1,034	1,104	1,092	1,053
12	891	703	769	717	820	727	794	886	906	936
Ungraded .	6,214	5,901	6,122	6,625	6,807	6,698	7,325	7,668	8,164	8,264
Total.	19,576	18,279	18,464	19,104	19,850	18,750	20,362	21,633	21,577	21,644

Note: A home-based private educational program is a program of educational instruction provided to a child by a child's parent or guardian or by a person designated by the parent or guardian. These programs must provide at least 875 hours of instruction each school year and must offer a sequentially progressive curriculum of fundamental instruction in reading, language arts, mathematics, social studies, science, and health.

Source: Wisconsin Department of Public Instruction, Home-Based Private Educational Program Statistics, "Enrollment by Grade" at https://dpi.wi.gov/sms/home-based/statistics [March 2021].

Wisconsin charter school enrollments, 2020–2021

CESA[1] district	Total students			American Indian	Asian	Black	Hispanic	Pacific Islander	White	2 or more
	Total	Female	Male							
1	25,067	12,369	12,698	57	2,166	8,748	7,747	11	5,517	821
2	8,002	3,825	4,177	37	222	714	1,150	1	5,285	586
3	380	194	186	1	1	3	15	—	347	13
4	1,024	535	489	5	6	22	41	—	894	56
5	1,253	667	586	3	4	10	51	—	1,141	44
6	6,056	2,965	3,091	19	328	215	519	3	4,682	290
7	2,030	983	1,047	14	56	89	392	—	1,330	149
8	163	80	83	14	—	2	6	—	135	6
9	2,127	1,025	1,102	19	35	48	55	5	1,907	58
10	1,711	826	885	21	17	26	82	—	1,482	83
11	2,320	1,015	1,305	57	25	83	133	—	1,967	55
12	728	363	365	18	6	3	28	2	647	24
Total.	50,861	24,847	26,014	265	2,866	9,963	10,219	22	25,334	2,185

—Represents zero.

1. Cooperative Educational Service Agency.

Source: Wisconsin Department of Public Instruction, Wisconsin Information System for Education Data Dashboard at https://dpi.wi.gov/wisedash/download-files/ [March 2021].

AGRICULTURE

Wisconsin's comparative agricultural production, 2019

Commodity	Unit (1,000)	United States Production	Leading state	Wisconsin Production	% of U.S.	U.S. rank
All commodities	Dol	369,723,116	California	11,217,432	3.0	8
Livestock and livestock products	Dol	175,993,463	Texas	7,901,939	4.5	6
Crops	Dol	193,729,653	California	3,315,493	1.7	18
Dairy						
Milk production.	Lbs	218,382,000	California	30,601,000	14.0	2
Cheese, total (excluding cottage cheese)	Lbs	13,137,243	Wisconsin	3,363,863	25.6	1
American.	Lbs	5,232,242	Wisconsin	1,003,082	19.2	1
Cheddar	Lbs	3,736,742	Wisconsin	712,595	19.1	1
Italian	Lbs	5,670,525	Wisconsin	1,698,941	30.0	1
Mozzarella	Lbs	4,494,583	California	1,110,363	24.7	2
Dry whey, human food	Lbs	961,792	Wisconsin	285,831	29.7	1
Livestock and poultry						
Cattle and calves, all[1]	Head	94,413	Texas	3,450	3.7	9
Milk cows[1]	Head	9,335	California	1,260	13.5	2
Hogs and pigs, all[2]	Head	79,048	Iowa	365	0.5	18
Sheep[1]	Head	5,200	Texas	81	1.6	19
Milk goats[2].	Head	440	Wisconsin	82	18.6	1
Chickens	Head	532,498	Iowa	9,699	1.8	15
Broilers	Head	9,177,200	Georgia	58,500	0.6	20
Mink.	Pelts	2,704	Wisconsin	1,016	37.6	1
Honey	Lbs	156,922	North Dakota	2,162	1.4	16
Eggs	Eggs	113,253,400	Iowa	2,163,100	1.9	15
Crops						
Corn for grain	Bu	13,617,261	Iowa	443,220	3.3	9
Corn for silage	Tons	132,807	Wisconsin	18,200	13.7	1
Oats.	Bu	53,148	North Dakota	6,480	12.2	2
Soybeans	Bu	3,552,241	Illinois	79,430	2.2	13
Wheat, winter	Bu	1,304,003	Kansas	9,600	0.7	21
Forage (dry equivalent), all.	Tons	83,214	Texas	6,135	7.4	7
Hay (dry only), all	Tons	128,864	Texas	2,784	2.2	18
Potatoes, all	Cwt	422,890	Idaho	28,220	6.7	3
Cherries, tart	Lbs	262,000	Michigan	9,100	3.5	4
Cranberries	Bbl	7,917	Wisconsin	4,670	59.0	1
Maple syrup	Gals	4,180	Vermont	270	6.5	4
Cabbage, all	Cwt	21,706	California	1,325	6.1	8
Carrots, all	Cwt	49,803	California	1,601	3.2	3
Sweet corn, all.	Cwt	62,966	Washington	8,645	13.7	3
Green peas, all	Cwt	5,038	Washington	1,087	21.6	3
Snap beans, all	Cwt	16,557	Wisconsin	6,223	37.6	1

Note: Wisconsin is also a leading state in the production of turkeys, ducks, and ginseng; Wisconsin's rank is not available for these commodities.

Bbl–Barrels; Bu–Bushels; Cwt–Hundredweight; Dol–Dollars; Gals–Gallons; Lbs–Pounds.

1. January 1, 2020 inventory. 2. December 1, 2019.

Sources: U.S. Department of Agriculture, National Agriculture Statistics Service, "2020 Wisconsin Agricultural Statistics" and U.S. Department of Agriculture, Economic Research Service, "Annual cash receipts by commodity, U.S. and States 2008–2020F" at https://www.ers.usda.gov/data-products/farm-income-and-wealth-statistics/data-files-us-and-state-level-farm-income-and-wealth-statistics.

Wisconsin's net farm income

	2015	2016	2017	2018	2019
Value of agricultural sector production[1]					
($1,000)	12,982,418	12,188,098	12,616,321	12,002,756	12,467,413
Value of crop production.	3,289,689	3,560,163	3,233,167	3,388,945	3,020,703
Value of animals and products production	7,936,905	7,246,744	7,787,646	7,307,118	7,927,985
Farm-related income	1,755,824	1,381,192	1,595,508	1,306,692	1,518,726
Less: Intermediate product expenses[2]. . . .	6,889,773	6,904,954	7,157,586	6,571,586	6,963,664
Less: Contract labor expenses	26,761	22,903	34,138	23,320	48,193
Less: Property taxes	450,000	380,000	380,000	400,000	380,000
Less: Motor vehicle registration and					
licensing fees	13,489	17,308	16,238	12,614	14,997
Plus: Direct government payments.	305,627	285,304	134,422	300,846	501,461
Equals: Gross value added	5,908,022	5,148,237	5,162,781	5,296,082	5,562,021
Less: Capital consumption (depreciation). .	1,376,803	1,423,182	1,251,228	1,073,331	999,135
Equals: Net value added[3]	4,531,219	3,725,056	3,911,553	4,222,751	4,562,885
Less: Payments to stakeholders[4]	1,834,350	2,092,064	2,069,246	2,117,562	2,169,803
Equals: Net farm income[5]	2,696,868	1,632,991	1,842,306	2,105,190	2,393,082
Number of farms	66,600	65,700	64,800	64,800	64,900
Average net farm income per farm ($). . . .	40,494	24,855	28,431	32,488	36,873

1. Value of agricultural sector output is the gross value of the commodities and services produced within a year. 2. Includes purchases of feed, livestock, poultry, and seed; outlays for fertilizers and lime, pesticides, fuel and electricity; capital repair and maintenance; and marketing, storage, transportation, and other expenses. 3. Net value added is the sector's contribution to the national economy and is the sum of the income from production earned by all factors of production, regardless of ownership. 4. Includes compensation for hired labor, net rent paid to landlords, and interest payments. 5. Net farm income is the farm operators' share of income from the sector's production activities.

Sources: U.S. Department of Agriculture, Economic Research Service, "Value added by U.S. agriculture (includes net farm income)" at https://www.ers.usda.gov/data-products/farm-income-and-wealth-statistics/data-files-us-and-state-level-farm-income-and-wealth-statistics [December 2020]; U.S. Department of Agriculture, National Agriculture Statistics Service, "2020 Wisconsin Agricultural Statistics" at https://www.nass.usda.gov/Statistics_by_State/Wisconsin/Publications/Annual_Statistical_Bulletin [September 2020].

Wisconsin's agricultural cash receipts

Commodity	2016 ($1,000)	2017 ($1,000)	2018 ($1,000)	2019 ($1,000)
All commodities	10,736,456	11,318,453	10,953,765	11,217,432
Livestock, dairy, and poultry	7,163,569	7,827,608	7,340,192	7,901,939
Meat animals	1,737,302	1,968,757	1,875,008	1,812,338
Cattle and calves	1,639,375	1,846,035	1,754,534	1,662,302
Hogs.	97,927	122,722	120,474	150,036
Dairy products, milk	5,014,800	5,444,480	5,002,800	5,705,424
Poultry and eggs	245,772	275,255	340,563	265,549
Broilers	108,602	122,944	127,899	110,905
Farm chickens	353	166	262	219
Eggs	79,493	108,619	176,103	113,111
Miscellaneous livestock	165,696	139,116	121,821	118,628
Honey	8,939	8,370	6,770	6,464
Trout.	1,558	1,694	1,493	1,525
Mink pelts	39,812	40,908	27,414	22,255
Wool	238	215	198	187
Crops	3,572,887	3,490,845	3,613,574	3,315,493
Food grains	72,497	62,624	67,956	54,227
Wheat	66,765	55,760	59,576	47,657
Feed crops	1,396,351	1,410,534	1,587,319	1,497,294
Barley	NA	NA	294	613
Corn	1,305,917	1,308,075	1,465,229	1,352,550

Wisconsin's agricultural cash receipts, 2019

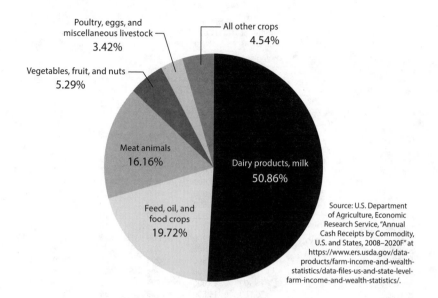

Poultry, eggs, and miscellaneous livestock — 3.42%

All other crops — 4.54%

Vegetables, fruit, and nuts — 5.29%

Meat animals 16.16%

Dairy products, milk 50.86%

Feed, oil, and food crops 19.72%

Source: U.S. Department of Agriculture, Economic Research Service, "Annual Cash Receipts by Commodity, U.S. and States, 2008–2020F" at https://www.ers.usda.gov/data-products/farm-income-and-wealth-statistics/data-files-us-and-state-level-farm-income-and-wealth-statistics/.

Wisconsin's agricultural cash receipts, continued

Commodity	2016 ($1,000)	2017 ($1,000)	2018 ($1,000)	2019 ($1,000)
Hay.	84,447	95,356	112,838	133,352
Oats	5,987	7,103	8,958	10,779
Oil crops	983,902	889,951	876,156	660,933
Soybeans	983,902	889,951	876,156	660,933
Vegetables and melons	449,273	462,438	432,797	456,500
Potatoes.	298,905	310,834	283,795	294,772
Beans, snap.	45,634	40,115	47,877	42,254
Cabbage	13,535	21,569	14,912	21,337
Carrots.	10,588	8,820	7,092	24,096
Corn, sweet.	48,958	44,863	40,181	33,470
Cucumbers.	9,210	7,168	21,141	16,431
Pumpkins.	6,254	11,023	2,791	12,869
Peas, green	13,007	14,363	11,811	11,272
Fruits and nuts	203,242	184,547	156,787	137,439
Apples.	21,819	26,297	NA	NA
Cherries, tart.	4,076	2,109	1,928	934
Cranberries.	177,347	156,141	154,859	136,505
All other crops.	467,622	480,751	492,559	509,100
Maple products	7,873	6,500	7,290	8,775
Peppermint oil.	4,407	3,774	3,565	NA
Mushrooms	2,693	2,738	2,527	NA

Note: Bold figures indicate category totals of the commodities immediately following and indicate categories included in next higher level of aggregation. Category totals may include amounts for specific commodities not listed separately or that are not listed to provide confidentiality to large producers in concentrated industries. Prior year's numbers have been revised to reflect updated source data.

NA–Not available.

Source: U.S. Department of Agriculture, Economic Research Service, "Annual Cash Receipts by Commodity, U.S. and States, 2008–2020F" at https://www.ers.usda.gov/data-products/farm-income-and-wealth-statistics/data-files-us-and-state-level-farm-income-and-wealth-statistics/.

Number, size, and value of farms in Wisconsin

	Number of farms	Farm land (1,000 acres)	Avg. farm size (acres)	Value of land and buildings Total (mil. dol.)	Avg. per farm ($)	Avg. per acre ($)
1935	200,000	23,500	117	1	6	53
1940	187,000	22,900	123	1	6	52
1945	178,000	23,600	133	1	8	61
1950	174,000	23,600	136	2	12	89
1955	155,000	23,200	150	2	15	101
1960	138,000	22,200	161	3	21	133
1965	124,000	21,400	173	3	27	155
1970	110,000	20,100	183	5	42	232
1975	100,000	19,300	193	8	84	434
1980	93,000	18,600	200	19	201	1,004
1985	83,000	17,900	216	17	204	944
1990	80,000	17,600	220	14	176	801
1995	80,000	16,800	210	17	218	1,040
1996	79,000	16,600	210	19	237	1,130
1997	79,000	16,500	209	19	244	1,170
1998	78,000	16,300	209	20	259	1,240
1999	78,000	16,200	208	23	301	1,450
2000	77,500	16,000	206	27	351	1,700
2001	77,000	15,800	205	31	400	1,950
2002	77,000	15,700	204	34	438	2,150
2003	76,500	15,600	204	36	469	2,300
2004	76,500	15,500	203	39	507	2,500
2005	76,500	15,400	201	44	574	2,850
2006	76,000	15,300	201	49	644	3,200
2007	78,500	15,200	194	58	736	3,800
2008	78,000	15,200	195	59	750	3,850
2009	78,000	15,200	195	57	731	3,750
2010	73,200	14,700	201	54	733	3,650
2011	71,200	14,600	205	57	796	3,880
2012	69,800	14,600	209	60	860	4,110
2013	69,800	14,600	209	60	858	4,100
2014	67,500	14,500	215	64	945	4,400
2015	66,600	14,400	216	66	984	4,550
2016	65,700	14,400	219	65	991	4,520
2017	64,800	14,300	221	70	1,075	4,870
2018	64,800	14,300	221	70	1,081	4,900
2019	64,900	14,300	220	71	1,091	4,950

Notes: "Farm" is currently defined as a place that sells, or would normally sell, at least $1,000 of agricultural products during the year. The actual number of farms in Wisconsin peaked at 199,877 in 1935.

Source: U.S. Department of Agriculture, National Agricultural Statistics Service, "2020 Wisconsin Agricultural Statistics" and prior editions at https://www.nass.usda.gov/Statistics_by_State/Wisconsin/Publications/Annual_Statistical_Bulletin [September 2020].

Nonirrigated cropland cash rents

County	2016 ($/ acre)	2020 ($/ acre)	% change	County	2016 ($/ acre)	2020 ($/ acre)	% change
Adams	74.00	91.50	23.6	Buffalo	121.00	122.00	0.8
Ashland	18.00	32.50	80.6	Burnett	44.00	67.00	52.3
Barron	72.00	89.00	23.6	Calumet	155.00	177.00	14.2
Bayfield	25.00	23.50	−6.0	Chippewa	95.00	98.00	3.2
Brown	181.00	183.00	1.1	Clark	87.00	110.00	26.4

Nonirrigated cropland cash rents, continued

County	2016 ($/ acre)	2020 ($/ acre)	% change	County	2016 ($/ acre)	2020 ($/ acre)	% change
Columbia.	179.00	176.00	-1.7	Oconto	110.00	118.00	7.3
Crawford	124.00	129.00	4.0	Oneida	NA	NA	NA
Dane	172.00	182.00	5.8	Outagamie.	108.00	142.00	31.5
Dodge	176.00	173.00	-1.7	Ozaukee	NA	NA	NA
Door.	81.00	107.00	32.1	Pepin	130.00	135.00	3.8
Douglas.	15.00	22.00	46.7	Pierce	135.00	142.00	5.2
Dunn	99.50	101.00	1.5	Polk	73.50	86.50	17.7
Eau Claire.	86.00	88.00	2.3	Portage.	52.00	62.50	20.2
Florence	NA	NA	NA	Price.	28.00	34.50	23.2
Fond du Lac	156.00	156.00	0.0	Racine.	133.00	134.00	0.8
Forest	NA	NA	NA	Richland	103.00	116.00	12.6
Grant	192.00	209.00	8.9	Rock.	182.00	195.00	7.1
Green	169.00	198.00	17.2	Rusk.	66.00	65.50	-0.8
Green Lake.	143.00	160.00	11.9	St. Croix.	103.00	108.00	4.9
Iowa.	199.00	175.00	-12.1	Sauk.	125.00	129.00	3.2
Iron	NA	NA	NA	Sawyer	35.00	44.00	25.7
Jackson	99.50	127.00	27.6	Shawano	97.00	108.00	11.3
Jefferson	156.00	176.00	12.8	Sheboygan.	107.00	117.00	9.3
Juneau	91.50	91.50	0.0	Taylor	83.00	85.00	2.4
Kenosha	152.00	164.00	7.9	Trempealeau	130.00	99.00	-23.8
Kewaunee	144.00	183.00	27.1	Vernon	129.00	134.00	3.9
La Crosse	132.00	139.00	5.3	Vilas	NA	NA	NA
Lafayette	227.00	217.00	-4.4	Walworth.	190.00	181.00	-4.7
Langlade	82.00	92.50	12.8	Washburn	56.00	57.00	1.8
Lincoln	44.00	57.50	30.7	Washington	120.00	119.00	-0.8
Manitowoc.	159.00	166.00	4.4	Waukesha	114.00	136.00	19.3
Marathon.	79.50	90.50	13.8	Waupaca	87.00	89.50	2.9
Marinette.	96.00	92.00	-4.2	Waushara.	56.00	63.50	13.4
Marquette	53.00	71.50	34.9	Winnebago	98.00	96.50	-1.5
Menominee	NA	NA	NA	Wood	65.00	82.50	26.9
Milwaukee	NA	NA	NA	Total.	131.00	138.00	5.3
Monroe.	132.00	124.00	-6.1				

NA–Not available. Data withheld to avoid disclosing details of individual operators.

Source: U.S. Department of Agriculture, National Agriculture Statistics Service, "2020 Wisconsin Agricultural Statistics" and prior editions at https://www.nass.usda.gov/Statistics_by_State/Wisconsin/Publications/Annual_Statistical_Bulletin [September 2020].

Wisconsin agricultural land sales

County[1]	Total agricultural land sales[2]				Land continuing in agricultural use, avg. cost per acre ($)		Agricultural land diverted to other uses, avg. cost per acre ($)	
	Number		Avg. cost per acre ($)					
	2018	2019	2018	2019	2018	2019	2018	2019
Adams	10	3	5,746	3,120	3,871	3,214	11,251	2,557
Ashland.	3	4	1,542	1,289	1,542	1,289	NA	NA
Barron.	27	24	2,503	2,836	2,502	2,836	2,600	NA
Bayfield.	9	4	1,458	1,131	1,458	1,131	NA	NA
Brown.	21	14	13,087	9,996	11,441	9,996	24,261	NA
Buffalo	11	3	4,317	3,951	4,319	3,951	4,250	NA
Burnett	6	6	1,741	1,870	1,779	1,870	1,427	NA
Calumet	14	16	10,707	9,558	10,631	9,558	14,308	NA
Chippewa	26	24	3,052	3,886	3,066	3,840	2,303	5,050

Wisconsin agricultural land sales, continued

County[1]	Total agricultural land sales[2]				Land continuing in agricultural use, avg. cost per acre ($)		Agricultural land diverted to other uses, avg. cost per acre ($)	
	Number		Avg. cost per acre ($)					
	2018	2019	2018	2019	2018	2019	2018	2019
Clark	25	18	4,596	3,939	4,619	3,939	2,100	NA
Columbia	13	12	7,218	6,926	7,218	7,014	NA	4,200
Crawford	15	8	3,525	3,724	3,529	3,724	3,452	NA
Dane	39	29	11,144	11,538	8,912	11,513	21,004	14,000
Dodge	21	19	7,573	6,474	7,091	6,474	23,000	NA
Door	6	7	4,145	4,036	4,145	4,248	NA	1,000
Douglas	2	5	1,219	1,116	1,219	1,116	NA	NA
Dunn	28	36	3,981	3,368	3,985	3,368	3,125	NA
Eau Claire	16	23	4,174	4,619	4,176	4,619	4,079	NA
Florence	2	NA	1,914	NA	1,914	NA	NA	NA
Fond du Lac	22	30	6,512	6,421	6,512	6,420	NA	6,600
Forest	NA	3	NA	1,619	NA	1,619	NA	NA
Grant	41	31	6,922	5,563	6,922	5,563	NA	NA
Green	13	18	6,098	5,545	6,095	5,545	6,200	NA
Green Lake	11	6	7,865	9,082	7,865	9,082	NA	NA
Iowa	31	22	5,270	6,180	5,270	6,180	NA	NA
Jackson	10	13	3,946	3,487	3,946	3,487	NA	NA
Jefferson	14	14	7,127	6,686	7,204	6,686	6,093	NA
Juneau	8	6	3,841	2,553	3,527	2,553	4,841	NA
Kenosha	11	7	15,189	10,977	11,250	10,977	24,828	NA
Kewaunee	5	8	6,677	5,636	6,677	5,636	NA	NA
La Crosse	16	12	4,653	5,343	4,675	5,343	4,113	NA
Lafayette	18	20	6,943	7,469	6,953	7,469	5,800	NA
Langlade	6	7	3,936	4,504	3,936	4,504	NA	NA
Lincoln	9	7	2,133	2,326	2,142	2,326	1,954	NA
Manitowoc	34	16	8,156	6,875	8,156	6,743	NA	7,500
Marathon	44	49	3,897	3,917	3,873	3,922	3,996	1,500
Marinette	8	7	4,472	2,615	4,503	2,615	3,000	NA
Marquette	9	8	3,406	3,722	3,406	3,722	NA	NA
Milwaukee	2	NA	15,829	NA	NA	NA	15,829	NA
Monroe	23	17	5,692	3,765	3,634	3,765	11,836	NA
Oconto	8	6	5,714	3,167	6,110	3,167	4,598	NA
Outagamie	16	13	8,191	7,288	7,888	7,319	15,931	6,000
Ozaukee	11	4	7,794	5,489	7,705	5,489	16,000	NA
Pepin	10	6	3,960	4,332	3,960	4,332	NA	NA
Pierce	16	10	5,139	4,734	5,175	4,734	3,247	NA
Polk	27	19	3,597	3,239	3,618	3,206	2,033	3,600
Portage	22	9	3,902	4,370	3,917	4,370	3,832	NA
Price	3	NA	1,322	NA	1,322	NA	NA	NA
Racine	18	10	12,282	8,803	7,468	8,803	21,866	NA
Richland	20	10	3,377	4,291	3,395	4,291	2,150	NA
Rock	16	17	7,875	7,457	7,109	7,457	24,772	NA
Rusk	6	11	1,956	2,021	1,972	2,041	1,795	1,314
St. Croix	35	16	4,818	4,255	4,524	4,255	7,253	NA
Sauk	30	19	5,398	5,225	4,480	5,225	24,786	NA
Sawyer	3	2	1,839	1,380	1,839	1,380	NA	NA
Shawano	23	13	5,965	5,193	5,971	5,193	5,000	NA
Sheboygan	18	19	6,018	6,267	6,018	6,267	NA	NA
Taylor	15	19	2,100	2,925	2,095	2,925	2,233	NA
Trempealeau	15	16	3,446	3,570	3,393	3,570	3,854	NA
Vernon	27	27	4,258	3,997	4,274	3,969	3,300	4,600
Walworth	16	25	7,990	7,872	7,990	7,788	NA	9,155
Washburn	7	6	1,864	1,783	1,864	1,783	NA	NA
Washington	14	9	9,194	8,069	9,194	8,069	NA	NA

Wisconsin agricultural land sales, continued

County[1]	Total agricultural land sales[2]				Land continuing in agricultural use, avg. cost per acre ($)		Agricultural land diverted to other uses, avg. cost per acre ($)	
	Number		Avg. cost per acre ($)					
	2018	2019	2018	2019	2018	2019	2018	2019
Waukesha	9	6	15,982	15,684	10,138	15,684	25,016	NA
Waupaca	13	23	3,914	4,591	3,914	4,633	NA	2,942
Waushara.	6	4	3,109	3,707	3,109	3,879	NA	2,600
Winnebago	25	14	6,361	6,058	5,308	6,062	18,621	5,600
Wood	12	11	2,945	3,404	2,941	3,404	3,000	NA
Total.	**1,070**	**900**	**6,045**	**5,278**	**5,587**	**5,269**	**13,280**	**5,942**

NA–Not available.

1. Iron, Menominee, Oneida, and Vilas counties had no agricultural sales in years shown.   2. Includes land with and without buildings and other improvements.

Source: U.S. Department of Agriculture, National Agricultural Statistics Service, "2020 Wisconsin Agricultural Statistics" and prior versions at https://www.nass.usda.gov/Statistics_by_State/Wisconsin/Publications/Annual_Statistical_Bulletin [September 2020].

CONSERVATION

Fish and game harvested, 2019–20

Fish[1]		Coyote	59,823
Great Lakes trout[2]	117,430	Deer (with guns)	196,135
Great Lakes salmon[2]	125,620	Deer (with bows)	94,058
		Elk	10
Game and fowl[3]		Bear	3,679
Wild turkey	42,368	Duck	365,300
Pheasant	291,400	Canada goose	143,387
Ruffed grouse	162,325		
Gray partridge	0	**Furbearers[3]**	
Bobwhite quail	199	Woodchuck	5,797
Woodcock	51,138	Muskrat	169,280
Squirrel	218,783	Mink	4,634
Cottontail rabbit	73,482	Beaver	31,683
Snowshoe hare	5,320	River otter	1,661
Doves	50,007	Bobcat	789
Raccoon	116,226	Opossum	7,867
Red fox	5,009	Skunk	4,964
Gray fox	3,227	Fisher	555

1. Data based on 2014–15 diary survey estimating total fish caught (39,654,149) and total harvested (12,334,465). These are underestimates, because they do not include fish caught or harvested by unlicensed anglers, short-term license holders, or senior citizen discount license holders.   2. Data from Lake Michigan Creel Harvest Tables 2004–20 at https://dnr.wisconsin.gov/sites/default/files/topic/Fishing/LM_CreelHarvestTables2004-2020.pdf 3. Deer, bear, turkey, bobcat, otter, and fisher are all from hunter-registered harvest. Remaining data is from hunter surveys.

Source: Wisconsin Department of Natural Resources, departmental data, March 2021.

Fish and game stocked, 2019–20

Game farm pheasants released	77,751
Warmwater fish produced and distributed (includes fry)	20,284,618
Coldwater fish	7,825,163

Source: Wisconsin Department of Natural Resources, departmental data, April 2021.

Fish and game licenses and recreation permits issued

	2015	2016	2017	2018	2019	2020
Boats actively registered	623,796	618,043	630,134	619,319	609,957	625,273
Snowmobiles actively registered	213,325	200,529	223,938	214,661	211,624	229,118
All-terrain vehicles actively registered	320,758	366,987	382,029	400,285	418,345	447,917
Off-highway motorcycles actively registered[1]	NA	365	2,245	3,608	4,209	5,234
Gun deer hunting and license tags (including nonresident)[2]	515,869	499,312	488,826	472,370	460,314	454,394
Small game hunting license tags (including nonresident)[2]	134,391	129,857	120,103	109,155	109,943	120,213
Spring turkey licenses (including nonresident)[2]	94,056	96,469	93,689	87,429	86,047	90,313
Fall turkey licenses (including nonresident)[2]	14,663	16,006	15,298	21,767	21,114	25,240
Resident annual fishing licenses[3]	721,379	706,688	686,253	652,561	647,672	738,472

Fish and game licenses and recreation permits issued, continued

	2015	2016	2017	2018	2019	2020
Resident husband and wife fishing licenses	211,439	196,332	190,994	187,471	179,962	201,922
1-day resident fishing licenses.	8,290	8,784	10,566	9,767	9,616	10,912
Nonresident annual fishing licenses	114,847	120,309	120,563	113,594	113,380	132,288
Nonresident family annual fishing licenses.	64,706	57,530	54,324	53,548	53,080	58,883
15-day nonresident family fishing licenses	31,142	25,780	23,282	22,424	22,109	21,082
15-day nonresident fishing licenses	24,087	24,888	24,956	24,973	24,326	22,622
4-day nonresident fishing licenses	56,896	52,670	52,288	51,184	50,804	46,555
1-day nonresident fishing licenses	63,811	61,116	64,394	60,211	59,675	58,926
Resident sports licenses.	48,770	46,144	44,567	48,140	48,700	56,003
Nonresident sports licenses	3,600	3,022	3,147	3,403	3,344	3,630
2-day Great Lakes fishing licenses	37,411	39,751	37,837	36,174	34,412	32,947
Resident archer's licenses[2]	165,025	157,691	143,244	130,524	119,785	125,075
Nonresident archer's licenses[2].	9,077	9,204	8,928	8,782	9,452	10,879
Guide licenses (residents only)	1,552	1,188	1,592	1,789	1,790	2,019
Conservation patron licenses	47,965	50,231	51,889	52,633	52,590	55,805
Nonresident patron licenses	973	1,147	1,213	1,039	857	1,026
Resident crossbow licenses[4]	62,872	58,878	70,855	77,988	93,681	112,905
Nonresident crossbow licenses[4]	1,767	1,512	2,093	2,453	6,957	8,557
Elk licenses[5]	NA	NA	NA	10	10	10

NA–Not available.

1. DNR began registering off-highway motorcycles in 2016. 2. Includes mentored licenses. 3. Includes senior and junior fishing licenses. 4. Includes mentored licenses. Does not include upgrades. 5. The first Wisconsin elk season was held in 2018.

Source: Wisconsin Department of Natural Resources, departmental data, April 2021.

Department of Natural Resources funding sources

	2014–15 ($1,000)	2015–16 ($1,000)	2016–17 ($1,000)	2017–18 ($1,000)	2018–19 ($1,000)	2019–20 ($1,000)
Segregated funds	**362,115**	**412,607**	**432,415**	**427,135**	**455,533**	**453,407**
All-terrain vehicle registration fees	3,756	4,634	3,954	5,471	4,174	6,340
Boat registration fees	5,543	5,610	5,165	5,573	5,380	5,428
Dry cleaner fund	757	820	576	572	928	447
Endangered resources voluntary payments . .	549	1,218	1,688	1,422	271	650
Environmental improvement fund	1,358	1,404	1,408	1,729	1,752	1,661
Environmental management account	48,231	52,026	48,057	44,353	47,984	46,991
Federal aids	53,799	93,340	103,659	104,553	123,313	112,367
Fishing, hunting licenses and permits	60,273	56,787	59,181	60,932	57,476	67,116
Forestry mill tax.	97,208	99,721	109,699	98,883	103,166	101,545
Gifts and donations	751	620	641	932	953	798
Heritage State Parks and Forests Trust Fund . .	35	42	94	33	183	35
Nonpoint source account.	15,134	16,135	15,866	15,055	14,960	14,646
Park stickers and fees	13,974	18,676	19,068	21,605	23,001	22,700
Petroleum storage environmental cleanup fund	9,514	11,621	10,964	12,351	14,403	11,442
Program revenue[1]	35,283	34,614	35,280	36,634	39,724	43,525
Recycling fund	—	—	—	—	—	—
Snowmobile registration fees	2,981	2,696	3,737	3,873	4,370	4,162
Waste management fund.	198	66	18	438	307	134
Water resources account	11,982	12,006	12,893	12,306	12,744	12,991
Wisconsin Natural Resources Magazine	789	571	467	420	444	429
General funds.	**175,297**	**161,753**	**164,092**	**158,356**	**176,422**	**165,944**
General purpose revenue.	109,049	102,175	106,900	97,746	113,768	98,444
Program revenues	20,370	18,438	20,227	22,983	20,978	22,866
Program revenue—services	11,051	10,227	9,455	7,860	10,464	12,899

Department of Natural Resources funding sources, continued

	2014–15 ($1,000)	2015–16 ($1,000)	2016–17 ($1,000)	2017–18 ($1,000)	2018–19 ($1,000)	2019–20 ($1,000)
Federal aids	34,827	30,913	27,510	29,767	31,212	31,735
Total.	**537,412**	**574,360**	**596,507**	**585,491**	**631,955**	**619,351**

—Represents zero.
1. Includes all segregated expenditures in assigned or dedicated appropriations.
Source: Wisconsin Department of Natural Resources, departmental data, March 2021.

Department of Natural Resources expenditures

Program	2014–15 ($1,000)	2015–16 ($1,000)	2016–17 ($1,000)	2017–18 ($1,000)	2018–19 ($1000)	2019–20 ($1000)
Fish, wildlife, and parks (FWP)	**89,477**	**85,711**	**87,401**	**85,706**	**93,519**	**93,547**
Wildlife management	21,618	20,260	21,248	24,285	27,854	26,819
Southern forests	5,613	5,235	5,540	5,455	5,823	5,783
Fisheries management	27,384	26,060	25,509	26,322	26,441	27,943
Parks.	18,010	17,282	17,720	17,842	17,802	17,256
Endangered resources.	5,867	6,068	6,648	6,939	8,210	8,288
Facilities and lands	9,911	9,690	9,438	—	—	—
Property management	—	—	—	3,744	6,168	6,275
FWP program management	1,074	1,116	1,298	1,119	1,221	1,183
Forestry	**52,903**	**53,247**	**61,655**	**53,403**	**58,092**	**56,441**
Public safety and resource protection	**41,362**	**39,316**	**40,425**	**36,145**	**35,315**	**39,378**
Law enforcement	30,921	30,913	31,230	35,383	34,598	39,378
Integrated science services.	9,574	7,617	8,356	—	—	—
Enforcement/science program management.	867	786	839	762	717	—
Environmental management (EM)	**74,494**	**70,249**	**69,667**	**72,080**	**75,960**	**79,291**
Drinking and groundwater.	13,034	12,931	13,464	13,755	14,952	15,498
Water quality	26,444	22,427	22,922	23,299	27,044	27,104
Air management	13,722	14,049	13,366	10,911	13,166	13,009
Waste and materials management	7,434	6,962	7,106	7,159	7,376	7,225
Remediation and redevelopment.	11,461	11,348	10,529	15,689	12,159	14,985
EM program management	2,399	2,532	2,280	1,267	1,263	1,470
Conservation aids	**42,575**	**45,700**	**43,735**	**44,718**	**47,270**	**48,501**
Fish and wildlife aids.	1,565	1,578	1,367	848	1,862	1,516
Forestry aids.	8,561	9,869	8,571	8,005	9,611	8,091
Recreational aids	12,290	12,730	12,105	13,825	13,694	16,422
Aids in lieu of taxes.	15,308	16,916	16,975	17,140	17,229	17,325
Enforcement aids.	2,277	2,277	2,277	2,277	2,277	2,532
Wildlife damage aids.	2,574	2,330	2,440	2,623	2,597	2,615
Environmental aids	**33,630**	**34,643**	**35,803**	**35,669**	**38,090**	**33,961**
Water quality aids	6,093	5,807	6,839	6,260	6,307	6,269
Solid and hazard waste aids	21,446	20,163	21,103	20,829	20,162	20,411
Environmental aids.	5,067	6,373	5,912	6,509	9,011	5,677
Environmental planning aids.	232	172	294	365	303	285
Nonpoint aids	792	2,128	1,655	1,706	2,307	1,319
Debt service.	**110,109**	**115,815**	**116,781**	**105,634**	**123,473**	**105,167**
Resource	72,382	77,986	87,567	79,399	93,821	79,788
Environmental.	4,468	4,725	4,856	4,093	4,470	4,077
Water quality	29,845	29,598	20,766	18,737	21,282	17,901
Administrative facility	3,414	3,506	3,592	3,405	3,900	3,401
Acquisition and development	**10,743**	**13,223**	**9,479**	**9,690**	**9,276**	**9,873**
Wildlife	1,384	1,084	995	741	1,497	2,176
Fish	1,838	198	752	314	552	220

Department of Natural Resources expenditures, continued

Program	2014–15 ($1,000)	2015–16 ($1,000)	2016–17 ($1,000)	2017–18 ($1,000)	2018–19 ($1000)	2019–20 ($1000)
Forestry	918	5,324	1,572	285	314	1,070
Southern forests	317	361	379	327	233	475
Parks	3,625	1,746	2,310	1,639	3,492	2,649
Endangered resources	308	848	320	254	85	121
Facilities and lands	2,153	3,590	3,142	5,530	1,529	1,657
Property management	—	—	—	600	1,574	1,505
Law Enforcement	163	72	4	—	—	—
Water resources	37	—	5	—	—	—
Administration	**22,401**	**23,898**	**21,986**	**24,191**	**22,180**	**23,751**
Administration	1,707	1,648	1,906	1,437	1,486	1,593
Legal services	2,369	2,358	2,158	2,210	2,439	2,450
Management and budget	547	530	427	640	446	612
Facility rental	7,336	7,514	7,651	7,498	7,676	7,524
Nonbudget accounts	10,442	11,848	9,844	12,406	10,133	11,572
Internal services (IS)	**19,743**	**20,261**	**20,287**	**31,193**	**32,312**	**32,884**
Finance	7,035	7,633	6,837	6,893	6,329	6,396
Facilities and lands	—	—	—	9,164	8,064	8,338
Technology services	8,964	8,917	9,691	8,840	10,812	11,601
Human resources	3,744	3,711	3,759	2,686	2,900	2,645
IS program management	—	—	—	3,610	4,207	3,904
External Services (EX)	**39,970**	**72,298**	**89,170**	**87,062**	**96,464**	**96,527**
Watershed management	14,435	13,768	14,455	14,321	16,490	17,505
Office of communication	1,763	979	923	723	728	1,246
Community financial assistance	6,284	41,660	56,611	55,920	61,365	60,714
Customer & outreach services	11,207	9,758	11,143	9,957	10,473	10,047
Environmental analysis & sustainability	3,480	3,409	3,084	5,123	5,795	6,104
EX program management	2,800	2,724	2,954	1,018	1,613	911
Total	**537,407**	**574,361**	**596,389**	**585,491**	**631,951**	**619,321**

Note: Subtotals and total do not add due to rounding.

—Represents zero.

Source: Wisconsin Department of Natural Resources, departmental data, March 2021.

Department of Natural Resources land acquisition acres

Fiscal year	Northern forests	Southern forests	Natural areas	Parks	Wild rivers	Wildlife mgt.	Fisheries mgt.	Other	Total
2000[1]	496	110	3,301	3,705	16,135	11,800	2,808	136	38,489
2001	149	194	1,063	4,295	3,558	5,191	2,773	683	17,905
2002	5,525	208	3,174	1,349	607	4,997	1,595	258	17,713
2003	35,464	—	5,801	2,029	2,406	3,765	1,880	86	51,432
2004	4,132	159	1,747	3,060	2,132	7,513	1,177	156	20,076
2005	6,578	475	7,477	3,842	10,692	5,385	2,308	329	37,086
2006	18,799	103	2,592	1,823	767	6,022	957	414	31,477
2007	45,075	171	2,948	713	8,793	3,247	982	192	62,120
2008	8,722	12	2,288	1,641	2,589	6,515	915	454	23,136
2009	7,943	1,024	1,844	1,876	1,867	2,150	837	358	17,899
2010	8,547	37	3,498	1,000	818	3,767	785	73	18,525
2011	27,070	297	5,845	3,525	2,729	5,560	1,786	5	46,818
2012	10,866	—	1,804	619	184	892	587	7	14,958
2013	48,989	247	2,697	891	437	3,046	1,430	157	57,894
2014	10,283	144	1,346	204	147	4,267	87	283	16,761
2015	14,446	10	455	1,049	81	1,404	843	218	18,506
2016	22,340	92	245	358	4	6,671	358	85	30,152

Department of Natural Resources land acquisition acres, continued

Fiscal year	Northern forests	Southern forests	Natural areas	Parks	Wild rivers	Wildlife mgt.	Fisheries mgt.	Other	Total
2017............	7,285	44	1,040	359	146	990	355	12	10,230
2018............	20,816	1	4	17	21	844	444	3	22,150
2019............	14,392	—	—	108	—	356	339	10	15,205
2020............	—	—	—	412	69	322	182	—	985
Total............	**324,385**	**7,462**	**78,045**	**40,869**	**106,658**	**125,300**	**47,291**	**6,883**	**736,893**

—Represents zero.

1. The Stewardship 2000 program replaced the Warren Knowles-Gaylord Nelson Stewardship Program in 2000.

Source: Wisconsin Department of Natural Resources, Bureau of Facilities and Lands, departmental data, March 2021.

Department of Natural Resources land acquisition cost

Fiscal year	Northern forests ($1,000)	Southern forests ($1,000)	Natural areas ($1,000)	Parks ($1,000)	Wild rivers ($1,000)	Wildlife mgt. ($1,000)	Fisheries mgt. ($1,000)	Other ($1,000)	Total ($1,000)
2000[1].........	550	403	3,472	2,734	12,633	9,061	2,861	352	32,066
2001..........	533	873	2,156	8,605	739	4,251	5,247	420	22,824
2002..........	13,575	1,105	2,955	3,244	1,095	5,635	4,156	3,822	35,587
2003..........	7,680	—	3,603	4,105	3,807	3,908	3,976	117	27,196
2004..........	13,474	579	2,770	5,727	4,629	8,490	3,054	130	38,853
2005..........	2,418	3,050	4,993	16,693	3,591	8,164	5,034	401	44,345
2006..........	9,852	1,220	3,642	3,247	1,526	5,574	3,919	81	29,061
2007..........	20,147	1,081	4,039	6,760	15,864	7,227	3,529	254	58,901
2008..........	8,734	246	3,004	3,222	5,777	10,016	2,529	135	33,663
2009..........	6,534	11,325	1,849	8,069	3,729	4,250	2,236	128	38,120
2010..........	5,867	272	5,448	2,881	2,119	6,693	2,232	122	25,634
2011..........	12,974	2,023	7,153	4,762	5,416	10,144	4,277	35	46,782
2012..........	7,426	—	1,836	2,605	369	2,736	1,657	—	16,628
2013..........	17,412	796	900	3,955	490	5,333	1,660	—	30,546
2014..........	6,997	742	967	572	410	5,630	249	73	15,640
2015..........	1,154	30	782	884	899	2,315	1,390	40	7,493
2016..........	189	660	719	1,273	7	1,328	682	40	4,896
2017..........	213	250	2,148	74	520	192	369	—	3,767
2018..........	3	—	—	—	—	60	71	—	134
2019..........	4,341	—	—	86	—	176	462	1,100	6,165
2020..........	—	—	—	693	186	635	528	—	2,042
Total.........	**144,631**	**32,691**	**68,892**	**89,785**	**97,035**	**130,380**	**69,859**	**11,418**	**644,690**

—Represents zero.

1. The Stewardship 2000 program replaced the Warren Knowles-Gaylord Nelson Stewardship Program in 2000.

Source: Wisconsin Department of Natural Resources, Bureau of Facilities and Lands, departmental data, March 2021.

Highway mileage in Wisconsin, January 1, 2020

County	Total miles	State trunk system	County trunk system	Local roads (city, village, town)	Other roads (parks, forests)
Adams	1,451.56	91.45	226.57	1,133.54	0.00
Ashland	1,134.70	119.53	91.26	878.90	45.01
Barron	1,999.33	141.89	290.90	1,566.54	0.00
Bayfield	2,202.07	155.16	172.75	1,779.46	94.70
Brown	2,356.10	190.24	361.43	1,799.13	5.30
Buffalo	1,042.73	148.02	317.90	572.88	3.93
Burnett	1,573.59	106.38	220.05	1,206.20	40.96
Calumet	877.41	94.73	131.76	650.92	0.00
Chippewa	2,148.71	210.29	489.17	1,431.13	18.12
Clark	2,190.75	157.37	300.98	1,685.42	46.98
Columbia	1,740.09	277.92	357.23	1,103.95	0.99
Crawford	1,089.48	182.78	132.44	768.56	5.70
Dane	4,249.33	401.45	516.48	3,310.06	21.34
Dodge	2,077.20	238.15	538.56	1,282.71	17.78
Door	1,268.99	101.61	295.55	871.83	0.00
Douglas	2,094.84	161.60	336.72	1,500.89	95.63
Dunn	1,760.45	205.43	425.12	1,129.90	0.00
Eau Claire	1,600.86	150.08	420.53	1,012.31	17.94
Florence	554.24	66.89	49.12	379.25	58.98
Fond du Lac	1,794.08	199.56	384.14	1,210.38	0.00
Forest	1,110.79	152.41	109.06	777.17	72.15
Grant	2,129.74	259.11	310.36	1,559.32	0.95
Green	1,263.05	122.41	277.86	862.78	0.00
Green Lake	703.66	69.97	228.27	405.42	0.00
Iowa	1,321.02	169.74	366.87	783.15	1.26
Iron	802.31	114.00	67.26	557.88	63.17
Jackson	1,477.48	185.97	231.11	1,035.56	24.84
Jefferson	1,443.73	179.60	256.30	1,007.83	0.00
Juneau	1,529.89	191.96	234.17	1,091.65	12.11
Kenosha	1,104.75	116.78	248.58	739.39	0.00
Kewaunee	828.42	61.80	219.04	547.58	0.00
La Crosse	1,212.10	156.51	281.02	773.76	0.81
Lafayette	1,159.79	126.79	272.27	760.73	0.00
Langlade	1,159.36	143.36	271.04	736.75	8.21
Lincoln	1,321.64	155.51	270.74	868.14	27.25
Manitowoc	1,662.34	154.66	283.60	1,224.08	0.00
Marathon	3,387.10	276.56	614.34	2,489.72	6.48
Marinette	2,362.82	154.30	334.28	1,640.24	234.00
Marquette	860.61	87.46	237.22	535.86	0.07
Menominee	455.02	40.74	36.51	81.67	296.10
Milwaukee	3048.13	254.83	140.20	2,634.26	18.84
Monroe	1,733.62	238.33	344.02	1,063.70	87.57
Oconto	2,053.75	149.83	318.55	1,540.91	44.46
Oneida	1,723.31	159.56	171.18	1,352.21	40.36
Outagamie	2,024.83	186.89	343.77	1,486.67	7.50
Ozaukee	948.92	82.29	155.55	711.08	0.00
Pepin	462.4	48.58	154.72	259.10	0.00
Pierce	1317.82	164.19	248.68	899.47	5.48
Polk	1,989.28	159.22	331.37	1,488.40	10.29
Portage	1,904.93	157.75	433.85	1,313.33	0.00
Price	1,442.86	155.24	220.05	1,054.74	12.83
Racine	1,325.97	153.75	158.97	1,013.25	0.00
Richland	1,130.17	150.12	296.49	683.56	0.00
Rock	2,092.31	252.62	212.05	1,627.64	0.00
Rusk	1,243.36	105.26	255.13	859.85	23.12

Highway mileage in Wisconsin, January 1, 2020, continued

County	Total miles	State trunk system	County trunk system	Local roads (city, village, town)	Other roads (parks, forests)
St. Croix	1,951.55	205.07	334.48	1,410.32	1.68
Sauk	1,906.98	221.51	308.35	1,296.98	80.14
Sawyer	1,508.35	161.32	228.94	1,092.77	25.32
Shawano	1,766.27	178.83	293.58	1,252.36	41.50
Sheboygan	1,565.11	166.71	449.13	949.27	0.00
Taylor	1,458.08	110.22	248.37	1,081.75	17.74
Trempealeau	1,370.24	176.46	291.53	893.48	8.77
Vernon	1,655.45	214.03	285.22	1,153.68	2.52
Vilas	1,562.81	136.27	204.25	1,135.02	87.27
Walworth	1,538.27	216.11	193.25	1,128.91	0.00
Washburn	1,416.69	137.16	198.65	982.04	98.84
Washington	1,545.60	181.74	177.78	1,186.08	0.00
Waukesha	3,109.97	217.07	406.00	2,486.90	0.00
Waupaca	1,663.10	197.38	333.46	1,132.26	0.00
Waushara	1,331.28	132.32	333.46	865.50	0.00
Winnebago	1,581.61	168.01	217.46	1,196.11	0.03
Wood	1,798.37	185.88	324.22	1,275.66	12.61
Total	**115,673.52**	**11,744.72**	**19,821.27**	**82,259.90**	**1,847.63**

Source: Wisconsin Department of Transportation, Division of Transportation Investment Management, departmental data, October 2020.

Wisconsin road mileage, January 1, 2020

System	Miles	Percent
State trunk highways	11,745	10.2
County trunk highways	19,821	17.1
City streets	14,015	12.1
Village streets	6,728	5.8
Town roads	61,516	53.2
Park, forest, and other roads	1,848	1.6
Total	**115,674**	**100.0**

Surface	Miles	Percent
Bituminous or higher	91,578	79.2
Gravel or soil-surfaced	16,515	14.3
Sealcoat	5,726	5.0
Graded and drained	1,732	1.5
Unimproved	122	0.1
Total	**115,674**	**100.0**

Source: Wisconsin Department of Transportation, Division of Transportation Investment Management, departmental data, October 2020.

Wisconsin harbor commerce tonnage, 2019

Harbors[1]	Crude inedible materials (except fuels)	Coal and lignite	Primary mfd goods	Food and farm products	Petroleum and petroleum products	Chemicals and related products	Mfd equip., machinery, and products	Unknown or other
Lake Superior	22,924,783	8,306,580	181,089	1,860,755	57,154	44,871	391,513	—
Duluth-Superior	22,924,352	8,306,580	181,089	1,860,755	54,962	44,871	366,225	—
Bayfield	387	—	—	—	1,096	—	12,644	—
La Pointe	44	—	—	—	1,096	—	12,644	—
Lake Michigan	2,968,783	459,589	1,633,007	100,274	299,408	10,509	9,113	36,404
Milwaukee	1,587,757	—	1,056,884	100,274	59,957	—	1,926	28
Green Bay	1,233,847	441,055	324,110	—	237,788	10,509	—	36,376
Manitowoc	79,491	18,534	137,769	—	—	—	—	—
Menominee[2]	56,326	—	114,244	—	—	—	—	—

Wisconsin harbor commerce tonnage, 2019, continued

Harbors[1]	Crude inedible materials (except fuels)	Coal and lignite	Primary mfd goods	Food and farm products	Petro- leum and pe- troleum products	Chemi- cals and related products	Mfd equip., machin- ery, and products	Unknown or other
Kenosha	11,362	—	—	—	—	—	1,330	—
Detroit Harbor[3]	—	—	—	—	1,663	—	5,857	—
Total.	25,893,566	8,766,169	1,814,096	1,961,029	356,562	55,380	400,626	36,404

Note: Tonnage reported in short tons. One short ton equals 2,000 lbs.

— Represents zero; Mfd–Manufactured.

1. Harbors with reported commerce. 2. Includes tonnage handled at Marinette, Wisconsin. 3. Washington Island.

Source: U.S. Army Corps of Engineers, Navigation Data Center, Ports and Waterways (database), Calendar Year 2019, Region 3, at http://cwbi-ndc-nav.s3-website-us-east-1.amazonaws.com/files/wcsc/webpub/#/?year=2019&regionId=3 [March 2021].

Motor vehicles in Wisconsin, by type

Fiscal year (ending June 30)	Total	Autos	Trucks[1]	Trailers, semi- trailers	Motor homes	Buses	Motor- cycles[2]	Mopeds
1930.	819,718	700,251	115,883	X	X	554	3,030	X
1935.	722,797	597,197	116,912	5,634	X	498	2,556	X
1940.	874,652	741,583	123,742	5,144	X	675	3,508	X
1945.	828,425	676,978	139,591	6,484	X	1,489	3,883	X
1950.	1,157,221	921,194	209,083	14,124	X	2,465	10,355	X
1955.	1,369,636	1,108,084	227,367	21,643	X	3,337	9,205	X
1960.	1,598,693	1,303,679	246,353	31,502	X	5,184	11,975	X
1965.	1,867,223	1,517,397	269,771	44,017	X	7,218	28,820	X
1970.	2,205,662	1,762,681	317,096	64,065	X	8,178	53,642	X
1975.	2,737,164	2,096,694	425,854	91,609	X	11,897	111,110	X
1980.	3,417,748	2,509,904	558,840	102,256	17,071	13,775	205,786	10,116
1985.	3,372,029	2,310,024	765,852	72,289	17,195	10,325	176,023	20,321
1990.	3,834,608	2,456,175	1,045,583	123,061	21,095	15,081	149,268	24,345
1995.	4,285,753	2,464,358	1,391,374	207,042	22,554	15,593	161,762	23,070
2000.	4,703,294	2,405,408	1,813,385	214,344	24,427	15,587	160,920	17,977
2005.	5,226,584	2,347,042	2,216,863	342,879	22,598	12,478	249,979	34,745
2006.	5,326,157	2,361,853	2,281,988	364,024	22,406	13,174	246,307	36,405
2007.	5,428,629	2,357,616	2,333,538	396,229	21,147	13,516	266,036	40,547
2008.	5,499,872	2,381,911	2,370,655	410,737	20,209	10,736	260,220	45,404
2009.	5,532,953	2,340,991	2,396,470	417,031	20,039	12,685	291,164	54,573
2010.	5,525,794	2,333,029	2,416,295	426,092	19,615	13,376	269,316	48,071
2011.	5,564,794	2,300,243	2,445,056	434,782	18,792	13,745	296,808	55,368
2012.	5,551,411	2,274,596	2,473,072	447,195	18,535	14,169	274,553	49,291
2013.	5,671,185	2,276,007	2,548,029	460,542	18,187	10,598	301,477	56,345
2014.	5,697,808	2,255,966	2,609,402	479,237	18,584	12,615	275,120	46,884
2015.	5,823,555	2,229,199	2,703,329	502,301	18,766	13,324	303,577	53,059
2016.	5,870,311	2,192,295	2,802,029	525,513	18,760	13,739	274,787	43,188
2017.	5,985,094	2,132,984	2,919,745	546,535	18,779	14,138	303,541	49,372
2018.	6,047,860	2,080,739	3,050,820	571,827	19,005	10,164	275,301	40,004
2019.	6,195,594	2,019,545	3,197,066	596,396	19,282	12,525	305,278	45,502
2020.	6,072,320	1,886,351	3,245,480	604,370	18,199	12,896	269,431	35,593

X–Not applicable.

1. "Trucks" includes minivans and sport utility vehicles. 2. For 2020, the motorcycle total includes 96 autocycle registrations.

Sources: Wisconsin Secretary of State, *Biennial Report—1928–30*; Wisconsin Highway Commission, *Biennial Reports—1933–35, 1938–40*; Wisconsin Motor Vehicle Department, *Wisconsin Motor Vehicle Registrations—Fiscal Years 1944–45* through *1964–65*; Wisconsin Department of Transportation, *Wisconsin Motor Vehicle Registrations—Fiscal Year 1979–80, 1980*, and prior issues, and *Wisconsin Transportation Facts* (periodical); departmental data, February 2021.

Wisconsin motor vehicle crashes

	Total licensed drivers	Crashes[1]			Persons killed	Persons injured	Miles traveled (millions)	Fatality rate[2]	Fatal crash rate[3]
		Total	Fatal	Injury					
2001.	3,835,549	125,403	684	39,358	764	58,279	57,266	1.33	1.19
2002.	3,839,930	129,072	723	39,634	805	57,776	58,745	1.37	1.23
2003.	3,933,924	131,191	748	39,413	836	56,882	59,617	1.40	1.25
2004.	3,993,348	128,308	714	38,451	784	55,258	60,398	1.31	1.18
2005.	4,049,450	125,174	700	37,515	801	53,462	60,018	1.33	1.17
2006.	4,066,273	117,877	659	35,296	712	50,236	59,401	1.20	1.11
2007.	4,075,764	125,123	655	36,048	737	50,676	59,493	1.24	1.10
2008.	4,079,562	125,103	542	33,766	587	46,637	57,462	1.02	0.94
2009.	4,085,833	109,991	488	29,907	542	41,589	58,157	0.93	0.84
2010.	4,114,622	108,808	517	29,380	562	40,889	59,420	0.95	0.87
2011.	4,142,823	112,516	515	28,965	565	40,144	58,554	0.96	0.88
2012.	4,171,428	109,385	535	28,453	601	39,370	59,087	1.02	0.91
2013.	4,188,194	118,254	491	28,474	527	39,872	59,484	0.89	0.83
2014.	4,194,760	119,736	451	28,801	498	39,701	60,044	0.83	0.75
2015.	4,206,770	121,613	513	29,845	555	41,653	62,140	0.89	0.83
2016.	3,960,597	129,051	524	31,066	588	43,669	63,870	0.92	0.82
2017.	4,286,263	139,870	539	30,614	594	42,178	65,324	0.91	0.83
2018.	4,288,173	144,082	526	29,934	584	41,092	NA	NA	NA
2019.	4,296,646	145,288	511	28,791	551	39,723	66,341	0.83	0.77

NA–Not available.

1. A motor vehicle crash is defined as an event caused by a single variable or chain of variables. The property damage threshold for a reportable crash was raised from $500 to $1,000, effective January 1, 1996.   2. Number of fatalities per 100 million vehicle miles traveled.   3. Number of fatal crashes per 100 million vehicle miles traveled.

Source: Wisconsin Department of Transportation, *Wisconsin Traffic Crash Facts*; departmental data, December 2020.

Wisconsin motorcycle crashes

	Total registered cycles	Cycle crashes				Cyclist fatalities[1]		
		Total	Fatal	Personal injury	Property damage	Total[2]	No helmet	Helmet
2001.	201,143	2,285	69	1,928	288	70	53	14
2002.	198,495	2,184	73	1,794	317	78	59	15
2003.	225,181	2,512	98	2,099	315	100	74	24
2004.	221,982	2,423	81	2,015	327	80	60	18
2005.	239,938	2,680	91	2,277	312	92	69	22
2006.	291,534	2,441	88	2,065	288	93	69	24
2007.	322,505	2,788	102	2,331	355	106	70	26
2008.	327,938	2,829	86	2,318	425	87	66	19
2009.	355,487	2,345	82	1,912	351	82	51	27
2010.	343,878	2,426	97	1,959	370	98	72	23
2011.	361,893	2,331	79	1,877	375	80	69	5
2012.	340,268	2,630	107	2,110	413	112	82	25
2013.	367,474	2,150	84	1,705	361	83	60	20
2014.	337,637	2,101	63	1,696	342	67	43	21
2015.	365,878	2,221	80	1,724	417	81	63	14
2016.	334,950	2,250	78	1,733	439	82	62	17
2017.	363,094	2,206	73	1,741	392	76	45	27
2018.	331,356	2,075	78	1,609	388	81	52	28
2019.	340,640	1,806	81	1,369	356	82	53	29

1. Number of cyclists killed includes both drivers and passengers.   2. Includes fatalities where there is no data on whether the cyclist was wearing a helmet.

Source: Wisconsin Department of Transportation, *Wisconsin Traffic Crash Facts*; departmental data, December 2020.

Fatal crashes on Wisconsin highways and roads

	Total	Interstate	State	County	Local
2001	684	35	286	167	196
2002	723	44	310	171	198
2003	748	46	317	174	211
2004	714	47	298	155	214
2005	700	42	284	163	211
2006	659	34	294	128	203
2007	655	43	259	143	210
2008	542	32	225	119	166
2009	488	27	221	93	147
2010	517	32	230	105	150
2011	515	34	236	113	132
2012	535	26	242	103	164
2013	491	26	225	104	136
2014	451	23	198	85	145
2015	513	36	223	93	161
2016	524	31	211	110	172
2017	539	36	230	91	182
2018	526	30	235	108	153
2019	517	40	223	124	130

Source: Wisconsin Department of Transportation, *Wisconsin Traffic Crash Facts*; departmental data, December 2020.

Drivers involved in crashes, 2019

Age of drivers	Total licensed drivers		Drivers involved in crashes[1]		Drivers by type of crash[1]		
	Number	% of drivers	Number	% of drivers	Fatal	Injury	Property damage
14 and under	—	—	74	0.0	—	21	53
15	—	—	303	0.1	1	31	271
16	33,433	0.8	4,563	2.0	4	479	4,080
17	47,100	1.1	5,568	2.5	7	622	4,939
18	53,665	1.2	5,664	2.5	3	679	4,982
19	56,374	1.3	5,387	2.4	8	683	4,696
20	59,301	1.4	5,327	2.4	5	744	4,578
21	61,010	1.4	5,177	2.3	6	679	4,492
22	62,402	1.5	5,183	2.3	10	697	4,476
23	64,459	1.5	5,282	2.3	8	706	4,568
24	66,012	1.5	4,969	2.2	14	658	4,297
25–34	706,920	16.5	44,240	19.5	70	5,829	38,341
35–44	680,972	15.8	35,012	15.5	57	4,400	30,555
45–54	676,389	15.7	30,056	13.3	59	3,984	26,013
55–64	789,577	18.4	29,232	12.9	72	3,920	25,240
65–74	579,944	13.5	16,558	7.3	54	2,162	14,342
75–84	271,699	6.3	7,286	3.2	28	973	6,285
85 and over	87,389	2.0	2,072	0.9	12	274	1,786
Unknown	—	—	14,511	6.4	—	38	14,473
Total	**4,296,646**		**226,464**		**418**	**27,579**	**198,467**

—Represents zero.

1. Figure indicates the number of times a driver in this age group was involved in a crash. If a driver had more than one crash, the driver would be counted more than once.

Source: Wisconsin Department of Transportation, *Wisconsin Traffic Crash Facts*; departmental data, December 2020.

Possible contributing circumstances to Wisconsin motor vehicle crashes, 2019

	All crashes				Urban crashes				Rural crashes			
	Total	Fatal	Injury	Property damage	Total	Fatal	Injury	Property damage	Total	Fatal	Injury	Property damage
Driver												
Exceed speed limit	1,372	27	490	855	815	19	300	496	557	8	190	359
Speed too fast for conditions	8,225	18	1,204	7,003	4,867	13	723	4,131	3,358	5	481	2,872
Failed to yield right-of-way	9,610	16	1,185	8,409	5,628	11	681	4,936	3,982	5	504	3,473
Following too close	5,888	3	486	5,399	3,431	3	276	3,152	2,457	0	210	2,247
Improper turn	1,450	1	107	1,342	842	1	62	779	608	0	45	563
Unsafe backing	3,640	0	23	3,617	2,137	0	12	2,125	1,503	0	11	1,492
Failure to control	10,854	41	2,093	8,720	6,347	25	1,249	5,073	4,507	16	844	3,647
Ran off roadway	2,472	28	716	1,728	1,443	18	424	1,001	1,029	10	292	727
Disregarded red light	1,467	4	260	1,203	841	2	142	697	626	2	118	506
Disregarded stop sign	955	11	205	739	570	8	116	446	385	3	89	293
Disregarded other traffic control	398	6	81	311	228	4	48	176	170	2	33	135
Disregarded other road markings	193	0	28	164	117	0	16	101	76	1	12	63
Improper overtaking/passing right	367	0	31	336	214	0	18	196	153	0	13	140
Improper overtaking/passing left	411	2	44	365	243	1	23	219	168	1	21	146
Wrong side or wrong way	437	10	109	318	248	5	64	179	189	5	45	139
Failure to keep in designated lane	3,461	32	649	2,780	1,969	20	365	1,584	1,492	12	284	1,196
Operated motor vehicle in aggressive/reckless manner	1,068	12	248	808	639	10	157	472	429	2	91	336
Operated motor vehicle in inattentive, careless or erratic manner	5,176	15	770	4,391	3,025	8	439	2,578	2,151	7	331	1,813
Swerved or avoided due to wind, slippery surface, motor vehicle, object, non-motorist in roadway, etc.	613	1	97	515	357	1	55	301	256	0	42	214
Over-correcting/over-steering	642	7	171	464	379	4	101	274	263	3	70	190
Racing	43	2	11	30	18	1	6	11	25	1	5	19
Other contributing action	3,719	15	521	3,183	2,120	10	308	1,802	1,599	5	213	1,381
No contributing action	44,725	25	6,614	38,086	26,120	12	3,840	22,268	18,605	13	2,774	15,818
Looked but did not see	2,723	0	160	2,563	1,626	0	96	1,530	1,097	0	64	1,033
Unknown	10,395	43	573	9,779	6,132	26	332	5,774	4,263	17	241	4,005
Highway												
Backup due to prior crash	869	3	247	619	462	0	124	338	407	3	123	281
Backup due to prior nonrecurring incident	559	2	162	395	323	1	79	243	236	1	83	152
Backup due to regular congestion	3,724	1	1,034	2,690	2,894	1	809	2,085	830	0	225	605
Toll booth/plaza related	1	0	0	1	0	0	0	0	0	0	0	0
Road surface condition (wet, icy, snow, slush, etc.)	11,770	41	2,183	9,546	5,027	6	907	4,114	6,743	35	1,276	5,432
Debris prior to crash	112	0	22	90	47	0	9	38	65	0	13	52

Rut, holes, bumps	121	1	48	72	54	0	19	35	67	1	29	37
Work zone (construction/maintenance/utility)	967	7	241	719	537	2	124	411	430	5	117	308
Worn, travel-polished surface	4	0	0	4	2	0	0	2	2	0	0	2
Obstruction in roadway	332	0	71	261	156	0	31	125	176	0	40	136
Traffic control device inoperative, missing, or obscured	77	0	22	55	68	0	18	50	9	0	4	5
Narrow shoulder	106	3	26	77	31	0	5	26	75	3	21	51
Low shoulder	31	0	14	17	1	0	1	0	30	0	13	17
Soft shoulder	43	0	11	32	2	0	0	2	41	0	11	30
Nonhighway work	29	0	9	20	14	0	1	13	15	1	8	7
Loose gravel	144	1	83	60	25	0	11	14	119	1	72	46
Rough pavement	24	0	9	14	6	0	1	5	18	0	8	9
Other debris	158	1	24	134	76	0	14	62	82	0	10	72
Sign obscured/miss	14	0	1	13	8	0	0	8	6	0	1	5
Narrow bridge	7	0	3	4	2	0	2	0	5	0	1	4
Visibility obscured	559	3	159	397	312	1	84	227	247	2	75	170
Not applicable	538	1	69	468	289	0	29	260	249	1	40	208
Other	474	1	104	369	275	0	56	219	199	1	48	150
Vehicle												
Brakes	1,346	3	366	977	932	1	250	681	414	2	116	296
Exhaust system	28	0	12	16	22	0	12	10	6	0	0	6
Body, doors	541	0	123	418	445	0	99	346	96	0	24	72
Steering	384	1	94	289	253	0	61	192	131	1	33	97
Power train	173	0	44	129	99	0	29	70	74	0	15	59
Suspension	129	0	34	95	76	0	21	55	53	0	13	40
Tires	1,251	15	283	953	536	3	122	411	715	12	161	542
Wheels	358	0	78	280	204	0	50	154	154	0	28	126
Head lamps	144	1	49	94	104	0	35	69	40	1	14	25
Turn signals	63	0	15	48	32	0	9	23	31	0	6	25
Tail lamps	56	2	12	42	25	1	6	18	31	1	6	24
Stop lamps	39	0	13	26	22	0	8	14	17	0	5	12
Windows/windshield	214	0	55	159	133	0	39	94	81	0	16	65
Mirrors	74	0	14	60	55	0	12	43	19	0	2	17
Wipers	16	0	8	8	12	0	6	6	4	0	2	2
Coupling device/trailer hitch/safety chains	114	0	15	99	50	0	9	41	64	0	6	58
Disabled due to prior crash	80	1	33	46	41	0	14	27	39	1	19	19
Other disabled	158	0	49	109	96	0	28	68	62	0	21	41
Other	715	3	111	601	356	1	57	298	359	2	54	303

Note: Numbers represent the number of times a possible contributing circumstance was cited and not the total number of accidents.

Source: Wisconsin Department of Transportation, *Wisconsin Traffic Crash Facts*; departmental data, December 2020.

Mass transit systems in Wisconsin, January 2021

Urban bus	Rural/commuter bus	Shared-ride taxi[1]	
Appleton	Bay Area Rural Transit	Baraboo	Plover
Beloit	Dunn County	Beaver Dam	Portage
Eau Claire	Kenosha County[2]	Berlin	Prairie du Chien
Fond du Lac	La Crosse County[2]	Black River Falls	Prairie du Sac/
Green Bay	Lac du Flambeau Tribe	Chippewa Falls	Sauk City
Janesville	Manitowoc[5]	Clark County/Neillsville	Reedsburg
Kenosha	Menominee Regional Transit	Clintonville	Rhinelander
Madison	Oneida Tribe	Edgerton	Richland Center
Milwaukee County[2]	Oneida-Vilas Counties Transit	Fort Atkinson	Ripon
Monona[2]	Commission	Grant County	River Falls
Oshkosh	Ozaukee County Express[3]	Hartford	Shawano
Racine[3]	Platteville[3]	Jefferson	Stoughton
Sheboygan	Racine Commuter[3]	La Crosse County	Sun Prairie[6]
Superior[4]	Rusk County	Lake Mills	Tomah
Waukesha (city)[2]	Sauk County	Marinette	Viroqua/Westby
Waukesha County[2]	Sawyer County	Marshfield	Walworth County
Wausau	Stevens Point[5]	Mauston	Washington County
	Verona	Medford	Watertown
	Washington County Express[2]	Monroe	Waupaca
		New Richmond	Waupun
		Onalaska	West Bend
		Ozaukee County	Whitewater
			Wisconsin Rapids

1. Taxi services are privately contracted except for Grant County and the City of Hartford, where they are publicly owned and operated. 2. Privately contracted. (Note: The private service in Waukesha County is an inter-urban service. Waukesha (city) and Waukesha (county) have merged to form Waukesha Metro Transit.) 3. Privately managed. 4. Contracted with Duluth Transit Authority. 5. Moved to "rural" funding tier under WisDOT's criteria for service areas of less than 50,000 in population. 6. Sun Prairie also providing commuter bus service through contract with Madison Metro.

Source: Wisconsin Department of Transportation, Division of Transportation Investment Management, departmental data, February 2021.

Wisconsin urban transit systems

	Revenue miles (1,000)	Revenue passengers (1,000)	Operating revenue[1] ($1,000)
1950.	53,362	288,996	22,692
1955.	42,807	169,129	23,134
1960.	34,950	130,299	20,665
1965.	32,330	110,979	20,457
1970.	28,371	80,172	22,078
1975.	26,119	63,587	22,454
1980.	33,943	88,756	29,631
1985.	31,829	79,540	39,635
1990.	33,685	78,215	39,594
1995.	30,734	71,875	50,171
2000.	42,447	89,821	58,785
2001.	46,755	87,729	60,299
2002.	48,322	84,874	64,263
2003.	47,753	81,650	61,868
2004.	46,696	81,812	65,621
2005.	52,163	83,545	67,628
2006.	51,700	83,913	72,896

Wisconsin urban transit systems, continued

	Revenue miles (1,000)	Revenue passengers (1,000)	Operating revenue[1] ($1,000)
2007.	51,748	81,229	77,236
2008.	52,439	82,953	83,263
2009.	52,488	77,510	82,570
2010.	52,579	74,717	87,288
2011.	52,316	77,533	82,640
2012.	51,214	75,290	83,005
2013.	50,973	74,694	83,522
2014.	52,003	72,281	76,310
2015.	53,268	67,281	71,737
2016.	52,816	63,346	68,149
2017.	54,078	59,955	68,422
2018.	52,834	57,913	71,368
2019.	53,202	54,046	69,426

1. As recognized by the Wisconsin Department of Transportation.

Sources: Wisconsin Department of Transportation, departmental data through January 2021; (former) Division of Transportation Assistance *Wisconsin Urban Bus System Annual Report 1989* and prior issues.

Railroad mileage, usage, and revenue in Wisconsin

	No. of railroads	Mileage operated in Wisconsin[1]		Freight traffic			Passenger traffic		
		Road[2]	Track[3]	Tons (1,000)	Ton-miles[4] (1,000)	Revenue ($1,000)	Passengers (1,000)	Miles[5] (1,000)	Revenue ($1,000)
1920. . . .	35	7,546	11,615	100,991	9,052,084	92,826.00	20,188	960,569	28,646.00
1930. . . .	27	7,231	11,583	83,672	6,908,656	78,747	4,799	466,154	14,071
1940. . . .	22	6,646	10,484	87,980	6,910,647	69,941	3,952	445,938	8,201
1950. . . .	20	6,337	10,000	121,576	10,850,178	141,762	5,575	646,353	14,933
1960. . . .	18	6,195	9,625	93,475	9,096,855	134,065	3,127	383,457	9,800
1970. . . .	15	5,965	9,127	97,130	13,432,055	191,764	1,463	138,572	4,264
1980[6] . . .	21	5,192	7,990	101,008	14,727,522	453,977	174	1,122	54
1990. . . .	15	4,415	6,125	116,099	14,436,776	455,541	112	783	63
2000. . . .	12	3,548	4,956	151,573	21,321,266	580,678	NA	NA	NA
2001. . . .	13	3,699	5,107	158,881	25,922,949	700,258	NA	NA	NA
2002. . . .	12	3,688	5,095	NA	21,417,016	704,167	NA	NA	NA
2003. . . .	11	3,450	4,643	118,387	26,092,960	667,736	NA	NA	NA
2004. . . .	11	3,417	4,610	106,719	27,408,816	713,951	NA	NA	NA
2005. . . .	11	3,417	4,614	109,214	27,966,142	715,206	NA	NA	NA
2006. . . .	12	3,432	4,634	114,609	28,024,633	717,421	NA	NA	NA
2007. . . .	12	3,430	4,585	109,210	22,942,906	737,119	NA	NA	NA
2008. . . .	12	3,417	4,560	109,207	22,906,152	784,264	NA	NA	NA
2009. . . .	10	3,417	4,571	107,146	20,456,847	762,649	NA	NA	NA
2010. . . .	10	3,408	4,594	108,206	21,394,264	771,203	NA	NA	NA
2011. . . .	10	3,402	4,606	106,527	24,891,634	971,369	NA	NA	NA
2012. . . .	9	3,482	4,669	111,472	25,972,105	1,146,602	NA	NA	NA
2013. . . .	9	3,489	4,676	126,154	28,734,278	1,288,345	NA	NA	NA
2014. . . .	9	3,482	4,668	135,210	30,455,440	1,511,135	NA	NA	NA
2015. . . .	9	3,005	4,176	130,219	29,220,895	1,237,662	NA	NA	NA
2016. . . .	9	3,018	4,189	114,986	27,804,936	994,275	NA	NA	NA
2017. . . .	9	2,995	4,111	138,393	31,589,253	1,155,539	NA	NA	NA

Railroad mileage, usage, and revenue in Wisconsin, continued

Year	No. of rail-roads	Mileage operated in Wisconsin[1] Road[2]	Track[3]	Freight traffic Tons (1,000)	Ton-miles[4] (1,000)	Revenue ($1,000)	Passenger traffic Passengers (1,000)	Miles[5] (1,000)	Revenue ($1,000)
2018....	9	3,044	4,166	148,156	32,570,938	1,157,136	NA	NA	NA
2019....	9	3,036	4,156	135,129	31,242,722	1,140,078	NA	NA	NA

NA–Not available.

1. In order to avoid duplication, mileage shown is exclusive of trackage rights. 2. Road mileage is the measurement of stone roadbed in miles. 3. Track mileage is the measurement of track (2 steel rails) on roadbeds in miles. 4. A ton-mile is the movement of one ton (2,000 pounds) of cargo over the distance of one mile. 5. Passenger miles are the combination of the number of passengers carried on Wisconsin trains and the miles traveled by the passengers while within Wisconsin boundaries. 6. Intercity passenger service operated by Amtrak after May 1, 1971.

Source: Office of the Wisconsin Commissioner of Railroads, departmental data, March 2021.

Wisconsin airport usage by certified air carriers

	2018 Passengers	Enplaned freight (lb.)	2019 Passen-gers	Enplaned freight (lb.)	2020 Passen-gers	Enplaned freight (lb.)
General Mitchell International (Milwaukee)	3,548,817	79,010,065	3,374,073	75,874,000	1,309,967	74,298,000
Dane County Regional (Madison).	1,082,529	14,297,349	1,162,024	13,061,697	422,167	12,835,527
Green Bay-Austin Straubel International (Green Bay) . . .	360,107	10,978,393	386,737	10,805,803	190,282	8,203,186
Appleton International (Appleton)	324,840	155,695	347,263	174,403	144,316	165,176
Central Wisconsin (Mosinee) . .	128,181	771,232	141,123	619,262	56,782	638,756
La Crosse Municipal (La Crosse)	98,744	X	97,069	X	44,853	X
Chippewa Valley Regional (Eau Claire).	24,931	1,562,840	27,203	1,420,686	13,652	1,419,884
Rhinelander-Oneida County (Rhinelander)	23,734	X	24,268	X	10,086	X
Total.	5,591,883	106,775,574	5,559,760	101,955,851	2,192,105	97,560,529

Note: Wisconsin has eight scheduled air carrier airports. A certified air carrier is an airline that is registered by the Federal Aviation Administration.

X–Not applicable.

Source: Wisconsin Department of Transportation, departmental data, March 2021.

Number of landing facilities in Wisconsin

Type	2016	2018
Airports in the State Airport System (public use)[1]	97	97
Privately owned, public use airports	31	30
Private use airports	426	420
Heliports[2]	155	109
Seaplane bases[2]	27	16

1. Eligible for federal and/or state funding. 2. Public and private.

Source: Federal Aviation Administration data compiled by the Wisconsin Department of Transportation, March 2021.

NEWS MEDIA

News media correspondents covering the 2021 Legislature

Organization	Correspondents
Print/web	
Associated Press	Scott Bauer, Todd Richmond
Capital Times	Briana Reilly, Jessie Opoien
Daily Reporter/Wisconsin Law Journal	Michaela Paukner
Isthmus	Judith Davidoff, Dylan Brogan
MacIver News Service	Abbi Debelack, Lexi Dittrich, Bill Osmulski
Milwaukee Journal Sentinel	Molly Beck, Patrick Marley, Laura Schulte
Up North News	Julian Emerson, Pat Kreitlow, Christina Lieffring, Jonathon Sadowski
Wheeler Report	Gwyn Guenther, Trevor Guenther
Wisconsin Examiner	Melanie Conklin, Ruth Conniff, Erik Gunn, Isiah Holmes Henry Redman
Wisconsin State Journal	Riley Vetterkind, Mitchell Schmidt
Wispolitics.com	J.R. Ross, Stephanie Hoff, Adam Kelnhofer, Royce Podeszwa
Spectrum News	Anthony D. DaBruzzi
CBS 58/Telemundo Wisconsin	Victor Jacobo
Radio	
Wisconsin Public Radio	Shawn Johnson, Laurel White
Wisconsin Radio Network	Bob Hague, Raymond Neupert
Television	
WisconsinEye	Jon Henkes, Steve Walters, John Schroeder, Matthew Peters
Wisconsin Public Television	Frederica Freyberg, Zac Schultz , Andy Moore, Marisa Wojcik Will Kenneal ly
WDJT-TV (CBS 58) Milwaukee/ Telemundo Wisconsin	Emilee Fannon
WISC-TV (CBS 3) (Madison)	Naomi Kowles
WKOW-TV (ABC 27) (Madison)	Tony Galli, A.J. Bayatpour
WMTV-TV (NBC 15) (Madison)	Caroline Peterson

Source: Data collected by the Wisconsin Legislative Reference Bureau with the assistance of the Wisconsin Capitol Correspondents Association, February 2021.

THE WISCONSIN CONSTITUTION

Last amended at the April 2020 election

ARTICLE V—Executive

Section

ARTICLE VI—Administrative

Section

ARTICLE VII—Judiciary

Section

Article XIV—Schedule

Section

1. Effect of change from territory to state
2. Territorial laws continued
3. Repealed
4. Repealed
5. Repealed
6. Repealed
7. Repealed
8. Repealed
9. Repealed
10. Repealed
11. Repealed
12. Repealed
13. Common law continued in force
14. Repealed
15. Repealed
16. Implementing revised structure of judicial branch

PREAMBLE

We, the people of Wisconsin, grateful to Almighty God for our freedom, in order to secure its blessings, form a more perfect government, insure domestic tranquility and promote the general welfare, do establish this constitution.

ARTICLE I—Declaration of rights

Equality; inherent rights. Section 1. All people are born equally free and independent, and have certain inherent rights; among these are life, liberty and the pursuit of happiness; to secure these rights, governments are instituted, deriving their just powers from the consent of the governed.

Slavery prohibited. Section 2. There shall be neither slavery, nor involuntary servitude in this state, otherwise than for the punishment of crime, whereof the party shall have been duly convicted.

Free speech; libel. Section 3. Every person may freely speak, write and publish his sentiments on all subjects, being responsible for the abuse of that right, and no laws shall be passed to restrain or abridge the liberty of speech or of the press. In all criminal prosecutions or indictments for libel, the truth may be given in evidence, and if it shall appear to the jury that the matter charged as libelous be true, and was published with good motives and for justifiable ends, the party shall be acquitted; and the jury shall have the right to determine the law and the fact.

Right to assemble and petition. Section 4. The right of the people peaceably to assemble, to consult for the common good, and to petition the government, or any department thereof, shall never be abridged.

Trial by jury; verdict in civil cases. Section 5. The right of trial by jury shall remain inviolate, and shall extend to all cases at law without regard to the amount in controversy; but a jury trial may be waived by the parties in all cases in the manner prescribed by law. Provided, however, that the legislature may, from time to time, by statute provide that a valid verdict, in civil cases, may be based on the votes of a specified number of the jury, not less than five-sixths thereof.

Excessive bail; cruel punishments. Section 6. Excessive bail shall not be required, nor shall excessive fines be imposed, nor cruel and unusual punishments inflicted.

Rights of accused. Section 7. In all criminal prosecutions the accused shall enjoy the right to be heard by himself and counsel; to demand the nature and cause of the accusation against him; to meet the witnesses face to face; to have compulsory process to compel the attendance of witnesses in his behalf; and in prosecutions by indictment, or information, to a speedy public trial by an impartial jury of the county or district wherein the offense shall have been committed; which county or district shall have been previously ascertained by law.

Prosecutions; double jeopardy; self-incrimination; bail; habeas corpus. Section 8. (1) No person may be held to answer for a criminal offense without due process of law, and no person for the same offense may be put twice in jeopardy of punishment, nor may be compelled in any criminal case to be a witness against himself or herself.

(2) All persons, before conviction, shall be eligible for release under reasonable conditions designed to assure their appearance in court, protect members of the community from serious bodily harm or prevent the intimidation of witnesses. Monetary conditions of release may be imposed at or after the initial appearance only upon a finding that there is a reasonable basis to believe that the conditions are necessary to assure appearance in court. The legislature may authorize, by law, courts to revoke a person's release for a violation of a condition of release.

(3) The legislature may by law authorize, but may not require, circuit courts to deny release for a period not to exceed 10 days prior to the hearing required under this subsection to a person who is accused of committing a murder punishable by life imprisonment or a sexual assault punishable by a maximum imprisonment of 20 years, or who is accused of committing or attempting to commit a felony involving serious bodily harm to another or the threat of serious bodily harm to another and who has a previous conviction for committing or attempting to commit a felony involving serious bodily harm to another or the threat of serious bodily harm to another. The legislature may authorize by law, but may not require, circuit courts to continue to deny release to those accused persons for an additional period not to exceed 60 days following the hearing required under this subsection, if there is a requirement that there be a finding by the court based on clear and convincing evidence presented at a hearing that the accused committed the felony and a requirement that there be a finding by the court that available conditions of release will not adequately protect members of the community from serious bodily harm or prevent intimidation of witnesses. Any law enacted under this subsection shall be specific, limited and reasonable. In determining the 10-day and 60-day periods, the court shall omit any period of time found by the court to result from a delay caused by the defendant or a continuance granted which was initiated by the defendant.

(4) The privilege of the writ of habeas corpus shall not be suspended unless, in cases of rebellion or invasion, the public safety requires it.

Remedy for wrongs. Section 9. Every person is entitled to a certain remedy in the laws for all injuries, or wrongs which he may receive in his person, property, or character; he ought to obtain justice freely, and without being obliged to purchase it, completely and without denial, promptly and without delay, conformably to the laws.

Victims of crime. Section 9m. (1) (a) In this section, notwithstanding any statutory right, privilege, or protection, "victim" means any of the following:

1. A person against whom an act is committed that would constitute a crime if committed by a competent adult.

2. If the person under subd. 1. is deceased or is physically or emotionally unable to

exercise his or her rights under this section, the person's spouse, parent or legal guardian, sibling, child, person who resided with the deceased at the time of death, or other lawful representative.

3. If the person under subd. 1. is a minor, the person's parent, legal guardian or custodian, or other lawful representative.

4. If the person under subd. 1. is adjudicated incompetent, the person's legal guardian or other lawful representative.

(b) "Victim" does not include the accused or a person who the court finds would not act in the best interests of a victim who is deceased, incompetent, a minor, or physically or emotionally unable to exercise his or her rights under this section.

(2) In order to preserve and protect victims' rights to justice and due process throughout the criminal and juvenile justice process, victims shall be entitled to all of the following rights, which shall vest at the time of victimization and be protected by law in a manner no less vigorous than the protections afforded to the accused:

(a) To be treated with dignity, respect, courtesy, sensitivity, and fairness.

(b) To privacy.

(c) To proceedings free from unreasonable delay.

(d) To timely disposition of the case, free from unreasonable delay.

(e) Upon request, to attend all proceedings involving the case.

(f) To reasonable protection from the accused throughout the criminal and juvenile justice process.

(g) Upon request, to reasonable and timely notification of proceedings.

(h) Upon request, to confer with the attorney for the government.

(i) Upon request, to be heard in any proceeding during which a right of the victim is implicated, including release, plea, sentencing, disposition, parole, revocation, expungement, or pardon.

(j) To have information pertaining to the economic, physical, and psychological effect upon the victim of the offense submitted to the authority with jurisdiction over the case and to have that information considered by that authority.

(k) Upon request, to timely notice of any release or escape of the accused or death of the accused if the accused is in custody or on supervision at the time of death.

(L) To refuse an interview, deposition, or other discovery request made by the accused or any person acting on behalf of the accused.

(m) To full restitution from any person who has been ordered to pay restitution to the victim and to be provided with assistance collecting restitution.

(n) To compensation as provided by law.

(o) Upon request, to reasonable and timely information about the status of the investigation and the outcome of the case.

(p) To timely notice about all rights under this section and all other rights, privileges, or protections of the victim provided by law, including how such rights, privileges, or protections are enforced.

(3) Except as provided under sub. (2) (n), all provisions of this section are self-executing. The legislature may prescribe further remedies for the violation of this section and further procedures for compliance with and enforcement of this section.

(4) (a) In addition to any other available enforcement of rights or remedy for a violation of this section or of other rights, privileges, or protections provided by law, the victim, the victim's attorney or other lawful representative, or the attorney for the government upon request of the victim may assert and seek in any circuit court or before any other authority of competent jurisdiction, enforcement of the rights in this section and any other right, privilege, or protection afforded to the victim by law. The court or other authority with jurisdiction over the case shall act promptly on such a request and afford a remedy for the violation of any right of the victim. The court or other authority with jurisdiction over the case shall clearly state on the record the reasons for any decision regarding the disposition of a victim's right and shall provide those reasons to the victim or the victim's attorney or other lawful representative.

(b) Victims may obtain review of all adverse decisions concerning their rights as victims by courts or other authorities with jurisdiction under par. (a) by filing petitions for supervisory writ in the court of appeals and supreme court.

(5) This section does not create any cause of action for damages against the state; any political subdivision of the state; any officer, employee, or agent of the state or a political subdivision of the state acting in his or her official capacity; or any officer, employee, or agent of the courts acting in his or her official capacity.

(6) This section is not intended and may not be interpreted to supersede a defendant's federal constitutional rights or to afford party status in a proceeding to any victim.

Treason. Section 10. Treason against the state shall consist only in levying war against the same, or in adhering to its enemies, giving them aid and comfort. No person shall be convicted of treason unless on the testimony of two witnesses to the same overt act, or on confession in open court.

Searches and seizures. Section 11. The right of the people to be secure in their persons, houses, papers, and effects against unreasonable searches and seizures shall not be violated; and no warrant shall issue but upon probable cause, supported by oath or affirmation, and particularly describing the place to be searched and the persons or things to be seized.

Attainder; ex post facto; contracts. Section 12. No bill of attainder, ex post facto law, nor any law impairing the obligation of contracts, shall ever be passed, and no conviction shall work corruption of blood or forfeiture of estate.

Private property for public use. Section 13. The property of no person shall be taken for public use without just compensation therefor.

Feudal tenures; leases; alienation. Section 14. All lands within the state are declared to be allodial, and feudal tenures are prohibited. Leases and grants of agricultural land for a longer term than fifteen years in which rent or service of any kind shall be reserved, and all fines and like restraints upon alienation reserved in any grant of land, hereafter made, are declared to be void.

Equal property rights for aliens and citizens. Section 15. No distinction shall ever be made by law between resident aliens and citizens, in reference to the possession, enjoyment or descent of property.

Imprisonment for debt. Section 16. No person shall be imprisoned for debt arising out of or founded on a contract, expressed or implied.

Exemption of property of debtors. Section 17. The privilege of the debtor to enjoy the necessary comforts of life shall be recognized by wholesome laws, exempting a reasonable amount of property from seizure or sale for the payment of any debt or liability hereafter contracted.

Freedom of worship; liberty of conscience; state religion; public funds. Section 18. The right of every person to worship Almighty God according to the dictates of conscience shall never be infringed; nor shall any person be compelled to attend, erect or support any place of worship, or to maintain any ministry, without consent; nor shall any control of, or interference with, the rights of conscience be permitted, or any preference be given by law to any religious establishments or modes of worship; nor shall any money be drawn from the treasury for the benefit of religious societies, or religious or theological seminaries.

Religious tests prohibited. Section 19. No religious tests shall ever be required as a qualification for any office of public trust under the state, and no person shall be rendered incompetent to give evidence in any court of law or equity in consequence of his opinions on the subject of religion.

Military subordinate to civil power. Section 20. The military shall be in strict subordination to the civil power.

Rights of suitors. Section 21. (1) Writs of error shall never be prohibited, and shall be issued by such courts as the legislature designates by law.

(2) In any court of this state, any suitor may prosecute or defend his suit either in his own proper person or by an attorney of the suitor's choice.

Maintenance of free government. Section 22. The blessings of a free government can only be maintained by a firm adherence to justice, moderation, temperance, frugality and virtue, and by frequent recurrence to fundamental principles.

Transportation of school children. Section 23. Nothing in this constitution shall prohibit the legislature from providing for the safety and welfare of children by providing for the transportation of children to and from any parochial or private school or institution of learning.

Use of school buildings. Section 24. Nothing in this constitution shall prohibit the legislature from authorizing, by law, the use of public school buildings by civic, religious or charitable organizations during nonschool hours upon payment by the organization to the school district of reasonable compensation for such use.

Right to keep and bear arms. Section 25. The people have the right to keep and bear arms for security, defense, hunting, recreation or any other lawful purpose.

Right to fish, hunt, trap, and take game. Section 26. The people have the right to fish, hunt, trap, and take game subject only to reasonable restrictions as prescribed by law.

ARTICLE II—Boundaries

State boundary. Section 1. It is hereby ordained and declared that the state of Wisconsin doth consent and accept of the boundaries prescribed in the act of congress entitled "An act to enable the people of Wisconsin territory to form a constitution and state government, and for the admission of such state into the Union," approved August sixth, one thousand eight hundred and forty-six, to wit: Beginning at the northeast corner of the state of Illinois—that is to say, at a point in the center of Lake Michigan where the line of forty-two degrees and thirty minutes of north latitude crosses the same; thence running with the boundary line of the state of Michigan, through Lake Michigan, Green Bay, to the mouth of the Menominee river; thence up the channel of the said river to the Brule river; thence up said last-mentioned river to Lake Brule; thence along the southern shore of Lake Brule in a direct line to the center of the channel between Middle and South Islands, in the Lake of the Desert; thence in a direct line to the head waters of the Montreal river, as marked upon the survey made by Captain Cramm; thence down the main channel of the Montreal river to the middle of Lake Superior; thence through the center of Lake Superior to the mouth of the St. Louis river; thence up the main channel of said river to the first rapids in the same, above the Indian village, according to Nicollet's map; thence due south to the main branch of the river St. Croix; thence down the main channel of said river to the Mississippi; thence down the center of the main channel of that river to the northwest corner of the state of Illinois; thence due east with the northern boundary of the state of Illinois to the place of beginning, as established by "An act to enable the people of the Illinois territory to form a constitution and state government, and for the admission of such state into the Union on an equal footing with the original states," approved April 18th, 1818.

Enabling act accepted. Section 2. The propositions contained in the act of congress are hereby accepted, ratified and confirmed, and shall remain irrevocable without the consent of the United States; and it is hereby ordained that this state shall never interfere with the primary disposal of the soil within the same by the United States, nor with any regulations congress may find necessary for securing the title in such soil to bona fide purchasers thereof; and in no case shall nonresident proprietors be taxed higher than residents. Provided, that nothing in this constitution, or in the act of congress aforesaid, shall in any manner prejudice or affect the right of the state of Wisconsin to 500,000 acres of land granted to said state, and to be hereafter selected and located by and under the act of congress entitled "An act to appropriate the proceeds of the sales of the public lands, and grant pre-emption rights," approved September fourth, one thousand eight hundred and forty-one.

ARTICLE III—Suffrage

Electors. Section 1. Every United States citizen age 18 or older who is a resident of an election district in this state is a qualified elector of that district.

Implementation. Section 2. Laws may be enacted:

(1) Defining residency.

(2) Providing for registration of electors.

(3) Providing for absentee voting.

(4) Excluding from the right of suffrage persons:

(a) Convicted of a felony, unless restored to civil rights.

(b) Adjudged by a court to be incompetent or partially incompetent, unless the judgment specifies that the person is capable of understanding the objective of the elective process or the judgment is set aside.

(5) Subject to ratification by the people at a general election, extending the right of suffrage to additional classes.

Secret ballot. Section 3. All votes shall be by secret ballot.

ARTICLE IV—Legislative

Legislative power. Section 1. The legislative power shall be vested in a senate and assembly.

Legislature, how constituted. Section 2. The number of the members of the assembly shall never be less than fifty-four nor more than one hundred. The senate shall consist of a number not more than one-third nor less than one-fourth of the number of the members of the assembly.

Apportionment. Section 3. At its first session after each enumeration made by the authority of the United States, the legislature shall apportion and district anew the members of the senate and assembly, according to the number of inhabitants.

Representatives to the assembly, how chosen. Section 4. The members of the assembly shall be chosen biennially, by single districts, on the Tuesday succeeding the first Monday of November in even-numbered years, by the qualified electors of the several districts, such districts to be bounded by county, precinct, town or ward lines, to consist of contiguous territory and be in as compact form as practicable.

Senators, how chosen. Section 5. The senators shall be elected by single districts of convenient contiguous territory, at the same time and in the same manner as members of the assembly are required to be chosen; and no assembly district shall be divided in the formation of a senate district. The senate districts shall be numbered in the regular series, and the senators shall be chosen alternately from the odd and even-numbered districts for the term of 4 years.

Qualifications of legislators. Section 6. No person shall be eligible to the legislature who shall not have resided one year within the state, and be a qualified elector in the district which he may be chosen to represent.

Organization of legislature; quorum; compulsory attendance. Section 7. Each house shall be the judge of the elections, returns and qualifications of its own members; and a majority of each shall constitute a quorum to do business, but a smaller number may adjourn from day to day, and may compel the attendance of absent members in such manner and under such penalties as each house may provide.

Rules; contempts; expulsion. Section 8. Each house may determine the rules of its own proceedings, punish for contempt and disorderly behavior, and with the concurrence of two-thirds of all the members elected, expel a member; but no member shall be expelled a second time for the same cause.

Officers. Section 9. (1) Each house shall choose its presiding officers from its own members.

(2) The legislature shall provide by law for the establishment of a department of transportation and a transportation fund.

Journals; open doors; adjournments. Section 10. Each house shall keep a journal of its proceedings and publish the same, except such parts as require secrecy. The doors of each house shall be kept open except when the public welfare shall require secrecy. Neither house shall, without consent of the other, adjourn for more than three days.

Meeting of legislature. Section 11. The legislature shall meet at the seat of government at such time as shall be provided by law, unless convened by the governor in special session, and when so convened no business shall be transacted except as shall be necessary to accomplish the special purposes for which it was convened.

Ineligibility of legislators to office. Section 12. No member of the legislature shall, during the term for which he was elected, be appointed or elected to any civil office in the state, which shall have been created, or the emoluments of which shall have been increased, during the term for which he was elected.

Ineligibility of federal officers. Section 13. No person being a member of congress, or holding any military or civil office under the United States, shall be eligible to a seat in the legislature; and if any person shall, after his election as a member of the legislature, be elected to congress, or be appointed to any office, civil or military, under the government of the United States, his acceptance thereof shall vacate his seat. This restriction shall not prohibit a legislator from accepting short periods of active duty as a member of the reserve or from serving in the armed forces during any emergency declared by the executive.

Filling vacancies. Section 14. The governor shall issue writs of election to fill such vacancies as may occur in either house of the legislature.

Exemption from arrest and civil process. Section 15. Members of the legislature shall in all cases, except treason, felony and breach of the peace, be privileged from arrest; nor shall they be subject to any civil process, during the session of the legislature, nor for fifteen days next before the commencement and after the termination of each session.

Privilege in debate. Section 16. No member of the legislature shall be liable in any civil action, or criminal prosecution whatever, for words spoken in debate.

Enactment of laws. Section 17. (1) The style of all laws of the state shall be "The people of the state of Wisconsin, represented in senate and assembly, do enact as follows:".

(2) No law shall be enacted except by bill. No law shall be in force until published.

(3) The legislature shall provide by law for the speedy publication of all laws.

Title of private bills. Section 18. No private or local bill which may be passed by the legislature shall embrace more than one subject, and that shall be expressed in the title.

Origin of bills. Section 19. Any bill may originate in either house of the legislature, and a bill passed by one house may be amended by the other.

Yeas and nays. Section 20. The yeas and nays of the members of either house on any question shall, at the request of one-sixth of those present, be entered on the journal.

Powers of county boards. Section 22. The legislature may confer upon the boards of supervisors of the several counties of the state such powers of a local, legislative and administrative character as they shall from time to time prescribe.

Town and county government. Section 23. The legislature shall establish but one system of town government, which shall be as nearly uniform as practicable; but the legislature may provide for the election at large once in every 4 years of a chief executive officer in any county with such powers of an administrative character as they may from time to time prescribe in accordance with this section and shall establish one or more systems of county government.

Chief executive officer to approve or veto resolutions or ordinances; proceedings on veto. Section 23a. Every resolution or ordinance passed by the county board in any county shall, before it becomes effective, be presented to the chief executive officer. If he approves, he shall sign it; if not, he shall return it with his objections, which objections shall be entered at large upon the journal and the board shall proceed to reconsider the matter. Appropriations may be approved in whole or in part by the chief executive officer and the part approved shall become law, and the part objected to shall be returned in the same manner as provided for in other resolutions or ordinances. If, after such reconsideration, two-thirds of the members-elect of the county board agree to pass the resolution or ordinance or the part of the resolution or ordinance objected to, it shall become effective on the date prescribed but not earlier than the date of passage following reconsideration. In all such cases, the votes of the members of the county board shall be determined by ayes and noes and the names of the members voting for or against the resolution or ordinance or the part thereof objected to shall be entered on the journal. If any resolution or ordinance is not returned by the chief executive officer to the county board at its first meeting occurring not less than 6 days, Sundays excepted, after it has been presented to him, it shall become effective unless the county board has recessed or adjourned for a period in excess of 60 days, in which case it shall not be effective without his approval.

Gambling. Section 24. (1) Except as provided in this section, the legislature may not authorize gambling in any form.

(2) Except as otherwise provided by law, the following activities do not constitute consideration as an element of gambling:

(a) To listen to or watch a television or radio program.

(b) To fill out a coupon or entry blank, whether or not proof of purchase is required.

(c) To visit a mercantile establishment or other place without being required to make a purchase or pay an admittance fee.

(3) The legislature may authorize the following bingo games licensed by the state, but all profits shall accrue to the licensed organization and no salaries, fees or profits may be paid to any other organization or person: bingo games operated by religious, charitable, service, fraternal or veterans' organizations or those to which contributions are deductible for federal or state income tax purposes. All moneys received by the state that are attributable to bingo games shall be used for property tax relief for residents of this state as provided by law. The distribution of moneys that are attributable to bingo games may not vary based on the income or age of the person provided the property tax relief. The distribution of moneys that are attributable to bingo games shall not be subject to the uniformity requirement of section 1 of article VIII. In this subsection, the distribution of all moneys attributable to bingo games shall include any earnings on the moneys received by the state that are attributable to bingo games, but shall not include any moneys used for the regulation of, and enforcement of law relating to, bingo games.

(4) The legislature may authorize the following raffle games licensed by the state, but all profits shall accrue to the licensed local organization and no salaries, fees or profits may be paid to any other organization or person: raffle games operated by local religious, charitable, service, fraternal or veterans' organizations or those to which contributions are deductible for federal or state income tax purposes. The legislature shall limit the number of raffles conducted by any such organization.

(5) This section shall not prohibit pari-mutuel on-track betting as provided by law. The state may not own or operate any facility or enterprise for pari-mutuel betting, or lease any state-owned land to any other owner or operator for such purposes. All moneys received by the state that are attributable to pari-mutuel on-track betting shall be used for property tax relief for residents of this state as provided by law. The distribution of moneys that are attributable to pari-mutuel on-track betting may not vary based on the

income or age of the person provided the property tax relief. The distribution of moneys that are attributable to pari-mutuel on-track betting shall not be subject to the uniformity requirement of section 1 of article VIII. In this subsection, the distribution of all moneys attributable to pari-mutuel on-track betting shall include any earnings on the moneys received by the state that are attributable to pari-mutuel on-track betting, but shall not include any moneys used for the regulation of, and enforcement of law relating to, pari-mutuel on-track betting.

(6) (a) The legislature may authorize the creation of a lottery to be operated by the state as provided by law. The expenditure of public funds or of revenues derived from lottery operations to engage in promotional advertising of the Wisconsin state lottery is prohibited. Any advertising of the state lottery shall indicate the odds of a specific lottery ticket to be selected as the winning ticket for each prize amount offered. The net proceeds of the state lottery shall be deposited in the treasury of the state, to be used for property tax relief for residents of this state as provided by law. The distribution of the net proceeds of the state lottery may not vary based on the income or age of the person provided the property tax relief. The distribution of the net proceeds of the state lottery shall not be subject to the uniformity requirement of section 1 of article VIII. In this paragraph, the distribution of the net proceeds of the state lottery shall include any earnings on the net proceeds of the state lottery.

(b) The lottery authorized under par. (a) shall be an enterprise that entitles the player, by purchasing a ticket, to participate in a game of chance if: 1) the winning tickets are randomly predetermined and the player reveals preprinted numbers or symbols from which it can be immediately determined whether the ticket is a winning ticket entitling the player to win a prize as prescribed in the features and procedures for the game, including an opportunity to win a prize in a secondary or subsequent chance drawing or game; or 2) the ticket is evidence of the numbers or symbols selected by the player or, at the player's option, selected by a computer, and the player becomes entitled to a prize as prescribed in the features and procedures for the game, including an opportunity to win a prize in a secondary or subsequent chance drawing or game if some or all of the player's symbols or numbers are selected in a chance drawing or game, if the player's ticket is randomly selected by the computer at the time of purchase or if the ticket is selected in a chance drawing.

(c) Notwithstanding the authorization of a state lottery under par. (a), the following games, or games simulating any of the following games, may not be conducted by the state as a lottery: 1) any game in which winners are selected based on the results of a race or sporting event; 2) any banking card game, including blackjack, baccarat or chemin de fer; 3) poker; 4) roulette; 5) craps or any other game that involves rolling dice; 6) keno; 7) bingo 21, bingo jack, bingolet or bingo craps; 8) any game of chance that is placed on a slot machine or any mechanical, electromechanical or electronic device that is generally available to be played at a gambling casino; 9) any game or device that is commonly known as a video game of chance or a video gaming machine or that is commonly considered to be a video gambling machine, unless such machine is a video device operated by the state in a game authorized under par. (a) to permit the sale of tickets through retail outlets under contract with the state and the device does not determine or indicate whether the player has won a prize, other than by verifying that the player's ticket or some or all of the player's symbols or numbers on the player's ticket have been selected in a chance drawing, or by verifying that the player's ticket has been randomly selected by a central system computer at the time of purchase; 10) any game that is similar to a game listed in this paragraph; or 11) any other game that is commonly considered to be a form of gambling and is not, or is not substantially similar to, a game conducted by the state under par. (a). No game conducted by the state under par. (a) may permit a player of the game to purchase a ticket, or to otherwise participate in the game, from a residence by using a computer, telephone or other form of electronic, telecommunication, video or technological aid.

Stationery and printing. Section 25. The legislature shall provide by law that all stationery required for the use of the state, and all printing authorized and required by them to be done for their use, or for the state, shall be let by contract to the lowest bidder, but the legislature may establish a maximum price; no member of the legislature or other state officer shall be interested, either directly or indirectly, in any such contract.

Extra compensation; salary change. Section 26. **(1)** The legislature may not grant any extra compensation to a public officer, agent, servant or contractor after the services have been rendered or the contract has been entered into.

(2) Except as provided in this subsection, the compensation of a public officer may not be increased or diminished during the term of office:

(a) When any increase or decrease in the compensation of justices of the supreme court or judges of any court of record becomes effective as to any such justice or judge, it shall be effective from such date as to every such justice or judge.

(b) Any increase in the compensation of members of the legislature shall take effect, for all senators and representatives to the assembly, after the next general election beginning with the new assembly term.

(3) Subsection (1) shall not apply to increased benefits for persons who have been or shall be granted benefits of any kind under a retirement system when such increased benefits are provided by a legislative act passed on a call of ayes and noes by a three-fourths vote of all the members elected to both houses of the legislature and such act provides for sufficient state funds to cover the costs of the increased benefits.

Suits against state. Section 27. The legislature shall direct by law in what manner and in what courts suits may be brought against the state.

Oath of office. Section 28. Members of the legislature, and all officers, executive and judicial, except such inferior officers as may be by law exempted, shall before they enter upon the duties of their respective offices, take and subscribe an oath or affirmation to support the constitution of the United States and the constitution of the state of Wisconsin, and faithfully to discharge the duties of their respective offices to the best of their ability.

Militia. Section 29. The legislature shall determine what persons shall constitute the militia of the state, and may provide for organizing and disciplining the same in such manner as shall be prescribed by law.

Elections by legislature. Section 30. All elections made by the legislature shall be by roll call vote entered in the journals.

Special and private laws prohibited. Section 31. The legislature is prohibited from enacting any special or private laws in the following cases:

(1) For changing the names of persons, constituting one person the heir at law of another or granting any divorce.

(2) For laying out, opening or altering highways, except in cases of state roads extending into more than one county, and military roads to aid in the construction of which lands may be granted by congress.

(3) For authorizing persons to keep ferries across streams at points wholly within this state.

(4) For authorizing the sale or mortgage of real or personal property of minors or others under disability.

(5) For locating or changing any county seat.

(6) For assessment or collection of taxes or for extending the time for the collection thereof.

(7) For granting corporate powers or privileges, except to cities.

(8) For authorizing the apportionment of any part of the school fund.

(9) For incorporating any city, town or village, or to amend the charter thereof.

General laws on enumerated subjects. Section 32. The legislature may provide by general law for the treatment of any subject for which lawmaking is prohibited by section 31 of this article. Subject to reasonable classifications, such laws shall be uniform in their operation throughout the state.

Auditing of state accounts. Section 33. The legislature shall provide for the auditing of state accounts and may establish such offices and prescribe such duties for the same as it shall deem necessary.

Continuity of civil government. Section 34. The legislature, in order to ensure continuity of state and local governmental operations in periods of emergency resulting from enemy action in the form of an attack, shall (1) forthwith provide for prompt and temporary succession to the powers and duties of public offices, of whatever nature and whether filled by election or appointment, the incumbents of which may become unavailable for carrying on the powers and duties of such offices, and (2) adopt such other measures as may be necessary and proper for attaining the objectives of this section.

ARTICLE V—Executive

Governor; lieutenant governor; term. Section 1. The executive power shall be vested in a governor who shall hold office for 4 years; a lieutenant governor shall be elected at the same time and for the same term.

Eligibility. Section 2. No person except a citizen of the United States and a qualified elector of the state shall be eligible to the office of governor or lieutenant governor.

Election. Section 3. The governor and lieutenant governor shall be elected by the qualified electors of the state at the times and places of choosing members of the legislature. They shall be chosen jointly, by the casting by each voter of a single vote applicable to both offices beginning with the general election in 1970. The persons respectively having the highest number of votes cast jointly for them for governor and lieutenant governor shall be elected; but in case two or more slates shall have an equal and the highest number of votes for governor and lieutenant governor, the two houses of the legislature, at its next annual session shall forthwith, by joint ballot, choose one of the slates so having an equal and the highest number of votes for governor and lieutenant governor. The returns of election for governor and lieutenant governor shall be made in such manner as shall be provided by law.

Powers and duties. Section 4. The governor shall be commander in chief of the military and naval forces of the state. He shall have power to convene the legislature on extraordinary occasions, and in case of invasion, or danger from the prevalence of contagious disease at the seat of government, he may convene them at any other suitable place within the state. He shall communicate to the legislature, at every session, the condition of the state, and recommend such matters to them for their consideration as he may deem expedient. He shall transact all necessary business with the officers of the government, civil and military. He shall expedite all such measures as may be resolved upon by the legislature, and shall take care that the laws be faithfully executed.

Pardoning power. Section 6. The governor shall have power to grant reprieves, commutations and pardons, after conviction, for all offenses, except treason and cases of impeachment, upon such conditions and with such restrictions and limitations as he may think proper, subject to such regulations as may be provided by law relative to the manner of applying for pardons. Upon conviction for treason he shall have the power to suspend the execution of the sentence until the case shall be reported to the legislature at its next meeting, when the legislature shall either pardon, or commute the sentence, direct the execution of the sentence, or grant a further reprieve. He shall annually communicate to the legislature each case of reprieve, commutation or pardon granted, stating the name of the convict, the crime of which he was convicted, the sentence and its date, and the date of the commutation, pardon or reprieve, with his reasons for granting the same.

Lieutenant governor, when governor. Section 7. (1) Upon the governor's death, resignation or removal from office, the lieutenant governor shall become governor for the balance of the unexpired term.

(2) If the governor is absent from this state, impeached, or from mental or physical disease, becomes incapable of performing the duties of the office, the lieutenant governor shall serve as acting governor for the balance of the unexpired term or until the governor returns, the disability ceases or the impeachment is vacated. But when the governor, with the consent of the legislature, shall be out of this state in time of war at the head of the state's military force, the governor shall continue as commander in chief of the military force.

Secretary of state, when governor. Section 8. **(1)** If there is a vacancy in the office of lieutenant governor and the governor dies, resigns or is removed from office, the secretary of state shall become governor for the balance of the unexpired term.

(2) If there is a vacancy in the office of lieutenant governor and the governor is absent from this state, impeached, or from mental or physical disease becomes incapable of performing the duties of the office, the secretary of state shall serve as acting governor for the balance of the unexpired term or until the governor returns, the disability ceases or the impeachment is vacated.

Governor to approve or veto bills; proceedings on veto. Section 10. **(1)** (a) Every bill which shall have passed the legislature shall, before it becomes a law, be presented to the governor.

(b) If the governor approves and signs the bill, the bill shall become law. Appropriation bills may be approved in whole or in part by the governor, and the part approved shall become law.

(c) In approving an appropriation bill in part, the governor may not create a new word by rejecting individual letters in the words of the enrolled bill, and may not create a new sentence by combining parts of 2 or more sentences of the enrolled bill.

(2) (a) If the governor rejects the bill, the governor shall return the bill, together with the objections in writing, to the house in which the bill originated. The house of origin shall enter the objections at large upon the journal and proceed to reconsider the bill. If, after such reconsideration, two-thirds of the members present agree to pass the bill notwithstanding the objections of the governor, it shall be sent, together with the objections, to the other house, by which it shall likewise be reconsidered, and if approved by two-thirds of the members present it shall become law.

(b) The rejected part of an appropriation bill, together with the governor's objections in writing, shall be returned to the house in which the bill originated. The house of origin shall enter the objections at large upon the journal and proceed to reconsider the rejected part of the appropriation bill. If, after such reconsideration, two-thirds of the members present agree to approve the rejected part notwithstanding the objections of the governor, it shall be sent, together with the objections, to the other house, by which it shall likewise be reconsidered, and if approved by two-thirds of the members present the rejected part shall become law.

(c) In all such cases the votes of both houses shall be determined by ayes and noes, and the names of the members voting for or against passage of the bill or the rejected part of the bill notwithstanding the objections of the governor shall be entered on the journal of each house respectively.

(3) Any bill not returned by the governor within 6 days (Sundays excepted) after it shall have been presented to the governor shall be law unless the legislature, by final adjournment, prevents the bill's return, in which case it shall not be law.

ARTICLE VI—Administrative

Election of secretary of state, treasurer and attorney general; term. Section 1. The qualified electors of this state, at the times and places of choosing the members of the legislature, shall in 1970 and every 4 years thereafter elect a secretary of state, treasurer and attorney general who shall hold their offices for 4 years.

Secretary of state; duties, compensation. Section 2. The secretary of state shall keep a fair record of the official acts of the legislature and executive department of the state, and shall, when required, lay the same and all matters relative thereto before either branch of the legislature. He shall perform such other duties as shall be assigned him by law. He shall receive as a compensation for his services yearly such sum as shall be provided by law, and shall keep his office at the seat of government.

Treasurer and attorney general; duties, compensation. Section 3. The powers, duties and compensation of the treasurer and attorney general shall be prescribed by law.

County officers; election, terms, removal; vacancies. Section 4. (1) (a) Except as provided in pars. (b) and (c) and sub. (2), coroners, registers of deeds, district attorneys, and all other elected county officers, except judicial officers, sheriffs, and chief executive officers, shall be chosen by the electors of the respective counties once in every 2 years.

(b) Beginning with the first general election at which the governor is elected which occurs after the ratification of this paragraph, sheriffs shall be chosen by the electors of the respective counties, or by the electors of all of the respective counties comprising each combination of counties combined by the legislature for that purpose, for the term of 4 years and coroners in counties in which there is a coroner shall be chosen by the electors of the respective counties, or by the electors of all of the respective counties comprising each combination of counties combined by the legislature for that purpose, for the term of 4 years.

(c) Beginning with the first general election at which the president is elected which occurs after the ratification of this paragraph, district attorneys, registers of deeds, county clerks, and treasurers shall be chosen by the electors of the respective counties, or by the electors of all of the respective counties comprising each combination of counties combined by the legislature for that purpose, for the term of 4 years and surveyors in counties in which the office of surveyor is filled by election shall be chosen by the electors of the respective counties, or by the electors of all of the respective counties comprising each combination of counties combined by the legislature for that purpose, for the term of 4 years.

(2) The offices of coroner and surveyor in counties having a population of 500,000 or more are abolished. Counties not having a population of 500,000 shall have the option of retaining the elective office of coroner or instituting a medical examiner system. Two or more counties may institute a joint medical examiner system.

(3) (a) Sheriffs may not hold any other partisan office.

(b) Sheriffs may be required by law to renew their security from time to time, and in default of giving such new security their office shall be deemed vacant.

(4) The governor may remove any elected county officer mentioned in this section except a county clerk, treasurer, or surveyor, giving to the officer a copy of the charges and an opportunity of being heard.

(5) All vacancies in the offices of coroner, register of deeds or district attorney shall be filled by appointment. The person appointed to fill a vacancy shall hold office only for the unexpired portion of the term to which appointed and until a successor shall be elected and qualified.

(6) When a vacancy occurs in the office of sheriff, the vacancy shall be filled by appointment of the governor, and the person appointed shall serve until his or her successor is elected and qualified.

ARTICLE VII—Judiciary

Impeachment; trial. Section 1. The court for the trial of impeachments shall be composed of the senate. The assembly shall have the power of impeaching all civil officers of this state for corrupt conduct in office, or for crimes and misdemeanors; but a majority of all the members elected shall concur in an impeachment. On the trial of an impeachment against the governor, the lieutenant governor shall not act as a member of the court. No judicial officer shall exercise his office, after he shall have been impeached, until his acquittal. Before the trial of an impeachment the members of the court shall take an oath or affirmation truly and impartially to try the impeachment according to evidence; and no person shall be convicted without the concurrence of two-thirds of the members present. Judgment in cases of impeachment shall not extend further than to removal from office, or removal from office and disqualification to hold any office of honor, profit or trust under the state; but the party impeached shall be liable to indictment, trial and punishment according to law.

Court system. Section 2. The judicial power of this state shall be vested in a unified court system consisting of one supreme court, a court of appeals, a circuit court, such trial courts of general uniform statewide jurisdiction as the legislature may create by law, and a municipal court if authorized by the legislature under section 14.

Supreme court: jurisdiction. Section 3. **(1)** The supreme court shall have superintending and administrative authority over all courts.

(2) The supreme court has appellate jurisdiction over all courts and may hear original actions and proceedings. The supreme court may issue all writs necessary in aid of its jurisdiction.

(3) The supreme court may review judgments and orders of the court of appeals, may remove cases from the court of appeals and may accept cases on certification by the court of appeals.

Supreme court: election, chief justice, court system administration. Section 4. **(1)** The supreme court shall have 7 members who shall be known as justices of the supreme court. Justices shall be elected for 10-year terms of office commencing with the August 1 next succeeding the election. Only one justice may be elected in any year. Any 4 justices shall constitute a quorum for the conduct of the court's business.

(2) The chief justice of the supreme court shall be elected for a term of 2 years by a majority of the justices then serving on the court. The justice so designated as chief justice may, irrevocably, decline to serve as chief justice or resign as chief justice but continue to serve as a justice of the supreme court.

(3) The chief justice of the supreme court shall be the administrative head of the judicial system and shall exercise this administrative authority pursuant to procedures adopted by the supreme court. The chief justice may assign any judge of a court of record to aid in the proper disposition of judicial business in any court of record except the supreme court.

Court of appeals. Section 5. **(1)** The legislature shall by law combine the judicial circuits of the state into one or more districts for the court of appeals and shall designate in each district the locations where the appeals court shall sit for the convenience of litigants.

(2) For each district of the appeals court there shall be chosen by the qualified electors of the district one or more appeals judges as prescribed by law, who shall sit as prescribed by law. Appeals judges shall be elected for 6-year terms and shall reside in the district from which elected. No alteration of district or circuit boundaries shall have the effect of removing an appeals judge from office during the judge's term. In case of an increase in the number of appeals judges, the first judge or judges shall be elected for full terms unless the legislature prescribes a shorter initial term for staggering of terms.

(3) The appeals court shall have such appellate jurisdiction in the district, including jurisdiction to review administrative proceedings, as the legislature may provide by law, but shall have no original jurisdiction other than by prerogative writ. The appeals court may issue all writs necessary in aid of its jurisdiction and shall have supervisory authority over all actions and proceedings in the courts in the district.

Circuit court: boundaries. Section 6. The legislature shall prescribe by law the number of judicial circuits, making them as compact and convenient as practicable, and bounding them by county lines. No alteration of circuit boundaries shall have the effect of removing a circuit judge from office during the judge's term. In case of an increase of circuits, the first judge or judges shall be elected.

Circuit court: election. Section 7. For each circuit there shall be chosen by the qualified electors thereof one or more circuit judges as prescribed by law. Circuit judges shall be elected for 6-year terms and shall reside in the circuit from which elected.

Circuit court: jurisdiction. Section 8. Except as otherwise provided by law, the circuit court shall have original jurisdiction in all matters civil and criminal within this state and such appellate jurisdiction in the circuit as the legislature may prescribe by law. The circuit court may issue all writs necessary in aid of its jurisdiction.

Judicial elections, vacancies. Section 9. When a vacancy occurs in the office of justice of the supreme court or judge of any court of record, the vacancy shall be filled by appointment by the governor, which shall continue until a successor is elected and qualified. There shall be no election for a justice or judge at the partisan general election for state or county officers, nor within 30 days either before or after such election.

Judges: eligibility to office. Section 10. (1) No justice of the supreme court or judge of any court of record shall hold any other office of public trust, except a judicial office, during the term for which elected. No person shall be eligible to the office of judge who shall not, at the time of election or appointment, be a qualified elector within the jurisdiction for which chosen.

(2) Justices of the supreme court and judges of the courts of record shall receive such compensation as the legislature may authorize by law, but may not receive fees of office.

Disciplinary proceedings. Section 11. Each justice or judge shall be subject to reprimand, censure, suspension, removal for cause or for disability, by the supreme court pursuant to procedures established by the legislature by law. No justice or judge removed for cause shall be eligible for reappointment or temporary service. This section is alternative to, and cumulative with, the methods of removal provided in sections 1 and 13 of this article and section 12 of article XIII.

Clerks of circuit and supreme courts. Section 12. (1) There shall be a clerk of circuit court chosen in each county organized for judicial purposes by the qualified electors thereof, who, except as provided in sub. (2), shall hold office for two years, subject to removal as provided by law.

(2) Beginning with the first general election at which the governor is elected which occurs after the ratification of this subsection, a clerk of circuit court shall be chosen by the electors of each county, for the term of 4 years, subject to removal as provided by law.

(3) In case of a vacancy, the judge of the circuit court may appoint a clerk until the vacancy is filled by an election.

(4) The clerk of circuit court shall give such security as the legislature requires by law.

(5) The supreme court shall appoint its own clerk, and may appoint a clerk of circuit court to be the clerk of the supreme court.

Justices and judges: removal by address. Section 13. Any justice or judge may be removed from office by address of both houses of the legislature, if two-thirds of all the members elected to each house concur therein, but no removal shall be made by virtue of this section unless the justice or judge complained of is served with a copy of the charges, as the ground of address, and has had an opportunity of being heard. On the question of removal, the ayes and noes shall be entered on the journals.

Municipal court. Section 14. The legislature by law may authorize each city, village and town to establish a municipal court. All municipal courts shall have uniform jurisdiction limited to actions and proceedings arising under ordinances of the municipality in which established. Judges of municipal courts may receive such compensation as provided by the municipality in which established, but may not receive fees of office.

Justices and judges: eligibility for office; retirement. Section 24. (1) To be eligible for the office of supreme court justice or judge of any court of record, a person must be an attorney licensed to practice law in this state and have been so licensed for 5 years immediately prior to election or appointment.

(2) Unless assigned temporary service under subsection (3), no person may serve as a supreme court justice or judge of a court of record beyond the July 31 following the date on which such person attains that age, of not less than 70 years, which the legislature shall prescribe by law.

(3) A person who has served as a supreme court justice or judge of a court of record may, as provided by law, serve as a judge of any court of record except the supreme court on a temporary basis if assigned by the chief justice of the supreme court.

ARTICLE VIII—Finance

Rule of taxation uniform; income, privilege and occupation taxes. Section 1. The rule of taxation shall be uniform but the legislature may empower cities, villages or towns to collect and return taxes on real estate located therein by optional methods. Taxes shall be levied upon such property with such classifications as to forests and minerals including or separate or severed from the land, as the legislature shall prescribe. Taxation of agricultural land and undeveloped land, both as defined by law, need not be uniform with the taxation of each other nor with the taxation of other real property. Taxation of merchants' stock-in-trade, manufacturers' materials and finished products, and livestock need not be uniform with the taxation of real property and other personal property, but the taxation of all such merchants' stock-in-trade, manufacturers' materials and finished products and livestock shall be uniform, except that the legislature may provide that the value thereof shall be determined on an average basis. Taxes may also be imposed on incomes, privileges and occupations, which taxes may be graduated and progressive, and reasonable exemptions may be provided.

Appropriations; limitation. Section 2. No money shall be paid out of the treasury except in pursuance of an appropriation by law. No appropriation shall be made for the payment of any claim against the state except claims of the United States and judgments, unless filed within six years after the claim accrued.

Credit of state. Section 3. Except as provided in s. 7 (2) (a), the credit of the state shall never be given, or loaned, in aid of any individual, association or corporation.

Contracting state debts. Section 4. The state shall never contract any public debt except in the cases and manner herein provided.

Annual tax levy to equal expenses. Section 5. The legislature shall provide for an annual tax sufficient to defray the estimated expenses of the state for each year; and whenever the expenses of any year shall exceed the income, the legislature shall provide for levying a tax for the ensuing year, sufficient, with other sources of income, to pay the deficiency as well as the estimated expenses of such ensuing year.

Public debt for extraordinary expense; taxation. Section 6. For the purpose of defraying extraordinary expenditures the state may contract public debts (but such debts shall never in the aggregate exceed one hundred thousand dollars). Every such debt shall be authorized by law, for some purpose or purposes to be distinctly specified therein; and the vote of a majority of all the members elected to each house, to be taken by yeas and nays, shall be necessary to the passage of such law; and every such law shall provide for levying an annual tax sufficient to pay the annual interest of such debt and the principal within five years from the passage of such law, and shall specially appropriate the proceeds of such taxes to the payment of such principal and interest; and such appropriation shall not be repealed, nor the taxes be postponed or diminished, until the principal and interest of such debt shall have been wholly paid.

Public debt for public defense; bonding for public purposes. Section 7. (1) The legislature may also borrow money to repel invasion, suppress insurrection, or defend the state in time of war; but the money thus raised shall be applied exclusively to the object for which the loan was authorized, or to the repayment of the debt thereby created.

(2) Any other provision of this constitution to the contrary notwithstanding:

(a) The state may contract public debt and pledges to the payment thereof its full faith, credit and taxing power:

1. To acquire, construct, develop, extend, enlarge or improve land, waters, property, highways, railways, buildings, equipment or facilities for public purposes.

2. To make funds available for veterans' housing loans.

(b) The aggregate public debt contracted by the state in any calendar year pursuant to paragraph (a) shall not exceed an amount equal to the lesser of:

1. Three-fourths of one per centum of the aggregate value of all taxable property in the state; or

2. Five per centum of the aggregate value of all taxable property in the state less the sum

of: a. the aggregate public debt of the state contracted pursuant to this section outstanding as of January 1 of such calendar year after subtracting therefrom the amount of sinking funds on hand on January 1 of such calendar year which are applicable exclusively to repayment of such outstanding public debt and, b. the outstanding indebtedness as of January 1 of such calendar year of any entity of the type described in paragraph (d) to the extent that such indebtedness is supported by or payable from payments out of the treasury of the state.

(c) The state may contract public debt, without limit, to fund or refund the whole or any part of any public debt contracted pursuant to paragraph (a), including any premium payable with respect thereto and any interest to accrue thereon, or to fund or refund the whole or any part of any indebtedness incurred prior to January 1, 1972, by any entity of the type described in paragraph (d), including any premium payable with respect thereto and any interest to accrue thereon.

(d) No money shall be paid out of the treasury, with respect to any lease, sublease or other agreement entered into after January 1, 1971, to the Wisconsin State Agencies Building Corporation, Wisconsin State Colleges Building Corporation, Wisconsin State Public Building Corporation, Wisconsin University Building Corporation or any similar entity existing or operating for similar purposes pursuant to which such nonprofit corporation or such other entity undertakes to finance or provide a facility for use or occupancy by the state or an agency, department or instrumentality thereof.

(e) The legislature shall prescribe all matters relating to the contracting of public debt pursuant to paragraph (a), including: the public purposes for which public debt may be contracted; by vote of a majority of the members elected to each of the 2 houses of the legislature, the amount of public debt which may be contracted for any class of such purposes; the public debt or other indebtedness which may be funded or refunded; the kinds of notes, bonds or other evidence of public debt which may be issued by the state; and the manner in which the aggregate value of all taxable property in the state shall be determined.

(f) The full faith, credit and taxing power of the state are pledged to the payment of all public debt created on behalf of the state pursuant to this section and the legislature shall provide by appropriation for the payment of the interest upon and instalments of principal of all such public debt as the same falls due, but, in any event, suit may be brought against the state to compel such payment.

(g) At any time after January 1, 1972, by vote of a majority of the members elected to each of the 2 houses of the legislature, the legislature may declare that an emergency exists and submit to the people a proposal to authorize the state to contract a specific amount of public debt for a purpose specified in such proposal, without regard to the limit provided in paragraph (b). Any such authorization shall be effective if approved by a majority of the electors voting thereon. Public debt contracted pursuant to such authorization shall thereafter be deemed to have been contracted pursuant to paragraph (a), but neither such public debt nor any public debt contracted to fund or refund such public debt shall be considered in computing the debt limit provided in paragraph (b). Not more than one such authorization shall be thus made in any 2-year period.

Vote on fiscal bills; quorum. Section 8. On the passage in either house of the legislature of any law which imposes, continues or renews a tax, or creates a debt or charge, or makes, continues or renews an appropriation of public or trust money, or releases, discharges or commutes a claim or demand of the state, the question shall be taken by yeas and nays, which shall be duly entered on the journal; and three-fifths of all the members elected to such house shall in all such cases be required to constitute a quorum therein.

Evidences of public debt. Section 9. No scrip, certificate, or other evidence of state debt, whatsoever, shall be issued, except for such debts as are authorized by the sixth and seventh sections of this article.

Internal improvements. Section 10. Except as further provided in this section, the state may never contract any debt for works of internal improvement, or be a party in carrying on such works.

(1) Whenever grants of land or other property shall have been made to the state, especially dedicated by the grant to particular works of internal improvement, the state may carry on such particular works and shall devote thereto the avails of such grants, and may pledge or appropriate the revenues derived from such works in aid of their completion.

(2) The state may appropriate money in the treasury or to be thereafter raised by taxation for:

(a) The construction or improvement of public highways.

(b) The development, improvement and construction of airports or other aeronautical projects.

(c) The acquisition, improvement or construction of veterans' housing.

(d) The improvement of port facilities.

(e) The acquisition, development, improvement or construction of railways and other railroad facilities.

(3) The state may appropriate moneys for the purpose of acquiring, preserving and developing the forests of the state. Of the moneys appropriated under the authority of this subsection in any one year an amount not to exceed two-tenths of one mill of the taxable property of the state as determined by the last preceding state assessment may be raised by a tax on property.

Transportation Fund. Section 11. All funds collected by the state from any taxes or fees levied or imposed for the licensing of motor vehicle operators, for the titling, licensing, or registration of motor vehicles, for motor vehicle fuel, or for the use of roadways, highways, or bridges, and from taxes and fees levied or imposed for aircraft, airline property, or aviation fuel or for railroads or railroad property shall be deposited only into the transportation fund or with a trustee for the benefit of the department of transportation or the holders of transportation-related revenue bonds, except for collections from taxes or fees in existence on December 31, 2010, that were not being deposited in the transportation fund on that date. None of the funds collected or received by the state from any source and deposited into the transportation fund shall be lapsed, further transferred, or appropriated to any program that is not directly administered by the department of transportation in furtherance of the department's responsibility for the planning, promotion, and protection of all transportation systems in the state except for programs for which there was an appropriation from the transportation fund on December 31, 2010. In this section, the term "motor vehicle" does not include any all-terrain vehicles, snowmobiles, or watercraft.

ARTICLE IX—Eminent domain and property of the state

Jurisdiction on rivers and lakes; navigable waters. Section 1. The state shall have concurrent jurisdiction on all rivers and lakes bordering on this state so far as such rivers or lakes shall form a common boundary to the state and any other state or territory now or hereafter to be formed, and bounded by the same; and the river Mississippi and the navigable waters leading into the Mississippi and St. Lawrence, and the carrying places between the same, shall be common highways and forever free, as well to the inhabitants of the state as to the citizens of the United States, without any tax, impost or duty therefor.

Territorial property. Section 2. The title to all lands and other property which have accrued to the territory of Wisconsin by grant, gift, purchase, forfeiture, escheat or otherwise shall vest in the state of Wisconsin.

Ultimate property in lands; escheats. Section 3. The people of the state, in their right of sovereignty, are declared to possess the ultimate property in and to all lands within the jurisdiction of the state; and all lands the title to which shall fail from a defect of heirs shall revert or escheat to the people.

ARTICLE X—Education

Superintendent of public instruction. Section 1. The supervision of public instruction shall be vested in a state superintendent and such other officers as the legislature shall direct; and their qualifications, powers, duties and compensation shall be prescribed by law. The state superintendent shall be chosen by the qualified electors of the state at the same time and in the same manner as members of the supreme court, and shall hold office for 4 years from the succeeding first Monday in July. The term of office, time and manner of electing or appointing all other officers of supervision of public instruction shall be fixed by law.

School fund created; income applied. Section 2. The proceeds of all lands that have been or hereafter may be granted by the United States to this state for educational purposes (except the lands heretofore granted for the purposes of a university) and all moneys and the clear proceeds of all property that may accrue to the state by forfeiture or escheat; and the clear proceeds of all fines collected in the several counties for any breach of the penal laws, and all moneys arising from any grant to the state where the purposes of such grant are not specified, and the 500,000 acres of land to which the state is entitled by the provisions of an act of congress, entitled "An act to appropriate the proceeds of the sales of the public lands and to grant pre-emption rights," approved September 4, 1841; and also the 5 percent of the net proceeds of the public lands to which the state shall become entitled on admission into the union (if congress shall consent to such appropriation of the 2 grants last mentioned) shall be set apart as a separate fund to be called "the school fund," the interest of which and all other revenues derived from the school lands shall be exclusively applied to the following objects, to wit:

(1) To the support and maintenance of common schools, in each school district, and the purchase of suitable libraries and apparatus therefor.

(2) The residue shall be appropriated to the support and maintenance of academies and normal schools, and suitable libraries and apparatus therefor.

District schools; tuition; sectarian instruction; released time. Section 3. The legislature shall provide by law for the establishment of district schools, which shall be as nearly uniform as practicable; and such schools shall be free and without charge for tuition to all children between the ages of 4 and 20 years; and no sectarian instruction shall be allowed therein; but the legislature by law may, for the purpose of religious instruction outside the district schools, authorize the release of students during regular school hours.

Annual school tax. Section 4. Each town and city shall be required to raise by tax, annually, for the support of common schools therein, a sum not less than one-half the amount received by such town or city respectively for school purposes from the income of the school fund.

Income of school fund. Section 5. Provision shall be made by law for the distribution of the income of the school fund among the several towns and cities of the state for the support of common schools therein, in some just proportion to the number of children and youth resident therein between the ages of four and twenty years, and no appropriation shall be made from the school fund to any city or town for the year in which said city or town shall fail to raise such tax; nor to any school district for the year in which a school shall not be maintained at least three months.

State university; support. Section 6. Provision shall be made by law for the establishment of a state university at or near the seat of state government, and for connecting with the same, from time to time, such colleges in different parts of the state as the interests of education may require. The proceeds of all lands that have been or may hereafter be granted by the United States to the state for the support of a university shall be and remain a perpetual fund to be called "the university fund," the interest of which shall be appropriated to the support of the state university, and no sectarian instruction shall be allowed in such university.

Commissioners of public lands. Section 7. The secretary of state, treasurer and attorney general, shall constitute a board of commissioners for the sale of the school and university lands and for the investment of the funds arising therefrom. Any two of said commissioners shall be a quorum for the transaction of all business pertaining to the duties of their office.

Sale of public lands. Section 8. Provision shall be made by law for the sale of all school and university lands after they shall have been appraised; and when any portion of such lands shall be sold and the purchase money shall not be paid at the time of the sale, the commissioners shall take security by mortgage upon the lands sold for the sum remaining unpaid, with seven per cent interest thereon, payable annually at the office of the treasurer. The commissioners shall be authorized to execute a good and sufficient conveyance to all purchasers of such lands, and to discharge any mortgages taken as security, when the sum due thereon shall have been paid. The commissioners shall have power to withhold from sale any portion of such lands when they shall deem it expedient, and shall invest all moneys arising from the sale of such lands, as well as all other university and school funds, in such manner as the legislature shall provide, and shall give such security for the faithful performance of their duties as may be required by law.

ARTICLE XI—Corporations

Corporations; how formed. Section 1. Corporations without banking powers or privileges may be formed under general laws, but shall not be created by special act, except for municipal purposes. All general laws or special acts enacted under the provisions of this section may be altered or repealed by the legislature at any time after their passage.

Property taken by municipality. Section 2. No municipal corporation shall take private property for public use, against the consent of the owner, without the necessity thereof being first established in the manner prescribed by the legislature.

Municipal home rule; debt limit; tax to pay debt. Section 3. (1) Cities and villages organized pursuant to state law may determine their local affairs and government, subject only to this constitution and to such enactments of the legislature of statewide concern as with uniformity shall affect every city or every village. The method of such determination shall be prescribed by the legislature.

(2) No county, city, town, village, school district, sewerage district or other municipal corporation may become indebted in an amount that exceeds an allowable percentage of the taxable property located therein equalized for state purposes as provided by the legislature. In all cases the allowable percentage shall be 5 percent except as specified in pars. (a) and (b):

(a) For any city authorized to issue bonds for school purposes, an additional 10 percent shall be permitted for school purposes only, and in such cases the territory attached to the city for school purposes shall be included in the total taxable property supporting the bonds issued for school purposes.

(b) For any school district which offers no less than grades one to 12 and which at the time of incurring such debt is eligible for the highest level of school aids, 10 percent shall be permitted.

(3) Any county, city, town, village, school district, sewerage district or other municipal corporation incurring any indebtedness under sub. (2) shall, before or at the time of doing

so, provide for the collection of a direct annual tax sufficient to pay the interest on such debt as it falls due, and also to pay and discharge the principal thereof within 20 years from the time of contracting the same.

(4) When indebtedness under sub. (2) is incurred in the acquisition of lands by cities, or by counties or sewerage districts having a population of 150,000 or over, for public, municipal purposes, or for the permanent improvement thereof, or to purchase, acquire, construct, extend, add to or improve a sewage collection or treatment system which services all or a part of such city or county, the city, county or sewerage district incurring the indebtedness shall, before or at the time of so doing, provide for the collection of a direct annual tax sufficient to pay the interest on such debt as it falls due, and also to pay and discharge the principal thereof within a period not exceeding 50 years from the time of contracting the same.

(5) An indebtedness created for the purpose of purchasing, acquiring, leasing, constructing, extending, adding to, improving, conducting, controlling, operating or managing a public utility of a town, village, city or special district, and secured solely by the property or income of such public utility, and whereby no municipal liability is created, shall not be considered an indebtedness of such town, village, city or special district, and shall not be included in arriving at the debt limitation under sub. (2).

Acquisition of lands by state and subdivisions; sale of excess. Section 3a. The state or any of its counties, cities, towns or villages may acquire by gift, dedication, purchase, or condemnation lands for establishing, laying out, widening, enlarging, extending, and maintaining memorial grounds, streets, highways, squares, parkways, boulevards, parks, playgrounds, sites for public buildings, and reservations in and about and along and leading to any or all of the same; and after the establishment, layout, and completion of such improvements, may convey any such real estate thus acquired and not necessary for such improvements, with reservations concerning the future use and occupation of such real estate, so as to protect such public works and improvements, and their environs, and to preserve the view, appearance, light, air, and usefulness of such public works. If the governing body of a county, city, town or village elects to accept a gift or dedication of land made on condition that the land be devoted to a special purpose and the condition subsequently becomes impossible or impracticable, such governing body may by resolution or ordinance enacted by a two-thirds vote of its members elect either to grant the land back to the donor or dedicator or his heirs or accept from the donor or dedicator or his heirs a grant relieving the county, city, town or village of the condition; however, if the donor or dedicator or his heirs are unknown or cannot be found, such resolution or ordinance may provide for the commencement of proceedings in the manner and in the courts as the legislature shall designate for the purpose of relieving the county, city, town or village from the condition of the gift or dedication.

General banking law. Section 4. The legislature may enact a general banking law for the creation of banks, and for the regulation and supervision of the banking business.

ARTICLE XII—Amendments

Constitutional amendments. Section 1. Any amendment or amendments to this constitution may be proposed in either house of the legislature, and if the same shall be agreed to by a majority of the members elected to each of the two houses, such proposed amendment or amendments shall be entered on their journals, with the yeas and nays taken thereon, and referred to the legislature to be chosen at the next general election, and shall be published for three months previous to the time of holding such election; and if, in the legislature so next chosen, such proposed amendment or amendments shall be agreed to by a majority of all the members elected to each house, then it shall be the duty of the legislature to submit such proposed amendment or amendments to the people in such manner and at such time as the legislature shall prescribe; and if the people shall approve and ratify such amendment or amendments by a majority of the electors voting thereon, such amendment or amendments shall become part of the constitution; provided, that if more than one amendment be submitted, they shall be submitted in such manner that the people may vote for or against such amendments separately.

Constitutional conventions. Section 2. If at any time a majority of the senate and assembly shall deem it necessary to call a convention to revise or change this constitution, they shall recommend to the electors to vote for or against a convention at the next election for members of the legislature. And if it shall appear that a majority of the electors voting thereon have voted for a convention, the legislature shall, at its next session, provide for calling such convention.

ARTICLE XIII—Miscellaneous provisions

Political year; elections. Section 1. The political year for this state shall commence on the first Monday of January in each year, and the general election shall be held on the Tuesday next succeeding the first Monday of November in even-numbered years.

Eligibility to office. Section 3. (1) No member of congress and no person holding any office of profit or trust under the United States except postmaster, or under any foreign power, shall be eligible to any office of trust, profit or honor in this state.

(2) No person convicted of a felony, in any court within the United States, no person convicted in federal court of a crime designated, at the time of commission, under federal law as a misdemeanor involving a violation of public trust and no person convicted, in a court of a state, of a crime designated, at the time of commission, under the law of the state as a misdemeanor involving a violation of public trust shall be eligible to any office of trust, profit or honor in this state unless pardoned of the conviction.

(3) No person may seek to have placed on any ballot for a state or local elective office in this state the name of a person convicted of a felony, in any court within the United States, the name of a person convicted in federal court of a crime designated, at the time

of commission, under federal law as a misdemeanor involving a violation of public trust or the name of a person convicted, in a court of a state, of a crime designated, at the time of commission, under the law of the state as a misdemeanor involving a violation of public trust, unless the person named for the ballot has been pardoned of the conviction.

Great seal. Section 4. It shall be the duty of the legislature to provide a great seal for the state, which shall be kept by the secretary of state, and all official acts of the governor, his approbation of the laws excepted, shall be thereby authenticated.

Legislative officers. Section 6. The elective officers of the legislature, other than the presiding officers, shall be a chief clerk and a sergeant at arms, to be elected by each house.

Division of counties. Section 7. No county with an area of nine hundred square miles or less shall be divided or have any part stricken therefrom, without submitting the question to a vote of the people of the county, nor unless a majority of all the legal voters of the county voting on the question shall vote for the same.

Removal of county seats. Section 8. No county seat shall be removed until the point to which it is proposed to be removed shall be fixed by law, and a majority of the voters of the county voting on the question shall have voted in favor of its removal to such point.

Election or appointment of statutory officers. Section 9. All county officers whose election or appointment is not provided for by this constitution shall be elected by the electors of the respective counties, or appointed by the boards of supervisors, or other county authorities, as the legislature shall direct. All city, town and village officers whose election or appointment is not provided for by this constitution shall be elected by the electors of such cities, towns and villages, or of some division thereof, or appointed by such authorities thereof as the legislature shall designate for that purpose. All other officers whose election or appointment is not provided for by this constitution, and all officers whose offices may hereafter be created by law, shall be elected by the people or appointed, as the legislature may direct.

Vacancies in office. Section 10. (1) The legislature may declare the cases in which any office shall be deemed vacant, and also the manner of filling the vacancy, where no provision is made for that purpose in this constitution.

(2) Whenever there is a vacancy in the office of lieutenant governor, the governor shall nominate a successor to serve for the balance of the unexpired term, who shall take office after confirmation by the senate and by the assembly.

Passes, franks and privileges. Section 11. No person, association, copartnership, or corporation, shall promise, offer or give, for any purpose, to any political committee, or any member or employe thereof, to any candidate for, or incumbent of any office or position under the constitution or laws, or under any ordinance of any town or municipality, of this state, or to any person at the request or for the advantage of all or any of them, any free pass or frank, or any privilege withheld from any person, for the traveling accommodation or transportation of any person or property, or the transmission of any message or communication.

No political committee, and no member or employee thereof, no candidate for and no incumbent of any office or position under the constitution or laws, or under any ordinance of any town or municipality of this state, shall ask for, or accept, from any person, association, copartnership, or corporation, or use, in any manner, or for any purpose, any free pass or frank, or any privilege withheld from any person, for the traveling accommodation or transportation of any person or property, or the transmission of any message or communication.

Any violation of any of the above provisions shall be bribery and punished as provided by law, and if any officer or any member of the legislature be guilty thereof, his office shall become vacant.

No person within the purview of this act shall be privileged from testifying in relation to anything therein prohibited; and no person having so testified shall be liable to any prosecution or punishment for any offense concerning which he was required to give his testimony or produce any documentary evidence.

Notaries public and regular employees of a railroad or other public utilities who are candidates for or hold public offices for which the annual compensation is not more than three hundred dollars to whom no passes or privileges are extended beyond those which are extended to other regular employees of such corporations are excepted from the provisions of this section.

Recall of elective officers. Section 12. The qualified electors of the state, of any congressional, judicial or legislative district or of any county may petition for the recall of any incumbent elective officer after the first year of the term for which the incumbent was elected, by filing a petition with the filing officer with whom the nomination petition to the office in the primary is filed, demanding the recall of the incumbent.

(1) The recall petition shall be signed by electors equalling at least twenty-five percent of the vote cast for the office of governor at the last preceding election, in the state, county or district which the incumbent represents.

(2) The filing officer with whom the recall petition is filed shall call a recall election for the Tuesday of the 6th week after the date of filing the petition or, if that Tuesday is a legal holiday, on the first day after that Tuesday which is not a legal holiday.

(3) The incumbent shall continue to perform the duties of the office until the recall election results are officially declared.

(4) Unless the incumbent declines within 10 days after the filing of the petition, the incumbent shall without filing be deemed to have filed for the recall election. Other candidates may file for the office in the manner provided by law for special elections. For the purpose of conducting elections under this section:

(a) When more than 2 persons compete for a nonpartisan office, a recall primary shall be held. The 2 persons receiving the highest number of votes in the recall primary shall be the 2 candidates in the recall election, except that if any candidate receives a majority of the total number of votes cast in the recall primary, that candidate shall assume the office for the remainder of the term and a recall election shall not be held.

(b) For any partisan office, a recall primary shall be held for each political party which is by law entitled to a separate ballot and from which more than one candidate competes for the party's nomination in the recall election. The person receiving the highest number of votes in the recall primary for each political party shall be that party's candidate in the recall election. Independent candidates and candidates representing political parties not entitled by law to a separate ballot shall be shown on the ballot for the recall election only.

(c) When a recall primary is required, the date specified under sub. (2) shall be the date of the recall primary and the recall election shall be held on the Tuesday of the 4th week after the recall primary or, if that Tuesday is a legal holiday, on the first day after that Tuesday which is not a legal holiday.

(5) The person who receives the highest number of votes in the recall election shall be elected for the remainder of the term.

(6) After one such petition and recall election, no further recall petition shall be filed against the same officer during the term for which he was elected.

(7) This section shall be self-executing and mandatory. Laws may be enacted to facilitate its operation but no law shall be enacted to hamper, restrict or impair the right of recall.

Marriage. Section 13. Only a marriage between one man and one woman shall be valid or recognized as a marriage in this state. A legal status identical or substantially similar to that of marriage for unmarried individuals shall not be valid or recognized in this state.

ARTICLE XIV—Schedule

Effect of change from territory to state. Section 1. That no inconvenience may arise by reason of a change from a territorial to a permanent state government, it is declared that all rights, actions, prosecutions, judgments, claims and contracts, as well of individuals as of bodies corporate, shall continue as if no such change had taken place; and all process which may be issued under the authority of the territory of Wisconsin previous to its admission into the union of the United States shall be as valid as if issued in the name of the state.

Territorial laws continued. Section 2. All laws now in force in the territory of Wisconsin which are not repugnant to this constitution shall remain in force until they expire by their own limitation or be altered or repealed by the legislature.

Common law continued in force. Section 13. Such parts of the common law as are now in force in the territory of Wisconsin, not inconsistent with this constitution, shall be and continue part of the law of this state until altered or suspended by the legislature.

Implementing revised structure of judicial branch. Section 16. **(4)** The terms of office of justices of the supreme court serving on August 1, 1978, shall expire on the July 31 next preceding the first Monday in January on which such terms would otherwise have expired, but such advancement of the date of term expiration shall not impair any retirement rights vested in any such justice if the term had expired on the first Monday in January.

INDEX